Cornelius Cardew
(1936 – 1981)
a life unfinished

John Tilbury

Copula – an imprint of Matchless Recordings and Publishing

First published 2008 by:

Copula — an imprint of Matchless Recordings and Publishing
2 Shetlock's Cottages, Matching Tye, near Harlow, Essex CM17 0QR, UK

British Library Cataloguing in Publication Data

Tilbury, John Richard

Cornelius Cardew A Life Unfinished

ISBN 978-0-9525492-3-9 (hard cover)
ISBN 978-0-9525492-4-6 (soft cover)

Cover design Ian Walters

Typography: Maureen Asser and Kenneth Ansell at Wildcat Design, email wildcat1@ntworld.com
Printed by: CPI Antony Rowe, Chippenham, Wiltshire, SN14 6LH, UK

For all those who knew and loved Cornelius

'Those who resist the dream are not only madmen and enemies of society; they betray the part of light in their own humanity'. George Steiner

Contents

List of plates

Acknowledgements

Extracts from Cardew's scores are quoted by permission of Peters Edition, Universal Edition, Novello, and Danny Dark Records. For manuscripts, diaries and copious correspondence I am grateful to the Cardew family, to Sheila Kasabova, and to Ilona Phombeah née Halberstadt, for putting everything at my disposal. I would also like to thank the Cardew Estate, Seth Cardew, Alec Hill, Victor Schonfield, Sheila Kasabova, Tim Mitchell, Laurie and Brigid Baker, as well as the Darmstadt archives, for providing me with photos. No biographer could ever had such a comprehensive inventory of his subect's material legacy. I should also like to thank the Hinrichsen Foundation for their generous financial contribution at the very beginning of this venture.

A section entitled Acknowledgements is really an anomaly, for acknowledgements are made constantly throughout this book. Here I declare simply a recognition of the indispensability of so many people, without whom this book could never have been written – indeed, a recognition of co-authorship: people, interviewees, who have recounted often touching and revealing anecdotes about Cardew, not all of which, simply by virtue of the plenitude of material, I have been able to include. The reason for the existence of this anecdotal 'evidence' is that anybody who had even just a passing knowledge of Cardew was in some way affected by him. I am like the accountant who gathers all the evidence: tickets, bills, invoices, each with its own story attached to it; intriguing evidence of unheard-of locations, of speculative adventures, of secrets, and so forth. All this is presented in some kind of state of viability to a higher authority, in my case to the general public.

During this long haul, spanning a quarter of a century, assistance and encouragement from all the Cardew family, including Sheila Kasabova, has been unstinting. In relation to the early years in particular, his brother Seth has been a mine of sensitive, perceptive observations and has furnished me with indispensable information. And I recall his mother

Mariel, who, after her son's death, entertained and charmed my wife and me at her home in Barnes and introduced us to the secret pleasures of carrageen. More than anybody, of course, Stella Cardew and Sheila Kasabova have provided insights into Cardew's inner life. My conversations with them have been ongoing and no doubt will continue long after the publication of this book, as will my discussions with Cardew's two sons Horace and Walter, who have both responded so generously and thoughtfully to all my questions and requests. Stella Cardew's daughter, Emily Underwood, has also talked about her step-father with a most touching affection. And in the early stages of my research a trip to Holland to interview Cardew's first wife, Ruth Koenig, was made pleasant and comfortable by Ruth and her husband Michael, Cardew's friend and colleague from the Cologne days, who offered me hospitality and were exceptionally kind and co-operative. To all of these people I owe a huge debt of gratitude.

The response from those of his schoolfriends I was able to track down has been quite overwhelming: Gerald Hare, Neville Swanson, Graham Tew, Jonathan Varcoe, to name a handful, and in particular Canon Roger Job whose detailed account of life at the Choir School and at King's College, as well as his personal recollections of Cardew, have been invaluable in respect of both the material and mental states which obtained in the early school years. He brings to life so vividly those still war-torn days of the early fifties in a drab, shell-shocked Canterbury. David Sladen, a lifelong friend who was also at the King's School, read the first draft of this book and made helpful suggestions and constructive criticisms. Perhaps even more importantly, his regular, uninhibited outbursts of encouragement and praise have spurred me on when the going was getting tough. I would also like to thank Paul Pollack who had been a young teacher when Cardew was at the King's School and who remembered him well. He kindly conducted David Sladen and me on a tour of the school – much changed, of course, but with the occasional neglected hideaway which had somehow escaped or survived modernisation, much to Sladen's delight.

Musician, artist, writer, film-maker friends and colleagues have given lengthy interviews or have responded by mail – much of it extraordinarily moving: Frank Abbot, the Uruguayan composer/musicologist Coriún Aharonián, James Allen, Virginia Anderson, Richard Ascough, with his invaluable Scratch Orchestra archives, Ed Baxter, David Bedford, Richard Rodney Bennett, Hanne Boenisch, who made a magical film of the Scratch Orchestra, the late Susan Bradshaw, Greg Bright, the late Alan Bush, Carole Chant, Richard Churches, Victor Clarke, Robert Coleridge, the late Hugh Davies, the late Brian Dennis, the critic Paul Driver, Rod Eley, Psi Ellison, Howard Ferguson, his composition teacher at the Royal Academy, Michael Finnissy, Luke Fowler, who in 2006 made a film portrait from the perspective of the younger generation who did not know Cardew, Wendy Frankland, Lou Gare, Natalie Gibson, who provided me with some captivating love letters she had received from Cardew, John Gillard, Michael Graubart, Peter Greenham, Bryn Harris, Alec Hill, Nicholas Hodges, the composer and critic Bill Hopkins, Michael Horovitz, the composer and critic Adrian Jack, Chris Johnstone, Hans Keller, the late Bernard Kelly, the Canadian film director Allan King, Alex Kolkowski, who researched on my behalf into Cardew's stay in Berlin in the seventies, Takehisa Kosugi, Catherine Morley née Williams, Chris Hobbs, Patrick Hughes, David Jackman, Adrian Lee, John Le Grand, the critic William Mann, Jane Manning, Benedict Mason, Ian McQueen, Ian Mitchell, Paige Mitchell, Tim Mitchell, John Nash, Josephine Nendick, the Hungarian violinist János Négyesy, now residing in California, who has sent me his personal reminiscences of Cardew in Berlin in the seventies where he was politically active, Michael Nyman, Phillip Pilkington, the critic Andrew Porter, Phillipe Regniez and Gwyneth Baines, who provided me with the transcripts of all the interviews they had made, including Stockhausen, Feldman and Christian Wolff, for their 1986 film portrait of Cardew, Adrian and Frances Rifkin, Krystyna Roberts, Keith Rowe (a major contributor), Dave Ryan, Victor Shonfield, Vicky Silva, Julian Silverman, Dave Smith, the late Tim Souster, Jeffrey Steele, the late Bernard Stevens, Stefan Szczelkun, Alan Thomas, Noel Upfold, John White, Harry Peter Wilson-Wright, especially for his 'silent contribution' to *Schooltime Compositions* at the ICA on 23 March 1969, and Bob Woolford, who, in the early days, recorded much of Cardew's music-making.

In December 1985 Peter Devenport and Hugh Shrapnel compiled a comprehensive list of Cardew's songs, which includes arrangements of songs by other composers, as well as traditional songs. It also includes unfinished sketches. I have drawn on this in compiling my own list which, whilst including all his own songs, omits some other material, such as basic arrangements of songs by others, and numerous sketches. Needless to say I am greatly indebted to Shrapnel and the late Peter Devenport for their painstaking and conscientious work. My debt to Laurie and Brigid Baker is perhaps even greater; they have provided me with copies of the actual songs, many of which I had begun to despair of ever being able to retrieve. The number of 'missing' songs is now, I hope, negligible.

Cardew's colleagues at Aldus Books, in particular Ruth Midgley, also responded positively to my requests for their memories, and in particular I want to thank his employer at Diagram Visual Information Ltd, Bruce Robertson, and his wife Pat, whose friendship with, and fondness for, Cardew invariably overrode their professional relationship. I very much enjoyed hearing and recording their recollections, so warmly and endearingly expressed, at their flat in Kentish Town.

There is an equally imposing list from abroad:

In Austria Gerhard and Maria Crepaz from very early on recognized Cardew's importance, and during one of my many discussions with them in their flat in Hall in the Tirol they talked at great length and with much affection about the visit of the Scratch Orchestra in the early seventies and the profound impression Cardew made upon them at that time. And the composer and horn player Kurt Schwertsik, a close friend from Vienna, recounted delightful anecdotes which had been stored away in his memory bank and which he was only too pleased to share with me. (I should also mention the Czech composer/flautist, Petr Kotik, who promoted Cardew's work in Czechoslovakia in the sixties with some memorable performances).

And in Poland, unforgettably, the late Jósef Patkowski, musicologist, who was one of the first in East Europe to recognize Cardew's importance, and was certainly instrumental in facilitating Cardew's visit to Poland in the sixties. Just weeks before his passing, in 2005, we met in London and our conversation inevitably turned towards Cardew.

From Italy I must thank the dancer and dance teacher Francesca Astaldi, dedicatee of one of Cardew's piano pieces, whose hospitality I enjoyed on a visit to Rome. I also had the pleasure of meeting Goffredo Petrassi in Rome when he was already in his nineties; he spoke warmly about Cardew and could still recall aspects of his compositional style. Two fellow students in Petrassi's class, Claudio Annibaldi and Zoltan Peszko, whom he got to know well at that time, also provided me with recollections and observations which went to the heart of the matter. And I was fortunate in the early stages of my research to have met up again with Francesco Carraro, Mario Bortolotto (who was probably the first Italian critic to recognize Cardew's genius), and the composer/conductor, Marcello Panni. The young experimentalist Andrea Rocca, who resides in London, also provided me with some interesting insights into *Treatise*. And most recently, in 2006, Stefano Zorzanello in Sicily produced five radio programmes dedicated to Cardew's life and music.

A number of young French musicians have also been involved in interpretations of *Treatise,* including two female dancers, whose names I have forgotten, who created a beautiful choreography from pages of *Treatise*, and who talked about its composer with such intimacy, such warmth and respect; it was as if they had known him personally. Fortunately, the interview has survived on cassette and if they ever they come across this book I would like them to know how much I appreciated their contribution. And the Spaniard Enrique Brinkmann, who designed the exquisite cover for *Two Books of Study for Pianists*, sent me a cassette many years ago now in which he talks warmly of the unique personality that was Cornelius Cardew.

Cardew had a special relationship with Germany; he spent a considerable amount of time there both during the sixties and, although in rather different circumstances, in the seventies. He had, and still has, many friends and admirers throughout Germany. Karlheinz Stockhausen looms large in the early days in Cologne and I have drawn on the interview with him in the previously mentioned film by Phillipe Regniez. The artist Mary Bauermeister spoke to me on the phone with superabundant enthusiasm for Cardew, both as artist and man. I must also thank his close friends Michael von Biel, Hans G. Helms, Dieter Schnebel, Isolde Vostell and Ilse Schneider, who on various occasions and in diverse locations all imparted their thoughts and feelings about Cardew. Thanks, too, to Hanno Ehrler, who more recently has promoted Cardew and his work in Germany with radio programmes on which I have drawn. And heartfelt thanks, in particular, to Christoph Müller from Cologne who was one of the first to begin researching into Cardew's texts and recordings, and at the very outset of my own project generously and selflessly provided me with invaluable material.

Regarding his time in Berlin in the seventies my chief debt of gratitude must be to Alex Kolkowski, who alerted me to the existence and relevance of a number of people from that time and, moreover, tracked them down and put me in touch with them. All these comrades-in-arms, who include Erhard Grosskopf, Christian Kneisel and Thomas Kessler, have provided me with invaluable personal and anecdotal material. Ingrid Beirer from the Deutsche Akademie has been most obliging; Michael Haerdter was also helpful and generous with his contribution, notwithstanding the fact that during the political campaign (Bethanien) he and his colleague Nele Hertling would have been considered by Cardew to have been on the other (wrong) side of the barricades. To all these people I offer my heartfelt thanks.

In North America, too, Cardew had many close friends, and the mutuality of their relationships becomes clear as the narrative unfolds: composer Frank Abbinanti from Chicago sent me a cassette of his thoughts and memories, and composer David Behrman captivated us with his recollections when he visited our home in Deal. The artist George Brecht collaborated with Cardew on a number of projects when he was in London during the sixties, and the late Earle Brown sent me a wonderful cassette recording, characteristically warm and perspicacious, of his memories of Cornelius. Larry Austin, John Cage (who remained loyal to Cardew's memory, in spite of 'John Cage, Ghost or Monster'), Alvin Curran, Tom Johnson, Joan La Barbara, Renée Levine, Kathryn Gleasman Pisaro, Elliot Schwartz, Richard Teitelbaum, David Tudor, among many others, all delighted in remembering Cornelius and reminiscing – as did Morton Feldman, of course, who wrote so eloquently about Cardew, paying eloquent tribute to his extraordinary talents. And Frederic Rzewski was a comrade-in-arms who still relishes the opportunity to talk about his old friend. But most of all, perhaps, it was Christian Wolff, whom Cardew admired as a musician and loved as a human being; through all the political rough-and-tumble the warmth and integrity of their friendship never faltered. Christian provided me with recollections and insightful observations of inestimable value in a variety of contexts: royal and electronic mail, obituaries, recordings of conversations, including film interviews.

And I was the happy recipient of the hospitality of the 'Wolves' (as Cardew referred to Christian and Holly Wolff and their family) in their home in New England.

All these individuals have given me imaginative and unique insights into Cardew's character which I have attempted to weave together in the narrative which follows. I hope I have succeded in giving them due recognition, both formally and informally. To all of them, some of whom, sadly, are no longer with us, I owe an enormous debt of gratitude.

Back in Britain, and to those people, his political comrades, with whom, in the last decade, he lived and fought for a better world, and for and with whom, quite literally, he was prepared to sacrifice his life: Hakim Adi, Dalwinder and Satnam Atwal, Laurie and Brigid Baker, Chris Coleman, Michael Chant, the late Peter Devenport, the late John Maharg, Ian McGargle, Barbara Pearce, Geoff Pearce, Chris Thompson, Cath Walker, Penny Wright, are just a handful of comrades that I managed to meet and to interview. They all recalled the times with dignity and a certain pride which was absolutely justified and I thank them for their invaluable contributions. The late Hardial Bains, leader of the Canadian Marxist-Leninist Party, penned and delivered moving eulogies of Cardew. Regrettably, I never met him, but his contribution to our knowledge and understanding of Cardew as political activist is of inestimable importance.

Howard Skempton, with admirable and characteristic meticulousness, read the final manuscript, a taxing chore I would have thought, but one which he dispatched with a typical generosity of spirit. I am also greatly indebted to my friend Michael Parsons, an unpaid 'research assistant', who has been generous and selfless with his time and unfailingly patient and assiduous with my questions, queries and requests. Thanks, to, my lawyer son-in-law Trevor, who likewise stinted neither time nor patience to explain a legalistic nicety and advise accordingly. And on the production side heartfelt thanks to Ken Ansell and Maureen Asser, always infinitely considerate, tactful, tolerant. And to my son Jasper for keeping me, technologically, as up to speed as the task required, breaking off from his own work to guide me calmly and expertly through a procedure on the phone, when I had pressed the wrong key and had got myself into a technological pickle. For all these people I can only express my deepest appreciation.

Over the years I have gladly availed myself of advice – suggestions, corrections, criticisms – emanating from a variety of perspectives. All of it has received my most serious attention. But above all I owe a special debt of gratitude to my doughty editor, Harry Gilonis – for his quite intimidating eye and mind for detail, whether in respect of vocabulary, punctuation, stylistic consistency, clarity, interpretation, which however did not preclude a grasp of the broader issues. Occasionally, reservations were expressed, especially in relation to some of my more speculative, politically-orientated musings. After a lively exchange I would either take his useful suggestions and criticisms on board or we would simply beg to differ and leave it at that. And to my publisher Eddie Prévost, not only a great and much treasured friend with the patience of Job, but also a man whose resolute and unfailing commitment to this, some might say foolhardy project, has helped me, especially in the later stages, to see it through. I should also mention his editorial talents; reading though the final draft he has spotted anomalies and oversights which have escaped myself and even my editor.

Last (almost) but not least, and always, my daughters Faye and Rose and my wife Janice, cajoling and cursing, encouraging and praising, living my frustrations with me, the dilemmas and self-doubt, urging me on, convinced of the worth of something which has accompanied me for at least a third of my life span.

Inevitably, there will be errors and omissions which will come to light, which will be brought to my attention, no doubt within hours of publication, but ultimately I have only myself to blame for these. And despite the queue of contributors that populate my lists, I will have missed people who should have been thanked. And there are are several people, from various stages of Cardew's life, that at a late (too late) hour I realised I had not got round to intervewing. To these contributors my sincere apologies; perhaps in the course of time I will be able one way or another to remedy these omissions. Moreover, there are forgotten people who have described images (often fleeting) or moments which I have not documented and yet which are lodged in my memory and hover tantalisingly over parts of the manuscript, perhaps colouring a piece of narrative through an unfathomable pertinence.

And finally, the most important acknowledgement of all: my debt to the man himself, to Cornelius Cardew. A man who has accompanied me on this quest, whose ever present spirit has breathed life into these pages, and who has never allowed me to take the easy path, because to do so would have been a betrayal. Even so, too often the task has proved to be beyond me and I have failed. And not always for better.

Preface

This book has been a long time in the writing. People began to doubt its existence, and it achieved mythical status. At social gatherings at which I was present, especially with musicians, it would be a subject to be skirted round, to be alluded to, sometimes, with an enquiring but casual tone. For myself I learnt how to stonewall and divert. My predicament became the butt of a gentle humour, sometimes a source of embarrassment.

For over twenty years I have visited the book fitfully; until the last three years it was never allowed to interfere with my own music-making: practice, rehearsal, travel, concerts, teaching and lecturing, etc. Sometimes I abandoned it for months and it was not always easy to pick up the thread. The book was 'fitted in' to my life, never disruptive but always an insidious, nagging, but I think ultimately benign influence. I learnt this from Cardew; he never allowed one thing to dominate, to make unreasonable demands upon his time. He never seemed to prioritize in the way that most of us do. The reason for this was that every activity was endowed with equal significance: devising a new musical notation demanded the same care, the same attention to detail, the same concern and respect for human relations, as bathing the baby or preparing a picnic.

From time to time one particular friend would enquire, waspishly: 'John, have you finished your autobiography'? And there is more than a grain of substance to his quip. Cardew's qualities, as a musician, and as a human being, were immeasurably greater than mine, but through music our lives intertwined. I was not his Boswell, nor his confidant. We were fellow travellers on a journey which shaped and redefined our understanding of what is still, if only be default, referred to as music – a quest which both extended and blurred the horizons of our art.

Our relationship shifted its focus but never fractured. I remember visiting him at his flat in Camden during the mid-seventies when my frequent absences from London and his political exclusiveness seemed to have detracted from our friendship. The first thing

I noticed as I entered the living room was a photograph of myself on the mantelpiece. Perhaps I feigned more embarrassment than I felt ('you can get rid of that for a start') but I was genuinely surprised, and also touched and bemused, intrigued too, I suppose. At that time I was not a real comrade-in-arms, not immersed in the maelstrom of revolutionary politics to the extent that he was. I assumed that he would have regarded me as a bystander. But as far as I can recall the photo remained on the mantelpiece until he and his partner, Sheila Kasabova, moved to Leyton.

Throughout his life Cardew was preoccupied with matters of moral, ethical, social and, at the end, political import. To make connections between the latter and his compositions of the seventies would simply be an exercise in tautology, but the relationship between his non-musical preoccupations ('philosophy of life') and his compositions in the sixties is one of infinite subtlety and considerable depth; his life and work during that tumultuous decade must be conceived as a single narrative in which life and work intertwine. Primarily, I have sought to do what Ray Monk in his inspiring biography of *Ludwig Wittgenstein*[1] successfully brought off: to show what Cardew's work has to do with himself. However, on reflection, and with the aim of greater clarity for the reader, I decided after all to discuss those aspects of his compositions which are relatively autonomous under a separate heading: The Music.

In the later chapters, and for long sections, it may appear as if I have abandoned music in favour of politics. In fact, to all intents and purposes this is what Cardew himself did – or rather, he continued to compose, but music was assigned a supporting role. So from the mid-seventies onwards, to accommodate this change, I allow the music, which is often of an 'occasional', or 'utilitarian', nature, to emerge more or less chronologically within the narrative, where it is usually associated with, or generated by, some political exigency: an anti-fascist demonstration, new reactionary government legislation, or perhaps a celebration of an act of revolutionary heroism, or of a victory over the forces of darkness somewhere in the world. And we are constantly reminded of this in his writings from 1972 onwards by a freight of detailed, political analysis serving an ideologically-motivated agenda, with few and limited references to music. Rightly or wrongly I judged it would be a mistake to separate this music from its political *raison d'être*.

The fact is that whatever judgement we may pass on the momentous decisions that revolutionized his life in the last decade, his political commitment demanded 'politics first', and however disconcerting this may appear to the music-loving reader I hope that he or she will stay the course and reap, perhaps, an unexpected benefit. Much of this exegetic material I have gathered together in Chapter 16, entitled after Cardew's book *Stockhausen serves Imperialism*. The modern reader may prefer to scan and skim the contents of this chapter – unwisely perhaps, for embedded within the political jargon of Cardew's book are key thoughts which refer back to, and cohere with, concepts and notions, *critiques,* which preoccupied him throughout his life. In my various attempts to translate these ideas into a more accessible language I apologise in advance to those political sophisticates who may judge my efforts in this respect to be condescending, however well-intentioned.

Throughout this book I have stressed and insisted on what I regard as the *continuity* of Cardew's thought and actions, however much his political comrades have demurred on this issue. They have argued, if I am characterizing their disagreement accurately, that the qualitative change in his life in the seventies, through a decisive, *revolutionary* rupture with 'bourgeois' ideology, effectively derails my thesis of 'continuity'. The comrades have a point, but rather than rehearsing my counter-arguments here, I will allow them to unfold within the pages of this book in which I have tried to deal with the politics from the perspective of Cardew's personal imperatives and development; in any case, I am not equipped to unravel the complexities of the waxing and waning of the political Left in Britain, however much my sympathies lie broadly with it. I am not a political historian. Moreover, the situation is compounded by the fact that since the fifties and sixties, a comparatively short space of time, the social and economic relations between individuals have changed to such an extent that they are not easily recaptured.

My approach to the last decade is expository rather than critical. In attempting to 'explain' Cardew's actions during this period I may appear to some to be adopting the mantle of 'apologist'. It is true that I find myself in sympathy, still, with much of what he said and did in the last decade, although not enough for him to have regarded me at the time as a true comrade-in-arms; I was a 'petit bourgeois' supporter with many ideological shortcomings and on whom, therefore, he, as a communist, could not rely. This is my assumption; he never expressed these sentiments to me and to the end we remained good, and I like to think, close friends. So while I occasionally 'fellow-travel', I am often critical in a way that would have brought denunciatory criticism raining down upon me. Well, perhaps this is not such a bad relation for a biographer to have to his subject.

My preference has been to give Cardew a free rein − for example, in his analyses of contemporary capitalism, of working class culture, of folk music, and so forth, even adding elucidatory (supportive) comments where his views might be considered, in the contemporary context, highly contentious, or simply outmoded; hence the somewhat pedantic, aforementioned exegesis I allow myself in the chapter *Stockhausen serves Imperialism*. We may even take it upon ourselves, if we feel we are suitably equipped, to tear Cardew's arguments and theses to shreds, but in doing so let us pause to reflect on our own submerged and too often unacknowledged certainties with at least a degree of the same ruthless honesty with which Cardew scrutinized his own doubts.

Apart from the musical scores themselves by far the most precious extant documents are Cardew's Journals.[2] There are nine − most of them linen-bound, hardbacked, 7" by 9", lined writing books dating from 1952, when he was still at school, to 1974 when, for reasons to be explained later in the book, he ceased confiding his thoughts and feelings in this form. There is no Journal for 1969/70; we can only assume that he kept a Journal during those two years, but it has not survived. The contents of the Journals range from objective, descriptive narration to the deeply personal; there is analysis, and self-analysis; confessional texts and political statements. There are literary, poetic, and sexual references, as well as remembered dreams. There are copies or drafts of letters he may or may not have sent. There is spontaneity and calculation; vulnerability and impregnability; judgement and misjudgement. Cardew himself numbered the pages of the earlier Journals, from 1952 to 1962, but not thereafter. I have numbered the pages of most of the rest of the Journals, lightly in pencil, and this numbering is referred to in the footnotes in square brackets.

With the Journals I have enjoyed the dubious benefit of insider dealings. They act as an occasional but regular counterbalance to the inevitable fallibility of a biographer's narration and I use and quote from them liberally. Are the Journals an expression of youthful, middle-class vanity? Cardew came from a family and was educated in a manner which instilled into him a feeling of self-belief; in this sense he was typical of his class. Later in life, having jettisoned his middle-class *amour propre* he needed a new set of beliefs on which he could structure a new life. Thus, he had to *learn* self-doubt whilst the likes of his fellow musicians in the AMM (and myself) had to learn self-confidence, self-belief and, most importantly, self-esteem. We were not brought up to harbour expectations; rather, to express gratitude. And as young men we would certainly not have felt it incumbent upon ourselves to expose our feelings, and our judgements, in an ongoing Journal.

It may have been the case that Cardew's journals satisfied a psychological need; the need to confide in somebody, perhaps a mythical, ephemeral *persona,* (or an *alter ego?),* or soul mates like Agatha or Gladys from 'The Story of Agatha' (see Appendix 2). Certainly, the opacity of many Journal entries was contrived; Cardew was aware of the enigmatic quality in his *persona*, and its attraction. Yet they serve to illuminate the structure of his thought at certain moments in his life and, in particular, the nature of his sensibility; like Beethoven's sketchbooks the Journals express Cardew's most self-questioning and vulnerable moods. But all this was to change in the early seventies when, overtaken by the certainties of Marxism-Leninism-Mao Zedong Thought, Cardew became a soldier for communism. Now there is less spontaneity, less open vulnerability, and I shall elaborate on the reasons and explanations for these changes in the later pages of the book.

There are also two extant weighty ledgers (1961-4) containing all manner of correspondence, in alphabetical order, sometimes of artistic import, other times of a purely functional nature: a bill, a contract, an invoice, bank statements, publishing agreements, a formal invitation to a function, a formal communication from a public organization, etc. And there are many personal letters from family and friends. Is it not reasonable to presume that only a person with an unshakeable belief in his own historical destiny would have preserved such material as an invaluable source for future historians and biographers? These ledgers seem to be comprehensive (during this period Cardew appears to have kept all his correspondence — that is, letters written to him); they also contain some copies and/or originals of his own letters, or rather drafts of letters to people, the fair copy presumably filed or later discarded by the addressee.

Judging by the educational institutions that Cardew attended, public school and the Royal Academy of Music, he would be described as an 'educated' man, although it would be more accurate to say that he *used* the education that was available to him. As E. P. Thompson has written: this conventional concept of education 'involves submission to certain institutionally defined disciplines, with their own hierarchies of accomplishment and authority'.[3] However liberally one interprets this definition, Cardew would have remained outside it; even the paradox of his 'Communist Party membership' in the seventies can be explained, I believe, without compromising this view. For this can be seen as belonging to a tradition of intellectual 'dissent' in which alternative cultures were created in opposition to what Thompson calls 'the polite culture' — that is, a classical, intellectual culture associated in particular with Oxbridge and a relatively small elite. Reviewing these alternative intellectual traditions, from the eighteenth century onwards, Thompson reveals that they

> existed also — and especially in London — at the level of family traditions, and obscure intellectual currents surfacing, submerging and then surfacing again in little periodicals, or in chapels which fractured into several petty chapels, which invited new ministers or gathered around new voices, which knit up ideas and unravelled them and knit them up again throughout the eighteenth century. And we have to learn to see the minds of these men and women, formed in these kinds of collisions and voluntary associations, with more humility than patronage. Out of such an 'education', of informal traditions and collisions, came many

original minds: Franklin, Paine, Wollstonecraft, Bewick, Cobbett, Thomas Spence, Robert Owen. And it is in this kind of tradition that we must place Blake.[4]

And Cardew, too, in my opinion; except that for 'chapels' we should read political groups, heretical music-making with AMM, the Scratch Orchestra and associative organizations, and, just as importantly, we should remind ourselves that a significant component in Cardew's informal education was his exposure at an early age to non-European cultures. The continuation of Thompson's text is too relevant to omit:

In this tradition experience is laid directly alongside learning; the two test each other. There is nothing of our present academic specialization: thought may be borrowed, like imagery, from any source available. There is, in this tradition, a strong, and sometimes an excessive, self-confidence. And there is an insistent impulse towards individual system-building: the authority of the Church, demystified in the seventeenth century, had not yet been replaced by the authority of an academic hierarchy or of public 'experts'.

The correlation between Thompson's characterization of this alternative tradition and the trajectory and substance of Cardew's own life will, I trust, become transparent as the reader progresses through these pages.

I have dealt with some of Cardew's music at considerable length – indeed two works, *Treatise* and *The Great Learning* each commands a chapter to itself.[5] I am conscious of the fact that for some readers what appear, dauntingly, to be analytical incursions into technical zones will create apprehension, impatience, even irritation. However, there are certain compositions where I believe it is difficult, indeed unwise, to separate the technical from the *immanent* – works which, apart from their intrinsic worth, are springboards, or represent important shifts in the trajectory of his musical (and not only musical) life: *February Pieces, Autumn 60, Octet '61 for Jasper Johns,* and later *Schooltime Compositions* and the *Piano Albums.* Such works demonstrate Cardew's conviction that the fact of music as *human activity* – that music is not only reflective but also *projects* the possibilities of new (desirable) modes of human commerce – must never be lost sight of. For this reason I have dwelt on them, perhaps excessively, to tease out at least some of the multiple meanings, to hint at subtle contingencies and ambiguities, and to respond to the idealities to which Cardew's notations seem to aspire.

The free improvisation group AMM is dealt with at length, a whole chapter and more devoted to it, but invariably from the perspective of Cardew's participation and involvement.

I hope this does not create a distorted picture; as a current member I am conscious of the burden of responsibility. AMM was never the 'Cornelius Cardew Quintet' (see Chapter 7, footnote 24); it came into existence before Cardew became a member and continued to develop and thrive without him. In AMM there have never been soloists or leaders. I have not followed a strict chronology, dealing quite freely with aspects of AMM's activity and generally focusing on Cardew's contributions. I have not attempted even a potted history of AMM, with dates of 'gigs' and events, although I trust that much of the material will be of use to future musical historians. The later AMM falls outside the remit of this book and I have had to break off, frustratingly, at a point of crisis in the early seventies when both Cardew and Keith Rowe left the group. I have tried to mitigate the severity of this rupture by returning to a more general appraisal of the importance of AMM for Cardew's philosophy of music.

My book contains copious references to Cardew's scores and notations, and to specific features, and in most cases I have provided the relevant extracts.[6] With AMM, however, since the music does not exist in notated form, I occasionally refer the reader to recordings and CDs. This may be frustrating for those who do not have access to the recorded material, but I hope they will bear with me. In any case those who have experienced the music, both live and on CD, will attest to the inadequacy of a reliance on recordings.

Two final points, one of which came to me at a relatively late stage in the production of this book when I came across a letter to Cardew, dated 17 February 1964, from David Sladen, an old school-friend who remained close to him throughout his life:

> If a man leaves traces of himself, even in the form of pieces of his own handwriting, the traces are not him but of him. Him can be found only in personal acquaintance. One's relationship with another is selves-contained, an aura of inviolability. Writing a biography of someone you know well, or even reading one can be a jarring, if stimulating experience.
> 'When you know somebody you always, in a sense, know all there is to know'. Or, perhaps, all you *need* to know.
> Sure there's some point in collecting bits of knowledge about other people. But its not the same thing as *knowing* them.
> Different kind of knowledge. Art tries to recapture this knowledge.
> The other kind is called biography. They have different kinds of *truth*.

And the second point, not entirely unrelated to the first: I anticipate that some readers will be disappointed that I have not given adequate consideration to the family history and achievements, both on the paternal (Cardew) side, and on the maternal (Russell) side. My response would be to direct them to Michael Cardew's autobiography, *A Pioneer Potter,* and to Tanya Harrod's forthcoming biography of Michael Cardew, due to be published by Yale University Press in 2008.

Notes and references

1 I hope the reader will not become irritated by the frequent quotes from, and references to, Wittgenstein. The fact is that from his early twenties right up to his death Cardew read and studied Wittgenstein. Wittgenstein was his silent mentor – even during the political years when most writers and philosophers outside the Marxist/Leninist canon – and even many within – were dismissed as at best irrelevant and at worst counter-revolutionary by Cardew's political comrades.

2 Among the extant material there are also a dozen or more conventional diaries, with mainly appointments and addresses, and some manuscript books from his Royal Academy days.

3 E.P. Thompson, *Witness against the Beast* (Cambridge: Cambridge University Press, 1993), p.xiv.

4 Ibid. p.xv.

5 Regarding *Treatise* there are certainly many more avenues of fruitful enquiry than I have been able to deal with; for example, the possible relationship between *Treatise* and Kandinsky's theories of visual composition.

6 The musical examples references are formulated as follows: (1) number of chapter, (2) the chronologically listed number of the example in the chapter, and (3) where several examples are taken from within a single movement, or song, letters may also be used.

Abbreviations

Jrnl	Cardew's Journals	BH	Bryn Harris
RA	Ruth Aaronberg	DJ	David Jackman
CC	Cornelius Cardew	EP	Eddie Prévost
CCR	*Cornelius Cardew Reader*	MP	Michael Parsons
MC	Michael Cardew	KR	Keith Rowe
SC	Seth Cardew	HS	Hugh Shrapnel
IH	Ilona Halberstadt	HSK	Howard Skempton

1

Family Background, Childhood, School 1936–53

It was May Day, 1932, and a Sunday morning. A young woman emerged from the firewood shed behind the Greet Pottery, north of Winchcombe in Gloucestershire, where Michael Cardew had bought a field from which he dug clay.[1] With her thick dark hair worn in two long plaits, her large deep-set eyes, and graced with the complexion of the goddess Pomona, she might have been a gipsy. Undeterred by the frosty reception she received from Cardew, his brother Philip, and Philip's friend, ex-bouncer Bernard Cook, Mariel Russell sat down with them to unwrap and eat the sandwiches she had brought with her while her male company, unaccustomed to female unconventionality, sought to redeem themselves through verbal and gestural assuagement.[2] As they walked together to the field, in pairs – Michael and Philip, Mariel and Bernard – Mariel was impressed by the brothers' conversation, most of which centred on the character and structure of individual flowers and plants. When a thunderstorm broke the party dispersed; Philip and Bernard departed for London and Michael invited Mariel for tea in the hut and showed her the Pottery.

But what had brought Mariel to the Greet Pottery in the first place? Ostensibly her purpose was to seek out Michael Cardew who, according to her friend the art historian David Talbot Rice, had already gained the reputation of an eccentric but talented young potter. However, this was only partially the case; in fact, Mariel's motives were mainly musical, and had little to do with the art of pottery. She had acquired a recorder, and the potter Michael Cardew, a proficient recorder player who had performed with the Dolmetsch ensemble, had been recommended to her as a prospective teacher. Whatever her motive, whether she fulfilled a professional or private purpose, Mariel spent several hours of that May Day with Michael, charmed and no doubt flattered him with her attention and interest to such an extent that he arranged to see her again and thereafter began to pursue her in earnest. Michael Cardew describes their courtship:

It was the beginning of an intermittently tempestuous friendship which finally, after nineteen months, led to our getting married. All that summer we met often. She was currently working as the curator of the museum in Gloucester [having previously been working, for a brief period, at the Pitt Rivers estate at Cranborne Chase in Dorset], and living in two tiny rooms in a back street. When I went to see her in Gloucester we would sit up half the night talking; sometimes I slept on a sofa in the small living room. Once or twice she came over to Winchcombe, and on one occasion she made tea on the outdoor table in front of the hut for three or four local children who happened to be around. The way she presided over that tea table made me think, well! She puts on an act of being a rootless bohemian, but what a wonderful old-fashioned mother she would be if she ever had children of her own. Beano[3] used to tease me about my girl-friends, saying that I only considered each of them in the light of the question, 'Will she do?' Very gradually and with much reluctance I began to admit to myself that if anyone were to ask me if Mariel would 'do', the answer would have to be 'Yes'. Our long walks seemed to indicate that (unlike my other girl-friends) she did not mind my being poor and even actively approved of it. All the others had been unattainable in different ways, but in every case I had decided (unwarrantably, I dare say) that the insuperable obstacle was that I had been too poor.[4]

On Christmas Eve, 1933, Mary Ellen Russell and Michael Ambrose Cardew were married at the Winchcombe Parish Church, Gloucestershire. In a conversation I had with Mariel at her house in Lonsdale Road, Barnes, in south west London, sometime in the eighties and after her second son's death, she recalled walking across the fields to the chapel with the much-loved Nanny Mason (see below); Michael was accompanied by his brother Philip, whose contempt for the nuptial proceedings was even deeper than his own, and who was to be heard muttering under his breath, 'black magic, black magic', throughout the entire ceremony.

Certainly marriage did not alter their unconventional, bohemian lifestyle and they continued to live at the pottery in Winchcombe. In 1928 Michael Cardew had had a wooden hut built in the orchard behind his pottery so that he 'could move out of the pottery and no longer had to eat in the semi-darkness beside the *kang*. […] It was a good home for Mariel and me during the early years of our married life, and two of our three children were born in it'.[5] Their second son, and the subject of the pages which follow, Brian Cornelius McDonough Cardew,[6] began his life there on 7 May 1936.

In fact the hut was their home for many months of the year and they would frequently entertain artists and intellectuals who would visit them from far afield to discuss and argue into the night. These included the American scholar and collector, Henry Bergen ('the first American I had ever known', as Michael Cardew recalled), and the Catholic scholar and writer Dom Bede Griffiths.[7] They seemed to enjoy, even take pride in their relative poverty, but they were not without well-heeled benefactors who tolerated and sometimes encouraged their eccentricities.

The move from Winchcombe to Wenford Bridge, near Bodmin in Cornwall, on 1 June 1939, was a positive one, not only because the larger premises afforded them the extra space they needed, but because it had long been Michael's wish to live and work in Cornwall where the sky 'is given a luminosity by the reflections from the surrounding ocean, specially in the evenings […] For my father such things were the stuff of life – however subjective they appeared to others'.[8] Michael drove down in an old Jowett and most of the family's effects were transported by train. He and Mariel, with help from one or two of their new neighbours, 'worked from dawn to dusk between then and September, in a fever of activity' to render the buildings habitable, at least to their own humble standards.

The premises had been an inn – Wenford Inn; it had belonged to the St Austell Brewery and had been run by a Mr and Mrs Armstrong. Mrs Armstrong was an energetic lady ('a little dynamo') who used to cook and provide for the various railway and clay workers. Her husband preferred to chat with customers at the bar so that when his wife died he had no work experience whatsoever and could not cope with the responsibilities he had inherited. He eventually lost his licence because of a blatant disregard for hygiene and returned to his former trade as a stone-mason. The St Austell Brewery decided to sell the inn and early in 1939, while exploring the country on the western slopes of Bodmin Moor, Michael Cardew, on the recommendation of a friend, had called at the inn to assess its viability for conversion to a pottery. Mr Armstrong showed him around the house and the outbuildings, many of which were in an advanced state of decay. These comprised a brewhouse with a loft above it, a skittle alley, a blacksmith's shop, a stable with another loft, a pig's house and a cowshed; there was a garden at the back, three acres of meadow, and another small patch of rough land on the other side of the road beside the River Camel.

> The place seemed far too big and far too ambitious for us: I had been looking for something much smaller. But when I went to the St Austell Brewery and learnt that they were only asking £550 for the whole place (this being, as it happened, the exact amount of our capital), I no longer hesitated. I went to my elderly cousin Gilbert Chilcott, who was a solicitor in Truro and would therefore know how to get a mortgage, so that we should have a little bit of cash left for starting the

3

pottery. He insisted on an independent valuation – which decided that the property was only worth £350. In the end we got it for £500. I think my cousin was rather scandalized that I paid so much.[9]

Some weeks before the family left for Cornwall a group of refugee children had arrived, evacuees from the Basque country during the Spanish Civil War. Mariel was a member of a pacifist group, Peace Pledge Union, and had invited six children to come and stay with her and the family in Winchcombe. Somehow they were all accommodated at the pottery, with friends and neighbours helping and contributing generously. When the time came for them to return home the children managed to delay their departure by a week, after representation to the Refugee Committee. This relatively brief episode made a deep and lasting impression upon hosts and guests alike; Seth Cardew confesses that for a long time he cherished a wish to go to Spain and the Basque country to try and trace them.

A visit to Wenford Bridge created a lasting impression of a family, of a place, and a way of life. Yet the Cardews' home was never a haven from the wildness of the nature which surrounded it – rather it was part of that nature, stark and uncluttered like the moorland that lay a few miles to the east. There was no electricity – candles were used, and the family would often go barefoot; water from a stream was drawn from outside the kitchen window for drinking and washing purposes and they would share a tin bath in front of the fire. Hidden away in a small barn was a chemical toilet. Its character could not have changed substantially; some people still thought it was a pub; they would open the door, walk in, settle down in a chair, and order a pint.

But the material primitiveness was mitigated by a strong cultural presence: books in great diversity, fine pieces of pottery, music-making; in Seth Cardew's words, Wenford gave off a feeling of 'spartan erudition'.[10] This combination provided a home base which seemed secure and unshakeable, and undoubtedly stood the boys in good stead in later life. However, there were family tensions which often caused distress; above all, it was Michael Cardew's personality which dominated: irascible, quick-tempered, curmudgeonly, a self-willed man of great talent and considerable arrogance; a detached and censorious father, with a limited sense of humour, who, when he was in a good mood, smoking his pipe, could 'fill the house with sunshine', to everyone's benefit and relief – and yet who could, in a trice, wilfully destroy a congenial atmosphere by the sharpness of his tongue and his abrasive manner.

A word that rises to the mind in thinking of father is hubris. He feared neither god nor men in that he ate what he pleased in large quantity. Did what he pleased, said what he pleased – often to the great contradiction of what pleased yesterday, and sometimes most emphatically with stamps and kicks thrown in the presence of strangers [...] Really TENSION was his medium, and he revelled in it, whether it was dire atmosphere, or drama or physical strain.[11]

Michael's father, Arthur Cardew, had been a civil servant and a gifted amateur musician who loved the music of Haydn and venerated Mozart above all others. His mother, Alexandra, was also musical, a violinist, but whose main claim to fame lay in the fact that she had been the child photo model, Xie, for Charles Dodgson, alias Lewis Carroll. According to Seth Cardew, Alexandra Cardew, née Kitchin, doted upon her only daughter, Penelope, and showed little interest in her five sons: Christopher, Richard (who was killed in the first World War), Michael (born 26 May 1901), Philip and Alexander. Alice Mason was engaged as a nanny and virtually brought up the boys single-handedly. It is Seth's view that the consequences of such maternal rejection can have a devastating effect on sons, and did so in the case of his father: 'When a mother withdraws from her boys – denies affection, cuddles and whatever, they tend to be wary of feminine affection later in life. Nanny Mason was always being talked about, asked after, visited, but not Alexandra.'[12]

Nanny Mason had definite ideas about caring for babies; she claimed that it was wrong to go to a baby when it was crying and to try to pacify it; a baby has to exercise its lungs and if you fuss over it it somehow senses that something is wrong. It is perfectly natural, and necessary, for a baby to cry. Such was the child-rearing gospel according to Nanny Mason, and she remained in the Cardew household up to and including the time when Seth and Cornelius were babies.

By contrast with her husband, Mariel Cardew (born 30 March 1905) was a woman of immense charm, a warm and inspiring character, an engaging personality with the gift (which she shared with her second son) of being able to enthuse people to artistic creation and endeavour. Mariel was a raconteuse, *par excellence*, who could delight an audience as much by the witty manner of her delivery as by the humorous content of her stories. Her maternal guidance and influence remained with Cornelius into his later years (despite the profound differences which separated them in many matters); their long and frequent walks in the Cornish countryside, when he learnt from his mother how to make fires anywhere and in the most adverse conditions (a favourite hobby which he never tired of), probably as much as anything else nurtured and moulded the personality by which, in his maturity, he was recognized and admired. Mariel's 'bohemianism' was a style which many people associated with Cornelius, particularly in his twenties. Not that her zeal and devotion had always been rewarded with positive filial response;

on one or two occasions, for example, she had managed to persuade the boys to go to church but the 'ox-like expression on my mother's face during the sermons was enough to convince us that this was an exercise in humbug and hypocrisy'.[13]

Like her husband, Mariel was of middle class, though less conventional, stock. Her father, Thomas Russell, was a journalist who worked for an American advertising magazine. He and his wife Olga were pacifists, teetotallers, and active supporters of the suffragette movement, and as a young girl Mariel would accompany them on demonstrations and marches. She eventually went to Oxford where she read English Literature, Geography and Anthropology, before deciding that she wanted to paint. She and Michael were in fact contemporaries at Oxford but they never met there.[14]

War broke out and the only time a bomb dropped in that part of Cornwall was when Michael Cardew fired the kiln. These two acts were associated in the minds of the local people, some of whom were convinced the Cardews were spies; they lived like gypsies, poor people, when manifestly, to their neighbours, they were not. The pottery was in stark contrast to the well-scrubbed Cornish homes which surrounded them; there were no curtains and the barefooted children seemed to run wild. For some time the Cornish people mistrusted them and resented their presence; they were outsiders, transgressors, perhaps Nazi sympathisers. It was even rumoured that they were transmitting radio signals to the enemy; Michael and Mariel had been given a radio that so offended their artistic sensibilities – it was an extremely gross object – that they kept it out of (their) sight in a cupboard which they would simply open when they wanted to listen to something.

On one occasion in the early forties, a detective visited Michael Cardew. In an intensely spy-conscious society Michael Cardew's cut-glass English accent may have aroused suspicion of fascist leanings amongst the local people: Cornish patriots with broad Cornish accents. The detective does not seem to have been politically mature; the content of the various newspapers, journals and books were of less import than the fact that they seemed to have been written for intellectuals. The New Statesman and Nation (a left-wing weekly) was singled out as literature of dubious provenance although when Mariel assured the detective that the New Statesman was read by hundreds (corrected to 'thousands' by her husband) his suspicions abated. The relationship with their neighbours improved and matured; in the end the people of Cornwall took this incongruous and unfathomable family to their hearts.

Inevitably, village life had been disrupted and transformed by the war: blackouts, evacuees, encampments in fields full of homeless people (especially when Plymouth was bombed) who were eventually accommodated by Social Services, and on one occasion a platoon of soldiers found refuge and comfort in the pottery after night manoeuvres. After the US entry into the war Seth Cardew recalls a young American army officer who 'came to tea for several weekends to make drawings of the pottery and kiln. I fear he may have perished in the war as we never heard anything afterwards'.[15] He was a sanguine, friendly character who was intrigued by the pottery and by the plans for it that had been drawn up by Michael Cardew. Seth recalls that he and his brothers all took to this likeable stranger who came into their lives, briefly but memorably, and who made his mark.

The officer had been posted to Hengar Manor, a nearby stately home which had been requisitioned by the American army. They would exercise in their jeeps around the area and generally enjoyed a high profile. They seemed cool and calm; after an exercise the officer would call a halt and announce lunch-time; it was as if they were on a film set. Seth Cardew recalls that on a Sunday they would stroll around in their Sunday best enquiring of him and his brothers and friends, quite reasonably, whether they had any sisters. When Mariel called her boys in for lunch some of the soldiers, hearing a female voice, interpreted her command to her sons as an invitation to the soldiers – a presumption which was peremptorily dispelled by Mariel's appearance and the forbidding expression on her face.

Mariel also took in an evacuee, Via – a lovely girl in her early teens from the East End (of London) and of Italian parentage. Via was impressive, 'a great inciter to rebellion', in Seth's words, who encouraged the boys to disobey, tease and generally provoke their mother. Mariel claimed that the girl was having a bad influence on her children and Via was sent to another family in the neighbourhood. Yet they kept in touch and after the war Via, on Michael and Mariel's invitation, attended a private exhibition held at Philip Cardew's house in Regent's Park Road. She was, as Seth recalls, 'a fantastic dish'.

From 1940 Seth, Cornelius and Ennis attended the St.Tudy primary school, to which they were transported each day by the school bus. There were three classes, fifty children in all: Ennis was in the youngest class; his teacher was Miss Armstrong, the daughter of the publican who was managing the Wenford Inn before it was purchased from the St Austell Brewery by Michael Cardew. Seth and Cornelius were in the same, middle class; their teacher was a devout lady by the name of Miss Best, who radiated fair-mindedness. The oldest class was taught by the headmaster, Mr Wilcox. All three teachers lived in St. Tudy.

Ennis recalls his brother Cornelius from those times:

His charisma was also apparent early on. The bus from the nearest town (Bodmin) would stop in St Tudy for ten minutes or so before continuing to Wenford, St Breward and Camelford. One day coming home, Cor (aged about seven, I suppose) had been persuaded to read to somebody's child in the back of the bus. When the bus stopped and the engine was turned off in St Tudy Cor continued reading and all the passengers stayed silently listening to him finish the story. A magic few minutes of respect.[16]

In 1942 Seth and Cornelius left the St. Tudy school to join the Canterbury Cathedral Choir School where they remained until the end of the war when the school moved back to Canterbury. Ennis stayed clear of these upheavals; he was happy to stay where he was. One particular incident from those days reminds him of his brother's 'stoicism'; he and Cornelius and their mother were staying with a friend of Mariel's at an old farmhouse in Oxfordshire:

In the garden was a well with a hand rotary pump between the cogs of which Cor and I were squashing grass (to make green juice since you ask) and I was turning the handle while Cor fed in the grass. Of course eventually (no formal 'risk assessment' was required of your children's play in those days!) Cor's index finger became caught in the cogs. The momentum of the machine ensured that the tip of Cor's finger was well crushed – no recriminations and few tears as I recall. The finger was permanently disfigured.[17]

The Choir School had been evacuated to the village of St. Blazey, about sixteen miles from Wenford, and it occurred to Mariel that if her two older boys could sing there was a chance that the problem of their war-time education could be solved, as it were, on the doorstep. Encouraged by her friend Mary Varcoe,[18] who lived in Par, near St. Blazey, and whose son, Jonathan, was also to join the school, Mariel put forward both Seth, aged 8, and Cornelius, aged 6, for entrance auditions.[19] Although he had had little or no musical tuition, Cornelius responded exceptionally well in all the tests, was able to do whatever was asked of him, and was awarded a place. Whether Seth's acceptance was attributable more to his younger brother's talent than to his own efforts, as their mother suggested, may or may not have been the case, but in 1942 Seth and Cornelius left the St. Tudy primary school and became boarders at the Choir School in St. Blazey.

Choir practice under the choirmaster Mr Knight was conducted in St. Blazey church and the church services were no doubt enhanced by the Choir School choristers. The head teacher (from 1937-63) was the Reverend Clive Pare (known as Pedro to the boys); Mr Sage (Sago) was the organist/pianist and Miss Bridge (Bridget) instructed the boys in their singing, musical theory and individual piano lessons. The domestic staff consisted of 'three excellent women': Mrs Carne, Mrs Card (who was also the owner of the bakery where the school boarded) and Miss Rooke, who cooked all the school meals; the dishwashing was done by a rota of boys. In fact, both Mrs Carne and Miss Rooke, as matron and cook respectively, followed the school back to Canterbury where their Cornish accent was a soothing and reassuring balm to the boys from Cornwall.

At St. Blazey there were walks to old tin mines and clay works and when they were a little older some of the boys had bicycles. The school base was on the main street, the dormitories were on the top floor of a bakery; downstairs they had their supper and did their homework. Puckey's bus took them along the coast to Carlyon Bay Hotel where they had their lessons. They returned to St. Blazey for lunch; then singing practice in the afternoon, and evensong in St. Blazey church where the boys would take turns in singing at the Eucharist.

It is a strange, English educational anomaly that by virtue of being musical, a boy (never a girl), brought up by atheist parents[20] in a liberal, secular environment, can be thrust into an esoteric world of iconic religious ritual and discipline, into a structure through which control can be maintained and punishment meted out, and in which all human commerce is subject to the insidious influence of a latent sado-masochism. Or is there an exegetic programme whereby the new boy is made aware of the *meaning* (as opposed to the origin) of, for example, the daily, solemn incantation of texts which for the uninitiated, as Cardew had been, reflect an alien and forbidding other-world?

With regard to such schools (and to some families), where unbending strictures are imposed, one is tempted to speculate as to whether tolerance and a more relaxed approach might yield a more positive, more harmonious outcome. Paradoxically, in such schools a blind eye or a deaf ear *is* turned to more subtle, moral transgressions because, according to the school's ideological premises, they reflect precisely those traits necessary for a successful *rite de passage* in an ultimately hostile world: deviousness and disingenuousness, one-upmanship, ambition and me-ism, to name a few.

In 1942, at the age of forty-one and therefore probably overage in terms of military service, Michael Cardew went to the Gold Coast (later, after independence, Ghana) for the first time and stayed there until 1945. He had originally been asked by the Colonial Office to recommend a potter to fill a post that had become vacant at the Achimota College and had offered his own services. This was not only a turning point in his artistic career; it was virtually to rupture his relationship with his family. In a footnote to his father's autobiography Seth Cardew writes:

> My father's text gives no explanation for his readiness to take up the post in West Africa. However, from the context it appears likely that his motivation at the outset

was for the most part financial. Quite simply – the job offered a regular salary.[21]

Michael Cardew did not return to England until two years or more later, on his first ever flight, which landed at Bristol on the evening of 2 October 1944. A short chapter in his autobiography bears the title Home Leave, although he seems to have spent most of the time in the Midlands, Stoke-on-Trent and Derbyshire, on assignments related to his work.[22] After a brief period at home in Wenford, where he was waiting for sailing orders, Mariel accompanied him, with their youngest son Ennis, to Liverpool, whence he returned to Africa. They walked along the quay, waiting for embarkation orders – 'Mariel haunted by premonitions of unknowable future disasters which I tried in vain to dispel'.[23]

In October 1945 Michael Cardew wrote to his wife to tell her that he had decided to make his life in Africa ('I absolutely believe in this West African pottery idea').[24] And to compound matters he informed her that he had arranged for her 'allotment' to be terminated:

> But I must keep this money as capital for starting the new pottery, and then as soon as I begin to earn something I'll send you as much as I can, and consignments of the best pots when we make them. [...] If I come home now I should be miserable, and would be sure to make you and the boys miserable as well.[25]

In his later years Michael Cardew reflected on his decision and his motives; quite simply he had been overtaken by an obsession which made him

> absolutely selfish and totally impervious to any argument about what was just, or right, or proper. [...] Everything we do springs as much from our faults and failings as from our strength and courage, like fruits and flowers nourished by compost and dirt as much as by the sun and the rain.[26]

In 1948 he returned to Wenford where he remained for four years. In 1951 he was appointed by the Nigerian Government to the post of pottery officer, setting up a pottery and training centre at Abuja in northern Nigeria and working and teaching there for fourteen years. (In 1964 he was awarded the MBE.) Occasionally, when he was granted leave by the Nigerian Government, he would visit the family in England.

Prompted and encouraged by their mother the boys sustained their relationship with their father as best they could. On one occasion Seth found a pipe in the river, cleaned and dried it and sent it to his father explaining that it had cost him nothing – justification for what might otherwise have been regarded as an extravagant gesture. For the family was impoverished and the boys were all acutely aware of the lack of money. On another occasion, sometime after the end of the war, with Michael's return imminent, a welcome home fund was set up and fifteen shillings was raised by concerts which included their own pieces and arrangements: Mariel on recorder, Uncle Philip on viola, Seth on clarinet, and Cornelius on piano.[27] A banner was made and when Michael finally arrived the reception proved too much for him and he broke down and wept.

During her husband's long absences Mariel loyally endeavoured to nurture the image of their father as a great man, an artistic genius, in the boys' minds. (Cornelius himself, in later years, would describe his father to friends as 'a great man'.) In reality, the boys' relationship with their father grew ever more tenuous; their resentment for his lengthy absences, which were tantamount to abandonment, turning into indifference and even pleasurable anticipation of the holidays, returning home from boarding school, if they knew he would not be there. Life without father was sweeter – they could do without the tensions which Michael created and thrived on. Both Seth and Ennis, in particular, were alienated from their father by his abrasiveness and he could be cruelly scathing towards even his closest family. Cornelius, however, would rise to meet the verbal challenge head-on; his mind could be equally nimble and penetrating, his tongue as waspish as his father's. Cornelius, in fact, boasted two of his father's most outstanding attributes: an incisiveness of mind (a quality which in his later life he was to admire greatly in Lenin) and a determination to control one's own destiny, to lead one's life, to be true to one's own nature and talents regardless of other considerations. It was therefore not surprising that Michael's feelings towards his second son seemed to be unequivocally stronger and more positive. Ennis Cardew recalls Cornelius sitting up at night with his father, reading (by lamplight in those days) and exchanging paragraphs of their books with each other in a very companionable way. There was no such bonding with his other two sons.

After the war was over, in 1945, to supplement the meagre amount (in fact, half his salary) she was now receiving from Michael through the Crown Agents in London, Mariel taught part-time in Launceston and in Bude; her means of transport was a second-hand motor-bike – a 'dangerous and unreliable vehicle' according to Michael Cardew. She also developed a friendship with the writer Rumer Godden (both of them had young children); it was an important period in Mariel's life, when she became acquainted, through Godden, with the work of Ouspensky – who was still alive and living in London (although he died in 1947). It was also at this time that she was painting a portrait of an elderly lady in St. Tudy who was impressed by Mariel's talent and gave her one hundred pounds to study at the Byam Shaw Art School in London.

According to Stella Cardew (Cornelius's second wife and mother of his two sons), Michael Cardew was not authoritarian, rather pedagogical. He related to many people, including his own children, in the mode of teacher. He had a middle class upbringing; his parents were Edwardian who looked back in time. They were conscious of their illustrious backgrounds, were versed in the social graces, and this they conveyed more or less subtly to those with whom they came in contact. If Michael Cardew might be described as a patriarchal humanist, his wife had irrepressible, do-gooder instincts; they both respected the idea of class superiority. Their attitude to working class people and to other races (at least in Mariel's case) would have betrayed more than a hint of condescension. One assumes that, around the dinner table at home, at least some of this would have rubbed off on their sons, who may well have challenged some of their parents' observations, whilst taking others for granted. Certainly they would have been shielded from the more unrefined and defiant qualities of proletarian culture. However, Michael Cardew's view of the common man, especially in the wake of his experiences in Africa, would have been more respectful. It was his young African colleague and friend, Kofi Athey, who 'taught him to be human'; the people he lived and worked with in Africa were loving brothers who showed him how much he had missed in life: the complete antithesis to the English bourgeoisie from which he came.[28]

In January 1945 the Choir School moved to Canterbury, which, at that time, in the immediate aftermath of the war, was a run down, depressed and bomb-damaged town.[29] The Choir School itself, which must have been financed on a shoestring, was reasonably well maintained, although in winter – and in particular the bitter winter of 1946/7 – the dormitories were exceptionally cold. And in a country with badly insulated buildings and an almost total reliance on open coal fires (central heating was a virtually unheard-of modern luxury), the situation was exacerbated by fuel shortages and, in some places, considerable bomb damage.

And it was in wintertime during this post war period that many people were afflicted with an ailment known as 'chilblains'. And none more so than the young Cardew. Chilblanes caused swelling, soreness and cracking, usually attacking fingers, toes and ears. Cornelius's fingers, in particular, were badly affected. A contemporary, Gerald Hare,[30] recalls: 'I can see him now, wrapped in an overcoat, with heavy mittens on his hands, sitting down to the piano to practice; removing his mittens to reveal fingerless knitted gloves and courageously forcing himself through his pieces.'[31] Hare also recalls an occasion when his mother had invited Cornelius to tea in Canterbury. He was sat down at their 'battered piano' and asked to play Richard Addinsell's *Warsaw Concerto*, which he read through with consummate and persuasive ease, much to Mrs Hare's delight.

Cardew was also a member of Hare's 'patrol' in the school scout troop; one can only presume that a temporary obeisance to God and the monarch, and to a hierarchical structure which was probably not unduly oppressive, was a price worth paying for a few weeks in the year of camping, fire-lighting, climbing – in short, the simple, open-air life which he had enjoyed as a child and for which from time to time throughout his life he would experience cravings which he would acknowledge and describe in the Journals.

At the Choir School in Canterbury, according to Seth Cardew, the regime was typically harsh and the schedule became even more rigorous – a place where young boys were licked and kicked into shape, where caning was a standard punishment and bullying and being bullied a way of life. Seth recalls his brother at the Choir School:

> Cornelius was a slow dresser, slightly awkward at doing up buttons, tying ties etc. and also slow to rise out of bed. Consequently, he was often late, and was taunted for this, at which point he would weep, after blushing furiously. His nickname was Blubbus because he was always 'blubbing' [weeping]. He became violent when cornered by other boys, throwing everything (but everything) at his persecutors, and going for the eyes with scissors etc.[32]

Seth Cardew disliked the school with ever-increasing intensity, which he expressed in fighting other boys, and was eventually withdrawn on the headmaster's advice. He subsequently became a boarder at a grammar school in Midhurst, Sussex, where he was later joined by his brother Ennis. Cornelius, probably by dint of a greater commitment to music, managed to adapt and survive.[33]

In response to my request for his memories of the Choir School, and the King's School, Canon Roger Job, Cardew's contemporary, sent me the following lively and evocative account. I immediately determined that any kind of editorial intervention from myself could only diminish its compelling authenticity, although I have made some alterations in the sequence of his narrative. I begin with Roger Job's timetable – the day in the life of a chorister – and at the end of his account I add an outline of the structure and duties of the Choir:

7.30 Rising bell
7.45 Instrumental practice (there was a piano in almost every room)
8.00 Breakfast (cooked on Tuesdays, Thursdays and Saturdays)
8.35 Choir practice or 'aural' (theory of music: Cor would have had an advanced knowledge of this from a tender age)
9.25 (until Lunch-time) School lessons
There was a mid-morning break and we would be given milk or cocoa, before going out into the Precincts for a scrimmage. After the extensive bomb damage

there was plenty of room for us to let off steam. (Several of the houses on the south side of the cathedral were destroyed.)

1.30 Rest i.e. we went and lay down on our beds and read a book. I suppose the day-boys sat at their desks for a spell of quiet.

1.55 Choir practice and 3.00 Evensong or games. Cor did not shine at these.

4.00 Tea, consisting of bun and milk, then more unstructured leisure outside.

4.15 – 6.00 Lessons

6.15 Supper after which there was free time, except for those with fifteen minute spells of instrumental practice booked.

7.15 Junior bed-time (30 minutes later in summer term)

7.45 Senior bed-time (ditto)

Extra-curricular activities at the Choir School were usually arranged for the boys. We went to the cinema with fair regularity – I recall *David Copperfield*, *Oliver Twist*, *Great Expectations*, *Kind Hearts and Coronets*, *Swiss Family Robinson*. We also went occasionally to live theatre, at Milner Court etc.[34] Concerts in the cathedral. I recall Cor taking the part of Henry Purcell in Sydney Nicholson's opera for choristers plus two adults, *The Children of the Chapel*.[35] Each November the top four boys went up to London for a couple of nights to sing in the annual festival of St Cecilia at St. Sepulchre's church, Holborn Viaduct. Cor certainly did this in 1948 and 1949. We used to stay in a little hotel near Claridge's, where we revelled in the luxury of breakfast in bed. I think the wealthy Musicians' Benevolent Fund paid for these excitements. In 1948 evening entertainments included *The Marriage of Figaro* at Covent Garden and *Murder in the Cathedral* at the Lyric Theatre. The following year we were rather disappointed by Britten's *Let's Make an Opera*. It was too much like a long extra choir practice.

The boys were free – how different things were in those days – to go into the town, shopping in pairs after Saturday Evensong. Only the very newest boys were taken on Sunday walks. Members of the Thirty-Two, numbered 17-32, could go out into the town, again in pairs, on Sundays, either morning or afternoon.

The Choir School food was pretty good. ['The food was probably quite nutritious for the time, but rabbit stew, salty ham were never my favourites'.[36]] Miss Rooke, a Cornishwoman who had followed the boarders back from exile in 1945, did it all and there was a family feeling about it.

The food at King's was fairly awful. Central feeding was the chosen way, not eating in houses, and the results can be imagined.

We were too young to know much about relations between the Choir School and the town. There was certainly a fan club of the choristers. Our favourite play area was an area called Canon Macnutt's.[37] Occasionally it was invaded by town boys whom we called 'thugs'.[38]

As these depredations took place in our absence there was never a serious set-to. The RSCM [Royal School of Church Music] had a sort of undergraduate establishment at Roper House in St Dunstan's [the name of an area of the city]. Some of these young church musicians certainly took an interest in the boys. CP [Clive Pare, the headmaster] always seemed to remain remarkably relaxed. Clive Pare and Gerald Knight (the organist) certainly admired Cor's musicianship. There was a retired prep school headmaster from Sheffield called George Bernard Brinsley Johnson. He had bought a little house on the Stodmarsh Road close to the Sandwich Road and from September 1945 taught Latin in the top three forms. We used to rag him a bit, and I recall Cor's receiving a beating for cheek. A small incident sticks in my mind relating to Cor's last term at the King's School. 'Johnnie' [Brinsley Johnson], by now properly retired, would pole round the town regularly, take ex-choristers out to coffee or tea, giving them half crowns or even ten shillings when they were hard up, which was always. One day Cor and I were the recipients of his kind generosity. Cor said to him, 'You won't be telling your wife about this little get-together, will you?' The old boy was rather put out, and finally, under Cor's pressure, admitted he would probably not be telling his wife all about it. Cor had this streak of ruthlessness, a desire to get the better of people – not a very amiable trait. I was to be on the receiving end not much later when I stayed at Wenford Bridge.[39]

The 'Sixteen' (two rows of eight choristers – *Cantoris* and *Decani*) was the choir for high days and weekends and consisted of the most senior boys in the school; in fact, almost all the boys reached the 'Sixteen' in due course. The 'Thirty-Two' was also called the Merbecke choir (after the sixteenth century composer John Merbecke), which sang the one weekly service for boys' voices only; the same boys were divided into Tallis and Gibbons choirs for weekdays in term time. Both Boarder choir and Dayboy choir (the Choir School consisted of a more or less equal number of dayboys and boarders) sang through the school holidays, except for Easter and Christmas. A boy's position in the choir was determined by annual voice-trials; Cardew became 'corner boy' (a kind of 'lead' singer, chief chorister, to whom the other choristers could refer for entries, for example) while comparatively young, so that when his voice broke and he went on, in 1950, to the King's School, he had held the choir together for two or three years and had 'something of the air of a musical Commander- in-Chief'.[40]

The Choir School and the King's School were completely separate establishments, although they shared the same governing body – that is, the Dean and Chapter (a Dean, who was the chairman, and four Canons). The relationship between them seems to have been extremely flexible, such that the King's School would take new boys in any of the three terms, as it was deemed convenient or advisable, and presumably according to when a boy's voice began to break. Boys normally sat the Common Entrance exam to King's at the age of thirteen although many choristers, including Cardew, took it late. There were also academic scholarships although, given his reputation, it would have been surprising if Cardew had been the recipient of any award. Cardew took his 'O' level exams in the summer of 1952, after barely two years at King's, and 'A' level a year later in July 1953 where he attained a Distinction in English (in which he shone, according to his contemporaries) and a Double Distinction in Music.

At the King's School Cardew was placed in The Grange, a boarding-house on the south side of the Mint Yard, and he and David Sladen, who was to become a life-long friend, were in the same tutorial group, of around sixteen boys, with a Mr Mackintosh.[41] In 1952 they were moved to the senior part of the House, the Hall, a huge room with twenty or so desks in it. One entered by a side door; Cardew had a window desk on the right hand side. Subsequently, about nine boys, including Cardew and Sladen were put in a Study called The Lower Study which was separated from the main meeting room of the House, which was where evening prayers were held. The Lower Study was coveted by all the boys simply because it was very difficult for people in authority to enter it without announcing their approach, along the corridor outside, through the door, and then down the stairs inside the Study. So the boys had time to stop activities and put away articles and objects of dubious educational value and pretend that they were engaged in some legitimate academic pursuit. The Lower Study (or 'The Lower', as it was referred to) thus acquired a reputation; if you had the good fortune to be placed there, you automatically became a rebel.

A day at the King's School certainly bore resemblance to a day at the Choir School; in this respect there was a continuity which, presumably, helped the new younger boys to adapt. The day began with breakfast followed by a solidly traditional form of prayers lasting fifteen minutes or more in the Chapter House: a psalm sung to an Anglican chant, a scripture reading (Authorized Version) by a senior boy, and prayers recited (from memory) by the Headmaster. Lessons ensued until 1pm.

Most afternoons were devoted to seasonal sports: rugby, hockey, cricket, and occasionally athletics. Thursdays were given over to the CCF (Combined Cadet Force) although Ronald Smith's piano lessons took precedence even over the military. On Mondays, Wednesdays and Fridays there would be two fifty-minute periods of lessons after sports. On Saturdays, too, there would be lessons until lunchtime, followed by matches in the afternoon, sometimes against other schools.

Cardew would have systematically avoided the afternoon sports sessions, and the CCF, through his genuine and determined commitment to music. Afternoons would have been spent practising the piano and cello, taking instrumental and music theory lessons and his first steps in the world of musical composition. And in the evenings there would be regular orchestral practice sessions in which he would play the cello (his teacher was Nancy White). Supper at 7 pm was according to Roger Job the best meal of the day (although certainly way below present-day nutritional standards); private study (Prep) followed from 7.30 to 8.45 (9.30 for the older boys) and lights out, at 10 pm, was preceded by a bible reading and brief prayers. Sundays, naturally, saw a different programme; it is unlikely that Cardew would have attended the voluntary Holy Communion service at 7.45, although he would have sung in the cathedral service at 10 am, taken part in school orchestra practice from 11.15 until lunchtime, and would have sung again in Evensong at 6 pm.

David Sladen recalls Cardew's behaviour at school as 'stand-offish', rather than rebellious; his considerable maturity set him apart and he seemed to view the school with cynical detachment, self-consciously going his own way, leading his own life, refusing to identify with the normal, day-to-day routines of the House. Cardew's 1955 Journal seems to reflect back on this: 'Motto for the year. Be an observer rather than a participator: only participate under your own careful observation.' Rather than opposing the public school system to which, in any case, he was not entirely averse, he preferred to side-step it and to remain unaffected by its expectations. There were occasional clashes with the school authorities but in the main his considerable self-assuredness enabled him to stand aloof from it. Although he was essentially a loner – Sladen recalls him walking around with music under his arm, sloping off hands in pockets towards the music school – he had a small group of friends, some of whom, like Roger Job and Tim Clarke, had come through with him from the Choir School, while others, Ian Maitland, Graham Tew and one or two others, he had befriended later and they were not necessarily musical.

Maitland, Tew and Cardew belonged to a rebellious and intrepid brotherhood known as the 'stuntmen' for whom the cathedral building was the ideal challenge: 'Between the interior and exterior was a locked and forbidden warren of stairways and passages and enormous vaulted roof spaces filled with dust and cobwebs and pigeons and jackdaw shit.'[42] On one occasion the three stuntmen 'took the iron fire escape ladder route up the outside and across a narrow mossy plank bridging nave and transept at the corner of Bell Harry tower. This was a 'stunt'; we were 'stuntmen', sixty feet above the heads of watchful vergers'.[43] On another occasion, the stuntmen were hitch-hiking to smog-bound London when they decided to board a train, ticketless, from Woolwich Arsenal to Charing Cross. At the exit Tew passed through unnoticed; Cardew was stopped, but according to Tew, by the simple expedient of producing his post office savings book his fellow stuntman was allowed through – a ploy which clearly the ticket-collector had never previously encountered and which temporarily relieved him of his sense of civic responsibility.[44]

Ronald Smith, a virtuoso pianist of international fame, although still under thirty, began to teach piano at the King's School in the summer of 1951 and Cardew was one of those selected to take lessons with him.[45] According to Roger Job:

His playing went from strength to strength. I recall a memorable performance of Mendelssohn's *Andante and Rondo Capriccioso*. There was also a wonderful account of a chamber work, a trio or a quartet, but I regret I cannot now name it. Ronald of course groomed Cor for his Academy entrance exam. It was typical of Cor that he should have said he wished to play atonal Schoenberg pieces.[46] Very well, he was told, they must be memorized. And they were. There was some discussion about what might have been in the composer's mind when he wrote these works. Although the words would not conceivably have been used, I gather the answer was, the sex act, probably in sordid circumstances.[47]

At the King's School David Sladen recalls that Cardew would always stop playing if an unexpected visitor entered his room; it was as if an act of privacy, on which the cultivation of the relationship to the instrument depended and which he had no desire to share, had been interrupted. Already in his teens his attitude to music and music-making was unconventional, ascetic. The desire and need to play for someone was lacking; he balked at the idea of giving pleasure through his Art even if, in the Journals, paradoxically, he occasionally claims Taoist credentials. Richard Bennett (a friend and contemporary at the Royal Academy of Music) recalls that he seemed more interested in the ideas behind the music than the music itself – a view that is substantiated in Cardew's compositional practice in the sixties, in particular.

Already during his schooldays Cardew seemed to be conscious of himself as a special, unusually gifted person who was marked out in some way and who sought to express a gift which was palpable yet undefined, enigmatic. Certainly he did not project himself conventionally as an artist on whom an appropriate status should be accorded, even as a young man. Unlike his peers he had a profound understanding of what Art was, whether painting, literature, music. And he was a precocious reader, devouring Dumas and then Aldous Huxley well ahead of his contemporaries. Roger Job recalls that Cardew talked of 'mastering the art of prose-writing [...] Thought it would be a good idea to copy out a page or two of e.g. *Point Counterpoint* to see how it was done'.[48]

Certainly all this had been encouraged and instilled by an upbringing which was permeated by Art of the highest quality. At breakfast time in Wenford he held it in the shape of the mug from which he drank; in reflective moments its presence nurtured and refined the sensibilities; at night certain resonances would accompany him to bed. So Art was breathed in naturally, unconsciously, and Cardew was an 'unconscious' artist. Small wonder then that, in David Sladen's words, 'he treated Art lightly'; the idea of ambition, and the pursuit of reward, success, fame which fuels the 'bourgeois' artist's *raison d'être* was never part of Cardew's cosmology. One might ask therefore: to what extent was he actually 'a musician' in the accepted sense of that designation? My hope is that this book may provide some kind of answer. To say that in his teens he already demonstrated that he was intensely 'musical' seems inadequate. To recall, as some have, that he played the piano 'beautifully' evokes the sensuality associated with touch, of the instrument and of the human body; the erotic: Roland Barthes described the finger-pad as the most erotic part of the pianist's body. We are entering, perhaps, more meaningful territory.

By the time they reached the sixth form, Cardew and Sladen were close friends. Sladen recalls that Cardew did not work particularly hard; he certainly developed his intellect, learning to analyse and criticise English prose and excelling in English and History in his Advanced Level examinations. But he had no academic ambitions and seemed indifferent to examinations for which, in his case, a minimum of work would usually suffice.

Yet it was clear, and not least to himself, that he was more interesting, and had more artistic potential than any of his peers, a presumption which he (and Sladen) attributed to his upbringing in Cornwall. He boasted a maturity far in excess of his schoolmates which enabled him, with just sixteen or seventeen years of life-experience, to assess people and their various capacities and to grasp some of the realities which informed the world beyond the cloistered and repressive confines of the English public school. David Sladen's view was that Cardew should not have been at school; it was an irrelevance and he transcended it, merely observing the absurd rituals that his peers enacted at the bidding of individuals who themselves were the willing victims of an arbitrary (abstract) system.[49]

According to Sladen even the headmaster, Canon John Shirley (known to the boys as 'Fred'), could not disguise his scepticism in relation to the authoritarian structure which affected all aspects of life in the school. Cardew did not deliberately break rules and get into trouble by trying to undermine and compromise the system; it was a situation he had been placed in, but which was of no intrinsic importance. He simply paid no attention to it; he ignored it and went his own way. He even managed to subvert the school uniform which fortuitously lent itself to the teddy-boy style of dress which he favoured.[50] Roger Job recalls that the tie he wore boasted 'a huge, non-U knot' and he wore a ring of stunning vulgarity – 'really ugly'. In the schoolboy we can discern the lineaments of the mature man. According to Paul Pollak, a contemporary of Cardew, whose name he chose not to divulge, offered the *aperçu*: 'I recall Cardew as a classmate whose sense of social, or even mere human obligations, seemed almost wholly undeveloped.'

Towards the end of his school career he was seeing a local girl, whom he claimed to have slept with, and such a relationship, with a member of the opposite sex, would in itself have separated him from the majority of his public school peers. David Sladen recalls walking with him to St Martin's, a suburb of Canterbury, one night; they stopped and Cardew threw pebbles up at a window. There was no response; perhaps the girl was sound asleep, or was two-timing her schoolboy with somebody who had financial assets and prospects which Cardew could not match. In any case, Cardew's behaviour was completely beyond the public school pale. Even more heroic, according to the late Tony Wright, one of his music teachers at the King's School, was his alleged seduction of one of the school matrons; David Sladen had also heard this story, commenting ruefully, 'he was certainly sexually more mature than the rest of us',[51] but discounts it. Paul Pollack, who was a young teacher at the school at the time, insists that the notion was the result of an outrageous fantasy (on the part of Tony Wright or Cardew himself), with no possible relation to historical reality, although he concedes, or rather suggests, that Cardew may have found temporary release for his youthful libido amongst ladies lower down the pecking order of the School's auxiliary staff.

Cardew was regarded as being highly artistic, yet without being a conscious artist in any particular field, even music, although his musical performances at school earned him praise. Reporting the King's School end-of-term concert on 1 April 1952, *The Times* referred to 'Cornelius Cardew, another pianist with real feeling for the instrument'. His contemporary Roger Job recalls that Cardew was an 'outstanding musician', the 'best pianist in the school' and a 'first-rate sight-reader [...] I can still hear him playing through the Mozart sonatas each evening on the grand piano in the Third form room'.[52] He was also a competent cellist. Above all, at an early age he recognized Art and understood it.

David Sladen reflects, 'maybe he hated King's and stored up that hate'.[53] Perhaps his experiences there did in fact colour his view of society more than he admitted to himself at the time. Sladen's recollection is that Cardew was neither happy nor unhappy at school; after all, he had his small group of friends and admirers. Indeed, Ruth Koenig (his first wife) recalls his pride at having been a pupil at King's, along with a certain degree of 'snobbishness' about education. He would have been aware that such an education would provide easier access to the world for its privileged students. In this respect, in spite of himself, Cardew did benefit, materially and intellectually, from the education that he had received. Of course, one can argue, as he did, that the disadvantages seriously outweighed the advantages. And this is one of the recurring themes in the latter part, in particular, of this book.

The earliest surviving composition dates from his school days in Canterbury in the early fifties, part of a grandiose project for an opera based on Shelley's *Prometheus Unbound* in collaboration with David Sladen who, however, did not feel able at the time to take on the responsibility of librettist. Act 2, Scenes 1 and 2 exist in short score for solo voices, two pianos and parts for solo clarinet and solo cello – the latter written with a genuine feel for the instrument's expressive qualities. Here and there ideas for instrumentation are pencilled in. The few pages are of little musical significance but there are several bold, cadential phrases and imaginative touches; occasionally, a promising young composer emerges.

Cardew left the King's School in the summer of 1953 armed, or rather encumbered with a remarkable report written by Canon Shirley, the headmaster. It is a document which perhaps reflects more upon the writer and the institution and culture within which power, authority and respect were conferred upon him, than upon the subject – a seventeen year-old boy whom he damns in an extraordinarily savage act of excommunication. According to Roger Job, Canon Shirley had told him that the Headmaster of the Choir School, the Reverend Pare, had also been relieved when Cardew moved on: 'couldn't get rid of him soon enough'.[54]

> One of the most difficult boys I ever knew – shy, reticent, introvert, self-centred, obnoxious to most people; lacking graciousness and humility; got into some bad scrapes,[55] and everyone was glad when he left, for his sense of his individual worth made him rebellious; and he collected a small gang whom he made like-minded to himself. His brain was of brilliant calibre, but he could be bothered to work only at the things he liked and which came easy.[56]

Roger Job identifies two lesser scrapes:

> There was a famous occasion in the summer term of 1952 when Shirley put up a notice saying: Orchard robbers see me. F.J.S.
> There had been some quite large-scale cherry scrumping just outside the town. Cor was one of over sixty boys beaten on a Sunday afternoon. Some time later

Shirley was to beat him again for 'Playing the mandolin in prep'.[57]

Job also refers to some letters to him from Canon Shirley in which there are two references to Cardew: the first claims that the headmaster had 'a nice letter' from his recalcitrant student when he left school – presumably before Cardew had read the above-quoted report.[58]

In a much later letter, dated 16 January 1963, the mood swings yet again:

A very tiresome ex-chorister and OKS – most tiresome creature – before your time, I think; I didn't know what had happened to him – anything could, for I don't think he possessed a moral scruple – anyway, he has an article in today's Financial Times on some sort of very modern music.[59]

It was typical of Cardew that on leaving school the inconvenience of two years National Service (compulsory for any able-bodied young man at that time) was avoided not by confrontation (as a conscientious objector like his brother Seth, for example, whose registration was not accepted – an outcome which may well have served as a warning to his brother), but by the simple ploy of failing to sign on – a small but crucial act of submission on which the authorities relied for their conscription lists. In September 1953 Cardew became a student at the Royal Academy of Music (with some financial support provided by his parents), sharing a one-room bed-sitter with his brother Seth in Colville Square in west London until December 1954, when Seth was called up for National Service.

Notes and references

1 Michael Cardew left Oxford (Exeter College) in 1923 where he had been an average, half-hearted student with little or no enthusiasm for his subject (Greats had probably been chosen for him by his father). Since boyhood he had decided that pottery would be his life and this ambition sustained him during the four years of uncongenial academic study. Free at last he went to study and work with the potter Bernard Leach at St. Ives in Cornwall: 'I spent nearly three years (1923-26) at the Leach pottery, the most important part of my education as a potter [...] What I learnt there I certainly learnt profoundly; but almost painlessly, almost unconsciously, as if in spite of myself.' *A Pioneer Potter,* (Oxford: Oxford University Press, 1989), p.29.

2 Slightly less prominent in the reception committee were Sidney and Charlie Tustin, and Elijah Comfort; they were mainly farm labourers and fruit pickers from the Vale of Evesham – men who would turn their hands to any work associated with the land. They were also regarded as friends.

3 'Beano' was Katherine Pleydell – Bouverie, daughter of the Earl of Radnor; she was a close friend of Michael Cardew's and a fellow student at the Leach Pottery in the Twenties.

4 *A Pioneer Potter*, p.88.

5 Ibid, p.68.

6 Cornelius (Cardew) was an ancestor, a clergyman in Cornwall during the second part of the 18th century; McDonough was the name of a maternal uncle. The name Cornelius boasts a more remote, more exotic provenance: when Italian Jews, forced to rename their (Hebrew) children, were offered options by their Catholic rulers, the name Cornelius, with eli at its centre, became one of the most popular choices of Jewish mothers.

7 Alan Griffiths entered the Catholic Church and Benedictine Priory at Prinknash Abbey in Gloucestershire as Dom Bede Griffiths and described his experiences in his book *The Golden Spring* (London: Harvill Press,1954).

8 Letter from SC to JT, 1 January 1990.

9 *Pioneer Potter,* p.109.

10 'Both my parents used their clothes until, after much repair, and button replacements, they fell apart; and [they] lived frugally…' Email communication from SC to JT, 21 October 2004.

11 Letter from SC to JT, 14 May 1986.

12 Letter from SC to JT, 16 January 1991.

13 Letter from SC to JT, 14 May 1986.

14 Mariel's older sister Olga, who became Mrs Mansfield by marriage, 'was very taken with Cornelius as a child, and often sought out ways to help his career along as a choir boy, King's man and Royal Academy student, sometimes in the way of food parcels and maybe money presents too'. Email communication from SC to JT, 31 August 2004.

15 Letter from SC to JT, 1 January 1990.

16 Email communication from Ennis Cardew to JT, 16 February 2005.

17 Ibid.

18 'Mariel was one of my mother's best friends [...] a calm wise-woman type who inspired love in all who knew her. My mother was not the most assertive personality, she was a fine pianist and a very sensitive person and in Mariel she found someone without 'side' who genuinely cared for her friends. There were fairly frequent visits of Cardews to Varcoes and

vice versa. My father and Michael were great friends through love of music and knowledge of minerals. Mariel often said to us – we met her through the years both in Cornwall and in Barnes where we too were living – that she didn't understand Cor's music but she was there to support him in any way she could (What a wonderful example of motherhood.) Email communication from Mary Varcoe's son, Jonathan, to JT, August 2004.

19   During one of her visits to Wenford, a friend of Mariel Cardew, Elizabeth Perrett, who taught music at Mayortorne Farmhouse School for Girls in Wendover, Buckinghamshire during the war, gave instruction to Cornelius and Seth on how to sing for their entrance audition for the Cathedral Choir School. Clearly, she had instructed them well.

20   If there were any references to God in the Cardew household they would rarely have extended beyond Michael Cardew's exclamations, such as 'Allah ya kai mu' ('God Willing'), and were usually in a foreign tongue. Staple reading matter would have been *Iliad* and *Odyssey*, rather than the *Bible*.

21   *A Pioneer Potter,* p.120.

22   The beginning of 1945, on 29 January, saw the death of the beloved Nanny Mason who had been living in Michael's sister's house in Leatherhead, Surrey.

23   *A Pioneer Potter,* p.156.

24   Ibid, p.166.

25   Ibid, p.167.

26   Ibid, p.167.

27   Michael Cardew described Philip Cardew as 'easily my favourite brother'; his sons, too, admired and looked up to their uncle Philip. A charismatic, talented musician, with a penchant for fast cars, Philip Cardew abandoned the classical orthodoxy to become an established band leader and arranger. For most of his life he lived in an impressive five-story Regency house in Regent's Park Terrace, Camden Town. His nephews loved and admired him, wished to emulate him and to share his life-style. Mariel, who was intolerant of her brother-in-law's undisguised homosexuality, countered her sons' enthusiasm: 'Uncle Philip is not a happy man', she cautioned them.

28   Stella Cardew draws an interesting analogy: Michael Cardew saw Kofi Athey like DH Lawrence saw women: it was to do with earth and nature, grace and humanity.

29   Roger Job, one of Cardew's school friends, recalls a seedy junk shop in Palace Street whose proprietor was named Dirty Dick by the boys.

30   Gerald Hare attended both the Choir School and the King's School. He was a year older than Cardew but they were friends in the early years before their academic choices separated them and they eventually lost contact. Hare went on to become a nuclear physicist and worked for UK Atomic Energy and subsequently in nuclear medicine with Atomic Energy in Canada.

31   Email communication from Gerald Hare to JT, 16 November 2004.

32   Letter from SC to JT, 1 January 1990.

33   Not every past student from the Choir School and the King's School concurs with Seth Cardew's characterisations. According to ex-student Roger Job, whom I quote at length below, it would be a travesty to describe the Choir School as 'a miserable place, where sadistic bullying was the order of the day. [...] When there *was* an outbreak of bullying, ca. 1947, C. Pare [Clive Pare, the headmaster] came down on it like a ton of bricks'. Email communication to JT, 1 November 2004. Regarding sex there was certainly a degree of

commerce, of experimentation, between older and younger boys, although mainly between equals, that is, within peer groups. Such behaviour still seems to be generally regarded, rightly or wrongly, as part of the rough-and-tumble of everyday life at an English public school. There is no need to pursue the subject any further except perhaps to speculate to what extent Cardew himself was affected by it, then and in later life. Roger Job recalls hearing Cardew 'bemoan the fact that a monastic school environment promoted homosexuality' (Ibid), and there is, as we shall see, the occasional equivocal reference to his own sexuality in the Journals. As for bullying, none of his peers have any recollection of Cardew's involvement, either as perpetrator or as victim. He was probably too 'streetwise', too aware of the need to cultivate self-preservation in such an environment, to have been drawn into that particular symptom of public school culture.

34 Milner Court, named after Alfred, Lord Milner, was the Junior King's School at Sturry, just outside Canterbury.

35 'His character was a boyhood Henry Purcell and he had two main solos, one about home sickness with the plaintive refrain "Oh! I want to go home to my mother!" which broke the hearts of all the elderly ladies who were stalwart fans of the show. The other was a song set to the tune Lillibulero. [...] With his cherubic face and shock of hair, this quite devastated the same ladies'. Email communication from Gerald Hare to JT, 16 November 2004.

36 From a later e-mail from Roger Job to JT.

37 Canon Macnutt was a Chaplain to the Queen and a canon of Canterbury cathedral until 1945.

38 The relationship between the school and the town was characterised by a mixture of alienation, resentment, mistrust, curiosity; lines were drawn which could not be crossed – a kind of 'standoff': thus a boy could not leave the school premises unless he were in full regalia.

39 Email communication from Roger Job to JT, August 2004.

40 Letter from SC to JT, 1 January 1990.

41 Roger Job recalls that at the end of the summer term of 1951 his house master, Francis Voigt, informed him that he had been invited by the Archdeacon of Canterbury and his sister to lodge with them at 29 The Precincts, Chillenden Chambers. (This use of accommodation in private houses enabled the headmaster to squeeze more boarders into the school's premises.) Were there two boys he would like to take with him, Mr Voigt asked, adding with emphasis – 'not Cardew'.

42 Letter from Graham Tew to JT, 16 September 2004.

43 Ibid.

44 Cardew's propensity for risk and danger was one of his most formidable character traits; we shall encounter it time and time again, in different guises and contexts, throughout the pages of this book.

45 Ronald Smith (b. London, 1922; d. Kent, 2004). Pianist, composer; specialist in the music of Alkan, about whom he wrote several books.

46 Paul Pollak, who was a young teacher at the King's School at the time, recalls that it was after his teacher had introduced Cardew to the music of Schoenberg, according to Smith, that 'the rot set in'.

47 Email communication from Roger Job to JT, 10 August 2004.

48   Ibid.

49   However, his brother refutes this thesis; in an undated letter from the early sixties Seth Cardew wrote, apparently in response to a communication from his brother: 'Now to come to your retardment. Your attitude is based on the public school type to which you have been conditioned (I have also been conditioned, don't mistake me), and our problem, I have discovered, since we are both retarded, is that we are not able to form profound relationships with people.' Arguably, this *was* the case with Cardew. As we shall see, there were serious relations with women. But were they 'profound relationships', by which I mean a deep *mutuality* of empathy and feeling?

50   Roger Job's comprehensive description of the King's School uniform reads as follows: 'Canterbury Dress was worn for cathedral services on Sundays and on all formal occasions. It consisted of black shoes, grey or black socks, pinstripe trousers (various patterns were around), black jacket, white shirt, wing collar and black tie (not bow). For visits to the shops etc. boaters were *de rigueur*. To go into the town required the house master's permission. For school we wore the above, but with grey trousers. After lunch we could wear a blue school tie in place of the black tie. In the summer term, school blazers could be worn with a school tie after lunch. Scholars (like David Sladen) wore a gown. A Music Scholar like Cor did not qualify.' Letter to JT, 17 September 2004.

51   From a recorded interview with JT sometime in the eighties.

52   Letter from Roger Job to JT, 17 September 2004.

53   From a recorded interview with JT sometime in the eighties.

54   Letter from Roger Job to JT, 17 September 2004.

55   Graham Tew describes one such 'scrape', an attempted joyride, which took place one night in Canterbury and involved Cardew, Ian Maitland and Tew himself: 'The Sunbeam was parked in the cinema car park. It was the first unlocked car we came to. Which was unfortunate for two reasons. Firstly the driver, Ian, had no experience of steering column changes and would fail to find reverse when it really was needed. Secondly, as the car was approaching the exit, a friend of its owner just happened to be driving in. The entrance being narrow, the two cars were unable to pass, the other driver recognised his friend's car, and the three musketeers were forced to abandon vehicle, sprinting off into the night in separate directions.' The next day the headmaster accompanied the three boys to Canterbury police station. He assured the police that the boys would be dealt with in the appropriate manner, which would certainly have involved a beating.

56   Mariel Cardew described the headmaster bitterly as 'a sadist' – an opinion which she imparted to me in passing in one of our conversations and with which others, who knew him better, concurred; David Sladen recollects that whilst the Head was a complex and idiosynchratic personality, he did seem to like the boys who were rebels and would overrule some of the punishments that had been meted out by members of his staff, bizarrely protecting them from his own school. Curiously, he did value those pupils (including Cardew) who were eccentric or original in some way. Sladen's assessment may go some way towards explaining the headmaster's subsequent letter. According to Seth Cardew Canon Shirley wrote a letter of apology and reconciliation to his brother in the wake of his report, but it has not come to light. Roger Job confesses that the report came as a surprise: 'It overstates the prosecution case against Cor. Of that I am certain.' Letter to JT, 17 September 2004.

57   Email communication from Roger Job to JT, August 2004.

58   However, it appears that there was an intervening letter, between the head's report and Cardew's 'nice letter', which, as Seth Cardew recalls, 'mollified his previous salvos; I remember the situation in which Cornelius showed it to me; we were in the "School" room here [at Wenford] and lighting the stove that heated the room one cold day. I have the feeling it was written to him, and very much man to man; that he felt he may have mis-judged him following some conversation with another cleric who was more of an educationist than he was, and understood that sometimes, indeed often, talented people put the backs up of their elders by their manners which the elders do not consider to be sufficiently polite or subservient. Anyhow that was the flavour of the letter, which was then used to help light the stove'. Email communication from Seth Cardew to JT, 31 August 2004. Perhaps the 'nice letter' from Cardew was in response to this expiatory letter from Canon Shirley.

59   Quoted by Roger Job in the aforementioned e-mail communication, August 2004.

Cornelius Cardew a life unfinished

2

Royal Academy of Music 1953–57

Like the King's School, the Academy's influence on Cardew was probably negligible; he suffered the conservatism and exploited the liberalism by leading a dual existence – satisfying the demands the Academy made on him whilst pursuing his real interests, which were by no means only musical, and which offered excitement and excess. In this respect he was probably better equipped than most of his peers and, moreover, knew to what this faculty was attributable. 'I had a frugal upbringing (but with infrugal liberty, muculence etc. – and mental armament.'[1]

At the Academy he was to find kindred spirits: bold, restless young souls for whom the future of music lay beyond the walls of the Royal Academy of Music and the English musical establishment and, indeed, beyond the English shores. For the future was of no concern to the RAM – nor, for that matter, was the present; it stood as a fortress of Western musical history and pre-eminence in which the classical heritage was jealously guarded. The overthrow of tonality and its attendant risks, including the undermining of tried and tested criteria, was a foolhardy act spawned in continental Europe and therefore highly suspect.

Yet it was to just this foolhardiness that Cardew committed himself as a young, inexperienced composer. It is unlikely that he had received any grounding either in compositional technique or serial analysis before he came to the Academy, and his knowledge of the contemporary repertoire would have been decidedly sketchy. It was a mark of his single-mindedness and keen intelligence that when he left the Academy in July 1957 his understanding of the most recent serial techniques, as Karlheinz Stockhausen has remarked, was second to none.

In fact the study of serialism had been Cardew's overriding preoccupation at the Academy, in particular Webern and the post-Webern serialists: 'See Richard [Bennett] in the morning for quite a time and we talk about new serial techniques and about Webern, as usual.'[2] The manuscript books he was using at the Academy also bear witness to this; numbered I to VIII (although only III, IV, and VII are extant) they contain academic contrapuntal exercises, sketches for compositions, completed compositions, including the *Second String Trio* and the *Second Piano Sonata* (both serial), piano reductions of the aforementioned string trio and of Webern's *Variations*, op.30, numerous tone rows, their transpositions and segmentation, and analytical material.

From the beginning his progress was rapid although it was not only his compositional prowess and grasp of contemporary techniques which impressed, as his composition teacher, Howard Ferguson, recalls: 'But even more interesting to me was the sensitivity and instinctive musical understanding with which, during our lessons, he would play a Bach prelude and fugue or a Schubert impromptu.'[3] Cardew's Bach playing drew praise from many quarters,[4] including his brother Seth, a perceptive amateur musician who particularly admired his brother's ability to 'bring out the submerged rhythms'[5] in Bach's music in a way which few performers could emulate. Cardew's feeling for Bach was also recognized by Paul Steinitz; Cardew was a member of the London Bach Society Choir, which Steinitz had founded and conducted, and provided manuscript copies of a composite basso continuo part of several of Bach's double-choir motets (that is, determining what was the actual, real bass at any given moment), which have remained in use.

It would be an exaggeration to describe the student Cardew as an *enfant terrible* (a reputation he did acquire in musical circles, but later); there were several professors at the Academy, apart from his composition teacher, who recognized and encouraged his talents, but at that time the RAM was not an institution where unconventional talents were given full rein and could blossom. When Cardew and Richard Rodney Bennett, at the age of 19, gave the first English performance of Boulez's *Structures I* (for two pianos) at the Academy it might have been construed as an act of rebellion, except that the rebellion was probably not even noticed. Rather, it was his physical appearance that attracted attention: tall (around six foot) and slim, with long, curly hair (before anybody had long hair); he wore very rough tweeds and outsize jackets – one was a bottle green corduroy, with wide, padded shoulders, low pockets, sleeves a little too short. The garments appeared to be hand-me-downs: ill-fitting, 'home-made', yet were sported with a certain arrogance, in particular the dark red scarf, tied around bohemian style.

Bennett and Cardew were both members of a new music group formed at the Academy and which included, among others, Susan Bradshaw, Howard Snell, Ruth Aaronberg, Josephine Nendick (who, in fact, was studying at the Guildhall School of Music and Drama at the time), Julian Lee and Alan Cohen.[6] The group had no official recognition and independently organized concerts featuring their own music, the European avant-garde – in particular Webern and Boulez, and more traditional music, such as Poulenc and Copland. They also made contact with the Royal Northern College of Music in Manchester and collaborated with the contemporary music group there: among its members were Alexander Goehr, Harrison Birtwistle, Peter Maxwell Davies, and the pianist John Ogdon.

The Bennett/Cardew duo performed sonatas by Gieselher Klebe, Poulenc, and the novelist and composer Paul Bowles, and Cardew himself played the Copland *Piano Variations*. Throughout his life his accomplished piano playing was one of his greatest assets – he was also an excellent sight-reader – and was complemented by the propensity at all stages of his career to write for the instrument for which he felt such a strong affinity.[7] 'Then John [John Hewetson, a friend and General Practitioner in Southwark, South London] played me records [of Beethoven piano sonatas]. Schnabel op.101 and 110 and Fischer op.110. The Schnabel was terrific. Left me writhing.'[8]

But the obsession with serialism amongst Cardew's circle of friends at the Academy was such that most other musical matters were marginalised, although there was more to it than simply the acquisition and mastery of a new compositional technique. Centred in Darmstadt, in what was then West Germany, which Cardew visited whilst still a student at the Academy, the European avant-garde paraded some progressive slogans; serialism itself was associated with the scientific method, with progress and discovery; some apologists, such as the French composer/conductor Rene Leibowitz, claimed that the new compositional method was the equivalent of the classless society. John Cage observed that 'Schoenberg's method is analogous to a society in which the emphasis is on the group and the integration of the individual in the group'.[9] More traditionally-orientated composers, such as Benjamin Britten and Dmitri Shostakovich, who were not writing serial music, were for that reason not regarded as composers at all – were, in fact, figures of ridicule in avant-garde circles. The serialists received support and praise from high places; funds were made available and the leading protagonists were glamorous, charismatic and highly motivated.

Cardew's Journals from his Academy days abound with philosophical and aesthetic ideas and questioning; a pervasive high-spiritedness and lightness of touch do not detract from an underlying seriousness. Some of the attitudes and beliefs scattered randomly throughout the Journals take root, and their development and transformation help to plot the course of his musical and philosophical thought. 'I am on my way to Cornwall and liberty, which means so much to me, which I really love – the liberty to cut myself off, to be alone, and to communicate with nobody, except on M.S. paper.'[10] And as we shall see, no composer has given more consideration to the problems, to the art, of communicating on manuscript paper.

Yet when he chose to, Cardew could use words with economy and to telling effect; occasionally, in the earlier Journals there is a typical, incisive thrust – an illumination, which in later years became his trademark. And even close friends would be the butt of his *bons mots*: 'Ruth [Aaronberg] has put on the armour of John. She no longer has an Achilles' vagina.'[11] Or he would draw on his verbal resources to make a sardonic comment: 'Richard's [Richard Bennett] latest. It has a lovely sound, Corny!'[12] The jibe at Richard Bennett was not untypical; their friendship was not without an element of tension. There are affectionate references to Bennett in the Journals from the Academy days but at the same time one gets the impression that Cardew felt intimidated and irked by his friend's precocious talent; a competitive element seems to have crept into their relationship, at least on Cardew's side. He writes testily: 'I don't know why he [Bennett] takes lessons; it seems to me all he needs is to get it all down quickly before he gets killed. In a composer's world he might be called a Natural.'[13] Certainly Cardew admired and envied the fluency of Bennett's writing, but this was always tempered by criticism of its content – its lack, as he saw it, of a spirit of adventure. Here his own motives come under scrutiny:

I have been doing Richard an injustice, in my attempts to shirk his superiority. When his work has been technically impeccable I have criticized its content, or character. And when it has shown pronounced content I have criticized its technique, form or whatever (2nd Quartet 'chose forms that required no development section'). I do not mean to admit that my criticisms have been unjustified but that I have made them from the wrong motives – in an attempt to belittle him.[14]

And in a later entry he uses a precise musical example to vent his frustration:

Richard, Ruth and I go to the National Film Theatre to see supernatural *Dead of Night* film. In the queue Richard asks for ideas on tense music for his film. The scene in question is: Main crook goes into cafe to see girl, only witness of their robbery. She must be kept quiet. After $7\frac{2}{3}$ seconds she looks up and recognizes him. I suggested horns sustain high A + C minor third for $7\frac{2}{3}$ seconds, then clarinet and bass clarinet come in sfz with respectively bottom D and E flat major 7th. 7 November. I go and see what Richard has done. It is my idea, but so beautifully handled that I almost didn't recognize it. Horn holds middle D for $7\frac{2}{3}$ seconds, with violin doing agitated rhythmic figures on the same note. Then staccato chord from which emerges D an octave lower with cello rhythm and bass drum roll. It would be good if I could use my ideas as well as that.[15]

For Cardew, even in these relatively early years, the importance of Eastern thought, and in particular ancient Chinese philosophy, cannot be overestimated; according to Seth Cardew his brother's Sinophilia was handed down to him from his father who in turn had received it from his own father who, when he retired from the Civil Service, opened a shop in St. James' and sold chinoiserie. The abundance of quotations from Eastern sources in the Journals reveal the depth and range of Cardew's interest while his comments indicate the extent to which it was reflected in his music-making, in particular the integration he achieved into whatever instrument or sound-source he happened to be using ('at-oneness'), and his esteem for intuitive music-making on even the simplest level. There was already a striving towards directness, towards a subversion of the cultural intervention between ear and instrument, and in this he was both inspired and unsettled by the words of kindred spirits from distant cultures:

For Ruth.
'It is a wonderful experience to attain the object directly through the eye. Most people look through some medium, generally inserting something between the eye and the object. Some interpose their thoughts or their tastes, others their habits.' Soetsu Yanagi, *The Way of Tea*. Surely this is what Ouspensky calls 'identification'.

For Howard [Snell].
'He who would know before he believeth cometh never to the true knowledge of God.' ["nor only God", Cardew inserts here] 'It is the same with the beautiful' says Yanagi, "those who employ their intellect before they see are denied a real comprehension of beauty. [...]
If the eye is clear, it functions promptly. As it penetrates it is free of doubt. Doubt begets thought; thought bedims the eye. [...] Thus seeing is at once believing. [...] the revelation of the reality of the thing induces belief. People free of doubt are bold. The seers therefore make discoveries.
[...] If we are enslaved by Tea, we lose sight of true Tea. Unless we purify our eyes how can we keep Tea pure?
[...] Seeing led them (Tea masters Cha-no-yu[16]) to using, and using to seeing still deeper. Without using there is no complete seeing, for nothing so sets off beauty as right application.
[...] We might say they comprehended it in action. Tea is not a mere appreciation of beauty. To live beauty in our daily lives is the genuine way of Tea".

For me.
Why, since most of the opposite page [the left-hand page of Cardew's exercise book, i.e. the previous quotation] is directly opposed to my principles, does this seem so good to me? Does my principle embrace this, but stipulating the necessity of intellect after vision?[17]

It seemed good to him precisely because it opposed principles which he had temporarily adopted for a variety of reasons – curiosity, fascination, spirit of adventure, fashion – musical principles which, based as they were on the unassailable superiority and prestige of the intellect, served to legitimize the claim that their proponents, and they only, were the true heirs to the European classical legacy. The debate, such as it was, was therefore conducted on a purely intellectual basis, after which winners and losers, composers and non-composers were duly proclaimed.[18] The above quotation, which Cardew chose to include in the Journal, embodied a total negation of the prevailing ethos of the European avant-garde. By substituting 'hearing' for 'seeing', and 'ear' for 'eye', we arrive at a description of the principles which would inform much of Cardew's music-making throughout the sixties: his legendary performances of La Monte Young's music, the radical aesthetic forged by the sound explorations of AMM, and the experimental notations which focused on the twilight zone of the art of performance – the accidental, the half-intended, the blurred sound (in The Great Learning), which the Darmstadt avant-garde, through a dogged, intractable perpetuation of traditional notation, had sought to eliminate.

Occasionally, a spontaneous outburst of enthusiasm, of an intensity which he rarely expressed verbally, finds an outlet in the Journals; two broadcast talks by Isaiah Berlin, for example, met with his hearty approval, especially the second on Belinsky.[19]

God, it was good. Recorded in the lecture theatre this time, with storms of applause at the end, and laughter during the talk etc. – really wonderful. He discussed the underlying pattern and harmony underneath the sordidness of real life in those days – a view which Belinsky borrowed from Hegel. Followed by long talk with Ruth. She says she has faith in me. That makes 3 with Mama and me. What a multitude.[20]

The self-deprecatory exclamation at the end was not untypical of Cardew – nor was self-analysis. A student friend at the Academy had responded positively to some consoling words from him (she had failed to win a prize): 'Veronica says I always know the right thing to say. This is strange because only once in 150 times do I know the right thing to say.'[21] To another young friend, who had philosophically reached a suicidal position, he counterposed existentialism as a solution to the problem with words which have a prophetic significance in the light of his own death, and its manner: 'throwing oneself zestfully into reality, seeking a release from it by intense concentration on it, in detail from moment to moment. [...] I want my death to show something, to teach somebody something. Or at least to be recognized as a reasonable procedure and not an irrational whim'.[22] And at the end of a Journal entry on 9 August 1955 there is a positive, determined response to a litany of frustrations:

I am in a thorough mess, a tangle of negative emotions. Jealousy of Richard [Bennett] and his new theory, irritation with Cog [Percy Coggin, Methodist preacher and manager of the granite quarry at Wenford, and a devotee of the Cardew family] for his failure to play chess with me, inability to control my movements (I have hiccoughs and drop things), inability to listen to Ennis's back-chat, inability to concentrate on the Rhythm questions. Inability to express myself to my friends in letters, writing the first emotional blather that comes into my head. Tardiness in pursuing electronics. [...] Memo for the 10th. Seek to analyse all these failures and to correlate them.

Dreams, recounted in considerable detail, short stories and references to poetry and literature in general are a common feature in all the Journals. There is a further reference to Shelley, 'on re-reading *Prometheus Unbound*,' which ends: 'This couplet (*Epipsychidion*) must have been written for Dowland. Weeping, till sorrow becomes ecstasy: Then smile on it, so that it may not die.'[23] And a quote from Yeats: 'the best lack conviction; the worst is full of passionate intensity' evokes a comment: 'Impossible to describe the turmoil of emotions this disturbs.'[24] There is also mention of Sartre (*The Age of Reason*), Camus (*The Plague*) and Joyce's *Portrait of the Artist as a Young Man* from which 'the wonderful description of Hell' is singled out. Yet his passion for literature found only modest expression in his early compositions; between 1954 and 1968 there were just two settings, both from Blake's *The Book of Thel*: *Voice from Thel's Grave* for voice and piano (1957) and *Ah Thel* for mixed chorus (1962). The choice of poet, nevertheless, is a significant one and is only partially explained by an artistic compatibility; composer and poet shared concerns across a range of wider issues, both artistic and moral – in particular the dichotomy of impulse and spontaneity on the one hand and intellectual control and restraint on the other, and their perception of the reasoning faculty as potentially destructive of imagination.

Blake regarded human imagination as the essential divine quality by which God manifested himself in Man. This was almost equating Man with God and Art with Christianity. Blake had therefore reached the extremity of humanism, an attitude which seemed to his contemporaries, startled by so revolutionary a mode of thought, to be explicable only as a form of insanity. So complete an artist was quite beyond their comprehension.[25]

Both Blake and Cardew praised inexplicitness in art, and their own was criticised for it: Blake for his failure to achieve sufficient control over his reader's response, and Cardew for the failure of his notations to secure an accountable response from his performers. Both men regarded these 'failures' as virtues: 'The wisest of the Ancients considered what is not too Explicit as the fittest for Instruction, because it rouses the faculties to act.'[26] Blake's belief in the inseparability of art and morality would also be echoed in the humanism embodied in Cardew's notational experiments of the sixties ('people-processes' as Michael Nyman aptly described them); and the idea that participation is essential to finding value in life, even when it is destructive, is fundamental to the meaning of both *Thel* and to that of Cardew's own life.

Like Blake Cardew was fascinated by the possibilities of human perfection; like Blake he had no fear of human nature; he revelled in and was inspired by the limitless possibilities it encompassed, and throughout his life Cardew was drawn to the challenges and dangers of 'the road of excess' and to those, like Blake, like Burroughs, like Rimbaud, like Wittgenstein, like Lenin, who had chosen that same road, who had pierced the carapace of the 'historical crib' to reveal new vistas, new challenges for the human race.

Cardew's relationships with women are documented, particularly in the early Journals, with a degree of gentlemanly relish which rarely exceeds the bounds of good taste. There are constant references to women, known and unknown; women admired, loved, desired, unattainable, picked up, abandoned, pursued, analysed – women who appear briefly in his life but assertively and unforgettably like the two encounters on different occasions at the Oval station (in south east London):

But her mouth will always remain with me. It was the fullest, the most perfect and the most sensual I have ever seen. […] Oval seems to be my lucky station: the time before that on the escalator I met the Irish waitress from the Vienna Cafe Baker Street whose carriage I admire so much.[27]

Prospecting for women occupied a fair proportion of his time and energy. Several feature prominently – his love-affair with a lady employed at Dickens and Jones (a fashionable London store) fills several pages in the Journals and, like all the women he loved, Perdita seems to have been a lady of substance. 'The real reason I so enjoy her company is the taut physical domination she exercises over me. The beauty of it is that she exercises this power unashamedly yet restrainedly.'[28] And on 1 June another reference to Perdita:

It is an escape into a world of absolute blissfulness, in which depression and ordinary work-a-day miseries just vanish.[...] Perhaps I'd better not go out with her again, because she is 'going' with a man.[...] No – it would be definitely a bad thing to make a habit of this escape ladder. After all, she is a woman – not a ladder.

Occasionally, his mother's disapproval is recorded; in January 1955 she wrote to rebuke him for his dissolute life and lack of standards. A year later she was warning him that if he continued to live promiscuously with girls he would rapidly become a 'rotter'. 'Mummy's new year thoughts about me are becoming cyclic. I eagerly await the next fateful Christmas. Will I be at Wenford being ticked off about yet another girl.'[29] In fact, in the teeth of still more maternal opposition, one of these relationships would attain a more permanent status.

Cardew met Ruth Aaronberg, an attractive, vivacious young woman, at the Academy – a fellow student who had begun her course there two years before him and was studying the piano as a main subject with Max Pirani. She was born in Sheffield; her father, a Russian émigré from Vilnius, had escaped the pogrom in the early part of the century and had come to England with his whole family. During the blitz he moved to Worksop, in the Midlands, where he had a furniture shop. Ruth's mother was born in London (where her Polish father kept a grocer's), studied music and taught her daughter the piano. Mrs. Aaronberg kept an orthodox kosher household, faithfully celebrating the various festivals, although her daughter was sent to a non-Jewish school. According to Ruth it was a decision, a course of action, which served to validate and sustain her sense of alienation from her Jewish background, which she came to regard as something exotic and quite separate from her normal life-style. Her mother died when Ruth was young and her father assumed responsibility for her upbringing, which was not strict. He tolerated, though he did not approve, her non-Jewish boy-friends; her eventual marriage to a Gentile upset him, but he never reproached her.

Sometime during the year 1955 (Ruth does not recall which month) Cornelius and Ruth moved into a flat in Greville Road, Richmond, where they stayed until Cardew left for Cologne in the autumn of '57.[30] The Journals chart the vicissitudes of their youthful relationship with copious references: dates, visits, meals, parties, tiffs, deceits, broken arrangements, third parties, traumas, falling in and out of love. Ruth's opinions were noted respectfully, although her public school-educated partner would often mock her respectable, middle-class background; and while she was often a sounding board for his ideas – an ideal, ego-boosting female companion for a young male artist – there were clearly times when his superciliousness and self-centredness stretched her tolerance too far and she would turn the tables on him:

> I notice a distinct change in Ruth's attitude towards me. Perhaps her extremely low opinion of me is only a pose (but unfortunately justified on most counts). She used to think that my ideas on Bach should go without much question. Now she resentfully and bitterly questions all my ideas. [...] Not only Bach either, everything I think about or mention is open to this hostile criticism. [...] her contempt will take a lot of breaking down. That is, she used to think that everything I said I believed with my whole soul, and that everything I said I would do, I did. Failure in these respects she wouldn't mind in the casual friend. [...] but with me it takes the form of a reaction from her original picture. And to have fallen from impossibly high to an ordinary low is unforgivable because she can't see that it is no lower than 'ordinary'. In this she lacks common sense and self-criticism – since this vice of mine is no more than the virtue of so-called adaptability (see Chuang Tsu[31]) which she possesses in a high degree, the only difference between her and me being that she, in adapting her exterior, allows her interior to be affected too.[32]

Whilst acknowledging that her hostility is well-founded, he nevertheless cannot accept criticism from her – hence the *coup de grâce* arrogantly administered at the end of the quote, the argument *ad hominem*: her adaptability is a result of her feeble-mindedness, her volatility. Perhaps he was preparing himself for what seemed to him to be an inevitable end-of-the-affair with a self-vindicating analysis of their relationship.[33] Just the day before, 8 June, he had written in the Journals:

> I think it is all over with Ruth now since she seems to have some difficulty in getting any pleasure from me these days. She is engaged to a more highly-skilled libertine who practices the Caezza (or variant)[34] and has read many authorities. He is a wit and she seems to have fallen in love with him. He claims that his method is taken from Vanderveldt – remember to ask John (Hewetson) about this lubricious character.

Yet despite the stop-go nature of their relationship there was no doubting the strength of his feelings for her; the Journals betray an often obsessive attitude towards her and he would resent her absence if they were apart for any length of time. 'Ruth and electronics concurrent in my brain. Consequent inability to focus. What is required is a huge blind gesture. I hope I'll still be able to pick up the pieces.'[35]

As a young man his sexuality was often close to the surface and there are explicit references to sex rarely found in the later Journals.

I have kissed no fresh lips for two years come November. Consequently at the moment I feel Coitus nix. Maximum mystery lies in the mouth. Vagina is too secret to be really mysterious and too sheltered to be really beautiful. Coitus? In time it is fulfilment, but in space it is not so full as a kiss.[36]

But the description of an Indian sculpture of a couple making love (*Mithuna*) is vintage Cardew, the touches of humour enhanced by a studied detachment:

They are against a wall. He has it to lean against, and she leans against him (so presumably he 'thrusts his instrument into her by the back avenue' to use Mrs. Berkeley's expression).[37] Each stands on one leg (both right). His is slightly flexed to adjust height. She as it were 'sits' on his right hip. Her left leg doesn't seem to come into the picture, but his is lifted outwards – puppywise – so that his left foot rests on her right knee. Her right arm is twisted up behind his head thus, with her head thrown back their mouths are brought together. Her other arm in this sculpture rests on her right thigh but I suppose it could support his left ankle. His right arm is broken off but it looks as though the right hand rests on her right hip. His left arm comes under her armpit and the head caresses the left breast. The combined posture gives an incredible impression of sensuousness and ecstasy. Judith, hurry up and return so that we can attempt it (Allah ya kai mu[38]).[39]

The Journals contain several insightful remarks on form and expression, the ramifications of which would be of primary concern to him in his radical music-making during the sixties; reference is also made to Schoenberg's 'Criteria for the evaluation of music' – a subject he was to address in uncompromising fashion in his later years.

Today I was paid a compliment after my own heart. Julian [Lee] said he liked it.

('It is something one hasn't heard before.') So much more refreshing than Richard's [Bennett] perennial 'Yes, it has a good shape', whatever that may mean. [...] Shape: I think he means with a reversion to the first material at the end of the piece. If this is shape it is as ugly as a woman with a dead baby inside her. It seems to me that anything that comes back to the beginning again is so much wasted energy, merely an excursion, not a journey. A Recapitulation may be sublimated or debased or, if this effect is wanted, a fruitless cycle, but 'not, please not', just Recap. for its own sake, or to 'give it unity'.[40]

Another entry later in the year deals with the problem of musical repetition in another way:

The essence of poetry, or rather a good deal of poetry, relies for its poetic essence on repetition. This may be concised to a single word. Music up to Webern also relies on repetition for its poetic essence (or lets say coherence). This may be concised to the repetition of a single note in context, or related in some other way to the note it is essentially a repetition of. It is not good enough to repeat the note or phrase (or tone row) just so as to give it poetic essence – special attention must be devoted to the relation of the note or phrase to the note or phrase it repeats. (All this of course after matter has been introduced in between. What is the quality of this matter? Is it contrast? Or deviation? Or is it a psychic jump from which to return to repetition?) (Repetition must always be understood to include variation).[41]

Earlier in the same entry Cardew raises the question of content in music – the idea of music as the expression of the human soul. The answer is disappointingly non-committal: 'I am too young to be able to answer these questions. But unless I start work on them soon I shall never do it.' Yet there was always a commitment to poetic utterance, whatever his inability, or reluctance, to verbalise on such matters at that time, which, given the exclusively formal preoccupations of his masters and peers, would have been difficult to overcome:

Went to a wedding on St Michael's Mount and then on to St Ives to see Bernard, Eleanor, Betty, Michael and David Leach.[42] While sitting in Eleanor's porch I had a rare moment of peace and thought. The following, scribbled on the back of the Rhythm chart, was the result. Poetic fragment: When the wind drops Time slows to die in absolute stillness – the wind ceases, vibrating plants wave slower, there is no bird with wings to measure time. The only countable 'duration' is the beating heart and breathing. These merge with natural stillness – time ceases. Minims become breves, expanding into stillness. Ties – a tied breve into nothingness. Or to perish in action: a crescendo of vibrations or time measurements suddenly collapsing into obliviousness, or even a crescendo of vibrating so fast – so wide – to the point that the bigness of mobility becomes immobility (or so fast – so miniscule – to the point that the quickness of microscopic movement becomes stillness).[43]

I think we can reasonably presume that the personal thoughts and feelings Cardew chose to entrust to his Journals (and to posterity) are an accurate reflection of his concerns, both intellectually and emotionally, at that period of his life. If wider, public issues were ever discussed among friends, for whatever reasons they were deemed inappropriate material for the Journals; traumatic events such as the bombing of the Suez canal and the invasion of Hungary, for example, find no mention. Nor do the protests by Bertrand Russell and others against the preparations for chemical and nuclear warfare, although the subsequent formation of the Committee of 100 and Direct Action did inspire Cardew, probably for the first time, to support a radical, political cause.[44]

Meanwhile, less than a decade after the election of a Labour government with a huge mandate, the counter-revolution was rapidly regaining lost territories for the old ruling classes: new forms of privilege were emerging, the trend of post-war income redistribution was being reversed, and business was once more playing an active role in shaping the nation's life. Such developments, however, were of scant interest to the 'absolute beginners'[45] of the fifties whose abrasive self-confidence and disdain for the debilitating respectability and responsibilities of adulthood reflected a newly-emerging, autonomous youth culture increasingly obsessed with its own self-image. For a young, middle-class student, and in particular a music student, barely out of his teens, the social life of the New Conservatism, with its jazz clubs, cinemas and coffee bars, was entertaining, innocuous and sufficient; by contrast, the idea of plotting to overthrow the system and change the world at the Partisan coffee bar in Carlisle Street and the tireless propagation of the contents of Tribune and Universities and Left Review (later, in 1960, New Left Review), to which small groups of his peers (including myself) were devoting their lives, would have seemed decidedly unattractive and profoundly irrelevant; the real drama was in the heart-searching, the confessions, the insecurities and jealousies of one's private life.

Compositions 1953-56

The works that have survived from Cardew's student days at the RAM consist of numerous compositions for piano, including two piano sonatas, pieces for piano duet, two pianos, and for trumpet and piano, two string trios, a quartet for flute and string trio, a piece for soprano and string quartet, a setting of part of a Blake poem for voice and piano, and an orchestral version, *Microcosmos,* of the *Piano Sonata No.2.* None of these date from his first year (except possibly for the *Introduction, Theme and Variations, and Coda* for 2 pianos, which is dated simply 1954); nor have any sketch pads survived from that period.

In the first term of his second year he completed a string trio, dated October 1954; and a 'Viola movement', which has so far not come to light, is mentioned in a Journal entry on 20 January 1955: 'Apparently, Howard Ferguson told Richard that my Viola movement made an immediate impression on him, really beautiful – Cheers.' The trio, however, did not fare so well at a one-off composition lesson with Arnold Van Wyck (presumably deputising for Ferguson), who made short shrift of it.

In the year 1955 Cardew completed five compositions; three of them, *Short Pieces for Duet (for Ruth)*, *Piano Sonata No.1*, and *Fantasia for 2 Pianos*, interesting milestones though they may be in Cardew's development, are of insufficient merit to warrant our attention in the present volume, but the remaining two display a marked, qualitative leap forward to the extent that, to a modest degree, each has secured a place in the repertoire. For the first time there is stylistic coherence and continuity; the music seems to breathe more easily and his handling of serial technique is fluent and assured.

Three Rhythmic Pieces for Trumpet and Piano were completed in August 1955; in the first piece the music is finely poised, and the wide, sweeping trumpet phrases are elegantly and expressively drawn. The second piece is a trumpet solo: arresting, highly-charged music with an effective use of rhythmicized, repeated notes and bold, chromatic flourishes. The relationship between trumpet and piano becomes more intricate in the third piece; the linear style of piano writing persists and occasionally, as in the first piece, dramatic trills and tremolos are interspersed. The repeated note motif is developed and characterized in different ways through rubato, augmentation, pitch and dynamic variation, and ends the piece with a typical Cardew laconicism (Ex.2.1).

Ex.2.1. from *Three Rhythmic Pieces for Trumpet and Piano*, last 4 bars of the third piece.

The *Second String Trio*, composed between October '55 and January '56, and the less successful *Piano Sonata No.2*, completed in May 1956, were two essays in pointillism; the Trio, approximately four minutes in duration, aspires to a Webernesque intensity and concentration of material and demonstrates Cardew's mastery of an idiom which, at that time, incorporated the most advanced serial techniques. His teacher, Howard Ferguson, whom he held in high esteem and affection,[46] confessed: 'Before long he was producing pieces that I had considerable difficulty in trying to understand.'[47]

His sketches reveal the detailed scrutiny to which the various permutations of the row and its division into three and four note cells were subjected, as well as the application of the method to other aspects of the musical discourse, such as rhythm. Towards the end of the piece, for example, the pulse quickens and the music gathers momentum through an abrupt diminution of rhythmic values. Yet it is the idiosyncrasies, eluding or perhaps simply ignoring the exigencies of the serial method, which catch the ear and stimulate reflection. At the beginning of the work the initial chord (which later assumes importance as a four-note motif) is followed by a group of four repeated Gs, then three, two and one; the phrase ends with three B flats, establishing in the opening bars a strong feeling of G minor tonality and cocking a snook, right at the outset, at serial orthodoxy (Ex.2.2a).

Ex.2.2a. *Second String Trio*, bars 1-5.

Likewise, the work ends with 4 repeated Gs (Ex.2.2b):

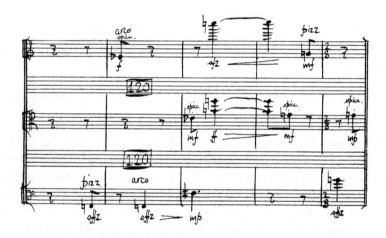

Ex.2.2b. *Second String Trio*, last 5 bars.

Of more significance, however, than any heretical gesture which the repetitions may appear to represent is the fact that the repeated note is a germinal idea which will feature prominently in Cardew's later works in a variety of guises: in *Autumn 60* specific pitches are offered to the ensemble which they perform simultaneously, though the attacks are not synchronized, producing a kind of hocket effect; in *Three Winter Potatoes* (1965) the pianistic device of repeated notes is used frequently; in *Volo Solo* (1965) the whole work consists entirely of strings of fast, repeated notes; and in *Solo with Accompaniment* (1964), a kind of slow-motion *Volo Solo*, length-of-breath notes (Solo) are repeated against a varied, constantly changing Accompaniment. This idea of the same note/sound heard and tracked in shifting, changing contexts, the perception of the metamorphosis of a sound through the passing of time, through mental and physical exhaustion on the part of the performer and listener, through the interaction of both subjective and objective, social and psychological, mental and physical determinants in the experience of music, would find its most radical expression in the mid-sixties in Cardew's marathon,[48] single-sound performances of La Monte Young's music and in the subtle and inventive notations, the 'people-processes', of *The Great Learning*.

Like the *Second String Trio* the *Piano Sonata No.2* demonstrates the self-conscious adoption of the technique of total serialism – although the two works do not bear comparison. The influence of Boulez's *Structures I* weighs heavily on this arid and graceless music; the poetic impulses which illuminate and enrich the string trio are suppressed through subservience to a compositional system which brooks no theoretical transgression. There are no heresies here, no idiosyncratic touches, no careless moments of poetic licence to relieve the harshness and unrelenting tedium of the piano writing which only a few months earlier had played such a dramatic and expressive role in the trumpet pieces. And Cardew himself added a telling postscript to the work by pencilling in harmonics (notes depressed silently and resonating sympathetically to sounded notes) at particularly vulnerable points in the score, perhaps in a last-ditch attempt to provide a bleak landscape with a modicum of warmth and sustenance. Could the same motivation have been behind his decision to make an orchestral version of the work, *Microcosmos*, or was the exercise undertaken in a detached spirit of curiosity and experiment? Certainly the orchestrated version is aurally more attractive, enhanced by the addition of a percussion part for two performers with a full complement of percussion instruments and, here and there, some well-judged textures and imaginative juxtapositions: a short section scored for solo instruments is a particularly effective choice midway through the piece.

These two works, *Second String Trio* and *Piano Sonata No.2,* were the only two works Cardew completed between September '55 and May '56. This may be explained in part by the fact that in April 1956 he passed his LRAM piano performance diploma examination, which would certainly have necessitated months of solid preparation. And with this achievement under his belt a new composition quickly materialised: *Fantasy for Mezzo Soprano and String Quartet* (completed June 1956), a serial setting of a poem by Howard Snell, reverts to the expressive lyricism of the trumpet pieces. It is a work of some merit; Cardew weaves a delicate web of accompanimental string sound, with dynamics and articulation precisely and purposefully notated, and shows an awareness of the emotional content and associations of key words in the poem. Wide leaps and dissonant intervals, reminiscent of Webern's Hildegard Jone lieder, characterise the ambitious vocal writing, although the somewhat pedestrian rhythmic movement is often at variance with the freedom and plasticity of the melodic lines.

Written nine months later, *Voice from Thel's grave,* a setting of the final section of William Blake's poem *The Book of Thel* for voice and piano, is an altogether bolder, and artistically more successful exercise. There is a more rigorous application of serial technique with tighter harmonic control, coupled with a greater rhythmic freedom and complexity, particularly in the relationship between voice and piano, which is more in the nature of a duo. The piano writing is technically more demanding, anticipating the pianism of the *Piano Sonata No.3* and *Two Books of Study for Pianists* completed the following year – swooping through registers across the whole range of the keyboard and creating a variety of textures. The vocal line, too, achieves a greater intensity and plasticity through melisma and elaboration, something he had begun to assimilate through his acquaintance with the works of Boulez, in particular *Le Marteau sans Maître.* (He was later to play the guitar part in the first English performance at the Wigmore Hall under John Carewe.) The dramatic content of the poem is well served; the piano creates an appropriate atmosphere in the opening bars: music shrouded in dark colours, and at the climax, 'Why a Nostril wide inhaling terror trembling and affright?', the piercing qualities of high percussive tones are effectively exploited (Ex.2.3):

Ex.2.3. from *Voice from Thel's Grave.*

For Cardew the final year at the RAM was a time of emotional turmoil; the relationship with Ruth Aaronberg had reached a make or break point and there was uncertainty with regard to his musical career. 'Awaiting a letter from Herbert Eimert[49] in Köln. If negative try Berio in Milan [Italian scholarship].'[50] The Principal, Thomas Armstrong, had persuaded him to stay on at the Academy until the end of the academic year, and in 1957 he was awarded the *Oliveira Prescott Gift* for composition. The response from Dr.Eimert was positive and he was subsequently in receipt of funds from the *Manson Bequest* (£300) as a contribution to his projected studies in Cologne; the tide had turned very much in his favour.[51] In a letter dated 20 August 1957, which contains an uncharacteristic trope that would not have been used in any other form of correspondence, Cardew informs his father: 'I am to go to the Electronic studio at Köln in October, and the Royal Academy, god bless them, have given me £300 for the purpose.' The phrase 'god bless them' jolts because it is uncharacteristic, but echoes his father's propensity for similar tropes: 'Allah ya kai mu', for example, he would interject. It is as if this respect, the awareness of the nature of his relationship with his father (mutual respect and admiration), necessitates a stylistic accommodation in which Cardew's normal mode is compromised.

In July 1957 Cardew left the RAM; he could have had few regrets. As Richard Bennett recalls: 'They were good times'.

Notes and references

1   Jrnl. 4 September 1955.
2   Jrnl. 3 February 1955.
3   Letter from Howard Ferguson to JT, 31 March 1986.
4   In fact, Cardew entered the RAM as a first study piano student; composition was his second study, although these may well have been reversed during the course of his period of study.
5   Letter from SC to JT, 14 May 1986.
6   Several of these students became distinguished professional musicians: Susan Bradshaw, pianist, critic, translator; Josephine Nendick, singer; and Alan Cohen, arranger and band leader.
7   There is some confusion as to who his piano teacher was. Ruth Koenig, a student contemporary, recalls only Percy Waller; but according to the RAM alumni database (25 August 2004) he had two teachers: Eric Grant and Frederick Jackson.
8   Jrnl. 26 January 1955.
9   John Cage, *Silence* (Connecticut: Wesleyan University Press, 1961), p.5.
10   Jrnl. 14 January 1955.
11   Jrnl. February 1955.
12   Ibid.
13   Jrnl. 24 January 1955.
14   Jrnl. 20 May 1955.
15   Jrnl. 6 November 1956.
16   Cha-no-yu: literally, Tea-of-hot water.
17   Jrnl. 20 August 1955.
18   Of course there are many echoes of 'the way of Tea' in European culture; for instance, Cardew might have stumbled across the following passage from Schopenhauer: 'Further we do not let abstract thought, the concepts of reason, take possession of our consciousness, but, instead of all this, devote the whole power of our mind to perception, sink ourselves completely therein, and let our whole consciousness be filled by the calm contemplation of the natural object actually present, whether it be a landscape, a tree, a rock, a building, or anything else. We lose ourselves entirely in this object, to use a pregnant expression. [...] It was this that was in Spinoza's mind when he wrote: *Mens aeterna est quatenus res sub specie aeternitatis* [The mind is eternal in so far as it conceives things from the standpoint of eternity].' From *The World as Will and Representation*, Vol.I, p.179.
19   This was probably a talk entitled 'Belinsky: Moralist and Prophet,' which appeared in *Encounter* 5 No.12, December 1955.
20   Jrnl. 2 February 1955.
21   Jrnl. 7 November 1955.
22   Jrnl. 14/15 February 1955.
23   Jrnl. 25 May 1955.
24   Jrnl. 4 July 1955.
25   Geoffrey Keynes, from the Introduction to William Blake's *The Marriage of Heaven and Hell* (Oxford: Oxford University Press, 1975), p.ix. [My emphasis added]
26   From one of Blake's letters to Dr Trusler, 23 August 1799.
27   Jrnl. 31 January 1955.
28   Jrnl. 27 May 1955.

29 Jrnl. January 1956.

30 Earlier in the year Cardew had left Colville Square and had moved to Robert Street in Euston, north-west London, not far from the RAM; there he rented a room in a run-down tenement building where fellow student Ken Brazier had also found accommodation.

31 The Chinese philosopher Chuang Tsu lived in the latter part of the fourth and first years of the third centuries; he was considered an important reference for an understanding of early Taoism.

32 Jrnl. 9 June 1955.

33 This also accords with a 'love-sick' letter sent around this time to Judith (Judith Edsell, a former pupil of his mother's at the City of London School), a simmering passion from pre-Academy days which had survived, suggesting that the idea of seeking comfort in the arms of another had already presented itself as a viable alternative to solitary confinement and temporary abstinence.

34 Caezza was a sexual practice advocated by the American seer and mystic Thomas Lake Harris in the mid nineteenth century whereby sexual intercourse could take place without movement or orgasm.

35 Jrnl. 8 June 1955.

36 Jrnl. 17 October 1956.

37 This lady remains a mystery to me.

38 'Allah ya kai mu' is an expression in Hausa meaning 'God Willing' which Michael Cardew had learned in West Africa. Hausa is the language of Northern Nigeria and is also the second language of much of West Africa.

39 Jrnl. 27 May 1955. From *The Art of India* (Phaidon, 1954), plate 122.

40 Jrnl. 24 January 1955.

41 Jrnl. 15 May 1955.

42 Bernard Leach, the potter, and his family.

43 Jrnl. 5 August 1955.

44 I cannot substantiate this assertion; it has been lodged in my memory for some time but I have no idea as to when and how I received the information.

45 A reference to Colin McInnes' influential book *Absolute Beginners*.

46 In the later years he was less generous to Ferguson, and, of course, to the Royal Academy generally. He did not receive the rigorous training in traditional harmony and counterpoint, in musical history, etc. that he subsequently felt he needed. The fact is, he would almost certainly have resisted this. Had he studied with the communist composer, Alan Bush, for example, it is unlikely that he would have lasted the first semester. Or would he have been impressed by Bush's politics and found Marxism twenty years earlier?

47 Letter from HF to JT, 31 March 1986.

48 Perhaps my characterisation of *Piano Sonata No.2*, penned in the mid-eighties, is a little severe. A number of musicians, including the composer Michael Parsons and the pianist Tania Chen, would take issue with me. However, my reservations remain, and so do my original words; in essence I hold by what I said then, some twenty years ago.

49 Herbert Eimert was the Director of the Electronic Studio at Cologne Radio.

50 Jrnl. 2 November 1956.

51 According to Ruth Aaronberg she and Cardew would stay up into the early hours trying to get the Nachtprogram from Cologne; on one occasion they managed to tune in and were astonished and delighted to hear Cardew's music.

3
Cologne 1957–61

Cardew arrived in Germany on 7 October 1957 to study at the Electronic Studio of the Westdeutscher Rundfunk with Karlheinz Stockhausen. Ruth had driven him from Richmond to London Airport whence he took a flight to Cologne. He took a room in an apartment on the Hohenstaufenring, and remained there until Easter 1958. Through the offices of the Principal of the RAM, Sir Thomas Armstrong, he had been awarded a grant of £300 (from the Manson Bequest) towards the cost of his studies; this was supplemented by a monthly allowance of £30 from his father until early 1959, when payments were discontinued.

The trajectory of his career, powered by an inner conviction and a Blakeian dedication to risk and excess, had borne him to what he considered at the time to be the most advanced outpost of Western musical thought and practice. His letters to friends and family in the early months exude a sense of intoxication, a breathless effusiveness which contrasts sharply with the laconic witticisms and self-indulgent philosophising to be found scattered throughout the Journals from the Academy days. For Cardew, at that time, the Cologne studio embodied a commitment to the new, the experimental, to risk-taking; it was something he felt he could identify with. He admired the pioneering spirit and single-mindedness of its leading practitioners; Gottfried Michael Koenig,[1] in particular, was singled out as a 'real conjuror with the machines [...] a real joy to watch'.[2] He was both fascinated and intimidated by the studio technology and the richness of material that it offered composers. In a letter to Ruth not long after his arrival Cardew had described in painstaking detail some of the idiosyncrasies of working with the tape machines; thus, in some instances it might be not only more practical, but also artistically more satisfying, to incorporate into a piece the imperfections generated by the technology – when an attempt to eliminate them would seem to be counter-productive. This practical work, however basic and unambitious, was deemed necessary, and Cardew embarked on an electronic piece for sine tones which seems to have caused him considerable frustration and ultimate disappointment: 'My piece is now ready, but it is quite horrible and impossible to like.'[3] Yet his determination to learn and master state-of-the-art technology was unshakeable and he would spend hours in the Studio 'to emerge with a splitting headache each day and go home and study German'.[4] The bulk of the work in the Studio seems to have been done by the long-suffering Koenig 'who is deified by all the others who just sit around and watch and chat'.[5] Composers who visited and used the Studio are mentioned in passing in the Journals and letters: the Italian composer Franco Evangelisti is described as 'one of the Darmstadt horrors, [who] has taken a paternal interest in me, and praises Koenig and his own music to me in execrable English'.[6] Others include Herbert Brün,[7] Mauricio Kagel, Roman Haubenstock-Ramati ('a rank positivist whose chief remark is "prove it"') and György Ligeti:

Ligeti is very aleatoric, and in the Studio nowadays the deathly hush can almost be seen as three or four people sit or stand in awkward positions endlessly shaking hats full of tiny tape-pieces and sticking them end to end. At the end of the day, when the results are played through, the tension is released in nervous hilarity.[8]

There are also references to some of the Studio's early achievements, such as Stockhausen's *Gesang der Jünglinge* and Koenig's *Klangfiguren II* ('huge and fantastic'). Yet within a short time his letters home betrayed a scepticism which, in the sanctified atmosphere of the Studio, it would have been prudent to conceal:

A young Dutch sculptress was brought into the Studio by one of the more objectionable inmates. The Hungarian Ligeti asked her what sort of sculpture she did. Her answer provoked a sensation: 'Realistisch', and followed it up with 'I expect that is something quite new for you.' (Laughter and General Confusion.) The next day Ligeti asked her whether she had really been in earnest! I quite sympathize with her quip (although she couldn't have known its appropriateness) because Ligeti does rather (tend) to have definitions for New Art. Whereas the very meaning of the word 'New' defies definition.[9]

Underlying the descriptions and observations of his daily routine in the letters there is a turbulence that finds expression in the aggressive thought, violent images and bizarre dreams which are recorded in the Journals during these early months in Cologne:

Fantastic dream identifying Ma (mother) with Christ. Scene set in a submerged Chinese rice field. I am Peter and just over the rise is a cardboard mountain to be moved. Ma (Christ) says it would be easy to move it but wrong – a trick. Here there is more confusion – a scene with Mussolini in which the cardboard mountain does actually roll forward. However this is not at all clear. Anyhow, Christ (Ma) and I have to make a journey across the desert. On the other side of a sketchy hedge, standing in two feet of water (I sit on the dry path), Christ must for some reason change for the journey. It is now that I realise that she is a woman and the whole identification becomes apparent. She is menstruating and wearing one of those old-fashioned white zwischenpolstern. Most curious – our journey is never made.[10]

There seem to be manifold references here, on various levels: to the role of his mother within the family constellation, to male/female identification, to creativity and, through the 'trick' and the 'cardboard mountain', perhaps to the fast-diminishing credibility, in Cardew's eyes, of the European avant-garde which was bedevilling and thwarting his musical development. Hence, perhaps, the desert, symbolizing loneliness, lack of creativity or of growth, dry intellectualism; and, having to cross the desert (initially), the idea of the lack of direction and purpose in his life.

In a Journal entry on 2 October he projects a scenario of his own madness and confesses to a 'preoccupation with failure'. Success is equated with the violence and conviction of the new music: 'Goodness is ingrowing, like a cancer; violence has the virtue of extraversion.[…] In order to reach a virtuous old age one must live viciously; those who live virtuously get slain by circumstance, before reaching it'.

There is desperation in these words; yet the dog-eat-dog sentiments were common enough in an ambience where the methods and aims of the European avant-garde had been elevated to the status of a religion (with the canonization of Webern and the appropriation and, in some cases, misrepresentation of his musical thought), and where the disciples defended and counter-attacked with the ferocity and intolerance of true believers. Had not Schoenberg himself been the advocate of belligerent competitiveness among artists?

I think (composers) are in the first instance fighters for their own musical ideas. The ideas of other composers are their enemies. You cannot restrict a fighter. His blows are correct when they hit hard and only then is he fair. Wagner, Wolf, Mahler and Strauss fought for (the) life or death of their ideas.[11]

In the fifties West Germany was the chosen battleground where blows rained down on the heads of the arch-enemies, in particular Benjamin Britten and Dmitri Shostakovich – figures of ridicule derided as primitive reactionaries. Hans Werner Henze describes his disillusionment: 'At the beginning it had looked as though we were all working together on a humanistic project, as if we were all brothers, comrades, allies. That was now gone. Slowly but surely we became, or were made into, competitors in the same market.'[12]

After the briefest introduction into this world, Cardew was already entertaining heretical thoughts and doubts: 'The most interesting thing here is to watch my landlady attempting to seduce me', he quipped in a letter to Seth, 29 October 1957. The mechanistic philosophy which underpinned European serial composition was anathema to him; its monstrous abstractions oppressed and violated the performer and singularly failed to reach and engage the listener, except those few critics, agents, impresarios and radio producers who now formed a new audience of experts, exercising their paternalism, distributing contracts, promoting styles and composers according to their individual penchants. 'Please don't sound so miserable', Ruth pleaded with him in a letter dated 28 January 1958, and thanking him for the flowers he had sent for her 22nd birthday, but the studio-based coterie of intellectuals, from whom, it seemed, he was still unwilling or unable to free himself, continued to irritate him.

The composer Konrad Boehmer, who was still at school at the time, recalls that during the discussions in the Cologne studio Cardew for the most part remained silent. At the end of the evening he would give Boehmer a lift on the back of his bicycle from which he would lead remarkable conversations on the subject of composition, and on theoretical and aesthetic issues. If he wished to make a particularly important point Cardew would look back to ensure that his young co-rider had fully understood. This he considered to take priority over road safety. In particular, as Boehmer recalls, he deplored the 'academicism' of the Cologne School; their notion of form was fatally flawed: a lifeless skeleton which through pitches and durations could miraculously be brought to life. He would draw an analogy: it was like seeing the human skeleton as the form of a body, with the blood, organs and muscles the material through which this 'form' was articulated. But form was not the mechanical sum of its parts; form was process, *Dynamis*. To help his young colleague grasp these ideas he directed him, typically, outside music; on the back of a copy of the piano piece *February Piece I* (1959) which Cardew had given Boehmer was inscribed: 'Molloy – S. Beckett', and shortly afterwards the book followed.[13] In an article for the Donaueschingen Festival in 1984 Boehmer describes Cardew's image: Long legs, gangling ('schlaksig'), anxiously bent over the handlebars, like an English country parson or doctor.

Cardew's admiration for Stockhausen, however, survived the profound misgivings he was experiencing towards the European avant-garde in general. In a letter to Ruth dated 9 November 1957 he wrote:

Since I have been here I have been rather an island in the sea of Stockhausen disapproval. I share with Koenig the opinion that the Piano Pieces up to 8 are the best things he has written, and that the first version of *Zeitmasse* is much better than the final version. […] In the evening I ate in the canteen with Koenig and we discussed Stockhausen's work and the proposed splitting up of piano piece 6 (I had protested about this to Stockhausen and got non-committal answers) and so we went back to the Studio and heard 6 complete (!) which is fabulous.

Stockhausen himself reciprocated these positive sentiments by employing Cardew as an assistant at the beginning of 1958 when the young Englishman returned to Cologne after the Christmas vacation. Cardew's knowledge and understanding of avant-garde compositional techniques, as well as his gimlet eye, had made a considerable impression on Stockhausen ('he knew my music so well that he could show me mistakes in the printed scores')[14] so that apart from run-of-the-mill copying and proof-reading Cardew was also entrusted with work of a collaborative, creative nature; for example, on *Gruppen*:

On Friday I started work for Stockhausen (Karlheinz to his friends). The day before he asked me what time I got up in the mornings, and I rashly answered 'any time'. So he said, 'be at my house at 9 am tomorrow', so I said 'I'll be there at 9.30' which is really not too bad. The first day I rashly started on the Drums part of the 3rd Orchestra, and I didn't finish it till 10.30 p.m. So far the only novelties he demands are thick bar-lines and correct crotchet rests – very trying. The score itself is huge and fantastic lasting 21 minutes and will be played on March 24th and another concert the next day.

Doing this work for Stockhausen is rather like a difficult apprenticeship. He insists on knowing what you think of works, composers, his scores, everything. In the last two days he has asked me outright for my views on Boulez, [Giselher] Klebe, Henze, Nono, Bo Nilsson (not here even now) Berio etc. etc. He, Stockhausen, is of course Führer and pronounces everything the others do as really 'too, too simple' to be worth listening to. He is always quoting Meyer-Eppler, information theory and the rest of it. […] In the parts we are writing he insists that several bars rest should be written so

instead of the normal

Why? Because in the old way there are 2 symbols, one with meaning and one without, that is, you have to refer back to the time signature to find the length of the bar. In his version both symbols are significant, you read first the length of the bar ━━ and then the number of times it must be counted! In Stockhausen it's an imposed discipline on his musical invention, and keeps its proper place – but he showed me a score by a friend of his, also a pupil of Meyer-Eppler, that consisted almost entirely of 'Information'. I felt that he had only written the music because there had to be done something which the players could be very efficiently and neatly told 'How To Do'.[15]

These comments elicited a thoughtful observation from Howard Skempton:

One of the things that Cornelius must have admired most about Stockhausen was his craftsmanship; his concern for precision in all matters. Information Theory acknowledges the opposition of efficiency and redundancy, and perhaps the necessity of both (e.g. a postcode is not enough!). Cornelius' example demonstrates Stockhausen's preference for efficiency.[16]

And throughout their collaboration Stockhausen's notations came under Cardew's sharp scrutiny (particularly in his role as interpreter), their idiosyncrasies sometimes approved, sometimes challenged and questioned – eventually to be subjected to the severity of Cardew's logic in a brilliant contribution to the Summer 1961 issue of *Tempo* magazine: 'Notation – Interpretation, Etc.' – a collection of forty 'remarks', broadly relating to the subject title, penned over a period of a year between the Springs of 1959 and 1960.

The relationship between the two men was an amicable one, based on mutual respect, and a letter from Stockhausen to Cardew, dated 16 March 1959, expresses warmth and solicitude: 'Leb wohl. Ich habe Dich ins Herz geschlossen, und das sollst Du ruhig wissen.' (Take care, and rest assured that I have taken you into my heart.) When she and Cornelius were short of money Ruth Aaronberg recalls how Stockhausen's wife Doris would feed them, and there is a reference to mealtimes with the Stockhausens in an undated letter to Ruth: 'The only embarrassing thing about working for Stockhausen is having to listen to Grace before meals, especially under the gaze of Suja, aged 4 (all the kiddies are sweet).' And there were stretches of a few weeks when Cardew actually lodged with the Stockhausen family.

Amongst his colleagues in the avant-garde, however, there was considerable back-biting and intolerance which would occasionally draw comment from him in the Journals or in letters:

> On one occasion Stockhausen had completely lost his temper with a fellow composer, Herbert Brün. [...] But the salient feature of the scene was the very clear representation of that aspect of religious mania that makes believers like Karlheinz demand, fully believing they have a right to, similar aspirations, and a strict adherence to these, from their fellow humans. The church militant in its worst guise.[17]

The same letter contains a paragraph which already expresses the profoundly antithetical relationship between the two men's attitudes towards musical composition: 'He (Stockhausen) throws out some remark which I am far from understanding, e.g. a composition must be an example, not a phenomenon. All my compositions which I regard most highly have to do with "phenomena": 1st Trumpet piece, 2nd Trio, 2nd Sonata, and Quintet.'

Nevertheless, Cardew would throw his own pieces into the lion's den where, more often than not, they would receive a mauling or – worse – would be barely sniffed at by Messrs. Koenig, Ligeti, and Stockhausen. The last

> seemed to think my (first) Sonata wasn't a bad piece at all, and looked at the score, discussed it and the performance quite reasonably, which was refreshing after the brief and freezing remarks he made some days ago about the Septet.[18]

Regarding the Piano Sonata No. 2 Stockhausen opined that

> One cannot any more write pieces that are 'fast' or 'slow' and he had the feeling that it could all be pushed together, that is, played faster, and the structure would be just as clear. But, rather sweetly, he said that during the performance he was paying more attention to me than to the music, and particularly at the point where he noticed the audience wasn't going with me any more, and he said he felt exactly as I must have been feeling, chilled in the spine, and he was impressed how coolly I went on. He said that with another pianist, the audience would have been whistling for the last quarter or third of the piece.[19]

Koenig and Ligeti were much harsher, and probably more accurate in their judgement: 'The first thought nothing much happened in it and noticed a few triads; the second said it was too empty.'[20] Perhaps Stockhausen's professional judgement was vitiated by fatherly, protective feelings towards his protégé, thereby sealing the fate of a relationship which had been doomed from the outset:

Karlheinz gave a not very coherent lecture about my music. (Actually, it was distributed over 2 half lectures.) And it is very strange to hear yourself being quoted. The words came out all obscure, unsympathetic, unhelpful from a mouth which was not built for them (not being my mouth). But the little piano piece I played as illustration went down quite well.[21]

Occasionally Cardew himself would be the butt of a jibe or would be thrown a bait, as when a young German literary intellectual commented how 'the English spoke no foreign languages and their own badly'. Despite this he would insist on asking Cardew the meaning of such phrases as 'bedad' and 'a long twister', to which Cardew's response was that he really did not speak English at all.

Cardew's letters to Ruth during the early months in Cologne suggest that her arrival was eagerly anticipated. He craved the warmer, more intimate, more merciful companionship of a woman, a need which on one or two occasions had been briefly and inconsequentially satisfied by intimacies with his landlady, Frau Pfeil – a plump, middle-aged, blonde divorcée who, according to Cardew, had made all the running (shades, perhaps, of the apocryphal intrigue at the King's School?). These would have been conducted circumspectly (a gentlemanly discretion in such matters was his trademark) although, typically, he considered it unnecessary, unworthy even, to conceal the relationship from Ruth who had subsequently complained in a letter to him at the beginning of 1958 that he and his landlady had 'made a fool of her'. Ruth was referring to her brief visit to Cologne in November of '57 and her self-perception was that of an unsuspecting participant in a *ménage à trois*. Cardew's facile response: 'One doesn't do that sort of thing to make a fool of someone', begged too many questions and merely added to her displeasure. Nor would she be spared his descriptions, often humorous, of casual encounters: the delicate initial probings, the feeling out of the potentiality of a relationship, the failure to materialize for this and that reason, and so forth. On one occasion, in a coffee bar, Cardew had engaged a young lady and her male companion in a conversation which soon began to flag. He had:

brought the subject of conversation round to art (gross geschrieben [in capital letters]) and lo, she painted. But my fantasies of Tachist studios and coffee at midnight came crashing to the ground when it turned out that she was illustrating a children's book, earning money by reducing maps, and living with her parents in a pre-fabricated house.[22]

Ruth's letters to Cardew express love and longing – restlessly anticipating their re-union; infused with youthful impatience they are sparkling, animated, fervent, occasionally fretful, sometimes consoling, often erotic, and with a barely concealed vein of desperation running through as if she were aware that it was all too good to be true. Describing a visit to the cinema in Hammersmith, west London, with Richard Bennett,[23] who had brought with him a letter addressed to her from Cardew, she writes:

He gave me your letter – we rushed in as the film was about to start, so it was all very tantalising as I had to wait until the lights went up for ice cream. And then I was scared that it would be obscene and that the people behind would see.[24]

Maybe, even now, it would be unfair to speculate on Cardew's reaction in a similar situation: nonchalantly slipping the letter into his pocket he would have settled down to the film without giving the letter any further thought until, reaching home and preparing to go to bed, it would have materialised out of his pocket and, all in good time, he would have opened it and savoured its contents.

Ruth returned to Cologne in March and she and Cornelius were married at the British Consulate in Düsseldorf (with the composer, poet and theorist Hans G. Helms and Gottfried Michael Koenig as witnesses) on 14 April 1958. Their marriage had necessitated a move from Hohenstaufenring and in a letter to his brother Seth, dated 7 April 1958, Cardew described the incident which finally precipitated their departure:

We went to Paris for a week – a good substitute for the ancestral home, if more expensive, and returned to find my landlady in our bed (3.45am. Good Friday morning) so after 2 days we are at the above address (Bayenthal-Gürtel 30 – the cellar of our early London days-dream.[25]

Cardew's daily routine was unaffected by married life; he continued to visit the Studio most days, using the Rundfunk's lunch vouchers to eat in the canteen where he would spend hours, especially before concerts, discussing music (serialism and electronic music) and modern literature with friends and colleagues from the Studio. Though the prevailing ethos amongst them was 'anti-establishment', political debate (in which Cardew rarely participated) was generally circumscribed by the theoretical writings of the Frankfurt School, in particular the work of Theodor W. Adorno[26], whose post-war positions, not surprisingly, had received short shrift from Marxists of a more militant, less speculative persuasion; indeed, Hanns Eisler's dismissive characterisation, 'they only want to be more clever than the bourgeois theorists, but they do not want to take issue with them',[27] was to become one of the key tenets of Cardew's 'anti-revisionist', revolutionary politics in the seventies. Paradoxically, for those followers of a school to whom the superstructural areas of society were of paramount importance, there seems to have been little inclination, at least until the sixties, towards considerations of the communicative (in particular), humanizing role of Art; indeed, those German victims of Nazism to whom such questions had been crucial (among them Eisler, Georg Grosz, Käthe Kollwitz, Bertolt Brecht) had become virtually *personae non gratae.* Furthermore, and more importantly, such concerns ran counter to the dictates of Western Cold War ideologues, for whom the abstract nature of modernism, with its eschewal of any *social* dimension, was the ideal foil to Socialist Realism.[28]

In a letter to his brother Seth on 8 November 1957 Cardew had allowed himself a rare but portentous incursion into the realm of politics and war:

I have met many people here who have had more or less frightful experiences in concentration camps, and I have seen the effects also. These are almost as quietly appalling as the following quotation from a correspondence between Auschwitz Extermination camp and I.G. Farben Chemical Trust (who write): 1. 'In contemplation of experiments with a new soporific drug, we should appreciate your procuring for us a number of women.' 2. 'We received your answer but consider the price of 200 Marks a woman excessive. We propose to pay not more than 170 Marks per head. If agreeable, we will take possession of the women. We need approximately 150.' 3. 'We acknowledge your accord. Prepare for us 150 women in the best possible health conditions, and as soon as you advise us you are ready, we will take charge of them.' 4. 'Received the order of 150 women. Despite their emaciated condition, they were found satisfactory. We shall keep you posted on developments concerning the experiments.' 5. 'The tests were made. All the subjects died. We shall contact you shortly on the subject of a new load.' There is a boy here whose mother's British nationality protected him during the war, but immediately after the war he was put in a concentration camp for 6 months by the Russians. To find a reason for, and a pattern in all this is not easy, but they are there. We can discuss it in England.

Cardew's reaction to this 'correspondence' is characteristically detached and analytical;

yet there is also a hint of the moral outrage ('quietly appalling') which fuelled his politics in the last decade, as well as a nod in the direction of the acceptance of a political dimension.

In Germany in 1958 the effects of the war, spiritually and physically, were everywhere evident and despite its pretensions Modernism could not transcend such a condition. Yet it represented a commitment to, and a trajectory into, the future, and it was to the future that an artist, and a German artist in particular, had to look, whether inspired by idealism or desperation; the newness, the untarnished originality and purity of the New Music and the New Art, was irresistible. Ruth Aaronberg recalls the excitement of the visits and expeditions at that time: to an exhibition at the Stedelijk Museum in Amsterdam with Cornelius and Koenig, a trip to Donaueschingen in her Citroen 2CV with Cornelius and the Swedish composer Bengt Hambraeus, and to the Brussels Exposition together with Karlheinz and Doris Stockhausen to visit the Philips pavilion, designed by Le Corbusier and Iannis Xenakis, and 'sonorized' by Xenakis and Varèse. In Düsseldorf they and their friends would foregather at the Galerie 22, owned by Jean-Pierre Wilhelm and Manfred de la Motte, who exhibited a number of influential, contemporary artists (including the French op artist, Victor Vasarely) and promoted performances by the Korean avant-gardist, Nam June Paik; in Cologne, too, there were a number of galleries and cinemas which boasted a similar commitment to the new and the experimental. And there were more light-hearted occasions such as Carnival time in Munich with Herbert and Manni Brün, and the jazz clubs, although these were expensive and consequently frequented less often than those that had been popular with Cardew and his circle in London.

Yet for all its new-found confidence and self-assurance, perhaps partly as a corollary of it, the relations embodied in the New Music were restrictive and coercive, especially between composer and performer; the latter found himself operating, as it were, in a strait-jacket, enjoined to execute ever more mathematically precise notations (for example, the 11/12 ratio at the beginning of Stockhausen's *Klavierstück I*), which in turn engendered a proportionally increasing 'inaccuracy' in performance; spontaneity, akin to subversion, was outlawed or, to put it from a different perspective, the performer's sole interpretative contribution was by virtue of the mistakes he made. Even Pierre Boulez, hardly an innocent party in the matter, had expressed alarm at the situation pertaining to Darmstadt, deigning to attribute a measure of responsibility towards bursting the serial bubble to John Cage.

Little is recorded in the journals during 1958, and nothing after 10 August. The marriage was already deteriorating and Ruth's anathema to the Journals (according to Cardew) restricted and finally curtailed further entries:

> Write an analysis of Ruth which at the same time is always demonstrating the connection between the literary vehicle and its load. Thus it should give me, through my relations as author to subject, a guide to my relations with her in every importunity of flesh and blood. Thus her state of prostration at my reading or writing this Journal, that is, having a secret, must be a mystery in the text − a secret that is only disclosed, either when everything necessary for its understanding has been said or gradually, as hints are dropped about its nature, details, implications, etc.[29]

Nor does the meeting with John Cage, David Tudor, Merce Cunningham, Earle and Carolyn Brown at Darmstadt in 1958, of momentous import to Cardew's musical development, find mention in the Journals; in fact, Ruth dates the beginning of the breakdown of their marriage from this time. For her marital ambitions were conventional − and she made no secret of them: a permanent home in England, children, a family life − all of which was far removed from the philosophies and life-styles of Cardew's new American mentors and, for that matter, was totally incompatible with his own proclivities at that time. In Ruth's view theirs was a marriage of convenience: 'I don't think we would have married if we hadn't gone to Cologne, but living in sin was terribly inconvenient in post-war Germany, and once married I got all these bourgeois ideas which − quite naturally − made Cor cut and run.'[30]

Yet, in the light of her husband's antipathy to bourgeois conformism and the conventions of monogamous marriage, Ruth's explanation − that their marriage was for the sake of convenience − is not wholly convincing unless, as the magnitude of the step began to dawn on him, his initial acceptance metamorphosed by way of indifference into an hostility, with more than a hint of desperation. A dream recorded in the journals on 3 March, and a letter dated 7 April to his brother Seth, only weeks before his marriage, suggest that deeper levels need to be plumbed. In the letter the ambivalence and complexity of Cardew's attitude towards marriage is expressed through a series of interlocking aphorisms − a 'poem' in which he allows the free play and interpretation of related ideas, ending with a cryptic, quadratic equation, where we may speculate, capriciously, that 'a' stands for art, 'm' for marriage, and 'C' for Cornelius:

> Marriage has nothing to do with Art, only with Imagination.
> Sex has nothing to do with Marriage, only with Imagination.
> Art is pure miscarriage.

Sex is pure mismarriage.
Imagination + Marriage have nothing in common except Carnage.
Carnage is a stimulant. It is also its own antidote
Other stimulants require antidotes that are also other.

$$\int \frac{dy}{dx} = \int 3a^2 + 2m + a - C \quad \text{multiplied or divided ?}$$

[Seth refers to this in a letter to me dated 16 January 1991.]

The dream begins with Cardew's encounter on a boat with a group of ten or eleven whores; some are women, some hermaphrodites, one is an old man, one is half human, half animal (a Lion-Goddess), and the most important, a monster. There is a struggle with the monster on the parapet of a high cathedral and finally, in a square, high room ('a cube of space') the monster is joined by a man and a woman and 'the dream plays itself in slowly widening circles of sadism, horror and sexuality'. Even the most cautious and sceptical of analysts must needs tread carefully in this welter of bizarre images: the whores perhaps a desperate, last-ditch resistance to his impending sexual dependence on a permanent partner; the hermaphrodites suggesting an uncertainty relating to his own sexuality; the monster symbolises a struggle with those internal emotions and drives which both repulsed and attracted him; the height represents his isolation; and the sadism characterising the end of the dream may well be a throwback to earlier childhood experiences (at school?). Certainly the horror, brutality and drama of the dream (which, however, he does not describe as a nightmare) reflects a life in turmoil which, despite his desperate strivings, he is unable to control. Perhaps his relationship with Ruth was indeed fatally flawed from the outset; their marriage lasted barely nine months. 'What really is this openness we lack? (of the heart)' he had once written to her, and she too had opined in a letter to him, dated 18 January 1958, that 'there should be more truth in our relationship, especially on my part. You keep things secret because (I think) it is an essential part of your nature to keep yourself inviolable. You dread being "possessed"'.

In December 1958 Cornelius and Ruth, accompanied by Koenig, returned to England to spend Christmas at Wenford, where they were joined by David Sladen, and where Cardew and Koenig had planned to work on a translation into English of Koenig's article 'Musik und Zahl'. Like many other visitors, Köenig was impressed by Wenford – chiefly the cold and damp, necessitating the illicit use of wood meant for the pottery kiln, and the absence of electricity.

Before returning to Cologne Cornelius and Ruth had arranged to spend a few days in Richard Bennett's flat in Hampstead. On the afternoon of 5 January Ruth returned to the flat from an appointment with the hairdresser – they had been invited to a party that evening – to find a brief note from Cornelius to the effect that he had left her. The note referred to their waning sex life and his own sexual ambivalence, though on such occasions explanations, written in haste and under considerable stress, are rarely entirely credible.

That evening, on the boat train to the Continent and with time to reflect, Cardew had already begun to pen his reasons – 'physical', 'mental' and 'social' – for leaving Ruth. He begins: 'Jan 5. 7.15 pm GMT. Waiting for the train – "flight" to start: Ruth. How many times must I write, say, think, that life is not possible with her. Impossible. Perhaps reasons will help.' Her physical imperfections (that is, her physical characteristics), including her 'prohibitive asthma, inescapable but unbearable', are then listed, followed by her 'mental' flaws and inadequacies; these include

> Constant jealousy, sulkiness[…], an over-developed proprietorality, fear of things being stolen. Inability to support disorder. Irrational responsibility, irresponsibility always rationalised and severely rationed. Perhaps more than anything, her climbing attitude for me.

Yet the urge to leave Ruth at that particular time had been comparatively moderate. On previous occasions there had been a greater intensity of negative feeling which he had overcome, summoning up an even stronger commitment to their relationship:

> Somebody preserve me from the 20x made mistake of returning with returning strength. No strength is enough to surmount that, however strong I become. It is a perpetual circle. I have the strength built up, I return, it works, it weakens me. I succumb, bell, round, recuperate. But it must be broken for good – don't stop recuperating, it's fatal. She's a drain.[31]

And there is much more; the sum total of her physical and mental frailties are mercilessly enumerated to the exclusion of all redeeming features – an unworthy, for him indispensable, exercise in self-justification.

The next morning the consequences of his actions – his decision to leave Ruth, her plight – force a new awareness on him; speculation concerning her state of mind, her changing relationships with their friends, her immediate plans. But there is no weakening of his resolve. ('She will not go to Oxford. So that must be my itinerary'.) On the contrary, love itself is denied as having ever existed in their marriage, and it is contemplation of the latter institution which predictably, towards the close of the Journal entry, elicits unequivocal condemnation:

> The negative death (of life, I admit, rather than music) brought about by acquiescence. The total lack of responsibility implied by simply saying 'yes' to things which represent, when analysed, a grapple or infiltration with or into 'the world' the 99 percent (of pretty heaummes [Cardew's attempt to simulate the bourgeois pronunciation of 'homes'!], incomes, interior decorating, 'holidays', the new car which is never as good as the old one).[32]

In an undated letter to Ilona Halberstadt, probably from around the same time, he wrote:

> A decision like mine to leave Ruth was necessary (way of life and way of thinking were mutually exclusive), but the action was certainly inevitable, but, if left unacted, meant the cessation of organic evolvement. The way of life would have ceased to be the result of the way of thinking. Corollary: Thought Atrophy. But (back we are at Nietzsche's 'Survival') I accepted the necessary.

For her part Ruth had resolved to pursue her husband and had set off the next day for Cologne, to their lodgings in Dasselstrasse, where a combination of emotional blackmail and mouth-watering meals secured her a few weeks grace but failed to save their marriage. They parted and Ruth found much needed comfort with her friends Manni and Herbert Brün who invited her to Berlin and found her a room in their Pension near the Kurfürstendamm. She remained in Berlin throughout February and made the decision to stay in Germany indefinitely. Friends in Cologne, in particular Koenig, rallied round and helped her to find employment, initially in the English section of the Radio Station and subsequently as an English teacher at the Berlitz School.[33]

Cardew in the meantime had returned to England, to the flat in Richmond, and remained there until the end of April, working 'in odd moments' on his piano piece, *February Piece I,* and adapting his article, 'The Unity of Musical Space' ('my final comment on my studies in electronic music!'), for *New Departures*, a new arts magazine founded at Oxford University in the summer of '59 by two students, Michael Horovitz and his old school friend David Sladen, and for which Cardew was enlisted as music editor. The circumstances were now very different; in Cologne he was neither a student nor an acolyte – he was Stockhausen's employee, with a recently broken marriage behind him. In England, without prospect or strategy, the Journals reflect a kind of regression to the changing moods, the restlessness of his undergraduate days through a variety of subjects, briefly embraced and quickly abandoned: philosophy and morals, human agency, Socratic thought, humour, chance encounters, overheard conversations, observed scenes in trains, parks, coffee bars, and on a bus where he was attempting to write a programme note: 'On the bus: I have to write to distract me from the woman, the warm pressure of the femme de trente ans, her softest arm. Boulez – rescue – your programme note must curb my corpuscular eruptions.'[34]

And, a few days later, a series of twelve questions: philosophical, flippant, humorous, ambiguous, surreal, vulgar. Yet for all their variety and opacity the juxtaposition and alternation of anecdotal material and musical analysis is consciously provocative, with the circumscribed world of serialism clearly losing out to the 'perfectly ordinary reality' which was to become the stuff of his meta-music of the sixties: *Treatise*, AMM and the Scratch Orchestra.

Feb. 29 (can it be March 1st 1959?).
I have a headache. The Reason?..:
Structures la, the series is used as a block, as material, and these blocks are transposed according to the intervals of the series.[35]

A crazy couple walking through the park. He was reading aloud in a boring voice with public-speech ups and downs, from *The Compleat Angler*. She, in pressed black slacks, a nice walk and maybe a plain face – she was too far away and in the wrong light really to see, but durchaus attractive – listened with an expression of utter boredom (I could see that much, anyway). They are now half a mile away, still at it – I can see them. I'm sure this has some bearing on the problem of ends and means.

No, scrub that: The elementary building block is a series of durations with a series of pitches having a constant attack and intensity. To obtain further material, the block is transposed in an order given by the intervals within the block (extrapolation).

It is hopeless – I am murderously attracted to people who seem unhappy.

Another 'idea of bliss': to carry a portable radio through the park – bringing music to the millions.

These blocks are then superimposed, making sections in various tempi with various densities. The constant factors (attack + intensity) correspond to the colours, '- – or take something of importance, such as – – – marriage', so that the various block-constructions appear variously multi- or mono-chromatic.[36]

The next day there is a brief after-thought – with a sting in the tail:

Shadow of that headache persists, – a touch of the sun? or of evil?
A Great disinclination for work.

Meanwhile, the eclectic nature of his reading material (he appears to pluck a book out of the air, randomly) is borne out by two Journal entries in close succession – the first from Plato's *Symposium*:

Today I read about that wonderful woman Diotima, who tells Socrates such wonderful things 'laughing'. The ultimate Socratic tactic 'Certainly not, O Socrates' is very efficacious since it contains, implicitly, the accusation of Sophistry, in its latter-day, debased sense.[37]

Five days later the subject is morals and the reference is John Stuart Mill:

Memo: discuss with David [Sladen] whether, in morals, there are cases where the difference between right and wrong is a quantitative one. I see now that I am not at all clear on this point. I should work at it. The result would be the purest John Stuart Mill. (Conceit is the mother of – – – ?)[38]

In March a brief visit to Oxford offered a welcome, if partial contrast to the buttoned-up earnestness, self-importance and competitive power-mongering of his Cologne circle. At the university there were the chance encounters, usually at parties, with kindred spirits – young, artistic, self-absorbed – who by dint of background and education exuded well-being and self-confidence, unrestrained in their cultivation of exotic tastes, relaxed in their unchallengeable superiority, and unaware of, or indifferent to, the banality of their own drawled presumptions. (Having been to Oxford… 'qualifies you for nothing, but prepares you for anything' was Michael Cardew's peremptory verdict on the great institution.) [39] Cardew records incidents and conversational fripperies from these parties, conferring significances where it is doubtful that any obtain, and allowing a somewhat disproportionate amount of space in the Journals to an account of a three-day infatuation with a Greek student:

conceived, incubated and born still on the evenings of the 13th, 14th and 15th of March (when are the Ides?) [. . .] Hauled out of sleep at 9pm by Anna Pialopulo – Greek Goddess who impresses me not at all until the party is reached and she discusses Arabic poem about love out of the blue. Seems not to know love at all. Later, her face dawns on me and I speak again – at 1am she and Ilona [Halberstadt] come back to David's [Sladen] for coffee, and I realise she must be seen again; a lift to town tomorrow, if she can swing it. On the way out David suggests she leaves some cigarettes – 'I have, surely.' [40]

Nevertheless, it *was* a time of change at Oxford; there was a small but significant increase in the number of students fron State schools and from abroad, while radical political debate, particularly within the Labour Club, reflected a wider concern with issues such as colonialism, nuclear disarmament and the position and role of women in society. Culturally, too, there were challenges to tradition; in her second year at Oxford Ilona Halberstadt, a St. Anne's philosophy student, together with fellow student Julian Silverman, founded the Oxford Contemporary Music Club, and it was she who invited John Cage and David Tudor to give a concert at the Holywell Rooms on 20 October 1958. Halberstadt had already met Cardew and Richard Bennett at the Dartington summer school in 1957 and it was on her initiative that Cardew, too, had come to Oxford.

In fact, they became close friends, and Ilona features frequently, and for a time obsessively, in Cardew's Journals. Her attributes seemed to satisfy his needs – she was elusive, anarchic (with Marxist tendencies), wayward (or as wayward as a female undergraduate dared to be in the nineteen fifties), with a somewhat irritating proclivity for the elliptical remark, possessed of an acute intelligence which matched and challenged his, and of powers of concentration which intimidated him, causing him to reflect on her advice and ideas with unusual consideration and respect:

In Oxford I had maintained that the failure of my relationships resulted from incapacity to withdraw, well and timelily. Now she [Ilona] puts it to me that my lack of withdrawal technique is merely a result of the fact that I am not involved. I reply that I stretch out my hand to someone, but should they start pulling I wish my hand to come off smoothly and easily. This is not non-involvement, but the wish to make the involution dispensable. But I do see what she means. Involvement in a permanent way is an involvement of an organic part of you, not an attachment.[41]

And on 5 April:

explain, as Ilona did to me, that a day's conversation in which we did not agree does not mean very much; it was stupid of me to try and persuade her she was wrong – if I had succeeded it would have meant she was insubstantial, which she certainly is not.

For Cardew, as for his Oxford peer group, the need to establish intellectual superiority, to partake in the games of one-upmanship in which intellects were vanquished and character and status summarily down-graded, was indisputable; in such contests any lowering of the guard would be interpreted as a weakness to be exploited ('Ilona. I must be sustained when seeing her, to match her utter concentration'.) Yet this perceived need to fight his corner intellectually was at odds with his attraction to the ethos both of the American Beats and of the New Departures poets and artists, whose non-conformism and extravagant behaviour he found congenial, indeed irresistible. In the Journals he indulges his fascination for railway stations – meeting places where arrival and departure points coincide and where there is constant flux and multi-directional movement, inspiring him to both poetic extemporization (at South Kensington station) and philosophical meditation: 'I felt like learning Tao, sitting cross-legged on a sheet of newspaper on Waterloo station this morning.' [42] Such action would not have been challenged by the poets, nor rationalised; it would simply have been acknowledged. On one occasion, in Darmstadt, the conductor Daniele Paris was shocked that Cardew had spent the night in the railway station, assuming that a state of impecuniousness had forced such drastic measures upon him. This may have been the case; more likely, he was simply indulging his penchant for stations and the life that is generated in and around them.

On 9 April 1959, the day before Cardew's return to Cologne, there is an exuberant reference to a visit to Gaberbocchus (and to an English nursery rhyme): 'Five, Five, the Ravers-O. Julian [probably Silverman], Mike [Horovitz], Anna [Lovell], Ilona [Halberstadt] and I took ? of a plumby bottle to Gabberbochers [sic] where there happened to be a great Experimental new film, for which I would quite like to have written the music.' [43] Mike Horovitz recalls the occasion and the film, which was *Food for a Blush*, made by Carole Russell, who was at the time a student at the Chelsea College of Art. Horovitz also recalls an excursion with the same party to Philip Granville's gallery, Lords, to listen to recordings of Kurt Schwitters reading his 'Ursonate'. Jazz venues such as Studio 51 in Great Newport Street, the Flamingo, Cy Laurie's and Ronnie Scott's Old Place in Gerrard street were also popular.

With the inauguration of Live New Departures the need for performance spaces for their own events became a priority and a number of venues (among others the Partisan, a coffee bar in Soho frequented by artists and people of left persuasion) were booked. The idea was to bring all the Arts together, to break down barriers which separated artists from each other so that, for example, both jazz and avant-garde music would be featured in the same evening; and in this latter respect, particularly, Horovitz recalls the central role Cardew played in the evolution of Live New Departures in the early years.[44] He would play Jimmy Yancey numbers on the piano, and also accompany the poets with his own, avant-garde music; Horovitz recalls Cardew accompanying his (Horovitz's) reading of his poems 'Sonata of Heaven and Earth', and 'Pieces of Air' – and a translation Cardew made into German of Horovitz's poem 'Hotwine' ('Glühwein'). These gatherings were joyful, celebratory, with humour an essential ingredient; on one occasion the Alberts, a comedy group with the brothers Tony and Douglas Grey and their dog, were driving from London to appear in the New Departures Ball at the Carfax Assembly rooms in Oxford when they picked up a hitch-hiker, by chance one Cornelius Cardew, who was bound for the same destination (although even his virtuosity is unlikely to have matched that of the Alberts, one of whose specialities was to play the trombone with his left foot). It was a remarkable coincidence, for in the back of their van, which the Grey brothers customarily used for delivering daily newspapers to railway stations, was a piano which they were transporting to the Carfax Assembly Rooms. Cardew opened up the piano and duly entertained his hosts and their dog, who was also in the back of the van, for the rest of the journey.

But it was the American writing and its New World energy which appealed to Cardew: more realistic, direct, fresh, vigorous, aural, closer to street life and therefore closer to real life, where you had to be quick on your feet.[45] In an undated letter to Ilona Halberstadt, written in the Spring of 1959, he refers to Kerouac's On the Road, a book which had fired the imagination of many of their peers:

> Key character of O.t.R. – Carlo Marx – Self-sufficient. Dean's relationship with him could reach a peak and pass it without tears (contrast Dean and Sal – 'we will be together always' later). The only one not to criticise Dean's actions and yet realizing that simply being Dean was not enough.

By contrast, the new, university-trained English poets' obsession with 'Collages rather than Colleges' reflected an English spirit of irony and detachment. Moreover, according to Horovitz, they had been tutored to be 'wily and devious'; and he quotes aptly from Eliot's 'The Love Song of J. Alfred Prufrock': 'Prepare a face to meet the faces that you meet.' Whereas the message of the Beats was 'to strip off all masks'.

On 10 April Cardew returned to Cologne with 'an open mind and a work-hungry spirit' to embark on what turned out to be a lengthy and sometimes enervating collaboration with Stockhausen on Carré, a new work conceived during Stockhausen's long flights over North America while he was lecturing there – a collaboration which was 'on the one hand, an expression of his altruistic desire to help me personally and, on the other, his solution of his problem of having more commitments than he could accomplish single-handed'.[46]

Cardew stayed with the Stockhausens for several days until his advertisement for accommodation was answered by a Ukrainian family in the Brüsselerstrasse. ('Every day I assiduously scan the local paper only to find offers of rooms to "2 solide Männer – separate beds".'[47] The rent was low, the husband and wife and three children made him welcome, and in a letter to his mother he even expressed relief not to be living with German people, a generalization which probably concealed a truer description of his sentiments – that he had found a haven, or so he thought at the time, from the unrelenting atmosphere of the German cultural milieu in which he circulated. ('The whole of Germany smells of fresh paint' he wrote, metaphorically, in an undated letter to Ilona Halberstadt.) In any case the links with the Studio and the majority of its 'inmates' were now tenuous and even the work on *Carré* is rarely mentioned in the Journals up to the end of 1959, and then in a disrespectful or negative vein: 'I cannot remember the last time I woke up and thought O God another day. But it almost happened this morning. Is this to do with the Stockhausen work?'[48] It may well have been – although there were redeeming features which Cardew acknowledged and elaborated upon later in his report on *Carré*. Inevitably, the work necessitated an even closer relationship with Stockhausen:

> Working daily chez Stockhausen from 3 p.m. until dinnertime; aided, irritated, confused, encouraged, and sometimes even guided by his own eagle eye, or his voluminous notes, or his random narrations as he worked on his own experiments for what later became *Kontakte* for piano, percussion and 4 track tape.[49]

At the same time, between April and June, he was writing his own *Octet 1959* and had taken upon himself the onerous task of learning the guitar part of Boulez's *Le Marteau sans Maître*, presumably for the performance at Dartington on 6 August.[50]

The Journals, however, are preoccupied with friends and events in England: Ilona, Anna Lovell, Richard Bennett (even more disparagingly), and Ruth, who by this time 'seems to be going places with Koenig'.[51] 'I am completely vacuous, suspended. Only *The Ginger Man* pulling my feet to the ground. Christ, when is the next train back to London?' he wrote to Ilona Halberstadt around this time, and the same letter continues with a fulmination against Sundays: 'How wrong was the immortal Karl Kraus (was it him?): "Es muss ein Sonntag sein." It must NEVER be Sunday, ever again.' And a quote from the author of *The Ginger Man*, J. P. Donleavy, is enlisted: 'Dear God, come down and settle in my heart on this triangular Sunday.'

Dreams, too, to which he always attributed significance without ever venturing into analysis, are recorded in remembered detail: a brief description of an orgy at Richard Bennett's flat which he abandons to go to Düsseldorf to renew his passport ('my passport is more important to me than my sex-life') and a more complex dream involving protagonists and venues in both England (Wenford) and Germany, starring the ubiquitous Anna Pialopulo in bed in Wenford and then transported, still in bed, to a strange town resembling Munich: Cornelius at her bedside, Ilona always close by, and an atmosphere involving young and old and high jinks.

The Journals themselves manifest interesting changes in style, and even handwriting, which Cardew himself commented on in an entry on Whitsunday, May 1959:

On reading early 1955. How did I lose my ability to write, think, clearly, logically. Where did I drop it? (where did I pick it up? at school?). It is economical, flowing – ideas are not repeated within a sentence, as so often happens now as a result of a stylistic whim.

There are two methods: either one works hard to find the mot juste, working from the premise that it exists. (This seems to result in the clear, economical early pages [...]) Or one invents words, recreates language for each new eventuality. Leads of course to confusion, because the checking process (a large part of language history in a sort of subconscious way) is missing. So, a gain in richness and colour against a decline in polish and delineation, definition (moulding, clarity, etc.)

The intention is different (prosodic).

But have my intentions changed?

What do I mean by this book?

A difficult question.

The early Journal entries do betray a scholastic influence constituting, as it were, a linguistic home-base, just as his lifestyle at the time was structured around the requirements of the Academy, and his compositional ideas and thought processes moved along the grooves of the musical avant-garde. This was no longer the case; he had cut himself adrift, at least of the European avant-garde, free of theory and fashion, in favour of an existentialist mode: sensuous, intuitive, pragmatic, the free flow and association of feelings and ideas, the here and now – to which his personality and background were eminently more suited. 'A nice morning: totally concerned with myself', was the way he signed off the above Journal entry. And, accordingly, his ideas relating to purely musical matters – brought about to a large extent by his meetings in Darmstadt with John Cage and La Monte Young – underwent radical change: 'Things that I would never in those (earlier) days have admitted had anything to do with music whatever – sound, for instance!'[52]

Somehow, in the teeth of an oppressive, European (German) conformity and within a repressive moral climate, Cardew's originality blossomed and began to imprint itself with wit and subtlety on the city's landscape, as the Austrian composer and horn player Kurt Schwertsik recalls:

> The very important part he played in my life began shortly after my arrival in Cologne in 1959. I was feeling somehow betrayed by the social graces of my musical heroes in that capital of New Music. I believed that an artist should live outside society altogether, or at least on its outermost fringes: a hermit or clochard. I worked quite hard to achieve that. One day in the Hohestrasse I caught sight of someone who had succeeded without trying. His loping walk, his dress, his entire demeanour – all different! Unmistakeably, at whatever distance, Cornelius Cardew. He never needed to avoid normal patterns of behaviour; he simply never came within sight of them. For instance: seeing a grubby old coat draped over a parked motorcycle to protect it from the Cologne weather, he took off his own coat, compared the two, meditated for a moment, and swapped them over.[53]

In Cologne Cardew was like a visitant who led a life of semi-vagrancy, a stranger with *Fingerspitzengefühl* in everything he touched, and of a fabled sensuality.

Schwertsik's first encounter with Cardew was in Vienna in the Autumn of 1959 at the flat of the Austrian composer/conductor Friedrich Cerha. Schwertsik recalls listening to Cardew practising and admiring his extraordinary ability to characterise individual chords through the subtle control and balancing of their constituent tones. (This was a feature of David Tudor's virtuosity which must have impressed Cardew during their work together on his, Cardew's, *Two Books of Study for Pianists* and which he himself subsequently developed in his own playing to an impressive degree.) The two men became acquainted and before long were good friends. They had much in common, not least in their attitude to the European avant-garde; for them the whole enterprise had degenerated, had become 'bourgeois', pretentious and academic, with much intellectual posturing, its credo littered with 'musts' and 'don'ts'.

> He [Cardew] was the first person I met in Cologne who talked sensibly about modern music; we agreed about the inconsistencies, the lies they were telling the whole time. All stemming from Adorno, arguments founded on 'logic'. Cornelius was the first not to have an ideological viewpoint but who would try to talk sensibly as a musician. Koenig (et al.) would say that if you played Beethoven's symphonies at the correct metronome marking they would sound like modern music, which was complete naiveté. Cornelius was never naive.[54]

On one occasion, Schwertsik recalls commenting to Cardew on his admirable

calmness, his equanimity, to which Cardew replied, 'Yes, but not under all circumstances.'[55] On another, Schwertsik was joking, disparagingly, about 'socialists on holiday';
Cardew retorted summarily, 'I'm a socialist.' Schwertsik's portrait of Cardew from the
Cologne days, as perceptive as it is captivating, is illuminated through the language of
the Journals – ever inventive, colourful, wayward; the observations subtle and now
perhaps kinder, as in an entry on 19 May describing his landlord with daughter:

But Oh the man-woman thing. How she loves him, and then he embraces, enfolds,
spreads his arms round his daughter, covers gently her face with his hand, shuts
out the light of the world, makes a womb for her. Oh Christ, the physical Lawrencian
emanation from this complex.

Places of desolation and mystery attracted him – the debris, the buildings destroyed
or half-destroyed by Allied bombing, their buried secrets and the enigmatic signals of
survival:

I wandered among the big machines and broken stones, and some shrubs are
creeping up. Next door there is an old ruined (bombed?) sort of church with a
back door saying 'Emil Boys – Kunstformer' and then hung up inside in a ruined
passage a note to say that he was now in a different part of the house and to
make yourself bemerkbar ['noticeable'], at the cellar windows in Piusstr. – signed
Boys. This I did and tried all windows (barred) and doors (locked or rusted or
nailed shut). Perhaps worth trying in the day-time. He must be found. What is a
Kunstformer? I must find somewhere to live before the police find me.[56]

And the same entry gives evidence of his continuing enthusiasm for more remote
cultures: 'Read Waley + Canto LXXIV [Ezra Pound]: the latter is a great long poem of
800 odd lines. Good indeed.'[57]

Presumably there was some irregularity relating to Cardew's residence with the Ukrainian
family and on 1 June he left them in what appears to have been a mutually beneficial
move. His landlord had already received complaints from other tenants that Cardew's
appearance frightened them – his extra-long hair, his unshavenness, the blue trousers,
the sandals and his dirty feet. 'I get looked at and laughed at quite a lot [...] due to the
paucity of passing, work-a-day wonders', he wrote to his mother.[58] The acrimonious
parting is recorded in some detail, with Cardew's eccentric behaviour – sitting on the
doorstep in the sun waiting for Stockhausen, with a bottle of milk and two rolls, and

wearing a suit – a calculated affront, so it would have seemed, to the conventional sensibilities of his landlady: 'Never wore it on Sundays, now he wears it and sits in the middle of the street in it. Komplet verrückt [Quite mad].' And the suspicious parents standing in watchful apprehension as Cardew, this foreign *Luftmensch,* seated among an entranced audience of children, sings a little – 'April in Paris' – and tells them of America, England, and Tower Bridge; 'there is nothing Mr. Corneliuvooni doesn't know'. After several hours it eventually transpired that Stockhausen's car had broken down; Cardew had to make his own way to Stockhausen's house whence, in the evening, he was driven to his new lodgings in Vogelsang, Gürlitzweg.

And the early summer days passed by, a succession of sleepless nights, 'raves' with the Stockhausens, the Kagels, the publisher Ernst Bruecher and his wife, and especially his two friends Haro Lauhus and Mary Bauermeister; discourse and debate into the night of teutonic length and complexity. And, in the Journals, sharing his attention to Raymond Chandler, Alfred North Whitehead and the numerous bars with their unpredictable juke boxes, were the minutiae of appointments, meetings and chance encounters with friends, bus conductresses, travelling families, boring writers, diplomats and photographers – recorded with detachment and gentle irony. So too, for the second time, was the status of the suit (in post-war Germany), which he wore on his first morning from Vogelsang by bus to Stockhausen's house, passing en route the cryptic domicile of the elusive Kunstformer, Emil Boys, and experiencing painful recognition and frustration. ('to be an Anzugmensch (suit person) – everyone looks at you with such respect').

In 1957 the artist Mary Bauermeister had come from Saarbrücken to Cologne where Cardew and the painter and photographer Haro Lauhus were among her first friends. Together they organised avant-garde concerts and events which took place in the huge studio that Mary Bauermeister had rented. Cardew, who by this time had many contacts in West Germany and internationally, drew up the programmes, Lauhus contributed ideas which were exhilarating if not always viable, and Bauermeister raised the necessary funds by selling her paintings; in fact, various offers of financial support materialised from a number of enlightened sources. The studio provided a base for a 'counter-culture' and the opportunity for the younger experimentalists to present their work to a curious, if wary, public; it also provided a roof and a number of mattresses for itinerants and those like the critic Heinz-Klaus Metzger (who slept in the bath) who preferred a more ascetic, unadorned way of living. In contrast, the IGNM Festival (Internationale Gesellschaft für Neue Musik) promoted those members of the avant-garde who had already achieved a degree of notoriety, or rather fame – Cage, Kagel, Stockhausen; its organisers (and sponsors) were not inclined to take risks with lesser, younger lights.

Cardew first mentions Pyla (Ilse Schneider), an artist friend of Haro Lauhus and Mary Bauermeister, in a Journal entry dated 21 June 1959. He was extremely taken with her; she, in turn, was somewhat disconcerted by the swiftness and boldness of his manner towards her. Nevertheless, she agreed to accompany him to Schloss Morsbroich, near Leverkusen, for the opening of an exhibition of Concrete Art (including works by the Swiss artist Max Bill), which seems to have impressed Cardew, although in the Journals he expresses regret that the work of the German aesthetician Max Bense had not been represented.

Cardew pursued Pyla in earnest, though not always conclusively; he was intrigued by her occasional remoteness, captivated by her whimsicality (the 'or perhaps not' or the 'perhaps it does' which ended each sentence); but there were subtleties which eluded him, and needs which his self-centredness prevented him from recognizing. The Journals record an evening together with Lauhus and Mary Bauermeister which ended awkwardly:

Walking my baby against her increasing reluctance. This is strange and stupid of me. Do I not want to be alone? I only want not to go home. More and more difficult, she aches, and so does the conversation. Finally, we do not understand each other, good night.[59]

On parting, a disused signal box in a goods yard seemed to offer him an overnight retreat, but before long he was ejected by a blue-uniformed railway official with a constant, minatory grin. He was taken away, and later released, by a stroke of irony, when his marriage to Ruth, now a legal resident, came to light and was deemed to legitimise his own status in the Federal Republic. A few hours later the same morning a visit to Ruth to clarify the divorce procedure provided an appropriate sequel; Ruth conducted the business from her bed and in the Journal Cardew describes the extreme sexual tension which they generated, attributing his own restraint to his dirty feet rather than to his exhaustion from the escapade in the goods yard, although he confesses to masturbating twice later in the day.

But it was the relationship with Pyla which now consumed him, and when, on one occasion, she fails to materialise for a date he reflects presumptuously on her 'probable lesbianism'. A week later, on 30 June, he refers in the Journals to an 'unforgettable day and night with Pyla... the girl I cannot harm'. Her unattainability fired him, just as the 'uncatchability' of music was for him its most precious quality. 'She does not need me, I do not need her. It is unnecessary and it is beautiful.' (Beauty as the image of transience.) And at this point there is an interesting change of tack as if the paean to the lack of (proprietorial) need between them had provoked a further, contradictory thought:

Riding his bicycle home, it begins to rain and Cardew dismounts in a clearing in a wood, sits down on some dead leaves and lets the rain come; 'the desire, love of something stronger than me [...] I seek it in a way in Pyla. But again her strength challenges, stimulates me to strength'. These private imperatives: desire, love of something stronger – a person, Nature – hover precariously on the periphery of human need and dependency, those very qualities which his initial thought appears to depreciate. Yet it is to this thought, clearly the more compelling of the two, though hardly as deeply-rooted, that he reverts: '2 creepers (parasites!) growing round each other, and yes, succeeding in growing in spite of the absence of the real tree on which to grow. Because of the growth, this absence becomes irrelevant.' For Cardew the absence of 'the real tree' meant the absence of a controlling and restrictive dependency and thus a condition of freedom and autonomy which he sought both in his relations with people – floating freely in and out of one another's orbit – and between musical structures where, like the autonomous parts of his *Two Books of Study for Pianists*, there may be strengthening and stimulation, even challenge, but never dependency.

A year earlier, in the summer of 1958, the same concerns had been anticipated in a letter to his brother Seth in which he described in some detail his project for an autonomous musical structure: a vibration in the air suspended and sustained through the 'repellent' qualities from itself: 'As if, from the contact with the various fixed "magnetic" poles these constellations had somehow acquired a sort of anti-magnetic field, built up by the structure itself, impenetrable to all except its own structural electrons, and unrelatable to any fixed medium'.

The project, originally conceived as an hour long piece for thirty-two players, was never realised or, most likely, was metamorphosed into the piano music of the late fifties – beginning with the *Two Books of Study*. As we have seen, the idea of the superimposition and interaction of autonomous entities relating freely to each other, rootless and independent, was at the time beginning to be of particular concern to Cardew, in both musical and human relations.

During the summer of 1959 ('the summer of *Le Marteau*') Cardew returned to England and the journals fall silent. Part of August was spent at Dartington and there was a visit to the pottery at Wenford with friends, including Luigi Nono, who was teaching composition at Dartington that year, and a young English pianist whom he had just met, informally, at Dartington, and who, some forty years or so later, was to become his biographer. There was also a reunion with Ilona Halberstadt, a young lady who continued to impress him: 'Ilona is the woman of the year; Ilona, the craziest woman after my own heart that I know. Why do, did, will I not take her?'[60]

Throughout 1959, that is, from the time he left Ruth and moved from one rented accommodation to another in Cologne, Cardew and Ilona Halberstadt exchanged letters with exceptional frequency. The mode is mostly improvisatory, the content often entertaining and amusing, sometimes flippant and inconsequential, and with an undertone of frustration, desperation even, which occasionally surfaces in the form of suicidal fantasies. References to writers and philosophers – Pound's *Cantos*, Büchner's *Wozzeck*, Donleavy's *The Ginger Man*, Whitehead, Sartre, Taoism, and of course, Wittgenstein – result in a kind of tug-of-war with concepts, as well as linguistic games, playing with words, meanings, sounds. If they occasionally demonstrate his (and her) brilliance, they also expose a vulnerability: 'This terrible reluctance to *send* my letters to you at all – they are so defenceless.' And in another letter, when he was lodging with the Stockhausen family, Cardew writes:

Wittgenstein, tell me what happens when I read the words 'I love you'. Does understanding them mean simply reading the words? Is the fact that I start sweating a symptom of my understanding? Why do I start sweating? Because, just (with conviction) Because.
She: I don't understand.[61]

Halberstadt's 'letters' consist mainly of cut-outs and newspaper cuttings, cryptic snippets of information on small pieces of cardboard, drawings, collages, scribbles, personal fragments; whereas for Cardew the message is most important – for her, perhaps, it is the medium.

Cardew returned to Cologne in September to join David Tudor and Siegfried Rockstroh in the first performance of Stockhausen's *Refrain* (playing celesta and antique cymbals) in the Berliner Festwochen on 2 October, and then to Darmstadt where he performed his own *February Piece I*, and the *Two Books of Study for Pianists* with David Tudor.[62] 'Tudor brings life to the Books, sight-reading with an appalling headache (he tells – it is not evident in his behaviour – so Wittgenstein?). With him the piece can really be worked on'.[63] This is the first reference to Wittgenstein in the Journals. David Sladen had given him a copy of the *Tractatus* and this was to provide the impulse for much of his experimentation with musical notation as well as for his writings on music, in particular his article 'Notation – Interpretation, Etc.', published two years later in *Tempo* magazine.
In a revealing description of the significance (for him) of performance Cardew refers to a concert in Vienna in which he and David Tudor played the *Two Books:*

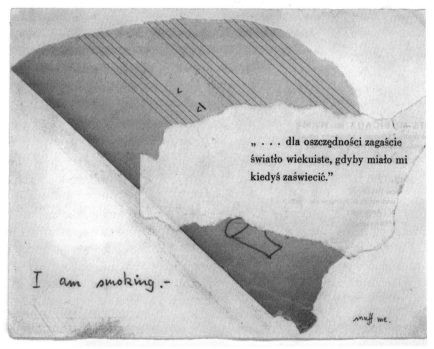

Collages: from Ilona to Cornelius (top), Cornelius to Ilona (bottom) originals: colour, 1959.

Back now in Cologne. After [the] Viennese concert where David and I once more scandalised with a new version of the scandalous books. But this time I refused to smile. Being on the stage is not being above anything at all. Yes, you woman with the whistle, come up here and I'll throw you down again – you dare wreck my piece? What have I wrecked of yours? [...] I fossilise up there – stiffened face. Yet somewhere down there is some warmth and in spite of all a happy crowd is gathering afterwards and I have to run to catch a train back here. And it is tearing silk to leave. [...] And outstretched Autographs. Full length Autographs and wonderful Hungarian, Czech and God knows Dollies. Everybody interested and Christ what do I live for if not this contact during and after concerts.[64]

Before the decade had drawn to a close Cardew had already assumed a position hostile to the European avant-garde (which was already beginning to feel vulnerable to the fresh winds blowing threateningly across the Atlantic, bearing subversion and heresy), dismissing what he regarded now as the pretentious and numbing dogma which pervaded at Darmstadt, mocking its supreme irrelevance, and even pitying its sagging, yet still earnest protagonists. A lecture by Pierre Boulez at Darmstadt in September 1959 inspired him to write a letter, *in situ,* to a girl-friend, Natalie Behr:

I think the man next to me thinks I am taking notes on a very complicated lecture in French by Boulez, which is going on now [...] That funny little man gabbling away in front of a blackboard with arrows and words like 'Morphology' 'Syntaxe' 'Statique' 'Dynamique' 'Critères sélectifs' etc. etc. I'm feeling like yelling CRAP at the top of my voice, but suddenly he looks rather sweet and vulnerable. 'Un ensemble conceptual.'. Yeah, Yeah, that's us! Great. Applause now so must stop.

At the end of October, under the pretext of a request to type the instructions for *Octet 1959*, another visit to Ruth (now living with Koenig) generated the same atmosphere of over-charged sexuality as on the previous occasion, and underlined the difficulty he was experiencing in extricating himself, emotionally, from the relationship: Ruth's commitment to another man simultaneously a deliverance and a provocation. A dream around the same time provided humorous relief, as well as an outlet for his sexuality, and is recorded in the Journals on 23 October with some relish and a Cardewesque lightness of touch:

A wonderful dream last night (this morning) of a clitoris of a quality I have not experienced. Size, texture, resilience, all tended to make it an end in itself. Entrance therefore did not occur. It seems to me I had the idea but turned it down. She was wearing a shirt of such a red as I have not experienced. A very delicious dream altogether. But the main thing was this wonderful clitoris – as though I dreamt only with the third finger of my right hand. A finger dream. That's right: My finger was dreaming.

And all the while, as winter approached, and he was living in a tiny dark room in Severinstrasse, bei Hölschermann, insistent images from the heady English days of recent months monopolized his imagination: 'And that crazy, gin-swilling, compulsive, criminal-type, accident-prone Welshman who brought Mike (Horovitz) and me down from Oxford this summer – Mike singing Trompete Lieder down Shaftesbury avenue and Anna [Lovell] sulking home.'[65] The days in Cologne were beginning to weigh heavily on him and he seems to have been living in a kind of emotional and intellectual limbo: 'I am seeking a self – la tête habitable, perhaps, or for a satisfactory spirit to inhabit my head which is already habitable, I imagine, in fact hospitable.'[66] Moreover, the relationship with Pyla had become strained ('she lacks sensuality, yes, simple direct perception […] she must learn to fill her life, and live it gladly'[67]) and occasionally other women drifted into his life which took on an existentialist character through an intensive and exclusive sensuality: 'The hole in the throat. Oodoo's throat – the drop of water and the incredible indelible sweetness.'[68]

It was his employer who, fortuitously and in a dramatic intervention, stopped the rot, jolting his protégé back into the world of responsible and rational action. On the eve of Cardew's departure, in December, to England Stockhausen sprang the idea of a new element he wanted to insert into *Carré* – episodes contrasting with the main material of the piece which would also necessitate considerably more work than hitherto planned and cause a delay in completion of some months.

Despite the extra work-load which accompanied him, it was with some relief that Cardew returned to England – to sources of inspiration, to the company of his English peers, to young people 'who paint and drive to India in jeeps', to ladies to spar with, analyse, love, always demanding of them, yet self-critical: 'Too often my sensations are those of a teacher: I have to learn, not teach. Ridiculous idea: to get you [Natalie] to show your emotions more strongly. It is lack of refinement in me. To teach you to express yourself more coarsely, that would coarsen you. Oh its so clear.'[69]

Natalie Behr, a student at the Royal College of Art, was the woman of the moment; Ilona, a fitful but unfading presence, and still, obsessively, Ruth, who in a dream had invited him to dinner, castrated him in his sleep, and served him his own 'fried' genitals. Cardew described the dream as 'the most horrible I have ever had, but it had no nightmare quality', and expressed the desire to discuss it with an analyst, whilst fearing the possible interpretations that could be put upon it. Yet the 'meaning' – surely the dawning on him of the inevitability of Ruth's rejection of him − seems to be less complex than those of previously recorded dreams.

I have already mentioned that I first made Cardew's acquaintance at the Dartington Summer School in the summer of '59. Soon after my return to London I received a phone call from him, the purpose of which was to ask me if I would be interested in taking part in a concert of music for one and two pianos with him. As far as I can recall, he had not heard me play (apart, possibly, from Schoenberg's op.19 which I may have performed, informally, at Dartington) but was, I suppose, impressed by my enthusiasm for contemporary music and unaware of my ignorance of it.

'Generation Music I' took place at the Conway Hall in London on 27 January 1960 and included music by Schoenberg (op. 19), Feldman, Cage, Wolff, and Cardew's *Two Books of Study for Pianists.* The novelty of the programme, as well as Cardew's growing reputation as a young composer to watch, attracted a reasonably-sized audience which included a number of prominent figures in contemporary music − composers Thea Musgrave and Richard Bennett, the pianist, Paul Jacobs; and there was a handful of jazz musicians (whom I had got to know as a national serviceman in Cologne where they were playing in the Kurt Edelhagen band), including Jimmy Deuchar and Ken Wray and their wives, who did not last out the concert but courteously waited for us in a nearby pub until it was all over. Neither could Richard Bennett find reason to enthuse:

> Der Cornelius gave a concert of really stunning boredom at the Conway Hall with another demented youth: Feldman, Cage, Cage, Cardew, Feldman. An audience of 70 sat transfixed with gloom while they produced, very slowly and laboriously, a series of small tired noises, not violent, not beautiful, not exciting, not even remotely interesting; the whole effect as soporific as an evening spent listening to the complete Methodist Hymnal.[70]

Despite its 'mixed reception' the same programme was subsequently taken to Oxford (on invitation from the Oxford University Contemporary Music Club[71]) and Cambridge Universities; earlier in January, prior to the 'Generation Music 1' concert at the Conway Hall, Cardew had taken part in a performance of *Le Marteau sans Maître* for the B.B.C.

In February Cardew returned to Cologne to continue work on *Carré*, from which there was still no respite, and to complete his piano piece, *February Piece II*, which together with Stockhausen's *Refrain* was included in a concert in Amsterdam during Easter. ('March 1960, finished last page (3000 odd notes) of rough score of *Carré* in a sun-filled library in Amsterdam'.) Kurt Schwertsik recalls that Cardew had nowhere to stay in

Amsterdam, probably because he could not afford accommodation, and that he and an American composer friend had smuggled Cardew into their hotel room whence, in the morning, he had beat his retreat while Schwertsik had skilfully distracted the proprietor's attention. They met up later in a café where Cardew was sitting with the omnipresent *Carré* on the table. Schwertsik also recalls the sequel to the concert when he and Cardew, together with Mauricio Kagel and some other musicians, were sitting passively and somewhat dispiritedly in a bar. After a while Cardew sauntered over to the juke-box, made what turned out to be an inspired selection of pop-songs and transformed the evening. An interest in popular music was not yet fashionable amongst the avant-garde at that time but Cardew had unerringly picked the right moment; the music immediately became the topic of animated and learned debate to which Cardew, a roll-up between the fingers, probably declined to contribute.

Around the same time he records a holiday in Terschelling, in the north of the Netherlands, with Natalie, and a brief visit to Brussels and Paris where they met up with David Sladen and his girl-friend from Oxford, Gretta. Natalie recalls a Miles Davis concert in Amsterdam: Cardew's determination, against great odds, to obtain tickets, the threatening ambience, as she perceived it, and the greenness of Miles' trumpet. But in Paris she was aggrieved when her lover magnanimously relinquished their room in Hotel Gît-le-Coeur to Sladen and Gretta and they moved into accommodation which was seedier, grubbier, infested with bed bugs and colourless ladybirds, and without even the consolation of a chance encounter with an avant-garde sculptor or a celebrated junkie. In the Journals, meanwhile, doubt and self-criticism surfaced as his relationships with his women friends, in particular, waxed and waned – doubt as to the adequacy of his love for Natalie and on 30 April, in Cologne, the mundane but pressing matter of his divorce provoked a further expression of self-recrimination: 'Got news calling me to my divorce in very depressing language, and it becomes like a mirror; suddenly I see the things I am and do and they are unaccountable, inexcusable.'

The relationship with Pyla continued fitfully, sometimes tearfully, and seemed doomed: a walk in the Eifel[72] at the dead of night, a cold hotel room, and a night huddled apart. Visits to and from Haro Lauhus and Mary Bauermeister were, as usual, enlivening – Cardew accompanying them, on one occasion, to Wuppertal for a lecture on the Philosophy of Money – but for several weeks, through May, he was consumed by a relationship which foreclosed on all extraneous thought and feeling: 'No lust for sound, none for silence, none for activity and for inactivity for which one should need no lust. I have none whatsoever. Lust for Nat. (Natalie)'[73] Two weeks later, in barely legible handwriting, there is a frenzied cry of anguish without precedent in the Journals – desperation, torment, a breaking apart: a manifestation of a profound love-sickness:

Is this now real love-tragedy? Or are her letters lost in the post? Last letter May 20th – only one need have got lost, or illegible address, or customs inspected. Oh let there be one tomorrow. Everything is too heavy. I can't write. Everything pressing me down down to a gravelly emotional deep – tearful dreaming in Kagel rehearsal. Of her sudden love for some pretty boy. Or realizing, Confucius serious truth thinking if you love me why aren't you here? And why wasn't I there? To hold you tight. To keep a hold on your roving eye 'and that is why…' The sun is shining, postman can't you come tomorrow with warm hands?[74]

Certainly there was a complex matrix of emotions raging at the time in which the relationship with Natalie was the rawest, the most vulnerable: his divorce (on 20 May), the enervating shadow of *Carré*, and the momentous decisions affecting his musical career. But it was his tormented obsession with a young woman which had finally precipitated the emotional crisis which now engulfed him – Natalie, a will-of-the-wisp, seemingly child-like, beautiful, popular – but 'half-awake, intellectually $2/3$, sexually $1/3$ … she will have no stomach for my music'. Such reservations would temper and circumscribe, if not his ardour, his commitment to other lady friends, but with Natalie they were irrelevant because, for a time, he was spellbound; her artlessness disarmed him and she refused or was unable to rise to the baits he threw. 'Any misery and poverty she takes and transforms – a realist whose reality is beautiful.'[75]

Four days after the trauma of 2 June Cardew penned the last Journal entry of 1960, not to resume until July the following year. It refers to *Carré* and is couched in bitter, resentful language:

82x Bridge of evil – copying it for the second time. No composer could have written this. Attacks of Nausea when attempting to copy it today and all because Karlheinz is afraid of musicians (orchestral) – doesn't trust them to respond to the prescription 'start low then play fast passage ending high' and such like. Today I composed a little on the Cycle of Cycles, and perhaps that is why this makes me so sick. I can only do it in peace when I am not a composer.[76]

Cardew's relationship with Stockhausen now hung on a thread – and a financial thread at that. The gap between the two men, aesthetically and philosophically, was unbridgeable; it was merely 'use-value' to each other which sustained the contact, and a few years later Cardew's outrageously provocative realisations of Stockhausen's *Plus-Minus* (with the American composer/pianist Frederic Rzewski) would provide final evidence, if indeed any were needed, of their artistic incompatibility and the fact that their paths, having once crossed, had not only diverged but were proceeding in opposite directions.[77]

The rest of the year saw Cardew constantly on the move and the Journals may well have found, materially, a temporary repose, perhaps in Richmond; they were never a constant travelling companion. His journeys began in July with a trip to Bagnols-sur-Cèze in the south of France where he had found useful employment deputising for Natalie, who was sick, as a 'nanny' for the children of Peter and Alison Smithson.[78] Then on to Marseilles where the copying of the orchestral and vocal scores of *Carré* was finally completed, the final chapter of a protracted involvement which had served only to quicken and intensify his sense of alienation from the European avant-garde in general and Stockhausen in particular.

In Venice in September he rewrote the verbal introduction to *Two Books of Study*, meeting up with David Tudor again, and then moved on to Vienna where he stayed for six weeks with Kurt Schwertsik and his mother – writing in the morning and then, always just at the right time, as it seemed to Schwertsik, he would stop to buy provisions and cook, simply and expertly. Two compositions, *Arrangement for Orchestra* and *February Piece III*, the former an arrangement of the latter solo piano work, were completed, and some sheets of working notes on *Carré* were soon given a new function – as writing paper. In a letter to Natalie from Vienna he expresses his relief: 'This all symbolizes the job I've just finished. All over now. I'm light as air lighter [...] Beauty will someplace sometime catch up with everyone each of us.' And this was Cardew's damning conclusion in his post mortem on *Carré*:

> The thing that makes coherent performances of the monumental works of the past possible is the unshakable conviction of the validity of the composer's indications. This enables the conductor to rest assured that if he unpacks the piece with sufficient care and respect, the present will be discovered inside, intact. With Carré, it seemed that not even Karlheinz was convinced of the validity of the indications in the score, and was therefore more inclined to lay down the piece like a law; an arbitrary law, easily disfigurable by heavy-handedness. I do not pretend that it would have been easy to let the piece play itself – to assist (a complex and imponderable mingling of active and passive functions) at its birth or self-demonstration or what you will – but I think it would have been rewarding. [...] I am of course offering only my own personal and prejudiced and exaggerated impression when I say that the life of the piece was nurtured up to the point when each orchestra was rehearsing separately in the concert hall and rehearsal rooms of the radio, but that thereafter it was bullied into an atavistic maturity, realizing only a fraction of its musical potential.[79]

In the Autumn Cardew was back in Venice for a performance on 23 September of

Stockhausen's *Refrain,* and October saw the first performance of his own *Autumn 60*, with Heinz-Klaus Metzger (piano), John Cage (piano), Kurt Schwertsik (horn), the composer (guitar), and Benjamin Patterson (conductor), also in Venice, where he was enjoying the congenial company of a number of friends and colleagues, including, along with Cage and Metzger, Earle and Carolyn Brown (who were all staying with Peggy Guggenheim), Sylvano Bussotti, and Nam June Paik, whose extravagant presentations were, at any rate for Cardew, an antidote to the acute boredom from which he would profess to suffer during performances of music by other composers.

In fact, there were a number of more informal concerts, including another version of Cage's *Variations I*, this time for horn and guitar by Schwertsik and Cardew, and a street-performance in the early hours of the morning of La Monte Young's *Poem for Chairs, Tables, Benches, Etc.- (or other sound sources)* (1960). Cardew and Schwertsik created havoc of a more spontaneous nature by hiring a rowing boat, buying provisions, and setting out on an excursion to some of the islands. The return journey took them into the Grand Canal where they vied for space with the gondolas and vaporetti and other, even more intimidating, vessels. As Schwertsik recalls, Cardew rowed smoothly and purposefully whilst he, Schwertsik, navigated, in fear and trembling, until Cardew disembarked at the Rialto to buy teas for his mother. For Schwertsik the trauma continued as he tried to seek calm and refuge in a side canal before eventually picking up Cardew and negotiating the last stage of their journey. The two mariners finally arrived at Peggy Guggenheim's residence where they were greeted by the amiable Earle Brown who happened to be looking out over the Canal and had spotted their approach.

Cardew and Earle Brown returned to Cologne for a concert at Mary Bauermeister's studio[80] and then to England for a brief visit before Cardew left for Hamburg for the first performance of *Carré* on 28 October. And there were engagements – talks and performances of his own music – in Cologne and Bremen. It was a busy time although it did not deter him from seeking out cheaper and slower means of transport. A few paragraphs in an undated letter to Natalie Behr headed 'Hook of Holland trying to pick up a lift towards Hamburg' convey the distance that now separated him from his professional assignment in Hamburg:

Il pleut (oh Holland!) everywhere.
Everyone is driving to Amsterdam which is really out of my way.
Funny feeling of being back in my element, travelling – the road runs away from you and you just breathe and move. Conversations are like black mountain pools where I don't know my way around – don't know how deep they are, or how cold.
Difficult to plunge in.

Hitching is different – conversations take place on the shingly surface, or, if deep, impermanent…

In La Monte Young's 'Poem' in Cologne a few days ago I had 2 durations to fill; in the first I smiled and in the second I changed my shirt.

John (Cage) opened letters, read them, tore them up small, and threw the pieces out of the window.

David Tudor roasted cloves, cinnamon, peppercorns, and mustard seeds in that order making a wonderful smell.

Christian Wolff went to sleep.

Ben Patterson practised the double-bass part of *Tristan and Isolde* and Helms did some typing. […]

What is the point of hitchhiking when I go and spend 18/- for lunch? Well, that's the point of hitchhiking, so that you *can* spend 18/- for lunch.

Hamburg – 'the scene' is indescribably chaotic! Therefore Love Cornelius.

Most of November was spent in England where the two-week trial of Penguin Books at the Old Bailey had just ended. Penguin Books had been sent for trial under the Obscene Publications Act for attempting to bring out an unexpurgated paperback edition of D.H. Lawrence's last novel, *Lady Chatterley's Lover*. Such sociological and political phenomena would probably have amused Cardew – it amused the whole country – but he would have remained supremely detached from and indeed ignorant of the underlying tensions that had brought about this confrontation between Imperial England and the new liberal forces that were beginning to flex their muscles.

December found him back in Cologne for a performance of Cage's *Variations I* in a version for horn, piano and various accessories with Schwertsik at Mary Bauermeister's studio (in Schwertsik's recollection 'a resounding success') And then with Pyla – a renewed but temporary lease of life together – to Barcelona and south-west of Barcelona to Peniscola, where he worked on his *Third Orchestral Piece* (which he would complete before the end of the year in England).

In a letter written to me, dated 3 April 1991, Pyla recalls an incident in Peniscola when Cardew returned home one evening in fisherman's attire; he had exchanged his shirt, jacket and trousers with an old Spanish fisherman. However, such was the stench that permeated his newly-acquired clothes that the next morning they were obliged to go into town to redeem and refine his wardrobe with some additions in which the aquatic element was more discreet, more symbolic. But let us compare Pyla's account with Cardew's description of the same episode in an undated letter written to Ilona Halberstadt at the time:

2 nights ago I got raving drunk on Absinthe in a bar and changed all my clothes with a young builder – beautiful jacket, shirt, and hat, and ancient dungarees pants which were so cold I had to go to Benicarlo and buy corduroys yesterday.[81]

They hitch-hiked back to Paris from the Spanish border, anticipating a quicker arrival by travelling separately. Earle Brown had donated to Cardew an old Mercedes car which he had left in a parking lot at the Deux Magots.[82] Despite the fact that they arrived two weeks later than had been arranged, it was still there. From Paris they drove by night through the Ardennes to Cologne. The conditions were icy, there was barely any tread left on the tyres (according to Brown there had never been any tread) and Cardew had no driving licence – a traumatic journey to which Pyla attributes a kind of nervous breakdown which she suffered soon after. The same vehicle took them together with Isolde Koch to Wenford where they spent Christmas with the Cardew family.

In the new year Cardew and Pyla spent some days together in London where Pyla tried, unsuccessfully, to find employment as an illustrator. She also made the acquaintance, through Cornelius, of Stella Underwood. After 'the saddest of partings' she left him to return to Cologne.

Compositions 1957-60

The relative paucity of compositions in the period from October '57 to December '60 can be partly, perhaps mainly, attributed to an accumulation of circumstances, though not all of equal weight: in the early months in Cologne the hard practical work of familiarizing himself with the Studio technology, and of learning the German language to a high level of proficiency, inevitably precluded the degree of single-mindedness necessary for musical composition. Moreover, as we have seen, the hypercritical ambience in which he lived and worked, and the ethical precepts that underpinned it, had given rise to a cluster of ambivalent feelings in which scepticism and alienation were always close to the surface.

During the latter part of 1958 the deterioration of his marriage had led him to a reappraisal of his personal life, and the cathartic effect of the American invasion of Darmstadt in the same year had raised philosophical and aesthetic issues which previous musical procedures and systems were not able to confront. The radical content of the new American music – its freshness and temerity – coupled with David Tudor's prodigious musicianship had made a deep impression on both Cardew and Stockhausen and was the catalyst not only for Cardew's early indeterminate pieces but also for Stockhausen's first moment-form works.

In 1959/60 the enervating influence of *Carré*, which had become an endless and often disagreeable chore, and the peregrinations and performances throughout Western Europe, particularly in 1960, had taken their toll and had combined to frustrate Cardew's compositional ambitions – although the search continued for modes of expression and notational systems which could emblematize the new spheres of musical experience which the manifold and profound implications of, in particular, Cage's aesthetics had opened up to him: the 'autonomy' of musical sounds, experiential as opposed to clock time, the aural perception of musical structure and, perhaps most importantly, the relationship between composer and performer and its expression through the adoption of new ways, radical and experimental, of notating music. The time/space relations expressed in Christian Wolff's notations, for example, stimulated and intrigued him in the way that they would occasionally lead to 'impossible' performance situations, so that the player might find him/herself in the position of having to play 3 tones in 0 seconds! 'Groping for the ungraspable is the most satisfying of modern pastimes, where the satisfaction lies in the fact that satisfaction is impossible', he wrote in March 1958. Such philosophical indulgences had already prompted a cautionary note from his friend Howard Snell the previous month:

> I heard a recording of your Quintet from Dartington. Perhaps you overestimate the value of a note as note. Its simple enough for a certain cast of mind to contemplate the stillness in space, and the colour thru time; but audiences aren't philosophers. On this level words wont go (as a medium) further than asking for a bus fare.[83]

And Richard Bennett, as we have seen, was to cast similar aspersions, though less politely, in his response to the Conway Hall concert in January 1960.

Yet it soon became apparent that the limits of Cage's influence on Cardew were perhaps more significant than its presence. More profound levels of inspiration lay elsewhere, in the same continent. Rather than the audacious refusal by John Cage to be bound by the European canon, by constraints and thresholds, in his compositional odyssey – it was the bravado, the spontaneity, the sensuality of the American Beats, their uninhibited life-style and the music they worshipped, jazz, which fired Cardew. ('Ammons drives the beat, Johnson is driven by it, Meade Lux Lewis rides it' Cardew noted in the Journals.[84]) And during the Cologne period his inimitable *persona* (which Kurt Schwertsik so admired) had embodied these characteristics in a unique way. It was during these restless, emotionally-turbulent years that the seeds were sown for his musical preoccupations over the next ten years. Time and again in his article 'Notation – Interpretation, Etc.' Cardew highlights not only the creative role of the performer but, more significantly, the mutuality of the relationship between composer and performer:

'This means devising a human notation rather than a musical one; that is to say, placing more emphasis on the human aspect of notation.'[85]

The *Piano Sonata No.3* was completed in March 1958; strictly speaking, it belongs to the pre-Cologne period, having been composed at least in part during the summer of '57. The surviving manuscript comprises two movements, marked I and II, although in October 1980, when his interest in the piece would have been minimal and his memory of it hazy, Cardew responded to a request for information pertaining to the work with a few dismissive paragraphs in which he refers, if somewhat vaguely, to a third movement:

> The third movement has left no impression on my memory, either in composition or performance. The only evidence at hand of its existence is the fact that although the second movement is optional in performance and was in fact omitted by David Tudor in the Cologne premiere, the performance as I recall it was definitely not of a single movement work.[86]

Piano Sonata No.3 represents the summation of Cardew's serial preoccupations (which extended barely a few months into his Cologne period); its pedigree is irrefutably that of the European avant-garde – the rich sonorities and harmonic language of the first movement reflecting the influence of Stockhausen's *Klavierstück XI* (a work much admired by Cardew at that time) and of the second part of Boulez's *Structures I*, with which Cardew was familiar through study and performance. The opening and very ending of the second movement feature the use of harmonics, though not as extensively, nor as effectively as in the *Two Books of Study*. But the music flows effortlessly, at times brimming over with a youthful exuberance; some of the piano writing, especially in the latter part of the work, displays a dashing virtuosity which does foreshadow the rampant pianism of the later works. Towards the end there is a striking parallel with the grace note technique which adorns *Klavierstück VI*, although the grace notes in the Stockhausen piece were the result of a substantial revision, and the composer's new version did not appear until 1961 (Ex.3.1a-b).

Ex.3.1a. *Klavierstück VI*, p.36.

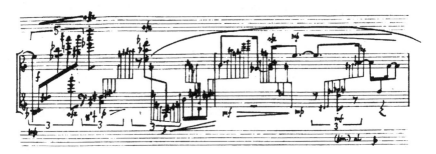

Ex.3.1b. *Piano Sonata No.3*, p.16.

The only other work to be completed in 1958 was the *5 Books of Study for Pianists*. Cardew's initial preference was that in all renderings of the material the different Books, whether 2,3,4 or 5 in number, should be played simultaneously, not successively, so that the work is always in one movement. The first two Books were subsequently published in 1966 by Peters Edition as *Two Books of Study for Pianists* and were first performed by the composer and Richard Bennett, 'to a mixed reception', at Darmstadt in 1959. Books 3 and 4, where the sounds are produced mainly inside the piano (pizzicato and mute effects) were never performed publicly and the manuscripts have so far not come to light. On 13 April 1970 Cardew had written to a friend, David Pinder, that the manuscripts were lost. 'Any information leading to their recovery will be gratefully received.' Book 5, which uses the piano "purely as orientation", was later reworked for piano solo and incorporated into the collection *Four Works*, published by Universal Edition, under the title *Memories of You*.[87]

The material for *Two Books* consists of various categories: single notes, double notes, aggregates, short groups of notes executed as fast as possible, periodic groups and harmonics; its organization in the score is consistently random, though its realization is leavened, at least in theory, by a degree of spontaneous choice allowed to the performer. The mobile character of the material and the application of a scale of six dynamics (between *ppp* and *fff*) invites comparison with Stockhausen's *Klavierstück XI*, but in their modes of procedure for the performer the two works differ considerably. In *Two Books* the tones are presented like a string of beads: the strings are fixed at both ends (these represent points in time) and the beads (sound events) on a particular string are fixed in their order but mobile along the string (that is, the rhythms in which the sounds are presented are free) and hence flexible in their relation to beads on other strings. The pianists have to handle up to nine strings simultaneously. The piece is therefore a study for the pianists not only in the rhythmic presentation of sounds in time (unlike *Klavierstück XI* where the rhythmic value of each tone is precisely notated) but also in combining sounds from several groups in counterpoint, and then combining these sounds with those produced by the other pianist. To elucidate what actually occurs in the interpretation of the piece, Cardew constructs a metaphor in the form of a (Wittgensteinian) 'game':

Imagine a table with 9 piles of photographs (neither of the pianists has to cope with much more than 9 lines simultaneously, and dense passages of 7, 8 or 9 lines only last for brief periods). Each pile contains photographs of a different subject field: landscapes, portraits, group-photographs, machines, etc. Now imagine the following story-making game: each pile is to remain covered until a particular time; at that time the first photo in that pile is to be uncovered (then that pile comes into action). As a photo is uncovered it has to be incorporated into a story; after it has been incorporated and played its part in the story it is discarded. Gradually, as more piles are uncovered more and more photos come into play. Some can be amalgamated (e.g. a portrait can be regarded as an enlargement of part of a group-photo, or a machine can be imagined as being housed in one of the barns in a landscape photo, etc. etc.), whereas others, depending on the progress of the story, will seem at variance with one another and present obstacles. In such a case, one photo might be incorporated first (leaving the others for later consideration) and then discarded, and perhaps the photo underneath will provide a better combination with the other photos. In the course of play some photos will be exhausted (e.g. machine photos will no longer be available), and others will be activated, providing new material (photos of antique furniture, or something). Now imagine someone else playing the same game at another table, and your story having to fit in with his in a kind of counterpoint, and you will have an approximate idea of what the pianists are doing in *Two Books of Study for Pianists*. They invent nothing, but their imagination must be constantly active.[88]

Two Books prefigured, if tentatively, a new departure; Cardew himself described the work as 'a very dubious piece (I, of course, can like it, despite all) and has become rather an object of experiment',[89] and the problems it raised would have been discussed and argued in more abstract and generalized language with his German colleagues in Cologne. The following damning *post scriptum* after one of his deliberations on *Two Books*, for example, would undoubtedly have served to enliven and extend the discourse: 'I don't wish to excuse the triviality of the effect by referring to the complexity of the intention.'

In *Two Books* Cardew addresses the concept of 'spontaneity' (which had been skirted around in European avant-garde circles) more consequentially than, say, Stockhausen in his 1956 *Klavierstück XI,* allowing the performer to enjoy a greater or lesser degree of freedom of interpretation according to his or her taste and ability: the performer may disperse the sounds spontaneously, 'improvising' from the score or, if preferred, in a more or less flexible version of a particular Book.

Cardew's intention was that in performance, whether prepared or quasi-improvised, 'the pianist's musical attitudes and background are revealed quite formally, not quasi-inadvertently as in more conventional music'.[90] In fact, this seems to have been wishful thinking on his part, for the constraints on the performer, not only those imposed by the stopwatch but also by dint of the technical demands of the music, preclude any expression of perceptible 'attitude' or background; it would be hard to imagine an 'idiosyncratic' realisation/performance of *Two Books* – even by David Tudor or the composer himself. Paradoxically, Cardew's own contribution to performances of *Two Books* tended to enhance its abstract qualities, its autonomy and purity, just as his performances of Cage's *Winter Music* and *Music for Piano* did: 'Tones must be allowed to be tones' – Cage's stark dictum had no more persuasive and eloquent advocate. Yet even in later years, in the late seventies/early eighties, when his concerns were focused elsewhere, he recognized, albeit in a negative manner, the improvisatory quality of *Two Books*, criticising it rather harshly as 'laboured spontaneity'[91]

Cardew's reference to 'attitudes' and 'backgrounds' appertains more properly to those works composed in the wake of *Two Books*, beginning with *Autumn 60* and *February Piece II*. Despite the licence it encourages performers to exploit and enjoy, *Two Books* obstinately maintains allegiance to another aesthetic mode where the subjective preferences of the performer, whether in Boulez's *Structures I* or Cage's *Music of Changes*, are strictly denied any interpretative role; both the European and the American avant-garde, with one notable exception, shared this antipathy towards improvisation and it was this, above all other issues, which determined and secured Cardew's role as outsider throughout the sixties. The exception was Earle Brown, whose *December 1952*, a quasi-improvisational work based on graphic 'stimulae' for an unspecified number of players, was for Cardew a seminal work (Ex.3.2).

Brown's pioneering involvement in the amalgam of improvisational spontaneity and compositional structure must have been a crucial influence in Cardew's development at the time. Brown ascribed his own development as a composer to the inspiration derived from his music-making as a professional jazz musician and from the spontaneity exhibited in the creative procedures of artists such as Alexander Calder and Jackson Pollock. But he also admired artists for whom structural concerns were paramount: Ad Reinhardt, Barnett Newman, Mondrian, among others.

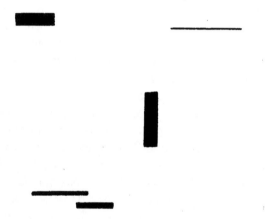

Ex.3.2. detail from *December 1952*.

To all intents and purposes Cardew had by this time settled accounts with the dominant West European compositional method − total serialism − after the briefest of affairs; he had experienced what he considered to be its vast imposture at first hand. In *Two Books* the isolation of tones, the feeling of discontinuity, the wayward harmonic language are clear evidence that the new American aesthetic had taken root in 'European' music, and Cardew was one of the first Europeans to grasp both the nature and the far-reaching extent, psychologically and socially, of its implications for the avant-garde. Cardew's originality lay in the fact that out of this he was to create music and music-making utterly different from that of his American mentors.

It was typical of Cardew that his preoccupation with the notion of musical spontaneity should have been rooted in more generalized concepts; analysing what he regarded as a contradictory viewpoint held by a friend he wrote:

She acts on two levels: conscious of implication, the future (responsibility), but within this consciousness acting spontaneously. But this is a contradiction; one cannot act spontaneously while referring it to a course which one imagines is 'right' from the long-term view. Having once been able to conceive of a 'right' course, spontaneity degenerates into mere perversity."[92]

There is a clear analogy here with the *Two Books* although Cardew balks at applying the same purity of definition, the same harsh logic to *Two Books* as he does to the behaviour of a young lady he is attempting to seduce.

On 11 June 1959 a late night discussion with Haro Lauhus and Mary Bauermeister revolved around the idea of spontaneity:

Liberation from History etc + then also from the immediate past + the future, birth + death. Towards a real spontaneity. Great efforts and flights of the imagination. Where is it that I disagree? Because the real acoustical music is of course electronic. And I have so little sympathy with Vasarely etc. which is a real optische Malerei.

There was a dilemma for Cardew here, which he recognized. He attempts to equate 'real spontaneity' with pure, that is, dehumanized actions ungoverned by human history; but in terms of music such a quest for purity necessitates the repudiation of instrumental tones – because of their stubborn refusal to shed their historical and cultural associations – in favour of abstract, electronic sounds. In October 1959, adopting an even more extreme position, disabusing spontaneity of the idea of intention, he submitted: 'Mistakes are the only truly spontaneous actions we are capable of.'[93]

Yet for Cardew such abstract, idealized notions of spontaneity not only produced undesirable results (electronic music and op-art), it deprived spontaneity of free, flesh and blood human agency; and it was precisely his restoration of the fragile and unreliable performer – desirous, active, free and imperfect – back to the hub of music-making, which set him apart, in the early sixties, from both his European and American peers. Cage shared Cardew's antipathy towards electronic music but his solution was to de-personalize 'musical' tones, to free them from historical thrall through the ingenuity of his notation, the persuasiveness of his aesthetic convictions and, crucially, through the denial of the performer's background and predilections. In his quest for an inviolable objectivity Cage identified with the serialists; they too had sacrificed the 'background reference', 'the primary level of articulation' on which tonality depended, to operate on a single level, whittling away those individual particularities with which tones, in the tonal system, had been endowed through reference to a cultural (as distinct from a 'natural') grid. And, as a corollary, in demanding a quasi-mechanical precision of performance, the serialists had marginalised interpretation, with its inherent threat to composer, and had forfeited the idea to which Cardew was committed – the enjoyment and assimilation of the same thing in a changing and developing guise. It was the issue of *referentiality* more than any other at that time which separated Cardew from his avant-garde peers, both European and American: this is clearly demonstrated if we compare Cage's *Music for Piano* and Stockhausen's *Klavierstücke I-XI* with Cardew's *February Pieces*; Cardew had no wish to control the listening psyche, to obliterate uncomfortable, intrusive, 'irrelevant' levels of meaning and reference.

The logic of Cardew's musical hierarchy, in which spontaneity had assumed a paramount role, naturally impinged on his attitude towards structure, which he refers to as 'feeling of structure' – that is, a listener's impression of a time structure – downgrading it in an analysis of *February Piece I*:

> Concerning the 'feeling of structure' in this piece. The notation
> for durations (!) almost forces you towards an 'organic' structure, by suggesting
> that something should coincide with the end of the note. The ceasing of one note
> generates the attack of another (legato). The other notation used in the piece for
> durations (., $\overline{.}$, $-$, $-$) tends on the other hand to boost the 'feeling
> of structure'; for these signs say nothing about where – at what point *in the
> music* – the note should cease, and in consequence it seems to cease arbitrarily
> (arbitrariness is characteristic of the 'feeling of structure').[94]

For Cardew the notion of organic form, 'necessary form', was crucial; it was antithetical to the 'feeling of structure' which he regarded as an attempt to dissipate, break down, extend the 'now' of organic form, to bring a time factor to bear on the only thing outside time: *now*. It was a formal contrivance which exaggerated the temporal discrepancy between concept and phenomena created in performance by the muscular translation of the mental into the acoustical. 'Towards a music without structure!' he proclaimed. [...] 'The "feeling of structure" is not a very important *feeling*, I should say, and it is therefore fine if a note goes, say, flat or sharp at the end of a breath. It gives an apparent reason for stopping (the *real* reason, after all).'[95]

Time and again Cardew returned to *nowness*, and insofar as his music-making (especially, as we shall see, with AMM), and indeed his whole life, was a celebration of 'nowness', he was a child of his time. As Arnold Hauser observed: 'The time experience of the present age consists above all in an awareness of the moment in which we find ourselves: in an awareness of the present.'[96] The way we experience 'nowness' and the insidious nature of its influence was an area of compositional research in which some of Cardew's most significant contributions were made. Paragraph 7 of *The Great Learning*, for example, offers a radical manifestation of human susceptibility to musical influence (a time-honoured fact of human life recorded through innumerable myths: the trumpets of Jericho, Orpheus and his lute, the singing of the Sirens), particularly in relation to experiential, as opposed to clock time – a work in which time is indeed made to 'fly, crawl, and stand still' in varying degrees and successions.

> The relationship between clock and experiential time is in any case problematic, as the latter is constantly subjected to a combination of contracting and expanding tensions, difficult for a composer to control, but easy for him to influence.[97]

Such concerns were the stuff of his article for *New Departures* magazine and were undoubtedly stimulated during work on a translation of Stockhausen's article, 'How Time Passes', for *Die Reihe*.

The three *February Pieces* are Cardew's first masterworks; written during 1959-61 they exemplify the extraordinary fecundity which he was to apply over the next decade to the art of composition, and to notation in particular. In *February Pieces* Cardew achieved the utmost differentiation, the refinement, the exactitude which the European avant-garde composers had demanded and singularly failed to accomplish in the pointillist scores of the fifties, where the ever-increasing exactions of the (traditional) notation engendered a proportionally increasing inaccuracy in performance. 'The indeterminacies of traditional notation became to such an extent accepted that it was forgotten that they ever existed, and of what sort they were.'[98]

What Cardew evolved in *February Pieces* was a notation of extreme subtlety and originality, yet traditionally based, where fidelity to the text was possible – a notation of the way in which instruments are actually played. The problem of 'the composer's intention' was circumvented by coalescing 'intention' and notation:

> There is no intention separate from the notation; the intention is that the player should respond to the notation. He should not interpret in a particular way (e.g. how he imagines the composer intended) but should be engaged in the act of interpretation.[99]

February Piece I and *February Piece III* are related through the audible recurrence, again and again in each piece, of the same seven tones (which form a chromatic scale from B flat to E). In *February Piece I*, though the function of the remaining five tones differs, their role is to nourish and enliven the seven prominent notes; whereas in *February*

Piece III they spring from the salient tones and multiply, 'like the leaves from the root of a tree'. The tree analogy is apt for although, like roots, they are essential, the seven tones in *February Piece III* are unobtrusive; it is the colour of the music, its potent and dramatic 'nowness', rather than its structure, that the listener experiences. Harsh, chordal attacks of great intensity pierce the air, like flashes of lightning that blind the eye – leaving a faint after-image on the retina. In the same way the chords vanish to expose a faint residue, the resonance and interplay of overtones; for the use of harmonics is much more ambitious than in *Two Books* and the impression at times is of an electronic quality. The chordal aggregates are complex and the result is a shifting mosaic of legato sound, where the player is constantly integrating and balancing tones; textures change, now spectacularly, now imperceptibly (Ex.3.3).

Ex.3.3. *February Piece III*, p.8.

By contrast, in *February Piece I* the ear is engaged linearly by tones which are joined and embellished by characteristic flourishes, swift passages, and occasionally a brief succession of regular (periodic) chords (Ex.3.4).

Ex.3.4. *February Piece I*, p.8.

As an admired and sought-after performer of contemporary music Cardew was constantly being reminded of the problems relating to the notation of music and would often discuss the idiosyncrasies and inconsistencies which fellow composers exhibited in their work. A rehearsal of Stockhausen's *Refrain* (1959) with the composer was the subject of critical comment and analysis in the aforementioned *Tempo* article. In *Refrain* the length of a sign relates to the length of the sound it represents (time-space notation); moreover, its thickness determines the dynamic. Yet such a notation over-simplifies and distorts the relationship between dynamic and length of sound; a contradiction exists between Stockhausen's 'drawn' notation and the reality of the properties of sound in decay:

> The sound of a piano decays rapidly at first, and then much slower, so that if we postulate that *mf*, *mp*, *p*, *pp*, *ppp*, *pppp* are 6 evenly placed dynamics, the sound takes longer to decay from *ppp* to *pppp* than it does from *mf* to *mp*. Everybody knows this, and Karlheinz in particular, but his notation has misled him – in his drawing of the sound he has used a straight line diminuendo.[100]

In the same article Cardew describes his own solution to the problem of notating the relationship between duration and dynamic in *February Piece I*:

> One feature of the piece is the method used for controlling the length of tones: a tone is struck at a particular dynamic, and is released when it has reached another. So for example, the length of a tone is the time taken by this particular tone to make the diminuendo from *mf* to *pp*. Such tones are sometimes accompanied by a sign meaning e.g. 'relatively long', and it becomes clear that our interpretation of the signs *mf* and *pp* will also have to be relative, and we come up against the question: 'are the dynamics controlling the durations, or are the durations controlling the dynamics?' Neither, for the player controls both, that is he controls their interaction. This is the real meaning of such signs as 'long', 'loud', etc.: their function is to put the player in a position where he is conscious of himself, of his own experience of 'long', 'loud', etc. He is conscious of what he is doing and of the capacities of the instrument at which he sits. The function of such signs is to bring the pianist to life. The piece is also so devised that the pianist can respond correctly (to the stimuli which are the signs) under any circumstances. These circumstances include size and quality of instrument, hall, pianist, audience, etc.[101]

February Piece II was completed in September 1960 and is dedicated to Isolde Koch, a painter friend from Cologne. If a residual influence of the American and European avant-garde is perceptible in the other two *February Pieces*, the second February piece severs all links by virtue of the pervasiveness of an aesthetic which was anathema to both Stockhausen and Cage (though not to Earle Brown). In *February Piece II* the demands made on the performer are of a different order; by allowing the performer a degree of influence in respect of harmonic colouring (individual tones and chords may be freely overlapped) and, in particular, by relaxing control over the rhythmic flow, Cardew imbues the music with a freer, improvisatory spirit which invites the performer to assume a more creative role. Moreover, he or she is encouraged to respond spontaneously to the notation, a performance mode which prefigures the experimental notations, particularly *Treatise*, of the middle and late sixties. The result is a curious, compelling, heterogeneous continuum; weird juxtapositions, spontaneous outbursts, fleeting references to other musics, past and present; a hypersensitive music which haunts and disturbs the memory reflecting, like a Joycean monologue, a mysterious, fantastic, disintegrated existence (Ex.3.5).

Ex.3.5. *February Piece II*, p.10.

This kaleidoscopic picture of human agency at large (the spontaneous quality of the music) in a chaotic, incomprehensible world is the expression, to quote Hauser again, "of a desire to bring unity and coherence, certainly in a very paradoxical way, into the atomized world in which we live. Art is seized by a real mania for totality".[102]

In a letter to Natalie Behr, dated 23 September 1960, Cardew refers to his performance of one of the *February Pieces*, probably *February Piece II*, in Venice:

> A rather unhappy experience to play this sad private music to people who know of so few things outside criticism. But John [Cage] liked it, though I felt like a cloud-burst while playing it. And then afterwards to play Feldman sent peace and goodwill into me, like a long drag of opium or something I imagine.[103]

In between the first two February pieces Cardew completed his *Octet 1959* which, in its rhythmic characterisation, bears a strong resemblance to *February Piece I*: the same quality of sustained sounds, occasional short bursts of acceleration, flourishes, and brief successions of periodic tones. The predominance of extreme registers, too, is common to both works: in the *Octet* through the choice of double bassoon, bass clarinet and double bass, piccolo and E flat clarinet, in addition to the oboe, flute in G and violin.

In April 1959 Cardew wrote to his mother:

Have just written, I think, a wonderful piece for 8 instruments (an Octet!), which will, I think, be an agonizing experience to listen to, because it pushes the extremes hard most of the time, resulting in a very tense sound, whereas compositionally it is extremely relaxed and plastic.

An agonizing experience to play, too, he might have added, for although the same notational method as for *February Piece I* is used, it is far less successful when applied to the relationship between players in collective music-making (Ex.3.6).

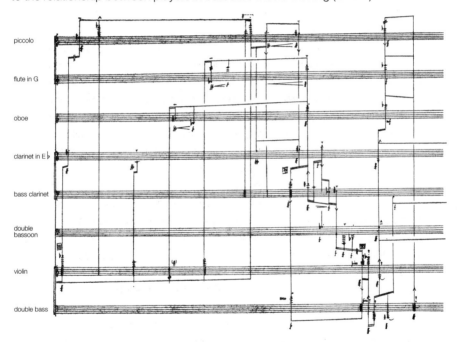

Ex.3.6. *Octet 1959*, p.13.

Cardew's aim was a rational, economical notation with the elimination of irrelevant or 'passive' signs (there are no bar-lines, no metric divisions) and with a limited number of rules. Yet the mode of performance engendered by the notation is uncharacteristically inelegant; a technocratic exercise in which the overriding demand for precise synchronizations and split-second co-ordinations inhibits the performer and circumscribes his or her creative response, as was the case in so much of the avant-garde music of the fifties.

There are few references to the *Octet* in the Journals, and perhaps the initial enthusiasm briefly expressed in the letter to his mother may be taken with a pinch of salt. There is mention of copying it and of a performance in Vienna, the prospect of which had excited him, but it was never featured in any of Cardew's concerts in the sixties; certainly its instrumentation and the demands it makes on the players limit the possibilities for programming it: 'a piece which protests violently at instrumental limitation, and yet uses them like mad' he wrote to Ilona Halberstadt. And elsewhere he writes.

I am reworking my *Octet*, which means I am thinking of you, because while I was writing it the remainder of my mind and body was engaged with you.
Lord, they can't take that – 'association' – away from me.[104]

Perhaps he subsequently regarded it as an aberration, or at least an anachronism, for it belongs to a world with which his collaboration on *Carré* at the time provided the only tenuous link, apart, that is, from his participations as a performer. On 6 May 1959, at the end of an account of an unsettling dream, he remarked with heavy irony: 'And my Octet continually disturbed me the while, weightily banal and infinitely insistent'. And yet, later in the year, a letter to Ilona Halberstadt dated 18 October reveals a persistent concern, even affection, for the work suggesting that, after all, it had not been written off:

Imagine an animal walking through a fine mesh grid – like radar – the animal is 'screened'. Internal organs come and go. The meshes are of varying flexibility – they can respond to what they are screening – dwell on features.'Octet 1959' screens a family of animals in this way.
Do not attempt to recognize the animals – they are extra-terrestrial.

Thereafter silence ensued, as if *Octet 1959* had been still-born.

In the latter part of 1960 Cardew produced three orchestral works, the first of which, *Arrangement for Orchestra*, was completed in late summer in Vienna (where he was staying with Kurt Schwertsik and his family), and bears the dedication 'for Natalie'. *Arrangement for Orchestra* is, in fact, an arrangement of *February Piece III* and aspires to the subtle dynamic differentiation and overall complexity of the piano piece through a meticulous instrumentation where all the parameters of each individual sound, in particular timbre and register, are given careful and imaginative consideration. Thus, the three degrees of 'piano' (softness) in the following extract from *February Piece III* are arranged for double bassoon, alto saxophone and cellos, with the higher dynamics given to the more penetrating sounds (Ex.3.7a-b).

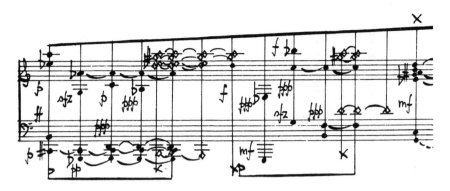

Ex.3.7a. *February Piece III*, p.2.

There are no *crescendi* or *decrescendi* prescriptions in the orchestral work, and only two dynamic markings: *p* and *f*; in the piano piece a scale of eight degrees, from *ppp* to *fff* is applied to all the attacks with occasional *crescendo* and *decrescendo* markings occurring over a succession of 'quavers' as a kind of shorthand. In the orchestral work (where the beat, naturally, is highly flexible), to facilitate co-ordination these 'quavers' are translated into a conventional system of bars of unequal lengths – roughly corresponding to the varying durational values of the 'quavers' of the piano piece. Each section of *Arrangement* is treated by Cardew as a single sound entity; the shifting kaleidoscopic canvas of *February 61* metamorphosed into an orchestral mosaic of stunning coloration.

The second of the three orchestral pieces, *Autumn 60*, was Cardew's first wholly original contribution to experimental notation and a harbinger for the coming decade. It was composed, 'in its essentials', on a long and uncomfortable night train journey from Vienna to Venice, in the company of Kurt Schwertsik. Four days later, in October 1960, it was premiered in the Academia by Heinz-Klaus Metzger (piano), John Cage (piano), Kurt Schwertsik (horn) and the composer (guitar). The performance was conducted by Ben Patterson. 'How our music is conditioned by the way we live', he quipped, with reference to the genesis of *Autumn 60*, during a seminar for the Cambridge University Heretics' Society in the early sixties.[105]

Autumn 60 was a landmark in Cardew's compositional career, a radical new departure, the essence of which was the ever-increasing importance Cardew had come to attach to the freeing and refining of the relationship between composer and performer – a relationship in which the latter, through the exclusion in the total serialism of the fifties of 'all possibility of interpretation in any real sense'[106], had become the victim of a gradual process of brutalization. Stockhausen, too, had sought to mitigate performer-abuse and meet grievances through a strategy of concessions which, however, still left him breathing down the performer's neck. In his Report on *Carré* Cardew wrote:

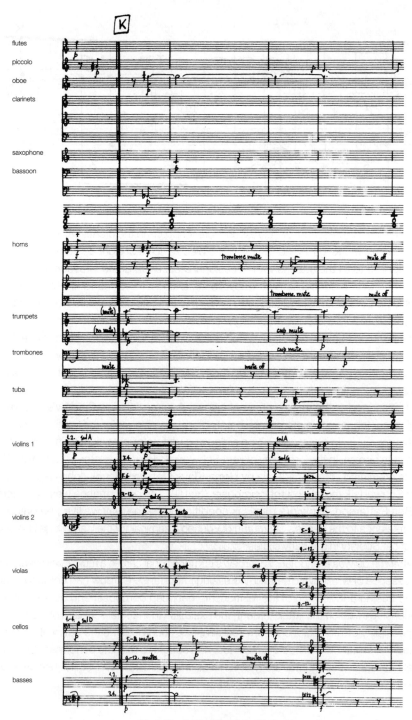

Ex.3.7b. *Arrangement for Orchestra*, p.9.

I think Karlheinz does want his music to be a certain way, and it is as a result of this that he has constantly exerted his personality in coaching performances of his works (indeed performances in which he had no hand have been exceptions; even the Glasgow performance of *Gruppen* was modelled on a tape-recording of a performance in which Stockhausen was the principal conductor); thus he has evaded the necessity of finding an adequate formalization of his ideas.[107]

In the *February Pieces*, as we have seen, Cardew had begun to explore the subtle indeterminacies of the composer/performer relation within the limits circumscribed by traditional notation; but the time-honoured mutuality of the relationship, as he saw it, could only be restored and enhanced by widening, and to a degree altering, the terms of reference: 'A notation should be directed to a large extent towards the people who read it, rather than towards the sounds they will make.'[108] For Cardew indeterminacy was not simply a case of displacing an inflexible, unyielding compositional mode – total serialism – with one which was more malleable, more responsive to his, and the performer's, needs; it was a choice which reflected deep-seated, ethical considerations (which invariably underlay his musical discussions) – an expression of the vital thread of humanism which throughout his life illuminated his musical activities, making for a continuity which overrode the stylistic changes, however radical, which marked his development. With his espousal of indeterminacy creative freedom was extended to performers through notational systems – and this is the nub – which impressed upon them the weightiness of their responsibility whilst at the same time circumventing the embarrassments of self-indulgence and vulgar spontaneity of which Cage had complained.

In January 1966, in an introduction to *Four Pieces* (*Autumn 60, Material, Solo with Accompaniment, Memories of You*), published by Universal Edition, Cardew wrote:

It is not possible for a conductor to distribute the parts for *Autumn 60* among orchestral musicians and then get up on the rostrum and conduct the piece. The very fact that the parts and the score are identical implies that a higher degree of interest and involvement is demanded of the musicians. They have to acquaint themselves with the musical principles underlying the work; they have to investigate the range of possibilities opened up by the score. And finally they have to accept the responsibility for the part they play, for their musical contribution to the piece. [...] Nobody can be involved with this music in a merely professional capacity.

The qualifying 'merely' already hints at what Cardew had come to regard as the enervating effect which 'professionalism' has on a musician's life: the cash nexus which determines and limits the range and scope of his musical activity, the debasement of much music-making into a chore and, in the extreme case of contemporary music, the disaffection from which too many of his performer colleagues continue to suffer; in short, the violation of the relationship between a musician and his art.[109] And it was this degeneration (as they saw it) which led Cardew, and others, to abdicate their position as leading protagonists in the field of contemporary music to seek and create new and meaningful outlets for their creative talents within modes of music-making outside and often in opposition to the mainstream. Cardew returned to this theme in a review of a Stockhausen lecture at the ICA in which he attacked the conditions under which professional musicians operate. ' "Normal professional conditions" are inimical to creative music-making. Surely a pianist like Richter would be insulted if one were to refer to him as a "professional" pianist.'[110]

Cardew described the genesis of *Autumn 60* as a unique and sudden inspiration: a sound, a large number of musicians, some of whom were doing similar things to each other; others were doing different things though there were certain characteristic qualities common to all. It was a phenomenon he had associated, in an undated text from the early sixties, with Mozart… 'the whole symphony in your mind, every detail in a fraction of a second'.

His compositional task was to devise a system of notation commensurate with an accurate realisation of his original aural conception. The result was a work for orchestra consisting of sixteen sections (lettered A to P) of varying lengths, and separated by breaks; each section comprises a number of measures comprising 1,2,3 or 4 beats. Each beat is assigned a number of indications (up to 8): instrumental names, pitches, dynamics, durations, articulations and modes of attack (pizzicato, mute, glissando, tremolo, etc.); the performer is invited to observe all but two, any two, of these indications (and where a beat is assigned as many as seven or eight indications his ingenuity is stretched to the full). Underneath the given material a stave is left empty in which the performer writes his version (Ex.3.8).

Ex.3.8. *Autumn 60*, p.11.

By responding to the notation, the would-be performer enters into a creative dialogue with the composer. Furthermore, without this proper state of preparedness, already in rehearsal, his part will lack conviction and vitality, and he will not achieve the necessary freedom in his reaction to what other players are sounding; for what is crucial and requires the highest degree of concentration, discipline and awareness, is the way in which a performer spontaneously integrates his part into the whole. In performance each musician is free to enter at any point during the conductor's beat, which is free in length; that is, the tempo can change within as well as after each beat, which may be clear or ambiguous. Perhaps even more important is the option, if the musician considers his (prepared) sound inappropriate at a given moment, not to play at all. For when the rules which govern the piece have been properly assimilated the musician will realise that his contribution to the music need not be so ardent, so persistent; rather it is his silence and the occasional flash of his imagination which may best enhance the quality of the music and its accessibility.

An interesting perspective on the notation of *Autumn 60*, from a composer's viewpoint, is expressed by Howard Skempton:

> *Autumn 60* achieves precision in two ways. Free from context, a musical symbol is remarkably precise. Take, as examples, cresc. symbol or portamento symbol. In context, they can be vague and thus liable to be treated with scant regard. *Autumn 60* avoids this danger by making the performer responsible for the precise placing of these precise symbols. Responsible, but free. Cage would say, 'free without being foolish'. I am sure that Cornelius was much influenced by *Variations I*, in which Cage achieves absolute precision, for example with regard to dynamics, without 'telling people what to do'. We could argue that such precision is literally meaningless, but that's another matter! [111]

The conductor's role is truly virtuosic by virtue of the infinite range and variety of colours, textures and chordal aggregates which the score encourages him to draw from the ensemble. Conventional, melodic phrasing yields to an arbitrary horizontality; the conductor exploits the musicians' sounds (without being responsible for them), bringing the casual and the emphatic into relation, shaping the material, rendering it intelligible. He must be receptive to this mingling of the necessary and the fortuitous, integrating what happens by his hand with what happens in spite of it, and aware of certain formal principles through which the composer secures the quintessential nature of the resultant sound; for example, all signs have their peak of density so that a particular symbol will occur frequently in one section and sparsely in others. And the conductor can add a further degree of refinement (or stress!), determining the character of a section by suggesting, for example, that the musicians play in a low register, or play their material as fast as possible, or omit this or that sign.

Appropriately enough, at the Cambridge University Heretics' Society meeting, a clash of tastes occurred between the conductor, Cardew himself, and members of the ensemble whom he had criticized for indulging in references to nineteenth century music in their performance.[112] His contention was that this had resulted from a superficial, if not perverse reading of the score – obeying the letter though not the spirit; but his audience boxed him into a difficult corner from which he attempted to escape, not altogether convincingly, by shifting responsibility from himself as composer onto himself as conductor: 'When I conduct the piece, I surrender to my tastes'. Taste and 'correctness' may sometimes be at odds, though not in this particular case – he was treading on dangerous ground!

Cardew showed no preference for any particular instrumentation for *Autumn 60* (more often than not it was a question of availability and commitment of musicians, as was the case for its Venice premiere) and a performance using eighteenth century instruments (which, apparently, had taken place) had equal validity with any other instrumental combination. Where Cardew did express preference was for a larger number of players, so that a more homogeneous sound and more general features would emerge rather than the individualistic features and divergent interpretations which characterise performances by small ensembles. 'The piece gets closer to my conception of it as you have more players', he told his audience in Cambridge. This 'conception' is illuminated in the aforementioned Introduction to the published work written several years later. In *Autumn 60*

> the number of possible solutions for even a single beat far exceeds the number of musicians that can be got together for a performance, and if all the possible solutions were presented simultaneously the result would in any case be an undifferentiated mass of sound. Thus the criterion of a good performance is not completeness (that is, perfection), but rather the lucidity of its incompleteness. Any performance is a kind of documentary relic (more or less revealing) of the composer's conception.

Of course, a larger group, say a normal-sized orchestra, also presupposes an increase in the number of defaulters – that is, those musicians unwilling to undertake responsibility for the creation of their part with the necessary degree of scrupulosity – and when the occasion arose Cardew would meet these players half-way, writing out for them which notes were to be played and leaving them free to attend to their precise placement. For performances directed by Mauricio Kagel Cardew went even further, writing out a score and adding parts to the collection as and when they were required for concerts with different instruments. So that when Schoenberg's *Pierrot Lunaire* was performed in Zagreb the same combination of instrumentalists was able to perform *Autumn 60*; likewise in Leeds and Boulez's *Le Marteau sans Maître*. Yet Cardew harboured mixed feelings about such compromises:

> This runs counter to the original idea, and I have noticed in these performances that the players have regained as often as not their usual attitude to contemporary music, that is, 'we play it, but don't blame us for what it sounds like', which is exactly the attitude which these pieces try to circumvent.[113]

Cardew held that the substantial difference between the manifold performances of *Autumn 60* (and other works, too) would serve to enrich the work without undermining its identity, which, assuming probity of interpretation in sufficient cases, would remain intact. His vision was that across continents, indeed across centuries, variously and imaginatively, musicians would plumb the infinite resources of *Autumn 60*, would respect the subtle messages of its originator, would cherish the spirit of spontaneity it celebrates. In a Cologne Radio broadcast on *Autumn 60* in the early sixties Cardew drew an interesting analogy:

> There is one more point I would like to make about the freshness that one imagines will be characteristic of the piece if each time it is played it is different. When we admire the freshness of a great jazz musician's performance – a musician whose recordings we have known and loved for years – what we are admiring is the new life that is given to something which is already present in us, namely through the thorough knowledge we have acquired from these recordings. This example is a good one; when a jazz musician records an improvised solo, there are many things that he does on the spur of the moment, and we would be hard put to it to say exactly what he did play. But the record remembers, and so do his fans – they get to know every quirk and squeak of a particular recording. One assimilates the material (a particular player's treatment of a melody, for example, and the sound he makes) and also the player's style. Then when one comes to hear him in a live concert, everything he plays seems familiar, and yet fresh; it has the vigour of spontaneity. This would have passed one by in many cases if one had not this familiarity acquired through the recordings. One can also appreciate the difference when one hears the same melody played by someone else. It is not a prototype that one should get familiar with; this gives one very little. The knowledge of how something is written down, for example, is very little help.

Unlike many composers and musical theorists Cardew did not baulk at discussion of such issues as the content, reception and function of music. At the Heretics' Society seminar, in response to the questions, 'What is music written for? Is it written to be played or to be listened to?' Cardew answered pithily: 'For neither. Music is written to express.' The use of the intransitive form here is apposite; for Cardew (at that time) what music expresses is intangible, 'uncatchable', and thus defies object status. In the Cologne Radio broadcast he began:

> What are the characteristics of this music we have just listened to? What emotions has it aroused? (It would be unjust to deny these, merely because it is a piece of contemporary music.) What impressions does it create? These are the appropriate questions to ask with regard to this piece, and also about many other pieces of so-called indeterminate music, since they appeal directly to our sense of hearing. The sounds are generated directly and spontaneously by the musicians themselves. Thus we cannot ask – what plan is hidden behind these sounds? Or – what is this piece about? There is no by-passing of the sensual impression of the sounds themselves.

Cardew then attempts to locate the source of what we experience as a pervasive and excessive melancholy, a mournfulness intensified by the funereal slowness and regularity which had characterised many performances of *Autumn 60*. And yet such qualities do not necessarily originate in the score – even the downward glissando sign is not necessarily associated with lamentation, and in any case appears too infrequently to be influential. Cardew's diagnosis of this exaggerated, at times histrionic, sadness is directed specifically to to the constant and exclusive dirge-like use of a limited range of tones: F, G flat, A flat, B flat and D flat. For whenever one of these tones is indicated several performers will use it, and from within the admixture of attacks, durations and timbres, its pitch can be discerned and its recurrence registered in the memory. An aura of past and remote musics, of pre-tonality, surrounds these five quasi-pentatonic tones whose choice was not only conscious, but calculated:

> The choice of notes is in my opinion the prime function of the composer, and the hard core of feeling that abides in the relations between notes will survive the most wilful treatment of dynamics or tempo. The reasons for this fundamental belief of mine are many and various; first and foremost I have experienced the fact that tones have emotional content, and on the theoretical side one can deduce the experience post facto from the interaction of the overtones subconsciously – we do not actually hear the overtones, but they are always present in what we

hear – they take us unawares and give rise to those inexplicable and apparently spontaneous impressions that go to make up an emotional response.[114]

In the Introduction to *Four Works* the choice of pitches in *Autumn 60* is seen clearly to have been determined by the role which Cardew assigned to them. *Autumn 60* and its companion pieces *Solo with Accompaniment, Material, and Memories of You* are described as 'seeds' which,

> besides containing growth mechanisms orientated towards the future, also bear hereditary characteristics linking them with the past. So it will be found that the pitches given in *Autumn 60* – and in the nature of things pitches will often predominate – are almost pentatonic.

We may speculate on these future performances, and on the development of the piece across centuries of communitarian music-making in which perhaps even the tones themselves, and their pentatonic character, take on unimaginable significations. These musical references to a familiar, but not always comforting, past are used to offset the ephemeral nature of the new music and to leaven the uncertainty of an unknown future which Cardew saw as a necessary condition of our time:

> The musicians in pieces like this are faced with a situation which they cannot grasp. They do not know what they are doing. So many factors are unknown that there is a terrible feeling of insecurity. There is a great pattern inherent in lack of confidence. Hesitancy may be the expression in some cases of a great and natural delicacy, but here it springs from unknowing, uncertainty as to what is expected of one. This slows down one's reaction time; one hangs on to each beat as to a last refuge, and each changeover to the next seems like a perilous journey. This applies equally to the conductor – he does not know what sound to expect, and when it comes he strives to assimilate it, seeking in it the answer as to how to proceed. In the performance he is somewhat frantic with anxiety, whereas to us, calmly listening, each beat seems long and we are able to plumb the morbid tensions in each sound, before the next one takes place. The thick, succulent chords that hold on and on, notes get added, some disappear, various other changes occur, but the sound is prolonged, drained to the last drop, because the musicians are reluctant to abandon a context which they have managed to grasp. This is what gives it such a mournful character these long, fluctuating chords. So many of them are so long that this gives them the semblance of regularity, however unevenly spaced they may actually be in time. Thus the

mournfulness we experience when listening to it is our sympathetic response to the agony experienced in the performance.[115]

Cardew insisted that the hesitancy and feeling of insecurity that compromised performances of indeterminate music were transitional phenomena; that his experiments, and those of his colleagues, would soon begin to show results; that the fund of experience gained would help to create more authentic, more compelling versions of experimental pieces, and that the fashion for complexity of sound would disappear. Certainly, the latter prognosis was vindicated by subsequent developments during the sixties and into the seventies; the vogue for (serial) complexity indeed waned as its leading protagonists suffered a crisis of confidence, and it was eventually overtaken and marginalised by the disarming artlessness, the raw vigour and, crucially, the sheer popular appeal of Minimalism, a mode of composition to which Cardew himself contributed through propagation, in the sixties, of the works of La Monte Young (in particular) and Terry Riley, as well as through facets of his own compositions. Yet 'complexity' survived, reasserting its musical credentials convincingly enough to be deemed worthy by musical theorists, two decades later, of its own, brand-new label: New Complexity. Ironically, a complexity of ends, though not of means, an unanalysable profusion of detail, is precisely what distinguishes much of Cardew's work in the sixties – from *Autumn 60* to Paragraph 7 of *The Great Learning*. And it was a richness which Cardew foresaw, rather than contrived, as we shall see in the succeeding chapters; by which I mean that he understood that a structure would yield certain results. He was conscious of the implications, as well as the inherent limitations, of the sound material to which in some cases he would grant a considerable autonomy. From the outset, in all these compositions, his vision was clear.

It was natural that Cardew should have clung to his predictions throughout a decade in which the utopian aspirations of experimental music and the democratic ideals enshrined within its practice became part and parcel of the political and artistic currents which swept along large numbers of the younger generation in many parts of the world, and not least in Western Europe and the US. The stakes were high: 'new ways of thinking and feeling', new initiatives, new freedoms – the New Man no less; yet vitiated by uncertainty, irresolution, doubt, in short by a lack of nerve which finally precipitated the disintegration and dispersal of the 'new art' into channels of activity which were therapeutic, entertaining and approved – a process which continued unabated, untouched by the more exotic, revolutionary spasms of the seventies, into the eighties when interpretations of experimental music indeed became more confident, more *chic*, superior even, eclectic and post-modern, though hardly more authentic. For these performances had sacrificed the unpredictability, the rawness and sensuality, the thrill of those of the earlier pioneering decade; they had jettisoned risk and spontaneity, had become more 'design-conscious', less disruptive of conventional sensibilities, celebrating the end of history and accommodating the needs of a battered bourgeois culture to the manner born; music-making spawned of a socio-political *degeneration*, as Cardew came to regard it, and against which he was to direct some of his most violent and uncompromising polemics in his later years.

Autumn 60 was a seminal work, of great subtlety and sophistication; yet Cardew expressed dissatisfaction with what he saw as its limitations, for it was still a musical score giving instructions for the production of, and purporting to represent, *the sound*. These uncertainties and misgivings had already found expression in Journal entries and talks which were gathered together in the *Tempo* article. Cardew was all too aware that sound has a 'logic' of its own, which a logical notation cannot specify except through a crude approximation; that, paradoxically, if a composer wishes to write a logical music he must forget about the sound.

And like both Blake and Wittgenstein Cardew believed in a logic of the imagination which was quite separate from the logic of concepts. Christian Wolff was the admired exponent of a 'logical notation', which described *how* rather than *what* to play. With its encroachments into the hitherto taboo psychological and social domains of music-making, the score of *Autumn 60* was an important step in this direction (Cardew once remarked that *Autumn 60* had taught him about the psychology of musicians!). And five years later, as a member of AMM, Cardew and his friends were to pioneer a mode of direct and spontaneous music-making to which the idea of notation, whether traditional or graphic, was a supreme irrelevance.

Within a few months of completing *Autumn 60*, during a visit to Peniscola in Spain with Pyla in December, Cardew began working on his *Third Orchestral Piece*, in which he reverted to traditional notation, albeit in an unconventional and exploratory mode; the quest continued for the elusive balance between artifice and spontaneous musical expression. Clearly, he believed that a creative approach to notation – such as he admired in Feldman's work – could still yield the kind of music-making towards which he had been gravitating.

> Here in Peniscola, a lovely name for a little crooked village where I live in a little crooked house painted pale blue and freeze and write some lovely music for Orchestra, in which everything is free but remember 'real freedom lies in the recognition of one's responsibilities' as the instructions warn all conductors of 3rd Orchestras all over the world 'as elsewhere'.[116]

The score consists of seventeen sections lettered A – Q (compared to sixteen in *Autumn 60*) with precise instrumentation. The order of the sections is free and an individual section may be repeated over and over. Unlike *Autumn 60*, pitches for each individual instrumental part are given throughout (the player does not choose his own note), and any note may or may not be played. Likewise, the frequent instructions – *col legno, sordini, cup mute, sul ponticello,* flutter tonguing, etc., as well as dynamic indications, may or may not be observed. In a broadcast talk on the music of Christian Wolff, Earle Brown and Morton Feldman for Cologne Radio in the winter of 1962 he was to extract one of the rules for the *Third Orchestral Piece* for comment on a semantic nicety during a discussion of indeterminate notation:

> Once, in the instruction concerning the performance of an orchestral piece of mine, having specified that certain notes could either be played or not, I went on to remark that 'together with the freedom either to play or not to play a note, must come the freedom to play more or less, that is, softer or louder, longer or shorter'. But where is the 'must'? I was immediately asked. Where indeed; obviously it is inconceivable that a note should be played either loud and long or not at all. But the 'must' remained, for it soon became clear to me that it was not a logical 'must', but an aesthetic 'must'. For aesthetic reasons, reasons concerned with the music itself, I felt it necessary that there should be available a whole gamut of possibilities between the presence of a note and its absence. This whole gamut was not available for every note; some were marked soft, others short, and beyond these there was a sign for the borderline case between presence and absence, that is, a sign meaning extremely soft and extremely short.

Cardew exercises more control over the conductor's beat than in *Autumn 60*; 'no beat should be twice as long or short or more than those on either side of it', and more influence on the overall rhythmic features: there are just four rhythmic entrances or positions – on the beat, just after the beat, between beats, just before the beat, allowing for infinite latitude and creating considerable rhythmic complexity.

Yet each bar is provided with a generalised rhythmic profile (unlike *Autumn 60*) which is not compromised by the durational freedom given to individual tones or by the rhythmic irregularities generated by individual choice. Furthermore, every bar in the piece contains a number of synchronised attacks, something which *Autumn 60* does not specify.

In *Autumn 60* the spontaneity of the performer is less 'pure', by virtue of the fact that each part is considered and prepared beforehand and is therefore subject to the idiosyncrasies of taste and musical background. The *Third Orchestral Piece* requires no such preparation; the decision-making is telescoped, often faster, split-second, 'purer', influenced by the engulfing sound, the moment, rather than by the exigencies of pre-conceived material. Unlike *Autumn 60,* the *Third Orchestral Piece* does not feature a scalic 'row', but some sections have features in common, and when notes are sparse the harmonic profile maintains its identity from one realisation to another.

Such considerations, and those concerning overall balance of orchestral colour are the prerogative of the players; they take care of the sounds while the conductor is responsible for the form – 'of the house that Jack built', as Cardew describes it in his introduction to the score. Perhaps the most intriguing of Cardew's seven rules of interpretation for the *Third Orchestral Piece* is that which anticipates a characteristic feature of a work composed nine years later – Paragraph 6 of *The Great Learning* – and which defines a mode of attack common in musical practice but ostracised by musical notation: 'Hollow notes are on the borderline between being played or not.'[117] It is instructive to compare this with a performance note for Paragraph 6: 'An "optional" sound can mean […] an accidental or incidental (glancing) type of sound, or a quasi-accidental sound, or no sound at all.' Ideas germinated over a long period; a relatively marginal feature of an early work would become an essential feature of another work a decade or so later.

In a letter dated 5 May 1961 to the committee of the Warsaw Autumn Festival regarding the *Third Orchestral Piece*, Cardew described his piece as

> an investigation into chosen sounds (these are not outlandish), and an attempt to find what might be described as the music in sounds. If the music expresses a feeling of tenderness for the material, then it is a true picture of my experience at the time of writing it.

All composers at work conceive their music at various levels of elaboration but ultimately there is a point of no return, of completion. By contrast, Cardew's indeterminate works of the sixties contain growth mechanisms orientated towards an 'unknown future'; there is no such 'end product' simply because there is an infinite number of possible elaborations which he preferred should bear distinguishing historical marks of identification.

For Cardew, the new music – Indeterminacy – contained obscure yet irrefutable indications of future ways of thinking, perhaps of feeling, too. This was not perceived in any literal sense, had nothing of the grandiosity of his later political projections; rather it was theoretically primitive, ill-defined, as yet unformed, subject to organic laws undiscoverable except by living and breathing them; and he harboured the romantic belief that such nebulous and profound messages could be conveyed directly to the senses through the creative generation of sounds. Moreover, it became increasingly evident that the seriousness of the assertion could only be tested and measured in relation to the *social role* which music exercised and enjoyed. It was the continuing elevation of this role which marked the trajectory of Cardew's musical career throughout the sixties, and which was to culminate in the creation of the Scratch Orchestra.

Notes and references

1   Gottfried Michael Koenig (b. 1926). Major electronic music theorist and composer. Worked at the Westdeutscher Rundfunk electronic music studio in Cologne, 1954-64; taught at the Cologne Musikhochschule (electronic music, composition and analysis).

2   Undated letter to RA.

3   Undated letter to RA.

4   Letter to RA, 10 October 1957.

5   Ibid.

6   Ibid.

7   Herbert Brün (b. Berlin, 1918; d. 2000.) Theoretician and composer of primarily electronic and computerized music. For many years taught at the University of Illinois at Champaign/ Urbana; became Professor Emeritus in 1987.

8   Letter to RA, 7 February 1958.

9   Letter to SC, 8 November 1957.

10   Jrnl. 29 October 1957.

11   *Arnold Schoenberg: Letters*, ed. by Erwin Stein, (London: Faber and Faber, 1964), p. 265.

12   Hans Werner Henze, *Music and Politics: Collected Writings 1953-81* (Ithaca, NY: Cornell University Press, 1982), p.38.

13   In one of his letters to Ilona Halberstadt from the late fifties Cardew refers to 'a sucking stone', a typically enigmatic yet unforgettable incarnation from Beckett's *Molloy*.

14   From the film *Cornelius Cardew 1936 – 1981*. Directed by Phillipe Regniez. Arts Council of Great Britain 1986.

15   Undated letter to RA.

16   Letter from HSK to JT, 20 February 1991.

17   Undated letter to RA.

18   Letter to RA, January 1958.

19   Letter to RA, 3 March 1958.

20   Ibid.

21   Undated letter to Mariel Cardew from Darmstadt 1958 on the eve of a performance of Cardew's *Two Books of Study* by the composer and Richard Rodney Bennett.

22   Letter to RA, 3 March 1958.

23   Bennett himself wrote copious letters to Cardew, and to Ruth, when they were in Germany: 'Dear Mr. and Mrs Cardew' he would begin, and proceed engagingly and often dismissively; camp, self-parodic, waspish and witty, with the odd tit-bit of titillating gossip, as well as the occasional insightful diversion (for example, on Boulez's latest compositions), before signing off: Edie Purbright (Mrs).

24   Letter from RA to CC, 20 February 1958.

25   Bayenthal-Gürtel was in Marienburg, a smart Cologne suburb, but they were there only briefly before moving at the beginning of May to Bonnerstrasse, where they remained until August. Another move took them to Dasselstrasse 54 and Frau Haas, where they stayed until the end of the year.

26   In a letter to Cardew (one of the few in English), dated 1 January 1958 Stockhausen recommends a text 'which requires utilization of all perceptual qualities your intellect governs. Adorno, who has been analysing so many areas of our daily life, surely will affect

your thinking capacities in an extensive, a grand way. The results, the transpositions of crucial[?] [word not clear] understanding onto your own creational level, should stimulate your creational powers – and that we want, we demand of you: a composition'. However, the sheer irresistibleness of Stockhausen's testimony, the aura of certainty which envelops his words, may well have ensured that Cardew never read a single paragraph of Adorno for the rest of his life. I may exaggerate, but I cannot recall any mention of Adorno in the Journals, nor any serious, live discussion of his work. However, at the beginning of his stint in Cologne, presumably in order to become *au fait* with the ideological inclinations of the circle into which he had been thrust, he did ask Ruth to bring a copy of Adorno's 'Modern Music is growing old' ['Die Alten der neuen Musik', now translated as 'The Aging of the New Music'] to Cologne with her. It was an interesting, even reckless exclusion, and in the light of his later political involvement, perhaps a fatal one.

27   Hanns Eisler, *Gespräche mit Hans Bunge* (Leipzig: VEB Deutscher Verlag für Musik), p.40.

28   The high modernism of the early 20th century, which had at first been associated with a critique of the establishment centred in Paris, was hi-jacked by the CIA, institutionised and re-centred in New York. In her book *The Cultural Cold War – the CIA and the World of Arts and letters* (New York: The New Press, 2000), Frances Stonor Saunders documents the evidence of the CIA's manipulative cultural undertakings during the Cold War. Ms. Stonor claims that many artists, including leading American painters, were willing, unwilling or just plain ignorant dupes of the CIA agenda. With the benefit of this particular hindsight one cannot resist the question: had Cardew's colleagues in the Studio in those heady days in the late fifties become aware of the role that not only their fellow American artists (including musicians), but also they themselves, were playing in the cultural cold war, how would this have effected the tenor of their arguments and, by corollary, their musical practice? Perhaps, like some of the American artists, there were also Europeans who were aware of the nature, and motives, of their sponsors, and blithely went along with it.

29   Jrnl. 5 December 1957.

30   Letter from RA to JT, 24 June 1990.

31   Jrnl. 5 January 1959.

32   Jrnl. 6 January 1959.

33   Ruth and Cornelius had studied German together at Berlitz for a short time.

34   Jrnl. 28 February 1959.

35   This refers to the 1957 work by Pierre Boulez, an extremely rigorously serialist piece.

36   Jrnl. 29 February 1959.

37   Jrnl. 26 February 1959.

38   Jrnl. 2 March 1959.

39   Letter from SC to JT, 14 May 1986.

40   Jrnl. 13 March 1959.

41   Jrnl. 19 March 1959.

42   Jrnl. 21 March 1959.

43   Gabberbocchus (derived from Stefan Themerson's Latin translation of Lewis Carroll's Jabberwocky), at 41a Formosa Street, Maida Vale, in west London, had functioned both as a press and as an arts community centre. The moving spirits behind it were two exiled Poles, Stefan and Franciska Themerson. They were both avant-garde film-makers in Poland

but, unable to continue this in London, turned to other genres. He wrote poetry, criticism and novels; she drew and created stage designs. They published their own work and that of kindred (mainly European) spirits, including Jarry, Apollinaire and Schwitters.

44   Horovitz recalls an occasion in Wales, a Live New Departures event, where a prestigious grand piano had been hired. Cardew spent much of the time seated at the piano in silence; a plaintive call from a member of the audience – 'can we have the Alleluia chorus' – seemed not to faze him, though it probably assuaged the palpable tension and (perhaps?) hostility that had been building up.

45   Ironically, Cardew had criticised one of the New Departures playwrights, John McGrath, mildly and in passing, for his political orientation.

46   'Report on Stockhausen's *Carré*', *Musical Times* October-November 1961. (*CCR*)

47   Undated letter to IH.

48   Jrnl. 29 May 1959.

49   'Report on *Carré*', from the *Musical Times.* (*CCR*)

50   Cardew once confided to a friend that he had learnt the guitar part of *Le Marteau* because he knew that very few guitarists were able to play it, whereas it was, in fact, the *only* piece he could play.

51   Jrnl. 12 May 1959.

52   Jrnl. 28 April 1959.

53   *Tempo* magazine, March 1982.

54   From a recorded conversation between KS and JT, 27 February 1992.

55   Zoltan Peszko recalls a concert at the University in Rome in the mid-sixties with Cardew and Bussotti when, because of the malfunctioning of the contact microphones, only a few ill-defined, acoustic sounds could be discerned by a bewildered audience. But what impressed Peszko was the equanimity with which Cardew, both during and after the event, accepted the situation – his simple conviction that there could be no legitimate objections on either philosophical or aesthetic grounds.

56   Jrnl. 24 May 1959.

57   Arthur Waley (1889-1966): English Orientalist and Sinologist. Both Waley and Pound translated Confucius's *Great Learning;* Confucius features in Pound's *Canto LXXIV*, and indeed throughout the *Cantos*.

58   In an undated letter (possibly the second half of 1959) to IH he writes: "Being thrown out of a reception because not wearing a suit, almost makes me forget the beauty of Boulez's *Visage Nuptial*."

59   Jrnl. 21 June 1959.

60   Jrnl. 24 October 1959.

61   Two undated letters to IH.

62   His friend and colleague in the Studio, Gottfried Michael Koenig, expressed his admiration for the *Two Books,* which must have been heartening for him at that time.

63   Jrnl. 24 October 1959.

64   Undated letter (probably from 1959) to Ilona Halberstadt.

65   Jrnl. 24 October 1959.

66   Jrnl. 10 November 1959.

67   Jrnl. 5 November 1959.

68   Jrnl. 22 November 1959.

69   Jrnl. 20 December 1959.

70   Letter from RB to RK, undated.

71   Through the good offices of Ilona Halberstadt, who was President of the Club.

72   The Eifel: a region of forests and small villages between the river Moselle and the Belgian border.

73   Jrnl. 16 May 1960.

74   Jrnl. 2 June 1960.

75   Jrnl. 3 May 1960.

76   Jrnl. 6 June 1960.

77   In Italy and elsewhere the 'myth' has been created that Cardew had 'ghost-written' substantial parts of Carré, although Cardew always denied that he had had any creative input in the composition of the work. However, this may have been simply because he did not wish to be associated with it; or, at least, he was anxious that his contribution to it would be judged as minimal by future musicologists.

78   Peter and Alison Smithson were the first English exponents of 'brutalism'; the first 'new brutalist' building in England, a school in Hunstanton, was created by the Smithsons in 1949. While a student at the Royal College of Art Natalie Behr had taken a room in the Smithsons' house (which, as she recalls, many years later, was full of beautiful chairs) in return for looking after their children. The architect George Kasabov (about whom we shall hear more in the latter part of this book) had come into the common room at the Royal College to pin up the Smithsons' advertisement. Before he was able to do so Natalie offered her services and was subsequently offered the job.

79   'Report on Carré – part 2', Musical Times. (CCR)

80   The concert took place at her studio, Lintgasse 28, am Altermarkt, on 6 October and included Cage's Cartridge Music and Music for Amplified Toy Pianos, Paik's Etude for piano and La Monte Young's Poem. The participants were Cage, Cardew, Helms, Paik, Ben Patterson, Bill Pearson, Kurt Schwertsik, and David Tudor.

81   It is indeed a cautionary exercise for a biographer to compare two (let alone three or four) accounts of the same event. I offer no comment save to remark on the metamorphosis, some thirty years later, of the young builder into an old fisherman, and that whereas the later account makes considerable play of the memorable 'fact' of the odour, the earlier description makes no mention of it at all. The fact that many of the recollections of my sources for this book are similarly separated by ten, twenty, or even thirty years from the events in question must be deeply unsettling for both myself and the reader. Our only solace is that all biographies are subject to the same treacherous conditions.

82   A bar on the Left Bank frequented at that time by existentialists and followers of Jean-Paul Sartre.

83   Letter from Howard Snell to CC, 18 February 1958.

84   Undated. Meade "Lux" Lewis, [Albert] Ammons, [Pete] Johnson were boogie-woogie pianists; performed solo and as the Boogie-Woogie Trio. They recorded and did radio broadcasts in the thirties and forties.

85   Tempo Magazine, 'Notation – Interpretation, Etc.' note 12, p.26. (CCR)

86   Tudor's recording on Hat Hut Records, Piano Avant-Garde, (hat Art CD 6181), from 20 September 1958, comprises the aforementioned movements I and II, as published by Peters Edition.

87 This collection also includes *Autumn 60, Solo with Accompaniment,* and *Material.* They were subsequently published separately.

88 Jrnl. 1 September 1964.

89 Letter from CC at Brüsselerst, Cologne to MC, 3 May 1959.

90 Previously quoted letter from CC to David Pinder, 13 April 1970.

91 Stockhausen compared *Two Books* to Beckett: crawling with colossal effort through never-ending mud, 'and (corollarily) the overpowering consciousness of immediate environment (particles of mud), i.e. not only who one is sitting next to, but musically: past and future – even within the piece itself are obliterated, not relevant. (He was hardly critical, just it was foreign to him)'. Undated letter (probably from 1959) from CC to IH.

92 Jrnl. 19 March 1959.

93 'Notation – Interpretation, Etc.' note 15, p.26. (*CCR*)

94 'Notation – Interpretation, Etc.' p.28, note 24. (*CCR*)

95 Ibid. p.26, note 19. (*CCR*)

96 Arnold Hauser, *The Social History of Art*, 4 vols (London and Henley: Routledge and Kegan Paul, 1962), vol.4, pp.230-31.

97 *New Departures* magazine 1959: 'The Unity of Musical Space', p.55-56. (*CCR*)

98 'Notation – Interpretation, Etc.' p.22, note 5. (*CCR*)

99 Ibid. p. 27, note 22. (*CCR*)

100 Ibid. p. 29, note 26. (*CCR*)

101 Ibid. p. 27, note 22. Cardew even suggested that players with small hands might 'recompose to the best of their ability the places where the stretches are too big'. (*CCR*)

102 Arnold Hauser: op. cit., p.225.

103 Cardew always regarded his music as being 'available,' intuitively comprehensible to enquiring ears and minds.

104 From an undated letter (late summer/early autumn 1959) to Ilona Halberstadt.

105 The Cambridge Heretics Society was established in 1909 as a society for junior and senior members of the University, with the aim to encourage 'free and radical discussion of religious, ethical and philosophical problems'. H. G. Wells, Bertrand Russell, Virginia Woolf and Ludwig Wittgenstein were among those who addressed it. The latter used the opportunity to deal with the various misunderstandings which had arisen in relation to the *Tractatus.* (*CCR*)

106 'Notation – Interpretation, Etc.' p.22, note 5. (*CCR*)

107 Cardew played the Glockenspiel in the first performance of *Gruppen* in Cologne on 24 March 1958.

108 'Notation – Interpretation, Etc.' p.26, note 13. (*CCR*)

109 In a paper delivered at a conference at Bretton Hall College (University of Leeds) in March 1994 and published in the *Contemporary Music Review,* Volume 15, Parts 3-4, I alluded to Cardew's strictures in relation to 'professionalism': 'In particular, 20th century Western compositional modes have to be re-assessed, modified and, where necessary, jettisoned. Their embodiment of an outmoded and discredited system of cultural values involving human control techniques (notations), an alienated labour force (professional musicians), and a reactionary social function (patronage and funding strategies) is recognised, implicitly, by the development of 'survival strategies' – new, creative modes of 'self-invention' – within and through improvised music.'

110 Cornelius Cardew, 'Composed Laughter', *New Statesman,* 10 December 1965, pp.943-944. (*CCR*)
111 Letter from HSK to JT, 20 February 1991.
112 Among those performing on that occasion were the clarinettist Tony Pay (Corpus Christi) and the conductor David Atherton (Fitzwilliam House), who was playing bass clarinet.
113 From an undated draft (almost certainly for a Cologne Radio talk), handwritten in the 1959-1962 Journals. (*CCR*)
114 From the previously mentioned Cologne Radio broadcast. (*CCR*)
115 Ibid. (*CCR*)
116 Letter from CC to IH, December 1959.
117 Rule of Interpretation 3 for the *Third Orchestral Piece.*

(*CCR*) Also found in *Cornelius Cardew A Reader*

4

Stella and the Americans 1961–62

The will to make things true, to create a truth.[1]

Seth Cardew and Julie Guyatt suffered one of those frustrating relationships, common among young people, which never attained a mutuality; their attraction for each other would alternate and each time desire from the one would meet with indifference from the other. Early in 1961 Seth and Julie had arranged to meet for lunch in the West End. Julie, who was working at Longman Publishers at the time, had for some reason decided that it would be appropriate for a third party to be present, and had invited Stella Underwood to join them. However, whatever the secret ambitions and devious ploys of the two leading protagonists had been, it was the chance meeting of the minor characters, one with a walk-on part, and their reciprocation which, as the day unfolded, revealed a potentiality which was to prove irresistible to both of them.

It was a pleasant day, spring-like, and Cornelius Cardew arrived at the restaurant for the purpose of borrowing a shirt from his brother – a purpose which was soon to be relegated to an irrelevance as the party moved from one coffee bar to another throughout the afternoon. Stella recalls that much of their conversation revolved around America and American cars, a topic prompted by the disclosure of Cornelius's plans to emigrate.

From then on Cardew was a frequent visitor to Stella at her flat in Redcliffe Square, appearing and disappearing without warning – to Cologne, to Paris to participate in a performance of Kagel's *Sonant*, and in February, nearer home, to Bernard Miles' Mermaid Theatre for a repeat of the two piano programme given at the Conway Hall the previous year, with myself the second pianist. And it was perhaps a sign of the seriousness of his feelings, if not of his intentions, that Stella and her two children, Emily and Gabriel, were invited to tea to Mariel Cardew's house in Richmond, where Cardew had been living. Or it was merely expedient that Stella and his mother should meet since his ailing grandmother was about to move in to her daughter's house and would need his room. The simplest and most convenient solution for Cardew, indeed for everybody, was that he should move in with Stella, which he did without fuss. The temporary convenience, in particular, suited him, for the plan to emigrate to the United States was still uppermost in his mind and in March he left for Liverpool, whence he would sail to America.

Even in 1961 it would have been more usual, more conventional, to make the journey by air, but the relatively lengthy sea journey would have enhanced the sense of adventure, and of rupture from the European cultures from which he sought release. And he would have relished the exposure to the elements: the ocean spray, the air, the accompanying birds and fish, the rhythm of the waves, the feeling of immense distance and space – Nature at closest hand. By contrast the aeroplane provides cocoon-like protection from nature, its function to minimise the inconvenience of distance. For the air-traveller nature is marginalised to the extent that it is neither benign nor threatening. If he suffers apprehensions which distract him from the purpose of his journey they would probably be concerned with the infallibility, or otherwise, of the technology bearing him to his destination.

For Cardew at that time the image of America was conjured up by his musical contacts – Cage, Tudor, Feldman, La Monte Young, Jazz – and through the literature he had been drawn to and inspired by: the (fifties) Beat Generation and its quintessence in Kerouac's *On the Road;* and William Burroughs, of course. In New York, and only in New York, the younger painters were beginning to attract attention, admiration and money from speculative collectors, afficianados, and hangers-on. Even the CIA had begun to recognise their potential in America's titanic quest to subvert and overthrow the Soviet empire.[2] Politically, the liberal John F. Kennedy was in the White House and although brutal forms of racism were still rife, particularly in the southern states, the Civil Rights movement was gathering momentum. The political establishment was still committed to Keynesian economics and amongst ordinary working people a relative optimism prevailed. To the (probably negligible) extent that such factors might have influenced him, Cardew would have responded positively to America's image and reputation as a 'progressive' democracy, even if his awareness of class society, let alone class struggle, would have been vague and superficial.

In fact, the journey was not made and his stay in Liverpool brief; he would have frequented the clubs and pubs around the docks, touting for a passage, perhaps for work, though it is hard to imagine, as Stella has suggested, that he played the piano in such establishments for he was totally unversed in the art of musical entertainment. If his enthusiasm had begun to wane it was undoubtedly because, in the recesses of his mind, there was a nagging insistence, which could no longer be suppressed, that he had mistakenly abandoned a relationship, albeit in embryo, to which he was far more committed than he would allow himself to admit. The pie-in-the-sky romanticism of an American odyssey finally lost out to the reality of a woman he had begun to love, and he expressed his feelings in a briefly-worded postcard to Stella which also alerted her to his return – a message she confesses she received with some embarrassment, conscious that its intimate words would have been read by the postman.[3]

Stella Underwood, née Sargent, was the daughter of Walter and Winifred Sargent. Her father was a cabinet maker who worked for Willis and Sons, the organ builders; her mother was secretary to the editor of the *New Statesman and Nation*, Kingsley Martin, although she had no time for socialists, regarding them as inadequate people driven by envy and frustration. In the fifties both Stella and her twin sister Freda had been Fine Art students at the Royal College of Art, their work much admired by staff and students alike. Freda was the more flamboyant, ambitious, career-wise, and therefore, ultimately, more successful – the recipient of various awards and prizes, including the RCA Gold Medal and the Abbey Major scholarship which took her to Rome.[4]

Stella had a room in the philosopher Richard Wollheim's large house in Pelham Crescent, South Kensington, in return for occasional duties of an *au pair* nature, and in her second and third years at the RCA gave birth to Emily and Gabriel, on 9 October 1953, and 6 September 1954, respectively. The father, who eventually became her husband, was John Underwood, a gifted sculpture student of immense charm and (like Freda Sargent) darling of the RCA teaching staff. A Byronic mystery man who led a nomadic existence and who would occasionally be sighted along the corridors of the RCA, Underwood nevertheless abandoned sculpture on leaving the RCA to become an art photographer. Stella Cardew recalls their first encounter in a small room in the College where models were painted; the room was cluttered with furniture – the model in the middle – with Underwood, dead-pan, of earnest expression, clambering over tables and chairs from model to palette to canvas in a delightfully comic routine.

According to an old friend, Victor Clarke, Underwood was an intensely dissatisfied man for whom 'impermanence was a fetish', and who had raised unpredictability and irresponsibility to the level of an art form – yet whose talent and charisma had bewitched his peers at art school. Clarke recalls an occasion in the early fifties when he and his girl-friend Jane Hampton, with Stella and John Underwood, visited Freda in Paris, where all talented and aspiring young artists would gather at that time. They found accommodation in the Rue de Seine, in the Hotel Louisiane – a tall, narrow, grey building with balustrades, boasting a bohemian clientele and round baths, which harmonized perfectly with the tastes of the English visitors.

Underwood and Clarke contrived to receive a commission to decorate a well-known night-club, La Rose Rouge. Previously run by the actress Anouk Aimée and her husband, Nico Papadakis, La Rose Rouge was a favourite haunt of a number of established stars, including Marlon Brando, Juliette Greco, Charlie Chaplin, Myrna Loy and Rex Harrison; it enjoyed a reputation for discovering and promoting new talent as well. Clarke recalls that it had moved to new premises, which presumably accounts for the commission. Underwood's proposal, to decorate the venue with huge photographs of Egyptian sculpture, had met with the enthusiastic approval of the lady who ran the establishment; or, perhaps more likely, she too had fallen prey to Underwood's charm. There were a number of meetings and an agreement was reached, whereupon Underwood, as was his wont, disappeared for a week or more, and the project was scotched.

In October of 1953, after the birth to Emily, Stella and John Underwood moved into a house in Regents Park which belonged to the writer Colin MacInnes. The house was cold, damp and in a dilapidated condition, but on her return from hospital her room had been decorated by Freda, John and their friend Peter Mosely; Freda's individual contribution was to cover the walls with stencil dots, an artistic act of sisterly solicitude which was much appreciated by Stella, who continued to attend the RCA, leaving the baby in the care of Underwood's sister, Jean. Meanwhile, Underwood and Mosely were making films, successfully and above all remuneratively, which enabled John and Stella to move into a pleasant flat in Lancaster Gate, by which time they had married and a new baby, Gabriel, had arrived, in September 1954. Underwood was rarely at home or, if he was, he would be in his studio developing his photographs. Stella recalls that after their marriage there was very little communication between them; Underwood began to work for *Vogue* magazine, became very much part of the Chelsea set, socializing, drinking, womanizing, fathering more children and accumulating debts; he eventually eloped with a neighbour − a brief and ill-fated affair which ended, according to Stella, when they both contracted influenza and separated.

Meanwhile, the lease on the flat in Lancaster Gate had expired and neither Underwood nor Stella made any attempt to find new accommodation. For Stella these were bleak and desperate days and she finally moved to a hotel room in Paddington, for six weeks − where one of the children contracted measles − and then to a depressing boarding house in Primrose Hill. Some friends, who were clearly concerned by these turn of events, suggested to Stella that she went to Ibiza where the climate was congenial, where day-to-day living was cheap, and where she could pick up the pieces of her life and recover her equilibrium. She and the children stayed in Ibiza for about a year. On their return she rented a flat in the Old Brompton Road, South Kensington, where they remained for nearly two years, until 1960, when they moved into the small basement flat in Redcliffe Square, Earls Court.

The energy and enthusiasm with which Cardew took up the challenge of domestic responsibility, and moreover assumed the role of father to Stella's two children, gives pause to question Ruth Koenig's analysis of his attitude towards such matters in general and their own marriage in particular. Clearly, it was not the prospect of children which had made her husband 'cut and run'. In any case, the life he was to share with Stella, for a decade, was very much of their own making and owed no allegiance to received social norms. There were some concessions to conventionality – the children were educated as a matter of course within the state system, for example – but for the many visitors to their home in Redcliffe Square in the early sixties it was the unique ethos of the family life that Stella and Cornelius created which made an indelible impression. Neither of them aspired to the bourgeois trappings and concomitant life-style which for Ruth had probably seemed to be an unavoidable, even desirable consequence of marital status.

And Stella, beautiful and original, was an inspiration to Cardew, as well as ground support in a musical climate which, though different, was as uncongenial as Cologne, and where the protective diffidence and hauteur he had cultivated on the continent would often intimidate and provoke his company. With Stella he was kept close to the family pulse and to roots of feeling; the intense and pervasive intellectualism which bedevilled relations within his circle in Cologne and, to a lesser extent and differently, with his peers at Oxford and the RAM was relegated to a more humble standing. The highfaluting disquisitions of a mainly abstract nature gave way to parental talk and discussions centred on the realities of family life: the needs of the children and the constant attention their growth and development demanded. And it was Cornelius, in the early months, who looked after the children while Stella eked out their existence through a variety of teaching jobs, in schools, remand homes, and evening classes – an advanced girlishness belying an iron will and seriousness of intent. She recalls that he preferred to stay at home, miraculously able to write music and practice the piano whilst consumed in a hubbub of domesticity. But the old guitar he had bought was condemned by their friend, the guitarist Julian Bream; it made his fingers sore and Bream insisted that he should dispose of it.

Through Stella he met many new people, although he was never able to give his heart to her friends and colleagues from the worlds of Art and Advertising; it was evident to her that outside his own personal experience and circle of friends his knowledge of many areas of life was extremely limited. 'Settling down at last' he wrote under April 1961 in the chronology of events listed at the beginning of one of the Journals. It was as if, after a surfeit of travelling, on a circuit which was draining and ultimately unrewarding, he had gratefully accepted the opportunity to put down roots. The trips to the continent continued but more often than not he would take Stella and the children with him – the professional engagement more a pretext for a family outing. In April a visit to the South of France needed no such pretext: Stella's brother-in-law, the Columbian painter Alejandro Obregon, had bought a house in Alba, a small village in the Ardèche, west from Montélimar across the Rhône, which over the years had become a haven for Parisian artists and writers, and at that time still boasted a small, artistic community. They travelled separately – Stella and the children from London, Cornelius by car from engagements on the continent – and had arranged to meet in a hotel on the Belgian coast, according to Stella's hazy recollection of the occasion, probably in the vicinity of Ostende, whence they drove to Alba.

The house had been empty for years and the early part of the summer was spent cleaning, making it habitable. These were happy days and Cardew also found time to work on the *Third Orchestral Piece*, presumably some revisions in preparation for its first performance in Warsaw the following September; and whatever the fate of the condemned guitar he managed to write a short guitar piece, *for Stella*. Meanwhile, the faithful Daimler was parked in a field, covered in grass seed and hay, to melt and blister under a relentless sun, and then to be coaxed into action again, in June, for the return journey – via Paris, where they had been offered overnight accommodation by the then Principal of the Royal College of Art, Rodrigo Moynihan.

Stella recalls the hesitancy and reluctance with which the beady-eyed concierge admitted them, no doubt apprehensive of the acts of vandalism which this ragtag and bobtail family of foreigners might perpetrate against the array of modern masterpieces which adorned the Moynihans' studio. Stella, too, entertained fears: that Cornelius might be provoked to avenge the appropriation, as he saw it, of contemporary art by Academia (by a professor) through a violent act of redemption; to maim the paintings would be to liberate them. No such violation occurred, however, and the next morning they left for England.

A visit to Paris in June saw the concurrence, for Cardew, of two contrasting and symbolic events: the one associated with a past he had renounced – a 'disastrous tour' arranged by an old friend, Haro Lauhus, performing in Cologne, and on 20 June, in Paris, on a Pleyel piano, at the Salle de l'Ecole Normale de Musique. The other event an exhilarating representation of the issues of aesthetic and philosophical import which now preoccupied him: an exhibition of paintings, sculptures, drawings and lithographs by Jasper Johns at the Galerie Rive Droite. The explosive irruption of the new American painting into Europe fired Cardew's musical imagination, just as Cage's radicalism, a few years earlier, had inspired him to attain more profound levels of inventiveness and creative thought. As we shall see, the experimental notation that had been inaugurated in *Autumn 60* was to be taken a stage further in *Octet '61 for Jasper Johns* (subsequently referred to as

Octet '61), a work written in spontaneous response to the Paris exhibition and dominated, like the paintings, by the pervasive presence of Arabic numerals.

And it was the brief return to Cologne that witnessed a further severance with the past when the concluding chapter, the epilogue rather, of his relationship with Pyla was finally written. On the night that Cardew was leaving Germany, Pyla and a mutual friend, the American musician, Ben Patterson, had come to see him off; the three stole on to a Rhein tourist boat, emptied a bottle of schnapps between them, and Cardew was deposited, with some difficulty, into the train. Patterson accompanied Pyla home and they were to stay together for another seven years.

Yet the revelations of the Johns paintings in Paris and the creative outpouring they generated did not preclude a mindfulness of matters which were equally pressing, if of a more mundane nature – in particular the necessity of securing a regular means of income. Translating work, from German to English, had come his way: a book on chess for Thames and Hudson and a Concert Guide (a long term project for which he had also been given editorial responsibilities and which he was still working on in May '62; there were also contributions to music magazines, including the *Tempo* Magazine article, 'Notation – Interpretation, etc.', and his reports on Stockhausen's *Carré* for the *Musical Times* (in the October and November 1961 issues), some piano accompanying for London County Council evening classes, and the occasional Workers' Educational Association lecture. But it was irregular, free-lance work, and the financial rewards, though sufficient to meet the cost of a second-hand upright piano and a Daimler purchased from friends to replace the old Mercedes which he had abandoned that summer in Cologne, were modest and, in any case, inadequate to meet the family's needs. A longer-term view was sought and in October 1961 Cardew enrolled as a student at the London College of Printing in Holborn on a one year typography course, which he attended two days a week. And it was the acquisition and refinement of this skill which was to provide him with essential income for lengthy periods of his life over the next 15 years. Nor could it have been undertaken reluctantly; maps and cartography, for example, had always interested him and, as we have seen, the signs and symbols of musical notation held a fascination for him; it was his typographical appreciation of the 'form' of numerals which enabled him to extract them from the Johns paintings and incorporate them, as the essential ingredient, into a musical notation: a transmigration from one Art to another.

The course at the London College of Printing was run by John Gillard and was attended by students from vastly differing backgrounds and who were engaged in a variety of employments during the rest of the week. The majority of them wanted to work in publishing houses, or for magazines, or to become assistants in design houses. Gillard had already heard of Cardew through his friend Denis Duerden, who had been in West Africa where he had befriended Michael Cardew, and who possessed a large collection of Cardew's pottery. Coincidentally, Gillard had known Stella and Freda Sargent, who had been a year ahead of him at the Beckenham School of Art in the early fifties, and whose work he had greatly admired.

At the College of Printing Gillard and Cardew struck up an immediate friendship. Cardew's commitment, his serious attitude – not only to his typographical work, but to more general matters which, as Gillard recalls, they would discuss over tea in a local 'greasy spoon' – and his outstanding intelligence made a profound impression on Gillard. Cardew could identify immediately all the relationships in a grid and soon developed an awareness of the parallels between typographical grids and structures and musical forms, and of their implications for his experimental notations. And it was on Gillard's suggestion, in the spring of 1962 and towards the end of the course, that Cardew went to see the designer Edward Wright, a meeting which resulted, in due course, in Cardew's employment at Aldus Books and the beginning of a lengthy, if detached and sporadic, association with the world of publishing.

The course, demanding and energy-sapping as it was, had nevertheless served its purpose and Cardew had even managed to take time off from his College work to produce, by the end of the year, a *First Movement for String Quartet*, which he dedicated to Sir Thomas Armstrong, Director of the Royal Academy of Music (who had commissioned the work for a fee of fifty guineas), and his own piano version of *Octet '61* (which later became the first of the *Three Winter Potatoes*). A visit to Redcliffe Square in December from Kurt Schwertsik is recorded in the journals and in the new year Cardew's talent as a vigilant copyist was again pressed into service for the parts of Mauricio Kagel's *Heterophonie*.

On a single leaf of paper, headed '17 Jan 1962' the date, apparently detached from the main body of letters and journals, the delicate tensions between domesticity and creativity, which he never saw as a crudely antithetical relationship, found expression in a brief essay:

> The washing up just finished, after seeing Ben home after reading to him and the children from *Treasure Island* (Ben inspires me to read properly; he listens) after carrying an awe-inspiring armful of wood to dump on the way to bringing Emily back for the Reynold's Television after cooking and eating spaghetti with the 2 boys after expiating the boredom of the afternoon by translating one paragraph, now is the time to write. If what I were thinking about were a work of literature now would be the time to sit down and write on. The white wine opened in expectation of the guests, even a glass poured and set, the oven on in preparation

for the ready chicken, the salad dressed, now is the time to take a seat – not the armchair by the fire but the straight one next to it away from the fire, full on, table and paper and wine and tobacco and ashtray and fruit at my left elbow, and the book of Steakhouse matches that came from where? – and listen to my scratchy pen in expectation of the night.

But what I am thinking about is not a work of literature, so writing on is out. It is not even a piece of music; there is nothing to be continued, nothing to be pushed ahead, steadily. There is just the mood to do just that. The physical condition is right for forging ahead, but not for starting something, not even a piece of music; the time for that was yesterday and I didn't take it far enough for it to be possible to continue it; that will need an extra, full start. The time is right for writing on, the chairs and table set, the gramophone waiting; before the guests come, and Stella with her chicken, there is a nice little bit of time for taking it just that beautiful little calm stretch further, to fill the gone day with satisfaction, the consciousness of supremacy over pen and paper, the materials of my heart, silly organ.

The last two words appear almost as an afterthought and yet they provide an ironic twist, a belated antidote to a domestic rhapsody, as well as recalling the unsettling cadences which at that time brought many of his pieces, like *February Pieces*, to their conclusion. His frequent resort to irony would often be leavened by a quirky, irresistible humour: in an undated letter to Ilona Halberstadt, written during a concert of 'half-baked music' which apparently had recently become mildly fashionable on the European market, he refers to 'old lady next [to] me, started making feverish notes as soon as the music began. I saw what they were: "collect alarm clock, take in overcoat + jacket; paper handkies". Etc. All reasons, stimuli, for me to write away the time. But tinkle tinkle, I cant properly think(le)'.

Another Generation Music concert, this time at the Wigmore Hall on 2 June 1962, reaffirmed Cardew's commitment to indeterminate music and experimentalism: a demanding programme of music by the American composers John Cage, Morton Feldman and Christian Wolff, and a trio of younger composers – Griffith Rose, Cardew himself, and a young composer from Hamburg, Michael von Biel, whom Cardew had admired and befriended.[5]

Through the initiative of von Biel these three, with the German violinist Egon Mayer, had come together to form The Generation of Music Ensemble which, to all intents and purposes, was the first musical group to which Cardew had belonged since his student days at the Academy.[6] Certainly, during his stay in Cologne he had taken part in many ensemble performances, and often with musicians for whom he had the greatest respect – David Tudor, John Cage, Kurt Schwertsik, to name but three – but these more often than not were ad hoc arrangements with musicians passing through or in brief, temporary residence. Cologne was a mecca but also a battleground, as we have seen in the relation between the Cologne music establishment and the artists who gravitated towards Mary Baumeister's studio; certainly, the city's mystique, the aura which seemed to surround it, and not least its flair for aggressive self-promotion, drew people to it, visitors and observers from far-flung places; but the ethos was competitive rather than collaborative and hardly conducive to a long, patient haul undertaken by kindred spirits living in proximity, such as would be the case with the successful, collective music-making groups (Musica Elettronica Viva and, in particular, AMM) which would make their mark throughout the decade. Nor could The Generation of Music Ensemble hope to live up to the grand designs of its manifesto; its individual members, despite their nomadic existence, were based too far apart, such that regular playing sessions would have been impossible. Yet how else could 'a high degree of awareness exercised [...] by each interpreter individually and in relation to the group[...] and the ability to react spontaneously within situations that are familiar and yet always fresh in detail' be acquired? [7] And there are echoes in the group's manifesto of Cardew's antipathy towards 'professionalism', which he had expressed in various talks and texts, particularly in relation to performances of *Autumn 60* and *Octet '61*:

> This ensemble has been formed with the idea of creating a nucleus of performers who will not rely on a facile talent for getting through a performance on two rehearsals, but on the acquisition of this skill, and a wide experience of its application, not to mention that firm understanding of and devotion to the music itself, which is essential for the valid interpretation of any music.

A statement of intention which is so earnest, so high-minded, rarely inspires confidence; too often the loftiness of the intention seems to be in inverse proportion to the efficacy of its practice: practice bearing such an intolerable burden is doomed to failure, and the purity and assertiveness of intention serves only to highlight the inadequacy of its practice. When practice is free of such pressure, when the demands on it are looser, only then can practice flourish, even exceed theory's most radical expectations. Such would be the case, as we shall see, with AMM, whose extraordinary practice developed untrammelled by theoretical precepts and pressures, by *intention*. Moreover, its members had inhabited similar urban neighbourhoods over a long period, were subject to the same environmental culture which 'builds up a communal fund of subconscious experience in the inhabitants of a city'.[8]

The Times reviewed the concert with detached amusement, describing it as an ISCM festival fringe concert, pointing out that the official business of the day had been a boat-trip to Hampton Court, and ending with a paragraph singling out Cardew's 'musical professionalism'(sic) as a welcome respite from the ear-abusing items which had made up the rest of the programme:

> One of their number, Mr. Cornelius Cardew, actually played the piano instead of attempting to demolish it, and his performances of his own and Morton Feldman's pieces went beyond mere belligerence towards the condition of music; there was a musical professionalism to be met here.[9]

Indeed, 'the condition of music' which Cardew's performances expressed would almost certainly have gone beyond the comprehension of *The Times'* music critic and, of course, had nothing to do with 'musical professionalism'. Cardew was not immune to the unrelenting adversity of the critics, though it is doubtful whether he would have bothered to keep tabs on reviews of his concerts; it would certainly not have affected the compositional path he had chosen to pursue and he would have maintained a stoical front at all times – there was no chink in the armour. Stella, for her part, was perplexed by the negative response not only of critics but of sections of the audience who would walk out or express their antagonism verbally, and she had concluded that Cornelius was ahead of his time.

Yet in some official circles there was recognition of his talent, and in June, the month of his marriage to Stella, Peters Edition published *February Pieces*, a decision which was certainly on the recommendation of Dr Hans Swarsenski, who was responsible for copyright, various editorial decisions, and contemporary music, including the acquisition of new composers. Swarsenski was a gentleman who prided himself, with some justification, on his wit and musical knowledge and who was clearly fascinated by Cardew's *persona*.[10] Cardew, like William Blake, belonged to that zone of Anglo-Saxon culture which for many Europeans is as irresistible as it is unfathomable. Swarsenski found Cardew's manner and appearance disconcerting, too much in the popular style and inappropriate for a young composer of serious music. 'The trouble with Cardew' he once said to me, 'is that he is not a Beatle.' The inference was that Cardew had assumed the air of a rock musician, which was not an accurate observation simply because Mr. Swarsenski was out of his depth in such matters.

Later in the year The Generation of Music Ensemble surfaced again, in Cologne, with two concerts in Mary Baumeister's Atelier on 26 and 28 September. In a letter dated 12 September Michael von Biel writes that he is 'banking' on Cardew to come, and to perform in *Octet '61*, von Biel's *Book for 3*, as well as in Feldman's *Three Hands* and

Cage's *Variations I*. Appearances by the Ensemble seem to have been fitful and there is no further reference to it in Cardew's journals, though it may well have continued to function without his further participation. In any case, by October he was an employee at Aldus Books and there would have been far less scope for the life of itinerant musician which he had enjoyed over the last five years. Now the demands of domesticity preoccupied him and his marriage to Stella on 29 June 1962 was perhaps further testimony to his commitment to her and the children.

The wedding was conducted by a chubby, bespectacled registrar at Kensington Registry Office. There followed a reception with about eighty people at their flat in Redcliffe Square whence with a smaller party of guests they drove off in a convoy of eight or more cars in appalling weather to an elaborate dinner in the Kent countryside. This had been arranged by their friend, the Canadian film director, Allan King, who had around that time commissioned some film music from Cardew.

Two weeks later Cardew wrote a letter to a Herr de Delas, a gallery owner in Cologne, including photos of Stella's paintings and a lengthy, intelligent exposition of her Art, and with the proposal that he might call in on his way to Poland for the Warsaw Autumn Festival in September [11] – in stark contrast, as we shall see, to his dismissive attitude towards her paintings on a later occasion. In September Cardew's *Third Orchestral Piece* received its premiere at the Warsaw Autumn Festival of Contemporary Music by the Cracow Philharmonic Orchestra under Andrzej Markowski. Cardew himself attended the performance and on his return from Poland expressed his disappointment in a letter to his mother:

Warsaw itself was a bit cold and dreary, and the performance of my piece was something of a fiasco. Staunch friends supported me; however, I felt very little loyalty to myself, even – it just seemed like a bad piece. However, most pieces set out under a cloud of self-criticism, and some have proved themselves later. It takes experience to play an orchestral piece convincingly, of course; and not only experience of new music, but experience of this piece. So I console myself, and am less downhearted now. [12]

Somehow the piece managed to transcend the composer's doubts and misgivings: towards the end of the year Cardew received a letter from Jack Gottlieb, assistant to Leonard Bernstein, Director of the New York Philharmonic. Apparently, Bernstein had expressed interest in the work but had found some of Cardew's instructions 'confusing'. Gottlieb proposed a meeting with Bernstein or himself to iron out the difficulties with a view to the possible inclusion of the work in the NYP's 1963/64 season. Whether the meeting materialized is not known; in any event, Bernstein never conducted the work.

Meanwhile, and of more pressing concern, a letter from the Administrative Editor of Aldus Books, a Mr. Frame-Smith, had confirmed Cardew's employment as Assistant Art Editor for a mutual three-month trial period starting 1 October 1962. His immediate superior, the Art Director, was a Mr. Bruce Robertson. In the event of more permanent employment a salary of £750 per annum was offered; during the three-month trial period 'a minute's notice can be given on either side', thus providing both parties with the option of a 'speedy getaway'. Cardew was immediately informed of his first assignment: the title *Man in Society,* and he would be working with Bruce Robertson.

Aldus books, situated in Fitzroy Square, off the Euston Road, was owned by one Wolfgang Foges, a Viennese Jew who had fled the Nazis and had found sanctuary in England. Foges's purpose was to produce popular educational materials for the public at large, and to that end had enlisted a number of prestigious names on to his editorial board: Jacob Bronowski, Arthur Koestler, Lancelot Hogben, Bertrand Russell, and the naturalist, James Fisher. Aldus Books subsequently became a subsidiary of Doubleday, an American company, and the majority of the books were distributed through American Book Clubs and in general sales. This accounted for most of the work that Cardew was involved in during his time at Aldus Books.

The inspirational designers involved in the project included the Italian Germano Facetti, who subsequently became Art Director for Penguin Books, Edwin Taylor, later to become Art Director on the *Sunday Times*, the Hungarian, Felix Gluck, and a host of enthusiastic and creative designers who together produced the prototypes of what subsequently became popular non-fiction books: the 'coffee-table' book. This was the team of visualizers and designers which Cardew was to become part of when he joined Aldus Books in October 1962, although at the time his uncompromising intellectualism and high-flown aesthetic ideals would have made it impossible for him to have accommodated the unadulterated commercialism which pervaded at Aldus books. For Cardew art should not, could not, talk down to people; it occupied the highest ground, and if people were unable to comprehend its message such a state of affairs could not be mitigated by the crude stratagems of the coffee-table popularizers. What he would have regarded a decade later, in political terms, as cynical (bourgeois) opportunism, he now dismissed with disdain and detachment – artistically meretricious, and politically (in so far as politics affected him at all) irrelevant. As for the job itself, Cardew possessed all the necessary technical skills which he could deploy without any burden of association with the end-product. Most importantly, it was a regular source of income – adequate to sustain the family life to which he was now wedded.

Bruce Robertson recalls that Cardew's presence at Aldus Books was welcomed by his co-workers; his aptitude for mathematics, his precision, fitted him for those menial tasks – such as the scheming and organization of charts and diagrams – which his colleagues regarded as tiresome, professional chores; naturally, the work they enjoyed and merited demanded flair and imagination, as well as a degree of skill, which, by dint of their training at various art schools around the country, they felt able to provide superabundantly. Yet, according to Robertson, it was the routine aspect of the work which Cardew seemed to enjoy: sitting quietly, casting off the copy, ensuring that all the captions fitted, devising time lines and flow charts. But he was also involved in work at a more detailed level, in organisational diagrams: contents lists, bibliographies, indexes, structural diagrams, all of which were part of the body of the book. And the assemblage of typographical detail required care, fastidiousness, scrupulosity, diligence – skills and attitudes which Cardew had developed so single-mindedly during his involvement with the musical avant-garde: the copying and realisation of modern scores, the invention of new notations, the deciphering of complex instructions.

Throughout the late fifties (virtually from the early months in Cologne) and into the sixties the shift in the trajectory of Cardew's musical aspirations, borne of a new, visionary (utopian) perspective, reflected a deep-seated reaction to the new ways of thinking and feeling, to content and meaning, to the idealism, both moral and philosophical, that seemed to infuse the new American music. 'There is no room for the policeman in art', Cage had said in one of his polemics against the Europeans, and Cardew was one of the few artists not only to grasp the social implications of Cage's declaration but to act fearlessly upon it. And yet, much as he admired Cage's compositional techniques (he once described Cage's *Variations I* as a 'giant step forward'), it was the latent 'democracy' embedded within Cage's scores that particularly impressed him, with their calculated risk-taking and open invitation to participate in a process in which traditional definitions of music were challenged and subverted.

When a student once asked Morton Feldman, cognisant of the importance that Feldman attached to the actual pitches that he wrote, how he accounted for the occasions when he did not specify a particular note, Feldman replied that in that particular instance he had heard all the available notes, so that it did not constitute a 'gap' in his hearing of notes – rather, a 'blur'. It was precisely the open-endedness of the Americans' music, the incompleteness of their vision, their 'blurred' conception of truth which for Cardew produced the 'only honest utterances of our time'. Their music inhabited the creeks and backwaters of musical expression with no pretensions to the status of 'artistic masterpieces' – a negation of individualism and subjectivism, of art as the expression of an unmistakeable, inviolable 'personality'. Rather, it comprised fragmented 'notes and commentaries' on reality, reflecting sometimes environmental sounds, sometimes the principles of nature, including the vagaries of human activity, drawn together through the application of 'chance' operations, innocent of purpose. Not that Cardew challenged the validity of the 'artistic masterpiece', but it was a temporary validity bestowed by history which the profound antagonisms and fragmentation of contemporary life could no longer accommodate. To modern minds

> the truth was a 'blur', and if it were not a blur it would not be the truth. The philosopher Wittgenstein holds – as I understand him – that the truth is not an explanation, but lies away, somewhere, in an indescribable region which can however be apprehended by us simply by a scrutiny of the various concrete facts, all of which lie plainly exposed to our eyes.[13]

This was how Cardew rationalised the equivocalness which characterised the New Music; and all the while Wittgensteinian thought loomed ever larger in both his philosophical and his musical concerns, particularly in relation to 'indeterminacy': plurality of interpretation; flexibility of meaning based on context; rule based procedures; the questioning of preconceived assumptions about composition – an omnipresent force, a guide, a constant forewarning against the consequences of flawed logic and of self-deception, a subtle and chastening influence on a furious imagination, an intellectual and moral yardstick by which a projected course of action could be judged/justified/verified. Yet the references are still discreet, respectful, and relatively sparse, as if he were still unable, or unwilling, to give verbal expression to the profound relationship he had been nurturing, and for some years, with Wittgenstein's philosophy.

A 'series of blurs, of varying kind and density', was how Cardew characterised the pieces that Christian Wolff was writing at the time – *Duo for Pianists I and II* (1957-8), *For Pianist* (1959), *Trio II* (1961), *For 1, 2 or 3 People* (1964):

[Wolff] indicates, for instance, 4 notes from 'a' ('a' being a set of pitches given at the outset), one of them transposed up or down an octave, 2 of which are pizzicato, and one of them pianissimo.

This provides an inexhaustible field of possibilities, but nevertheless a limited one, one that you can grasp. In the same way one can write a set of notes without specifying their durations, tempo, loudness, instrumentation, etc. and still be able to recognize them. [...] The composer accepts (John Cage designates this courageous, others naive) all the possible versions within the field as being equally valid. The performer then chooses what he will play, and if he's anything of an interpreter he will express himself in his choice, himself and thus also, his conception of the piece. If the interpreter feels himself in a quandary as to what to play then he had better refrain from performing the piece until he is no longer in a quandary (similarly the composer who is in a quandary as to what to write).[14]

In the same broadcast one of Wolff's pieces, *For Prepared Piano* (1951), elicits an interesting, if rare, point of comparison with Stockhausen's *Kontrapunkte*, and Cardew exploits the occasion to refute a fashionable argument, clinching his thesis in style with a typically Cardewesque metaphor:

the formal concept (that of a gradual transition from alien to familiar sounds) seems to have a lot in common with Stockhausen's 'Form as Process'. The form of Stockhausen's *Kreuzspiel*, for example, consists of the process by which each of the elements exchange their positions; what was high at the start is low at the end, and what was low at the start is high at the end, and the point where they cross ('kreuzspiel') signalizes some important structural shift. The form of his *Kontrapunkte* is based on similar procedures: the beginning is characterised by rapid fluctuations over the whole range (of timbre, pitch, loudness, duration, etc.) in which, in the nature of things, the extreme areas are necessarily prominent; and the end is characterised by a [word illegible] of change within a narrow medium range (all instruments have dropped out except the piano, the dynamics tend to stick within the range *pp-mf*, the pitches gambol around in the lower register, showing only a vague (though insistent) profile towards middle C, and the motion has become a constant interplay of the various groupings of semiquavers, either simple or dotted, or as triplets or quintuplets).

Stockhausen's detractors can dismiss both these forms, that of *Kreuzspiel* by saying that nothing is accomplished by turning an 'x' back to front, its form remains the same, and that of *Kontrapunkte* by saying that the piece is just a long petering-out, from the complex and varied sounds of the opening to the uniformity of the close. And this is also a criticism that can be levelled at Wolff's piece. It equates interesting with unusual, the sounds become less interesting the fewer preparations that are heard, and consequently the piece becomes more and more boring as it progresses. This criticism is a manifestation of a fallacy that is becoming more and more widespread, and that is that unfamiliar things are more interesting than familiar things. The argument being that familiarity with an object exhausts the object, we know all there is to know about it, and it holds nothing further for us. Nothing could be more mistaken. The less we know about an object, the more primitive the concepts by means of which we try to grasp it. Take for instance flight: when people first started making aeroplanes, they made complex structures of wood and canvas; perhaps they thought it would be something like sailing, but lightness was the primary consideration. But as the sensation of flight became more familiar, would-be fliers became aware of the real problems of aerodynamics and concentrated their attention on design and the disposition of weight and surface. What happens in Christian's piece is somewhat similar. The sensual intoxication of unusual sounds is progressively denied the listener, and as the sounds become more usual, so the listener is invited to penetrate more deeply into them. In this way something unfamiliar is brought home.[15]

For Cardew, as indeed for most composers, the question of 'form' was of paramount importance, and something to which he returned time and again. A Journal entry opens with, if not quite a definition of form, at least an unequivocal expression of his attitude towards it:

The 'form' of a piece is really its meaning – the way it makes sense as it goes along (form as movement). Klee apparently created about 20 pictorial forms and all his pictures are expositions of one or another or combinations of these basic formal ideas. Try and find similar formal propositions in your own work: first the conglomerate sign – (the meaning deriving from interaction of the components) *Autumn 60*, *Octet '61*. Then, the rigid rods which 'attract' constellations of material which adhere plastically to the rigid. Third: ??? No more spring to mind. They should.[16]

In his writings and talks from the early sixties Cardew would frequently expound on the antithetical relationship, as he saw it, between the American and the European avant-garde. In the Cologne Radio broadcast it was clear, right from the outset, where his sympathies lay:

Christian Wolff, Earle Brown, Morton Feldman, lumped together as the three most significant pupils, friends, of John Cage. Yet how different they are and how different from their teacher. One could say that they had received the perfect education from their teacher, that education whose sole visible result is a certain freedom of thought, rather than the adoption of a particular way of thinking. Free thinking leads to honesty and truth, but also to isolation. If the distance between Wolff, Brown and Feldman is greater than that between Stockhausen, Boulez and Nono, it is because their minds are livelier, their conclusions more far-reaching and, furthermore, arrived at with greater frankness. The three Europeans are certainly more ambitious, their concepts larger, their forms more extended and their sense of direction more consciously developed. But they lack perspicuity, or far-sightedness; they are avowed revolutionaries and therefore concerned with what they reject. History, on the other hand, is the arrival and assimilation of elements from outside, ideas God knows whence. The Indians certainly didn't know where Columbus came from, and the Europeans certainly did not realise that their most valuable contribution to Indian culture was the horse, which the Indians were later to use in defending themselves against the proverbial cowboys. However that may be, our position in Europe is now the reverse, and having so long been in the habit of exporting ideas and other manifestations of culture, and exporting them about by force, we are now on the receiving end, and very difficult we find it to assimilate the ideas that come to us from America and other places which are now virtually on our doorstep. Never mind, perhaps it will turn out thus: that the more passionately we reject these ideas, the more powerful they will be in us when we finally do assimilate them, as of course we must, and on our own terms so to speak.

The music of Cage, Brown, Feldman and Wolff inhabited a different universe, no less, which in turn reflected a 'state of mind, of being' – a sound universe whose logic remained completely obscure to those who could not, or would not enter it. It was only through a profound identification with this sound world that one could comprehend the decisions that were taken and the conclusions that were reached within it. Moreover, Cardew emphasized the importance of context:

> In water, the fish communicates, it lives and it may be that often the music of Wolff, Brown and Feldman is out of water in our European concert halls. But we must find water in which they can live, which seems impossible since until we find it we cannot understand what they are saying. [17]

In his *Lecture on Something* John Cage describes this 'state of mind' in a reference to Feldman's music:

> Feldman speaks of no sounds, and takes within broad limits the first ones that come along. He has changed the responsibility of the composer from making to accepting. To accept whatever comes regardless of the consequences is to be unafraid or to be full of that love which comes from a sense of at-one-ness

with whatever. This goes to explain what Feldman means when he says that he is associated with all of the sounds, and so can foresee what will happen even though he has not written the particular notes down as other composers do.[18]

This essential at-one-ness Feldman attributed to his long relationship with Cage; the 'self-permission' to pursue unflinchingly a radical course of action in which one believed:

What it really amounts to is whether you want to be in the work, in the medium, or outside it. [...] I feel that Cage and myself are in the work. I feel that Stockhausen and Boulez are out of it. And it becomes a question of temperament; I would like to go even further and say that if you want to be out of the work you want to be out of life.[19]

Feldman felt strongly the need to grant more autonomy to sounds. In his *Last Pieces* (1959) Feldman's instruction 'Durations are free' seems to be directed at the notes themselves, rather than to the performer – 'hold for as long as you can', he seems to be saying, 'nothing is going to cut you off'. So the overtones of the component notes in a chord are given ample time to argue things out amongst themselves. For the performer the balance of notes within a chord becomes uneven since in the attempt to play extremely softly the imperfections in the instrument become apparent, take their toll. The listener's ear, meanwhile, is led down and down, deeper into the deepest recesses of the chords. Yet Feldman recognized the contradiction which lay at the heart of the exercise:

I began to feel that the sounds were not concerned with my ideas of symmetry and design, that they wanted to sing of other things. They wanted to live, and I was stifling them. It is not a question of a controlled or decontrolled methodology. In both cases it is a methodology. Something is being made. And to make something is to constrain it. I have found no answer to this dilemma. My whole creative life is simply an attempt to adjust to it. There is very little concern, very little involvement with anything else. It seems to me that, in spite of our efforts to trammel it, music has already flown the coop – escaped. There is an old proverb: "Man makes plans, God laughs." The composer makes plans, music laughs.[20]

In rehearsal Feldman would help his performers by describing the sounds as 'sourceless'; he wanted them to take on that precious quality of transience, of *uncatchability* (Cardew's word), to be free but not arbitrary, elusive but compelling – a perception which evokes an old Taoist dictum: 'The greatest music has the most tenuous notes.' A few years later Cardew was to give characteristically ironic expression to the same notion:

> Music is vagrant; it has no fixed abode. It's a menace to society. It needs cleaning up. The impossibility of abolishing music. Its omnipresence. Its uncatchability. Perhaps after all we have to step down and let music pursue its own course.[21]

For Cardew, notation had become the very antithesis of such a definition, with an increasingly censorial role in twentieth century music which had to be challenged, exposed, transformed; or, and this was the radical option which Cardew would choose with the AMM, notation had to be abandoned altogether, forced to step down so that music could 'pursue its course'.

The 'dilemma' – to which Feldman sought constant creative adjustment – provoked Cardew, however, to a more Homeric response, which was to take him yet another significant step away from his mentors, as we shall see in our discussion of AMM music. For Cardew, if sounds were to be freed to pursue their own course it could not be by means of 'calculation', of compositional methodology, however sophisticated (as in the scores of Cage and Feldman); quite the contrary, he came to believe that it was rather through the spontaneous generation of sounds in freely improvised music – within a whole gamut of degrees of control between accident and intentionality – that music could aspire to, even if it could never achieve, the desired state of autonomy.

In Cage Feldman identified a man who

> always wanted to go out into the world. He was always creating situations where the world could enter into him, where he couldn't distinguish which was the centre, life or him. [...] And so for me the real is not the object, the real for me is not the compositional system, the real for me is to what degree, almost in Kierkegaardian terms, I can exist, I can plunge, I can leap into this thing which I call life, which I call the environment.[22]

Cardew, too, had recognized the 'the musical composition of the world' and, as we shall see, with AMM would indeed take the plunge – into life – discarding the 'compositional system' which bedevilled and embarrassed his peers and former mentors, and in doing so left them behind, shaking their heads in incredulity.

'I don't think anyone ever wrote about my early music as beautifully as Cornelius did... .and he played it beautifully' Feldman recalled.[23] Indeed my own first and abiding memory of Cardew the musician was his performance of Feldman's music at the aforementioned Conway Hall concert at the beginning of 1960. Those floating, sourceless sounds, which he played with an unerring sense of timing, with an artistry that was as persuasive as it was unconventional, evoked an emotional response quite unlike any other I had experienced in listening to music:

> Feldman's music springs from a state of mind, of being; an attitude embedded in a particular atmosphere. What goes on in this atmosphere, the decisions taken in it, the conclusions reached in it, the logic of any activity within this atmosphere escapes us if we cannot enter into the same atmosphere.[24]

This 'atmosphere' is surely related to Feldman's attitude to musical space; for where, as it seemed, so many composers were busying themselves filling space, whether on manuscript or acoustically, for Feldman the creation of space remained throughout his life a central preoccupation. This was a reaction (as I interpreted it at the time), in part, to the growing pressure and congestion of contemporary life. For myself, as performing musician, this satisfied not only a musical need, but also a socio-psychological one.

In the Cologne Radio broadcast Cardew makes more specific references to the music:

> Almost all Feldman's music is slow and soft. Only at first sight is this a limitation; I see it rather as a narrow door, to whose dimensions one has to adapt oneself (as in Alice in Wonderland) before one can pass through it into the state of being that is expressed in Feldman's music. Only when one has become accustomed to the dimness of light can one begin to perceive the richness and variety of colour which is the material of the music. When one has passed through the narrow door and got accustomed to the dim light, one realises the range of his imagination and the significant differences that distinguish one piece from another. [...]
> Feldman sees the sounds as reverberating endlessly, never getting lost, changing their resonances as they die away, or rather do not die away, but recede from our ears, and soft because softness is compelling, because an insidious invasion of our senses is more effective than a frontal attack, because our ears must strain to catch the music, they must become more sensitive before they perceive the world of sound in which Feldman's music takes place. [...]
> I see Feldman as the first composer to break free from the dogma and dreary theorizing that has enshrouded new music for so long. Feldman has evolved a language that is capable of expressing his ideas in all their freshness and intensity; it is not a synthetic language dictated by any lame need to justify atonal music or the serial idea or any other theoretical concept, such as that the 12 notes have equal rights, or that noise is as important as notes, etc. etc.

Cardew gave the European avant-garde short shrift; its exclusiveness, its zealous control and limitation of the influx of extraneous ideas, its erection of a system as intimidating as it was inflexible, its emphasis on rejection rather than assimilation – all this he had found profoundly alienating, and it is not hard to imagine the overwhelming sense of relief and wonder that he must have experienced when, through the prodigious performances of David Tudor, he encountered Feldman's music for the first time – a music-making which appeared to have escaped the tyranny of 'meaning' which the European avant-garde had sought to impose.

And yet the enormous significance of these performances – aside, that is, from the compositional material which they presented – lay as much in the uniqueness and originality of Tudor's supreme pianism, a pianistic technique born of a profound identification with Feldman's music and singularly appropriate to the expression of Feldman's revolutionary aesthetic. Tudor's break with traditional 'pianism' was as definitive and as necessary as that of the great jazz pianists – Art Tatum, Bud Powell, Thelonious Monk, Bill Evans.

Ironically, at the same time the revolutionary serialists had annexed aspects of traditional performance practice, pressing them into the service of a spurious musical 'progress'. In particular their music was characterised by the continuing acceptance of, and dependence on, a *received* instrumental sound, the execution of which is taught and honoured in our music colleges and which bears an aesthetic which intervenes at the most crucial stage of music- making – at the very point of production – to reproduce a quality of reassuring familiarity and respectability. In the hands of executant experts the authority of this 'received' sound can legitimize and sanction even the most brutal extravagances of modernism, including the grotesque serial edifices spawned through Darmstadt in the fifties.

And herein lies the world of difference between Morton Feldman, in particular, and his European peers; because through the infamous softness and slowness of his music and a radical commitment to the muscular, physical and essentially sensual qualities of the art of performance Feldman refines an aesthetic of musical *pleasure* which negates the attempts at expressive reduction and control our conservatory training operates. When David Tudor, or Cardew, played Feldman what the listener experienced, with such intensity, was the fingerpad, 'the only erotic part of a pianist's body' [25] – the limb as it performed – and the resulting sound was raw and thrilling, of a quality which defied Institution, Criticism and Opinion. With too many performers one is all too conscious of a 'polite culture' intervening between body and instrument.

Feldman once remarked how so many professionals seemed frightened of their instrument, somehow alienated from it. In stark contrast, with Tudor and Cardew one sensed an *at-oneness*, an ability to bridge the gap between player and instrument;

the playing seemed to come from the inner body. 'Through David Tudor I could appreciate the spirit in which he performed. I have a fundamental conviction that every honest utterance makes sense.'[26] Tudor and Cardew were virtuosi (which has nothing to do with velocity or 'petty digital scramble') by virtue of the extraordinary sounds they drew from the piano, and by the infinitesimally differentiated degrees of control they exercised. Their performances steered a hazardous course generating risk and excitement: the phrasing and articulation 'situational', determined spontaneously by the idiosyncrasies of individual sounds at particular moments, by ambience and acoustics, by the imperfections in the instrument and the dimensions of the room.[27]

Extreme sensitivity of touch is of the essence in a performance of Feldman's music: in the piano pieces the depressed key is gently eased back to position to minimise the obtrusive sound of the key mechanism (I recall Cardew demonstrating this to me in a rehearsal); time is allowed for the minutest of harmonics to resound, and at the ends of phrases fingers steal away from the keys noiselessly and elegantly like dancers vacating the stage. Cardew would execute such movements with supreme elegance. This purification of the art of performance, in which all redundant cultural baggage had been jettisoned, constituted a kind of training-ground which, as we shall see, would lay the foundations of his music-making with the AMM.

Throughout their relationship Cornelius and Stella were avid and eclectic readers, sharing books and reading to each other in bed; George Borrow's *Wild Wales* and *Lavengro* were two of the earliest books they read together. As Stella recalls, they loved the descriptions of the countryside: the Romanies in their tents, the Armenian man (*Lavengro*) who loved languages and lived like a gipsy. And Belle the gipsy girl who reminded Stella of the Scratch Orchestra girls.

Yet their reading tastes did not always find common ground – especially in the early days. In the debate which raged over the novels of William Burroughs, for example, Stella sided with those for whom *The Naked Lunch* was the creation of 'a third-rate, degenerate mind'. Cardew, on the other hand, admired the work, for a number of reasons, not least its virtuosic use of language, but above all for the extreme nature of its content – its obsession with the unthinkable and the unspeakable, its monstrous disregard for conventional sensibilities; and in its anti-authoritarianism Cardew recognized a kindred spirit. Formally, too, it was innovative – 'you can cut into *Naked Lunch* at any intersection point' (Burroughs), just as phrases from one of the *February Pieces* could be folded into either of the other two. Moreover, Burroughs' own characterisation of his literary style in *The Naked Lunch* evokes the atmosphere of *February Piece III* (1961): 'The word cannot be expressed direct.... It can perhaps be indicated by mosaic of juxtaposition like articles abandoned in a hotel drawer, defined by negatives and absence....'[28] Perhaps Cardew responded to its purported humanism or, in his exploitation of obscene material, to Burroughs as heir to the Marquis de Sade, another taboo writer who had fascinated Cardew. And, the books aside, perhaps he respected a gentle, kindly man who had treated him courteously when Cardew and Ilona Halberstadt visited Burroughs (whom Ilona had met previously in London) in the Hotel Gît-le-Coeur in Paris in February 1960 – a meeting, however, during which a silent and unforthcoming Cardew adopted the ploy of anonymity, ignoring or deflecting the older man's expressions of mild and unthreatening curiosity about his young guest.

The French Symbolists attracted Cardew, particularly Rimbaud and his vision of the Poet's awesome mission. In *Une Saison en Enfer* Cardew recognized the progenitor of *The Naked Lunch*; like Burroughs' addiction to The Sickness, Rimbaud's life, too, became a hell where art, culture and human society were deprived of all meaning, and his last days were spent in agony, his leg amputated, in a Marseilles hospital. A wild, destructive rage is a frequent feature of Rimbaud's poetry: 'Merde pour la poesie' was how the founder of modern poetry responded to news of his fame, and this would be mirrored by the vehemence of Cardew's rejection of his own momentous contributions to contemporary music in the sixties. Both Rimbaud and Cardew abandoned Art for the banalities of commerce and politics respectively; it is the contiguity of their earlier, artistic concerns which offers, perhaps, a more fruitful area of study. The symbolist movement emphasized the need to create rather than to inherit forms, saw the world as crisis-ridden and fragmentary just as, one hundred years later, and beginning with the *February Pieces*, Cardew's indeterminate works from the early sixties challenged contemporary notions of form, digested a welter of aural imagery from everyday reality to create a sensation of newness – a revolutionary language of transcendental content, and culminating in the timeless, epiphanic moments, Pater's 'exquisite pauses in time', which characterised his music-making with AMM.

Jean Genet's *Les Bonnes*, from the late forties, provided further congenial reading matter – to Cardew if not to Stella. The eroticism and libido of the rituals and fantasies acted out by Claire and Solange would have elicited a strong response – as would the idea of bisexuality conceived as a conflict between the masculine and the feminine features of the self, a theme which occurred not only in Cardew's dreams but which also surfaced at times of emotional stress. He would have empathized with the complex love/hate feelings underlying a text based on the impossibility of establishing any form of positive interrelations, except in the world of fantasy and dreams. Those features of the play which concerned the Marxist critics, particularly in the sixties and seventies, would have had to wait another decade before assuming importance for Cardew: the socio-historical aspects, the conflicting aspirations of the underprivileged classes and their need for destruction and revenge, for example, although he may have responded to the idea of the revolt of the underdog. But the economic relationship between Madame and her two maids (one of feudal bondage) and the idea of slavery, with its political overtones – these aspects of Genet's work would have been beyond the realm of his experience; he would not have possessed the analytical tools to confront political issues of this kind.

It is worth reminding ourselves, at this point, that during this period literary works which seemed to offer a preponderance of sexual activity between the sheets were considered a threat to public morality – copies of the eighteenth century novel *Fanny Hill*, for example, were confiscated by the police, acting on advice from the Director of Public Prosecutions. For Cardew the stuffy conservatism of Adenauer's Germany was now matched by the overweening hypocrisy of the English Establishment, and this was as much part of the sixties decade, albeit the early years, as the riotous anarchy that challenged it and forced it into abeyance and temporary retreat.[29] As the year 1962 drew to a close, frustrations and tensions surfaced; his rejection of the avant-garde, in which he could see no future, intensified his position of isolation for which the haven of family life was only partial consolation. Stella felt her role to be that of mediator between Cornelius and the children, fearing that he would tire of them while they, in their turn, might become over-dependent on him. And the fact that she was now pregnant with his child may well have added to her anxiety. Cornelius loved and cared for Emily and Gabriel with intelligence and imagination – perhaps it was his status as step-father which allowed these faculties to function more easily – although it is a notoriously ill-defined role and if they were behaving in a particularly tyrannical fashion he would conjecture it was because they sensed they were 'without a master'.

And there were always visitors – often impromptu because it was known that Cornelius and Stella would always welcome and accommodate the unexpected – and guests who might have been invited at short notice, spontaneously, to lighten their mood, avert a tiff. 'Of all Stella's recurrent remarks "I wish something exciting would happen" is the most enervating. Because what it means is that she wants to have a slanging match!'[30] On holiday with the family in Dartmoor in the same month Cardew echoes Stella's dissatisfaction: 'I want a man in my arse and a woman on my dong. I just want everything! Life here (Dartmoor) is very burdensome – Stella is furious with the cold, and consequently refuses to consider sex, though this is a fast way to warmth.'[31]

Occasionally, and typically still, a shaft of humour bursts through into the pages of the Journals, as on 18 December:

At lunchtime Tim (Clarke) said of a person in front, walking along, 'Here's a sturdy pair of legs in a sturdy pair of boots'. She turned into RADA Drama School.

'Ah, a drama student.' 'She'll go a long way with that pair of legs' I said, and Tim, simultaneously, our voices in counterpoint: 'She won't get far with that pair of legs.' We were in perfect agreement.

A page in the Journals is headed 'Dec 1 '62 Lecture for Cambridge – "Aesthetics of Chance"(!)' and comprises a sketch of the lecture in note form. The exclamation mark seems to express an ambivalent attitude towards chance, an unwillingness to commit himself to this or that definition, which is underlined by the self-depreciating introductory sentence that follows: 'No philosophical speculations as to the existence or non-existence of chance – I lack the necessary profundity, or time and energy, concentration.'

Of course, he had over a long period given considerable and profound thought to 'chance' and in particular to the subtle implications of its use in musical composition – there was no lack in this respect and he knew it – but such speculation was contingent upon a life-style to which he had no access and, when all was said and done, no real inclination. For the Cambridge lecture a pragmatic approach was adopted:

We just take 2 pieces that are supposed to be governed by chance:
Cage – *Variations*,
Stockhausen – *Momente* (?)[32]
and see what happens to them.
Describe the enigmatic score. The way one is instructed regarding it. What one actually does with it before performance. What happens in a performance. Criteria of good performance. (Form and movement).

And nobody could have been more eminently suited to such an exercise than Cardew himself, and in raising the issue of 'criteria' in relation to performance he was addressing an area of musical aesthetics which was highly contentious. In Cage's *Variations*, if tones 'are allowed to be tones' and if one tone is as good as another, then it is the attitude of the performer which is crucial, not only during performance but during preparation and pre-preparation. (In a later chapter we shall see how ideology came to inform Cardew's critique of *Variations 1*, embodying rather than replacing his earlier reservations.) Cardew knew, for example, how much the powerful impact of Cage's *Variations* owed to the flair, stunning aural imagination and sheer boldness of choice which David Tudor's performances exhibited. At the end of the Journal entry he is quite specific: 'Cage does not so much rely on chance, as on the heightened tension of a performance.'

Two weeks later a fanciful idea is recorded in the journals:

An opera with Piero [Heliczer].[33] Perhaps voices with just prepared piano. For extensive scene shifting: big clusters, and shift the preparations! (pedal down).

A very delicate piece. Lucid music.

Write him.[34]

Then follows, in brackets, what is perhaps a comment on, or a response to, the idea:

[Answer: Bessie Smith – great! with 4-note blues.]

Tailpiece:

In a Journal entry on 23 November 1962 a 'Private Eye-type' comment in the *Spectator* magazine on the *Guardian* initially provoked irritation and moral indignation, not for its substance but for the impurity of its motivation. The writer had remarked that whereas in its Manchester days the *Guardian* had upheld the view that 'comment was free – facts were sacred', since it had moved to London it now functioned on the principle that 'comment is free, but facts are expensive'.

Cardew's perception was that if the *Guardian* had deteriorated then the joke should communicate a feeling of frustration, of disquiet, rather than the unadulterated pleasure, the *Schadenfreude* of the hack for whom the decline of the *Guardian* was excellent copy since it gave him the opportunity to 'make his crack'. It is easy to attribute such sentiments to a naiveté in the ways of the world – which was not uncommon in Cardew at that time – but for him it was further proof of the unscrupulous and demeaning nature of 'professionalism': its dishonesty, its all-too-ready compromises, its commercialisation of reality – which he had already encountered and criticised in the musical world.

The anagram in the following paragraph lightens but does not weaken the weight of sentiment expressed: 'The statement "facts are sacred" seems to represent a position from which it would be impossible to fall far. Better "facts are scared" – [to] show their faces these days – they know they will be hacked to pieces!' In fact this was all tangential to the main thrust of his thought on 'facts', which was of a more general, philosophical nature:

Abandoned – finally I re-arrived at the unshakeable conviction that facts have no independent existence. One can say this or that happened, but already [there is] a meaning, a field of explanations and comments implicit in the statement of fact. Chuangten's little circles of earth are useless, and yet given the whole expanse of earth they undoubtedly serve him well. Compare: 'X fell off the cliff into the sea and was killed. There was a high wind blowing' and 'X was blown off the cliff into the sea and was killed'. There is nothing sacred about either of these versions of a set of facts. It is often the comment − or the choice of context that makes a statement of fact true or false.[35]

Compositions 1961-62

For a few weeks in the spring of 1961 the house in Alba had provided a congenial home base for Cardew and his new family, and his first composition since the completion of the *Third Orchestral Piece* the previous December was in the manner of a private celebration, a love-poem perhaps: a guitar piece on a single page with the inscription *for Stella*; an essay in guitar writing of great subtlety and delicacy in which the full gamut of the instrument's possibilities is explored. The lure of America had receded, the extravagant project to emigrate laid to rest, and his restlessness abated; indeed, the new life he was about to embark upon was the antithesis of his life-style in Germany, and of that of the American artists and musicians he so admired, for whom the single-minded pursuit of their artistic objectives was all-consuming and would certainly have precluded any other responsibility as demanding and on-going as the rearing of a family (apart from Christian Wolff, father of four [36]). But with Cardew, putting Emily and Gabriel to bed, or taking them for a walk, or engaging them in an activity of a joyful and creative nature, would be endowed with the same degree of imaginative commitment and originality as the act of composing a piece of music. True, the same could be said of David Tudor, except that Cardew's world embraced a greater variety of concerns; a less exclusive, less protected life-style and therefore more exposed to the insidious influence of convention and habit. Moving in with Stella Underwood, an English woman seven years his senior, and her young family, was less a change of heart, more a radical change of circumstances, and together they were to forge an existence which subverted bourgeois conventionality where it is most vulnerable, from within the family, and to an extent that none of his peers on either side of the Atlantic could have matched. Many of them, as Kurt Schwertsik had observed, were simply too busy cultivating the social graces, wheeler-dealing their way into prominence and favour in the bosom of avant-garde musical circles. 'You should coiculate [sic], John' − I recall Morton Feldman's well-meaning and friendly advice in Venice during a Biennale in the sixties where he had taken to hobnobbing with the influential and the affluent, securing promises of concerts in fashionable and exotic venues.

The improvisatory quality of the solo guitar piece, *for Stella,* is clearly analogous to that of the *February Pieces*; throughout the sections the player is invited to explore the variety of basic shapes and patterns, the possibilities for harmonic and rhythmic inflections, and to balance this against the more formal, composed parts of the score. These are elegant, finely-wrought phrases of considerable plasticity (with echoes, perhaps, of the guitar part of *Le Marteau sans Maître,* which Cardew had performed on several occasions), with bitter-sweet harmonies reminiscent of the lute fantasies of John Dowland. Its overall structure owes more to *Autumn 60*; both pieces are in sixteen sections of varying lengths, marked A to P, so that the resulting impression is of a compositional amalgam of *February '61* and *Autumn 60* (Ex.4.1).

Ex.4.1. *Guitar Piece for Stella,* sections A-E.

However, there is no hierarchical system in terms of the frequency of individual tones (as there is in *February Pieces*), except in the last section, P, where each of the twenty-two chords contains an F and two of them contain two Fs: a succession of chords beginning with four, five and six tones and gradually thinning out to one, two and three tones. Nor is the order of the events determined – this is left to the player whose brief, as in *February Pieces,* is virtually to improvise on the material: 'Play with these pieces. Over and over. Change anything. Add and take away.' Of course, a perverse reading may well take the indication 'change anything' to extremes, but the instructions are surely an invitation to *edit* – adding, subtracting, changing, repeating ('over and over', too, has a more insistent ring to it) according to the flair, taste and skill of the individual instrumentalist. Some sections lend themselves to this treatment more than others; some are self-contained and self-sufficient, others are open-ended, inviting intervention, whether elaborative or reductive. So that rather than intimidating and discouraging the would-be performer, the virtuoso demands of section B, for example, can be neutralised by discreet omissions and substitutions. Despite his fascination for the hazardous and the unpredictable, it is unlikely that in this instance it was Cardew's aim to provoke or tempt the performer to heroic failure, although the occasional 'impossibility' (shades of Christian Wolff) which this little piece presents can create sweat and stress in even the most experienced and skilful of performers.

The guitarist, Adrian Lee, who has frequently performed the piece, has remarked on how the choice and appropriateness of a particular tone quality is determined by the polyphonic nature of much of the material. Another guitarist familiar with the work, Alan Thomas, has observed that

in attempting to best render the polyphony and voice-leading of the work, the player discovers a sometimes bewildering variety of technical approaches to any given passage. [...] Individual choices of fingerings and string selection can lead to quite different sonic results. [...] Maintaining legato in melodic lines over large position jumps is a particular challenge. At the extreme, a successful approach to the final chordal section (P) stands as a supreme test of the art of fingering on the guitar.[37]

Unlike the two works either side of it, the guitar piece breaks no new ground; there was no back-tracking – rather a marking time, a consolidation, a relaxation into familiarity, a brief period of respite from the exhaustion of the radical changes which had propelled his more recent work into aesthetic and philosophical domains which were still relatively uncharted.

Whereas the guitar piece gives off a strong sense of personal expression, of intimacy, in the Octet '61 there is no such exposure of sentiment, no identification with the composer's dispositions and feelings (which one is aware of even in Autumn 60, with its modal colouring); here, by contrast, the subtle nuances of interpretation are given free rein through a further development and enrichment of Cardew's notational experiments. Octet '61 jettisons the traditional precept of compositional identity; rather it is an incitement to act:

If the most important function of a composer were the stimulation of an interpreter this piece would be a composition. The stimulation of the interpreter is a facet of composition that has been disastrously neglected. Disastrously under-stimulated performances of contemporary music are the result (for here, past glories cannot act as stimuli). When performed, the piece may be judged as a musical experience (sounds brought together by human agency) and thrown down the drain. No one is to blame. My reputation is free to suffer. This piece is not gilt-edged.[38]

The influence of Wittgenstein is clearly discernible here, especially the self-deprecating end of the preface to *Philosophical Investigations*:

If my remarks do not bear a stamp which marks them as mine, – I do not wish to lay any further claim to them as my property.
I make them public with doubtful feelings. It is not impossible that it should fall to the lot of this work, in its poverty and in the darkness of this time, to bring light into one brain or another – but, of course, it is not likely.
I should not like my writing to spare other people the trouble of thinking. But, if possible, to stimulate someone to thoughts of his own.[39]

And the genesis of the paintings, *0 – 9*, on which *Octet '61* is based, is described by Johns in words which clearly relate to Cardew's musical conception:

I learned that there was the possibility of making something which didn't have to filter through judgements that one made about what one was doing; that one could set out to do something and do it. The paintings that followed immediately, which were paintings of targets and numbers, gave me the same opportunity – to feel removed from the work, neutral toward it, involved in the making but not involved in the judging of it.[40]

And Johns' response in an interview with Vivien Raynor might equally have been referring to the notation for the *Octet*:

My work is in part concerned with the possibility of things being taken for one thing or another – with questionable areas of identification and usage and procedure – with thought rather than with secure things.[41]

Like the paintings of Jasper Johns, *Octet '61* inhabits a region of indeterminate meanings and ambiguities. In the Cologne Radio broadcast on the music of the American avant-garde Cardew elaborated on this:

> The idea of indeterminate music – where some details (sometimes a great many) are left to a performer or an editor, conductor, or what have you, where the composer gives, in fact, an incomplete picture – poses a large number of problems. Mozart, to pick an example from the blue, had a sharp vision, a sharp eye, a sharp mind – and sharp ears. [...] In Mozart's time the truth was something spiritual but definite; in our time the truth is something material but vague.

Yet for all Cardew's empathy with Johns' intellectual position, it was the sheer physical impact of the paintings (and he already possessed a typographer's appreciation of the form and individuality of numerals) which inspired him to write his *Octet '61*:

> I wrote the piece after seeing an exhibition of paintings by Jasper Johns in Paris in June 1961. Most of the paintings consisted of the whole series of Arabic numerals superposed.Each number was of a size to fill the canvas, and none of them were more obtrusive than the others, except temporarily. The outlines of the numbers form a complex network of lines on the canvas, breaking it up into thousands of small areas of different shapes and sizes and it was this aspect that he painted. Thus, on the surface, the painting appears as a screen of small brightly coloured patches – some paintings were executed monochrome, some in a limited range of colours – some with various different materials like a collage – but the ones I remember most clearly are those that looked like a vivid patchwork of dazzling colour. Then, when the eye has absorbed this violent onslaught, out come the numbers, singly at first then gradually all are there.[42] Thus the vivid assembly of colours achieves a marvellous plasticity as it becomes identified with one or other of the numbers.

> Numbers, what a significant choice of subject. An abstract concept designated by a concrete image which is identifiable for everybody – the interpretation of the numbers is free. And this is the case also in the *Octet '61*. The numbers that are used in the signs are the negative element, the colourless fluid, that binds the various musical signs together into a suggestive musical image.[43]

For all their surface similarities, the notations for *Octet '61* and *Autumn 60* differ radically; the *Octet* is more experimental in that each of the sixty signs is formed of a configuration of elements which *suggest* interpretative solutions, whereas in *Autumn 60* the signs occur in list-form and dictate an interpretative procedure. Not that the performer is left entirely to his own devices in the *Octet*; most of the signs incorporate specific tones (a far wider range of pitches than in *Autumn 60*, in fact) and many of the constituent symbols refer to traditional meanings and associations (which Cardew lists at the beginning), drawing from a common reservoir of basic musical signs, and providing 'sufficient context for a concrete interpretation of at least one sign by almost any musician' (Ex.4.2).[44]

Ex.4.2. Extract from *Octet '61 for Jasper Johns*.

This reliance on aspects of traditional notation in *Octet '61* demonstrates that even in his most radical compositions Cardew was still addressing the interpreter/musician; by referring to 'almost any musician' he clearly intended to cast the net wide – his strategy to draw as many musicians as possible into the orbit of experimental music and to accommodate their needs and abilities, providing them with a testing-ground where ideas which currently concerned them could be tried out. Like Cage, what he was asking of his collaborators was good faith, for which he was prepared to pay a high price – his reputation 'free to suffer' from well-meaning versions of stunning banality. Yet such calamities were few and far between; as David Bedford has recalled, 'the empathy of the performers, channelled into producing a coherent piece of music despite sometimes sketchy and sometimes paradoxical instructions, was often remarkable'.[45] If, initially, the unconventional appearance of the score might alienate the trained musician, closer inspection would reveal that it was by no means musically arcane and intimidating – except insofar as it presupposed an acceptance of creative responsibility. In *Octet '61* there is no prescription; the signs suggest, sometimes persuasively, sometimes indifferently; the interpreter may not resort to a claim of absolution – 'I was only carrying out orders'.

In *Octet '61* the performer is confronted with the immediacy of a graphic image which is precise and unique; an arrow, for example, may be relatively large or small, placed in a specific way on the stave with its own characteristic slant, combined suggestively, elliptically, with the other signs involved in any particular event, pointing towards it or away from it, or inextricably fused within it. There are at least four such arrows at 9, 13, 46 and, more speculatively, 59 – and a better trained, more imaginative eye than mine may well find more − all of which have to be distinguished from the bold arrow at 35 which may only be interpreted once in any performance of the piece. Such peculiarities may be pored over, but not necessarily in the methodical way which *Autumn 60* demands, for the signs of *Octet '61* attempt to create a feeling of freedom: freedom to respond subjectively to the notation, freedom of association, freedom from the dogmas and taboos of modern music; *Octet '61* stands at the threshold of 'free' improvisation.

Yet Cardew hesitated, unwilling at that juncture to cross the threshold: 'Playing from the score is not recommended except for experienced performers'[46] − and he rejected the idea of a spontaneous response to the score − that is, of spontaneous performance. For Cardew at that time 'experienced performer' meant 'experienced reader', an eagle-eyed musician with extreme agility of thought and movement such as he admired in David Tudor. The crux was that the player was presenting a sound image which he himself had created; no matter how he had tackled the problem of the signs, and how long it had taken, his interpretation of them was emphatically his own. 'Self-expression' − an historical, if contentious, entitlement to performers at which the post-war modernists on both sides of the Atlantic had baulked − was a particular nettle which Cardew was keen to grasp: 'I have also said that self-expression for the performer was not enough. I have since come to the conclusion that, whether it is "enough" or no, it goes a very long way, and it must of all expressions be demanded and called forth.'[47]

Formally, *Octet '61* is cyclic − 'start anywhere, joining the end to the beginning or the beginning to the end if you are reading backwards' − and is based on the same general principles as *Autumn 60*; that is, at certain points in the piece specific signs occur with greater frequency, so that as the work unfolds one detects a shift of emphasis first in one direction, then in another, and so forth. This idea of the graphic presence and recurrence of certain symbols − whose reference is unspecified − took root in Cardew's work, and the development of these symbols and the elaboration of the relationship between them, within the context of a musical notation, was to become a significant feature of his compositions in the early sixties.

Of the sixty signs which comprise *Octet '61* two are singled out in Cardew's introduction to the work as enjoying distinctive, prescribed features. The arrow incorporated into sign 35 is interpreted once only, and is assigned the meaning 'out, away; something completely different'. The interpretation of this sign, according to Cardew's instructions, constitutes the essential identity of the piece which 'will be known and remembered (if at all) as "the piece where something peculiar happens in the middle"'. This characterisation is immediately followed by a contradictory presumption that 'any composer or potential composer interpreting the piece and wishing to take the problem of form on his own shoulders will probably interpret either at the beginning or the end'. And for those interpreters for whom the question of 'form' assumes an importance which overrides, or at least matches other considerations, there is another (unnumbered) sign which Cardew suggests may be used to provide uncomplicated solutions to such problems, easing the conscience of the performer into the bargain:

 This sign may be used 'anywhere and as often as desired' and Cardew suggests that the interpreter make

one short characteristic version of this sign and use it as punctuation. Break the piece down into a series of statements separated by this sign. Or, if several players are taking part, one of them can interpret this sign, and only one, and this is the only sign he can interpret. All procedures can be legitimized. [48]

In December 1961 Cardew completed his own version for piano solo of *Octet '61* which later became the first of the *Three Winter Potatoes*. In the accompanying notes on interpretation to the score of the *Octet* Cardew offers a proposition which is at the same time prescriptive and equivocal: 'Not necessarily for piano.' He and Ilona Halberstadt had clearly discussed this formulation and the effect of its ambiguity on would-be interpreters:

Yes, the "hardness of the logical 'must'," but you are wrong to isolate it for this reason. Anything softer is 'should'. But Oh the softest, softest approach from the other direction: 'not necessarily' makes everything clear.[49]

And in another undated letter to Ilona there is simplification: 'Perhaps is my word. I had hoped you would understand it as an integral part of any assertion I have ever made.'

A detailed study of Cardew's version demonstrates the need for careful scrutiny of each sign. As he himself pointed out, the meaning of the numerals is more fluid, more elusive; they enjoy a neutrality which is denied to the more musical signs. Kurt Schwertsik recalls that Cardew was unhappy with his (Schwertsik's) version of the sign denoting 'something completely different', the sign which for Cardew constituted the essential 'identity' of the piece. This exaggerated concern for 'identity' led him to a solution that seems tantamount to a panic measure. He himself admitted it was a brutal ploy, partly mitigated by the context in which it appears. A screw is inserted between the strings of middle D which at the moment of preparation during performance usually produces a grating (and therefore memorable!) sound. However, once in position it creates a mellow tone-mixture which is heard quite unobtrusively each time the D occurs, thus colouring the music which follows it.

Cardew's backhanded response to Schwertsik's own realisation – 'you've gone to a lot of trouble' – was a veiled criticism: it was too contrived, too exclusive. By contrast Cardew's version exemplifies a freedom of spirit; in particular Schwertsik admired the bold and original use of triads and tonal references, of familiar chords and progressions and their associations.

Ignore their 'associations' (whose associations?) and they are conspicuous by their absence. But to 'acknowledge' them can be treacherous. It is no longer just a question of cocking a snook at tradition: one can 'accept' them (like Cage) but they have the habit of turning the tables on you, of holding you hostage. Yet its just this ambivalence that is their charm.[50]

Cardew characterised the idiom of his own version as 'harmonic', and yet it is totally independent of the formal functions of tonality; such that whereas the chords he uses have a familiar ring to them, the hierarchical system in which we are used to hearing them has been disconcertingly but refreshingly subverted. The rhythmicisation of the material he describes as 'spontaneous, as in the sense in which one can say that the rhythm of speech is spontaneous'. This he achieves by a method of notation which is sufficiently flexible, producing a kind of controlled rubato: the crotchet unit is 'variable' and the rhythmic subdivisions within it are expressed thus: notated crotchet = on the beat; semiquaver rest + dotted quaver = just after the beat; quaver rest + quaver = suspended between beats; dotted quaver rest + semiquaver = just before the beat. It is a method which lends itself to the essentially rhapsodic nature, the spontaneous flow, of the music. It must have satisfied him; a few years later he was to employ the same method for his 1964 ensemble piece *Material*.

Cardew's piano version, the first *Winter Potato*, begins with the sign 10; the piece thus ends with signs 1-9. In his introduction to the *Octet* Cardew furnishes examples (signs 1-6) with explanations (a 'partial key') (Ex.4.3):

Ex.4.3. From the introductory notes to *Octet '61 for Jasper Johns*.

Although this sequence bears a strong resemblance to his own performing version, published by Universal Edition some months later, slight alterations and modifications were made to the excerpt which appeared in *Octet '61*.

Cardew's own version of *Octet '61* betokens not only the originality of his harmonic language but also the sharpness of his ear: the care and precision with which chords are balanced and weighted, the colouristic use of octave doublings and transpositions (as we have seen, a characteristic feature of many of his compositions), and the awareness of the importance of pitch range and texture to harmonic considerations. Already in the early sixties Cardew's harmony had broken all the longstanding taboos of modern music that had been enshrined in Darmstadt – not, as in the case of Cage, through the randomisation of the compositional procedure, but by a high-risk recipe – the abandonment of 'system', whether serial or aleatoric which, in one sense, because it could offer no theoretical defence, left him far more exposed, but in another sense, because of his uncompromising advocacy of intuitive choice, put him beyond the pale of received criticism. Cardew's first *Winter Potato* was both an affront and a challenge to musical theory in the same way that Feldman's compositions were at that time; and it was imbued with a magical, unfathomable *musicalness* which seemed to disarm all criticism or at least to render it irrelevant. Cardew had indeed 'flown the coop' and was to embark on a musical odyssey from which there was to be no turning back.

With Cage the greater individual responsibility that his work demanded was nevertheless circumscribed according to his prescriptive notations. Cardew's notations, by contrast, invited the interpreter to choose his or her own terms, although he never flinched from the enormity of the consequences that such radical action would bring in its wake.

The greatest music is always explicit − like Webern, if you dig him.
In *Octet '61* I realise that explicitness has been sacrificed. In this research it is
always necessary to sacrifice trusted concepts.
As long as there is no blur in the thinking…[51]

And such sacrifices were never made without a rigorous inner debate; each thought,
each step exposed to scrutiny and analysis of Wittgensteinian intensity:

Compare the composer who has arrived at a point where really any one note will
do, so long as it is a single note, simply writes the figure 1, realizing that perhaps
in the performance there may be valid reasons for the player to choose one or
another note; compare him with the composer who reasons, 'well, since any
note will do, it doesn't matter which one I write, so I'll write this one', thus evading
the responsibility of writing what he heard, which was no particular note, and
denying the performer the possibility of choosing spontaneously, which might
have served, by his hesitancy, or air of decision, or of seeking, to create the right
atmosphere for the piece.[52]

And, four years on, his commitment to indeterminacy showed no signs of abatement:

a real interest in contemporary music implies an interest in something which is in
a state of flux, that is risky, or in other words a piece of raw material, which has
a vitality which is not perfectly defined. Listening to the first performance of a new
composition this is the most exciting element − nobody knows exactly how it's
going to influence the situation, you don't know what aspect is going to be
powerful.[53]

The *First Movement for String Quartet,* completed December 1961, in which the influence
of Stockhausen and Cage is now residual, elicited the following observations from Howard
Skempton:

Formally speaking, Cardew's *First Movement* might just as appropriately have
been entitled Last Movement. Which reminds one of Feldman. There is a richness
in this piece equivalent to that which Cardew found in Feldman's work of this
time. There is the same feeling for material; the same 'touch'; the same
achievement of substance through careful, moment-to-moment decision-making.
The emphasis is on flexibility. The notation acknowledges the need for rubato.

Regularity on paper opens the door to variability of tempo, phrasing and dynamics. And yet the notes for interpretation advise us that 'the four players are as one instrument'.

So this *First Movement* is as much a commentary on the social aspects of string quartet playing as an exploration of colour and texture.[54]

1962 was a comparatively lean year, with the completion of just two works, and in June the Journals note: 'Film work for Allan King. £180'. *Ah Thel*, a part-song for mixed choir and optional piano accompaniment, was composed during the summer, published by Novello in July 1963, and appeared as a supplement in the *Musical Times*. A miniature masterpiece, it is over in less than two minutes and yet manages to express the timeless quality of Blake's poem – the words are based on a part of *The Book of Thel*, the same poem he had used some years earlier in a setting for solo voice and piano.[55]

Ah Thel is like a watery bow And like a parting cloud, Like a reflection in a glass, Like shadows in the water; Like dreams of infants, Like a smile upon an infant's face; Like the dove's voice, Like transient day; Like music in the air Ah gentle may I lay me down And gentle rest my head And gentle sleep the sleep of death And gentle hear the voice Of him that walketh in the Garden in the evening time

The tempo is 'slow and erratic, ruminative throughout'. The opening phrases, fragmented to begin with, float upwards, each time reaching for the soprano G, the highest note the sopranos sing – the harmonic dissonances telling, fleeting (Ex.4.4).

The music is reflective, sensual, and eminently singable, with the occasional spoken phrase cleverly integrated into the texture. In the last two phrases the soprano G assumes an even greater prominence and in the penultimate phrase – 'and gentle hear the voice of him' – new chords are introduced and there is an acceleration in the harmonic rhythm. In the final phrase the voices sing just two or three notes, independently of one another, as the music regains its equilibrium, the melodic semitones of the inner parts providing a poignant accompaniment to the more consonant outer parts (Ex.4.5).

Ah Thel honours the great English choral tradition but, in Howard Skempton's inimitable gloss, 'Cardew toes the line only to leap in the air.'

Movement for Orchestra was completed in December of 1962. It is written for a largish orchestra, mainly by virtue of the fact that it requires two 'string orchestras' – ranged symmetrically either side of the conductor, with the two groups of violas meeting in

Ex.4.4. *Ah Thel*, first two systems (without Cardew's piano accompaniment).

the centre – which Cardew exploits to produce a rich and complex web of string sound. It is a curious phenomenon – almost as if Cardew wanted to move back into the world of the European avant-garde. As John White has pointed out, the work is a prime example of the kind of orchestral music that was being produced at that time: meticulously laid out, delicately scored effects requiring the specific skills which contemporary music had begun to demand of performers. One particular feature of the piece are the 'gruppetti', flourishes of a varying number of fast notes – between two and eight – which act as up-beats into the succeeding phrase. In the uncompromising dissonance of its harmonic language it is one of the most consistently, one might say perversely dissonant pieces that Cardew ever wrote, even if it cannot be described as a 'serial composition'.

Ex.4.5. *Ah Thel*, last two systems (without piano accompaniment).

The free, atonal idiom in which it was composed was employed to vastly different effect in both the *First Movement for String Quartet* and *Ah Thel*. Moreover, unlike both of these pieces *Movement for Orchestra* is tightly coordinated rhythmically, and even when the texture becomes more sparse, there is no relaxation of control. There are moments of high drama, with extreme, almost theatrical contrasts of dynamic, and textures are built up pictorially. And yet there is hardly any structural development; the piece seems to be cast in 'moment' form and the music grows and changes organically. *Movement for Orchestra* looks back to past concerns, to the Stockhausen of *Zeitmasse* and *Kontrapunkte,* to his own *Piano Sonata No. 2.* Was it the anticipation of a course of study with Petrassi which prompted him to move back into the mainstream? With the benefit of hindsight we know that it was his desire to improve upon his orchestral writing that took him to Petrassi the following year. Yet for all his self-doubt as a composer for the orchestra, *Movement* contains some impressive pages.[56] In the *Musikalische Jugend* of November/December 1963 Helmut Kirchmeyer writes of Cardew's great success with his *Movement for Orchestra* at the Palermo Festival in Sicily – 'one of the surprise packages of the Festival'. At the end of the year Cardew muses on his two most recent orchestral pieces:

> Down in Dartmoor, looking into the fire is like a fugue; the solid lines of pieces of wood like subjects that gradually begin to burn. Later the inner parts begin to glow…
>
> But back here in the flat the room is full of the sounds I wrote here 2 summers ago, and this is useful for the scoring I am doing. Look around and all the lovely imagined sounds of the *Third Orchestral Piece* are there, available.[57]

Notes and references

1   Journal, 19 April 1962.
2   Vide Frances Stonor Saunders, *The Cultural Cold War – the CIA and the World of Arts and letters.*
3   Yet the idea to emigrate did not completely evaporate; he was still hankering after an opportunity. Later in the year, in a letter dated 27 October, John Cage suggested individuals and organisations (mainly academic) whom he might contact. Whether he followed these up we do not know; but he remained in England.
4   At that time the RCA boasted a host of young talents, both students and members of staff: among them John Bratby and the 'Kitchen Sink' artists, Robert Buhler, David Hockney, John Minton and, of course, Freda Sargent.
5   In the early sixties, when von Biel was staying in London, in Holland Park Avenue, Cardew arrived unannounced one day. Somehow von Biel's reputation as a talented avant-gardist had reached Cardew. The main purpose of the visit was to discuss the idea of promoting concerts of avant-garde music in London and elsewhere. Von Biel recalls that Cardew was 'very English', polite, well-bred, somewhat aloof, and with a trace of decadence. Von Biel sensed an air of desperation, not because of an apparent lack of money, but rather through a barely disguised desire for fame.
6   As we have seen, the first Generation Music concert was that given by Cardew and myself at the Conway Hall on 27 January 1960, which suggests that the appellation of the music ('generation'), if not that of an ensemble, originated with Cardew.
7   From the Ensemble's manifesto printed at the back of the Wigmore Hall programme.
8   From a lecture delivered at the University of Illinois on 25 February 1967, quoted in full below.
9   *The Times*, 4 June 1962.
10   A letter to Cardew dated 7 August 1963 shows Swarsenski in good form: 'Your friend, the poet Michael Horovitz, paid me a visit, the aim of which remained concealed behind his weighty explanations. Perhaps you know what he wanted, and can tell me?'
11   Stella Cardew has no recollection of this (Autumn 2004).
12   Letter from CC to Mariel Cardew, 6 October 1962.
13   From the 1962 Cologne Radio broadcast on the music of Christian Wolff, Earle Brown and Morton Feldman.
14   Ibid.
15   From Cardew's handwritten draft, undated, in Jrnl. 1959-62.
16   Jrnl. 24 November 1962.
17   From the 1962 Cologne Radio broadcast on the music of Christian Wolff, Earle Brown and Morton Feldman.
18   John Cage, 'Lecture on Something' in his *Silence*, pp.129-130.
19   Interview with Morton Feldman in *International Times*, no.3 (14-27 November 1966). *International Times* was launched at the Roundhouse in north-west London on 15 October 1966. It was London's first weekly underground newspaper.
20   From 'A Compositional Problem', in *Give My Regards to Eighth Street, Collected Writings of Morton Feldman* (Cambridge, Mass: Exact Change, 2000), pp.110-111.
21   Jrnl. 25 February 1965.

22   From the aforementioned *International Times* no. 3 interview.

23   From Phillipe Regniez's 1986 film *Cornelius Cardew 1936 – 1981*.

24   From the previously quoted Cologne Radio broadcast on the music of Christian Wolff, Earle Brown and Morton Feldman.

25   Roland Barthes, 'The Grain of the Voice', from *Image – Music – Text,* Essays Selected and Translated by Stephen Heath (Glasgow: Fontana/Collins, 1977), p.189.

26   I am sure Cardew wrote this, but I cannot locate or remember the source. JT.

27   Nowadays, fifty years on and in an age of designer performances, the rough edges of non-conformity are smoothed out – even in Feldman's music; too often, a vulgar, enervating rationality obtains.

28   William Burroughs, *The Naked Lunch* (London: Paladin Grafton Books, 1986), p.98.

29   Of course, national attitudes towards sex, and reputations too, are part of folk-lore. In Britain it became a major tourist attraction: *No Sex, Please, We're British* was a long-running West End farce which foreign visitors found irresistible.

30   Jrnl. 18 December 1962.

31   Jrnl. 23 December 1962.

32   Reasons for the question mark are open to speculation. JT.

33   Piero Heliczer (1937-93), poet, film-maker, publisher and musician. Cardew became acquainted with Heliczer and his work through Michael Horovitz and *New Departures.*

34   Jrnl. 17 December 1962.

35   Ten years later, addressing the question of factual objectivity, Cardew had this to say about 'facts': ' "Ambiguity" or "tolerance and ambiguity" is advocated in education. Implying that facts are indefinite in some way. Obviously we can interpret facts in many different ways, we can see them from different angles. But this does not mean that a fact does not function and affect reality in a definite way. Our aim is to see objective facts in an objective, all-sided way. We must realise that a given fact can be good for one class and bad for another, without being in any way "ambiguous".' Jrnl. 1972, p.151.

36   'While working with David Tudor on *Burdocks*, he said that he could see the results of having small kids around – my music had loosened up.' Christian Wolff, *Cues, Writings and Conversations* (Cologne: Edition MusikTexte 1998), p.162.

37   Email communication from guitarist Alan Thomas to JT, 21 December 2004. His performance of *for Stella* can be found on Matchless Recordings, MRCD45.

38   From the notes accompanying the score of *Octet '61 for Jasper Johns*, published by Peters Edition.

39   Ludwig Wittgenstein, Preface to *Philosophical Investigations,* (Oxford: Basil Blackwell, 1991), p.viii.

40   From a film, *U.S.A. Artists No.8: Jasper Johns (with interviews of the artist and Leo Castelli)* directed by Alan R. Solomon, produced by Lane Slate.

41   From *Art News*, vol.72, no.3, March 1973.

42   Morton Feldman, too, had remarked how the new American painting had 'made me desirous of a sound world more direct, more immediate, more physical than anything that had existed heretofore'. From the sleeve notes for a recording of *Durations* by Morton Feldman, (Time Records No. 58007).

43   From the Cologne Radio broadcast on *Autumn 60* and *Octet '61 for Jasper Johns.*

44   From the Introduction to the score, published by Peters Edition, 1964.

45 From *Performance* magazine, April-May 1982.
46 From the instructions in the published score.
47 From preparatory notes for the aforementioned Cologne Radio programme.
48 From the instructions to the published score.
49 Undated letter to Ilona Halberstadt.
50 John Tilbury, *Ark* 45 (Royal College of Art magazine) Winter 1969.
51 Jrnl. 17 February 1963. The entry is headed, 'for lecture on Indeterminacy'.
52 From the Cologne Radio programme on Wolff, Brown and Feldman (1962).
53 David Bedford and Cornelius Cardew, 'A Conversation', *Musical Times*, March 1966, pp.198-202.
54 From the programme notes for a concert at the Purcell Room in December 1991 marking the tenth anniversary of Cardew's death.
55 In Stella Cardew's opinion, Cardew did not understand Blake's poetry and she assumed, at the time, that the piece would not turn out well.
56 I am indebted to John White for his thoughtful observations on *Movement for Orchestra*, which he kindly passed on to me.
57 Jrnl. 27 December 1962.

Cornelius Cardew a life unfinished

5

Italy, Family Life and Buffalo 1963–66

'Jan 1st 1963 Horrible New Year' – the Journal begins. A New Year's party of supreme vulgarity, attended by 'craven rogues', and where the 'soft buds' of a new affair are wantonly crushed, engenders a New Year's morning 'of such straightforward perfect depression as I cannot remember experiencing before'. And as we have seen, on many occasions, Cardew would seek to purge his consciousness of the negative effects of such an experience by means of the written word – thinking it through, writing it out, drawing conclusions and making resolutions, although in this case the cloud had already begun to lift by lunchtime, and by evening the whole question had become academic and therefore most unlikely to sustain his interest. Yet such an indeterminate outcome seemed to him somehow inadequate; the contradictions thrown up by the party dissolved, but not resolved, and he had been left 'no better off'. Of course there were much deeper conflicts at play at that time which the grossness and artificiality, the hyperbole of New Year's Eve would have exacerbated; his radical experimentation had reached a point of no return, he had sacked the temple of traditional notation but the spoils remained, to be recycled, redistributed; the task, which he, the composer, would have to undertake alone – 'the agony of being too far out' – weighed heavily on him.

A good man watches, experiences, the complete devastation of his private world and *survives*. Then he moves back into the real world and grasps it with his mind. So he recreates it, and it is no longer private. It is everybody's world and he grasps it instinctively with his mind.[1]

Later in the month he elaborates the theme:

To do something constructive you have to look beyond yourself. Humanity in general is your sphere, (not 'people'). Self-expression lapses too easily into mere documentation. ('I record this is how I feel'). You should not be concerned with yourself beyond arranging a mode of life that makes it possible to remain on the line, balanced, 'dead centre'. Then you can work. [2]

And within a few months, typically, the stark metaphor of 'the line' had found musical expression, or, more accurately, expression in musical notation as a central line in relation to which a musical 'life' evolves. And without this 'line' there would have been no *Treatise*.

In the early sixties the idea of the necessity of relinquishment, of letting go, was central to Cardew's musical philosophy; if such sacrifices were considered both foolhardy and unnecessary by Cardew's peers, for him it was axiomatic that out of the violent rejection of received ideas radical new musical practices would be born. Moreover, it was normal, even desirable, initially to hold erroneous views and misconceptions. 'What everybody really wants is to make a fool of himself. But few are intelligent enough to do it.'[3]

Cardew displayed, cultivated even, a detachment from current affairs, including those on which he might have been expected to have a viewpoint, such as the 'Lady Chatterley' trial, during which the remnants of fifties' conservatism and hypocrisy fought their last stand. Nor did the burgeoning world of Pop with its attendant drug culture distract or influence him.[4] Outside his own compositional and music-making projects, which now loomed large, his immediate ambitions were modest, quaint even, and could not measure up to the new demands and enticements of contemporary society – nor, for that matter, at least in Europe, of contemporary music.

By the beginning of the new decade Capitalism, sensibly, had relaxed its image and gained a new lease of life; its new cultural icons – the pop groups, the fashion innovators, the film makers – merged to dominate the decade and create the phenomenon of 'the sixties'. The Beatles – slick, self-conscious, but with a casual air and a knowing spontaneity – secured the fascination and allegiance of a global audience in a manner which seemed effortless, while in the films of Antonioni cool, vacuous young women floated across the screen as the audience watched entranced, sedated by an unfathomable symbolism. It was easy come, easy go; instant gratification was enjoyed as much in the discarding as in the acquisition, whether of a new single or a pair of paper knickers. 'Nowadays', wrote Cardew, 'I see that everything is presented so seductively. Bach is played with ethereal beauty. Women in the cinema'.[5] And in the Journals, on New Year's Day, he had set up a simple agenda:

Program for the year – things I wd like to do.
Learn a little mathematics.
Travel again and play my music and so forth.
Be a dustman.
(Weather the baby).

What an adolescence I am going through.

In March William Burroughs was in London and Cardew and Stella were invited to a 'Burroughs and Co séance' (in Earle Brown's description) on 28 March, attended by a number of young American beat poets. Stella recalls that Cardew said little, sat quietly in observational mode – as usual, maintaining a certain distance, inhabiting that inviolable space which always seemed to envelop him.

A few months later he writes a reminder to himself – this time of a musical, more concrete, nature:

Remember to write orchestral piece of long flying, but rigid and rock-hard lines. Firm foundations make it possible to leave the ground.[6]

It might seem incongruous that the idea of a traditionally-rooted orchestral piece originated, and persisted, at a time when Cardew had embarked on the most grandiose, the most abstract, and the most experimental composition of his entire career; it was as if, as a composer, he were leading a double life, uncharacteristically hedging his bets, as it were. By the time the orchestral piece, *Bun No.1*, of 'rigid and rock-hard lines', received its first performance, in Rome in the summer of 1965, *Treatise* was already well underway, displaying, moreover, a multiplicity of 'lines' of striking character, some bold and dramatic in their trajectory, some elegant and graceful, others hesitant, uncertain, dilatory.

Treatise notates ideas, not sounds, although the notation may lead to sounds, even orchestral ones – just as it may lead to choreography and dance. For Cardew it was a rich and limitless source whence new sounds, new relationships between sounds, between sounds and players, between players, could be quarried, generating new modes of music-making. As we shall see, most of the works written contemporaneously with *Treatise,* between '63 and '67, bear some kind of relationship to it – sometimes quite precise and analytical, as with *Bun No.2,* sometimes of a teasingly arcane nature, as with *Volo Solo.*

It was during this period, soon after Cardew had started working for Aldus Books, that he entered into a relationship which was to continue, *sine die*, into a future without claim or obligation. There were chapters which opened and closed; there were quiescent periods and temporary cessations because of some inner imperatives, or because of the force of circumstances – when he was away for a lengthy period, in Italy or in America, or Germany. It was a relationship which waxed and waned but which could not be extinguished and which in the final years achieved a condition of consummation and equilibrium.

Sheila Muir recalls meeting Cardew and Stella, who was pregnant with Horace, at a party in Notting Hill Gate in the early part of 1963. The host was an American friend who had been at the Central School of Arts and Crafts with Sheila and who at the time was taking guitar lessons with Cardew. Some months later chance circumstances brought them together again; both had found employment with Aldus Books, he as a graphic designer and she as a picture researcher, working on the same floor though not sharing the same art editor. However, they would contrive brief assignations in the post-room, which was in the basement, where they befriended the post-boy, Gwigwi, a black South African musician who had come over with the Musical *King Kong* and had been granted political asylum.[7] It was here that the rudiments of a long relationship were established; right from the beginning there was a strong mutual attraction. Sheila recalls that she had never experienced such a depth and intensity of feeling for anybody else. She cannot describe their relationship sequentially; it was as if she had known Cornelius for as long as she had known herself. Twice a year she would use the change in time in order to create an extra hour to have with him.

During their extended lunch hours Cardew and Sheila would take the bus or the tube somewhere – often a premonitory visit to East London – and would go for long walks, especially by the river. Sometimes they would walk and talk, sometimes they would just walk, just being together; sometimes they would find the occasion to make love. Sheila recalls Cardew's intense awareness of, and sensitivity to, the environment through which they moved, to its sounds – whether the noise of scraping machinery or the impact of rain on different surfaces – although the wider, political dimensions of world events and the deliberations and pronouncements of the world's tribunals were never discussed. Sheila recalls that Cardew was witty, playful, rebellious, spontaneous; a providential library would inspire reference to a poem (such as, on one occasion, 'The Marigold'[8]) which they would look up and read together.

If their relationship was enclosed and self-centered it was because circumstances demanded that it should be under self-imposed strict control: Cardew was married and Sheila was living with George Kasabov whom she eventually married, in 1966. Kasabov was unaware of his partner's extra-marital relationship although had he been told it is unlikely that he would have intervened; he himself had cultivated a romantic attachment for a considerable time while he was living with Sheila. In any case, Cardew had intimated that he did not want Sheila to discuss their relationship with Kasabov. As in many such affairs there was an insistent moral cutting edge and as a corollary of morality – feelings of guilt.[9]

The baby was due in June, and for the last six months of her pregnancy Stella had rented a room where she could paint every day. The room was conveniently situated on the other side of Redcliffe Square near the Bousefield school which Emily and Gabriel attended. Cardew showed no interest in what she was painting and although they frequently and lengthily conversed, and on a wide variety of subjects, painting and music were never discussed. Stella recalls only one incursion into her work when she was taking her paintings around a number of London galleries and Cornelius accompanied her. One of the gallery owners, Krane Calman, expressed interest and proposed an exhibition provided that Stella would return to him with paintings that were not of gravestones – the Brompton cemetery had become an obsessive theme for her. When she was asked to add her name to some of the paintings she duly signed 'Stella Cardew'. On returning to their van Cardew immediately expressed his disapproval: 'How could you put my name on your pictures?' He clearly did not want the name of Cardew to be associated with Stella's paintings of grass and gravestone; for him the theme was trivial and the activity itself, that of easel painting, was outmoded.

One can interpret the insensitivity and arrogance of his reaction in a number of ways; it may well have reflected a deeply embedded class attitude; we know from his first wife, Ruth, that he was discretely proud of his family tree, of the roster of family achievements, and of his upbringing and education; he guarded his parentage jealously, even from his wife, who could boast no such lineage. Cardew's background was his capital; by the seventies, of course, it had become a liability. Or he was expressing incredulity that Stella's, in his view, modest and outmoded easel paintings might be associated, through her autograph, with the work of his father and himself.[10]

Occasionally, there are mildly critical references to Stella in the Journals, often insightful and shedding light as much on *their* relationship and his own attitudes as to any shortcomings on her part. 'Stella judges humanity without human sympathy. Yet she bemoans her lot; she would rather be in the position of any of the judged, rather than in the one she happens to occupy. Or perhaps she just judges the men.'[11] Certainly, financial insecurity was an endemic condition for the Cardew family, even if, from time to time, he was able to augment his income from Aldus Books with a certain amount of freelance work: copying parts for two of Stockhausen's works, *Momente* (1962-64), for which he received £45, and *Punkte* (1952, revised 1962), and the occasional concert review for the *Musical Times* which in January took him to Cologne for a small festival, two concerts, of contemporary music: 'A festival consists of two things: concerts and personalities', the review begins, with a touch of irony. This particular festival seems to have centred on two 'personalities' – Luigi Nono and Earle Brown – for whose music Cardew showed differing degrees of sympathy, though he was on good personal terms with both men. Cardew remarks on the striking quality of Nono's expressionism, which he regards as even more extreme than the early works of Berg and Schoenberg, and how the 'loose emotion' which Nono's music arouses is now gathered together and directed towards a definable and desirable objective – the intensification of sympathy for, and 'humanitarian indignation' at, the plight of oppressed peoples, so that the 'timpani rolls become gunfire, the soprano's high notes the cries of suffering humanity, and as such they are beautiful, very moving, and immediately comprehensible'.[12] Yet stripped of these associations, Nono's music, in Cardew's view, was insubstantial, relying on those musical features which he had continually overplayed in his earlier music, with little innovation. It was not Nono's ideological message that he found wanting; it was the inadequacy, and perhaps the inappropriateness of the music which provoked him to such a damning judgement. Nono's music displayed all the brash self-confidence, the exclusiveness and hyperbole of gesture, of a European avant-garde which had long been anathema to Cardew. It was also the music by which the progress of contemporary music was measured and by which trends could be estimated, just as financial trends are assessed on the Stock Exchange (Hanns Eisler had made a similar analogy). And international festivals were the natural habitat for such indulgences.

Cardew's preference for Brown's music is expressed unequivocally in the second part of the review: his 1962 piece *Available Forms II for Large Orchestra*, *Four Hands*, played after the Nono, proved to be a

> much more complex and stimulating musical experience. Brown was for many years associated with John Cage, and it may have been from him that he inherited a profound conviction that devising experiments and learning from the results is one of the most rewarding of human pursuits.[13]

Such partisan attitudes, on this occasion in relation to Nono and Brown, were by now predictable – Cardew had long made up his mind about the merits and demerits of the avant-garde, and the review reflected the entrenched position which, in this respect, he now occupied. In *Available Forms II* the two conductors, the 'four hands', move independently through the material and their spontaneous interaction 'ensures a constant awakeness on the part of the musicians and audience'; the rough and ready coincidences of sonorities and rhythmic structures, the frantic efforts of the musicians to keep abreast of the musical events, interpreting the manual signs given by their conductor and acting accordingly – this was music-making at its most exhilarating: 'a gust of fresh air sweeping through the audience. Some gasped, and some giggled, but all were shaken off that cultural pendulum that swings between limiting concepts of aesthetics and ethics'.[14]

Earle Brown enjoyed the review, appreciated its perspicacity and originality, and in particular the analogy that Cardew, in lively and irreverent form, drew between his piece and a game of poker. The 'available forms' – the wide variety of formal configurations from which performers may choose – he compared to the framework of a game of poker in which full house, straight flush, two pairs and so forth are available configurations within the pack of cards. As in poker the material that each conductor is dealt 'has a fixed position in a hierarchy of possibilities, yet their potential value depends to a large extent on the way they are exploited; with subtle betting, three aces can be better than a straight'.[15]

Some years earlier, in an undated letter to Ilona Halberstadt, Cardew had written scathingly of Nono's lecture at Darmstadt:

Gigi's [Nono] lecture was a disastrous occasion. He is the naïvetist of all time. A very personal attack on Cage, and the whole on the level and in the tone of a Hyde Park Corner Political Harangue. 'His freedom (long pause) is freedom (long pause) (then very fast) to be dead.' Bravo Bravo shout all the reactionaries, who suddenly feel themselves justified for not having bothered to think about or understand what they hear. 'He is free in the sense that a stone is free.' Gigi goes on. Very nice, what fun Polemics are. 'But think of the context' I felt like shouting. 'It's fine to talk of communication, responsibility, etc. but it is your responsibility to your communication that it should be as little as possible misunderstood. You must be conscious of the type of mind you are communicating with.'

Stella gave birth to Horace (named after Horace Silver, the American jazz pianist) on 10 June 1963 at home in Redcliffe Square. The baby was delivered by a Dr. Huntington with Cornelius in attendance. Within a few days John Underwood, Stella's ex-husband, called in and was a frequent visitor until the Cardews left for Cornwall, for Wenford, which had been vacated by the rest of the family for the summer period. Underwood was at a loose end, without a partner; his third marriage had collapsed and he was now making films prior to his departure for Africa where his children Emily and Gabriel were to join him for a holiday later in the year. 'Another Ode by Horace', he would observe, administering a benison of parturition while Horace gurgled quietly, and they would all laugh.

But in Wenford the tranquillity of their stay was soon to be shattered on one dramatic evening when a neighbour suddenly alerted them that the pottery barn was on fire. Buckets of water were thrown onto the roofs of the adjoining buildings and since there was no phone in the pottery Cardew had to drive up on to the moor to the nearest phone to call the fire-brigade. Stella's concern was that the inferno threatened to devour the whole premises and would eventually reach and destroy the pottery itself. However, by dawn the fire was finally extinguished, the pottery itself unscathed.

Stella recalls that for Cardew it had been a distressing experience; his parents' home and work had narrowly escaped total destruction and he felt himself responsible. In fact it had been the children, Emily and Gabriel and their friends, playing with matches, who had caused the fire. Within a year the barn was rebuilt, out of the same material and designed as Michael Cardew had specified, with a splendid gallery. For him the fire had positive consequences, although uncharacteristically his wife was less forgiving and would occasionally and not without bitterness refer to the paintings of hers that had been destroyed.

In a letter dated Sunday, 4 August 1963, his father wrote to him from Africa:

The want of capital is an old complaint in the Clan Cardew [...]The hard fact remains: art is impossible without Capital (that is, income!) [...] It is a perennial paradox: you can't devote yourself to Art unless you have that magic unattainable heavenly thing, a "Private" or "Independent" income (As if any income was Private!! – or independent!) because if you have to slave for a salary for your income, your energy, if you are an honest man, goes into earning that; whereas nothing but the cream of first fruits will do for creative work – yet, the possession of a private income invariably seems to narrow a man's genius and emasculate his style. An insoluble problem: public or private patronage is the only way Art can be helped.

As we shall see, Cardew spent most if not all of his life refuting his father's theory. He took his domestic responsibilities very seriously and managed to scrape together just enough for the family to survive; he was never able to devote himself entirely to his Art. Indeed, one could say he invested as much *creativity* into his family relationships as he did with his compositions and music-making. He simply refused to recognize that the relationship between Art and Life was antithetical, that the one excluded, or somehow detracted from the other. Art and Life coalesced.

In London, meanwhile, Cardew had left Aldus Books, albeit temporarily, and was busy enlisting friends and colleagues for a Little Festival of New Music at Goldsmiths' College on 6 July. The performers listed in an advertisement in the *Musical Times* included Fred Turner, Michael Garrett, John Cale, Griffith Rose, Enid Hartle, Robin Page, George Macunias, Tomas Schmitt, Emmett Williams and Cardew himself. Macunias and Williams were members of the Fluxus group.[16] Page was a painter and friend who would contribute to many of Cardew's projects in the sixties, and the Welshman, John Cale, would shortly leave for America where in 1965 he would co-found, with Lou Reed, the Velvet Underground rock band.[17]

The Festival comprised two concerts on the same day, at 2.30 pm and at 7 pm. Admission free. The content of the evening programme, in particular, had now moved even further away from the received definitions of music, further certainly than that of the concerts with Michael von Biel at the Wigmore Hall the previous year, to which the afternoon concert still bore some relation: Cage's 1951 *Music of Changes* (probably in part), Cardew's *Autumn 60*, Cage's *Concert for Piano and Orchestra* with *Aria*, and Michael von Biel's *Book for Three*, which had also been performed at the Wigmore concert.

The evening concert was virtually a *Fluxus* event, featuring pieces by George Brecht – *2 pieces for string quartet*, George Macunias – *Solo for Violin*, Nam June Paik (whom Cardew knew from Cologne) – *String Quartet*, Emmett Williams – *Counting song*, and three pieces by La Monte Young – *Piano Piece for David Tudor #2, Piano Piece for Terry Riley #1* (1960), and *Composition 1960 #3*. Cardew had already met Young in Germany and was to introduce the American's work into many European countries with performances which have become legendary, in which his listeners were shaken off the 'cultural pendulum' – as in Earle Brown's *Available Forms* (1961) but more violently – and feats of sheer physical endurance were achieved by performer and audience alike. *Piano Piece for Terry Riley #1* involves pushing the piano up to and, if possible, beyond all obstacles, including a wall. 'The piece is over when you are too exhausted to push any longer.' (Young's instructions.) The demand for supreme stamina, for fortitude, for a heart of oak, on the part of the performer is characteristic of many of Young's pieces at that time and Cardew would certainly have regarded these qualities as virtues to be encouraged and nurtured and, on occasions, displayed publicly. *Piano Piece for David Tudor #2* is less spectacular but demands more concentration as the listener is required to focus to an extreme degree while the performer attempts to open and close the piano lid without making a sound. There is anxiety, too, as the performance progresses and failure, perhaps humiliation, seems to beckon.

The notion of 'failure', as one of the aspects of the psychology of performance, and not only musical performance, frequently elicited Cardew's thoughts and comments; on 6 September, Gabriel's ninth birthday, a reflection in his Journal on the nature of anxiety, also associated with performance activity in general, concludes with a pointed reference to his relationship with Stella:

> To eliminate all one's own anxieties is not the only problem: after that one has to acquire immunity to everyone else's anxieties. I note e.g. that the baby (Horace) is by no means immune to those of Stella and I. However, I feel I am more free than I used to be of Stella's.

Here Cardew aspires to a condition of detachment which he had long admired in Eastern philosophy, yet which is also considered an English trait by some commentators; his 'English' *persona* had often elicited observation and comment, especially from non-English critics, and finds expression a little further on in the same Journal entry:

> Yesterday evening listened to Matthew Arnold on the Radio. All English romantics have this lovely feeling for the country. Almost as though only England had a land which could really be home and one's mother and mistress and everything. Dwelling at peace in the bosom of the English landscape, everything is seen in proportion; and 'the spark is awaited from above' quite rightly. The English landscape is safe; safe for everyone, and therefore an excellent point of departure for lyric poets. Aware of their nest between the 'melancholy din' and 'suck and roar' of the cold North Sea on the one hand, and the 'raving Atlantic' on the other. Perhaps here exists the only true sadness about world affairs, for only here can they be seen detachedly for what they are. Though all too often they are simply not known.

The emotional response to things 'English' – there is both warmth and pride in these words – is also a response to the idea of roots. In his music-making, too, Cardew was concerned with 'putting down roots' and there are many references in his writings to 'seeds' and 'growth', to organic form; the latter part of *Treatise* is full of tree images and the Confucian text for *The Great Learning*, as we shall see, contains many similar references. But if his Englishness was the very spring and source of his creativity, the 'class content' of his upbringing and education was ultimately more influential, as he himself came to recognise in the later years.

In October 1963 Cardew departed for Sicily for a performance of his *Movement for Orchestra* given by the Sicilian Symphony Orchestra under Daniele Paris at the Palermo Festival.[18] From Palermo he flew to Rome to meet Stella and the children who had arrived from London for a short break. Despite his dissatisfaction, as he expressed to Stella, with the rehearsals and performance of his own work, in his review of the Festival for the *Musical Times* he was generous both to the Sicilian Orchestra and to their conductor. The organisers of the festival were praised, too, for the boldness of their programming and the high profile given to the most recent accomplishments in new music; at the very beginning of the festival, in the opening concert, the audience was precipitated into an awareness of the present with works by Ligeti (*Atmosphères*), Roland Kayn (*Schwingungen* 'für fünf Klanggruppen'), Aldo Clementi (*Informel 3*), Franco Evangelisti (*Random or not Random*), and Kagel's theatrical piece for actor and tape (*Antithèse*). Cardew's gift for identifying, in a few sentences, the essential features of a work and for bringing the seemingly peripheral into focus is exemplified in this one-page review in the December 1963 issue of the *Musical Times*. What interested him, invariably, were those works which broke through the barriers of conventional definitions of music, such as a highly theatrical piece for cellist and tape, *Per Arco*, by the Italian composer Guiseppe Chiari:

> In the first part we hear from the loudspeakers a continual crashing and squealing
> – the sounds of war – and only after this is over does the soloist, who has been
> sitting motionless, begin to express his feelings – protective, desperate, tender
> and nostalgic – for his instrument. It was a macabre duet between the player
> and his cello, with the bow performing a strangely serpentine and evasive role,
> sliding through the hands and fingers of the cellist with a quickness that suggested
> it wanted to slip away into a quiet corner, there to await with equanimity the
> extinction of its dual master.

The soloist was Italo Gomez, the moving spirit behind the Florentine 'Società Cameristica Italiana', a group which had evolved 'a phenomenal technique in the performance of new music' and which was much admired by Cardew. Other compositions, according to the review, were not so fortunate in performance, due mainly to lack of rehearsal facilities, and there were occasions of near farce: before Sylvano Bussotti's *Torso* the audience were obliged to wait for over an hour while a search was conducted for the conductor's missing music stand. Cardew clearly appreciated the open and lively atmosphere which permeated the Festival and the fact that it heralded 'the emergence of a group of young Italian musicians proliferating a rich undergrowth around the two tall bare trees of the Italian avant-garde establishment – Luigi Nono and Luciano Berio'.[19]

Cornelius and Stella rented a small house in Ansedonia, some 100 kilometres north-west of Rome. Cardew had been awarded an Italian Government scholarship for Goffredo

Petrassi's Corso di Perfezionamento in Composizione at L'Accademia Nazionale di Santa Cecilia in Rome – a two year course, 1964/1965, which ran from February 1964 to June 1965. After the Palermo concert Cardew had decided to stay on in Italy where he had a number of engagements. He was also able to take possession of the house in Ansedonia and prepare it for the family who were to join him at the end of January '64.

The image of Ansedonia that Stella has retained in her mind's eye is of a barren hillside adorned with expensive, secluded villas and overlooking a spectacular bay with a long white stretch of sandy beach. Their accommodation was characteristically stark: a small, one storey, stone house which probably also served as a functional summer holiday home. There was no heating, save for a single fireplace, and they would make fires with driftwood and fir cones. Such resourcefulness in the face of adverse circumstances was to the manner born for Cardew – a legacy from his Cornish childhood – and under his tutelage the family drilled itself into a spartan way of life.

But Stella Cardew was not happy in Italy and suffered an acute sense of displacement and disassociation; unlike her husband she was incapable of outwitting circumstances. The house was situated in a deserted spot on an unfriendly terrain and she felt desperately insecure. And because of her lack of Italian she had no friends, nor even acquaintances. She was marooned and would experience distressing panic attacks when she was left alone with the children, two or three times a week, while Cardew was in Rome, or elsewhere – meeting people, networking, performing. Nevertheless, every morning she would paint while Cornelius, with his gift for husbandry – for everything had to be negotiated on an extremely tight budget – would organise the domestic requirements such as shopping and taking the children to school, all of which he accomplished effortlessly, with unobtrusive speed and efficiency. On one occasion, however, he fell ill with severe stomach pains; this may have been due to his insistence, according to Frederic Rzewski, on buying the cheapest fish from the fishermen in Orbetello, a small Mediterranean port at the end of the peninsula, just a short drive from their house, where they would shop once a week and where the children went to a small, local state school. Apart from the fact that it was all they could afford – supplemented with daily helpings of pasta – Cardew had theorized, inscrutably, that the cheapest fish was also the best fish. Marcello Panni recalls that the choice of food would involve a discussion with the whole family, including the smallest. Everybody had their say and everybody's whims and preferences had to be somehow accommodated. It was exemplarily democratic.

A Journal entry from 4 September makes it clear that Cardew's Italian sojourn had been planned well in advance: 'Mem: in Italy this winter do not be an amateur skater on the ice of contemporary music (again); send roots into the ground.' Contemporary music was a pursuit he had been unable to slough off; his antipathy towards the European avant-garde did not preclude a continuing, if detached involvement – as a professional critic and, from time to time, as performer. It was natural then that he should hesitate to cut himself off from his friends and colleagues in the profession, although it was becoming increasingly difficult to maintain a musical relationship with them, especially with those whose allegiance to the avant-garde, whether as leaders or acolytes, seemed to be unshakeable. It was therefore to composition itself, and in particular to his *Treatise*, that he continued to apply himself – in virtual isolation, for his radical experimentation in the field of musical notation had led him into aesthetic, philosophical and indeed moral territory where few would follow.

There was also the occasional foray into more modish areas of experimentation. The Spanish artist, Enrique Brinkmann, who designed the cover for Cardew's *Two Books of Study for Pianists*, recalls a conversation in Piazza Navona when Cardew described his experience with the drug LSD, pointing to the fountain and explaining, by way of example, how the water and rock formations would be perceived differently. When Cardew suggested that Brinkmann should attend one of his concerts under the influence of LSD Brinkmann declined. Nevertheless they became good friends and the Spaniard was happy to provide Cardew with a roof over his head for a few weeks. The family had gone back to England and Cardew was looking for a *pied-à-terre* in Rome for the duration of the Petrassi course.

On the world stage 1963 had seen the assassination of Kennedy; in Britain it was the Christine Keeler affair and the humiliation of Government minister John Profumo which, for a few weeks, had provided entertaining headlines in the media and provoked an effusion of public ribaldry.[20] Such events were of as little concern to Cardew as they were to the majority of his peers who were already too busy creating their own culture, a culture sited well away from the seats of middle-aged power and influence. In any case they were aware that their elders 'had lost control of themselves, of their class, of their generation, of their countries'.[21] According to Stella her husband took no interest in current affairs; he never read newspapers nor listened to the radio.

The beginning of 1964 saw Cardew back in London, briefly, for a concert in January at the American Embassy under the auspices of the Park Lane Group.[22] The programme was shared with the violinist Egon Mayer and the percussionist Eric Allen, with Cardew performing in all pieces except for Stockhausen's *Zyklus* (for solo percussionist). The remainder of the programme consisted of Ives' *Three-Page Sonata* and *4th Violin and Piano Sonata*, Cage's *Water Music*, Feldman's *Extensions 1* for violin and piano, Cardew's *Treatise* (selected pages) performed on violin and piano, and La Monte Young's *Composition 1960 #7* in which the performers are instructed to hold an open fifth, the notes B and F#, 'for a long time'.

On his return to Rome, in February, to join Petrassi's composition course Cardew was befriended by a young Hungarian participant, Zoltan Peszko; he and Cardew would attend the sessions together, normally twice a week, on the sixth floor of via Vittoria 6, near Piazza di Spagna, in 'an indescribably beautiful room' (Peszko) with a breathtaking view of the city. Each tutorial was divided into two: the first part was spent scrutinising compositions they were currently working on, and in the second half they would analyse and discuss works by other composers who were of interest to them. Peszko recalls that Cardew took along some scores of Stockhausen and, somewhat surprisingly at that time perhaps, but also prophetically, some pieces by Hanns Eisler. Each session would be followed, quasi-ritualistically, by an espresso coffee in a nearby bar where Cardew and his new friend could relax and talk more informally.

Cardew's main project, on which he would be assessed at the end of the course the following year, was his orchestral piece *Bun No.1*, which in fact was a version of an earlier work from 1960: *Third Orchestral Piece*. However, around the same time, early in 1964, he received a request from Mauricio Kagel for a chamber orchestral work for a concert in Brussels. *Bun No.1* was temporarily abandoned and *Bun No.2* was duly completed in Ansedonia in April – in less than 8 weeks. In the same month he completed *Material*, this time a transcription, rather than a version, of the *Third Orchestral Piece*, as well as resuming translating work on Willi Reich's biography of Alban Berg, which had been commissioned by Thames and Hudson.

None of this, however, apart from the translation, provided funds to alleviate his financial situation, which was worsening. Struggling to cope on his £8 a week scholarship even Cardew's resourcefulness and thrift were stretched beyond the limits. In a letter to Mauricio Kagel he asked if a commission fee for *Bun No.2* might be negotiated with Belgian Radio. Kagel's solicitous response confirmed, however, that there was no possibility of a fee – at best an invitation to the performance – but listed a few ideas for Cardew to consider and perhaps to follow up: a Nachtprogramm for Herbert Eimert at the Northwest German Radio, a letter to Hans Otte at Bremen Radio, who would be sympathetic and possibly useful, or simply to earn money by copying the parts of his own piece.

Bun No.2 occasioned a number of problems right from the outset. Hans Swarsenski, his publisher at Peters Edition, objected to Cardew's insistence on a high trumpet in G (or piccolo in B flat) on account of its scarcity (which he judged would put the most severe limitations on the work's inclusion in the repertoire), and to what he described as an unreproducible orchestration page, which was duly omitted from the first three printed scores. Cardew had, in fact, given the matter due consideration, seeking out Kurt Schwertsik's advice on orchestration in general and on the capabilities and possibilities of the trumpet in particular.

During the first part of 1964 family life in Ansedonia remained unchanged except that now, as well as his domestic preoccupations there were regular visits to Petrassi, to which, according to Peszko, he showed a serious commitment. As with every Cardew household there was a constant flow of visitors; colleagues and friends from Rome would often appear, including Frederic Rzewski – twice, once with family, Klaus and Isolde Koch, his old friends from Cologne, his father Michael and brother Ennis and, in March, Kurt Schwertsik. However unfavourable their own circumstances were (and in Ansedonia they were particularly cramped), Stella and Cornelius invariably welcomed, fed, entertained and succoured all manner of variously motivated travellers, some of whom were no more than tangential acquaintances who had been given their address – an open house where people would pass through after a chat and a cup of tea, or a convivial evening meal. Or they would stay on for months. Schwertsik recalls that at the time he was considerably weighed down by domestic tribulations and had decided to visit Cardew – a temporary respite when he could sit quietly, in congenial company, discussing art and music over a few glasses of wine. He had even taken the expedient of alerting them by telegram and arrived in a relaxed and expectant mood. However, the house was empty, though unlocked. Schwertsik made himself at home and waited; when night fell he chose a bed and went to sleep, only to be woken at a late hour by Cardew, accompanied by Klaus and Isolde Koch.

Stella's unhappiness may well have prompted feelings of resentment towards Cornelius which, according to him, she expressed through a variety of psychological ploys. And yet these veiled resentments seemed to bind them together and in the Journals he traces the tensional morphology of their relationship, with its occasional skirmishes, through which we can map the gradually changing features of its emotional landscape. (There is an echo in these comments of the battle of wits between Clarissa and Lovelace – Cardew notes *Clarissa* in the Journals; perhaps he was reading Richardson's book at the time.)

Throughout his life there were many romantic attachments and entanglements, as well as the occasional 'louche assignation'. Towards Stella his behaviour for much of their time together was solicitous, even uxorious. He craved the ministrations of women; he enjoyed feminine wiles and commerce and had access to a range of female sensibilities. It sharpened his own sensibilities; perhaps it made him a finer person. Foreign women responded to what they perceived as his English nonchalance behind which he seemed to obey some inner tangle of tensions and energies. If he were ever guilty of impropriety he would have acted with discretion; the two are not necessarily incompatible. He would have covered his, and his lady friend's, tracks. His female admirers were legion.

A Journal entry from Ansedonia contains an analysis of a difference of opinion with Klaus and Isolde Koch which, like so many of his remarks and comments, insinuates a whole range of philosophical complexities:

> What Klaus and Isolde refuse to accept is a logic based on dependence. They are pragmatic rationalists and economists. They say it limits Emily if she is not capable of walking down to Daniela's on her own. There is nothing against this limitation. Sure it may turn out to be a matter of life and death one day whether she can exist on her own or not, and maybe she will die because she can't. But that is her code and she is faithful to it.
>
> Stella *needs* company. Klaus and Isolde can say 'but she doesn't need to have this need'. But why shouldn't she have this need? It is a need which keeps her in contact with *facts*, with the realities of fear and loneliness which are the roots of our human condition. Denying fear and loneliness they are on the road to non-humanity. Heroic yes and praiseworthy too − fighting the limits, reaching them and exceeding them − very fine. But do not dogmatically lay it down that we all have to be independent and self-sufficient, even as far as lies within our power. No, you may even set yourself the task: cultivate dependency, make yourself insufficient. Refuse to be competent and efficient − these things do not deserve your whole energy. Not in themselves. This way you may be able to strike a balance and see in both directions.
>
> The good educationalist works from within the material drawing it out, he does not impose the pattern he has chosen on 'ungrateful material.' [23]

Ungenerously, one can interpret this as a piece of disingenuous sophistry to justify his frequent absence from the family; a recital of words, self-indulgent ratiocination. For underlying these shafts of analytical brilliance may be the need for self-justification when he is visited by guilt feelings; for they are also injunctions to himself. He is in Rome and elsewhere; Stella is lonely. He is unable or unwilling to satisfy her need for company; he therefore rationalises and idealises her state of loneliness. Stella would voice every passing anxiety and it was in his gift to take the measure of her feelings, of the tenor of her behaviour, her cosmology. Although he would criticise her for her pliancy, her inability to take the world's measure, he seems to have accepted it; in her he recognised a state of latency which most husbands prefer to deny. He was willing to try to understand Stella psychologically, but his own self-centeredness prevented her needs from ever assuming a centrality in their relationship. Whilst he identified her 'weaknesses', he failed to recognise her considerable strengths (which in some respects outweighed his own), in particular and crucially her struggle to accommodate the relationship between art and everyday, 'ordinary' reality: the unyielding, unforgiving demands of her own profoundly artistic temperament, and the undeniable claim for recognition and fulfilment of a considerable

1. Mariel Cardew with her sons (l-r) Seth, Cornelius and Ennis, August 1945

2. Mariel and Michael Cardew, September 1934

3. Wenford 1954

4. Cornelius Cardew, Wenford 1949

5. Mariel Cardew and Jonathan Varcoe, early 1940s

6. Canterbury during World War Two

7. (l-r) Cardew, James Skinner, Peter Freeman, Richard Osborn and Roger Job, Canterbury 1948-49

8. Cardew at King's School, Canterbury 1952

talent, weighed against the reality of child-birth, of the physical, emotional, and merciless demands of raising children, of their uninterrupted, unmitigated proximity, and, irresistibly, of the indescribable joy and delight with which their extraordinary presence can expose and undermine the pretensions of Art.

Cardew's reputation as a performer had preceded him in Italy and his expertise and flair as an interpreter of contemporary scores was well-heralded and frequently in demand – in Cologne he had already befriended Franco Evangelisti, who was one of the founder members of the Nuova Consonanza group.[24] On 13 June 1964, in Rome, as part of the second Nuova Consonanza festival Cardew's *Octet '61 for Jasper Johns* was performed in the Teatro delle Arti by the Società Cameristica Italiana, and on the next day Cardew and Frederic Rzewski gave the first performance of Stockhausen's *Plus-Minus*. At the time Rzewski, whose home was in Rome, was residing in Berlin as a recipient of a German Academy of Arts scholarship and had returned to Rome temporarily to prepare *Plus-Minus* with Cardew.

Plus-Minus was written 'for composers' and evolved out of Stockhausen's composition course in Cologne which attracted a growing flock of young composers from around the world. Not surprisingly Cardew and Rzewski treated *Plus-Minus* as a challenge rather than an opportunity, manipulating Stockhausen's material and stretching his rules to the limit; in particular Rzewski's approach to the 'given' pitch material was confrontational, using every opportunity to eliminate it and develop an entirely separate and 'autonomous' character for the piece. Cardew's strategy was to aim for extremes – between maximum simplicity of unadulterated pitch material and the rich complexity of three transistor radios tuned respectively to atmospherics, speech and music. The result was that

> after four or five minutes' flight over something that was quite recognizably Stockhausen country we found ourselves emerging into vast spaces of uncharted virgin steppe, a landscape of almost Wagnerian grandeur, and we experienced a feeling of elation (it must be remembered that this grew up only gradually through a number of very sticky rehearsals) and an invigorating sense of unlimited freedom.[25]

However, Cardew's description in the *London Magazine* gives no indication of some of the more unconventional and provocative aspects of his interpretations of *Plus-Minus*; one member of his audience recalls that on one occasion Cardew was propelling paper aeroplanes into the audience. Stockhausen himself is reputed to have enjoyed some performances and been angered by others; knowing the two protagonists as he did, he could hardly have expected anything else.

In the same month an open-air concert on the terrace of the Forte Belvedere in Florence, organized by Guiseppe Chiari and the Gruppo Settanta, premiered pages 57-60 and 75-79 of Cardew's *Treatise*. The pages were played as two separate sections lasting 1½ and 4 minutes respectively. The performers were an illustrious group comprising Rzewski (piano and auxiliary sounds), Mauricio Kagel (reading aloud), Italo Gomez (cello), Sylvano Bussotti (percussion) and the composer (whistles).

Cardew also found time, and inspiration, to complete a short piano piece, conceived as music for dance for a friend, Francesca Astaldi. In fact, in a letter to Signora Astaldi the following year he wrote that it was originally intended to be one of a series of dance pieces and 'turned into just one little piano piece − but I am afraid it is very difficult to play! I don't know of anyone in Rome to recommend to play it to you. But there it is with my love, and gratitude'.[26] Cardew had been introduced to Francesca Astaldi in Rome where she ran a dance school, Centro Internazionale di Danza (C.I.D.). Primarily to boost his meagre income he would play for her classes and stay on at the Studio in via del Babuino, to which he was given a key, to work on his compositions, which at that time − the first half of 1964 − would have included *Treatise*, the two *Buns* and the aforementioned piano piece (which in fact became the third of the *Three Winter Potatoes).*

The Astaldi family were extremely solicitous towards Cardew; they would offer him lunch, a piano was always available for him − for he liked to practice regularly − and generally they kept an eye on his well-being. But of particular interest is the fact that, according to Francesca Astaldi, they would often improvise together, for this was probably the first time that mention of him as an 'improvising musician' has been recorded. In fact, there was another occasion in Rome, during the summer of 1964, where Cardew was involved with 'free improvisation', as recalled by the American composer Larry Austin. He had co-founded the New Music Ensemble in Davis, California, which had begun experimenting with 'free improvisation' in the summer of 1963, and had brought tapes of their concerts to Rome:

> The day came for the first session of the Italian group. I retain a vivid impression. Cornelius Cardew came to observe, heard the group and, in the later part of the session, joined in. Franco [Evangelisti] was an ecstatic priest of the session. We had lots of keyboards … pianos, organs …It was a huge ensemble. I played flugelhorn and string bass. There must have been ten people …[Aldo] Clementi, [Ivan] Vandor, Evangelisti, [Bill] Smith, [John] Eaton, John Heineman, Cardew, [Alvin] Curran, Mario Bertoncini, myself.[27]

There may also have been occasions for improvisation at the Live New Departures events in the late fifties but they were most likely to have been contributions of a private nature, smothered and largely unheard in a hubbub of jazz and poetry readings and ravings. Whereas in Francesca Astaldi's studio in Rome there would have been a clarity and focus, a clearly defined accompanimental function; his music would have been exposed, and listened to – if only by a lone dancer. And Signora Astaldi recalls that Cardew's music-making heightened her awareness of the quality and power of sound – and of silence, too.[28] They would sit quietly and wordlessly together, and he might break the silence with a quietly-spoken observation which was always illuminating, the silence merely masking an ever-active and penetrating mind:

> We have to find our experiences in living, not in going to concerts or watching dances. Sure, they too are living, if we go to them, but we must not seek out a particular part of life for our experiencing. If we stay still there is a great deal of living going on around us already; and we have been moving around a lot. [29]

Their relationship, which was an artistic one, was relatively brief, their meetings irregular; Cardew had many commitments and was often away.

But what does all this, and *Treatise* especially, have to do with Cardew's decision, at the beginning of 1963 or even earlier, to study with Goffredo Petrassi? [30] What need was there for this translation to another place? Was he seeking some kind of validation? For the young Italian composers who knew of Cardew through his already established reputation in the avant-garde, as a member of the fashionable Beatles generation who had put bourgeois values to flight, it was simply a manifestation of English eccentricity; this was the only possible explanation for what appeared to them a bizarre decision. In fact, the reasons were probably rather more prosaic, pragmatic: firstly, his financial situation in England was dire, and the opportunity to take the family away to Italy, as the recipient of a small monthly grant, was attractive (a reason which was openly acknowledged in conversation by both Cardew and Petrassi); secondly, it was precisely because Petrassi had no connection to the European avant-garde that he was considered the ideal teacher; his musical and compositional pursuits and interests were quite different to those of Cardew, and this would have been recognised by both men. Cardew appears to have had neither the time nor the inclination to write 'new pieces' for Petrassi; as we have seen, even the piece submitted at the end of the course was a version of a previous orchestral work. Cardew's compositional quest at the time was for a music which was based on new aesthetic premises, and which did not yet exist; the means towards compositional ends remained undefined and whatever solution lay ahead it was his own private affair.

And yet if his purpose had little to do with the art of (traditional) musical composition he seemed genuinely convinced that as far as writing for the orchestra was concerned there was much to learn from Petrassi, and in this respect he would have manifested polite obeisance to the Italian maestro. 'I go to Petrassi not to learn a skill, but to learn a feeling. To develop a feeling for the orchestra. Why the orchestra? Because that is the field of composition where the most can be notated.'[31] And there were few practitioners more knowledgeable of the manifold new possibilities for the large, modern orchestra, nor more skilled in their deployment, than Goffredo Petrassi.

And so the sessions passed without nod towards the avant-garde – except for the occasional score that Cardew took along – and in general all phenomena pertaining to the avant-garde were relegated to an inconsequential status. In any case Cardew's own involvement with the European avant-garde was diminishing; for him it was now a world of low definition. The by now tenuous links were maintained by virtue of his role as performing mercenary who viewed the antics of his European peers with a cynical detachment, an attitude which had certainly informed his performances of *Plus-Minus* and which, in his *London Magazine* review of his involvement with the work, he did little to disguise.

Now and again, as Zoltan Peszko recalls, there would be a temporary breakdown in communication; in stark contrast to his teacher, for example, Cardew's perception of other music at that time was totally devoid of any historical perspective and this would occasionally manifest itself in the lessons. In a discussion of a work of Charles Ives, in whose music Cardew showed particular interest during the first year, Petrassi pointed out that a particular, relatively important, flute part could not possibly be heard within the context which Ives had placed it. Whereupon Cardew offered a solution whereby a microphone could be positioned to amplify and project the said part. The fact that such a 'solution' would have been inconceivable in Ives' time was for Cardew an irrelevant detail, of consequence only to musicologists and historians. Petrassi listened to Cardew's suggestion in utter disbelief.

On an early summer's day in 1964 Cardew and his family boarded the train in Rome to return to London. The arrangements for their departure had been made in good time and the journey began with a sense of both relief and anticipation, at least on the part of Stella. An hour or two north of Rome the train stopped at a station and Cornelius announced that he was getting out and returning to Rome, abandoning Stella and the children to continue the journey without him. Despite its dramatic effect, the apparent spontaneity of the action was not entirely convincing. According to Stella, his mother, who was at the station in London to meet them, did not seem surprised that her son had not made the journey. Had she been forewarned? Had Cornelius asked her to meet and help Stella and the children? Yet such an impulsive decision would not have been out of character; nor was it without precedent. Of course there would have been reflection, deliberation, self-analysis, for days perhaps, or for hours, and then – seize the hour, or the moment, and act boldly, decisively, however discomfitting the immediate consequences. And what lay behind his precipitous action? Perhaps the reason was one which Stella could not have accepted. Rather than lying he simply created a situation where explanations and discussions could not be accommodated. Was there a relationship in Rome which he was unwilling to sever? For although he would return to Rome, to Petrassi's course, the following February, there are relationships which can barely survive absences of hours, let alone a separation of seven or eight months. We can but speculate; the incident was never subsequently discussed, nor even mentioned in the Cardew family.

Whatever his business in Rome, it was suspended, or abandoned, or finished by the end of June, for the first half of July was spent with Kurt Schwertsik and his family in Vienna where Cardew began to sketch out some notes on *Two Books of Study* for a Cologne Radio Nachtprogramm, though this was not scheduled until the following January. Schwertsik was one of Cardew's closest friends and they saw eye to eye on many musical matters; with Schwertsik there was no need for Cardew to moderate his language, to curb his intensity of expression in discussions on the European avant-garde; Schwertsik was even more scathing in his criticisms and denunciations than Cardew. In a projected but unrealised article entitled 'Why is the music of Stockhausen, Boulez and Nono so easy to understand?'[32] Cardew describes its purpose: 'To display its primitiveness. Kurt should do Boulez. I Nono and Evangelisti Stockhausen, and the articles should be published simultaneously declaring an Anglo-Austrian-Italian Axis against the Franco-German-Venetian 3rd Empire.'[33] Yet Stella Cardew recalls that in the same breath her husband would both disparage Stockhausen and defend him as the greatest living composer. Boulez, too, according to Stella, he held in respectful awe although the Frenchman was never regarded, as Stockhausen had been, as a 'comrade-in-arms'. 'Everything Stockhausen has written is on a level of intensity sufficient to penetrate all self-imposed barriers of esoteric thinking and technical complexity' Cardew wrote in a review entitled 'Composed Laughter' for the *New Statesman* on 10 December 1965. Though strong, Cardew's admiration for Stockhausen during the sixties was always stinted, as we have seen in some of his letters from Cologne in the late fifties as well as in his report on *Carré*.

In a Journal entry on 10 July, in cheerful and flippant mood, he sets out a general plan of action for the next two years:

Just for the record and to see how far it will be in my power to execute it;
Rest of 1964. Get money by fair means or foul.
1965 first half. Finish Petrassi's course. (Leonardo's birds and Variations)
second half. Go back to Aldus while I finish *Treatise*.
1966 – still at Aldus (if they still exist).
September, take up as music teacher in a school in London.
Take out life insurance and make a will.
(E&G 12&13, Horace 3, Me 30, Stella 38?)

The idea of a teaching career could only have been prompted by urgent economic considerations; at the time he simply could not conceive of earning a living in music in any other way and many of his English peers had come to the same conclusion. Whether he would have been able to knuckle down to the demands of a University music board for school examinations is questionable; by now his views on music and music-making and, as a corollary, musical education were too radical, too uncompromising to be able to be accommodated within the normal school syllabus. A few years later he did take on some piano teaching at Latymer Upper School in Hammersmith but it was short-lived; his appearances became spasmodic and the head of music deemed it was not possible to retain him. By mutual agreement they parted company and this was probably the nearest that Cardew came to becoming a school teacher.

After Vienna Cardew continued his journey northwards to Darmstadt – ineluctable still, even to Cardew, though conveniently en route to London. For however alienated he felt from the ethos of Darmstadt, it was a relationship which he could not afford to sever. The musicians on whom he relied for performances of the piano works, of *Autumn 60*, of *Octet '61*, of *Material*, even of *Treatise*, would still foregather, every summer, at Darmstadt – Kagel, Maderna, Rzewski, Otte, Bussotti et al. – where his ideas would at least receive consideration, in open forum, and his compositions a hearing; at that time he had really no other outlet. In general, however, the reception was unsympathetic, if not downright hostile, as when he performed his own *February Pieces*. The repressive climate which pervaded throughout the fifties had softened but the critical shroud that inhibited spontaneous response had not dispersed and a defensive intellectualism still held sway. The intense sadness, the spontaneity, the privacy, of Cardew's music met with incomprehension, and even his admirers were left behind, non-plussed, when his notational experiments entered a more abstract phase and he became even more reticent about his aims.

For Cardew *Treatise* was the musical, or rather compositional corollary of his increasing isolation. In the *Treatise Handbook*, dated December '63, a consideration of 'colouring' *Treatise* leads in typically mercurial fashion to deeper levels of analysis:

Colouring *Treatise*. Two quite different uses of colour: to clarify and to express. Colouring *Treatise*, is one trying to clarify the notation, the design of the piece? Does it need clarification? What is there to explain? That such and such elements are combined in such and such ways?

Surely it is more as though one were trying to express the (subjective) effect that the design has on one. And one is trying to express this effect back through the design.

I should try and invent a concrete case: the design affects me in such and such a way, and I use it in such and such a way to express this affect that it has on me, etc. etc. The fact that this idea makes me feel tired is suspicious. Cannot the design simply stand on its own, and then I just choose to make music besides?

Because: Psychologically the existence of the piece is fully explained by the situation of a composer who is not in a position to make music. The question to be put: 'If he cannot make music (circumstances do not allow) what can he make?' The answer: '*Treatise*'.[34]

This dilemma, and Cardew's rationalisation of it into a highly abstract score would have received short shrift at Darmstadt where he detected a 'Certain lack of seriousness – a desire, not only on the part of organisers but also of composers, merely to amuse and entertain a capricious and difficult public.'[35] His review of the 1964 Darmstadt summer school in the *Musical Times*, characteristically entitled 'Modern Music has found its feet but on what low ground', seeks to identify the 'lack of seriousness', locating it in compositions and performances alike. Describing an interpretation of Berg's *Three Orchestral Pieces Op.6* given by the Südwestfunk Orchestra under the direction of Ernst Bour, he writes:

In 1929 Berg revised the instrumentation and applied Schoenberg's principle of marking out the main and the subsidiary voices, the remainder being relegated to the accompaniment. Bour's interpretation exaggerated this tendency almost to the point of simplicity, with the results: (a) loss of richness and real power in sound, and (b) an inexplicable form (since a complex form cannot be made comprehensible by suppression of important details, that is, by being made simple). The general tendency that this represents, and which could be observed retrospectively in the Ferienkursen [Darmstadt summer courses] as a whole, is a desire for superficial clarity rather than depth and richness of expression.[36]

This dichotomy also informs his criticism of Kazimerz Serocki's *Sinfonische Fresken* (1964):

> I was struck by the work's 'honesty' (a very English expression: an 'honest' man is one who does not try to camouflage his shortcomings; in fact by presenting them prominently he contrives to make them appear virtuous) and by the high craftsmanship of its execution (a modern work in which it is possible to really hear every single thing that is happening in the orchestra is a rare phenomenon − in fact it is rather suspicious). This is the music of Outer Space as Stan Kenton might conceive it (but without Kenton's rhythm). Varèse is the father of this music of extraordinary, static sound effects; but Varèse's music generates great intensity, which suggests an intuition of hidden psychological drives. Serocki's piece on the other hand was pathetically obvious and not powerful at all − just very smoothly effective.[37]

What did impress Cardew at the time was the marked improvement in the standard of performance in comparison with those which he had attended in the middle and late fifties. The performances given by the International Chamber Ensemble under Bruno Maderna were in Cardew's view of an exceptionally high quality, both in terms of ensemble work and individual playing. Milton Babbitt's twelve lectures on 'The Structure of Musical Systems', which ranged from Schoenberg's *Fourth String Quartet* to psycho-acoustical perception problems of computer music, were also singled out for the seriousness and excellence of their content. And yet for Cardew the virtues of Darmstadt could not mask its irrelevance − at least to his own overriding concerns − and his review ends accordingly:

> Yes, the Darmstadt Summer School has become an excellent Academy, and problems like Notation and Electronic sound are competently handled in a rather academic way. What has got lost is the vital interest in new and serious experimental music.

On the 27 July Cardew arrived back in England to spend a relatively quiet and uneventful summer. In a rare utterance of Romantic persuasion and purpose, he wrote: 'Love is the origin of fruit. Making love is the only way to have children − and we must be constantly on our guard against the nightmare of artificial insemination.'[38] In August, following Mauricio Kagel's advice perhaps, he had completed a commission from Hans Otte at Bremen Radio: *Solo with Accompaniment*, for unspecified instruments, which earned him a much-needed fee of £150. In September he returned to the talk which he had begun the previous July: a Nachtprogramm for Cologne Radio that also occasioned a renewed assessment of *Two Books of Study*, which was to be included in the programme. Six years had elapsed since its composition and in a Journal entry on 9 July 1964, Cardew reflects on his initial thoughts on *Two Books*, in particular in relation to audience reception:

> *Two Books* were composed without considering the effect on the audience – merely trying to set up a mode of music-making. But just the same, in the course of writing it a few general ideas came up about how the piece might be 'received'. Given the listener's mind as an open white blank (which is never the case), the mind has to be shuttered like a camera so that it can focus on specific music. So in the first notes I imagine the shutter flaps noiselessly sliding over one another until they discover the right aperture.

Now, with numerous performances of *Two Books* behind him, and with at least three other pianists – Richard Bennett, David Tudor and myself – he was now able to take a broader and more advantageous view:

> How different was the activity of the pianists as I originally envisaged it. I imagined each one responding to the other in some clearly defined way: opposing him, supporting him, contradicting and commenting, depending on which elements he had available. And then the other, while providing material for the first player's commentary, is actually commenting on his commentary in just the same way as the other. I had the idea that this would be carried on spontaneously in performance, as though each particle of material was an articulate event that could exist on its own. Later it became clear that such spontaneity appears terribly laboured in performance, the minimal silences for reflection weighing heavily on the listener's ear and destroying all sense of continuity.[39] To correct these disadvantages would require a prohibitive degree of saturation in the material on the part of the performers, and faculties of concentration and fast reactions which would put the task outside the capacity of most humans. The procedure that I now favour consists in each pianist making a more or less complete version, collecting and collating individual elements into articulate but malleable phrases and aggregations adapted to combinations with whatever the other pianist may do, which may be estimated on the basis of the elementary material that he has at his disposal. Thus, these phrases and aggregations can be given the last little push towards making sense in the actual performance (guided by the experience of rehearsals). Only after that amount of instructive work on the

part of the pianists can the spontaneous crystallisation of the elements in performance be expected to occur. But this amount of instructive work on the part of each pianist does produce an interesting adjunct to the piece's general effect: the pianistic styles of the two interpreters are manifested in their ordering of their respective materials, and the piece takes on the character of an argument between two people, each with his own distinctive associations, modes of thinking and phrasing. From these remarks it is clear that there is no direct relationship here between what the composer 'sich denkt' (thinks to himself) while composing the piece, and the effect that the music has on an audience – indeed there is no direct relationship between what the composer 'thinks' and what is heard in performance. [...]

And what has the composer composed if he has no direct influence on the effect of the music? What I composed in this piece – the image that hovered in front of my mind's eye – was a 'musizierweise' (mode of music-making). I invented a way of making music and limited it to such an extent that musicians without constructive ideas of their own are in a position to adopt this 'musizierweise'. And, as in many of my pieces, my aim was not merely to invent some artificial and contrived way of making music, but to invent one that really works and is autonomous (if it wasn't autonomous, it would not be worth putting into a score-form), that is, not *invent*, but express a thought about music in general – what it is, and the way it is made. (Although; God preserve me from asserting that everything the musician does is music – rather all his faculties are musical; music is his way of experiencing). 'Music in General' is only a manner of speaking; actually, I am convinced that Everyman's music is peculiar to him.[40]

There is much food for thought and comment here: firstly, the idea of the pianists spontaneously reacting to one another – 'opposing', 'supporting', 'commenting and 'contradicting' – illustrates just how far Cardew's philosophy of music was sited from that of Cage. Moreover, whereas the silences between events in, say, Cage's *Winter Music* can be indulged simply for what they are – unintended sound or ambient sound, in *Two Books* the silences are imposed upon the structure by the exigencies of performance ('silences for reflection').

And the reference to 'musizierweise' is of particular consequence: it is as if *Treatise* was already germinating in the earlier work. In *Two Books*, as in *Treatise* (albeit in a more abstract, or rather metaphorical way), Cardew is not just expressing musical ideas, he is also expressing ideas *about* music, 'what it is, and the way it is made'. With *Treatise* he took a radical step forward through his realisation that the provision of discrete tones was surfeit to his intention – more, was incompatible with his understanding of what music-making is. With hindsight he recognised, paradoxically it might be said, that in *Two Books* the deployment of tones had simply been inadequate to express the range and depth, the logical consequence of his musical thought at that time. *Two Books* looks forward to *Treatise*, *Treatise* looks back to *Two Books*; there is a thread, a continuity.

The afterthought at the end of the above Journal extract is typical of Cardew: a simple sentence, the penultimate, which cuts deep into meaning, expressing Cardew's belief in music as life-experience, that music is the musician's way of experiencing, that music engages all our faculties, and that we musicians must be infused with the *spirit* of music if our utterances are to engage our listeners. It brings us back to Blake and his importance for Cardew; both artists strove to wrest the idea, and practice, of 'spirituality' from religion.

And the final sentence, in the light of Cardew's later political views, when his purpose was to inspire a unified 'class' response to his music, encapsulates a 'liberal' philosophy of music which in the last decade he criticised with considerable vehemence. For until that time he had always harboured a strong antipathy to the idea of a controlled response to music. On 13 July 1964, amongst the notes on *Two Books*, we find a brief, questioning reference in the Journals: 'All music directed towards making an effect is entertainment music? Music that plans an emotional response is entertainment music. Entertainment music is Ohrenschmaus (food for the ears)? None of these define it.'

And all the while it was the music and art of his American peers, with their occasional appearances in London, that continued to inspire him, offering meaty if temporal sustenance in a mean-spirited English artistic climate dominated by a musical establishment immured within a safety-first mentality spawned by complacency and intolerance. Whereas in its relation to the European avant-garde the English musical establishment vacillated between awe and mistrust, its intractable hostility to Cage, which assumed the status of an artistic principle, could not be moderated. In September 1964 a challenging review of the Merce Cunningham Dance Company at the Phoenix Theatre in London appeared in the *Musical Times*. In it Cardew draws attention to the fact that pieces of music by Cage, Feldman, La Monte Young, Wolff, Toshi Ichiyanagi, and others, 'all unwaveringly rejected or ignored by our more powerful pundits of musical taste (William Glock, Hans Keller, Peter Heyworth, etc.) have slipped, without protest and with a high degree of acceptance from the ballet press, into the ears of the ballet public, and been *enjoyed*'.

Having now completed his translation for Thames and Hudson of Willi Reich's book on Alban Berg he was now offered more work, from October, for a salary of a basic £60 a month for an initial six month period. The first book was by the German author Herbert Frank entitled *'Die das "Neue" nicht fürchten'*, and subtitled *'Managers der Kunst'*. The book deals with the modern art movements of the last hundred years from the perspective of the dealers, patrons and museum directors – a theme that certainly in the later years Cardew would have found of particular interest. In the mid-sixties it was simply a means of acquiring desperately needed funds and he accepted the offer with both resignation and relief. Other translation work occasionally came his way – as when Peters Edition commissioned him to translate the text of Ligeti's *Aventures,* which Ligeti was pleased with and wrote thanking him. Domestically, as the children grew older, there was an even greater strain on their meagre financial resources and adjustments had to be made; in September Emily, the oldest of the four children, started her secondary school career at the City of London School for Girls, where Mariel Cardew was teaching Art, and this would certainly have entailed further expenses. 'Memo. Music is dying and I can't save it' was the mournful entry in the Journal on 29 October.

Nevertheless, work continued on *Treatise* unabated, with another seven pages completed in November, as well as a new graphic composition *Memories of You* – a work which, according to Cardew, I premiered, although neither of us could remember the occasion. An entry in the Journal on 2 November recalls Feldman and his frequent analogies between (his) music and fine art: 'To make music like a painter, who weighs the colour on his brush before folding it into the picture.' And there were concerts including his own music: *Octet '61* at the Institute of Contemporary Arts with David Bedford, Peter Greenham and the composer, and the premiere at Brussels Radio of *Bun No.2* for Orchestra under Mauricio Kagel.

In the Preface I have referred to the two large ledgers from 1961 to 1964 and their general contents. As one would expect many of the letters are from fellow musicians and musical organisations, usually relating to musical performances and scores: among them the BBC; Sir Thomas Armstrong, Principal of the Royal Academy of Music; John Cage – a very down-to-earth, prosaic letter from Stony Point, dated 30 May 1962, complaining about 'blindness, arthritic pains in wrists and feet, congestion in the lungs, economic difficulties'; lively, affectionate and funny letters from Earle Brown, who was also producing records of American and European avant-garde music; rather formal letters from Morton Feldman and David Tudor – the beginnings of what were to become significant and close relationships; letters from the Polish conductor Andrzej Markowski (who conducted *Third Orchestral Piece* in Warsaw); and various communications from fellow composers, including Sylvano Bussotti, Mauricio Kagel, György Ligeti, Gordon Mumma, La Monte Young, as well as the poet Michael Horovitz and myself. There are warm, motherly letters from Mariel; two or three affectionate, grandmaternal letters from Mariel's mother; letters from his brothers – Seth's affectionate and occasionally combative, the seafaring Ennis's in travelogue style from all points on the compass, but with brotherly solicitude; and, when he was away for a longer period than normal, loving letters with detailed accounts of domestic life from Stella, in which the desperate need for more funds to help make ends meet was a constant motif. And yet, scrutinising the bank statements between July 1961 and March 1963, the maximum overdraft (briefly) was around £40, and for much of the time their account was in the black.

Of course, there were a number of other far more prolific correspondents whose letters were kept separately by Cardew himself and to which I refer from time to time throughout these pages: his first wife Ruth, Richard Bennett and Ilona Halberstadt wrote copiously, if not obsessively, and although many of Cardew's letters have not survived (those to Richard Bennett, for example), he seems to have responded with equal alacrity. Cardew enjoyed writing and from early on cultivated an engaging style which captivated many of his correspondents, including some to whom he was relatively unknown.

The New Year, 1965, began with a flurry of concerts; at the end of January the Director of the Rheinische Musikschule, Hugo Wolfram Schmidts, invited Cardew and Frederic Rzewski to Cologne for two two-piano recitals at the Wallraf-Richartz Museum, and there were also two Nachtprogramme for Cologne Radio which featured music by Ives and Cardew's *Two Books of Study*. The first of the Museum concerts included works by Rzewski, Chiari, Pousseur, and La Monte Young's *Two Sounds* which, predictably, infuriated some, but entertained and refreshed the more speculative members of the audience, who listened and observed in relaxed appreciation as Rzewski scraped a tin lid across walls and windows, an activity which was punctuated by brief, piercing cries emitting from a loud speaker.

Cardew's inscrutable performance skills stood him in good stead in what appears to have been the last item in the concert – Giuseppe Chiari's *La Strada*, in which he sat at a desk occasionally dipping his pen into an inkwell. This and other mundane activities gradually emptied the room, according to one eye-witness. Certainly the response was confused and critics seemed subsequently unable to decide whether outrage, scorn or irony should have been the appropriate response; one audacious member of the audience even went so far as to ask whether the composers took the audience for fools. The second concert eschewed such antics and for the most part, in works by David Behrman, Morton Feldman, Michael von Biel and Cardew himself, Rzewski and Cardew sat at their respective pianos. As to their interpretation of Stockhausen's *Plus-Minus*, in the second half of the concert, the music critic of the *Köln Stadt-Anzeiger* preferred to keep his own counsel, although he was at pains to explain that the score absolved the composer from all responsibility for the resulting 'sound-in-performance'. The Journals also mention a Michael von Biel concert in Aachen (January 1965), and although the distance from Cologne to Aachen is only seventy kilometres we can perhaps assume that Cardew did not make the journey solely to be a member of the audience. This, after all, was a reunion of like-minded, musical colleagues who had pioneered the experimental music programmes in London in 1962 and Cardew's reciprocal participation in Aachen would have been more than welcome.[41]

In between the German concerts, in a Journal entry on 31 January, Cardew's poetic imagination and inventiveness finds expression in what is clearly a love poem, although the object of the prose-poem remains a matter of speculation:

I compass
You my North Pole
My needle swings in response to temporary proximity of lesser magnets.
Under normal conditions it points directly at you. Your all-pervasive magnetic current – the hot spot wrapped in instantly melting ice – tugs at my needle, inducing a tingling flow of particles.
As my stream disappears into the ground, I am happy in the thought that it is seeping back to you.

And on 7 February a list of 'principles' in the Journal reminds, enjoins him to 'forget' the general but to 'remember' the particular:

Principles
1. Forget.
Forget facts – they're no use.
Forget what you see hear etc.
Forget the jokes that are told you (why? so that they are still funny next time).
Forget what you understand, for it's finished.
Forget what you learn.
Forget your name and identity.
Forget your loves and hates.
Forget your interpretations.
Above all forget what you translate.
Forget this message.

Remember your front door key.
Remember your wife's weak points (so as not to keep on touching them).
Remember your children's birthdays.

Remember how awful it was before you were married.
In fact remember all your sufferings.
Remember to shut the door when you go out.

This reads like an ode to the practicalities of life, to day-to-day obligations and duties, to the need for creating a simple *modus vivendi*, to the sanctity of the present. 'Forget' connotes the negation of theorizing, intellectualizing, labelling, harbouring, bearing grudges, living in the past, property-owning, self-expression. Human beings adopt these stances, singly and in combination, thus diminishing and impoverishing their lives. And finally, 'Above all forget what you translate'. Does this refer to his translating work? Or is 'translate' used more abstractly? The 'above all' elicits further speculation and is a typical provocation.

Cardew arrived back in Rome in February to resume his studies with Petrassi. The family had remained in England and he rented a room in Via della Pace of typically spartan bias; a pervasive and unrelenting discomfort, freezing in winter, with a shared toilet at some distance along an endless passage – it suited him well. Peszko, too, rejoined the class but saw less of his colleague socially during this period, although Cardew would occasionally visit Peszko and his wife nearby in Via Giulia. Cardew was introduced to several of Peszko's Hungarian friends, among whom was the pianist Szuszanna Sirokay – dedicatee of the second *Winter Potato*. By the end of the month he had completed *Bun No.1*, his assignment for the Petrassi course, *Volo Solo* – I had rashly asked him to write a virtuoso piano piece – and had finished his translation assignment, Frank's *Managers der Kunst*.

And all the time *Treatise* continued to represent a condition of latency and would materialise in a number of mutations, including *Volo Solo* and *Bun No.2*. Occasionally, Cardew would express his dissatisfaction with these 'transcriptions'; fundamentally, at any rate in relation to his own artistic imperatives, he doubted the efficacy of traditional notation – 'the writing down of music is in process of disintegrating'. In fact, after *Volo Solo* and until the political music – a period of around six years – he found only occasional use for it (as in parts of *The Great Learning*) and within a matter of months this radical departure from the compositional mode was to be hastened and vindicated by his music-making with AMM.

In a Journal entry, 14 February, St.Valentine's Day, he pens his response to a recent dance performance:

Teatro di Movimento. It's nice to see girls dancing. But why do they always fall into such expressive conventionalism? It is the same with Bussotti. And then nowadays it is not sufficient just to show something like a demonstration (like my piece for Petrassi); something has to actually happen on the stage or in the music like in Cage, Christian (Wolff), La Monte etc. In fact today that seems to me really the only interesting thing. Perhaps there is still room for the demonstration that is totally unrelated and unreferred (as far as possible). But not much.

A very empty-eyed feeling today – after writing to Stella.

The second half of this paragraph is perplexing. The characterisation of *Bun No 1* as a piece in which something is 'shown', 'demonstrated', is to contrast it with the music of Cage, Wolff and La Monte Young in which things 'actually happen'. Yes, in Cage one follows a sequence, wide-eyed and open-eared, of unpredictable aural events – of greater or lesser sonic interest. Similarly with Wolff, except that there is the significant addition, in his works of the sixties, of a dynamic interaction between players – an added bonus for the alert listener. La Monte Young's early minimalist pieces, featuring the bowed disk or the sustained perfect 5th, are more difficult to perceive in this way; of course something 'happens' to the sound in its course: it changes, through human agency or frailty, through the objective nature of the sound source itself, and so on. A La Monte Young piece is best described as a 'happening' – something that continues, the end is not legible in the beginning – as opposed to a sequence of events (Cage and Wolff).

But wherein lies the essential difference between these examples and *Bun No.1*? Cardew implies that nothing happens in *Bun No. 1* – that it relates, pertains, to nothing. Perhaps the idea of 'demonstrating', 'showing' something, refers to Wittgenstein. 'What *can* be shown *cannot* be said.' *Tractatus* 4.1212. Perhaps *Bun No.1* is a 'demonstration' piece which cannot 'say' anything in the sense that is normally expected of a piece of music. An orchestration of an abstract idea, of a process? Of *Treatise*? A metamusic?[42]

Thus, given Cardew's preoccupations at the time, when the editor of the *Musical Times*, Andrew Porter, gave Cardew a book on notation to review for the March 1965 issue he may or may not have realised that such a commission was tantamount to an incitement to an act of damnation even if, in this particular case, with faint praise. The very title of the book, by Gardner Read, *Music Notation: A Manual of Modern Practice* set it up for the most penetrating and uncompromising critique by a master practitioner of the art of deciphering and creating contemporary musical notation. And the editor of the *Musical Times*, an admirer of Cardew's work, was well aware of this.

In Cardew's view the book defaulted on several important counts, to the extent that its very title was rendered inaccurate and the author was immediately taken to task for his claim in the Introduction that 'in automatic command of this basic technique, the notator or performer should be able to solve the crisis of a new idea with a modicum of logic and common sense'. For Cardew, however worthy the qualities of logic and common sense, such solutions – if indeed any existed – were far more dependent on intuition, insight and imagination, and Gardner's proposition provoked a string of rhetorical questions from him:

And how can the practical musician solve the crisis of a new notation? What about the ideas that the notation itself inspires and fosters? And what about the beautiful concept of 'paper music', meaning a notation that is in itself eloquent and expressive – and autonomous, and hence the solace of composers who have to make do with few performances, like Anton Webern (or is the scarcity of performance a direct result of the fact that his works are limited or even damaged by any 'mere' interpretation?)? And what are the forces behind the recent outbreak of unconventional and even non-musical systems of notation, and what changes are they producing in the world of musical sound? [43]

However, as Cardew acknowledged, this was not the brief which Gardner set out for himself; his book was a manual of modern conventional practice and such questions did not concern him, although they 'would make an absorbing and difficult book – a book that would bring down vituperation, contempt and ridicule on its (hypothetically) unsuspecting author's head'. The review continued and ended in an ironic vein:

Our reverence and esteem are reserved for books like this one by Gardner Read, who has painstakingly and even warmly performed a fundamentally boring and unrewarding task, thus fully earning him enormous credit and the gratitude of music teachers everywhere [...]
Altogether a book to help young composers win prizes.

Stella's letters to Cornelius in Italy are tender and loving, mostly describing her domestic life and the children, their foibles and predispositions. She writes about their school and future education, about the possibility of a loan from the London County Council to buy a house, and that with more space she would be able to paint again. Several times she writes of their love for one another and the joy she derives from this – 'the sweetest music to my ears'. And yet a barely concealed desperation vitiates the crumbs of comfort and optimism with which she seeks to convince her husband that 'everything is alright'.

On 15 February there are more references to Stella and music in the Journal:

I have to watch my step, when so many aspects of my experience begin to fit into a single theory, namely that to acquire the necessary intensity of sensibility to something you have to be withdrawn from that something. e.g. My sexual sensibility to Stella is heightened by my absence from her.

My reluctance to involve myself with great music of the past, and also my lack of desire to go around digging the 'culture' of Rome (except in so far as it is expressed in the air – i.e. that I am breathing the same air that stimulated that culture).

That Beethoven found his most intensely and sensually beautiful sounds as he got deafer and deafer and less able to actually enjoy them.

Stupid Theory.

Ten days later, 25 February, he parodies the musician's – or music lover's – penchant for self-referral:

"I'm just a musician"
"I'm not just a musician"
"I'm not necessarily a musician"
"I'm more of a musician than a — "
"I prefer being a musician"
"I am a musical person" (v.Clarisse)[44]
"I have a weakness for music"
"Music is my life"
"Music is the road to salvation"
"Music makes life bearable"
"The Musician in me"

There is also more evidence in the Journals at this time of his continuing absorption in Wittgenstein's work; in fact, Wittgenstein now motored his existence to such a degree that it had reached a point where, in some perhaps arcane and inscrutable way, it had to be objectified. Wittgenstein's philosophy now assumed a centrality in Cardew's life, as we shall see in our discussion of *Treatise*. On the 21 February some brief passages from the *Remarks on the Foundations of Mathematics* are quoted without comment:

W. *Foundations of Maths*. p.180e. 'It might be said: Experiment – Calculation are poles between which human activities move.'

Cardew then turns via Wittgenstein to Gödel, mathematician and logician, for further amplification of his concerns:

> p.177e 'It might justly be asked what importance Gödel's proof has for our work. For a piece of mathematics cannot solve a problem of the type that troubles *us*. The answer is that the *situation*, into which such a proof brings us, is of interest to us. "What are we to say now?" – That is our theme.'

Gödel had deduced that it is impossible to prove the consistency of a formal system, which contains the arithmetic of natural numbers, within the system itself. Thus with Cardew's *Treatise* the original rules must be jettisoned when a new situation, that of actual performance, propels the work into a new dimension.

> p.180e 'I have asked myself: if mathematics has a purely fanciful application, isn't it still mathematics? – But the question arises: don't we call it 'mathematics' only because e.g. there are transitions, bridges from the fanciful to non-fanciful applications? That is to say: should we say that people possessed a mathematics if they used calculating, operating with signs, *merely* for occult purposes?'

And on the 27 February there is more philosophical speculation:

> One idea keeps coming back to me. Unlike many it is easy to remember. It remembers itself.
> That our unhappiness and frustration is one of the more profound and beautiful things in life and has therefore to be cherished accordingly ie. Don't try to evade suffering. (that is cutting off your nose to spite your face?)
> But seek it out? That is very disgusting:
> Ah, here is another opportunity to suffer!
> But really we suffer from our loves and pleasures most of all. And that is supposed to be delight. So where does the suffering of loneliness and pain stand? They are supposed to be misery – perhaps that is why they are profound and beautiful.

The unremitting desperation which Stella's letters from London expressed prompted further reflection on the same theme:

> Unhappy?
> Unhappiness is the one thing that keeps me going. If I wasn't unhappy I'd be dead.

When I think of Stella I think of her in tears, in a panic, unable to cope, dreading the future, wondering what is going to happen.

Seeing her thus I get sad, melancholic, bitter and even alcoholic. She should write gay happy letters of how full her life is – then I too might be able to take some interest in my surroundings.

Killing thoughts.

My unhappiness is so profound that I can't even express it. And of course one must not express it to other people: if there's one thing worse than self-pity its other people's pity. So you better just accept their indifference.[45]

And with the advent of the Roman spring his mood had not changed, though now finding a poetic, rather than a philosophical expression, for his condition:

Night and day
The agonizing night swishing around me.
In the day, in the silence between thunderclaps the wailing of children becomes audible.
I and my window rattle.[46]

For Stella there was temporary solace when Ennis Cardew took a room in the neighbourhood and paid her and the children frequent visits. Ennis, who was then a merchant seaman, the first mate on a liberty ship, had arrived in Southampton to collect his Master's ticket and had been injured in a road accident when returning with friends from a social gathering. He suffered severe leg injuries and spent a considerable time in hospital. Stella would invite him for supper and his genial company would divert her thoughts, raise her spirits.

March had seen Cardew back in London to provide music for the Canadian director Allan King's film *Great Escape*, for which he received a fee of £150. The experience prompted the following thought, jotted down in pencil and undated on a scrap of paper: 'What sound does the film-director hear in his mind when – watching the fine-cut of the film he is making – he suddenly cries "Music" at a particular point?' And *Autumn 60* receives a cryptic mention ('*Autumn 60* programme on "what composers hear"') – a reference, perhaps, to the situation of the conductor of *Autumn 60* as he elicits music from the ensemble without knowing precisely what sounds will ensue?

On 24 April Cardew participated as recitalist in the Third Nuova Consonanza Festival at the Teatro delle Arti in Rome with a wide-ranging programme of mainly experimental music: Joel Chadabe's *Three Ways of Looking at a Square*, Christian Wolff's *For Prepared Piano*, his own *February Pieces*, George Brecht's *Incidental Music*, Charles Ives' *Three-page Sonata*, Earle Brown's *Four Systems*, and a part of Michael von Biel's *Book for Three*.[47]

His inclusion of a Fluxus piece, Brecht's *Incidental Music* (performed, incidentally, during the interval), is an indication of his continuing concern for 'metamusics', for performance pieces which operate in 'twilight zones between the different media'. George Brecht's 'events' – which was how Brecht preferred to describe his pieces – originated in the New School for Social Research in New York where Brecht had attended John Cage's classes in experimental music. 'The pieces turned out quite theatrical when performed, as interesting visually, atmospherically, as aurally, though they were performed with as much economy, with as little fuss, as possible.'[48]

Incidental Music is one of the 'events' which make up Brecht's *Water Yam* – a work which Cardew performed on more than one occasion, with a balletic grace and elegance, and in which his impeccable display of relaxed concentration, unflappability and sheer nerve would invariably serve to heighten the extreme tension built up during the performance. Another of Petrassi's students, Claudio Annibaldi, recalls describing to Petrassi and his students the next morning the 'perfect aplomb' with which Cardew performed. Cardew, who was also present at the gathering, remained silent during Annibaldi's account: 'smiling gently'. The score reads as follows:

INCIDENTAL MUSIC

Five Piano Pieces,
any number playable successively or simultaneously, in any order and combination, with one another and with other pieces.

1.
The piano seat is tilted on its base and brought to rest against a part of the piano.

2.
Wooden blocks.
A single block is placed inside the piano. A block is placed upon this block, then a third upon the second, and so forth, singly, until at least one block falls from the column.

3.

Photographing the piano situation.

4.

Three dried peas or beans are dropped, one after another, onto the keyboard.[49]

5.

The piano seat is suitably arranged, and the performer seats himself.

Summer, 1961. G. Brecht

In his description of *Water Yam* in the aforementioned *Volo Solo* programme Cardew clearly prefigures his own verbal scores of the late sixties – in particular *Schooltime Compositions*; it is significant, for example, that he stresses its educative potential (see Appendix 1).

The American composer, Alvin Curran, though not a student of Petrassi, saw Cardew frequently during this period; they would meet in bars, eat together, and Cardew would visit Curran in his apartment in Trastevere on the Tiber river, enlisting his help in copying the parts of *Bun No. 1*.[50] Curran had arrived in Rome the previous year, having read music at Yale, and recalls that by that time Cardew had already attained mythological status within avant-garde circles – a man with a unique cast of mind who had boldly and single-mindedly rejected the prevailing mores, and whose compositions and music-making were seen and admired as a constant and refreshing infraction of current musical laws. In retrospect, Curran regards Cardew affectionately as his teacher, and it was on the streets of Rome amongst the flotsam and jetsam of artists and intellectuals and hangers-on, during 'nights of cheap meals and cheap drink', that the relationship was born and nurtured. Cardew's insight, and foresight, at that time, were manifest not only through the medium of conversation, with its frequent shafts of brilliance, but through the infinite resource of his notational experiments and the originality, the waywardness, of his practical music-making.

Curran recalls that in the early part of the summer of 1965 he had been invited to contribute a composition to a concert organized by the American Academy. The piece was for violin, clarinet and piano and Cardew played the piano part, music of a transcendental complexity – as was the custom in contemporary music circles in Italy at that time – which he dispatched, after a dram or two of whisky, with supreme nonchalance and prodigious accuracy.

'Integrity for him lay in a refusal to clarify his intentions'. Thus Anita Brookner describes one of her characters. Cardew, too, rather than explaining what he meant, preferred to 'blur', or sometimes to illuminate, to *demonstrate* through the creation of original musical artefacts and live performance. Curran recalls Cardew showing him pages of the nascent *Treatise* and soliciting his opinion, asking him how he would interpret such and such symbols; and Curran, taken aback – for to him these notations were quite outlandish – would hazard spontaneous responses, including extravagant and improbable suggestions, which Cardew would duly and silently note. These sessions also served to disabuse Curran of much of the theoretical clutter he had accumulated and to which he had become temporarily wedded through his musical education; they inspired him not only to search for and explore new musical horizons, but to a commitment to being, in his own words, 'a full-time, life-time outsider'.

Cardew's second *Winter Potato* was completed in May and performed for Maestro Petrassi and his class. (Howard Skempton attributes its expansive nature to Cardew's sojourn in Italy and 'his susceptibility to the blandishments of Italian cultural life'). Together with the two earlier pieces, from '61 and '64 it formed the *Three Winter Potatoes* which were later published, in 1966, by Universal Edition. The three pieces are dedicated individually 'for Andrew Porter' (No.1), 'for Szuszanna Sirokay' (No.2), and 'for Francesca Astaldi' (No.3), the name appearing at the end of the piece – although at the beginning of the published score there is a dedication as if for the work as a whole: 'gratefully dedicated to Barbara and Allan Bryant, music lovers'. The Journals also record a payment: 'Pno Piece for Allan Bryant (£50)' – which clearly refers to the *Winter Potatoes*.[51]

May also saw a brief return visit to London to discuss some reviewing assignments with Andrew Porter and to participate in a concert of Experimental Music organized by myself at the South-West Essex Technical College where I held a lectureship.[52] The concert consisted of four works: La Monte Young's *Poem for Chairs, Tables, Benches, etc.*, Michael von Biel's *World II*, Cardew's *Solo with Accompaniment* and *Treatise* (pages 89-106); the performers were John White (tuba), Roger Smalley (piano), David Bedford (accordion), Clem Adelman (saxophone), the composer (guitar and conductor) and myself (piano).

The College boardroom made an excellent venue; its heavy Directors' desks, exuding ennui and self-importance, pushed and dragged across the impressive, largely uncarpeted floor in *Poem*, produced sounds of astonishing richness and penetration.[53] And, inexplicably, it housed a splendid Steinway grand piano which was never moved from the boardroom and therefore rarely played. The concert was announced in the pages of the *Financial Times*, accompanied by a text provided by Cardew who, presumably, had managed to persuade the music editor of the cultural significance of this event in Walthamstow, East London, a worthy but cheerless locality which for its readers would have conjured up rather intimidating images of working-class probity and William Morris socialism. Cardew's text began in declamatory style – more appropriate to a town crier of old than a contemporary, bourgeois newspaper:

> In Walthamstow tomorrow afternoon at 2.20 a concert of Experimental Music is to take place. It is the latest in a long straggling series of such concerts in this country. It is a sign that the seed of a new kind of musical life planted here by the American composer, John Cage, in 1956, is still growing, albeit in rather out-of-the-way places.[54]

The strategy could be likened to a guerrilla campaign where members of the band made occasional sorties into enemy territory, caused disruption, even made recruits, before withdrawing to base to reassess and refine tactics; the analogy is not too extreme. Cardew's Walthamstow text was both a statement of intent and an expression of a growing concern for the audience, for the social implications of music-making in general and experimental music-making in particular; it recognized that it was incumbent upon the practitioners of the New Music to address the problem of communication – not that the music itself had to become necessarily more immediately accessible, but that it was important to create optimum conditions under which the listener could *experience* the music. A particular stumbling block was the fact that concerts of Experimental Music often included works which were radically different from one another, each of them providing more food for listening and thought than could readily be assimilated in a single evening.

> The audience's neurotic response is thus explained: no sooner had they begun to get their teeth into one set of problems and sensations, than a completely different set would be set before them [...] This means that their (the compositions) best chance of creating understanding in an audience is to expand freely in an unlimited amount of time. And since different performances of the same piece can be very different in character (if different musicians are performing, for example) each piece should be performed a number of times.[55]

For Cardew the repertory idea, borrowed from the theatre, provided the ideal solution; thus a repertoire of twenty compositions, for example, could be booked for a two-month season at a London theatre, each composition receiving three performances spaced over two months. Unfortunately, even in the heady days of the mid-sixties such an ambitious and profligate scheme would have been given short shrift by theatre impresarios. Comparable series of concerts did take place – several years later in the heyday of the Scratch Orchestra – but venues were diverse and scattered, determined by a complex matrix of idiosyncratic choices, circumstance and necessity.

Back in Italy the twin themes of solitude and love persist, inspiring on three separate days in June a page of 'poetry' in the Journal:

12.VI.65.

The Same

So I rebel against the international world of Pleasure.
Solitude is my rebellious act.
What is its power?
It disintegrates my capacity to enjoy.
What wd I be saying if I was at the Ritz, drunk, with a lovely black girl in a grass skirt?
The Same.

16.VI.65.

Eyes

Beautiful green brown puddles that children drown [?] [word unclear] in.
Wide black pupils through which you look straight into a brain seething with mindless desire.

24.VI.65.

Homemade

Love
is the bread
we live on.

To make love
is to eat it,
toasted,
with butter and jam.

In the first poem the intense feeling of solitude is all the more dislocating for being two-fold. Certainly he missed the family and family life to which there is no doubt he was committed and which nurtured his 'capacity to enjoy'.[56] But there was also an artistic solitude; *Treatise* had created this condition from which, for a person of Cardew's integrity, there could be no retraction; he had reached this point in his musical career through the fantasy, the vision, and the continuity, of his musical thought, through which, and in all manner of circumstances, his music-making was driven and its viability and consequence tested. And *Treatise* could only be superseded by an act of comparable boldness of imagination and ambition which, in 1966 and before its completion, it was. The second 'poem' seems to be addressed to somebody in particular, somebody absent, for whom the mind and body craves, whilst the third is a simple, homely paean to love.

On 4 July the Journal spawns a lewd image, which is described precisely and with considerable relish: 'Girl enters bank with big Alsatian (or something). Bends over to write a fat cheque. Dog takes opportunity to lick and snuffle at her tight-jeaned arsehole. She quivers, straightens, cashes cheque, and both exeunt.'

Petrassi's course ended in June although the final students' concert took place a month later, on 15th July, when *Bun for Orchestra No. 1* received its premiere by the Orchestra dell'Accademia Nazionale di Santa Cecilia under Daniele Paris in a large auditorium in the via della Conciliazione. Claudio Annibaldi recalls being disappointed; it was far less radical than he had expected – or perhaps he had been unable to recognize its radicalism; in any case Cardew was never one to confirm expectations. After the concert there was a dinner in a restaurant in via della Lungara attended by, among others, Petrassi and his wife, the student composers, the conductor, and the composer Mario Bertoncini. Annibaldi, who was present at the concert, remembers Cardew neither at the concert nor at the dinner after the concert, although he was certainly at the final rehearsal. According to Annibaldi this may well have been the day before (or earlier?); Cardew could have left Rome on the same day and did not attend the actual concert. The following reflections in the Journal, dated 15th July, seem to indicate that they were written in England.

Taking Horace down to Rachel every day, in her front yard a spell seems to descend on me. I am twice as slow as other people in reacting, unable to take in the situation – Rachel has washed her hair, elastic bands still in push-chair, Horace labouring upstairs, now his back is turned I ought to be half-way up the street already – meanwhile another parent has been (bearded, I remember), deposited his child and left again in what seems like the space of a second. Only in the zebra crossing leading to Hollywood Road, in sight of home, do I pick up speed again – and hurry back to write this. Down there I seem to 'lose track', like in a piece of music where everything suddenly goes away.

Perhaps it is *Treatise* doing this to me.

And yet the Journal states that on 23 July Cardew left Rome to return to London, his by now customary itinerary taking him first to Vienna – doubtless for a few days with Schwertsik – then to Cologne, and finally home. Did he then return to Rome for a few days sometime after the 15? But why the need to return to England for an equally brief period after the final rehearsal? Why miss the first performance? There is no mention of any commitment in London during that week in the Journal.

It is difficult to assess Cardew's Italian experience, mainly because it was subsumed within the *Treatise* experience. He seems to have maintained a distance from Italian culture,[57] apart from the language, which he learnt for mainly practical reasons: the necessity of dealing with everyday domestic requirements, especially when the family were with him. And gregarious as he was it would have been difficult for him, indeed uncharacteristic, to have resisted the allurements of Italian and specifically Roman life. Musically, it was an exciting period in Italy; the avant-garde was flourishing – despite, or perhaps because of, the calculated opposition from a conservative musical establishment – and much discussed in the mainstream press; moreover, the Palermo Festival had established itself as one of the leading contemporary music festivals in Europe. As well as musicians Nuova Consonanza in Rome included poets and painters, and composers such as Scelsi, Evangelisti, Pennisi, and the conductor Daniele Paris were prominently active in the organisation. However, the influence of the American avant-garde was still marginal at that time and the jealously-guarded European identity of Italian music would have been anathema to Cardew. The 'two tall bare trees of the Italian avant-garde establishment', Luigi Nono and Luciano Berio, reigned supreme, unchallenged.

In England there was social change, too, manifesting itself in the development, diffusion and exploitation of, in particular, the youth culture, where quick and easy money could be made. Yet again, in the spring and summer of 1964 and 1965, the Establishment had overreacted – this time to the visit to Clacton-on-Sea and to Brighton of around one thousand 'Mods'. Mods were really about style, rather than moral disorder, and with a less fearsome image than their deadly rivals, with whom they were often paired in the public imagination – the visually more intimidating 'Rockers'. Mods displayed a slick elegance and a dandy element; continental *chic* – and they were largely apolitical. It was a fashion-based phenomenon which Cardew probably did not even notice.

Pop music was now at its zenith and had sealed its dominance within the youth culture; it was the era of Beatle-mania, of the Rolling Stones, The Who. Classical musicians responded, too, and were pleased to be rubbing shoulders and occasionally working with fashionable rock musicians – as, for example, the composer David Bedford did. Yet despite the fact that through the children and their friends he had easy and continuous access to it – Gabriel, in particular, was *au fait* with all the latest trends and possessed many records – Cardew showed no interest in the popular music of the time, rarely venturing outside the orbit of jazz, which he loved: Charlie Parker, Thelonius Monk, Ray Charles, Billie Holliday and the great Blues artists. Nor for that matter did he ever buy records of classical music; his purchases were invariably of jazz.

Can this indifference (or was it a stronger sentiment, a more considered, if unformulated, critique?) to popular music be explained? Since there is no recollection within circles of friends and family of any discussion of the phenomena of pop culture at that time we can only speculate. It is unlikely that he heard the music other than on disc and radio; his experience of it would therefore have been inadequate, hardly authentic. A few years earlier, as a young bachelor, he may have regarded the venues as opportunities for venery pursuits – the (sexual) pleasure principle – but this was no longer viable. Hearing and over-hearing the music from Gabriel's room it probably struck him as musically meretricious, tame even, and therefore not worth a second thought. Yet its omnipresence and unavoidability, its insistent role in family life may have provoked thoughts in relation to its function, and in this respect his analysis and critique would have been both harsh and radical, even anticipating the reasons for his denunciation of (capitalist) popular culture in the seventies. Furthermore, in his own stepson he had the advantage of an on site case-study, although Gabriel's casual attitude to school at that time would not necessarily have invoked Cardew's censure.

The adherents of pop he would have identified as enfeebled consumers, addicts, victims; pop diminished the sense of human agency, of *leading* one's life, and for Cardew that would have been its greatest heresy. It inculcated delusory (bourgeois) ideas of freedom, galvanising the young into febrile, energetic movement, to a condition of animality, thereby holding them in bondage. Pop music was an agent for entrenchment – not change, and could therefore never lead to discovery, let alone revelation. It released a latent pagan energy which could always be contained, controlled, manipulated; its volatility disguised a deadening conformity, a quiescence; pop music was *reflective* of a society in which it would not, could not, intervene creatively or confrontationally. Even its apparent excesses were modulated, marketed, sold. Thus might the argument have run.

My own feeling is that Cardew found pop music's manifold deceits and contrivances irritating, even objectionable: a sham spontaneity, synthetic emotion (professional soulfulness), its theatricality – the 'pool of light':

The theatrical situation arouses disgust in me. The stage world is lit from one side only. A thin gaudy veneer is all that is necessary to reflect the light, a thin film of colour, like a flower child's cloak concealing decomposing undergarments and undernourished flesh.[58]

Yet I think it is unlikely that its commercialism would have been an issue for him – as it became in the later years when his analysis was all-round and more penetrating; after all, Cardew enjoyed and admired much American movie music – commercial music, *par excellence.*

The summer of 1965 began peacefully and uneventfully with the family in Cornwall, where they were joined by Stella's sister Freda. The oppressive reality of a worsening economic condition, which loomed large as late summer approached, was alleviated by a cluster of engagements in the autumn: in September, the Scottish artist Mark Boyle[59] organized a performance of pages 45-64, 74, 89-127 of *Treatise*, work in progress, at the Theatre Royal in Stratford, East London,[60] and there followed, for Cardew, three concerts in Holland, including Stockhausen's *Plus-Minus*, with Rzewski. There was also a commission, in September, for music for a TV film entitled *The Girl who loved Robots*, written by Peter Everett and produced by Kenith Trodd.

However, the family's financial insecurity was compounded by a protracted dispute with their landlady at Redcliffe Square which was coming to a head and eventually precipitated a move. For the house to be profitably sold Stella Cardew, who was a rent-controlled tenant, had to be persuaded to vacate the property. Irked by the Cardews' reluctance to comply with her wishes the landlady, a psychoanalyst by profession, in a combative mood somewhat at odds with the ethical code of her vocation, had resorted to the threat of coercive action, although this eventually gave way to the more liberal, more efficacious tactic of financial inducement, and for a few hundred pounds the Cardews agreed to move out.

While Stella and the children remained in Cornwall Cornelius and Freda returned to London to flat-hunt. They finally decided on a large, newly-refurbished, seven-bedroomed, top-storey flat nearby in Nevern Square which, at £21 a week, necessitated a financial commitment they could ill afford. The family moved in on 20 October together with a posse of lodgers who occupied the three large bedrooms at the end of the flat and whom, as Stella recalls, they never saw – so capacious was the accommodation, which also boasted a huge sitting-room with a red carpet, one old chair and a piano, as well as a large kitchen and two bathrooms. The economic strain was not the only disadvantage; the flat looked out onto the busy Warwick Road and Stella recalls that at first the traffic noise was such that she could barely hear herself read to the children, although after a few months its insistence had somehow secured it an acceptability and she rarely noticed it. And there were attractive features such as the stately lift, all glass and brass and with a rope handle, which moreover boasted its own permanent operator – a solicitous, portly Scottish caretaker, who zealously supervised all comings and goings into and out of the Mansions.[61]

Stella recalls a considerable density of physical activity at the flat at Nevern Square; despite its expanse, it always seemed crowded. The feeling of claustrophobia was aggravated by frequent bouts of tension. People of a variety of dispositions stayed with them, some of whom seemed to be suffering from multiple privations and cramping emotional disabilities, such that the flat, or at least a sizeable part of it, was encompassed about with clouds of heart-searching, regret and discontent. Inevitably, it created a dispiriting situation that was deleterious to family harmony. Nor could they escape for, say, two or three hours, to find solace and a relative solitude simply in another place; a lack of money meant that Cornelius and Stella rarely went out together, except to the occasional concert when Mariel Cardew or a friend would baby-sit for them.

Musician friends were frequent visitors, casually or pre-arranged; and however parlous their situation, however frugal their day-to-day living, Stella would magically rustle up something to eat. The Cardews were notoriously welcoming and companionable hosts and their household exuded a comforting beneficence. And there were longer-term visits from friends and family whose presence they welcomed and appreciated: Freda and her young son Matteo, who seems to have been a disruptive influence, stayed until Stella gave birth to her third son, Walter Emery, on 14 February, and their German friends Klaus and Isolde stayed for a comparable period; Klaus practical and brotherly, Isolde beautiful and talented – though they, too, were not altogether happy with their relationship and each was probably speculating around, even planning, a future without the other. Another guest, Enrique Brinkmann, recalls an occasion when Klaus Koch, a sensitive, genial man, in a spontaneous act of generosity, gave Cardew his Braun record player – an expensive, state-of-the-art piece of equipment at that time, a sacrifice which demonstrated a warmth of feeling and admiration for Cardew.

Stella was burdened with an exhausting routine of cooking (she was the lone cook), housework, feeding and looking after her own and often other children, tasks which she accomplished for the most part single-handedly. To add to her travails her son Walter had contracted a virus during birth, and at two months had to be taken into hospital. At five months – a delicate, frail baby – he was receiving physiotherapy and Stella had to take him to St. George's hospital in Tooting two or three times a week. It was later discovered that he had a heart problem. Her morale was further undermined by, perhaps contributed to, the fact that Emily and Gabriel were unsettled at school; Gabriel's education at Holland Park Comprehensive was blighted by drug-taking and chronic truancy while Emily had decided that she wanted to change schools; marooned in a traditional, academically-orientated girls' public school, to which she felt profoundly unsuited, she envied the degree of freedom, both physical and spiritual, that her brother and his peers seemed to enjoy at Holland Park. She eventually left, attended Dartington Hall boarding school in Devon for less than a year, then a comprehensive school in Putney, South London for a similar length of time, before returning to the City of London school where she finally completed her schooling. Education for Emily had been an extremely unhappy, traumatic experience.

From time to time Stella would reproach Cornelius for his apparent indifference to her plight; his reaction would be to withdraw further from the family and, in response no doubt to private imperatives, to compose, thus asserting a jealously-guarded territoriality of spirit. And yet he did enjoy many aspects of family life, like the occasional picnic with the children and friends in Nevern Square or Holland Park. And when Emily needed help with her school homework he was always generous with his time. He also encouraged her in her interest in Native American culture, bringing home presents from his visits to reservations in the United States. In particular Emily recalls a photograph, relating to The Battle of Wounded Knee, of the frozen bodies of massacred Sioux Indians which she and Cornelius would return to again and again. Aldus Books, too, had begun to publish books on the subject, including a pictorial history of the Native Americans. Cardew could be very good with children; he would introduce them to adventure and encourage them to explore and question – especially in the summer months in Cornwall where the sea and the countryside would inspire thoughts of risk and danger and where he was, literally, in his element.

For all this, and notwithstanding Cardew's extra-marital relations, of which Stella had intimations, and possibly knowledge, he and Stella continued to enjoy a warm, close relationship and a precarious harmony was maintained. Stella recalls that Herman Hesse was a writer for whom they both felt considerable affinity at that time (like Hesse Cardew was deeply sceptical of the substance and trajectory of European Art); Stella valued especially *Narcissus and Goldmund*, her husband admired *The Glass Bead Game*.

During this period, and subsequently, Cardew's relationship with Sheila Kasabova continued to occupy him, to which the frequent veiled references in the Journals bear witness. She would attend his concerts and performances, suffering the anonymity the situation demanded, forced like all mistresses to lead a shadowy, conscience-stricken existence. She too was aware of his infidelities, at home and abroad, but if Cardew was often dissimulating, he was also careful not to commit any major indiscretions, although occasionally, overcome by a quietly destructive candour, he would reveal hurtful details.

The year ended with a move aimed at securing a temporary respite from economic hardship and instability: in December Cardew returned to Aldus Books who, happily, always seemed willing to offer him employment, and on this occasion at an annual salary of £1150.[62] Allan King's film *Great Escape*, with Cardew's music, was shown on TV, and in the Journals Cardew notes the completion of *Three Winter Potatoes*, presumably with some revisions since the three individual pieces are dated December '61, May '65 and June '64 respectively. December was also enlivened with a visit by Stockhausen, which is noted briefly in the Journals.

Artistically, the early part of 1966 was an extremely fruitful period for Cardew. He had begun playing with AMM and had been offered some teaching at the Leeds School of Art which was a particularly lively place at that time. As well as the English painter Patrick Hughes and the Canadian Robin Page, whom Cardew greatly admired, the American artist George Brecht was also teaching there. Brecht was worldly-wise, world-weary, kind and warm. Cardew admired Brecht's thinking about art, as we have seen through his performances of Brecht's work, and enjoyed his company which, if he had not consumed too much alcohol, was a delight.[63] Brecht was a ruined voluptuary; he was not vain, nor self-seeking, unlike some of his peers. He was not a star, although one day he might well acquire a legendary status.

There were also notable performances of Cardew's work at that time: in April *Volo Solo* and *Treatise* with David Bedford and myself at the American Artists' Center in Paris; a premiere of *Solo with Accompaniment* in Bremen in May; and in June Peters Edition published *Two Books of Study for Pianists*. There were also more performances, in Germany and France, of *Plus-Minus* with Rzewski. I recall the April trip to Paris: David Bedford and I duly arrived at Nevern Square whence Cardew was driving us to Heathrow in his Mini. However, he was unable to find his passport, which, methodically and calmly, he continued to search for long after, as it seemed to Bedford, Stella and myself, the last possible time of departure for Heathrow. When he finally came across it we had 20 minutes to get to the airport, which Cardew achieved with some miraculously fast and cool driving.

During this hectic period he had somehow managed to hold down his job with the ever tolerant, ever accommodating Aldus Books, whom he left, again, in September, in anticipation of an invitation to spend some months in the US, and just before a visit to Poland, with Bedford and myself. Joined by Zygmunt Krause we performed extracts from *Treatise* at the Warsaw 1966 Autumn Festival. There were also two lectures, at Ravensbourne and Kingston Schools of Art, and a commission for some music, with AMM, for Allan King's film, *Warrendale,* which was recorded on 20 October but was not used. In fact, no music was used.

A week later, on 26 October, Cardew flew to the US to take up the temporary post of 'Creative Associate' at the Center of the Creative and Performing Arts at the State University of New York at Buffalo. The invitation had come through the offices of the American composer/conductor, Lucas Foss who, with Allen Sapp, was co-director of the Center. Due to Cardew's severely limited finances and the bureaucracy involved in obtaining a visa his arrival was subject to a number of postponements which were beginning to discompose the Center's administration, in particular Renée Levine, who was the co-ordinator. However, on receipt of a letter from Cardew explaining and apologising for his delay in arrival Ms Levine recalls that the letter was 'so perfect, so sophisticated, so funny in context that I just fell under his spell right then and there'.[64] When he finally arrived, well into the fall, he found accommodation in the Victor Hugo apartments on Delaware Avenue where a number of creative associates, including David Tudor and Frederic Rzewski, had stayed.

One of his first assignments was a symposium which took place in the Albright-Knox Art Gallery: Webern's Legacy. The panellists were Maryanne Amacher, Cornelius Cardew, Henri Pousseur, Allen Sapp, Niccolo Castiglioni, and the moderator was Lukas Foss. By this time Cardew's relation to the European serialists, including Webern, was barely luke-warm. In the discussion the opinion that the reason for Webern's influence was 'the spiritual convalescence which was needed after the war' is attributed to Cardew by a Buffalo-based web-site which provides a summary of the debate. The phrase 'spiritual convalescence', or rather its use by Cardew, does not ring true to these ears, although he may well have put forward the thesis that non-musical reasons could explain Webern's status and influence in post-war Germany. We have only to remind ourselves that he was deeply immersed in *Treatise* at that time, with its rich source of psychological, social and philosophical implications. The web-site summary is brief, offering an extremely truncated version of what may well have been an interesting discussion. Part of the argument seems to have revolved around the issue of 'determinism' – Pousseur suggesting that a true understanding of Webern's music leads to 'mobile form', to a liberation of the performer, rather than towards the determinism exemplified in Darmstadt during the fifties. Cardew disagreed: 'The idea that the performer is a machine is a naïve idea that comes from Webern.' [65] Webern, in his view, was the bearer of that intolerable guilt – the subsequent creation of those monstrous edifices whose ineluctable and implacable presence dominated Darmstadt programmes and eventually, in the latter part of the decade, precipitated a crisis, an impasse, which even its leading practitioners, such as Pierre Boulez, had to acknowledge. None of this, however, prevented Cardew from performing the *Kinderstück* (1924) and accompanying Ethel Casey in some of Webern's songs in the Symposium, a task he would have achieved skilfully, with conviction, and with no hint of the 'machine' in either his bearing or his execution. Of course, it was a familiar repertoire, one that he would have been called upon to perform on numerous occasions over the previous decade.

His first project was a performance, or rather two performances, of the reworked pages of *Treatise*, pages 1-44: 1-20 at the Allbright-Knox Gallery in Buffalo on 17 December 1966; and all 44 pages at the Carnegie Recital Hall in New York City three days later on 20 December. Then on a bleak, wintry Buffalo night in March, to a sparse audience, he presented a recital of piano music by Feldman and Terry Jennings [66] at the University. Renee Levine recalls: 'It was a gem. Very intimate, thoughtful, understated – as though we were in his library or studio. He had no airs onstage.'[67] Yet Cardew was not happy in Buffalo; a barren environment (it seems that he did not take advantage of the glorious surrounding countryside), the city cold and ugly, the people unresponsive to his work – all of which he was prepared to tolerate for the small financial rewards it offered. Nor would he have taken to American university life. Throughout his stay he maintained a taciturn presence, missing his family and writing home most days, full of misery and complaints. However, he did manage to spend Easter at home in London and on his return to the US gave two performances, in Buffalo and New York, of Stockhausen's *Plus-Minus*.[68]

In Nevern Square Stella Cardew was experiencing her own problems about which she complained bitterly to Cornelius in her letters.[69] Yoko Ono and her husband Tony Cox, presumably on Cardew's casual invitation, had come to stay, and although initially Stella had welcomed Yoko as a soul-mate, a woman artist, she had become quickly disillusioned, disconcerted in particular by what she felt was their exaggerated and unseemly preoccupation with money.[70] This response was perhaps a little ungenerous since Yoko Ono's projects, such as her 'bottoms' film, did require financial support and she and her husband spent considerable time and energy in fund-raising, at fashionable venues and parties where the rich and infamous would foregather, leaving their young daughter for Stella to look after: Stella was probably politely asked the favour and she, equally politely, consented. However, when the child contracted pneumonia the networking did not abate; Stella's role became that of nursemaid and she grew resentful. She was already preoccupied with her own four children, one of whom was suffering from ill health, and two from maladjustment at school. Nor did her two guests make any financial contribution towards their stay, in a situation where Stella was weighed down by a constant lack of money to provide even the most basic needs for her own family. Stella asked them to leave but they stayed; finally, Cardew wrote to them, and they left.

For Cardew the first few months of 1967, in Buffalo, saw the completion of *Treatise* as well as the publication, by Universal Edition of *Four works*: *Autumn 60, Material, Solo with Accompaniment*, and *Memories of You*. And in April he produced his only purely verbal composition, written for AMM: *The Tiger's Mind*. On 8 April the first complete performance of *Treatise* took place at the Commonwealth Institute in London, the first of four concerts of Experimental Music presented by Michael White. The second concert, with pianists Zygmunt Krause, David Bedford, Cardew and myself consisted of music for four pianos by Terry Riley, Earle Brown, John Cage and Morton Feldman; the third comprised experimental works by George Brecht, John Cage, Toshi Ichiyanagi and La Monte Young; and the fourth was a concert of improvised music by AMM.

After the series Cardew returned, briefly, to the US, and penned the following entry in his Journal:

23.IV.67. Buffalo last landing.
Pinpoint the mechanisms – true or false – that I'm dimly perceiving.
Being in Buffalo alone was/is the basic guilt. I feel guilty about it because the necessity of being here alone is not proved. (*Treatise* did not make it necessary to be here alone – I could have worked on it – not equally intensively, but adequately – with Stella and family here). So I had to provide a necessity for being here alone. Otherwise succumb to the meaninglessness of my aloneness. This I did. So the guilt escalated to another sphere. Have I burned my boats? No, but the boat I was/am in has flared up by spontaneous combustion. So I'm to be fried, and no land in sight.

A different approach.
Brought up as a moral man. Spent years trying to acquire real moral fibre – live correctly according to moral law. This has been disintegrated by the years with Stella, living according to instinctual law.
Now exposed to the same hazards that Stella has had all her life – at the mercy of momentariness. 'Events' the only authority, etc. etc. Even in music now – I am waiting to see what my hands will do next, what will be the next thing my mind will curl itself around. But inevitably with a nostalgia for my past morality. Hence the insupportable guilt. Hence incidentally my feelings of inadequacy with AMM now, who are all working on their moral fibre.

On 5 May Cardew was back home in Nevern Square, this time permanently, two days before his thirty-first birthday. The same month saw another complete performance of *Treatise*, this time at York University, thanks to the initiative of a thriving and adventurous music department under Wilfrid Mellers. Having completed *Treatise* and now enmeshed in improvisation, the act of composing required a tremendous feat of will and imagination; improvisation was consuming his responsibility for the resulting sound-in-performance.

Meanwhile the clandestine relationship with Sheila Kasabova continued; daring and experimental, it was occasionally interrupted by mutual consent because they felt it was the right thing at the time. Sometimes it was simply through Cardew's absence, perhaps a tour of America, or somewhere abroad. On more than one occasion they tried to finish the relationship once and for all. Sheila insists that it was not as if she had chosen to have a relationship with Cardew; no strategy was involved in either initiating or pursuing such a state of affairs. But there was always a moral edge; so that an aura of guilt – from which they were never entirely free, even when they finally committed themselves to a life together – hung in the air. Sheila would often attend Cardew's performances but found this painful: the unknown person in the shadows, unable to celebrate his music openly as she wanted. Moreover, like Stella, Sheila was also aware that Cardew was attracted to, and had relationships with, a variety of women. It was a situation which continued for several years.

Notes and references

1   Jrnl. 1 January 1963.
2   Jrnl. 24 January 1963.
3   Jrnl. 1 January 1963.
4   Although he did experiment with LSD for a brief period while he was in Rome studying with Petrassi.
5   Jrnl. 3 March 1963.
6   Jrnl. 21 April 1963.
7   Roughly during the period 1945-60 Gwigwi Mgebe had been an important figure in the organisation and development of black African music in Johannesburg and its surrounds.
8   'The poem you ask about is "The Marigold" by George Wither, written in 1684 [...] Try as I could I could not find the poem, which I remembered as being in a collection of metaphysical poets, I think [...] Ironically I have now come across it again, copied out and accompanied by a little pressed and now faded wild marigold (which I picked in Sicily), in an old note book of my own I was going through.' Email communication from SK to JT, 21 May 2005.
9   See chapter 16 for more on Sheila Kasabova's (née Muir) background.
10 After some reflection I have rejected a more benign interpretation – that Cardew's concern was that by signing her work with her maiden name, 'Sargent', Stella would have more strongly secured their identity as *her* paintings. On the other hand, to contradict my speculative thesis in the main text, there could have been a strain of jealousy, relating back to the acclaim she received when she was a student at the Royal College.
11 Jrnl. 13 January 1963.
12 *Musical Times,* March 1963. Actually, these words are describing an earlier work, *Il Canto Sospeso* (1956); the piece performed at the Cologne festival was *Sul Ponte di Hiroshima*, which in Cardew's view, 'does not differ essentially from Nono's earlier music'.
13 Ibid.
14 Ibid.
15 Ibid.
16 Fluxus was an informal, international group of avant-garde artists working in a wide range of media, active from the early 1960s to the late 1970s. Fluxus members included artists such as George Macunias, George Brecht, Dick Higgins, Alison Knowles, Nam June Paik, Takehisa Kosugi and Emmett Williams, and there were many others of comparable status associated with the group. Many of them had attended Cage's experimental music course at the New School of Social Research in New York in 1958. Cage's idea of the coexistence and interaction of multifarious activities had found expression in his collaboration with Merce Cunningham and Robert Rauschenberg and led to a redefinition of 'music'. 'Artists, anti-artists, non artists, anartists, the politically committed and the apolitical, poets of non poetry, non-dancers dancing, doers, undoers, non doers: Fluxus encompasses opposites.' From V TRE 3, Fluxus newspaper New York (1964); unsigned manifesto, probably penned by Macunias.
    And Michael Parsons writes: 'It (Fluxus) was concerned (among other things) with a kind of art which would merge almost imperceptibly with everyday life: with redefining perception of ordinary objects and events, and with reassessing the value of common materials, activities and situations. There was a prevailing interest in the use of chance, in games,

puzzles and paradoxes, in inversions of conventional use and value which owed something to Dada and Surrealism, in particular to the work of Kurt Schwitters, Man Ray and Marcel Duchamp.' From 'The Scratch Orchestra and Visual Arts'; *Leonardo Music Journal* Vol.11, 2001. German translation: *44 Lacher und Komisches Gehen: Das Scratch Orchestra, Fluxus und die visuellen Künste;* Positionen 45/46, November 2000 / February 2001.

17   Andy Warhol heard the group at the *Cafe Bizarre* in Greenwich Village and they started working at *The Factory* with Warhol and the singer Nico early in 1966. John Cale, whose association with La Monte Young predates the Velvet Underground, created the music for one of the group's most celebrated pieces: Sister Ray.

18   At the same Festival Cardew took part in a performance of Dieter Schnebel's *Glossolalie* under Mauricio Kagel.

19   *Musical Times*, December 1963.

20   Christine Keeler was a call-girl whose favours had been enjoyed by both the British War Minister, Profumo, and the Soviet Attache, Ivanov. Mr Profumo was taken to task for what was deemed, probably unreasonably, a breach of security, and forced to resign. The British Press capitalised on the affair in unbridled fashion; the scandal, which also allegedly involved members of the aristocracy, the royal family, Rock-n-Roll musicians and film stars, was on everybody's lips and there was a proliferation of quotes and jokes.

21   Roger Hutchinson, *High Sixties* (Edinburgh: Mainstream Publishing, 1992), p.33.

22   The Park Lane Group was founded in 1956 in Park Lane House in London. Its principal aims were to provide a prominent central London platform for highly talented young artists and to present events of special interest. This policy of creative opportunity has been continued for 49 seasons with 'excellent results'. In a somewhat quaint and formal letter the Chairman of The Park Lane Group, John Woolf, reminded Cardew that a fee of 10 guineas had been agreed and, in a *post scriptum*, that 'Dress for the concert will be either dinner jackets or tails.' Whether or not Cardew observed the latter stipulation nobody seems able to recall.

23   Jrnl. 22 May 1964.

24   Nuova Consonanza was formed at the end of the fifties by a group of Italian composers, resident in Rome, who in 1960 organised the first Settimana Internazionale di Nuova Musica in Palermo, described by Franco Evangelisti at the time as an 'anti-music' festival free of any political engagement – in an obviously critical reference to Luigi Nono. The group of mainly young musicians included Mario Bertoncini, Mauro Bortolotti, Antonio De Blasio, Franco Evangelisti, Domenico Guaccero, Egisto Macchi and Daniele Paris. The group existed for nearly thirty years, exerting a considerable influence on Roman musical life through its initiatives in introducing a wide range of contemporary music into the city's concert halls, galleries and studios.

25   Cornelius Cardew, 'Stockhausen's *Plus-Minus*', *London Magazine*, April 1967, pp.86-90.

26   Letter to Francesca Astaldi, 10 December 1965.

27   Larry Austin, 'Forum Improvisation', Reprint from *Perspectives of New Music,* Fall-Winter 1982, Spring-Summer 1983, Vol. 21, nos. 1 & 2, 27-33 (p.28).

28   'The silence of "now" is the ultimate bliss' Cardew wrote to Ilona Halberstadt on 20 October 1959.

29   Jrnl. 26 June 1963, Florence.

30   A letter from the British Council, dated 27 February 1963, acknowledges receipt of Cardew's

application for a scholarship to study in Italy. On 25 April he received confirmation that he had been awarded an '8 month scholarship'.

31 Jrnl. 26 June, 1963.

32 Clearly, this is an ironic reference to Alban Berg's article: 'Warum ist Schoenbergs Musik so schwer verständlich?' Written for the composer's 50th birthday (special number of the *Anbruch*, August 1924). English translation: *The Music Review*, Cambridge, August 1952.

33 Jrnl. 9 July 1964.

34 *Treatise Handbook*, p.vi. (*CCR*)

35 Jrnl. Entry headed 'Darmstadt July 64'.

36 *Musical Times*, September 1964, p.674.

37 Ibid.

38 Jrnl. 16 July 1964.

39 Soon after the beginning of the Mermaid performance of *Two Books* a lone voice in the audience entreated us to 'get on with it'. Other members of the audience may not have been experiencing the same degree of impatience and frustration. Since that time, 1960, the notion of silence as a contributory and integral element in music-making, especially in free improvisation (AMM), has been embraced by performers and listeners alike. And it is perhaps not without significance that the person beseeching us to greater urgency was himself a composer whose peremptory intervention may well have been prompted as much by an aesthetic presumption as by psychological discomfort. What I am suggesting, with the benefit of hindsight, is that Cardew's response and stance need not have been so defensive.

40 Jrnl. 1 September 1964.

41 When I contacted Michael von Biel sometime in 2004 and asked him, he could not remember whether Cardew had taken part in the concert, although he thought it was likely, given the circumstantial evidence in the Journal.

42 My attempt to 'demonstrate' relations between *Bun No.1* and the *Third Orchestral Piece* may well fail to contribute meaningfully to the above discussion; at best it may serve to thicken the plot.

43 *Musical Times*, March 1965, p.195.

44 The arcane reference here is presumably to Richardson's *Clarissa* – a book Stella Cardew recalls her husband was reading around this time – although according to my own routine familiarity with the work there was nothing of significance that I could detect in terms of Clarissa's musical prowess.

45 Jrnl. 6 March 1965.

46 Jrnl. 13 April 1965.

47 Michael Parsons, who was in Rome at the time and attended the concert, recalls that Cardew strolled casually on to the stage, cigarette dangling from his lips, with the casual informality of a jazz musician, and paying little attention to the audience.

48 George Brecht, from the programme for my own *Volo Solo* series of concerts October/ December 1970.

49 In some later editions this was elaborated, as Harry Gilonis has reminded me: 'Each such seed remaining on the keyboard is attached to the key or keys nearest it with a single piece of pressure-sensitive tape'. However this does not appear on the original *Water Yam* card.

50 Alvin Curran; composer, performer, co-founder of Musica Elettronica Viva (MEV).

51   Allan Bryant; musical instrument inventor, performer, co-founder of Musica Elettronica Viva (MEV).
52   Porter also persuaded Cardew to undertake to draw, write out, all the music examples, from both the classical and the contemporary repertoire, for the *Musical Times* during the middle to late sixties.
53   Referring to a performance of La Monte Young's *Poem* Michael Parsons recalls 'Cardew hearing "rich orchestral mixtures, like cellos and French horns", in a version performed on the wooden floor of the concert hall at Morley College, London, in 1969.' From 'The Scratch Orchestra – Performance/Interpretation' by Michael Parsons, published in German in *Positionen* 26, February 1996 pp.8–13: 'Wer Künstler werden will, melde sich', Das London Scratch Orchestra.
54   *Financial Times*, late May 1965.
55   Ibid.
56   By this time Stella was attending an Infant Teacher's induction course for graduates run by the London County Council and was expecting their second child.
57   Giacinto Scelsi was one of the few Italian composers whom Cardew held in great esteem. He had even mildly reproached Petrassi during one of their meetings for not doing enough to support Scelsi and his music, even intimating that the Roman musical establishment – of which Petrassi was a respected pillar – had contrived somehow to sabotage Scelsi's career. Petrassi responded diplomatically, insisting that he personally had no influence in respect of the promotion or otherwise of Scelsi and his music.
58   'Sitting in the Dark', *Musical Times*, March 1968, p.233. (*CCR*)
59   Mark Boyle (b. Glasgow, 1934; d. 2005) gained notoriety in the 1960s for numerous happenings and projection events, including the experimental liquid light project for The Soft Machine, produced collaboratively with his wife Joan Hills and others of The Sensual Laboratory. In August 1968 he began *Journey to the Surface of the Earth* (ICA, London 1969) – a project to make 'multi-sensual presentations' of 1000 randomly selected sites on the earth's surface. They (together with their children) continued to exhibit as Boyle Family (Scottish National Gallery of Modern Art, Edinburgh 2003).
60   The participants on this occasion were Kurt Schwertsik, the jazz saxophonist John Surman, guitarist Keith Rowe, percussionist Peter Greenham, the composer and myself.
61   The Mansions were home to a number of wealthy people; the young Christopher Hobbs, Cardew's student, recalls being astonished by the fact that Sir Robert and Lady Dashwood Strettell occupied the ground floor.
62   At the time, in the mid-sixties, the status of this salary was comparable to that of a newly-fledged college lecturer; I was earning the same amount for my lectureship at South-West Essex Technical College.
63   In 2005, or possibly 2004, Patrick Hughes sent me a review he had written of a performance by Cardew of George Brecht's *Gap Event* at the Leeds Institute Gallery on 18 February 1966: 'After the interval we saw and heard and participated in two most delightful pieces. First Cornelius Cardew gave an impeccable performance in George Brecht's *Gap Event*. Cardew spent several minutes on the shiny lino floor of the Institute Gallery drawing a line in chalk, during which time we could see some very odd holes in the HEELS of his shoes, as if made by burning coals. The chalk drawing... set the audience in an expectant mood. When he had finished the line he honked a hooter attached to a radiator at his side

of the room, then dashed to twirl a football rattle attached to a table at the opposite wall, dashed to honk the hooter, and went on at great speed trying to reduce the gap between these two sounds until he was exhausted. He must have made twenty crossings.'

64   Letter to from Renée Levine to JT, 24 July 1994.

65   Cardew himself may well have fallen victim to the malign influence of performances of Webern at that time which were notoriously cold and 'academic'. (The musicologist, Hans Keller, would refer, ironically, to 'Saint Anton'.) The pianist and critic Peter Stadlen's recollections of Webern's approach to his own music, in particular the piano *Variations*, suggest quite a different attitude towards the performer, and far removed from the metaphor of the 'machine'.

66   American composer and saxophonist Terry Jennings was born in 1940 in Eagle Rock, California. A student, associate and friend of La Monte Young he is best known for his minimalist keyboard music, although Michael Nyman, in his *Experimental Music,* also draws attention to his string writing. He died in San Pablo, California, in December 1981.

67   Letter from Renée Levine to JT, 24 July 1994.

68   Meanwhile, I had given the first broadcast performance of the *Three Winter Potatoes* for a BBC Invitation Concert, on 1 November, and in December the work was published by Universal Edition.

69   Even in his absence, or perhaps because of Stella's welcoming 'open house', Nevern Square continued to be a meeting point for artist and musician friends, and I recall an improvising session there with Evan Parker and myself around that time.

70   Cardew's perspicacious review, in the *Financial Times*, 29 September 1966, of Yoko Ono's performance at the Africa Centre, had not been particularly flattering, although he had proceeded with caution, and occasionally irony: 'But my conviction of the uplifting quality of the [her] work began to waver in the celebrated "Cut piece" which followed. It was impossible to disentangle the compulsion of the audience to cut and Yoko Ono's compulsion to *be* cut. In cutting off pieces of her clothing, members of the audience show unmistakeable signs of artistic striving, and she for her part is equally unmistakeably striving towards a kind of nerveless detachment, so that all emotional interplay is precluded. As the piece progresses one becomes aware of another kind of nudity underneath the clothing of her skin, and this inner amorphous nude shape is visible only in her eyes, fixed unwinkingly on the audience.' (*CCR*)

(*CCR*) Also found in *Cornelius Cardew A Reader*

Cornelius Cardew a life unfinished

6
Treatise 1963–67

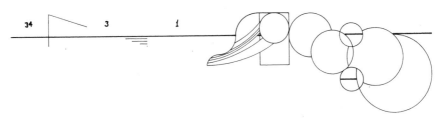

Ex.6.1. *Treatise*, p.1.

'It is impossible for me to say one word in my book about all that music has meant in my life. How then can I hope to be understood?'[1]

My age of romanticism is over. Sensations, moments, drop away. My desire is to experience long-term continuities as beautiful. In the *Treatise* to create the coherent code which expresses the truths we do not know and cannot live up to. To dismiss Bodmin Moor and the girl around the corner as beings without future. To pursue the lonely adventure of the spirit, to draw nourishment from the life of the land and the continuity of family life. To be aware of the psychological groundings of your musical strivings (being timid, physically, as a boy, I became bold in spirit), and still leave the ground. (When did I write that it is only possible to leave the ground if you are on it?)[2]

In a Journal entry on 18 November 1966, when he was in Buffalo, Cardew describes the genesis of *Treatise:*

Treatise. I've always been preoccupied with huge abstractions. I was 23 when I first came across Wittgenstein's *Tractatus*; right from the first sentence, handwritten by Slad [David Sladen] as a foretaste before he gave me the book, 'The world is everything that is the case', it made a deep impression on me. The name

Treatise (from *Tractatus*): – a thorough investigation. Of what? Of everything, of nothing, like the whole world[3] of philosophy. I started work on it in 1963 and have worked on it inconsistently ever since. In that time it has lost some of its abstract quality; autobiographical aspects have crept in. But then there are autobiographical wisps to be read into Wittgenstein's *Tractatus* – the whole takes on a slight autobiographical slant in view of his later rejection of parts of it.

Cardew began working on *Treatise* during the first months of 1963, 'on the basis of an elaborate scheme involving 67 elements, some musical, some graphic; the fusion of two professions'.[4] In its final version, drawn and measured on a grid, it clearly owes much to the fact that for much of the time he was employed as a design assistant at Aldus Books. In a BBC talk preceding a broadcast of a part of *Treatise* on 15 January 1966 he acknowledges the important influence that working at Aldus exerted upon him:

While there I came to be occupied more and more with designing diagrams and charts and in the course of this work I became aware of the potential eloquence of simple black lines in a diagram. Thin, thick, curving, broken, and then the varying tones of grey made up of equally spaced parallel lines, and then the type – numbers, words, short sentences like ornate, literary, art-nouveauish, visual interlopers in the purely graphic context of the diagram.

Yet for a work which displays such virtuosity and panache, it emerged tentatively; Cardew confessed to having no idea, initially, as to the outcome, and progress was fitful. Paradoxically, it was the musical elements and their integration which created the greatest obstacles; it was the 'apparent musicality' of p.99, for example, which he described as 'a stumbling block that impeded my way for some time to come.'[5] Somehow these 'idiosyncratic' musical signs, these 'interlopers', seem to have been a source of equivocalness, even embarrassment, to him; they impinged on the visual content disproportionately to their relative importance as indices for many of the basic elements. Yet such traditional indicators as *treble clef* and *forte* were considered indispensable and they litter the score; in relation to conventional musical notation *Treatise* is an act of de-construction rather than rejection. There is historical and stylistic sedimentation scattered throughout the score as well as expressive, visual gestures of an immediate, inspirational or suggestive nature. In other words, the notation is an attempt to embody the way people actually experience structure in music. And the way a composer notates delimits his creative imagination; the force of Cardew's creative imagination broke the fetters of a musical language which for him had become obsolete and suppressive. Perhaps he felt that the superabundance of traditional symbols on page 99 were in some way threatening, that they might assume a dominant role, forcing a more referential, less creative mode of interpretation, upon the performer. Be that as it may, the consequent on page 100 is a master-stroke; rather than an arbitrary cessation of these signs Cardew simply allows them to wither and dissolve into new shapes of similar dimension, so that there is no feeling of dislocation – a brilliant exercise in damage limitation.

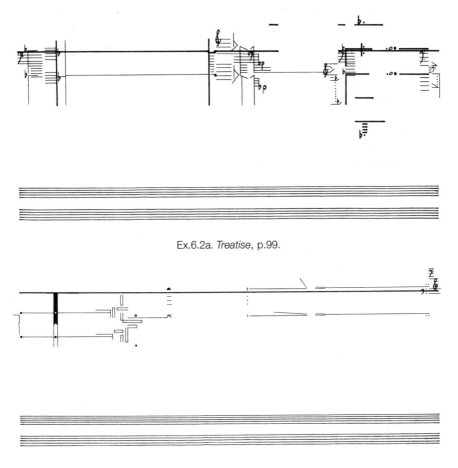

Ex.6.2a. *Treatise*, p.99.

Ex.6.2b. *Treatise*, p.100.

Whatever the problems presented by page 99, they do not appear to have been exaggerated. Around eighteen months elapsed between the first ninety-nine pages and their continuation as late as December 1964, when seven separate, that is, non-consecutive, pages were put into freehand fair copy. And it was at this juncture that

Cardew decided to abandon freehand drawing in favour of the drawing instruments with which he had become familiar and adept at Aldus Books. By October 1966, when Cardew arrived in Buffalo, he had completed pages 45-143 and the piece was beginning to assume its final shape, although the first forty-four pages were still to be revised. During the early months of 1967, still in Buffalo, Cardew drew the final fifty pages and *Treatise* was submitted to the Gallery Upstairs Press for publication.[6] Some years later he was to recall his execution of those last pages:

It was surprisingly poignant coming to Buffalo again, really golden in the sunset. The sun sets over Lake Erie and has to struggle with all the smoke of Bethlehem Steel, which makes it red as red. Especially my old favourite the phallic library, its tip gleaming with coloured mosaics that I don't remember being there before. I remember sitting on the lakeside in freezing sunshine sketching out the last 40 pages or so of *Treatise*. Then I put the library in when I was re-doing the beginning, but for some reason I laid it on its side![7]

The Gallery owner, Ed Budowski, showing both foresight and alacrity, published *Treatise* before the year was out and it appeared in accordance with Cardew's wishes without any introductory material or instruction 'to mislead prospective performers into the slavish practice of "doing what they are told"'.[8] In fact it was the sheer length of *Treatise* as much as anything else that militated against the provision of an interpretative system; and because of the exhaustive manner in which the signs are treated it was assumed, at least by a sanguine and trusting composer, that performers would devise their own methods of interpretation, as their study of the work progressed.

Ideally, then, we should while composing strive to eliminate all mere interpretation, and concentrate on the notation itself, which should be as new and as fresh as possible (hence less likely to arouse preconceptions in the interpreter – though if you have a good interpreter isn't it likely that his preconceptions will be good too?) and should contain implicit in its internal structure, without any need of any instruction, all the implications necessary for a live interpretation.[9]

Several years later, in 1971, the publication by Peters Edition of the *Treatise Handbook* did not really compromise his earlier position in relation to performer instruction, although the Journal of Working Notes, with which it begins, and the numerous aphorisms which spice it, provide a fascinating insight into Cardew's developing ideas on musical notation – as well as an indication of the extent to which these were influenced by his on-going study of Wittgenstein's writings.

The Graphic Material of *Treatise*

The topography of *Treatise* may be divided into four distinct categories: abstract shapes (of which circles, squares, rectangles are the most prominent), signs associated with conventional musical notation, numbers, and a horizontal middle line which divides each page into two equal parts. Nearly all the symbols are drawn with either of two pen-widths, the thicker width being used throughout for the middle line.[10]

I posit four categories; yet even this most general description may be regarded as contentious: for example, by including the two empty staves which Cardew provides at the bottom of each page underneath the graphic material, Brian Dennis insisted that there are five categories. Dennis's view is strengthened by the fact that at one point these prosaic and seemingly functional staves are themselves subjected to idiosyncratic treatment. In the middle of page 25 the graphic symbols actually encroach upon the upper stave and for two inches the top two lines (of the stave) are missing. Furthermore, in the *Handbook*, p.v., Cardew himself proposes that the two staves be read as part of the score, 'as being suggestive for beginners'. But even if we acknowledge an arcane quality in the presence of the two lower staves, in practice they have been regarded either as an irrelevance (by non-readers) or at best as a useful space (for experienced readers) where material can be traditionally notated as and when required; for example, where specific tones are to be featured on a page. (This in fact is how Cardew uses it in his own annotated copy of the score.)

The symbols constituting the (four) categories are deployed throughout the one hundred and ninety-three pages hierarchically; that is, a specific stretch of the score will feature a particular symbol, or a combination of symbols will predominate, while other symbols will appear only spasmodically, playing a more dominant role in another section; or a symbol, having fallen into desuetude, will be marked by its absence. It is a method of structuring material which Cardew employs in a number of works (see my analysis of *Autumn 60*), through which the form of the work falls naturally and conveniently into sections which in turn sub-divide into smaller units, into short pieces perhaps, and into phrases and tropes which can be regarded as self-contained and yet belonging, fitting within a context. In Cardew's indeterminate works, as we have already seen, the originality of the notation serves to bring the question of musical 'structure' to the surface and the listener is aware of the resulting music 'as a token of something that exists in some sense independently of the sound; it means not so much hearing the sound as hearing the composition through the sound'.[11] Conversely, as readers we may 'hear' *Treatise* through the notation; as Richard Barrett has observed, an involvement with *Treatise*, as performer or simply as reader, leaves us with the strong impression 'that there *is* a sonic analogue to what is on the page, that it will remain forever just out of reach, but that something about *Treatise* consistently makes musical sense'.[12] In so far as it 'provides a unique context within which sound can be heard as musically meaningful'[13] *Treatise* is a composition. But can our concept of 'composition' accommodate the perpetual tension which *Treatise* creates between the presumption of a formal ('compositional') representation of sounds, and the desire to unleash sounds, to give them free rein, and to reveal a latent aspiration to sing of other worlds?

I have broken *Treatise* down into eight sections on the basis of the frequency, scope and visual presence of the particular symbols which characterize them: Section 1: pages 1-19. Section 2: 20-44. Section 3: 45-88. Section 4: 89-126. Section 5: 127-144. Section 6: 145-164. Section 7: 165-178. Section 8: 179-193. Not that I am underestimating the roles of other symbols whose appearances are more fitful; it is simply that to me their functions within a particular section appear to be of lesser significance. In other words I am interpreting, rather than describing, the form of *Treatise*. The exercise is a subjective one – just as an initial classification of the graphic material depends as much on the visual awareness and imaginativeness of the reader as on the objective features of the signs themselves. Nor am I concerned with the far-reaching modifications and transformations which a symbol undergoes; for example, there is an extraordinary range of graphics under the generic heading 'stave'. At this initial stage what I am trying to do is to build up a knowledge and understanding of the score by adopting a simple, perhaps over-simplified, system of classification.

Of course, it is tempting, and would be reassuring, to analyse *Treatise* into *seven* sections, which would conveniently correspond to the seven sections of Wittgenstein's *Tractatus*. In fact, it would not be a difficult undertaking, although I suspect that it would be no less arbitrary than my own interpretation, with the crucial difference that I am not seeking a particular outcome. However, the attraction is undeniable and one could argue persuasively that the final two and a half pages of *Treatise* are a perfect notational exemplification of the famous seventh section of the *Tractatus*: 'Whereof one cannot speak, thereof one must be silent.' [14] Brian Dennis drew attention to this 'final cadence' of *Treatise*:

> On p.191 the 'lifeline' stops and after two beautifully drawn loop designs the staves emerge as shown: the top stave is hand-drawn (apart from line 2), the bottom is ruled (apart from line 2) and the process continues for two more pages of empty staves, identical except for the minute fluctuations of the composer's unguided hand (Ex.6.3).[15]

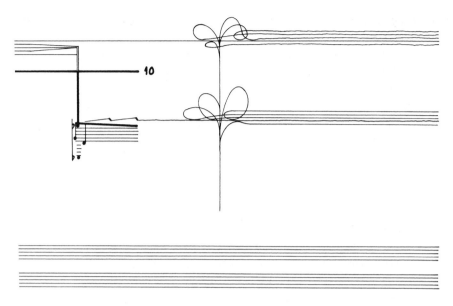

Ex.6.3. *Treatise*, p.191.

Keith Rowe and myself took advantage of a succession of long flights in North America to try and identify the 'sixty-seven' elements, some musical, some graphic, which, according to Cardew in the *Handbook*, constitute the score of *Treatise*. The problem was compounded by the extraordinary fecundity of the score and the elusiveness of the signs which constantly combine and change in bewildering fashion, contributing to an exhilarating and vivifying impression of movement in the notation. So it was partly in desperation that we agreed that an approximate figure, say between sixty and seventy, would be acceptable. However, our first count was far too general and amounted to less than thirty. It was clear that what we had included in the 'circle' category, for example – say a crescent shape or incomplete circle – needed to be grouped separately; our problem was a conceptual one. So we had to redefine the limits for each group of elements – that is, to decide what to include, what to exclude, in order to achieve an appropriate taxonomy. For example, the elements ⌐ ⌣ could be subsumed either into one category, or each could belong to a separate category; the target figure of around sixty-seven indicated that the latter would be the most expedient choice. Similarly, and more obviously, the nine (and only nine) numbers which Cardew uses in *Treatise* – 1,2,3,4,5,6,8,10,34 – needed to be categorised separately into ones, twos, threes, etc. Thus the target figure itself became a key, determining factor in our method of taxonomic classification. Conversely, the practicalities of interpretation may subsequently demand that it is precisely the interrelatedness of categories, rather than their separation, that is of consequence, and they may then be grouped under a single, generic heading – say 'circle derivatives', or 'numbers'.[16]

Like Wittgenstein, his private mentor, Cardew was concerned with the nature and limitations of language and logic and with the relationship between the structure of language and the structure of reality. Musically, or more specifically, in terms of musical composition, these concerns were expressed in the correlation between the way music is notated and the nature of the actions and sounds it generates. In *Treatise* Cardew created a notation which embodied his needs and aspirations at that time, freeing him from the cramping disability which, in the light of his own experience, the system of traditional notation seemed to impose on compositional thought. There seemed to be no limits to Cardew's musical horizons or, if there were, they extended outside and beyond the locus of compositional theory and practice (and the imagination) of his peers and colleagues. At the time of *Treatise* tensions had already begun to show and Cardew's relation to the avant-garde, both the European and the American, had reached a breaking-point. Whatever similarities seemed to exist between Cardew's indeterminate compositions and those of his peers, on both sides of the Atlantic, they were in essence superficial, or at least, inconsequential. Significantly, neither the European nor the American musical avant-garde, with very few exceptions, had sought to subvert, or even to question, the prevailing composer/performer relationship of Western art music, which reached its most extreme expression in post-1945 serialism – a relationship marked by an increasing dominance in the role of the composer, whilst the compliant performer assumed a 'technocratic' role, as a kind of 'systems-expert'. Even Cage, for all his radicalism, could not relinquish it. By contrast, what was of primary concern to Cardew was to evolve a way – rather than a method – of notating music which could express the subtleties and nuances, the indeterminacies, and above all the mutuality, of the composer/performer relation.

Treatise was the culmination of a trilogy of works (with *Autumn 60* and *Octet '61*) in which this essential, human dialogue was re-opened, explored and refined. Rather than prescribing sounds Cardew sought to stimulate, provoke and inspire through a visual score of astonishing scope and imagination which sometimes subtly, sometimes flagrantly impinges on the performer's sensibilities, serving not simply as a measure of the performer's intellectual capacity, digital dexterity and viability, but also of his probity, of his virtuosity, courage, tenacity, alertness and so on. And for Cardew, drawing *Treatise* was an integral part of the compositional process; he was aware of the psychological drama generated through the performer's relation to the (drawn) notation in the act of interpretation.

A composer who hears sounds will try to find a notation for sounds. One who has ideas will find one that expresses ideas, leaving their interpretation free, in confidence that his ideas have been accurately and concisely notated.[17]

Cage's notations, too, concern themselves with ideas but I would baulk at describing their interpretation as 'free' in the sense that Cardew meant 'free'. Certainly Cardew's admiration for Cage's scores was unstinting and he would frequently cite Cage's *Winter Music* and *Variations* as works where the notation is a consummate expression of the ideas – where there is no element of 'blur'. Howard Skempton shares Cardew's enthusiasm for *Variations I*:

> That a score so starkly pure and simple is capable of yielding results of extraordinary richness and complexity is proof that Cage's work, at its best, is successful in its aim of imitating nature in the manner of its operation.[18]

Yet in the light of Cage's own musical philosophy such enthusiasm begs the question. From the performer's point of view isn't Cage treading the same familiar ground? Isn't it the case that Cage is providing specific instructions for the performer to follow: the procedural rules which accompany the score – in this instance a sequence of mechanically-derived readings and measurements? At a certain point the performer's artistic creativity and ingenuity *is* engaged, but it is too late, and his sense of alienation from the score is undiminished. *Variations I* belongs to the composer, it is leased to the performer under certain conditions. Certainly, Cage was not a man to claim proprietorial rights over anything, and yet in terms of his own philosophical credo might it not be argued that his compositions under-achieved – for all their exhilarating iconoclasm? And might it not also be argued that his oft-cited objection to 'idiosyncratic' performances of his works (and to those of his musical associates, as we shall see in a subsequent chapter) was somehow a derogation from the moral teachings and the idealism embodied in his writings? By his insisting on the criteria for making judgments of performances, isn't the 'freedom' which Cage championed severely compromised?

The importance of Cage's involvement with Eastern philosophies has been comprehensively documented, by himself and others, and cannot be overstated; but equally important, it seems to me, is the fact that Cage was also a product and exemplary model of American Individualism. Seminal, indeterminate works such as the *Variations I-VI* and *4'33"*, in which he ignored artistic taboos and boldly crossed frontiers into outlawed territory, are strikingly emblematic of the American pioneering spirit. These prodigious and audacious works owe at least as much to the ethos of individualism – individual risk, individual discovery – as they do to Zen, and it is this indispensable quality, together with patronage, marketing and availability, which has ensured that Cage's compositions have remained essentially within the mores of Western musical practice and has helped his music to compete successfully in the perennial quest for sponsorship and exposure.

Treatise, I submit, embodies a different set of relations; most importantly it is a negation of the egocentricity that lies at the heart of Western artistic orthodoxy. *Treatise* does not wholly belong, either to Cardew or to those whose lives it nourishes and inspires; it is offered and shared unconditionally, untethered to any rules or laws of musical composition or any other 'figments of the musicological imagination.' What Cardew proposes to the performer in *Treatise* is no less than a voyage of 'self-invention' (to borrow from Eddie Prévost): 'What I hope is that in playing this piece each musician will give of his own music – he will give it as his response to my music, which is the score itself.'[19] And it was the ethos of 'self-invention' which became the categorical imperative of Cardew's revolutionary musical thought and practice in those heady years of the late sixties – with AMM and with the Scratch Orchestra.

Some Remarks on the relation of *Treatise* to Wittgenstein's philosophy

Cardew had been acquainted with Wittgenstein's philosophy for over three years before he embarked on *Treatise* and although Wittgenstein's name is rarely mentioned there is a freight of oblique references to Wittgensteinian thought both in his writings (*Notation – Interpretation, etc.*) and in his compositions (*Autumn 60* and *Octet '61*) during the period 1959-62. Yet it is unlikely that the extent of Wittgenstein's influence on Cardew and the debt which his musical and compositional practice owes to Wittgenstein can ever be accurately measured; those of us who have taken the first tentative steps have floundered in a sea of speculation, observing connections where probably none exist and overlooking the obvious and the significant. This is certainly the case with the present writer, but of this I am certain: that the plot will thicken and the discoveries by people more knowledgeable, more perspicacious, both about music and about philosophy, than myself, will create lines of enquiry which will yield results of far-reaching and unimaginable consequences.

Rather than plunging headlong into the analytical fray let us begin modestly with a broad and intuitive, if unremarkable, impression which several commentators have entertained; it is, after all, largely on the basis of intuition that the performer proceeds with *Treatise*. Let us take the imposing, middle line of *Treatise* – the 'lifeline' which runs throughout the piece and whose occasional distortions and absences are as meaningful as its majestic presence – and suggest an analogy to the single, sweeping line, metaphorically speaking, of Wittgenstein's *Tractatus*. In fact, the analogy is too pat; track the middle line of *Treatise* and by the time we reach page 30 the comparison begins to jar; Cardew's 'lifeline', for all its qualities, shows a vulnerability which is entirely absent in the *Tractatus,* with its continuity and clarity of purpose. Cardew's middle line occasionally falters, deviates, and even disappears – and with it our analogy. Let us therefore broaden our perspective and cite other, less contentious correspondences – not least, the striking coherence which both works exhibit. For Cardew this meant a kind of graphic logic in which each and every sign was appropriate to the context in which it appears (this he described as 'diagrammatic writing'), a stylistic imperative which determines the process of refinement which they undergo; in *Treatise* the presence and characterisation of a sign in a given context never seems arbitrary. *Treatise* is informed with an organicity both of motion and structure.

Yet we should not get carried away with the idea of the pre-eminent role of 'logic' in *Treatise*; an important (contradictory?) feature of the graphics is precisely its non-homogeneity; compare, for example, the precise shape and connotation of the neatly-drawn bass clef signs, notes and accidentals just four pages earlier on page 186 with the wild, impulsive gestures – like missiles propelled into the air causing two birds to take evasive action – which dramatise page 190. And signs are often juxtaposed with other signs; or signs are fused, as we saw in *Octet '61* (Ex.6.4a).

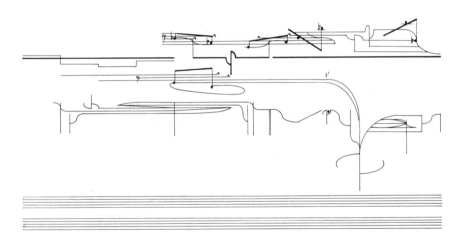

Ex.6.4a. *Treatise*, p.186.

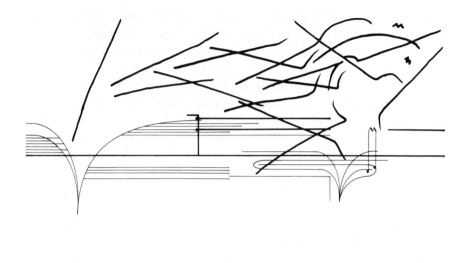

Ex.6.4b. *Treatise*, p.190.

What is significant is that these spontaneous gestures which characterise page 190 appear towards the end of *Treatise*, and it was in 1966, when *Treatise* was nearing completion, and when he was already a fully-fledged member of AMM, that Cardew expressed the view that an improvisatory character was essential to *Treatise*. This was a clear shift in his thinking for which a newly-discovered, serious commitment to free improvisation was a key, contributory factor. Initially, he had insisted that the score must govern the music; it was not an arbitrary jumping off point for improvisation, although this, in fact, is what it became for most interpreters; the majority found it simply more practical, and less daunting, to adopt an impressionistic attitude towards *Treatise*. Yet as late as 1970 Cardew still seemed unsure as to the precise nature of this 'improvisatory quality'. On the one hand he did not consider *Treatise* 'improvisatory', and yet 'it does seem (using hindsight) to have pointed in the direction of improvisation. A square musician (like myself) might use *Treatise* as a path to the ocean of spontaneity'.[20] Michael Parsons has drawn an interesting comparison between Cardew's change of heart in relation to *Treatise* and Wittgenstein's earlier and later views on musical notation. In the *Tractatus* Wittgenstein talks of the notation as being an exact analogue of the sound: the idea that for every element in the notation there is an aural correspondence. Thus the structure of the musical notation corresponds exactly to the structure of the sounds which it represents. This representational theory is perfectly exemplified in the theory and practice of serialism, where the score is expected to represent an exact picture of the sound. (And there is a broader relationship in the way that the elaborate formal structures of the serial works of the fifties express both the purity and the artificiality of the *Tractatus*.)

Despite his insistence, initially, on the authority of the score – something which he stresses several times in the Working Notes in the *Treatise Handbook* – Cardew recognized that Wittgenstein's representational theory, at least in respect of the musical score and its realization, was flawed. In the *Tempo* article there is a reference to it dated as early as July 1959, which would have been around the time that David Sladen presented him with a copy of the *Tractatus*:

> Suppose the player to behave as follows: he reads the notation and makes himself a picture of the sound (in his mind – the hypothetically imagined sound). He then attempts to reproduce this picture in sound; he plays, and then listens to the sound he has made; he compares it with the picture of the sound he had in his mind beforehand, and he may make a few changes, reducing the most glaring discrepancies, releasing wrong notes quickly, reducing the notes he finds too loud, etc. etc.[21]

And just as Wittgenstein later objected that the picture theory was deficient because it did not take into account the way language is actually used, so for Cardew the concept of the 'hypothetically imagined sound' was 'dubious'. 'On what basis does the player imagine the sound?' he asked. 'On the basis of his understanding of the notation? But the process of imagining cannot be included in the notation!'[22] Could a notation be devised which at least took into account the way instruments 'actually are played'? This in turn raises the question: what mental and physical processes are actually involved in playing?

In an earlier note in the *Tempo* article he had identified 5 stages in the production of music: 1. What is written. 2. Information gleaned by the player from (1). 3. The player. 4. The action to produce the sound. 5. The sound. What strikes one immediately here is the world of distance which exists between stage 1 and stage 5, both of which are referred to as 'the composition'. Significantly, the player is found mid-way between the two – the midwife who delivers the notation into the world of sound – and there are myriads of uncertainties (indeterminacies) between conception and birth. So the role of the notation in determining the 'sound' may be crucial, but it is also limited.

In many cases we do not imagine the sound on the basis of the notation, but on the basis of our previous experience, that is, (too) while practicing the piece, and therefore the 'imagined' sound has no particular claim to correctness at all, and therefore a comparison of the actual sound with it has no sense whatever.[23]

As we have seen, in *February Piece 1* Cardew attempted to circumvent the problem of the performer's 'imagining' by excluding it – just as the European serialists had: 'He (the performer) should not interpret in a particular way (e.g. how he imagines the composer intended) but should be engaged in the act of interpretation.'[24] But is the performer really 'engaged in the act of interpretation' – or he is simply engaged in doing what he is told? Despite its efficacy and sophistication the prescriptive nature of his notation for *February Piece 1* belonged to a compositional mode which he had found wanting, and in the *Tempo* article, some three years before he embarked on *Treatise*, he already expresses a deepening scepticism of the role which the representational apparatus of traditional notation is still expected to play in contemporary music. Cardew was more aware than most of the limitations which the constraints of the western notational system imposed on compositional thought – not least by the mere fact of sitting at a desk with a sheet of manuscript paper impressing its image on the mind's eye.

But to return to Michael Parsons' comparison: around 1929-30, when he was beginning to reconsider his earlier theory, Wittgenstein's view of musical notation had begun to shift:

Later (in MS 107, p.243) [this refers to the unpublished MS of 1929] Wittgenstein notes that musical notation can be thought of as a set of instructions for acting in a certain way:
'Die Sprache der Notenschrift [ist] eine Anweisung für das Spielen eines Instruments'.
Thus musical notation provided Wittgenstein with an interesting example of how a symbolism can be part of a complex which includes human activities guided by this notation.[25]

And right at the outset of *Treatise*, in February 1963, (*Handbook,* p.iii) Cardew had expressed the same idea: 'Notation is a way of making people move.' So in both cases a fairly rigid, representational relationship is dismantled. Rather than representing a reality, the notation intervenes; its role is dynamic, creative, and the way notation is actually used becomes the crucial factor, just as the use of language became central to Wittgenstein's later philosophy. In the later work Wittgenstein regards language as a part of human life; this is the context in which language should be examined – in the way that it 'meshes with life'. Its complexities of form and function have no independent basis outside themselves; their justification can only be met within language and its place in our lives. He refused to construct systemic philosophical theories and he rejected the pseudo-scientific treatment of non-factual modes of thought, defending their claim to independence. His aim was simply to assemble the facts about language and to wage a continuous war against what he saw as the bewitchment of the intellect.

If we can posit an analogy with Wittgenstein's repudiation of his earlier work, it would reside, I believe, in Cardew's rejection of serialism (the representational theory) in favour of graphic notation, or even in his abandonment of notation altogether in favour of improvisation. Here are where the most profound correspondences can be sited, rather than in his politically-motivated position during the seventies. During his apprenticeship in Cologne Cardew, too, had concluded that to theorize was to falsify, and throughout the seventies he was to pour scorn on what he regarded as the pseudo-science which had permeated theoretical discussion in Darmstadt during the fifties.[26] For Cardew it was not the scientific 'validity' of musical theories that was of importance or relevance; it was the way in which any musical manifestation affected the lives of those who practised and listened to it. He was sceptical of the usefulness of 'science' when we try, for example, to describe the impression a piece of music makes on us; it might be necessary to enter other areas of discourse, but rarely science. Like Wittgenstein he held the view, at that time, that the aesthetic creations of the human mind enjoy a precious immunity from scientific analysis.

Notwithstanding its title *Treatise* clearly reflects Cardew's simultaneous preoccupation with both the earlier and the later Wittgenstein. Moreover, it can be argued that *Treatise* does express their chronology: the forward trajectory, the flow and continuity of the graphics, the more abstract, pristine quality of the geometrical shapes of the first two sections (pages 1-44) suggest the bold, majestic sweep of the *Tractatus*; by contrast, the later sections of *Treatise*, with their 'autobiographical wisps', correspond more to the anthropocentrism of the *Philosophical Investigations*, with its 'short, sharp observations, interspersed with arresting questions, and startling dialectical volte-faces.'[27] In the latter pages of *Treatise*, in particular, copious musical equivalents are to be found, and to the sensitive and perceptive interpreter a recognition of these correlations will have meaningful consequences. By the time *Treatise* was nearing completion Cardew's attitude towards it was decidedly anthropocentric:

> Each player interprets the score according to his own acumen and sensibility. He may be guided by many things – by the internal structure of the score itself, by his personal experience of music-making, by reference to the various traditions growing up around this and other indeterminate works, by the action of the other

musicians working on the piece, and – failing these – by conversation with the composer during rehearsal.[28]

For Cardew insight into the way of (musical) life of musicians was crucial to any understanding of the art they practise. He was deeply interested in the 'stream of life' within which musical utterances found expression, just as Wittgenstein would try to draw us away from words and sentences to consider rather the occasions on which we use them, the context which gives them a particular meaning.[29] Despite his frequent references in the earlier pages of the *Handbook* to the supremacy of the notation, Cardew now seemed to be suggesting that in the act of making music the score has no more 'authority' than any other parameter. For in *Treatise* the notation does not depict, or attempt to depict, an existing sound 'reality'; it is there to inspire, even incite the performer in order to bring about a music which does not yet exist. In fact, this was a view he had reflected upon even in the early months; on 28 September 1963 he remarked that in *Treatise* 'the score seems not representational. No rules of representation. Except the central line represents perhaps the performer or a single line of thought'.[30] Notation could not be simply a representation of sounds any more than linguistic forms comprise solely statements of facts.

Rules and Rule-making[31]

'I tell you, no virtue can exist without breaking these ten commandments. Jesus was all virtue, and acted from impulse, not from rules.'[32]

In *Treatise*, by prescribing no rules at all, Cardew brings the question of 'rules' to the surface; the performer is invited, by implication, or by default, to provide his own. Of course, different modes of procedure presuppose different perceptions, but even in the most spontaneous and wayward of interpretations (for example, where the performer responds to perceived changes in audience behaviour) rules and attitudes towards rules are invariably involved. It is the absence of *prescribed* rules which makes *Treatise* such a radical departure.

The rules which we are therefore obliged to invent for *Treatise*, sometimes as we go along, rarely provide a fixed and immutable point of reference. Even in group realisations, where it may be desirable for some kind of consensus to be reached, our collectively-agreed rules allow for divergent, individual interpretations; paradoxically, what gives such musical practices their stability is a consciousness of the limitations of whatever rules are applied, and of the need for flexibility. Some interpreters set great store by the rules they adopt and try to hold to them systematically; others, whilst adopting rules, cannot resist flouting them – sometimes for the sake of convenience, sometimes through mental laziness, sometimes through a fiercely-held conviction that rules (even home-made ones) are meant to be broken – interpreters such as Janice Tilbury to whom a return date stamped on a library book is an intolerable act of authoritarianism. 'Rules and regulations ruin our true appreciation of nature and our powers to express it', Goethe opined in *The Sorrows of Young Werther.*[33]

In one way or another the rules we adopt, whether purposefully or half-heartedly, and their application, reflect our perception, our *understanding*, of *Treatise*; more broadly, they relate to and are determined by our practice, by the way we lead our lives; they are not plucked randomly out of the air. Through his creation of a notation which was about 'making people move' Cardew had to address the fundamental issues of why and how people *humanize* sounds, just as Wittgenstein had brought all the great philosophical questions which have arisen out of the various discourses to the same level from which philosophy started – ordinary human life. One may even conceptualize a musical language which has no rules at all, an internalised language embedded in life, in human activity.

In the early sections of *Treatise*, in particular, there is a lucidity and explicitness which invites, if not demands, the application of a system of rules. In the *Handbook*, in an elaborate interpretation of the various triangles which appear in the score, Cardew shows how precise information relating to the morphology of a sound can be derived by the systematic application of rules.[34] There is also a detailed description of a method he devised for determining tones from each appearance of the 5-line musical stave. This was for a Swedish trombone quartet who were to have taken part in a performance with the composer and other musicians in the *Warsaw Autumn* Festival in September 1966; for some reason their appearance did not materialise. Some performers would regard this process as intolerably pedantic but it does demonstrate the detailed extent to which Cardew felt it was possible to interpret the signs and thereby to determine the minutiae of sound production.

Flexibility in the interpretation of rules was something which Cardew admired in the music of Christian Wolff. In Wolff's scores the signs do not represent sounds; they create situations in which the performers act, and the instructions consist mainly of suggestions as to how the players interact. Rules have to be modified, altered, or simply jettisoned in order to deal with the 'impossible' situations which arise from time to time during the course of a Wolff piece: playing five tones in zero seconds, for example! 'One can establish a hierarchy among rules and make general decisions about which rule takes precedence (where two rules seem mutually exclusive). Alternatively one can decide for each particular situation which rules are binding.'[35] Thus, *mutatis mutandis*, the rules are obeyed differently according to the circumstances. With the music of Christian Wolff it is as if one is interpreting the rules, rather than the notation; rules and notation coalesce.

Cardew clearly enjoyed these problems, not least because logic seemed to be under threat from art. In the following quote from the *Tempo* article he seems to be expressing the same anthropological attitude to logic which had impressed him in the *Philosophical Investigations*: 'Compare "that seems natural" with "that seems logical" with "there is a sort of severe logic in it" meaning it's not natural but it's "right".'[36] In the context of human affairs logic appears less intractable, even vulnerable. For Cardew the source of all rules and rule-making, of all necessities, is *in ourselves*; rules and their application are derived from our practice, our *modus vivendi.* In music they are derived from the requirements, the needs, of our music-making, not according to some external, musicological canon. At the same time he warned against what he described as 'lapses into constant evasions': when the going gets tough we simply abandon the prevailing method of interpretation and adopt another. Yet he did not condemn these 'evasions' out of hand; they must be 'watched and conscious'. As a last resort consistency – that is, a self-imposed, unbending rule or set of rules – may be jettisoned, but not in a cavalier fashion, and certainly not as a recipe for anarchy. For it is assumed that new rules, perhaps rules that contradict the deposed rules, are substituted. Cardew recognized the necessity of rules – but not their supremacy; rules are dispensable.[37] The subtleties of the notation/performance relation in *Treatise*, for example, transcend the rules:

> The notation should put the player on the right road. He can rise above the notation if he works through the notation. Interpreting according to the rules should lead him to the identity of the piece; this grasped, he may slough off the rules and interpret freely, secure in the fact that he knows what he is doing – he knows the piece.[38]

On Interpreting *Treatise*

As we have seen, several years before he embarked upon *Treatise* Cardew had already turned his back on what he dismissed as the coercive formalism of serialism in favour of the nuances of the particular case, of indeterminacy; indeed, some of the ideas which were developed during the *Treatise* years, 1963-7, had been anticipated as early as 1959 in the *Tempo* article:

> One point is, that every sign should be active (compare the barlines in Feldman

and Boulez). Here are openings for indeterminacy, or freedom for the player: he must decide which signs he will give activity to, or allow to act. The composer can bring this about in a variety of ways: by overloading the player with so many rules that they begin to contradict each other; or by using the same sign in a variety of contexts where it *cannot* mean the same (paradoxical notation); or by giving no rules whatever and obliging the player to seek out just such rules as he needs or as will make sense of the notation. (This last is very important, and often seems the case with Feldman.) All these are psychological obscurities directed at the player in the hope of waking him up.[39]

Of course, the indeterminacies which Cardew lists here are associated only with the *interpretation* of signs; the signs themselves should not be indeterminate: his view at that time was that a notation was not a drawing, even though a drawing might suggest an interpretation.[40] Significantly, in the latter stages of *Treatise*, in particular, the notation does become more impressionistic; I have already touched upon the importance of AMM with respect both to the transformation of the graphic content, and to Cardew's own attitude towards the work.

It is worth reminding ourselves that when Cardew joined AMM, in January 1966, *Treatise* was still a year before completion; dramatically, he was plunged headlong into a situation in which the making of music would reach an unparalleled level of intensity and would inspire a depth of personal commitment which he had previously never experienced. In the *Handbook*, on p.xi, he refers to the influence of his music-making with AMM on *Treatise* and identifies this change of perception:

Before that [joining AMM], *Treatise* had been an elaborate attempt at graphic notation of music; after that time it became simply graphic music (which I can only define as a graphic score that produces in the reader, without any sound, something analogous to the experience of music), a network of nameless lines and spaces pursuing their own geometry untethered to themes and modulations, 12-note series and their transformations, the rules or laws of musical composition and all other figments of the musicological imagination.

In fact, the 'untetheredness' of the network produces more than 'something analogous to the experience of music'; it launches the reader/interpreter into the unknown, into speculative realms hitherto deemed unimaginable, into metaphysical abstractions – all far beyond the province of mere personal experience. In a lecture (untitled) at the University of Illinois on 25 February 1967, just at the point of the completion of *Treatise*, Cardew refers to the 'infinite variety of possible sounds', and their notation:

Like vectors – space filled with lines going in all possible directions, each extending to infinity at both ends. One line is for instance piano sounds. This would rather be a big cluster of parallel lines representing all the pianos so far. Intersecting these are the lines of the millions of people who play all these pianos. Other clusters of lines are the other instruments. Along the lines are the infinite gradations of loud and soft, and the infinite subdivisions of pitch. Amidst the maze of infinite lines there are infinite intersections, or points of identity – the sound of this pen striking the table is identical with the sound of the table being struck by the pen. All lines also extend as planes in time (since time of occurrence can also be a significant variation – e.g. the horn player entering a bar late is a very different sound from when he enters at the right time). And so on and so on. Finally it seems as though there must be almost an infinity of dimensions in which sounds can vary. Timbre, pitch, loudness, duration, time of occurrence, place of origin, orientation of hearer, acoustical environment, etc. etc.

Here Cardew seems to be positing a kind of science-fiction notation, a musical space journey for the intrepid musician-traveller across vast expanses of space-time; the multi-lined staves of *Treatise*, which notate a calculus of piano sounds across the whole keyboard, representing the idea of 'all the pianos so far' and the infinite number of pianists that played them. A truly intoxicating projection.

'Sounds – ideas; reading *Treatise* is a twilight experience where the two cannot be clearly distinguished.'[41] Cardew proffered diverse descriptions of *Treatise* ('a travelogue in the land of composition'), as if he were seeking to establish an identity for the work in his own mind. For the would-be interpreter some are particularly useful: 'an articulated network', for example, implies that something, say the interpreter's performance material, should be referable to the network of signs which constitutes the whole work. Like a grid *Treatise* is placed over the material and allowed to 'work' on the sounds. The sounds are placed at the mercy, as it were, of the signs, which act both upon each other and on the sound material: interfering with, modifying, changing, distorting. And however much one attempts to 'control' this relationship, the signs insist on assuming a certain autonomy – or what Cardew calls 'authority'.

So the interpreter devises and freely connects up his musical language with this pre-existing structure, this 'articulated network'. In making these connections he has certain options, but the structure itself is permanent and unchangeable. And whatever signification it is decided that an individual symbol should bear – and the meaning of a sign *is* the role it plays (the role assigned to it by the interpreter) – its interpretation is contextually dependent, as is the case, of course, with all notated music.[42] Moreover, since the rules which connect interpretation to score can never be described exhaustively, the information they embody is often transmuted beyond the point of recognition.

Yet assigning 'meaning' to each and every sign can become a tiresome, cramping exercise; its intellectualism stultifying. Sometimes an obdurate hieroglyph refuses either to yield a sound or to relate in some way to one; the reader must remain patient in the hope that eventually he/she will be able to coax it into an intelligible response. Often it is the context which will suggest an interpretation, a point Cardew makes in the notes for *Octet '61*. Pedantry, however well-meaning and incorruptible, soon leads the reader into one cul-de-sac after another, forcing him to abandon his interpretation in a state of moral crisis. Perhaps what Cardew wanted to demonstrate in *Treatise* was the incompatibility of the permanent symbolism of notation and the transience of sound.

The relationship between the signs and the 'resulting' music cannot, in my view, be described in purely symbolic terms; one can prepare oneself for *Treatise* but one cannot sit and work it all out. What one can do is to react emotionally, spontaneously, irreverently to the notation while still following, or rather observing, a set of rules which one has devised, none of which necessarily involve a specific symbolism. This corresponds to the way in which improvising musician Eddie Prévost (of AMM) approaches a group performance of *Treatise*:

> Without having any preconceived ideas about what I will play – except by virtue of the instrumentation I will apply – I immerse myself within the sounds of the music unfolding, reading the score as if it were a visual representation of the music. I then engage in a dialogue with the other players, using the inspiration of sounds and symbols to add my own voice. These are, of course, simultaneous readings (they always are).[43]

In *Treatise* the reader is swept along, sometimes at breath-taking speed, by the visual expression of 'long-term continuities'; for example the stave, free of traditional constraints, will take off in unpredictable, vertiginous flight, now contracting, now expanding, twisting and turning, disintegrating, fragmenting, now orderly and undemonstrative, now riotous and violent, exploding into fragments like a display of fireworks. Then, suddenly, a particular element catches our eye; we follow it, it seems to offer a temporary stability, an orientation. Or it incites us to extravagancies; the pulse quickens, and we are driven, page after page, towards a climactic expression. And then it disappears, leaving us marooned in unfamiliar territory. And yet, by following it, using it, by our *commitment*, we have validated it. Through it we have been moved to make music. For many performers it is the morphology of the signs in *Treatise* and their broad trajectories as much as any symbolic meaning which is attached to them that governs and stimulates interpretation. Like living forms they grow, expand, metamorphose, splinter, vanish, are revitalised – just as real sounds behave. As if *Treatise* were a kind of notational naturalism which resists symbolic representation, or renders it, at least in part, superfluous.

To read and act upon a notation can be a liberating experience; a notation can posit the unthinkable, the unimaginable, the unplayable, the unperformable, just as Cage's and Wolff's notations sometimes do. In *Treatise*, too, the signs expand the normal field of reference of traditional notation beyond the received definitions of 'music'. *Treatise* cannot be circumscribed by purely musical references; *Treatise* invites us, irresistibly, to play, to sing – but also to dance (dancers have been inspired to choreograph their readings of *Treatise*), to perform, to act, to move; ultimately, to *self-invent*.[44] With *Treatise* Cardew wanted to incite the performer to risk, to transgress, not through an 'accident' thrown up by the score, as in Cage, but through the re-definition, the re-invention, of her own consciousness.

To 'sight-read' through *Treatise* is an exhilarating experience (John White described reading through *Treatise* more soberly as 'a music lesson'); for there is no time to think, to imagine, to prepare the sound beforehand. The relation is kinaesthetic, the notation more an incitement to act than to imagine – or rather, action and imagination coalesce to defy notational control, however subtle and persuasive. Thus, and here reservations surface, sight-reading through *Treatise* the sound is created less on the basis of the notation, more on the basis of the player's previous (playing) experience; the performance is thereby closer to improvisation. But as source material the past is always treacherous; it can turn the tables on the indulgent performer, hold him hostage; the bedrock of past experience is too easily accessible, too comforting, dissuades the performer from leaving the ground, from flying and discovering. So although in the more spontaneous context of 'sight-reading' the signs enjoy less authority, their mere presence is crucial; intervening, checking, moderating, reducing/subverting the insidious purchase of subconscious habit – their influence recorded instantaneously, or not at all.

If Cardew did not completely abandon notation, he had nevertheless, with AMM in 1966, discovered a way of making music where the question of notation was simply bypassed. ('But one cannot "write" sound; the best one could do would be to "sound" the sound'.[45]) Rather than creating an elaborate metaphor, Cardew chose to *illustrate*, just as Wittgenstein 'abandoned theory, and all the glory that theory can bring on a philosopher (or musician), in favour of an illustrative technique'.[46] But that position had been reached by a tortuous route; the primacy of notation had been instilled in him, in all of us, and he had become a brilliant practitioner; in Western musical culture reading was a prerequisite of making music, and Cardew was one of the finest 'readers' of his generation.[47]

Early interpretations of *Treatise*

The performance practice of *Treatise* was developed empirically, and Cardew's initial experiments were carried out with composers and instrumentalists from the field of contemporary music – highly trained music readers whom he quaintly described as 'square musicians': among others were Frederic Rzewski, Mauricio Kagel, Sylvano Bussotti, Roger Smalley, John White, David Bedford, Kurt Schwertsik, Peter Greenham and myself. Our attitude to notation might have been described as casually, or rather unostentatiously, reverential; after all, it was through notation that the superiority of Western music had been unequivocally established, and we carried that heavy burden on our shoulders as we strove, dutifully, to give musical expression to *Treatise*. Moreover, we recognised the Western artistic conventions which seemed to inform the formal characteristics of *Treatise*; to those of us familiar with late-romantic music we could identify the gradual build-up of symphonic proportions, extending over two of my eight sections (pages 127-164), which culminates in a monumental climax of Brucknerian grandeur. This features black circles, increasing in frequency and magnitude until one of them, the largest, covers almost half a page, completely obliterating the central line which had gamely held its position until that final cataclysmic moment.

In Western culture the musical work is hypostatized as an entity in itself. Music is non-representational, abstract; we analyse its inner structure and formal relations. Preparation for *Treatise* was therefore dominated in the early realisations by a search for rules, and the necessity to hold by them. The rules were implicit and their discovery and application would reveal at least some of the secrets of *Treatise*. Rather than a creative reading of the score, it became an exercise in scholarship, trying to match the fastidiousness of the score with a method of reading which was as ingenious as it was meticulous. But the tools we were using were often inappropriate, inadequate for the symbolization of the new modes of expression which Cardew sought to elicit from interpreters. Our performances carried a surfeit of historical and stylistic sedimentation through which we sold *Treatise* (or its composer) short. We were unable to shed a proclivity for the clichés of contemporary music and, in some cases, of jazz, our fingers and the shapes in our hands programmed by the obligatory repetition of time-honoured figurations. In particular, we were the precocious children of the avant-garde; we were familiar with the most recent works of Cage, so that when Cardew suggested grouping symbols together and reading them in relation to 'time-lines' – through which various parameters of the sound could be derived – we knew that he had Cage's *Variations* in mind. Christian Wolff's scores, too, were for us an invaluable source of interpretative ideas. In our creative imagination the notational systems and performing practices, the 'representational apparatus' of the avant-garde were influential as well as delimiting factors.

An unfortunate consequence of this was that we tended to interpret *Treatise* as a succession of events (despite the fact that Cardew had criticised the predominance of 'event' parameters in the two earlier experimental works: *Autumn 60* and *Octet '61*): a mechanical one-thing-after-another mode of procedure antithetical to the seamless flow which characterises numerous sequences of pages in *Treatise*. In the *Handbook* Cardew forewarns against this mode of interpretation, positing two basic sets of parameters: event parameters and happening parameters; and he considered it to be of primary concern for the interpreter to identify and distinguish between these parameters: 'Events: something short, compact, homogeneous that we experience as complete (though we may only experience a part of it) and as one thing. Happenings: something that continues, the end is not legible in the beginning.'[48] By circumscribing symbols, by our concern for beginnings and endings, we forced our chosen signs into the 'event' category.

If it is true that *Treatise* generated considerable interest and commitment on the part of those who chose to involve themselves in it, it can also be said that some performers felt frustrated and sceptical; in Buffalo Cardew's experiences with *Treatise* were not the happiest, probably because his own attitude towards it was shifting into an ambivalence which the performers sensed, and which probably undermined their confidence in their own contribution. For the two American performances he demanded an ever-increasing number of rehearsals and whereas on the one hand he would make precise demands from them, on the other he was unclear, perhaps unsure, as to what he wanted. If he wanted to create an 'authoritative' first version, this was not the right way to go about it. It seems to me that one has to live with *Treatise* for some time, just as the AMM lived with AMM music over the years, nurturing and refining it. Here, Cardew's 'city analogy' is a good one, for all its limitations, because it exemplifies the depth and extent of commitment which musical interpretation demands:

Entering the city for the first time you view it at a particular time of day and year, under particular weather and light conditions. You see its surface and can form only theoretical ideas of how this surface was moulded. As you stay there over the years you see the light change in a million ways, you see the insides of houses – and having seen the inside of a house the outside will never look the same again. You get to know the inhabitants, maybe you marry one of them, eventually you are an inhabitant – a native yourself. You have become part of the city. If the city is attacked, you go to defend it; if it is under siege, you feel hunger – you are the city. When you play music, you are the music.[49]

Cardew's documentation of early performances of *Treatise*, 1964-7, affords many insights not only into his own attitude to the work, but also into the idiosyncratic attitudes and anomalies of behaviour of those who were involved as interpreters: Rzewski's interpretation of the middle line exclusively; John White's precedent for 'perverse readings' by reading ascending lines as descending intervals; the composer's own interpretation of the five-line system as a chord which is transformed according to rules connected with angles created in the course of the stave's growth and development. More importantly, there were certain collective solutions arrived at in those early performances which were handed down and became part of a 'tradition' in subsequent realisations of *Treatise*. The frequent appearance of numbers, for example, has tended to be interpreted as note/chord repetition; that is, each player repeats his/her chosen note 'x' number of times, resulting in the repetition, 'x' times, of a random chord. The numbers enjoy a degree of separateness, normally occurring in breaks in the score:

> The numbers are included at the pauses for the reason that: any act or facet of the conception or composition of the score may have relevance for an interpretation. [...] It is the fact that there were 34 blank spaces before the first sign put in an appearance.[50]

This is an interesting, if perplexing, note because it is one of the few references, in the *Handbook* or elsewhere, to the compositional method which Cardew employed in *Treatise* and suggests that his statistics for the appearances of individual signs were subject to a random procedure. Whatever 'method' was employed here Cardew treated it on at least one occasion in cavalier fashion; in the Buffalo performance in December 1966, according to the *Handbook,* ' the number 34 at the beginning was reduced to 17 and the performance began with 17 pianissimo chords each lasting 17 seconds'.[51] No explanation is given. Perhaps 34 pianissimo chords was considered excessive by the musicians; perhaps there was a revolt; to save the concert Cardew had to compromise and the relation of 17 to 34 was close enough for him not to lose face.

Keith Rowe is not the only interpreter who regards the first 5 millimetres of *Treatise* – in which the number 34 appears – as possibly the most important detail in the whole work: a hurdle which has to be negotiated right at the outset before access to the work is obtained, and it is tempting to see this conundrum as a deliberate ploy on Cardew's part to discourage the faint-hearted. For Rowe it reflects Cardew's attitude to performance, or rather to pre-performance (as he recalls it in those early AMM days): the thoughts calm and focused, the mind relaxed, alert, open. 34 – a significantly large number (the largest) in the context of *Treatise* – it creates a sense of gravitas right from the beginning, reminding Rowe of the poem which was used in a poster advertising a *Tiger's Mind* performance on the last day of 1967:

I lay my harp on the curved table,
Sitting there idly, filled only with emotions.
Why should I trouble to play?
A breeze will come and sweep the strings.[52]

And which is echoed both in Lou Gare's 'poem', an example of notated Scratch Music which is printed in Cardew's anthology, *Scratch Music*:

I lay down my saxophone on the curved table,
Why should I trouble to play,
It is such hard work, and there
aren't any breezes about today.

And by Hermann Hesse:

[…] the whole world might be no more than a breath of wind playing over the surface, a ripple of waves over unknown depths.[53]

For musicians involved in both reading and improvising, it is instructive to contrast playing *Treatise* with improvising; in improvisation the stimulus to play and continue playing is generated from within, in response to the music as it unfolds, and the music develops organically; in *Treatise* the listener is intensely aware of a *third force*, an authority which impinges upon the music-making, obliging the performer to stop playing where he might prefer to continue, or to go off on a new tack where he might prefer to remain where he is, or suddenly to introduce a contrasting instrumental technique at a juncture where it feels inappropriate. Eddie Prévost illustrates this 'third force' in more personal terms; for that reason, perhaps, his words produce a stronger, more lasting resonance. Whereas the investigative mode and dialogue are the dominant features of improvised music (at least, we should add, in Prévost's preferred practice), with *Treatise*

tracking the score, allowing its presence, history and associations to permeate the music, inevitably means that in an intellectual and an emotional way I am still engaging with Cornelius. It is a tangible way in which I can continue to invite him to enter my musical Life.[54]

With *Treatise* the characteristic flow of much improvised music is rarely allowed to establish itself, or rather, when the score flows, as *Treatise* often does, then the music is encouraged to flow, but only as long as the score allows. And even in those pages where the feeling of movement and flow is strong, small disruptive signs will occur to throw the music temporarily off balance – which was most likely the composer's intention. Thus for the listener there can be a disorientating feeling of arbitrariness, of insecurity or, more positively, of unexpectedness; the influence of the score appears now benign, now malevolent.

By offering accessibility as well as extreme complexity Cardew's *magnum opus* demonstrates its inherently democratic nature. No performer is turned away; through *Treatise* everyone can make music – from the tentative beginner to the awe-inspiring David Tudor – bringing a musical utopia tantalisingly within reach.[55] For whatever its illustrious status in the field of composition, *Treatise* does not belong to that category of arcane 'modern' scores. One does not pore over the score in order to intuit Cardew's 'meaning'; it means what the performer, or would-be performer 'sees'. As Eddie Prévost remarked, 'an interpreter of *Treatise* is drawn to the work because there is something within its weft and warp which fascinates'.[56]

Treatise is a long, complex story which needs to be sifted. Some of its pages might appear excessively challenging and the interpreter may feel intimidated, overwhelmed – as if Cardew had created a kind of Frankenstein's monster. Worse, a feeling of frustration and failure can accompany a post-mortem of a performance. My own long relationship with *Treatise* evokes a feeling of inadequacy: a failure to do the work justice. Others share this feeling: the composer/performer Richard Barrett writes of 'exquisite frustration' accompanying his efforts to interpret *Treatise*, while composer Brian Dennis confessed to being 'thoroughly inhibited' from attempting any realization at all. And in Buffalo too, even the performing elite, whose expertise was hired on a regular basis by individual composers, could no longer understand, let alone contribute to the kind of music-making that works such as *Treatise* demanded. The musicians were bemused; they were being asked to do things, to make decisions, which had never been within their remit; for even with Cage's scores they were told what to do. Indeed, as we have seen, after *Treatise*, perhaps disillusioned by the results of his collaborations with professional musicians, Cardew distanced himself even further. But if *Treatise* was the culmination of his career as an avant-garde composer, it also carried within it the seeds of destruction of his relationship to the avant-garde.

Other Compositions 1963-67

'Pieces occur at the meeting points of different worlds. They form the ice between the cold air and the colder sea. Copper and cheese produce the Gorgonzola. We rust if we stick our necks out and become interested in the air; this rust is our music, it flakes off (like the shine after copulation).'[57]

Treatise did not dam up work on other projects; in fact at least two of the works from that period probably owe their existence to *Treatise*. Of the eight compositions Cardew completed between 1964-65, *Bun No.2 for Orchestra* (April '64) and *Volo Solo* (February '65) refer directly to *Treatise*, whilst both *Solo with Accompaniment* (August '64) and *Memories of You* (November '64), with their use of experimental notations, relate to *Treatise* in a number of ways. Of the remaining works, three – *Material* (April '64), the third *Winter Potato* (June '64) and *Bun for Orchestra No.1* (April '65) – all derive from the earlier *Third Orchestral Piece* (1960), whilst the second *Winter Potato* (May '65) is a version for solo piano of *Autumn 60* – altogether further proof of Cardew's propensity, to use Romain Rolland's phrase, to 'bake many cakes from the same batch of dough'.

In a relaxed and amiable interview with David Bedford, which appeared in the March '66 issue of the *Musical Times* under the title 'A Conversation', Cardew's questions are searching but not intimidating; Bedford, after all, was a comrade-in-arms, one of the few English composer friends who partook enthusiastically in performances of Cardew's indeterminate pieces: *Octet '61*, *Solo with Accompaniment* (on several occasions) and *Treatise*. During their conversation Cardew raised the question of metric notation and the importance of 'pulse' in music. In his work with school children Bedford was experimenting with space-time notation, attempting to wean them away from a reliance on 'beat' and the inflexibilities of metric notation. Cardew, however, was sceptical:

I think possibly you're underestimating the immense power of rhythmic music – traditional music with regular pulse. To ask them at one fell swoop to abandon that and think in terms of durations is a rather more far-reaching decision than appears at first sight.

He then asked Bedford whether his use of a basic unit of a second could be considered to constitute 'anything like a beat'. In his reply Bedford affirmed: 'I do regard the second as a beat, but as a personal beat which may be slightly different for each player during the piece.' In his advocacy of a 'personal beat', an inner pulse free of outside coercion and control (the baton), free of the mechanical constraint of an imagined metronome, Bedford could not have found a more sympathetic and understanding audience. Several of Cardew's works at that time featured the idea of a variable pulse, variable according to inner needs and fallibilities: in *Solo with Accompaniment*, for example, the regular production of a length-of-breath tone – if the soloist is a wind or brass player – constitutes a physical determination and constraint of 'pulse'.

Bun No.2, completed in Ansedonia in April 1964, is for chamber orchestra with enlarged brass section and percussion, and with idiosyncratic and generous use of the snare drum. It comprises six sections, each of which is marked either Falsch or Richtig as follows: Falsch (1), Richtig (1), Falsch (2), Richtig (2), Falsch (3), Richtig (3), and consisting of 9, 37, 17, 14, 14, 33 bars respectively. In the introduction to the printed score Cardew states that, ideally, the piece should be performed twice in the same programme, though not consecutively. Moreover, the two performances should differ in that the first interpretation should contain only those (three) sections headed Richtig, while the second interpretation should omit nothing. Cardew also requires that a number of notes overlapping ends and beginnings of sections – that is, are common to both – should be omitted; these notes are written within square brackets. Thus the 'purity' of the 'Richtig' interpretation is sealed. The fact that the omission of the Falsch sections in the first interpretation is prescribed so fastidiously, as well as the designations themselves – 'Right' and 'Wrong' – suggest a mutually exclusive relation, although even after repeated hearings of an indifferent cassette recording of the first performance the essential nature of the relation does not yield itself, at least to these ears, with any degree of certainty; indeed, the three Falsch sections seem as sharply contrasted as any Falsch/Richtig comparison.

The Relationship to *Treatise*

In the introduction to the score Cardew writes:

> With the exception of the passages marked FALSCH (2) and FALSCH (3) the piece is based on pp.45–51 (middle) of Treatise. In a way it represents an analysis of that passage of Treatise.

Cardew's choice of the word 'analysis' (i.e. 'to examine in detail in order to discover meaning, essential features, etc.') to characterise his treatment of *Treatise*, and the derivation of *Bun No.2* from it, is in itself an important guideline for any attempt to decipher their relationship. But if Cardew's quest in these few pages was a short voyage of discovery, it was also his intent, as we have seen in our discussion of *Treatise*, not only to discover, but to *create* meaning. This, of course, renders the exercise a highly speculative one, particularly in view of Cardew's idiosyncratic mix of the contrived and the spontaneous in his own interpretations of *Treatise*. An adopted system, rigorously pursued for, say, a section, might suddenly be abandoned, overridden by new features demanding a new interpretative mode. Yet we may reasonably posit that throughout *Bun No.2* the frequent, sustained chords acquire their harmonic movement by means of the same elaborate system which Cardew later includes and explains in the *Handbook* (pp. xi-xii). Here he describes how intervallic progression can be derived from individual geometrical shapes and how the dynamics can be determined by the spacing of the 5-line stave – the narrower the softer. This 'rule' may well have been incorporated into his orchestral realisation.

By contrast there are correspondences of a quite different kind, some quite humorous in their literalism. For example, the two small complete triangles in the middle of page 47 of *Treatise* (Ex.6.5a) are almost certainly instrumental in eliciting the exposed triangle tones in bar 32 of *Bun No.2* (Ex.6.5b).

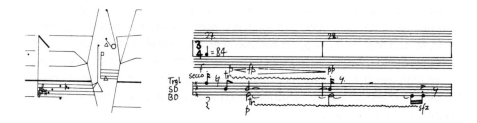

Ex.6.5a. *Treatise*, p.47.   Ex.6.5b. *Bun No.2*, p.8, bar 32 (percussion part).

Having identified these correspondences, they can then act as landmarks of coincidence between a *Treatise* symbol and a specific feature in the orchestral score; for the rest one can only apply creative intelligence and imagination to speculation as to the correspondences between the two works, and hope for the best. Even at the beginning of the exercise, where no guesswork is required, it is difficult to determine the relationship with exactitude: How and why does the profusion of parallel lines at the beginning of page 45 of *Treatise* correspond to the fastidiously notated double bass parts and the wind chord and triplet rhythm in bar 1 of *Bun No.2*?[58]

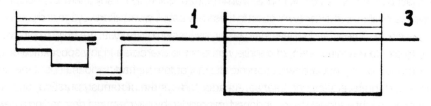

Ex.6.6a. *Treatise*, p.45.

Ex.6.6b. *Bun No.2*, bars 1-2 (two-piano version by Dave Smith).

In bars 1-2 of *Bun No.2* the same harmonic structure is used for each phrase, with freer, more expressive material superimposed. With a stretch of the imagination we can see how the shape of these two phrases might correspond to the beginning of page 45 of *Treatise*: we can posit the stave as denoting the (brass) chord, with the thick lines representing its constituent parts (the tiny line representing the tenor trombone's two grace notes); the break in the middle line corresponds to the triplet rhythm while the short thick line below the break represents the low (piano) B flat; the number 1 represents the pause.

This is fine as far as it goes but one quickly encounters contradictions, even when we pursue what would appear to be a promising area of speculation: the correspondence of the six numbers, 1, 3, 1, 1, 3, 1 on pages 45/6 of *Treatise* to the six pause marks which occur in the first six bars of the orchestral piece. But the next numbers 1,1,1, do not appear until towards the end of page 51, the end of the section of *Treatise* on which the orchestral work is based. Meanwhile *Bun No.2* is punctuated throughout with a superabundance of pause marks. So my interpretation of the relationship between numbers and pauses is quickly found wanting.

Of course, it is not difficult to 'construe' instances of correspondence, but it is when a more rigorous and ongoing analysis of the relationship is attempted that we flounder in a sea of compromise and self-deception; perhaps it is no more than the lineaments of the relationship between the two works that can be determined with any degree of confidence.[59] Or perhaps my linear approach is too routine, too predictable, and therefore doomed right from the outset? Ultimately, there is a feeling with *Bun No.2* that the music is straining at the notational leash, urged on by its fascination with *Treatise*, to which it is in thrall; Cardew had reached a stage where traditional notation was too restrictive to the impulse of his thought. According to Stella Cardew he had 'serious doubts' about *Bun No.2* and was 'very unhappy at rehearsals'. After the performance in Brussels on 12 December he refused to take a bow amidst considerable embarrassment. Just a few weeks earlier, on 3 November, he had written self-analytically:

Making orchestra transcription of *Treatise* (for instance) is not undertaken for the sake of public recognition, but simply surrendering to the vulgar desire to hear what I imagine. The technique of performance is losing its hold on me (I mean 'the way music is made' as a kind of philosophical enquiry). I remember with gratitude how a similar preoccupation with systems of notation relaxed its grip on me some time ago. Not that I lost interest; simply the threat of an obsession was removed.[60]

And on 19 September he penned an equivocal, presumably ironic, reference to *Bun No.2* which was also deemed worthy of inclusion in the *Handbook:*

Bun for Orchestra: '...for all those who give up halfway, the fainthearted, the soft, those who comfort their souls with flummery about the soul and who feed it – because the intellect allegedly gives it stones instead of bread – on religious, philosophic and fictitious emotions, which are like buns soaked in milk.' (Musil)[61] This bun is a stone bun soaked in milk.[62]

For Cardew conventional musical notation had become dangerously routine; its advantages and virtues were taken for granted, while its disadvantages and severe limitations, because they were ignored, insidiously imposed themselves on musical thought. In Western music, and in contemporary music in particular, notation had fettered the musical imagination, blunted musical sensibilities, and inevitably music itself had suffered, imprisoned within a prescriptive and controlling system. Yet it was precisely to this 'system' that he had wilfully subjected some pages of *Treatise* in a vainglorious exercise to objectify his desire – and 'vulgar' because it betrayed the ethical purity of the idea of *Treatise.*

In *Material*, for any ensemble of harmony instruments, as in the *Third Orchestral Piece*, of which it is a transcription, the players initially follow the same route through the sections and the beats are synchronised – that is, imposed by a conductor or 'imagined' metronome marking – so that a characteristic movement and flow is established between the players. In *Material*, however, at a certain agreed stage in performance, sections may be freely counterpointed; synchronization is abandoned, the beat thus becomes variable and, in the context of an ensemble, the resulting increase in rhythmic complexity gives the music an extra dimension. Yet somehow the feel of the beat is maintained, fighting for its very existence in a sea of rubato.

As in the orchestral work, Cardew notates huge, chordal conglomerates from which the performer selects pitches; thus change may be effected according to individual taste and contemporary practices and fashion. There are also what Cardew describes as 'hereditary characteristics' linking it with the past (just as we saw in *Autumn 60* with its pentatonic scale): rhythmic pulsation, and the development, through a subtle notational device, of the rubato idea provide that link.

In the case of the elegant *Solo with Accompaniment*, completed in August 1964, a satirical gloss may conceal its true significance. Here, the relatively simple solo part is thrown into relief by an extremely busy accompaniment – an ironical comment on a traditional relationship.[63] The solo part consists essentially of one note of medium-low register (relative to the instrument used) selected by the soloist and held for as long as possible – that is, length of a breath, or of a bow – and repeated *forte* an indeterminate number of times. The note is similarly repeated, but *piano*, at the octave above. At a certain point the soloist interprets a 'matrix', taking as little or as much time as he wishes; this normally has the effect of a cadenza, which perhaps is how Cardew envisaged it.

The accompaniment part consists of a number of 'matrices'; the parameters of the basic elements in a matrix wax and wane according to the composer's complex system of notation. The way these elements are supposed to function in relation to one another is best described in terms of magnetism:

> Elements in a diagonal relation attract each other; elements in a vertical or horizontal relation repel each other. Differently put: Elements on the same diagonal axis can combine and multiply together; elements on the same horizontal or vertical axis are mutually exclusive and must not be allowed to occur in combination.[64]

Thus, for example, in Matrix 10 'p' can combine with 'z' but not with '5' or '8'; 'f' can combine with '5' but not with '8'.

Ex.6.7. *Solo with Accompaniment*, matrix (10).

The various symbols which occupy the matrices refer to basic elements such as specific tones, intervals, rhythmic features, durations, dynamics and a number of unconventional sounds including auxiliary percussion material, vocal sounds and various kinds of unorthodox instrumental sound production such as piano preparation and the dismembering of wind instruments, the exact nature of which is left to the performer. There is also a group of numerals, 0-9, which are assigned to a set of ten categories selected by the performer. Cardew's own suggestions in the score are purely musical – tremolo, chromaticism, legato, etc. – but in the Introduction he recommends that these numbers should 'refer to qualities that can change according to a changeable musical climate – just as objects yet to be discovered or invented will one day change the shape of *Memories of You*'. (See below)

In his examples of the interpretation of matrices Cardew demonstrates how to negotiate danger zones, no-go areas and blind alleys; he discusses the subtle implications of rules and the flexibility needed in their interpretation, stressing the need for alertness, and for foresight to avoid difficult situations where the interpreter finds himself in a 'moral quandary'. Such situations may be avoided or indulged, persisted in; the resolution of such problems, ultimately, depends on the interpreter's 'convictions in the moral matter'. Typically, Cardew throws the responsibility of making and breaking rules on to the performer, thus raising the stakes by elevating the status of the mere performer (including the professional) to that of moral agent – bringing sounds to life and nurturing them whilst excluding and cutting off others. The composer's role is to ensure that a balance is maintained 'between cogent explicitness (necessary to galvanise the player into action) and sufficient flexibility (in the symbols and the rules for their interpretation) to permit of evolution'.[65]

Solo with Accompaniment is a 'process composition' and as such may be compared to Stockhausen's *Plus-Minus* which, through study and performance, Cardew knew intimately. Certainly Cardew's 'solo' and 'accompaniment' material may be regarded as analogous to Stockhausen's idea of 'central sound' and 'ancillary notes'. As in the 'central sound' of *Plus-Minus* Cardew's 'solo' defines the work's formal identity and process, while Stockhausen's 'ancillary notes', like Cardew's 'accompaniment', stand in a decorative relation to the 'central sound'/'solo'. And in both works there is the possibility for polyphonic treatment; in *Solo with Accompaniment*, for example, several accompanists may combine. It is in the treatment of the matrices/material that significant differences obtain; where there is systematic accretion or erosion of material in *Plus-Minus*, in *Solo with Accompaniment* the matrices find musical expression through mutual exclusion or combination and fusion of the elements.[66]

As one sits down, rule book in hand, keeping in mind the musical characteristics assigned to the various elements, making rational decisions, and after the completion of one matrix moving to the next – *Solo with Accompaniment* is, in Howard Skempton's words, a 'celebration of pedantry'. In the Journals Cardew writes:

Memo 1.9.64.

Giant step forward from dot notations of the kind used in *Solo with Accompaniment* to Cage's notations of *Music Walk* or *Variations* type. The pedantry of dot notations.

The limit on the player's thought as a continuous process.

The dot – a tiny, atrophied sign which for Cardew aptly symbolized that subjugation of sound to system, to logic, which obsessed the European avant-garde in the fifties.

Like *Solo with Accompaniment, Memories of You*, composed November 1964, abandons traditional notation altogether; indeed, *Memories of You*, as Cardew points out in his Introduction, 'even dispenses with the tempered scale, except insofar as this is represented symbolically by the presence of a piano' (Ex.6.8a).

Memories of You might best be regarded as an homage, a nostalgic reflection on Cardew's musical past with particular reference to a composer whose influence shaped his early career. Less generously, we might charge Cardew with musical plagiarism – an accusation which the following extract from Cage's *Concert for Piano and Orchestra,* with the instruction 'Notes give place of performance with respect to piano', would seem to support (Ex.6.8b):

In *Memories of You*, too: 'Each circle gives the location of a sound relative to a grand piano.'[67] Cardew then adds refinements to the Cage model: 'Sounds made at floor level are indicated by •' and 'sounds made above floor level are indicated by ○', creating for the performer a compelling spatial configuration. Furthermore, Cardew's prescription that a sound 'should begin and/or end at the point indicated' encourages the performer to explore and exploit the performing space. In this respect, as the British painter, musician and performance artist, David Ryan, has observed,

> Cardew's spatial notation of location both frees and disciplines the approach to making sound. For example, the idea of moving towards, and ending a sound at a particular spatial point suggests extreme concentration, and this for me is the key to the piece.[68]

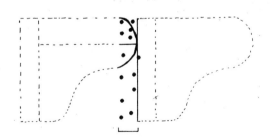

Ex.6.8b. *Concert for Piano and Orchestra* – John Cage.

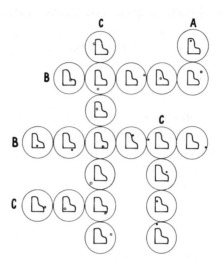

Ex.6.8a. *Memories of You*.

Ryan, who has performed the work on several occasions, also draws an interesting comparison with Cage's notation. For whereas the latter exists within 'a teeming excess of notations' in the *Piano Concert*, Cardew's discrete, self-contained notation, with its precise demarcation of space, provides a location, a creative site where the action unfolds in and around the piano, which itself assumes a kind of sculptural presence throughout.

A further refinement is Cardew's use of three, freely-chosen auxiliary objects which not only serve to characterise the sound world through which the piece moves, but also adds a new dimension to the piece. The performer selects the objects although Cardew sets the tone in the printed score through his own suggestions, which are everyday, prosaic: side drum or bass drum stick, matchbox, comb, hand, glass ashtray, plastic lid. These objects and the sounds they generate and extract are in stark contrast to those associated with the noble grand piano, the 'great warhorse of the Western classical tradition' (Ryan), which stands centre stage, in silence. Or almost silent, for Cardew suggests that 'the pedal may be engaged throughout the piece', thus enhancing, or rather betraying the pianoforte's hypersensitivity – the various activities which in one way or another impinge upon it, generating delicate resonances, so that a kind of magical, protective aura surrounds the instrument.

As David Ryan has pointed out, *Memories of You* is not 'conceptual' in the way that, for example, much of Fluxus Art was; it is a supremely *practical* exercise. Cardew's intention was to challenge the imagination and ingenuity of the would-be performer to create music – and this is wholly typical – within the most severe limitations, and with the most impoverished means; in this respect it foreshadows the tasks he was to set performers in *The Great Learning* where likewise, discipline, integrity, and a 'virtuosity of restraint' are of the essence.

Some time during the latter part of 1964 (or possibly earlier) I wrote to Cardew commissioning a 'virtuoso' piano piece;[69] I cannot remember what prompted such a foolhardy overture but in an introduction to a performance of the work (occasion forgotten) I recalled that my idea at the time was for a piece which would impress 'aunts and impresarios who love to see the fingers flying about'. I described it as, indeed, a virtuoso piece 'with a vengeance' which had a 'curative effect' on me; never again would I make such a foolish request.

Alvin Curran recalls seeing the completed work at Allan Bryant's apartment on the Campo dei Fiori in Rome; a small, incredulous group of musical colleagues and friends perusing the score, its monstrous demands on the instrumentalist(s) the cause of consternation and probably a hint of scepticism. Perhaps *Volo Solo* should be considered a conceptual piece – the virtuosity is in the mind, not in the fingers; it has the outlandish quality of a set of variations by John Bull; in a felicitous turn of phrase Howard Skempton has referred to its 'flamboyant theatricality'.

As we have seen, many of Cardew's pieces are versions, reworkings for different forces, of other works or, more subtly, of other works seen in different perspectives: *February Piece III* and *Arrangement for Orchestra*, *Octet '61* and the first *Winter Potato*; *Bun No. 2* and *Volo Solo* and *Treatise*, *Material* and the *Third Orchestral Piece*, and so on. In the preface to the printed score Cardew reveals that *Volo Solo* 'contains (with a few trivial alterations connected with the gaps, which figure in *Treatise* as numbers) the entire formal scheme of *Treatise* transliterated into well-tempered pitches'. Just as the scheme of *Treatise* consists of 67 graphic elements, so *Volo Solo* deploys 67 well-tempered, and functionally distinct, pitches. (On the 88-key piano there are therefore 21 tones missing from a keyboard version, mainly from the extreme outer registers.) To correlate the pitches with the graphic elements we would need not only to determine the 67 pitches which constitute the raw material of *Volo Solo*, but also to identify the 67 graphic elements, the delimitation of which, as I have shown in my discussion of *Treatise*, are subject as much to imaginative speculation as to analytical precision. As in other works of this period, such as *Autumn 60*, Cardew deploys the 67 elements in such a way that certain individual pitches or pitch areas will predominate at any given time; that is, they are not totally randomised.

Volo Solo, 'for a virtuous performer on any instrument', consists of 68 (*sic!*) 'events', separated by pauses, ranging from single notes and short groups to long and complex passages spanning a wide range of the keyboard; most of the longer groups are characterised by strings of repeated notes. The performer endeavours 'to play as many of the written notes as possible, and to play them as fast as physically possible. The instrument should seem to be breaking apart'.[70] In a letter to me from Italy, dated 11 March 1965, Cardew comments:

> One instruction that I finally decided to omit was 'Speed is of the essence'. I left it out because of course I don't want everything sacrificed to speed, but actually if you wish you may leave out a few extra notes for the sake of neatness and speed (that is, I don't want it to sound too un-pianistic − but then again not too pianistic!)
>
> Apart from that: the combination pedalling-dynamics should be handled with interest. Another omitted instruction was 'low dynamics as a precaution against exhaustion'. Aim at low dynamics and in long passages the instrumental sound will build up to forte of its own accord. In fact that is the way I envisaged the long passages: the piano is playing and you are sitting there holding the terminals and getting electrocuted.
>
> One other thing: think of it as (remember that it is) a tonal piece. Most of the high notes are occurring all the time, so when the bass shifts you can seek out opportunities to *modulate* (don't overdo it!) (Don't add any notes − except split ones). Naturally I haven't been into this in detail (that is, the modulation idea) − it was just one of those things I had vaguely in mind.

As in other Cardew works, the act of *performing* plays a crucial role in areas normally considered the composer's responsibility. In *Volo Solo* the actual stress which Cardew's performance instructions induce may well alter the performer's perception of the tonal characteristics of individual groups and sequences of groups; that is, exhaustion can influence phrasing, dynamics and, of course, note selection and omission, which in turn will affect the consequent tonal relationships. Thus, in determining when these relationships occur, and how they are modulated, performer stress plays an important *structural* role; it is, as it were, composed into the piece.

Of course, one can also 'edit' on the basis of taste; musical taste and pianistic limitations or prowess (aesthetics and technique) can and often do form a mutually-determining relationship; the technically problematic may appear inelegant in performance and is therefore deemed undesirable; and there are degrees of risk: the impossible, the extremely difficult, the demanding, the awkward, the unpianistic, the superhuman, etc., which have to be weighed against aesthetic judgements and demands.[71] Through this kind of intervention the performer actually influences the *identity* of a composition:

And the most important matter for the performer to decide is: which instructions are interpretative (an interpretation provided gratuitously by the composer) and which ones are essential to the piece, i.e. are actually notations in their own right, in which case they must naturally be respected.[72]

In *Volo Solo* the characteristic repeated tones set up tonal centres, juxtaposed (bitonality) and sometimes overlapping, which are further strengthened or contradicted and weakened by the surrounding, if fleeting, harmonies. This process is further complicated by the fact that the player has the option, or is often obliged, to omit notes and groups of tones. Tonal centres may be discovered, chosen, created, but they are not prescribed; rather what Cardew notates is tonal *potentiality*. Thus, hierarchical relationships between tones are set up; that is, within a group/phrase certain notes achieve relative (tonal) importance. Of course, this is just one element among several, including Cardew's imaginative suggestions for registral colour, which serve to characterise and drive the music.

And for the listener his/her experience is enhanced by the way elements almost involuntarily move in and out of focus; the ear is in a constant state of entrancement, and bewilderment, as it seeks to track the music. For whilst it may rest temporarily on a string of repeated notes, their unpredictability and volatility, as well as the shifting context in which they occur, mean that both ears and wits need to be sharp. From time to time, throughout the piece, a short phrase of one or two tones, even a lone G sharp or chord, may afford moments of welcome repose for the lost listener, and performer, to find their bearings. Yet even these can be rendered marginal by the unexpected brevity or the subversive role of the pauses which separate them. The performer's choice of pause lengths between groups and of sustained tones at the ends of groups also create tonal pointers or ambiguities which can suddenly disrupt the listener's sense of tonal orientation and alter her perception of the music.

Finally, and perhaps most radically, the choice of instrument(s) (melodic/harmonic) will have far-reaching consequences for the resulting music; compare the omission of numerous impossible pitches in, say, a performance on solo clarinet with a performance for two pianos where virtually all the notes can be accommodated if desired (Ex.6.9):

Ex.6.9. *Volo Solo*, p.9, middle system.

In the clarinet solo version, that is, without the repeated low B flats, the lower range notes create a strong feeling of G sharp minor tonality. In the two piano version the insistent B flat quickly asserts itself, at least to my ears, as a tonal centre overriding the tonal implications of the inner parts, although through careful control of dynamics and pedalling, which the composer himself recommends, it would still be possible, in the two-piano version, to create and nurture the G sharp minor 'feeling' with the B flat as a discreet pedal point on the supertonic: for the performer such considerations are of the essence.

Many pieces (*Volo Solo* is one) contain internal implications some of which (not all) the composer is aware of. These he describes in his instructions. But there may be other implications which require that certain instructions should be waived and others observed.[73]

Towards the end of this text Cardew reaches a radical and, for the performer, a somewhat unsettling conclusion:

none of the instructions to the piece are essential, they are all interpretative, even the very title itself which might be taken to imply that it must be played by someone 'alone'. But no, I can very well imagine it being performed by several players. So none of the remarks that surround the piece are essential. In fact the most useful instructions are those which make it plain under what conditions the notation itself is not binding (i.e. when notes may be omitted, etc.)[74]

So despite its title, *Volo Solo* ('I fly alone') may be performed by a number of disparate instruments simultaneously; in fact, it was first performed by Cardew and myself on piano and prepared piano at the American Artists' Centre in Paris in February 1965, thus setting a precedent for a 'perverse' interpretation. Similarly, even the explicit instruction borne by the piece's subtitle, 'for a virtuoso performer on any instrument', may be ignored, according to Cardew, by the enthusiastic and well-intentioned amateur, which would confirm that, after all, speed and virtuosity are not essential to the piece. The tempo instruction, 'as fast as physically possible', will therefore vary considerably between performers and performances.

'Phrasing and dynamics are free', and the 'free' choice from the given pitches (as in other Cardew pieces from this period: *Autumn 60, Octet '61, Material* and *Solo with Accompaniment*) will inevitably create highly differentiated interpretations. Nor does the well-tempered scale, chosen 'purely as a matter of convenience', escape the contingent status; indeed in the aforementioned first performance of the piece Cardew abandoned it by preparing his piano with all manner of objects – plastic, metal, rubber, cloth, etc., such that the 67 well-tempered pitches were transformed beyond recognition.

At the end of 'On the Role of the Instructions' *Volo Solo* is represented as signalling the end of Cardew's use of traditional notation:

> I hope I have made it clear that the writing down of music is in process of disintegrating. *Volo Solo* is evidence of the far advancement of this process at the present time, but I hope this will not prevent virtuosi and others all over the world from turning over its crumbling leaves during the short and precious duration of its half-life, on the off-chance of deriving insight, edification or at least enjoyment from playing these notes that are not 'binding' (whatever that may mean), and perhaps even communicate something of this to a completely hypothetical and unlikely listener. It is a widely accepted doctrine – and I accept it myself with almost indecent alacrity since my survival depends on it – that even the meanest and most imperfect creature may be the unconscious bearer of a seed which, if by chance it fall on fertile ground, may take root and grow, and contribute, even if only infinitesimally, towards making Everything All Right.[75]

Indeed, within a few months Cardew was able to demonstrate the versatility and adaptability of his 'indeterminate' works. Commissioned to provide music for Peter Everett's TV film, *The Girl who Loved Robots*, in September 1965, Cardew produced a score consisting of juxtapositions and superimpositions of two recently composed works, *Material* and *Volo Solo*, which he and I performed on two pianos.

Bun No. 1 for Orchestra, completed 13 April 1965, was written during Cardew's studies with Petrassi and was submitted to a board of examiners in whose presence it was performed. A favourable response would entitle the student to a 'diploma di perfezionamento in composizione', which Cardew duly received.

Bun No.1 relates to both the *Third Orchestral Piece* and to *Material*. But whereas *Material* is a transcription of the *Third Orchestral Piece*, *Bun No.1* is the composer's own 'version' of it – a work in which, as we have seen, there is considerable leeway for both players and, in particular, conductor. Whether the board of examiners knew it or not – and they probably did not – *Bun No.1* was therefore not a new composition; it was an exercise which enabled Cardew to satisfy academic requirements whilst at the same time maintaining a detachment which did not preclude a mild curiosity: how satisfactory, or unsatisfactory, would a more prescriptive notation of the *Third Orchestral Piece* be? The points of discussion with Petrassi would certainly have revolved around Cardew's use of the orchestra, around matters of a practical nature; as he himself expressed it, Cardew's professed purpose in studying with Petrassi was 'to learn a feel for the orchestra'. Certainly, Petrassi would have been unimpressed by Cardew's undisguised antipathy to traditional, formal concerns – an attitude which the formlessness of *Bun No.1* exemplifies unequivocally. It is important to bear in mind that during his studies with Petrassi Cardew's overriding commitment, as a composer, was to a philosophy of music which was sited far beyond the limits of their teacher/student relationship. His *Treatise*, begun just before the beginning of the first semester, would not have been mentioned, even in passing. During their sessions together Cardew would have maintained a protective observance of his own interests; he knew what subjects could be gainfully broached and discussed and those which could not, and to that extent he was in control.

Bun No.1 consists of six sections which are played without a break – the total duration is around 17 minutes – and each section features and elaborates two or three of the seventeen sections which constitute the *Third Orchestral Piece* (the opening of *Bun*, for example, is based on sections A and B of the earlier work). The music is articulated skilfully and elegantly and displays a profusion of detail, not least in the string parts which are often sub-divided and treated soloistically. Clearly, Cardew's aim in *Bun No.1* was to represent the total individualization of the orchestral instruments – an important feature, perhaps the most important, of the *Third Orchestral Piece*. In one long, sustained phrase near the beginning the second violins are divided into ten solo parts and there are ten successive entries. The string writing is occasionally extremely thick, with frequent use of harmonics, and at the beginning of the score Cardew requests that as many as possible of the double basses should have five strings.

The music is highly coloured throughout, the orchestration ranging from extreme density to a pointillistic, often kaleidoscopic, texture. The fifth section is an exquisitely scored version of the last sections of the *Third Orchestral Piece*, featuring the juxtaposition of the minor 3rd of N and the major third of O, and their superimposition in Q – a clear reference to Cardew's notes to the *Third Orchestral Piece* in which he suggests that the four sections N, O, P and Q 'can build up a total sound. For example, all the sounds of N and O can be sustained, and then P and Q can occur inside this total sound' (Ex.6.10a-b).

A more detailed examination of the relationship between *Bun No.1* and the *Third Orchestral Piece* would be a rewarding exercise. A sensitive, imaginative interpretation of the latter could, in theory, produce the music of the former. Yet by composing a version of it Cardew derogates from the earlier orchestra work by eliminating crucial, distinguishing features. What characterises the *Third Orchestral Piece* is a comparative lack of synchronised attacks whereas in *Bun No.1* all the sounds are coordinated by the conductor. In the earlier work the musicians move together, *en masse*, but their relationship to the conductor's beat is freer, and the responsibility towards their own individual sounds is greater – to the extent that they have 'the freedom to play or not', to make 'the sort of sound that leaves you in doubt as to whether it was there or not, and if it was there, as to whether it was by accident or design'. Such instructions are the stuff of a music-making whose psychological basis distinguishes it sharply from conventional orchestral playing (including *Bun No.1*; perhaps Cardew had taken into consideration the fact that the *Bun* was to be submitted to a panel of examiners.) These were still central issues for Cardew, and had remained unresolved.

In *Bun No.1* there are no high points; at the end there is a feeling of attainment and completion rather than struggle and collapse. It is a work of sobriety rather than excess, which does not, or should not derogate from its undoubted elegance; an exercise in retrospection and damage limitation perhaps – how the *Third Orchestral Piece* might have sounded on that (for Cardew) depressing occasion in Warsaw in the Autumn of 1961?[76] Yet inadequate performances of his music rarely provoked his criticism, however deep his sense of frustration and disappointment. Ultimately they were his responsibility, and his alone, and as such were therefore matters of deep, personal concern. If the musicians involved were unable or unwilling 'to move' in the way he had anticipated there was no point in blaming them. It is not surprising that few composers have had a better relationship with performing musicians than Cardew; nor have there been many composers who have commanded more respect from players than Cardew, who have been able to impart the subtlest, the most tenuous of musical ideas to musicians with comparabl efficacy.

Ex.6.10a. *Bun No.1*, bars 275-81.

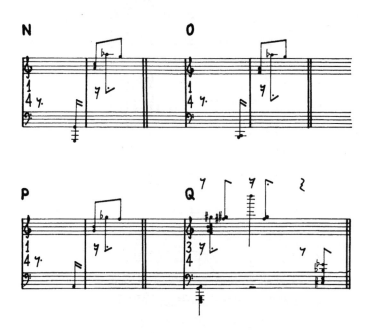

Ex.6.10b. *Material* (transcription of Third Orchestral Piece), sections N, O, P, Q.

When I once asked Cardew how he came to choose the title *Winter Potatoes* he replied that it was because 'they had been lying underground for some time'. Doubtless in Italy while he had been busy with the two *Buns*, although the first of the three *Potatoes* was completed three years earlier and they are probably related simply by virtue of the fact that all three are solo piano versions of other pieces: *Octet '61*, *Autumn 60, and Material*.

The fact that all but two of the sections of *Material* can be played by a single keyboard player without omitting notes may have prompted Cardew to create his own version for solo piano in June of 1964: the third *Winter Potato*. A letter to the dedicatee, Francesca Astaldi, reveals his purpose:

Dear Francesca,

A small Christmas greeting. The third piece is inscribed to you because I thought of it originally as a dance for you, with the dance movement taking place in the regular little gaps between the sounds: [77]

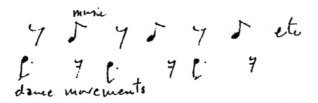

Ex.6.11. from letter to Francesca Astaldi.

The third *Winter Potato* is a short chordal piece, rather like a postlude, the chords ranging from a simple perfect fourth to highly complex aggregates for which the source work offers rich pickings. Cardew feasts on the rich material, sometimes gluttonously, occasionally fastidiously, eye and ear roving freely but with intent in and out of the sections. A short repeated motif in the middle of the piece, reminiscent of early Feldman, introduces a moment or two of whimsy which is wholly characteristic (Ex.6.12a). Here Cardew allows the tones from section M of *Material* to accumulate through repetition, superimposition and octave transposition, the range widening, the texture thickening (Ex.6.12b).

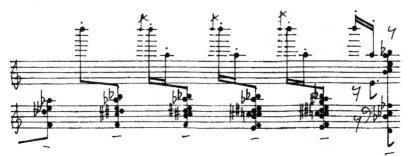

Ex.6.12a. *Third Winter Potato*, middle system.

Ex.6.12b. *Material*, section M.

In stark contrast the opening phrase of the third *Winter Potato* extracts a single line from the first three bars of section I from *Material*, which consists of a sequence of huge chords (Ex.6.13a-b).

Ex.6.13a. *Third Winter Potato*, first 7 notes.

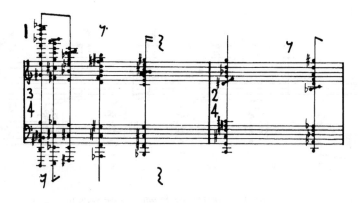

Ex.6.13b. *Material*, section I.

The second *Winter Potato,* completed in May 1965, is a compendium of twentieth-century pianistic techniques: Ravel, Scriabin, Messiaen, Stockhausen, Cage – though there is never specific reference to any of these composers. Rather there are occasionally fleeting evocations as the music unfolds, in Michael Parsons' words, 'in a relaxed and elastic sequence of loosely connected phrases and irregular bursts of activity, each with its own shape and gestural character' (Ex.6.14a).[78]

Ex.6.14a. *Second Winter Potato*, first system p.2.

And thirty years earlier Bill Hopkins acknowledged the 'mastery with which the piece's structural periods are varied'.[79] Cardew's skill in formal matters was often overlooked by critics who were usually too busy focussing on his iconoclasm. The notation is fastidious and demands extreme precision of articulation from the performer: neat hand movements are required to depress notes silently and rapidly and there is also frequent use of the middle (sostenuto) pedal for which Cardew gives precise indications (Ex.6.14b).

Ex.6.14b. *Second Winter Potato*, first system p.1.

Howard Skempton is one of several composers and critics to have been impressed by the sheer brilliance of the piece and has suggested that the expansive nature of the second *Winter Potato* might be attributed to the fact that it was written while Cardew was in Italy studying with Petrassi.

> Three Winter Potatoes are remarkable not least for their exuberance. Cardew, like most composers of any real quality, was fascinated by virtuosity. He once suggested (in conversation) that there should always be something impossible in a piece.[80]

Listening to, practising, performing and recording *Winter Potatoes* over the years, it finally dawned on me, during the evening of 11 September 1997 – some thirty years on – that the (pentatonic) character of the pitch material bears a strong affinity to that of *Autumn 60* and that these given pitches are given prominence in the piano version. Moreover, the sixteen structural periods of the second *Winter Potato* correspond to the sixteen sections, A–P, of *Autumn 60*. Significantly, this revelation came to me as I racked my brains to find at least a modicum of relevant, if prosaic, information to impart through analysis and comparison. To what extent then, in the piano piece, does Cardew observe the rules for *Autumn 60*? For if Cardew enjoyed inventing and following rules it was also the case that a pedantic application of the rules was invariably mitigated, and sometimes circumvented, by imagination and ingenuity – qualities he encouraged from all performers of his music. And this is certainly true of this piano version of *Autumn 60*.

Generally, the principal rule in *Autumn 60* is observed – that is, the use of some, and the exclusion of other indications – as are the individual meanings assigned to the indications. But Cardew's exhilarating freedom of approach relegates the rules to a walk-on role; they are accommodated, subsumed into the music and occasionally treated in cavalier fashion. The following example is a microcosm of all the virtues which Cardew brings to bear on his piano transcription of *Autumn 60*. Here the first beat of section P of *Autumn 60* corresponds to the first six crotchet beats of the passage quoted from the second *Winter Potato:*

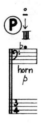

Ex.6.15a. *Autumn 60*, first beat of section P.

Ex.6.15b. *Second Winter Potato*, third system, p.6.

Thus, according to the rules, two of the indications, in this instance horn and III (3 beats), have to be 'ignored'; the rest – the B flat, the harmonic, the descent, the dynamic *p* and the medium duration – are all incorporated within the phrase.

By contrast, at the beginning of the two pieces, sections A and B of *Autumn 60* and the first two measures of the *Winter Potato,* there already appears to be an anomaly:

Ex.6.15c.   Ex.6.15d.

Autumn 60, sections A and B.   *Second Winter Potato*, first two bars, first system, p.1.

In A the pizzicato and the exaggerated attack indications are negated, whilst the *piano* and pitch indications are observed. However, in the next measure only the viola indication is negated, whilst the remaining three indications are observed. And throughout the piano version there are other such anomalies where, typically, musical imperatives override notational exigencies.

Cardew's works from the 'Italian' period are in many respects backward-looking – self-imposed exercises, versions of earlier works, like the *Three Winter Potatoes*, where he seems to be testing the viability of music conceived under different circumstances and with a less radical aesthetic and social agenda. Yet it is unlikely that this music could have had a role to play in the new musical world taking shape in Cardew's imagination. With the benefit of hindsight we can see that these works from the mid-sixties represent Cardew's swan song to the avant-garde, or rather that part of it which still courted recognition, favours and patronage from the musical establishment through music festivals, publishing houses, radio stations, Arts funding bodies, etc. One or two modest commissions would come his way and from time to time comment would be passed on his activities, but in general it was considered that his involvement with the AMM (from 1966), and the Scratch Orchestra (from 1969), in particular, had taken him beyond the pale.

Notes and references

1   Ludwig Wittgenstein. From *Recollections of Wittgenstein*, ed.Rush Rhees (Oxford, 1984), p.160.
2   Jrnl. 4 September 1963.
3   The word 'white', in brackets and with a question mark, is written above 'whole world', with a different pen and presumably at a later date.
4   *Treatise Handbook* p.i. (*CCR*).
5   Ibid, p.i. (*CCR*).
6   In November 1966, just a few months before its completion, Cardew was the recipient of an Arts Council grant of £600 for his *Treatise* project.
7   Letter from CC to SK, dated 11 January 1975.
8   *Treatise Handbook*, p.i. (*CCR*).
9   From 'On the Role of the Instructions in the Interpretation of Indeterminate Music', ibid. p.xv. (*CCR*).
10 Keith Rowe recalls that in drawing *Treatise* Cardew used the early German rapidograph which had two widths and was capable of extreme precision.
11 Nicholas Cook: *Music, Imagination, and Culture* (Oxford: Clarendon Press, 1990), p. 35.
12 *New Music 87*, ed. by Michael Finnissy and Roger Wright (Oxford University Press), p.24. (*CCR*).
13 Nicholas Cook: *Music, Imagination and Culture*, p.41.
14 Ludwig Wittgenstein: *Tractatus Logico-Philosophicus* (London: Routledge, 1990), p.189.
15 Brian Dennis, 'Cardew's *Treatise* (mainly the visual aspects)', *Tempo* Magazine no.177, June 1991, pp.10-16. (*CCR*).
16 Brian Dennis pointed out the hierarchic ratio of the tally of numbers: 1(96), 2(27), 3(19), 4(9), 5(7), 6(1), 8(1). 34 is the first number and 10 the last, and both occur only once; he detected the possible influence of Stockhausen here. But Cardew's fascination with numbers was broad-based; the work of Jasper Johns and Wittgenstein, whose *Remarks on the Foundations of Mathematics* Cardew had studied, could also have been reference points for the particular use of numbers in *Treatise*.
17 *Treatise Handbook*, p.iii. (*CCR*).
18 Skempton and I agree that he sent me this gloss in a letter but neither of us can remember when, except that it was almost certainly sometime during the 1990s.
19 *Treatise Handbook*, p.x. (*CCR*).
20 *Treatise Handbook*, p.i. (*CCR*).
21 *Tempo* Magazine, 'Notation – Interpretation, etc.' p.23, note 8. (*CCR*).
22 'Notation – Interpretation, etc.' p.24, note 8. (*CCR*).
23 Ibid, (*CCR*).
24 Ibid, p.27, note 22. (*CCR*).
25 Merrill B. Hintikka and Jaakko Hintikka, *Investigating Wittgenstein* (Oxford: Basil Blackwell, 1986), p.238.
26 'It was all lies' was Kurt Schwertsik's *cri-de-coeur*, echoing Cardew, in a conversation we had in an Indian restaurant sometime in the early nineties.
27 David Pears, *Wittgenstein* (Fontana/Collins, 1971), p.113.
28 *Treatise Handbook*, p.xii. (*CCR*).

29 'Many of the remarks of the *Tractatus* have a proverbial quality that calls to mind the mystical writers of old China. Indeed a remark by one of these, Lieh Tzu – "is it likely that long short, loud soft, can entirely represent the true scheme of things" – applies well to Wittgenstein's return to philosophy'. From a talk prepared in England for a forthcoming US tour. Jrnl. 12 September 1967.

30 *Treatise Handbook*, p.iv. (*CCR*).

31 In the following section I am indebted to Sophie Hampshire for the many pertinent and illuminating remarks she makes in her thesis 'Language, Representation and Rules: a study of Wittgenstein's theories of language and their relevance to visual art and music'. Undergraduate Thesis for the London Institute (1991).

32 William Blake: *The Marriage of Heaven and Hell* (Oxford University Press, 1975), Plate 23.

33 Regarding 'rules', the Italian composer/performer Andrea Rocca used them to construct the broad edifice of a piece based on page 92 of *Treatise.* However, he felt free, and without compunction, to jettison them at a later stage of the creative process when elements were introduced which were quite independent of the score – what he described as 'inflorescences of the main plant'. From Brief Notes on *Infant Love Song.* Andrea Rocca, July 1994.

34 Wittgenstein also makes use of triangles as examples in the *Philosophical Investigations* (Oxford: Basil Blackwell, 1991), p.200.

35 'Notation – Interpretation, etc.' p.25, note 11. (*CCR*).

36 Ibid., p.26, note 16. (*CCR*).

37 'And is there not also the case where we play and – make up the rules as we go along? And there is even one where we alter them – as we go along'. *Philosophical Investigations*, Part I, 83.

38 'Notation – Interpretation, etc' p.31, note 32. (*CCR*).

39 Ibid., p.23, note 7. (*CCR*).

40 According to Stella Cardew this was the basis of his objections to her own suggestions; he would not tolerate the indeterminate blurs and smudges which appealed to her more painterly imagination. Interestingly, her most striking contribution to the pages of *Treatise*, specifically page 190, which is reproduced above, was not censored, precisely because it dramatically enhances the more 'autobiographical' nature of the later stages of the work. Moreover, they had nothing to do with aesthetic considerations; Stella's graphic gestures were made in anger and frustration; they erupted out of domestic strife.

41 *Treatise Handbook,* p.vii. (*CCR*).

42 Wittgenstein talking about chess: 'Let us say that the meaning of a piece is its role in the game.' *Philosophical Investigations*, Part 1, 563.

43 From a letter to JT, 2 June 1994.

44 For a performance at Morley College in 1969 the artist Tim Mitchell created a wooden relief structure based on one page of *Treatise.* During the performance, by Cardew's Morley College students, the sounds of Mitchell's sawing and drilling were incidental, 'chance', by-products of his interpretation. Thus, in this version the 'music' was consigned, arbitrarily, to a secondary, accompanying role.

45 'Notation – Interpretation, etc.' p.22, note 4. (*CCR*).

46 *Treatise Handbook,* p.xvii. (*CCR*).

47 1966 was a momentous year, the first since Cardew became a student at the Royal Academy

that produced not a single composition. In 1967 a single work: *The Tiger's Mind,* which comprises solely a written text. 1968 saw another purely text piece, *Schooltime Special,* and *Schooltime Compositions,* a note-book of ideas including some references to traditional musical notation; and in April Paragraph 1 of *The Great Learning,* which does include a relatively conventionally-notated section for organ solo.

48   *Treatise Handbook*, p.iii. (*CCR*)

49   Ibid, p.xvii. (*CCR*)

50   Ibid, p.iv. (*CCR*)

51   Ibid, p.xii (*CCR*)

52   Attributed to Po Chü-i (772-846). Included in *A Treasury of Asian Literature*, ed. by John D. Yohannan (Meridan, Penguin Books, 1994).

53   Hermann Hesse, *The Glass Bead Game* (Harmondsworth, Middx: Penguin Books, 1972), p.487.

54   Letter from EP to JT, 2 June 1994.

55   Without a *utopian* core perhaps no meaningful artistic endeavour can advance?

56   See note 54.

57   Jrnl. 13 January 1963.

58   For the latter example I have used Dave Smith's transcription of the work for two pianos.

59   Perhaps it was Cardew's intention that the relationship, like many of his amorous intrigues, should be a private affair, should remain arcane, unfathomable. But in that case why the titillating disclosure of the relatively short section of *Treatise* on which the orchestral piece is based?

60   *Treatise Handbook* p.vii.(*CCR*)

61   Robert Musil (1880-1942), Austrian novelist. The quotation is from Part 1, Chapter 13, of his novel *The Man without Qualities*.

62   *Treatise Handbook,* p.vii. (*CCR*)

63   *Solo with Accompaniment* was commissioned by Hans Otte, musical director of Bremen Radio, and composer of paradoxically 'simple' long pieces such as *Das Buch der Klänge.* The first performance was to be given by Severino Gazzelloni and Frederic Rzewski in a programme including works by Dieter Schnebel – *Anschläge-Ausschläge,* and Bruno Maderna – *Amanda.* However, the Schnebel piece arrived too late, and Maderna was unable to finish his piece in time. In the event it was decided not to invite Gazzelloni for just the one piece, and *Solo with Accompaniment* was performed by another duo: Karl-Bernhard Sebon and Bernhard Kontarsky.

64   From the Introduction to the printed score, p.7.

65   Cornelius Cardew, from the Introduction to *Four Works*, January 1966, published by Universal Edition. (*CCR*)

66   In the aforementioned issue of *Performance* magazine, David Bedford describes his experience with Cardew's indeterminate pieces: 'Speaking as a performer in many of Cardew's early works it must be said that the experience was totally rewarding. Our creativity was constantly being challenged [...] It should be pointed out that none of Cardew's works ever gave total freedom to the performer. The instructions were a guide which focussed each individual's creative instinct on a problem to be solved – how to interpret a particular system of notation using one's own musical background and attitudes.'

67   From the introduction to the score, published by Universal Edition.

68   At my request, sometime in the late nineties, neither of us can remember precisely when, David Ryan sent me 'Some thoughts on *Memories of You*', from which this quote is taken.

69   'Commission' is perhaps too imposing a word; I simply asked him. Throughout our long friendship there were never any 'financial arrangements'. In any case, neither of us ever had any money.

70   From Cardew's instructions in the score.

71   We are reminded of Webern's celebrated insistence on a 'technically problematic' rendering of a phrase in the second movement, bars 12-13, of the piano *Variations.*

72   'On the Role of the Instructions in the Interpretation of Indeterminate Music'. *Treatise Handbook,* p.xv. (*CCR*)

73   From 'On the Role of the Instructions in the Interpretation of Indeterminate Music'. *Treatise Handbook*, p.xiv. In his letter to me these 'internal implications' are clearly what Cardew was referring to with his reference to the 'modulation idea'. (*CCR*)

74   Ibid, p.xvi. (*CCR*)

75   Ibid, p.xvi. In the seventies he did return to traditional notation, but by then his musical and social needs and aims were quite different. (*CCR*)

76   It must be said that not all of those present on that occasion, including myself, shared Cardew's negative response to either the piece or the performance. Perhaps *Bun No.1* does have something of the 'hardness' of Zen art, which reminds us of Cardew's counsel to himself, in April 1963, to write orchestral music of 'long flying, rigid and rock-hard lines'; it certainly has a coolness, and a sense of equilibrium.

77   Letter from CC to Francesca Astaldi, 10 December 1965.

78   From Michael Parson's sleeve notes to the CD *Cornelius Cardew piano music 1959-70*, released on Matchless Recordings (MRCD 29), 1996. (*CCR*)

79   GW (Bill) Hopkins (b. Stockport, England, 1943; d. 1981), British composer/critic. From his review in the *Musical Times,* August 1967.

80   Letter from HSK to JT some time during the 1990s.

(*CCR*) Also found in *Cornelius Cardew A Reader*

7
AMM 1965-71

'AMM is like a cradle: however violent or destructive you feel, it holds you, it won't let you hurt yourself'.[1]

In the Autumn of 1965 a young guitarist, Keith Rowe, was introduced to Cardew by Alan Cohen, an old friend and fellow student from the Academy days. The introduction was not without motive; its main purpose was part of Cardew's strategy to cast the net wider in his search for musicians who would respond positively and creatively to the challenge of his indeterminate notations. In this instance he was hoping to recruit Rowe, a jazz musician with the Mike Westbrook band, to participate in a performance of some pages from *Treatise* at the Theatre Royal in Stratford, east London. Another jazz musician, saxophonist John Surman, was also invited, presumably to offset the four remaining 'square' musicians in the ensemble: the composer and horn player Kurt Schwertsik, the percussionist Peter Greenham, the composer and myself. The event was organised by the artist Mark Boyle for the Institute of Contemporary Arts; *Treatise* was the sole musical item on the programme.

Rowe, in turn, invited Cardew to some improvising sessions with fellow jazz musicians at the Royal College of Art.[2] 'I think it had been a lifelong ambition of his [Cardew] to play in a jazz band and we were the next best thing.'[3] This jocular remark may have been nearer the truth than Prévost realised at the time; for years Cardew had collected jazz records and had taken vicarious pleasure in listening to jazz. For apart from some Jimmy Yancey transcriptions at Live New Departures events in the early sixties, and the occasional private indulgence behind closed doors, Cardew always fought shy, for whatever reason, of the jazz performance arena. Perhaps he was in awe of the prodigious and unfathomable talent which jazz musicians seemed to possess. Like secret avatars they practised their art with an ease and fluency which transcended the limits of his own education and experience. If, indeed, AMM (the cryptic acronym under which the group still performs) represented for him 'the next best thing' he would have appreciated the irony at the heart of these exchanges; for inviting Cardew was also a strategic ploy on the part of Rowe and his colleagues in their resolve to break with the strong emulative impulse to play like their black American heroes.[4] And in order to do this the jazz idiom itself had to be subverted and for some improvising musicians eventually discarded altogether.[5]

Both Rowe and saxophonist Lou Gare had been members of the Mike Westbrook band where Rowe's disconcerting habit of dropping bars and playing in different keys had created havoc.[6] Stimulated by recent memories of his Art School education in Plymouth Rowe would create guitar tablatures from Paul Klee drawings:

I'd get the part from Mike Westbrook, get some idea of what the music was like, find a picture that I thought was appropriate and glue it onto the opposite page of the chart. I would play from the picture and the others would play from the dots.[7]

As we shall see, Rowe continued to experiment with analogies with Fine Art well into the seventies. Such idiosyncratic behaviour, however 'creative', was inimical to Westbrook's artistic aims at that time and inevitably precipitated Rowe's, and Gare's, departure from the band, to the satisfaction and relief of all concerned. Eddie Prévost, who had worked in bands with Gare, was the drummer in the early Royal College of Art sessions, and another ex-member of the Westbrook band, bassist Lawrence Sheaff, soon joined them. What they embarked upon, in those heady days of the mid-sixties, was no less than a musical voyage into the unknown, and the fact that they were creating their own music – music without a clear trajectory and to which no limits, no agenda, had been set – intensified the strength and determination of their commitment.

In performance various strategies were adopted: Rowe, for example, would record pop songs – 'Barbara Ann' by the Beach Boys and 'Lightning Strikes' by Lou Christie were particular favourites – twenty or thirty times in succession, and play them back at full volume – a proto-punk performance and a direct, unambiguous use of popular material which Rowe had admired in the paintings of Roy Lichtenstein. This idea of the creation of a 'Wall of Sound', of maximum volume, often in complete darkness, which totally enveloped the performing/listening space, was a critical feature of a slowly emerging aesthetic within which the beginnings of what Eddie Prévost has identified as a 'practice of self-invention' could be discerned. For this welter of sound tested not only the ingenuity and imagination of the musicians, but also their tenacity and fortitude; it was like a sparring partner, a self-imposed trial. Incarcerated within the Wall the musicians were forced to adopt, to discover, to invent means of musical survival. Thus they could fight the Wall through comparable volume, or they could contrive to outwit it through subtle and deft placement of even the tiniest of sounds – a strategy which was to stand them in good stead in AMM's maturity; or they could use it to distil the sounds they were making in an act of patient and fastidious refinement. Ultimately, each one of them had to come to terms with it, to develop a relationship to it. Eddie Prévost would rise to the challenge in heroic, if foolhardy manner: a relentless snare-drum roll continued to the point of total exhaustion.[8] And the musicians learnt an important lesson: that it was impossible to emerge from the Wall unscathed; attitudes brought to it would be dismantled, transformed, invalidated. Out of it, paradoxically, came the search for the transparency which renders discourse and argument unnecessary, as well as a propensity for silence (or near silence) – the multifarious uses of which became over the years a distinguishing feature of AMM performances. Not silence, perhaps; rather a holocaust of tones, and embedded within the debris the rich and complex sediment of a new sound world.[9]

Cardew joined AMM in January 1966 and there was an immediate sense of compatibility; a providential, as it were, meeting of minds, or rather, of sensibilities. Perhaps for the first time, in Europe certainly, he encountered artists as audacious and uncompromising, as dissenting, as himself; musicians who had already entered uncharted territories and who would risk all in the making of each performance: vagrant, sometimes threatening music; an omnipresent, uncatchable, free music. A period of extraordinary acceleration ensued – Cardew's presence and greater experience creating a breadth and sense of authority within the group, as well as serving as a confidence-booster. The intuitive nature of the music-making, unfettered by formal considerations, was something which he had experienced briefly and certainly more cautiously in the improvisatory sessions in Francesca Astaldi's dance studio in Rome in the earlier part of the decade but this was an altogether much bolder enterprise, with wider implications and of deeper musical significance. For Cardew it meant the freedom to indulge his musical proclivities without embarrassment, to act spontaneously without composer demur – free of the role of technocrat which so much contemporary music had conferred on performers, free from the tyranny of baton and barline, free of the disaffection from which too many of his performing peers were suffering. The exhilaration in the unmediated act of spontaneously making a sound free of notational prescription was irresistible:

> For a cameo picture of what I have found in AMM that I haven't found before is just the fact that I can go there and play, and play exactly what you want, and that's something I've always wanted to do.[10]

Even the Journal entries just prior to joining AMM seem to have been affected, their style and content aphoristic, economical, speculative – as if words were to give way to sounds, and formal contrivances displaced by spontaneous gesture; it was as if through some sixth sense he had divined AMM music:

> Words, words, an endless stream of them. I swallow them in German and spew them out in English. They come to fill even my dreams, seeking out the remotest corners of my life with their monotonous drone, so that I am never free of them. No wonder I don't like conversation. And such futile words. They drive out the sounds, drive out the songs, they take over the pleasures and infiltrate the sensations. When will I be rid of them?[11]

Six years earlier, in a letter to Ilona Halberstadt dated 18 October 1959, he had referred to Wittgenstein's plaint: 'So in the end when one is doing philosophy one gets to the point where one would like just to emit an inarticulate sound.'[12]

At the time it was his translation work, a debilitating chore, which intensified the extreme antipathy and the resentment he felt towards the word as transgressor; and it was in the long, wordless sessions with AMM that this particular need, the need to be rid of words, and other unwieldy furniture, was to be satisfied. 'It would be possible to imagine people who had something not quite unlike a language: a play of sounds, without vocabulary or grammar. ("Speaking with tongues")' Wittgenstein mused.[13] Twenty years later such a 'play of sounds' had become part of Western contemporary music practice, the leading protagonists, AMM, engaged in a kind of human archaeology, digging depths which words cannot reach.

The weight and consequence of Cardew's influence can be gauged by comparing the Mercury Theatre recording of 27 November 1965 – just weeks before Cardew joined AMM – with the Elektra recording[14] some six months later, by which time Cardew was a fully-fledged member. In the first part of the Mercury performance there are moments when the listener is conscious of a judicious choice and sensitive placement of sounds, of a higher or rather more profound level of consciousness, presageful of the later AMM music; this has already travelled an appreciable distance from jazz. Yet one senses a hesitancy, a lack of (self) confidence; there is a refreshing 'musicalness', but without the majestic sweeps and decisive musical gestures which were to become the distinctive features of AMM music in the late sixties.

In the louder, faster section which ensues in the second half of the recording the music is less successful. Energy and youthful vigour do not compensate, in this instance, and to these ears, for the loss of sharpness and focus. There seems to be a loss of nerve as the music regresses into self-indulgence and seeks dubious refuge in automatism: a kinaesthetic, mechanical mode of playing which, if the intention was to free their sound-creating actions from the habits of jazz (and this was an important part of AMM's agenda at that time), was wholly inappropriate and oppressively counter-productive. Instead the music hustles, asserting itself unforgivingly until, running out of steam, it degenerates into a kind of self-parody: an indulgent philistinism – heavy lidded, glazed eyed and swollen lipped – brings the music to an abrupt end.[15]

From time to time, though increasingly rarely, this manner of playing would emerge and temporarily usurp the music-making; it was as if AMM had to disgorge itself of unwanted matter, as in group therapy, before moving on to a new plane. Yet there was much that was positive which did take root and was nurtured from those early sessions; and in the first half hour of the Mercury recording the seeds of future development can be clearly heard and felt. Given the essentially exploratory and experimental nature of AMM's music-making at this stage it is perhaps not surprising that they were not able, nor even disposed, to sustain this quality throughout their performance.

It has always been a characteristic of AMM that their concerns outside the music should be brought inside. On the opening track of the Elektra recording of 8 June 1966 there is an unambiguous reference to aspects of Eastern culture; the music has a ritualistic, quasi-religious aura about it, enhanced by the long, sustained sounds of Prévost's bowed cymbal and the gong-like punctuations and evocation of ringing bells of Cardew's prepared piano – a celebratory tintinnabulation which foreshadowed by almost twenty years the later piano works of Morton Feldman: single notes, chords, brisk flourishes, repeated tones and chords, rich and resonant, of extraordinary beauty and variety, allowing the balance to change as the multiple string and percussion drones become more insistent and new elements come into play. And the clear relation to both Gagaku and Feldman, in the same stretch of music, is emblematic of the cross-cultural terms of reference which have continued to inform AMM music.[16]

In AMM there are invariably moments of gentle humour, usually unpremeditated and instantly appreciated – like the manic music box effect on track 1 of the Elektra CD and the radio critic's fortuitous and barely audible reference to English folk music. The transistor's habit of introducing felicitous incongruities into the music is a constant source of bemusement and delight: 'I can drink most men under the table' boasts a male voice in the middle of a quiet, meditative passage, and as the same voice utters the words 'brandy tasting' the music stops peremptorily. The transistor interjections can be remarkably apposite: 'they had struck up an understanding' declares a political commentator during a dialogue between two instruments, and then just for an instant, during a weighty passage, the word 'gravitas' is given appropriate focus. 'In the Realm of Nothing Whatever' (track 4) begins with a tortured melody of squeaks – its beauty and eloquence a tribute to AMM's versatility – which is subsumed into the ensuing hurly-burly. The track ends with Cardew's brief, eloquent piano solo, beginning with declamatory pizzicati tones which lead to what sounds very much like a prepared piano version of phrases from his earlier solo piano composition: *February Piece II*. In the Elektra recording, for the most part, the musical gestures are bolder, more authoritative, and the phrasing is more finely honed. There is a stronger feeling of commitment to the 'sound' of the music, and of *conviction*, so that the music is given breathing space and allowed to take its time. And a greater richness and complexity; a soundscape which embraces an infinite range of sounds and ideas, a kaleidoscopic tapestry swishing and swirling across a wide acoustic and cultural spectrum. Yet, like the Mercury performance, this quality, at least to these ears, is not sustained – and for the same reasons. The last half hour, with some memorable exceptions, is musically less convincing; the degree of creative investment seems considerably diminished. In a vain attempt to compensate, the music surrenders to a freneticism which both irritates and bores – a regression to the atavism of the final section of the Mercury recording. Interestingly, in these earlier sessions Cardew's playing was far more assertive than in those a year or two later when he was prepared to let others take the initiative. It was as if he had been trying to install self-belief in his fellow musicians, to spur and embolden them to continue to pursue the radical path they had chosen and not to look back – a tactic which soon became unnecessary. As Eddie Prévost recalled in a conversation with Keith Rowe and myself in Rotterdam in 2001 (we think): 'Cornelius convinced me that the music was serious. He invested so much intensity, so much meaning into it.'[17]

In an illuminating text accompanying the re-release of the Elektra recording on CD, more than twenty five years later, Prévost elaborates on the thirteen aphorisms that constituted the sleeve notes of the original album. These remarks, in turn piquant and weighty, also indicate the degree of self-awareness that AMM had attained, and their consciousness of the wider implications of the kind of music-making to which they had committed themselves.[18] Because of the central position it occupied in their lives AMM sensed a moral dimension to their musical activity; intuitive music-making could be neither perceived nor practised in purely aesthetic terms. Gradually a host of related considerations impinged on their sensibilities and the whole future of the group hinged on how these problems were to be resolved.

'The reason for playing is to find out why I want to play'; this maxim from the Elektra sleeve note has an awesome potentiality which AMM explored to the limits. It was not surprising, therefore, that the narrow, syntactical framework within which improvising jazz musicians normally operate was deemed inadequate and was rejected by AMM; what replaced it had no 'musical', theoretical basis, though there were certainly historical, if remote precedents. 'Playing the changes' was supplanted in favour of a non-theoretical, anthropocentric mode; a fragile reliance on human *virtue*, no less, such as mutual respect, individual integrity and forbearance – a 'philosophy of music-making' ('virtues that a musician can develop') which Cardew, by then a fully-fledged member of AMM, expounds in 'Towards an Ethic of Improvisation' in the *Treatise Handbook*. And as a corollary the music began to develop a dialogical emphasis which in turn demanded a higher degree of concentration and led to a uniquely *collectivist* mode of playing. For AMM a meaningful musical dialogue came to depend above all on a deep-seated rapport between the musicians, to the extent that the full burden of meaning of an individual contribution was made manifest, even to the contributor himself, only by reference to the total sound aggregate at any given time, to the context of *collective* music-making.[19]

'Mutual understanding grew to a pitch that I have never experienced in concert-hall music', Cardew asserted during a lecture delivered at the University of Illinois on 25 February 1967:

Much more potent at present are the varieties of popular music that flower in different cities. Liverpool, London, Detroit, New York and Los Angeles are all producing beat music with a very wide sale, but only the cream is exported. Standardization converts the cream into a crust but underneath this crust the differences are still strong. Evidence for this is provided by radio programmes: English, German and American radio programmes (to quote only those I am familiar with) are widely divergent in style. All this environmental culture builds up a communal fund of subconscious experience in the inhabitants of a city. The rapport that exists amongst members of AMM, for example, is very much deeper than anything that could develop with the musicians of my acquaintance during my 8-month stay in Buffalo. And this factor is particularly vital in improvisation. I theorize that the more obtrusive an environment is, the more profound is the sense of community uniting its inhabitants. In a village dominated by an enormous, noisy factory operating continuously ten hours a day with a one-hour break for lunch, all the inhabitants and particularly the children would be permanently affected by the specific patterns of frequencies and dynamics set up by the factory. In musical terms the link that such a common reference provides would be enormously valuable – as a point of departure. This shows the terrible fallacy of the all-star orchestra idea, which regularly circulates amongst contemporary performers. It is not that brilliance cannot tolerate the presence of brilliance for fear of losing its shine; any good musician longs to find other musicians who are his equal. The error lies simply in supposing that any two players can match up without the link of a basic common experience, the more basic the better.

With the musicians of AMM there was indeed 'a basic common experience'; moreover, there were common attitudes, common aspirations, common feelings, which informed and strengthened their music-making. Above all, it was the feeling of *solidarity* that Cardew enjoyed, something which would have been denied him by the competitive ethos of his background and education: '…in the group there's a terrific solidarity. It's terrifically reassuring to feel that Lou is backing me'.[20]

Yet Cardew's relationships within the AMM were not without tensions and unease. On occasions he gave the impression that he felt a certain insecurity in AMM, although the others regarded his position as invulnerable and such thoughts would not have entered their heads. As we shall see with certain members of the Scratch Orchestra, where Cardew stepped outside the circle of relationships in which he had been brought up and educated – English public school, the Royal Academy of Music, his Oxbridge chums, the high-flying German intellectuals in Cologne, people of great breadth and ease, his touch and even his cool occasionally deserted him. He had not met the likes of Keith Rowe, Eddie Prévost and Lou Gare, young men brought up in the school of hard knocks – nor had he even a nodding acquaintance with the kind of lives they had been forced, through circumstances, to lead: Prévost, a working-class lad from a single-parent family in Bermondsey in south east London; Rowe, working class, brought up by his aunt in Plymouth, who managed to go to Art School and left to become a dockyard worker; Gare, from Rugby in the Midlands and a similar background, who used to have his clarinet lessons from a peripatetic teacher on the premises at Rugby public school until somebody, no doubt mindful of the school's best interests and fearing that this could be the thin end of a wedge, objected to the school authorities. Gare recalls describing to Cardew his efforts, on leaving Art School, to secure employment, any kind of employment, and how, eventually, he found a job in a printing firm. Apparently, Gare's resourcefulness, born as much of economic necessity as of any genetic coincidence, and which he regarded as a matter of course, impressed Cardew to an extent which surprised Gare. Gare's attitude and resolve reflected socio-economic and cultural circumstances which at that time were beyond the limits of Cardew's own experience. He would not have comprehended that for Gare, Prévost and Rowe the economic necessities imposed, had always imposed, a strategy for survival which demanded an acceptance of compromise, a stoical resilience, and an attitude to life which was more fatalistic than heroic. *Class* was Cardew's Achilles heel, as it was for many of his middle-class peers; if, in his youth, and as Ruth Koenig attests, his artistic, bohemian/middle-class family background was a source of pride, in the last decade he came to regard it as an embarrassment, a stigma, the cause of a nagging guilt, and we shall see how he attempted to resolve these deep personal conflicts through a political activism and an ideology for which 'class', in all its manifestations, was the central issue.

Thus, when Cardew became part of AMM the trajectory of his life changed, and the seeds of much of his later work, both musical and political, were sown during this period. Joining AMM was his first meaningful encounter with working-class people, or rather, young men from a working-class background: a 'deprived' background would have been the sociologically-correct description, although all three could no doubt point to the warmth of human relations which they enjoyed during their childhood which more than compensated for their material deprivations.[21] Cardew had no knowledge or understanding of their roots, their family life, the material conditions in which they had been brought up – nor would he have considered this of any relevance to their relationship with him. Ilona Halberstadt recalls how he would pour scorn on any reference to class – class attitude, class consciousness, etc., and this was reflected in the insensitive and intolerant way he would react, on occasions, to the needs and idiosyncrasies of the other members of the group. Eddie Prévost recalls an occasion at Lawrence Sheaff's house when he, Prévost, had proposed a simple format whereby an AMM performance would consist entirely of duos. Cardew was extremely dismissive, rejected the idea out of hand, and was generally impatient with Prévost's hesitancies in relation to the direction AMM was taking. Prévost was both hurt and undermined, and for a time laboured under the impression that Cardew regarded him as a redundant member of the group.[22] As for the sentiments of the other members of AMM, while they welcomed and respected Cardew's presence they were also apprehensive of its implications, and for good reason; they were conscious of his previous concerns, his commitment to composition, and his status. There was the suspicion that he might position himself, like the sun, at the centre, and they would orbit around him – just as had been expected, in those early years, as part of the natural order of things, of his young women friends; AMM would simply glide along in the slip-stream of Cardew's activities.

This initial ambivalence towards Cardew's role found pointed expression in the first aphorism in the Elektra album sleeve notes:

> Does group direction, or authority, depend on the strength of a leading personality, whose rise or fall is reflected in the projected image, or does the collation of a set of minds mean the development of another authority independent of all the members but consisting of all of them?

Whoever penned this particular contribution, it seems to me that it is a barely disguised reference to the perceived relationship at that time of Cardew to the other members of AMM, and to the inherent risks of such a relationship[23]. Prévost recalls these uncertainties in his elaborations on the original Elektra sleeve notes: 'Concern about what a 'group' meant and the danger of it being a tool for one individual's thinking always lurked beneath the surface.' Cardew was a bearer of musical experience and knowledge of the most recent developments in new music and his very presence enhanced the group's self-esteem; he was also a Trojan horse, infiltrating the bourgeois notion of 'natural' superiority and leadership, even if unconsciously, through which AMM would indeed become the Cornelius Cardew Quintet! [24]

Such concerns were quite justified; AMM was evolving an ethos of collective creativity which was anathema to the world in which they lived and made music; in the presiding culture 'collectivism' was seen as a threat against which the susceptible individual had to be on constant guard. And in a world in which innovation and radical change in any field was perceived to be by virtue of the efforts and achievements of dominating, talented, and above all ambitious individuals, the notion of collective accomplishment would have been treated with both scepticism and hostility. The necessarily antithetical relation of the 'individual' to the 'collective' is one of the principal canons of bourgeois ideology, and the disparagement of collectivism, especially in Art, was for AMM, at that time, intimidating:

> We naturally wondered whether individuality was at risk, though ironically I suspect we were not fully conscious at this stage of what individuality actually could be like. If it was anything like the so-called 'freedom' and 'security' we felt in everyday life – then who needed it [...] And through discussion and work we came to recognise that a new creative and social experience based on collaboration was more liberating than imprisoning – despite having to deal with the background aversion to collectivism that oozed from every crack in our culture.[25]

This 'freedom' and 'security' were an attractive, though ephemeral, dividend in the package of benefits which had been bestowed upon the British people after the Second World War through the creation of the Welfare State. The butt of Prévost's ironic remarks was the paternalistic ethos underlying a political agenda which demanded, in return, conformity, docility and gratitude – a deal which many of the young Jack-the-lads, especially those who inhabited the new working-class ghettos, were unwilling to strike. A post-war, working-class anti-hero emerged, to be fêted and mythologized through literature and film in the fifties and early sixties. Rendered mutinous and angry by broken promises and the numbing routine of daily life, and fuelled by an aggressive individualism, he vowed 'to beat them at their own game', often – in literature if not in real life – through the expedient of seducing the boss's wife and marrying his daughter.

Perhaps Lou Gare, Eddie Prévost and Keith Rowe were temperamentally unsuited to such capers; but if their sense of alienation was comparable to that of their more volatile peers, as Prévost has attested, it manifested itself quite differently; for their own music-making strategy evolved on ethical precepts which allowed of no accommodation to the prevailing culture. AMM learnt to survive and to maintain their integrity through a constant and discreet nurturing of their own individuality – through a rigorous, demanding process of *self-invention*. Paradoxically, it was they, for all their need to loosen their class allegiances, who in a more profound sense remained true to their working-class roots. For AMM it was *by virtue* of collectivism, not in spite of it, that one's individuality could thrive and blossom. And this was not a conclusion they had drawn on the basis of theoretical discussion and argument; they discovered, or rather re-discovered it, embedded deeply within the quiddity of their practice. Moreover, what AMM music taught its participants was that the expression of 'individuality' had nothing to do with control or power; indeed, it was not even necessary for the individual authorship of their musical contributions to be identifiable.

For Cardew, initially, the relevance of these concerns to the music and, indeed, to his own life-experience, was marginal. How could it have been otherwise? Since childhood, for all his parents' ostensible liberalism and bohemian life-style, he had spent years of claustration in essentially upper-middle and middle class educational institutions, including seven years immured in a public school, where he had been bred to intellectual one-upmanship, exposed and subjected to a relentlessly competitive ethos, and where he had endured the bizarre rituals, the excesses and repressions, the grotesqueries, which have long been associated with the more traditional models of the English educational system. Nevertheless, it was felt that membership of such schools ensured a boy, or a girl, a *rite de passage* through life from which all manner of incalculable advantages and privileges would flow. And parents with the financial means and an uncomplicated view of life considered such a prospect for their scions both fitting and desirable.

Yet Cardew's early years at home would have been quite out of kilter with his initial experiences at public school. As we have seen, he enjoyed access to non-European cultures; revered artefacts and books from Africa and the East graced the Cardew household. Within the bosom of family life there were constant reminders of worlds and peoples whose lives and art revealed profound and enigmatic alternatives, extraordinary vistas which fired the imagination; and the freight of references to Eastern thought, in particular, in Cardew's journals from the fifties, give an early indication of the far-reaching significance of these encounters. Inevitably, through a protracted, Eurocentric education – which at that time still treated non-European cultures as no more than 'exotica' and with considerable condescension – these impulses were controlled and his enthusiasms directed into more intellectually viable, that is, European cultural channels which, let it be said, he explored with initiative, gusto and a typical eclecticism – as we have seen: Sterne and Joyce, de Sade, Rimbaud and Genet, Hesse, Benjamin and, of course, perennially, Ludwig Wittgenstein. Yet there were other sources of inspiration and influence which were even more precious, and it was through his passion for jazz and the Beat poets and novelists, as well as his involvement with the American avant-garde in music and painting, that he was able to maintain his tenuous links with non-European culture and, indirectly, with Oriental philosophies. If the Europeans fed his intellect during this period, the Americans had access to his soul.[26]

So that when Cardew joined AMM, in 1965, it was as if he had finally returned, like a prodigal son, informally and somewhat hesitatingly but, as if by instinct, with a powerful sense of home-coming, to modes of thought, codes of behaviour, ethical precepts which he had first encountered as a child at Wenford, and whose source were the great Chinese and Indian classics. It is no exaggeration, I believe, to say that with AMM Cardew re-discovered himself. As an improvising musician he discovered modes of expression which symbolized new spheres of psychic and social experience; within AMM music he recognised a dimension of an ethical reality which embraced freedom from egocentricity, a sensitivity to the (musical) needs of others, and which validated the dissolution of the dichotomous relation of the individual to the collective. AMM was for Cardew a moral force and he came to recognize the profound social and philosophical implications of what it was doing, the consequences of which were to surface and consume him several years later when a cluster of socio-psychological issues reflected upon his preoccupations in the seventies – among them intra-class relations and attitudes, and the moral imperatives of duty and sacrifice.

But in the mid-sixties there were more immediate consequences of his membership of AMM which related specifically to his work on *Treatise* and more generally to the entrenched and unquestioned role of the composer in contemporary musical life. In AMM, and for Cardew in particular, the very absence of the 'composer' threw these matters into sharp relief. With *Treatise* Cardew had set himself the task of deconstructing musical notation in an attempt to lay bare the essential nature of the human relations embedded within it. The musical score represents a property relation – the composer *owns* the score; but it also embodies another more important relation, a relation *between* people, that of the composer to the performers. Moreover, through bar-line and baton, through the *notation*, the composer also governs the relationships between performers. I have dealt with these issues more fully in the chapter devoted to *Treatise* but it might be useful, in the context of his membership of AMM, to remind ourselves at this stage of the background to this compositional marathon, and in particular of Cardew's on-going involvement with the European avant-garde.

As an interpreter of European avant-garde music (although in truth the word 'interpreter' is a misnomer in this context), Cardew had experienced at first hand the constraints it imposed upon the performer. In the fifties, in order to secure the 'objectification' of his composition, the European avant-garde composer had sought to purge his music of 'impurities' by minimizing, ideally by eliminating, the indeterminacies which existed between notation and its realisation. These indeterminacies manifested themselves mainly through the agency of the interpreter: his background, taste, competence, mental and physical health, and so on; in short, the performer's 'creative' input had to be dissolved. A corollary of this relentless pursuit of super-objectivity was a commodity fetishism for which total serialism was the ideal vehicle: an ultra-refinement of the composer's 'intention', itself circumscribed by the series and its permutations, and an obsession with the perfection of an ideal object where the performer was enjoined to reproduce mathematically-precise notations. Thus, the performer found himself playing in, as it were, a straight-jacket, training his limbs to accommodate the exaggerated and increasingly unreasonable demands of the notation which, ironically, engendered a proportionally increasing inaccuracy in performance. The performer had become a technician to whom all choice of expression and any measure of spontaneity were denied; the relationship of composer to performer had become an unequivocally coercive one: the performer was simply carrying out a sequence of commands.[27]

During the heyday of serialism what the performance of a composition demanded was expertise, know-how and an indifference to the end-product; the performer made the sound but was not required to identify with it. From the point of view of the professional musician an extremely tenuous line separated indifference from cynicism. If he loathed the music, at least he appreciated the payment; meaningful musical relationships gave way to the cash nexus. It was a fact of musical life which Cardew, the professional performer, knew only too well – the embodiment of what was for him an outmoded and discredited system of cultural values involving human, that is, performer 'management' techniques (notations), a cynical and alienated labour force (professional musicians), and a regressive social function (patronage and funding strategies).[28] The experimental and improvised music of the sixties was part of a general reaction against these values, a defiant riposte to the alienating forms, as well as the minutiae, of everyday bourgeois commerce which in turn reflected the social and cultural ethos which sustained them.[29]

Yet if collective music-making was a 'sixties phenomenon', for AMM, and a number of other groups and individuals, it seemed to exemplify certain qualities, certain virtues, that could not, simply by virtue of changing times, be relinquished; virtues whose substance and indispensability, as the latter part of the 20th century became engulfed in a blaze of capitalist triumphalism, could not be gainsaid. Leapfrogging the calamitous decades which were to follow in which first the communists, in the early seventies, then the capitalists, in the late eighties, promised a glorious future for mankind, AMM in the late sixties began to develop a 'fortress' aesthetic, an alienation *strategy*, which embodied the 'virtues' they had identified in their own 'musica practica' and which was informed by multifarious interests and preoccupations, from a wide range of cultural sources, which surfaced and assumed a degree of prominence at particular stages of the group's development. Some of these pursuits were retained for relatively long periods of time, while others were more quickly discarded.

> At various times such areas of interest as continuo playing, the use of programmatic elements, Buddhist thought, electronic treatments, silence, the performing environment, Chinese ideograms, acoustic work, the use of volume, the cello players, the radio players, those studying Gurdjieff and Ouspensky, all played an important role.[30]

Not that these concerns ever formed a monolith; rather, interests introduced by an individual, or perhaps two or three members, would overlap – as, for example, in 1970, when Prévost, Rowe and Cardew attended Chinese classes together at the Working Men's College in Crowndale Road, north London, near Mornington Crescent tube station, and Gare practised transcendental meditation. Such diversity was comfortably accommodated, filtered through and undoubtedly enriching the music.[31]

In AMM there was no exclusive agenda, and none of the high-flown theorizing which inveigled receptive young minds to indulge in serialist summers in Darmstadt. Rather there was a curiosity, an openness to all ideas, none of which, even those which enjoyed most purchase, were allowed a dominating role. Passion and deep respect were tempered by level-headedness and a deep-rooted, inalienable scepticism of any claims to indisputable eminence, whether in materialistic or other-worldly guise – as was the case with their relation both to jazz and to Buddhism. Their admiration for John Coltrane and Charlie Mingus, for example, did not necessitate the assimilation into their music-making of Coltrane's licks or Mingus's riffs; nor did their feeling of empathy with Tibetan monks take on a formal expression through dress and appearance, eating and sleeping habits and prayer routines. They had neither the inclination nor the capacity to become Buddhists in the manner of some of their peers, but they had opened their hearts and minds to a religious tradition in which they perceived both wisdom and commonsense; it entered their music-making and they felt at ease with many aspects of its teaching.[32]

Certainly, Eastern thought was a constant, though never obsessive, preoccupation for AMM, and in some form or other its on-going influence continued to manifest itself into the seventies. Sometimes the sounds themselves would echo an Eastern aesthetic, the quality of the music recalling the zithers, the bamboo flutes and the stand drums of ancient Chinese music; but of greater significance was the gestural quality and feeling of ritual in AMM's music-making.[33] To perform the simplest musical task the appropriate attitude, the right presence of mind, was deemed essential; an instrument or sound source would be ritualistically appraised and reappraised before use. There would be an awareness of the sound-producing gesture, and of the fact that the resultant sound was not simply the 'end-product', the goal of an hierarchically-ordered series of actions, but was itself just one of several stages of a complex, seamless process, in which the performer was engaged.[34]

With AMM there was a shift of emphasis onto the physical and sensuous aspects of the art of performance such that an essential part of the pleasure which AMM communicated to the listener was a feeling of intimacy with the physical production of the sound: their closeness to their instruments, to the sources of their sounds. 'The shape of the drum is possessed in my person (in the form of the ear).'[35] In Western classical music-making this sense of identification is rare because of an unequivocal cultural intervention that exercises a censorial control over the very grain of the sound, so that a 'received' tone is produced of an aesthetically approved quality, authenticated by the long-established traditions of conservatory training. As a corollary, fear, rather than love, is an all-too-common relation of instrumentalist to instrument in Western culture.[36]

In AMM's improvisations (and, for that matter, in Cardew's compositional processes) new 'voices' were being generated, emerging, as it were, unbidden from the cracks and crevices within the music-making: intonations which were incompatible with a notational system based on equal temperament and the isolation of discrete pitches; a way of making music which subverted the basic tenets of Western musical practice.[37] This was in part a consequence of the way in which AMM would differentiate between levels of control of the sound, all of which – the intended, the half-intended, the accidental, the makeshift – were granted legitimacy. An unintended sound could be regarded, unambiguously, as a 'mistake', which a player would either quickly abandon or cover up; or he would contrive to make it seem appropriate by spontaneously creating a context for it. Conversely, just as an 'intended' sound might be accompanied or neutralized by extraneous noise, so 'intent' could accompany and validate noise. This idea of 'letting-go' of conscious control was, of course, an aspect of Zen to which the AMM had responded so positively. Eddie Prévost proffers an example of his own Taoist sympathies in the early days:

I adopted a very direct percussive version of the casting of yarrow stalks (though one suspects it might make some of the more sensitive Taoists wince), grasping a handful of drum sticks high above my head and then allowing them to fall onto the snare drum in some aural divinatory equivalence. In short, it was always clear that becoming master musicians required reference points much more diverse than 'musical'.[38]

Such mystical preoccupations, however intrinsic to the group's development, were not exclusive; as we have already noted, a sensitivity to the trajectories of contemporary Western art created viable parallels with, in particular, the visual arts. The reassessment of an instrument's potential, attributed to the influence of Eastern thought, would often lead to unorthodox practices in ways analogous to the American Abstract Expressionist painters; just as Jackson Pollock's canvases had been laid on the floor and the high fidelity of the fine brush jettisoned, Keith Rowe's guitar was placed flat on the table and the conventional performance techniques abandoned in favour of experimental methods – the guitar 'prepared' with bolts, coins, knives, steel rulers, and the bow used for the characteristically long sounds, producing a variety of new and outlandish resonances. Victor Schonfield describes the range and quality of Rowe's sound world in *Town Magazine* in April 1966: 'Sounds like those made by flocks of birds, dogs, sirens, rain on a tin roof, buzz saws, bubbling lava, giant insects ripping and slashing at steel doors, or electrified cats and babies.' For AMM a guitar, a piano, a drum were sound sources to be exploited rather than instruments to be played; AMM was deconstructing, in practice, just as the philosophy was emerging in the theoretical field. A hands-on, re-inventing ethos was the guiding, dominating 'mode of procedure' in AMM music: 'to play as if there had never been any such thing as music before'. Conversely, a glass ashtray and a windowpane were not simply passive objects, part of a 'non-musical' environment. Elegant and purposeful gestures would uncover their expressive potential, transforming them into 'musical' instruments emitting sounds of extreme complexity and intensity. Nor would a room be viewed simply as a performance location, but rather as an active component or contributor; for every environment houses particular sounds and its contents would evoke a common curiosity – what do they sound like? In some sense the music would actually be derived from the room in which it was taking place – its shape, acoustical properties, the view from the windows, as Cardew pointed out in the *Treatise Handbook*. The time of day or night, too, was sometimes an influential factor, just as in Indian music where there is specific music for particular times of the day, reflecting a sensitivity to the changing characteristics of the twenty four hour cycle.

Sometimes, a found object, possessed of a certain undefinable potential, would become part of the AMM inventory, transported from home-base to venue and back, and treated with care and affection. Long chains, which Cardew would swish around;

a sledgehammer, which he would also wield in dramatic and menacing fashion; and stones were all part of his instrumental repertory in the later years. Some of the objects which cluttered AMM's performing space could be extremely cumbersome, like the water drum Cardew brought back from an Indian reservation; and of elephantine bulk, such as Eddie Prévost's wine barrel which he had rescued from destruction at an Italian restaurant in the Strand in London; and the steel gong which was cut down to size so that it could be transported by a Renault 4 (at least three members of the AMM owned a Renault 4), with two circular sheets of steel fitted between the wheel arches. A multi-purpose discovery – the top of it, when suspended, was a smooth patch, filed down to accommodate hours of bowing – the gong would be used outdoors, placed on some rocks, as a useful surface on which to fry eggs. Marked with a tomato stain which nobody chose to erase, tempered by fire and water, it led a weather-beaten existence, at each playing its sound unpredictably unique.

> Mystique. In choosing an instrument take the plainest, commonest, sturdiest and keep it a long time. Lecture exposing the means employed by musicians to preserve their mystique (??)[39]

In Cardew's mind this 'mystique' was associated with a certain kind of conventional, instrumental virtuosity for which he felt a healthy mistrust. All too often virtuosity would become an alienating force, an intimidating power, competitive by nature, which served only to detract from the listener's experience of music. Yet Cardew would not necessarily use the word 'virtuoso' disparagingly; in the *Treatise Handbook* (p.xv), he describes virtuosi as 'people who are able to perform magic on their instrument'. But here magic is not associated with speed and power – rather with control, and Cardew's terms of reference are more likely to have been the 'virtuosity' of David Tudor; it was the extraordinary quality of the sounds which Tudor extracted from the instrument rather than their velocity which impressed him. What mattered was what came from the inner body and from the imagination, not from petty prestidigitation.

AMM music, virtually from its beginnings, was clearly distinguishable from that of its peer groups. The juxtaposition of individual musical statements and the solo/accompaniment relation, which had survived from jazz in most of the new free improvisation groups, was supplanted in the AMM with what Evan Parker has defined as 'laminar techniques': the creation of a layered texture through the accumulation and superimposition of individual contributions; a slowly shifting sound of extreme complexity ('a single vast sea of ambiguous and shifting colours' in Roger Sutherland's description[40]). A further striking feature of AMM music at the time (already alluded to) and a corollary of its collectivist mode of music-making – one which members of the audience would often remark upon – was the fact that it was often impossible to perceive which gestures were producing which sounds. Was the source of a constant drone a bowed metal disc or an organ sound or some electronic contrivance? Sometimes the only way the performer himself could determine the nature of his own contribution would be to stop his activity and try to identify the difference; thus the musician's own relation to the music he was creating took on a speculative aspect. For Cardew the psychology of music-making – the various states of mind in which musicians practise their art – was a constant source of fascination and reflective thought. A brief, Wittgensteinian comment, before Cardew joined AMM, exemplifies these concerns: 'What we *do* is important – not only what we have in mind. Often what we do is what tells us what we have in mind… Having in mind is a strange matter anyway.'[41]

For those in the audience who were unacquainted with Cage's experiments the strangeness of AMM music was enhanced by the bizarre and startling nature of the sound material itself: the piano preparations (bolts, screws, rubber, plastic inserted and wedged between the strings), the battery-operated cocktail mixers, oscillating rulers, the various appendages to small motors activating the guitar strings, the rubber 'superballs' which could coax expressive screeches and squawks from a medley of surfaces, and the numerous 'found objects' – some of which, as we have seen, acquired talismanic status. But in particular it was the introduction of the transistor radio, in the manner of the abstract expressionist, combine painting, which provided the element of shock and displacement. Just as Robert Rauschenberg would drip paint around the found object embedded in his canvas, so Keith Rowe would splash sounds around those emitting from the radio: a Byrd Mass, a political discussion, a quartet or a quiz. And whereas Cage would *use* the transistor, in a more formal, aleatoric way, Rowe would *play* it, normally and appropriately with his left hand – the hand with which the conventional guitarist discovers and creates melody – seeking out and selecting material, rejecting what was deemed inappropriate at any given moment: *improvising* – a mode of music-making to which Cage, we should remind ourselves, was extremely resistant.[42] Keith Rowe was without doubt the magnet which, initially, drew Cardew into the AMM – a formidable and uncompromising personality which Cardew found hard to fathom. David Tudor aside, perhaps, another performer, there was no other musician whom Cardew respected more.[43] At the time Rowe's grasp of Art was intuitive, spontaneous, non-analytical; for Cardew it was the perfect foil, and a necessary antidote to the spurious intellectualism which had overtaken many of his peers in the world of contemporary music.

For all its single-mindedness and seriousness of intent AMM's week-by-week musical activity was as contingent upon the vagaries of urban existence as other aspects of its day-to-day living were. To survive, the music needed to be both flexible and resilient; it also needed to draw on a deep well of self-belief – the 'monstrous egotism' without which the artist's vulnerability becomes too exposed. Thus, during the second half of the decade AMM responded to, occasionally succumbed to, technological encroachment, to the creative input of new members, to the works of Cage and other avant-garde composers (with whom, through Cardew and occasional participation, it came to enjoy a more formal, and practical, acquaintance) and, most crucially, as we shall see later, to the creation of the Scratch Orchestra. At critical junctures there were significant changes of focus and emphasis occasioned by the influence of these and other factors, changes which obtruded upon the music in various ways, disturbing and shifting the delicate balance of relationships, both aesthetic and psychological, which had been fine-tuned through weeks and months of music-making. The music changed – it sounded different; or rather, sifting the music from a distance one can identify aspects which had changed, some quite radically. Yet what emerged still bore, in essence, the same content; the core of the music remained somehow inviolable.

By the spring of 1966 AMM had enlisted the services of Victor Schonfield[44] as their manager:

My main responsibility was simply to make sure the group had a place to play for nothing without being interrupted. Listeners were always welcome free of charge, but only as long as they did not interfere; interference was also welcome, but only from within the group. When I brought Ornette Coleman, Lou asked us to leave the room, as we were talking, and the time that Steve Lacy sat in, Lou asked him to stop playing. (By contrast, when I got Barry Miles to bring Paul McCartney he just listened, though when I asked him afterwards how he liked it he said they went on too long).[45]

Between May and September, in their weekly sessions in the music room at the London School of Economics, the group had already entered a new phase: conventional, acoustic instruments were dispensed with to be replaced by a proliferation and diversification of sound sources. Gare put aside his saxophone and used bric-a-brac and various percussion sounds; Prévost began to experiment with pitched instruments, while Rowe, Cardew and Sheaff (and occasionally Prévost) involved themselves in amplification both of small, indeterminate sounds, and of conventional instruments, including two cellos. These changes were brought about, essentially, by the expression of individual needs and proclivities (notwithstanding the collective premises of AMM's overall development), through various preoccupations and influences, as well as by the availability of new technological gadgetry. In particular, the use of contact microphones for the amplification of unfledged 'small sounds' served an aesthetic which had informed a number of Cage's scores in the sixties – compositions such as *Cartridge Music*, which Cardew had performed with Cage, Tudor, Wolff and others at Mary Bauermeister's studio in Cologne in October 1960 – and which goes back as far as the early forties with his *Imaginary Landscape 2* and 3.This new emphasis in AMM's music-making on ambient sounds – drawing attention to them, making them audible by means of contact microphones, 'playing the environment', bore witness to the influence of Cage, through Cardew, on the AMM – even if their paths soon diverged. For Cage the structuring of these small, 'non-musical' sounds by chance operations was aesthetically desirable and socially necessary; the resulting music was more 'interesting' and the procedures initiated by the notation 'altered the awareness' of the performers. Left to his own devices the performer would indulge his taste, idiosyncratically, for this or that sound, forcing the music to conform to inbred modes of expression and to certain recognised aesthetic conventions, thus circumscribing and channelling the listener's perception. But Cage's notations, by 'freeing' the sounds from the attentions of over-enthusiastic egos, act both as a liberating agent and, paradoxically, as a constraint.

However, in the music room at the London School of Economics AMM demonstrated an aesthetic which represented a radical departure from Cage. In these sessions the sounds were not simply 'heard', brought into focus and tendered to the listener in a condition of pristine objectivity. Rather, the AMM musicians were *tracking* the sounds, in the way that a hunter tracks an animal and in doing so gains knowledge and gradually his attitude towards the hunted becomes a relationship *with* the animal. Something analogous to this occured in AMM music; an attitude towards the sound matured into a relationship *with* it, and since AMM had granted a relative autonomy to sound the relationship was a mutual rather than a controlling one; or more accurately, perhaps, a mutually-controlling one. This relationship to the sounds one tracks becomes a commitment, a commitment based on a kind of trust, trust in the manner in which these sounds are made into music, are *humanised*. Cage appears to deny this humanising process to his musicians; the responsibility they are given is tightly circumscribed by prescribed procedures about which the ideal (Cage) performer can have no 'view'. Hence, the dangers inherent in AMM music-making play no part in Cage's cosmology.

Yet, paradoxically, for Cardew and Rowe the idea of 'notation' was easily accommodated within AMM's 'meta-music'; moreover, it could be just as constraining and just as liberating as those with which Cage discomposed the musical world in the late fifties and sixties. But it was not one that could be drawn on manuscript paper nor, indeed, on any paper at all. In an illuminating paragraph in 'Towards an Ethic of Improvisation', Cardew discusses the kind of 'notations' which were bread and butter to the AMM musicians:

> Once in conversation I mentioned that scores like those of La Monte Young (for example, 'Draw a straight line and follow it') could in their inflexibility take you outside yourself, stretch you to an extent that could not occur spontaneously. To this the guitarist [Keith Rowe] replied that 'you get legs dangling down there and arms floating around, so many fingers and one head' and that was a very strict composition. And that is true: not only can the natural environment carry you beyond your own limitations, but the realization of your own body as part of that environment is an even stronger dissociative factor. Thus it is that the natural environment is itself giving birth to something, which you then carry as a burden; you are the medium of the music. At this point your moral responsibility becomes hard to define.[46]

This 'playing the environment' requires a subtle awareness, a heightened sense of one's immediate surroundings, more – an *identification* with one's surroundings, one's source material, and the ability to respond creatively and with imagination to every nuance, to every intimation of change in a constantly shifting matrix of sound. This sense of identification with sounds, of *being* the sounds, was what impressed Cardew and bound him for so many years to the AMM:

> The difference between making the sound and being the sound. The professional musician makes the sounds (in full knowledge of them as they are external to him). AMM is their sounds (as ignorant of them as one is about one's own nature.)[47]

'…music heard so deeply/That it is not heard at all, but you are the music/While the music lasts'. In the *Four Quartets* T. S. Eliot seems to be poeticising Cardew's thesis. Perhaps there was a conscious reference to Eliot here; Cardew was familiar with Eliot's work and such a compelling formulation of his thoughts would have etched itself in his memory.

For musicologists AMM's radical aesthetic placed it beyond the pale and it was largely ignored. AMM, in its turn, was unperturbed by the music establishment's disapprobation, although Eddie Prévost deigned to offer a relaxed defence:

> Maybe its not 'music' according to the convention, but it is certainly a new 'sound-using' activity, laden with new meanings and cultural implications that differ from what has gone before. I'm inclined, at the moment, to think of it as a 'meta-music'.[48]

The fascination, if not the obsession, with amplification, and the ubiquitous contact microphones, remained a feature of AMM's music-making (and of many other experimental groups) for almost two years, the accessibility of the tiniest sounds and the sense of discovery and unpredictability overriding the inherent limitations and drawbacks of the technology. For if these amplified sounds were novel and occasionally arresting they were also crude, often an inexpedient substitute for aural imagination, creating a one-dimensional homogenizing sound-quality which had begun to pall. At some venues, such as the gallery in Kingly Street, central London, in the first months of 1967, the volume had reached an ear-splitting level, the audible rendered inaudible; such a predicament could no longer be tolerated and gradually it was superseded by a music-making of a more differentiated, polymorphous character.

By the time of the concert at the Crypt in the Lancaster Road Methodist Church, North Kensington, in west London, on 12 June 1968, AMM had begun to recognize that the technological means and know-how (the pervasive use of electricity) which had served the music over the last two years were now incompatible with the newly-encroaching, shifting artistic perspectives. There had also been changes in personnel: Lawrence Sheaff had left the group in 1967 to be replaced in April 1968 by one of Cardew's students from the Royal Academy of Music, the 17-year-old Christopher Hobbs.[49] The American composer Christian Wolff had also been part of the group for the duration of his sabbatical year in Europe, 1968, though he did not take part in the concert at the Crypt.[50]

In attempting to describe the recording of the Crypt concert we encounter from the very outset a teasing equivocalness; for the music cannot be said to 'begin' – rather the listener's attention is gradually and unevenly engaged by sonic phenomena, of varying degrees of characterisation, which impinge upon it: indeterminate rumblings and noises engulfed in long breaths of sustained sounds, harsh electronic interventions, controlled and half-controlled feed-back, and in the background an insistent accompaniment of percussion. ('An AMM performance has no beginning or ending. Sounds outside the performance are distinguished from it only by individual sensibility'.[51]) But as I continue with this description it behoves me to remind the reader that what I am actually doing here – as somebody who may well have been in the audience (I cannot remember) – is *imagining a performance*; the CD, to which I am listening, is functioning simply and imperfectly as an *aide-mémoire* as I 'witness' the events of an AMM performance, however impressionistically, in my mind's eye. The listener, as opposed to the witness, misses out, crucially on the nature of the performing action (where it is visible) and its relationship to the resultant sound(s), misses out on the subtle interrelationships between the spontaneous music-making and the context in which it occurs:

> What a recording produces is a separate phenomenon, something really much stranger than the playing itself, since what you hear on tape or disc is indeed the same playing but divorced from its natural context. What is the importance of this natural context? The natural context provides a score which the players are unconsciously interpreting in their playing. Not a score that is explicitly articulated in the music and hence of no further interest to the listener as is generally the case in traditional music, but one which coexists inseparably with the music, standing side by side with it and sustaining it.[52]

What would have absorbed the watchful listener on that summer's day in the Crypt were the various shades and intimations of control exercised by the musicians in relation to the sounds they discovered, produced, tracked. And by corollary there were nuances of intention (which Cardew was to incorporate into the score of *The Great Learning*) which embodied the attitudes of the musicians towards the sounds they heard, identified, created – attitudes which ranged from the non-committal to the committed, from the casual to the meticulous, from embarrassment to fascination. At times the sensitive listener might have detected a kind of collective diffidence, or half-heartedness, on the part of the musicians towards a particular sequence of sounds. Yet diffidence is a human attitude; why should it not find expression in a musical narrative?[53] And on that day at the Crypt it did, when a succession of desultory, half-intended, semi-controlled frictional sounds was echoed and transfigured by Lou Gare's saxophone.[54] And in an extreme compression of historical time, these mutate into a choir of farmyard animals, or perhaps larger, wilder animals, or even prehistoric humans – creatures expressing themselves, accompanied electronically by modulated drones.

The Crypt music is vibrant, full of life and character, the product of a riotous, collective imagination tempered by a seriousness of intent. Eloquent phrases call to each other across vast ravines and coalesce into slowly shifting, harmonic blocks, creating incidences of exquisite dissonance. In its train the music bears odd associations and memories: a penumbra of sensations. The listener is presented with a vast spectrum of tones and timbres from the ineffably sweet to sounds, it would seem, of malign intent: ne'er-do-well sounds, miscreant sounds. These undergo a process of humanization – or dehumanization, when the music takes on an ominous cast, invested with meaning which may be malevolent, like one of the evil characters who from time to time struts across Shakespeare's stage. Occasionally, an unexpected sound shatters the aura so tortuously and painstakingly achieved by the musicians and threatens, momentarily, to disrupt the musical continuity and flow – perhaps a cry of anguish or a peremptory drum flourish, surprising through its incongruity, but which is then embraced, welcomed, followed, contextualized, and the music changes. The sounds hum, throb, grate, ring and sing; evanescent, 'romantic' sounds redolent of a bygone age are juxtaposed with the rebarbative emissions of a brutal industrialism – the ultra-refined married to the super-crude. And every so often ornaments, tropes, phrases of rarefied, vestigial beauty; the music becomes blurred, a shroud of the softest vibrations; each sound tenuous but compelling. And finally silence, and the players immured within it. In one extraordinary sequence human activity seems to cease; we are enveloped in an apocalyptic phenomenon of nature, a blizzard of grey noise – to which Roger Sutherland was surely referring in his review in an LMC newsletter: '... it is as if the musical terrain has been devastated, the harmonies eroded by massive frictions and the rhythms pulverised into the dust of raw vibration'.[55] The musicians simply abandon the scene, leaving behind an elemental soundscape which brooks no human intervention; there seems to be a consensus amongst the musicians here – no interference. A primitive melody is whistled on an instrument of ancient origin and some of the musicians potter around testing this or that against a sustained string sound of calm beauty, motorised by some Heath Robinson contraption.[56] From time to time a press review would challenge the validity of these phantasmagoric soundscapes: is it music? Cardew's own reply was characteristically stark: 'The answer is that it is music because I am a musician, and I have always played music and this is what I play now.'[57]

In the autumn of 1968 Cardew had begun his Experimental Music class at Morley College where there seems to have been a disinclination towards the use of electronics amongst the participants, and their almost exclusive preference for acoustic sound would be carried over, the following year, into the Scratch Orchestra. Perhaps it was by virtue of an overlapping membership – of Morley College, of AMM, and of the Scratch Orchestra – that such predilections also found purchase in AMM: Lou Gare returned to his violin and saxophone – for him it was refreshing to re-discover the 'musicality' of musical instruments, Cardew to the cello and prepared piano, Prévost to his drum kit.[58] As a consequence there was now a greater refinement in the music, more differentiation in the overall sound production, which had become less amorphous, more honed, more specific. With a burgeoning self-confidence which the preceding years of radical musical praxis had instilled in them, individual members now sought to explore new approaches to their musical instruments and began to develop their own self-contained areas of sound activity. Not that this tendency towards individual autonomy heralded a departure from established practice; the assimilation of the individual musician into a total soundscape remained an essential feature of AMM's music-making. In fact, the relationship between private imperatives on the one hand and the priorities of a collective music-making on the other had always been fluid, though never to the extent that the relationship became one-sided and an imbalance obtained; if the pendulum swung, it always swung back. Engulfed within those densely saturated, wall-of-sound, collective soundscapes which had characterised the music in the early days, AMM had learnt that the virtue of *selflessness* could lead, propitiously, to individual discovery and self-realisation.[59]

The extant recordings of AMM sessions from the early seventies from Roger Sutherland's invaluable collection, by which time the Scratch Orchestra was in full flow, betray an assimilation of influence rather than any change of direction or even emphasis.[60] Although there are palpable, some might say attractive and welcome, surface differences, AMM's praxis remained, essentially, intact. The music from this period seems more straightforward, with less gadgetry and fewer contrivances; the sound is predominantly acoustic, instrumental, with the transparency of chamber music – which was what it was – and for this reason, perhaps, required greater control, and certainly an awareness of the issue of balance between instruments. Not that this return to idiomatic instrumental playing bespoke a regression into conventionality; Cardew's pianistic figurations are still highly idiosyncratic and the simple, expressive cello phrases are often boldly and impressively microtonal. It was simply the case that the acoustic instruments (plus electric guitar), rather than the electronics, bore the weight of the musical content.

Listening to these recordings one can discern the concerns and preoccupations of the group at the time, and the way these relations find expression in the music, even if their assimilation is not always convincing. In one set, from a recording early in 1970, long sequences of repeated tonal chords on the piano probably bear witness to the influence of the Scratch Orchestra and perhaps minimalism (the Scratch Orchestra had given several spiritedly inaccurate performances of Terry Riley's *In C*). Later in the same set a drone-like continuum based on the repetition of a dominant 7th chord, reinforced by the stentorian tones of Cardew's vocals and elegantly elaborated by Gare's tenor saxophone, creates an aura uncomfortably close to that of the soft-centred, 'beautiful music' (predecessor of the more contentiously labelled 'New-Age' music, described by Stella Cardew, in a moment of inspiration, as 'soppy music') which would invariably provoke scathing and dismissive comments from Cardew. Elsewhere, some relentless percussion playing by Eddie Prévost displays a startling and brutal atavism of the kind which occasionally overtook the Scratch Orchestra. In general, and here I am expressing an opinion, AMM's music from the early seventies seems most successful when it is quieter, epigrammatic, more reflective. Though not as spectacular and cataclysmic as the Crypt music there is a restlessness, a striving towards an undefined yet irresistible *immanence*; the music is searching, not so much within itself, but beyond itself.

Whatever the extent of change and development, both subtle and overt, brought about by extraneous factors, by individual predispositions, or simply by the passing of time, the regularity and frequency of AMM's music-making sessions between 1965 and the early seventies, which were held irrespective of the size or presence of an audience, ensured a continuity of purpose which has remained the hallmark of the group's remarkable musical odyssey over a period of nearly forty years. How did this strength of purpose and the ethos which nurtured it manifest themselves in practice? What was it like to perform in the AMM? What was the role of the listener? What was the nature of the relationship of the listener to AMM music and indeed to the musicians themselves?

For AMM it was axiomatic that every performance was characteristic of its time and place; conversely, to each location AMM would have brought something uniquely of itself. The mutuality of the group's relationship to its environment is reflected in the inspired simplicity of David Ilic's trope that AMM's albums are 'as like and unalike as trees.' On each and every occasion the recognisability, the continuity, of AMM performances was expressed both visually: the stage encompassed about with diverse objects, appurtenances, some placed on the floor, some suspended; and aurally: the music laminating, slowly and unevenly, and creating, at its several peaks, a breathtaking diapason of sound. Lou Gare's text, 'Subjective view of an AMM session', which appeared in a brochure contained in the LP box set (the Crypt session) and later reprinted in the CD booklet, encapsulates the spirit of AMM's performances, for which there were no formal presuppositions, no consciously adumbrated formal organisation. If such a performance strategy were adopted by an individual it was never (and is still not) disclosed to other members, and in any case would probably have had to be abandoned or at least modified, too seriously compromised by a complex of contingencies during performance to be of any consequence. What did exist was a kind of unwritten covenant embodying a moral code of musical practice which could not be abrogated. In Gare's text there are explicit references to this code, particularly in relation to the psychology of improvising and the range of feelings it spawns. Cardew would certainly have admired Gare's words for their directness and honesty. They do not attempt to explain the music in any way, but rather to identify what it means to play in AMM. The text is concerned with Lou Gare's experience, his feelings and reactions. It is in no way explanatory.

I arrive at the place, probably we have played there in previous weeks.
Mostly we play once a week. The place is familiar then.
Some or all of the other players are there.
We chat a bit, set up equipment, tinker with things. Small sounds go on.
The playing increases as we get involved in listening, searching, trying to perfect
a sound, an action.

The lights go out, or sometimes stay on but usually very low – almost dark.
In the dark it is like having your eyes shut. All the sounds seem to go inside.
The sudden shocks of loud noise jolt one into alertness.
The energy flows through the body.
I think – a sound isn't good – it doesn't fit – we've heard it before – but all the time I'm playing.
And then something happens and I'm listening very closely – it's beautiful and sharp and falls away, everyone is maintaining it, a slight change comes in, it alters, breaks down, picks up again.
It makes me laugh – I work hard – I can't go on – it's too difficult, why don't they stop – but I play all the same.
Just for an instant, or slightly more I'm right on the brink so to speak.
It is good just to listen. I don't know what to do.
Keith is playing fantastically tonight.
Why is Eddie lying on the floor?
I can't hear Cor.
Why doesn't Christopher turn that thing off, whatever it is?
I shall go deaf if this noise goes on much longer.
Why doesn't someone turn the lights on – I hope they don't, don't stop.
I can't bear it.
One is tossed this way and that – and I don't move.
It would be nice to play in this.
It is very quiet.
I must have been sitting here for a long time, my ankle hurts.
The silence goes on for what seems like a long time.
The lights come on.
Cor is still playing the cello.
There are one or two or more people in the room as well.
It seems as though I can't listen – it has to come to me.
We chat a bit, make arrangements, discuss business, say goodbye.

'Chat a bit, make arrangements, discuss business,' but was there no discussion of the music? All the AMM members had a feel for words, and in the early months the radical nature of their music-making, which had exposed them to both adulation and ridicule, had created a need for verbal boosts and comradely reassurances from one another. For a time, perhaps a few months, there was discussion and discriminating analysis of the effect of the music; at informal get-togethers ideas and opinions, likes and dislikes, were freely expressed although, not surprisingly, in view of his antipathy at that time to words and conversation, Cardew rarely attended these meetings, which were held separately. Whatever opinions he held, he preferred to keep his own counsel. Eventually, these discussion sessions were dropped; a six-hour journey to a venue, and a six-hour journey back, would pass with no mention of the music.

Cardew enjoyed raw sound (just as he enjoyed nature) and was comfortable in those blurred areas between sound and 'music'.

> It is not the exclusive privilege of music to have a history – sound has history too. Industry and modern technology have added machine sounds and electronic sounds to the primeval sounds of thunderstorm, volcanic eruption, avalanche and tidal wave. Informal sound has a power over our emotional responses that formal 'music' does not, in that it acts subliminally rather than on a cultural level. This is a possible definition of the area in which AMM is experimental. We are searching for sounds and for the responses that attach to them, rather than thinking them up, preparing them and producing them. The search is conducted in the medium of sound and the musician himself is at the heart of the experiment.[61]

This states a clearly anthropocentric position; for all the commitment to sounds, for all the deference to the power of 'informal' sound, the sounds discovered, created, synthesized by the AMM do not acquire an autonomous existence; but nor are they a vehicle for 'self-expression'. What they embody is human potentiality, the idea of 'becoming': self-invention. '[...] even though they may have some beauty in their own right. What the sounds embody for me is everything I am not, which is the reason I keep playing. If they reflected me, it would be time to give up'.[62] For AMM meaning can be invested in any sound; furthermore, there is codification in the sense that meanings become attached to certain kinds of sounds. What gives a sound 'meaning', as Eddie Prévost has asserted, may well be 'perception, intention and organisation' on the part of the performer, but for the listener it is the interaction of the aesthetic, moral and social considerations underpinning the music-making that asserts the music's humanism and enriches and diversifies its 'meaning'. I am not suggesting that these concerns preoccupy the listener during the music-making; rather, that they may subsequently become the object of reflection. In AMM's music-making the mutuality of improviser and listener acquired a status which paralleled that which Cardew had sought to express, in his experimental notations, between composer and performer. The objective was broadened from finding personal meaning and satisfaction to making the occasion significant for the listener who – initially disregarded and marginalised by AMM – became part of this process of 'self-invention'. This is the core of the whole problem: Creation? Expression? Discovery? But there is no contradiction between them. At its best AMM is involved, in a balanced way, in all three.

AMM never offers the listener gratification; in fact it offers nothing − a point which is beautifully illustrated by the text from Kwang-Sze in the sleeve notes to *The Crypt*. See Appendix 3. Rather, it invites the listener to listen attentively and creatively, to experience imaginatively. For the listener seeking perceptual gratification − and nothing more − there is frustration and disappointment, for it is precisely the freedom of imagination that AMM offers which plays havoc with the listener's expectations. Rather than proffering meanings, AMM seeks to initiate 'performances' of meanings by the listener, and through its non-exclusion of environmental sound to facilitate and strengthen the non-dualistic quality of listening.[63] There is no hidden, formal agenda, no inner circle membership; no insider dealing as an admission ticket for listener participation and comprehension. What the music demands of us − and it *is* demanding − is that we transcend the cultural references which both dominate and inhibit our perceptions; that we rise above our conditioning and the vulgar determinism which seeks to rationalise it. With AMM there is no formal blueprint, no overall unifying form; the form of an improvisation is never prescribed; it *unfolds,* spontaneously, freely, and in its wake bears a train of meanings which impinge in diverse ways – aesthetically, psychologically, culturally − on the sensibilities of both performers and listeners. For the listener the overall shape of an AMM performance 'remains just out of grasp, like the kind of landscape that is simply too powerful to assimilate in its entirety'.[64]

As we have seen, in the *Tempo* article, 'Notation − Interpretation, etc.', Cardew had reflected on the incompatibility of 'structure' and 'musicality': structure as an external constraint on musicality, the arbitrariness of structure as opposed to an 'organic' music-making ('If there is to be structure, let it, like Mozart's, be invisible!'). In AMM musical structure and form are contingent upon the physical characteristics of hearing (how sounds are heard), the artistic predispositions of the musicians (the sounds chosen, or ignored), the sound-producing and creative skills of the musicians (how sounds are focused, phrased, projected), and the degree of listener commitment and imagination (how the sounds are perceived). In his book *Music, Imagination, and Culture* Nicholas Cook comes close to describing formal perception of AMM music:

It is the web of individual connections between its various components that gives it formal coherence. In other words, the form inheres not so much in the influence of the whole over the experiencing of the parts as in the influence of each part over the experiencing of other parts. And this constitutes a much more diffuse conception of formal organization than the one that is embodied in most theoretical and analytical approaches to musical structure.[65]

But even this only takes us part of the way; for long stretches of The Crypt, for example, as listener one is not concerned with 'connections' of any kind. Naturally, this makes great demands on the perceptual, or rather the creative faculties of the listener. AMM is a multi-potential music which exists in myriad listener realizations, like an open, non-prescriptive text. It cannot be reduced to the 'atomized multiplicity' demanded by conventional musicological analysis, in which the illusion is spread that hearing notes, intervals, and note-rows is to hear 'music'.

The commitment to improvisation, the insistence on its relation and relevance to the non-musical world, if such a separate world exists, was shared by all the members of the AMM, whose radical mission was to recognise the 'musical composition of the world' no less. 'My attitude is that the musical and the real worlds are one. Musicality is a dimension of perfectly ordinary reality', Cardew wrote.[66] In Cardew's texts there are many instances where he posits the dissolution of the dichotomy between musical reality and 'perfectly ordinary reality'; indeed, his entire compositional odyssey may be viewed as an elaborate strategy to achieve this in practice. Metaphors from nature abound in his writings: 'Drifting through life, being driven through life. No, best is to lead your life. Similarly in improvisation – like a yachtsman utilise the interplay of natural forces to steer a course.[67] Nor does Eddie Prévost separate the musical from the non-musical; and he, too, uses metaphor from the same source: 'I always looked at the music in terms of an encounter with the world; fighting your way out of a storm.'[68] The cellist Rohan de Saram, who played in AMM in the late eighties/early nineties, also reflected on the relationship between 'living' and improvising:

In an improvisation you have to be prepared for all sorts of directions that are unseen and also for taking away your sense of direction. Maybe you personally would like a certain direction but somebody else does something and the direction alters. So that in itself is very close to life, I think, more so than a written composition. Life is a continual interaction between what one person would like and what is imposed on them from outside.[69]

The final section of 'Towards an Ethic of Improvisation' bears the subtitle 'Virtues that a musician can develop' and Cardew lists seven: Simplicity, Integrity, Selflessness, Forbearance, Preparedness, Identification with Nature, and Acceptance of Death. Many of these virtues, if not all, bear directly on his experience as an improvising musician; the fourth virtue, Forbearance, reads:

> Improvising in a group you have to accept not only the frailties of your fellow musicians, but also your own. Overcoming your instinctual revulsion against whatever is out of tune (in the broadest sense).

Clearly, the idea that making music embodies certain human qualities – and that the nurturing of these qualities, through music, is paramount – again reflects the Eastern influence:

> For the Chinese zither, or qin, was traditionally the instrument of the scholar; it was played in order to concentrate the mind and achieve a certain type of self-control. Virtuosity and acoustic gratification were disdained; what mattered was not the sound of what was played, but the moral and intellectual qualities it embodied.[70]

As a performer Cardew embodied all these virtues; an hieratic *persona* – his sheer presence in the performing arena has often been remarked upon: the calmness before playing that emanated from him, the inscrutable manner in which he seemed to appraise, and reappraise, a concert venue, its *genius loci*, from the moment of entering it. When performing his physical bearing was immaculate; posture at the cello impeccable, and the sweeps of the bowing arm would be executed as if he were conscious of the shapes and angles they created. Sitting cross-legged in front of the AMM steel gong the choreographic elegance of his gestures would enhance the visual aspect of the performance; clarity and intensity of sound would be matched by fluency and grace of movement. Economy, sensitivity and awareness went hand-in-hand in Cardew's improvisations, qualities he maintained however indulgent, frenetic or threatening the music which enveloped him. In such situations he would roll a cigarette and light up; and then, when it seemed that he had altogether lost interest in the proceedings and torpidity had overcome him, he would suddenly be galvanized into action: a sudden access of inspiration – a large gesture such as bowing the tam-tam – would lead the music into new regions or even, at a stroke, totally transform it.

Keith Rowe recalls that the most important thing he learnt from Cardew was when, and how, not to play. 'To play and to arrive at the state where you no longer need to play'.[71] You could stop playing, you could look around, change the position of your instrument. You could leave, have a coffee, and return to the fold refreshed and sharp. Such licence was acceptable and natural because of the radical time scale of AMM music-making: an 8pm. start may have been a necessary expedient for the organisers and custodians of the venue, but the music had already begun. And when the instruments were finally put away the music continued into the night; it was part of a continuum, a recognition of 'the musical composition of the world'.[72] The effect that this had, both on the performers and on the audience, was that the *experience* of time was revolutionized. Single phrases would be stretched out into several minutes length or more; sections of oceanic proportions and rhythmic sequences corresponding to rhythms of sleep, for example, would have a disorientating effect on both player and listener: as Rowe puts it, 'often we didn't know what time of day it was'. New notions of time would influence the playing variously: Cardew would spend lengthy periods during the sessions playing long notes and chords on the cello, interspersed with singing and smoking – music-making quite alien to Western musical practice but which sat comfortably with the traditions of more remote cultures.

> Playing in AMM sometimes produces a state where you feel sounds in a completely different way from usual…Seeing as if for the first time this reddy-brown object with all the strings going away to the left, and a bow going across the strings on the right hand side, and interwoven amongst the strings various little things, on the top of that a plastic lid, and you just watch the sound happening. That's something you don't normally do.[73]

In 1968, during an AMM sojourn in New York city[74], a visit to a native American reservation in New York State made a deep impression on Cardew, and his subsequent performances bore overt references to Native American culture. Keith Rowe recalls how Cardew would sit at the piano, straight back, hands on knees, rarely approaching the keyboard, and then suddenly breaking into song, sometimes recognizable, but often just vocalise, a kind of transcription for voice of what he might have played on the cello. The singing would be strong and resonant – few notes, occasionally great leaps in pitch; for Cardew all playing was an extension of singing. Music is erotic, we speak of 'music-lovers' and when it sings we recognise its erotic quality. In AMM

> the ambiguity of figure/ground relationships means that listening by the audience, as well as by the performers, becomes constructive. Hearing and feeling (or feeling as hearing), because they are close for the musicians, become close for the audience. The music is not projected outwards, is not a form, however subtle or beautiful, of harangue. Rather the listener is drawn into the music. Emotions are immediate and close to those of new experience (which the performance, after all, is).[75]

Cardew's performances would often incorporate ritualistic elements; in a concert in Berlin a painting from Native American history – *The Battle of Wounded Knee* – provided the inspiration. Cardew enjoyed planning sequences of actions which would produce situations of chance and risk, as we have seen with his performance of George Brecht's *Incidental Music*. He had a penchant for suspending objects with pieces of string or thread or rope and then experimenting with the sounds by means of a variety of bought, found and home-made beaters. He liked to create tensions which would accumulate and intensify throughout a lengthy passage of music; he was interested in the question of human control and, more importantly, of human fallibility. Of course, in a sense all the AMM performances were ritualistic if the reference of the word 'ritual' can be widened to embrace the idea of extending and deepening the ways of examining the environment and our place within it: what the environment might do to you, and what it might do to your music. Lou Gare, who at the time was interested in Zen, recalls trying to heighten his awareness at the moment of arrival at each venue: he attached bells to the sling of his saxophone to remind him of this task.

The sense of arrival ceases to exist when one is always arriving places. The 'feeling of arrival' needs time – we must stop somewhere, to have arrived there.
And is the 'feeling of going' an adequate substitute?
And is the 'feeling of going backwards' as satisfactory as that of going forwards?
Is future time the only interpretation of 'forwards'?[76]

For every member of the AMM it was the totality of the experience which was overriding; as soon as you embraced the idea that *any* sound could be music, then it was but a small step to the idea of incorporating perceived movement, gesture and environmental reaction into the total experience.

Inevitably, in the late sixties such attitudes were invariably attributed to the influence of drugs: members of AMM were assumed to be drug-takers by many who had themselves succumbed to the pervasive and convenient clichés of the day. In fact, there were no drug users in the AMM and they quietly and undemonstratively resisted the drug culture; when the ubiquitous joint was passed round AMM always declined.[77] As Eddie Prévost has pointed out, alcohol, rather than drugs, was the escape route of the culture in which he was brought up; 'getting pissed on a Friday night' was the norm for his peers in Bermondsey. The mind-expanding antics of psychedelia were never part of AMM's lifestyle; they were not interested in any form of escape from where they were; on the contrary, they were looking for and investing meaning in the everyday objects and phenomena that were all around them, striving to capture the 'whatness' from the commonplace, as Stephen explains in *Portrait of the Artist as a Young Man*. And it was part of AMM's quest to discover and raise the untenanted and the discarded to great heights.

In the aforementioned lecture for the University of Illinois in February 1967 Cardew draws an interesting comparison between his compositional 'method' and free improvisation, in which he seems to be suggesting that a compatibility exists – that they are not, as Eddie Prévost has suggested, mutually exclusive:

I compose systems. Sounds and potential sounds are around us all the time – they're all over. What you do is insert your logical construct into this seething mass, a system that enables some of it to become audible. That's why it's such an orgiastic experience to improvise – instead of composing a system to project into all this chaotic potential, you simply put yourself in there (you too are a system of sorts, after all) and see what action that suicidal deed precipitates.

It is a profound irony that Cardew's involvement with AMM and improvised music began at a time when his mastery of the misconceived, misused art of musical notation had, with *Treatise*, reached a peak. For while he was seeking to refine the art of notation, his actual music-making, with AMM, drew him ineluctably to its abandonment. For a time they coexisted, uneasily; for performances of *Treatise* could not measure up to the extraordinary soundscapes of AMM's world. Musically, *Treatise* lived in the shadow of AMM and it was the fabulous visual presence of the score which alone guaranteed its unassailable position in contemporary music. An imaginative, silent, lone reading of *Treatise* was an experience which even an AMM performance could not surpass; it was through *Treatise* that Cardew clung on to notation. He was still convinced of the broader significance of notation as a paradigm of communication between people, rather than as a crude and unwieldy symbolization of sounds (as I have tried to show in my discussion of *Treatise*). Of course, the notion of 'communication between people' itself begs unsettling questions, for if Cardew devised a system through which notational control mechanisms could be loosened, it was never his intention that they should be relinquished altogether. 'Control is essential to authority' Eddie Prévost has reminded us, and the bug of 'authority' had bitten deep into Cardew, however generously one chooses to interpret manifestations of it at crucial stages of his career: the Scratch Orchestra, *The Great Learning* and Confucianism, and Leninism.

Yet there are other kinds of 'compositions' which may be interpreted by musicians, such as the 'environmental notations' which, as we have seen, Keith Rowe 'reads' in his recognition of 'the musical composition of the world'. In itself, however, this is no more than the sonic expression of a primordial, solipsistic relation to the limitless source of raw material that the world provides, and as such has no social corollary. Musical notation, however, whether neumatic, as in the Middle Ages, or graphic, as with *Treatise*, embodies the notion of music as *social activity*; it prescribes, as in classical music, or implies, as in *Treatise*, certain social relations which an aural sensitivity to the environment *per se* does not necessarily engender. For AMM the means and principles for the socialisation of sound-making were acquired not through compositional notations, which they rejected, nor through the contemplation of 'perfectly ordinary reality', however wondrous, but through *social intercourse*, and through the profound and complex demands it makes of us.

For Cardew traditional notation, and the system of equal temperament in particular, was a strait-jacket which had forced music to behave as it did, segmenting musical space into discrete steps and creating a music which was accessible to Western rationalisation. For Cardew's peers the supremacy of the Western notational system, even when it was not present, could not be questioned. In Berio's words, 'even today, of all things that can happen when improvising, it seems to me that it's those elements which establish a relation with a more or less explicit idea of notation that make sense.'[78] Most composers, including Cage, view music hierarchically; composing is simply the highest form of musical life: 'It is better to make a piece of music than to perform one, better to perform one than to listen to one [...].' Cage was unequivocal.[79]

But AMM music bears no relation to the received notion of musical notation whatsoever; indeed, as Christian Wolff has observed, it would seem to be impossible to conceive of a functional notation for AMM music – except, perhaps, *The Tiger's Mind*: a verbal, narrative 'composition' (discussed below) which clearly relates to Cardew's music-making with AMM, and which was an attempt to create a notational context in which musicians could find hints, pointers, images, metaphors, that might draw them into the orbit of AMM's 'meta-music'. The 'sense' that Berio refers to exists only within the remit of the stave, of 'notation', and as such is the prerogative of the composer. For him and for many of his peers musical 'sense', then, is what the composer, and the composer alone, dispenses; beyond the stave only 'no-sense' exists.

In AMM music the musician cannot refer to a formal context; he is in the throes of creating one – one, moreover, that is aurally perceptible, which is how he demonstrates his musicianship – just as much as by his ability to perform persuasively on a musical instrument. Furthermore, in AMM the structural role which notation assigns to, for example, discrete pitches is assumed by other elements; structural definition is achieved characteristically in AMM by the use of laminal techniques – textural layering and juxtaposition. The status of intonation, too, has to be reassessed if, as is often the case with AMM, the objective status of the 'semitone' as a structural entity is abandoned; the 'tuned' piano has no more, and no less legitimacy in AMM music than an 'untuned' one, so that radically different approaches to tuning, within the group, often attain a structural significance. As we have seen, as far back as 1959 Cardew wrestled with the composer's problems of sustaining the impression of a time-structure, especially in relation to the expression of what was for him a desirable musical form. One might argue that for Cardew AMM music constituted a resolution of the problems, as he defined them, of 'structure', a period of reckoning during which the issue of structure was finally laid to rest.

Cardew stressed the uniqueness of an improvisation:

> Written compositions are fired off into the future; even if never performed, the writing remains as a point of reference. Improvisation is in the present, its effect may live on in the souls of the participants, both active and passive (that is, audience), but in its concrete form it is gone forever from the moment that it occurs, nor did it have any previous existence before the moment that it occurred. So neither is there any historical reference available.[80]

Yet because of its directness, its immediacy, improvisation is often perceived simply as something musicians do when they arrive on stage, as if by default, without sheets of manuscript paper. They invent nothing, they simply access their memory bank.[81] But just as thought has preceded the mark on the manuscript paper in the composer's studio, so before he emits a sound the improviser has trained and prepared himself; he has reflected on the new musical problems that have arisen; he has pondered and perhaps rejected the 'reformulation of successful modes'; he has recalled the unresolved tensions of previous performances; he has considered the relationships with other players: in short, he has engaged in musical thought. A particular improvisation is one of many possible consequences of these considerations; spontaneously and publicly, they are given temporal musical expression.

There is a pertinent and illuminating analogy here; which Cardew surely identified in Norman Malcolm's *Ludwig Wittgenstein: A Memoir*, a book he read and re-read to the end of his life; for the way that the audience is drawn into this process (of improvisation) is demonstrably comparable to the way Wittgenstein would engage the audience in his Cambridge lectures.[82] Wittgenstein's lectures were

> drawn from his thoughts about the problems with which he was wrestling at the time and delivered without notes and with very little preparation for the occasion. He was really thinking aloud, and he might succeed in pushing his

investigation of a problem beyond the point that he had reached in his meditations outside the lecture room, so that his audience would witness the difficult, and sometimes painful emergence of his new ideas. They also took part in the process, because he drew them into the discussion and dealt with their objections. He conducted the meetings with deep seriousness and relentless determination never to be satisfied with incomplete or superficial solutions and he made very great demands both on his audience and on himself.[83]

The AMM audience, too, witnesses the evolution and deployment of 'problem-solving techniques' to negotiate each unforeseen moment, to ride the rapids of uncertainty. And the heuristic quality of Wittgenstein's lectures is echoed in Cardew's own characterisation of AMM performances:

We are searching for sounds and the responses that attach to them, rather than thinking them up, preparing them and producing them. The search is conducted in the medium of sound and the musician himself is at the heart of the experiment.[84]

Talking/playing, thinking/listening and searching, discovery of meanings; these constitute the quiddity of a Wittgenstein lecture, and an AMM performance. More, the unpredictable acting-out and interacting of these constituents spontaneously determine the form. Clearly, if the 'meaning' of the lecture/performance cannot be predetermined, nor can the form; for the form develops organically – its appropriateness, its efficacy, its compatibility with the content depending on the sensitivity, intelligence and experience of the protagonists.

The Times newspaper critic Max Harrison, reviewing an AMM concert at the Purcell Room on 30 January 1984, wrote:

This ensemble has over the years acclimatized us to a large spectrum of fresh sounds and sound relationships. That is enough, I think, and the gentlemen of AMM ought not to worry about morality, certainly not about sociology.

What had miffed Harrison was a sentence in the concert programme which flew in the face of received musicological opinion: 'Collective music development arises out of dialogue and the constant inter-action of aesthetic, moral and social considerations.' Is it then simply a case of a group of aurally-aware people making 'fresh sounds and sound relationships'? In respect of AMM certainly Cardew did not think so; the musician himself, he insisted, is 'at the heart of the experiment' and a critic who approaches this music must therefore do so anthropocentrically.

For Cardew, and for his fellow musicians, AMM music was a kind of commentary on a society, or rather on what it was like to live in that society; but it also investigated, sifted, and created the possibilities for transcending it. It was not a gloss or an embellishment; rather an antidote, or a point of rest, a release from the frenetic conformism of contemporary life, a strategy for survival. Jazz was an inspiration, not a model, for AMM because of the relationship it had to its soil, to its community, and through its contributions within and for that community in America. For jazz, and for AMM, the test is the authenticity of the commentary, the level of profundity, the depth and psychological consequences of its impact on the audience. 'Improvisation', Cardew wrote, is a 'spectator sport, where the subtlest interplay on the physical level can throw into relief some of the mystery of being alive.'[85]

Without doubt joining AMM was one of the major turning points in Cardew's career; an indefinable, 'uncatchable' music, it reached beyond the circumscribed agenda of conventional musicological discourse and asked fundamental questions about, and of, the art of music. It thus freed him to make any sounds and to husband them, to enjoy the beauty of adventitious sounds and to develop a 'sound aesthetic' free from competitiveness and intellectual game-playing. What excited and exhilarated him in AMM's music-making was that sudden access of spontaneous inspiration that can transform a performance: *Duende*. 'All arts are capable of *Duende*', Lorca wrote,

but where it finds its greatest range, naturally, is in music, dance and spoken poetry, for these arts require a living body to interpret them, being forms that are born, die and open their contours against an exact present.[86]

Time and again, throughout Cardew's life, the intrinsic qualities of the improvisatory mode impinged not only on his compositions and music-making but also on the way he conducted his life: spontaneity, freedom of expression, the uncatchable, the transient, 'being' and 'nowness', and not least its inescapable moral basis (the seven 'virtues'). For Cardew the western notion of 'musical thought' was intellectually circumscribed, that is, it was *western* musical thought, and as an improviser with the AMM he had rejected the prerequisites of Western compositional modes – scholarship, precedent, form, deliberation; his commitment now was to new aesthetic priorities with a different constellation of responses.

The story of AMM goes on – and I shall pick it up again at a later stage in this book – but by now, the early seventies, the narrative has been overtaken by new developments with comparable demands on our attention; it is these which I address in the following chapters.

Sextet – *The Tiger's Mind* (1967)

Since becoming a composer 1966 was the first year, indeed the only year, in which Cardew did not complete a single composition.1967 saw the publication of *Treatise* but this apart his sole contribution to the repertoire that year was *The Tiger's Mind* – a verbal, narrative 'score': such was the impact and consequence of his participation in AMM and the demanding schedule for the final drafting of his epic graphic score during that period. In the September 1967 issue of the *Musical Times* Cardew placed an advertisement for a projected performance of *The Tiger's Mind* the following month. Would-be participants were invited to write in, 'stating what character they were interested in and in what way they interpret it'. The brief text ended on a sobering note: 'No fee is offered, no guarantee of acceptance.' Although there seems to have been little or no response the performance duly took place at the Electric Garden venue in London, Daypiece on 30 October, Nightpiece on 12 December, with the participation of just a few friends: including AMM, the Royal Academy students, Christian Wolff (who interpreted the Tree), Howard Skempton (who interpreted the Mind), and a female dancer (who interpreted Amy). The text, *The Tiger's Mind*, reads beautifully and demonstrates Cardew's poetic flair, the characters etched with an economy of expression and felicitous turn of phrase:

Daypiece
The tiger fights the mind that loves the circle that traps the tiger. The circle is perfect and outside time. The wind blows dust in tiger's eyes. Amy reflects, relaxes with her mind, which puts out buds (emulates the tree). Amy jumps through the circle and comforts the tiger. The tiger sleeps in the tree. High wind. Amy climbs the tree, which groans in the wind and succumbs. The tiger burns.

Nightpiece
The tiger burns and sniffs the wind for news. He storms at the circle; if inside to get out, if outside to get in. Amy sleeps while the tiger hunts. She dreams of the wind, which then comes and wakes her. The tree trips Amy in the dark and in her fall she recognizes her mind. The mind, rocked by the wind tittering in the leaves of the tree, and strangled by the circle, goes on the nod. The circle is trying to teach its secrets to the tree. The tree laughs at the mind and at the tiger fighting it.

Cardew follows the text with a page of 'interpretative' guidelines, which are only loosely prescriptive (memorization of the text is recommended) and act rather to stimulate the imagination and galvanize the performer into a creative response. Procedural methods and the way in which the roles are allocated are suggested but not insisted upon. The

THE TIGER'S MIND

NIGHTPIECE Lou Gare Susan Gittins
Robin Thompson Samuel Richards Keith Rowe
Eddie Prevost Christian Wolff Paul Rutherford
Cornelius Cardew Colin Wood Christopher Hobbs
Hugh Shrapnel David Conway Bernhard Living
Laurence B Crawley Howard Skempton

43 King Street WC2 Tuesday 12th December 1967
I lay my harp on the curved table, Sitting there idly, filled only with emotions. Why should I trouble to play? A breeze will come and sweep the strings.

number of characters – 6, and the shifting ambiguity of their relationships may refer to Pirandello, an author Cardew admired and enjoyed. Amy is clearly the central character; she is the only one who 'should never be duplicated' unless, unavoidably, by some procedural quirk. The page of interpretation is followed by notes on the six characters which are 'intended primarily to encourage and assist prospective performers in the assumption of their roles'.

In his lecture for the University of Illinois on 25 February 1967, a week after its completion, Cardew informed his audience:

This is the first time I made a composition that expressly requires improvisation. Wind-music can be constructed, and so can circle-music, tree-music and mind-music, but Tiger-music has to be improvised and the same goes for Amy-music.

Interestingly, the insistence on the improvisatory nature of Amy-music and Tiger-music as opposed to the possible 'construction' of the remaining characters' music, which Cardew expressed in the Illinois lecture, does not appear in the printed score. The reasons for this distinction are clear enough but he must have realized that the imposition of such refinements was doomed to be ignored. Amy's human qualities and the Tiger's animal instincts are enough to separate them substantially from the insensate Tree, the insubstantial Wind, and the abstract Circle. And the Mind? 'The mind itself is never in danger', Cardew notates; 'only its user […] The mind is a nonentity – hard to recognize'. In performance Cardew would play his cello which he regarded as a 'tree-instrument', depriving or protecting other instruments. Sometimes he would joke: eat an apple; drink water.

It may be both edifying and diverting to speculate on the pedigree of the 'notation' for The Tiger's Mind; certainly the role-playing conjures up children's games and the Tiger itself perhaps relates to Kipling's Jungle Book – which Cardew had surely read, although his is a vulnerable and more benign Tiger. Or to Blake's burning Tyger, a symbol of spiritual energy. And there are also clear references to English nursery rhymes and games: The House that Jack built and The Cow with the Crumpled Horn which jumped over the Moon, especially, and the 'paper/scissors/stone' game.

After a performance (of Daypiece) Cardew noted his impressions in the Journals (undated):

Shape of a day is represented only by this, that at noon a certain level of musicianship was attained and then this deteriorated again to the end.

At the end we are left simply with the people as they are – they lose their connections with their objects. Lou is Lou not Amy. Maybe this should be: not how does Amy stand out from the natural environment that the piece sets up, but how do I stand out from the natural environment.

The Story of Agatha
See Appendix 2

The 1967/8 Journals include a text, written in red pen, undated and untitled, which was probably composed in the summer of 1967. The narrative has a dream-like quality, comparable to a number of dreams which Cardew recorded, but is described at the beginning as 'really a sexual narrative' and is clearly a product of the unconscious imagination. Perhaps a more accurate description would be an 'erotic narrative'; there is fantasy, intoxication and an intense sensuality which demand a more provocative, a more wanton choice of epithet. *Treatise* had not long been finished and an irregular succession of performances, stretching back to the summer of 1964, had punctuated Cardew's musical activities over these three years – a counterpoint, a poor relation perhaps, to his music-making with AMM, which began a little later.

Both *Treatise* and the AMM exemplified, in consummate manner, the fact of music as essentially a communication, not from, but between people: an unequivocal rejection of those modes of human intercourse based on control and manipulation. In their development of improvisatory and collective music-making they created not only alienation strategies for the present, but also visionary alternatives for the future. But who would respond to the moral imperatives which Cardew's strategies and visions embrace? Do such people exist and if so, where are they? With such speculation Cardew's narrative begins: 'I am assuming that anyone who finds interest or profit in my story is for that reason alone a member of what I call my tribe.' The members of AMM, of course, belonged to this tribe, or perhaps the tribe was an extension of AMM, for when Cardew joins the expedition the post to which he is appointed seems to bear a relationship to his membership of AMM. Yet he expresses embarrassment, as if he still did not feel that his apprenticeship to AMM had been fully served.

The planet of the narrative, it seems to me, emblematizes AMM and its ethos, and an interesting comparison can be drawn between this text and that of *The Tiger's Mind*. But if *The Tiger's Mind* is a literary metaphor for AMM, this narrative is a poetic intensification of the metaphor. Significantly, in both the leading protagonists are women; unlike the *Scratch Orchestra* the AMM was, and still is, an all-male preserve. The strong, dominating female presence characterises both *The Tiger's Mind* and this narrative, even if the latter is perhaps somewhat compromised by the ambiguity of Gladys's and Agatha's gender. Yet they are not portrayed as hermaphrodites, the ambiguity does not lie in a male/female dichotomy; it is as if a third gender, neither male nor female, but somehow artistic, inhabits the planet and takes part in acts of procreation. In view of Cardew's ambivalence, at least as a young man, towards his own sexuality this is perhaps not surprising. As we have seen in his parting letter to Ruth and in his dreams, for example, such equivocal feelings did occasionally surface.

The creatures Gladys and Agatha are a transmogrification of AMM; they are sensitive to touch, to environment, into which, chameleon-like, they merge. Much of Cardew's imagery is musical; the creatures' 'phrased' walking is like a language, corresponding to the irregular, randomized rhythms of AMM, while the ritualistic preparation and consumption of liquid sustenance and their simple home – a cave with a fire – echoes typical features of Cardew's upbringing and domestic life. Like AMM the music-making sessions with Gladys and Agatha last a very long time, and as the music drifts beyond his control Cardew is transported by its unique and extraordinary quality. His 'at-oneness' with whatever instrument he happens to be playing is taken a stage further on the planet: the body grows and develops according to the exigencies of music-making – hence, the ridged arms for the string instruments and the aperture for wind instruments. If Gladys and Agatha are members of Cardew's 'tribe' they are nevertheless ill-at-ease with the human species in general. Agatha represents an outlet, or rather an inlet, for Cardew's sensuality. She is special, unique; she sings while Cardew, ear 'glued to her navel' listens entranced to the endless outpourings of exquisite melody. The kaleidoscopic nature of this fantastical being characterises her ineffable presence, her ever-changing colours accompanying her music. In a strange way these ephemeral creatures, with their extraordinary inventiveness and magical qualities, seem to look forward to the Scratch Orchestra. At the end of the narrative Agatha presents Cardew with a child, their child – 'a sweet friendly organism I had no difficulty in relating to'. At the moment of conception Agatha is perceived as an awe-inspiring mirror of nature with whom an extraordinary physical union is being enacted.[87]

In a Journal entry on 10 June 1967 penned the following poetic reference to Agatha:

A Musical Novel

Full of Nature and Love.

ending

I took up my sax and wrote

Dear Agatha,

≡≡≡≡≡≡≡≡≡≡ ⟶ 10 pages of melody.

x   x   x   x

To this I received no reply.

Notes and references

1   Members of AMM can all recognize this quote. But none of us can attribute it.

2   Between June 1965 and October 1970 there was an impressive roster of weekly meetings at a variety of venues which were only changed when they withdrew their hospitality; they were all free of charge. In the early days the Royal College of Art had made a room available to AMM, for almost a year, before they moved to the music room at the London School of Economics (LSE), from May to September 1966; from January to April 1967 at a gallery in Kingly Street in central London; at the Lisson Gallery in Marylebone from July to October 1967; in Langtry Road in north-west London, in a tiny house used as a studio by an acquaintance, the novelist and television director David Benedictus (who was away at the time), from January to May 1968; from June 1968 to May 1969 at the Arts Laboratory in Drury Lane; from July 1969, for at least a year, they met every week at The Place, a large building (associated in particular with dance) near Euston station, and they continued to play there, though not on a regular basis, until May 1971. Except for The Place the sessions were private, admission by invitation only. There were also numerous engagements of a more formal nature: at the Institute of Contemporary Arts, the Commonwealth Institute, the Conway Hall, Camden's Roundhouse, the Queen Elizabeth Hall, the BBC – in fact most of the major venues in London, as well as modest tours of the US, Canada, the Netherlands, Belgium, Denmark and Germany.

3   Eddie Prévost, from an interview with Trevor Taylor in *Drums and Percussion*, August 1974.

4   'A feature of Jazz's history is the lionization of (especially) black American jazz musicians in Europe – a welcome and justified response, given the way black musicians were usually treated in the US. But heroism and 'otherness' turned agreed aesthetic objectives into conventions, sometimes no better than the rigidities artists have striven to escape.' Edwin Prévost, 'Improvisation: Music for an Occasion', in *No Sound is Innocent* (Harlow UK: Copula, 1995), p. 176. Yet by adopting an emulative style, many European jazz musicians seemed to have found a haven – though invariably an unhappy one – in which their musical talents could find expression.

5   Other musicians who had struck out on their own included John Stevens, Trevor Watts, Derek Bailey, Evan Parker and Paul Rutherford. Stevens and Watts, in particular, were central to the influential Spontaneous Music Ensemble (SME) which performed regularly at The Little Theatre Club in Monmouth Street in the West End, where, on the odd occasion and in a spirit of solidarity, they invited AMM to play.

6   Rowe recalls that at the time the main influences on the Westbrook band were the later Ellington – in particular the Duke's unifying use of literary themes – and the Charlie Mingus big band with its frequent use of riffs. Certainly the band was very much within the mainstream of modern jazz.

7   Keith Rowe, interview with Kenneth Ansell in *Wire Magazine*, Issue 11, January 1985.

8   In an informal, recorded discussion one evening somewhere in central France in the Spring of 1990, on the way to a concert in Switzerland, Keith Rowe remarked that in his experience only Frank Butler, an American jazz drummer, could produce a snare drum roll comparable to that of Eddie Prévost.

9   It was by dint of its sheer volume that AMM was still regarded by many in the mid-sixties as a 'fringe' pop group and appeared on one or two occasions on the same bill as Pink

Floyd (whose manager, Peter Jenner, was one of the producers of the LP AMMMUSIC) – at the UFO Club in Tottenham Court Road – and with Cream at the Roundhouse in Chalk Farm, north-west London in a day long event which also featured Geno Washington and the Ram Jam Band. It is unlikely that the other musicians had ever heard of AMM; at the Roundhouse the promoter refused to pay AMM on the grounds that they had 'only been tuning up'. AMM's manager at the time, Victor Schonfield, did eventually manage to prise a token fee from some administrative source or other.

10   From David Sladen's interview with Cardew and Keith Rowe, printed in the ICA bulletin, March 1966.

11   Jrnl. 7 February 1965.

12   *Philosophical* Investigations, Part 1, 261.

13   Ibid, 528.

14   *AMMMUSIC – 1966*, RēR /Matchless Recordings.

15   This value judgement, written several years ago, may seem excessively censorious and, perhaps, then and now, 'out-of-touch' and 'out-of-depth' (like Palestrina's biographer describing a punk concert), but I have not yet reached that philosophical condition, that state of 'enlightenment', where an opinion is *merely* opinion. Hence my (foolhardy) decision to allow these particular thoughts to take their chances in the public domain. In fact, Victor Schonfield describes this music as 'free jazz', adding in a note to me, 'though I do not necessarily disagree with your account'.

16   According to Keith Rowe it was Cardew's bold and imaginative use of prepared piano which inspired him and other members of the group to experiment with their own instrumental inventory.

17   It was around the time of the Elektra recording, July 1966, that the Canadian film director, Allan King, approached AMM with the idea of a collaboration on a film about a home for disturbed children: *Warrendale*.

18   In fact, not all the aphorisms were contributed by AMM members; at least one was by Victor Schonfield.

19   Of course, the same applies to the contribution of a member of the second violins in a Mozart symphony. Yet, however sensitively played, the individuality of such a contribution is of a much lesser consequence within the whole than that of an AMM musician. If the second violinist's part is essential (and we are discussing Mozart's second violins!), it is also subordinate and clearly prescribed; what is required is not creativity and imagination, but aural accuracy and technical expertise.

20   From David Sladen's interview printed in the ICA bulletin, March 1966.

21   I am conscious of the contentious nature of these distinctions and comparisons. Cardew, too, suffered 'deprivation' as a child in Cornwall; living without running water and electricity. But this was the result of a conscious decision on the part of his parents to lead their lives in a particular way. It was their choice, just as the beautiful art objects and books they surrounded themselves with were the fruits of conscious, calculated and informed choice. Of course, it can also be argued that those children sent at some considerable cost to celebrated boarding schools might be considered emotionally and even socially 'deprived'.

22   If, indeed, Cardew ever harboured such an opinion in the early days, it was certainly short-lived; there was subsequently, and until the end of his life, ample evidence of Cardew's deep affection and admiration for Eddie Prévost, as man and musician.

23   These aphorisms were created at a brain-storming session at Keith Rowe's flat in Stockwell, south London. Cardew was not present and did not therefore contribute to the Elektra sleeve notes.

24   It was assumed by many superficial observers that the music and the direction the group had taken was evidence of a 'strong personality', an individual 'guiding force', which was probably Cardew; Cardew was the putative leader of AMM. The natural collectivist sentiments which the music exemplified were more or less ignored. For example, in a review of AMM's first album in the *Musical Times*, August 1967, G.W. (Bill) Hopkins) opined that 'Cardew's is an expert and closely knit group', while *Jazz Journal*, July 1967, called AMM 'The Cornelius Cardew Quintet'. On a tour abroad there was a further twist in the tail, as Victor Schonfield recalls : 'Money entered the picture only occasionally, most notably when AMM was invited for several days to Berlin in December 1969. This gave us a chance to fix a couple of extra gigs in Denmark on the way back. We all (AMM, me and my wife) went off in the AMM van through bitter winter weather deep into East Germany, then out again to Aarhus […] The final date of the tour was a Danish Radio concert in Copenhagen where we were greeted by posters that proclaimed "AMM − leder Victor Schonfield". It took me some time to live that one down.' From the sleeve notes to the CD *Laminal*, released on Matchless Recordings (MRCD31) in 1996.

25   From Eddie Prévost's sleeve notes − 'AMM − a few memories and reflections' for the re-release on CD of the LP AMMMUSIC − co-released in 1989 by RēR Megacorp and Matchless Recordings as AMMMUSIC − 1966.

26   'Americans' refers here, of course, to those relatively small segments of American culture which survive and flourish outside the mainstream, for which Cardew had no sympathy whatsoever.

27   In a programme note for his concert of contemporary piano music at the Haro Lauhus gallery in Cologne in the early sixties Cardew makes explicit references to the inadequacies, as he saw them, of musical notation: 'These notations (of Feldman, Cage, Wolff, Brown, La Monte Young, Stockhausen, Kagel, Bussotti and myself) show great diversity, richness and imagination, but I see them as inessential to the process of producing music. I have attempted to dispense with formalisation as far as possible in the music of my own which I will play […] I realise that a notation leads to sounds, but sounds also lead to sounds, and their connection is implicit, and evades the qualitative leap (from sign to sound) which lends modern music its 'profound obscurity'.'

28   I have already touched upon the issue of 'professionalism' in the discussion of *Autumn 60*. Even then, at the beginning of the sixties, Cardew was already experiencing misgivings about the role which professional musicians were expected to play in our musical culture.

29   Free Improvisation was one of the most influential and pervasive manifestations of (musical) dissent. As Derek Bailey remarked, 'you couldn't walk down Oxford Street without bumping into at least 30 or 40 free improvisers − it was rife, not to say plagued'. *Perspectives of New Music*, Vol.21 nos.1 and 2 (fall-winter, 1982/ spring-summer, 1983), p.51.

30   Kenneth Ansell, *The Wire*, No. 11, January 1985.

31   According to Eddie Prévost 'the Chinese studies helped AMM to develop perspectives, strategies and techniques to encourage leaps away from conventional teachings and meanings, and the traps within them'. 'AMM and the Practice of Self-Invention', in *No Sound is Innocent*, p.16.

32 Although Keith Rowe did come perilously close for a time when he joined a Buddhist commune in Clapham in south-west London and became a militant vegetarian.

33 The African, or Afro-American influence in relation to, for example, the importance of body and dance rhythms is of marginal significance in AMM music. And yet there *is* emphasis on the consciousness of the body in performance, and a subtlety of movement which is more akin to the movements of, for example, Tai Chi, which Eddie Prévost has practised on a daily basis for many years, and Aikido, which Lou Gare practices. Perhaps there is an inner body rhythm to which AMM music responds. This would also account for the generally slower momentum of AMM music in comparison, say, to the 'pointillism' of some improvising groups.

34 On the piano, especially, this 'end-product' has more the quality of a 'by-product' because once the action has been made (which action/s?) to produce the sound, the sound tends to free itself of your control. In a text I contributed to the Royal College of Art Magazine, *Ark* 45, Winter 1969, I described a performance of a piece by the Japanese composer/ violinist Takehisa Kosugi which demonstrated the complexity of this process. The piece consists of performing any action as slowly as possible. 'I decided to perform the action to produce the note B flat on the piano as slowly as possible. Several problems presented themselves, the most taxing of which were how, where, and when to begin, and at what point to end. By using this slow motion procedure a simple reflex action turns into an inhibiting dilemma. For example, was it possible to perform the action to produce the sound without performing the sound? If I sounded the B flat, would not that be an "excess"? Does the action begin when my hand is at rest on my leg, or from the moment I approach or sit at the piano?'

35 Cardew noted down this quote from the Taoist writer Thien Thung-Hsiu which he had read in the chapter on Physics in Joseph Needham's *Science and Civilisation in China* (Cambridge: Cambridge University Press, vol. 4, Part 1, 1962), p.209. Joseph Needham embarked on his magnum opus in 1954; seven volumes in eleven or more parts were projected. Since his death in 1995 assistants have continued the project, although it has yet to be completed.

36 In a BBC Radio 3 discussion with the pianist Roger Woodward and the cellist Christopher Gough preceding a broadcast of his *Piano and Orchestra* and *String Quartet and Orchestra* on 28 August 1980 Morton Feldman made the point that 'it's amazing how many professionals are actually frightened by the instrument they themselves, allegedly, have mastered'.

37 Bruno Nettl makes an apposite point in relation to Western ethnomusicologists, describing them as victims 'of an analogue of the Whorfian hypothesis, according to which thought is regulated by the structure of language; musical hearing on the part of Westerners may be profoundly affected by the characteristics of Western notation'. Bruno Nettl, *The Study of Ethnomusicology: Twenty-nine Issues and Concepts* (Urbana: University of Illinois Press,1983), pp.78-9.

38 *No Sound is Innocent*, p.20.

39 Jrnl. 30 December 1968.

40 *New perspectives in Music*, (London: Sun Tavern Fields, 1994), p.208.

41 Jrnl. 6 April 1965.

42 Rowe's technique of 'playing' the transistor radio was certainly the precursor of the later developments of 'scratching'; that is, 'playing' the turntable.

43 I am conscious that in singling out and eulogizing an individual there is a danger of creating a misleading impression. Moreover, it is an expedient which is at odds with AMM's own 'self-perception'. Listening to the Elektra recording, for example, or the later recording from the Crypt – always assuming a favourable disposition towards the music, as well as to Rowe's playing – one can equally apply superlatives to the contributions of the other members of the group. But I felt it was important to draw attention to what Eddie Prévost has often pointed out – that artistically, and perhaps on a purely personal level too, Cardew's relation to Rowe was somehow special.

44 During the mid-nineteen sixties Victor Schonfield became known as a free-lance jazz journalist with a particular interest in the newer fringes of jazz: in the UK musicians such as Bobby Wellins and the Mike Westbrook Orchestra. He also promoted the first European concert of Ornette Coleman, for which he was blacklisted for a time by the Musicians' Union for contravening the exchange regulations for foreign musicians. In the latter part of the sixties he became involved in organising concerts of jazz, free improvisation and contemporary experimental music (as the director of Music Now, which he founded in 1968 'at Cardew's behest'): John Stevens and the Spontaneous Music Ensemble (SME), Derek Bailey and Evan Parker (Music Improvisation Company, which also included Hugh Davies, with live electronics, and the percussionist Jamie Muir), the Scratch Orchestra, Christian Wolff, Cornelius Cardew, John Tilbury and the Japanese group, Taj Mahal Travellers (with Takehisa Kosugi). Schonfield organised Sun Ra's first European tour, which left Music Now heavily in debt. Partly to try and recoup losses he also promoted a concert by John Cage and David Tudor at the Albert Hall in 1972, a venture which made matters worse financially.

45 Victor Schonfield, from the sleeve notes to *Laminal*, pp.8-9. Another report, by Chris Fox, claims that McCartney added 'a simple ingredient to the discordant melange by running a penny up and down the coils of a steam radiator at his side'. *Rubberneck*, November 2000.

46 *Treatise Handbook*, p.xviii. The title of the piece by La Monte Young is *Composition 1960 #10*. Rowe's reference to dangling legs appeared first in David Sladen's interview in March 1966. (*CCR*)

47 Ibid., p.xx. (*CCR*)

48 Prévost recalls saying (or writing) this but cannot remember the particular occasion, except that it was probably sometime in the early nineteen-nineties.

49 Lawrence Sheaff had been an integral part of AMM, a committed member of the group, and his departure, which was in unfortunate circumstances, is documented, though not fully, by Eddie Prévost in his sleeve notes to the RēR / Matchless CD of *AMMMUSIC* – 1966). There is much mileage that can be extracted from this sad event, though it would be beyond the remit of this book. Suffice it to say that the affair does not seem to have been settled honourably and it would appear, admittedly from some distance, that AMM, for all its loftiness of purpose and seriousness of aim, was capable of acting with extreme insensitivity towards those who, in its eyes, had transgressed. It had apparently not yet learnt to apply the 'virtues' which informed its 'musica practica' to the moral rough and tumble of everyday existence.

50 The complete session of the Crypt concert, a 2 CD set, was released on Matchless Recordings MRCD05.

51   From the sleeve notes to *AMMMUSIC* – 1966.

52   'Towards an Ethic of Improvisation', *Treatise Handbook*, p.xviii. (*CCR*)

53   But to give artistic (musical) expression to 'diffidence' does not necessarily mean playing diffidently (which is what I am suggesting in my characterisation of a section of AMM's performance); when Debussy prescribes 'un peu gauche' at the beginning of his piano piece, *Jimbo's Lullaby*, he is not asking the pianist to play in a 'gauche' manner.

54   Lou Gare's playing was much admired by Cardew – it seemed to convey an inner strength, an integrity, an immoveable quality; it exuded a warmth which was comforting.

55   From Roger Sutherland's review in the *London Musicians' Collective News*, May 1992, p.24.

56   At the time of writing, the autumn of 2004, I am informed by Eddie Prévost that the Crypt CD remains the most sought after of all of AMM's recordings.

57   From the film *Cornelius Cardew and the Scratch Orchestra – Journey to the North Pole*, by Hanne Boenisch. Produced with support from the Munich Academy for Film and Television, and Bavarian Television, Munich, in 1971/72. Cardew had made this remark some years earlier, in March 1966, when he and Keith Rowe were interviewed by David Sladen.

58   Keith Rowe's relation to amplification was different since the amplifier was an integral part of his instrument; Rowe, was, and still is, an 'electric' as opposed to an 'acoustic', performer.

59   The recording from 16 December 1969 in Aarhus, Denmark, which is included in the *Laminal* box set (Matchless Recordings MRCD31), is an invaluable document in that it exemplifies this new tendency, acting as a bridge between the music of *The Crypt* and that of the AMM sessions (some recorded by Roger Sutherland) from the early seventies.

60   Roger Sutherland (1948-2004), who was also a member of the Scratch Orchestra, attended most of AMM's concerts during the early seventies, and recorded many of them. We need to remind ourselves, however, that these recordings, invaluable though they certainly are, are only a very rough equivalent of how the music *actually* sounded.

61   *Treatise Handbook* p.xviii. (*CCR*)

62   Eddie Prévost in the *Melody Maker*, 5 June 1971.

63   'Through the power of an ever new internal logic, each work will rouse the listener from a state of passivity and make him share its impulse, so that there will no longer be a difference of kind, but only of degree, between inventing music and listening to it.' Claude Lévi-Strauss, *The Raw and the Cooked* (London: Jonathan Cape, 1971), p.26.

64   Steve Lake, from a *Melody Maker* review of *The Crypt*, published sometime during 1976. This quote also appears on the back of the Matchless CD version of *The Crypt*.

65   Nicholas Cook, p. 65. In any case the question of the listener's perception of form is highly contentious. It has been shown that the 'look' of a work on paper, say Webern's *Piano Variations*, Op.27, bears little or no relation to the listener's experience of it.

66   *Treatise Handbook*, p.xx. (*CCR*)

67   Ibid.

68   Prévost remembers saying this but cannot recall where and when; I have included the quote on trust!

69   From an interview which appeared in the February 1990 issue of *Wire* magazine.

70   Nicholas Cook, p.7.

71   Aphorism IX from the sleeve notes for *AMMMUSIC* – 1966, RēR /Matchless Recordings.

72   'Artistic thinking these days is an endless process of finessing. Without interest.' Cardew
      jotted down in an undated Journal entry. For him too many composers had sacrificed
      commitment to a mindlessly proliferating activity.

73   From the ICA bulletin, March 1966.

74   In New York AMM performed at the Steinway Hall on the 6, 7, 8, 9 March. On one occasion,
      while they were setting up, Mark Boyle appeared; he was doing a light show for the Soft
      Machine who were touring with Jimi Hendrix as a backup group. After the performance
      Boyle suggested they should all go to a bar where Hendrix would be playing. In the early
      hours of the morning Hendrix appeared and performed for an audience which consisted
      of the AMM and a few fortunate punters, including the composer Earle Brown and the
      saxophonist Charles Lloyd, who were either in the know or who happened to be in the
      right place at the right time.

75   Paige Mitchell,' High Culture and the Nature Concert', p.8 of a pamphlet included with
      AMM's LP *The Inexhaustible Document.* It is also included in the CD reissue (Matchless
      Recordings MRCD13).

76   From a letter from CC to Ilona Halberstadt, dated 20 October 1959.

77   There was one exception: Cardew could not claim the same degree of purity and
      abstemiousness; he occasionally smoked, and according to several sources experimented
      with LSD when he was in Rome.

78   *Luciano Berio, Two Interviews with Rossana Dalmonte and Balint Andras Varga* (New York,
      London: Marion Boyars, 1985), p.82.

79   'Forerunner of Modern Music' (1949), in *Silence* (Cambridge, Mass., and London, 1966),
      pp. 62-66 (p.64).

80   'Towards an Ethic of Improvisation', p.xvii. (*CCR*)

81   A crude, formal device which some composers and critics have ascribed to the practice
      of contemporary improvised music is that of excitement and relaxation – the music
      invariably following the same curve of invention. This description, however, bears no relation,
      for example, to the performance at the Crypt on which I have elaborated above, nor does
      the music comprise what Pierre Boulez describes, dismissively, as a 'sequence of negations':
      a section in a high register followed by a section in a low register, long sounds juxtaposed
      with short ones, or silences, and so on. (And there are other improvisers, notably Derek
      Bailey, to whom this mode of improvisation is anathema.) On the contrary, arguably it is in
      composed music that one often finds such sequences; for many teachers of composition
      these 'negations' are an intrinsic feature of Western aesthetics.

82   I am not, of course, comparing contents; but the investigation of a problem, whether
      philosophical or musical, was in both cases conducted *publicly,* and as a kind of drama.

83   *Wittgenstein*, D. Pears, p.16.

84   *Treatise Handbook*, p.xviii. (*CCR*)

85   Ibid. p.xvii. (*CCR*)

86   From Lorca's lecture: *Juego y teoría del duende* ('Play and Theory of the Duende').

87   We are also reminded of Laurence Sterne's marvellously inventive descriptions of the
      inhabitants of the planet Mercury in *Tristram Shandy*, a book Cardew greatly admired.
      Indeed, the jaunty style of Cardew's narrative itself evokes Sterne's masterpiece.

(*CCR*) Also found in *Cornelius Cardew A Reader*

8

The Royal Academy of Music, Morley College, and the Founding of the Scratch Orchestra 1967–69

'Musicality is a dimension of perfectly ordinary reality'.[1]

As a performer of contemporary music in the early/mid sixties – apart from the occasional broadcast or appearance at a festival, when it was usually a matter of an acceptable and desperately needed financial remuneration – it was Cardew's legendary performances of the music of La Monte Young[2] and, in particular, his improvisatory music-making in AMM which reflected, as we have seen, an existential need for a profound reappraisal of the function and purpose, of the *status*, of musical composition:

> 20th Jan 67.
> Reflection before a performance. A musical score is a logical construct inserted into the mess of potential sounds that permeate this planet and its atmosphere. That puts Beethoven and the rest in perspective![3]

Both theoretically and in their praxis, in the radical, psychoacoustic exploration of musical aesthetics, which also embraced audience receptivity, La Monte Young and AMM were involved, independently, in similar areas of research and experimentation, and we can identify common influences – especially, as we have seen in our discussion of AMM, from Oriental philosophies – which manifest themselves analogously in their respective musics. Through AMM Cardew had discovered that Improvisation is no less than 'a practical and secular method of making contact with the flow of existence'.[4] Cardew's marathon performances of Young's *X for Henry Flynt*, where the pianist repeats a large piano cluster, fortissimo, 'x' number of times,[5] made the same kind of demands on stamina and served the same aesthetic purposes as many AMM performances. 'You would be playing and it was deafening, but at the same time very quiet and still within yourself; or playing something very quiet could be very loud because of the nature of the concentration.'[6]

And when the European avant-garde sought, on occasion, to harness such immoderation to serve its own agenda, Cardew was sceptical and dismissive: the opening of Stockhausen's *Klavierstück IX*, for example, where the 228 repetitions of a chord spawned by a compositional technique still in thrall to serialism, and which could never have been assimilated into the music of La Monte Young, or for that matter Cage (unless occasioned by an irreversible application of chance operations), is described by Cardew as 'a weak, aesthetic version of the piece *['X'] for Henry Flynt'*.[7]

Cardew had first met La Monte Young in Darmstadt in 1959, an encounter which for Cardew was 'decisive'.[8] In a record review entitled 'La Monte Young and Marion Zazeela', written 24 June 1970, but which remained unpublished, Cardew stresses the consequence of Young's appearances in Europe:

The musical world has not been the same since [...] La Monte Young's single-minded absorption in the few principles that he considers vital, his concentration on tuning, purity, simple mathematical relations, and his adherence to Kant's idea of the 'sublimity of long duration', has resulted in musical experiences of great power and profundity...

Certainly, the twin influence of the Americans John Cage and La Monte Young was of tangible import in Cardew's development, although in the light of his subsequent musical and social concerns during the latter part of the sixties Cardew's debt to the Americans, though not his commitment to their music, is a good deal less than is still generally recognised.

For all its reductionism Cardew's characterisation of the two Americans' music, in the same review, is authentic, well-judged:

Young's music is religious, heavy, ecstatic, incense-laden, engulfing, mystical, (Indian), whereas Cage's is light, joyful, spontaneous, erratic, irritating, intellectual, (Chinese). (Please accept these epithets as impressionistic and superficial: they do not set out to delimit the range of these two composers' work.)

For some of his followers the ontological, mystical quality of Young's music presupposed a higher purpose – to sober or quiet the mind, thus rendering it susceptible to divine influences; but to European, more sceptical, or at least more secular ears, the richness and complexity of the sound was enough: the music appealed aesthetically and people found beauty in it. In his lecture at the University of Illinois on 25 February 1967 Cardew proffered a further comparison of his American mentors:

From Cage you learn that all sounds have life; from David Tudor you learn that this life can be nourished; from La Monte you learn that you can totally identify yourself with this life of a sound. It is something so big and powerful that you surrender yourself to it, instead of feeling obliged to protect something that is intrinsically fragile and weak. At this point the term sound has to be abandoned, and the term Music steps in to take its place.

In an article in the *Musical Times* Cardew describes La Monte Young's 'One Sound' and the particular context in which he and a few friends experienced it:

For a whole half-hour it struggled through the poor loudspeaker of the tape-recorder in a North London pub, drowning the television, driving away custom, boring its way into the minds of two aged and tenacious drinkers and the indulgent barmaid and her baby. Truly, to locate the pulse of new music in London requires more than a monthly rifle through the *Bulletin of the Institute of Contemporary Arts* [...] The one sound that I heard in the Islington pub was actually very beautiful, and got progressively more beautiful through the half-hour that the tape lasted. It took four people to produce it: La Monte Young and his wife Marion Zazeela (voices), Tony Conrad (violin), and a three-string viola drone provided by John Cale, a Welsh musician who was responsible for introducing the tape into this country. Both voices and instruments were amplified electronically to the point of virtual unrecognizability. Variations of timbre and texture were produced by tuning and intensity of the various partials of a single fundamental tone. The result was rich enough to colour an evening, which is something, and indeed I can still hear that sound in my mind now, with its guttural tremors as the microphone slides back deep into La Monte's throat. What does it mean? One of the aged drinkers pointed over at us listeners and said well look at them; it obviously means something. And credit that old man's imagination in recognizing this, for it means something on a much more profound level and much more profusely than the 1000 words of this article, to take a banal example. Like the chaotic and obsessive utterances of a schizophrenic, which may or may not mean something explicit to the professional analyst, yet even to us ordinary laymen they 'mean' that man's condition in a way that moves us more (or should) than any merely artistic or intelligent attempt to shake the foundations of our complacent normality.[9]

In Wittgenstein's later philosophy every kind of utterance is supplemented with an account of its surroundings and of its place in our lives.

There are also many cases in which he says that it is impossible either to analyse or to give any general account of what people mean when they use a particular form of words. They mean what they say.[10]

Similarly, AMM 'meant what they played'.

There is no doubting La Monte Young's affection for Cardew, although his considerable self-absorption would have made it difficult for him to perceive of the English composer outside and beyond the role which their relationship now demanded of him: musical disciple and business agent; Cardew was a bearer of the good news and a procurer of engagements. For his part Cardew tried to honour his genuine commitment to the music whilst at the same time keeping the composer at arm's length, which was an onerous task. For Young was constantly visited by an anxiety that his works were being relayed to the public in a perfunctory and inappropriate fashion. Moreover, his extreme attitude towards his own compositions and tapes is reflected in the conditions which he laid down, in the form of a contract, and which he imposed even on those friends, like Cardew, who were unstinting in their admiration and propagation of his work.

A contract drawn up by Young for the loan of a tape, of *Sunday Morning Blues,* which Cardew signed on 4 May 1967, contains an injunction that the tape be returned 'immediately on demand'; that Cardew 'agrees not to perform the Tape or the actual music recorded on the Tape, publicly or for profit'; that he 'agrees not to permit any copy of the Tape or the music on the Tape to be made on tapes or records or any other form of reproduction'; that he 'agrees not to perform the Tape or any of the music recorded on the Tape at private gatherings where it has been previously announced that the Tape shall be performed'; that he 'agrees not to permit any kind of performance, copy or reproduction of the Tape or the music recorded on the Tape, without the express written consent of the composer'; and so forth, presumably on pain of restitution. It is a curious anomaly that the composer of *Octet '61*, of *Treatise*, the 'father' of Scratch Music, in which 'no rights are reserved', should have agreed to be party to such a contract, although Cardew appears to have adopted a characteristically relaxed attitude to its demands over the subsequent years, as can be seen from a letter which Young wrote to him, dated 3 December 1967: an admonishment for Cardew's imprudent, somewhat cavalier distribution of copies of tapes, although the tone is gentle and conciliatory:

I really appreciate all the different people you have been putting in touch with me regarding my music, but one word of caution: Please don't let anyone else have any copies of my tapes that you have. A Mr. John Gosling, who seems to be a nice enough chap, has written to me regarding my work, to which you introduced him. He adds that he has obtained copies of two of my tapes, *Sunday Morning*

Blues and *The Bowed Gong* from you. Please understand that I gave you these tapes because of my deep feeling for you and your work and because of your many efforts on my behalf.[11]

Cardew had already defended La Monte Young publicly in a brief conversation with the musicologist and critic Hans Keller in a BBC *New Comment* programme on 19 December 1963. A less unflappable interviewee might have been discomposed by Keller's insidious interviewing technique where, through a carefully considered sequence of questions, the aim is to secure admissions and concurrences which undermine and ultimately invalidate the interviewee's presumed position. Cardew meets Keller's probing with a characteristically dead bat, occasionally dispatching a challenge with inscrutable ease: Keller's thesis that a piece of music must contain 'variation, contrast and continuity', for example, is shown by Cardew to apply in every regard to *'X' for Henry Flynt*. When Cardew draws attention to the fact that the piece, rather than communicating, causes the audience to react in a number of ways, Keller contends that Cardew is thereby equating *'X' for Henry Flynt* with a 'natural event'· Cardew concurs, but with the reservation that 'human agency', too, is involved: 'a human being is sitting on stage sweating and striving after perfection – as all performers should'. Keller pursues his argument, somewhat pedantically, by suggesting that Cardew is comparing the experience of 'a beautiful mountain, plus a little bit of sweat' with that of a piece of music, and he may well have been wrong-footed by the manner in which Cardew grasped this particular nettle: 'I think it is very rare that a piece of music arouses more than a beautiful mountain in the average listener.' The starkness of this statement, with its reference to the aesthetic endowments of natural phenomena, prefigures *The Great Learning* and Cardew's music-making with AMM, with their assimilation and exploitation of 'natural sounds' and their recognition of the joy and wonder which such phenomena may inspire in both participant and listener.

It may well have been the case that right from the outset of the interview Cardew and Keller were talking at cross purposes; the incompatibility of their relative positions virtually precluded a meaningful debate. Keller's theory of music presupposes a circumscribed cultural context in which the 'experienced' listener responds, evaluates, makes judgements, on the basis of pre-knowledge, of expectations. Cardew's premise was that 'experiencing' *'X' for Henry Flynt* does not involve the exercise of judgement; first and foremost, as with the music of Cage, one listens, distinguishes and remembers sounds without any predisposition. Aesthetic judgement, and enjoyment, take place, as Wittgenstein recognised, in an 'enormously complicated situation'. 'It is not only difficult to describe what appreciation consists in, but impossible. As he said, to describe what it consists in we would have to describe the whole environment[12]; and 'in order to get clear about aesthetic words you have to describe ways of living'.[13]

For Keller musical logic is culturally rooted; Cardew would have agreed with this, but would have extended the definition of 'culture' beyond musical 'language games' and the arousal of culturally-determined expectations which are either fulfilled or confounded. Furthermore, Keller's theories presuppose the priority of a (Western) musical logic in which *intelligibility* is a *sine qua non*. Cardew's music-making challenged the foundations of the intellectual authority which Keller posited; he would have argued, for example, that the 'incoherence' which Keller dismissed could indeed function aesthetically: AMM *creates* moments, even stretches, of 'incoherence' – musical utterances which *can* be grasped, enjoyed, but not through the listener's application of a circumscribed, historically-determined 'musical logic'.

Considering, or perhaps precisely because of the seriousness of the issues raised, the tone of the Keller interview, on both sides, was mild; at no point did the temperature rise above the norm. Perhaps there was too much mutual respect, or too little time to develop their arguments or, as I have suggested, their respective philosophies of music were simply too far apart for there to have been any possibility of a meaningful reciprocity. Yet given that the psycho-analytical territory into which the discourse seemed to be moving would have been far more favourable to Keller – it was an area, after all, to which he constantly referred in his writings – one might have expected him to have adopted a rather more robust approach. For all his undoubted charm Keller invariably displayed an intellectual arrogance that would have deemed it imperative that Cardew, or anybody else for that matter, should be worsted in debate. Perhaps the fact that he was thwarted on this occasion, either by the effectiveness of Cardew's strategy (the trapdoors which Keller opened were easily sidestepped), or by his own uncharacteristic failure to create and drive home an advantage, was still gnawing at him when a decade later he launched a sustained and vitriolic attack on Cardew's politics in the journal *Books and Bookmen*.

The perennial problem of liquidity, especially in terms of subsistence money for the family, beset Cardew remorselessly, and this was compounded by the fact that the very nature of his music and music-making precluded any consideration of the cash nexus. As Stella Cardew recalls, although her husband would invariably act with thrift and foresight in pecuniary matters, he rarely earned more than the minimum, and often less. Yet the negative material and financial implications and consequences of his musical projects – *Treatise*, AMM, the Scratch Orchestra, *The Great Learning* – would not have weakened his resolve. Just as for Wittgenstein a person can only be a 'good philosopher' if he is a 'real human being', so too for Cardew being a good musician is being a 'real human being'. There are many references in his music and music-making at that time to this on-going preoccupation with the concept and practice of 'morality': in the journals he mentions the 'moral fortitude' of AMM, in the *Treatise Handbook* there are the 'seven virtues', and in *Schooltime Compositions* (1968), which I discuss below, the references are again quite explicit. Like Wittgenstein (and Blake) Cardew's view of morality was based on integrity, of being true to yourself – a morality that was not imposed from without by a religion or a political party, but which came from within.[14] Moral fortitude was utterly relevant to the conduct of one's (musical) life. Morton Feldman, a perceptive observer of music in England, referred to this 'morality' in an informal conversation in New York in 1967:

> Any direction modern music will take in England will come about only through Cardew, because of him, by way of him. If the new ideas in music are felt today as a movement in England, it's because he acts as a moral centre.[15]

Howard Skempton experienced these concerns at first hand when he visited Cardew on a number of occasions, beginning in the summer of 1967 for, ostensibly, composition lessons. Replying to an introductory letter from Skempton Cardew wrote that he had decided not to give lessons on a weekly basis, but rather consultations whenever a prospective pupil felt that he or she had something to discuss. Furthermore, the price would be 'adjusted with a view to ensuring that this condition be fulfilled'.[16] Already we can sense Cardew's discomfort in translating a human relation which could not be quantified – the imparting of musical knowledge and experience – into a pecuniary one. And Skempton attributes the relatively high fee, at that time, of £5 per session, to a fundamental reluctance on Cardew's part to give composition lessons.

Cardew and Skempton arranged their first meeting at a concert of Karlheinz Stockhausen's music at Broadcasting House on 2 June 1967. Cardew introduced Skempton to Stockhausen (they had already corresponded) who asked Skempton if he was planning to come to Cologne. Skempton replied that he had decided not to go to Germany and had arranged to have lessons with Cardew. 'I opted for fantasy and spontaneity, rather than German rigour', Skempton recalls.[17] He was attracted to Cardew's 'light touch', to the man and his music – specifically *Octet '61* and the four works published by Universal Edition: *Autumn 60, Material, Solo with Accompaniment*, and *Memories of You.*

Initially, for the first two or three lessons, Skempton travelled down to London by train from his home in Ellesmere Port in Cheshire. Then he moved to London, enrolled as a student at Ealing College, and rented a room in Acton, in west London. He remembers leaving his first meeting with Cardew 'armed with a pile of La Monte Young scores and documentation, and including a tariff of performances – the shorter the performance the greater the cost'.[18] The sessions were informal and open-ended; Skempton would produce scores and they would discuss them. However, since the pieces were 'pretty nebulous', as Skempton recalls, there was not much to say; years later Cardew confessed to Skempton that he had had to work very hard during their sessions together, which numbered around eight in all.

Cardew would speak his mind; what he said would therefore lodge itself in the memory, and Skempton recalls how he would learn a great deal from just one or two apparently off-the-cuff remarks. On one occasion he was told, bluntly, that he gave the impression of being a dilettante. 'That hurt and I had to stop and think. If you are working in isolation its very easy to become self-deluded.'[19] It also upset Skempton when Cardew declared that he felt he had very little to teach him; Skempton was aware that this was what teachers would say to students with no talent. But it was Skempton who had underestimated his own ability; Cardew quickly recognised the fact that the young composer had already established what he wanted to do: the creation of a fairly constant sound with occasional features. And he admired some of Skempton's early pieces; in particular *A Humming Song*, which Skempton had completed before he began his lessons with Cardew.

Cardew invariably stressed the importance of relating composing to performance and was therefore strict about presentation; he felt it was 'bad manners' to present a score in a perfunctory way. At the same time he criticised Skempton for what he called his 'mannerisms': underlining titles, adding date of birth, decorating the front page, putting a cover on the score and doodling on it – even if it did demonstrate a seriousness of intent, a certain pride, a celebration of what had been achieved, however modest. Skempton recalls that Cardew never attempted to direct the course of work in any way, to impose a style, or to encourage his pupil to pursue a particular compositional path; as a teacher he was completely open-minded. The essence of his teaching was that everyday experience could be turned into music; that a composer could derive and extract ideas for composition from the most unlikely sources: from relationships with people, and from things and events, and that this experience could be translated into musical notation, as he himself had done with *Treatise*.

This notion of the ubiquitousness of music, and of the inexhaustible sources of musical inspiration and meaning, he had nourished for a long time; he admired it in the art of David Tudor, and in the AMM where 'musicalness' was recognised and cherished as a 'dimension of perfectly ordinary reality.'[20] 'My attitude', Cardew wrote in the Journals on 11 July 1967, 'is that the musical and the real world are one.' By 'real world' Cardew was referring as much to the interior world of the imagination, to the creative world of the mind, to human relations and interaction, as to the volatile, external world of business, politics and art. As we shall see, *Schooltime Compositions*, in particular, is a work of an untrammelled, creative instinct, demonstrating a profound commitment to the 'moral' dimension and to the idea of 'the world as musical composition'.

Cardew continued to pen his thoughts on music, both in his Journals and for external publications, but in terms of his own compositional activity he was finding it increasingly difficult to verbalise the situation he had reached, to project it intellectually. 'This is our life – why profane it with words!' he rationalises, with a hint of desperation.[21] Nevertheless, on 11 July he began to write what appears to be an introduction to *Treatise*, possibly for use in a forthcoming short lecture tour in the US.[22]

Finding myself presently in the middle of an extended idle moment, like being in a bubble in the middle of nowhere, it seems like a good time to try to establish my intellectual whereabouts, by means of a 'now whereas earlier' routine. This is an admission that things have changed. Earlier when I sat down to write an article I felt I was trying to get and give a clear view of a topic; by analysis and pointing things out I hoped to uncover the logical structure of various musical activities. Now I feel that such logical structures are neither here nor there – they have a glossy transparent quality such that you can either see them or see through them (not see them) according to your will. And as with the glass in a window, if you focus on the glass the view behind is lost, or at best and on a bright day it becomes flat and blurred. At this point my longings tell me that beyond these logical panes is the land of music, or rather the land of composition. To know it or understand it you have to live in it and work in it; to describe it you write music, but to explain things in it you have to leave it. This is what my longings tell me, longings aroused by writing this article. That is, for the purposes of this article I *wish* the subject 'composition' could be postulated in this way. It provides a starting-point for a way of talking.

Treatise has provided a starting-point for a number of ways of talking, and what follows is a collection of elucidatory notes (some were programme notes, some were working notes; my aim in presenting them here is to provide a kind of 'Basic *Treatise*' course for the benefit of potential interpreters)...

Now, ways of talking are two a penny and really easy to come by, however difficult and interesting they seemed earlier when they were not recognized as merely ways of talking. 'Ways of talking' are analogous to 'means of earning a living': earlier this was a real existential problem, now it is simply a matter of 'getting a job'. 'Things have changed' is wrong; it is my attitude to things that has changed. Well, maybe 'things' *have* changed, but it is the change in my attitude that is my legitimate topic of conversation, and it is within the bounds of possibility that my change in attitude has changed 'things'. Better: my attitude is one of the myriad things that is moulding our musical environment. (This is an example of the widespread − and heroic − tendency to read dignity into our chosen occupation, however mean)...

September 1967 was a fruitful month: on 4 September a section of *Treatise* (which was shortly to be printed in Buffalo by The Gallery Upstairs Press) was recorded by the BBC, and there were two performances of *Solo with Accompaniment*: at Danish Radio by Ed Yadzinski and Jan Williams and at the Warsaw Autumn Festival by Yadzinski and Lukas Foss. There is also an intriguing reference in the Journals to a performance of La Monte Young's *Poem* in Bingley, Yorkshire (initiated, one assumes, by Cardew) which lasted two days, from 3pm on 26 September to 5pm on 28 September. In *Poem* random digits determine the duration of the performance, number of events and their individual lengths; the 'content' of each event is decided by the performer: preparing a meal, darning a sock, playing the harmonium, taking a nap; the choice is infinite.

Of more immediate economic significance, if mundane in other respects, was Cardew's full-time re-employment, from September, by Aldus Books. Rather more unexpected was his engagement as a composition teacher by the Royal Academy of Music, albeit on a tenuous, part-time basis of one two-hour session a week. This was brought about thanks to the initiative and resolve of an Academy student, Philip Pilkington, pianist and heir to the Pilkington glassworks, who managed to convince the Principal, Sir Thomas Armstrong, of the benefits of the appointment to the Academy and its students. Nevertheless, it was apparently considered prudent not to broadcast Cardew's presence so that only the alert and neoteric student would have known that this particular path of compositional study could be pursued.

Pilkington and the seventeen year-old Christopher Hobbs had been members, as schoolboys, of the Northwood New Music group, in Harrow (a borough west of London), and it was through his friend that Hobbs learnt of Cardew's imminent appointment at the RAM. At his entrance interview Hobbs requested specifically to study composition with Cardew, with whom he had had no previous contact but had heard playing with AMM at the Conway Hall the previous year. Hobbs recalls their first meeting at the Academy: to celebrate the occasion he had presented a kind of greetings piece − based on Cardew's own *Memories of You* − in which the performer followed a prescribed circuit around the piano, at the end of which he would produce a sound. Cardew's reaction to the performance gave little away; perhaps he was unimpressed by what was intended by Hobbs as a modest tribute to his new teacher; or he simply needed a little time to take the measure of his first and only student − a bright young chap, fresh from school and keen as mustard to make his mark. Hobbs recalls that after a few noncommittal remarks and 'fairly inconsequential questions' the matter was closed. At each session Hobbs would present whatever he had written, or was working on, and recalls, like Skempton, that Cardew's primary concern was the appropriateness and clarity of the notation and the practicalities of performance; he was particularly interested in loopholes, notational nooks and crannies into which a sceptical interpreter might crawl to subvert the composer's perceived intentions. Clarity was of the essence and if there were ambiguity it had to be a conscious, thought-through ambiguity, an intentional 'blur', and not as a result of composer complacency and condescension. Eventually these individual lessons ceased and Cardew was given a composition class of several students which took place on Wednesdays, around lunchtime, probably from 1pm to 2pm. Aldus Books was a short walk away (Christopher Hobbs would often accompany him) so that he was able to fulfil both commitments comfortably, although it did mean that every Wednesday he would take a somewhat extended lunch break from Aldus which may or may not have been noted by his employers. After a few months the number of students began to increase as word of Cardew's presence and accessibility at the Academy became known. One of the first to join Hobbs was Robin Thompson who was indignant that he had not been informed of Cardew's availability by the authorities and immediately demanded a transfer from Lennox Berkeley. Hugh Shrapnel joined the class around the same time, and soon after Richard Reason, a combative student who always spoke his mind. Another student who attended the class was Diana Gravill; she was (also) a conceptual artist who, with Nicholas Rochford, founded and ran the progressive bookshop, Compendium Books, in Camden High Street in north London.

Hobbs recalls that his attendance at the Academy was sparse; apart from the Wednesday lunchtime sessions his only other commitment was his percussion lessons with Patricia Brady, which went through into his second year, enabling him to take a job in a small firm near the Angel in north London which made radio microphones. This had been arranged through Bob Woolford, a sound engineer who at that time recorded many avant-garde and experimental concerts, including Victor Schonfield's prestigious 'Music Now' series, *The Tiger's Mind* performance, and AMM at the Crypt. Hobbs and a few other rebellious spirits had exploited a simple fact of Academy life – that if you did not register for a class on the first day of the Academic year the authorities did not know that you were absent from it. (Cardew had avoided National Service through a similar ploy, the beauty of which lay in its simplicity.)

Shrapnel recalls that Cardew pursued his aims without nod to the traditional methods of teaching. He was not interested in pointing out miscalculations, such as the inaudibility of a notated sound in a particular context; Cardew's view was that these were technical matters and the student would, through experience, find out for himself sooner or later.

Furthermore, for Cardew, to correct or seek to improve in some way, even to re-write, a given phrase, or stretch of music, would have begged too many questions. The twin issues of criteria and taste are too complex because they can only be addressed by reference to the cultural context – to the way of making music, to the mode of living – in which an infinite number of factors are involved: every judgement is informed, consciously or unconsciously, by a cultural bias. 'To describe a set of aesthetic rules fully means to describe the culture of a period.'[23]

And the problem is compounded by the fact that Cardew's own musical philosophy, particularly within the vortex of AMM, was itself subversive of the dominant culture. The audio-technical question as to whether a particular instrument can actually be heard at a given point in the score – the kind of detail on which a conventional composition teacher would have focused – is rendered irrelevant where the 'intention' is for the player simply to be observed playing, or occasionally heard playing, or imagined to be heard playing; that is, where the duality of performer/listener is perceived in a more complex, and more subtle relation, as was the case in AMM.

For Cardew, notational intelligibility and integrity was paramount, and we are constantly reminded of this while we track and chart his compositional odyssey. He taught his students that in deliberating over a score they were discussing a relationship between composer and performer, rather than between composer and listener – which he considered to be unrealistic. For the culturally-rooted listening experience is subject to a calculus of influences and the number of 'senses', 'meanings', of a piece of music is infinite. That *fact*, for Cardew, was something to accept, to enjoy and to celebrate. Wittgenstein was surely referring to this in his Aesthetics lecture when he reminded his students: 'I very often draw your attention to certain differences, e.g. in these classes I tried to show that Infinity is not so mysterious as it looks.'[24]

Cardew's classes at the Academy may not have constituted 'a course in composition' – that is, in the conventionally accepted sense of both 'course' and 'composition'. But he would prevail upon the infinite resources of his imagination so that what was guaranteed was a challenging indeterminacy; each session was a unique event which would bring forth unforeseen, unimagined potentialities and moments of pleasure and enlightenment for everybody. And yet Christopher Hobbs' impression (possibly mistaken) was that Cardew did not particularly enjoy these composition classes, that he was a teacher *malgré lui*. Be that as it may, it would, however, have been uncharacteristic of him to have allowed a session to become routine, a painless exercise in passing the time of day. With an air of relaxed seriousness he would challenge preconceptions: What is music for? How does it relate to people? What are the realities of performance? But he was also conscious of the fact that it was important that he himself should be sensitive to the student's own cosmology; for in exorcising the devils one can also disturb the angels. (Cardew would probably have expressed this conversely; it was the devils in his students he would have wished to protect.)

For Cardew's students the spontaneity and unpredictability of the sessions were not least a necessary antidote to life at the Royal Academy which was hedged about with all manner of petty, unwritten rules – bound in some unfathomable way to traditional Academy etiquette – which were enjoined in particular, it seemed, upon the part-time staff. On one occasion, when Cardew, Shrapnel and Hobbs had gone into one of the organ practice rooms to rehearse an organ duet one of them had written, an obdurate porter came into the room to inform them that it was not allowed to have more than one person on the organ at the same time. Organ duets could therefore not be permitted and they had to stop.

To the hackneyed inflexibilities and stifling conservatism of the Academy Cardew counterposed stratagems inspired by his own interior visions of the role of music-making – a role which, as the ancients had warned, might threaten subversion, danger and the ruination of society. On one summer's day he left the room and locked the students inside, taking the key with him. Eventually, by means of insistent and penetrating noise (music?), including shouting out of the window, the students managed to attract the attention of somebody outside; porters arrived to unlock the door and release the occupants. Inevitably, reports of the escapade came to the attention of the authorities. Each member of the class was summoned, in separate hearings, firstly to give their account of what happened, and secondly to try and offer an explanation for 'Mr. Cardew's extraordinary actions'. A recalcitrant Richard Reason insisted that it had been one of the most instructive composition lessons he had ever had. In Hugh Shrapnel's words, 'it made us think; what were we doing at the Academy? It was a kind of metaphor for our condition there'. Characteristically, Cardew never subsequently mentioned the episode.

On another occasion Cardew maintained an unannounced, complete silence for the duration of the session. No words were spoken – as if by a (tacit) agreement on the part of all the members of the class to participate in the 'experiment'. In both these instances Cardew was testing the resourcefulness and determination of the students to make music under whatever conditions, and whatever the obstacles and limitations – just as some of them were soon to experience in the Scratch Orchestra, and later on political demonstrations.

Of course, Cardew's attitude and behaviour alienated him even further from the Academy authorities, and when he tried to mount an ambulatory concert, using all the rooms in the building, his plans were blocked and the project never materialised. Hobbs recalls that Cardew's students were routinely failed in their composition examinations and attempts were made to expel them from the Students' Union on account of their supposed political affiliations, presumably (in 1968) with their brothers and sisters in the

European, and American, universities.[25] In fact, like Cardew, most of them had no affiliations whatsoever and were probably not even members of the Musicians' Union.

Cardew's description, in the aforementioned 1962 Cologne Radio talk, of the influence of John Cage on fellow Americans Christian Wolff, Morton Feldman and Earle Brown ('a certain freedom of thought, rather than the adoption of a particular way of thinking') clearly demonstrates the extent to which Cage's philosophy of music informed Cardew's teaching at the Academy. And it was this 'freedom of thought', rather than any consciously rebellious attitude, that lead to what were regarded as infractions of the rules and regulations, just as it had at the King's School. Cardew's students agree that there was never any kind of inculcation in his sessions, nor talk of revolution – social or musical – either with individuals or with larger groups. On the contrary, for Cardew integrity lay more often than not in the refusal to clarify one's intentions. As a rule he would ask questions of a general, or occasionally personal nature, the responses to which would sometimes generate comment and discussion. Most crucially and, for his students, most memorably, he was capable of decisive and challenging *actions* which, for the Academy authorities, would have put him completely beyond the pale.

Wittgenstein's comments give pause for thought: 'What I am doing is also persuasion. If someone says: "There is not a difference", and I say: "There is a difference" I am persuading, I am saying "I don't want you to look at it like that".'[26] This particular lecture ends: 'How much we are doing is changing the style of thinking and how much I'm doing is changing the style of thinking and how much I'm doing is persuading people to change their style of thinking. (Much of what we are doing is changing the style of thinking).'[27] Cardew, too, was 'persuading people to change their style of thinking', and he had expectations; he wanted bold, *consequential* thought and action from his students; he had no time for velleities or the pursuit of trivia.

The tenor of Cardew's behaviour in his class suggested that he preferred to maintain a certain distance from his Academy students; at the same time his attitude towards them could not really be described as formal; perhaps the lack of an expedient age difference – he was barely ten years older than his students – made him feel slightly ill-at-ease: too old to claim peer status, too young to represent a remoter authority. On one occasion he invited Hobbs, Thompson and Shrapnel to dinner at his home in Nevern Square. It turned out to be a rather uncomfortable evening; nobody seemed willing to talk, to commit themselves. Cardew would not, could not have initiated the small talk, perhaps some light-hearted banter, that would have relaxed the students and into which, or after which, matters of more weight and substance could have been introduced. On another occasion, in the summer of 1969, when several of his students were leaving the Academy and it was their last session together, he rather awkwardly suggested that they should go to the pub; he would buy them a drink. This overture, and its consequences, suffered likewise from the same lack of informality; at that time, and in those particular circumstances, he seemed incapable of routine, conventional conversation for conversation's sake. Yet it may well have been the case that Cardew himself was not uncomfortable in these situations; there are many entries in his Journals during this period referring to the inadequacy of words; perhaps his apparent reluctance to converse was more a consequence of motive and calculation than embarrassment ('Whereof one cannot speak, thereof one must be silent.'). Might it have been simply the case that the students were unable to cope with his unconventionality? It was in Cardew's gift to communicate – all his students would attest to this – but he would have considered a mere recital of words to be inappropriate, and probably counter-productive.

Michael Parsons recalls being extremely impressed at his first encounter with Cardew, sometime in 1967. Parsons had been commissioned by a BBC periodical, *The Listener*, to write an article on Cardew. He arrived at Nevern Square to find his interviewee in the middle of a meal: fish. Cardew acknowledged Parson's arrival with a brief greeting and with epicurean relish went on eating his fish, wholly and exclusively concentrated on the act of eating for half an hour or more; there were no concessions to the presence of a visitor, nor hint of affectation; an atmosphere of agreeable neutrality prevailed. Others have remarked on Cardew's propensity for maintaining silence in company and I have already referred to his visit with Ilona Halberstadt to William Burroughs apartment in Paris, where he assumed throughout an air of silent inscrutability.

On 12 September 1967 Cardew began the first draft of a lecture, incorporating the themes of virtue and vice, which he would deliver during a US tour the following November. The need for musicians to develop strength of character, to nurture virtues – and sometimes vices, too – was for Cardew a *fact* of musical life.

> I am trying to think of the various different kinds of virtue or strengths that can be developed by the musician. In Europe it might also be of interest to investigate the possible vices and weaknesses lying in wait to ambush the valiant and unsuspecting musician on his way to heaven, since in Europe these are rampant, but here in the New Country I would consider it ignoble, on the assumed argument that what your minds don't wot of, your hearts wont yearn after and your hands lustfully grasp at. This delivery of mine is miraculous: From America Columbus brought us back syphilis, or Death through Sex, and there is no reason why the compliment should not be returned, with myself the humble vehicle, in the form of serialism, or Death through Music. In both cases we are dealing with a message of love, of which sex and music are two of the broadest facets. The

love traffic between our two continents has always occurred as it were between the lines of the history books – love nestling under the wings of more aggressive encounters – White Slavers, Star-smiling Hollywood, the GI baby problem etc. etc. But enough of Love and Death; in the case of serialism the damage has already been done; Schoenberg is the bearer of that intolerable guilt. Rotting branches on the tree of American music are even now dragging down and destroying fresh green talent in Columbia and California and all places beginning with C.

The temptation to exploit the fading reputation of serialism proved irresistible on more than one occasion; the following quote is taken from what was originally a section of 'Towards an Ethic of Improvisation', entitled 'Folklore and the Merits of a Localized Music', but was not included in the final, published version:

Since the war Folk music has become dissipated and internationalized (at least in Europe and America), to the point that one can hardly call it Folk music. This fate can be compared to the heroic pseudo-scientific universalism of serial music; in the early fifties at that time you were quite likely to hear serial compositions by a Bulgarian, a Japanese and a South African in the same programme and be virtually unable to tell the difference between them. At that time serial music was not available on disc, so we may attribute the effect to the pervasiveness of the idea. However, death in a vacuum is not a happy thought and around 1960 many of the more reputable composers were beating a hasty retreat, taking with them just as much of the original as they were able to carry. Nono went into political music, Stockhausen into the grand operatic tradition, Boulez into impressionism and a glorious career as a conductor.[28]

For Cardew the internationalization of an indigenous folk music led inevitably to a weakening of its roots in its local culture. These roots and the environmental culture which they generate, and of which they are part, create 'a communal fund of subconscious experience in the inhabitants of a city'. In Cardew's view this was what contributed to the strength of AMM music-making:

The rapport that exists amongst members of AMM, for example, is very much deeper than anything that could develop with the musicians of my acquaintance during my 8-month stay in Buffalo. And this factor is particularly vital in improvisation. I theorise that the more obtrusive an environment is, the more profound is the sense of community uniting its inhabitants.[29]

Such a 'theory' negated the idea, fashionable at that time, of the 'all-star orchestra': a collection of brilliant performers, gathered together for series of concerts and concert tours, but who lack a basic, common experience.

AMM music could never combine with the improvised music of La Monte Young, although I hold that music in very high esteem, because the two groups are conditioned to a great extent, much more than is generally supposed, by the very obtrusive local environments of London and New York respectively.[30]

Immediately on his return from the US, on 21 November, Cardew took part in a performance of his *Material* at the BBC studios in Maida Vale, and towards the end of the academic autumn term joined forces with the American Fluxus artist George Brecht, who was living in London at that time, for a week's course at the Leeds School of Art. He continued to promote experimental music vigorously; in December a concert at the US Embassy offered a mixed programme which included, among other works, Britten's early *Sinfonietta*, Earle Brown's *Novara*, a work by Elliott Schwartz, and Cardew's *Solo with Accompaniment*.[31]

1968 began with an intensification of the Communist Tet offensive in Vietnam. Cardew was not directly involved in the anti-war movement; it is unlikely that he would have been one of the ten thousand hard and soft Left activists, liberals and 'flower' people on the Vietnam Solidarity demonstration on 17 March, although he would probably have broadly supported its aims. Even the issue of racism, which had become not only pressing but also, through the assassination of Martin Luther King in April of that year, newsworthy, failed to galvanise him into political action – unlike the London dockers and the Smithfield porters who were inspired to march in support of the Conservative Party right wing M.P. Enoch Powell within days of his infamous 'rivers of blood' speech on immigration in Birmingham on 21 April.

At that time Cardew's reservations, I suspect, would have been on pragmatic grounds – that the demonstrations were gestural politics, satisfying the participants' subjective, psychological needs, and did very little to further the cause of the Vietnamese people. Orthodox left opinion would have characterised this argument as a jaded, liberal-conservative formulation to justify opposition to the 'politics of protest'; it was routinely exploited by those who believed that support for the Americans was necessary, if politically embarrassing. Cardew did not support the US action but he may well have harboured doubts in relation to the motives, the clarity of purpose, the integrity, of many of the participants in the Anti-war movement.[32] The mass demonstrations gave a superficial and misleading semblance of unity in the face of the enemy; in reality there were countless 'enemies', and the most lethally dangerous were often, so it seemed, embedded within the revolution itself – undermining, splitting, subverting. Each political (and artistic) group or faction promoted and defended its own 'revolutionary' agenda and this would often seem to take precedence over the much-trumpeted claim of a 'united front'. John Cage, too, at that time, regarded demonstrations as 'negative' acts; he preferred to act 'positively', through collaborative music-making, through Art, in order to change people, or rather so that they should be freed to change themselves. In an interview in 1972 he expresses his view, concluding with a Hegelian flourish:

> And I think we can state that the power structure is dying because it cannot make any inspiring statements about what it is doing. I think that the protests about these things, contrary to what has been said, will give it the kind of life that a fire is given when you fan it, and that it would be best to ignore it, put your attention elsewhere, take actions of another kind of positive nature, rather than to continue to give life to the negative by negating it.[33]

This was how Cardew would have assessed the social function of his own compositions and music-making at that time; and in their radical utopianism he and Cage reflected one of many revolutionary perspectives of the sixties. The locus of their creativity was inviolably within the world of music and their concern was to forge a radical aesthetic, a new philosophy of music, which would render the past an irrelevance. Such a revolution 'against history', even 'against their own personal history', as Morton Feldman once said, would be a more potent force, in their view, than the confrontational stance in relation to the past that the Marxist students had adopted.

Moreover, for Cardew the idea of *detachment*, and of self-regard, was still part of his personal cosmology; he was blessed with a gene that had ordained his uniqueness and he had no desire to assort with the political masses. He could not have agreed to the terms of acquiescence that they demanded, with everybody reading from the same text. If, perhaps, somewhere within him, in a state of latency, a yearning to face the world on *its* terms was biding its time, such speculation would have been vanquished, at that time, by issues of interiority, by the scope and intensity of an unsullied (philosophical) idealism. These comprised multiple alternative universes in which 'Art', as we have seen in the Keller interview, would not necessarily have enjoyed a status of pre-eminence.

Cardew's music-making, because of the broadness of its scope, its all-embracing nature, satisfied whatever social involvement he felt he needed; he was powered by the momentum of his own artistic imperatives. If any attempt were made to force a political commitment from him he would have echoed the words of Karl Kraus: 'If I must choose the lesser of two evils, I will choose neither. Politics is what a man does in order to conceal what he is and what he himself does not know.'[34] Of course, many of his close friends and colleagues were political activists and when the politically-orientated Anti-University invited him to teach there from February 1968 he accepted, again juggling with the timetable so that he could continue to honour his commitments at Aldus Books.[35] However, his appointment was short-lived, terminated, ironically – bearing in mind the 'revolutionary' circumstances – because his students claimed he refused to teach them anything (it was rumoured that, English romantic that he was, he read Shelley to them). His dismissal, however, did not prevent him from securing an engagement for AMM at the Anti-University on 4 April.

By this time the European students' climacteric revolt was in full flow; on 7 May, Cardew's thirty-second birthday, police with dogs were called in when students at Essex University broke up a meeting addressed by Dr T.A. Inch from Porton Down, an establishment where, it was alleged, experiments in chemical warfare were being carried out. In London, inspired by the action of the students at the Ecole des Beaux-Arts in Paris, students and staff at Hornsey College of Art began an occupation which resulted in a number of expulsions and dismissals. And a similar fate befell the instigators and sympathisers of protests at the Guildford and Croydon Colleges of Art. In the US there were the Weathermen[36] bombings and more turmoil when, in June, Robert Kennedy was assassinated. In Eastern Europe the armies of the Warsaw Pact countries moved into Czechoslovakia in order to depose the Dubcek government and restore Soviet control in a country where the perceived likelihood of a Western takeover could no longer be ignored by the Soviet authorities.

Cardew's music-making remained unaffected by these events; it neither changed nor flagged. Indeed, this period of barely five years, from 1966 to 1970, saw the completion of arguably his finest achievements, the summation of his work as an avant-garde composer: *Treatise*, his music-making with AMM, *The Great Learning* and *Schooltime Compositions* – the latter receiving its premiere at the International Students' House in Great Portland Street in a Focus Opera Group [37] production directed by the composer on 11 March (Day School) and 12 March (Night School), 1968. And in May there were a number of 'vintage performances' in a series of four concerts entitled Sounds of Discovery, presented by Music Now, which began on 18 May at The Royal Institute Galleries with a programme devised by Christopher Hobbs and consisting of Terry Riley's *In C* (1964) and La Monte Young's *Death Chant* (1961). The second concert, at the same venue the next day, was given by the Rome-based improvising group Musica Elettronica Viva (M.E.V.) and the third took place at the International Students' House. This was a concert dedicated to music by the American composer Christian Wolff, who also directed, and consisted of four works: *Play* (1968), *Trio 2* (1961), *Septet* (1964), and *Edges* (1968).

The last, a graphic score, was performed by AMM, who themselves gave the final concert at the Queen Elizabeth Hall on 23 May.

During this period, from the mid-sixties, the bedrock of Cardew's musical life, as well as informing his private imperatives, was undoubtedly AMM, which offered both solidity (and solidarity) and danger, and through which he was now making music in another dimension. And in an undated reference to AMM in the '67/'68 Journals he notes:

> Something about the strongest things being not commercially viable. Commercially viable in the age of technology means reproducible in unlimited numbers or broadcastable. A music that is local in inspiration and interest is therefore not commercially viable.

All of his activities, including composing and his domestic responsibilities, had to be woven in and around his commitments to AMM; if he did prioritise, this was where his priorities lay. Musically he could rely on AMM in a way that he could not rely on *Treatise*. *Treatise* was vulnerable, for all its sophistication and conceptual brilliance; it needed to be explained, despite his reluctance, or at least introduced, to musicians in some way. More significantly, in the light of his experiences with AMM it had begun to take on a remoter significance. Perhaps it is not surprising then, given his reservations, uncertainties and frustrations in relation to his *magnum opus*, that most of his musings and writings from this period were on *Treatise* and were gathered up, refined, and edited, to appear in the *Treatise Handbook* where they would receive characteristically eloquent and occasionally arcane expression. These were the vectors which carried his musical philosophy into the next decade where it was to be reassessed and, during the last decade of his life, repudiated.

There was also domestic upheaval and insecurity around this time: his relationship with Sheila Kasabova had entered a quiescent phase: a loosening of their entanglement. She herself, throughout their relationship, had been living with a man, George Kasabov, whom she had married in 1966 and to whom, on 28 February 1968, she bore a daughter Anna. At home in Earls Court the character of Nevern Square was changing, for the worst according to Stella Cardew; the rents were being raised and many of the families there, including the Cardews, were forced to move, making way for a more affluent, and more cosmopolitan, class of tenants. The Cardews, however, benefited from a stroke of misfortune which befell Cornelius' younger brother Ennis. On receipt of compensation monies for an accident he had suffered Ennis obligingly provided the £5000 down-payment, on an interest-free loan basis, for a house which Stella had found and set her heart on, impressed by the congenial surroundings and its closeness to Barnes Common. She and Cornelius washed it down, cleaned and painted it, and on 25 September 1968 the family moved in to 112 Elm Grove Road, Barnes, in south-west London. Despite the fact that Cardew was often away, usually with AMM, and that she was still taking their youngest son Walter to the hospital for treatment regularly, Stella remembers the early days in Barnes as happy ones. They all loved the Common, where they would often take picnics, and it became an integral part of the family's day-to-day existence, an extension of their home but also, especially for Stella, a temporary haven from the duties and responsibilities associated with domesticity.

Morley College

In the same month as the move Cardew began an Experimental Music class at Morley College; the sessions took place on Fridays from 6pm to 10pm.[38] The situation was clearly preferable to that which obtained at the RAM insofar as it afforded a propitious opportunity to initiate members of the class into the world of experimental music with compositions of his own choice and without the obligation of dealing with the students' own work. It was not, after all, a composition class. This aspect of class activity could therefore be controlled and would evolve according to the partialities of individual participants and to the needs of the class as a whole. Cardew would have argued that exposure to the music of La Monte Young, Cage, Wolff, George Brecht, as well as his own, would in the long run benefit everybody, including those with compositional ambitions; he was convinced of its educational value, in the broadest sense. As far as the Academy students were concerned, and particularly in relation to the current political and social turmoil which was engulfing many parts of the world, the RAM had probably already been deemed a supreme irrelevance, and when Cardew advised them to join the Morley class, most of them duly did so. Cardew had already suggested to Howard Skempton that he should discontinue individual lessons and attend the Morley sessions.[39]

Moreover, it was at Morley College where the rudiments for several lasting relationships were laid down. The class included, among others, Michael Chant, Tim Mitchell, Michael Parsons, Carole Finer, Wendy Darling, Psi Ellison, Judith Euren, David and Diane Jackman, and Bryn Harris; together with Skempton and the Academy group these were later to form the nucleus of the Scratch Orchestra. They came from manifold backgrounds, not all musical, and joined the course for a variety of reasons and by a number of circuitous routes. Marjorie Wardle, who attended regularly, was the oldest and one of the most enthusiastic members of the class. She would have been described as 'middle-aged' and may have looked out of place amongst the more colourful members of a younger generation; but she wrote experimental pieces of equal, if not superior merit, and brought a much needed quota of common sense to the proceedings. Nor was she afraid to ask unsettling questions and had on one occasion opined that a vocal piece by Academy student Hugh Shrapnel was too long and too un-differentiated. Some years later the composer agreed that her criticisms had been entirely justified. Carole Finer recalls that she had been 'overwhelmed' by performances in London by the Merce Cunningham Dance Company, so that when she noticed an advertisement in the London College of Printing, where she was teaching at the time, for classes in experimental music at Morley College, she immediately enrolled. There were other connections, too; Finer had been taught Art at the City of London Girls' School by Mariel Cardew and had been a close friend of Judith Edsell, one of Cardew's girl friends at that time.

At the first meeting Cardew took along his cello and talked about it; perhaps his aim was to alleviate the anxiety which often surrounds the playing of a musical instrument: fear occludes creativity and celebration whereas in a benign and indulgent atmosphere of calm concentration even the most modest of utterances can compel respect and admiration. This was followed by a performance by John White and himself of White's *Cello and Tuba Machine*, a work of some considerable length which would have taken up most of the session. At one stage members of the class were asked to introduce themselves, and then to each one the question was posed as to whether they considered themselves to be a music-lover. Wendy Darling, who was a student at Essex University at the time, recalls feeling that the question was 'loaded', with an intimidatory edge, as if being a lover of classical music and a member of Cardew's Morley class were somehow incompatible. For whatever motives, or reasons, nobody confessed to being a 'music-lover'. She has remained rather less generous, or perhaps more objective, in her appraisal of Cardew's *persona* and behaviour in the Morley classes, laying the burden of accusation on him for a number of 'authoritarian' impositions. And she succeeded in maintaining a degree of detachment and even scepticism which, particularly in the heady days of the Scratch Orchestra, was both unusual and, with hindsight, invaluable – even if her reservations were never expressed publicly at the time. At Morley she was faintly amused by the fact that as a matter of course Cardew would sit at a particular desk, always on an eminence, as it were – a quaint, incongruous strain of authoritarianism which was to carry over into the Scratch Orchestra. And yet for Carole Finer Cardew's paternalism was mitigated by a strong democratic strain. Certainly, for most participants his authority insinuated itself into the class, or perhaps was conferred upon him; and if the majority perceived this, few objected to it. It was to be the same with the Scratch Orchestra; their acceptance of his authority was a concession, perhaps, which the music-making validated; the importance of the music was overriding and therefore justified their pliancy.

Normally, the first hour and a half of the class would be spent working on something: discussing, preparing.[40] Then there would be an extended coffee break of between thirty and forty-five minutes, after which they would spend at least an hour, sometimes two hours, making music – usually a performance of some kind, whether improvisation or pieces for which the first half may have been used for rehearsal and preparation. Among the works performed were La Monte Young's *Poem*, Cage's *Variations 1*, and one of the pieces from Stockhausen's set of verbal scores *Aus den sieben Tagen*. The score of *Variations 1* was far too expensive for anyone to buy; Cardew explained the procedure, demonstrating from his own copy of the score, so that participants could prepare their own version at home and bring it along the following week; the printed score was thus relegated to the status of unnecessary luxury object. If participants were encouraged to play an instrument it was also made clear that a viable music-making could be created without recourse to musical instruments; Carole Finer, for example, would take along her banjo, which she could not yet play.[41] In any case Cardew rarely commented on performances at Morley College (some of which were open to the general public); those who expected advice, criticism or evaluation would have been disappointed. There were no stated criteria; whatever happened was self-justifying.

One evening Psi Ellison, who was a student at St. Martin's School of Art, decided to arrive late, his pockets stuffed full of marbles. As he entered the room the group were sitting together with their instruments – rehearsing, performing, discussing, engaged in purposeful activity, the faculties concentrated. Ellison tripped, perhaps deliberately, and the marbles splattered and scattered everywhere; it was a sign and portent, an act of creative disruption which was to become Ellison's trademark in the Scratch Orchestra, his chosen activities always militating against the risk of an unwarranted gravitas which might, from time to time, have overtaken the Orchestra. On this occasion the group's equilibrium was quickly restored, the calm mood again intensifying around them as they continued with their chosen task and Ellison gathered up his marbles.

Cardew's individual contributions could be equally, if less spectacularly, provocative, wrought by both the liveliness of his imagination and his performing acumen. At one of the sessions he announced in the break that he was going to perform a solo for the class; what materialised, for half an hour or more, was a kind of percussion piece. The sound source was a relatively simple construction: peas or dried beans rolled down a slope, dropping on to an amplified metal container (a saucepan?) and generating tiny sounds, isolated and subtle, which, as Michael Parsons recalls, 'seemed to have a life of their own' – the creation of a musical world of high definition in which rawness was combined with sophistication.[42]

One can draw an analogy with Psi Ellison's marbles 'piece': Cardew's piece was framed, the formal relationship (distance and separation) between performer and audience maintained; the indeterminacy and quiet anarchy of the beans offset by the palpable intentionality embodied in Cardew's simple act of provisioning. In Ellison's piece the separation of 'performer' and audience is blurred; there is no demarcation. Nor could there have been any recognition of intentionality although, knowing Ellison, some of his Morley class audience may have surmised it. Almost certainly, Ellison's intention was to create a brief mayhem; and the intention was disguised by the theatricality of the 'accident'. In fact, both pieces were highly theatrical, and a clearly delimited sound-image – a staccato clatter of a number of small objects on a hard surface – was common to both.

David Jackman describes the Morley class as 'a learning zone'; Cardew, the enabler, seemed to be granting unspoken permission to do whatever one wanted, to experiment and to take risks. And by January 1969 he was encouraging participants to bring along their own compositions; on one occasion they were asked to write pieces for each other. A spirit of collaboration and experimentation prevailed; people felt overwhelmed by the welter of new ideas coming from a variety of sources and directions. It was a period of joyful discovery, of risking all, of *doing*.[43] The mind was concentrated but there was never any sense of travail; for most of the participants the sessions were totally absorbing.

The structure of the Morley sessions, as well as the admixture of a relaxed informality and an awareness of the practicalities, and demands, of music-making, prefigured the Scratch Orchestra meetings. Of particular significance was the creation of a number of 'Activities' which were clearly harbingers of the Scratch Orchestra's repertoire. And there were other modes of music-making which mark the Morley group as a nascent Scratch Orchestra. Of these the most important were probably the improvisation 'rites' which became one of the 'repertory categories' included in the Scratch Constitution and which were invariably included in Scratch Orchestra events. And the Morley classes would occasionally throw up social and psychological problems which had to be dealt with; these experiences would also stand members in good stead for life in the Scratch Orchestra. One young man insisted on playing loud clusters on the piano, continuously and inconsequentially, during the improvisations. Several exasperated members of the class decided one evening to 'mute' the piano by stuffing it with hay and sacking before the session began. The young man took umbrage and left the class.

At the beginning of the New Year a pocket diary contains some interesting jottings, particularly in relation to his project, incubating in his mind and now beginning to take shape, for a second Paragraph of *The Great Learning*, in which the performers would drum and sing:

Just be yourself, and listen to the sound of it.
Choosing a drum! Like in love; a good girl is one who gives it back.
You strike the drum and the sound comes back to you in waves, lifting the spirit.

At the beginning of the second term at Morley College (January 1969) Cardew introduced Paragraph 2 of *The Great Learning* to the class and distributed drumming and singing parts. This became the main project for the term and from the outset everybody was urged to acquire a drum and to recruit friends and acquaintances to swell the numbers. The class embarked upon what turned out to be an extremely arduous task: drilling themselves to memorise all the twenty-six rhythms which accompany the singing; furthermore, Cardew's original idea was that the performers should drum and sing simultaneously. It soon became apparent that for the majority of participants such a level of virtuosity was beyond their reach and Cardew's new proposal of two separate groups of singers and drummers was greeted with relief and gratitude. This was the form it took in the final version, completed towards the end of January. Drumming in general took off and became a popular pastime with the Morley group; almost immediately Howard Skempton produced his *Drum No.1*, motivated by demand and inspired by the memory of the performance of Terry Riley's *In C* the previous year in the Sounds of Discovery series:[44]

Any number of drums.
Introduction of the pulse.
Continuation of the pulse.
Deviation through emphasis, decoration, contradiction.

Several opportunities arose, or rather were created by Cardew for performances of the first completed Paragraphs of *The Great Learning*. These included the first performance of Paragraph 2 at the Leeds College of Art on 16 March, and there were further performances at the Philharmonia in Rome in April (according to his Journal), and on 10 May a performance of Paragraphs 1 and 2 in Highgate church. In February he was invited to Norway for a series of four lectures and there were a number of invitations for solo concert appearances, including a recital in Cardiff on 9 April (the day after the completion of Paragraph 7). There was also some teaching at Maidstone School of Art, certainly on the recommendation of Gavin Bryars, who was on the staff there. Many experimental and avant-garde musicians, including Michael Parsons and myself, had found employment at art schools in the late sixties, rather than music schools, where the whole experimental ethos was anathema to the authorities and indeed to most of the staff. As Tom Phillips has recalled, Liberal and Complementary Studies Departments in Art Schools and Technical Colleges were 'a mask which concealed all kinds of virtues'. At the time there was considerable political and artistic upheaval in the art world; the experimental musicians were the natural allies of the art students and, in many cases, of the staff, too.

The beginning of the third term at Morley was taken up with rehearsals for another four concert series presented by Victor Schonfield and Music Now, this time at the Roundhouse in north London. The first and third concerts, on 3 and 8 May, were given by the Sonic Arts Union from the US: Gordon Mumma, David Behrman, Robert Ashley and Alvin Lucier, who specialised in theatrical performances of their own live electronic music. The second was a mammoth seven-hour concert, on 4 May, which again consisted of English and American experimental music and included Paragraph 2 of *The Great Learning* (then called *The Great Digest*), Eddie Prévost's *Silver Pyramid*, Christian Wolff's *Stones*, and Christopher Hobbs' *Voicepiece*. Cardew had asked Howard Skempton to provide a piece which could be performed simultaneously with *Voicepiece* and Skempton duly obliged with a short piece entitled *Scumbling*, a kind of drinking song in which the four male singers – Hobbs, Cardew, Parsons and the composer sat around a table and partly sang, partly spoke, eight times, the composer's own brief Latin text. As Skempton recalls the piece created an atmosphere of such hilarity amongst the musicians that they were unable to perform their parts with any reasonable degree of accuracy and conviction.

By comparison George Brecht's low-volume, candle-lit *Candle Piece for Radios* was a relatively solemn affair, as were performances of Terry Jennings' *String Quartet*, with David Aherne on violin, Tim Souster on 2nd violin, Allan Cutts on viola and Cardew on cello, and, minus Souster, La Monte Young's *String Trio*. The *piéce de resistance* was undoubtedly Cage's *Atlas Eclipticalis*, performed by Tom Phillips, Gavin Bryars, Christopher Hobbs and myself. Hobbs recalls that this particular reading of *Atlas Eclipticalis*, which lasted for the entire seven-hour duration of the concert, resulted in an extremely sparse music, giving performers ample time for drinking and socialising between sounds. At the bar one of us would suddenly glance at his watch and then excuse himself in order to go and fulfil his artistic obligation by performing a sound – to return shortly after to finish his drink.

By the spring of 1969, perhaps earlier, Cardew was already formulating his ideas for a more permanent, possibly more cohesive, yet more heterogeneous group of people for the propagation of experimental music. In the wake of his experiences at Morley College, particularly with Paragraph 2, which had encouraged him, it seemed a propitious moment. On Sunday 4 May, during the morning rehearsal of Paragraph 2 at the Roundhouse that same evening, Cardew announced that the inaugural meeting of the 'Scratch Orchestra' would take place on 1 July at St. Katherine's Dock, near Tower

Bridge – then a complex of relatively cheap studio places designed for young artists. A provisional manifesto had been prepared and Cardew's 'A Scratch Orchestra: draft constitution' appeared in the June edition of the *Musical Times*, thanks to the boldness and foresight of its editor Stanley Sadie, whom Cardew knew. This was prior to an advertisement in the *International Times*, presumably all part of the same recruitment campaign, written at home in Elm Grove Road and dated 12 June, which begins with a characteristically modest, slightly apologetic, assumption: 'I might be wrong, but I think you may be interested in joining the Scratch Orchestra'. The aim of the meeting was to discuss '1) what exactly membership is likely to involve, 2) any amendments to the Constitution, 3) a possible schedule of the orchestra's activity this autumn, and 4) further ideas, including finance and promotion'.

Embedded in the mythology of the Scratch Orchestra is the notion that it was founded by a trio of Cardew, Michael Parsons and Howard Skempton; Parsons recalls that some time in early 1969 Cardew did specifically ask Skempton and himself to be co-founders and the three of them met on several occasions to discuss the planning and co-ordination of the work. A small number of people have been privy to an embellishment: that the trio subsequently became a quartet, and the fourth member, Christopher Hobbs, withdrew because at the time he could not afford the £5 fee which it was agreed each founder member should contribute. There may be more than a grain of truth in the latter version but it is nevertheless misleading. Hobbs recalls an occasion after a meeting at Morley College when Cardew proposed the idea of a Scratch Orchestra bank account and asked whether there were any individuals present who, along with him, would contribute five pounds towards opening the account.

Now the only two people on that evening who had five pounds were Howard Skempton and Michael Parsons. Therefore the three of them put in five pounds each and opened the Scratch Orchestra bank account and therefore, when you read of the founders of the Scratch Orchestra, it is those three because they literally founded its bank account, but there were a lot of other people who were around at the time: myself, Bryn Harris, Hugh Shrapnel, and others; Diane Jackman, David Jackman, Carole Finer, Michael Chant, Phil Gebbett; various others who I have probably forgotten who were equally attentive to the needs and ethos of the Scratch Orchestra but who did not on that evening have five pounds that they could pledge to put into a bank account. So when you read that those three people founded the Scratch Orchestra, one shouldn't think that those three people got together in a sort of enclave and said, 'Hey, let's form a

Scratch Orchestra!' That wasn't the case at all.[45]

At the meeting, which attracted around eighty people, Cardew elaborated on his concept of a 'Scratchbook', and 'Scratch Music', as well as proposing the idea of a 'Research Project'; clearly, his intention was to instil in his audience the desirability of certain virtues in relation to music-making. His manner, or rather his approach, at St. Katherine's Dock might therefore be described as 'teacherly', enjoining prospective Scratch Orchestra members to go away and think, imagine, prepare, create, soberly and conscientiously, and to assemble their ideas verbally and visually in a Scratch book. And to this praiseworthy and edifying end a commitment to research would be beneficial. At the same time he wanted to make it clear that despite these prescriptions

nobody as yet knows what the orchestra is, and that they can make it what they like, that it probably isn't a sublime organism on a higher plane telling us what to do, but just us making music together. That if anyone finds they simply don't know what to do, they should just sit and listen.[46]

The second item on the agenda was as follows:

Each person should make a note of the first playing session, at the Docks (same room) on September 30th at 6.30 pm. On that date they should be ready to rehearse Scratch Music (i.e. come prepared to play at least one accompaniment), and at the same meeting we'll decide programmes for the first series of concerts.

Cardew was never coy about money; he estimated that the projected November concerts would cost around £150 and suggested that each member, according to their means, should contribute £2 or more. He also encouraged people to consider ways of raising funds for the Orchestra and, where appropriate, to take the initiative on an individual basis. Finally, people were also asked to leave their names and addresses so that they could be notified of further meetings. The convivial atmosphere of the meeting was further enhanced by Cardew's choice of a piece by Christian Wolff, entitled *Drinks*:

Put into various containers something people enjoy drinking. When you like, make sounds (for which you may use the containers). The containers may be refilled at any time.

At this point we need to pause, to retrace our steps in order to identify the vectors that carried Cardew's musical philosophy forward to its present stage. At Morley College the idea had developed of a musical collective to which a variety of musicians and non-musicians, enthusiasts, contributed according to their abilities and aptitudes. The repertoire, on the whole, was prescribed by Cardew and comprised mainly the avant-garde 'classics'; the emphasis was still on 'music' and 'musical' scores.

With *Schooltime Compositions*, completed several months before the Morley class began, Cardew had already achieved the crucial breakthrough: received definitions and notions of 'music', 'musicality', 'musicalness' are questioned and reassessed, thereby challenging and unsettling traditional and hidebound perceptions of what constituted a 'musical' performance. Leafing through its pages the Scratch Orchestra's debt to Cardew the composer becomes visually exposed; for virtually the entire repertoire of the Scratch Orchestra is embodied in this little booklet of intimate, cryptic notations which is manifestly the precursor of the 'Scratchbook', by which, at least initially and in the early days of the Scratch Orchestra, Cardew set great store. Like its progenitor, a Scratch book comprised visual and verbal expressions and inventions, *notations*, which opened up new aesthetic horizons through which the performer is motivated to transcend contemporary canon and practice to create a 'Scratch music'. Cardew's *Schooltime Compositions* was the chrysalis from which the Scratchbook, and Scratch Music, emerged. And out of this the Scratch Orchestra created a *musica practica*, more – a *modus vivendi* – which was wholly original. The Scratch Orchestra symbolized the *socialization* of *Schooltime Compositions* – a process for which the Morley class, and the work there on Paragraph 2 in particular, was the catalyst and which received formal representation in Cardew's 'Draft Constitution'.

The title, *Schooltime Compositions*, was not a mere quirk of Cardew's imagination; nor was it randomly acquired from the shelves of a schools' stationer. The connotation of an educative function for these little pieces was a conscious expedient and provides the palpable link with Cardew's conception of a 'Scratch Orchestra'. The 'draft constitution', as we have seen, was probably drafted around the time of the ICA performance and the ideas and suggestions for music-making which it presents seem to derive, in large part, both from the *Schooltime Compositions* themselves and, what is most likely, from Cardew's experience of the performances at International Students' House and the ICA (which I discuss below), in which several prospective Scratch Orchestra members did take part.[47]

In *Schooltime Compositions* Cardew subtly defines the areas – emotional, physical, psychological, and historical – in which the performer operates, although there is no question of his *controlling* the interpretation, either directly or by some back-door ploy involving 'chance operations'. And yet, paradoxically, for all its intangibility, in *Schooltime*

Compositions the ultimate 'authority' of the composer is still maintained, if tenuously; the composer provides the material for the 'opera' roles in the same way that Cardew had provided material for the performer in, say, *Autumn 60*. In *Schooltime*, as in all compositions, the composer presumes to harness the sensibilities, skill and ultimately the complicity of others to establish his, the artist's, priority. And it was his desire and intention that, irrational, intuitive and evanescent as these pieces appear to be, their performance was to be controlled by aesthetic judgement, taste and criticism; reflection, not indiscrimination, was to be the guiding principle. Nor were they necessarily improvisational; performances were usually measured and formal, although performers would often be provoked by the pieces to ignore Cardew's artistic preferences altogether. David Jackman recalls he could 'make neither head nor tail of the score' and simply used it as a prompt to do what he wanted; this was the 'permission' the score seemed to him to be granting.

In the Draft Constitution, by contrast, the emphasis is on self-provisioning – in Scratch Music, in the Popular Classics, in the Research Projects, and in the Improvisation Rites. Even the 'compositions', their own or by others, which the Scratch Orchestra included in their programmes, were vehicles for music-making or performance of a less focused nature. The status of 'composition' in the Scratch Orchestra was no higher, or lower, than any other category in the Draft Constitution; Cardew's experiments with composer/performer relations brought him to their coalescence. For the first time, in an act of self-immolation, Cardew posits the extinction of the composer. Or, less cataclysmically, the hegemony of composition is overthrown; composition is reduced to the ranks.

In creating the Draft Constitution Cardew's purpose was to create a performing group which was drawn from the widest spectrum of society. To do this he needed something which was inspirational and at the same time down-to-earth, viable. The Constitution was prescriptive in so far as its purpose was to initiate collective, creative activity. At the same time he wanted this most radical 'composition' to embody the idea of, not the inaccessibility of creative freedom, but rather an awareness of the extreme difficulty of its attainment. Indeed, for Cardew it was the consciousness of the tortuous path to any condition of enlightenment which was more important than the attainment itself, another hypothesis which he shared with Wittgenstein and which is certainly rooted in his readings of Eastern philosophies. Hence the notion of 'training' in his references to the Draft Constitution and the rigour with which he prescribes the various categories. Cardew, as far as I remember, never used *Schooltime Compositions* with the Scratch Orchestra. There was no need; virtually from the outset the Scratch Orchestra, on the basis of the Draft Constitution, was producing its own 'schooltime compositions'.

Yet might it not be argued that the Draft Constitution itself was Cardew's composition, and that the seeds of its destruction were sown within it? Like Frankenstein Cardew created a monster, a benign monster, but one he could not control. The Draft Constitution was meant to embody not so much an 'authority', as a guide, a referent, which also embraced the desirability, to put it no stronger, of *discipline*, towards which it was expected that a flexible and not entirely subversive attitude would be adopted. Since for Cardew discipline could never be imposed from without he was walking a tight-rope from which he surely knew, sooner or later, he would fall. This was what fuelled Cardew's monstrous imagination; and there could be no safety net.

Throughout his life Cardew grappled with the profound complexity of human relations which the concept of music embodies: in particular the duality of artist and audience, and the presumptuousness which is at the heart of it. 'Art is about aristocracy and subversion' Anita Brookner wrote with crystalline honesty, a dictum written on stone tablets and laid down by Western Art orthodoxy which Cardew – and perhaps this is his most revolutionary contribution – challenged and sought to subvert.[48] Whereas in *Schooltime Compositions* the performers are characters in an opera who discover their roles, in and through the Scratch Orchestra its members discovered, not roles, but parts of themselves – or rather they *self-invented* parts of themselves through those rare and precious revelatory experiences which participation promised and occasionally delivered. The notion of 'aristocracy' and 'subversion' was too prosaic; for Cardew, with the Scratch Orchestra and *The Great Learning* his aims were to transcend the most fundamental precepts of Western Art and in particular that of the artist as aristocrat. The Scratch Orchestra was an expression of the universality of Art; Art as a way of life. As Keith Rowe said of the AMM: 'you can't either play music or live your life. There's no division between the two'.[49]

On 23 March 1969, a year after the first performance, an all-day performance of *Schooltime Compositions*, from 11.30 to 22.00 hours, took place at the Institute of Contemporary Arts.[50] This was both multi-layered and diffused, even less focused than the earlier performance at the International Students' House (which had also foreshadowed, in the richness and opacity of its content as well as the extreme flexibility of form, both the spirit and letter of Scratch Orchestra performances), and still closer, perhaps, to the essential nature of the Scratch Orchestra – closer, and yet in one crucial consideration incongruent with it. For on the recording of the ICA performance the sound, the music, has an impermeability and luxuriance, a projection and sense of conviction not associated with early Scratch events in which many of the performers, unlike those in the ICA performance, were inexperienced and tentative. On this occasion, *Schooltime Compositions*, like *Treatise*, had been off-loaded into safe harbour, into the hands of mainly experienced, performance artists – the same expert hands into which both the European and the American avant-garde, with a degree of circumspection and worldliness not unrelated to their instinct for artistic self-preservation, had entrusted their own music. By contrast the Scratch Orchestra comprised a motley constellation of performance novices, essentially unversed, the young and unfledged: clerks and civil servants, housewives and traffic wardens, tax accountants and labourers, students and laboratory technicians, computer analysts and teachers, who had discovered the Scratch Orchestra through varied and circuitous routes, whose relations to music and musical instruments were oblique and insubstantial, whose talents were latent, untapped, whose participation was unprescribed and unpredictable, who represented the vast unknown of infinite human resources, and who had turned up at St. Katherine's Dock on that fateful day.

The performance at the ICA (Cardew, stoically, was performing with a strained back) resembled a market or bazaar (without the cash nexus), creating an aura which stimulated a wide range of shifting relationships involving performers and public, as individual members of the audience moved around observing, pausing, questioning, participating, moving on – the whole bathed in an atmosphere of informality and in this respect prefiguring the nature of subsequent Scratch Orchestra events.

The beginning of the recording is evocative of AMM, some of whom were taking part in the performance: the long, bowed sounds, the high-pitched whistling, the deftly placed percussion sounds, the purposeful screeching effects ('Song of Pleasure'?); and in the background a dense, continuous sound, which may have been a rendering of the AMM maxim 'Every noise has a note'. The residual sounds of visual interpretations can occasionally be identified by those who were present and whose memories are still functioning reliably – such as the painter Tom Phillips' typewriter and 'Little Flower of the North'. Phillips interpreted 'Little Flower' as representing 'hair' and projected slides of snippets of his own hair onto a screen. This was accompanied by himself typing out the phrase 'Little Flower of the North' over and over, as a schoolboy might write out lines.

Harry Wilson-Wright moved around the spacious performing arena recording stretches of music of varying lengths according to his disposition and whim: bird calls, bird song, and the sound of happy children, all of which suggest 'Song of Pleasure'. So does a beautiful saxophone solo (Lou Gare?), which is joined eventually by other reed instruments (Michael Parsons' saxophone and Alec Hill's clarinet?). And just as Bob Woolford's high-fidelity stereophonic recording of the International Students' House performance was 'a legitimate by-product of the composition', so Wilson-Wright's roving microphone constituted an 'interpretation' of Schooltime Compositions which may or may not have accorded with the impressions of others who attended and participated in the event. Individual members of the audience could not have focused, separated and excluded to quite the degree that Harry's microphone does; the performance was far too diffuse. Nor would Cardew have necessarily approved Harry's interpretation (or Bob Woolford's the previous year); he may even have had reservations about the viability of recording the events. For what Cardew disliked about the theatre, as he expressed in his piece 'Sitting in the Dark' for the *Musical Times*, was precisely the dependence on focus and exclusion, this fascination for 'manipulations in a pool of light'. The theatrical aesthetic excludes too much, is too prescriptive, and the same problem blights most audio recordings. Moreover, the microphone, like the pool of light, encouraged the manipulators and attention-seekers; Cardew preferred the 'twilight' of Scratch performances where all occurrences were bathed in the same pervasive but temperate light.

Beginning with the first performance of *Schooltime Compositions* in March of 1968 and culminating in the founding of the Scratch Orchestra in July of the following year, it had been a momentous period for Cardew. Not surprisingly, for most of the remainder of the summer Cardew's musical activities were in abeyance; he and the family escaped to France and camped in the Ardèche where it was dry and extremely hot. Stella recalls that there was a series of deep rock pools coming from an underground river. And there were old mulberry trees, five feet tall and hollow, which they would fill with stones and dry material and set light to, and they would explode across the valley. On the mountainside there was scree and Cornelius and the children would rub stones together and throw them to see which ones would make a sound. All of this represents a desire, a need perhaps, to return to the roots of musical practices and clearly relates to *The Great Learning*; Stella remembers Cornelius sitting outside at a table writing music – sketches, perhaps, for further Paragraphs. Occasionally they would entertain friends who had managed to track them down, among them her old College friend, Craeg Tarrant, and a young Australian composer who had come to study with Cardew. Soon he would return to autumn in England where the newly-formed Scratch Orchestra awaited him; it was to be a watershed, not only in his own life, but in the lives of many of those who joined him and who participated in his quest.

Compositions 1968

Of the compositions completed after the second *Winter Potato*, that is, from May 1965 to April 1970, none of them could have been accommodated within the avant-garde establishment, either in Europe or in America. In 1966 Cardew's only composition was the music he wrote for Allan King's film *Warrendale* (but which was not used – nor did King use any other music); 1967 saw the completion of *Treatise* and *The Tiger's Mind,* a verbal composition written for AMM. *Schooltime Compositions* (1968) is a booklet of ideas, thoughts and experimental notations written mainly for friends and colleagues, *Schooltime Special* (1968) is essentially a practical introduction to improvisation, conceived probably for an educational assignment at a college; and *The Great Learning* (1968/70) is a work of unwieldy length for trained and untrained musicians which at the time was associated with the *Scratch Orchestra*. All of these creations were too fluid, their definition of time/space too open, and, what was for professional musicians particularly problematic, in *Schooltime Compositions*, as with *Treatise*, there was no prescription; both were printed and distributed without any accompanying notes on interpretation; the performer was left to sink or swim. In fact, during the period 1966 to 1970 Cardew made more music than at any time in his life. And it was through his membership of AMM, in particular, that his music-making blossomed and flourished; AMM had become the main recipient and beneficiary of his musical energies. It is to the compositional achievements of these years that we must now turn our attention in a little more detail.

Schooltime Compositions (1968)

In the Spring of 1968, as a result of a commission by Michael Sargent of Focus Opera Group, a new composition surfaced. Cardew's 'Opera Book' – as he describes it in the printed version – was to be performed with operas by György Ligeti, *Aventures & Nouvelles Aventures*, and Mauricio Kagel, *Sur Scène*, on the same evenings: 11 and 12 March. By now, Cardew had a full-time job and a young family, which not only affected, but also enriched his work, specifically *Schooltime Compositions*, which in a charming and creative manner reflects a concern for children and their needs: 'play each phrase to make the preceding phrase seem as though it had been played by a child' is an instruction separating two melodies in the appendix, and there are childlike epithets added in the appendix to the 'keyboard' piece: 'pretty', 'kind', 'nice' – such conceits found echoes in the Scratch Orchestra, within whose orbit children played and grew. And in its juxtaposition of playfulness and sobriety *Schooltime Compositions* presages the ethos of the Scratch.

Some of the notations encapsulate Scratch activities through visual imagery, like the aforementioned 'Little Flower of the North' (Ex.8.1):

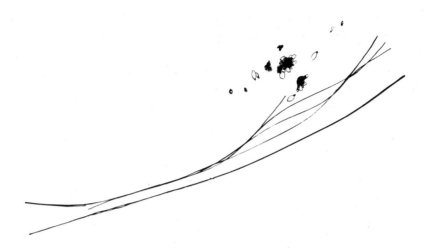

Ex.8.1. 'Little Flower of the North' from *Schooltime Compositions*.

others through verbalization, like 'Desire' (Ex.8.2):

Want to do something; Do it.
Do something without wanting to
Do something wanting not to
Be done to
Be done

note 1: Perform all or none of the instructions
note 2: Instructions are to be followed only by
qualified person

Schooltime Compositions takes its title from the little booklet whose cover betokens both an American (Grade) and an English (10/-) origin. It is essentially a notebook: of 'observations, ideas, notations, hints, diagrams, concepts, scientific experiments, geometric analogies – some direct, some oblique, mostly presented as "facts" with no covering instructions'.[51] In this respect *Schooltime Compositions* resembles *Treatise*, although the differences are of greater significance. An interpretation of these 'facts' requires a commitment and flight of the imagination and, concomitantly, a restraint (unlike *Treatise*?) on the intellectual ingenuities. Arnold Hauser has noted that whereas with T.S. Eliot and Paul Valéry the primary foundation is always an idea, a thought, a problem, with Joyce and Kafka it is an irrational experience, a vision, a metaphysical or mythological image. Paradoxically, *Schooltime Compositions* seems to embody both these ideas: 'Decide: which pieces are finite and which infinite'.[52] *Schooltime Compositions* are about feelings, and attitudes – the mind cannot fathom them. The senses leap ahead; a matrix draws out 'an interpreter's feelings about certain topics or materials. [...] They point to the heart of some real matter, mental or material'.[53]

Their apparently arcane nature is due not to incoherence of thought on Cardew's part, but rather to the calculated suppression of explanatory links. Just as Blake had referred to the capacity of children to 'elucidate' his visions, so it is to the musically innocent that Cardew addresses these notations; it is they who, unburdened by the weight of a censorial, protectionist musical education, might draw meanings and create live performances out of these drawings and texts.[54] In *Schooltime Compositions* the different matrices

> grew around such things as words, melody, vocal sounds, triangles, pleasure, noise, working-to-rule, will and desire, keyboard. [...] Some matrices serve as a measure of probity (cf La Monte Young's 'Draw a straight line and follow it'); others as a measure of virtuosity, courage, tenacity, alertness, and so on. [...] The interpreter knows the general area of his potential action; he wishes or has talent to play, or sing, or construct, or illumine, or take exercise of one sort or another. He can draw out his interpretation in that direction. The interpreting route from matrix to action is what determines the condition he arrives in, the spirit in which he undertakes his action.[55]

The intended educative function of the work is made clear not only by the texts in the *Musical Times* ('Sitting in the Dark') but also by scrutiny and consideration of the compositions themselves.

Some of the *Schooltime Compositions* suggest a more formal treatment; they demand a measured, considered approach, and the kind of preparedness and awareness that characterised the later Scratch Improvisation rites. And references to the past, such as the use of archaic objects and artefacts from folk culture, were common to both: Scratch member Daphne Simmons' grandfather clock, and the use of a 'bamer'[56] in 'Making A', for example, which consists of a list of quite explicit instructions, as if one is following a recipe. (In the appendix a list of 'ingredients' are listed as in a recipe book.) This *feeling* for the past, rather than a sentimental nostalgia, invariably found characteristic expression in Scratch contributions. If, as Psi Ellison has suggested, the Scratch was creating a new folk music, then a continuity with the past was natural. The Scratch Orchestra was not self-conscious about its ostensible modernity; it mined the past as much as it observed and invented the present.

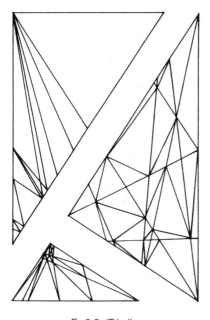

Ex.8.3. 'Triad'.

The very first composition is untitled (Ex.8.3): three diagrams of super-imposed triangles recalls the importance of triangles in *Treatise,* and especially in the Appendix where Cardew provides detailed 'guidelines for systematic interpretations of the triangles' under the title 'Triad'.

The 'keyboard' piece originally bore the title 'Phrygian Octave for Emily' (Cardew's step-daughter). The words superimposed onto some of the 'keys' suggest qualities of sound: arid, spectral, remote, etc; in the Appendix simple, homely epithets are added to each of the white notes of the mode: loyal, pretty, kind, nice, etc., words describing positive, human qualities such as would be familiar and meaningful to a young, teenage girl (Ex.8.4). Underneath this drawing, smaller in dimension, there is another drawing of the Phrygian octave, but in this version two staves are drawn across the upper part of the keys suggesting the possibility of some kind of harmonic accompaniment.

The 'make x words' piece (Ex.8.5) can be approached quite literally and systematically: construct a crossword, read words across as melody, words down as harmony.

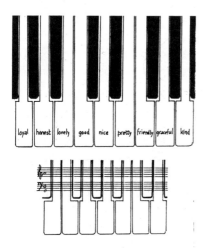

Ex.8.4. From the Appendix (keyboards).

Ex.8.5. 'making xwords'.

Song of Pleasure

I am rowing a boat on a lake. The sounds – the regular breathing, the small creaking and thudding sounds of the oars in the rowlocks, the water lapping and sucking at the belly of the boat, the occasional passing bird– all combine to make a song of pleasure.

Ex.8.6. 'Song of Pleasure'.

'Song of Pleasure', too, may be treated literally, naturalistically or metaphorically: hire a rowing boat at the Serpentine in Hyde Park and record the sounds. Or simply imitate the sounds. Or disregard the text and create your own 'song of pleasure' (Ex.8.6). The Scratch Orchestra loved outings and open air performances. 'Were we to succeed in refining a certain "aesthetics" of musical pleasure, then doubtless we would attach less importance to the formidable break in tonality accomplished by modernity.'[57]

The 'mechanical device', for which Cardew provides two detailed sketches, is the kind of challenge which a mechanically-minded art student would have risen to at that time. Cardew had many artist friends and was in great demand at art schools around the country. The untitled 'hands', too, would have met with a positive response in the art colleges (Ex.8.7). Or is it an echo of Stockhausen's advice to Ruth Cardew a decade earlier in Cologne to 'cultivate her sixth finger'? Or a reference to virtuosity? Or finger shadows?

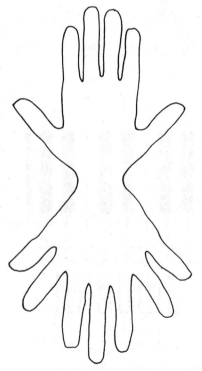

Ex.8.7. no title provided.

In 'Vocals' the extensive range of the pitches notated suggests squeaks and grunts as well as sung tones, juxtaposed with sounds of kisses.[58] 'Every noise has a note' is an homage to AMM and to Lou Gare, in particular, who coined the phrase. How to get ('musical') sound from a particular instrument or object; in AMM you would cultivate having an eye, and an ear, for a potential 'instrument'.

The aforementioned text 'Sitting in the Dark' appeared together with an 'explanatory' second part which Cardew added at the request of the Editor of the *Musical Times*, Stanley Sadie. It was intended as an introduction to the first performance of *Schooltime Compositions* at the International Students' House. And yet, typically, the cryptic nature of Cardew's 'explanation' contrasts oddly with the directness of these little pieces which echo George Brecht's aforementioned *Water Yam* and look forward to the Scratch Book; with both a sensory connection with the pieces is essential. There is no narrative in *Schooltime Compositions*, nor does Cardew resort to the illusory; and the use of everyday objects, as we have seen, is common to both *Schooltime Compositions* and *Water Yam* in which the domination of musical instruments in music-making is challenged. Objects, such as in 'Making A', for example, would reveal hidden resonances more appropriate to the kind of 'music' which Cardew was seeking.

In his article Cardew professes an antipathy to both opera and the theatre. The theatrical situation and its supreme artificiality aroused 'disgust' in him; he mistrusted attention-seeking actors performing their manipulations in a pool of light. By contrast it was the concealed objects and furtive movements offstage and backstage which intrigued him, whilst he preferred a more oblique relationship to the onstage narrative. Whereas his music had reached the point where it excluded nothing, the theatre seemed to exclude too much. In contrast to theatrical lighting, in his text Cardew exalts twilight; twilight allows things their own definition; twilight enhances sensuality.

Unlike the productions of the Ligeti and Kagel operas Cardew's work, as it is recalled in the memories of participants, did not use the stage – or it was used peripherally. So there was no conventional separation of performers and audience. Cardew's intention was that it was through the pieces and their interpretation, rather than through their presence on stage, that the performers become characters in the opera. The characters are not pre-ordained, the process is that of discovery, but more importantly of self-discovery and self-invention; the characters are 'real-life' characters involved in a process of self-revelation.

The core belief of this process is according to Cardew a 'musician's optimism'; that at any time the 'divine afflatus' can manifest itself; that a revelatory experience is possible. And revelation expands consciousness:

It may suit our momentary need to pretend we know the meaning of words like 'music', 'musical', 'musicality' (I am keeping this consciously on a linguistic level) but in a musician's behaviour is expressed the knowledge that they are bottomless pits that not only defy definition and analysis but present no angle to them.[59]

This can occur through a transcending of 'music': music as simply an awareness of 'the other' – as a child in the womb becomes aware of what is not itself through hearing. The present deafens us to the myriads of musics that have yet to be revealed; words like 'music', 'musicality', 'musicalness' (whose meanings, in *Schooltime Compositions*, Cardew seeks to extend and redefine) are circumscribed, in thrall to both history and culture, attached to prevalent norms in a relationship which cannot be breached.

Schooltime Special (1968) encapsulates Cardew's philosophy of musical education: the world as material for musical composition; and the moral dimension of music as an expression of human relations. The piece consists of four groups of questions, each group focussing on a particular stage in the process of music-making. In the first group, group A, each question is posed in terms of the potential performer's desire or lack of desire to participate: 'Do you want to […]? Do you want to leave the room?' If a person wishes to take part, the only contribution expected of him/her is *one* sung, played, made or heard sound. (Notice that the desire or willingness to 'hear' a note or noise qualifies one as a participant.)

In the second group of questions the performer is invited to characterise his/her sound in some way. The third group of questions concerns the effect that the music is having on each individual performer and Cardew notates corresponding, interpretative responses. Finally, in the fourth group, Cardew's notation raises more general issues for the performer, such as commitment – encouraging the performer to explore, enhance, change, indefinitely extend the music – and morality (relationship to other performers and self-reliance).

Notes and references

1   *Treatise Handbook,* p.xx. (*CCR*)
2   One such performance took place in Paris where members of the audience absented themselves for an hour or two for supper and then returned to see how he was getting on.
3   *Treatise Handbook,* p.vii. (*CCR*)
4   Prévost, *No Sound Is Innocent,* p.107.
5   Not everyone would describe the piece exactly as Cardew does. However, if any musician could claim authenticity of performance of *'X' for Henry Flynt'* then it would have been Cardew (not forgetting David Tudor), and I would direct the reader to Cardew's essay 'On the Role of the Instructions in the Interpretation of Indeterminate Music' in the *Treatise Handbook,* pp.xiv-xvi, in which he refers to it, p.xiv, as 'a remarkable case of a piece that consists of no notations, and performing instructions that no one can agree upon'. (*CCR*)
6   Keith Rowe, interview with Kenneth Ansell, *The Wire,* No. 11, January 1985.
7   'Stockhausen's *Plus-Minus',* London Magazine,* April 1967, p.89. (*CCR*)
8   According to Stella Cardew her husband was in awe of La Monte Young's guru-like persona; he was an admirer, rather than a friend, and was gratified if Young showed him any recognition.
9   'One Sound: La Monte Young', from the *Musical Times,* November 1966, pp.959-60. Again, we are reminded of Wittgenstein who insisted that something was indicated by the propensity of human beings to talk nonsense. (*CCR*)
10   D. Pears, *Wittgenstein,* p.179.
11   John Gosling was a fine art student at the Kingston School of Art in the mid-sixties.
12   Ludwig Wittgenstein, *Lectures and Conversations on Aesthetics, Psychology and Religious Belief* (Oxford: Blackwell, 1966), p.7.
13   Ibid., p.11.
14   In the seventies this view would be severely compromised, though not entirely jettisoned, by the encroachments of Party morality.
15   'Conversations without Stravinsky', in *Give My Regards to Eighth Street, Collected Writings of Morton Feldman,* ed. by B.H. Friedman (Cambridge, Mass: Exact Change, 2000), p.52.
16   Letter to Skempton dated 17 May 1967.
17   From a recorded conversation with the author sometime in the nineties; neither of us can remember either year or location.
18   Ibid.
19   Ibid.
20   *Treatise Handbook,* p.xx. (*CCR*)
21   Jrnl. 28 April 1967.
22   In fact the second part of the text, which I do not include here, was used more or less verbatim in the *Treatise Handbook,* p.xx, to describe the sixth 'virtue': *Identification with nature.* (*CCR*)
23   In Wittgenstein's *Lectures and Conversations on Aesthetics* [...], p.8 footnote 3, which Cardew would doubtless have read, James Taylor paraphrases a Wittgenstein remark which is particularly apposite here.
24   Wittgenstein, *Lectures and Conversations on Aesthetics, Psychology and Religious Belief,* p.27.

25   Hobbs recalls that the attempted expulsion came about when some of the group distributed Chairman Mao's Little Red Book in the student common room.

26   *Lectures and Conversations*, p.27.

27   Ibid. p.28.

28   The artist/writer Stefan Szczelkun, later to become a member of the Scratch Orchestra, makes a similar and more general observation on Western Art music: 'music lost its social connection in two ways: First local accents accruing to music were wiped out. The music was no longer in flux and could not respond to changing conditions. It became inert and bound up with a romantic bourgeois identity. Secondly, as the Aesthetic was elaborated it required increasing technical skill to perform which required highly trained professional musicians. Music production was therefore dissected from social life and moved to State academies. The aesthetic concept of musical excellence moved out of the realm of common experience.' '25 Years from Scratch' in *Noisegate* Vol 1 No 10 (London ISSN 1367613X, 2002), pp.21-29.

29   From the aforementioned draft lecture, 12 September 1967.

30   Ibid.

31   The concert took place in the Embassy auditorium, and according to Elliot Schwartz, to whom I am grateful for bringing this event to my attention, was very well attended.

32   I am surmising; I do not recall Cardew ever expressing these views, but I believe they would have been in character at the time.

33   Richard Kostelanetz, *Conversing with Cage* (Omnibus Press, 1989), p. 265.

34   From 'A trial involving sexual morality' quoted by Frank Field in *Karl Kraus and his Vienna* (London: Macmillan, 1967), p.56.

35   The Anti-University, an off-shoot of the Free School in New York, was founded early in 1968. It was set up in seven rooms in 49 Rivington Street which were rented from the Bertrand Russell Peace Foundation. Artists, sociologists, politicians across the Left spectrum were represented: anarchist, anti-academic, anti-establishment.

36   The Weathermen was an anarchist group which first appeared in Chicago, June 1969, at an SDS (Students for a Democratic Society) conference; they were associated with bombings in Chicago and New York later in 1969 and early in 1970.

37   Focus Opera Group (1963-1975) was founded by Michael Sargent; the aim was to put on three or four small-scale contemporary opera or music theatre productions each year, mainly in London.

38   Morley College, situated near Waterloo Station in south-east London, was, and still is, a much respected and admired Adult Education establishment which boasts a strong musical tradition. Amongst its musical Directors and teachers can be counted the composers Peter Racine Fricker and Alexander Goehr, and the pianist and Controller of Music at the BBC, William Glock.

39   Somehow his composition class at the Academy continued but after the foundation of the Scratch Orchestra, from the Autumn term1969, Penny Jordan seems to have been his only student.

40   In Christopher Hobbs recollection the sequence, if not the content, was different: 'At least for the first six months the classes began with improvisation, the idea being that as you arrived so you joined in. [As was to be the case with the Scratch Orchestra meetings.] I think this period was followed by Cardew talking – parish notices, that kind of thing'.

Email communication from Christopher Hobbs to JT, dated 20 October 2005.

41 Some thirty years on Carole Finer now plays the banjo reasonably well and with great enthusiasm, attending banjo players' conventions as far away as Nevada in the US. Her experiences at Morley College seem to have done her no harm, may even have been the catalyst for her subsequent and lasting commitment to the instrument.

42 And by contrast, on another evening, Cardew performed a number of Howard Skempton's piano pieces including *A Card for Hilary* (a young lady whom Skempton admired), *September Song, A Humming Song, Loop No.4 and Music for Clavichord*.

43 Tim Mitchell recalls 'being very enthusiastic about apparently inconsequential things. Cornelius set us a task at Morley College to prepare and present some meaningless activity. I remember Howard [Skempton] counting – up to something like 5000, I think. It was like being given a new freedom – permission to put a great deal of time and energy into something which had no meaning beyond itself'. From the programme for '25 years from Scratch', an event celebrating the twenty fifth anniversary of the Scratch Orchestra. It took place on 20 November 1994 at the Institute of Contemporary Arts in London and was presented by the London Musicians' Collective.

44 According to Skempton Cardew was 'more impressed by that piece than he was by any piece of mine before or since' (from a conversation with J.T.) and it subsequently became a great favourite with the Scratch Orchestra, a feature of many Scratch events. *Drum No.1* also appears in the *Nature Study Notes*, the first of 152 rites.

45 Christopher Hobbs, as quoted by Virginia Anderson in *British Experimental Music: Cornelius Cardew and His Contemporaries*, Master of Music thesis, The University of Redlands, California, August 1983, p.52.

46 From a typewritten sheet headed 'Agenda for the meeting on July 1st 1969'.

47 In the Journals the draft introduction to *Schooltime Compositions* contains a reference to Bob Woolford's participation in the first performance at International Students House, which is omitted in the printed edition of the work: 'The equipment used by Woolford in his interpretation was high fidelity stereophonic recording equipment including radio microphones and hence the tapes made by him are a legitimate by-product of the composition.'

48 She (Anita Brookner) might be referring to the 'superiority' of Art in relation to the mundanity, and often the banality of life (actual living) itself and its (Art) ambitions towards the transcendent. Or/and she might be echoing Schoenberg's famous dictum: if a work 'is art, it is not for all, and if it is for all, it is not art'. As for subversion, I take it this refers to the (Adornite) notion of art as a 'worm of subversion'. That is, that whilst the presence and high profile of Art in a society is regarded as a measure of the degree of 'civilisation' that society has attained, at the same time Art can (should) be a destabilizing element, creating discomfort, challenging received orthodoxies.

49 *The Wire*, February 1995.

50 The event was tape-recorded, insofar as such an event can be recorded, by Harry Peter Wilson-Wright, who aptly described this invaluable documentation as 'my silent contribution to the event'.

51 Michael Nyman, *Experimental Music* (London: Studio Vista, 1974), p.101.

52 Jrnl. undated, but sometime during 1968.

53 *Musical Times*, 'Sitting in the Dark', March 1968. (*CCR*)

54   As performance art there is an obvious debt to Fluxus where the subject matter was creativity itself. Cardew had organised and participated in Fluxus-inspired events from the early sixties. Some of the *Schooltime* pieces bear resemblances to the Fluxus repertoire, not least in their symbiosis of playfulness and seriousness of intent (cf. the Scratch Orchestra).

55   *Musical Times*, 'Sitting in the Dark'. (*CCR*)

56   What is a 'bamer'? Presumably some kind of receptacle. At the time of publication I had still not uncovered the mystery of its substance and provenance.

57   Roland Barthes, 'The Grain of the Voice', in *Image – Music – Text*, (London: Fontana/Collins), p.189.

58   In the first performance *Vocals* was performed by a small chorus directed by Michael Graubart.

59   *Musical Times*, 'Sitting in the Dark'. (*CCR*)

(*CCR*) Also found in *Cornelius Cardew A Reader*

9

The Scratch Orchestra 1969

The history of music took a whole new direction with the Scratch Orchestra. That movement carried along everyone who participated in the Scratch. No one was untouched by it. It crystallised a mood for change of its times, and in turn changed the direction of lives. Its function as a musical construct for changing people's lives abides in the memory and is imprinted in the musical culture.[1]

Scratch Orchestra Meetings

After the first rehearsal at St. Katharine's Dock on 30 September 1969 the Scratch Orchestra began to meet at The Place, a versatile building which AMM had also used.[2] The first group of Scratch Orchestra concerts was preceded by a number of 'playing sessions' where tentative explorations into Scratch music were initiated and where the form and content of the forthcoming events was discussed and decided upon. These took place in Studio 6 at The Place, in Duke's Road, opposite Euston station, on Monday evenings from 6 to 8pm, starting on 13 October and continuing through to the end of November. The first four meetings in 1970 were also held there and it was used intermittently until the summer of 1971 when a room in the Lamb and Flag pub in Covent Garden was rented.

A simple procedure was adopted whereby each member of the Orchestra, starting with the youngest and ending with the oldest, devised a concert.[3] And it would be incumbent upon him or her to determine the venue, content and essential nature of the event, to which every individual member would have been expected to give their full support, both materially and morally, however excessive, or outrageous, the demands on mental and physical stamina might have appeared to be. In fact, there was initially some resistance to the idea that the first programmes should be decided by the youngest members. Cardew, however, expressed his reluctance to drop the idea of some privilege accruing to youth; furthermore, did other, older members want to programme concerts anyway? 'Personally', he wrote on a scrap of paper dated 20 October 1969, 'I prefer to keep the rule'. 'So do I' added Michael Parsons and the rule was carried, if by default; nobody came up with a better idea.

At Scratch Orchestra meetings, from the outset, the role of words was delimited to a clearly defined, practical purpose – that of determining and discussing the nature and content of a forthcoming event, which may or may not have involved actual rehearsal ('playing'). The sessions were focused and purposeful with only the occasional brief skirmish – usually on purely technical matters. An outsider would have been impressed by the diligence and resoluteness with which the Scratch Orchestra went about its organizational business; there was no time, nor inclination, for pettifogging. Where there was disagreement there had to be compromise, and in this respect members did not always defer to Cardew's wishes. (In performance, of course, this clarity of purpose would often give way to an engaging spirit of improvidence).

The agenda for each meeting was invariably set by Cardew who would sit with a hand-written list of points to be raised and discussed. Many of these 'agendas', often scruffy pieces of rough paper, have survived in various cardboard files and demonstrate not only the extent of Cardew's commitment to the Scratch Orchestra but, more significantly, his control over all aspects of Scratch commerce: thus, he would concern himself not only with the overall artistic content of projects and the long-term planning of the Orchestra's future, but he would also undertake the most menial tasks, including routine administrative duties (for which, it must be said, there was never a shortage of volunteers), with a sharp eye for the inconspicuous, the smallest detail. And in all these accretions of duties he was admirably methodical and painstaking.

Howard Skempton has drawn attention to Cardew's astonishing industry in the early weeks and months of the Scratch Orchestra during which time he worked selflessly, without concession. Apart from the Draft Constitution he initiated the *Nature Study Notes*, which involved an enormous amount of work – writing out all the Improvisation Rites and preparing them for publication; the eventual form of the *Scratch Music* book was also his own design. These were all key contributions which have become part of Scratch Orchestra mythology and it redounds to his credit that he never made heavy weather of it (at least, he never gave this impression); perhaps he was unwilling to delegate responsibility for a highly personal, artistic project by which he had set such great store. And at the same time, and to which I have already referred, there were the more mundane matters, such as sending out newsletters to all the members (if somebody turned up to a meeting they were automatically put on the mailing list).

A Scratch meeting would invariably begin with a low burden of continuous playing – often, but not always nor in every individual case, of an improvisatory nature, into which the innocent latecomer would merge spontaneously and discreetly. This was known as Scratch Music, a discreet music-making which exemplified the Scratch philosophy and was a conscious antithesis to the sixties fashion of attention-seeking and worldly blandishment.

The Repertoire

The Scratch Orchestra repertoire constituted a mental and emotional pabulum for its members, and from the minds and imaginations of these free-spirited people the Scratch Repertoire poured forth – even if, as we have seen, Cardew himself had attempted to circumscribe it by means of his proposal of 'Categories'. At the time, an abundance of contrasting trends and movements were introduced and represented democratically, and on an equal footing, and it seemed unlikely that the Scratch Orchestra's programme would get bogged down in artistic internecine conflict where one faction would be played off against another. And yet right from the outset the Draft Constitution was regarded by some members, and outsiders, as a controlling ploy, a 'composition' within which the seeds of its own destruction had been sown. Let us consider each of the five categories in turn: Scratch Music, Improvisation Rites, Compositions, Popular Classics, and Research Project.

Scratch Music

Tune a brook by moving the stones in it.

JN15 (John Nash's rite) on page S from *Scratch Music.*[4]

As we have seen, a Scratchbook and Scratch Music were ideas which Cardew had put forward at the very first Scratch Orchestra meeting at St. Katherine's Dock. For some members, but probably less than half, the Scratch Book was important because it represented the visual and literary area of the Orchestra's activity,[5] although non-musical representation was in fact present in other categories as well – in the Improvisation Rites, for example, and in the Research projects in particular. A Scratchbook was intended as a kind of *vade mecum* which accompanied one on every occasion:

> Your Scratchbook is your own personal, private document, and as such anything at all can go in it. However, the original idea of a Scratchbook was that it should contain Scratch Music at one end and Research at the other.
> The aim of the Scratchbooks was to establish concern and continuity […] [Scratch Music is] thoughtful, reflective, regular, treasuring the transitory idea; it is also about privacy and self-sustenance.
> Scratch Music – its performance – is about 'live and let live', peaceful

cohabitation, contributing to society, meaningless and meaningful work, play, meditation, relaxation.[6]

Scratch Music, in Cardew's view, was 'good for the soul,' and that, essentially, was its *raison d'être*.

Yet there never was a 'pure' Scratch Music in the sense of Cardew's definition in the Draft Constitution, which was far too prescriptive for most Scratch Orchestra members. Cardew's somewhat ambitious and ultimately unrealistic idea was that every day each individual would notate something which carried the potential to generate a 'musical' performance (he himself was probably the only member of the Scratch Orchestra to have followed such a rigorous and demanding routine to the letter);[7] Scratch Music, as an emanation from the Scratch Book, was short-lived and was superseded by a freer improvisational mode unencumbered with the notational (accompanimental) prescription which Cardew had written into the Draft Constitution. Yet its influence was far-reaching, and without it the Scratch Orchestra would never have achieved its uniqueness.

In particular, Scratch Music exemplified the idea, the ideal, of collective music-making, of shared experience, within which the individual voice would gain confidence and blossom; it was aptly described as a kind of 'training' programme for those who wished to participate in the Scratch Orchestra. Scratch Music was essentially a hybrid consisting of various improvisational and semi-improvisational modes, and as such it was one of the most characteristic of Scratch Orchestra activities. Leafing through the pages of *Scratch Music,* visual images and recollections spring to the mind's eye, and there are constant reminders of *Schooltime Compositions*, the indisputable 'mother' of Scratch Music (vide p.384 below, and 'Improvisation Rites' for an explanation of the 'mother' reference).[8]

'Notated' Scratch Music was a compendium of notations which initiated or embodied some kind of performance of an accompanimental or soloistic nature. Bryn Harris succinctly defines the original Scratch music as 'an exercise in a compositional approach to music'. And yet, conversely, Scratch Music was also a subtle and effective way of weaning composers off notation, liberating them from the insidious influence of the five-line stave. Scratch Music had enormous potential; it was the progenitor of many musical styles and phenomena which followed it; it was a sharing, subtly ambient music to which the listener could attend with varying degrees of focus. The flightiness of its details concealed an underlying seriousness of which even its members were not wholly conscious. Hugh Shrapnel recalls:

Scratch Music was often strikingly beautiful. There was a Scratch Orchestra *sound* which was unmistakeable – the result of many individuals 'doing their own thing' (in '60s parlance), but united by a common purpose; no self-indulgent egoists, but a community of people each contributing his or her sound on an equal footing to the whole.[9] The result was a complex and delicate polyphony of noises and notes. This fine balance between individual purpose and collective will in the Scratch Orchestra is perhaps a clue to the subtle and searching character of Scratch Music at its best.[10]

Cardew stressed the accompanimental nature of each notation but also its potential as solo material. In other words the individual had to be conscious of the needs of others whilst being prepared to strike out alone, to take a lead.

Cardew contributed seventy-four examples to the anthology in *Scratch Music;* these date from 29 May 1969 to 4 December 1970 and there were certainly many more, both within this period and subsequently. According to the dated list in *Scratch Music* some twenty of these were conceived in May/June 1969, in other words prior to the formation of the Scratch Orchestra and when he was preparing the 'draft constitution' for publication in the June edition of the *Musical Times*.

The lineage linking Cardew's Scratch Music with *Schooltime Compositions* is clear; groups of the examples in *Scratch Music* are generically connected to individual pieces from their progenitor. The practical procedures associated with the creation of art objects, drawings, assemblages, collages, 'mechanical devices' – and involving glue, paint, sellotape, crayon, proofing paper, etc. – are rife, in fact one third are of this kind; while another third relates specifically to sound and musical notation, to musical colleagues and influences. The remaining third comprises maxims, tropes, solitary words, of an abstract, speculative nature; in all there are references to an astonishing variety of human psychology and commerce.[11] Here are just five examples of Cardew's Scratch Music:

Examples:

1) CC16 20.6.69 Glued on: A plane tree leaf pointing downwards, maybe 2 cms across. **Content** Under a plane tree. (audible) Wind. (audible) Thought.[12]

2) The following is Cardew's description of a piece of his own Scratch music, still unrecovered.

CC43 21.8.69 Between two pages about a dozen leaves from a diseased tree, each leaf in a different stage of decay. The two pages are taped together with masking tape.

Content Progress of a disease. Progress of a mechanical thought. Progress of
a consuming love. (the following is added in pencil) plus: progress of a calculation
error / progress of a lying word / progress of a mesalliance / progress of a vendetta
/ progress of a destroying fire / progress of an erosion (These not readily
performable except as film, projections, etc.)
Irreversible processes[13]

3) Scratch Music 14.1.72

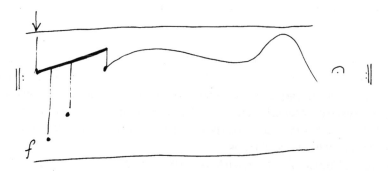

↓ = cue, alternately from an event in the environment
and from a sound from another player.
The figure needn't be identical each time.

4) CC52 14.9.69 Content[14]

Virtuosity

Develop a skill

Legerdemain

eg. in the handling of a sledgehammer

Able		properly
	to do something	more or less
Unable		not at all

5) CC29 21.7.69 Content Find or make a peak or vantage point. Survey past and future from it.[15]

Disappointingly, at the date of completion of this book only six more examples have come to light; these are dated from 27 September 1971 to 11 February 1972, which suggests that they were among the last, if not *the* last, that Cardew wrote. Example 3 above belongs to this group.

Improvisation Rites

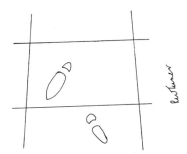

BH25 (Bryn Harris's rite) from *Scratch Music* , page O.[16]

Cardew's collection of Scratch Rites was invariably referred to as Nature Study Notes; this was because the original hard-back exercise book in which the various Rites were gathered and to which everybody was encouraged to contribute, was, like *Schooltime Compositions*, from an English educational source and bore the title *Nature Study Notes* – a not entirely inappropriate title either. In fact, as we have seen, the Improvisation Rites originated in the Morley College class, so that some of the rites predate the Scratch Orchestra: for example, the second rite in *Nature Study Notes*, CCIR2:

Initiate an improvisation in the following way: All seated loosely in a circle, each player shall write or draw on each of the ten fingernails of the player on his left. No action or sound is to be made by a player after his fingernails have received this writing or drawing other than music.

This was Cardew's rite although it was 'fathered' (see below) by Richard Reason's 'Games for Musicians'.

Although Cardew divided the Scratch repertoire into categories, in performance these categories invariably overlapped and merged; Scratch Music might have been mistaken for an Improvisation Rite which might have been mistaken for a Composition (even though Cardew insisted, in the Draft Consitution, that 'an improvisation rite is not a musical composition; it does not attempt to influence the music that will be played; at most it may establish a community of feeling, or a communal starting-point, through ritual'), and Popular Classics were more often than not simply unrecognizable. The archaic nature of many of the rites, their innocence and quaintness, enhances the idea of lineage, as if the Rites are, indeed, part of a 'folk tradition'; many of them are

> accompanied by a pedigree naming one or more of the following: the Mother (her initials are at the head of the code name), who wrote it down as a rite; the Father (F), who provided the idea; any other relatives the Mother sees fit to recall; and an Ancestor (A) or Archetype, identifying the basic human or non-human state, activity or event the rite bears on.[17]

Thus, (mother) Bryn Harris's Improvisation Rite BHBR140 reads as follows: 'Have a battle. (Try to avoid fatalities).' In the 'Notes' section at the back of *Nature Study Notes* the explanation reads: '[...] Father: Beethoven. Ancestry: Military music.' (140 is the number of the Rite in the *Nature Study Notes* collection).

If the Improvisation Rites were Cardew's idea they were certainly 'fathered' by Confucius. In Chinese humanistic philosophy the combination of Rites (*li*) and music were essential to the regulation of man's behaviour and emotion:

> The early kings were careful about that which might affect the heart. They instituted *li* to guide the mind and music to harmonise the sound, the government to unify the actions, and penalties to restrain the evils.[...] To know music is to be versed in *li*. One who knows music and is versed in *li* is said to possess virtue; virtue is but music and *li*.[18]

The Rites varied between the elaborate and time-consuming, and the minimal: the New Zealander Philip Dadson's Rite, for example, consisting simply of the prescription that everybody should shout the word 'porridge'. And not a few of the Scratch Rites embody a moralistic view:

> If you have something to give, give it. Don't hesitate to give, yet choose the time or space.
> If you have nothing to give, receive. By receiving, you are under no obligation to give, yet it is better to give than to receive. Stop making music when you please, but don't stop giving.[19]

The ritualistic elements in *The Great Learning* and in Cardew's contributions to AMM music have already been referred to; in the Scratch Orchestra these 'ceremonial' procedures, which could be either stimulating or restraining – or both, certainly deepened the feeling of community, of awareness of, and respect for, others. Most importantly, the Rites were acts not only of self-communion, but of communion with the past; Psi Ellison went so far as to regard them as the regeneration, renewal and development of an urban folk art. They were, as it were, reliquaries for ancient thoughts and dispositions whose echoes and resonances found expression in the ludic, as well as the poetic impulses which seem to have inspired many of the Rites, such as Bob Guy's Red Indian Rite (BGRIR63): 'The group chooses a suitable outdoor site and waits for rain. Meanwhile improvisation takes place in an attempt to induce rainfall.' And Hugh Shrapnel's rite: 'Sit Tight Rite Tonite.' And on 31 July 1971 Brian Dormer Taylor, of Surbiton, whom so far nobody can recall, typed in the middle of a white sheet of A4: 'Make a flute out of the bones of sadness. Play a brittle tune of subtle melancholy'. And I can remember at least one performance of Howard Skempton's Big Leader Rite (HSIR8):

The group assembles, one of the members being elected BIG LEADER. When there is silence, the BIG LEADER makes a sound, as short and quiet as possible. He is then challenged, the challenging member attempting to produce a sound even shorter and more quiet than the first. In the midst of great celebration the challenger becomes BIG LEADER.
The process then continues until all members have had a chance of becoming BIG LEADER. The challenger who last becomes BIG LEADER is named as the SUPER BIG LEADER. There is great celebration; drinking, music, etc.

Subsequent to the relative popularity of Skempton's Rite the following conventions arose, possibly according to Scratch performance practices: '1. Any challenge must first be announced. 2. It is generally accepted that the challenger always wins. 3. Nobody is allowed to become BIG LEADER more than once.'[20]

In Cardew's own Rites there are many references to *The Great Learning* – the compositions in Paragraph 5, the invitation to solo improvisation in Paragraph 4, among others. Any paragraph from *The Great Learning* might be mistaken for an 'Improvisation Rite', although little of *The Great Learning* and relatively few Rites might be mistaken for 'free improvisation', even if, in a flush of realism, Cardew concedes at the end of his definition of Improvisation Rites that 'free improvisation may also be indulged in from time to time'(just as it is in Paragraph 5). A large number of the Rites, like the BIG LEADER rite, are prescriptive and organised, like games and some of Christian Wolff's music.

Perhaps more than any other category the Improvisation Rites characterised the essential nature of the Orchestra. And Scratch Music? Is this why Cardew wrote, in the latter part of 1970:

> Think about: Rites and Scratch Music are vessels that catch ideas that would in the normal course of events be thrown away and forgotten, sometimes definitely rejected. So should they be discontinued? Does this depend only on their usefulness?[21]

Just as in the Scratch Orchestra there was an extraordinary admixture of discipline and indiscipline, so in the Rites periods of extreme quiet and concentration would be juxtaposed with behaviour of a riotous nature, as at the end of the Big Leader Rite.

Compositions

Following the founding of the Scratch Orchestra there was a rapid accumulation of compositions and it was Scratch policy that every contribution should receive due consideration and, invariably, at least one performance. The Scratch compositions tended to be motivated primarily by social considerations; notations would be brief and to the point, no frills – capable of being grasped by musicians and non-musicians alike.

At the end of a circular letter to Scratch Orchestra members at the beginning of 1970 Cardew wrote: 'A small prize (5 Weights[22]) is offered for information leading to the identification of the composer of *The Balkan Sobranie Smoking Mixture* performed at Ealing [Town Hall] on December 6th.' The composer was the nineteen year-old Greg Bright, of a lugubrious, bleached look, and a connoisseur of good tobacco. The piece was a vocal/speaking composition which became a Scratch favourite. Bright's compositions were much admired by Orchestra members; they were original, appealing, and displayed an irresistible quirkiness. Some of us, including Cardew, thought he was, or could have become, a talented composer.[23]

In fact, he went into designing mazes, which he would not have regarded as separate from his Scratch activities, as a letter to Cardew, dated 21 April 1971, indicates. At the time he was designing and digging a maze somewhere in the vicinity of Glastonbury in Somerset and the letter is a charming, humorous description of his toils in the Wiltshire soil – an account which must surely have warmed the cockles of Cornelius's heart:

> Dear Cornelius, I enclose, please find a piece of Scratch Music (The Labyrinth) and a composition – 'Labyrinth II'.[24] The Labyrinth is suitable to be used in conjunction with 'Labyrinth II'. Yesterday and all last night it pissed down. Trickles

of water entered the tent. Yesterday I didn't even shift a spadeful. It was all paperwork. I drew some of the Labyrinth and wrote some more 'Labyrinth I'. I enjoyed immensely a hot cup of Horlicks. Sardines today.[…] Today the 'Grateful Dead' paid a visit to my dig. They interrupted a melodic line I was piecing together as I broke the turf. Consequently it's flown from my mind… Lord! A Health and Heather. Tricky to roll, but a smoke of such charm and delicacy. A smoke in a million. I recall reading a book by Jagjit Singh. (Dr Jagjit Singh, General Manager of the South Eastern Railway, Calcutta, was born at Amritsar in 1912).[…] I think today's day 10. What's happened? Well, for one thing there's been the horse eating my tent but today I built with tremendous effort a long trench about 50 feet right across to keep them out.

In Labyrinth II a paper labyrinth is placed on the head of a large drum. A 'Tracer', using a match stick, traces his or her way through the labyrinth. This is done without pause or break so that the eyes may water and the forehead sweat. A group of 'Watchers' watch and listen to the Tracer's activity, occasionally sipping from a glass of water, closing their eyes in concentration. One of the 'Watchers' signals the passing of time with an occasional sound, such as from a gong, but in any case suitable to the proceedings.

Such a 'composition' – with its original setting, its accommodation of bodily functions, in this case drinking, its quietly focused but unobtrusive sounds, its ritualistic flavour, exemplifies the essence of the Scratch ethos. And there were a number of compositions by non-Scratch composers which Scratch members found especially congenial. One such piece was the Japanese composer Toshi Ichiyanagi's *Distance*, in which performers would separate themselves from their instruments and with considerable ingenuity contrive to operate them.[25]

And yet, for the idealists in the Orchestra – those of us who regarded the Scratch Orchestra as a magic carpet which transported us into other worlds – 'composition' represented an outmoded aesthetic, too closely associated with the idea of prestige and proprietorial kudos. Composition for us was at best no more than a springboard, one of many, for 'musical' activity. A handful of compositions did catch the imagination, or were encouragingly negotiable for all, and they would become Scratch 'repertoire'. One such work was Michael Parsons' *Mindfulness of Breathing*, a Buddhist meditation in which a low sung drone accompanied length-of-breath tones spanning a perfect fifth.[26] The use of the voice was exploited to the full in a number of contrasting compositions: *Mindfulness of Breathing*, for example, would pair, in satisfying fashion, with Howard Skempton's *Fish Talk*: 'Breathe in silently. In breathing out, produce distortions. Lips/tongue hard/soft long/short. If appropriate, kiss.'

Skempton's *Drum No.1*, quoted above, received enough performances to warrant inclusion in the Popular Classics category. Its popularity was understandable, for *Drum No.1*, in a sense, was emblematic of every Scratch performance, embedding individual predilection and choice within a reassuring collective. And there were simple compositions by members to whom conventional musical notation was not a complete mystery, like Diane Jackman's *Cottleston Pie/Pooh Music No.2* for voice, strings and oboe. Some of the composers contrived, often successfully, to involve and incorporate the multifarious skills and aptitudes of the whole Orchestra. Michael Chant's *Beautiful Music* was such a composition in which the choice of playing 'any drone' is offered to 'anyone', and appropriate material is offered to 'music readers' and to 'music non-readers', as well as the opportunity for anyone to provide on percussion the sound of 'crashing thunder'.

Cardew's Note at the beginning of the Draft Constitution was etched in the minds of the majority of Scratch members:

> The word music and its derivatives are here not understood to refer exclusively to sound and related phenomena (hearing, etc.). What they do refer to is flexible and depends entirely on the members of the Scratch Orchestra.[27]

Hence, for example, Carole Finer's *Magic Carpet* enjoins the Orchestra to 'hover, rest, fly, move away from the ground'. No reference to sound here.

CF7 on page T from 'Scratch Music'.

However, nearly all members of the Scratch Orchestra possessed sound-producing objects or instruments of some description and, as I recall, enjoyed and exploited the opportunity to focus their attention and actions on the production of sounds. Chris Robbins' *pocket music* stipulates instruments that are small enough to fit into a pocket: kazoo, jews harp, recorder mouthpiece, etc. And many compositions accommodated this proclivity for sound-making with small instruments and objects which most members shared.

Throughout its brief but charitable existence the Scratch Orchestra assembled an impressive inventory of unusual instruments and sound-producing objects; toy instruments, in particular, were popular – emblematic, perhaps, of the child-like innocence of the Scratch Orchestra, especially in the early days. And if the compositions were occasionally outrageous – like Alan Brett's *Whoopee!* – they were usually viable, if only to the Scratch Orchestra. (In *Whoopee!* the performers are asked to jump up and down, only making sounds while airborne.) Often, composers would take into account the context of performance, including location, which was rarely a concert hall, and their notations would encompass manifold opportunities for far-reaching spatial projections of sound, in time and space: 'Performing area should preferably be quiet, spacious and irregular in shape. A church or cathedral would be ideal', Hugh Shrapnel writes at the end of his *Space-Time Music*.

Not all the Scratch compositions were indeterminate; there were a number of pieces written for various string ensembles – conventionally notated compositions conceived for the small number of competent string players in the Orchestra or for other musicians who could read music and possessed instrumental skills. Ed Fulton's *Violin Music 5* for solo violin and piano, for example, is a sophisticated, Feldmanesque piece which only performers versed in contemporary music would be able to negotiate. Pieces such as this and Christopher Hobbs' *String Trio* were performed in Scratch Concerts but their inclusion demanded an awareness of the context in which they could reasonably function. These 'traditional' scores, including those that were fairly easy to read and perform, received relatively few performances; many of the Scratch members were either unable or unwilling to involve themselves in 'reading' of this kind. In any case, for alert ears and eyes there were all manner of visual stimuli which surpassed the cramping hieroglyphics scattered about manuscript paper. In general, the status of Scratch compositions (except, it must be said, for *The Great Learning*) was no different to that of the other categories in the Draft Constitution, although one or two, such as *Drum No.1* and, briefly, Ketelbey's *Bells across the Meadows*, did achieve talismanic status and were therefore performed more frequently. The singer for the latter – I am fairly certain it was a Scratch concert in Cornwall – wore a red rose against a black dress and waxed suitably sentimental. Cardew did not approve; I suspect he found it trivial.

Popular Classics

On 7 July 1969 Cardew wrote:

> The Popular Classics idea is directed against a certain class of music lovers, aiming to outrage or otherwise awaken them. It represents an aggressive invitation to those who are saturated with the classics to the exclusion of the New to change their ways. (see p.255 of SBC (Sacred Books of Confucius): 'If music is delightful

and charming, it is dangerous, then the people will be riotous and negligent, mean and low.')[28]

The Popular Classics was in fact a relatively neglected, possibly undervalued category, even if it did provide some of the most exuberant and hilarious moments in the Scratch Orchestra's history. Perhaps the Scratch members felt intimidated by it; we recall that in the Morley College class no one would confess to being a 'music lover'. If such an attitude prevailed then it is highly unlikely that even a particle, a shred of a page of Brahms' Requiem, let alone Schoenberg's Pierrot Lunaire, would have found its way into a Scratch concert. There would have been an inhibiting degree of ignorance in relation to the music of Schoenberg, and probably Brahms, too, amongst the majority of the Orchestra, and those of us who were familiar with the works of Schoenberg would have harboured too much antipathy (or at least indifference) towards them at that time to have contemplated a creative interpretation in a Scratch event. Only those works with pizazz – such as Tchaikovsky's 1812 Overture or Piano Concerto No.1 would have inspired, and indeed did inspire the Scratch Orchestra into a posthumous collaboration: on 4 December 1970, at the Purcell Room, the Scratch Orchestra, with myself as soloist, presented the Tchaikovsky concerto. Simultaneously, we performed Hugh Shrapnel's Houdini Rite so that the problems we had with the virtuosic demands of the Concerto were compounded by the fact that we were bound hand and foot.[29] I was on stage battling manfully against the odds while the Orchestra, sitting in the audience, gamely and sportingly accompanied me. The 'particle' was a recording of those infamous opening bars which bellowed out into the arena. As the first phrase moved inexorably to the apocalyptic entry of the soloist I recall the crescendo of tinkling and whistling, abetted by Michael Nyman's trombone obligato, as the Orchestra, once again, strove to rise to the occasion.

According to Cardew, the category of Popular Classics was 'fathered' by Michael Chant. Chant regards (still) Cardew as the 'father'; he, Chant, was the 'mother'. An exchange of letters between Cardew and Chant fails to provide a conclusive answer. We are none the wiser.[30]

Research Project

Although in the Draft Constitution more space is devoted to this category ('an activity obligatory for all members') than any others, Cardew harboured doubts and misgivings about it:

Research is a function of intellect and so has little to do with music on the face of it [...] It would be wrong to abandon it entirely: exercise of the intellect is by no means something that musicians can dispense with.[31]

The educative function of the Research Project, at least in Cardew's mind, is evident from the Draft Constitution, in which its inclusion, according to Cardew, is 'to ensure its [the Scratch Orchestra's] cultural expansion'. But his insistence on imagination and experience in the conduct of research, rather than 'the mechanical accumulation of data', was probably superfluous; members of the Scratch Orchestra could not have proceeded otherwise.

The first Scratch event to be based on a Research Project was conceived by the American artist and friend of Cardew, George Brecht, and was entitled 'Journey of the Isle of Wight Westwards by Iceberg to Tokyo Bay'. It was performed at the Chelsea Town Hall on 15 November 1969. Michael Parsons, one of the participants, describes the Journey:

This was inspired by a proposal from Brecht & McDiarmid Research Associates for the translocation of land masses by harnessing them to icebergs, the latest in an increasingly ambitious series of 'translocation and delivery' projects on which Brecht had been working during the 1960s [...] The Scratch Orchestra's response to this proposal was a performance made up of a dense texture of divergent strands of aural and visual activity derived from the research of individual participants. Brecht himself delivered a lecture on various relevant geographical, oceanographical, sociological, economic and other aspects to be taken into consideration. Christopher Hobbs tolled a deep bell at regular intervals to warn of the island's progress. A collective painting on a long paper scroll evolved in response to the sounds of the performance, in reversal of the usual relationship between music and visual stimulus of a graphic score such as *Treatise*.[32]

Bryn Harris recalls Frank Regan and Roger Wright perambulating with their Uher tape recorder, generating feedback by pointing the microphone at the monitor speaker. Birgit Burkhardt was painting at the back of the hall and a duck call occasionally punctuated the proceedings. There was joyous celebration when the equator was crossed.

For some, like Michael Parsons, the Research Project had enormous potential which was not realised in the context of the Scratch Orchestra.[33] His own proposal for a Scratch Orchestra journey, for which his sole condition was that it should be 'undertaken in the spirit of the text', was regretfully and somewhat surprisingly not taken up, despite the provision of an introductory text which would surely have appealed to Scratch members' sensibilities:

> Danish clergymen had announced from their pulpits that to participate in expeditions to the North Pole would be beneficial for the eternal salvation of the soul. However they admitted that it was difficult and perhaps impossible to reach the Pole, and that not everyone could undertake such an adventure. Finally they announced that any journey – from Denmark to London, say, by ship – or a Sunday outing in a hackney coach, was in fact a real expedition to the North Pole.[34]

Early Performances

AUSTERE RITE

$$\text{Each player} = \tfrac{1}{2} \text{ a sound}$$

HWKempton

Skempton's 'Austere Rite' from 'The Book of Thoughts'.[35]

Scratch Orchestra performances consisted in the main of various assemblages of material derived from the Draft Constitution, and if they were invariably characterised by sound, they were rarely monopolised by it. Even the most frenetic sound activity would be offset, probably consciously, by visual presentations which would engage and stimulate the eyes of the audience.

Jackman's 'Symphony' from 'The Book of Thoughts'.

So there was always a certain amount of tension and contradiction between the musical and non-musical contributions. For the musicians what happened at Scratch Orchestra events was 'music' (we were, after all, an 'orchestra'), and as long as it was generally recognised as 'music' (which, with one or two exceptions, it probably was) they were prepared to stretch the boundaries to an almost limitless degree, it would seem. The question – 'is it music?' – could be answered, and usually in the affirmative, but on a purely subjective basis. In the publication *Scratch Music* Michael Chant suggests that the transition from 'activity' to 'music' takes place when 'a certain philosophical cast of mind' is present. But for the musicians a certain theoretical justification, borrowed in the main from John Cage, was necessary.

In his contribution to the programme for *25 Years from Scratch* Christopher Hobbs recalls:

The tapes I have heard of those early concerts give absolutely no idea of what it was really like to be there; and that pleases me. Even at the time it was obvious that merely listening to the sounds without being able to see their source (I think of Psi Ellison, soberly cranking up his gramophone for yet another rendition, on cracked 78, of 'You've got to have Money in the Bank, Frank'), or imagining those events which had no sound at all (I think of Birgit Burkhardt, festooned with small lights, inching her way around a terrifyingly narrow ledge high up in the gallery of the Round House) was a wasted exercise. Sorry, but you had to have been there. You can't eavesdrop on history in this case.

As a participant myself at this event, I do not recall Burkhardt's performance, and I suspect that each participant and each member of the audience would vividly recall different, unforgettable occurrences. We could agree only that a performance had taken place.

Despite their physical differences – differences of age of up to twenty years, differences in their individual attire and demeanour – on performance occasions the Scratch Orchestra would muster as a body, their diverse personalities masking a solidarity which, it seemed, could not be breached. The concerts were often quietly confessional, or acts of self-communion – the emotional tone subdued. The Scratch Orchestra was our work; our jobs were avocations. We would spread themselves across the performance area, sometimes knots of people strategically positioned depending on the requirements of the programme of events. And then we would, as it were, throw ourselves on the mercy of whatever audience there happened to be. And the venues at which the Scratch Orchestra played were as diverse and as unusual as the programmes we offered: churches and prisons, beaches and office blocks, the Festival Hall and the Derbyshire Peak District (on one occasion, and in appalling weather conditions), outside Caxton Hall for an Italian wedding, and incognito in the forecourt of Euston station during a power-workers' strike. Where fees were offered these were never distributed amongst the members of the Orchestra but by common consent were banked and used to promote further activities. The Scratch Orchestra did not set out to provide 'popular' music, but we did strive, in the most unorthodox ways, to *engage* people and to address their concerns, rather than their expectations. If our performances were often discreet, almost self-effacing in the way that we would husband the sounds which constituted our concerts, they could also be robust and exuberant, as the occasion or the piece demanded; Skempton's *Drum No.1*, for example, mentioned above, received many Dionysian renderings. For performance material the net was cast wide and the stuff of reality provided us with all our needs. The heuristic ethos of the Scratch Orchestra ensured an unpredictability in performance: a spontaneous, consensual flow of music, for example, might be punctuated by occasional, individual divagations into surprising territory, not necessarily of an aural nature, to which the response, if any, was never automatic or coordinated. Or a Scratch event, safely corralled within its own aesthetic, would modulate imperceptibly and dangerously into something unforeseen and beautiful, fuelled by an unshakeable belief in the authenticity of its utterances. Miraculously, an unwilled action, or a convergence of several unwilled actions would create something leading to discovery, even to revelation.

The Scratch Orchestra was unencumbered either with musical theory or, in many cases, with musical training of any kind. Objects, therefore, did duty for instruments; Daphne Simmons, an art student from the Kingston College of Art, would bring along a chiming, grandfather clock, and unerringly, at felicitous moments, she would release its tones, redolent of great grandparental memories – traces and evocations of a distant, anterior time. Or, brutally, the revving up of Psi Ellison's motorbike, brought defiantly into the performance space, would fracture the solemn near silence in which the performance had become enveloped. And the comb prongs neatly and briefly activated in George Brecht's *Comb Music*, a companion piece to the composition 'Plink' from Paragraph 5 of *The Great Learning*, recalling and contrasting with a more robust use of the comb (with paper) with which elderly gentlemen of a certain disposition might entertain their grandchildren. (Such is the versatility of the comb-instrument which the Scratch Orchestra exploited to the manner born.) As Christopher Hobbs has recalled: 'Whether delicate, soft and languorous in its quiet moments or amorphous, impenetrable and violent in its (more frequent) loud ones, Scratch Music, once experienced, was never to be forgotten.'[36]

The Scratch Orchestra was performance art *par excellence*; the anarchy and poetry of those extraordinary and often incomprehensible events defy documentation. To attempt to define the Scratch Orchestra in terms of 'what it played' would be a travesty, because the Scratch Orchestra transcended its repertoire; the very notion of individual composition, for example, was subverted and rendered meaningless. Like AMM the Scratch Orchestra would reify the most abstract and ephemeral notions into concrete sound. In its brief hey-day there was a transparency, a lucidity, which defied analysis, and even description.

Activities

It did not take long for some members of the Scratch Orchestra to break ranks; this took the form of an accumulation of what were known as 'Activities', 1001 of which are printed in Cardew's *Scratch Music* publication. 'Activities' did not constitute a 'category' in the original Draft Constitution, and like many of the contributions in *Scratch Music* very few of them involve the conscious production of sound. Occasionally, the distinction between Scratch Music and an 'Activity' seems to become blurred but on closer scrutiny the contrasts are in fact quite sharp: Scratch Music is often visually creative and complex; an Activity consists solely of a short text, a few words. Scratch Music often describes a process, gives a set of performance instructions as a reminder to the notater, so it is often quite practical; an Activity is usually more general, sometimes abstract: an idea, a whim, a saying, sometimes cataclysmic in its implications. Scratch Music can be extended and developed; an Activity is invariably briefly and concisely expressed. While most Scratch notations tend to be performance orientated the Activities are not necessarily so. Paradoxically, very few of the 'Activities', unlike Scratch music, acceded to the realm of 'action'; they remained 'conceptual', the spontaneous expressions of unfettered minds and imaginations. Similar distinctions exist between Activities and Rites; unlike the Activities, a Rite was normally a 'communal starting-point' for music-making of some kind.

There are at least two versions of the origin of the 1001 Activities: Carole Finer recalls being in a pub with various Scratch members; somebody suggested that they should write down 1001 things to do. 'So it went round and you had to think fast.' Hence the spontaneous nature of the Activities. The following, alternative version, by Psi Ellison, is probably the authentic one. According to Ellison the Activities originated out of an incident during the Scratch Orchestra's week at Wenford Bridge, Cornwall (which is recounted below), although he recalls that there were only 101 and suggests that Scratch Orchestra members subsequently provided additions which eventually reached the thousand mark. He remembers being surprised when he read in *Scratch Music* that there were so many. The following is a verbatim account of the drama from a letter sent to me by Ellison on 2 March 1997. Some twenty-seven years had passed but I am somehow perversely confident that Ellison's account is essentially accurate, although I confess I cannot recall the incident myself.

One day during our stay at Wenford Bridge, Greg Bright, Hugh [Shrapnel] and I set off to find the biggest hole in Europe, the Delabole slate quarry. Of course we were on motorbike and sidecar. On arriving at the quarry everything seemed shut down and derelict but the actual hole was impressive and we went for a walk around the top. It was then we came across what looked like a bell suspended from a tripod. On striking it the sound was remarkable so we decided that it would make a good instrument to play in the Orchestra. Why not? So we hauled it back to the bike. 2 cwt plus the chain and heavily laden we drove back to the camp site. Excitedly we decided to suspend it by the chain from a tree only to witness the cops arriving within minutes of our doing so. I think they arrested us and under escort we had to drive the bell in the sidecar back to the police station at Bodmin. We were to learn that the bell was in fact a nose cone from a second world war shell and the quarry owner who happened to be a bomb disposal expert had given it to the quarry to act as a device for telling the men in the bottom of the hole to stop for lunch and what have you. He saw us remove the bell that afternoon because his house overlooked the quarry and he was a local magistrate. You can imagine we were in the shit well and truly. After lots of questions we were released pending a magistrate's hearing in a few weeks. At that hearing we elected to go for trial at the county court. We had several appearances at different courts spending time in cells and being treated like a bunch of yobbos who had vandalized the High Street. I think there was that sort of trouble in Bodmin during the summer.

It was on a trip down to court in a van that the 1001 Activities came into being. We were in the pitch black travelling through the night from London to Bodmin ready to appear in court by 10 am, laughing until it hurt. I in fact got arrested a second time one night whilst waiting for a train. I had no money to buy a ticket and I was banking on trying to jump the train Greg and Hugh were coming down from London on. I was on Salisbury station. The train was due at 3am. I fell asleep. The railway police carted me off and handed me over to the civilian police. I asked them to take me to Bodmin for the court appearance. They let me go and I went back to the station. I remember waiting on the other side of the barrier and running like fuck down the platform as the train drew in hoping to catch a glimpse of Greg and Hugh to get the fare off them and foil the police. I saw them and they had some money and all was well. The actual court appearance was as you can imagine a farce. Firstly the barrister we had hired in London sent down a junior who knew nothing about the case so we fired him and decided to defend ourselves, all within minutes of the start. Everybody farted on, and the judge seemed sympathetic to our case. We were given a Conditional Discharge and Told Off. For some reason it didn't stop there. Once again we were on the motorbike all three of us after the case, heading for the station and the cops pulled us over and escorted us to Bodmin Road station whence they set about looking for drugs and giving us a hard time. They let Hugh get on the train, I suppose he looked the most harmless. After taking the bike apart they demanded a total exit from Cornwall never to return again. They reminded me of French police. At least we had a good laugh. At some point in all this the cops turned up at my parents place with a warrant and suggested that I had been in possession of a chain and lump of metal implying grievous bodily harm. My Dad never got over it.

Many Scratch events had equally bizarre origins and consequences, born out of everyday existence, the quotidian, which was raised to a higher level of significance by an irrepressible freedom of spirit. The following thirteen randomly selected Activities are printed in the section entitled 1001 Activities in *Scratch Music*:

Tap Dance
Sacrifice a brown paper bag (sheep's bladder)
Do brass rubbing (not necessarily brass)
Imagine you're at a concert starring Judy Garland
Let your shadow follow you, give it a few words of encouragement
Avoid a Corsican

Surreptitiously enter sleazy joint
Use gold dice to decide whether or not to inform your client that he has to appear
in court on Tuesday
Vamp
Blanch at a vulgarity
Be left holding the baby
Listen to Vivaldi in Ironmongers shop.

Some of the Scratch composers and musicians tended, and still tend, it seems to me, to marginalise, to downgrade these 'extra-musical' activities; in fact, they were in a sense the true essence of the Scratch Orchestra. I believe Cardew himself recognised this even if he did not always appreciate (or approve) the anarchic nature of many of the 'interpretations' which would often quite unpredictably, and sometimes disruptively, burst onto the scene.

The Groups [37]

The Scratch Orchestra was not monolithic; within it members who shared certain proclivities, who admired certain gifts and idiosyncrasies exhibited by other members, formed groups, off-shoots, some short-lived, others seemingly indestructible, which would operate both under the aegis of the Scratch Orchestra and independently of it. These groups celebrated a number of genealogies which partly overlap – Dada, Vaudeville, Chaplin and Keaton, Slapstick, Cage – thus covering an extremely wide range of artistic, social and philosophical interests and activities, as their very titles suggest:

David Jackman's Harmony Band played improvised music; in 1971 the group consisted of David and Diane Jackman, Carole Finer ('I loved being in that band. It felt comfortable the way we played together') and Tim Mitchell. By mid-1972 Penny Jordan and Chris May had joined the band and Tim Mitchell had left. The music was generally quiet, sparse and 'a little tentative'. Occasionally, compositions by members of the band were performed. There were several concerts in 1971, including three at The Place, as well as many private sessions in group members' homes, in some of which Michael Chant took part. Jackman disbanded the Harmony Band at the end of the summer of 1972.

Private Company was founded by Michael Chant and included Scratch members Stella Cardew, Carole Finer and himself, as well as poets, such as Bob Cobbing, and artists from outside. The participants contributed their 'concrete poetry, spontaneous painting, philosophical speculation and private imagery to create mixed-media performances with a ritualistic atmosphere (candlelight, drinks, special cakes, etc.)'.[38] They performed regularly at the Poetry Society, at the Herne Hill Art Gallery, and at the ICA. At one concert Chant and Finer wore costume – black cloaks; a questionnaire, with answers provided, was compiled by Michael Chant and distributed to members of the audience.

The title 'Comet' (Comprehensive Omni-Media Entertainment Troupe) metamorphosed (degenerated) into *Come,* to *Come Dancing*, to *Cum*. The group, which included, variously, Bryn Harris, Deryk Barker, Richard Ascough, Carolyn Rogers, Catherine Williams and myself, started with a free advert in *Private Eye,* a first gig at the Wandelconcert, a second at the Chelsea Art College, and its final appearance at The Crypt in Holland Park. It was short-lived.

PTO (Promenade Theatre Orchestra) was a quartet of trained musicians: John White, Chris Hobbs, Alec Hill and Hugh Shrapnel. The members provided their own disciplined music, much of it using systemic processes, such as bell-ringing. The group met on Sunday afternoons and accepted regular professional engagements.

Dave Smith and John Lewis met at teacher training college in 1970 and formed the Smith/Lewis Duo. By 1973 they had moved to London and were presenting their two keyboard programmes with music by colleagues – Michael Parsons, Howard Skempton, Christopher Hobbs and Richard Ascough, American minimalists (in particular Terry Riley), as well as their own compositions (these included Smith's arrangements of Hanns Eisler and Albanian music). Their last public performance was in 1977.

CPE – Chris May (recorder), Phil Gebbett (flute) and Ed Fulton (violin) – were in their early twenties and all in the same year at Imperial College (London) studying physics. May joined the Morley College experimental music class in September 1969 and subsequently became a member of the Scratch Orchestra to which Gebbett and Fulton were more loosely affiliated. In the main, CPE favoured conventionally notated music, whether baroque arrangements or their own modernist compositions.

The Shrapnel Wood and Metal Band was formed by Hugh Shrapnel specifically to perform in the historic 'Beethoven Today' concert at the Purcell Room in 1970. Shrapnel had heard Beethoven's *Ecossaise in D* on the radio and was immediately won over by it's 'primitive quality'; he arranged it for the Scratch Orchestra wind players who premiered the arrangement in the aforementioned concert. It was Michael Parsons who later suggested to Shrapnel that the band should be revived under the title 'Shrapnel Wood & Metal Band', and it subsequently performed regularly in Scratch Orchestra concerts. The regular line-up was Alec Hill (clarinet), Hugh Shrapnel (oboe), Chris May (recorder), Dave Smith (tenor horn) and Bryn Harris (drums) 'with others joining in at odd times'. The Band's repertoire consisted of popular classics – arrangements (mainly by Shrapnel himself and Dave Smith) of composers such as Beethoven, Sousa (*Liberty Bell* was a special favourite), Ezra Reed and Gershwin; there were also arrangements of 'hit' songs such as 'It had to be you' (sung by 'the splendidly outrageous' Sue Gittins). The Band differed both from the Portsmouth Sinfonia and the Scratch Orchestra's own renditions of popular classics in that the arrangements were 'straight' and the music recognisably close to the original (allowing for the rather limited and uniquely balanced line-up). Moreover, the Band had its own 'sound' – primitive, raucous, rather like an out-of-doors rustic village band. Independently of the Scratch Orchestra it appeared in several concert venues, including the prestigious Purcell Room.

As Michael Parsons has suggested, these last four groups exemplified a more controlled and determinate compositional and performance style, a trend which may well have been a counter-reaction to the indeterminacy and anarchy which characterised much of the Scratch Orchestra's activity, as well as the increasingly free and improvisatory tendencies in Cardew's own work (in AMM and *The Great Learning*).

At the other end of the artistic spectrum were the anarchic Slippery Merchants which included Psi Ellison, Judy Euren, Stefan Szczelkun, Greg Bright, Bryn Harris, Catherine Williams, Hugh Shrapnel, and Birgit Burkhardt.[39] The inaugural Slippery Merchants event, entitled Afternoon Teas, took place at the Zees Arts Gallery in Chiltern Street, W1 between 10 and 16 October 1970 with Szczelkun, Ellison, Euren, Williams, and assisted by Cardew and others.[40] It comprised various evening events: on one occasion Cardew appeared and spent the whole evening building a cobweb out of cotton over the window, while Bryn Harris was cooking locusts. (Fried locust was on the supper menu.) At the time Harris was working as a pest research officer and had brought along a tankful of locusts to the event; Harris was breeding locusts by day and eating them by night. A number of people, anxious to join in the spirit of experimentalism, sampled some locust and remarked that they tasted like salt and vinegar crisps. However, all this was subsidiary to the main idea: the serving of afternoon teas consisting of black cakes and different kinds of teas. Judith Euren made fairy cakes and dyed them with black food colouring. Ellison had located a source of stale cakes in Camden Town and he would arrive at the gallery laden with boxes of stale (but apparently edible) cakes. The Slipperies would accost insouciant passers-by and invite them to partake of free afternoon teas. Judith Euren was pleased with her cakes which she distributed and dispatched to various parts of the world. One went to the station-master at Tokyo station; another came to rest not far from the Gallery on a huge porcelain jar on a pedestal outside a chemist's in Baker Street, where it remained for years. Stone-like it neither rotted nor disintegrated.

During the course of the week Ellison was building a huge, spatial, real cake with candles that filled a room in the gallery, while in the corner of the room Catherine Williams was building a bed, or rather a mattress, of jelly on which she would lie and rest. In another corner there was a little cupboard where Greg Bright spent most of his time. Bright was a loner and a true dissident; if he felt disturbed by what was going on he would retreat into the cupboard until the activity abated. Nobody saw him but one could sense he was there. The week culminated in a children's party; the children duly arrived but would approach neither the cake nor the jelly sculptures. It was as if there were an invisible barrier, or perhaps they perceived it as a show or a match and they were mere spectators. Suddenly, one bold child emerged and approached the cake; the taboo was broken and within minutes there was total mayhem. The cake and the jelly were taken out into the street; the children rolled in it, threw it at passers-by and over cars; some of it may even have been consumed. The cake which had begun its life bright and sparkling became grey and gooey, in fact unrecognizable. Ellison recalls that it was an extraordinary event and that it took the Slippery Merchants a day to clear up the mess.[41]

According to Ellison the idea for the tea parties event went back to the Scratch Orchestra tour of Cornwall during the summer of 1970 (described in the next chapter). Cardew had given him '5 bob' to buy food for the whole Orchestra for Scratch member Ilona Halberstadt's birthday party. The only store where food or ingredients could be obtained was the local post office, which was also a general store. Ellison bought everybody an ice-cream cone, without the ice-cream, and some 'hundreds and thousands' confectionery to sprinkle on or into the cone. He obtained a piece of material and spread it out on the village green, placing the cones upside down on the 'table cloth' and sprinkling the 'hundreds and thousands' around each one. It was a (confectionary) theme with which Ellison continued to experiment, on one occasion icing his motor bike, as one would a cake. The BBC, who somehow had got wind of the 'event', arrived at the gallery to film the bike-icing, but Ellison quite belligerently ordered them to 'piss off'; he wanted no truck with the media.

One of the most daring and spectacular Slippery Merchant productions was 'a series of direct interventions in the educational system in the form of "School Raids": groups of performers in colourful 'wig-out' costume made sudden brief appearances in school playgrounds, disappearing equally suddenly without explanation'.[42] The idea was to disrupt the school day and give the children some excitement. The Slipperies selected six schools which were within easy reach of each other. At each school they left a ball on which was written part of an anarchic message; the idea was to unite the schools in some way, to make them interdependent. Greg Bright's costume was the most remarkable – a bird costume made out of coloured pieces of wood which were like multicoloured fish scales and which clacked when he moved; he also sported a head dress with a beak. Judith Euren was covered in multicoloured flowing ribbons from head to foot and Birgit Burkhardt had balloons sewn on to her clothes. And, of course, they all had musical instruments, including whistles, bells and a huge drum.

The Slippery Merchants would enter the school premises during lesson times and dance around the playground, which was usually empty. The children would see them through the window, become utterly distracted, and the lesson would come to an untimely end. Every raid would end with the school staff chasing the Slippery Merchants whilst the children looked on, cheering and encouraging the Slipperies – like a scene from one of the English Ealing comedy films. On one occasion the Slipperies got trapped at the end of the playground and had to scale a rather forbidding looking chain link fence. But they were never caught.

On another occasion their last visit of the day was a girls' school in Putney. When they entered the premises it was afternoon playtime so that the playground was densely populated with girls who, on seeing the Slippery Merchants, began screaming as if the Beatles had arrived. A female member of staff emerged from the school building and blew a whistle to try and restore order and calm. The intruders responded with their own whistling so that a kind of duet took place between the authorities and the anarchists, causing more hilarity and mayhem.

The Slippery Merchants disappeared as suddenly and as inexplicably as they had arrived. Nothing more was ever heard of them.

Notes and references

1   Michael Chant, "The Scratch Orchestra Remembered", from the programme for the event '25 Years from Scratch', 20 November 1994.

2   We should not overlook the fact that Cardew's work was still featuring in the more prestigious citadels of contemporary music. On 10 September 1969 *Arrangement for Orchestra* was performed under the Italian conductor and composer Marcello Panni at the Venice Biennale in La Fenice. Earle Brown's *Modules* was also performed, as well as Satie's *Parade,* in which Cardew performed the 'noises': tape machine and revolver. Unfortunately, as Maestro Panni recalls, in the performance the revolver refused to fire. Of course, one could speculate that it was Cardew who (creatively) refused to fire the revolver.

3   Michael Parsons has reminded me that in fact 'the procedure was interpreted flexibly and in a non-exclusive way: extra concerts were inserted into the age-related sequence on certain occasions'. Letter to JT dated 13 April 2005.

4   The quiet American John Nash was a prolific creator of Scratch Music and there are fifty examples in *Scratch Music.* They include miniature portraits, pencil drawings, games, collages, with occasional references to native American culture.

5   In my own recollection – I may be wrong – these non-musical areas did not achieve a meaningful degree of autonomy, aesthetically impressive though they often were; rather they served to invite, encourage, elicit, stimulate, inspire, provoke, foment *action* of some kind, usually within the context of Scratch performances. The Scratch Orchestra was 'performance art' *par excellence*; because the Scratch Orchestra's conception of 'music' (and Cardew's at that time) was so broad almost any such activity could be subsumed within it.

6   From the New Draft Constitution of The Scratch Orchestra, 1970, as printed in *Scratch Music, Edited by Cornelius Cardew* (London: Latimer New Dimensions, 1972), p.14. (*CCR*)

7   I myself invariably took part in Scratch music though I produced no Scratch Book or notation of any kind. Rather than notating the sounds my preference was for sounding the sound. Cardew would have called this 'Unnotated Scratch Music' or perhaps 'False Scratch Music', as he suggested in a short text written on 23 May 1971 which appears in *Scratch Music*, p.15.

8   There is, of course, one crucial difference: whereas *Schooltime Compositions* was written for others to interpret, Scratch Music belongs exclusively to its creator.

9   Catherine Morley née Williams recalls: 'The sound he [Cardew] wanted had a social character'. From a recorded interview with JT, 30 April 2005.

10 From a letter from Hugh Shrapnel to Richard Churches, dated 22 November 1997.

11 Of course, in respect of the twenty-five or so visual pieces, all we have are Cardew's own precise descriptions.

12 *Scratch Music*, p.74.

13 Ibid, p.76.

14 Ibid, p.76.

15 Ibid, p.75.

16 'BH25 180769 Two shoe prints drawn in outline on a noughts and crosses layout. At right, a signature. Content J.W. Turner.'

17 From the introduction to *Nature Study Notes*.

18   Li Chi *The Sacred Books of Confucius*, Book II: Rites and Music.

19   *Nature Study Notes*, PD31 (Philip Dadson).

20   *Nature Study Notes*, p.14.

21   *Scratch Music*, p.14/15.

22   'Weights' was a cheaper brand of cigarette.

23   'I recall a performance of a piece by Greg in 1972 – I think it was *Salts of Copper* for string quartet – after which Cornelius remarked: "I wish I could have written that."' Letter from MP to JT dated 13 April 2005.

24   The score of *Labyrinth II* is reproduced in the Appendix to *Scratch Music*, on p. 128.

25   In a Scratch Orchestra performance of *Distance* in April 1970 'scaffolding was put up and instruments were played by remote control with ropes, rods, tubes, missiles and other specially devised equipment'. Michael Parsons, 'The Scratch Orchestra and Visual Arts', *Leonardo Music Journal* Vol.11, 2001.

26   There are many examples of the influence of Eastern philosophy on Scratch activity and output, even if this tended to be overshadowed by Cardew's magnum opus, *The Great Learning*. Presentation 25 by David Jackman took place at the Unitarian Chapel, Highgate, in north London. Jackman recalls: 'Orchestra members each took one of the eight categories of sound which are found in Tibetan Ritual Music: moaning, bass moaning, sharp tapping, soughing (as of a great wind), ringing [...] I forget the rest. The "rule" was that each player should stay with their chosen category and perform without pause for *two hours*. I conducted/encouraged from the pulpit. The performance was exhausting and exhilarating.' From a letter to JT dated 22 December 2004.

27   *Scratch Music*, p.10.

28   From a type-written sheet containing advice, suggestions, questions, etc. for Scratch Orchestra members.

29   Somewhat against my better judgement I have allowed my editor, Harry Gilonis, to persuade me to direct the reader to page 115 of Michael Nyman's *Experimental Music* which reproduces a photograph of myself performing the *Houdini Rite* on another, later occasion.

30   Michael Parsons suggests that the 'popular classics' category in the Scratch Constitution may have originated in the experiments in the early days at Morley College, such as four instrumentalists standing around the piano sight-reading through a Beethoven sonata and not bothering or being capable of the necessary transposition.

31   From a typewritten sheet, dated 20 September 1969.

32   Michael Parsons, 'The Scratch Orchestra and Visual Arts', pp.5-11.

33   Perhaps it was one of the areas short-circuited by the political developments, as were other potentialities; in any case, Parsons was to continue into the eighties with the Research idea, including his opera *Journey to the North* Pole, and many old Scratch Orchestra members participated in his projects.

34   From an essay by Jorge Luis Borges: 'Kafka and his Precursors', included in a collection of writings titled *Other Inquisitions 1937-52*, Clarion Books (New York, 1964) pp.106-108.

35   Skempton's 'Austere Rite' is abstracted from 'The Book of Thoughts', a hardback writing book similar to those used by Cardew for his journals. 'The Book of Thoughts' is in fact a compendium of Scratch Orchestra repertoire with contributions from a relatively large number of members. It was lent to me by David Jackman who cannot recall how he came by it.

36   From *25 Years from Scratch*, p.37.
37   Some of these groups outlived the parent body and continued well into the seventies. After disbanding Harmony Band David Jackman has continued to make music, mainly CD production.
38   From a Private Company publicity leaflet.
39   In fact, Ellison never regarded the Slippery Merchants as a 'sub-group'; his view was that they were part of the Scratch Orchestra and their performances and activities were 'scratch' activities. Stefan Szczelkun, on the other hand, says of the Slippery Merchants: 'It was a loose formation and not a members group'. 'The Scratch Orchestra', in *Noisegate* 10. pp.38-39.
40   According to Bryn Harris Cardew had finger-written the word 'slippery' on the misted-up window pane of the Zees Arts Gallery and somebody added the word 'merchants' underneath; this was how the name Slippery Merchants originated. There may well be other accounts, of equal charm and persuasiveness, possibly apocryphal, of the origin of the name Slippery Merchants, just as we saw with the anecdotal 'evidence' in relation to the Scratch 'activities'. In Scratch Orchestra mythology imagination would often take precedence over 'truth'; there seemed to be few qualms.
41   Ellison likened the experience to that which occurred when the Scratch Orchestra was camping in Anglesey, North Wales (which I describe in the following chapter). He draws the comparison with the behaviour of the boys in William Golding's *Lord of the Flies*.
42   Michael Parsons, The Scratch Orchestra: 25th Anniversary, in *Resonance*, Vol.3 No.1, Winter 1994.

(*CCR*) Also found in *Cornelius Cardew A Reader*

Cornelius Cardew a life unfinished

10

The Scratch in Cornwall and Anglesey 1970

The first Scratch Orchestra Concerts

Up to and including August 1970 the Scratch Orchestra averaged over three 'presentations' a month, culminating in a series of village concerts in Cornwall and North Wales. The venues included Town Halls, BBC studios, art schools, colleges, universities, theatres, arts laboratories, galleries, public houses, concert halls, political rallies (Nuclear Disarmament and the Chicago Eight), churches, parks, and village halls and greens. The first four Scratch Orchestra concerts took place in November 1969 at the Hampstead, Islington, Chelsea and Ealing Town Halls on the 1, 8, 15 and 25 November respectively. A further concert, Presentation 6 by Fran Green, at the Acton Town Hall in west London, took place on 1 December and was televised by the BBC. And on Saturday 6 December, between 5 and 8 pm, the last concert of the year, Presentation 5 by Victoria Ellis, was given in the refectory at Ealing Technical College, where Howard Skempton was a student.[1]

Prior to these concerts, at the beginning of October, a 'Music Walk', initiated by the Rome-based group Musica Elettronica Viva (MEV), provided a useful introduction for a fledgling Scratch Orchestra into a kind of music-making which required a political and social awareness as well as the ability to make music in adverse, even threatening, circumstances. The following handwritten report by an unknown participant describes the event in precise detail.

Members of the S.O. whose telephone numbers were available in the file were contacted at very short notice and asked to take part with Musica Elettronica Viva in a Music Walk on the afternoon of Saturday October 4th 1969. About 35 people, including perhaps 10 or 15 of the S.O., came together at the New Arts

Laboratory at around 2.30 p.m. and soon afterwards set off at a leisurely rambling pace towards Euston Station. After playing in the station forecourt for about 10 minutes the walk made its way down Woburn Place, round Russell Square, past the British Museum, down Shaftesbury Avenue and Charing Cross Rd. to Trafalgar Sq. An escort of 4 or 5 policemen joined the walk in the lower part of Charing Cross Road and led it across the east side of Trafalgar Sq. After brief discussions in which the police said they could not allow us to play in the square itself, it was agreed to continue down Northumberland Avenue to the Embankment, play for 10 minutes in the garden by Charing Cross bridge and then disband. Continuous improvised music was played during the walk, to an estimated audience of 5000 people. The walk ended at 4.30.

The walk could be regarded as a pilot project for street music in London. Individuals or groups of players from the S.O. might like to play street music at chosen times and places (e.g. on Hungerford Bridge between 7 & 8 p.m.; at Speakers Corner on Sunday afternoon; at Piccadilly Circus in the rush hour – for more experienced players). Players could report times and places of playing, and their experiences, to the S.O. afterwards. Information about reactions from public and police, which will be useful to future street players, could be collected.

A few suggestions – maintain anonymity if possible – do not collect money unless you really need it – don't collect it for the Orchestra – street music is an end in itself. Respect the rights of other street musicians who may be working for their living.

Don't argue with the police if they try to move you – you can't be charged with playing music in the streets, but you can be charged with obstruction. So if asked to move, go and play in another place – or keep moving.

Attitude of police to the walk: It was a mistake to allow the walk to fall under police control. Although they did not try to stop it, by escorting it out of the square they effectively contained it and imposed a pattern not chosen by the walkers themselves – that is, they turned it into a procession. This could have been avoided if players had dispersed. As it was we did not have the confidence or experience in this kind of work to move away from the group and continue playing – so it was easy for police to take control. With more experience players will not need to stay together all the time. If we had dispersed we could have realised our original plan to play in Trafalgar Square.

9. Cardew with Ruth Aaronberg, late 1950s

10. Cardew, late 1950s

11. In Italy, mid-1960s (l-r) A.N.Other, Richard Teitelbaum, Cardew and Zoltan Peszko

12. On stage (l-r) Morton Feldman, David Tudor (crouching) and Cardew, location and date not known

13. Cardew, early to mid-1960s

14. Cardew in Berlin circa 1970

15. Cardew with tabletop electronics

16. Cardew in Italy, 1975

This was probably the first of many outdoor events involving the Scratch Orchestra. The most significant part of the report is contained in the final paragraph – an interesting portent of later Scratch Orchestra political involvement: that we must always be prepared to resist or somehow circumvent tactics, strategies, sometimes traditions, whose aim is to force us to behave compliantly by limiting, undermining and ultimately controlling our freedoms.

The Hampstead Town Hall concert, tickets 10/- at the door, was a landmark simply by virtue of the fact that it was the first Scratch Orchestra concert: Presentation No.1, devised by Christopher Hobbs. I myself can recall very little of the occasion, and those Scratch members who were also present and apparently prominent at the event, and whom I have interviewed, have responded with disconcertingly contrasting, and sometimes even conflicting, accounts. Even the content of the programme is in dispute: in Cardew's typewritten circular to members, dated 4 October, three items are listed for the Hampstead concert: 'Rite No.50' from *Nature Study Notes*, Christopher Hobbs' *Two Compositions, 21 May 1969*, and The Nuns' Chorus from *Casanova* by Ludomir Rózycki. A completely different programme, handwritten in pencil by Cardew on a sheet of exercise paper and undated, is elaborate and precisely timed, to the second: interpretations of Sinding's *Rustle of Spring*, presumably as a Popular Classic, are separated by various Improvisation Rites, a silence of 21 minutes and a composition: *She was a Visitor* by the American composer Robert Ashley. However, according to Virginia Anderson 'Hobbs remembers only that the [Scratch] members were allowed to do anything as long as they used random procedures in their performance.'[2] The only way to explain the conundrum is to assume that the two programmes listed above were individual programmes devised by two Scratch members; the second, *Rustle of Spring* version certainly seems to be following Hobbs' instruction to use 'random procedures'. Right from the outset, this provided a salutary lesson, if indeed one were needed, for a foolhardy individual who had taken on the responsibility of documenting the Scratch Orchestra's activities.

We should not be surprised by this. Our memories have the habit of playing tricks on us, although as we get older events from the distant past can often be remembered in sharper focus than recent occurrences: a contretemps at primary school is vivid in the mind's eye whereas one may have difficulty in remembering what one had for breakfast a few hours earlier in the day. Perhaps it really is a question of the relative significance or insignificance of what one is trying to recall? Moreover, and this is particularly germane to the present discussion, with the mental act of remembering one is dealing with a highly selective process. The kaleidoscopic character of Scratch Orchestra events meant that each participant, or audience member, took away a unique and unassailable impression which was lodged in the memory. When I interviewed individuals who were present at the Hampstead Town Hall on that first day of November 1969, it was as if they had all been to different concerts – such was the disparity in their accounts. Nor does the microphone serve in the quest for objectivity – although what we hear on David Jackman's tape recorder, switched on and off at random moments and in different parts of the venue (again, it would seem, following Hobbs' instruction), presumably does bear some resemblance to the overall soundscape created on that occasion. There are two extant, short, recorded excerpts: one from the middle of the concert, the other from the later stages; in both the texture is rich, layered, with sustained instrumental sounds; wind instruments playing melodic fragments – improvised or remembered – create the impression of an Ivesian polyphony; a dog, or person, barks intermittently; the male voice predominates (there is no audible female voice), from a radio, and 'live' from the hall – the delivery declamatory, perhaps a reading of a poem or text; a cymbal is dropped (rather than struck). The second, shorter excerpt is dominated by Psi Ellison's 'wind-up' record player; Frankie Lane's rendering of 'Walking My Baby Back Home' seems overpowering; then by stylistic contrast, but equally loud, *The Dam Busters* – Eric Coates' patriotic march inspired by British heroism in the Second World War. (According to Bryn Harris this was an extract from *Bridge over the River Wye*, a post Goon Show collaboration between the Goons and some other comedians.[3]) Harris recalls singing along with its famous 'big tune' and has reminded me that the 'Teddy Bears' Picnic' was also among Ellison's contributions that evening. A visual, or rather architectural feature of the concert was a large construction which had been erected by Tim Mitchell in the middle of the performing space. It was a kind of scaffolding under and on which people would perform.

The Hampstead Hall concert was filmed by a young man interested in the Scratch Orchestra, but when the film was processed, because it had been so dark at the venue, it turned out completely black with no features whatsoever; nor did it have any sound. The film-maker was apparently overjoyed by his success. It was the first, but not the last, doomed collaboration which the Scratch Orchestra enjoyed during its (relatively) brief existence.

Presentation No.2, the Islington concert, tickets 5/- at the door, was devised by the nineteen year-old Frances Booth (few people now remember her; it may have been her only contribution to Scratch history); the word 'shape' was her sole indication for the content of the event.

The Chelsea Town Hall concert already broke the mould in so far as it was devised, not by a teenager (the name Pauline Maloney had initially been listed but does not appear in Cardew's circular of 4 October), but by the American artist George Brecht, who was living in London at the time and was aged at least forty.

Incongruously, as the Scratch Orchestra prepared for the Ealing concert, the last of the first four presentations, a demonstration of fascists protesting against 'coloured immigration' paraded past the Town Hall. The nineteen year-old Paul Irvine, another individual who eludes the memory and whose presentation it was, was equally parsimonious with his instructions and preferences: his only requests being that it should last three hours and that it should include Bach's *Toccata and Fugue in D Minor* (presumably, as a Scratch Orchestra Popular Classic). On 29 November, on a sheet of A3 paper, Cardew noted down the economic reality of Scratch Orchestra concerts: Receipts from Presentations 1- 4 (the Town Hall concerts): £37; Expenditure: £100; with the sole comment: 'Most successful ticket price 10/-'.

The year 1970 began with a concert on Sunday 11 January, from 5 to 7 pm, at the New Arts Laboratory, a disused fire station in Robert Street, near Euston Station (the street where Cardew and his brother Seth had lodged when Cardew was at the Royal Academy). This was Scratch Orchestra Presentation No.8, entitled 'Scrapbook for 1960', and was compiled by Bevan Jones, whose instruction to the Orchestra was simply 'Play scrap music'. Jones had also indicated his preference for a 'popular classic'. As usual Cardew was quick to respond and in a circular to Scratch members he wrote: 'the backroom boys in that department have come up with: "Gustav Mahler (1860-1911) was played a lot in 1960, the centenary of his birth. Anyone wishing to contribute to the popular classic on Jan 11th should get hold of a scrap of Mahler's music and produce it in the concert".' Appropriately, the concert also included a performance of Cardew's *Autumn 60*, prepared and conducted by Howard Skempton; among the participants were Michael Parsons and the composer himself. Skempton recalls that the performance was undertaken with due seriousness, at a very slow tempo, and lasted a good forty-five minutes. Cardew himself described it as 'authentic' although such compliments were often backhanded; Michael Parsons has recalled that you could not take what Cardew said at face value; there were always contradictory implications. The event was also notable for the presence of Karlheinz Stockhausen who was brought along by the composer and BBC producer Tim Souster. Stockhausen was not recognised by the majority of Scratch members; Stefan Szczelkun approached the German maestro with an inflated balloon, artlessly inviting him to 'feel its vibrations'. In an individual performance involving word repetition Howard Skempton referred to an idea from psychology which emerged in 1960; the term 'semantic satiation' indicated, apparently, that if a word was repeated often enough it would lose its meaning.

The Scratch Orchestra meetings following Presentation 8, on 19, 26 January, 2 and

9 February (all Monday evenings) continued to be held at The Place. And then in April a clutch of concerts: The Roger Smalley Memorial Concert, Presentation 11 by Bryn Harris on 24 April at St. John's Church, Smith Square; Rocks, Presentation 14 by Diane Jackman on 16 April at the St. Pancras Town Hall; and Prize-winners Concert, Presentation 15 by Howard Skempton at the same venue on 30 April.

An important contribution from the non-musicians, specifically the visual artists, in the Scratch Orchestra was the introduction of outdoor, or environmental, events. As is evident from the list of venues Scratch Orchestra performances tended to take place indoors – something which was taken for granted by the musicians. An all-day perambulatory concert in Richmond on 16 May, devised by Stefan Szczelkun, broke the mould and brought the Scratch Orchestra into direct, conscious contact with an environment which most of us used frequently but in a conventional, routine manner. The following text is Szczelkun's own description of the day:

The Richmond Journey concert, on Saturday the 16th May 1970, followed a route through the landscape designed to compose an allegorical sequence.

We began by breaking the claustrophobic shell of capitalist normality: Richmond High Street was to be disrupted! We would then pay respects to our ancestors before climbing up through the residential district – recruiting deadened office workers. Our swollen ranks would proceed to the top of the hill, to the ancient Royal Park, to celebrate our connection to an earlier arboreal past and to reclaim the heights. After a break to eat we would descend through the steep Thames meadows and follow the great river on to our destination – that benign archive of the earth's flora, Kew Gardens. Here the whole journey would end with a formal group photograph taken by a local photographer and dispersal. The allegory consisted of an image of growth, flowering and seeding linked to ideas of political renewal. This was to be realised through a series of movements comparable to those in a symphony, which would explore a sequence of moods and emotions. Each stage of the journey was scored by a different individual to meet the overall plan.

The first stage, to start at 11 am, was composed by Psi Ellison and Judith Euren. A study of the High Street had inspired 14 optional instructions including such apparently innocuous things as 'either shout or whisper in conversation' or 'as a group stand and stare in a shop window – hum automatically'. But the final instructions were more radical: 'produce imbalance in Dickins and Jones' and 'sever Marks and Spencer with a quick march in chain formation holding hands'.

The 'imbalance' was easily produced by such activity as rolling on the floor and came to a head when a balloon exploded just as the whole staff were becoming disorientated. Quite harmless but unbelievably dramatic in its effect! Anyway we escaped this excitement to the next stage which was choreographed by Birgit Burkhardt.

Behind the Magistrates' Court in Paradise Road was an old graveyard and passageway called the Vineyard. Birgit arranged a sort of double helix 'spiral' with musicians in the inner spiral and 'dancers' in the outer spiral. As far as I remember there were about 12 to 16 of us at this time. The next node of the route map was my own: 'Awakening the residential area'.
The graveyard of the living? make enquiries... door to door.
knock/ring/tinkle/chime/footsteps/quavers/faces/voices/slam shut/road.

This was a difficult score as it threatened to fragment the group – we struggled on up the hill. The next stage was a release from this tension as we entered the old landscape of Richmond Park. 'Eating Rites' from the Scratch Publication *Nature Study Notes* (ACSR64) and other pieces were directed by Daphne Simmons.[4] A complex piece by Michael Chant reflected the concentric rings of tree growth.

After refuelling we descended through the terrace gardens towards the river Thames using a score by Greg Bright which demanded: 'No conversation... Remember 3 or 5 things from the journey and say them at any time... 3 or 5 handclaps'. This suddenly became very magical as we then encountered a large group of Scratch Orchestra members waiting for us in the steep meadow. We silently went on to Greg Bright's light hearted but intense 'Field Spiral'. His score suggested: 'As each person joins the spiral they should play on flutes, whistles etc... Remembering nursery rhymes'. We then followed the towpath without any playing to Kew Gardens. The Kew score was a series of instructions from *Nature Study Notes* (DJBR98, DJAC92, HSBR34) along with 'Sticks' by Christian Wolff. The journey ended with the group photograph and dispersal.[5]

Cardew did not participate in the Richmond concert, nor in an event in the forecourt of Euston station on 23 May; he was in the US and Canada, from 12 to 31 May, on a lecture tour – an indication, perhaps, of the measure of independence which the Scratch Orchestra rank-and-file had already attained. But on 13 June he was back to take part in a concert for children by his Morley College Experimental Music Class. This was organized by Howard Skempton and the programme comprised an Improvisation Rite, Michael Chant's *Pastoral Symphony,* and Cardew's *Schooltime Special.*

Howard Skempton recalls that at one point Cardew stood up on a chair, removed his waistcoat, turned it inside out and put it back on. The principal of the school was most impressed because it was done with such grace and slowness; 'Cornelius always gave himself time'. And (probably the same piece), in a concert recorded by the BBC Cardew was involved in another extremely slow-motion activity. The work was Takehisa Kosugi's *Anima 7* (1964) – 'perform any action as slowly as possible' – and Cardew had chosen to take his cello out of its case with immaculate pacing and control. Skempton recalls that it was like a normal action that had been slowed down rather than someone trying to achieve a slow motion; in other words the morphology of movement was perfectly balanced from start to finish.

Stella Cardew recalls that her husband was often away during this period which, because of the stressful domestic situation, made life difficult for her; she needed his support. Her eldest son Gabriel was having, and creating, problems at school and was virtually out of control – a situation which Cardew seemed to view, and tolerate, with a detached equanimity. Yet it would be wrong to impute an indifference to family life to Cardew; as we have seen on many occasions he could be a caring and considerate father and step-father, very capable of dealing with the children's diversely exigent temperaments, and a loving and thoughtful husband and partner. Stella recalls that he would conscientiously organise a baby sitter so that she could accompany him to Scratch Orchestra meetings and concerts. His relationship with his step-daughter Emily was a good one; his affection for her was reciprocated. He was conscious of her needs, her frailties, and when he was at home he would walk with her across Barnes bridge in the morning to Hammersmith, and she would take the tube to the City of London girls' school where, for several years, her schooldays were fraught and deeply unhappy. Emily recalls an occasion when late at night, perhaps in the early hours, she and her step-father climbed over into Hyde Park and took a boat out onto the Serpentine. She remembers that he drew her attention to the movement of the oars and the water lapping against the side of the boat. Perhaps this gave him the idea for 'Song of Pleasure' from *Schooltime Compositions*, or he may have been interpreting the piece.

Life in Barnes seemed to play upon deep altruistic and familial currents within him. According to Stella Cardew her husband loved Barnes Common where the whole family would often take their tea. Eating together round the dinner table, already a fast-disappearing tradition of family life, was for Cardew a comforting, indeed civilizing routine which he would try, against the odds, to maintain; perhaps it explains why he set such store by the ritual of communal eating in the Scratch Orchestra. And yet cracks were beginning to appear in their relationship which Stella did not, or perhaps simply refused to recognise. His ongoing relationship with Sheila Kasabova showed no signs of abating and created a play of shifting affective states within him which undoubtedly created tensions and distress at home.

The first year culminated in the first Scratch Orchestra tour, from 27 July to 7 August: a series of village concerts in and around Cardew's childhood home in Cornwall, and on the island of Anglesey off North Wales. Cardew himself had made all the travel arrangements; a Mr Keith Webber from Blisland, North Cornwall, supplied and drove the coach. Cardew also organised the provisioning of comestibles at the camp site, the basic appurtenances for living in the open air, as well as a method and style of a communal life, simple and democratic, which was successfully adopted for other tours. In his circular to Orchestra members prior to their departure he describes these arrangements:

Five families or individuals (Cardew, Keith Rowe, D&D Jackman, Bryn Harris, Sladen) who are used to providing for a number of people will bring cooking equipment and basic supplies (salt, sugar, oil, etc) sufficient for a group of 7 or 8 people. They should also bring enough food for 7 or 8 people for the first weekend (bread, cheese, jam, vegetables, tea, soup, whatever). (Money spent on this will be recoverable from a communal purse: everyone puts in £1 to start with and when that's all used, they put in another one, and so on.) The rest congregate around these nuclear providers.

All the domestic requirements are listed; the needs of the children, too, are accommodated: 'And for each concert evening a volunteer couple will be needed to see the children into bed.' At the bottom of the letter he adds a typical touch: an aptly chosen Chinese poem from the 4th century A.D.

He thought of the Way as he went out of the capital.
Oaths he swore forty-eight.
And took the Great Vows to succour all creatures.
Oh, how subtle is the Pure Land!
Those who come to it are all earth's finest flowers.
In whom can we trust in our declining years?
To make the most of mutability we must set off at dawn.

As part of the publicity for these concerts a press release drew attention to a recent film of the Scratch Orchestra which had been shown on BBC TV and had been discussed by representatives of various fields of music: Jimmy Page (star of the Led Zeppelin pop group) and Roger Smalley (Composer in Residence at Kings College, Cambridge) were enthusiastic, while Bernard Herrmann (composer of Alfred Hitchcock soundtracks) was less charitable; he declared that it made him 'want to jump into the nearest river'.

The Scratch Orchestra camped in a field adjacent to Cardew's parents' home, the pottery at Wenford Bridge, some ten miles north of Bodmin. The landlord, Michael Cardew, showed his generosity by donating half a large wheel of cheese to the Orchestra, an expensive luxury at that time which few of us had ever enjoyed. The village venues blessed with a visit and performance by the Scratch Orchestra were the village hall in Blisland, the youth club at St. Breward, the village hall in St.Tudy, and an International Youth Camp at Porthpien near St. Austell. On the whole the villagers were well disposed towards this happy, harmless, colourful and eccentric group of people marching around the village, announcing their presence with a full-blooded rendering of a bellicose rhythm from Gustav Holst's *The Planets* (Popular Classic). On Blisland Common the Scratch Orchestra stood among the trees and silently performed Takehisa Kosugi's piece *Anima 7* ('perform any action as slowly as possible'), each performer peeling an orange. Psi Ellison recalls that the 'action' took on a strangely surreptitious character, as well as heightening the perceptions; one felt one was being watched, as if the whole village were spying on our activity.

The visit to the International Youth Camp, however, was a discouraging set-back; greeted with sullen teenage hostility, and without the necessary socio-psychological skills and resources to initiate some kind of *rapprochment*, the Scratch Orchestra was out of its depth. In truth, for most members the tour was a temporary encampment in alien territory; the 'concerts' were sorties into the unknown and at the end of the day the pleasure and inspiration derived from them was usually tinged with a measure of relief. Not surprisingly then, as Wendy Frankland recalls, some of the Scratch members, who were on leave from work, lapsed into 'holiday mode', and Cardew would occasionally 'assume the air of a bemused and slightly exasperated schoolmaster trying to control his unruly charges'.[6]

From Cornwall the Scratch Orchestra travelled north to Anglesey in North Wales where they camped for just under a week, from 3 to 7 August, in a field at Talyllyn, Capel Coch. This site had been suggested by relatives of Scratch Orchestra member Carole Finer, and as in Cornwall a number of village hall concerts were organised. Michael Chant's '17 people play simultaneously at one piano' was performed and televised by Harlech TV and, by way of contrast, a concert in a church consisted of one-minute solo performances by each Scratch member. Unfortunately, the event had to be curtailed when some younger members of the audience, impatient of what they perceived as makeshift and unconvincing offerings, began to stone the Orchestra. 'Stoning', with its rather stark, biblical and medieval associations, would perhaps be an overportrayal of what happened. The children were actually lobbing small stones, pebbles, into the midst of the Scratch Orchestra which, one would suppose, was dangerous enough.[7] Carole Finer recalls that Lou Gare rescued the situation by getting up and improvising beautifully on his tenor saxophone, much to the delight and relief of the assembled congregation.

In Anglesey such hostility, or rather lack of appreciation, was in fact rare; the local people welcomed the Scratch Orchestra, gave them advice, offered them lifts and generally created an atmosphere of tolerance, warmth and friendliness. Who knows what they really felt about the strange, quixotic sounds that their guests insisted was music? Who knows what recollections and memories, if any, they may still harbour of those days of invasion when the calm, rigorous routine of rural life was temporarily subverted, or at least destabilised, by an assortment of foreign (English) hippies? At the end of the week, in order to thank the local people for their hospitality, the Scratch Orchestra invited them to the camp site, a field owned by a Farmer Jones, for a last feast. And as they approached the site an emanation of a commingling of cuisines greeted them, as well as the spectacular camp fire which the Scratch Orchestra, under Cardew's guidance, had so expertly built and tended. There was ample food, which the villagers sampled and savoured – especially Carole Finer's local baked apples with brown sugar and butter; overtaken with feelings of guilt, perhaps, Finer had felt the need to compensate for some of the music they had inflicted on the villagers. (What the villagers did not know was that the feast was actually a performance of Michael Chant's *Pastoral Symphony*. The 'activity' prescribed in the score was 'feasting'.)

In the evening the concert included a performance of a piece written jointly by Hugh Shrapnel and Michael Chant which was subsequently given the title *Two Harmoniums*.

This piece had been composed specifically for the two rather worn foot-pedal harmoniums which had been discovered in a Wesleyan Chapel by Chant and Shrapnel whilst on a walk. The two parts were written separately and were played together for the first time in the concert. The part written by Hugh Shrapnel consisted of held diatonic chords indicated by a series of numbers whilst Michael Chant produced a fully notated harmonic expansion of a Rolling Stones' song.[8]

An even more adventurous project, organized by Scratch Orchestra member New Zealander Philip Dadson, was an exchange with a group in New Zealand; on 20 August 1970 the London Scratch Orchestra and the Scratch Orchestra in Auckland performed a simultaneous concert, each at their respective home-base – or rather, the London Scratch Orchestra, beginning at 9 am BST, was playing in a barn on its camp-site at Capel Coch in Anglesey, while the New Zealand Orchestra, beginning at 8 pm local time, was playing in the University of Auckland Library Building (Room B 28). And there were prescribed moments when the English were listening to the New Zealanders and vice versa; timings were therefore crucial. In Anglesey it was pouring with rain; the doughty Scratchers struggled out of their tents down to the barn at the end of the camping field. A flag was used to indicate beginnings and ends of sections of music.

New Horizons: September 1970 to May 1971

Howard Skempton describes the Scratch Orchestra's second year as a period of consolidation.[9] This is only partially true, for there was also growth and change. Moreover, seeds of discontent were discernible before the more obvious manifestations during the two weeks in the northeast of England the following year. In the summer and autumn of 1970, inspired perhaps by the success of Stefan Szczelkun's perambulatory concert in May, a sizeable number of Scratch members developed an interest in performing in more unconventional locations, as opposed to the earlier Town Hall concerts: a summer concert on the boating lake in Regent's Park on 11 July; an open air concert (with no audience) at Biggin Hill, south of London, where a natural amphitheatre had been discovered and the Scratch Orchestra, half on one side, half on the other, called across to each other; and a slightly dangerous element was introduced: performing in public in the metropolis, at Euston station and on the London Underground, without the public's knowledge. This in turn led to the idea of activity of an interventionist nature: at the National Gallery one Saturday morning, at a given signal, a brief, collective shout ruptured the relative silence. Howard Skempton recalls that he was standing next to a large, voluptuous Rubens. The shouters also included Michael Parsons, Michael Chant (whose idea it was) and a reluctant David Jackman, who gave the signal. On the same day David Jackman's 'pigeon event' was enacted at Trafalgar Square where drawings were made with pigeon seed and the pigeons would alter and finally eliminate the drawings by devouring the seed. A variation on Jackman's 'pigeon event' was the subversive seed-planting at Kew Gardens where Scratch Orchestra members smuggled seeds into the gardens and scattered them, some randomly, some with careful forethought.

Danger of a different kind permeated the 'Beethoven Today' concert at the Purcell Room on 25 September 1970, organised by Michael Chant, Michael Parsons and Howard Skempton (Cardew was away in Berlin with AMM at the time): an idiosyncratic celebration of the Beethoven bicentenary, whose *pièce de resistance* was Michael Chant's performance of the *Diabelli Variations*, which took place in a specially designed plastic booth (or tent), simultaneously with unconventional, even heretical, renderings of other works. (In accordance with the fire regulations the Purcell Room management insisted on inspecting a sample of the material out of which the tent was to be made and, somewhat unexpectedly, gave their permission.) Chant provided the following characteristic programme note:

> Art is to truth as company law is to individuals.
> The Diabelli Variations will be performed as 33 variations on a waltz by A.Diabelli by Beethoven. You'll find that after the theme and the first few variations the music repays close attention. One of the variations later on is a fughetta which can usefully be discussed in demonstrating ideas in the language of music. Linking a fuga to the final 'tempo di menuetto' variation is a fairly slow passage reminiscent of the passage linking the reprise of Sergeant Pepper's Lonely Hearts Club Band to A Day in the Life.
> 'I will definitely come, If not arrive as well.'

CPE + 1 (Chris May, Phil Gebbett, Ed and Lesley Fulton) played an arrangement of part of Beethoven's *String Quartet Op.18 no.1*; the Shrapnel Wood and Metal Band played an arrangement of an *Ecossaise in D*; guest composer Gavin Bryars contributed an arrangement for double-basses of the Heiliger Dankgesang slow movement from the *String Quartet* op.132; John White played excerpts from the Piano Sonatas on the tuba (that is, the first note in the left hand of each movement of each of the thirty-two sonatas); and Bob Cobbing read a poem on the name 'Beethoven' with amplification and electronic accompaniment. Three of the symphonies were represented: the last movement of the Ninth was interpreted by the Scratch Orchestra 'and chorus', with Howard Skempton the 'boldly inaccurate' baritone soloist, who also sang two of Beethoven's Scottish folk arrangements accompanied by Spencer Allman on portable organ; the *Pastoral Symphony* received a more considered treatment, as a Scratch Orchestra 'popular classic', by the London New Beethoven Ensemble, conducted by Howard Skempton, who also provided the following instructions: 'Each player prepares his own part from the score of the *Pastoral Symphony* by Beethoven.' Skempton's programme note ends ominously: 'In the Trio section of the third movement and in parts of the Fourth movement (Storm) and Fifth movement (Shepherd's song) more concerted playing is called for.' Laurie Baker contributed an arrangement of the *Ode to Joy* for double basses; the performers included Gavin Bryars, Sandra Hill, the arranger himself, and one or two other double bassists whose names were not recorded. The tempo was extremely slow, like a tape played back at less than half speed, although the pitch remained inviolate. During the interval a tape realisation prepared by Christopher Hobbs and Gavin Bryars of material from the *Eroica* symphony was played, and there were readings from Beethoven's letters by artist Tom Phillips. The 'Beethoven Today' concert also marked the London debut of the Portsmouth Sinfonia, formed that same year, with Beethoven's *Fifth Symphony*. This ensemble of mainly art students from the Portsmouth Polytechnic introduced variation through sheer, unabashed incompetence – not, as was the case with the Scratch Orchestra, by anarchic design.

One of the most radical, and memorable interpretations, a representation of Beethoven, the man himself, was by Scratch member Catherine Williams who, blindfolded, with a stick, groped her way in and around the audience, many of whom were most solicitous, guiding and assisting her. When asked subsequently why she had portrayed the great man in this way – although scholarly questions of this nature were rare in the Scratch Orchestra – she retorted: 'Well, Beethoven was blind, wasn't he?' The anomaly is easily explained: if deafness was the devil's affliction for a musician, then for an artist, like Williams, it would have been blindness. A section of the audience, however, who were expecting a more conventional, more reverential occasion, voiced their disapproval, some even demanding their money back. Yet it was undoubtedly a joyous occasion and one which demonstrated that the Scratch Orchestra was eminently capable of mounting an ambitious event without Cardew's involvement. The critics were unanimous in their condemnation, with one exception: the *Daily Telegraph* critic, Anthony Payne, noted with appreciation 'its fascinatingly dislocated procedures'.

From here on, until the end of the year, there was a gathering momentum, a proliferation of Scratch Orchestra concerts and events beginning with the aforementioned 'Afternoon Teas' event at the Zees Gallery between 10 and 16 October. During November and December there were many performances and presentations, not all of them in London; the Scratch Orchestra participated in festivals at the Universities of Leeds and Essex, and in a concert on 8 December entitled 'How should it be played', devised by Michael Parsons, Adrian Rifkin and Robin Mortimore, in the Exhibition Hall at Portsmouth Polytechnic in conjunction with the Portsmouth Sinfonia (including works by Christopher Hobbs, Michael Parsons, Howard Skempton, as well as readings from the *I-Ching*). Greg Bright's Presentation no.7, which included a forty minute version of the Velvet Underground's 'Sister Ray', took place at the Goethe Institute on 11 December; and on 29 December a Masked Ball at the Chenil Galleries in southwest London, devised by the Slippery Merchants, provided a colourful finale to the Scratch year. Following the Goethe Institute concert Cardew wrote to Howard Skempton:

I enjoyed immensely your performance of Song of Pleasure [from *Schooltime Compositions*] at the Goethe Institute. At the reception afterwards there was a kind of fastidiousness in your refusal to accept the various roles allotted to you in the Masked Ball which almost enraged me. Re-reading Malcolm's memoirs of Wittgenstein has now inspired me to take you to task. Of course there can be no 'guilt' attached to your fastidiousness any more than to a long nose or virtuosity; nevertheless I felt the emanation from you of a huge indifference to something fundamental to music as a vocation, namely the obligation to actually be there when the music is made, when the waves go out and physically swirl around the various animate and inanimate objects in the environment. Just as the conscientious father has to actually be there while his wife conceives the child. Or as Pierre Louys says: 'O femmes, femmes, if you want to be loved, be there, soyez la'. I can't remember it in French.[10]

At a Scratch Orchestra event at Chelsea School of Art Psi Ellison recalls a vending machine outside the hall which he decided to operate as part of his performance. Miraculously, of its own volition, as it were, it began to make an incredible noise, to the amazement of all those in its vicinity who assumed, wrongly, that Ellison had 'treated' the monster in some way. As well as dispensing cans it suddenly began to take an active part in the concert. There was also a tug-of-war with a fortuitously discovered length of rope.

A particularly auspicious occasion was Alan Brett's Presentation no.10 at the Queen Elizabeth Hall on 23 November, which was recorded by the BBC and broadcast, in part, on 30 December. The concert was entitled 'Pilgrimage from Scattered Points on the Surface of the Body to the Brain, the Heart, the Stomach and the Inner Ear', and was inspired by the science-fiction film *Fantastic Journey* (starring Raquel Welch) in which a group of doctors and scientists is miniaturised in order to travel in microscopic capsules into the internal passages of the human body. The Scratch Orchestra had been to see a private showing of the film earlier in the year, on 11 July, in the Starlight Cinema of the Mayfair Hotel near Green Park underground station, preceded in the morning by Judith Euren's Regent's Park Boating Lake concert. The 'pilgrimage' was the second Research Project based on the 'journey' theme (the first was the aforementioned Isle of Wight to Tokyo Bay concert almost exactly a year earlier at the Chelsea Town Hall) and the collective imagination of the Scratch Orchestra rose to the occasion in style with outrageous proposals and demands of considerable prodigality. There was much discussion and a number of differing opinions concerning the ultimate destination of the journey. Richard Ascough suggested visiting all the organs, including the brain, and that various popular classics, chosen for their perceived association with particular organs, should be performed: thus, Christopher Hobbs performed the bassoon part of Mahler's *Symphony No. 6*, associated with the brain, from beginning to end. And the *1812 Overture* provided the perfect match when it was recalled that Napoleon had once remarked that an army marches on its stomach. As Michael Parsons recalls:

The performance began with [Parsons'] *Mindfulness Occupied with the Body* (which uses passages from the 4th century 'Visuddhimagga' by Buddhaghosa), which was gradually swamped by a rising tide of diverse interpretations of the journey theme, some of them rather obliquely related, with light projections, a game of ping-pong (organised by Cardew) [in which the spurious aim was to contrive the score 18-12], and the intervention of an anarchic and disruptive sub-group of Slippery Merchants[11] who appeared in motor-cycle racing gear, upside-down suits and other improbable costumes.[12]

The concert ended with Richard Ascough's *Rationalisation of Realisation*, with Roger Sutherland continuing to bow his cymbal after the piece had finished, insisting, in Ascough's recollection, on 'his right to do whatever he wanted'. According to the programme notes, compiled by Bryn Harris, the entire performance was to be governed by one of the rites from *Nature Study Notes*. The rite, HSTPR41, was conceived by Howard Skempton and read as follows: 'Each player divides himself into three equal parts.' By the end of the concert most of the large audience had left; somehow the Scratch Orchestra had usurped the audience's place. Like an indestructible army of benign ants they invaded and finally drove the audience away, occupying the audience space, breaking down artificial barriers and iconoclastically transforming the concert hall into an area of free activity unfettered by tradition and convention.

During the first half of 1971 Scratch Orchestra meetings continued at The Place on a regular basis and concerts/presentations were relatively frequent. Hugh Shrapnel's Presentation no.18, Excursion to the Seaside, on 6/7 February 1971, involved a trip to Dorset in the south of England and a concert on a beach near Corfe Castle. Reasonably enough, Shrapnel had anticipated inclement weather and had in his mind's eye relished the image of the Scratch Orchestra performing stoically in harsh and difficult conditions. In fact, much to his chagrin, the weather was glorious.

Shrapnel's programme consisted of Michael Chant's *Nature Study Notes* MC12 (in which 'stone throwers' throw stones to miss the 'improvisers' and cause no damage, with a vigour proportionate to the intensity of the sound), Greg Bright's *Salts of Copper*, for wind band, and ended with Walter De Maria's environmental piece *Beach Crawl*: starting in a huddle, spreading out over the beach, but not losing contact, making sounds, responding to other sounds, imitating natural sounds, using found objects, coming together at the end when materials would be gathered for a fire on the beach. However, access to the beach was by way of a perilous cliff descent which only the Slippery Merchants with one or two acolytes ventured to negotiate, and successfully. From somewhere the strains of Greg Bright's *Salts of Copper* could be detected; a trumpet sound wafted up from beneath the cliff and other sounds came from different levels. Two astonished ramblers passed by, and Psi Ellison recalls it was the first and only time he found himself thinking about 'the audience'.

As night fell they (that is, the 'Scratchers' minus the 'Slipperies') made their way to a seven-hundred year-old tiny chapel perched on a cliff top at St Aldhelms Head where they took shelter, suffering extreme cold, until morning. It was typical of Scratch enterprises: frequently difficult, always uncomfortable and demanding a stoical approach to life; Carole Finer recalls that she opted to spend the night in probably equal discomfort in her Mini. Down below on the beach the Slippery Merchants prepared for the long night. Cigarettes of any kind were essential; Bright, we recall, was a connoisseur. So any kind of found paper – tissues or toilet paper – was stuffed with whatever tobacco and exotic vegetation they could muster between them, and wound and bound with bits of string found in their pockets and thread extracted from the fabric of their clothes. The resulting weed, they observed, resembled the bound gaiter of the Norseman – hence the inspired new brand name: Norseman's Leg. The only edible (?) substance they found on the beach was sea kale, which they cooked in sea water and which was unbearably salty. This was followed by Norseman's Leg, to round off the meal, as it were.

In the morning, as dawn broke, and at some distance from the shore, a shoal of dolphins swam past. Before attempting the hazardous journey back, scaling the cliff, they ranged round on the beach collecting nails which Ellison, in entrepreneurial mode, calculated that he could sell to a scrap merchant. The Slippery Merchants, that is, Psi Ellison, Judith Euren, and Stefan Szczelkun would seek out, or rather stumble across, survival techniques and strategies; they had precious little money and lived in vans – Psi and Judith in one, Stefan in the other. Occasionally they were joined by Greg Bright and his guitar-playing, long-red-haired, hippy sidekick, Andy Allen. They survived on whatever edible material could be found in the locality: wild fruit such as blackberries – cooked, if necessary, in whatever vessel they could find (perhaps a discarded baked beans tin), and making a fire with whatever combustible material they could find. When forced by circumstances to buy, they would select the cheapest food on the market, such as pigeon food, for example, which they boiled up and which metamorphosed into a rice-like substance. The meals were named Clap (main course) and Bub (pudding).

In a Radio talk for the BBC sometime in 1971 (which in fact was never broadcast), in which he expresses his misgivings in relation to recorded music, Cardew recalls the Excursion to the Seaside concert:

Alan Brett was playing a Bach Sarabande at the top of a cliff in Dorset. From half a mile away down by the water's edge I identified the melody quite positively as Holy Night. In fact, I suppose the melody in question was by a composer called 'Wind', and a composer called Wind would despise any such concept, or is it a deity, as 'high fidelity'.

Some Scratch events seem to have attracted unlikely celebrities: on 25 February, at the Ealing Town Hall, a concert devised by Greg Bright and entitled Balkan Sobranie Mixture, was given, apocryphally, in the presence of Balkan Sobranie Mixture representative Charles C. Redstone (wishful thinking, perhaps, on the part of Greg Bright). On 30 April Scratch Presentation no. 22, BOTTLE MOMMY by Dave Gregory, took place at the City of London Polytechnic Students' Union. In his circular Cardew writes (according to Gregory's instructions):

This concert is to be unrehearsed, but each member is to prepare in advance and bring to the concert 25 graphic playing parts (8 inches by 10 preferred). These will be pooled and distributed on the night. 'Graphic' is understood to mean: Interpretation not governed by a system of rules or conventions.

On 13 May a Promenade Concert (Wandelkonzert) at the Goethe Institute began with a Scratch Orchestra favourite – George Brecht's Comb Music (playing the prongs) – and ended with Paragraph 3 of The Great Learning, for voices and large instruments, with the participants dispersed up and along the Institute's impressive staircase. In between, guest groups Intermodulation[13] and Gentle Fire[14] and various individuals and sub-groups within the Scratch Orchestra (PTO, Harmony Band, AMM, Wood and Metal Band, CPE, Ex-Slippery Merchants, John Tilbury, Cum, Private Company, Gavin Bryars with a group of Portsmouth students) presented their own programmes. The following two days saw two more Scratch events: Frank Reagan's presentation 21 at Nettlefold Hall, a Community Hall in Norwood, southwest London on 14 May, and a Walk in Primrose Hill, Hampstead organised by Catherine Williams on 15 May. The proximity to each other of these events would have made no difference to the Scratch Orchestra's level of commitment. A good turnout on each occasion would have been guaranteed.

Moreover, the various independent groups within the Scratch Orchestra continued to be active: a concert at The Place on 29 April by Dave Jackman's Harmony Band, Michael Chant's Private Company at the Wigmore Hall on 6 May; and performances of The Great Learning continued to be a staple element in the Scratch Orchestra's repertoire: on 15 and 16 February Paragraphs 2 and 7 were recorded at the Chappell's Studios in New Bond Street for Deutsche Gramaphon, and on 17 April Paragraphs 1 and 4 were performed at St. Pancras Parish Church, Euston Road, as part of the Camden Festival. A seemingly insignificant event, but of considerable portent, took place on 1 May, May Day, which Cardew describes in his later collection of essays, *Stockhausen Serves Imperialism*:

> Tilbury and Rowe had gathered a small group of members to participate in the May Day procession of the workers in Southampton. When it came to it they put away their drums and whistles as mere pathetic encumbrances and participated in the demonstration more honourably as ordinary people supporting the workers' cause.[15]

It was probably the first foray into political activism by the Scratch Orchestra and was a salutary warning to those of us who had begun to imagine a future for the Scratch Orchestra in the political arena.

All these events, from the first Town Hall concerts in November 1969 up to and including the northeast tour in June 1971, represented (in my view) the essentially anarchic, apolitical character of the Scratch Orchestra with which some of the composers had become frustrated and dissatisfied. John White, who was not a member, but certainly an admirer of the Scratch Orchestra, had set up a kind of composers forum which acted to some extent as a foil, a counterbalance to Scratch anarchism. He insisted on a more disciplined approach to performance and this attracted a number of Scratch Orchestra composers, including Alec Hill, Michael Parsons and Howard Skempton, all of whom contributed to White's series of Sunday afternoon concerts at the New Arts Lab. This satisfied the needs of those composers whose work required rehearsal, a different level of discipline, and certain skills such as the ability to read music, which many in the Scratch Orchestra did not possess (and nor did they desire to acquire it). By contrast, Cardew was interested in the dissolution of structure, and in improvisation, even if he did pay homage to White's systemic machines in Paragraph 5 of *The Great Learning*. And, of course, he was quite capable of getting inside them (his experience as a performer of La Monte Young would have been invaluable in this respect), and performing them, as we shall see in subsequent pages.

Attitudes to Audience

The Scratch Orchestra never baulked at the demands which were put upon it, however fanciful or immoderate they were, and however ill-equipped the Orchestra was to meet them. The Scratch Orchestra harboured the obstinate belief that no obstacle – whether artistic, social, or logistic in nature, was insurmountable. And it would achieve its ends, if necessary, by a variety of ingenious and even devious means. Thus, where the incongruity of its presence in certain venues would provoke reaction, the equable and inscrutable spirits of the Scratch Orchestra were able to withstand any audience excesses or hostility unflinchingly. And a disposition towards a quiet geniality on the part of many of the members would diffuse what might have appeared as a potentially threatening situation. To the disinterested observer the Scratch Orchestra probably gave the impression of a heterogeneous collection of insouciant, amiable young people.

Encompassed about with clouds of unknowing, the Scratch Orchestra was generally quite incurious of its public; its relationship to its audience was necessarily fluid and changing, depending on the circumstances: the venue, the degree of presence and focus. It was not always the intention to project a presentation, so that the Scratch Orchestra might operate from within an audience, inseparable from it, as in performances in public places such as the London Underground and the National Gallery. In such situations there might only be oblique references, hints, to 'performance'; just for a fleeting moment or two the public might be conscious of being an audience, although the assumption or imposition of such a role would be too brief to effect a real change of consciousness. As Michael Chant has remarked, 'It has been said that the Scratch Orchestra was its own audience. There was a truth in that, and not only in the negative sense. The concept of an audience as passive consumers was alien to the Scratch.'[16] Psi Ellison recalls that he would occasionally drop out of the proceedings, withdraw from the performing space and simply listen and observe as a member of the audience, and to enjoy 'some of the most extraordinary music' he had ever heard.

Everything was in motion; so much was happening in a variety and multiplicity of dimensions; movement and flux were of the essence in Scratch Orchestra performances. One can remember the events which generated the music but not the music itself; the music was 'uncatchable', though its mark was ineradicable. Like primitive art some of the Scratch activities were shrouded in mystery and performed in secret or with extreme discretion, as if they wanted to conceal rather than proclaim. The activities of the Scratch were neither abstract, nor allusive; their main quality was elusiveness. Their performances hovered between presence and absence, focus and dissolution, art and life, the heightened and the mundane. In a newspaper interview two months after the Scratch Orchestra tour of the Northeast, Cardew told the reporter, Elizabeth Hodgkinson:

We're trying to work out whether we have a future, and in time we shall settle down. The kind of music we play is very English.[17] We don't go in for electronic sounds and computer music as they do in America. Partly because we can't afford the equipment, partly because it would need someone to look after it full time, but mainly because we play primitive music.[18]

Ten years earlier, in Cologne, Cardew had referred to the subtle ambiguities which varying levels and forms of communication can engender:

The picture of myself as the old musician on the Hohestrasse playing so slowly on the mouth organ from his wheelchair. The melody has become so rich for him that each note is incredibly drawn out and wavering (no doubt impassioned). This slowness tempts me too. Although the passers-by, even at normal walking pace, can never hear more than 2 consecutive tones because they take so long and so never know – they never know what it is dass da vorgeht [what is happening there].[19]

Yet the blithe indifference which the Scratch Orchestra exhibited to public reaction in the early months masked an idealism which motivated and sustained its forays into unknown Cornish villages and intimidating civic centres in Newcastle. From the outset many Scratch members had quietly cherished the idea of the voluntary involvement of 'ordinary people' in Scratch activities. It reflected a deep-seated belief that, given the encouragement, inspiration and leadership, a person, any person, people like themselves, could rise to both artistic and political challenges. Indeed, audience response to the Scratch Orchestra was often positive; in the Northeast, in particular, as we shall see, where for the first time the Scratch Orchestra had incurred the displeasure of the political establishment, people would often gather round, volunteer to take part and generally help to create a convivial atmosphere. The Scratch Orchestra performed in diverse environments: some congenial, some hostile or indifferent. David Jackman recalls a concert at Morley College (he thinks) when his piece *Blocks* was performed. At one point the actress 'Wendy Craig stormed out of the audience, paused at the door and shouted "Rubbish!" A great compliment.'[20] The responses it evoked were occasionally problematic, in a way that responses to conventional concerts are not. And it was Cardew's view that it is through difficulty and danger that we learn – and so does our audience. Integration into the fabric of life, in whatever capacity, and at whatever risk, was throughout his life a maxim which Cardew never betrayed.

The Ethos of the Scratch Orchestra

Each and every Scratch Orchestra concert had distinguishing features; each was unique in some way. At the same time there were unifying factors which made the concerts recognisable as Scratch events – the bearing, the demeanour, the attitude towards playing and performing: the 'ethos'. The two events that have been described in detail – the early street music event initiated by MEV and the perambulatory concert in

Richmond – were both recorded by a participant probably immediately or at least soon after the event had taken place, when the details and chronology were fresh in the memory. Yet such 'stocktaking', as exemplified in the account of the collaboration with MEV, was rare in the Scratch Orchestra. We were involved in our own timeless present; past concerts, even those of the recent past, did not concern us. Nor really did the future, so that a meeting could have as much significance, sometimes more, than the concert for which it was a preparation; a meeting was just as capable of providing illuminating moments, flashes of inspiration, and of springing surprises, sometimes of an outlandish nature. The Scratch Orchestra represented an overwhelming immanence, suffused in a spirit of anarchy. In its discreet libertarianism, in its forays into the unknown, beyond the boundaries, certainly of music, perhaps of Art in general, the Scratch Orchestra was indeed a child of the sixties.

In a 1958 lecture entitled 'Communication', John Cage begins with a list of questions. Provocative though they are, the medium of written text renders these ideas speculative, passive; their latency a subject for intellectual entertainment:

> Which is more musical, a truck passing by a factory or a truck passing by a music school?
> Are the people inside the school musical and the ones outside unmusical?
> What if the ones inside can't hear very well, would that change my question?
> Do you know what I mean when I say inside the school?
> Are sounds just sounds or are they Beethoven?
> People aren't sounds, are they? etc.[21]

All these questions – and more besides – were thrust into the vortex of Scratch Orchestra praxis where they were exposed, not to polite debate, but to risk and annihilation.

My own memories are warm, pleasant, blurred; few Scratch members, if any, can now describe, with reasonable accuracy, a particular concert. More than thirty-five years on, when two or three members endeavour to describe the same event the result is an impressionistic, often entertaining but usually unreliable, recall. What one *can* do is to describe a composite, fictitious concert comprising a cluster of memorable/memorised, yet often fleeting moments and situations from the Scratch Orchestra's concert repertoire. What I have tried to do, with the help of fellow Scratchers, is to describe the Scratch ethos by recalling details and images, by evoking feelings from whatever thirty-five year-old-plus source. Conversations with Scratch members – who from time to time, for no apparent reason, will suddenly recall a moment which for him/her is invested with a remote, indefinable significance – will raise a smile, create a warm feeling, or a pang.

The legacy of the extant repertoire and programmes, photos, letters, notes, brought to life by sketchy, arbitrary but still vivid recollections, is an invaluable source on which I have had the good fortune and privilege to draw.

The late Brian Dennis, a composer, himself a member of the Scratch Orchestra between 1970 and 1973, compared the Orchestra to the Nature Theatre of Oklahoma, described in the last chapter of Kafka's unfinished novel *Amerika*, in which 'Everyone is welcome! If you want to be an artist, join our company! ('Jeder ist willkommen! Wer Künstler will, melde sich!') The problem with Dennis's comparison lies with the interpretation of the word 'artist'; whereas for the good folk of Oklahoma an artist was one who played, sang, acted, wrote, painted, sculpted, or composed, the notion of 'art' and being an 'artist' had for the Scratch Orchestra become blurred, even contentious. Not one single member, I would argue, joined the Scratch Orchestra in order to establish their credentials as an artist, let alone to *become* one. On the contrary, for some of us it was rather a case of shaking off the artist tag, and of questioning the nature and status of art in bourgeois society. As we shall see, the consequences of such a course of action would lead Cardew, and others, into a position of political entrenchment from which 'the nature and status of art' was subjected to reappraisal, redefinition and, subsequently, to a revolutionary political agenda which denied any form of artistic licence.

Yet in the early days, if the Scratch Orchestra was apolitical and anarchist in its world-outlook, it was certainly not anarchic in its organisation – thanks to Cardew and his Draft Constitution. The latter's 'legalistic tone' may have irritated some, like Eddie Prévost, but it did help to focus the mind towards an 'aim' – that of collective music-making. This, in turn, involved practicalities, administrative decisions; venues had to be booked, programmes and rehearsals agreed upon. Participants had to commit themselves to the consequences, the realities, of collective decision-making, and they had to exercise discipline appropriate to the task in hand. Conversely, the collective was bound to accept and act upon the ideas and (concert) proposals of an individual. And whether there was a sudden, whiplash enthusiasm for a project or simply a sensitive and discreet forbearance, the commitment could not be compromised; in the Scratch Orchestra the relationship of the individual to the collective was not an antagonistic one. There was no imposed discipline; there was therefore no stress, no pressure, no criticism of or from others; nobody felt vulnerable. If irritation or disapproval were felt, it was rarely voiced. The freedom for an individual to be embarrassing and vexatious, to be anti-social, to be a pain in the neck, to be *him/herself*, was considered somehow inviolate.[22] So there was no criticism of a colleague who did not in some way 'measure up'. Rather you would strive to overcome your sense of disapproval, your qualms, or you would attempt to change a situation you found intolerable through a positive sentiment or action – something in which Cardew himself was a past master.

One of the more extreme situations, a formidable test of the Scratch Orchestra's 'moral fibre', arose during an excursion to the Peak District in Derbyshire where, at a certain location, stones possessed of unique sound-producing qualities were supposed to be found. The expedition, which comprised a number of Scratch Orchestra members and their families, and AMM, followed Cardew to an idyllic river bank where he had suggested they should put up their tents. However the river warden arrived – a stout lady 'in a butch uniform', as Carole Chant (née Finer) recalls, brandishing a stick in a rather intimidating fashion – and informed them that camping was not allowed at that spot. Signs had in fact informed campers and nature-lovers of this prohibition but it had never been in Cardew's gift to observe such injunctions, particularly in the countryside. The doughty Scratchers duly packed away their tents and equipment, drove away and waded across a shallow part of the river to an approved site where they would camp for two days in incessant rain and bitter cold. According to Carole Chant the stones were found and their sound-producing qualities were indeed unique. Eddie Prévost recalls simply that no stones were found.

The Scratch Orchestra was graced with a remarkable, comforting tolerance, wherever it happened to be. Tensions between people did exist but in general the atmosphere created was relaxed, unhurried, and congenial. And on the camp-sites in particular: the slow grace and calm with which people went about their business, savouring involvement in their own timeless present, like secret avatars, accompanied by the occasional musical sound emitting from within a tent or beyond in a field. I remember two occasions on the tours when, together with Alec Hill, we brazenly exposed our preference for a more sybaritic life-style in bed-and-breakfast accommodation. When we arrived at the camp-site in the mornings, relaxed, replete and dry after a good night's sleep and a hearty breakfast, the bedraggled campers would greet us warmly and unrestrainedly, offering porridge and coffee, like monks to some weary and deserving pilgrims. If an occasional wry comment on our feeble-spiritedness passed the lips of a camper it would be in essence gentle, humorous and without malice.

The Scratch camp-sites exuded an atmosphere of well-being (a buttress against the world) and after an eventful day there would be an agreeable feeling of lassitude. Occasionally, but rarely, this sense of well-being would be disrupted; Carole Chant recalls being kept awake at night and distressed by a couple in a neighbouring tent, whose relationship was on the brink of extinction and who would argue and row, only to emerge in a truce for early morning breakfast, which they ate and enjoyed harmoniously. Psi Ellison claims that a 'dark side' did exist within the Scratch Orchestra, and cites telling instances. He recalls a night during the tour of Cornwall when he ventured into a field adjacent to the camp site and began to ring his handbell to the sheep, first from a tree and then amongst them, a performance which he sustained into the early hours of the morning. The sound was continuous but, according to Ellison, not loud. However, some Scratch members, and in particular David and Diane Jackman, were extremely incensed, emerged from their tents and began to rail against him, shouting abuse. But it was Ellison's conception that the Scratch Orchestra never slept; he was *performing* – the Scratch Orchestra's *raison d'être*, after all – and expected due consideration. In a discussion he and I had many years later Ellison made the following pertinent observation: if, he recalled, an all-night Scratch Orchestra concert had been planned, 'democratically', or if it had been agreed that a concert might or should be disrupted, then this was accepted; but if such 'disruptions' should happen spontaneously, as in Cornwall and at the Queen Elizabeth Hall concert, where there had also been some unforseen shenanigans, people would allow themselves to be upset and would demonstrate their antagonism to the unplanned disruption.

At the *Fantastic Journey* QEH concert (described above) the Slippery Merchants were using selections from the 1001 Activities, very successfully, for disruptive purposes: to subvert. Instead of interacting, or even in some way of trying to upstage the Slippery Merchants, some Scratch members allowed themselves to react in a negative and mildly intimidatory manner. In the light of these reactions Ellison began to feel that he was regarded more as a threat to the 'well-being' of the Scratch Orchestra than a contributor to it, and was therefore uneasily accommodated; he felt he was on the margins. Of course, one cannot gainsay Ellison's responses; one cannot deny their authenticity. But nor can one dismiss the frustration of those Scratch members whose thoughtfully and lovingly prepared and executed sonic contributions were rendered irrelevant by (hypothetically) the noise of a motorcycle. However, I do believe that the majority of the members of the Scratch Orchestra, perhaps all of them, regarded, and still regard Psi Ellison, with his charm, flair and unpredictability, to have been at the core of the Orchestra. If one thinks of the Scratch Orchestra, and if one names names, then sooner rather than later that of Psi Ellison joins the roster. Perhaps he could have viewed the frustration, irritability and even hostility which some of his contributions aroused amongst fellow Scratch members with a greater measure of equanimity – as Cardew would have done.

Collectively the Scratch Orchestra embraced a wide spectrum of aesthetic and cultural preferences so that even the purist, he or she who performed and lived according to the spirit and letter of the Draft Constitution, by force of circumstances, would occasionally lapse. There would be distractions: the occasional, spontaneous venture into the art of burlesque, mocking musical cameos, personal peccadilloes of a slightly embarrassing nature – all of which created, irresistibly, an atmosphere conducive to musical transgression which Cardew would accept, albeit with some misgivings and mild indications of disapproval. It was a truly heterogeneous group, an unlikely blend of artistic extravagance and excess with an appearance, a façade, of intellectual and emotional restraint. In this sense it exuded an 'Englishness' – or rather certain facets of what is still commonly identified as 'English'.

If the 'pleasure principle' appeared to play an important part in its brief and eventful life, the Scratch Orchestra also shed an aura of inscrutability and chastity never to be entirely confounded; there was no saturnalia, no flouting of sexuality, none of the 'permissiveness' with which the sixties had become associated. In the Scratch Orchestra there was an apparent cessation of vice, at least in its more carnal, more histrionic manifestations. A German film-maker, Hanne Boenisch, who with a small crew joined the Scratch Orchestra during its tour of the northeast of England in the summer of 1971 and filmed its activities, sensed a thwarted sensuality; she was astonished at the apparent lack of promiscuity in the Scratch Orchestra, where prurient concerns were discreet and private, indulged within the confines of the tent and normally with the same partner. Ironically, it was a German member of the Scratch Orchestra, Birgit Burkhardt, who made the most pertinent and insightful observations on the subject in a recorded interview with Boenisch sometime during the northeast tour. I paraphrase her German:

> Whereas in our society the Erotic is confined within the boundaries of Sexuality, in the Scratch Orchestra the sense of Erotic is diffused into a more general 'pleasure-principle'. If the Erotic is limited to the idea of Sexuality or, more precisely, to sexual gratification, some would say sexual success, then immediately the idea of anxiety obtains: Sex (the Erotic) as status symbol.

It was this more diffuse, subtler eroticism, experienced through all the senses and to which the whole body, the whole person, is susceptible, which Scratch performances, especially in the Rites, exploited. This Rite by Cardew is one of many examples:

> Commence improvising discontinuous music. In the gaps in your playing: without masking their expression, allow your eyes to wander amongst your fellow players. On meeting the eyes of a fellow player: play in accordance with their expression.[23]

Nor would one have associated the Scratch Orchestra with an overt conviviality; even on the camp sites individuals and small groups of families or friends would create a nestling quality, keeping themselves to themselves. There were no festive beggars' banquets, no late night drinking and roistering. Occasionally the Slippery Merchants and other small groups would provide moments of bizarre humour and craziness, and of provocation, but they rarely threatened to be a seriously disruptive force domestically. As we have seen, apart from Psi Ellison's concert for sheep, such behaviour normally found its fullest and most spontaneous expression in Scratch concerts and events.

The sense of communality in the Scratch Orchestra, of an undemonstrative togetherness, was strong; the ethos was collective, or rather it was understood that the individual lived and enjoyed life, not in spite of, but through others: a libertarian socialism would have been the most accurate political tag. Yet the bond was inspired and nurtured through art, not politics, and by a profound confluence of ideas and attitudes so multifarious that the Scratch Orchestra could never have been described as a 'school'. 'Perhaps a brotherhood more than a school', Hugh Shrapnel reflected; 'a "school by default" because we were outsiders spinning off into deep space; we had to cling together'.[24]

The ethos of the Scratch Orchestra found a natural and congenial habitat in the camp-sites; for many members travelling and living together for a few weeks was one of the most attractive bonuses of membership and served to create bonds and cement relationships.[25] But not everybody took the idea of togetherness to such extremes; many members did not take part in the tours. This could have created divisions, a feeling of exclusion amongst those, the majority in fact, who were disinclined or unable through circumstances to tour. But an individual's relationship to the Scratch Orchestra could not be measured simply by a record of attendance; the fact that a member's appearances at meetings seemed to be rather casual did not necessarily detract from his or her sense of commitment; it was simply expressed in a different way. And educationally too, with its emphasis on 'mixed-ability' music-making, its general indifference to instrumental prowess, and in its belief in equality of access to creativity, it reflected the kind of approach that some musicians/composers involved in education had adopted in the classroom.

Yet in some respects it was also a precursor of the revolutionary decade that was to follow. As we shall see, its activities led the Scratch Orchestra into confrontational situations with the State (as at Newcastle) which – even if a few (very few) members were prone to infraction – it had not sought, but through which it (or a part of it) moved rapidly towards the adoption of a more overtly political perspective. It is arguable, as others have pointed out, that the Scratch Orchestra was always 'political'; it concerned itself with questions of its own internal democracy, of leadership and decision-making, of human relationships, of the content and function of its agenda. All these were issues long before its 'politicisation', even if there was no formal discussion (discussion was felt to be an impediment to action). It was the emphasis on *musica practica* and Cardew's influence in this respect, in particular, which determined that these questions had to be resolved through direct, hands-on music-making rather than intellectual debate. There were the occasional petty arguments, expressions of frustration and resentment, but it was the activities – concerts, performances, events – which gathered everybody together and united them. This was undoubtedly brought about by Cardew, and it was a remarkable achievement.

This lack of discussion and therefore of intellectual debate in the Scratch Orchestra, which was generally accepted and approved, at least for a time, reflected Cardew's own distrust of verbalization; he admired 'words' for their inscrutability, their multiplicity of meanings, as in poetry for example, rather than as a tool for rational explanation and persuasive communication. Stefan Szczelkun makes the following pertinent observation:

> At the time there was an antipathy to documentation of almost any sort but the level of family snaps and mementos. It was thought that the work should have an effect directly and not through myths generated by slick documentation. Documentation was seen as a prime cause of inauthenticity of the conceptual art world of the time, a sort of cop-out from facing the force and effectiveness of the work itself. The idea was that our environmental work should have a direct effect on the environment rather than a cultural effect via documentation presented in the art world. Any art directed towards establishment approbation would simply be absorbed, filtered and drained of power.[26]

And of course it was precisely through the use (and abuse) of 'words' – by critics, pundits, experts, through *interpretation* – that such a process of neutralization would achieve its aim. Several years earlier, in 1964, Susan Sontag had penned a similar reproach in her essay 'Against Interpretation':

> Interpretation takes the sensory experience of the work of art for granted, and proceeds from there. This cannot be taken for granted now. Think of the sheer multiplication of works of art available to every one of us, super-added to the conflicting tastes and odours and sights of the urban environment that bombard our senses. Ours is a culture based on excess, on overproduction; the result is a steady loss of sharpness in our sensory experience. All the conditions of modern life – its material plenitude, its sheer crowdedness – conjoin to dull our sensory faculties. And it is in the light of the condition of our senses, our capacities (rather than those of another age), that the task of the critic must be assessed.

> What is important now is to recover our senses. We must learn to see more, to hear more, to feel more.

Our task is not to find the maximum amount of content in a work of art, much less to squeeze more content out of the work than is already there. Our task is to cut back content so that we can see the thing at all.

The aim of all commentary on art now should be to make works of art and, by analogy, our own experience – more, rather than less, real to us. The function of criticism should be to show how it is what it is, even that it is what it is, rather than to show what it means.

In place of a hermeneutics we need an erotics of art.[27]

Naturally, a considerable amount of textual material from the Scratch Orchestra has survived and, as I have already emphasised, has been an invaluable source of material for this book. Most of it falls into two distinct categories which have nothing to do with the kind of documentation Szczelkun describes: firstly, written material, often in note form, of a practical nature – instructions and information for the Scratch Orchestra (much of it by Cardew himself) pertaining to venues, travel, concert repertoire, etc., and secondly, the profusion of artistic texts: verbal scores, graphic material, 'notations' of all kinds. There was never any written assessment of what we were doing; no articles, papers, essays or the like, and for the reasons – if any were ever demanded – that Szczelkun outlines. This would have been the general view in the Scratch Orchestra and resonates with Christopher Hobbs' recollections quoted previously: 'Sorry, but you had to have been there. You can't eavesdrop on history in this case.'

There were certainly many artistic movements from the twentieth century (as well as individual figures, like Cage), which impinged upon the Scratch Orchestra; there are echoes of sixties guru R. D. Laing in its work, of painters like Richard Hamilton and the American Abstract Expressionists, and there were certainly elements of the 'flower power' culture in it. But the influence was of an informal nature, through a general receptiveness amongst members to new artistic currents, rather than a more aggressive pursuit and adoption of newly fashionable trends. Resonances of the Fluxus movement, for example, may be discernible in some areas of Scratch Orchestra repertoire and activity; like the Fluxistes, the Scratch Orchestra 'found beauty in accident and created an evanescent and improvisational art based on silent music, invisible creation, and chance utterance'.[28] But even a cursory comparison of their artistic and social practice demonstrates that they were quite different phenomena. Fluxus claimed to embrace artists and non-artists alike, yet its membership consisted predominantly of people who were then, or who have become since, artists, professional artists, successful artists: Wolf Vostell, Takehisa Kosugi, Charlotte Moorman, Yoko Ono, to name a few. After its inception in the early sixties it operated as an international troupe of, as it were, wandering minstrels and artists, mainly in northern Europe and New York, of no fixed abode. By contrast, the Scratch Orchestra was more 'homely', a family with a definite, collective identity, a strong patriarchal influence, and with a home base in London. Moreover, it really did involve 'non-artists' and in this respect was more inclusive, more informal, and more radical than the Fluxus group; in its inclusivity, its anti-elitism, it was very much a child of its time. And yet if the Scratch Orchestra was 'of its time', it was also an antidote to much of what was considered to be representative of the sixties. So that it was not merely a 'passing phase', a flimsy, bogus 'alternative' which was swept away with contempt by the new political realism. The Scratch Orchestra 'collective' came into being to satisfy deep-seated social, and psychological needs.

Equality of status was assumed in all Scratch Orchestra performances. By contrast, to be a member of Fluxus one had to boast certain artistic credentials; for all its (indisputable) claims to radicalism the perception of Fluxus was that of an artistic 'intelligentsia', a collection of creative misfits, uncompromising rebels, charismatic individualists who had no collective project like *The Great Learning* to bring them together. Perhaps, too, the choice of the word 'Orchestra' affirms a disjunction, one from another; for whereas, as Jeff Rian observes, Fluxus 'was a style of art and performance that was *engendered by words* and packaged using a support network of descriptions – the conceptualist's tender'[29], I think it is true to say that *sound* was at the heart of the Scratch Orchestra's 'style of art and performance'. Art student Psi Ellison recalls that in the Scratch Orchestra he was always highly conscious of the aural aspect, of the incidental sounds that his activity was generating. Sometimes these sounds were accompanimental, peripheral, but on occasions they would take over and assume a more dominant role.[30] Yet there were objections to the Scratch Orchestra's formally expressed 'musical' status; Scratch member Alan Brett, unhappy with the term 'concert' and its cultural and historical associations, made the following suggestion:

In order to meet the want of a better word than 'concert' to describe the Scratch Orchestra's expression of its function in a public sphere, might I suggest the word 'Parley' as a more suitable synonym for a performance? That is, a meeting together. (In his home in Whitefriars, in 1672, a violinist called John Bannister is generally acknowledged to have given the first music concerts that were 'open to the general public for a payment at the door'. One of the concerts was advertised as – 'A Parley for Instruments'.)[31]

There might have been a positive response by Scratch Orchestra members to this suggestion had it been aired at a meeting. Perhaps Cardew felt the idea was not substantial enough; I do not recall it ever being mentioned. Brett also suggested that the Orchestra might extend its influence by setting up 'Scratch Chamber Orchestras' in the provinces and creating a 'National Scratch Orchestral Society' or a 'National Federation of Scratch Orchestras'. This proposal, as far as I know, found no seconder, but there have been over the years a variety of initiatives, by individuals, groups, and larger bodies, in various parts of the world, which owe their existence to the Scratch Orchestra. Some of them, like the Portsmouth Sinfonia, have achieved considerable notoriety, and in 1969 the *émigré* Scratcher Philip Dadson set up a Scratch Orchestra in Auckland, New Zealand.

The educative function of the Scratch Orchestra, in the broadest sense, was regarded by Cardew, and other members too, as central. Yet such an 'education', if education it was, bore no resemblance to any known school or department of music, and in this respect can be compared to Cardew's classes at the Royal Academy of Music. Scratch members and artists David Jackman and Psi Ellison, on their own admission, had no idea what they were doing and why they were doing it. It was precisely the intuitive quality in the Scratch Orchestra's music-making which was its most precious quality, and the unfathomable beauty, the 'uncatchability' of some of the resulting music defied both musical and historical analysis. Philip Dadson's *purposeless work 1*, from the *Scratch Anthology of Compositions*, exemplifies this aspect of the Scratch ethos in uncompromising fashion:

> Sweep the length of a beach. Any number of sweepers
> begin; one hundred are fine, one is sufficient…
> Follow your nose
> at your pace
> as a current. There is no obligation to finish the
> distance…
> end instead when you have
> finished with sweeping.

Of course, the pedigree for this type of composition goes back some years before the formation of the Scratch Orchestra but it was a kind of activity which Scratch members would have found congenial and, in its 'purposelessness', worthwhile.

In stark contrast, by the end of the sixties the whole modern movement had been high-jacked by style, success, stardom. The obsession with style and image meant a high degree of contrivance, of self-consciousness, of the elevation of super-egoism – an egocentricity which fed off the media hype. Stardom in the guise of rebellion, particularly in pop music, but also in fine art, was desirable, marketable, irresistible: this was the 'New Aristocracy'. Anything deemed drab or shabby was an embarrassment, even if drabness and shabbiness still characterised the condition and life-style of many people; oppression and deprivation were just as rife in many parts of the country. The majority were mere onlookers, viewing and sometimes trying to imitate the 'stars' – what Jeff Nuttall has called 'lookism'. The Scratch Orchestra were certainly not 'onlookers', but we were shabby, unselfconscious, essentially unmarketable, except as a weird and temporary phenomenon which the media referred to *en passant*.

The Scratch Orchestra was very much part of the counter-culture ethos of the late sixties, even if at the time we rejected the notion of 'belonging' to anything; certainly, what was in artistic and media circles regarded as the 'avant-garde' (Stockhausen, Boulez, Cage) was anathema to members of the Scratch Orchestra. We were looking, but we were looking the other way; our performances were the antithesis of the fantasy world of the 'discotheque' culture – a dream environment of flashing lights, exotic costume and loud sound. (Although mistrustful of modern technology, the Scratch Orchestra recognised and occasionally revelled in its extreme vulnerability and unreliability.) The Scratch Orchestra performed in civic squares and railway stations in natural light and ordinary clothes in the real world. Incidents and events which might have been overlooked, taken for granted, were invested with meaning: choosing a camp site, preparing a meal, collecting stones for a performance of Paragraph 1; all these actions/activities would have an air of ritual and quiet dignity: a fusing of ends and means antithetical to the expediencies and manipulations which inform and drive capitalist society. Yes, of course the Scratch Orchestra was political.

And with hindsight one can recognise the benign influence of Eastern philosophy through Cardew and possibly other members of AMM (all of whom were associated with the Scratch Orchestra to a greater or lesser extent), and there would have been others in the Scratch Orchestra who were conversant with, and sympathetic to, such ideas. 'The Four Integrative Methods of Bodhisattvas'[32] – giving, kind speech, beneficial action, and co-operation – informed the Scratch Orchestra's activities and relationships and were especially evident in the preparation for concerts and on tours: music as a social, and humanising activity.

From a psychological perspective, as Michael Parsons has observed, there is also a childlike quality in the way in which the Scratch Orchestra related to the world. In early childhood sensations are undifferentiated; that is, they are all part of an interwoven network of experiences of equal significance. And, as a corollary, there was a strong ludic impulse which gave free rein to fantasy and inspired much of the Scratch Orchestra's more spontaneous, anarchic activity.

The experience of the Scratch Orchestra, at least of its first 2 years (its golden age) now seems like a second childhood. This feeling is not merely due to such Scratch phenomena as a craze for snake whistles, but the emphasis on *doing* without bothering about the how or why. Everything – a sound, a sight, an action, no matter how 'ordinary' – was held, with child-like wonder, to be an amazing experience: tapping on floorboards, a fire burning, a popular melody. (Some things really were amazing, such as actual snow pouring onto the stage from an opened stage door during a Scratch Orchestra performance at the Oval theatre, London.[33]

Cardew observed all this and learnt from it; for him the Scratch Orchestra was a completely new and magical phenomenon. He was as much intrigued and inspired by the 'Scratchers' as they by him; it was an irresistible combination.

But how innocent, how 'child-like' are children? Recalling William Golding Psi Ellison recounted an episode from the Scratch Orchestra's week in Anglesey. Ellison decided one evening to play the medieval fool, or rather, as it developed, the village idiot. This he achieved with such conviction that the children became fearful, wild in their incomprehension. Gradually they all began to gravitate towards him, shouting abuse at him and trying to hurt him, jumping on him, kicking him viciously, all of which he took as far as he could. But then they took up axes as if to destroy him and he quickly assumed his normal self. For the children Ellison had not been acting; he had become 'possessed' and it was as if they were engaged in an act of exorcism. The incident at the Zees Gallery tea party described previously, though not as threatening, also revealed children in a less-than-innocent, intimidatory role where adults became helpless, bemused onlookers.

In the late sixties politicians and most forms of authority had been discredited; rampant individualism and the insatiable drive for profit led to an ever-increasing pollution of the environment as well as an undermining of the community ethic. The big commercial concerns had identified how and where their interests could best be served and acted accordingly – swiftly and ruthlessly. The political reaction to this was spontaneous but ill-prepared; the leading protagonists were no longer pop stars and media people, they were politicians of contrasting hues from Enoch Powell to Bernadette Devlin to Tariq Ali, the last leading figure in the anti-Vietnam war demonstrations in London. But if these charismatic figures made the headlines it was the right-wing backlash, especially in the U.S. – the 'hippie' murders, master-minded by Charles Manson in California in August

1969, the systematic elimination of Black Panther leaders and the continuing genocidal atrocities perpetrated against the Vietnamese people – which was a truer portent of the political landscape which was to dominate into the twenty-first century. There was no democratic control of the new technology; more and more distractions and trivia were offered to compensate for the powerlessness which people felt when faced with issues of real importance. Change was frenetic, uncontrollable – especially by those it affected most. Liberalism had been found wanting, unable to bring about the radical, socially-orientated changes in society it had promised.[34] The 'progressive' values championed in the earlier part of the decade, an expression of the extension of both economic and artistic license, had been abandoned or subverted with alarming ease, had degenerated into psychedelia, unreality and escapism, in which popular music played a key role.

The Scratch Orchestra reacted to the new situation by means of various modes of artistic 'dissent' – survival strategies which were eventually deemed ineffectual by some of its most prominent members. What it could not resist was the ideological onslaught, which caught it unawares, unprepared, desperately vulnerable. If the Scratch Orchestra displayed a naivety, it was not in relation to its 'audience', but rather in its understanding of the role of a political establishment which seeks to monitor and control all aspects of people's lives; and it was the painful realisation of this and other limitations which, as we shall see in the following chapters, persuaded a relatively large number of members to embrace a political solution: their view, which was totally at variance with that of many other members, was that Art cannot circumvent a hostile environment; it has to confront it. Art is not simply an act of individual creation; it expresses a dynamic social relation. And, in a series of painful, indeed harrowing meetings and confrontations in the months that followed, the arguments were fought over to a bitter conclusion. By the end of the sixties there was already considerable disillusionment, and sheer exhaustion. At the beginning of the seventies, like many of its generation, the Scratch Orchestra was to turn to revolutionary politics.

If the Scratch Orchestra was, as some have posited, Cardew's 'composition', then the analogy with Frankenstein and his monster presents itself to the imagination; the Scratch Orchestra, like the monster, was ultimately uncontrollable. Because of its very nature it could never have existed on an even keel, which was why the attempt at its politicization, its *rationalization*, as we shall see, foundered and brought destruction in its wake. The Scratch Orchestra could not be directed; its affirmation of idealism could not be politically channelled; the utopianism inherent in its manifesto would find no purchase in the necessary expediencies of Leninism. In the Scratch Orchestra, as in AMM, there were fragments and resonances of a variety of doctrines: Confucian, Buddhist, Hindu, Maoist, and many others, obscure and newfangled, of a rarefied and exotic nature;

and there are instances of discernible influence in every area of Scratch activity – not least in Scratch music itself.

> The ceaselessness of Scratch Music would be emphasised. Scratch Music is the basic music of the world, going on everywhere, all the time. Nothing that is not Scratch Music except regular Western musical compositions since CPE Bach.[35]

But the Scratch Orchestra never followed a single doctrine – until the point when, significantly, like AMM, it broke up.

Like its older half-brother, Fluxus, the Scratch Orchestra looked into and listened for the spaces between things – a free-range art which posited music-making as a truly life-enhancing, life-fulfilling activity which freed and enabled ordinary people. At a time when the individual and the collective were (and still are) seen as an antagonistic relation, where the idea of any collective action was deemed anathema to society and to art, we can reflect on the Scratch Orchestra and the pinnacles of its musical activities, such as *The Great Learning.* And in this sense it was subversive and revolutionary.

Individual Members

The reader may well have been discomposed by the fact that since the arrival of the Scratch Orchestra I have allowed its members to run riot throughout these pages; they seem to have taken control, impinging themselves upon my memory, reminding me how things really were in those heady days, insisting on their autonomy and thus resisting my foolhardy attempts to control and direct my narrative. I too, like Cardew, was no match for their irrepressible spirit of anarchy; I too became the 'bemused onlooker'. The reason for my indulgence is based on my contention that personal contributions by Scratch Orchestra members lend a colourful authenticity which the worthiest and most conscientious labours of scholarship cannot achieve.

Members of the Scratch Orchestra were in the main socially indefinable, displaced from the class into which they had been born; some had regular, full-time jobs as scientists, civil servants, teachers, and of course there was a sizeable contingent of students. And there were drifters, outsiders, the trajectory of whose lives was uncertain, and for whom there seemed to be no credible cultural or artistic tradition to which they could turn. In fact, the Scratch Orchestra was representative of a large number of people across the length and breadth of the country who, suspicious of political rhetoric and unimpressed by the gloss and vacuousness of the 'swinging sixties' were seeking and creating, if modestly, alternative modes of human commerce, of production without possession, action without self-assertion, development without domination. And yet, during what Howard Skempton has described as the 'honeymoon period' there had been no indication of the great political awakening which was to overtake the Scratch Orchestra and rend it asunder. Politics was never discussed – there was no need; consensus on this and many other issues was reached tacitly, or we simply begged to differ. Appreciation, too, was usually expressed wordlessly in the Scratch Orchestra through gestures, attitudes, *commitment*. In any case it would have been impossible to describe what appreciation consisted in; there could be no 'theory of appreciation'.

In respect of Scratch Orchestra membership, there was a relatively high turnover: a fringe of people who took part in three or four concerts and moved on, and a nucleus of twenty or more stalwarts, most of whom had been members of the Morley College class.[36] At any one time the Orchestra might have boasted a membership of fifty or sixty people, at one point closer to one hundred; they came from a variety of social classes and backgrounds and contributed multifarious skills, all of which were somehow put to good use. Who were these people? And what induced them to join the Scratch Orchestra? Certainly their presence signified a need on their part, but it was what they gave, individually and collectively – the myriad subtleties of their discreet and often unknowing contributions – that was of such inestimable consequence. The following list of Scratch Orchestra members emanated from a simple mental procedure – choice is not the right word – whereby, casting my mind back some thirty years, I simply and passively allowed individuals to drift into my consciousness, to appear before my mind's eye. In other words, they are people who, one way or another, have etched themselves into my personal history. In one or two cases, which will be evident, I have allowed my curiosity to get the better of me and have sought to follow up, to delve, to amplify and elaborate the impressions which emerged more or less subconsciously so as to put, as it were, more meat on the bones of memory. The order of presentation was randomly determined, except that the individual members are separated by gender; this is because I wanted to consider the Scratch women's contribution collectively as well as individually.

As Scratch members with good memories may attest, my descriptive notes are impressionistic, highly idiosyncratic, and therefore fallible, if not in some cases woefully inadequate. Moreover, I have certainly omitted some of the more worthy and unassuming members whose faces I knew well but with whom I exchanged only a few pleasantries from time to time.

Michael Chant

Sometime in the mid sixties Michael Chant had written to Cardew, who did not reply. Undeterred, Chant presented himself at the flat in Nevern Square one day in his shabby pin-stripe suit with accessorial umbrella – 'a walking embodiment of a Verlaine character', as Stella Cardew recalls. At the camp sites, at meal-times, the usual rustic fare steaming invitingly in the pot, Chant would always appear as from nowhere, standing back slightly from the thronging Scratchers, lurking undemonstratively but insistently with plate in hand, Cardew's huge camp fire lighting up the evening gloom. According to Stella Cardew her husband 'couldn't fathom' Michael Chant; it is therefore not without significance that Cardew ends his *Treatise Handbook* with Chant's brief but searching critique entitled 'Responses to Virtues, for Theorizing'. Moreover, their political allegiance drew them into ever closer contact during the last decade where, perhaps, political confidences were exchanged which would never see the light of day.

Michael Parsons

Co-founder of the Scratch Orchestra, composer, Oxford classicist, of Cardew's generation. A thoughtful man of fine intelligence, cast in the mould of the best liberal traditions, Parsons wisely forbore to take sides during the political upheavals. He always spoke with quiet candour and would offer words of moderation at critical moments.

Howard Skempton

Co-founder of the Scratch Orchestra, the terseness of his musical utterances belied a verbal volubility, especially on the phone. His lodgings, in Acton and then Ealing, were models of frugality: a bed, a table, a wardrobe, a standard lamp. There were a few personal accessories: a portable radio, a record-player, a jar of Marmite. Skempton rented the Ealing bed-sitter for eleven years, undeterred by the fact that the central heating was off during the day, hot water was rarely available, except from a kettle, and sound of any description was frowned upon. Having only one set of clothes (including one pair of shoes which he replaced discerningly perhaps once a year), he would wash them on a daily basis, a routine which caused considerable friction with his landlady.

Chris May

A self-effacing, beautifully limpid young man who played the recorder expertly and who, on graduating from Imperial College, worked for the Ministry of Defence. May contributed prolifically to the Scratch Music repertoire, in which he displays a penchant for torn and pierced diagrammatic drawings.[37] Understandably, during the political turmoil which overtook the Scratch Orchestra in the seventies he severed his connections and disappeared without trace.[38]

Bryn Harris

Harris was a live wire, a friendly soul and a dedicated member of the Scratch Orchestra. He worked at the Anti-Locust Research Centre (which later became the Centre for Overseas Pest Research) and, according to Stella Cardew, was 'a thorn in Cornelius's flesh'. In fact, one sensed that Harris held Cardew in high regard but he seemed to be the kind of person who found it difficult to learn from anybody. So that in all the demands and challenges that life presented Harris was self-taught. The Scratch Orchestra's 'wild card', an artist in *lèse-majesté*, Harris would direct the occasional, irritating squib at Cardew, openly criticising and attacking him at meetings; one of the few who did. These criticisms would be pushed aside, occasionally somewhat peevishly, ignored, and probably had no purchase as far as the other members were concerned. Some of us, too, had been the butt of Harris's mocking disrespect.

Typically, Harris produced a parody of *The Great Learning*, entitled *Mass Medium*, which was also, perhaps largely, intended as a 'friendly' satire on Confucianism and religious ceremony in general. It was never performed by the Scratch Orchestra, although not because of any general antipathy towards it; it simply suffered the same fate as many other Scratch compositions: there were simply too many to be accommodated even in the Scratch Orchestra's prolific concert schedule. According to Harris Cardew did not take kindly to *Mass Medium*, although the suggestion that Cardew was piqued by Harris's contribution to the composition category is probably an exaggeration; he is more likely to have been dismissive of it. Perhaps it did cause a further deterioration of their uneasy relationship, although for his part Harris was too restless, too mercurial, to bear grudges.

Frank Regan

Another quiet, unassuming young man who was unfashionably interested in (home) electronics; his characteristic, sonic contributions are easily identifiable on tape, even amidst the hubbub of the Queen Elizabeth Hall concert.

Psi Ellison

Psi (Peter) Ellison was anti-authoritarian to the core, as we have seen – a philosophy he has upheld in a principled way all his life. He could always be relied upon to countermand any prescriptive communications from Cardew or anyone else. Like his girl friend Judy Euren Peter Ellison had been a student at St. Martin's School of Art in London. They and their friend, Scratch member Stefan Szczelkun, had two vans in which they lived and travelled around; they were among the first of the 'new-age travellers'. They had no 'home'; for some months Ellison squatted in a clothing shop in Deptford, in south-east London. Bedizened in extravagant or quirky garb, their 'performances' were a minefield of unpredictability. Ellison was one of the most beguiling, and most radical, members of the Scratch Orchestra, as his Scratch Orchestra Presentation no. 20 demonstrates:

> Each member of the orchestra equips themselves with a record player and one copy of the sound track to the film *West Side Story* together with one copy of the sound track to the film *The Sound of Music*. For one hour play the record of *West Side Story*. When not playing, listen. Interval 20 minutes. For one hour play the record of *The Sound of Music*. When not playing, listen. Playing may be accompanied by mimed words and actions. To take place in an Office Block.[39]

Richard Ascough
A competent flautist and Trade Union official who assumed and continues to this day to carry out the curatorial role in the Scratch Orchestra.

Alec Hill
An Oxford graduate, with a D.Phil. in Nuclear Physics. Hill worked for the Central Electricity Generating Board. As early as 1962 he had made contact with Cardew, inviting him to the University Contemporary Music Club. A staunch member of the Scratch Orchestra with an engaging sense of humour, Hill weathered the political storms and remained to the end. An excellent clarinettist.

Many Scratch Orchestra members, including original members, had been visually trained – that is, they had attended Art School. These included Tim Mitchell, Daphne Simmons, Psi Ellison, Judith Euren, Stefan Szczelkun, Stella Cardew, Lou Gare, Carole Finer, David Jackman, Tom Phillips, Keith Rowe, Raha Tavallali, and Catherine Williams. Indeed, the Fine Art contingent may well have constituted a majority although the fluidity of membership makes such a supposition hard to substantiate. Certainly their profile was high and it was they, more than any other group, who created the Scratch image and ethos. In the sixties art education had been a pioneer in conceptual, environmental and performance art, and this had contributed to the breaking down of barriers between the various disciplines which in turn was to become a feature of Scratch performances.

> It is clear in retrospect that experimental music generally, in Britain as in America, has owed much of its distinctive character to the influence of new developments in the visual arts. The principles of indeterminacy and open form, juxtaposition and simultaneity, the emphasis on sound as material and the use of systems all reflect an extended awareness of visual and spatial concepts, offering a radical alternative to the conservatism of most other forms of contemporary music, still largely bound to narrative models of linear development and expressive rhetoric. It was this influx of ideas from outside the musical mainstream which enabled the Scratch Orchestra to break away from traditional notions of order and continuity, and to realize briefly its Utopian vision of an all-inclusive and non-hierarchical form of social music-making, illuminated by the spirit of irreverent humour, discovery and invention.[40]

Tim Mitchell

A delightful man and a true 'poet', possessed of lethal good looks and charm, and one of the unsung Scratch heroes – heroic because perhaps of all the original Scratch members he has remained faithful to both the letter and the spirit of the Scratch Orchestra. On 30 May 1971 Mitchell's Scratch Orchestra Presentation no. 29 (Osmosis) was featured at the Bedford Square 'Book Bang' Festival. The concert, which was one of the most radical of Scratch Orchestra events, took place in an eighty feet diameter 'Big Top' and included George Brecht's 'Gap Event', for which the instructions are:

> missing letter sign, between two sounds; coming together.[41]

Here Mitchell demonstrates this continuity of Scratch activity:

> In some ways I've been doing versions of 'Gap Event' ever since: one version lasting many years has involved exchanging water between two rivers, the Thames and the Itchen. I've spent a lot of time during the last two years trying to do a large drawing of the Long Man of Wilmington in grass turfs attached to the chalk at the base of Beachy Head. There was also a beach event which I did with Bob Trotter, 'tied up/tide out', in which I was tied to a breakwater while the tide gradually came in. He disappeared for a while and came back just in time, as the water was already up to my chest.[42]

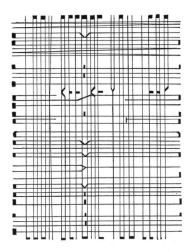

Tim Mitchell's drawing (TM32) on page Y from 'Scratch Music'.

Stefan Szczelkun

The driving spirit behind many of the Scratch Orchestra's most radical presentations; from the outset, his sharp intelligence and intellectual grasp of the political implications of the Scratch agenda, and not least his Polish bulk and indomitability, made him an impressive figure.

David Jackman

Gave off a morose and uncompromising air which did not allow him to suffer fools gladly. And yet, like Cardew, he had the gift of *enabling* people, of opening doors to artistic expression. He gathered a small group around him which he named, appropriately, Harmony Band.[43]

David Jackman 7/2/70 from 'The Book of Thoughts'.

Women were a minority in the Scratch Orchestra but there were several important and influential female members within the Visual Arts contingent (although the visual artists rarely functioned as a group):

Stella Cardew's drawing (SC28) on page I from 'Scratch Music'.

Catherine Williams

A gracile young woman, a kind of precursor of the pop singer Kate Bush, although Catherine Williams did not actually sing. Some Scratch Orchestra members felt that Cardew looked askance at her and people like her, regarding them as somehow *distrait*, peripheral. If this were so, he was quite wrong; her slightly fey exterior concealed an extremely determined and articulate individual, with considerable performing acumen, who had the ability, and occasionally the inclination, to discompose Cardew. Yet in his publication *Scratch Music* he singled out a piece by Catherine Williams entitled *String Games* – for women, which involved the weaving and forming of patterns from a single ball of string:

> It is interesting that Williams' contribution to the present book, though much of it falls outside most definitions of Scratch Music, is the most progressive in that it deals with mass movements, with unanimity, something that the Scratch has definitely not yet arrived at.[44]

Jenny Robbins
The youngest and most loquacious member of the Scratch Orchestra. I remember encouraging and helping her with her 'O' level music exercises, some of which we performed in a Scratch concert. She worked as a store detective and later as a traffic warden (one of the first). Her brother Chris was also a Scratch member. His travels took him away from London for longish periods but he kept in touch, even offering advice and criticism from a distance. In 'The Book of Thoughts' there is evidence of a gentle humour:

The Rite of Springs

Slowly destroy an old mattress.

A. [Ancestry] Rubbish dumping

Raha Tavallali
A young Iranian art student, a genuine voluptuary, whose beauty was a violent presence at many gatherings.

Daphne Simmons
Another art student, from the Kingston College of Art in south-east London. At once insouciant and yet knowing she shared a flat with two other female students. Daphne was delightfully offbeat; she and her friends cooked quirky meals which they prepared in an atmosphere of hilarity, and with a tinge of hysteria. On the one occasion that I was invited for a meal – there were just the four of us – I sat for a considerable length of time alone in their communal living/dining room until they all emerged from the kitchen bearing laden dishes for which, somewhat disconcertingly, they offered in advance profuse apologies. But it is the memory of Daphne's performance on the grandfather clock, and her impeccable sense of time/space as she released its tones, which for me secures her place in the annals of Scratch history.

Judith Euren
Had been a student at St. Martin's School of Art in London. She was a strong-minded, creative young woman whose talents may haved suffered a mite because she was in thrall to her lover Psi Ellison. In their early twenties, they were an utterly original and beautiful couple.

Stella Cardew

Quiet, painterly, motherly – because she invariably had her children with her. Yet the implications of her muted contributions, whether visual or verbal, were often far-reaching, sometimes provocative, unsettling. When Stella spoke, we listened. *Scratch Music* contains many of her captivating visual ideas and prescriptions:

> Content. Accompaniment. Rubbings – say four rich squares. Pinking method press the insects into very soft beeswax ground – remove – bite and print. Get newspaper aluminium sheets – scratch through the chemical on the back. Engrave with a burr.
>
> Stella Cardew (SC12), from 'Scratch Music'.

Her two youngest children, Horace and Walter, grew up within the orbit of the Scratch, their presence at meetings and on camp sites, along with other Scratch children, emblematic of innocence and domesticity.

Carole Finer

A lecturer at the London School of Printing and the same age as Cardew. More recently Finer (now Carole Chant) confided in me that at Scratch meetings and in concerts she would occasionally experience bouts of intolerance which, however, she felt at the time it would be inappropriate to express. In particular, she regarded Bryn Harris as an incorrigible nuisance who seemed to use performance, and in particular volume, to draw attention to himself. (In fairness to Harris he was not the only member to use volume, on occasion, in what might have been considered an anti-social way.)

According to Finer feminism was not an issue in the Scratch Orchestra; women were treated as equals (after all, equality was built into the Constitution) and she 'never felt excluded on that count'. There was sexism, of course, but in her opinion it never became problematic (the term 'male chauvinism' had not yet become part of the everyday language of sexual politics). The men were the leaders, Finer recalls; they planned and made decisions that influenced the day-to-day, week-to-week life of the Scratch Orchestra. The women could do what they wanted but they rarely initiated things outside their constitutional obligation or option to devise a concert. They had not been brought up to be assertive; they waited to be told, to be given permission. Of course there were exceptions; and the profile and *presence* of these young women – Catherine Williams, Judith Euren, Birgit Burkhardt, Ilona Halberstadt and, ironically, Finer herself – tends to weaken Finer's characterisation of the Scratch women. I doubt whether she herself would have been regarded in that pale and protected light by other Scratch members.

It seems to me, looking back, that the Scratch women occupied the space they needed and made contributions of great originality, according to their own feminine sensibilities. Perhaps what Finer is saying is that through their upbringing and societal pressures at that time their sights were lower, their sense of 'freedom' was more limited. But what these women achieved was to transcend historical determinism through their artistic contributions, their collective imaginations; without them the Scratch Orchestra would have been inconceivable. Interestingly, while she did not feel intimidated by 'sexism' Finer recalls a sense of exclusion in relation to what she describes as the 'professionals', that is, the professional and conservatory-trained musicians such as Cardew and myself and those who studied with Cardew at the Academy.

> The idea that I could be a musician and so could anyone if they wanted to be, was one of the best things ever to happen to me. And working with other people was a revelation since I had come out of Art School training with the belief that Art was a lonely and private pursuit.[45]

In the Scratch Orchestra there were sophisticates, like Tom Phillips, and there were the unstudied; and there was Greg Bright of an ocular melancholy and soulful poet's face, maze-builder extraordinaire; and Christopher Hobbs, wise far beyond his seventeen years; and there was Keith Rowe: a portentous figure who became irradiated by the blast of a great political revelation which was to bring about the disintegration of the Scratch Orchestra. Nobody can recall much about Fran Green, except that she wore green (boots). There were the effete and decorative, the degenerate personalities, hangers-on – though few and insubstantial – and noble specimens of an impressive animality. And there were those rather shadowy members content with a discreet position in the half-light, whose curiosity had brought them to this relatively modern pass, and the various young women, *ingénues*, and a cadaverously thin young man, who would glide along in the slip-stream of the Orchestra's activities.

And the scions – Horace, Walter, Jasper, Johnny and Olly et al who on Scratch camping expeditions would run around the site, with pagan energy and bliss, all in their own way showing an intense appetite for life and latching on to any Scratch person who would lend them an ear or entertain them.[46] In particular the Irishman, the late Bernard Kelly, was a great favourite. Like the Pied Piper wherever he went children followed him; they loved his eccentricity, his irreverence, his unpredictability. Kelly will continue to enliven the pages of this book, appearing, typically, at the most unexpected moments.

And there were many more Scratchers who would make fleeting entrances and exits, playing enigmatic cameo parts, who are still, to this day, lodged in the mind's eye; some of those previously mentioned will appear again as key figures as the Scratch Orchestra story unfolds.

Cardew's persona and role in the Scratch Orchestra

In a conversation with David Sladen he and I were regretting that we did not challenge Cardew, that we too easily accepted what he said and very rarely attempted to extract more than he seemed prepared to reveal. In fact, he rarely talked about himself, except, of course, in the Journals, in which, as we have seen, autobiographical conceits abound. Nor was he interested in the (his) past. Perhaps his lack of verbal self-expression betrayed a certain defensiveness, a vulnerability, uncertainty, even fear, fear of exposure? Stella Cardew identified weaknesses which were concealed or protected by a carapace formed of 'charisma and originality'. Sheila Kasabova holds that Cardew was 'of his generation [...]. It was very hard for him to talk about his personal feelings. He could be his personal feelings but he couldn't easily speak about them'.[47] As a corollary perhaps, he could be pre-emptively and brutally sarcastic, which was intimidating. I recall a conversation during the early sixties between Sladen, Cardew, his wife Stella, and myself, when he suddenly decided that Stella should be excluded: 'Slad's line of argument is far too subtle for you [Stella] to understand' – or words to that effect. Stella had presumably expressed reservations in relation to Sladen's 'argument'. Needless to say, neither Sladen nor I rose to Stella's defence – not that she needed it; she probably grasped the essence of what was being said only too well.

Both inside and outside the Scratch Orchestra Cardew was seen by some as an hieratic figure, a benign priest who kept his own counsel and who spread about him an aura of calm and purposefulness. He was ascetic without being puritanical; he never practised self-indulgence, and apart from his attire (at the RAM and in Cologne) he was not extravert. Like Anita Brookner's creation, Fibich, Cardew took naturally 'to the pleasures of sobriety, of extracting the essence from the example, of attaining and completing, rather than striving and collapsing'.[48] A friend, Krystyna Roberts, recalls that he 'always seemed to be rolling, smoking or relighting those nasty little cigarettes he attempted to smoke; head cocked to one side'. There was warmth and tenderness, too. And a giving nature; he gave spontaneously and as a matter of course. At the same time there was detachment; there seemed to be an inner need to keep a distance between himself and others, to create a space around himself which was impossible to invade. It was as if he sought to maintain a certain territoriality of spirit. His shyness was sometimes mistaken for aloofness. In fact, he was extremely empathetic; there was a plenitude of feeling.

To others, perhaps of a younger generation, his character was less remote, even avuncular. Cardew's centrality was acknowledged by everybody; he was the 'unofficial leader' (even AMM did not escape the embarrassment of such a perception by some commentators), and it is probably true to say that, particularly in the Scratch Orchestra, he enjoyed and cultivated the leader status, even if there was a not insignificant number of members for whom the notion of an 'authority' was always problematic. Acceptance of his leadership was therefore attendant upon its invisibility, or rather upon people turning a blind eye. What is irrefutable is that the Scratch Orchestra would not have existed without him; Cardew was the patriarch, a father figure, and when, as he perceived it, authority was required he would assert it. Sometimes it was difficult to intuit his meaning. A seemingly chance remark would often insinuate a web of complexities. But people would defer to his 'calm wisdom'. His influence was incalculable.

Because of the ultra-democratic nature of the Scratch Orchestra there were always those, like the Slippery Merchants, who would oppose any manifestation of authority as a matter of principle. Nevertheless, even they could not deny that it was Cardew who determined and organised, overall if not in detail, the Orchestra's agenda. A kind of balance was achieved because a sufficient number of members accepted the necessity of both authority and anarchy, an insoluble contradiction which each individual, in their own way, had to come to terms with. And there was another, slightly rarer breed of Scratch Orchestra members: those who perhaps were able to distance themselves and saw Cardew in a more sceptical and less flattering light as somebody who always managed to maintain a protective observance of his own interests. In their view he was the Orchestra's Godfather, or at least a *grand seigneur* who could rely on the majority of members to recognize his authority and whose imprint the Orchestra bore. 'It was almost as if he were using his authority in order to subvert everything but himself. And started to lose control of it when people realised that subversion could be applied to his role as well.'[49]

Cardew did have a magical side, but at the same time he was extremely practical. So whilst he was profoundly aware of the notion of 'otherness', he was also vibrantly involved with the fibrous content of real life. Christian Wolff tells a story which, in its spontaneity and lack of sentimentality, is quintessentially Cardew, as well as reminding us of the fires he and his mother uses to build in the Cornish countryside:

We once came, it was a birthday party for one of his children I think, Walter, and [it was] a cold day and he had a fire which was going down and there was no more wood and he walked over to a chair and simply took the chair apart and fed the fire with the pieces of his chair and remarked 'I never liked that chair very much'. And it was obviously the right thing to do, we were all warm for another hour or so. It was very nice.[50]

According to Carole Chant Cardew exhibited a chauvinistic attitude towards women, and was certainly paternalistic towards both men and women. The Scratch Orchestra he regarded as (beautiful) children and treated them as such. Some of the men resisted but the women, 'being half in love with him', allowed him to get away with it. Attracting his attention was in itself gratifying; progressive (feminist) ideas and impulses would be temporarily held in abeyance. Certainly, he existed on an eminence, which enabled him to view the Scratch Orchestra's activities with a degree of detachment and equilibrium. Though not always; Stella Cardew recalls that there were times when he was very much the 'amazed onlooker', a shade nonplussed, even fearful at moments of wilful playfulness, disarray and anarchy. But if he suffered anxieties he rarely betrayed them; indeed, he enjoyed the promise of excess which Scratch meetings and performances offered ('The road of excess leads to the palace of wisdom', Cardew's early mentor William Blake had declared). And it redounds to his credit that no immoderation, no hyperbole, in whatever direction, was ever censured in the Scratch Orchestra – until, that is, its metamorphosis into a politically motivated and controlled agit-prop group. (Psi Ellison has reminded me, however, that he would occasionally be rebuked, in the friendliest fashion, for not paying attention!)

So if Cardew was a catalyst, he was also a 'restrainer'. During a performance of Paragraph 5 of *The Great Learning* at the Cecil Sharp House on 21 January 1971, the improvisation which constitutes the second half of the Paragraph seemed to be getting out of hand. A small group clustered around the piano were hammering at the keyboard in mindless fashion. Cardew left the performing space and sat down in the audience quietly smoking a cigarette. At a certain moment he got up, wandered over to the piano, casually but purposefully closed the lid and went back to his seat in the audience. The music instantly changed, evaporated; the ceasing of the piano din affecting the other participants' music-making and thus radically changing, at a stroke, the content of the music. Through that one decisive (authoritative?) action, the music, the whole atmosphere, changed.

In a documentary file there is a typewritten text, headed '5.69 onwards', which sets out the ethical precepts on which, in Cardew's view, the Scratch Orchestra should base its music-making and which would embody its *raison d'être*, no less. The 'Documentary file' was a repository, provided by Cardew, for texts of a poetic, philosophical or practical nature, and for visual material which was deemed in some way, however arcane, relevant to the perceived needs of the Scratch Orchestra. The content varied from the sublime to the facetious: Michael Chant had slipped in two photographs of Lenin, one with, one without hair. The text in question consists of advice and definitions; it seeks to clarify. Occasionally, Cardew seems to be addressing himself, reminding himself of his own private imperatives, his own duties and responsibilities. The significance of this statement, its visionary quality, lies in the fact that it represents clearly and unequivocally Cardew's philosophy of music when his musical career was at its zenith; it embodies, *in toto*, the experience of four distinct but related, coextensive spheres of musical activity embracing almost a decade: *Treatise*, AMM, *The Great Learning* and The Scratch Orchestra. For this reason it is reproduced here in full:

The Scratch Orchestra needs an inspiring literature. It needs inspiring touches.

The aim of the S.O. is to generate a broad plunging and lively river of musical activity which quantitatively will possibly not be able to compete with the commercial and canned music output, but will far surpass it as regards candour, intensity and spontaneity.

Oppose any suggestion of a regular concert scene or regular playing. Work in bursts on the principle of expansion and contraction; be available for action at short notice.

Collect relevant texts (e.g. texts on music from the *Book of Rites* (Confucius), and the description of the dwarf's music from Chapter 1 of *The Hobbit*) for inclusion in the Documentary file. Promote production, not only of music but of books, pictures, buildings etc. [the word 'friendship' is added here in pen]

Don't entirely neglect a) that music can be a sobering experience rather than an intoxicating one (although exuberance, ecstasy, excitement and sensuousness can all feature in Scratch Music), b) that music can delight the mind rather than excite the senses, and c) the educative function of music (it can break down prejudice, stimulate and refine the mind, activate and mould opinion, renovate the people through joy and revolution).

Concert forms can range from a strict routine of many items lasting 2 or 3 minutes to entirely free and unplanned in every respect, as AMM.

The possible necessity for a code of behaviour (not ethics) for concerts: There are two states: 1) Stillness, 2) Participation. Natural behaviour (chatting, moving around, tuning up, etc.) can form part of 2, that is, should be used as a positive activity, not just to while away the time *between* activities.

No censure of the behaviour of other members (of course such behaviour will be privately censured, but don't give behavioural expression to such censure). This requires study. I don't want to exclude ordinary destructive participation, like drowning out a sound you don't like, etc but maybe just keep censure and dislike separate: Don't censure what you dislike; don't dislike what you censure.

On a broader level this also means: don't exclude anyone wishing to join the S.O. It is a classless orchestra.

The aim of the Scratchbooks is to establish concern and continuity.

Beauty in action is the easiest of attainments; *anything* can be beautiful in action. Beauty in repose is not so easy. Beauty in the mirror is the hardest of all − in fact impossible: the act of looking in the mirror tends to ugly. That's why it's so good to play, even if the playing is minimal. Avoid so-called self-expression. Try rather to express something else − an instrument, a relation, a melody. Express yourself only in the sense that you express a letter (make yourself faster? spend more on yourself). Dressing in the morning you express yourself. Running to catch a bus that would otherwise leave without you; that's expressing yourself, etc. etc. Of course it's not *necessary* (or only for a certain sort of person).

Work on the problem of communications within the orchestra.

The S.O. is not a secret society, nor a flock of sheep. It is an orchestra. Does that imply a certain measure of discipline? It implies a kind of spontaneous mutual respect, which is the same thing only better. Such that if the desire arises we can all play together, 'sudden and sweet'. But before this discipline comes the opening up of the musical channel in people, such that confronted with one thing we can do something else − render it in performance. (A gathering of people *performs* that gathering?) Confucius defines: 'Music is the heart's response to the external world'. Almost like letting the external world play you like an instrument. (This also requires work, there are dangers here). Confronted with the external world we get feelings and ideas. Traditionally the ideas arise in the brain, and the feelings in the heart. It is therefore (following Confucius) our feelings rather than our ideas that we should externalise in the form of music.

We are so constituted that heart and brain affect each other mutually (in Science terms: heart can send extra blood to the brain, brain can by mental effort accelerate or retard the heart) so there is no danger of being at sea on an uncontrollable flood of feelings.

Don't confuse stillness and rigidity (see above)

By all means use the S.O. as a vehicle for your individual work (if applicable – and how could anything not be applicable? – well, we'll see).

What can be played, we'll play; what can't be played, we'll think about.

No leader in the S.O. We all face the same way – outwards (NB any circular rite can display this outward-facing). The Constitution is a composition – not the dogma of a leader (composing could probably be viewed as an essentially dogmatic activity). An obligation with regard to the constitution may be felt and followed but should not be forced upon oneself. There are other obligations: to be human, and for every member to feel free to do what he wants – in full confidence that what he wants is in accord with 'Heaven's wants' (Confucius). The elements of the Constitution – Scratch Music, Popular Classics, Musical Journeys – should be given a try just like any other composition submitted by a member of the orchestra.
However, try not to fall over backwards for the sake of democracy.

Hidden among the leaves of the 'Documentary file' is a handwritten concert proposal, unsigned but almost certainly by Cardew. The item in question, the concert proposal, may never have received a performance, but its thoughtful composition, its gentle unconventionality and charm, the purity of its conception encapsulates all that was original and captivating about the Scratch Orchestra; an archetypal Scratch event except that few achieved such a coherent and persuasive balance of form and content. The title, 'Amy climbs the tree', already suggests a relation to *The Tiger's Mind*.

Venue: Any wooded spot (e.g. on Barnes Common).

All performers to be up trees.

Time: An autumn evening.

Programme: Tchaikovsky: *Nutcracker Suite*.

Cardew: *The Tiger's Mind*.

Wolff: *Sticks*

plus numerous other compositions and improvisations.

Part 1 lasts one hour. In it Tchaikovsky's *Nutcracker Suite* should be drawn on by all as the popular classic. *The Tiger's Mind* (each player chooses one sentence involving the tree and works on it continuously or intermittently). Improvised Music on a conventional musical instrument (each person to use one instrument only). Sounds and actions involving nuts and nutcrackers to be freely used. At least one journey to another tree.

String Music (using string of any material, including nylon wire, guts, chain etc., and on any scale, from hair to hawser.) Each player must contribute something to this music each time he catches sight of someone else doing it.

Programming for Part 1 is free for each person individually. When otherwise unoccupied collect dead wood for Part 2.

Part 2 begins with silence, then all play *Sticks* by Christian Wolff. When this piece comes to a natural end either the concert may end, or an individual may call for further music, either from Part 1 (e.g. by shouting 'let's play more String Music' or 'let's play the regular musical instruments') or other pieces – these may require some discussion. In any case, one suggestion is to be used at a time, and rendered concertedly. Further suggestions can follow after one has been rendered.

It was certainly the case that for some members of the Scratch Orchestra Cardew's saws and homilies – many of which receive prominence and emphasis in the above texts – were a source of irritation; yet they were generally taken to heart and there is no doubt that they did inform the essential character of Scratch Orchestra events. The importance of his frequent caveats on 'freedom' – that an individual's 'free' actions should not be deleterious to the well-being of other Scratch members – was generally recognised, even if in practice it was occasionally overlooked. The texts which were deemed 'relevant', worthy of inclusion in the Scratch Documentary file, shared a profound and unshakeable belief in the moral basis of music. Among the Chinese texts included is a Taoist text by Kwang-Sze which describes a music which 'proceeded according to (the principles of) propriety and righteousness, and was pervaded by (the idea of) the Grand Purity'. (Such was the significance of this text for Cardew that he included it in Paragraph 5 of *The Great Learning* both as an illumination of the power of music, and as a restraining influence. See Appendix 3).

The wisdom of the Greeks was also enlisted in support of the educative function of music in a section abstracted from Plato's *The Republic*.

Socrates: Then, from the start, in their earliest play the young will be kept to law and measure through music, because when their play isn't so, it's not possible for them to become serious law-respecting men.[51]

In tandem with music Socrates had advocated the pursuit of gymnastics but Cardew correctly concluded that care of the body could not have been written into the Scratch Orchestra Constitution.[52] At most it could have been smuggled into the repertoire through a Rite – perhaps one celebrating the virtues of *Health and Efficiency*[53] – or, more ambitiously, through Bevan Jones' verbal proposal for a Research Project on Hygiene. There were also Hindu texts of a general religious and philosophical nature contained in the Documentary file, probably placed there by Cardew, although there were several members of the Scratch Orchestra who would have deemed such literature worthy of inclusion. Most importantly, all these stress the communal nature of music and, apart from *The Hobbit* (although perhaps it is implied), the ethical basis of music-making.

As a corollary which flowed from his insistence on the moral basis of music, it was inevitable that any discussion of the Scratch Orchestra's relationship with the public should have been of concern to Cardew. His view was that in order for the Orchestra's influence to be effective and beneficial it was essential that it should have faith in, and commitment to, its own members' proposals; Cardew was never one for half-measures. Asked in an interview whether it would be possible that something could weaken or change the spirit of the Scratch Orchestra Cardew's reply was both illuminating and prophetic:

Political agitation could weaken it – could weaken it very much. The idea that music was exclusively sound would weaken it in my opinion. I think one of the most interesting things about the Orchestra is the fact that there are people working in the visual arts, people engaged in perfectly ordinary jobs, working with computers, all kinds of things like that.[54]

In the same interview Cardew expressed the opinion that it was not within the structure of the Scratch Orchestra to serve a political end – a situation which in a matter of months he was to regard as an essential weakness.

The weight of responsibility which the Scratch Orchestra imposed on Cardew may have given him a gravitas which masked his more light-weight virtues and which was enhanced by the long, black, extremely heavy, German army leather coat he was prone to wearing at that time. I was with him when he bought it in an Amsterdam flea market for fifty guilders (about £5) and in fact purchased one (but dark green in colour) for myself.[55] For some unaccountable reason I remember the words of the middle-aged lady vendor as we completed the transaction: 'You have a new coat there', she rasped at us in a thick, guttural Dutch accent. This caused me to speculate on the fate of the previous owner – a young Nazi officer, perhaps, whom the end of the war, or death, had dispossessed of such an impressive garment. Psi Ellison also recalls a pair of extraordinary boots which Cardew used to wear, although from a different and even more speculative source.

Irony and detachment lent Cardew's gentle humour an unmistakeable quality, as in his circular advertising the Scratch Orchestra's interpretation of George Brecht's Research Project: a 'Musical Journey' (described above):

> In the light of the time at our disposal (being 63' 41") it has been decided to exceed Brecht and McDiarmid's modest proposal to move the Isle (of Wight) west to Portland Bill (a point well within the visible horizon) and undertake a journey (still west, but to Tokyo Bay) that will not be viewable in its entirety from any point in the Cartesian cosmos. (There may well be points in the Riemannian from which the whole would be viewable; in the present state of research we are not competent to judge.) Such a journey will also present a far greater number of problems to the imagination, the solution of which may be of great value in future research.

Cardew had the ability to harness the talents of others and to give them a sense of – not direction, that would be too prescriptive – but of purpose and, most crucially, of self-belief; he never showed deprecation, even when he must have felt it. Some Scratch members refer to Cardew's generosity of spirit as an abiding memory – 'very open and accepting', in Richard Ascough's words; he was an internationally famous composer but there was no 'side' to him. He was always remarkably generous with his time to everybody, and in equal measure; no priority was granted to age or status. He was never 'too busy' or 'in a hurry' – and he bestowed his own talents with remarkable munificence. He was discreet and subtle with Scratch Orchestra members and therefore was an exemplary teacher.

In concerts his fearless presence vouchsafed a strength and conviction of performance. As John White once remarked to me: 'If your were waiting in the wings to go on stage, and Cornelius was there with you, you knew that *everything would be alright.*' And endorsed by Christopher Hobbs: in performance his reserve, his serenity, 'was made kinetic, transformed into an acute sensitivity to other people's moods and actions, which made him a great interpreter and a joy to perform with'. And always the expression of immense patrician calm to comfort and inspire the less experienced members of the Scratch Orchestra, releasing capacities which might otherwise have been forever walled up; so that from some remote corner of a venue a plangent cry of self-discovery might well up and issue forth. Or in a moment of disarray and confusion, of collective self-doubt, Cardew, sitting with his cello in a space which seemed impermeable, would make a decisive gesture – though never a repressive one, nor even necessarily an obtrusive one; but nevertheless one whose eminence we all recognised, and to which we responded. In Psi Ellison's words he had 'a kind of Buddhist centre; when all of us were astray, anxious and worried, you would look round and he would be in calm control, completely focused'.[56] He always preferred a musical exchange, which for him was stronger than verbal communication: you do something (musical), I do something, then you do something, and so forth. If he was paternalistic, as Carole Chant has suggested, he could also be very kind and understanding, and would always do what he felt had to be done (the moral imperative) regardless of dangerous, and sometimes literally, that is, physically, dangerous consequences. (On a mountain hike, for example, going on ahead, testing the terrain.)

Sometimes the Scratch Orchestra would meet in out-of-the-way places and Cardew and Stella would bring Horace and Walter along. One asks oneself to what extent his attitude towards composing and music in general was influenced by having young children and working and functioning in their company – just as (as David Tudor observed) Christian Wolff's was. He must have learnt the value of working with the innocent. He treated children as equals, as few adults can; he would give them the rein but always with moral guidelines. He taught his children to be as intrepid as he was, sometimes allowing them to experience a degree of danger which other parents would not have sanctioned.[57] Once in Cornwall he watched as they dived off the rocks into a rough sea. When one of them got into difficulty he immediately plunged in to the rescue.

During the Scratch Orchestra years family responsibilities were always present and occasionally Cardew would give way to domestic impulses. It was interesting, and for some of us humbling, especially at that time, to observe the considerable degree to which he integrated and intertwined his domestic arrangements and private life into his musical work and commitments. This was a corollary of the fact that he viewed the Scratch Orchestra as a microcosm of society – perhaps, universally, as a symbolization of the 'human condition'. The Orchestra was an 'oracle' which one consulted; but what one gleaned was cloaked in ambiguity and paradox; one had to work hard to interpret its message. It was important, too, to set it problems, to make demands, although the Scratch Orchestra would sometimes be found wanting and could not always measure up to the idealism which infused Cardew's expectations.

As we question the Orchestra, so the Orchestra also seems to have a questioning role in the larger context (e.g. it makes people wonder why they went to a concert, etc.). The main thing is to develop sensitivity of communication. Why don't people feel able to do what someone wants them to? The careless way things are simply dismissed as irrelevant − that's what gets me down.[58]

And on a scrap of paper on which he had been working out the Scratch Orchestra accounts he jotted down, in a moment of inspiration: 'Happy thought: Invite an anthropologist to spend a year with the Scratch Orchestra.'

Cardew enjoyed sparring and grappling with the various personalities in the Scratch Orchestra; and the attainment and exercise of authority and leadership, of being a teacher, stimulated and invigorated him. Yet it was just this 'teacherly' quality in the Draft Constitution that served to alienate some people − and not only Eddie Prévost. It is a strange paradox that the letter and spirit of the Draft Constitution was in some respect out of kilter with the ethos of the Scratch Orchestra itself, or rather with what the Scratch Orchestra was to become. (If, indeed, as has been suggested, it was a 'control strategy', it failed; ultimately, as we shall see, Cardew lost control of the Scratch Orchestra to become merely a 'participant'.) The wording of the Draft Constitution has in places a somewhat stilted quality − Prévost has referred to the 'legalistic tone' − and it therefore created misunderstanding in the minds of those who encountered it without prior knowledge of Cardew the man and his musical activities. Richard Ascough, for example, describes how he ventured to his first Scratch Orchestra meeting in trepidation, believing that some kind of audition awaited every newcomer. Is this surprising if Ascough, a young man not long out of a suburban school, had read the last paragraph of the Draft Constitution, and in particular the sentence: 'A meeting to confirm the draft constitution and initiate training should precede the summer recess'? This sounds more like an advertisement to join somebody's private army. There is also a resonance of public school, sixth form, academic pedantry in some of the language, and it reads as a po-faced, or is it tongue-in-cheek, prescriptive, almost dogmatic, document − a gift for the satirist. And yet, as Eddie Prévost has pointed out, there is such a delightful irony in 'so formal a document (published in the *Musical Times*!) legislating for such (subsequent?) nonconformity'.[59]

Whether or not the Draft Constitution was Cardew's 'composition', and despite the formal quaintness of its language, it was certainly a catalyst for the multifarious activities which the Scratch Orchestra invented, initiated and engaged in. But if the Draft Constitution was Cardew's 'composition' did it not then renege on his previous, painstakingly-cultivated relations to the performer – in the challenging notations of *Schooltime Compositions* and *Treatise*? Or, in the light of his experience with these profoundly experimental scores, did he feel the need to recoup some compositional losses? Was he in some subtle and devious way pulling in the reins? In other words is the Draft Constitution an ironic re-establishment of the compositional *control* which he had consciously and almost wilfully relinquished in the works which led up to the Scratch Orchestra? I think not. The Constitution was drafted with a freight of practical imperatives in mind, most of which he had accumulated in discussions, rehearsals and performances of his indeterminate works, of which *Schooltime Compositions* was the ultimate conduit to his conception of a 'scratch orchestra'. Moreover, the relationship between Cardew's works cannot be expressed simply in terms of their chronology; as we have seen in the works from the early sixties there is a sense of interrelationship, of interdependence, so that a piano work, *February '61*, will be followed by an orchestral version, *Arrangement for Orchestra*, and the *Third Orchestral Piece* is followed by a piano transcription, the third *Winter Potato*. And then there are the more problematic and arcane relationships to *Treatise*: *Volo Solo, Bun for Orchestra No.2*.

With the creation of the Scratch Orchestra, for the first time in his life, it was as if Cardew had 'lost control' and was swept along by events which he had unleashed but over which he could exert little or no restraining influence. When and how did this occur? My own view is that it was that fateful moment when the Pandora's Box, in the form of the Draft Constitution, was opened up to the world. From then on, to change metaphor, the helmsman fell victim to the huge buffeting waves and the violent and unpredictable winds which would finally overcome him; he could no longer 'utilise the interplay of natural forces to steer a course', to *lead* his life. As we shall see he was unprepared for the developing crisis, unable to play a significant role in the changes which were rapidly enveloping a large contingent of the Scratch Orchestra.

Perhaps *The Great Learning* was, as it were, a last ditch attempt to hold the Orchestra together; it was an instrument through which he sought to maintain influence, and respect. Through it, for a time, the Scratch Orchestra cohered; we were all reading from the same text. As we have seen, beginning with Paragraph 2 at Morley College, there were many performances of individual Paragraphs and the Scratch Orchestra responded with commitment and enthusiasm. But even his *magnum opus* would ultimately be sacrificed to the demands of a new political agenda which was beyond his experience; he was simply out of his depth. Even if he did recognise the seriousness of intent of the new political direction he was unable to play a contributory role. Painfully, he withdrew, to take stock, to assess the viability of his position in the Scratch Orchestra. And this was compounded by, or perhaps was a reflection of, a domestic situation which had also reached a crisis point.

So it now behoves us, at this critical juncture, to pause to consider and reflect upon a work in which we can discern echoes and resonances of earlier unresolved issues as well as pre-figurations of later concerns, which looks both backwards and forwards in Cardew's life and in doing so establishes a continuity which helps to clarify the meaning, and demonstrate the significance, of decisions taken both early in his life and in the final years.

Notes and references

1 We see already that the number of a presentation does not necessarily correspond to a chronological order; in the above cluster of events Presentation 5 was preceded by Presentation 6. There were various reasons: for example, a concert might have had to be postponed while a suitable, alternative venue was being sought and confirmed.

2 Virginia Anderson, *British Experimental Music: Cornelius Cardew and His Contemporaries*.

3 The Goons, with Michael Bentine, Spike Milligan, Harry Secombe and Peter Sellers, was a weekly comedy radio show which acquired cult status.

4 There is an error here. ACSR64 is by Alvin Curran, with the description: Sitting Room Song. And I cannot find any 'Eating Rites' in *Nature Study Notes*.

5 This version of Stefan Szczelkun's text differs, usually trivially, from that in *Noisegate* Vol.1 No.10 pp.37-38.

6 Undated letter from Wendy Frankland to JT, probably from the mid-nineties.

7 Although I had been in Cornwall, I was unable to make the trip to Anglesey and am therefore relying totally on the memories of others for this account.

8 Richard Churches, *From Improvisation to Revolution; a History of* the Scratch Orchestra (1969-1972) – *its Origins and Development up to and including the Period of Discontent*. There was also a part for chapel bell, which was rung by Andy Allen; according to Chant Allen ignored the composer's indications and simply improvised.

9 The first and second Scratch Orchestra years – 1969/70, 1970/71, to which Scratch members refer, correspond to the dates of the academic year September to July, originating in Cardew's Morley College class which had provided an important nucleus of enthusiasts for the Scratch Orchestra. The three tours, to Cornwall and Wales, to the Northeast of England, and to Munich and Austria, all came at the end of an academic year, that is, during the summer vacation period. For some members the tours were their statutory two-week holiday from work.

10 From a letter from CC to HSK, dated 20 December 1970, 'the eve of departure for Cornwall'.

11 It was through these 'interruptions' by the Slippery Merchants, in particular, that the ludic impulses of the Scratch Orchestra would find wayward and uncontrollable expression.

12 From 'The Scratch Orchestra – Performance/Interpretation', published in *Positionen* 26, February 1996 pp.8–13: 'Wer Künstler Werden Will, Melde Sich', Das London Scratch Orchestra.

13 Intermodulation was a Stockhausen-influenced, live electronics ensemble. Founded in Cambridge in 1968 its members were Roger Smalley, Tim Souster, Peter Britton and Robin Thompson.

14 Gentle Fire started as an improvising group at York University around 1968; specialised in indeterminacy, verbal scores, improvisations, using conventional acoustic and electronic instruments, circuitry, found, constructed and invented sound sources. Members of the group included Hugh Davies, Graham Hearn, Stuart Jones, Richard Bernas and Michael Robinson.

15 Cornelius Cardew, *Stockhausen Serves Imperialism* (London: Latimer New Dimensions Ltd, 1974), p.108, n.10. (*CCR*)

16 From *25 years from Scratch*, p.35.

17 Of the Scratch Orchestra David Jackman once remarked: 'It was so English – like a

knitting circle with instruments. […] It was totally unaggressive.'

18   From *The Northern Echo*, 26 August 1971.

19   Jrnl. 25 October 1959.

20   From a letter from David Jackman to JT dated 22 December 2004.

21   Section III of the text 'Composition as Process', collected in *Silence*, p.41.

22   As we shall see, this 'liberalism' was later identified as the Achilles heel of the Scratch Orchestra and was relentlessly exploited by its 'political' members.

23   *Nature Study Notes,* Improvisation Rite CCTG22.

24   From a recorded conversation with the author sometime in the mid-nineties.

25   Not everyone would concur with my generalization here: Some thirty five years on Catherine Morley (née Williams) recalls that "when it came to their 'social selves', they [the Scratch Orchestra] went into denial." From a recorded interview with JT on 30 April 2005.

26   From '25 Years from Scratch' in *Noisegate* No.10, p.22.

27   'Against Interpretation' in *A Susan Sontag Reader* (London: Penguin Books, 1979), p.104.

28   From an article by Jeff Rian, 'Fluxus, Flux On', published in *Flash Art* no. 167, November/December 1992, p.55.

29   Ibid, p.56.

30   When I once asked Ellison whether, during the days of the Scratch Orchestra, he regarded what he was doing as 'music', he evaded the question.

31   From a letter from Alan Brett to CC, dated 7 January 1970.

32   These are referred to in *Shōbōgenzō: Zen Essays by Dōgen*, translated by Thomas Cleary. (University of Hawaii Press, Honolulu, 1986).

33   Hugh Shrapnel, from *25 years from Scratch*, London Musicians' Collective 1994.

34   As early as the late fifties, in one of the letters to Ilona Halberstadt, Cardew proffers a brief and provocative gloss on liberalism: 'Bored with liberalism; substitute – Cynicism (necessarily?).'

35   Note by Cardew, dated 'Summer 1971', in *Scratch Music*, p.15.

36   The Morley class continued well into the seventies, maintained by the same nucleus which had joined the Scratch Orchestra and more or less on the same lines – improvisatory sessions and work on specific projects – but with a rotating class leader to which the authorities, perhaps with some justification, objected. For a time it functioned as a 'club' but its politicisation as part of the cultural arm of the Marxist-Leninist party, supported by Cardew and other members of the Scratch Orchestra, resulted in its closure by the College authorities.

37   Cardew seems to have appreciated May's contributions; a generous number of them are included in *Scratch Music*.

38   Felicitously, Chris May emerged from his self-imposed exile in the nineties; he has taken part in concerts of Cardew's music and has responded cordially to my request for his recollections of the Scratch Orchestra.

39   For a member of the audience the experience would have been comparable to the much-publicised sixties 'happening' where the audience was invited into a coach and then taken to a performance of Agatha Christie's *The Mousetrap*.

40   Michael Parsons: *The Scratch Orchestra and Visual Arts*, 1995.

41   Another (anonymous) Scratch version of Gap Event has survived: 1. Open grand piano. 2. Place objects between all consecutive notes of piano. 3. Close lid.

42   From *25 years from Scratch*, p.38.

43   See also my discussion of 'The Groups' in chapter 9.

44   *Scratch Music*, p.12.

45   Carole Chant, from a recorded conversation with the author sometime in the nineties.

46   Horace and Walter were the sons of Cornelius and Stella Cardew; Jasper was my son with my then wife (now Zuzanna Nash) and Johnny and Olly were the sons of Tim and Barbara Mitchell.

47   Zoltan Peszko, the Hungarian composer/conductor, recalls that Cardew was rarely communicative, often silent. There was never any false charm but he possessed a powerful charisma; he was generous in spirit, helpful, with no concern for money or financial gain.

48   Anita Brookner, *Latecomers* (London: Grafton Books,1988), p.5.

49   Anon. I cannot recall the author of this observation that I noted down, presumably some years ago. But I think it is an accurate reflection of an aspect of Cardew's relationship to the Scratch Orchestra and therefore warrants inclusion.

50   From an interview with Christian Wolff, sometime during 1985, for Philippe Regniez's film, *Cornelius Cardew 1936 – 1981*, commissioned by the Arts Council of Great Britain, 1986.

51   *Plato's Republic*, tr. I. A. Richards (Cambridge University Press, 1966), p.72.

52   In fact, as we shall see, a class in gymnastics was offered in the Scratch Orchestra Summer School the following year.

53   *Health and Efficiency* was a naturist magazine, perhaps the oldest in Britain; during the fifties it was probably the only publication where one could enjoy photographs of semi-naked people.

54   From an undated interview with the German film director Hanne Boenisch in the wake of the June 1971 Northeast tour.

55   From 7 – 14 March 1970 Cardew, Christopher Hobbs and myself, sponsored, if I remember correctly, by Gaudeamus Foundation, had given several concerts in the Netherlands. My unreliable memory tells me that our repertoire included works by Cardew, Hobbs, Terry Riley and the Dutch composer and improvising pianist Misha Mengelberg.

56   From an interview with JT on 28 September 1996.

57   They were certainly not over-protected; they were all brought up in what Eddie Prévost has called the 'Cardew School of Hardiness' – a spartan mode assimilated by Cornelius at an early age.

58   From an undated text.

59   From *25 Years from Scratch*, p.38.

(*CCR*) Also found in *Cornelius Cardew A Reader*

Cornelius Cardew a life unfinished

11

The Great Learning 1968–70

'The greatest music has the most tenuous notes'.[1]

In a short talk for the BBC on 21 July 1970, in which he introduced a performance of Paragraph 1 of *The Great Learning,* Cardew expresses the antithesis to Western ambition and complacency in a way which I find strangely moving:

> Failure is an interesting topic; I read recently that one African tribe attributes the creation of the world to God's failure to hold everything together in one piece; his grip wasn't strong enough and it just whirled out of his hand. Then I read in *The Naked Ape* that such a tribe of so-called primitives is itself a failure; it has failed to evolve technologically. Another example: the American composer La Monte Young says that if his music does not transport you to heaven he is failing. Everyone is failing; our entire experience is this side of perfection. Failure exists in relation to goals; Nature has no goals and so can't fail. Humans have goals and so they have to fail. Often the wonderful configurations produced by failure reveal the pettiness of the goals. Of course we have to go on striving for success, otherwise we could not genuinely fail. If Buster Keaton wasn't genuinely trying to put up his house it wouldn't be funny when it falls down on him.

Accordingly, through its kinship with nature, the music of *The Great Learning* never fails, except, perhaps, in relation to the demands of the word, the Confucian text. In Cardew's finest achievements of the sixties – *Treatise*, AMM, *The Great Learning*, the Scratch Orchestra – there is an acknowledgement, a celebration even, of human fallibility, which not only sets him apart him from the majority of his contemporaries in the late sixties but also aggravated his relationships with them. Notions of 'failure', and 'democracy', informed Cardew's artistic credo, just as, conversely, they fly in the face of received Western thought – especially in respect of artistic endeavour and achievement. The greatness of Mozart, it is assumed, lies in his perfection, his ineffability and flawlessness; what is admired about an artist is his exclusiveness. One recalls Schoenberg's much-quoted adage: if a work 'is art, it is not for all, and if it is for all, it is not art'.[2] For many of Cardew's peers the consequences of his position – philosophically, aesthetically and musically – were threatening, cataclysmic, and there was no longer any possibility for discourse. For Cardew, as we have seen, flux and uncertainty constituted the essential *Zeitgeist* of the late twentieth century and as a corollary time-honoured categories of the Western musical and compositional canon had to be jettisoned.

In 1968 Macnaghten Concerts[3] commissioned Cardew to write a piece for the Cheltenham Festival. Cardew's decision to base his composition on a Confucian text reflected the broader context of an affinity with Eastern philosophies – a predisposition which can be traced back to his youth, if not further. We know that Michael Cardew was interested in Confucianism, and the influence of his father may well have aroused Cornelius' curiosity as a boy. Through his grandfather, too, with his shop in St. James', if only by way of family anecdote and hearsay, Cardew might have glimpsed more artistic, more extravagant forms of sinophilia. This preoccupation with Chinese art and philosophy seems to have been a family trait passed on from one generation to the next.

In the sixties the composers and musicians for whom Cardew felt the most admiration and empathy were those whose work and performance practices were most clearly mediated, in various ways, by Eastern influences: John Cage, La Monte Young and AMM. And with AMM the focus was sharpened to the extent that Chinese philosophy and language became subjects of formal study. Joseph Needham's *Science and Civilization in China* was a work to which the members of AMM often referred and at one stage a project to purchase the complete Needham was discussed, although it never came to fruition. The financial burden of such a commitment would at that time have been too great, and a simple alternative was adopted: Keith Rowe has in his possession photocopies which Cardew made and stapled together of thirteen non-consecutive pages from the fourth volume, 'Physics and Physical Technology', of Needham's *magnum opus*. These provide an invaluable insight into the way in which ancient Chinese attitudes towards sound and the social function of music, as well as the infinite subtlety of their approach to the production of sound, had influenced Cardew's music-making with AMM (and the other members, too), and a few years later the whole ethos which these attitudes and performance practices embody was to inspire and inform Cardew's own *magnum opus*.

One such practice which Cardew abstracted from Needham was the description of a vibrato technique termed 'yin' which existed in more than ten varieties:

> Remarkable is the 'ting-yin', where the vacillating movement of the finger should
> be so subtle as to be hardly noticeable. Some handbooks say that one should
> not move the finger at all, but let the timbre be influenced by the pulsation of
> the blood in the fingertips, pressing the string down on the board a little more
> heavily than usual.[4]

On the same page Needham notes that 'even today an expert Ch'in player will himself remain intently listening long after a note has become inaudible to other listeners'. And later he remarks that 'the musician or scholar with almost miraculous ability to detect small differences of tone was revered'.[5] Elsewhere the Chinese scholar Chu Tsai-Yü's instruction for playing the pitchpipes is quoted: 'The thoughts must be serious, the mind peaceful, and the will resolute.'[6] It was Cardew's conviction, too, that the right presence of mind, the correct attitude, were essential to perform even the simplest action.[7]

Among the pages selected by Cardew there are also passages describing the practical usefulness of sound: the morale of an army, for example, could be divined on the basis of the quality of the sounds produced on the pitch-pipes by the shaman during the tense moments before battle commenced. Less portentous, the capacity of a domestic vessel would be checked by the pitch of the tones produced when it was struck.

Another practice which Cardew shared with the Chinese – although, in fact, it can be found amongst folk musicians from many diverse cultures – was the utilization of everyday objects as musical instruments. Until recent times the Chinese had used the rice pestle and mortar as a percussion instrument in the classical orchestra, just as buskers playing the spoons can still be seen in the streets of London at the beginning of the millennium. Cardew upheld the tradition with wit and flair: tables and chairs, transistor radios, ash-trays and coins were among the battery of objects he used; rough-hewn noises would be juxtaposed with delicate and intangible wisps of sound in his performances of Cage, his own music, and in his contributions with AMM. And this investigative practice – the discovery and redeployment of 'found objects' – is demanded of participants in *The Great Learning*. In Paragraph 1 'whistlers provide themselves with the wherewithal to whistle; all natural and mechanical means are permissible, from a broken tooth to empty bottles'.[8] In Paragraph 4 the use of a wand and a cushion is prescribed; sleigh-bells (!) and beans in a tin are also suggested as appropriate sound-producing material. And the dramatic possibilities inherent in Crash, Bang, Clank music in Paragraph 5 are highlighted by Cardew's provocative reference to the sounds of machinery. These are all explicit examples, but throughout the score of *The Great Learning*, embedded within the notation, a heuristic, creative approach to music-making is implied.

In particular it was the importance that the ancient Chinese attached to the social function of music which, in the late sixties, reflected Cardew's own musical priorities and at the same time distanced him from many of his European avant-garde contemporaries. During the early part of his musical career the idea of the autonomy of music would have been consonant with his own private cosmology (in 1960 he had quoted Cage's famous dictum, 'tones must be allowed to be tones', in the programme note for the first Generation Music concert at the Conway Hall), but the very nature of his subsequent musical activities subverted the notion that music existed somehow independently of people's thoughts and feelings – of their hopes and expectations, of their fears. In his music-making with AMM, and in particular with the Scratch Orchestra, the depth of his rapport with fellow musicians was such that he could not fail to be aware of the psychological and sociological bases of their musical strivings. What was common to all of them was a concern with the human response to sounds, with the associations which sounds evoke – in short, with music as a moral force. Just as the Chinese scholar had expressed centuries earlier: 'So when the man of breeding listens to the timbre (of different sorts of instruments) he does not listen merely to their clanging and tinkling, but he is also sensitive to their associations.'[9]

Cardew never entered into anything lightly, but nor was a serious preoccupation ever allowed to degenerate into an obsession; commitment was tempered with a degree of detachment, by appraisal and reappraisal. His method of study was idiosyncratic and eclectic, such that the possibility of his becoming a 'scholar', even less an 'academic', could never have arisen. However deeply he penetrated Chinese thought, however illuminating his responses, he extracted from it according to a range of personal needs – musical, social and psychological – which informed his artistic credo. It would therefore have been surprising, given the depth and substance of his involvement with Chinese culture and philosophy, if in some respect his own creative work had not been affected by it; moreover, he would have had to come to terms with the far-reaching implications of such a relation. The fact that he did so with a work of unprecedented ambition, and on a vastly expanded scale, is evidence enough of the profound influence which at least one important area of Chinese philosophy – Confucianism – had exerted on him. Clearly, his choice of text reflected more than simply a general interest in Chinese thought, especially when, at the time, one might have supposed that other Chinese writings would have better suited his musical concerns. As I have suggested, it is unlikely that there was any scholarly basis for his search for a viable text; this would have been governed more by his artistic impulses. And the same impulses would have led him to his choice of Ezra Pound's translation of *The Great Learning*.

During the seventies Cardew confessed to having fallen victim, as a young man, to the 'wildness and contradictoriness'[10] of Pound's work; it fascinated and beguiled him. A more informed approach might have steered him clear of Pound and his idiosyncratic translations, a choice which may also have been influenced by Cardew's fondness for twentieth-century poetry during this period – in particular the works of the French poets, Verlaine, Mallarmé and Rimbaud. But to have used Confucius and Pound as the basis for a musical composition in 1968, bearing in mind the prevailing mores amongst his peers at that time, would seem to have been an act of political and literary *naiveté*. As one critic commented: 'One can place about as much faith in his [Pound's] economic ideas as in his translations of Confucius.'[11] Cardew may well have been impressed by Pound's rigorously authoritarian position; moreover, his own aloofness from politics, his cultivated disdain for any kind of political commitment at that time, meant that for him Pound's fascism, and the idiosyncrasies of his translations, were of supreme irrelevance.

Perhaps the content of a letter from Howard Snell, his friend and colleague from the Royal Academy days, was still lodged in his memory, disabusing him of any doubts he may have entertained:

> Ezra is a good deal better than most people will allow. Also he's not a fascist. All he did was read bits of *Cantos* over the Italian radio in 1939 and 41, also saying that Mussolini's economics were better in some respects than Western capitalists' were.[12]

We can infer from this that Pound and his poetry had been discussed – Snell himself was writing poetry at the time – and that Cardew had possibly expressed some misgivings, or at least reservations, in the light of Pound's support for Mussolini and his anti-Semitism, neither of which receive mention in Snell's letter. Moreover, in view of Pound's admiration for Confucius, and for *The Great Learning* in particular, it is likely that Cardew had already encountered Pound's translation, more than a decade before his commission from Macnaghten Concerts in 1968, and had been impressed by Pound's analyses of Chinese history.

> In the 'Chinese' *Cantos* he [Pound] provides a panoramic view of Chinese history to show that the problems of civilisation recur, and that the most successful Chinese societies were those which upheld Confucius's ideas.[13]

Confucianism had continued to be a dominating ethic, a strong and influential tradition in China well into the twentieth century, and even after the 1949 revolution. The Confucian solution to society's ills was moralistic: Confucius advocated a return to virtue – if necessary at the expense of material gain – and to the correct observance of the ancient rites. For Confucius the highest good inhered in the mind; it was locked within, so that the central theme of *The Great Learning* is self-cultivation – not in an egocentric sense, but in accordance with the accepted social norms. Confucianism addressed itself to the dualism of the individual and society and sought to achieve a delicate balance. Confucius stressed the paramount importance of good government and his teaching was therefore directed towards the rulers whose good example the ordinary people were expected to emulate. The people were to be cherished and cared for, but they were also to be instructed and led; the hierarchical order could not be undermined or threatened. Thus, the 'virtuous man' was essentially an 'aristocrat' wielding power over the populace.

Cardew would have felt comfortable with much of this doctrine, bred to it within the English class system as a member of an élite to whom power and government were a matter of course and for whom the introspection and detachment which Pound's translation throws into relief were a corollary of its own *Weltanschauung*. But above all it was to the *moralism* at the heart of Confucian philosophy that Cardew responded; such notions (like the seven 'virtues' from the *Treatise Handbook*) permeated his own music-making at the time, with the Scratch Orchestra and with AMM, who, he reminded himself, were 'all working on their moral fibre'.[14]

I have touched upon Cardew's creative reading of texts in previous chapters – the way that he would mine texts for pointers, revelatory insights and illuminations, which the author him/herself may not have been conscious of. On the evidence of his treatment of *The Great Learning* – the eclecticism of his approach to it – his relationship to Confucianism was a complex one, and precluded an all-embracing identification of his own work with Confucian ideology. This anomaly was furthermore compounded by the multifarious reactions to Confucius' text, many of them negative, within the Scratch Orchestra, which in turn highlighted important contradictions between text and music, and text and performance. For many of us in the Scratch Orchestra the first chapter of *The Great Learning*, and Confucianism in general, simply begged too many questions.

At this juncture we should remind ourselves that only Paragraph 1 was composed before the formation of the Scratch Orchestra. The remainder of the work was written during what Howard Skempton has described as the Scratch Orchestra's 'honeymoon period': 1969/70. Indeed, as we have seen, it was largely through the necessity to recruit people for a performance of Paragraph 2, thereby augmenting Cardew's composition class at Morley College, that the Scratch Orchestra came into existence; the histories of *The Great Learning* and the Scratch Orchestra are indissolubly interwoven and interdependent. *The Great Learning* has to be viewed, therefore, within the context of the birth and development of the Scratch Orchestra, with which it is roughly coextensive.

In this respect Bryn Harris, Scratch Orchestra stalwart, has contributed some pertinent observations, pointing out that the demands on the performers of the three Paragraphs composed first – 1, 2 and 7 – are more straightforward than those of the later Paragraphs. Thus the level of self-discipline required of the 'untrained musicians' in Paragraph 6 increased considerably 'in accord with the needs apparent in the newly-assembled Scratch Orchestra'. Moreover, by the time Paragraph 4 had been completed, six months after Paragraph 6, Harris recalls that the Scratch Orchestra, for better or for worse, had established its own musical identity, such that most members had abandoned Cardew's category of 'Scratch music' and were expressing their musicality or their own idiosyncratic attitudes towards, and understanding of, music in Scratch concerts with scant reference to Cardew's original Draft Constitution. In Paragraph 4 the rigour associated with Paragraph 6 is abandoned.[15] Furthermore, Paragraph 3, the last but one Paragraph to be completed, in its use of notated parts for bass instruments – which constitute, literally, the 'roots' of the piece, and from which it derives its essential character – is a work which really fell outside the scope of the orchestra. And as an indication, perhaps, of Cardew's disillusionment with what he regarded as the Orchestra's lack of substance and development, Paragraph 3 provides support for Harris's thesis.

With Paragraph 5, however, probably the last to be completed, Cardew seems to have returned to the fold with a score in which he set out to accommodate every individual and collective aspect of Scratch Orchestra practice at that time. In doing so he demonstrated, conclusively, his commitment to the Orchestra, whatever misgivings he may or may not have felt. Paragraph 5 'reflects what I understood to be the internal structure of the Orchestra at the time of composition' Cardew wrote in a programme note for a performance of Paragraph 5 at Cecil Sharp House in London on 21 January 1972. It was a conscious attempt to come to terms with the needs and demands of the Scratch Orchestra, its outlandish admixture of talent and anti-talent, whilst at the same time sustaining the educative impulse which was central to his purpose. Throughout Paragraph 5 the various attributes of the Scratch Orchestra – including a penchant, by some, for activities of a risible nature – are skilfully deployed; for some Scratch members it was a cathartic release, induced by a score which was a synaesthetic celebration of the manifold talents and predispositions of the entire Orchestra. At the same time what constituted for Cardew the essential core of the Paragraph, indeed of the whole work, was intended as a built-in, sobering influence – a point on which he expounded in the previously referred to interview with Hanne Boenisch in the wake of the northeast tour in June 1971:

But the theme in *The Great Learning* that I find the most important is what is actually central to the text: that self-discipline is the only discipline; that you discipline yourself, and for the person who is disciplined himself, the whole world is in order. He emanates order. So in our chaotic or confused Scratch Orchestra concerts the person who is there in the middle of it, still and controlled, he emanates order through that confusion.

And of course, the person in the middle – still, calm and controlled, emanating order – was invariably Cardew himself, and it was through the presence and quality of his performing, and his manifest integrity, that he stamped his authority on the proceedings. The Orchestra's collective pragmatism allowed them to accept Cardew as an 'authority', as 'Emperor', and although he would often delegate responsibility, and even at a later stage offered to abdicate, nobody was willing to take his place.

The Boenisch interview offers invaluable insights not only into Cardew's relation to *The Great Learning* but also into his relationship with the Scratch Orchestra:

Cardew: I probably go a lot further than a lot of people, upholding these [Confucian] principles.

Boenisch: That means avoiding problems around you, doesn't it?

Cardew: Yes, it does. It really means not to dislike. To be so secure in your position in the world that things don't disturb you. You can go into them without being disturbed.

Boenisch: Well, whenever something makes you unhappy that comes from outside, from your environment, you still have to behave with 'propriety' and 'righteousness'?

Cardew: I believe that things that make you unhappy come from inside you; I don't think they come from the environment. I think everything comes from inside you. But this is maybe a rather specialised view. I'm certainly not immune to the unpleasant effects of the environment. When in the night mosquitoes bite I think my unhappiness comes from the outside environment. But then again I think, well, if I was inwardly correct the mosquitoes wouldn't dream of biting me. So, there you are (laughs).
There are other principles in *The Great Learning*, like – love the people, that I think are very important: 'To watch with affection the way people grow.' One way in which the Scratch Orchestra differs from a conventional concert is that the Scratch Orchestra doesn't dominate the audience in the way that in conventional concerts the audience is dominated by the music. So, my feeling is that we should

have an affectionate attitude to the audience, not a lecturing [hectoring ?] attitude.

Yet notwithstanding Cardew's solicitous attitude towards the Scratch Orchestra, from the outset there were difficulties and obstacles in relation to the text of *The Great Learning* which some members and friends of the Orchestra were quick to seize upon. Some felt bound not to ignore what they regarded as the negative aspects of the text – such as the overt authoritarianism and the overriding importance given to the hierarchical structure of the family. Some, with just a hint of malice perhaps, 'interpreted' parts of the text, and its use, in the light of their experience in the Scratch Orchestra: the 'virtuous man', the aristocrat, wielding power over the populace 'for their own good', described all too accurately the relationship which some perceived to exist between Cardew and the Scratch Orchestra. Scratch member Phil Gebbett gave a brief presentation drawing attention to the essentially 'reactionary' nature of Confucianism, and there was unequivocal and perhaps unexpected dissent from even closer quarters when Eddie Prévost once remarked, 'you can't be a Confucian and play in the AMM!' For some observers the Scratch Orchestra and Confucianism were just as incompatible. Bryn Harris' characterisation of the inherent irreconcilability of text and music is expressed in appropriately political terms: Cardew was trying 'to vitiate Confucianism with Democracy, to amalgamate a philosophy based on a tribute-paying society with the bourgeois, democratic, socio-economic formation'.[16]

The jarring of the text/music exegetic relationship and the tensions it created are particularly evident in Paragraphs 4 and 5: in 4 the participants and audience are exhorted to 'rectify their hearts' and to 'discipline themselves'; in 5, having attained this 'self-discipline', they can now 'set their own houses in order'. The culmination of these textual exhortations is a free improvisation which constitutes the second half of Paragraph 5 and normally lasts at least an hour. The goal, then, as expressed through the music-making, is 'freedom' and I recall that in the prodigality and kaleidoscopic bedlam of Scratch Orchestra performances, the kind of freedoms expressed through wit, humour, contrariness, riotous imagination, and the occasional inspired musical gesture, would have found no place in the Confucian orthodoxy. Each member, and Cardew was no exception, was as adept and willing to expose a lack of aptitude in any particular domain as to demonstrate his or her prowess in another. Such 'freedoms' – and in any case 'freedom' is arguably a misnomer in the context – could not be attained within the rigid, hierarchical framework of Confucianism in which texts are obeyed and rules are followed; a certain comfort and security yes, but not individual freedom – western, 'bourgeois' style, with its latent associations of guilt and anxiety.

Perhaps I, too, in this interpretation of Confucianism, have fallen victim to an 'orthodoxy'. For when Confucius asked his disciples what they would do if they had authority in the state, Pound's paraphrase in 'Canto XIII reads:

> And Tian said, with his hand on the strings of his lute
> The low sounds continuing
> > after his hands left the strings,
> And the sound went up like smoke, under the leaves,
> And he looked after the sound:
> > "The old swimming hole,
> "And the boys flopping off the planks,
> "Or sitting in the underbush playing mandolins." [17]

Asked who was right, Confucius said they had all answered according to their nature, hence correctly; but, sighing, said that he was with Tian.

Nevertheless, at the time of planning and writing Paragraph 5 Cardew would have been cognizant of the fact that the relationship of the Scratch Orchestra's musical and philosophical ethos to the demands of Confucianism, as they interpreted them and in respect of *The Great Learning*, had reached breaking point. His expedient, characteristically extreme, is to effect a dramatic intervention half-way through Paragraph 5; the Confucianism which has reigned unchallenged throughout the previous four paragraphs is suddenly confronted and (temporarily) overthrown: a *coup d'état* which has been thoroughly prepared – as Cardew explains in the score:

> It should be understood that the entire paragraph is an improvisation rite [...]. No formal components (not even the Ode Machines or the Action/Number Scores) should be allowed to overrun this point of rest and spill into the improvising part. They are all a prelude to an accord to the 'prescribed spontaneity apparent in Nature'.

And this is followed in the score by the 'Firelighting Component', an 'inspirational text' through which Cardew allows the confusion and irrationality of the world outside to invade and disrupt the sacred domain of Confucian thought. This Taoist text expresses, and encourages expression of, doubts and questions; it invites consideration of the dichotomy of order and spontaneity, for example, and is itself replete with images of a wild and headstrong music, a music which corresponds to the 'spontaneity apparent in Nature'.

It is easy to understand how both Confucianism and Taoism exerted influence on Cardew; the essence of each was manifest in Cardew's own personality. On the one hand his propensity for dogma and authority, purity and orthodoxy (Confucianism), to which his preoccupation with the writings of Wittgenstein and later the political doctrines of Marx and Lenin bear witness; on the other hand his visionary spirit, his passion for the writings of Blake, Burroughs and the Beats, for the spontaneous, the intuitive, the poetic, his music-making with AMM, and his delight in the 'carefree flight from respectability and responsibility' (Taoism).[18] At different stages of his career one might seem to hold sway, but never to the complete exclusion of the other; rather he contrived a miraculous balance, and in the heat of intense, sharp-edged, goal-orientated political activity in the last decade he could still write an inscription to one of his piano works: 'Try and let it float.'[19]

The Great Learning is the first of four texts which constitute the Confucian School of Philosophy: *The Great Learning,* the *Mean, Analects, and Mencius*. The so-called Four Books were compiled by the Sung scholar Chu Hsi in the twelfth century AD and were used as a basic primer in Chinese education, continuing to exert a considerable influence on Chinese thought well into the twentieth century. *The Great Learning* is an essay of some one thousand seven hundred and fifty words in eleven chapters, and was written around 260 BC by a pupil of Mencius (390-305 BC), one of the chief disciples of the Confucian doctrine. The first chapter of *The Great Learning*, on which Cardew's work is based, is attributed to Confucius himself (ca.600 BC). It divides into seven paragraphs, and these form the basis of Cardew's composition. And of the numerous European translations of the text Cardew was particularly attracted to that of Ezra Pound.

Paragraph 1 of Cardew's *The Great Learning* received its first performance at the Cheltenham Festival on 9 July 1968 by the Louis Halsey Singers.[20] However welcome this Macnaghten Concerts commission may have been as temporary and brief alleviation of a financial situation which was always critical, it was also an inducement to return to worlds with which he was experiencing increasing disenchantment – the world of the trained, professional musician and, in particular, the world of the contemporary music festival. Having tasted both frustration and disillusionment with performances of *Treatise* with classically trained, professional musicians, he was now again on the periphery of the music establishment whose recognition of him, with one or two notable exceptions (among them Sir Thomas Armstrong, Principal of the RAM, and the critic Andrew Porter), had never been more than token. Such a relation was not surprising; nor did Cardew himself ever voice any complaint about the lack of official patronage. Rather he valued and cultivated his independence, his status, as 'outsider'. His own creative agenda and the more circumscribed aspirations of a liberal musical establishment and its client artists had by this time already reached a state of incompatibility, and the attitude of many critics, too easily forgotten in the passage of time, had become hostile and intolerant.

After the Macnaghten commission there were to be only two more positive gestures from established musical bodies before Cardew's death thirteen years later: the performance in the Albert Hall in July 1972 of a revised version of Paragraphs 1 and 2 of *The Great Learning* in the Promenade Concerts series – a not altogether successful venture, as we shall see – and a further commission in 1981, the year of his death, from New Macnaghten Concerts for a two-piano work which was performed at the Wigmore Hall by Susan Bradshaw and myself.

In the following extract, written sometime in 1967, Cardew expresses the dilemma he experiences *vis-à-vis* the musical profession:

I see no possibility of turning to account the tremendous musical potential that musically educated people evidently represent, except by providing them with what they want: traditionally notated scores of maximum complexity. The most hopeful fields are those of choral and orchestral writing since there the individual personality (which a musical education seems so often to thwart) is absorbed into a larger organism, which speaks through its individual members as if from some higher sphere.[21]

Completed on 31 April 1968, Paragraph 1 was, indeed, commissioned by 'musically educated people', but the notation and the demands made of the musicians lie outside traditional conventions. Furthermore, to add insult to injury, as it were, the Louis Halsey Singers were not even required to sing; their role consisted in reciting, and playing stones and whistles.

The opening of Paragraph 1 is a master-stroke; no characteristic motif, no orthodox presentation of a tone-row, no *Klangzauberei* to bewitch and impress the listener's ear; simply a minor third on the organ, *p possibile*, accompanied by a clatter of stones: a compelling evocation of pre-history. Within a matter of seconds of the commencement of this seven-hour work Cardew encapsulates the ethical purity of the Confucian text by the simplest means, and the immediacy of communication is quite remarkable.

By contrast the ensuing organ solo is grandiose: a multi-layered, slowly-shifting texture emerges, necessitating the use of wedges, or weights, to keep the keys depressed while the player is occupied on another manual, and at a different register. The writing is bold, but always idiomatic, and the instrumental lay-out is entirely practical. In his instructions to the organist Cardew indicates the particular stylistic treatment he favours: 'Approach the instrument's idiosyncrasies: isolated notes coming from widely separated pipes, false tunings obtained by gradual pulling out and pushing in of stops.'[22] The apparent contradiction between the swift and dextrous movements of the organist shifting the wedges/weights on the one hand, and the relatively slow tempo of the music as experienced on the other, is resolved by virtue of the fact that it is precisely by dint of the sheer number and complexity of the actions that the organist achieves the desired pacing of the music – an interesting example of the subtlety of thought which informs Cardew's notations. Even so, lest the performer should feel overwhelmed by the profusion of detail Cardew concludes his instructions with quite specific advice in relation to phrasing:

> Avoid the impression of continuous and laboured concentration. Actions are to be performed briskly in groups, separated by pauses for relaxation and listening. Such pauses are generally not indicated in the score and are at the discretion of the player.[23]

The final and longest section of Paragraph 1 consists of an alternation of whistling solos and reciting chorus. The performers are divided into whistlers and speakers; each individual whistler – having provided him/herself with 'the wherewithal to whistle' – chooses his/her tone and sustains it, taking a breath where necessary. The whistlers take it in turns to interpret a solo, temporarily abandoning their sustained tone, and each solo alternates with a recitation of the text by the speaking group. (This mantric interpretation of the text corresponds to Ezra Pound's own instruction 'to keep re-reading the whole digest until he understands'.[24]) Constant throughout is the whistle cluster, a backcloth to both recitation and solo, which gradually and imperceptibly shifts and changes as one by one each whistler returns to the fold after soloing, but with a new sustained tone.

A distinctive feature of *The Great Learning* is Cardew's acute awareness of the physical, spatial and acoustic properties of sounds; the grain of the sounds he selects always seems uncannily attuned to both the musical and the textual context.[25] In Paragraph 1 the dynamic quality of the individual solos superimposed on the dematerialized, static quality of the whistle cluster expresses both the (spoken) notion of 'the way people grow' and that of 'coming to rest'. Time and again Cardew demonstrates his unerring ability to weigh up the claims of the individual parameters for degrees of autonomy; where, in the part for whistles in Paragraph 1 for example, the exact notation of pitch would be a cramping irrelevance, the desirability of the utmost refinement in phrasing and pitch inflection is expressed through a precisely drawn notation of considerable inventiveness and sophistication. These notations are directed at the player; they are an incentive to play or improvise in a certain way – that is, with particular musical objectives in mind, rather than a conventional symbolization of specific tones. Cardew had access to subtleties of musical thought which few attain; he was able to penetrate to the quiddity of a musical utterance and to create its notational equivalent or, as in the case of *Treatise*, a kind of visual metaphor (Ex.11.1a-b).

Ex.11.1a. From the whistle notation in Paragraph 1.

By contrast it is the pitch material, precisely notated, that is the crucial component in the organ solo. Embedded within the dense clusters which permeate the texture there are often conventional triads and other recognisable and familiar harmonies whose tonal references and implications, despite the slow tempo and engulfing dissonances, colour the music in a quite striking manner. In the final sentence of the organ solo, for example, a slow harmonic progression can be discerned: C minor, D major, C minor tonalities, and a final resolution in E flat major at which point the whistling and recitation enter:

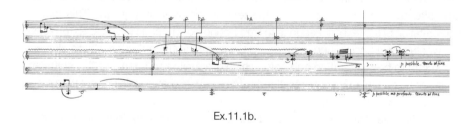

Ex.11.1b.

Against this background other events can be discerned, both as foreground melodic material, and as a reinforcement of the upper harmonic partials.[26]

After the final whistle solo the speakers recite the text for the last time; a Chinese bell rings (though this is optional), and the chorus of whistling disintegrates. The organ is switched off and the last chord, with an eerie, melancholy cry, dies away.

As we have seen, the first draft of Paragraph 2, completed in January 1969, was presented by Cardew to his Morley College composition class in the same month. A weekly regimen was instituted, allowing little time for other activities. The overwhelming sound of the drums soon convinced Cardew that a larger body of singers was required; these would be divided into groups and to each group a drummer would be assigned. The 'singers' comprised a heterogeneous congregation, some of whose vocal abilities would have found natural expression in a church choir, while others would have been more at home on the football terraces. Musically and socially this admixture of trained and untrained musicians, of diverse talents and inclinations, was ideal.

To what extent did Cardew consciously tailor the musical language of Paragraph 2 to meet the needs of this largely untrained group of performers? For he was no longer creating music for performance by an avant-garde elite, for experts well versed in the complexities of modernist techniques on whom he continued to rely, with misgivings, in his performances of *Treatise*. In Paragraph 2 the musical language does seem to have been determined by social considerations; the adventurous harmony which informs the organ part of Paragraph 1 is abandoned in favour of a traditional pentatonicism: melodic material which is eminently negotiable for 'non-singers' (Ex.11.2).

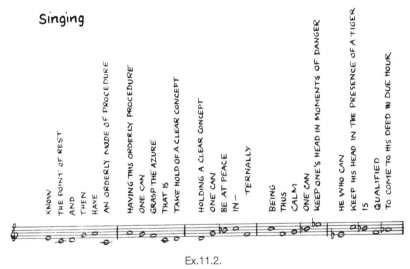

Ex.11.2.

Through a unique deployment of traditional and archaic patterns of musical rhetoric, whose associational meanings have been built up through centuries of usage and development, Paragraph 2 touches upon mythic and collective levels of experience and was a bold, apparently regressive departure in Cardew's on-going re-definition of music and music-making. Yet there are, or seem to be, specific contemporary references: Howard Skempton describes Paragraph 2 as 'an homage to Terry Riley'; certainly in its use of repetition and modality it recalls Riley's *In C* and *Keyboard Studies*, written several years earlier, although the Confucian text, the heroics demanded of the singers, and the sheer volume generated by the drummers, together create quite a different listening experience.

The text is sung five times, using the same melodic material, except that each repetition is sung a semitone higher so that by the end of the piece the tessitura of each singer appears to have been extended, or rather, shifted upwards. There are twenty-six drum rhythms so that each successive sung tone is accompanied by a new rhythm; the wild and exuberant noise of the drumming drives the voices on, the notated pitches impelling the voices inexorably into ever higher regions. In performance

the five or more chorus groups, widely separated in space, each with its own lead singer and drummer, move through the vocal part, each at a rate determined by the collective breath-length of the singers in that group and the leader's timing of the entry of each new note; starting roughly together, they gradually diverge, and as one group forges ahead and another falls behind, a freely canonic structure emerges, generating harmony and counterpoint across the space.[27]

The staging of Paragraph 2 encourages the audience to be mobile; the listener may move, using the space and experiencing changing foci as the sound of a particular group recedes, or emerges, or merges with that of another. The drum rhythms are usually sharp and dominant, sometimes indistinct, as a rule overwhelming but occasionally overwhelmed within the general hubbub. The critic Bayan Northcott found the conclusion 'in its primitive way rather a noble noise',[28] and a professional colleague referred to 'the strength, vitality and even ebullience of this wild but happy music'. The groups end independently, the drummers continue to drum until a signal; and with a deafening silence, the music stops.

The text of Paragraph 2 embodies a clear purpose and is cast in cumulative form, and yet in performance the text and music might seem to be at variance. For the required moral fortitude expressed so unequivocally in the text is compromised in the music in various ways. Like the text the music is exhortatory but the performer (human) responses to it have tended to drag a whole gamut of complex and ambivalent feelings and reactions in their wake. The music neither expresses nor interprets the text; rather it creates a psycho/sociological situation in which the text is exposed to the idiosyncrasies, the vagaries, the unpredictability of human behaviour. The idea, for example, of the endless cycle of striving and failing and its acceptance is surely central to the musical performance of Paragraph 2, but it is hard to identify such notions in Confucius' text. Cardew liked to tell the story (which had been told to him by Michael Parsons) of the Buddhist monks who would practise their chanting by a waterfall, the sound of which was so strong it could not possibly be drowned by the relatively weak sound of the voices. But the monks would nevertheless be inspired to reach new levels of vocal perseverance and prowess. Likewise in Paragraph 2 the singers struggle manfully but vainly against the irresistible force of the drumming, although in many cases it is unlikely that their relationship with the drumming maintains the same degree of equanimity as that of the monks towards the waterfall. Some singers have confessed to feelings of resentment towards the drummers because the drumming rendered the execution and maintenance of both note and word more difficult. For some singers the drumming engendered feelings of 'helplessness' and 'weakness', which Western culture finds inappropriate; the negative connotations of 'failure' are too strong. Such 'impurities' find no place in the text.[29]

On completion of Paragraph 2 Cardew initially used the title *The Great Digest* – 'Digest' implying rather a systematic and comprehensive compilation of facts. Significantly, in the light of his experience of working on the piece and performing it, he changed the title to *The Great Learning*; perhaps because 'learning' implies the acquisition of knowledge through self-discovery and experience – a central theme of the musical work.

Paragraph 3, for large instruments and voices, was completed on 14 July 1970. The text, which is the most succinct of all the seven Paragraphs, consists of three short sentences.[30] As the structural basis for his composition Cardew uses the metaphor of 'root and branch' so that the relationship between text and music is quite specific (Ex.11.3a-b). The instruments lay down and share a low, ruminant A flat which underpins the entire paragraph and from which root and branches emanate: a heavy ground swell of freely chosen, slowly ascending scales and arpeggios of varying intervals, wide or narrow, regular or irregular.

14. Some ascending scales

Ex.11.3a.

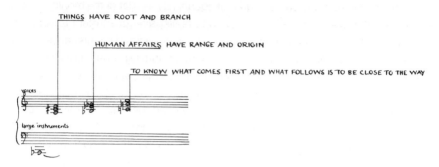

Ex.11.3b.

When it is (collectively) felt that the instrumental sound has established itself, the first word, 'things', of the first sentence is sung, the singers selecting one of the three given notes of an A major chord. (To secure a particular pitch a singer may avail him/herself of an auxiliary instrument; for example, a bell or pitch pipe.) By asking the singers to repeat the word 'over and over' Cardew exploits the energy locked within the basic harmonic unit – the major chord which, in a sea of instrumental dissonance, is consolidated and projected until it achieves recognizability and 'clarity' (Ex.11.3b). The singers may then move, individually, into the next phase in which they select from the instrumental tones they can hear that are within their vocal range. The singers are not required to read, but they do need to listen acutely in order to identify and separate singable pitches from a morass of instrumental sound, and to sing and sustain those tones in the context of a highly dissonant instrumental 'accompaniment'. The chosen tones are used to complete the remainder of the sentence and when this treatment of the text is completed the instrumental sound is repeated as before: the low A flat and slowly ascending tones. The next two sentences are treated in the same way, but with a different triad.

'All playing is an extension of singing; the voice and its extensions are the musical dimension of men, women, children, and animals' Cardew wrote.[31] And whence singing? For it is as if Paragraph 3 is sited in pre-history; the vibrating low A flat evokes a huge, slumbering pre-historic mammal, whilst the ascending instrumental scales suggest a metaphor for the primeval sounds of nature to which, at first mimetically, man's dawning consciousness seeks to relate. What is clear is that Cardew is not concerned here with the traditional, emotive representations of concerted choral delivery; the individual is not moulded into the collective, there is no synchronised breathing, no control of dynamics, no expressive reduction according to the demands of a specific culture (say, of the English choral tradition). Cardew's aim is not a culturally standardised sound where the grain of the individual voice has been neutralised, its disposition towards unruliness suppressed. On the contrary he exploits these differences to enhance the life and immediacy of the sound. In Paragraph 3 the listener can identify different individual qualities, rough and smooth, pure and croaky, trained and untrained, bourgeois and proletarian. What Cardew achieves is a miraculous balance between the individual and the collective, between composer's concept and plan and performers' abilities and predilections.[32]

Paragraph 4 was first performed at St. Pancras church in the Euston Road, north London. Completed 10 April 1970, when the activities of the Scratch Orchestra were at their zenith, Paragraph 4, for chorus and organ, reflects the ritualistic quality, already strong in Paragraph 1, which characterised many Scratch performances at that time. Dave Smith draws attention to this feature of Paragraph 4 in the programme note to the Almeida Festival performance: 'Brings La Monte Young's *Death Chant* to mind! It's very ritualistic and there's a lot of repetitive and ethnic music with that quality. And watching people beating cushions increases the effect.'

The chorus part is divided into seven sections – corresponding to the seven lines of the text – each of which is accompanied by the organ. A coda, during which the organ is silent, brings the Paragraph to a close. The chorus sits in crocodile formation, usually on the floor, and performs in canon, declaiming the syllables of the text at regular beats – the tempo for each section having been chosen by a leader. At each entry of the voice part one member of the chorus, whoever volunteers first, has the option of standing up, moving around, while performing an improvised version of the text – whispering, speaking, shouting, singing, keening, etc., although Cardew permits only one improvisation to a section.

The chorus accompanies each syllable by striking a 'sonorous substance' with a 'wand' (any kind of beater) – two expressions borrowed from a description of the music of the Arabian Nights Entertainment. Following tradition 'sonorous substance' may have referred to a cushion; in Paragraph 4 Cardew suggests that the phrase may be interpreted to mean anything that produces a satisfying sound when struck (or that one derives satisfaction from striking) with the 'wand'. The wand, too, may play an even more dynamic role if, for example, it is found to produce a satisfying sound in its passage through the air. In the second, fourth and seventh sections rattles or jingles are placed on the sonorous substances; these are not struck but should reverberate in sympathy when the sonorous substance is struck.

The declamatory sections alternate with interludes for notched or ridged, guero-type instruments which are stroked, rubbed, scraped with the wand according to a notational system similar to that for the whistling in Paragraph 1. The notation is therefore interpreted by each member 'according to his lights'. However, Cardew does cite the main variables that the notation may control: 1) speed of stroke, 2) force of stroke (pressure), 3) position (hilt to point) of the wand in stroking. And the guero may also be struck, 'laterally, longitudinally, etc. as suggested by the vertical strokes in the notation'. When the declamation of the text is completed and the organ falls silent, the coda is performed; all the 'guero' material is repeated, again in canon but now without reference to a beat.

Paragraph 4 is thus a development of Paragraph 1; the successive whistle solos of 1 are paralleled by the superimposed guero 'solos' of 4. (It also relates to Scratch Music in the way that an individual soloist can emerge, temporarily, from the collective.) In both cases individual, quasi-improvised contributions are performed within a strictly imposed framework. Moreover, both encourage and nourish an attitude of respect for nature, for natural sounds, creating fresh and instant awareness of their physical, spatial, and acoustic properties.

The organ part

The organ part is extremely demanding; several staves of chords are read simultaneously and freely superimposed with the proviso that (Ex.11.4.)

> the events on each individual stave should occur in the written order, without overlapping. The staves in each section are introduced in the written order, but thereafter the counterpointing of staves is free […]. Overlapping of events from different staves may be cultivated. Strong contrast between events participating in such overlaps is desirable.[33]

> According to Robert Coleridge

> the score creates impossible demands: trying to make sense of these very disparate events, and actually following the rules whereby events in a single system should not overlap. To make a continuity out of this is quite difficult.[34]

Ex.11.4.

In the second edition of *The Great Learning* there is an intimidating addendum: 'Rather than make a version [...] the organist should attempt to play spontaneously, reading from the score.' Coleridge opines that such an exercise 'would demand a brain like a computer or the brain of a chess grandmaster who also has to see the long-range implications of each move'.[35]

The technique implied for the organist is to use correspondences of tones between staves (chords with shared tones) to allow for gradual harmonic changes via pivotal tones which constantly vary their structural function. This procedure is not unlike that of Paragraph 7 where the held tones of the singers, sometimes subtly, sometimes disconcertingly and even dramatically, change their structural, harmonic function – or rather, it is changed for them by the slowly shifting context in which they cohabit.

With such freedom of choice for the performer the question of stylistic consistency, or inconsistency, is another consideration with which the organist is burdened, even if Cardew on one occasion had encouraged an anxious composition student, one Howard Skempton, to 'put everything he liked into a piece'! After all, some interpreters might also be tempted to put in things they do not like. And why not? One solution is to look at Cardew's own answers to these questions: *Three Winter Potatoes* and *Material*, for example, do embrace everything, from clusters to triads and diatonic fragments; and it is this heterogeneity that constitutes a large part of their fascination, their poetry. It might be tempting, for example, to exploit the rich, sensuous qualities and intrinsic beauty of individual chords from the organ part and to create combinations and progressions according to taste (as in *Material*), even if the generally dense texture makes it difficult to throw refinements of detail into relief. Furthermore, the subtlety of Cardew's notation obliges the performer to come to terms with his own musical preferences, in a sense to justify them; chords with strong tonal associations – dominant seventh chords, Neapolitan, added sixth chords, provoke action either on their behalf, as it were – by bringing them to the fore – or by negating their associations and implications through ectopic juxtapositions and superimpositions of other chords. Similarly, a sequence of three repeated chords may be treated simply as periodic reiterations, or points of rest, or may be broken up by enclosing material from other systems between repetitions of the chord. More radically, specific organ techniques could be used to obscure pitches in much the same way that preparations in the piano can distort pitch.

The overall duration and sheer massiveness of the organ events in Paragraph 4, together with the occasional, penetrating vocal sounds, makes the projection of detail well-nigh impossible. Exquisite refinements, sounds of undemonstrative beauty, are inevitably lost within the exhilarating hubbub of this music in a manner which, like the voices at the waterfall in Paragraph 2, recalls many processes in nature. And this was precisely Cardew's intention, which the score and instructions subtlety safeguards. 'Work on the (organ) piece!' Robert Coleridge wrote to me, 'is a 'Great Learning' in itself'.[36]

Paragraph 5 received its first performance at the Cecil Sharp House on 21 January 1971. It had been commissioned (a fee of £100 had been agreed) by Macnaghten Concerts (as had Paragraph 1) although the work may well have been completed, in its general outline, before the idea of a commission had arisen. Paragraph 5 is the most diverse and complex Paragraph of *The Great Learning*, bringing together a multifarious assortment of visual and musical elements, including gestures, activities, games, songs and free improvisation. As we have seen from Cardew's programme note the relationship to the Scratch Orchestra is quite explicit, and in Paragraph 5 he sought to create an appropriate musical language, or rather musical notation, for a whole range of activities which would have been considered, certainly in the music world, to belong in an entirely different province of art, if indeed art was what it was. 'The musician's pursuit is to recognize the musical composition of the world (rather as Shelley does in Prometheus Unbound).' This unequivocal statement appears towards the end of 'Towards an Ethic of Improvisation',[37] and was to find its ultimate expression in Paragraph 5 of *The Great Learning*. Cardew's artistic manifesto was taken up with gusto by the Scratch Orchestra; uninhibited and pragmatic, unconstrained by theoretical concerns, they responded to Cardew's score to the manner born.

Paragraph 5 begins with a 'Dumbshow', a visual translation of the graphic elements which make up the Chinese characters of the text into gestures derived from a hybrid of American-Indian sign languages evolved during the nineteenth century for communicating with whites. Cardew had no qualms about this kind of eclecticism; his artistic needs would always override cultural correctness. As we have seen, his approach to world cultures was never hidebound, nor academic; it was imaginative and creative, crossing boundaries of time and space with untroubled ease.

The Dumbshow highlights the gestural qualities of performance which Cardew had explored and projected with AMM music; it was the image of the body as received by the audience which concerned him. The Dumbshow is enacted as a kind of ritualised instruction embodying the educative ethos of *The Great Learning*; thus, 'the players divide into groups of seven or eight and each sits as if in a classroom'. The text for Paragraph 5 consists of seven sentences, each of which is realised in the Dumbshow through gesture: the first performer (teacher) interprets the first sentence while the second performer (pupil) watches. He or she in turn interprets the first sentence for the third performer while the first performer continues with the second sentence, and so on until all the performers are involved, both as teachers and pupils. Cardew includes a proviso that those who think they will be relatively slow in performance should go first while the quicker interpreters hold back, thus ensuring that all the players finish at roughly the same time – or at least embarrassing discrepancies will be avoided. What is conveyed to the audience is the idea of the cherishing and handing down of knowledge.

The Dumbshow comprises a range of bodily movements from the subtlest and tiniest to the broadest: cast eyes vaguely about, narrow the eyes, waggle the fingers, shake the hands like foliage, sway the arms as in wind, make little firework explosions. And there is mime: 'pretend to lift a pail of water'. Speed of movements, too, may be prescribed, such as a deceleration following a swift thrust forward, and although there is no formal 'music-making' in the Dumbshow, certain gestures are accompanied by vocal sounds of an indeterminate nature. Cardew's poetic imagery (the 'notation') is designed both as an *aide-mémoire* and as a stimulus for the performer's imagination, encouraging grace and elegance in the movements. And yet the instructions also require commitment and discipline in respect of their memorisation and precision of execution; Cardew exercises considerable control over the performer's movements. From sentence 3:

EITHER: Left hand strikes mouth several times (mouth position as for silent yell) followed by right hand flicked violently forward at shoulder level, as if throwing heavy dart or shaking off sticky dough. OR: Left fore-finger (other fingers are held by the thumb) nail against lips; Flip the finger (remainder of hand keeping still) several times against the lips, then slide it over to left cheek, turning hand so that nail now faces outwards. Suddenly throw it forwards with whole hand, opening the hand en route.

Throughout the Dumbshow each sentence features a 'centrepiece' which effectively divides it into two more or less equal parts, demonstrating Cardew's concern for structural clarity. The characteristic 'centrepiece' comprises small movements around the face accompanied by facial expression and whistling. The end of the Dumbshow has a comic ring: the performers cover their ears with their hands, fingers pointing down the neck, and then walk around on their heels 'for as long as you feel inclined', rather like a children's playground game.

The Dumbshow is followed by eight, short, verbal compositions ('verbal', that is, in their notation); each of the compositions is preceded by a recitation, in chorus, of the whole text pertaining to Paragraph 5. The compositions, which appear to bear little or no relationship to the text, nevertheless constitute a carefully considered preparation, a kind of training ground, for the ensuing improvisation. They are entitled: *Crash Bang Clank Music, Loud and Soft Laughter Music, Mountain Top Music, Silent Music, Beautiful Sound Music, Bowed Sound, Plink* and, optionally accompanying *Plink, Tube Train Stopped Between Stations*. The titles themselves provide a realistic indication of the character of the music whilst the ensuing 'notations' abound with imaginative ploys to generate the appropriate music:

> *Mountain Top Music*. Mostly winds. Taking off. Flying high. 'Blow your problems and solutions to the four winds.' In the middle get quiet but none the less blowy for that. Think of mountain contours all around 'cutting the horizon fold over fold'.

And at the end of *Plink* the following preparation is suggested:

> Spend time with the Masters of Plink in their hierarchy: Hugh Shrapnel, Christian Wolff, Webern, God. And on their work.

Cardew's intention was that individual members of the Scratch Orchestra would provide performance versions of these pieces; indeed, he seems to have had certain people in mind for particular compositions: Greg Bright for *Crash Bang Clank Music*, for which Michael Brawner also provided an imaginative and highly detailed version, and Hugh Shrapnel for *Silent Music* and, possibly, bearing in mind the dedication, *Plink*. After the final composition and recitation there ensues the Improvisation Rite, which is the core of the Paragraph.

An interesting obligation adhering to this basic structure is that each performer should for one of the seven compositions, any composition, become a member of the audience. If Cardew was ever questioned on his purpose for this instruction, it has hitherto not come to light. Perhaps he felt that the idea of 'taking a breather', of stepping back and adopting the role of 'passive' spectator would act beneficially upon the performer's attitude towards the music itself, and towards his fellow performers. After each recitation Cardew thus provides three alternatives: a composition, sitting it out, and the so-called Action/Number scores. And 'a decision once made must be allowed to run its course until the next recitation'.

Theatrical elements threatened, more often enhanced, many Scratch performances and they had to be accommodated. Cardew duly provided optional 'Action and Number Scores', to run parallel with the seven compositions, in which the emphasis is visual and the performers interpret by way of gestures, game-playing, the working out and presentation of relationships, and so forth (Ex.11.5a). Each sentence of the text is represented by lists of words comprising objects, activities, parts of the body, parts of the room, instruments, etc: streamer, COINGAME, LEGWORK, floor, drum, dumbshow/LIGHT, guero, handgame, swoosh/whistle, overhead, are some of the ideas provided for sentence 1.[38] The performer reads through, choosing and accumulating words from which actions are invented and superimposed; an activity may be discarded in favour of another, or activities may be continued in parallel for as long as it is practical. As Bryn Harris has pointed out, all five senses can be satisfied in Paragraph 5, including taste (the word 'mouth' appears) where the distribution of food might be incorporated. The action and number score component of Paragraph 5 clearly relates to the Scratch Orchestra's '1001 Activities'.

To accommodate a wider context, which the Scratch Orchestra's activities invariably embraced, Cardew also provides a sketch – a human body superimposed on two circles – with the title Topography:

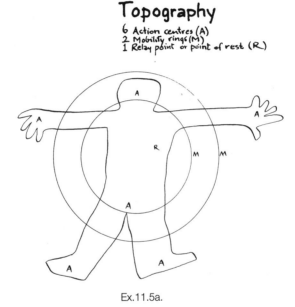

Ex.11.5a.

The various reference points marked on the sketch provide possible locations in and around the performing space; routes for audience circulation, and what Cardew describes as 'relay points' or 'points of rest' where, for example, centres of information might be set up where 'someone in touch with the action can inform the curious as to what goes on', or a central point whence activities can be coordinated, or terminated.

Of the remaining 'optional' material the ten 'Ode Machines' – ten unaccompanied 'songs' – provide a profuseness of highly expressive monody which may be sung throughout the first half of the Paragraph – that is, up to the improvisation (Ex.11.5b-f). The performance of the Odes is staggered so that they all end roughly at the same time: the longest Ode is the first to begin and the singer with the shortest Ode starts last. 'Ode Machine 1' is the only one which may accompany the Dumbshow.

In the programme note for the performance of Paragraph 5 at Cecil Sharp House on 21 January 1972 Cardew describes the origins and treatment of the Ode Machines:

In the book *The Great Learning* the ten chapters are a commentary on the amplification of the teaching of the first chapter. Sprinkled through these chapters are quotations from the Book of Odes, supposedly a collection made by Confucius himself of all the poetry extant at that time (6th century BC) that he considered worthy to survive. There are 305 Odes in the collection, and passages from ten of these are quoted in *The Great Learning* in support of the principles outlined there. Taking these ten Odes in their entirety, leaning on a number of existing translations, I have translated them and arranged them for singing in such a way that one breath is used for each character of the Chinese text [...]. The term 'Ode Machines' refers first to the mechanical nature of the composition techniques used in writing them and second to their function as a device for time measurement (through the unit one breath equals one character of a poem) laid over the whole structure.[39]

In fact, Cardew's use of his Ode Machines in Paragraph 5 differs considerably from the way in which quotations from the Book of Odes are 'sprinkled' throughout Confucius' work. If all ten Odes are used in a performance of Paragraph 5, or even, say, six or seven of them, they tend to establish a strong dominating presence throughout the whole of the first half of Cardew's composition. By contrast Confucius' use of the Odes in his *Great Learning* is far more circumspect; their role is more a supportive one.

The notion and practice of 'machine' music tickled Cardew, but whereas he wanted thereby to write 'dangerous compositions' Michael Chant had argued that machines are 'safe'. Cardew riposted (in a letter to John White):

I wonder what machines he was thinking of. Certainly in my hands no machine is safe. I still have a deformed fingernail from playing a machine with my brother at age 10 or so.
But I know what Michael means.[40]

In the same letter Cardew wrote: 'I hope you can accept the dedication of these highly imperfect mechanisms', – a clear, respectful reference to White's own *Tuba and Cello Machine* (which they had performed together) and other 'machine' compositions by him. Inspired by White's example Cardew experimented extensively with his own machine music, and the resulting Odes, both for the performer and the listener, are fraught with difficulties of every kind. For the singer an impeccable breath control is demanded to express the varying phrase lengths in convincing fashion whilst the listener, lulled briefly into a sense of diatonic predictability during a phrase, is jolted out of a nascent aural complacency by a sudden jarring and disorientating chromaticism. Each Ode can stand as a separate, unaccompanied melody; the finely-wrought linear structure has no need for harmonic accompaniment.

Ode 1 is the longest, around one hour in duration: a lengthy *recitativo arioso*, expansive and majestic. Each sentence is repeated four times, while each of the four musical repetitions is a variant, maintaining the shape and mode of the first statement; the setting is mostly syllabic. Michael Parsons has drawn attention to the isorhythmic treatment of the material in Ode 1; that is, while the rhythm is repeated for each line, the pitches change.

Ex.11.5b.

Most of the musical phrases in Ode 1 suggest a tonal centre: one note, or perhaps two or three are given prominence. The lines are eminently singable; there are no sequences of dissonant intervallic leaps such as to be found in serial vocal music (as in Cardew's early settings of Blake). Indeed, the middle part of Ode 1, where the poet vents his anger against the rulers, is mostly monotone and the ending is based on diatonic chords.

Ode 2 is the one Ode which does not use conventional notation. Single, drawn lines are assigned to individual words and phrases which are sung in one breath. Sometimes a word or phrase stands alone, in which case the singer improvises. (It is interesting that Cardew draws a distinction between 'reading' the lines and improvising. For many musicians the whole Ode is an exercise in improvisation.)[41]

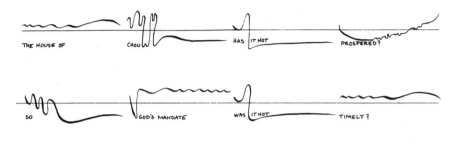

Ex.11.5c.

Ode 3 has a clear structural definition; moreover, the music catches the spacious nature of the imagery: nature, mountains, forests, pine trees – an added challenge to the singer's interpretative skills and imagination. The systemic (machine-like) mode of procedure is exemplified by the two phrases below – the beginning of the first verse and the beginning of the third:

Ex.11.5d.

The contrast between Odes 3 and 4 is strongly marked: whereas the structural basis of the melodic content in Ode 3 is triadic, most of Ode 4 consists of descending, scalic, melodic lines:

Ex.11.5e.

In Ode 5 most of the phrases consist of one or two two-note chords, the singer oscillating freely between the given tones. Where tones are outside the singer's range Cardew suggests the use of instruments to play the 'offending' tones, or simply to omit them whilst the remaining tones are reiterated staccato.

In Ode 6 Cardew introduces an innovation. At frequent intervals a vowel sound in a word is prescribed a number of repetitions: thus, in the word 'Dove', notated Do(4)ve, the o-sound is sung four times (without glottal stop). 'Each repetition should start gently below pitch and rise to correct pitch'.

In Ode 7, a narrative where the poet pleads with his lord, most of the phrases consist of simply one length-of-a-breath tone.

Cardew's Odes do vary considerably in respect of musical language, melodic content and tensional morphology. In Ode 8, for example (the only one written in the bass clef, although any Ode may be transposed to suit any voice), the melodic lines are florid, often several notes to a syllable, with unexpected twists and turns to take the ear by surprise. By contrast Ode 9 is modal and Ode 10 is based on triads of C, E minor and G; this enhances the idyllic nature of the text which describes the girl going to her new home, to organise her boudoir and, of course, to keep an eye on her house-maid:

Ex.11.5f. From Ode 10.

Michael Parsons has commented that the structural coherence of the Odes is an unexpected feature at a time when Cardew appeared to have turned his back on such concerns. Perhaps his intention in creating such a clear macrostructure in Paragraph 5 was to offset the chaos and latent anarchy which informs its content; certainly, these formal considerations enhance its ritualistic character. By contrast, in the works immediately preceding *The Great Learning*, from the mid-sixties, Cardew was concerned more with structural fragmentation, with 'deconstruction'; the infinitely variable microstructures were born out of chance and musical spontaneity and contingency, and these, in turn, determined the macrostructure. There may well be philosophical abstractions underlying these processes but there is no overall structural projection, no 'grand scheme' – as there is in most of the Paragraphs of *The Great Learning*.

Cardew's intention is that the Dumbshow, the recitation of the text, and the compositions, are by way of preparation for the improvisation, the duration of which should be roughly equal to the whole of the preceding section. The discipline and commitment which the Dumb Show demands, Cardew anticipated, hoped, would be a useful and necessary training for the second and final part of Paragraph 5. So the function of the first half of the piece is to clear the space, as it were, internally and externally, for spontaneous music-making, which for Cardew constituted the core of the Paragraph. The feeling for the physical space is acquired through the movement and gestures of the Dumbshow and, if they are used, the Action, Number and Topography scores. And through the eight 'verbal' compositions that explore separate and distinct categories of sound-production (including silence), his aim is to adumbrate the main areas in which spontaneous music-making might develop, to help the performer, through exploration and experimentation, to prepare him/herself for the music-making which lies ahead. All this seems to parallel Confucius' scheme in his *Great Learning*: the last ten chapters are a commentary and amplification of the teaching of the first chapter. The point where all these composed and semi-composed elements come to an end is the halfway point of the performance; what follows is improvisation.

The central point in the text of Paragraph 5 is the sentence 'They disciplined themselves', and Cardew constantly drew attention to the way in which, ideally, text and music complemented each other.

> I see such self-discipline as the essential prerequisite of Improvisation. Discipline is not to be seen as the ability to conform to a rigid rule-structure, but as the ability to work collectively with other people in a harmonious and fruitful way. Integrity, self-reliance, initiative, to be articulate (say, on an instrument) in a natural, direct way; these are the qualities necessary for improvisation. Self-discipline is the necessary basis for the desired spontaneity, where everything that occurs is heard and responded to without the 'aid' of arbitrarily controlled procedures and intellectual obscurity.[42]

There are no guidelines for the improvisation save for one short phrase: 'A dense forest that presents no obstacle to the mind or eye (or other sense)', and the aforementioned Taoist 'inspirational text': Firelighting Component.[43]

In the heat of the moment it is not always possible to heed Cardew's wise words, but if there is often self-indulgence and fecklessness in performances of Paragraph 5 there are also instances of joy and humour, as well as the occasional fleeting yet timeless moment which seems 'to point to the heart of some real matter, mental or material'. Much of the music of *The Great Learning* does have a solemn character – a gravitas – as befits a music which carries a Confucian burden of social responsibility. Not until the collective improvisation is reached do we become aware, as performers and listeners, of an intoxicating world of the spirit, a world in which the previous restraint is abandoned and the music can spill over into indulgence and excess. As Iris Murdoch put it, 'The absurdity of art, its funniness, its simplicity, its lucidity connects it with ordinary life and is inimical to authoritarian mystification.'[44]

In Paragraph 6, as in Paragraph 5, the essential 'virtue' is expressed quite explicitly: 'From the emperor down to the common man, simply and all together, this self-discipline is the root.' (This idea of 'the root', expressed in Paragraph 3 and also at the beginning of Paragraph 7, is crucial to the whole work.) It is also designated for 'untrained musicians', but whereas the focus in Paragraph 5 is broad, Paragraph 6 demands a high degree of concentration within a delimited area; the performer's attention is concentrated precisely on the sound, on the quality of the sound, on his/her relationship to the sound, on sounds produced by others, and on environmental sounds. In particular Cardew wanted performers to be aware of the different levels of control which may be exercised over any chosen sound – that is, of different degrees of intentionality.

More than a year before the completion of Paragraph 1, Cardew developed his argument in his own inimitable fashion:

> Someone will probably want to object that the same sound produced with two different attitudes nevertheless remains the same sound and hence is the same in its effect, that is, it strikes the ear the same both times. And here of course I am forced to become metaphysical since I lack the necessary scientific reading to be able to tell you how the ear is struck differently from inside the head due to faster-than-light transmission of sub-atomic particles to vital nerve-centres in the brain – and make you believe it. So I take the plunge – a sound made intentionally has the characteristic of being intended; the same sound made accidentally has the different characteristics of accidentalness – regardless of whether you hear it as the same or different.[45]

And in Paragraph 6 these 'different characteristics' are given expression through the notation:

> A 'sound', with no qualifying adjective, means a rather definite type of sound with a certain amount of presence. Sounds are generally shortish and rather quiet.'Optional sound' can mean a sound (as above), or an accidental or incidental (glancing) type of sound, or a quasi-accidental sound or no sound at all.[46]

Cardew's intention was that however meretricious the quality of an 'accidental' sound may seem, it may be momentarily nurtured, focused upon, embraced, *contextualised.*

> 'Isolated' always implies the option of making a sound or hearing it [...]. 'Synchronised sound' means make a sound simultaneously with another player. In cases of failure to produce a properly 'isolated' or 'synchronised' sound, there is no limit to the number of attempts that may be made, but there is no obligation to make more than one.[47]

Clearly, the precision demanded in the synchronisation of a sound with that of another performer involves a finer degree of intentionality than that demanded in the production of a 'glancing' sound – say if I casually knock a pen off the table with my elbow. But to what extent is the resulting sound of the pen falling on whatever surface *intentional* in the sense that the carefully intended synchronisation of two sounds is? In the former case the willed action produces an unwilled sound; in the latter the willed action produces a willed sound. Or was it in the former instance a case of producing an intentionally unwilled sound? Cardew was concerned with the subtleties of the *physicality* of the human production of sound: the way the hand travels over the keyboard; the same sound blown from a deep breath contrasted with one produced without especially taking a breath; listening or not listening to what you are playing. And he wrote of the *poetry* of performance.

The overall effect of the music of Paragraph 6 is a quiet, sparse, and above all, extremely concentrated deployment of sound. Not only is the character of each individual sound (or constellation) indicated, but also the number of sounds to be produced. Listening attentively, hyper-conscious of the slightest contextual shift, each player moves through the instructions at his/her own pace; a network of interrelating sounds and groups of sounds is created, the player/listeners hearing through the intervening silences with concentrated awareness of each others' actions and, of course, of any environmental intrusion.

The debt to Christian Wolff is clear in Paragraph 6: the intensive listening, the use of environmental sounds as well as performers' sounds, the morphology of the music. But in his characterisation of the sounds Cardew refines the music a stage further; the 'outward' listening of Wolff's music of the sixties is balanced by a 'subjective' orientation – the players' *intentions* now subject to a sophisticated, notational control which in Paragraph 6 intervenes between the player and the objective sound-world to whom he/she constantly refers and relates. Paragraph 6 was written at the same time as the formation of the Scratch Orchestra; it was as if Cardew was providing a study piece to meet the needs of the newly-formed Orchestra, focusing on the idea of collaboration with fellow performers, mutual need, and interdependence.

Paragraph 7, for any number of untrained voices, is the only Paragraph for voices alone and it is perhaps not without significance that its composition coincided with the launch of the Scratch Orchestra Draft Constitution. The whole piece is based on a procedure of listening and responding to others, of direct, unambiguous communication between people, without any instrumental paraphernalia; it requires no previous musical experience and is accessible to everyone. Each 'singer', beginning with a freely chosen tone, sings the first word for a specified number of lengths-of-a-breath, and then, moving around the performance space and beyond it, chooses for each successive word or phrase a new tone from amongst those being sung by the other participants. For the most part the dynamic is soft so that the unique character of each voice is emphasized; individuality is expressed through the collective.

Cardew provides here a unique solution to the problem of creating music for a large, heterogeneous group of trained and untrained singers, in which all can participate on an equal basis, by giving them a framework through which individual responsibility and choice, as well as a sense of community and interdependence, are given meaningful expression. The emphasis is on developing individual technique within a strictly ordered procedure; Michael Nyman reflects that the unitary scores of both Paragraphs 6 and 7 'provide for a personal ritual threading through a communal network'.[48] But whereas Paragraph 6 consists of a series of space-defining, space-creating gestures, Paragraph 7 creates a vast, limitless, aural space evoking the idea of the sublime.

For many performers the passing-on and taking-on of tones between people seems to embody certain ethical principles; it reflects the desired balance between individual and collective needs. Margaret Quail, who took part in a performance at the East London Late Starters Orchestra weekend in Kemsing, Surrey in 1991, describes her own experience which was shared by many others:

I experienced a tremendous sense of well-being with Paragraph 7. From the start I felt 'at one' with everyone in the room. In a strange way personal identity became unimportant – also the past and future and everyday concerns. As I took another person's note I felt I took on part of them and in turn the person who took my note took a part of me. In this way the people in the room seemed to possess a shared identity. At the end the one remaining person seemed to be both himself and everyone.[49]

Michael Nyman is another performer for whom the 'procedural' notation of Paragraph 7 is a striking example of Cardew's compositional sagacity:

> One of my most beautiful musical experiences came from taking part in a performance of this piece in a low-lit Portsmouth Cathedral.[50] Sounds fanned out in space and time as singers, standing still or circulating in a slow procession, passed on their sounds to someone in close proximity, and with great reverence, picked up sounds in the same way.[51]

The music as heard is not fixed in the score, but arises out of the differences in individual lengths-of-breaths, vocal abilities (and disabilities) and characteristics, as well as subjective preferences for this heard tone rather than that one: a variegated tapestry of vocal sounds. As Michael Parsons has written: 'It does not exist in an ideal realm of aesthetic perfection, but in the here-and-now, in the physical, acoustic and human circumstances of each particular and unique performance.'[52] In Paragraphs 3 and 7, for example, there is no attempt, through training, to achieve a technique and style of singing flattened out into a received method of vocal delivery. Moreover, like *Treatise*, the music is informed with an organicity, a seamlessness, both of motion and structure; a microtonal 'mistake' by an individual attempting to simulate the pitch of a heard tone disturbs the fulcrum, the temporary equilibrium, by creating a subtle leverage through which the music modulates (?) imperceptibly into a new 'harmonic' region.

Paragraph 7 begins with a random vocal chord, and just as the human embryo is first aware of otherness through the sense of hearing, the individual singer's first chosen tone is gradually enveloped in myriad relationships with other sounds whilst at the same time struggling manfully to retain its own unique identity. Finally it is relinquished; future development, and survival, depends upon others and viable alternatives are sought after. During the course of the piece (usually around ninety minutes) the wide spectrum of relationships narrows, slowly and naturally, tensions created and resolved; the last small group exchange tones until the sole remaining singer concludes the work – the initial cluster of maximum complexity finally resolved on to the extremity of a single unison.[53]

In the Almeida Festival programme Dave Smith describes Paragraph 7 as 'La Monte Young for the people – no need for just intonation! The effect is not dissimilar. I would have thought that this "beautiful sound" element is present in other Paragraphs as well.' The reference to La Monte Young and to the ineffableness of the 'sound' of Paragraph 7 gives us pause to consider Cardew's remark in his aforementioned article on the American composer in the *London Magazine*, April 1967: 'Subsequent developments have shown that the two 'giants' (Stockhausen and La Monte Young) had at least one vital weakness in common: an enormous susceptibility to the seduction of pure sound'. In respect of this 'weakness' it is tempting to draw a comparison between one of these 'giants' and Cardew, as Smith does, but I am not convinced that the comparison bears closer scrutiny; their differences seem more demonstrable, more conclusive, than their similarities.

In Young's music, the listener becomes engulfed within the sound and, as it were, surrenders to it in an act of faith. For only then does the revelatory experience become accessible. The sound is idealised; its purity symbolized by the primacy which is attached to tuning; it is the bearer of an unfathomable, chrome-gloss message. Its quasi-religious aura is enhanced by an oppressiveness – Cardew uses the words 'heavy' and 'incense-laden' – and it is the extraordinary materialization of the overtones which rewards the humble listener with feelings of ecstasy. The sound is precious, it is also vulnerable; its originator harbours protective feelings towards it, a possessiveness which is enshrined in a financial contract which in turn embodies the composer's rights. It is *his* sound.

By contrast, as Howard Skempton reminds us in the same programme note, Cardew was always 'essentially a humanist, a materialist'. The 'sound' of Paragraph 7 is impure, afflicted by the imperfections and weaknesses of ordinary mortals; their abject failure results in flawed tuning. The performers are involved in *doing* – they are not *being done to*. Moreover, both performers and listeners may step outside the performance space, metaphorically and literally, to bring their critical faculties to bear on the music, or simply to switch off.

The note-to-note morphology of most Western music, and its cultural significance, is of secondary importance in Cardew's work; in *The Great Learning* Cardew notates a way of making music which is orientated towards the performers who are producing the sounds rather than towards the sounds themselves.[54] Moreover it takes into account the essentially human aspects of music-making; Michael Nyman's description of the notations for *The Great Learning* – 'people-processes' – is brilliantly apposite. Without an assimilation of these 'processes', an 'analysis' of *The Great Learning* could not 'explain what is significant in [the] music while circumventing the human experience through which such significance is constituted'.[55]

Cardew enjoyed the challenge of taking laws and rules from other disciplines and converting them into musical form;[56] one of the most compelling features of the notation of *The Great Learning* is his use of Chinese ideograms, which are disassembled as lines and squiggles in Paragraphs 1, 4 and 5. And in the 'optional material' for Paragraph 5, two options, an Action Score and a Number Score, are derived from transcriptions of the Chinese text. Eddie Prévost provides the background to Cardew's fascination for Chinese as a non-phonetic language:

The [Chinese] calligraphies were a fascinating combination of visual references and language components, in which the origins of words and compound phrases could be traced back to drawings of physical objects. For example, the character for pen 'bi' (in phonetic 'pin yin') was written as 筆. It is based upon the radical for 'wood', of which pens were made. Gradually, through usage and development – the change from pointed wood ink applicator to brush – the ideogram became abstracted until perhaps only a scholar could know its original source. Chinese poetry thus depended as much upon brush style as upon literary content, until no real distinction was thought necessary. These kinds of connections – and the thought processes behind them – intrigued and influenced AMM (certainly they had an effect upon how Cardew came to view graphic notation), and was perhaps part of a growing interest in Chinese culture which had originally been stimulated by Ezra Pound. Cardew's *magnum opus The Great Learning* owed much to this field of inquiry.[57]

The notation for the whistle solo in Paragraph 1 and the guero parts from Paragraph 4 is derived from the shapes and sounds of the Chinese ideogram. (The choice of chords in Paragraph 4 may have a linguistic basis; perhaps they are based on Chinese characters – as in Paragraph 2 – bearing in mind the way they reappear in transposition and inversion.) The notation of the whistle solos is a horizontalization of the individual strokes of each Chinese character in turn, and in creating an appropriate calligraphy Cardew certainly had these sound sources and their expressive potential in mind. What is striking about the notation is its 'musicalness'; the calligraphy, imaginative and suggestive, generates music: phrases of varying lengths and shapes to which the individual, wayward tones lend character.[58] And the same notational style for the gueros in Paragraph 4, an unequivocal compositional decision, suggests a transcription of the material from Paragraph 1, or at least some measure of conformity to it. Moreover, as we have seen in our discussion of Paragraph 5, the Chinese characters were the source for further experimentation and cross-fertilization.

Comparing the notation of Ode 2 from Paragraph 5 with that of the whistling in Paragraph 1 and the gueros in Paragraph 4, Ode 2 is more undulating, less thrusting. In Paragraphs 1 and 4 the phrases consist of many differentiated 'attacks' whereas in the Ode for each breath the singer is concerned with a single, usually undemonstrative attack – the beginning of the breath – and that one sound may undergo changes in pitch, timbre, dynamic, intensity, etc., depending on how the singer responds to the morphology of the particular line. The striking characteristic of the notation for Ode 2 is that each breath is characterised by one drawn line which may or may not pursue an adventurous course. Whereas the phrases in Paragraphs 1 and 4 embrace a multiplicity of lines shooting off in various directions: denser, visually more complex, without the pristine quality of the Ode. Clearly Cardew's notations were designed with the particular instrument – whistle, guero, voice – very much in mind, and he wanted each instrumentalist/ singer to respond to the *musicalness* of the notations.

In his article on *The Great Learning* in the November 1971 issue of the *Musical Times* Brian Dennis illuminated uses of the ideograms in Paragraphs 2 and 7 (Ex.11.6a-b):

> The ideogram remains the essential source, however, and this example from Paragraph 2 shows how the longs and shorts of the characters are translated into rhythms:

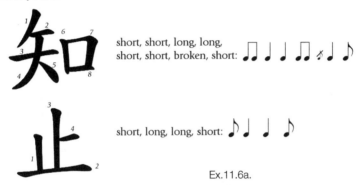

Ex.11.6a.

The simplicity of numbers provides the control for Paragraph 7 [...]. Each word or phrase is sung softly for the length of a breath as often as indicated.

    sing 8   IF
    sing 5   THE ROOT
    sing 13 (ƒ3) BE IN CONFUSION

    (ƒ3 = any 3 repetitions should be loud)

The numbers are derived as follows:

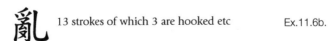

Ex.11.6b.

Although Cardew never succeeded in completely jettisoning the Western notational system (in fact such a clean sweep was never his intention), he believed that as long as music was in thrall to the system – that is, the division of music into discrete rhythmic and intervallic values, the constraints of Western notation would continue to exercise a cramping effect on contemporary compositional thought. The subtle, microtonal movements which are of the essence in Paragraph 7, for example, cannot be reduced to the 'atomized multiplicity' on which, ultimately, musicological analysis depends. In any case, in *The Great Learning* Cardew's concern was not 'compositional reality'; rather, to use Morton Feldman's words, it was 'acoustical reality'.

'Music is based upon the response of the human heart to cerebral things.'[59]

Writing from the critic's perspective, in his review of Paragraphs 1 and 2 Bayan Northcott's speculative, sensitive musings go to the heart of the matter:

How real are the distinctions between 'form', 'content' and 'style' which we bandy about? Does the hierarchy of values that they imply actually relate to the music we hear, or do they after all merely get in the way of the direct experience, already conditioned and limited by private factors such as age, temperament, the rest of our musical experience and our notions of 'historical' background? For once I ask myself whether we ought, indeed can, do more than 'turn in' or 'turn on' – to deploy already somewhat tarnished terminology from elsewhere – to the nature, the revealed sensibility of the individual, of the individual piece, without comment or judgment.[60]

For both Confucius and Cardew music was a moral training and should therefore ultimately be morally beneficial. Thus in Cardew's *magnum opus*, a work so exalted in tone, people are encouraged, *through the notation*, to adopt certain attitudes towards the sounds they produce, and towards each other. In this respect Cardew stayed true to the essential spirit and purpose of the Confucian scriptures.

Such is the incorruptible latitude of the score (*The Great Learning*) that each participant ideally fulfils the roles of performer, listener, critic and composer. This incorruptibility, which is coupled with a meticulous generosity, derives from Cardew's personal acceptance of the principles laid down in the Confucius text on which *The Great Learning* is based and the way in which they are translated into direct, non-symbolic musical terms (on a more profound level than the accepted banality of 'expressing the text in music'). Not only does this subtly help one along the road of 'correct behaviour' during a performance, it beneficially affects one's mode of procedure in everyday life.[61]

And just as it was Confucius' purpose, through his school of philosophy, to unite a kingdom, so Cardew wanted to gather together and unite people, to inspire in people the desire to make music, as well as the self-belief that they were capable of doing so. And yet, at the same time, within the same work, there is a (Taoist) *celebration* of sounds, sights, smells, touches, and Cardew encourages us to focus in different ways; there are different shades and different degrees. If, as Nicholas Cook proposes, 'a musical culture is, in essence, a repertoire of means for imagining music', then Cardew's invaluable contribution is that he has expanded that repertoire.

In *The Great Learning* art merges with everyday reality; the 'monstrous egotism' (in Anita Brookner's words) of the artist is diffused; so that the music is not saying simply 'listen to me'; the performers are not saying 'look at us'. As Iris Murdoch put it, 'Moral change comes from an *attention* to the world whose natural result is a decrease in egoism through an increased sense of the reality of, primarily of course other people, but also other things.'[62] And the enactment of this 'moral change' may be witnessed during the course of a performance of *The Great Learning* when moments of moral disorder, such as may occur in the improvisation in Paragraph 5, where the music founders on the rock of egoism, may undergo metamorphoses through the guidance of Cardew's wise words. Freedom lies in the consciousness of this relationship: 'It is rooted in watching with affection the way people grow' proclaims the very first sentence of *The Great Learning*, a principle which is touchingly prefigured in a Journal entry ten years earlier:

Oh yes, kissing her (Natalie) ear she said it went right down to her foot. But I didn't notice the tenseness or shiver in this tiny movement. I am becoming insensitive to such things – this is what I must really work on – watch people again as though for the first time.
Especially the tiny, tiny expressive movements, actions, of non-externalised people. Perhaps in this way I can achieve an interest in them.[63]

The structural organization of the individual Paragraphs is there not to satisfy a musicological penchant for analysis (such an analysis leaves too many questions unanswered) but for phenomenological purposes. The aesthetic pleasure derived from *The Great Learning* depends on an appreciation of a way of making music and, to a degree, a way of listening to music which lie outside the terms of reference of Western cultural rationalisation.[64] For this reason the presuppositions which critics and listeners often bring to a performance of *The Great Learning* are either an irrelevance or an obstacle to comprehension and enjoyment.[65] Nor can *The Great Learning* be performed in a purely professional capacity, and cannot therefore be evaluated and quantified in a way that professional performances are. Cardew's music does not fit well with the demands for an average culture:

> Such a culture, defined by the growth of the number of listeners and the disappearance of practitioners (no more amateurs), wants art, wants music, provided they be clear, that they 'translate' an emotion and represent a signified (the 'meaning' of a poem); an art that inoculates pleasure (by reducing it to a known, coded emotion) and reconciles the subject to what in music *can be said*: what is said about it, predicatively, by Institution, Criticism, Opinion.[66]

In *The Great Learning* Cardew seems to have uncovered older, buried traditions, incorporating them into an incomparably freer, personal vocabulary and creating a sound-world of quite extraordinary originality. *The Great Learning* achieves its immense power not through a self-conscious, unsuspecting reliance on the new technology – as many composers had attempted – but, with an astonishingly imaginative backwards leap, by an audacious act of regression into a primeval world of 'informal sound', and it is this which gives *The Great Learning* its unanalysable uniqueness. Any knowledge acquired through enculturation and musical training which the listener may bring to *The Great Learning* is therefore useless; *The Great Learning* contains no genetic trace of a previous music.

Yet this 'regression' is not an escape; there is no idealisation of the past, no sentimentality, no nostalgic longing for an Arcadian haven (although occasionally such images may have presented themselves in the Scratch Orchestra). *The Great Learning* is not about history; it is about the future. Like other major works of Cardew it is idealist, utopian – 'the truth of tomorrow' in Victor Hugo's romantic formulation. 'Utopista' was Goffredo Petrassi's unequivocal response when I asked him if he had been surprised to hear of Cardew's politicisation. And in the *Eighteenth Brumaire of Louis Bonaparte* Marx wrote: 'The social revolution of the nineteenth century cannot draw its poetry from the past, but only from the future.'[67]

And yet much of *The Great Learning*, and in particular Paragraph 7, does seem to occupy a metaphysical space; and in so doing it encroaches on the domain of spirituality normally associated with religion. Thus art wrests spirituality from religion; spirituality is not the private property of religion. Except that Cardew's *The Great Learning* offers no pat answers, no miracles (as religion does), nor does it offer solutions (as ideologies and Confucianism do). Art demands commitment and sacrifice; it involves risk, but promises nothing. *The Great Learning* says with Iris Murdoch: 'The world is not given to us "on a plate", it is given to us as a creative task'.[68]

In the aforementioned introductory talk to the broadcast recording of the first performance of Paragraph 1 at the Cheltenham Festival Cardew remarked:

> If music was a purely aesthetic experience I don't think it would occupy the central place it does in our affairs. It must make waves in the environment and have repercussions beyond the concert hall.

This reference to his musical credo was prompted by the furore which the work had created amongst the public on that occasion. The audience had split into two factions, 'participating' through vocal approval or dissent. The composer and critic Justin Connolly describes the socio-psychological aspects of the audience reaction in a manner which echoed Cardew's own response to the noisy proceedings:[69]

> It was evident from the behaviour at Cheltenham of the rowdy minority who, taken unawares by the absence of a programme note and the customary explanations, felt obliged to believe themselves the victims of some sort of hoax. They reacted readily enough, but with anger born of incomprehension rather than with enlightenment proceeding from understanding of the situation. They accordingly modified the nature of the piece itself by superimposing upon its slow circular motion certain finite gestures, such as indignant and noisy exits, sporadic hand-clapping, and bursts of angry conversation. By thus adding to the work spatial and timbral dimensions which served to emphasise their initial judgement that it was insufficiently 'interesting', they were able to re-compose the piece while at the same time giving expression to their feeling that its very passivity was a function of their mounting aggression towards it.[70]

Despite his reputation as a controversial figure, the *enfant terrible* of English music, Cardew, in fact, was never confrontational; *épater le bourgeois* was never part of his social or artistic agenda. What his music does, at its best, is to sharpen social and psychological contradictions, so that from confronting the music the audience finally arrives at confronting itself – as it did at Cheltenham.[71]

Cardew swam against the tide, and in his profound misgivings in relation to contemporary Western modes of music-making, even amongst the famous and the fashionable, he was not alone: Bartes says, 'Concurrently, passive, receptive music, sound music, is become the music (that of concert, festival, record, radio): playing has ceased to exist; musical activity is no longer manual, muscular, kneadingly physical'.[72] The contemporary instrumental technician completes the process and 'relieves the listener of all activity, even by procuration, and abolishes in the sphere of music the very notion of *doing*'.[73] Moreover, Cardew's music-making, certainly from the beginning of the sixties, was founded on a rapport between musicians and non-musicians in which the cash nexus played no part; it betokened a human need and was regarded by participants as a life-enhancing activity, no less. The first-and-last-performance syndrome and the atrophy and despair into which the social function of music had sunk were for Cardew depressing features of the world of contemporary music into which he had plunged, with vigour and idealism, as an enquiring, talented student in the fifties, and on which he would eventually turn his back to become an implacable critic and opponent.

Whether word or deed, for Cardew everything was an exercise in worth. Phenomena found unattractive or devoid of significance were summarily relegated; conversationally, he was incapable of persiflage. There was no small talk; rather, there was no talk, no conventional framework within which one's relationship to him could begin and develop. The poet Michael Horovitz, an old friend, recalls that conversation with Cardew was 'never routine', and sometimes 'uncomfortable'; however mundane the topic he always 'raised consciousness'. Any indifference or smugness would fade away, leaving a new scrutiny in its wake, the quotidian enhanced, enriched. Sitting with him in a coffee bar, a fleeting image or gesture, a tiny yet compelling detail would freeze in the memory.

Cardew was interested in essences; in any conversation or activity he would seek out the *root* (like Wittgenstein, whose relationships with people were invariably confrontational and raw). People would be forced to question themselves, which is what he achieved with his music: we recall the reception of Paragraph 1 at Cheltenham. Most of us devise our personal stratagems in order to compromise, to accept the unacceptable, to accommodate a (social) system we have rejected intellectually and emotionally a thousand times. Cardew refused to do this.

John White remembers an afternoon at Cardew's flat in the mid-sixties, around the time of the *Treatise* performances. White was commenting and elaborating on the differences between Schoenberg and Webern, as students were wont in those days, and Cardew was responding with observations and opinions. At the end of the afternoon, as White prepared to take his leave, Cardew pronounced verdict on the afternoon proceedings: 'well, that was a waste of time', or something equally dismissive. White was taken aback and probably felt deflated and a touch resentful; clearly, Cardew had been fielding White's commentaries on serialism as if he had been talking about the weather.

Finally, let us return to the broadcast talk in which Cardew's radical attitude towards music-making finds expression in his own reaction to the Cheltenham affair – and in his afterthoughts. Just as we should cultivate our own individual responsibility socially and politically, and only rely on our own judgement, so the audience at Cheltenham had every right, in Cardew's view, to act upon their judgement of a piece of music, and he applauds their lack of 'politeness'. The political dimension had already begun to emerge and in the vocabulary of his peremptory summing-up there are overtones of violence which clearly foreshadow his later commitment to revolutionary politics: 'When you find a certain situation intolerable you can attempt to change it, or terminate it.'

Notes and references

1   A Taoist dictum.
2   Arnold Schoenberg, 'New Music, Outmoded Music, Style and Idea' (1946), from *Style and Idea: Selected Writings of Arnold Schoenberg,* ed. Leonard Stein, trans. Leo Black (Berkeley, CA: University of California Press, 1984), p.124.
3   In the sixties, the decade of *The Great Learning*, the Macnaghten Concerts was the oldest existing English organisation for contemporary music. It was founded in December 1931 by three young female students: Iris Lemare (conductor), Elisabeth Lutyens (composer), and Anne Macnaghten (violinist), with the principal aim of promoting contemporary English composers of all schools by presenting concerts featuring their music.
4   Needham, *Science and Civilisation in China*, vol.4 p.132.
5   Ibid., p.184.
6   Ibid., p.139.
7   I recall a week in the summer of 1971 when the Scratch Orchestra was camping on some waste land outside Newcastle; a vision of Cardew has remained with me from that time – sitting in a field with his cello, playing a succession of simple phrases with consummate grace and elegance.
8   From the performance notes in the score of *The Great Learning.*
9   Needham, vol.4, p.153.
10 *Stockhausen Serves Imperialism,* p.96. (*CCR*)
11 John Harrison, *The Reactionaries* (London: Gollancz, 1967), p.112. It has to be said that not everybody is so dismissive of Pound's translations: '…literal accuracy isn't all there is to a translation of poetry, and Pound's Chinese translations are certainly the most influential in English in the twentieth century'. Harry Gilonis, in an email communication to the author in December 2005.
12 Letter from Howard Snell to CC, dated 4 November 1957.
13 John Harrison, *The Reactionaries*, p.134. In relation to the broader debate over Pound's fascism we should bear in mind that these were two young men barely out of their teens, who were making exciting discoveries and impetuous judgments, as well as dubious alliances.
14 Jrnl. 23 April 1967.
15 Harris offers an interesting speculation: 'To me, this (Par.4) is the weakest piece; at the risk of being accused of psychologism I believe that Cor was somewhat disheartened by the failure of the S.O. membership to respond to his initiatives described in the Draft Constitution, e.g. Scratch Music, Research Vectors, etc.' Letter to JT sometime during the summer of 1984.
16 From an undated letter to the author written sometime during the summer of 1984.
17 *The Cantos of Ezra Pound* (London: Faber and Faber, 1987), p.58. This text is essentially the same as the edtion which Cardew would have been using in the late sixties.
18 Several years earlier the late Bill Hopkins made a particularly pertinent observation in his previously mentioned review of *Three Winter Potatoes*: 'Cardew was compelled to weigh up the claims of artifice (selection and ordering) against those of the spontaneity which for him represents musical truth.' *Musical Times*, August 1967.
19 Taoism and Confucianism can be usefully contrasted although there have been periods in Chinese history where they have overlapped. Essentially, Confucianism believes in the

perfectibility of man, that through education and the correct upbringing a human being can learn to think and act rationally, logically, and can serve his fellow humans in the appropriate manner. For the Taoist the human point of view is irrelevant, and he regards ethical judgments as arbitrary. A mystical communion with nature is important for the Taoist for whom the spontaneity of nature is something to be emulated in human behaviour.

20 The Louis Halsey Singers was founded by the composer/conductor Louis Halsey in 1967.

21 *Treatise Handbook*, p.xix. (*CCR*)

22 From the performance notes in the score of *The Great Learning*.

23 Ibid.

24 *Stockhausen Serves Imperialism*, p.97. (*CCR*)

25 '*The Great Learning* appears to come to rest at a point of redefinition of the natural, concrete, real physical properties of (sounding) things. These properties make themselves felt as though totally independent of "composition".' Michael Nyman, 'Cornelius Cardew's *The Great Learning*', *London Magazine*, December 1971/January 1972. (*CCR*)

26 I am grateful to Robert Coleridge, himself a gifted interpreter of Cardew's organ music, for these apposite, analytical observations.

27 Michael Parsons: From the programme for the performance of *The Great Learning* at the Almeida Festival, London, in July 1984. (*CCR*)

28 Bayan Northcott, 'Modern Proms', from *Music and Musicians,* 21 November 1972.

29 The first public performance of Paragraph 2 was given at the Round House in Chalk Farm, north London on 4 May 1969.

30 There is some doubt as to the translation of the text for Paragraph 3. It is not by Ezra Pound.

31 Jrnl. 2 July 1967.

32 In the performance at the Goethe Institute on 13 May 1971 the idea of growth and ascent was expressed spatially through the use of the extensive staircase: the groups of singers and instrumentalists strategically situated from bottom to top.

33 From the performance notes in the score of *The Great Learning*. Cardew also suggests that, 'if the forces are available, suitable individual staves may be picked out and allotted to homogeneous groups of sustaining instruments (strings, woodwind, brass, saxes, electrical)'.

34 Undated letter to the author some time during the mid-nineties.

35 Ibid.

36 Ibid.

37 *Treatise Handbook,* p.xx. (*CCR*)

38 A word in capital letters indicates a priority of some kind. And notice the reference ('guero') to a previous Paragraph, Paragraph 4.

39 Cardew conceived the idea of a Symphonic Ode Machine, an instrumental version of the Odes, which he proposed to Howard Skempton as a 'co-authored piece' sometime in 1971. In a note to Skempton Cardew sketched out a format with suggestions for scoring and characterisation of the individual Odes: Ode 1 to be harmonized; Ode 10 for Strings in wide-spaced octaves; the possibility/desirability to change the timbre within an Ode; scoring to be simple and transparent.

40 From a letter to John White, dated 14 March 1971.

41 Harry Gilonis has drawn my attention to the fact that the notation for Ode 2 does not appear to be derived from the Chinese text. For example, Bernhard Karlgren's *The Book of*

Odes (Stockholm: The Museum of Far Eastern Antiquities, 1950) shows the character for king, 'Wang', the second ideogram in the opening stanza, to be wholly vertical or horizontal, and bears no resemblance to Cardew's own drawing.

42   Towards an Ethic of Improvisation, *Treatise Handbook,* p.xix. (*CCR*)

43   Fire-lighting seemed to take on an almost ritualistic significance for Cardew, as anyone who observed him on camp sites will attest. The Scratch Orchestra Documentary file contains a lengthy Zoroastrian text on the consecration of sacred fires and fire-temples, presumably placed there by Cardew, in which sixteen different kinds of fires are identified.

44   Iris Murdoch, *Metaphysics as a Guide to Morals* (London: Penguin Books, 1992), pp. 90-1.

45   From the lecture for the University of Illinois on 25 February 1967.

46   From the performance notes in the score of *The Great Learning*.

47   Ibid.

48   *London Magazine*, December 1971/January 1972. (*CCR*)

49   Letter to JT dated 5 March 1991.

50   This performance, in which the composer himself participated, took place on 11 December 1969 in St. John's Cathedral, Portsmouth, and was 'directed' by myself. Cardew had visited the Fine Art department at Portsmouth Polytechnic on 3 December to rehearse the Paragraphs to be performed: 1, 2, 6 and 7. Somewhat ambitiously, a circular advertising rehearsals as well as the actual performance estimated that 'three hundred performers are required for the piece to reach its full potential'. (It is unlikely that any performance of *The Great Learning* has been able to muster so many participants, although the desirability of large numbers for the work has generally been accepted over the years. If a hundred is reached this is invariably considered a more than adequate number.)

51   *London Magazine*, December 1971/January 1972. (*CCR*)

52   From the programme for the performance of *The Great Learning* at the Almeida Festival, London, in July 1984. (*CCR*)

53   Mark Rothko once wrote: 'We favor the simple expression of the complex thought. We are for the large shape because it has the impact of the unequivocal'. *Mark Rothko* (London: Tate Gallery Publishing, 1996), p.69.

54   Cf. *Notation – Interpretation, etc.*, p.26. (*CCR*)

55   Nicholas Cook, *Music, Imagination and Culture*, p.241.

56   One wonders to what extent Cardew may have been influenced by Hermann Hesse's *Glass Bead Game* ('a mode of playing with the total contents and values of our culture'. *The Glass Bead Game* (Harmondsworth, Middx: Penguin Modern Classics, 1973), p.18.) We know it is a book he much admired and which contains many tropes, precepts, and theses which can be applied meaningfully to much of Cardew's work and with which there are many levels of accordance.

57   *No Sound Is Innocent*, p.15. However, according to Harry Gilonis, Cardew, following Pound, greatly exaggerated the pictographic element of Chinese characters. The vast majority of ideograms are abstract, and most uses of pictographic elements are irrelevant to meaning (language being *oral*).

58   Keith Rowe has referred to the 'gestural quality' of Cardew's drawings of the Chinese characters.

59   From Confucius' *Book of Rites* (*Li chi*). The *Book of Rites* constitutes the fourth Confucian Classic.

60 *Music and Musicians*, November 1972.

61 Michael Nyman, *London Magazine*, December 1971/January 1972. (*CCR*)

62 Murdoch, *Metaphysics as a Guide to Morals*, p.52.

63 Jrnl. 19 December 1959.

64 For example, *The Great Learning* does not feature what Barthes called the paroxysmal development of contrasts in intensity, the opposition of piano and forte, 'the historical importance of which is perhaps not very clearly recognized, it characterizing after all only a tiny portion of the music of the world'. Barthes, p.151.

65 Dominic Gill, for example, complained that Paragraph 5 had 'little electricity, little tension of contrast or development'. *Financial Times*, 24 January 1972.

66 Barthes, *Image – Music – Text*, p.185

67 As quoted in *Marxism and Art,* edited Maynard Solomon (Detroit: Wayne State University Press, 1979), p. 47.

68 Murdoch, p.215.

69 The fact that Cardew approved Connolly's review is indicated by his inclusion of it in the programme for a performance of part of *The Great Learning* (though not Paragraph 1) at the Simon Fraser University in Canada on 19 May 1970.

70 *Tempo* no.86, autumn 1968, pp.16-17.

71 The following possibly apocryphal anecdote was, if I remember correctly, recounted to me by the late Tim Souster: After the Cheltenham performance an elderly gentleman, who looked like a retired colonel, pushed through the crowd in the artists' room to confront the composer. He grabbed Cardew's hand and said, 'Thank you, Mr. Cardew, what a relief to hear your music after all this horrible modern stuff.' It is the unpredictability of Cardew's music which so often produces unpredictable responses.

72 Barthes, pp.149-50.

73 Ibid., p.150.

(*CCR*) Also found in *Cornelius Cardew A Reader*

Cornelius Cardew a life unfinished

12

Scratch Criticism and Self-Destruction 1971–72

'The contemporary artist may abhor the moral vacuum in modern bourgeois society, but in the end he not only reflects it, he expresses a powerlessness towards it.'[1]

A Diversion: May 1971

The *Tuba and Cello Machine* was the first of John White's thirty or more machine pieces, described by Victor Schonfield as 'the most private, esoteric, numbing and entropic piece I have ever experienced'.[2] This had already received a number of London performances: at the Anti-University in April 1968, at Morley College the following September, in Blackheath in March 1970 (cello part only), at St. Pancras Town Hall in April 1970, and at the New Arts Laboratory the following July. For the Queen Elizabeth Hall performance, on 17 May, it was decided that a number of rehearsals, or 'training sessions', were necessary. Cardew would visit White at his home in Wimbledon, not so much to learn the notes but rather to inhabit the piece, and they would play through a section for two or three hours or more twice a week – 'like getting used to living in a space suit'.

In his wisdom Cardew understood what was necessary; it was he who had initiated this mode of preparation. In the months leading up to the concert Cardew and White corresponded, tracking the progress of the project and en route expressing hopes and betraying anxieties. The letters are agreeably relaxed, a light-hearted tone mediating the underlying seriousness which informed all Cardew's utterances on music – an on-going, pleasurable application which, on the day of the concert, was printed in the two-booklet programme: Cardew's letters in one booklet, White's in the other. As the letters indicate, Cardew clearly relished the prospect of performing White's *Machine*, even speculating on the possibility of a world tour. In the second letter (of seven) his enthusiasm spills over as he presents an extended deconstruction of the work, at the same time providing evidence of the kind of qualities in a piece of music that he looked for:

It's the mutual inaccessibility of the worlds of tuba and cello that is part of what's 'real' in your piece. What I said on the phone about my talk to Paul Patterson[3] – how these 2 being large instruments, they have very overloaded spectra, especially in the higher reaches, and how the partials in these higher reaches are all out of true because of the actual dimensions of the column of air, and the calibre of the string that is vibrating. (The small sections cannot vibrate in simple harmonic motion because of their thickness.) So as the piece progresses attention focuses more and more on the conflicts and resolutions amongst these upper partials, so much so that we as players lose our capability of tuning the actual fundamental notes we are bowing or blowing. So – all Machine music representing a decay process anyway – we start with the two worlds in reasonably good alignment as far as most arbitrary criteria go, and gradually drift apart. The coming together as successive non-ordinary planes is what the rest of the piece is about. I wish this could be put in words of one syllable, and without any technical data.[4]

This may well have been the last time that Cardew wrote about, or discussed music in this manner. Such preoccupation with 'technical data' was about to be superseded by a completely different set of criteria determined by the new political imperatives. In a letter written three weeks later it is the hazards of performance which concern him:

In the old days (La Monte Young, etc.) a bow could last a minute and all kinds of things could happen in it. So much could happen *within* it that it didn't seem terribly important how it began or ended (anyhow, usually at the end of the bow one would simply just turn around and come back again). Now with these new-fangled 7 or 8 second bows with their flat, steady sound, this question of attack and ending of the sound has got itself under the spotlight. Much to my embarrassment. More skill is required. More concentration. Will it ever end? Meanwhile these faulty starts and stops make very interesting listening material for me.
I keep thinking of the *regular* hazards out there in the second hour or so: the uninvited vibrato, irrecoverably bad tuning (being able to hear the right note in your head, but having a sinking feeling that it doesn't exist on your instrument) etc. This is an area where the domain of Machines and the domain of Scratch Music almost touch. Scratch Music – at least in my conception – could be like some sort of decomposing machinery.[5]

As the concert date became imminent and their voluble correspondence drew to a close Cardew had this to say in his penultimate letter on 21 April:

> This correspondence. There is no common ground (whatever that cliché amounts to). We certainly do not communicate – simply project our attitudes on cue. And we have agreed to respect each other's cues. So it is in the composition – a confrontation of 2 signalling entities. Occasionally by chance they strike the same note. Occasionally by miracle certain changes take place in the upper reaches of the spectrum [...]. So I've completed a circle, a very bulging, irregular circle. Anyway, these letters have provided a graceful counterpoint to practising the piece. Obviously they're not directed at you. They're simply a by-product of the machine which we may attempt to feed back into the system at some promising-looking point.

As for White's letters, as might be expected the strands which he wove into this counterpoint are of equal quotability, his famed wit and humour providing episodes of contrast and timeliness: 'Playing bar billiards with Christopher Hobbs has become a very musical occupation. It is all to do with maintenance and preservation. If one can keep playing legato despite the exigencies of alternate breaks all will be well.'[6] And in another letter, two weeks later, White lets the cat out of the bag, propelling us back to the heady days of *Treatise*:

> Your letters have communicated to me as much as the talks we've had over this rehearsal period, and remind me of early rehearsals and performances of your *Treatise*, when I reckon my musical education actually began. When people talk about the impossibility of playing *Treatise* I find it hard to think in general terms. All that comes to mind is the feeling of awe at having been in on the early days when the great impossibilities hadn't yet occurred to anyone. All of my Machines are the wayward and prodigal sons of *Treatise*. (I wonder how many other wild oats got sown by *Treatise* when you weren't looking!)[7]

May '71 to December '72

The new welfare and dole did allow many to survive on a subsistence level and provide an unofficial and completely unorganized cultural opposition. Unfortunately the class oppression required that they 'give up' their previous class affiliations and adopt a shallow, ill-fitting and confusing middle-class label. As the oppressor definition of working class was of someone without intellect or taste, then those with an Art degree could no longer 'therefore' be part of this class! It was from the ranks of those would-be sacrificial art lambs that many of the non-musician Scratchers came.[8]

A cluster of Scratch presentations followed hard on the heels of the QEH concert: on 19 May an all-day event entitled 'Scratch Below' involved random appearances on the tube and in subways. A 'Demolition Site' event on 22 May, in which a group of children from a local estate participated, and 'merge with Highgate Cemetery' on 29 May, were both organized by Birgit Burkhardt. And on 30 May Tim Mitchell's Scratch Orchestra Presentation No. 29 took place at the Bedford Square Book Bang Festival.

On 12 June (two days after AMM's performance at the Queen Elizabeth Hall) Jenny Robbins' Scratch Orchestra Presentation No. 24 took place in the Metro Club in Notting Hill in west London. Described as a 'youth club for immigrants', it was a venue where, the previous week, a 'riot' with the police had resulted in several arrests. A display board of telegrams and messages from various black liberation movements around the world expressed sympathy and militant solidarity. Even taking into account the Scratch Orchestra's unworldly approach to social matters at that time, the programme that Jenny Robbins, a working-class girl herself, had devised was, in the context, a perfect exemplar of chalk and cheese: her own niminy-piminy *Toy Symphony*, played with toys, musical and otherwise; Alan Brett's *Whoopee*, in which sounds are made only when the performers are airborne; Howard Skempton's *Drum No.1*; and a selection of pieces played by Hugh Shrapnel's Wood and Metal Band. It was not the case that Robbins had misjudged the audience and the occasion; such was her unsullied idealism that she had blithely not given a thought to either. Through the doorway of the Metro Club we had entered into a world in which our profound irrelevance was starkly and painfully exposed.

Shrapnel recalls that the Scratch Orchestra performed upstairs on a balcony quite separate from the main auditorium and stage, such that most of the audience were probably not even aware of its presence. Those that were, according to the few vague accounts that have survived, seemed to have been nonplussed, singularly unimpressed by our peripheral contribution. But at least they adopted an attitude of benign neutrality towards us, for which we were grateful. Our belief that by dint of 'good intentions', or of wish fulfilment, we could draw people, any people, into our orbit, was dealt a crippling blow. We were, quite simply, out of our depth.[9]

Predictably, both events were seized upon by the Marxists/Communists, a small but articulate minority (which included myself), as further evidence of the Scratch Orchestra's pie-in-the-sky idealism: the Scratch Orchestra was an 'unprepared irrelevance' with nothing to offer the working-class; nor could we while we clung to an irrational, anarchistic ideology which, among other idiosyncrasies, included, in Hugh Shrapnel's words, 'the elevation of incompetence to the highest of human aspirations'.[10]

Nevertheless, the experiences in Southampton and Notting Hill notwithstanding, on Saturday 19 June 1971 the Scratch Orchestra set off northwards for a series of concerts which had been funded with a grant of £150 from Northeast Arts through the agency of its music officer, Kevin Stephens. Cardew and his family, Birgit Burkhardt and Hanne Boenisch (who was to make a film of the tour) had already visited the area in and around Newcastle during the Easter period to reconnoitre and prepare the groundwork: choosing a camp-site and checking out the concert venues. Two large vans, one belonging to Stefan Szczelkun and Judith Euren, the other, a VW Microbus, belonging to Cardew, were provided as transport. Some Scratch members preferred to travel independently, a few by car. On arrival we set up our tents on a derelict piece of wasteland that resembled a bomb-site rather than a camp-site, and which had been rented from a local farmer by Cardew and his advance party in April. The first week comprised a series of planned presentations; the second week, although unplanned, it was assumed would also involve concerts and events – depending on the renewed energy and resourcefulness of individual members in coming up with ideas and specific proposals. A third week was set aside as a holiday for those who could afford the time and money.

The first concert was scheduled for Monday 21 June at the Newcastle Civic Centre, in the open air but under cover; a nearby fountain failed to soften the character of an area dominated by concrete. The second concert, on the next day, was to take place in the Durham Castle Courtyard which, as it transpired, was an open-air bandstand site in an eerie, deserted park close to a railway station. On Thursday 24 June the venue was the Sunderland Art School Courtyard, a quadrangle with arched walks, and on the next day we travelled some forty miles south to appear at the Dovecot YMCA centre in Stockton-on-Tees. On 26 June we would return to the Newcastle Civic Centre for the final presentation. The content of these five concerts was determined by an ingenious method devised by Michael Chant for using up the proliferation of proposals and to which he gave the title 'Dealer Concerts'.

When the Scratch Orchestra arrived at the Newcastle Civic Centre for its inaugural presentation the first person to greet us was a Civic Centre porter. The following is Bryn Harris's colourfully evocative description of what ensued:

We were to perform in front of the Centre, using only that area defined by a security operative who was the true embodiment of the concept of 'jobs-worth'. Said official, noting our interest in the acoustic and contemplative opportunity offered by an area of concrete ground relief partly screened off from our playing area by a wall of vertically placed and horizontally spaced concrete bars, advanced upon us. 'That back there' he hurried to advise the newly politically-activated Keith Rowe, 'is STATIC! All STATIC!' At the time Keith was very taken with this unusual application of the term. Clearly the space was out of bounds to us; perhaps our music would corrupt its barren waste. That though, was just the start [...]. As the first Dealer Concert got underway, he adjured us to 'pack up and go, quick', for 'the skinheads are coming off the moors'. There would be carnage! We stayed,they came; their spontaneous, friendly and chaotic behaviour mingled with and co-catalysed the pseudo-chaos of our dealings. A minor mess was caused, our entire stock of toilet rolls for the tour was plundered and dispersed, football style, to the winds [...].The now near paranoid security man summoned the fuzz.[11]

During the proceedings the said operative had noticed an area thronged with people who appeared to be engrossed in one particular part of the Scratch Orchestra's presentation; he pushed his way through to satisfy his curiosity. What met his vision were a few toilet rolls, strewn around on the ground, which had 'dirty', four-letter words and rough, rather inexpert representations of nude females drawn on them. In the Dealer concerts Cardew had 'drawn' a piece by Greg Bright for which the instructions read: 'Act as obscenely as you can until the authorities intervene.' Although it is unlikely that the obscene words, or even the titillating nudes, were outside the experience of a council worker in the heart of Newcastle, the security operative expressed disgust and ordered Cardew to get rid of the offending material; Cardew duly and promptly obliged. However, not content with this modest measure of control, the mortified official, in a no doubt strongly-worded report to his superiors, then contrived to have the Scratch Orchestra's next concert at the Civic Centre, the following Saturday, cancelled on the grounds of 'blatant obscenity'.

In no time the news of the Scratch Orchestra's transgressions reached the ears of the owner of the land at Prudhoe,[12] on the outskirts of Newcastle, where the Scratch Orchestra was camping. Fearing, presumably, that the corrupt and immoral character of his tenants might well reflect upon his own reputation he summarily evicted the Scratch Orchestra from his property; the supplications of Bryn Harris and Jenny Robbins for understanding and forgiveness were to no avail. The press seized on what they regarded as the saleable ingredients of the affair – salt-of-the-earth, decent working-class (the security operative) versus incomprehensible, degenerate modern art (the Scratch Orchestra) – and made hay for a day or two with considerable factual licence. One report claimed that the Scratch Orchestra had been 'booed off the stage' on an evening when in fact no concert had taken place, nor indeed was any booing or similar vocal disapproval registered at all. A newspaper article headed 'Drummed Out – Prof's Toilet-roll Orchestra' reported:

The audience were surprised when the 25 members turned up with only two drums between them. But they were stunned when the performance began. For most of the orchestra spent most of the time writing four-letter words on pieces of toilet paper, it was claimed last night. They then scattered them among the audience, which included children. City architect Mr. George Kenyon, who refused to allow the orchestra to perform again, said last night: 'The amount of blatant indecency displayed was intolerable'.[13]

A more graphic account focused on the bearing and demeanour of Cardew:

A man dressed in an ankle-length leather coat and wearing a beret was playing with plastic cups and writing obscene words on toilet paper. I saw a group of children playing around his feet. It turned out to be Cornelius Cardew, a modern composer and leader of the Scratch Orchestra. Mr. Cardew described himself as a Professor of Composition at the Royal Academy of Music in Marylebone. But an Academy spokesman said: 'Mr Cardew is not a professor in the sense that he has a chair and a department. He is simply a part-time teacher of composition. He has only one pupil and I understand she is in hospital'.[14]

When it transpired that the Scratch Orchestra was neither sensational nor pornographic the Press dropped the story with the same alacrity with which they had seized upon it. Northern Arts, however, like the landowner no doubt fearful for its good name, acted with indecent haste in publicly disassociating itself from the Scratch Orchestra (with the honourable exception of its music officer[15]). Scratch meetings were convened to discuss reactions and strategy, as well as the wider issues raised by the authorities' actions. Eventually a new, more congenial site was found in a pastoral setting with running brook, and the remaining concerts, with heightened Scratch resolve, went ahead as scheduled.

There are few memories of the subsequent events; presumably they have been eclipsed by the dramatic occurrences at the Civic Centre and the ensuing, partial disruption of the Scratch Orchestra's remaining programme. Some members recall the concert at Stockton-on-Tees where a BBC crew was filming and a flock of reporters and photographers, perhaps anticipating further scandal, had foregathered. When one of the reporters attempted to interview Cardew he responded in an 'automaton' style, speaking and moving slowly and mechanically according to the demands of a piece he was performing. There are several such cameo scenes which have survived in one form or other, including a photograph of myself, reproduced in Michael Nyman's book, bound hand and foot in an interpretation of Hugh Shrapnel's Houdini Rite at the Durham concert (to which I am frequently drawn attention).[16]

The 'tour' of the Northeast not only provided important lessons for many individual Scratch Orchestra members (most of whom had assumed that the overall public and 'official' response would be comparable to that of the previous tours, in Cornwall and Anglesey), it was also a turning point for the Orchestra as a whole. For the first time it had been confronted by organs of State power and forced to compromise, if not capitulate. It had not expected such an immoderate and gratuitous reaction to its presentations, however unconventional these may have seemed, and was therefore quite unprepared. Its defences were easily breached because it had erected none. Of course, it is arguable that had the security operative taken a more relaxed attitude towards the proceedings the Scratch Orchestra visit would probably have passed by peaceably without demur. However, the consensus which emerged and solidified at the meetings, and which was undoubtedly influenced by the analytical approach of the small 'Marxist' contingent (principally Keith and Carrie Rowe and myself), perceived familiar and characteristic attitudes and responses emblematic of a wider context of Anglo-Saxon hypocrisy and mean-spiritedness; furthermore, the official hostility had been compounded by a cynical manipulation and exploitation of ignorance and prejudice by the civic authorities and the Press. There were political lessons to be drawn and the Marxists seized the opportunity.

For Cardew, a confluence of factors, not all associated with the Scratch Orchestra and its recent travails, had precipitated the emotional turmoil which now engulfed him. He was becoming more and more estranged from Stella, and his on-going relationship with Sheila Kasabova was a source of both joy and guilt, for he feared the consequences for his children.[17] Physically and metaphorically distanced, for the first time, from the rest of the Scratch Orchestra (he and Stella had pitched their tent somewhat removed from the rest of the campers), he seemed a woebegone figure, existing in a state of limbo, filled with self-doubt and dismayed by the nascent criticism of his own status and role (as leader) in the Scratch Orchestra. But in particular it was Keith Rowe's remorseless recital of political mantras, the incontrovertibility and potency of which Cardew was beginning to recognise, even though, or perhaps because, it seemed to challenge the very core of his selfhood. For it heralded an ideological pilgrimage which was to last for the rest of his life, a quest for which the instrumentalities conferred upon him by education and upbringing were inadequate, and irrelevant.

This was the critical juncture, on a camp site in the northeast of England, the turning point which changed lives and none more so than the subject of this book; when the 'politicisation' of the Scratch Orchestra, or rather the struggle *for* politicisation, began and rapidly intensified. Keith Rowe, armed impregnably with the thoughts of Chairman Mao, would proselytise into the night with those willing to listen and argue. And many did; perhaps it was not surprising that, in particular, those who had been involved in the study and practice of ancient Eastern philosophies, like Rowe, should have been intrigued and beguiled by a contemporary manifestation which was gathering momentum in many parts of the world: Maoism. Certainly Cardew was impressed by Keith Rowe's extraordinary behaviour, which was both focused and unyielding, and which was without doubt the catalyst that eventually coaxed Cardew out of his antipathy to politics and thrust him into the maelstrom of revolutionary activism.[18]

In this respect the Scratch Orchestra did mirror the way in which political and social ideas and aspirations developed and changed during the sixties – from the Hippies and 'flower power' of the earlier part of the decade to the more sophisticated, if flawed, political radicalism of the late sixties and seventies. Both movements, in their own way, wanted to turn the world upside down. Until Newcastle the Scratch Orchestra were never banner-wavers; the overwhelming majority lacked any kind of theoretical motivation and harboured no ideological presumptions. There was an immanence of innocence, though not naivety (except in narrowly-defined, political terms), which belied any notion of provocation or disingenuousness in our public presentations. The Scratch Orchestra comprised a multitude of life styles; in our attitudes and behaviour, our *mores,* we were more akin to New Age travellers. Now all this was to be overthrown; the old Scratch Orchestra represented values which the new ideology was to put to flight; and the multifarious alternative universes which it had embodied would be collapsed into a strait-jacket of political rectitude.[19] As Stella Cardew has opined, by the end of the northeast tour everything was so fractured, so chaotic, that to a significant number of Scratch members politics was the only logical course – or seemed to be.

Discontent

The Scratch Orchestra's politicization was preceded by a recital of palpable discontent which was given written and democratic expression in a 'discontent file' which Cardew opened entirely on his own initiative, an extension of the Documentary file which, as we have seen, had already attracted some irreverent and controversial insertions. 'Different parties', he wrote in a communication to the Scratch Orchestra dated 11 July 1971, significantly just two weeks after returning from the Northeast, 'think our present activities are not musical enough, not social enough, not disciplined enough, etc. etc. A number of expositions of such critical views could be duplicated and some sessions devoted to harmonizing them. Is definition necessary?' There was a huge irony at the core of Cardew's proposal; far from being a harmonizing balm, the 'discontent' meetings which ensued later in the summer were, without exaggeration, traumatic, and relationships were damaged and even terminated in some cases; some of the repressed misgivings had been harboured for too long.[20] Grievances were rehearsed publicly and the numerous contributions to the 'discontent file', and to the 'sessions' in particular, presented what seemed to be irremediable problems. By now there were multiple zones of doubt and self-doubt; ambivalent feelings had surfaced in relation to what appeared to be happening to and within the Scratch Orchestra and a profoundly inharmonious atmosphere prevailed.

What kind of discontent was expressed? Was there a common thread which ran through the contributions and which would have provided a unity of purpose in respect of change and development? Some contributions regretted the lack of concentrated and focused work and preparation, and of knowledge and use of contemporary technology; for others there was too much discussion, not enough rehearsing, not enough energy and determination, too many mundane, uninspiring concert proposals. We were going nowhere. Many expressed the opinion that Cardew's shoulders bore too much bureaucratic responsibility, but there had been no serious consideration of different organisational structures. Some members felt that the Scratch Orchestra was self-indulgent; we were reminded, if we needed to be reminded, that an audience had not materialised – not even a 'cult' audience, which might have enabled the Scratch Orchestra to develop; we were playing for ourselves. Yet for a significant number of Scratch members, it has to be said, such concerns and their implications were irrelevant.[21]

Other members, like Richard Ascough, believed that there were a number of 'discontents' which might well have brought about the eventual demise of the Scratch Orchestra, irrespective of the politics, because they seemed to reflect a more general malaise and frustration; the 'crisis' was a result of the Scratch Orchestra's own internal contradictions. Psi Ellison identified what he regarded at the time as a contradiction between those who could perform proficiently on an instrument and those who could not. It seemed to be Cardew's view, according to Ellison, that only those who were able to demonstrate a seriousness of intent through the hard-earned acquisition of an instrumental skill could then abandon it and abuse it, could play the fool and belie their skills – like the clowns of the Russian circus.[22]

Bryn Harris locates the origins of discontent in Cardew's doomed attempt to effect an amalgam of authoritarianism and democracy in *The Great Learning*. Indeed, one might argue that the Confucian ideology 'exactly mirrored the social relationships within the Scratch Orchestra'. This seems to me to be an imaginative and thoroughly plausible reading of the situation within the Orchestra; perhaps it was indeed Harris' perceptiveness in this respect that embarrassed and irritated Cardew. Everybody recognised the fact that Cardew was the patriarchal figure but few, if any, were prepared to acknowledge that this was an issue that sooner or later would have to be resolved. At that time many of the commune groups in England, and elsewhere, foundered for exactly the same reasons. Nobody wanted to identify the patriarchalism, and when somebody did, there was acute discomfort. Scratch Orchestra member Phil Gebbett, who had studied Confucianism in depth, had come to the same conclusion as Harris; that in the Draft Constitution Cardew was attempting to establish himself as 'My good Lord' – a leader to be respected and emulated. Nevertheless, whatever gloss one chooses to put upon the relationship between Cardew and the Scratch Orchestra, there is no doubt in my mind that it was the sheer scope and magnificent grandeur of his *magnum opus* which sealed Cardew's dominance within the Orchestra.

For others, and in particular the composers, it was important that questions pertaining to the social role of music, and by corollary 'audience', should be raised. Here Michael Parsons refers to an earlier Scratch Orchestra performance at the Queen Elizabeth Hall on 23 November1970: Pilgrimage from Scattered Points on the Surface of the Body to the Brain, the Heart, the Stomach and the Inner Ear.

> The problem with performances of this kind was that it was almost impossible to define sufficiently intelligible and communicable criteria for 'musical realization' of the Research Project. In the absence of any clearly defined rules, this was largely dependent on obscure forms of analogical ingenuity or the subjective free-association of the individual performers. Uniquely inspiring and memorable as these occasions were to those who participated in them, audiences remained mystified in the presence of impenetrable collages of sound and activity with no apparent internal cohesion. It was out of such contradictions that the seeds of internal dissent grew, eventually leading to the orchestra's disintegration.[23]

Parsons recollects that the development of 'systemic' music and art, in which some Scratch Orchestra composers – Christopher Hobbs, Michael Nyman, Howard Skempton and Parsons himself – became involved, was itself an implicit critique of the Scratch Orchestra's more anarchic tendencies, although this was 'from a formal and aesthetic perspective relatively independent of the then current political considerations'. These two differing tendencies might well have developed and enriched the Scratch Orchestra but in a relatively short space of time, as we shall see, an exclusively political agenda effectively outlawed the anarchic elements and denounced the compositional experiments as irrelevant, if not reactionary.

The composers, presumably through their theoretical knowledge and, relatively speaking, instrumental expertise, were seen to be in an advantageous position; but from the point of view of the composers themselves such 'advantages' were neither here nor there; their allegiance to the Scratch Orchestra was far more deeply rooted. I believe it is no exaggeration to claim that for them membership of the Scratch Orchestra was a turning point, not only in their own, individual musical development but, as Michael Chant has observed, in the trajectory, potency and meaning of their individual lives. Yet for some, it transpired, the composers were the 'careerists', silently accused of exploiting membership of an avant-garde group, led by a composer of international standing, which would become infamous, if not successful, in some measure. (And, without question, the Scratch Orchestra, since its demise, has achieved legendary status.) The composers were suspected of having their own, totally separate agenda which they sought, through the leader and fellow composer Cardew, to impose.

Perhaps the composers did regard the Scratch Orchestra as a kind of forum or workshop where ideas, subliminally or by osmosis, could be adapted and translocated into their own compositions. And why not? As long as they realised that for many of their friends and colleagues the Scratch Orchestra was something quite other. If it *had* been their (unconscious) aim to impose a different, and in some respects alien, agenda they singularly failed to do so; the music remained free, improvisatory (anarchic?) and with no concessions to musical conventions – which, one concludes from Michael Parsons' strictures quoted above, is why the composers set up their own systemic music ensemble.

One or two members had already begun to drift away from the Orchestra, unable to deal with the instability and tensions which threatened to undermine and even destroy it, and Cardew was anxious to avoid any further fragmentation. In a letter to Howard Skempton dated 28 July 1971, about a month after the experience in the Northeast, he begins with a mild rebuke: 'You must really make more contribution of energy towards a better world and less towards warding off disaster! Do you have any contribution to the Scratch "Green Paper" of discontent? It will be a weighty document.' And the letter ends with another political reference: 'It would be good to hear from you. There has been so little contact one gets the impression you are taking Holy Orders or embracing the Revolution. I'd prefer the second alternative, but that's just me.'[24]

On 31 July Cardew wrote to Skempton thanking him for cheques (for the Scratch Orchestra), apologising in passing for having 'attacked' him in his previous letter (which he had forgotten), and asking Skempton to write some music for Act 1 of the Opera, *Sweet FA*. *Sweet FA* was the result of a collaboration of several members to write an 'opera' based loosely on the experiences of the Scratch Orchestra in Newcastle.[25] It was not intended as a realistic description of these events – rather it put forward a number of 'viewpoints' representing different attitudes towards the Scratch Orchestra and its role in contemporary musical life and within society at large. Not surprisingly the two dominant views were those held by the 'revolutionaries' on one side, and the 'hippies' on the other: this was the way that the Maoists had simplified and caricatured the situation in the Scratch Orchestra. Not only was it the first attempt to create political music, it also succeeded in alienating a large number of Scratch members, including David and Diane Jackman, Psi Ellison, Judy Euren, Stefan Szczelkun, Chris May, Greg Bright, Christopher Hobbs, and Michael Parsons, all of whom virtually boycotted the project.[26] The Scratch Orchestra was now, de facto, split into two opposing factions and although it continued to meet and prepare for concerts and presentations, and a precarious co-existence survived for a while, the differences were now profound and irreconcilable, even if they were not yet formally recognised. That would take a few more months; it was a dispiriting, joyless time.

Yet Cardew's attitude towards the Maoists was still ambivalent at this stage, the summer of 1971, even if his closeness to Keith Rowe, both as a member of AMM and as friend, ensured that the political agenda would not abate and would in fact increase in intensity. They met frequently, spent much time together, socially and on tour, and Rowe, the conduit of Party orthodoxy in both AMM and the Scratch Orchestra, took every opportunity to keep politics to the forefront. The 'purity' of the Maoist line, the perceived rejection of the cynical compromises of *realpolitik*, the moral imperatives embodied in the *Communist Manifesto* – this was 'philosophy in action' and for Cardew ultimately irresistible, even if it was preceded by much agonizing.

Cardew had introduced democratic ideas into the Scratch Orchestra but it was essentially paternalistic; such was the stark and incontestable paradox which lay at the heart of Cardew's 'composition'. If he were the 'leader' – and there could be no denying that he was – then it also has to be said that it was with the complicity of the overwhelming majority of the Scratch Orchestra; we understood that without Cardew the Orchestra would not have come into existence. Cardew was by no means impervious to the criticism which had surfaced in the Scratch Orchestra, and he realised that his role as guiding spirit was in a parlous situation, compounded by the fact that one half of the Scratch Orchestra was out of kilter with the other half. Now there was an animus against him, or at least there was a disenchantment, which was beginning to spread; it was felt that as 'leader' it was he who was responsible for the crisis which threatened to bring about the demise of the Scratch Orchestra, even if there was still a reluctance to voice the criticism openly and explicitly.[27]

The 'Discontent' meetings

Aided and abetted by fellow Scratch Orchestra members, I am recalling opinions, attitudes, feelings that *were* expressed at that time, verbally and in writing by individuals. Of course, one must exercise extreme caution now in respect of people's memories of their experiences of what were, thirty-five years ago, harrowing events; I am referring in particular to the two Discontent meetings. Some of the accounts are conflicting, not just in the recollection of minutiae of varying significance, but in the way that the meetings, and their *raison d'être*, were/are perceived and subsequently rationalised. But then there never was a consensus in the Scratch Orchestra; agreement as a necessary basis for action was reached through Anglo-Saxon pragmatism and compromise rather than by a spurious conversion to a 'unity of purpose'. So that when I refer above to the attitudes of 'non-musicians', for example, this is a rough generalization which has had to survive a number of stubborn exceptions.

Nevertheless, there *were* creative perspectives which, in the view of Ellison, Finer, Jackman and others, the 'literate' musicians did not recognize, and it was felt by many that Scratch Orchestra activities were tilted too far in their favour – to the 'note' as opposed to the 'noise' and the 'meta-music' of the non-literate composers. Many Scratch musicians (including Eddie Prévost and Keith Rowe of AMM) did not read music; nor had they any desire to learn. When various autonomous groups emerged (in which competent reading was a pre-requisite), and took part in Scratch Orchestra events (such as Hugh Shrapnel's Wood and Metal Band), some members did feel excluded, resenting what they perceived as a two-pronged threat: from an increasing reliance on the musical score, and from the burgeoning political agenda.[28] On one occasion, in September of the previous year, Carole Finer did voice her objection – to the aforementioned 'Beethoven Today' concert at the Purcell Room. For one thing, she complained, it had subverted the rota system (from the youngest upwards), and had therefore jumped the queue. Furthermore, expressing a resentment that was probably felt by others, Finer insisted that the 'musicians' were 'pulling rank'; it was 'just for the musicians'.[29] In fact it was not strictly a Scratch Orchestra concert; the Portsmouth Sinfonia had been invited to take part, for their London debut, and the poet Bob Cobbing also contributed.

On 17 August Cardew sent another circular advertising two Discontent meetings on 23 and 24 August at Catherine Williams' flat in St.George's Terrace, just off Primrose Hill, Regent's Park. The second meeting was in fact postponed and took place on 11 September in a small upstairs room at the Conway Hall in Red Lion Square in Holborn. At the first meeting I presented my own Marxist analysis, the cornerstone of which was a lengthy quote from Christopher Caudwell's essay on D.H. Lawrence: 'Study of a Bourgeois Artist'. In essence my contribution hinged on what I perceived as a contradiction between the aspirations and ideals of the Scratch Orchestra on the one hand, and its actual practice, and the consequences of its practice, on the other. In other words, I posited a fundamental disunity of theory and practice as the principal source of discontent and frustration in the Scratch Orchestra: in theory we believed in gregariousness and integration, in practice we were isolationist and parochial; in theory we rejected the musical establishment while in practice we applied for, and received, support (Arts Council grants, BBC television and South Bank appearances); in theory we wished to be an inspiration to people, in practice we appeared to many as a pessimistic symptom of a system in decay, or simply an irrelevance to the burning issues of the day; and so on. The Scratch Orchestra, I suggested, was trapped in the classic anarchist's dilemma: we willed one thing, and caused its opposite.

The Caudwell piece, in particular, seemed to crystallise the thoughts and feelings of a considerable number of Scratch members, including Cardew, and even some of those who subsequently resisted and bitterly regretted the Marxist 'take-over'. Others were thrown into perplexity and haplessness by the severity of the critique and its implications:

> But art is not in any case a relation to a thing, it is a relation between men, between artist and audience, and the art work is only like a machine which they must both grasp as part of the process. The commercialisation of art may revolt the sincere artist, but the tragedy is that he revolts against it still within the limitations of bourgeois culture. He attempts to forget the market completely and concentrate on his relation to the art work, which now becomes still further hypostasised as an entity-in-itself. Because the art work is now completely an end-in-itself, and even the market is forgotten, the art process becomes an extremely individualistic relation. The social values inherent in the art form, such as syntax, tradition, rules, technique, form, accepted tonal scale, now seem to have little value, for the art work more and more exists for the individual alone.[30]

I argued that if our relation to Art, both as individuals and collectively, was to be of any serious consequence, we had to come to terms above all with the *moral* issues which such a commitment raises. It was a challenge of the kind that the American painter Philip Guston had presented and taken up some years earlier:

> So when the 1960s came along I was feeling split, schizophrenic. The war, what was happening to America, the brutality of the world. What kind of man am I, sitting at home, reading magazines, going into a frustrated fury about everything – and then getting into my studio to adjust a red to a blue. I thought there must

be some way I could do something about it. I knew ahead of me a road was laying. A very crude, inchoate road. I wanted to be complete again, as I was when I was a kid […]. Wanted to be whole between what I thought and what I felt.[31]

For the second Discontent meeting it had been agreed beforehand that everybody in turn should have their say: Michael Parsons raised the question as to whether the Scratch Orchestra should seek an external audience or concentrate on its own needs. Brian Dennis asserted that it was external activity, exposed to public scrutiny, that attracted new people, whereas others felt that the Scratch Orchestra had no need for new members. The point was made that the good thing about the Scratch Orchestra was that things were done for their own sake and in response to whatever social situation it found itself in. With a thinly disguised reference to the perceived threat of a political 'coup' an obdurate David Jackman insisted that decisions affecting the Scratch Orchestra should only be made at meetings which were fully representative. Diane Jackman threatened to resign if the Scratch Orchestra became 'political' while others claimed that what was needed was a more democratic structure. Several members expressed the desire to get back to a 'normal' situation, somehow to make emotional reparation; unpredictable and malign cosmic configurations were also blamed for the current plight. Bryn Harris read out excerpts from John Cage's *Silence* and *A Year from Monday*, perhaps as a kind of palliative; but it was a forlorn wish. As the atmosphere became febrile David Jackman and Psi Ellison led a spirited, emotional revolt and it became painfully obvious that the huge divides that were developing dispelled all hope of compromise and reconciliation. If the Scratch Orchestra was not actually destroyed at the Discontent meetings, it was disfigured to an extent that would eventually make it unrecognizable. The ever-increasing silences between contributions became pregnant with malaise and despair. Unspoken, unspeakable thoughts began to occupy the space as the Scratch Orchestra lapsed into a state of inanition.

The meeting was finally thrown into complete disarray when Cardew seemed to be demanding the exclusion of Bryn Harris from the Scratch Orchestra when the plans which he was putting forward as the basis for future Scratch Orchestra activity were met with demands for outright rejection by Harris and David Jackman. There was uproar; that a member of the Scratch Orchestra could be excluded by another member, even by a majority consensus, was unthinkable. Cardew had badly misjudged the moment and matters deteriorated even further when he offered to stand down and 'hand over the reins' (these may or may not have been the actual words), to Ellison and Jackman, who both bridled at Cardew's presumptuousness in assuming the right and authority to 'hand over' the 'leadership' of the Scratch Orchestra, however benevolently, to anyone.[32] A highly emotional Ellison burst into tears and left the meeting while an envenomed

Jackman denounced Cardew's autocratic behaviour. Perhaps he should have been deposed there and then but few at the meeting would have been prepared to take such radical action. Amidst all the emotional confusion, the disorientation, glimmers of rationality surfaced to rescue the status quo. Yes, despite (or through?) Cardew's 'subtly autocratic' domination the Scratch Orchestra had benefited, however embarrassing and untenable this relationship subsequently became. The relatively high profile of the Scratch Orchestra owed much to Cardew: his contacts in the music world, the respect he enjoyed in certain sections of the media and in art institutions, particularly abroad, and the prestigious venues at which, from time to time, the Scratch Orchestra appeared. But all this was now in jeopardy; Cardew's authority was threatened, by the leftists on the one side, and by the anarchists and liberals on the other. The former proposed radical change, danger, cataclysms and, of course, new and more decisive modes of authority and leadership. The latter were united solely by their implacable opposition to the politicisation of the Scratch Orchestra.

In her admirable contribution to the Discontent file, Catherine Williams refers to her own personal experience. Although she found the 'controlling situation' in the Scratch Orchestra 'repressive', she admits that she had 'voluntarily submitted to [it]'; in fact, 'my "repression" *could* have been totally justified, in view of a "common good" [...] a trendy acquiescence in individual non-assertion has surrounded me like a fog'.[33] But the 'common good' was now being challenged by 'a more realistic ideology'. She then asks:

> But if the group [the Scratch Orchestra] has been self-deceived, for a long, or a short time, then the same group could still make similar mistakes. The situation *seems* more lively, under new pressures, but is the group therefore any less capable of mistakes, as it goes about constructing new departures from within itself? [34]

Williams goes on to propose the liquidation of the Scratch Orchestra, reasoning: 'Liquidation *could* involve repudiation of our former working condition, our name and constitution, but *not* the immediate imposition of a corporate identity'.[35] Catherine Williams' analysis of the crisis situation that had arisen in the Scratch Orchestra was measured and objective – a mature document which few, if any, other contributions could match. With reference to the Discontent file Cardew himself seems to recognise this, as well as the progressive content of the pieces she had devised:

> The most radical critique came from Catherine Williams, who suggested the liquidation of the Scratch. (It is interesting that Williams' contribution to the present book [*Scratch Music*], though much of it falls outside most definitions of Scratch

Music, is the most progressive in that it deals with mass movements, with unanimity, something that the Scratch has definitely not yet arrived at.)[36]

David Jackman has pointed out that if we consider the various twentieth century visual art movements – Dada, Surrealism, among others – they all lasted, as coherent movements, around two years, like the Scratch Orchestra. He takes a more relaxed, philosophical view of the discontent and break up of the Orchestra. With so many strong individuals, each developing in their own way, though initially on the basis of common ground, it would now seem to have been inevitable, with the benefit of hindsight, that tensions would arise, that individuals would voice their frustrations and that a process of disintegration would set in.

Perhaps, as Psi Ellison has suggested, there is a time-scale for groups working together intuitively and spontaneously: the Scratch Orchestra, 'in terms of unspoken, undiscussed, irrational activity', had run its course. The time had come for the Scratch Orchestra to assume conscious responsibility for what it was doing.

But there was still the need for reflection and for some weeks Cardew bided his time. The stakes had been raised, a seriousness of intent made explicit and before long Cardew himself, after much agonising, had grasped the political nettle. In the end, and not surprisingly, the challenge of the twentieth century's revolutionary mission had proved irresistible to him. Our 'opponents', for whom the very language used by the leftists was alien, were given neither time nor space to collect their thoughts and reply – it was a *fait accompli*.

Alexandra Palace [37]

Right from its inception, as we have seen, there were in the general and common attitudes of the Scratch Orchestra – such as its opposition to the unbridled consumerism of the 'swinging sixties' – auguries of the political concerns which would eventually overtake it. The construction of a cottage, the basic structure of which was designed by Scratch member Stefan Szczelkun, for the International Art Spectrum Exhibition at the Alexandra Palace in August 1971, was further evidence of a political gravitation, as well as being quaintly emblematic of the Orchestra's quixotic ideals. The aim of the Exhibition was to 'expose the breadth and excitement of the current London situation in a way that is not done in the normal exhibition circuits'; for the Scratch Orchestra it was an opportunity to create some down-market art: a 'medieval' cottage which was meant to be functional, that is, habitable(?), simple, unostentatious, and democratic – a worthy demonstration of the results of collective endeavour and of Chairman Mao's insistence on 'self-reliance'.

In other words, it was a 'political' statement; a tongue-in-cheek 'primitivism', its very presence a 'sore thumb' and in stark contrast to the individualistic and modish artefacts that pervaded the Exhibition. Despite the traumas of the Discontent meetings a nucleus of Scratch members had come together to pool ideas and resources, and for a brief period a precarious and temporary harmony prevailed. Even the Slippery Merchants continued to participate, offering people rides at a small charge around the exhibition in a wheelbarrow (a typical piece of Scratch irony, subtly and effortlessly materialised).

The Scratch Orchestra had originally requested 'a two-storied building approximately the dimensions of a country cottage with front and back gardens which would accommodate a library, a Prints and Drawings Room, a Studio, an Office, a Kitchen/diner, a Music Room, a Garden'. When this request was turned down it was decided that we should construct our own accommodation, reflecting the Scratch ethos of relying on our own efforts rather than the advice of opinionated experts, of achievement against the odds, and of resourcefulness – ideas which were rooted in Scratch Orchestra practice, and Cardew's in particular, long before Chairman Mao's Little Red Book had established itself as an indispensable point of reference. Scratch Orchestra members found themselves doing things they never believed themselves capable of. (Carole Finer brought along her electric drill which had always intimidated her and thus had never been used.)

The cottage was constructed, according to a plan drawn up by members of the Scratch Orchestra, from 'easily available materials', that is, materials which cost next to nothing or, preferably, nothing at all.

Space within the cottage would be subdivided by wattle screens and a first floor, extending across half the floor area, would be supported on a scaffolding frame (This pattern is derived from a typical medieval cottage type). Materials for the outer walls would be matured timber framing infilled with wattle screen on the upper level and with old doors in the lower. The roof would be of canvas supported on standard prefabricated roof trusses.[38]

In a circular to Scratch members, which admirably demonstrates his eye for detail as well as his grasp of the project as a whole, Cardew wrote:

No funds have been provided for materials; *we* have to find, collect and deliver to Alexandra Palace virtually all the building materials. These comprise essentially a lot of 4 by 2" timber; a variety of infill materials such as old doors, wattle fencing, corrugated iron, etc.; floor covering 1000 sq. ft. of matting, underfelt, carpet, etc; roof-covering, large tarpaulins […].

The interior furnishing will also be provided by us. This is a preliminary list of what will be needed, and we need to know in advance who can provide which items: Crockery (6 of everything, Bookcases (2 or 3), Electric Cooker, Desk or Bureau, Vacuum cleaner, Plan chests and portfolios, small wardrobe, Chest of drawers, Easel, Standardlamps (4 or 5), Tables (2 or 3), Chairs (about 10), sofa, cushions (many), a small library of 100-200 books.

Altogether, each Scratcher should think of contributing to this project under 4 headings: 1) material for the 'fabric' of the building, 2) a piece of furniture (reclaimable afterwards), 3) Books (3 or 4) & cushions (reclaimable afterwards), something else.[39]

Cardew himself, ever resourceful, spotted some underfelt outside an Earls Court hotel, in west London, which was being refurbished. He took it home, 270 sq. feet of it, cleaned it, and donated it to the cottage.

The venture was not without its moments of frustration and anxiety. No doubt mindful of the history of Alexandra Palace the authorities deemed the structure to be a fire hazard, which meant that the imminent opening of the cottage was in serious jeopardy. The indomitable Carole Finer made haste to a theatrical props shop she knew in Covent Garden, called Keeps, for some special paint, and the cottage duly opened and survived for the two week duration of the Exhibition, as an *objet d'art*, it must be said, rather than a dwelling place or quiet, temporary haven. Visitors approached it gingerly and entered it with a degree of trepidation; for some the Scratch Orchestra's propensity for risk and failure was, under the circumstances, disquieting, so that the informal presentation of Scratch events tended to happen around rather than in the cottage: Tim Mitchell exhibited his 'Refuse Collection' of art work, including etchings and paintings, by Scratch Orchestra members; and two scenes from *Sweet FA*, the Scratch Orchestra's 'opera', were also recorded and used later for live performances.

In his 'History of the Scratch Orchestra' Rod Eley quotes Michael Chant's scathing dismissal of the Alexandra Palace event: 'The Orchestra could pull together sufficiently to build a fire hazard, unfit for human habitation, and then withdraw to write its discontents. It became apparent that, like the cottage, the Orchestra was just a shell without any real substance.'[40] Ignoring the incorrect chronology (the 'discontents' had already been penned and aired before the construction, or even planning, of the 'fire hazard'), the cottage was never intended to be 'fit for human habitation'; it was a symbolic act, and a harbinger of the Scratch Orchestra's ultimate politicisation: a *statement* that even in the most difficult and extreme circumstances, for which they are not prepared, people should rely on their own initiatives and efforts, however flawed. Yet the project did betray a regressive, Arcadian strain, exemplified by Cardew's atavistic proposal to his son Horace that he should take his clothes off and appear naked in front of the cottage – an outrageous suggestion, even for a five or six year old, and Horace refused point-blank.

Overlapping with the Alexandra Palace Exhibition was the Scratch Orchestra Summer School which took place over five days, 30 August – 3 September, at The Place in Euston. Instrumental and singing classes were offered, as well as composition, mathematics, visual arts, history, Marxism and gymnastics. In fact, it was an exercise in self-education since the classes were led and attended, in the main, by Scratch Orchestra members and friends. In retrospect the Cottage and the Summer School may be seen as last-ditch attempts to hold the Orchestra together without compromising either its newly adopted political agenda or its traditional anarchist roots. The wealth of expertise in various fields embedded within the Scratch Orchestra, which never surfaced during meetings or concerts, was a revelation: Michael Chant's knowledge of mathematics, for example, was demonstrated in his fascinating lecture on the Zeno paradoxes. Michael Parsons recalls Cardew doing hand-stands and rolls clumsily but with great determination in Tim Mitchell's gymnastic class: 'It was strange to see him doing something badly'.

The Alexandra Palace Exhibition was arguably the last major event of the original Scratch Orchestra, in the sense that individual members used the space and room to perform in their various idiosyncratic ways. Those aspects of Mao Tse-tung Thought that could be accommodated within a liberal/anarchist world outlook were, at least temporarily, a source of inspiration, just as they had been to John Cage; that is, it *was* a liberating philosophy as long as its authoritarianism could be held at bay. Cardew came to regard such a position as superficial and untenable, and if he hesitated before deciding on a course of action which was to alter the course of his life profoundly, indeed cataclysmically, I do not believe that he would have balked at the question of *authority*, and of Party authority in particular.

The Id Group

The Scratch Orchestra Ideological group was a worm of subversion, the chrysalis from which the political faction emerged and through which the politicisation of the Scratch Orchestra as a whole was eventually achieved. The 'Id Group' was set up after the second Discontent meeting had taken place at the Conway Hall, and the first Id Group meeting took place at Birgit Burkhardt's flat in Hargrave Park, north London on 11 September 1971. Those present included Burkhardt, Alec Hill, Bryn Harris, Keith Rowe and myself (there may well have been some others), most if not all of them stalwart members of the Scratch Orchestra who were broadly sympathetic to the analysis that I had put forward at the first Discontent meeting and to the proposal for further discussion of the issues raised. A recent consensus suggests that Cardew was not present but joined the group not long after its inception, although probably more out of curiosity than conviction at that time.[41] Significantly, an equal number of prominent members were dismayed by this development and took no part in the Id Group discussions.

The political orientation of the group was made manifest at the first meeting where it was agreed that a course of study and discussion of Mao Tse-tung Thought should be embarked upon, beginning with the three seminal works: 'On Practice', 'On Contradiction' and 'Talks at the Yenan Forum on Literature and Art'. The last text was deemed to be of particular relevance; it raised the question of the function and purpose of art in an unequivocal fashion and, as I recall, provoked much discussion (for example, to what extent, if any, can political ideas such as 'democracy' be applied meaningfully in a musical context). Apart from any political bearing these meetings in the early seventies may or may not have had on the ultimate demise (or revivification) of the Scratch Orchestra, most of the participants agree that they were lively, impassioned, serious, and remain to this day of inestimable value to those of us for whom the relationship to art is an on-going preoccupation and which continues to exercise a profound influence on our lives. That such an uncompromisingly prescriptive artistic agenda as the 'Yenan Forum' text (to which I shall return in due course) could have generated a debate of such richness and complexity is a measure of the seriousness, perhaps too of the *unreasonableness*, of the demands it made of us.[42] It was precisely the rigour, one might say the *crudeness*, of these texts, with their intimidatory challenges and watchwords (such as 'revolutionary utilitarianism'), which inspired and galvanised us into action. Mao's intention was to wrest art from the philosophers and from the aestheticians, to demand its participation in the class struggle, and thereby, in his view, to *elevate* it: art became a matter of life and death. As one of the subtlest thinkers of the twentieth century wrote: 'There are many people to whom a dialectician means a lover of subtleties […] Crude thoughts belong to the household of dialectical thinking precisely because they represent nothing other than the application of theory to practice: its *application* to practice, not its *dependence* on practice.'[43] Or as Cardew expressed it some years later: 'on matters of principle there are no shades of grey'.[44]

For better or for worse the Id Group did succeed in injecting new purpose, new life into the Scratch Orchestra and Cardew subsequently went so far as to claim that it saved the Orchestra from liquidation. But equally it could be said that the new direction actually hastened the Scratch Orchestra's final disintegration, causing disruptions in the social fabric and undermining the strong sense of cohesion; certainly, not a few members would take this view. For David Jackman 'the eventual intrusion of an irrelevant authoritarian politics was a disaster. The friendly co-operation gave way to mutual suspicion and paranoia, and the ugliness of rampant ideology held sway. It was time to depart'.[45]

At the time of the Northeast tour Cardew had not been sympathetic to the political proselytizing through which Keith Rowe, in particular, was seeking to engage Scratch members in 'ideological struggle'. Not that he was unfamiliar with Rowe's fervour and tactics; as we shall see, there was an on-going debate in AMM which had already reached a high level of intensity through the closeness and relative frequency of the encounters. Rowe was a supporter of the Communist Party of England (Marxist-Leninist), a small Maoist group whose ideological purity and uneqivocalness had made a deep impression on him. At that time the Party's role was primarily to disseminate the thoughts of Chairman Mao, in the light of which the Scratch Orchestra's contributions to contemporary culture were dismissed as inconsequential and ultimately reactionary.

When the Id Group was set up in the Scratch Orchestra Cardew felt uneasy; compromised by political ignorance he initially remained aloof from it and for a short while, with one or two other doubting friends and colleagues, resisted membership. However, the Id Group and the malaise it had created in the Scratch Orchestra intrigued, rather than repelled Cardew, and the manifest seriousness of intent attracted him. If he began to identify with Marxism, or more precisely Maoism, at this stage – or at least to be drawn towards it – it was not only because it seemed to crystallise and illuminate his own thoughts and feelings about the *role* of art in society, which had been central to his own *musica practica* during the preceding decade; of possibly even greater significance was the fact of his attraction to the Confucian idea of a wise and benign authority, which found a natural bedfellow in Leninist Democratic Centralism. Maoism was the new *Great Learning*, dispensing leadership, authority, order and justice.

And yet, I do have some doubts about the potency and exclusiveness of the role of philosophy and ideology in respect of Cardew's politicisation. Of course, the Chinese connection goes back to his childhood, to his grandfather's shop in St James', and Eastern philosophy was a moral point of reference throughout his student years, as we have seen from the innumerable references in the Journals and letters. In the sixties, with AMM, he took Chinese lessons and towards the end of the decade this fascination for Chinese culture reached its apogee with the creation of *The Great Learning*. The significance of all this cannot be underestimated. But in respect of the European philosophical tradition, and in particular Marxist thought and priorities – to which he had been exposed already in the late fifties/early sixties through his close friend, Ilona Halberstadt – there seems to have been little purchase; her forays into political exegesis were met with negative, dismissive responses. Forty years on, at her house in Deal sometime towards the end of 2004, Halberstadt posited that it was the providential entry, at a crucial juncture, of an *artist* into Cardew's life (and one for whom he had enormous respect), bearing the message of cataclysm and revolution, of visionary praxis, which was of far greater significance than that of the intellectual cut and thrust of political debate. If Confucianism was a bridge to Leninism, then Keith Rowe was the conduit into the revolutionary politics of Maoism. This was the decisive factor which changed Cardew's life. We may pose the question: Would he, could he, have reached the Party through another route? I cannot answer this.

In due course, in a matter of weeks rather than months, Cardew formally joined the Id Group and his politicization began in earnest as he participated in, and contributed to, the group's analysis of the history of the Scratch Orchestra and its current situation. He would have concurred with the 'Id's' criticism of the Scratch Orchestra's 'aimlessness', its woolly 'anti-ideology', as well as with its glib characterisation of Scratch audiences as small, indulgent, elitist cliques searching for diverse forms of escapist entertainment. The Scratch leftists criticised their colleagues for seeing the world as a medley of surfaces on which, through the multifarious and unrestricted range of its activities, it would somehow leave its imprint. In one of the Id Group's numerous statements from the early seventies (in this case undated), which Cardew would have supported whole-heartedly, the totality of its opposition to bourgeois society finds uncompromising expression:

> Finally the enemy manifests itself insidiously in the realm of ideas; reactionary, anti-people, anti-revolutionary ideas and doctrines that are widely promoted within the superstructure of monopoly capitalist society – that is, institutes of higher education, universities, art colleges, intellectual and artistic circles, TV, the press, etc. These institutions do not exist in some sort of vacuum, functioning as the moral guardian of the system. They exist in a bourgeois society precisely in order to serve the political and economic needs of monopoly capitalism: the idea that art is first and foremost a means of self-expression, the notion that therefore whatever serves self-interest is valid; the popularisation of drugs, sex, transcendental philosophies as an antidote to this wicked world, and so on and so forth. Consciously or unconsciously, the function of all these ideas and theories is the same – to mystify capitalist social relations, to obscure the laws of motion and change, to attempt to stave off revolution, to hold back history.[46]

By the end of the year Cardew's attitude to the Scratch Orchestra was decidedly detached; he viewed them now as a group of harmless experimentalists whose existence was of marginal significance:

> Scratch seems like a flea circus on the chest of the body politic. A flea is completely ineffectual to destroy the body (except by some strange fluke). A virus works much more effectively. For this reason I should get back inside the musical

community and work from in there. Does going back in there preclude continuance of the Scratch?[47]

The last sentence is interesting because it suggests that Cardew still felt that the continued existence of the Scratch Orchestra depended on him; without him the Scratch Orchestra would cease to function. And this, in a relatively short space of time, turned out to be the case. For Cardew the Scratch Orchestra was now deemed an irrelevance; musically and socially its impact had been minimal. The correct strategy for the progressive musician – that is, the politically conscious musician – was to work within the profession, rather than in some ephemeral group, hovering virtually unnoticed on the perimeter.

The Id Group, now the self-appointed caucus responsible for monitoring the political correctitude of the Scratch Orchestra, continued to meet fortnightly at the flats and houses of its members, as well as in pubs, to the end of the year and into the new year. On 21 December 1971 we issued a statement to members of the Scratch Orchestra in relation to our participation in a projected performance of Paragraph 5 of *The Great Learning*, sponsored by Macnaghten Concerts:

> The Id Group was set up in the wake of the 'discontent' meetings to seriously consider the work of the Scratch, its social function and context and also the nature of its audience with regard to what was being communicated and to whom. In the light of these facts, and concerning the current performance, it is necessary to point out that while the ideas expressed in the work do not obviate its performance, in some cases they are no longer pertinent to our present ideological standpoint.

It was true that Confucian ideas were no longer 'generally accepted as a guiding principle for the Orchestra's activity', but had they ever been? The Scratch Orchestra went along with *The Great Learning* as an inspiring piece of avant-garde art in which we could all participate.[48] Much of the Confucian philosophy embedded within it they took with a pinch of salt and probably opposed; one did not have to be a member of the Id Group to have reached such a conclusion. Not surprisingly, for many Scratch members these Id Group communications were high-handed, factitious and alienating; it had even been suggested that Scratch Orchestra activity should be suspended for several months, apart from two outstanding engagements in January 1972: Paragraph 5 of *The Great Learning* at Cecil Sharp House (which, clearly, had been agreed upon) and a concert in Liverpool. The overtly political agenda which emanated from Id Group meetings was perceived as a threat to Scratch values and *modus vivendi*, an intolerable imposition of an alien (Maoist) ideology – which it was, and was met with fierce hostility and total rejection from a number of individuals.

But for Cardew it rapidly became a commitment, freely, even wilfully chosen, driven and exalted by political and philosophical certainties, which led to a relocation of the site of his daily existence, and to the outward transfiguration of his personality – an ennobling mission into which he was to throw himself heart and soul. As for the remaining majority of the Scratch Orchestra, in the wake of Cardew's defection it foundered on the rock of anonymity and, more importantly, through lack of true purpose – proof, perhaps, that it was, after all, his name and reputation as much as the activities of the Scratch Orchestra itself which assured it, for a time, its notoriety. In a perceptive analysis of the crisis which now engulfed the Scratch Orchestra Rod Eley had already warned of the danger that a small number of people armed with a well-organised set of views – at least on the level of rhetoric – might try to stampede the rest of the group (of individuals) into some kind of narrow orthodoxy, temptingly presented in the form of a 'programme for action': 'it would be foolish to train a wild natural growth by wrapping it round frames and weeding out offshoots which don't seem to harmonise with some narrow conception'.[49] If those that resisted the political juggernaut appeared less coherent it was because they mistrusted the idea of a consistent 'world outlook' (unlike the Id Group they did not enjoy the 'benefit' of a consensus), and of any political panacea to solve their own or the world's problems. They did not believe in the promise of 'answers' and 'solutions'; the questions they would have wished to pose would in any case have negated the idea of a question/answer, problem-solving, political agenda, and of the efficacy of, and therefore justification for, violent revolution – and even of the possibility of a rational society free of exploitation and injustice. Theirs was a philosophy of an existential quietism, in some cases of nihilism; perhaps, in lighter moments, of gradualism and reformism. 'The strength of the Scratch Orchestra lies in its heterogeneous character; people have such individuality and personality. Superficially this might appear a weakness, but surely it is respect for individuality that binds it together.'[50] Eley's remarks may have been intended as a last-ditch tribute to the old Scratch Orchestra but the on-rushing tide of events swept it away; what he had provided was an epitaph. The Party's tactic was to tarnish this 'individuality' by associating it with bourgeois ideology (ie by confusing it with *individualism*), and by cynically exploiting the self-doubt which was common to many.[51] Its overall strategy was total control over its members and unquestioning obedience to the Party line.[52]

As Eddie Prévost opined some twenty-five years on:

Simplifying political programmes or manifestos inevitably reduces meaning. If music is used to aid simplification then it contradicts its role, which is to enrich.

So with socialism. And, as with socialism, when art has to be commodified then it is time for it to withdraw to somewhere where it exists 'for its own sake'.[53]

This is precisely the route which some Scratch members, such as David Jackman and Psi Ellison took, although Prévost's proviso, echoing the thoughts of previous eminent thinkers on the philosophy of Art, and an expression of a personal conviction nurtured within AMM, was intended as a reminder of the temporality and therefore, in the long run, of the untenability of such a strategy: 'If humanisation is our ultimate goal, "art for art's sake" can only be justified as a tactical withdrawal.' [54]

Perhaps there were Scratch Orchestra members who really believed, and still do believe, in its indestructibility; that the activities and ethos of the Scratch Orchestra would continue *sine die*. Indeed, there is much evidence to support this thesis, from the on-going Scratch activities of original members and the fascination for the Scratch Orchestra mythology which is shared among members of younger generations. In the following extract, whilst recognising and accepting the demise of the Scratch Orchestra in its original form, Cardew refers to this idea of continuance and continuity through the vector of 'a more subtle principle', through the necessity, as he saw it, of 'search', through a transfiguration into a more profound relation:

The original structure of the Orchestra seems to be approaching exhaustion. This is no cause for unhappiness. As Howard Skempton says 'The honeymoon is over. The Profound things stand before us' (or some such sentiment). […] A more subtle principle is called for; far removed from the practicalities of Bank Accounts and Archives, publicity and concert management.
The discovery and communication of a source of inspiration (for me this source was People – previously I'd never worked with people), this was such a happy accident – it led inevitably to the logical necessity of 'search' as the first term ('search, discovery and communication'). […] The lack or decay of shared inspiration has made itself felt. We await too passively this new subtle principle. Is it a new route to the same old source, or the same old route to a new source or a new route to a new source (of inspiration)? We have to sniff the breeze and follow our noses.[…] As Hansel says to Gretel while he is transfigured into a deer: 'When I hear the sound of those horns I feel as if I could fly!' [55]

'I'd never worked with people.' Cardew had worked only with 'musicians' – even the AMM were mere musicians. Art, music, had to be transcended and therefore, as a necessary first step, artists and musicians had to be jettisoned or at least reduced (or elevated) to the ranks. The trajectory to a philosophical transfiguration, materialised into an anthropomorphic political activism through which artistic artefacts are stripped of their comforting and reactionary roles, is hinted at here by the wilful separation of 'people' and 'music,' the latter with its banal practicalities, dishonest utterances and delusory function.

Something was over. Perhaps this was the moment when the Scratch Orchestra finally shed its old identity; the friendships, relationships forged over two years were forfeited in a quest for a politically planned and prescribed, *utopian* future. The anarchic house style was deemed obsolete; it led nowhere and created no viable end product (the cottage at Alexandra Palace was deemed an exemplary study in futility). During the Scratch Orchestra's brief existence the time-honoured questions concerning the role and purpose of art, indeed of all human endeavour, *had* been raised; for two years it had sought, and found, refuge from the terror of the implications of such concerns: that Scratch activities had no intrinsic meaning, that there were unknown judgements pronounced upon us, by Dialectical Materialism, by Freud, by God, and that we had merely been assigned meaningless bit parts in the Grand Order of things.

For Psi Ellison the crux lay in the fact that the political faction in the Scratch Orchestra could not, or refused to, come to terms with these questions, and therefore could not survive them. Rather it capitulated to an abrasively presented, take-it-or-be-damned solution and agenda of dubious provenance, whose English adherents, the Communist Party of England (Marxist-Leninist), may have been driven as much by their own frailties and limitations, by their own psychological imperatives, as by their historic mission, boldly proclaimed on their banners, to liberate 'the oppressed and working people of the world'. In the main the Scratch Orchestra acted intuitively; so that, according to Psi Ellison, when it was asked to account for its past activities, to articulate its *raison d'être*, to act 'consciously' within a political framework which was quite alien, or at least unfamiliar to it, there was a calamitous loss of nerve. Some sought refuge in the certainties of Mao Tse-tung Thought; others retreated into a cocoon-like existence to suffer alone. Perhaps it was the fear of loss through consciousness, just as people are afraid of psychoanalysis: they do not want to know or understand what they are doing. But can a group of people act forever on that premise?

The Scratch Orchestra fractured, like an earthquake; the lives of many individuals were disintegrating. For many there was a kind of crisis, in terms of a future perspective for (artistic) work and the decisions which the trajectory of their private lives demanded. Cardew had rejected bourgeois culture before he became a communist; it had destroyed all continuity (which he could have read many years ago in the *Communist Manifesto*); there was little or no tradition which people could uphold or take part in and what had survived, particularly in relation to working-class culture, was now dismissed as an outmoded irrelevancy. There was a burgeoning rootlessness, and not just in the Scratch Orchestra.

The Scratch Orchestra was the apogee of Cardew's musical career and has attained mythological status. If we balk at the common perception of Cardew as the Orchestra's 'leader' we can feel comfortable with the notion of him as its teacher. And this is certainly how he himself perceived his role; already in his Draft Constitution there is a strong educative impulse.[56] And the influence of Chinese culture, in which the teacher is a necessary and revered member of society, is reflected in the importance he attached to teacher-pupil relations. Of course, such a relation is fraught with problems of a disquieting nature. Cardew was more aware of this than most; he understood that the teacher cannot prescribe, cannot impose discipline, and he sought, like Wittgenstein, to plot the limits of teaching. Cardew demonstrated through behaviour, inspired through example and language (his scores), encouraged through acts of solidarity, and he knew when to withdraw and remain silent. For Wittgenstein, to be a philosopher is to philosophise, not to pass on 'results'. Analogously, this is how Cardew the musician worked with the Scratch Orchestra; individual artistic autonomy was the *sine qua non* at the heart of his praxis.[57]

To his credit, and as a measure of his perspicacity, Cardew prophesied an outcome for the Scratch Orchestra which would be beyond his, and any individual's, control. For the Scratch Orchestra's inaugural meeting he wrote:

> Make it clear that despite all these plans and projects nobody as yet knows what the orchestra is, and that they can make it what they like, that it probably isn't a sublime organism on a higher plane telling us what to do, but just us making music together.

It is true that Cardew exerted more influence than any other individual by dint of his extraordinary powers of imagination and seriousness of intent, but in the end he had to let go. And this he did by going off on a political limb.

In the fifties and sixties if any attempt had been made to force a political commitment from Cardew, he would have echoed the words of Karl Kraus: 'If I must choose the lesser of two evils, I will choose neither. Politics is what a man does in order to conceal what he is and what he himself does not know'.[58] Such an attitude to politics was deeply ingrained, as his old friend Ilona Halberstadt attests. All her Marxist reasoning, her references to 'class' in particular, were summarily and scornfully dismissed. In particular, Marxism's claim on science would have been an obstacle: 'Nothing is more *conservative* than science,' Wittgenstein once said. 'Science lays down railway tracks.'[59] This fundamentally would also have been Cardew's position as a political innocent who had never been a member or supporter of any political party or group. His antipathy to political debate had survived into the seventies and would not be easily overcome. One evening during the period of political upheaval and disaccord, as Carole Finer was driving him home from a Scratch meeting, Cardew observed: 'Yes, it's all very well – the Yenan Forum, but the likes of you and me, Carole, don't want to get involved in politics.'[60]

Notes and references

1   Source of quotation unknown.

2   From Victor Schonfield's 'Notes for Richard Churches' (undated). A response to Churches' history of the Scratch Orchestra.

3   The composer Paul Patterson was born in 1947. He studied trombone and composition at the Royal Academy of Music and subsequently returned to become Head of Composition and Contemporary Music. In 1997 he was appointed Manson Professor of Composition.

4   8 March 1971.

5   27 March 1971.

6   8 April 1971.

7   23 April 1971.

8   Stefan Szczelkun, *Noisegate* 10, p.24.

9   With hindsight there may well be counter-arguments to my bleak analysis, but at the time it was a dispiriting experience from which little if any consolation could be salvaged.

10 My own view now, looking back on affairs in which I played a not insignificant role, is that it was rather a case of regarding 'competence' as irrelevant, which is not quite the same thing. The Scratch Orchestra had experienced for themselves that to produce a remarkably beautiful sound – 'a vast but subtle and delicate polyphony of noises (and notes)' (Shrapnel) – neither skill nor even competence was a prerequisite. If the Scratch Orchestra lacked knowledge of the rudiments of music, it was certainly not lacking in an intuitive understanding of the rudiments of artistic creativity.

11 Letter to Brian Dennis, 6 July 1994.

12 According to Harry Gilonis the chief industry in Prudhoe is the manufacture of paper tissue; he perspicaciously links this fact to the abundance of toilet rolls in the Scratch Orchestra's presentation at the Newcastle Civic Centre.

13 From the *Sun*, 25 June 1971.

14 From the *Daily Telegraph*, 26 June 1971: '4-letter musicians get art director's support' by Tim Beaumont.

15 Northern Arts Director, David Dougan, whilst claiming to stand by the Association's decision to help fund the Scratch Orchestra's visit, nevertheless attempted to disassociate his organisation from the event at issue: 'We cannot condone in any way what happened and had we known beforehand, which was impossible because of the spontaneous nature of their performance, we should have had the obscene item stopped'.

16 *Experimental Music*, p.115.

17 'To be in love with someone else than the woman you happen to live with is to condemn yourself to a lifetime of meaningless longings' he wrote in the Journals on 1 November 1971 in America.

18 Ironically, neither Cardew nor Rowe had the slightest 'political' instinct – and in a sense the Party of which they both became adherents was not 'political'; it was ideological, moralistic, authoritarian, even 'religious', but not conventionally political, which was why it dismissed all other (political) parties.

19 Throughout this section I have tended to play fast and loose with the terms 'Maoist' and 'Marxist'. Of course, they are by no means interchangeable and whereas all Maoists would regard themselves as 'Marxists', few Marxists, then and now, would regard themselves

as 'Maoists' – indeed, many would deny that the Maoists were Marxist. I would hazard a guess that Birgit Burkhardt (a German, significantly) and myself were the only members of the Scratch Orchestra who had not been politicised through contact with Mao Tse-tung Thought and its disseminators, the Communist Party of England (Marxist-Leninist). Ideologically, most, if not all of the Scratch Orchestra members who espoused Communism (to a greater or lesser degree) at that time, and many did not, would have been 'Maoists'. Although I admired and supported much of what was happening in the Peoples' Republic, I had a more orthodox pedigree of membership, as a teenager, of the Labour Party and subsequently the British Communist Party (the 'revisionist' Party, as the Maoists labelled it). I was therefore never above suspicion.

I have been urged, by my editor, to use the terms 'Maoist' and 'Marxist' 'precisely'! This would, in my view, be an unbearably tortuous and ultimately fruitless exercise. For example, one would have to deconstruct the various (opposing) Maoist 'lines' and somehow accommodate them all in the course of any discussion. As for Marxism and Marxists, where Iris Murdoch attempts to rescue Adorno from Marxism, Hannah Arendt tries to do the same for Walter Benjamin. But the crux of it is surely twofold, as Maynard Solomon expresses it in his anthology *Marxism and Art*, p. 543: 'For the superstructure is often the refuge of the pseudo-revolutionary dialectician, who is Marxist in all but two things: the theory of the state and the desire to change the world'.

But let us return to the subject of this book. It is *his* thoughts and *his* actions which are, or should be, our concern, and there is an abundance of both within these pages. As his life unravels each of us, including myself, will make sense of it according to our own life experience, and he will also be labelled variously: Maoist, Marxist, Utopian, Romantic, etc.

20   Richard Churches has suggested that intimations of discontent were already tangible during the week in Anglesey: 'Carole Finer in particular felt an "oppressive gloom" at the Chapel Concert; having genuinely expected great things of the orchestra she found herself disappointed.' *From Improvisation to Revolution; a History of* the Scratch Orchestra (1969-1972) – *its Origins and Development up to and including the Period of Discontent.*

21   Michael Chant's remark in '25 Years from Scratch' bears repetition: 'It has been said that the Scratch Orchestra was its own audience. There was a truth in that, and not only in the negative sense. The concept of an audience as passive consumers was alien to the Scratch.'

22   I personally lurked and occasionally made sounds. I rarely, if ever, displayed my pianistic abilities, preferring to hide my light under a bushel, and this has been criticised by Scratch Orchestra members and others – why hide it? It wasn't so much hiding – I felt that any form of traditional pianistic virtuosity was irrelevant and inappropriate; indeed, what I cherished from my formal training most of all was the 'musicalness' which my first teacher had instilled in me with her injunctions that everything must sing and that intense and tenacious listening was the *sine qua non* of musical performance.

23   Michael Parsons, 'The Scratch Orchestra – Performance/Interpretation' .

24   In an interview with Paul Driver on 6 July 1981 Cardew recalled that 'Howard Skempton wouldn't go along with Maoism and I respect him a great deal'.

25   In fact, the first version of *Sweet FA*, in five Acts and lasting nearly an hour, was written by Cardew himself. Much of it lies well beyond the instrumental and vocal capabilities of the Scratch Orchestra, which probably explains why a new version (or versions) of parts

of the opera were created by other Scratch members (in particular Michael Chant) who exhibited a more realistic attitude towards the performance potential, at least *vis-à-vis* traditionally notated music, of the Scratch Orchestra.

26   *Sweet FA* was entered for the composition prize of the City of Geneva, which might explain why Cardew was initially anxious to take full responsibility himself. It failed to win a prize.

27   Later, on reflection, it was conceded that the reality was the fact of our own individual and collective limitations and frailties.

28   The issue of the attitude towards notated music was reflected in Jenny Robbins' *Toy Symphony* which to the trained musicians was endearingly simple and naïve, whereas for the non-readers it would have been most frustrating not to have been able to participate in a work which was composed on such a simple level.

29   By 'musician' Finer was referring to those who had had a more than rudimentary musical training – in most cases at Music College – by contrast with the 'non-musicians' who had had little or no musical tuition. Clearly these are not entirely satisfactory designations but for the sake of continuity I shall use them (sparingly) throughout this exposition of a critical stage in the Scratch Orchestra's history.

30   C. Caudwell, *The Concept of Freedom* (London: Lawrence and Wishart, 1965), pp.11-13.

31   Robert Storr, *Guston* (New York: Abbeville Press, 1986), p.53. In Harold Rosenberg's words: 'Guston is the first to have risked a fully developed career on the possibility of engaging art in the political reality.' Harold Rosenberg, 'Liberation from Detachment,' in *De-definition of Art* (New York: Macmillan, 1972), pp. 130-140. Guston's longtime friends and admirers felt 'betrayed', as was the case with Cardew, and both men suffered for their indiscretion at the hands of critics and fellow artists alike.

32   To release the Orchestra from 'the domination of my subtly autocratic, supposedly anti-authoritarian leadership'. *Scratch Music*, p.12.

33   Catherine Williams, 'A baby fighting with its bedclothes can strangle itself': her contribution to the Scratch Orchestra Discontent file, dated 21 July 1971.

34   Ibid.

35   Ibid.

36   *Scratch Music*, p.12.

37   Alexandra Palace was opened for the first time in 1873. It provided the Victorians with a recreation centre in a congenial environment and has always housed museums, displays of painting and sculptures, and exhibitions. However the Palace has suffered much from ill fortune; it was burnt down just sixteen days after opening, and was rebuilt and opened again after two years. In July 1980 another fire destroyed about half of the Palace. It was known as 'The People's Palace' and is situated in Alexandra Park in North London

38   From a single typewritten sheet, unsourced, entitled Scratch Orchestra Cottage.

39   Circular letter from CC to the Scratch Orchestra, dated 11 July 1971.

40   From *Stockhausen Serves Imperialism*, p.28.

41   I should remind the reader that my sources for such information consist of extant sheets and scraps of paper exhibiting various degrees of perishability which I have rescued and culled from cardboard files. These contain type-written and hand-written (in pen or pencil) information which can no longer be corroborated; too much intervening time has elapsed and memory can no longer be relied upon. However, although the details (exact date and number of people present on a particular occasion, for example) may not always be correct,

the general accuracy of this narrative, both in letter and spirit, would – I hope – be attested by those who were participants and contributors during those heady days.

42   I recall E.P. Thompson, in a TV programme not so long before his death in 1993, comparing the 'very high quality of political discussion' that was frequent in the ('Stalinist' as he described it) British Communist Party with his experiences as a member of the Labour Party – 'an organisation absolutely designed to defeat thought of any kind'.

43   Walter Benjamin, 'Brecht's *Threepenny Novel*', an unpublished article collected in *Understanding Brecht* (London: Verso, 1983), p.81.

44   From 'The Role of the Composer in the Class Struggle', transcribed from a handwritten text delivered as a talk, probably 1978. *(CCR)*

45   From *25 years from Scratch*, p.38.

46   Of course, many people, on the basis of their own experience working within these institutions, shared the same antipathy; they knew that many university professors and head teachers, NHS administrators, TV executives, press barons and their journalists, business executives and company directors, as well as artists and arts administrators, were driven and sustained by raw, personal ambition. By 'human nature', in fact. The new ideologues were assuring us that there was no need to feel guilty, for example, about greed; human greed was natural and therefore good.

47   Jrnl. 29 November 1971.

48   In Carole Finer's view the decline of the Scratch Orchestra began when it tried to sing properly, to be squeamish about texts, and to engage in ideological 'struggle' after each concert: 'We can't sing. We only roll marbles around a saucepan lid'.

49   Letter from Rod Eley to CC dated 26.9.71.

50   Ibid.

51   At this stage we need to sharpen our focus in relation to the concept of 'bourgeois'. In previous chapters, in particular the chapter on Cologne, the word 'bourgeois' has looser, sociological connotations, occasionally synonomous with 'middle class', or perhaps extending to the idea of an expression of 'social contempt'. In the final chapters, the communist period of Cardew's life, the word 'bourgeois' is associated, more aggressively, with the idea of an (exploiting) *class*, with the political theories expounded by members of that class, with bourgeois *feeling,* bourgeois *thought,* bourgeois *ideology* and *art,* etc. This refers, of course, to a contemporary, late twentieth century bourgeois class, not to the perception of an historical, nineteenth century bourgeoisie.

52   Interestingly, and perhaps disconcertingly for some readers, Rod Eley became one of the Party's staunchest supporters and apologists, contributing a forthright and spiritedly correct analysis of the history of the Scratch Orchestra, and its demise, at the beginning of Cardew's book *Stockhausen Serves Imperialism*.

53   Edwin Prévost, *No Sound is Innocent,* page 34.

54   Ibid.

55   From a text on two handwritten sheets, stapled together, dated 2 June 1971.

56   Among the manifold documents that have survived are photocopies of pages from Plato's *Republic*, including Socrates expounding to Glaucon, in Book 3, on the need for 'good education', which makes 'good citizens', and 'good citizens, helped by good education, become better than they were, handing on better and better natures, as with other animals'. Clearly, Cardew felt the need to extract such pages for reference and use.

57   And in the last decade Cardew's insistence on the necessity for a revolutionary vanguard, a political aristocracy which would be the bearers of good news, would create a profound irony.
58   From 'A trial involving sexual morality' quoted by Frank Field in *Karl Kraus and his Vienna*, p.56.
59   Ray Monk, *Ludwig Wittgenstein The Duty of Genius,* (London: Vintage, 1990), p.486.
60   From a remembered conversation sometime in the mid-nineties between Carole Chant née Finer and the author.

(CCR) Also found in *Cornelius Cardew A Reader*

Cornelius Cardew a life unfinished

13

Maoism and the Art Schools

The successful artist in our society is a true 'flower of evil'[1]

As we have seen, Cardew's initial involvement with communism came about through the imposing and irresistible example of Keith Rowe, a supporter of the relatively newly-fledged Communist Party of England (Marxist-Leninist), founded formally on 25 March 1972, whose influence cannot be overestimated. As Eddie Prévost and others have posited, my own Marxist analysis put forward at the Discontent meetings in August of the previous year, intellectually and even morally persuasive though it may have appeared to some, would not of itself have brought about the cataclysmic consequences for the Scratch Orchestra or for Cardew himself. It was Maoism, with its ardour, its unyielding fundamentalism, and the aura of infallibity it exuded, as expressed in particular through the force and energy of Keith Rowe's personality, rather than European Marxism ('revisionism'), that had bump-started Cardew out of his antipathy to all things 'political' and had ultimately won him over to the revolutionary cause. As radical, experimental artists, going back to the mid-sixties and to *Treatise* and the early days of AMM, there had always been a mutual admiration and strong empathy between the two men and this relationship was now to find consuming expression in a political arena for which neither had previously shown the slightest disposition.[2] For Cardew (and probably for Rowe, too), during this period, there had been a profound realisation, if not revelation, of a reality to which he had been blind – a political awakening of the kind which the American painter Philip Guston had described (as previously quoted). Like Guston, Cardew did not seek an ironic detachment, which disconcerted friends and colleagues could more easily have related to – quite the reverse; what he desired was a greater sense of identification with the political ideas that now were beginning to grip him and with which he could make common cause. And it was the way that these revolutionary ideas could be expressed, or rather served, by art, by music, that was to dominate his compositional thought and practice throughout the next decade. What Cardew sought, in Harold Rosenberg's felicitous phrase, was 'a liberation from detachment'.

Cardew's political conversion, and the travail it involved, can only be understood, it seems to me, as epiphenomenal to deeper issues. Like Wittgenstein Cardew sought to fuse the personal with the philosophical: music as need and as responsibility – the ethical and the social, both aspects of the supreme 'duty to oneself'. He never scrupled to perform what he deemed was necessary; incorruptibility depended entirely on the qualities that had been nurtured within oneself. However daunting external matters seemed to be, nothing could be of greater concern than one's *self*. In the seventies the task he set himself, to 'turn the world upside down', was monumental; to many, including friends, it was senseless. Wittgenstein would have damned such a reaction for its superficiality: 'Might it not be better to perish unhappily in the hopeless struggle against the external world? But such a life is senseless. But why not lead a senseless life? Is it unworthy?'[3]

But was Cardew gifted *politically*? Probably not – that is, not in terms of conventional, bourgeois parliamentary democracy. Perhaps, *vide* Hamlet's speech, he could have acquired political greatness, although it must be said that there is no evidence of any real originality of political thought; nor was he, according to my own limited experience of his political activism, a convincing public speaker. He had to learn to relate to people – for which his brother Seth blamed their public school upbringing. His writings pale in comparison with those of Hanns Eisler; there is none of the tough dialectical thinking of Walter Benjamin, whom he read and admired earlier in his life. It was as if the agonising had been done, the plans laid; the job in hand was realisation, revolutionary *praxis*. Politics offers action, while inaction leads to atrophy. Like Wittgenstein Cardew's view was that what is problematic in life can only be solved by changing the way you live. Mere wisdom is 'grey'. There is no point in merely thinking 'correctly'; one has to act, one must change one's life, and in so doing change oneself. And what is necessary in action is passion.

So why the Communist Party of England (Marxist-Leninist), the Maoists, rather than any other left-wing group or Party? How was it that the CPE (M-L) was able to create (for some) such a plausible image of itself? In the case of Cardew this decision, which was taken after considerable, and often harrowing, debate and heart-searching, and which cost him relationships, friendships, even his musical 'status' in the eyes of some, reflected deeply-rooted psychological imperatives born of an individual life experience of extraordinary intensity.[4] Initially, one of the most compelling reasons for its attraction, I would suggest, was the fact that the Maoist party seemed to repudiate 'politics' in the traditional sense, just as Cardew and most of his colleagues had in their pre-political existences. And through the rejection of traditional (bourgeois) politics – with its corruption, its routine resort to expediency, its willingness to compromise and to sacrifice any human value or belief – the (Maoist) Party seemed to have occupied the *moral* high-ground; it had adopted a purer, more abstract language, and referred constantly to the more generalised and positive human qualities of heroism, selflessness, courage, incorruptibility, optimism, as well as – and this was especially important for Cardew – the (romantic) acceptance of risk and danger, of *sacrifice,* which the Great Proletarian Revolution in China had demanded and inspired. In this respect, and probably in this respect only – that is, the moral emphasis and the idealism – Cardew recognized the projection of a kind of society which the Scratch Orchestra, his own creation, in its brief utopian haven, and for fleeting and ineradicable moments, had experienced and enjoyed. He trusted his impulses, strong as they were, and acted upon them. At the time, in the early seventies, it was instincts, or feelings, and practices, rather than beliefs, which motored his existence. It was not so much the vaunted 'truth' and 'invincibility' of Marxism-Leninism that motivated him, it was the explosive and revolutionary potential embodied within its praxis. As John Maharg, an old Scottish comrade, put it: 'Marxist-Leninist politics fulfilled something in him, that he felt was missing'. With Marxism-Leninism Cardew scented a victory over uncertainty.

Members and supporters of the Communist Party of England (Marxist-Leninist)) dressed soberly and wore grave, earnest, and occasionally beatific expressions, the latter on utterance or contemplation of the thoughts of Chairman Mao. The seemliness of their attire, the purity of their political aspirations, their crusading zeal, and their unswerving loyalty to the Chairman made them appear, at least to themselves, unstoppable. Naturally, they would entertain no doubting Thomases amongst them; heretical thoughts were exposed and exorcised in tense, comminatory meetings. One of the most seriously debilitating acts perpetrated by the Party – one which had ruinous consequences for the intellectual life of its members, as well as for Cardew's own political development and understanding of Marxism and the Marxist tradition – was the index which the Party drew up, unofficially, of renegade communists: 'revisionists', Trotskyites, Castroites, social-fascists, anti-Leninists – the list seemed endless. These were all *personae non gratae*, whose thoughts and deeds were condemned in essays informed by a self-conscious political rectitude in a publication entitled *Literature and Ideology*.[5] Indexed communists and Left sympathisers included such luminaries as Christopher Caudwell, Noam Chomsky, Georg Lukács, and all those Left writers and intellectuals who had opposed Stalin. For Cardew and Rowe it meant that they were denied access to a wide area of Marxist thought, including some of the most subtly creative writers, such as Walter Benjamin and Bertolt Brecht, to name but two.

At the outset Cardew's political *persona* was a makeshift with no foundation, 'a blank sheet of paper' which, of course, was to the Party's and perhaps to his own advantage, too. Up to that time the ideological issues for him had been exploratory; he could not impose his argument because he was still debating within himself. Like a religious sect the Party attracted those unadulterated souls who were eager to join the upward movement towards the light, towards world revolution, to which aim the truths of Mao Tse-Tung Thought represented an unimpeachable authority. In accordance with the image of itself which the Party wished to project, Cardew dressed soberly: a tweed jacket with nondescript jeans and occasionally a white shirt. His footwear was slightly less conventional; he preferred boots to shoes. In the later years, at Party events, he took to wearing a suit, one which had followed him from pillar to post since 1957, and a tie, believing, perhaps, that such attire bespoke a proletarian gravitas. Nevertheless, whilst the Party welcomed and nurtured political innocents like Cardew, for a long time it kept him at arms length. At the beginning of 1972 he would have been regarded by the Maoists as a 'progressive composer' (rather than a 'communist' composer) – that is, a composer broadly sympathetic to the Party's aims but without the political knowledge, sophistication and, above all, without as yet the conviction and certainty, the ideological rectitude of what the Party would describe as 'a true communist'.

Far from alienating Cardew, however, as it did some who ventured into the Party rank and file, the very immoderation of its political philosophy, the extremes to which its leaders would push themselves and their supporters, emotionally and intellectually, the sheer unreasonableness of their demands, the puritanical discipline, the fervour, the intensity of their commitment, the fearsome logic of their programme, in short their *utopianism* – much of this corresponded to his own moral imperatives; and some aspects of it, though less extreme, he had already encountered and experienced in various guises during his career: at public school, in Cologne with the serialists, the AMM, the American avant-garde, the Scratch Orchestra, all of which were stages in a personal quest. Moreover, as others have remarked, the Maoist emphasis on 'self-criticism' would have appealed to Cardew, stirring up and nourishing middle-class feelings of guilt whilst at the same time animating the desire to worst his old middle-class friends in political argument. He was still riven by doubt and wanted to repair, through politics, what he regarded as the significant omissions in his education.[6] One of the most insidiously persuasive of the manifold Maoist slogans stated: 'Make self the target of revolution, and the broad masses the target of revolutionary propaganda.' In my view it was this precept as much as any other, with its emphasis on motivational purity, on *selflessness*, that impressed Cardew and finally drew him into the Party ranks. It is there, starkly, at the beginning of Paragraph 7 of *The Great Learning*: 'If the root be in confusion nothing will be well governed.'

In many respects Cardew's knowledge of, and enthusiasm for, ancient Chinese philosophy of the arts may have facilitated his 'conversion' to Maoism. Maoism was an extension of his Confucianism: the 'virtuous man' (the Party) wielding power over the masses for their own good (an abstract concept of considerable potency), and I recall that, in particular, it was Rowe's constant reference to the 'correct line' as the *sine qua non* basis of cultural as well as political activity – without which all good intentions were doomed to futility – that exasperated members of the Scratch Orchestra. If the Party comrades were quick to dismiss the analogy as superficial and even perverse, given the Chinese Party's crusade against Confucianism, it seems feasible to me that in the early stages Confucianism was a bridge, rather than an obstacle to Cardew's politicisation.[7] For example, Li Chi's statement in Book 2 of *The Sacred Books of Confucius* that 'the ways of music and of government are closely related' sits comfortably with Mao's precept that the aim of cultural and educational work is 'to transform the thinking of the masses,' although it has to be said that in the earlier text there is no mention of 'aim', nor of 'transforming'. Characteristically, Mao was proposing a much more prescriptive relationship between art and politics.

Cardew's public school background, too, would have nurtured the idea of an elite, if not a Party, to 'lead the masses'. As a child and young man, in school history books and certainly from the mouths of his masters at public school, his youthful ears and mind would have been exposed to the nonchalantly expressed saw, or quip, often in passing, relating to the inadequacy of the 'common man' (particularly he from Africa and the subcontinent), and the obligation either to exploit him, or to give him guidance, depending on the degree of liberality which the utterer's ideological standpoint would allow. The idea of the proletariat taking its destiny into its own hands, of establishing a dictatorship to serve its own needs, would have been unmentionable, indeed unthinkable.

For Cardew, Marxist-Leninist ideology established itself not as an 'alternative' within the wide spectrum of the Left, but rather as an opposition force upholding the communist principles which, in the opinion of the Maoists, all the other groups and parties had abandoned in the wake of Khrushchev's denunciation of Stalin at the Twentieth Party Congress in January 1956. Cardew did not seek out a communist party; he did not 'select' the Party from a number of political options; in Stella Cardew's words the party to which he ultimately committed himself body and soul came along in the 'river of life'. The purity of its ethos, its unassimilability into mainstream politics, struck a deep chord in him. Above all, the Party was *dangerous*. Without purity and danger, in Stella Cardew's opinion, Cardew 'would have had nothing to do with the Party'.[8]

For the origins of the English Maoist Party we have to cross the Atlantic to the University of British Columbia in Canada where, on 13 March 1963, a charismatic Indian from the Punjab, Hardial Bains, founded The Internationalists, initially a small Maoist group but which grew in numbers and influence to spearhead a new communist movement.[9] Between 1-15 August 1967 an historic Necessity for Change conference was held in London, which also saw the formation of the English Internationalists, attended by hundreds of revolutionaries from Europe, North America, Asia and Africa. In preparation, Bains wrote a pamphlet entitled *Necessity for Change* in which he presented a philosophical repudiation of the consumer culture of modern capitalism. Subsequent to the conference a significant number of the Internationalists, including Hardial Bains, decided to reorganize on the basis of Marxism-Leninism-Mao Tse-tung Thought:

> Through putting into practice the line of the conference, the English Internationalists prepared the ground for the formation of the English Communist Movement (Marxist- Leninist) which in turn further developed the conditions for the emergence for the first time in England of a genuine revolutionary proletarian party, the Communist Party of England (Marxist-Leninist).[10]

In 1968, the Necessity for Change Institute of Ideological Studies was set up with Hardial Bains as Director. According to the organisers the inauguration of this Institute was inspired and motivated by events in China, and in particular by the Great Proletarian Revolution. Like millions of other young revolutionaries of the day they saw Mao Tse-tung's Cultural Revolution as a titanic struggle against the dogmatism and bureaucratism of the old communist movement. They believed that Mao had discovered a method for ensuring the constant renewal and revolutionization of the communist movement, and that Mao Tse-tung Thought represented the re-establishment of Leninism in the communist movement. The aims of the Institute were clear: to develop a comprehensive critique of US Imperialism, to combat the incipient fascism which was gradually spreading its influence in all areas of bourgeois life – not least in the universities themselves, to uphold the thesis of the primacy of the economic base, to recognise the importance of the political and cultural superstructure in supporting this base and reflecting its needs and, most crucially, to stress the dynamic and revolutionary role that ordinary people can play in changing society by participating in the class struggle.

The Institute set up branches in North America and in Ireland, and in 1971 began a series of introductory talks in London which several members of the Scratch Orchestra, including Cardew, Rowe and myself, attended. On the week-end of the 4/5 December 1971 a two-day conference under the title 'Seek Truth to Serve the People' was organised by the Progressive Intellectuals Study Group, under the leadership of the English Communist Movement (Marxist-Leninist). It was held in a room at the University of London Students' Union in Malet Street and the programme of talks and seminars was as follows: The Present Orientation of the Revolutionary Intellectuals' Movement; Doctors in Class

Struggle: Two Lines in the Science of Medicine; Fascist Anthropology – On the theories of Robert Ardrey, Konrad Lorenz and Desmond Morris; The Red Detachment of Women: Film of Revolutionary Ballet from China; Two Lines in the Natural Sciences; Bourgeois Theories of Doom – on the modern fascist theories of nuclear holocaust, pollution and over-population; The Role of Literature in Class Society; *Chairman Mao is the Bright Red Sun in Our Hearts* – a revolutionary film from China. A slogan writ large on an imposing banner, behind which the conference expressed its unity of purpose, proclaimed: Integrate Theory and Practice! Organize to Change the World! Uphold the Wide-Scale Dissemination of Invincible Mao Tse-tung Thought!

Some meetings had already taken place, including one in November under the title Alan Sillitoe and David Mercer: Traitors to the English Working Class, which attracted a small but militantly enthusiastic audience. In contemporary British literature in the fifties and sixties, and in particular in the English theatre, many writers had taken the working class, and working class culture, as a political subject for their work. Apart from Sillitoe and Mercer there were John Arden, John Osborne, Harold Pinter, Arnold Wesker, and others. These writers, if they wrote sympathetically, wrote with a degree of detachment and in some cases with cynicism: the working class not as heroes and fighters, but also as victims, fall-guys, sometimes as collaborators. Not as 'gravediggers' of the bourgeoisie, not even as the vanguard for socialism, and with little or no consciousness of their own 'historical destiny'. Thus, the new 'kitchen sink' drama was upheld by some critics and commentators as a salutary, 'social realist' antidote to leftist 'romanticism'.

The Maoist ideologues were unimpressed and insisted that clear criteria had to be applied: What is the attitude of the writer to the working class? How do these works of literature relate to the history of the working class and what contribution do they make to its progress? And the ultimate acid test: which class does the writer serve? The conclusion drawn at the time was that many of these writers were indeed 'traitors to the English working class'. It was argued that the working class needed positive images; it needed encouragement and inspiration in order to come to the self-realisation that radical change was both desirable and viable; and that to show corrupted, compromised fallen heroes, whether they were drawn from real life or not, could only militate against the prospect and desire for revolutionary change. Few, if any, writers were able to conform to the circumscribed agenda of the Maoists and were therefore condemned to suffer the same fate as all those artists who had failed, or were failing, to fulfil the tasks which historical materialism demanded of them.

On 28 January 1972, a talk entitled Two Lines in Medicine: Medical practice in Imperialist Britain and the People's Republic of China compared, followed by a discussion, was given in the London University Union building. An introductory statement set out the speaker's agenda:

In Britain we have the hoax of 'socialist' medicine: 'medicine for all'. But detailed investigation into the training of doctors, the currently sponsored research programmes and the actual practice of medicine in this country, reveals that the precise opposite is the case: ultimately medicine serves only the ruling class and the interests of the ruling class.

This, some might have said at the time, somewhat harsh characterisation was contrasted with medical practice in the People's Republic of China where, guided by Mao Tse-Tung Thought, 'doctors and patients both actively participate in the prevention and cure of injury and disease, so that already in China all manner of miracles have been performed'. The hyperbole expressed here will evoke a variety of responses, and not necessarily of scepticism and ridicule, but the titles of the talks reflect quite accurately the ideological climate that existed at the time, as well as the militant and uncompromising positions that people took up. Cardew attended many of these meetings, responding initially with curiosity and interest, and eventually with enthusiasm and whole-hearted commitment.

In the early days of his political activism Cardew would have felt an acute sense of displacement for he was woefully inexperienced in such matters; there was no background of political membership or allegiance in his youth, as there had been for some of his friends and colleagues, including myself: Young Socialists, Young Communists, Socialist Labour League, the New Left Review group, CND and so forth.[11] Conscious of his political inadequacies, during the first half of 1972 Cardew embarked on a programme of self-study, reading the Marxist classics and encouraging members of the Id Group to do likewise. In summarising parts of *Capital*, sections of Lenin's *Materialism and Empirio-Criticism*, Lenin on Marx, paraphrasing Marx's definitions of 'surplus value', commenting on them extensively in the Journals – and all the while reproducing the sententious Party propaganda – Cardew was educating himself. The point, of course, which he would have grasped better than most, was not simply to study them, but also to apply the principles of Marxism, to combine study with revolutionary practice. 'Not criticism but revolution is the driving force of history', he read in the *German Ideology*.

During the early seventies, whilst strengthening his ties with the Maoists, Cardew continued to develop his work within the Scratch Orchestra, many of whose members (the Id Group) shared his enthusiasm for a political programme that had succeeded in alienating and excluding an equal number of sceptics and dissenters. Much of this period was spent challenging received notions about music and about art and culture in general, discussing and analysing the nature of our audience, its psychology, its class nature, attacking the avant-garde as individualistic, elitist and fragmented, indifferent to the situation in the real world, the nadir of a (bourgeois) culture in a state of decay, and, not least, in Cardew's case, criticising and repudiating his own works. Issues discussed at these meetings included the ideology of Paragraph 5 of *The Great Learning*, the nature of class exploitation, Mao's 'Yenan Forum' text, the need to define 'proletarian music' and eventually to produce it, and the necessity of returning to tonality and to 'tuneful' music. The latter generated further discussion around the notion of 'content' in music and of 'free' and 'spontaneous' music-making and its degeneration as evidenced, in the ears and minds of the Id Group, at recent Scratch meetings. The relationship of the Id Group to the Scratch Orchestra as a whole was also discussed and, most ominously, the necessity for each individual 'to remould his/her world outlook' – that is, 'to get beyond our petit bourgeois background and upbringing' – was considered to be of paramount importance, a *sine qua non* for the aspiring revolutionary.[12] Cardew was educating himself as a Marxist, as a revolutionary communist, an *activist*, for whom the unequivocal language of class warfare was the language of everyday discourse. Under the title 'the role of music in the proletarian revolution' he notes:

> Music as organized violence. (Shouting (singing), hitting, scratching).
> A music whose function is to *arouse* the masses. Lessons of Bagpipes, and early Chinese military sonic diviners. Our music must be understood by our own people, it must arouse the masses, our friends, strike terror into our enemy, the bourgeoisie (that is, because they can't understand it). The reason they can't understand it is because it is not based on commodity value, etc?[13]

The 'terror' that Cardew refers to is caused by conscious, mass, collective action, and the 'music' is an integral part of a political tactic or strategy. That is its sole function; it is hard to believe that we are discussing 'art' here.[14] Cardew's sentiment and the language in which it was couched would be considered by many as crude, shocking. We have noted Walter Benjamin's recognition of the necessity of crudeness ('crude thoughts'); in other words, cogitative refinements can be a deterrent to action (see chapter 12, p.538). In *Treatise*, for example, the sheer (visual) subtlety of Cardew's thought processes can both inspire and inhibit music-making. The 'referral of theory to practice' in performances of *Treatise*, the duality of what appears to be the 'idealism' of the score versus the pragmatism which underpins and guides the performer's choices, is for the musician a humbling experience; we begin dutifully, even confidently, with a process of ratiocination, yet burdened with the expectation that every decision must lead to (musical) action. It transpires that our interpretation is shot through with inconsistencies, such as the inevitable infractions of any rules we think up. Such was also the experience of the revolutionary, armed with Mao Tse-Tung thought, whose purity and invincibility likewise manifests itself both as inspiration and as an awesome responsibility for the lowly foot-soldier.

Philosophically there was much in the Marxist canon that Cardew would have responded to: the world as a complex of processes, everything in flux; 'in dialectical philosophy nothing is final, absolute, sacred' he wrote down in his notes and summary of Lenin's article on Marx. And there are clear pre-echoes of these ideas in his indeterminate works from the sixties. In the sleeve notes to the CD of Cardew's *Chamber Music 1955-64* [15] David Ryan highlights the 'restlessness' which lies at the heart of Cardew's early works and 'his tendency not to shy away from conundrums and contradictions'; so that, for example, the criterion of a good performance 'is not completeness (that is, perfection)', as Cardew wrote in his introduction to the published version of *Autumn 60*, 'but rather the lucidity of its incompleteness'.

But Cardew's new political agenda was impatient of such philosophical reflections and self-indulgences; pragmatism reigned. Musical compositions must either implant or illustrate Party doctrine, and judged by this yardstick it was deemed politically correct that his own previous compositions should come under scrutiny. Was there anything 'progressive' in them that could be salvaged? Composing for the Scratch Orchestra, for example, had thrown up a number of models of social organization, in particular *The Great Learning*. 'Of course, on scrutiny *The Great Learning* may turn out to be feudal or worse in its social organization', Cardew wrote in the 1972 Journals (undated), 'but I have a feeling there are at least some progressive notions in it'. He was right, of course, but such ambivalence was not tolerated by the Party ideologues, whose adamantine stance on cultural matters was made painfully and embarrassingly manifest during both private and public debate. So rather than trying to extricate 'progressive notions' from a suspect piece of music, why not simply abandon it to its fate and compose a work which wins the unequivocal support and admiration of the Party? For the Party, in its ignorance, *The Great Learning* was unnecessarily problematic, and for Cardew himself it was an albatross which would ultimately be damaging to his political aspirations. The argument might have run as follows: *The Great Learning* might be regarded as a paradigm of an affirmative, humanistic culture which, however, through its beauty and idealism, anaesthetizes the stress and anxiety of life under capitalism, thereby standing in the way of a realistic perception of society. The song is thus invalidated in and through the culture that sings it. For the communists the task had to be approached more directly and with more clarity: the *mores* of bourgeois society had to be exposed and ruthlessly attacked. [16]

Some undated notes in Cardew's 1971/72 Journal (probably early 1972) under the heading 'The Composer and his Public – the avant-garde solution' exemplify his ongoing preoccupation with socio-political aspects of music: the composer cannot simply avoid the 'depravity of the media' and its corrupting influence; he should actively oppose it. He should experience the 'heroism and high morale' of the Republican minority in Northern Ireland, for example; he should seek not fame and fortune, rather he should aim to inspire people to rebellion and to grasp their destiny in their own hands. Cardew cites the 'straw composer' who becomes successful without ever coming into contact with his audience: prestigious commissions on the one hand, polite audience applause and indifference on the other. Elsewhere in the same Journal, undated, Cardew gives himself an assignment:

Find a new music event in early March. Go to it. Talk to people in the audience. Talk to the composer and the musicians. Take notes on that and your own reactions. Read the reviews. Expose the whole set-up.

Cardew's political conversion had an unnerving effect on his friends and admirers. If there were few recriminations, there was, nevertheless, a deep well of disappointment and disbelief amongst a number of them for whom Cardew's repudiation of his own achievements, in particular, was tantamount to an act of betrayal. In the Scratch Orchestra attachments had been cemented – with David Jackman, Psi Ellison and a number of others – but these relationships were allowed to freewheel into a condition of disenchantment, frustration and even anger. Those Scratch members who had been left behind – that is, had not *actively* espoused his own brand of leftism – he considered a benighted group: lost, disorientated and without purpose, left to bewail their insalubrious fate over which a pall of bitterness had been cast. Naturally, the critics inveighed against him, much as they had done when he was an 'experimentalist'; now he was exposed on another flank – the political – whence more scorn and ridicule could be poured on him. As for his old colleagues in the avant-garde, they were nonplussed, but their liberalism disallowed them from excommunicating Cardew, some claiming that the very outrageousness of his actions consolidated and even enhanced his status as an avant-garde artist, even if it were now his old avant-garde friends and colleagues who were the ones that were being outraged.

Six months after the Newcastle debacle, Cardew set out his attitude to those portentous events in a letter to Hanne Boenisch:

I think what I said has been borne out: the politics has weakened the Scratch. It has alienated a number of (artistically) important members. I see it as a good thing now; before, I was afraid of it, or thought 'it wd be a pity'. It is a demoralization that precedes the building of good morale on a solid basis (ideology rather than personality). Weak in the sense that we have hardly done any playing – only lots of discussions and meetings with occasional rather half-hearted playing.[17]

Initially somewhat sceptical, Cardew was later to recognize the importance of the presence of Boenisch and her film crew in Newcastle; she doggedly pursued the Scratch members with questions relating, in particular, to the perceived social significance of what the Scratch Orchestra was doing and thereby began to break down the 'discussion taboo'.

In a Journal entry headed 'Tactics in handling the other Scratchers', Cardew defines and elaborates the Id Group's role in the Scratch Orchestra. One can imagine that the condescending heading and the pervasive tendentiousness of the piece would have caused offence to many of the less politically-enlightened members of the Orchestra. Yet its tone is thoughtful and conciliatory and it is interesting to be reminded of the priorities which Cardew and the Id Group had decided upon in their relation to the rest of the Scratch Orchestra. I quote the entry in full:

One can argue with people night after night trying to shake their convictions or convince them of something different, and get nowhere. This is the great weakness of what Keith [Rowe] calls 'Convince-me politics': that the person you can convince to be Communist in a short time will probably be equally easily convinced about something else a few weeks or months later; you can't keep people under constant surveillance as to what they are to come in contact with. It comes down to an old slogan: you can't educate people; people have to educate themselves. What we *can* do is provide the materials for them to educate themselves on. It's our hope to produce revolutionary propaganda works of very basic education, using mostly singing, which people can easily take in and digest in their own time, and which also have a powerful emotional impact.

'Providing materials for people to educate themselves' within the Scratch Orchestra is a different matter. Obviously the same material we present to the public will pass through their hands; we'll all be learning it together, so that's one part. But the most important is to try to provide a practical model for the other Scratchers. That people in the Id Group come forward to take responsibility, that they air their views at meetings (without interrupting others of course), that they are there on time, and that they get things done. This cannot fail to make an impression on other Scratchers. In fact we must serve as a shining example (as far as is in our power). We must not batter people with violent arguments and thus make enemies of those who are really our friends and have a lot to contribute, even though they may have no wish to join a political grouping. Working together on the basis of solidarity, and working together is hard when heated arguments are in the forefront.[18]

In his letter to Boenisch, as we have seen, Cardew had already referred to the debilitating effect that the introduction of politics had had on music-making in the Scratch Orchestra. To rectify the situation Cardew's proposal in 'Tactics in handling the other Scratchers' was that 'appropriate' material should be provided initially in the form of revolutionary songs which would be rehearsed and presented to the public. If the Scratch Orchestra members were to take up these songs and commit them to public performance it was essential, Cardew argued, that the Id Group gained their respect, however grudging, through example. The problem, which Cardew did not address in his brief text, was that these arguments, discussions and debates, which dominated Scratch Orchestra meetings and relations, were conducted from entrenched positions, particularly on the Maoist side, whence it was assumed that resistance to their arguments was evidence of an innate conservatism, or of an inability to see the world objectively, or of a lack of imagination and vision, or even of sheer bloody-mindedness. It would not have occurred to the Maoists that this repudiation reflected a perception of an untenable thesis, of a flawed logic, of a profoundly alienating aura of 'correctness' and 'certainty'. This was more often than not how their own position was characterised by dissenters.

The thorny question of what kind of music a politicised Scratch Orchestra should and could develop was one which Cardew grappled with for some time. It was not in his nature simply to abandon a (visionary) project, which he had invested so much of himself in, when unforeseen difficulties arose and the going got tough. On the contrary, it was the kind of challenge he relished and would rise to meet. Accordingly, in the aforementioned Journal entry, 'On reading Lenin on Marx', with its reference to music as 'organized violence' whose function is to 'arouse the masses', there are some sketches of lyrics, probably for two songs. The first is a eulogy of the productive achievements of the working class: Built skyscrapers, aeroplanes, trains, motorways. Dug mines, tilled the earth, harvested the fruit, produced the goods. And this is contrasted with the parasitism, lies, corruption and hypocrisy of the bourgeoisie. The other lyric, entitled Prison, deals with the theme of the 'victims of the bourgeois state'. In the same section of the Journals Cardew also reflects on the attitude of the Scratch Orchestra towards the provision of 'entertainment', or rather, towards the 'entertainment industry':

I don't think any musician in the Scratch would care to identify himself with the goals for artists put forward by the bourgeoisie. Our tendency has rather been in the opposite direction – a puritanical rejection of any goals and bourgeois goals in particular, and an (alienated) disdain for doing anything at all (say book illustration or film music) in support of the existing system. This is the root of the aloof attitudes that we encounter in the Scratch. If we write film music, we tend to try and fulfil the requirements with as little effort and outlay as possible. (This parallels the 'British workman' as caricatured in the popular press, whose working day if he had any say in it would be 90% tea break). This attitude is pessimism, the idea that there is nothing to work for; it is a manifestation of the decadence of the capitalist system we live under. With the knowledge that society must, can and will be changed, our pessimism will disappear and we will be able energetically to participate in this change.[...] The system encourages you to engage in meaningless work (supposedly neutral but actually in the service of Capital) to relieve the economic pressure and hence take the sting out of your revolutionary sentiment. But this does not work – because we are conscious of the demoralizing effect of meaningless work and many of us *prefer* economic distress to such insidious demoralization.[19]

A little further on in the Journals there is a proposal concerning the survival and development of the Experimental Music Catalogue which was 'founded by the composer Christopher Hobbs in 1969 to provide an essential service: the distribution of compositions which don't offer musical publishers adequate opportunities for commercial exploitation'. The proposal is somewhat over-ambitious, involving renting an office and employing part-time clerical and editorial staff, as well as securing a loan. As an alternative Cardew suggests it may be possible for the EMC to function under the aegis of a sympathetic, conventional publisher. But such a publisher never materialized.[20]

Meanwhile, the Scratch Id Group, on which Mao's 'Talks at the Yenan Forum on Literature and Art' continued to exert considerable influence, would meet on a regular, fortnightly basis, independently of the Scratch Orchestra as a whole. Looking through the proposals and statements, suggestions and recommendations by individual Id Group members, certain common attitudes and needs are seen to have emerged: a sense of guilt in respect of an acknowledged political naivety and ignorance; the need to cast off all association with 'bourgeois', that is, middle-class, artistic pretensions and endeavour, and the ethos of 'individualism, authorship and originality' in which it is rooted; to integrate with working class people; the need to study the Marxist classics and to consider their practical application in contemporary Britain; and to develop a music and music-making that is relevant and useful to these aims. Such was the content of the Id Group meetings at which Cardew was an attentive listener and incisive contributor. It was also recognised that the time-scale for such a programme would extend over many years; indeed, over a lifetime. These were all issues raised by Mao in his 'Yenan Forum' talks and give a clear indication of the extent to which Mao Tse-tung Thought was now informing and shaping the new political agenda of the Scratch Orchestra.

For Cardew himself the key issue at this stage was that of integration within the working class. His notes on an Id Group meeting on 18 January 1972 to discuss 'Talks at the Yenan Forum' end:

The message of Yenan is clearly: We must associate with, talk to, study, know deeply, live with, make intimate friends amongst, work with the working class. Our attitudes to this are various: Michael Chant is uninspired, Rod (Eley) is inspired for the future, I would love to but feel my work is 'music', etc. etc. We will slide out from under it. In practice, we do regard our petty bourgeois comrades and friends as more important than workers, etc.

All these ideas were consciously, but circumspectly, introduced into Scratch Orchestra meetings, and for a time the new political material coexisted with the old repertoire. Cardew supported this but also drew attention to the fact that there was still too little actual music-making at meetings:

Generally: In the Scratch not many people seem to bring instruments. Should this be regarded as a fault to be remedied ? Or regarded as a sign of the Scratch's present stage and acted on (that is, by writing pieces that don't require instruments)? Should Scratch music be revived? (At least it's a form where everybody knows they're supposed to play.)[21]

By now Cardew had begun to adopt a more critical stance towards the music and its performance. The function and status of criticism, previously virtually non-existent in the Scratch Orchestra, was now a potent and occasionally unsettling feature at meetings and did little to allay the increasing 'discontent' which was now directed mainly at the activity of the Id Group. Certain stalwart members no longer attended – including founder-member Howard Skempton, Greg Bright and Stefan Szczelkun – which left members like Psi Ellison and Judy Euren feeling isolated and vulnerable.

In the Journals, dated 6 January, Cardew noted down his reflections and conclusions on a long conversation he had had with Ellison. The latter expressed his opinion that the Scratch Orchestra's present inability, or refusal, to countenance unpredictable contributions from members such as himself was a dereliction of an important aspect of what he had understood as the Scratch 'ethos'. 'Unpredictability' had always been the essence of his own performances and since he felt himself to be a member of the Scratch in perpetuity, as it were, this for him constituted a crisis situation. He found the recent meetings trivial and small-minded and all he could do was to look on appalled. When Cardew suggested that Ellison should work with the Scratch Orchestra towards improvement as a whole, the concept of 'improvement' seemed alien to him. Cardew ends the note: 'I think he creates the pettiness and triviality by his aloof attitude. It was a long conversation, but I didn't really find it encouraging'. Clearly, there was an unbridgeable gulf between the two men, both psychologically and ideologically. In some ways Ellison was extremely close to pre-communist Cardew; he did believe in the ideas of positive action, of helping, giving, contributing, sacrificing (something which has characterised Ellison's whole life), but there could not be a reward, a goal, a happy ending – or even the prospect of 'improvement'; the world may change, Ellison would have agreed, but human beings merely substitute one flawed system for another.

On 21 January Paragraph 5 of *The Great Learning* was performed by an augmented Scratch Orchestra at Cecil Sharp House in Camden Town as part of the fortieth anniversary celebrations of Macnaghten Concerts. On the day following the concert Cardew jotted down two lists of comments: 'What was good about it' and 'What was bad about it'. The first list, somewhat routine, includes the beginning and the end of the improvisation, and individual contributions within the piece as a whole, such as the 'sustained aggression' of *Crash Bang Clank Music*, and the discipline of *Bowed Sound* and *Silent Music*. Most of his criticisms refer to the composition itself rather than the performance, and reflect, partly, the nagging 'guilty conscience' of the 'bourgeois artist' who has seen the error of his ways and is now grappling with the newly emerging criteria for 'good' and 'bad' which the political imperatives demand. In particular Cardew took exception to the multi-layering technique he had adopted for the ten Ode Machines which, in the Cecil Sharp House performance, rendered them 'incomprehensible'. Cardew's close friend, composer Michael Parsons, takes issue:

'The songs are incomprehensible': again a confusion of criteria seems to be involved; a retreat from the experimental idea of overlaying independent vocal lines, falling back (perhaps?) on a more traditional idea of comprehensibility (audibility of words, coherence of each vocal line etc.). This sounds like a critical intellect trying to hinder and obstruct the imagination, or to 'censor' the intuition, in retrospect; the build-up and interweaving of melodies in performance of the Ode Machines is actually one of the most interesting and 'experimental' features of the work.[22]

As far as textual comprehensibility is concerned it would seem that Cardew is on weak ground here; for most opera-lovers, for example, even aficionados of Lieder recitals, incomprehensibility of the text, as it is sung, is virtually taken for granted. If one wants to know what the singers are singing about, read the synopsis, read the poem. The criticism of the songs contains another strangely couched reference to a political idea for which the Scratch Orchestra as a whole felt a particular empathy: 'Sinister leaning on professional quality to provide continuity to carry our own efforts'. I presume that Cardew is referring here to the 'professionals' who sang the Odes throughout half the duration of Paragraph 5 and who provided a 'received' sound quality – that is, a conservatory-trained vocal style which functioned, Cardew appears to be suggesting, as a kind of musical safety net for his vulnerable composition and the unpredictable performances it invites – a direct contravention of the Maoist idea of 'not relying on experts'. The dumbshow is likewise subjected to Cardew's criticism, and yet the extraordinary body language, expressive of a subtle poetry, and of humour too, reaches and affects the audience in manifold ways. Perhaps he was referring to this when, in response to some misgivings expressed in relation to a possible performance of the dumbshow in Scandinavia several years later by Michael Parsons and Howard Skempton, he reassured them with the kind of saw which he would occasionally deliver in pre-revolutionary days but which, in its abstract generality, and in the context of the mid-seventies, would have been quite unexpected: 'Once you have established that you are human beings, you can do whatever you like'. The explicit permissiveness embodied in this response, in 1976, seemed to be quite out of character, as if he had momentarily relaxed his ideological guard. Of course, one can also interpret these words as a heavily ironic criticism directed at his two 'liberal-bourgeois' friends; one certainly cannot discount this possibility. Given his entrenchment at the time in 'anti-revisionist' dogma (in particular the 'bourgeois' idea of a 'human nature' which transcends the class struggle) such a response, ready and apposite, would have simply demonstrated how adept he had become in dealing with 'bourgeois mythology'. Moreover, his criticisms of the Cecil Sharp House performance of Paragraph 5 do specifically refer to a 'permissiveness' which he regarded as deleterious to the overall effect of the work, of any work, in the public arena. He therefore questioned 'the assumption that it's alright for people to go off on their own into Action and Number Scores'. And he did intervene at one stage during the improvisation – when some extremely indulgent (permissive) 'piano-playing' was in full flow – by simply getting up from his seat (in the audience), moving seemingly casually, but with intent, towards the offending contribution, and closing the piano lid. It was a sign for all; the improvisation regained its earlier discipline and was brought to a close with a general awareness of the subtle demands which free collective improvisation makes on participants – of the (frequently stressed) need for self-discipline: the sine qua non of creative, intelligent music-making.

Then on to Liverpool for a Scratch Orchestra concert at the Bluecoat Gallery (Bluecoat Arts Centre) on 26 January 1972 in which Michael Chant's revised version of *Sweet FA* received first performances in a combined opera/ballet version.[23] Cardew with one or two others performed his *10,000 nails in the coffin of Imperialism*, a robust offensive across the bows of bourgeois art, but a companion piece, John White's *The Chairman's Enemies' Favourite Things*, was withdrawn at the last minute by the composer due to a 'fit of pique' sustained as a result of Cardew's leading question to the audience at the beginning of the interval: 'How many of you consider that you possess a truly working-class world-outlook?' Here White is quoting Cardew some thirty years after the event, but he insists that the word 'truly', which he found particularly jarring, was certainly used by Cardew. And there was more disruption, again from within the performing group itself, when during a performance of Cardew's *Soon* (a setting of a text of MaoTse-Tung), Sue Gittins began to scream in protest whilst managing simultaneously to recite Blake's *Tyger*. One of my duties as member of the Id Group had been to observe and analyse the effect and impact of *Sweet FA* on the audience. Significantly, what struck me, and the general audience in particular, was the fact that the 'Maoist' contingent looked 'military', 'fascistic', and decidedly less happy than the contingent of Scratch 'hippies' who had been type-cast and had therefore applied themselves to the manner born. With its crude, normative designations of 'good' and 'evil', of 'correctness', of 'progressive' and 'degenerate', the libretto for *Sweet FA* was appropriately served by a musical performance of unsurpassable feebleness. Blinded, and deafened, by the Party slogan 'Put politics in command' the Party faithful and its supporters, like the Id Group, continued to compromise our artistic judgement compliantly, with an alarming otherworldliness.

Cardew, meanwhile, continued to respond to invitations to perform and conduct workshops: at La Sainte Union College in Southampton, arranged by the composer and educationalist George Self, and a lecture on Scratch Music at the University of Sussex. AMM, too, was stuttering on, beset by destructive tensions, but if Eddie Prévost and Lou Gare were sooner or later to be left to their own devices, the situation in the Scratch Orchestra was quite different and, at the time, certainly more encouraging from Cardew's political perspective. It was in the Scratch Orchestra that his energies were to be expended to more positive ends despite the parlous situation, created by the political coup, which threatened its continuing existence. So at a Scratch Orchestra meeting on 2 February Cardew quite consciously raised the stakes by proposing a new manifesto 'stating our present state'. This was to be circulated with the question: 'Are you in it or not? No reply means no.' Clearly, Cardew's aim was a more disciplined, more committed, more *political* Scratch Orchestra. Psi Ellison recalls that it was the first occasion on which Cardew gave free, outward expression to the authoritarianism which later, as a Party functionary, was to engulf him. The need to control became manifest and what he had previously tolerated, sometimes admired and even relished in Scratch Orchestra members like Ellison, qualities and values which in the minds and opinions of many in the music world he himself and his music-making had become associated with – freedom of the imagination, unpredictability, artistic dissent, anti-authoritarianism – these were now caricatured as reactionary expressions of an anarchic tendency and denounced as 'counter-revolutionary'; such antics no longer had even a nuisance value. Ellison found himself adrift in hostile surroundings, redundant and unwanted; before long he was to sever his connections with Cardew and the Scratch Orchestra. He and Judy Euren left London and settled for a time in Wales.

Between the 14 and 25 of February Cardew was invited to devise a project for students at the Bradford College of Art. The development of the project and reactions to it are recorded in some detail in the 1971/72 Journals. The musical compositions Cardew introduced to the students were all from the Scratch Orchestra's repertoire and involved drumming (Howard Skempton's *Drum No. 1*), the use of water and stones (David Jackman's *Georgina Cries* and Greg Bright's *Place*), and vocal pieces (Paragraph 7 and *Loud and Soft Laughter Music* from Paragraph 5 of *The Great Learning*, Alvin Curran's *Processional*, Robert Ashley's *She was a Visitor*, and Skempton's *Fish Talk*). All the practising and rehearsing of the pieces was interspersed with a considerable amount of discussion and Cardew also contributed a lecture on Marx. Cardew noted that all the discussions, on whatever topic, were dominated entirely by whichever member(s) of staff happened to be present; the students were not encouraged to express themselves and when they did their contributions were more often than not treated dismissively. Not surprisingly the students came to the conclusion that discussions were 'a fruitless exercise', whilst the staff came to the conclusion that the students were 'apathetic'.[24] Cardew also identified

a larger problem in working with Art students; the problem of individualism and originality. They find it hard to accept 1) to all do the same thing (say in a piece of music) and 2) to do the same thing over and over (as is necessary in rehearsal). (This problem is also present in the Scratch Orchestra.)[25]

A concert including some of the pieces that had been suggested by Cardew took place. The aim of the concert, or more precisely Cardew's aim, was 'to awaken political consciousness in the College, and create a happy [*sic*] positive atmosphere'. The aims were made more explicit by the display of banners with political slogans which presumably Cardew himself had proposed: Music is Collective Violence, Art for Whom?

etc. A discussion of the concert was organised for the next day in which twelve people took part (more than Cardew had anticipated) and which included two members of the teaching staff: Albert Hunt and Joe Dolan. Cardew's idea, according to his Journals, was to discuss the possibilities of the formation of a performance workshop, on a permanent basis, and/or a political Study group, depending on the response of the students present. He also wanted to initiate debate on more general issues. As so often happened in such discussions the various left-wing factions were soon at each others' throats. When Albert Hunt drew a comparison between Stalin's 'annihilation of millions of peasants' and Hitler's 'extermination of the Jews' Cardew questioned Hunt's motives in 'bringing up such analogies', while Hunt was outraged by what he perceived as Cardew's willingness to act as Stalin's apologist. The meeting broke up inconclusively, for which Cardew blamed himself, although a date was fixed for a Political Study Group meeting. A few days after his return to London he noted:

> Something wrong with my analysis at present. I keep saying we must do this, we must do that. 'We must compose.' 'We must get action.' If it's not coming there's no point in calling for it all the time. It shows my low level of consciousness. So what is actually happening? Political consciousness is rising. Bureaucracy is rearing its ugly head. I'm out of work and short of money.[26]

Such were the arguments and responses which bedevilled countless meetings that Cardew organised or attended in the subsequent years. His support for Stalin in particular, (following the Party line), invariably proved to be a step too far – a highly contentious issue which, during his many confrontations, drove many leftists and left sympathisers into a veritable frenzy. Many of these 'comrades' were broadly sympathetic to Cardew's views but he left no room for concessions, for compromise, for manoeuvre, for the slightest degree of scepticism (even regarding the role of Stalin).[27] The 'correctness' of the Party line was inviolable and therefore everything which emanated from it was beyond criticism. Small wonder then that in many of his appearances he found himself in a state of siege. And yet, it might be said, to have exalted Stalin, who in the course of his life, like many politicians of all persuasions, committed and condoned many crimes, does not necessarily reflect upon Cardew's own conduct, anymore than to believe in an omnipotent God who has surveyed such crimes without lifting a finger damns the religious believer to a delusive life of futility and failure.

Throughout this period Cardew's personal life was in turmoil. Regarding his financial plight, this was a condition which by now, through long experience, he was able to deal with through a variety of ploys – buying time, using contacts, scraping bits and pieces together, living from day to day (manageable on one's own but unmitigated and energy-sapping with a wife and four children). A concert with the Steve Reich Ensemble at the Hayward Gallery on 4 February had offered some economic respite, as did a Workshop and Concert at the Birmingham Arts Lab two days later, a lecture for Birmingham University on 7 February, a BBC recording with Reich on 9 February and, a little later, on 8 March, a lecture for the Chelsea College of Art. None of these engagements would have offered him remuneration of any substance but they helped to keep the wolf from the door and he would have set his sights no higher. March was an auspicious month for starkly contrasting reasons: while AMM was breaking apart, on 25 March the joyous occasion of the foundation of the Communist Party of England (Marxist-Leninist) would certainly have gladdened his heart, even if at that stage, as a rank-and-file supporter still to prove his worth, he would not have been privy to the formal celebrations of the Party élite. That was to come.

A more contentious issue, which was to engage the Scratch Orchestra in acrimonious debate and sharpen existing divisions, was a projected performance at the end of March of Christian Wolff's *Burdocks*. In a Journal note on 21 February (which reads as a draft circular to Scratch members), clearly already mindful of the opposition to it within the Scratch Orchestra ranks, Cardew somewhat disingenuously comments: 'Many of us have admired and respected Christian's music over the years and I find it impossible to believe that it is completely contentless.' [28] In the years which followed, when political involvement, and maturity, had taught him the necessity for incisive thinking, such a lame, speculative remark would have been summarily dismissed by Cardew. (We may compare this remark with his unequivocal criticism of Wolff's work, and Frederic Rzewski's, in *Stockhausen Serves Imperialism*, which will be discussed later.) But there is probably a personal agenda here: Cardew was still not politically self-confident enough to risk rupturing his relations with composers such as Wolff and Rzewski who were, broadly speaking, political comrades with whom he was on close personal terms. At the time of the *Burdocks* performance, despite the outward appearance of certainty and conviction, he was still beset by nagging, unanswered questions, by a residue of inner doubts.

For whatever reason(s) Cardew desperately wanted the *Burdocks* concert to go ahead, but at a Scratch Orchestra meeting at Frank Abbot's flat early in March his arguments were received with scepticism and even derision by many Scratch members, and he was given a rough ride by an Id Group which was gaining in terms of political consciousness, establishing a bedrock of political certainties and which, I think it would be fair to say, had much less to lose. The Id Group expressed its opposition to *Burdocks* on the grounds that the reasons for doing it were purely circumstantial, that it was indisputably an 'avant-garde' work of art and as such the Scratch Orchestra should have no truck with it. In a heated discussion Cardew defended *Burdocks*, probably more out of loyalty to Christian Wolff, a close friend, than from a deep-seated conviction of its potential for revolutionary 'consciousness-raising'. Certainly he marshalled his arguments persuasively – as one would have expected of him, citing formal aspects in the realisation of the score, such as the 'divided leadership' (autonomous groups working coextensively), with its implications of coordination and cooperation, and insisting that it could be transformed 'to meet the needs of the masses'. But his contention, that if *Burdocks* were an 'imperialist work' then imperialism would support its composer, received short shrift, and was rejected as sheer sophistry. Keith Rowe, emboldened by an unassailable sense of political correctness and therefore, at the time, not one to mince his words, denounced *Burdocks* as a work which 'overwhelmingly supports imperialism'. In contrast to Rowe's uncompromising stance, Michael Parsons, in support of *Burdocks*, maintained that in terms of audience it was the alienated, petit bourgeois class that the Scratch Orchestra was most qualified to reach – an opinion to which probably a majority of Scratch members at that time would have subscribed. What did clearly emerge out of the meeting, and the previous ones, was that within the Scratch Orchestra the contradictions were sharpening.

At a subsequent meeting, on 20 March at his own house, Cardew argued that 'we should all think what we would like to find out from the audience. If a piece is to be considered it must be condemned by the audience, not by our intellectual judgement alone'.[29] Cardew here is still, though not for much longer, referring to 'audience' in an abstract way, thus side-stepping the thorny crux of the problem: the *class nature* of the audience and the necessity for the Scratch Orchestra, as 'petit bourgeois' musicians and artists, to 'remould its world outlook' by integrating with and serving the working class, thereby creating a *new* audience, with impeccable proletarian credentials, for its concerts. This was the 'Party line' and it was certainly an important contributory factor to the ultimate disintegration of the Scratch Orchestra. 'Integrating with and serving the working class' was a pledge of (unquestioning) loyalty, and obedience, no less, to a handful of unimpressive (or to be more generous, ordinary) individuals who comprised the self-appointed Central Committee of the Communist Party of England (Marxist-Leninist). Thus, a confluence of factors, revolving around the performance of a piece of music, had brought things to a head. Cardew himself, torn between loyalty to a much loved and greatly respected friend, and the imperatives of what he was now beginning to see in a positive light as a strict, uncompromising, political allegiance, was still searching for a viable and acceptable compromise. Such a compromise was reached, more out of respect for Wolff, and for Cardew, still, than for the arguments advanced in favour of the music, and the *Burdocks* performance, directed by the composer, went ahead as planned on 28 March at the Cecil Sharp House in Camden. In an interesting Journal entry headed 're Howard's [Skempton] criticism of our approach to *Burdocks*', Cardew offers further elaboration of his defence:

'Our compositions are for now, not for posterity'. Everything is in a process of constant change: compositions too. Crystallised at a certain stage into written form they nevertheless cannot remain still and unchanging in a constantly changing context – psychological, technical, political etc. When you play a piece of music you bring ideas to it. This is inevitable (and hence desirable). If my ideas cancel out the ideas of the piece I am playing so much the worse for both of them – the ideas should support each other and give substance to each other.[30]

In fact, rehearsals of *Burdocks*, led by Cardew, had begun several weeks earlier, on 29 February, and with characteristic meticulousness Cardew had worked out a schedule which, despite the problems surrounding the projected performance, received conscientious support and commitment from the majority of Scratch Orchestra members. Section III, in particular, seems to have fired the imagination: 'Each player makes about 511 sounds, each one different in some way.' In one realisation a bowl of water was filled and struck by a beater; between each strike a small amount of water was removed by Scratch member Chris May with a pipette. In another ingenious interpretation a large number of homemade instruments were struck by a variety of beaters.

The concert was promoted by Victor Schonfield and Music Now and was the last Scratch Orchestra event to be supported by the Arts Council. The Orchestra was joined for the occasion by a number of mainly contemporary music groups – including AMM, Gentle Fire, Mouth of Hermes (directed by Frank Denyer), the Portsmouth Sinfonia, PTO, and sub-groups of the Scratch Orchestra: cpe, CUM, Harmony Band. The event began with an arrangement by Cardew of the 'Chorus of the Hebrew Slaves' by Verdi, which Cardew described in his programme notes as 'an allegory of the plight of the modern composer, isolated from the broad masses in the Establishment's Ivory Tower of New Music'. Typically for that period, and probably part of the deal Cardew had struck with the Id Group, a pre-arranged (political) discussion took place during the interval, most of which consisted of prepared contributions covering a wide spectrum of opinion from members of the Scratch Orchestra; these included Frank Abbott, Sue Gittins, Bryn Harris and Cardew himself. Somewhat incongruously, but characteristically, it was also decided to include some interval songs: Howard Skempton performed his own 'Not Very Long Song', Michael Parsons sang 'The Willow' by Ivan Hume Carter, Brian Dennis contributed a song by Dowland, and the Wood and Metal Band provided a rendering of 'I wanna be loved by you'.

The *Burdocks* affair had clearly rankled; Cardew had been attacked by his comrades, accused of disingenuousness in the way that he had conducted his argument, and although the concert was a success Cardew's standing in the Scratch Orchestra had again been compromised. Just two days after the concert, 30 March, in a letter to Alec Hill, a Scratch member sympathetic to the political developments, Cardew adopts a somewhat high-minded stance in an attempt to regain political credibility: 'I feel we should go into it in more detail. Generalities are not sharp enough to smash the bourgeois cultural superstructure'. Was his suggestion to 'go into it in more detail' really motivated by the desire to 'smash the bourgeois cultural superstructure' or, with the clear reference to the need for intellectual rigour, was he simply attempting to continue to argue the case for *Burdocks* in retrospect, as it were, and to justify his stance? The imputation to his Scratch comrades of lightweight intellectual argument ('generalities') echoes a tactic which was often used at the Maoist meetings: 'No investigation, no right to speak', was one of the Party's more maledictory slogans – an effective way of inculcating a culture of self-doubt and, as a corollary, self-censorship within the Party rank and file.

The 'left' influence on the Scratch Orchestra was now strong but there was still no formal alignment with a particular group or Party; this unalignment was regarded as both a weakness and a strength, depending on one's point of view. Until the question of the group's political identity could be resolved, one way or another, the Scratch Orchestra would remain intact, ideologically amorphous but with some pretensions – mustering for the occasional foray into political activity of a more general mind, such as demonstrations. Members would seek support for projects according to their propensities: Birgit Burkhardt and Bryn Harris, for example, had become interested in working with children. Burkhardt found inspiration in the American teacher and writer, Ivan Illich, while Harris was influenced by a book by Neil Postman and Charles Weingartner: *Teaching as a Subversive Activity.*

Meanwhile, Keith Rowe, who was then closest to the Maoist party, exploited the ambivalence and instability which had virtually immobilised the Scratch Orchestra (certainly in relation to its actual music-making) to continue to push hard for closer Party affiliation. This was never expressed formally; rather, Rowe would canvass for opinions from individuals whom he considered to be broadly sympathetic to the Party's political programme. His proposal was that these members would become part of a prescribed membership and attend exclusive meetings; those interested parties who wished to attend meetings for the first time would only be admitted after careful vetting beforehand. Seriousness of intent was paramount; portentously, he reminded the group that the lives of many of those engaged in revolutionary politics, past and present, 'do not have a natural end'. According to Rowe this tight-knit group should be armed ideologically with the 'correct political line' — 'correct' because it was the embodiment of 'invincible Mao Tse-tung thought', loyally and rigorously applied in England by the Communist Party of England (Marxist-Leninist).[31]

Few of Cardew's friends and colleagues in the music world shared his new revolutionary perspective. A letter from the American composer Tom Johnson rejects Cardew's request for his recent composition *10,000 nails in the coffin of Imperialism* to be included in a subsequent issue of the magazine *Aspen* as 'just too out of keeping with the issue as a whole'. Johnson concludes his letter in telling fashion: 'I hope AMM Music will be in this country again before too long. I look forward to the next time I will be able to hear your fine work together.'[32] And he apologizes for being so tardy in returning the score of *10,000 nails*. Cardew would have received this with a rueful sigh; at the time, embroiled as he was in the furore over *Burdocks*, not only was his kudos at a very low ebb, particularly in the Scratch Orchestra, but old friends, including those abroad, were tending to back off, to distance themselves, and even to make thinly disguised overtures to him that he should return to the fold.

And yet for educational and art institutions, and the media, Cardew's reputation as a maverick composer made him a desirable temporary presence: a Maoist on the loose for a day or two, marauding through the minds of the inhabitants of the Institution, ruffling a few feathers, provoking apathetic students to stir themselves — something the lecturers themselves were unable to achieve. Naturally, the Institution invariably survives, its liberal credentials demonstrated and vindicated; a little psychological repair work, some reassurance, perhaps, in the wake of Cardew's visits, was all that was required to re-establish business as usual. Yet not all such forays into institutional life were so easily accommodated. The 'John Cage; Ghost or Monster?' talk, which was commissioned by Hans Keller of the BBC Music Section and appeared in *The Listener* on 4 May 1972, to this day continues to 'make waves in the environment and have repercussions beyond the concert hall'. (I discuss this in the chapter 'Stockhausen Serves Imperialism' wherein it is reprinted.) And April had seen a lecture on the Scratch Orchestra at the ICA and a collective refusal by a majority of the Orchestra to participate in the ICES festival (International Carnival for Experimental Sound), promoted by Harvey Matusow, in London in August. The reason for the boycott was Matusow's alleged misdemeanours during the McCarthy witch-hunting period in the fifties.[33]

Both within the Scratch Orchestra and domestically there was ongoing emotional turmoil: Gabriel had left home; Emily was suffering from long-term depression and, for several years, bulimia. Walter was going to school but was still fragile and needed physiotherapy. Stella, as a constant and dependable presence, stoically bore the brunt of all this, but she was fearful for her children and desperately unhappy; to make matters worse, tensions between her and her husband were mounting. As for the Scratch

Orchestra, the politicisation of every issue ensured that positions became more entrenched and the possibility of any rapprochement ever more remote. In a letter to Alec Hill Cardew criticises the 'opportunist' line of Dave Jackman for 'wanting to be in ICES but on our own terms?'[34] At a meeting of the Scratch Orchestra on 17 April Michael Chant put forward the idea of a 'united musical front' which would embrace all Left musicians. Predictably, this was opposed by Keith Rowe on the grounds that without a clear and firm political line such a loose federation of artists would soon run into difficulties. By contrast, he argued, 'democratic centralism' unites around clear objectives. And he may or may not have added that a key tenet of democratic centralism was the authority of the Party and its acceptance by Party members and supporters. Furthermore, rather than attempting to attract more people into the Scratch Orchestra, which Cardew had favoured, Rowe insisted that at this stage the opposite was necessary: to close ranks. It was not long before Cardew was won over to this view.

By now the focus of the Id Group, as opposed to the Scratch Orchestra as a whole, was politically much sharper; from being a group set up to analyse the nature and social function of the Scratch Orchestra it had become, *de facto*, a cultural organ of the CPE (M-L). Its brief now was both wider and more controlled. Looking back over the 'literature' that has survived from this transition period this can be seen clearly from the content and language, the 'Partyspeak', of the manifesto which Cardew himself submitted for approval by the Id Group on 13 April 1972:

This group has been formed to study Marxism-Leninism and learn how to use it to attack the cultural superstructure of imperialism, in particular music in England. Our immediate concern is to raise the level of political consciousness of the Scratch and mould it into a united and well-disciplined organ of propaganda and a sharp weapon of attack against the cultural superstructure. Our role within the revolutionary movement is: to serve the proletarian revolution by 'doing battle in the realm of ideas', by creating public opinion in favour of communism and against imperialism, capitalism, metaphysics, bourgeois idealism, revisionism, etc. etc., and thus helping to create the right conditions for the revolution. The necessity for the existence of the Id Group is demonstrated by the number of things we lack for the accomplishment of any of the tasks listed above. We lack a thorough knowledge and understanding of Marxist principles, of the method of dialectical materialism, of the history of the communist movement and the lessons to be learned from it. (To uphold and study and praise Trotsky is to depreciate the work of Lenin; to denounce Stalin is to promote revisionism).

The statement ends with the above-quoted Maoist slogan: 'Make self the target of revolution, and the broad masses the target of revolutionary propaganda'.

The specific task of the Id Group then was to study and analyse its 'adversary': the English musical establishment. Cardew listed the main areas: classical music, pop music and background music, and their sub-divisions. Each member of the Id Group would be responsible for gathering and sifting information from an area with which he or she was most familiar. [35] Throughout the statement the political and ideological shortcomings of the Id Group are referred to; this self-deprecatory tone was typical. Through the Maoist cult of 'self-criticism', now in full swing in the People's Republic of China, the Party was able to feed off, and exploit, the self-doubt which had been instilled through the relentless flow of its propaganda; the strategy was to strip and cleanse members ideologically. Troubled by feelings of guilt and inadequacy, striving to 'remould their bourgeois world outlook' ('we must isolate the enemy as it exists inside our own heads') – Party members and supporters were thus more susceptible to Party demands and discipline. They were bourgeois sinners who needed to expiate their misdeeds under the guidance of the Party. Only when they were better equipped with Mao Tse-Tung Thought could they begin to do effective battle with the bourgeois ideologists.

Yet within the Id Group there were those who had palpable reservations in relation to both the content and the tone of the manifesto. In particular, the issue of Stalin and his 'contribution' was a constant thorn in the side of supporters who were less starry-eyed than Party members in their assessment of the Soviet leader.[36] Nevertheless, it was agreed that we should participate; to deepen understanding of our chosen profession and to show solidarity with our brothers and sisters in that profession seemed to be an honourable course of action to pursue. Significantly, those Scratch Orchestra members who embraced the Party and its ideology with the most enthusiasm, with a whole-heartedness and ardour which it seemed that nothing could dampen, were those who had had no previous political experience: membership of a political party, political youth groups, discussion groups, attendance at demonstrations, and so forth. On the contrary, like Cardew they had disparaged the very notion of political affiliation, of collective mobilisation and protest. So that the political *innocence* of Cardew, Rowe, Michael Chant, Hugh Shrapnel, Peter Devenport, to name but five musicians who for a number of years devoted many hours of their lives to the Party, was quite remarkable in its comprehensiveness, its wholesomeness, its utter irreproachability. The few, very few, in the Scratch Orchestra who did belong or had belonged to a group or party and had experienced and suffered the exigencies of political life – the twists and turns (sometimes u-turns), the back-tracking, the degeneracy into pragmatism, cynicism and ultimate disillusionment – we had been irreversibly tainted by 'revisionism'.

I recall an occasion, probably in the early seventies, possibly later, when Cardew accused me of keeping, or hiding, Communism from the Scratch Orchestra. In possession of fundamental truths that by circumstance, or upbringing, or education, had been denied to others, it was as if I had wilfully prevented the spread of these truths by my feeble-minded taciturnity or, worse, by a lack of 'character'; I should have been proselytizing, spreading the gospel. I suppose my view of the need for revolutionary change was not 'absolute', not cataclysmic enough; ultimately I lacked faith. We *must* act, I believed, *even if we may not be right*, whereas the Maoists, like a religious sect, acted on the basis of *certitude.* And such a fundamental difference must have impinged upon our attitudes towards our own actions and motivations. Here was the rub: when Keith Rowe debated with the Scratch Orchestra in Newcastle, or with the Id Group in a London flat, his arguments were underpinned by a cluster of well-rehearsed *certainties,* some of them 'reasonable', if debatable, and some of them highly contentious (that the 'dictatorship of the proletariat' will, *inevitably*, be established according to the 'laws of history'). Such a routine, involuntary recourse to certainties, against which, by their very nature, there could be no argument, was an invaluable boon to people who, up to just a few months previously, had not given these weighty issues a thought. For those of us who had come from a different (left) political culture, the retention of a degree of scepticism, of doubt, was natural – a kind of safeguard against, for example, an over-enthusiastic adoption of extreme and violent means. And yet to act only with extreme circumspection, or to use doubt as an excuse for inaction is itself, perhaps, a form of moral cowardice. And if I compare my own commitment and contribution to socialism with that of Cardew, who worked day and night for 'the cause', my own efforts pale into shameful insignificance. But ultimately, are not good intentions, even heroic endeavour over a long period, judged by results? We are no closer to the 'dictatorship of the proletariat'; it has been forestalled; the capitalists have outgunned and outwitted us. Perhaps, as some of his comrades have insisted, the 'timing was wrong'. And yet, when we survey the moral trajectory of Cardew's life any reference to 'goals' seems trite because the means, *his* means, were imbued with such passion, fire, and *poetry*, that it was as if the goal, the ends, were rendered arbitrary, irreparably diminished, by the intensity of the ever-present, the *now.* At the end of his essay, 'Towards an Ethic of Improvisation', death itself is expressed as a virtue to be striven for and cherished. It is an extraordinary text, precluding any encroachment of the religious agenda whose insidious influence still, in our contemporary cultures, carries a disproportionate weight in any debate which bears on the issue of death – but which here, in Cardew's text, is treated purely philosophically. So that death is linked to life, not after-life, which Cardew did not believe in. The meaning of death is to be extracted from the unceasing flow of life, not from speculation about, or certainty of, the 'hereafter'.

The desire always to be right is an ignoble taskmaster, as is the desire for immortality. The performance of any vital action brings us closer to death; if it didn't it would lack vitality. Life is a force to be used and if necessary used up. 'Death is the virtue in us going to its destination.' (Lieh Tzu).[37]

But to return to the canon, aside from the obvious – that is, the presence and pervasive influence of a formal Party (CPE M-L) – there is no doubt that the long-term commitment to a messianic socialism by Cardew and his colleagues was inspired and sustained above all by the discovery and study of the Marxist classics, and not least by the passion and moral outrage which are given such eloquent expression in Marx's early writings and in the *Communist Manifesto*, in particular. For Cardew, no other writer, with the possible exception of Wittgenstein, influenced him more than Lenin, whom he read and studied with great intensity of purpose, and to whom there are constant references in his letters, articles and speeches.

The American composer Steve Reich seemed not to be fazed by Cardew's new political stance, inviting him to join the Steve Reich Ensemble for concerts of his music in Europe at the beginning of May. There followed, on 8 May, a lecture ('on Criticism') at Sussex University, presumably a version of that which appears in *Stockhausen Serves Imperialism*. In fact, Cardew recorded 'on Criticism' the next day, 9 May, for the BBC, but it was never broadcast (on the grounds of its 'irrelevance'). Perhaps, in the wake of the furore surrounding his talk on Cage the previous month, the BBC decided on reflection that it would be prudent to give Cardew's inflammatory pronouncements a wide berth. (I return to this issue in the chapter 'Stockhausen Serves Imperialism'.) By contrast, my idea of approaching an old people's home in Islington – I was living in Highbury, in north London, at the time – arose out of the perceived need in the Id Group to integrate into working class communities ('serve the people'), to find and perform music that was unsentimental, 'progressive', and which would appeal to them. A date was agreed; the 'old people' were a delightful audience – relaxed, informal and appreciative. Mostly, we performed songs, including the 'Red Flag', and chatted about the old times. A refreshing experience, although I believe Cardew was absent on this occasion.

Cardew's three-day stint at the Cardiff College of Art, on 10, 11, 16 May, was a re-run, with some differences, of his visit to the Bradford College of Art the previous February. Clearly, the educative nature of his work at that time, whether in institutions or on the streets, had become paramount, and this was reflected in his decision to spend considerable time and energy in producing a report, dated 3 June 1972, of his visit to Cardiff, prefacing it 'with some more general remarks about teaching in art schools'.

Formally, Cardew decided to begin the course with an introductory talk followed by a political discussion. The musical programme (rehearsals and concert) would constitute a conclusion – a wordless, artistic presentation emanating from the complexities and contradictions of the issues thrown up and debated during the course of Cardew's visits. In Bradford it had been the reverse; perhaps he had hoped that an initial discussion would pave the way towards a more 'enlightened', and perhaps more disciplined, approach to the music-making. In fact, the result was a stultification of the artistic (musical) element, to which Cardew refers at the end of his report:

> The political ideas are so wide-ranging and large, that our musical capacity to represent them seemed inconsiderable. The impression is created that the artistic presentation is irrelevant. The idea that we should desist until we know what we are doing is growing on me.

The talk began contentiously enough, under the provocative slogan 'fine art students; a potential propaganda network'. Not surprisingly, this premise was met right from the outset with resentment and hostility from the majority of students. Cardew's attempted justification during his talk – 'lying propaganda must be countered with truthful propaganda' – would have cut no ice with the students. Propaganda is propaganda; 'truthful propaganda' is an oxymoron. But as was the case at Bradford it was the staff who took up the gauntlet – in particular, to defend art school education against Cardew's scathing attacks. The Director of Studies, Tom Hudson, insisted that art schools were offering the best education in the world; Cardew argued that it was still orientated towards 'success' and a respected and envied position in bourgeois society. 'The successful artist in our society is a true "flower of evil"', he wrote damningly in his report. Hudson, a fiery character, would have relished the confrontation, and as a committed educationalist had a personal stake in the argument. In the Journals Cardew noted Tom Hudson's view 'that I have thrown away my artistic power. This is necessary. Power cannot simply be redirected; it grows (like a culture) in a specific environment for a specific purpose'.[38] Nor did the concert fare better – a mishmash of half-baked ideas which had no chance of seriously engaging an audience. In fact, the only successful contribution was an event entitled 'Art Criticism' devised by Graham (along with David and Noreen), one of three 'firmly leftwing students'. Graham's idea was to initiate public criticism of some civic modern sculpture in Cardiff by asking passers-by to express their views; the artist(s) in question would thus be confronted with 'public opinion'. Graham also wanted to highlight the financial agreements underpinning the project and to present the whole package, to a mainly student audience, as an image of their future as artists – given a measure, that is, of success and recognition. So when it transpired that one of the sculptors of the civic sculpture was involved in a press conference on the day of the College concert Graham's idea received a new impetus. His suggestion then was to translocate the conference (together with civic dignitaries, drinks, reporters and the Stuyvesant sponsors) to the College where, as part of the concert, it would be subjected to on-the-spot public criticism. Cardew recalls in his report that this idea was fiercely opposed by several members of staff while the Director of Studies argued against the idea on the grounds that the concert was intended to consist of Cardew's work with the students. Cardew himself, for different reasons, also spoke against it; he feared the students would be outnumbered and 'literally outclassed' ('maybe it was too bold for me'), reduced to making an ineffectual protest resulting in defeat and disillusionment. Finally, it was agreed that Graham's item should be presented in the concert as originally planned; in Cardew's words:

> without using any music or other fine art media, without using any original artistic material, yet [it] managed to achieve 'audience participation'; it stimulated criticism, and it had political content. Under the slogan 'This is your future', Graham showed slides of the civic sculpture in front of the castle wall (an abstract tubular steel and wire affair). Meanwhile two speakers read out the comments of the first 40 passers-by who had been asked what they thought of the sculpture. Almost without exception they thought it was rubbish. Then Graham asked me to state an alternative path for artists, and I brought out Marx's saying about how philosophers used to be content to understand the world, but now it was their business to change it. Connecting this with art I said the artist could no longer be content with decorating the world, he had to change it, that revolution is the change required and artists should form propaganda teams to further revolution. Then Graham asked the audience members to comment and took the microphone around to those wishing to speak. Here at least the atmosphere had that kind of attentiveness that we associate with an appreciation of art.[39]

Many people in the audience broadly supported the point which Graham was attempting to make. Resistance rallied around comments made by the lecturers; one insisted that the public response to the sculpture did not indicate the *potential* response. In his report Cardew dismisses this point with a somewhat crude caricature of a serious contribution: 'Though the crowd can't appreciate modern art there's an elite that can. Really he's accusing the passers by of philistinism'. Or possibly not. The idea of a 'potential' response may simply reflect the idea that much art, including classical art, cannot, should not, be judged and evaluated on the basis of what appears to have been little more than a 'consumer survey' in which the outcome is predetermined: ask the questions in such a way as to achieve the desired result. Let us suppose that those people had been persuaded to sit down with the artist and to look at the sculpture, unhurried and focused; let us suppose that they had been encouraged to express themselves rather than to supply a pat answer. Would they then have been all so brutally condemnatory?

In Cardew's view the concert failed for 'lack of a definite political line'. (He also noted that the public criticism after the event was dominated by what he describes in the Journals as 'Moving Being' negativism.[40]) There were too many contradictory ideas; a propaganda team 'has to accept a political line unitedly, and make propaganda for that line'. Yet for many of the students there seemed to be a contradiction at the heart of Cardew's political agenda. 'Because Marxism sees everything as changing, it is fundamentally opposed to dogma, to any insistence on "eternal truths", or a changeless "human nature"', he informed his Cardiff audience. And yet to achieve the ultimate goal the individual had to subscribe to the 'Party line', to suppress reservations and doubts, and to join up in a quasi-military campaign which demanded obedience and sacrifice. (In his introductory talk Cardew proclaimed: 'Socialist Construction can rise from the blazing ruins of Capitalism'.) For most, if not all the students, such a prodigious commitment was unthinkable; less heroic, less worthy perhaps, they would have gladly settled for a more assuasive, more indulgent *modus vivendi* in return for modest concessions to self-interest and self-delusion. The discontented individualist may be attracted to the romance of guerrilla warfare but he will reject the discipline of a regular army. That same individualist, in Cardew's view, might respond to the call for revolutionary activists but he would baulk at the idea of integration with the working class. In any case, at English art schools in the seventies 'individualism' was taken for granted and to prefix it with the epithet 'bourgeois' would have been met with blank incomprehension. Cardew discusses the idea in his report and I quote the passage in toto:

In the evening Tom (Hudson – Director of Studies) invites me to a Chinese meal with his two children. Conversation turns on China and the communist movement. The eldest boy is keen to understand the basis of the struggle against individualism. He realises that there are two sorts of individualism: 1) cultivation of uniqueness for your own ends, and 2) maximising your individual potential in the service of the community. The bourgeois justification for 1) (if cornered into expressing itself in social terms): if a man does well for himself, he will be in a better position to do good for society. (I think this is Tom's attitude). Against this many arguments should be brought. Prominently: anyone prosperous in a capitalist system is prosperous on a foundation of the hardship and suffering of others, and that doing well within a system inevitably means that your interest is identified with the preservation of that system, and to fight against the system would cause extreme psychological torture (something normal people don't willingly inflict on themselves). These are not really conclusive enough. It all echoes the Christian aphorism 'the rich man can more easily pass through the eye of a needle than enter the kingdom of heaven'. I'm obliged to leave this in the air.

Cardew identified artistic individualism (egoism) as a key issue, with the problem of the petit bourgeois artist's relationship to the revolution at its root. So that when Cardew proposed a performance of his arrangement of the 'Red Flag' there was 'considerable unwillingness'. In the report he writes: 'Various explanations are offered, mine being that many people are too snobbish to join in with a straightforward song with straightforward content; that is, they take a class stand against it.' By contrast, and predictably, the group took well to Paragraph 7 of *The Great Learning* and showed commitment in rehearsal. Cardew's usual insistence on criticising the work ('in relation to the revolution') after rehearsal would have created an atmosphere of confusion and resentment.

In his report Cardew draws comparisons between the kind of music-making which characterised the old Scratch Orchestra and that which serves the needs of the revolution. The low relief, ambient activity, the attitude of 'doing your own thing' and spontaneous participation, must give way to the new idea of sharp relief communication of political messages, of the 'Party line'. The problem was that neither the Scratch Orchestra nor the students at Cardiff possessed the musical skills to provide 'revolutionary music'. It was a task Cardew determined to address, on a longer term basis, with the Scratch Orchestra.

If the report demonstrated Cardew's political commitment, his *belief,* in a way which bespeaks other-worldly, redemptive, fundamentalist positions, it also referred back to a more recent artistic philosophy, both radical and secular: AMM and 'self-invention'. It, too, was all-consuming, revolutionary, though its agenda was less spectacular. But for the Party, and for Cardew, 'self-invention', or 're-moulding one's world outlook', as he stressed in his report, involved above all the necessity of integration with the working class. In the discussions with the students this prescription seems to have created considerable tension; Cardew identified a 'reactionary line (quite widespread) that integration with the working class is intensely difficult and unpleasant'. Noel Upfold (lecturer at Cardiff at the time) recalls that at one stage Cardew accused his audience (students and staff) of 'despising' the working class. Such an unforgiving stance, according to Upfold, served only to drive people back into entrenched positions.

From a political perspective, and in the context of a college of art, the brief which Cardew held in so uncompromising a fashion was quite unrealistic. Ironically, for one who was constantly reminding us all of the necessity of grasping what was happening in the 'real world', his own understanding and analysis of the real world of the art students was manifestly inadequate, his ideas mere 'wishful-thinking' which, to his credit, he acknowledged in his report. In the discussion after the concert, the 'confusion' which Cardew sought to dispel was for many students 'a necessary condition of our existence'. In the first paragraph of his report Cardew expresses his current orientation with artless elegance:

> This year, as a result of correctly giving political criteria precedence over artistic criteria in the various kinds of work that come my way, any difficulties have disappeared or been partially solved. Aimlessness, lack of motivation, fascination with abstractions – beauty, freedom, spontaneity – difficulties of communication, and of formulating vague notions of spiritual benefit; these considerations grow pale in the context of the task before us, namely the benefit of the people, the overthrow of imperialism and the decadent system of parliamentary democracy that supports it.

And later in the month we read in the Journals:

> Class stand The artist should think to himself: do I really want the revolution to come? (Or is it simply an 'inspiring' possibility to juggle with?) Genuinely desiring the revolution; this implies the correct class stand and a proletarian world outlook. Only from this point can the 'benefit of the people' really be considered. The people will benefit (in the long term) only through revolution. Making the revolution equals serving the people.[41]

This was now Cardew's position, clearly stated, and there would be no turning back.

Regarding the situation in the Scratch Orchestra Cardew's impatience was growing, and he even went so far as to consider delivering an ultimatum:

> I have drafted a resolution. If this resolution is supported by the majority of those present, it should be circularised to everyone forthwith. If it is not supported, then I'll resign from the orchestra. The only thing I would take with me would be the Prom of Paragraph 1, which I reserve the right to organise independently of the Scratch.[42]

No other member could have delivered such an ultimatum, and in such a peremptory manner, and got away with it.[43] The Resolution begins:

The Scratch Orchestra is suffering from four lacks.
Lack of organisation and leadership.
Lack of a dynamic strategy.
Lack of new ideas (compositions, projects, etc.).
Lack of a decent place to work.
Because of these lacks and the obvious impossibility of eliminating them by
any merely formal administrative measures it has been decided to put an end
to any regular activity of the Scratch Orchestra.

At a previous meeting on 23 May, the last at the George IV pub in Holmes Road,
Kentish Town, in northwest London, as part of the plan to relieve Cardew of most of
his administrative responsibilities, a committee of 'committed members' had been formed
(on a rotating basis) to ensure communication between members, to confirm dates,
times and venues of meetings and circularise information, to organise meetings by
providing an agreed agenda and chairman, to be responsible for publicity, to solicit
engagements, to sign cheques on behalf of the Scratch Orchestra, and to help collect
items of repertoire, documents, suggestions, etc. The initial list included Frank Abbott,
Tony Attwood, Cornelius Cardew, Brian Dennis, Bryn Harris, Alec Hill, Chris May, Michael
Parsons, Barbara Pearce, Jenny Robbins, Kevin Richards, Howard Skempton, Dave
Smith, and John Tilbury. A new, updated list contained some additions: Birgit Burkhardt,
Carole Finer, Sue Gittins and Hugh Shrapnel. Significantly, the committee contained
hardly any 'communists'; the majority might have been described as politically left-
inclined social democrats and socialists – that is, at that time, (lukewarm) supporters
of, or rather voters for, the Labour Party. However, there was considerable interest in the
Chinese revolution and Mao's writings; Cardew's enthusiasm for Chinese communism
would certainly have been an important influential factor and there were attempts to
forge cultural links with representatives of the Chinese government in London. A group,
'Composers Pool', was formed for the purpose of 'collective composition', and a
letter to a Chinese cultural association (possibly the cultural attaché), drafted by Michael
Chant, refers to the music from the Chinese ballet Red Detachment of Women which
had impressed members of the Composers Pool.[44] The letter had sought information
relating to the method of collective composition adopted for the ballet as well as
biographical information on a Chinese composer of revolutionary songs: Hsien Hsinghai.
The letter ends: 'One reason for our interest in Hsien Hsinghai is that his melodies sound
less foreign to our ears than many other revolutionary songs'.

Meanwhile, notwithstanding Cardew's reservations, individual Scratch Orchestra
members continued to make proposals for concerts and the rest of us would rally round.
Jenny Robbins' concert at the Conway Hall on 31 May still bore the stamp of the old,

pre-revolutionary Scratch and included her own *Symphony No.1* and *Melody in E minor*, two pieces by Tony Attwood, *Knaresborough Rhapsody* by Barbara Pearce, *Salts of Copper* by Greg Bright, and contributions from the Wood and Metal Band. The only distinguishing addition to Scratch Orchestra concerts at that time was Verdi's 'Va Pensiero' – thrown in for the sake of political correctness, a concession to the revolutionary imperatives which had now become irresistible.

Yet despite the debilitating lack of self-confidence, of direction, which had overtaken the Scratch Orchestra during this period, a letter dated 19 June 1972 from Anthony Perry of the North Kensington Amenity Trust to Victor Schonfield – who had organised the Scratch Orchestra's participation in a community event in the west London borough – paints a rather more encouraging picture:

> I am writing to thank you and all the members of the Scratch Orchestra most warmly for coming to play at the Westway Theatre last Saturday afternoon. It was a tremendous performance and very much enjoyed by everyone in the very large audience. I do hope that if we manage to keep the theatre open you may be able to come and play again in the future.

The Scratch Orchestra performance, entitled *In the Shadow of Westway*, was the brainchild of Tony Attwood; he and his wife had joined the Orchestra in 1971. It took place opposite Cambridge Gardens on a stage literally under the motorway, and clearly reflects the political agenda which by now informed most Scratch events. *In the Shadow of Westway* is a good example of the tradition period in which, while the approach to music-making is much the same, the music now accompanies an unambiguous political message: each of the thirteen sections is introduced by a collective shout – a slogan such as 'Why did they have to build the motorway', and 'No cars, No cars', alternating with militant drum rhythms. Much of the music is improvised, using 'cheap' instruments and a variety of sound effects and found objects, but the inclusion of renderings of folk and popular music – *Loch Lomond*, an anti-motorway song in D minor, Woody Guthrie's *Car, Car*, and the verse of *Over the Rainbow* – had by that time become a feature of Scratch events. One section comprises a series of statements: 'Some people are falling asleep on the motorway killing each other in fog; some people are falling asleep in factories worn out and tired by the slog; some schoolkids are falling asleep in their classrooms taught nothing that they can use', and so on. And finally: 'But some people together are fighting and struggling knowing and showing the way that this muddling mess that's called capitalism has risen and how to bring it all down.'

According to the programme the event also included an arrangement by Barbara Pearce, who was to remain a political stalwart, of Act V of the Scratch opera *Sweet*

FA, a choice which in itself demonstrates the paucity of political material at our disposal. The finale consisted of a trio of pieces of a typically scratch-like incongruity: the song 'Show me the way to go home', the hymn 'Abide with me', and a percussion improvisation. Nevertheless, as Mr. Perry's response makes clear, the Scratch Orchestra, yet again, and against all odds, with its quirkiness and disarming artlessness, had risen to the occasion.

By contrast the Id Group's visit to the Fine Art department at Portsmouth Polytechnic, 19 to 21 June, included an uncompromising programme of unyielding political music consisting of songs from China, Ireland, the US and Britain, as well as a song by Cardew denouncing the recently introduced Industrial Relations Act.[45] The concert ended with a rendering of the 'Internationale' (which was to become a customary feature of such presentations) and a heated discussion ensued involving, as usual, a disproportionate contribution from members of staff. This was almost certainly a re-run of the debate at the Cardiff College of Art: the same objections raised, the same sense of liberal outrage, and the same implacable response from the revolutionaries. An open letter to the Scratch Orchestra Id Group from Adrian Rifkin, lecturer in Art History, who had attended most of the events, voiced (from the 'left') a number of criticisms and misgivings in relation to the group's preparedness and effectiveness: some of the new words to the songs were 'patronising' in their attitude towards 'the masses'; and in the discussion comparisons drawn between the Maoists and the Jesuits by some of the staff (a common enough ploy by 'bourgeois liberals') could have been handled more adroitly, peremptorily – as could the question in relation to the 'scientific validity' of Marxism.[46] These were valid points but Rifkin's opportunistic challenge to Cardew to justify performing ('actively promote') 'elite bourgeois avant-garde music' (Steve Reich) around Europe was unfortunate: 'If they play it for interest, then can that interest be reconciled with Marxism? If for money, then how easily bought off?' In fact, Cardew was not 'actively promoting' the music; this was what the composer was doing. Cardew was *employed,* as a professional musician with the necessary skills. 'Interest' in the music did not come into it; nor for that matter did Marxism. Cardew had no regular employment at the time (unlike Rifkin) and had a family to support; presumably, he negotiated and received the 'going rate'.

All this continued to take its toll of Cardew's domestic life (the tenth anniversary of his marriage to Stella, 29 June 1972, is cursorily noted in the Journals); his total preoccupation with the political agenda meant that the family suffered considerable neglect even though (or perhaps because?) he attempted to involve them all in the 'culture' which the Party imposed. This included a pre-school nursery where, among other educational benefits, the infants were taught the basic tenets of (Maoist) political correctness.[47] The Party's demands were often unreasonable and always overriding;

this was a fact of life for the long-suffering families of Party members and supporters. At the same time, apart from any other financial considerations, the family had to be fed and clothed, and Cardew was attempting to meet these needs, precariously, as a jobbing musician. In June a talk on Stockhausen's *Refrain* for the BBC, again commissioned by Hans Keller (I discuss this in the chapter 'Stockhausen Serves Imperialism'), may have added to his revolutionary kudos but the payment would have been insignificant. In July concerts with Steve Reich in Spain, Ives' sonatas for violin and piano with János Négyesy, Feldman's *Pianos and Voices* and Cage's *HPSCHD* in Berlin would have been more lucrative but barely sufficient to make significant inroads into his overdraft. A letter to Josef Anton Riedl in Munich, dated 24 July, confirms the AMM split, informing Riedl, who presumably had expressed interest, that Cardew and Rowe now 'hardly ever' play improvised music. So that was another source of income which was now closed to him.

Cardew's notes for a Scratch meeting on 28 July include a number of revolutionary quotes and reminders intended no doubt to raise the morale of the troops and to galvanise them into revolutionary action:

> Revolution means the seizure of political power by the working people. A revolution is not a dinner party. A revolution is an insurrection, an act of violence by which one class overthrows another. Apply Marxism-Leninism-Mao Tse-Tung Thought in a living way to the problems of the present.

The violence and destructiveness of the language, its severity and remorselessness, was guaranteed, probably intended, to discourage the faint-hearted, the feeble-minded liberals; in fact, a considerable number of Scratch Orchestra members, including some of the original and most committed ones, had by now become disaffected and had drifted away or, more formally, like David Jackman, had sent a letter of resignation, in an embittered and angry tone:

> I resign from the Scratch Orchestra. I also withdraw any permission you think you might have to use any of my work in its performances. For me, the Orchestra's situation has become ridiculous and impossible. I've had enough.[48]

Others either disappeared, like Chris May – understandably, as he worked for the Home Office – or, in some cases, continued with their own artistic work on an individual basis. Regarding Cardew's 'conversion' there were chasms of dismay – and not only in the Scratch Orchestra. For many of his friends and colleagues his particular brand of politics was no less than a self-traducement, a blanket rejection of everything he had striven for and achieved. And he would have concurred with this. In his response to Jackman's letter of resignation, a day or two later, Cardew offered no concessions; characteristically, the points made go to the heart of the matter, with no hint of a willingness to compromise:

I don't want to win you over by flattery, but naturally I'm sorry that the orchestra should lose the support of someone who's musically strong. And I don't want to be a 'prophet of doom', but this strength will turn into a weakness (as it has in the case of Cage) if you just carry on with your art with the attitude that the rest of the world can go to the devil. The orchestra isn't in a ridiculous situation. You could say it is exposed to ridicule, in the sense that people taking a serious attitude are always open to ridicule, or that your position in the orchestra has become ridiculous and impossible. The orchestra's situation is good – it's grappling with change. Your phrase about 'withdrawing permission' struck a jarring note. 'Where do good ideas come from? Do they drop from the sky? No. Are they innate in the mind? No. They come from social practice' (Mao). Many factors, and many people, have contributed in the production of 'your work'. There is no basis for you to claim private property rights in it. If you've had good ideas and put them into a good and useful concrete form they will be used, and changed to suit changing needs. Whether you participate in and influence such use and such change is up to you.

Cardew's letter in turn elicited a lengthier, more considered though no less intractable letter from Jackman, in which he voiced the sentiments of probably a majority of Scratch Orchestra members at the time:

You're a great organiser of people, Cornelius, it's a genuine talent, but I'm not really interested in being organised anymore. For the sake of a musical situation perhaps yes, because I joined the Scratch etc. for the music, but for the sake of an alien political philosophy, no thanks. After all, I don't find it necessary now to impose my politics on others, why do you? [...] The difference between us is maybe this: you're interested in political power, whereas I'm more interested in personal liberation; you want absolute certainty whereas I just aim, in as much as I have any aims, for some happiness. We are and always have been pretty much divided. I don't see that changing. [...] I can't follow you into this awful, pious brand of socialism. That's just how it comes across to me. I've had my fill of religiosity in my own life, and I loathe it and react badly against it. Maybe that explains a few things.[49]

As far as we know Cardew did not continue the correspondence but given his own political agenda at that time it is not difficult to intuit his response to the issues of 'political power' and 'personal liberation' which Jackman raises. 'Whose personal liberation', he would have asked, 'and at what and whose cost?' And his own answer to these questions necessarily begged the thorny question of the exercise and, more insidiously, the *conferral of* (revolutionary) political power, with its implications and consequences.

In August a performance of self-accompanied songs at the Cardiff City Art Gallery prompted Cardew subsequently to write to Howard Skempton asking him to write a political song which he, Cardew, could add to his repertoire. There was also a performance of Cage's *HPSCHD* (in which Cardew had participated in Berlin the previous month) at the Roundhouse in London in which both Cardew and myself took part with an undisguised display of professional cynicism. I recall that Cardew's attitude was that of studied detachment; a job presented itself and he needed the money. Cage was understandably hurt: 'if they don't like it, why do they perform in it', he protested. It was a far cry from those heady days in the early sixties of commitment, comradeship and the pioneering spirit, when Cardew and I performed *Winter Music* at the Conway Hall in London and Cage performed in the first performance of *Octet '61* in Venice. And August was to witness further confrontation and conflict with the Establishment. The issue on this occasion was the projected performance of Paragraphs 1 and 2 of *The Great Learning* at the Royal Albert Hall as part of the Promenade concerts series.

The route to the Albert Hall performance was fraught with obstacles. Naturally, when the BBC originally approached Cardew about including part of *The Great Learning* at the Proms that year (1972), they had in mind the original version – indeed they were probably ignorant of the existence of a new, 'political' version. Cardew had no intention, however, of using the original version, a 'misunderstanding' which provoked an exchange of letters and a series of meetings between Cardew and BBC officials, including the Controller of Music, William Glock. Cardew kept all of this correspondence along with his own notes, which I chronicle below.

On 8 August Cardew presented the BBC with a programme note which in fact had been devised by the Id group. It read as follows:

'Works of art that do not meet the demands of the struggle of the broad masses can be transformed into works of art that do.' In the light of this statement by Mao Tse-tung we have embarked on the transformation of *The Great Learning*. The aim is to present the work in process of transformation rather than as a transformed object. Confucius' text has been newly translated; the music of

Paragraph 1 has been curtailed, slogans have been inserted to link the work with the current situation, and a short version of Paragraph 2 included at the end.

Paragraph 1: 'The Great Learning means raising your level of consciousness by getting right to the heart of a matter and acting on your conclusions. The Great Learning is rooted in love for the broad masses of the people. The target of the Great Learning is justice and equality, the highest good for all.'

Slogans: 'Make the past serve the present.' 'Revolution is the Great Learning of the present.' 'A revolution is not a dinner party; it is an insurrection, an act of violence by which one class overthrows another.' 'Apply Marxism-Leninism-Mao Tse-tung thought in a living way to the problems of the present.'

Paragraph 2: 'We know our stand and so our aim is set. Our aim being set we can appraise the situation. We appraise the situation and so we are relaxed and ready. We are relaxed and ready and so we can think ahead despite all danger. Thinking ahead despite all danger we shall accomplish our task.'

The 'stand' referred to in Paragraph 2 is interpreted as our class stand on the side of the working and oppressed people. The 'aim' referred to is the overthrow of monopoly capitalism and its replacement by socialism.

On 10 August Cardew received a letter from William Glock with the following objections: that the BBC had asked for and expected the original version of Paragraphs 1 and 2. There had been no indication beforehand that the 'transformed' version of the work would be performed. He concludes, 'I am afraid, therefore, that we cannot print the note you have sent, nor have slogans or banners; and, as I have said, we wish to ask for a performance of Paragraph 1 as it stood before the transformation you mention'. The next day Cardew penned a reply in which he stresses that 'it would be unthinkable for us to perform the piece in the original version'. He lists four reasons: firstly, the amount of work and effort invested in the transformation by a number of people; secondly, his personal obligation, having publicly attacked the works of the avant-garde, to apply the same criteria to his own works; thirdly, that historically, works of Art have always undergone developments independent of their creators and patrons and that he, Cardew, wishes to participate consciously in such developments; fourthly, that it is the responsibility of the artist to say to the audience what he believes to be true, that his attitude to *The Great Learning* had changed radically and he wished to communicate this. He ends:

Reading your letter I find no reasons are given against performing it (except that the BBC was not informed earlier, and that it has something to do with the political content). Obviously there are reasons, otherwise you would not have written to me. Perhaps you could let me know these reasons. I'll be at home most of Monday if you would prefer to telephone.

Of course, Cardew was right; the reasons for the BBC's objections were politically based; the text offended the liberal consensus that would have prevailed at the BBC at that time: art could not, should not carry a specific political message (other than a 'liberal' one), particularly of an extreme, revolutionary nature; an overt fascist message would likewise have been censored.[50] On 15 August a meeting with Glock took place; both parties, and in particular the BBC, were anxious to find a compromise. Glock insisted that the slogans should be omitted from the programme notes and performance, as well as the final paragraph elucidating the references to 'stand' and 'aim'. Cardew must have accepted this 'compromise', but after leaving the meeting felt, on reflection, that he had conceded too much and received too little. He phoned the BBC requesting that the following rejoinder should be included in the programme: 'The BBC, in accordance with its policy of not allowing the Proms to be used as a political platform, has removed the political content from the programme note and the performance'. It should also be borne in mind that Cardew was conscious of the fact that he had to justify whatever agreement he had struck with the BBC to a militant Id Group who were in no mood to accept any compromises at all. The next day the BBC phoned Cardew to say that the sentence was unacceptable and could not be included in the programme. Why did the BBC, in its illiberal wisdom, feel the need to dig in and adopt a high-handed attitude towards Cardew's request? Did they suspect Cardew's motives? Was it perhaps an attempt on his part to expose the liberal image which the BBC so assiduously cultivated of itself? Would the BBC not be accused of an unyielding authoritarianism? Would it not, at least, cause liberal eyebrows to be raised?

The Id Group's response was swift and uncompromising: that if this acknowledgement by the BBC was not included in the programme then it, the Id Group, would leaflet the Prom audience. This threat was conveyed to the BBC who immediately convened another meeting between Cardew and three BBC officials. Fearful that the BBC would invoke the contract (although if the concert had been cancelled all fees would still have been payable), Cardew asked Victor Schonfield to accompany him at the meeting. It was agreed that the proposed rejoinder should be replaced by the following footnote: 'By agreement between the composer and the BBC the political content has been removed from the above Note, written by the Scratch Orchestra Ideological Group, and from this performance.' Thus, the BBC's liberal image remained untarnished; there had been no intimidation, no arm-twisting; the composer himself had 'agreed' with the BBC on the course of action taken and an honourable settlement had been reached. In fact, a subsequent edition of The Listener quoted all the political slogans, together with a report of an attack on the BBC by Member of Parliament Anthony Wedgwood Benn, on the grounds that it was undemocratic.[51]

Not everybody in the Id group was happy with the arrangement, especially with the agreement that the programme notes should be divested of all political content; the performance was still in jeopardy. However, by a small majority a vote was cast in favour of participation. Bryn Harris claims that there had also been a degree of deception on Cardew's part:

> In order to save the show Cor led the orchestra to believe that he had fought hard to keep them (the banners) and that the agreement between the BBC and him included an obligation on their part to inform the audience of the censorship imposed. On the basis of the information from Cor we agreed not to leaflet the queues concerning that same censorship.
>
> In fact, there was no statement at the Royal Albert Hall, though a brief allusion to an agreement to exclude political slogans was made during the broadcast introduction. Many of the politically conscious members of the Scratch Orchestra felt that Cor had sold out in order to get a Prom performance. While, in retrospect, such an attitude was ridiculously dogmatic, at the time it effectively destroyed Cor's remaining hold on the Scratch Orchestra's loyalty.[52]

And what of the new version itself? In stark contrast to the first performance of Paragraph 2 at the Roundhouse in 1969 – 'a glorious sprawling cacophony of singing and drumming lasting over an hour, with groups positioned all round the hall and balcony',[53] the new version lasted a mere twelve minutes and the number of drummers was reduced to four (no doubt to ensure that the revolutionary message of the text would be both audible and comprehensible), thereby negating one of the original inspirations behind Cardew's initial conception of the piece – the idea of striving and failing ('failing better'), just as the monks in Michael Parson's account had failed to overcome the sound of the waterfall.

> Cardew hopes in this way to clarify the nature of the violence in the music which, he says, it took him some time to recognise. It is not, he says, a generalised, chaotic and fortuitous violence (this is how he now views the opulence of the first performance of the work), but a controlled and focused violence as it is exercised by the revolutionary class against the ruling class.[54]

On 18 March, in his 1973 Journal, Cardew writes dismissively of the venture: 'Its like trying to convert a sponge into a stone by drying it more and more. You get quite a hard little object, but you'll never break a window with it.' Significantly (but was it knowingly?), such a remark reflects negatively on Chairman Mao's own dictum ('Works of art that do not meet the demands of the struggle of the broad masses can be transformed into works of art that do') which had originally furnished the ideological justification for the 'transformation' of *The Great Learning*.

This was effectively Cardew's final involvement in the work; thereafter it would simply be *used*, when and where appropriate, as a 'negative' example of the degeneration into which the avant-garde had sunk. However, in an interview a few years later in which the composer/journalist Adrian Jack asked him which versions of Paragraphs 1 and 2 he would now prefer, Cardew replied:

> The original, because it engages the participation particularly of the players in the situation that existed then – which was the formation of the Scratch Orchestra. That was a genuine real life situation and in no way artificially constructed; through that experience it already shatters their notion of the conventional establishment. And because it's a loose organic kind of experience and not a tight frightening one, it gives you a more flexible basis to do future work on. If people have participated in that kind of activity they can feel the satisfactions there are in it and also the dissatisfactions there are in it – which are many. They can express what they feel about these reactions and on the basis of that move on to something else. I don't really believe that a bourgeois piece of music can be reformed. You can only adapt it, and the adaptation certainly wouldn't be better than the original.[55]

For those of us in the political camp – that is, the Id Group, still riven with western liberal doubt and scepticism, Cardew's idealism, as exemplified in *The Great Learning*, had been severely compromised by historical ignorance and political naivety. In relation to the Confucian text he had failed to ask the obvious questions: what 'actions' does a government 'unify', and to what ends? What are the 'evils' a government seeks to restrain and on what basis are 'penalties' instituted? 'Idealism', as we understood it in the Scratch Orchestra, could only function in an 'ideal' society, and the tribute-paying, feudal society which Confucius inhabited fell too far short even of our own imperfect, projected Western models. By the time of the Promenade Concert performance it was a position that Cardew shared with the Scratch Id Group and during the seventies, *The Great Learning* was destined to become the subject of scathing criticism by the composer himself, both publicly, at concert performances, and in self-immolatory talks and articles.

Notes and references

1   CC, from a report of his visit to Cardiff College of Art, 3 June 1972.
2   For some readers, and in particular those for whom the history of AMM is an intriguing subject, Keith Rowe's extreme politicization and subsequent lapse will in itself be a matter for speculation and conjecture, and will no doubt be raised and debated in Brian Olewnick's forthcoming biography.
3   Monk, p.122.
4   Cardew always opposed the theory, still used to discredit and tarnish the reputations of dissidents (in relatively recent times in the UK: Member of Parliament Tony Benn and the miners' leader Arthur Scargill), which, by psychologising (subjectivising) non-conformist behaviour, purported to explain opposition to the status quo (belonging to radical political parties, union militancy, simply holding radical, anti-establishment views) as the result of character flaws, mental aberration, problems in childhood, etc. Ironically, the treatment of dissidents in the former Soviet Union was criticised and attacked by the very same organs (the press) which sanctioned and often initiated such treatment in their own country.
5   *Literature and Ideology* was a quarterly magazine begun in 1969 and published by the Canadian and Irish Maoists. Its general aims are stated on the inside cover: '*Literature and Ideology* is sponsored by the Necessity for Change Institute of Ideological Studies, Dublin and Montreal, as part of the world-wide struggle against imperialism. The Institute wishes to encourage progressive intellectuals to participate consciously in the discussion and analysis of the political and social role of literature, art, and criticism. *L & I* welcomes articles from its readers and invites them to organize Study Groups in their areas. Ths publication does not intend to provide opportunities for exercising self-interest or self-cultivation.'
6   Like Cardew I also came to recognise the significance of selectivity and exclusion in the content of my secondary education in the late forties/early fifties. The fact of the exploitation and oppression of people around the world could not be hidden from us although it was rarely, if ever, a subject for discussion. At our respective schools, Kings College Canterbury and Latymer Upper in west London, as I recall, debates were either facetious or abstract; a detached, superior attitude was nurtured, where being more clever was more important than being more truthful. Cardew was right to criticise his education; and yet certain useful tools could be, and were, acquired – not least in order to withstand and survive the fierce, cut-throat *modus operandi* of bourgeois intellectual life.
7   Interestingly, in his captivating little book, *The Book of Tea*, Kakuzo Okakura refers to 'the communism of northern China which expressed itself in Confucianism'. (Boston & London: Shambhala,1993), p.37.
8   We can identify a personality trait here which he inherited from his father and which in the early years was nurtured and stimulated in his relationship to the Cornish landscape and nature (and, I suppose, expressed itself in some of his more daring escapades at school with the 'stuntmen'); it was as if everything he did had to contain an element of risk and danger. 'When a catastrophe tends to inevitability one should relax, and build up the strength to survive it; only when the chances are even should we struggle to avoid the crisis', he once wrote.
9   Hardial Bains (b. 15 August 1939; d. 24 August 1997) was the founder and leader of the Communist Party of Canada (Marxist-Leninist) until his death. Born in India into a communist

family in the Punjab, Bains became a member of the youth wing of the Communist Party of India (CPI). Dismayed by Nikita Khrushchev's criticisms of Stalin at the Twentieth Party Congress he broke with the CPI when it supported Khrushchev.

10   From the *Necessity for Change* pamphlet reprinted by the Leicester Student Movement for the Necessity for Change Institute of Ideological Studies (English and Irish branches) in 1972.

11   'I cannot help feeling that this was a rare period in which Cornelius was catching up with events rather than being at the forefront.' Eddie Prévost, email communication to JT, 9 January 2003.

12   The stigmatic 'petit bourgeois' appears frequently in the latter part of this book. Marx characterised it as a vacillating class, aspiring upwards to the ranks of the bourgeoisie proper but in reality being too close to the proletariat for comfort; individual members 'are being constantly hurled down into the proletariat by the action of competition' Marx and Engels wrote prophetically in the *Communist Manifesto*. In modern times and in a more complex and mobile society 'petit bourgeois' reflects a category to which it might be said that millions belong without demur – psychologically and ideologically less sure of the desirability of aspiring to join the rich, yet at the same time fearful of the consequences of individual 'failure'. As for the petit bourgeois Scratch Orchestra, there was little, if any, upward mobility; rather it would be more accurate to describe us as aspiring downwards.

13   From On reading Lenin on Marx. Jrnl. 25 January 1972 [p.27.] Cardew's war-like metaphor recalls the functions of music in mythology, which had always fascinated him; in ancient cultures the social function of music embraced war as well as peace and domestic love and harmony; the Great (Scottish) Highland Pipes (also known as 'war pipes'), for example, are reputed to be able to raise the morale of the Scottish soldiery whilst at the same time 'striking terror' into the hearts of the enemy. The English State called them weapons and treated pipers as armed troops if captured.

14   It is unlikely that at this stage Cardew was familiar with the Brecht/Eisler songs, although there are some hand-written lyrics in the Journals, presumably his own, which bear a strong resemblance to one of the songs from *The Mother*: 'Im Gefängnis zu singen'. And at the end of the lyrics three slogans are added: The Joy of productive work. Music as organized violence. Music for mass production.

15   Matchless Recordings MRCD45. (*CCR*)

16   This notion of the heresy of alleviating rather than intensifying (thereby bringing revolt closer) the condition of the oppressed is the theme of Brecht's *Measures Taken* which Cardew was later to work on with his Songs for Our Society class at Goldsmiths' College.

17   From a letter from CC to Hanne Boenisch, dated 12 January 1972.

18   Jrnl. 24 January 1972.

19   Jrnl.1971/2, [p.28].

20   According to Harry Gilonis EMC did have a little stall, for a time, in Dillons University Bookshop.

21   Note on a Scratch Rehearsal dated 4 January 1972.

22   Letter to JT, 13 October 1999.

23   Cardew remained sceptical of its viability opining that the previously criticised material (presumably his own version) had simply been 're-shuffled' without any real improvement. Some of his criticisms were of a technical nature, relating to tessitura and vocal arrangements,

and with the aim of encouraging further rehearsal and public performance.

24   I recall teaching at the Falmouth School of Art in the mid-seventies where it had been proposed that the installation of a sauna bath or an orgone box could be the answer to creative listlessness and depression amongst students, rather than my own prescription of several doses of Mao Tse-tung Thought. My presence there was probably regarded as no more than an unwelcome irritant. Mercifully for the staff, and many of the students, my visits were intermittent and relatively brief.

25   From Cardew's notes on the Bradford College of Art project in the 1971/72 Journals.

26   Jrnl. 1 March 1972.

27   I am referring here to his public *persona*. In his private, one-to one relationships Cardew was often conciliatory and empathetic; he was always a good listener. But his loyalty to the Party and the Party line was never compromised.

28   Jrnl. 21 February 1972.

29   Notes from the Id Group meeting on 20 March 1972.

30   Jrnl. 7 March 1972. In passing we may note the deterministic equation of 'inevitability' with 'desirability', a philosophical can of worms which, with my limited knowledge, I am unwilling to open. However, it is a question frequently raised, or at least implied, in the remaining pages of this book, particularly in relation to the status of 'proletarian revolution'.

31   The necessity for 'forward-thinking' Marxism, in relation to Maoist ideology, is exemplified anecdotally by a remark made by a Party comrade to Stella Cardew and her daughter Emily on a visit to their house in Barnes on 21 March 1972. Informed of Scratch Orchestra member Alec Hill's talk on Marx's early writings the comrade commented: 'That's Marxism backwards. What you need is Marxism forwards.'

32   Letter from Tom Johnson to CC, dated 22 March 1972. Johnson was also an influential music critic: The collection of his *Village Voice* pieces, *The Voice of New Music* (Eindhoven: Het Apollohuis, 1989) contains his sympathetic review of *Nature Study Notes*, pp.139-141.

33   The Matusow case had already been aired, somewhat comically, during the *Burdocks* concert which Matusow attended. I myself still retain the bizarre image of Matusow angrily pursuing Scratch Orchestra member, Bernard Kelly, around the hall, stumbling in and out and over rows of chairs and tables and instruments. Apparently Kelly had made a public allusion to Matusow's activities during the fifties and the American had taken exception. The *AMM at the Roundhouse* CD refers to Matusow as 'an ex-patriot American, he fled to London in the 1960s [...] running from [...] his involvement with anti-communist crusader Senator Joseph McCarthy'.

34   Letter from CC to Alec Hill, dated 30 March 1972.

35   Some years earlier, probably in the late sixties, Cardew had photocopied pages from Plato's *Republic*. Various arrows inserted at certain sections of the text seem to indicate ideas which he felt were of particular relevance and importance for him at the time. In his zealous attacks on popular culture during the seventies he may well have had Socrates' warnings, as expressed in Book 4 to Adeimantus, in mind: 'We have to keep new sorts of music away from us as a danger to society; because forms and rhythms in music are never changed without producing changes in the most important political forms and ways; at least, so Damon says, and I am with him'. Such ideas were to lie comfortably with Cardew's Maoism.

36   I recall that it was invariably the (Party's) inevitable reference to Stalin's 'inestimable contribution' as war leader and the 'heroism and sacrifices of the peoples of the Soviet Union in the fight against Fascism' which would serve, if temporarily, to silence criticism – an evocation which resonated comfortably with many of Cardew's generation who had lived through the war as children and for whom Joe Stalin had been a liberator, a comrade-in arms.

37   From 'Towards an Ethic of Improvisation', p.xx. (*CCR*)

38   Jrnl. undated, but entered during his stay in Cardiff in May 1972.

39   From the Cardiff report, dated 3 June 1972.

40   Moving Being, a multi-media performance company, was based in the Chapter Arts Centre in Cardiff for ten years. Presumably, one or more of their members were present at the concert and their contribution to the discussion had in some way irritated Cardew.

41   Jrnl. 20 June, 1972.

42   From a typewritten circular from CC to the Scratch Orchestra, dated simply May 1972.

43   Nobody I have spoken to can recall such an ultimatum ever being formally delivered.

44   The Composers' Pool was Michael Chant's idea; the Pool composed and performed its own material. A concert took place at the Commonwealth Institute for which they rehearsed at the College of St. Mark and St. John in the Fulham Road. It was a short-lived enterprise.

45   The Industrial Relations Act (1971) was legislation by the Tory Government of 1970-74. It was overtly hostile to trade union practice and provoked what was then one of the biggest demonstrations that London had ever seen.

46   I believe I was present at the event although I confess to being able to recall precious little, except, dimly, that one member of staff, in true liberal tradition, suggested (during a break) that what we should be discussing was the nature, that is, both the bad and the good, of Capitalism – a proposal which was greeted with scorn by those Id Group members and their supporters who happened to be within earshot.

47   One might argue that aspects of his Marxism-Leninism echoed the ideological moulding of his public school background, with its rituals, its Jesuitical predisposition to correctness, and its inculcation of a sense of duty and sacrifice.

48   From a letter from DJ to CC, dated 28 July 1972.

49   From a letter from DJ to CC, dated 1 August 1972.

50   At that time the Communist Party of England (Marxist-Leninist) would have argued that the 'fascist' message is pervasive in contemporary bourgeois culture, and insidiously present within liberal ideology where it is free to spread its message protected by the cloak of liberal tolerance and respectability.

51   At the time, Cardew and the majority of the Scratch Orchestra's 'political' members still believed in the ultimate 'reasonableness' of the powerful. However, experience teaches us that such 'agreements' are worthless; the noble principles of probity and 'fair-play' can be jettisoned by the Establishment without qualms. The liberal, mantric insistence on the *fact* of freedom from censorship in Western society in general, which has been transparently exposed in a number of cases, demonstrates an unquestioning, ideological conformity to an accumulation and concentration of shared tenets of which 'artistic freedom' is a particularly potent example. In 1984, in a *cause célèbre,* the Arts Council withdrew its grant from a performance of an adaptation of Brecht/Eisler's *The Mother* by John Arden, Margaretta D'Arcy and myself on the grounds of our support for 'terrorism' (that is, Irish republicanism).

52 Undated letter from BH to JT around May 1987. Harris himself later changed his mind, suggesting that Cardew was probably right; it was better that the work should be performed at the Proms than not at all.
53 From a review by Tim Souster in *The Listener*, 17 August 1972.
54 Ibid.
55 'Cornelius Cardew, interviewed by Adrian Jack.' From *Music and Musicians*, May 1975, p.32. (*CCR*)

(*CCR*) Also found in *Cornelius Cardew A Reader*

Cornelius Cardew a life unfinished

14

The Munich Olympics and Austria 1972

In 1972 the Organizing Committee of the Munich Olympic Games invited a number of artists and performers from a wide spectrum of the arts, including the Scratch Orchestra, to provide various forms of expression of contemporary artistic practice during the course of the Games; the Spielstrasse, a two hundred and eighty meter-long walk along the shore of the Olympic lake provided thirty performance stages for actors, musicians, dancers, pantomimists, circus performers and artists. Following on from Munich the Scratch Orchestra was also invited by two young Austrian concert promoters, Gerhard and Maria Crepaz, from Solbad Hall (near Innsbruck) in the Tirol, who boldly took advantage of the Scratch Orchestra's relative proximity to promote a series of Scratch events in their home town.[1]

The tour was organized by Carole Finer and myself. Around thirty-five of us, including two drivers and several children, met the coach at the Embankment entrance of Charing Cross station at 6.30 pm on Friday, 25 August and took the 11.30pm ferry from Dover. We had equipped ourselves with tents and various necessities; camping facilities had been arranged beforehand with the local authorities. Eating would be organized on a communal basis and generally life on the camp sites was to be run on similar lines to our previous tours in Cornwall and North Wales.

It was already dark when we arrived at the field allocated to us a few kilometres outside Munich. As we unpacked our camping equipment, and families and individuals began to stake their claim in various parts of the field, it soon became obvious that cows, rather than campers, were the regular occupants of the land. Undeterred we approached our tasks gingerly and with concentration; on completion an atmosphere of relief and conviviality pervaded the site and we retired to our tents in good spirits. The next day our morale received a further boost when we learnt that beer brewed by the monks at a nearby monastery was available at a modest price.

In Munich we had been allocated six performances on the Spielstrasse, a performance of Christian Wolff's *Burdocks* and a recording of a Scratch piece for Bavarian Radio, and an outdoor concert at a Polytechnic. Since our repertoire was still drawn, in the main, from earlier Scratch Orchestra material, the new political agenda was inadequately represented; there was an embarrassing lack of what the Id Group would have described as 'progressive' material. So, in a sense, we reverted to type, into the role of stereotypical Anglo-Saxon (and Irish) eccentrics and 'entertainers' with (self) parody and satire much to the fore. One of the six concerts consisted of arrangements of broadly popular music by the Wood and Metal band, Verdi's 'Va Pensiero' (one of the few 'progressive' items in our repertoire), and, by contrast, Irishman Bernard Kelly's impersonation of the 'final appearance' of the singer Elizabeth Schwarzkopf. Another 'humorous' act which left the mainly German audience perplexed was my own impersonation of the English entertainer George Formby, known for his saucy songs which he accompanied himself on the ukulele. On this occasion I sang 'When I'm cleaning windows', and was accompanied by Dave Russell on guitar and Carole Finer on banjo. There were also performances of a Handel sonata and some Irish jigs, as well as an improvisation. And it was here on the Spielstrasse that Hugh Shrapnel's endearing Wood and Metal Band gave its last performance; Shrapnel recalls the stark contrast between the surfeit of international glitz and commercialism (with huge banners along the boulevard proclaiming 'Life is Competition') and the ill-sorted and scruffy ranks of the Scratch Orchestra with our assemblage of strange and primitive objects, and diverse instruments and 'equipment' in various stages of disrepair. Yet the Wood and Metal band was popular with the Spielstrasse audiences who seemed to find its 'people's music' a welcome relief from the unrelenting encroachments and violations of renderings of current pop hits which saturated the environs. On another occasion a truncated 'Promenade Concert' (political) version of Paragraph 2 of *The Great Learning* was performed, as well as some political songs and improvisations. Michael Chant's *Beautiful Music* and excerpts from *Sweet FA* were also included.

If Cardew disapproved of these incursions into the world of light entertainment, and I am certain that he did, he sensibly did not express his feelings publicly at the time. Nor did he approve the strong anarchic tendency which had always enlivened Scratch events; but even now he still accepted every (or nearly every) transgression. Perhaps he did not want to drive out the devils for fear of disturbing the Scratch angels, some of whom had rediscovered an old lease of life and were enjoying and profiting from a feeling of imaginative self-determination – quirky, whimsical, untrammelled by threats of political censure and excommunication. Generally, there was a feeling of relief after the tensions and harrowing events which had gripped the Scratch Orchestra at home. Despite the ongoing political agenda there was the excitement and challenge of negotiating a different cultural environment; there were new experiences to be relished, and the inevitable lapse from time to time, though not often, into holiday mode. The Scratch Orchestra was in a stage of transition; it was in the process of jettisoning much of its repertoire, although a good deal survived simply by default (there was nothing else we could perform) and continued to appear in programmes in Munich, in Solbad Hall, and back in England in the following months. There was already a vague perception of the need for a more popular, and therefore more accessible, style of music, but imbued with revolutionary sentiments and ideas. The sources for the music, it was believed, would only be found within popular culture, including, and perhaps especially, that of the past. Within the Left generally the relationship between art and politics had always been a contentious issue. For some political groups rock music was perceived as an ally; it served to create a 'modern' image, it might even boost membership. For the Maoists contemporary pop music was too associative of bourgeois consumer culture; the messages it carried were essentially and indeed, in the Party's view, *consciously* reactionary.

A performance of Christian Wolff's *Burdocks* at the radio station in Munich brought the Scratch Orchestra sharply back to earth, provoking a furore of protest and condemnation from what would (still) have been considered at the time an unexpected source: the American avant-garde, in the persons of John Cage, Morton Feldman and David Tudor, expressed their combined opinion that the Scratch Orchestra's 'interpretation' of *Burdocks* was a travesty. At a certain point during the performance an incensed Feldman rose to his feet to denounce the performance: 'This is not the music of Christian Wolff' he informed the audience (or words to that effect – nobody can agree on the precise expression). There was considerable confusion, and excitement, at the end of the concert; sensing that this event had the makings of a *cause célèbre* people were taking photographs and gathering around the leading protagonists. The American pianist/composer Frederic Rzewski was also there but had adopted a more neutral stance. Scratch Orchestra member Richard Ascough sought out Cage, Feldman and Tudor for clarification of their objections and attempted to deal with them, where appropriate, in the light of his own involvement with the work. At the conclusion of his discussion Ascough re-joined a group of Scratch members and recounted the conversation he had had with the Americans. This was recorded on tape and what follows is taken in its entirety from this source.

The musical incident to which Feldman and Cage had taken particular exception, and which had driven Feldman to his public denunciation, was the inclusion of folk songs in number V of the ten pieces which constitute *Burdocks*.

The score consists of six 'wheels', each of which is divided by a number of 'spokes' between which are various instructions/suggestions for interpretation of a more or less explicit nature. There are numbers on spokes and on dotted lines between wheels

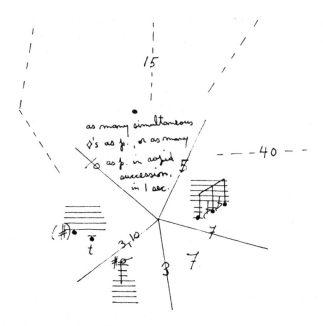

for which instructions are given. However, for the one instance of a number *between* spokes, the number 7, no instructions are given. Michael Parsons was the Scratch member responsible for this particular piece for the Cecil Sharp performance earlier in the year and in a circular to the participants he exhibits a considerable meticulousness of approach. With reference to number 7 he suggests seven notes, or sounds, or events – followed by two question marks implying, perhaps, the possibility of a more radical interpretation. Carole Finer decided to perform seven folk songs (including a dogged rendering of 'Charlie is my Darling') on the banjo, an instrument which she played passably well and which to this day she studies and practices conscientiously. Richard Ascough insisted there was nothing in the score to invalidate Finer's interpretation, whereupon Cage, Feldman and Tudor began to go through the score to find Wolff's instructions relating to number. When this failed to materialise Tudor concluded that there was a missing page which explained all these symbols. (No such page exists.) Cage then expressed disapproval of Bernard Kelly's interpretation (the reading (aloud) of a poem) of the last piece, number X, which states simply: 'Flying, and possibly crawling or sitting still.' 'Try, try again. Don't give up. Yes you can. I can't. You can. Take it easy' Kelly recited, in a section echoing Beckett. Cage objected (presumably) on the grounds that 'reading aloud a poem' was not in the score. Ascough recalled that in the London performance there had been a spoken 'commentary' (by Scratch member Sue Gittins) to which the composer, who was present, made no objection. Nor did the Americans approve of the sixth piece, which was conducted. Cage insisted that it should have been in different tempi. Ascough pointed out, correctly, that the score indicated that 'each player can (but need not) proceed in his own tempo'. The Scratch Orchestra chose to play number VI collectively, in the same tempo. Changing tack Feldman and Cage opined there that had been no intensity in the Scratch Orchestra performance; while the New York version had been very beautiful, the Scratch Orchestra's rendering was very bad. They seemed to dislike the relaxed approach to the piece (although some members of the audience expressed their appreciation of the Scratch attitude to music-making). The Americans insisted that it was not in the spirit of Wolff's music and furthermore it was suggested that Cardew and I had betrayed our 'special relationship'(!) with Christian Wolff. In effect they condemned the whole performance.

Right at the beginning of the concert, indeed before a sound had been uttered, feathers would have been ruffled. In his introduction (in German, but the gist of which would have been conveyed to the Americans) Cardew did not pull his punches; in particular his remarks concerning the 'ivory tower' condition of the avant-garde in general, and specifically in relation to the role of Cage, Feldman and Wolff, would have created a discomforting and alienating atmosphere. Clearly, this was the background, psychologically, against which the Americans had vented their anger on both Cardew and myself. Perhaps the most telling point emerged at the end of the discussion when Ascough, with a refreshing frankness, suggested that because of the profound debate that was ongoing in the Scratch Orchestra – which for many members had necessitated reassessments of (ideological) positions which hitherto had been taken for granted, and which had resulted in considerable soul-searching in respect of one's artistic activity – there may well have been differing levels of commitment from the participants. The seriousness of their situation was such that some members of the Scratch Orchestra were proceeding, in both art and life, riven by doubt, in a state of limbo; the direct (and often 'professional') commitment to the work of art had been supplanted by a recognition of a profound and stubborn scepticism, by an even more demanding and challenging commitment to a refusal of self-delusion: art could not simply be given a *carte blanche*. For some of us the questions about art had become unanswerable because the answers were unthinkable. Was then such a condition inimical to a meaningful and ethical engagement with art? Should the sceptic simply turn away leaving art to the believers? According to Ascough the Americans seemed to reject the idea of anything in transition, of flux and uncertainty, or rather they appeared to deny that such a condition could legitimately influence the *meaning* of the activity of making music. Ascough could not understand their objection, their refusal or inability to recognise the subtlety of the matter in hand. It all seemed lost on them. (Ironically, *Burdocks* itself was a transitional piece in Wolff's compositional development. 'Burdocks, sounds, can be unruly and messy.')[2]

Here I believe we are touching upon the essence of the divide which separated Cage and Cardew. Time and again Cage expressed a concern for the *inviolability* of the score, that is, of the work of art. This led to a protectiveness and a consequent preference for professionals, 'experts', rather than, say, a ragbag of students available at a given venue at a given time. In contrast, Cardew's music-making was based on the acceptance of human vulnerability, fragility and imperfection, of contingency. Whereas with Cage generally little or no spontaneous expression was permitted during performance, Cardew never denied the performer's history and background. He never exerted backdoor control whether by a mathematical series or by chance methods, but preferred to focus a performer's creativity on problems to be solved. True, Cage relished the charm of contingency in relation to nature, but seemed unwilling or unable to extend this to the wayward, foolhardy, fallible and unpredictable behaviour of human beings. What Cage offered us was a *conditional* freedom, freedom on his terms – the freedom politicians offer: do this and you will be free. It is therefore unlikely that Cage (or Feldman and Tudor for that matter) had ever worked with, made music with, (extra)ordinary people from all walks of life on a regular basis, and systematically, in the way Cardew had.

In an article in *Tempo* magazine at the end of 1973, by which time Cardew had renounced the avant-garde, Michael Nyman compares Cage with Cardew:

Through his evident isolation as a composer, Cage is still taking the steps towards the socialization of music. For Cardew, these steps have already been taken: the Scratch Orchestra, a successful experiment in such social music-making, lived and died while Cage was still scratching his head. [...]

Cage's current work with untrained musicians is conducted largely on the basis of the visiting guest composer spreading his gospel among students for a few days before moving on to another 'star' performance of one of his solo works. (In *M* Cage writes that 'Fame has its advantages. Anything you do gets used. Society places no obstacles. Also you become of some help to those who aren't famous yet.') Cardew, on the other hand, sank his individuality into conceiving, founding and, to some extent, shaping the Scratch Orchestra, adjusting his 'composer's individuality' to the varied needs and capabilities of a very mixed group of musicians, many of them untrained.[3]

The concert in Munich, despite the criticisms, was joyful, direct, disparate, and informal (coughs and sneezes were not suppressed) in the way that all Scratch Orchestra concerts were. (Of course, much of the preparation had been undertaken earlier in the year for the performance at the Cecil Sharp House in London.) There was much Scratch spontaneity and ingenuity (a limitless bestowal of Scratch imagination more than compensated for a limited instrumental range) along with a good measure of intelligence; the extant recording of the event demonstrates that the individual pieces were clearly distinguishable. Ascough recalled the parting remarks: when Cage said he would like to hear some real Maoist music Ascough disarmingly invited him to a performance of the Scratch opera *Sweet FA* which, fortunately for the Scratch Orchestra, Cage was unable to attend.[4] In fact, in just a week or two he was to hear some 'Maoist music' at a concert given by Cardew and myself in Venice, an account of which is given in the following pages.

The incident in Munich, and in particular Carole Finer's contentious use of folk music and the reaction it provoked, was reported to Christian Wolff some time later. He refers to this in a 1991 interview with Cole Gagne: '…I thought about it and discovered where that would have been possible. It wasn't recorded, so I haven't heard it and can't tell you, but I suspect that it's perfectly okay; especially given the nature of that particular group, that it would have been very beautiful.'[5] Elsewhere in *MusikTexte* Wolff describes the genesis of *Burdocks* and his involvement in the Scratch Orchestra's London performance:

I had an image in my mind (before having heard them) of the Scratch Orchestra, a varied community of musicians (classical, folk, experimental, jazz, et cetera), professional and amateur and non-musicians, joined in a populist-anarchist spirit.[…] I had also been affected by hearing a recording of Ba-Benzele Pygmy music, quasi improvised, polyphonically, by a whole community.[6]

Burdocks […] is an orchestra piece. It's a large group piece. It can be done by fairly few players, but the London performance especially used almost forty players. And that was a very different kind of situation. I thought it was fantastic. I mean it's one of the finest performances I've ever had.[7]

Nearly all the performers in Munich would have taken part in that performance at the Cecil Sharp House in March 1972 and were therefore extremely well acquainted with the work. David Tudor's insightful observation (previously quoted) also reflects the situation in the Scratch Orchestra where invariably there were 'small kids around'.

On 4 September the Scratch Orchestra left Munich for Solbad Hall in the Austrian Tirol. There was no fixed itinerary but we had been informed in advance by the organisers that there would probably be four or five concerts. The people of Solbad Hall, a homely, beautiful old medieval town some ten kilometres from Innsbruck, were taken completely by surprise. Catholic, deeply conservative, and with little knowledge of cultural developments abroad (even in neighbouring countries) – student occupations, debates, the political turmoil of the late sixties had all somehow passed it by. For some of its inhabitants such a state of affairs was the source of considerable frustration and resentment. To expose the obtuseness and hypocrisy which reigned at all levels of society, to cut through the absurdities which beset them in every area of life, to somehow circumvent or even to counter the prevailing ethos, Gerhard Crepaz, his wife Maria and their friends decided to initiate their own radical cultural programme. A small measure of financial support was squeezed from the local authorities and they then set about contacting and persuading interesting foreign and home-grown artists, known and unknown, to visit their town and to present their work in whatever form they wished: the emphasis was, and still is, on informality. The Scratch Orchestra's visit was part of this programme.

As in Munich the Scratch Orchestra was offered camping facilities, but in Solbad Hall a municipal camping site with a swimming pool was provided. The centre of town was within walking distance, the weather was good and the general atmosphere congenial. The first concert, which took place in the Pfarrkirche, consisted of Paragraphs 2 and 7 from *The Great Learning*. Such was the favourable impression that the work and its motley band of performers made on its audience on this occasion that two respected local businessmen, who were aware of the financial difficulties Gerhard and Maria Crepaz were facing, donated 1000 Austrian schillings[8] each at the end of the concert, which had inspired them to such a spontaneous act of generosity.

The second concert took place in the open air, mainly in the Oberen Stadtplatz (Upper Town square); a programme of 'popular music' included Sousa's *Liberty Bell*, a Beethoven *Écossaise*, some jazz arrangements, four dances by Ezra Read [9] and some Irish jigs, all of which would have been given an idiosyncratic Scratch interpretation. (Some of these pieces would have been performed by one or other of the sub-groups; possibly another 'last performance' by the Wood and Metal band.) The programme ended on a political note with four songs, including the 'Red Flag', and to finish, a spirited rendering of the 'Internationale'. Some young Austrians, who had been assisting the Scratch Orchestra, distributed the text of the 'Internationale' and on its completion unfurled the hammer and sickle. This visual provocation, together with a subversive text, enraged some local politicians who happened to be in the square at the time (although, according to observers of Austrian political culture, they had probably not recognized the song). The next day the whole event was branded by the local press as communist-inspired and Gerhard and Maria Crepaz were summoned to appear before a group of State cultural officials. In a short radio interview Gerhard suggested that singing the 'Internationale' in the Tirol would have the same consequences as singing the Tirolean national anthem in Red

Square; that is, neither could be construed as a threat to the status quo, for which reasonable supposition he incurred the hostility of both the Catholics and the local Communists.

The third concert took place in a cinema; *Sweet FA* was the main item but as on other occasions the show was stolen by Bernard Kelly's presentation: 'the last recital of Elizabeth Schwarzkopf'. Dressed all in black, with a black shawl around his head, Kelly lurched and tottered around the stage like a demented old woman, moaning and wailing. A drunken Jugoslav, a chance passer-by, joined Kelly and with Slavic intensity and abandon accompanied him on the guitar. The Solbad Hall street-singer Ernst Reich also took part in the concert, yet further indication of the inclusiveness of the Scratch Orchestra, of how it could embrace all eventualities and personalities within its all-encompassing sphere of activity. Children loved Bernard Kelly: his zaniness, his unpredictability. He seemed to have materialised out of another world, from the wonderful fairy stories their mothers and grandmothers had read them; they would follow him around just as the children of Hamelin had followed the Pied Piper, except that Kelly and his young acolytes remained within the confines of the town. In the church he would go barefoot and would lie down on the cold stone floor. He would create unexpected movements; to strangers he would offer a lifeless hand in greeting and then turn around in a sudden robotic movement, or he would slump to the ground in a huddle. His poem, inspired by the medievalism which encompassed us, was printed in one of the Scratch Orchestra programmes in Solbad Hall:

    sweep out the fountains
    they are stuffed
    cobble wobbles sprinkle tears
    in old Solbad Hall
    we broom the feudal spider web
    off the town's churchy ears
    vestment pills pop their stitches
    for the cracks to patter through

As an Irish republican Kelly set up a 'Free Derry Corner' Street Theatre piece in the town, for which posters advertising the event were displayed, on hoardings and lampposts. Members of the Scratch Orchestra, under the guidance of Carole Finer, helped to make a banner and contributed to the event in the evening by banging dustbin lids and whistling, just as the women of west Belfast would warn of the British army's approach. To add to the general mayhem firecrackers were provided by Austrian supporters while Scratch Orchestra members, dressed up, approximately but imaginatively, as British soldiers, 'attacked' the Town square and 'intimidated' the local people, much to the annoyance of some English tourists. Cardew himself, whilst empathising with the general spirit of the event, nevertheless was later critical of the lack of discipline and organisation which involvement in such a serious political and military struggle demanded. He was uneasy with Kelly's brand of libertarian anarchism; in Austria (and in Munich) Bernard Kelly was the particular thorn in Cardew's flesh for he represented, in Cardew's view, an ultimately reactionary political tendency to which too many of the Scratch Orchestra would still have been susceptible. But the enthusiasm and commitment which they showed in support of Kelly's 'cause' was no more, and no less, than they had demonstrated time and time again during those two heady years of Scratch musical activity at home in London. As we shall see, the matter was raised again in a brief correspondence between the two men later in the year.

The last concert took place in the Jesuitenkirche on 8 September. By now the Scratch Orchestra's 'reputation' had preceded it. In particular, a tantalising headline in a local tabloid, 'Scratch Orchestra girls do not wear knickers', was the subject of much gossip and speculation although, in fact, the characterisation could only have referred to one member, Birgit Burkhardt, who wore a flimsy, diaphanous night-dress and little else. Most of the other women wore ankle-length dresses and revealed very little of their bodies. The idea of sexual titillation informed none of the Scratch Orchestra's repertoire – nor, for that matter, and probably contrary to the mythology which rapidly gained credence amongst the good people of Solbad Hall and elsewhere, did drug-taking, with some inconsequential exceptions. For the last concert there was a wide range of expectations; some of the audience came out of curiosity, others came with preconceptions and were fearful; some, seeking 'action', were bent on provocation whilst others came out of a sense of solidarity with the Scratch Orchestra.

According to an extant programme, a single typed sheet, the programme consisted of Robert Ashley's *She was a Visitor* (a Scratch Orchestra favourite from the composition category), sections II and V from *Burdocks*, Terry Riley's *In C* (another favourite, which made excessive demands on Scratch skills), Hugh Shrapnel's *Space-Time Music*, and *Georgina Cries* by David Jackman.[10] At a certain point during the event two young men, possibly students, who had presumably anticipated a more traditional musical evening, began to remonstrate with Cardew: What does it mean? What is the intention? Is it art? And so forth – a familiar, if not hackneyed, sequence of questions. Cardew argued that the Scratch Orchestra was involved in a form of music-making which the young men clearly did not understand. This they refuted, continuing to raise objections and wrangle, and generally to monopolise and disrupt the proceedings. Cardew finally lost his patience and peremptorily brought the exchanges to a halt. Reverting to English he told the protestors they were stupid and that he had nothing further to discuss with them. Perhaps he had already learnt one important lesson from the Party: not to suffer fools and reactionaries gladly. But as we have seen, even before the communist decade and as a relatively young man, he could behave dismissively and arrogantly towards people who, as he perceived them, lacked brilliance and singularity.

By this time the tension was mounting and during the performance of *Georgina Cries* some Austrian psychology students burned a local newspaper (*Tiroler Tageszeitung*) in the middle of the church which was festooned with maize plants. This combination, together with the loud drumming of *Georgina Cries*, seemed to create an 'ecstatic' feeling which permeated the space and released the audience into a more participatory mood, such that it became difficult to determine who was performing and who was acting spontaneously. Nor was it possible to distinguish between members of the Scratch Orchestra and the Austrian students, who were similarly attired. At one point a priest appeared, white-faced and enraged, but powerless to restore order and equilibrium. Cardew maintained a central position in the space but said nothing. He would not have approved the anarchy that had engulfed the Scratch Orchestra's concert, but he would have adopted the role of observer rather than critic or peacemaker. Certainly, the situation had got completely out of control; a state of affairs reigned that had been perpetrated neither by the Scratch Orchestra nor by the organisers. It was simply the case, which Cage had demonstrated often enough, that given a 'free' situation elements in the audience would lapse into 'silliness'. Predictably, the 'consensus' (as publicised by the media) was that the Jesuitenkirche concert had been a huge scandal. And yet, equally predictably perhaps, there were expressions of support for Gerhard and Maria Crepaz; a local priest publicly praised their work: it was good and important.

In that summer of 1972 the invasion of the English 'travellers', 'hippies', with their children, together with a few young Austrian dissidents and some local dogs, did make a strong, perhaps lasting, impression. Some twenty years or more after the event I asked Gerhard and Maria Crepaz what had remained in the memory of the Scratch Orchestra's visit to Solbad Hall (now called simply Hall). I was particularly interested to know what kind of impression the Scratch Orchestra had made: as a concept, a precedent, a touchstone, an ideal, a 'composition'? What follows is based on a recording, freely translated from the German by myself, from 5 April 1994 at the Crepaz home in Hall.

For the Crepaz family these had been days of joy and pleasure. Gerhard Crepaz recalls with great affection the simple, idyllic life of the Scratch people. There never seemed to be any sense of anxiety or presumption; nor did the Scratch Orchestra indulge in those subtle forms of intimidation through which more self-conscious artists seek to maintain their distance. The Austrians admired how we would deal seriously, democratically and, when necessary, lengthily with every issue, large or small. ('What I learnt above all from the Scratch was that Democracy demands much more time than we had ever imagined'.) The chaos generated by the free and constant flow of ideas, as well as the accommodation of starkly contrasting personalities, sometimes put considerable strain on the democratic structure which underpinned social intercourse. Decisions were made collectively; at the same time it was important that nobody's individuality was threatened. Our hosts were intrigued and fascinated by the fact that in the Scratch Orchestra there were Stalinists, anarchists, and a man, Bryn Harris, whose (full-time) occupation was to look after locusts ('with the occasional health check').[11] The Scratch Orchestra exemplified both unity and heterogeneity; that was its genius.

Collectively the Scratch Orchestra created a self discipline – that is, a discipline *from within* that was rooted in a sense of an incontestable, if indefinable, sense of *purpose*. The Scratch Orchestra always arrived altogether and on time at the venues; to the Austrians this was as astonishing as it was admirable. The unconventionality of the Scratch Orchestra was not a superficial exhibition of 'otherness'; there were no ostentatious displays of provocation. The Scratch represented another way of life (*pauverismus,* as Crepaz termed it), or more accurately the *possibility* of another way of life, the surface manifestations of which – no concern for money, an acceptance of a low level of subsistence – for many conservative people in Hall, still living in the shadow of the trauma of the immediate post-war period, was threatening.

In particular it was the Improvisation Rites which caught the imagination of Crepaz and his family and circle of friends – how they seemed to overflow into Scratch life, enriching it and at the same time emanating from it. Certain anecdotes had been passed on: in Wales the Scratch Orchestra had suddenly and seemingly spontaneously emptied their pockets and given all their money to the audience. At the end of the concert the Scratch pockets had more money in them than at the beginning. What seemed to impress the Austrians was the idea of a pluralistic, *centreless* existence; that is, the recognition of the existence of many 'truths' rather than, say, a single Christian, or ideological, truth.

> We learnt this from you [the Scratch Orchestra]: the way to be really friendly. And Critique as Understatement. This one can detect perhaps through a small facial movement, the kind of smile. The really new and significant now manifests itself in private, occurring in small private observations which never reach the larger social consciousness. For the critics this would be incomprehensible; they inhabit the official world of music, they are still concerned with the great clichés of 'structure', 'musical material', 'originality'. [All those 'figments of the musicological imagination', as Cardew once described such phenomena.] It's a question of power and prestige rather than recognition and consciousness, of building Gods

and demi-Gods which will ensure their creator's survival in history. The cliché of the critic of cliché; cliché fights for supremacy with other clichés – a form of weakness of thought and consciousness. Cardew was right to renounce the false ideologies of Darmstadt.[12]

To the Austrians the impression Cardew made was of a man who was strict, serious, invariably friendly, yet always maintaining a certain distance from those who were not within his immediate circle.[13] For Gerhard Crepaz, echoing Goffredo Petrassi, Cardew was a (communist) Utopian.

The events in Solbad Hall brought the Scratch Orchestra tour to an invigorating close and on the morning of 9 September the majority of members (several had decided to spend a little more time in Austria and make their way home independently) boarded the coach for the homeward journey and arrived at Charing Cross the next day at 8pm.[14] Cardew and myself, accompanied by Hugh Shrapnel, Penny Jordan and Barbara Pearce, proceeded to Venice for the Biennale, where I had been invited to give a short morning recital of Cardew's piano music in the Sale Apollinee at the Teatro La Fenice on 12 September. The organisers and ourselves had agreed on a programme consisting of four works: *Two Books of Study for Pianists* (with Cardew), *February Pieces*, *Volo Solo*, and *Three Winter Potatoes*. However, in the light of the radical change in Cardew's music, the extent of which would have been unimaginable to the Italian promoters, Cardew and I decided that it would be wholly appropriate to include some of his recent, politically-inspired compositions: three 'piano songs'. To accommodate these and to ensure that the programme would not be too long we announced that the *Three Winter Potatoes* would be omitted. Furthermore we suggested that a discussion with the composer, myself and the audience should take place after the concert.

The new material was generously applauded and seemed to have been appreciated by a significant proportion of the public. The audience included a number of eminent figures from the world of music, including Cage, who must have followed, or preceded, us from Munich. However, the ensuing discussion, in Cardew's words, was 'like opening the floodgates of repressed feelings'. Many claimed that the concert was a 'provocation' – certainly, everyone was aroused one way or another – and of the four hundred or so in the audience perhaps as many as half, such was the passion and fury that overtook the occasion, insisted on contributing to the discussion, which was extremely heated and confrontational. (Hugh Shrapnel recalls the reaction of the English music critic Dominic Gill, 'who looked totally shocked and puzzled at the same time'.) My own feeling now (and probably at the time, too) is that the 'political' music in itself was not the cause of the furore which ensued; this could have been dismissed urbanely and without the slightest discomfort as a political gesture of little significance, or even as a temporary aberration on Cardew's part; or it could simply have been ignored, with attention focussed on the avant-garde music which constituted the bulk of the programme.[15] Cardew was well aware of this; hence his insistence on a discussion. What enraged people was the uncompromising and unforgiving tenor of our own (Cardew's and mine) brazen-faced, verbal contributions. These centred on the 'reactionary nature of the avant-garde', the 'essential parasitism of avant-garde composers', the 'total alienation of the avant-garde from the working class', and the 'exploitation of the working-class by bourgeois culture' – a propos of which I recall making the point that the only representation of the Italian working class at this event were the half dozen young men who had manhandled the Steinway grand piano from the ground floor up into the concert room. This was too much for one bejewelled, middle-aged Italian lady – a member of the aristocracy I was informed later – who made purposeful and threatening strides in my direction, waving an object of some substance above her head with the clear intent, as I perceived it in the heat of the moment, of striking a blow in the name of bourgeois culture. Either I sidestepped her attack or she was restrained – I cannot remember which – but I escaped from La Fenice unscathed.

Francesco Carraro, a friend and member of the organising Committee of the Biennale and a great admirer of Cardew's early piano music, was furious, his wrath directed at me in particular. I reminded him that I had mentioned the inclusion of the new material before the concert but he insisted that I hadn't. If I had, he would have refused, he told me. I suspect now that there had been some confusion or misunderstanding; I had probably not conveyed the essential character of the new pieces – certainly there had been no discussion. Sensing that if I were too explicit Carraro might have created obstacles, I probably acted disingenuously. He claimed that by omitting *Winter Potatoes* I had broken the contract but essentially I think his anger and suffering was because of what he felt was a personal betrayal: 'To hell with the audience, to hell with the Biennale. This is between John and me'.[16]

On 12 September, just a few days after the Venice concert and perhaps when he was already back in London, Cardew penned a summing-up in his Journal. His main reservation regarding our own role seems to have been that we should have been more in control of the discussion. This was a somewhat unrealistic view of the event which was, as I recall, from start to finish, uncontrollable. Cardew begins his notes in questioning mode:

Some questions. Do we want 'provocation' and its intensely emotional reaction? (lack of discipline). Was it right to organize the 'change of direction' in the concert behind the back of the administration? Is there any way of avoiding the situation (after the tension of a concert) of letting the initiative slip away, and being forced into defending yourself against attacking questions? What seemed to be under debate was our personal integrity and whether or not music could be revolutionary, rather than the revolution: do we want it, how can it be achieved. We should have applied an old principle: we ask the questions, the audience provides the answers. Good answers are supported and elaborated. Wrong answers (idealist or ill-intentioned) expose themselves as ridiculous.[...] However, some good points came out, and the struggle was 'fierce'. 1) Revolution affects all layers of society – you can't say a bourgeois salon is not the place for revolutionary politics. 2) On reflection: we should not fight this battle (in the avant-garde) as a losing battle. The avant-garde is weak – the last ditch of bourgeois culture. 3) So – keep it as legal as possible – not duplicate political programme notes behind the backs of the administration but through the administration, with their collusion. 4) The interpreter (a stranger – American 'capitalist' as he called himself) did well and supported our democratic right to say what we did, and also found we were doing what we did more or less correctly (that is, he was not antagonised by our style of work). (Is this important?) 5) Cage was very woolly about the revolution and attacked us as musically degenerate and humanly dishonourable (a dishonourable attack, this). 6) The need in bourgeois society (where all culture is more or less bourgeois) to state explicitly a stand against it – hence the necessity of words and music. 7) There was a lot of support for us.

In the wake of the Munich/Solbad Hall tour Cardew delivered a homily to the Scratch Orchestra which was schoolmasterly and earnest, rather patronising in tone, occasionally confessional, and which leant heavily on Mao Tse-tung's avuncular style in *Talks at the Yenan Forum* and his philosophical essays. The tone as much as the content would have appalled many ex-Scratch Orchestra members and probably embarrassed current members. He stressed the importance of discipline and strong leadership – as opposed to the weak, 'liberal' leadership style adopted on the tour, especially in relation to the disruptive, anarchist elements in the Scratch Orchestra, such as Bernard Kelly. Compositions such as *The Great Learning*, *Sweet FA*, *In C*, were all dismissed as bad music with one or two redeeming features. As evidence he cited Japanese members of the audience who had apparently claimed that *The Great Learning* reminded them of the devastation of Hiroshima and Nagasaki. He condemned the content and style of Scratch performances, its *modus vivendi*, its ethos, its spontaneity, imagination, outrageous and unpredictable behaviour, and proposed a moratorium on all Scratch activities in the public domain in favour of a period of disciplined study of traditional musical skills.[17]

Of course, the idea of acquiring 'skill' would have excluded many of the Scratch Orchestra's most inventive and imaginative members (Psi Ellison is the first who springs to mind), none of whom would ever have passed muster as 'musicians'. Nor had they any pretensions to such a status. The majority of Scratch Orchestra members were neither professionals, nor amateurs aspiring to be professionals. The flair that many of them possessed, to contribute a sound or a gesture, or to draw attention to a sound or gesture and to contextualize it, bore no relation to the hard-earned acquisition of musical skills. One of the many ironies was that despite all the political fervour, discussion and commitment, the performance of Paragraph 7 of *The Great Learning* in the Pfarrfirche in Solbad Hall, a work in which everybody, irrespective of their musical aptitude, participates on equal terms, was probably the musical high point of the entire tour, whilst with the performance of two extracts from a 'political' musical, *Sweet FA,* the Scratch Orchestra reached the nadir of incompetence.[18]

However, Cardew had already been persuaded of the necessity of grasping this particular nettle before the events in Munich and Solbad Hall. In a text headed 'Composing' the tone is conciliatory and encouraging:

> 'Driving a car is not difficult.' That's how I mean composing is not difficult. Obviously, not having driven before you can't just hop in, turn on the ignition (inspiration), and race around the countryside at high speed. There's a lot to be learnt, but none of it is unlearnable. Just so, composing is not difficult, but it has to be learnt. In the Scratch we have very good conditions for learning: a large body of people capable of performing different functions, some quite experienced instrumentalists to ask about instrumental writing, some quite experienced composers, and above all the experience of hundreds of public concerts behind us, some of which went well, others badly, but most somewhere in between.[19]

Friends of Cardew, most of non-communist persuasion, had expressed similar views, criticising the Scratch Orchestra for its tentative and self-conscious approach to their instruments and suggesting that they needed guidance and leadership from people like Cardew and myself who were 'doing a great disservice to the group by not giving them the advantage of your musical and performance knowledge'.[20] One can imagine Cardew's response a few years earlier: Why shouldn't they express tentativeness and self-consciousness if this is how they feel – that is, if their utterances of their condition are honest? There is an echo here of Cardew's defence of his step-daughter Emily when her timidity and lack of self-sufficiency was called into question by his friends Klaus and

Isolde Koch (see chapter 5, p.184). And wasn't the Scratch Orchestra predicated on the idea that *all* contributions, however modest, were valued on their own merits, and that people from a variety of musical, non-musical, non-artistic backgrounds would co-exist as equals with no hierarchy of skills and abilities? No-one is subordinate and each can create a personalized role. As the late Brian Dennis wrote: 'The Scratch Orchestra, initially at least, had the additional attraction of a feeling that "anything" could happen, "everyone was equal" and that "nothing mattered more than anything else", which pervaded the spirit of the 60s.' [21] And from the same source Carole Finer recalled: 'Everyone mattered, EVERYONE counted. We were all stars'.[22]

At this point in time, in the early seventies, Cardew would probably have accepted La Barbara's criticism: 'You are not a musical innocent and I believe you do some harm to the innocents by trying to be one of them.'[23] And yet in this respect I do not think that Cardew ever did do harm. La Barbara's advice was for Cardew and myself to form a separate (musical) leadership group, just as had happened politically. But her suggestion that the idiosyncratic, Scratch renderings of 'rhythmic figures' should be ironed out through tuition and training was against the ethos of the Scratch Orchestra. Like so many other observers and critics, she simply did not understand it:

Music has a great deal to do with confidence, whether writing or playing, and even beginners on instruments should make sounds with a great deal of energy and openness. [...] The only way to hear mistakes and acknowledge them. [24]

In fact some Scratch members did perform with 'a great deal of energy and openness', though not always with a great deal of attention to the world around them, and not necessarily with an awareness of the 'mistakes' (in particular the *nature* of the mistakes) they were making. For most Scratch members, 'making sounds' – whether aggressive or tentative, elegant or clumsy, defined or indeterminate, from an infinite variety of sound sources – concerned levels of control and degrees of intentionality; and it was the *contextualisation* of these sounds which (sometimes) constituted the defining *musical* act.

Each piece of Scratch Music should in theory be performable continuously (whether agonizingly or enjoyably depends on the type of person doing it and on the mood he is in) for indefinite periods of time [25]

Handed an instrument, or a familiar object, a Scratch member might have turned it upside down, exploring its potential without preconceptions – the same approach that Daphne Simmons adopted towards her grandfather clock (see chapter 9).[26]

1972 also saw the publication of *Scratch Music*, a book containing one hundred and sixty-four fragments and examples of Scratch material – a 'work of art' in its own right – laid out randomly on twenty-six double-page spreads, each having from 0 to 16 separate notations. The book begins with Cardew's brief introduction, which was clearly written last, ending epitaphically, with a final judgment: 'and some or all of the basic notions of Scratch Music may again be useful, but for now, as far as the Scratch Orchestra is concerned, Scratch Music is dead'.[27] This introduction is followed by earlier texts entitled 'Scratch Music – Early outlines and later notes', all of which, except for one by Michael Chant, are Cardew's own contributions. Of course, by the time of publication Cardew's attitude towards the Scratch Orchestra and Scratch Music had changed radically, so that although he is generous with his inclusion of earlier texts relating to Scratch Music, the tone of the introduction is critical – even if it manages to avoid being overtly polemical – and there were many in the Scratch Orchestra who would have taken issue with him on a number of his assertions. For example, the 'individualistic bias' ('doing your own thing') of Scratch music is described in the introduction as an 'inherent weakness', whereas in the 'Early outlines and later notes' he writes, in 1971:

> The superficially private and individualistic quality of Scratch Music must be seen in perspective. It fosters communal activity, it breaks down the barrier between private and group activity, between professional and amateur, – it is a means to sharing experience.[28]

In so far as Scratch Music consisted of a number of individuals performing discreetly and simultaneously with little or no regard for one another's contribution (which is reflected in Cardew's partly random method of selection and lay-out in the book) the criticism might have been justified. In fact, the ethos of the Scratch Orchestra ensured that any manifestation of 'individualistic bias' was usually accommodated and subsumed into the collective music-making. The Scratch Orchestra was too much like a family – though with fewer tensions than the average family – for members to disregard or be indifferent to what was being performed around them. Ironically, Cardew acknowledges this in the introduction when he writes:

> Very beautiful it was on many occasions, with latecomers simply tuning in to the sound environment of the room and adding improvised music to the general texture of interacting Scratch Musics. [29]

Another contentious point made in the Introduction is that 'Scratch Music never really caught on amongst the broad masses of the Scratch Orchestra [...] many people simply didn't understand what they were supposed to do'[30] – an uncharacteristic underestimation of the Scratch Orchestra's imaginative faculties and its artistic resourcefulness. It may well have been the case that individual members were not clear as to Cardew's own definition of Scratch Music, but collectively and wordlessly we created an undemonstrative, subtle, improvised music to which everybody in the Orchestra was committed and which was a feature not only of Scratch meetings, as Cardew describes, but of many public concerts and events. The fact that Scratch Music might have appeared indeterminate, furtive, cryptic, even conspiratorial to an audience more accustomed to a more palpable, more self-assertive, mode of music-making in no way diminishes from its artistic viability. It recalls a previously quoted Journal entry; here I simply substitute 'Scratch Music' for the word 'music':

> [Scratch] Music is vagrant; it has no fixed abode. It's a menace to society. It needs cleaning up. The impossibility of abolishing [Scratch] Music. Its omnipresence. Its uncatchability. Perhaps after all we have to step down and let [Scratch] Music pursue its own course.[31]

What is interesting in the *Scratch Music* collection is to note the subtle shift in Cardew's attitude towards Scratch Music as the political agenda took control.

In a circular to the Scratch Orchestra Cardew called for a meeting, on 25 September, to discuss and summarise the events in Munich and Solbad Hall. In the same circular an 'open meeting' of the Id Group, on 27 September, is advertised, as well as a party at Frank Abbott's flat in Balham, south-west London (where Alec Hill also lived for a while). Regarding the immediate future of the Scratch Orchestra Cardew proposed setting up a musical 'propaganda team' ('a musical equivalent of mass work') which would travel around (at week-ends) with an 'entertaining' programme of mainly socialist songs with the aim of initiating political discussion and thereby assisting in the task of winning over public opinion to socialism. He also recommended the development of 'more sophisticated musical forms' to engage the composers in the Scratch Orchestra whose interest might otherwise wane. The ultimate aim: to win over public opinion to socialism on a mass scale. Of course, we may assume here that Cardew was simply carrying out a directive from the Party; but at the same time I am convinced that he had no illusions with respect to the enormity of the task, the awesome power and influence of 'the enemy', and the huge odds against a significant measure of success. Against this scenario only the most radical political strategy could claim viability; for Cardew and his comrades it was risible that a 'communist' Party could be proposing, as an instrument of revolutionary change (as some were/are), the docile ballot box into which, every five years, a piece of paper is dropped, marked with a cross, with an earnest complacency and a considerable measure of self-delusion.

By October the Id Group had become a closed group consisting of ten people: Cardew, Stella Cardew, Rod Eley, Alec Hill, Carole Finer, John Tilbury, Tim and Barbara Mitchell, Frank Abbott and Keith Rowe, the latter as representative of the Communist Party of England Marxist/Leninist. The group was closed in the sense that it had taken it upon itself to decide whether a person should be asked, or allowed, to join. There was also an 'expanded group' (what remained of the old Scratch Orchestra), which occasionally met and included, among others, Bryn Harris and Michael Parsons. By now Cardew was totally committed to the CPE (M-L) line, unlike some other members, such as Frank Abbott, who was suspected of Trotskyite sympathies. At a meeting of the 'Central Ideological Group' on 1 October 1972 Cardew wrote, on a sheet of note paper: 'Put politics in command (music is of minor importance at this stage). Emphasis on ideological work, study. Build the Party. Build support for the general political line of the CPE (M-L)'. And at the end of his notes he makes the claim: 'Group is now under the leadership in the specific sense'. This is unclear. Was he referring to the Scratch and the leadership of the Id Group, or the Id Group and the leadership of the Party? Presumably the latter.

This is the context in which the remaining chapters of this biography are to be read and reflected upon. There is no deviation – by which I do not mean to say that there were no doubts but rather, above all, and to echo Brecht: how does one act?

> That the earth shall be made a common treasury of livelihood to all mankind, without respect of persons; and I had a voice within me which bade me declare it abroad, which I did obey, for I declared it by word of mouth wheresoever I came. [...] Yet my mind was not at rest, because nothing was acted, and thoughts run in me that words and writings were all nothing and must die, for action is the life of all, and if thou dost not act, thou dost nothing.[32]

I will not elaborate further; suffice it to say that much of the content of the succeeding chapters of this book will reflect, directly or obliquely, on Cardew's efforts, in the heat of his revolutionary praxis, to force such issues out of the realm of speculation and wishful thinking into the arena of day-to-day existence, where a titanic struggle, involving as a matter of course unimagineable sacrifices, is demanded of the overwhelming majority of the human race for their day-to-day survival. One might argue that his uncompromising nature was appropriate to both revolutionary politics and to art – in both of which he wanted to push back boundaries and explore extremes – but during the seventies, as a creature of impulse, politics demanded that his natural spontaneity should be curbed. Any action, any utterance, would be judged by the yardstick of a tightly circumscribed, political morality which, quite unequivocally, was based on an unflinching loyalty and obedience to the Party. For it was Cardew's firm conviction that without a revolutionary elite, a vanguard, without a *Party,* there could be no revolution. The Party was one of the mythic elements in his life.

> But who is the Party?
> Does it sit in a house with a telephone?
> Are its thoughts secret, its decisions unknown?
> Who is the Party?

> We are the Party.
> You and I and he – all of us.
> It is hidden in your clothes, it thinks in your head
> Where I live is its home, and where you are attacked it fights.[33]

In the same month, October, a contingent of the Scratch Orchestra, along with other British artists, was invited to perform at the Sonja Henie Foundation in Oslo as part of a 'British Culture' event organised by the British Council and our Norwegian hosts. The Foundation was situated in idyllic surroundings by the side of a lake and we were royally accommodated in an Oslo hotel whose gargantuan breakfast feasts have remained lodged in the memory. The Scratch contribution comprised a number of groups and individual contributors from within the Scratch Orchestra, as well as those associated with the Orchestra through dual membership, such as the Promenade Theatre Orchestra (Hugh Shrapnel, Alec Hill, Christopher Hobbs and John White), and AMM (Rowe, Prévost, Gare and Cardew, with Gare and Prevost playing as a duo). Among the other participants were Tim Mitchell, Frank Abbott, Colin Self and myself. Self, apart from participating in many of the collective Scratch events, was exhibiting some of his drawings in the main gallery. His work was mainly concerned with 'pop-art' themes, such as hot-dogs and other junk foods, and there were also some very detailed pencil drawings of B52 bombers flying through dramatically-lit night skies. Concerts and workshops were spread over the week: the Scratch Orchestra programme included the new, political versions of Paragraphs 1 and 2 of *The Great Learning*, Act II of *Sweet FA*, revolutionary songs, some instrumental works, a piano recital of works by mainly Cardew and Skempton, and improvisation.

The political members of the Scratch Orchestra – Cardew, Rowe, Mitchell, Hill, Abbott, Rowe and myself – determined to raise the political profile of the Scratch Orchestra contingent at every opportunity, to the embarrassment and discomfort of the rest. A workshop with Norwegian children was used to promote the thoughts of Chairman Mao and to initiate discussion with both the children and their parents, who understandably demonstrated a degree of anxiety, but no hostility, and relations remained good-natured and friendly. On another, more fraught occasion, probably during a performance of one of the paragraphs from *The Great Learning*, some Norwegian students tried to set light to a Marxist-Leninist banner which was being paraded. Coincidentally, the banner had already caused a fire-related incident which Tim Mitchell recalled in an interview sometime in April 2002. He and Alec Hill were in a basement workshop at the Sonje Henie Foundation cutting through lengths of timber to make bearers for the banners they had painted. They were making heavy weather of the task due to the bluntness of the circular saw that had been provided, and by forcing the wood through had caused the blade to smoke. Unbeknown to the two revolutionary workers this had activated an automatic smoke alarm on the other side of the lake. Emerging from the basement for a break they were surprised by the incongruous appearance of three fire engines racing along in the distance.

According to Mitchell, Cardew and I had managed to persuade a Swedish dance group from Stockholm to collaborate with us on a dance piece based on a quotation from Mao Tse-tung, 'A single spark can start a prairie fire' [34] (although I confess that I now have only the faintest recollection of the venture). Cardew enlisted the assistance of Mitchell – perhaps on the basis of his interest and proficiency in gymnastics – whose idea was that through the dissemination of the message in Mao's little red book the dancers' aimless and self-indulgent poses would be transformed into purposeful, consciously united and revolutionary movement. Mitchell, with typical self-deprecation and probably a measure of leg-pull, recalls that his efforts failed to convince the dancers and it was only thanks to my 'inspired intervention' that the project was rescued and successfully staged.

There seems to have been little fraternisation with the other British artists: Stuart Brisley spent much of his time naked, or near-naked, covered in mud and slime and crawling extremely slowly along a platform; he was thoroughly engrossed and did not respond to comments or questions. A performance group, Nice Style, headed by Bruce McLean, appeared in the main theatre every evening, strutting and posing to rock music. There was also a left-wing, agit-prop theatre group named 'John Bull Puncture Repair Outfit' with whom, however, no doubt for sectarian reasons, little contact was made. Hugh Shrapnel recalls the atmosphere of division and hostility which the political input generated; the insistence on the subservience of the music to the demands of revolutionary politics, in the context in which we had been invited to contribute, was an absurd position to have adopted and reflected the immaturity of a Marxist-Leninist Party which 'applied its (Maoist) politics to cultural work in a crude and dogmatic manner'.[35] There were heated arguments: Alec Hill's criticism of a Promenade Theatre Orchestra (PTO) performance as being excessively 'bourgeois' and 'subjective' was met with scorn and incredulity. In fact, the long discussions and arguments into the night precipitated the break-up of PTO, with Hill and Shrapnel on one side of the divide, and Hobbs and White on the other. Hill, in particular, took umbrage at White's refusal to take part in the 'revised' political versions of the Paragraphs from *The Great Learning*.

The Scratch Orchestra's 'political' contribution to the Oslo event clearly demonstrated our ineptitude in responding to the demands of a wider social context. Perhaps the lack of time forced us to adopt an opportunistic approach, relying on liberal goodwill and tolerance amongst the audience and participants to pursue an agenda which ultimately served only to alienate people even further. Within the Id Group itself there were misgivings as well as a degree of resentment at the high-handedness of a political 'élite' (in particular, I suspect, Cardew, Rowe, Hill and myself) which seemed to have lost touch with reality. Yet there was no formal 'post-mortem', no meetings to shed light, in retrospect, on our collective shortcomings, unlike previous occasions – the Art Schools, Munich, Venice – which for Cardew had provided experiences from which lessons could and should have been learnt. Perhaps, tacitly, it was decided to write off the Oslo affair from which only a few of us had emerged with any credit.

By now Cardew was an activist in musicians' union affairs, and in November he proposed a motion to the Union criticizing the BBC's parsimonious funding of jazz, and its discrimination against jazz in favour of (bourgeois) classical music. In his draft in the Journal he ends his proposal, typically, with a Party political point:

> Naturally we should protest against this, and naturally the BBC will respond with somewhat longer periods of inconspicuous airtime devoted to jazz and woolly intellectual attitudes to jazz. But we must be clear that such demands and concessions will not bring about a fundamental change.[36]

And a few pages further on, after some brief notes on music and ideology, he insists: 'Main thing: What has brought about this revolution in our thinking? The Party. Build the Party'. Again, the emphasis is on the idea of an elite dispensing wisdom, enlightening and leading the masses.

It was not only the liberals and anarchists who were expressing doubts and misgivings in respect of the Maoist take-over of the Scratch Orchestra; most of them, in any case, had long since departed. But there were others who, whilst they shared the revolutionary sentiments of the Id Group and agreed on the need for political activism, nevertheless balked at the lack of democratic procedures in the new Scratch Orchestra. A dissenting letter to Cardew from Jenny Robbins' brother Chris, who had moved to Edinburgh, deplored the idea of the Scratch Orchestra investing its money in order to protect it from devaluation; nor could he understand how the 'communists' could agree to such a proposal. (The communists, learning the art of *Realpolitik* from their Chinese comrades, probably put forward the proposal.) And with a veiled reference to the 'take-over' Robbins also stresses the need for collective control of the Orchestra 'by all its active members'. In another letter of dissent Bernard Kelly, the Irish anarchist who had so enlivened the tour of Munich and Austria, adopts a characteristically confrontational approach. Having recently attended a Scratch meeting he questions rhetorically, 'is the Scratch an evening institute in 19th century Marxism?', and expresses frustration and annoyance that his contributions on the tour were dismissed in a cavalier and superficial manner. He prefers to concern himself with the revolution in Ireland rather than the sterile politics of the 'old men in Peking'. He ends his letter contentiously:

> The fiend of Munich [Sir Alec Douglas-Home] is the latest fascist to be dined and feted by the Peking hosts. Yet these hosts spent ten years screaming at Russia. Today they plead with the Western fascists and honour them with their attendance. Why? Is this not a slap in the face of all revolutionaries around the world.[37]

Kelly hit a vulnerable spot; even some supporters of the CPE (M-L) were uncomfortable with the excessive hospitality which Peking appeared to lavish on Western reactionaries. Significantly, in his reply it is the only point which Cardew chooses to ignore. He begins:

> Many thanks for your letter. It looks as though you came to the Id group meeting expecting it to be a Scratch meeting, hence your antagonism to its 'form'. It's like accusing a tree stump of coldness and detachment if it refuses to shake hands with you.[38]

He then takes Kelly to task on both the tone and content of his letter: 'There was a tone of anger in your letter which you should save for the real enemy'. And then a reproach he addressed to many artists who opposed Marxism-Leninism-Mao Tse-tung Thought:

> I have an inkling of what's annoying you, and I don't see it as particularly political – its the distaste of the habitual 'lone wolf' for the collective approach. I'm

sure you'll dismiss this (rightly) as another gratuitous piece of arrogant 'wisdom'.

And in a flagrantly sectarian passage he invites Kelly to an Id Group meeting where Rod Eley

> will speak on the general topic 'social fascism' (socialism in words, fascism in deeds) and try to cover the main poisonous trends that try to wreck the revolution from within the left, so to speak: Revisionism, Trotskyism, Anarchism, Reformism, Terrorism, the Labour Party, etc. The aim is to draw out which of these lines we have to struggle against particularly, isolate them and wipe them out, so that we can achieve the necessary unity to go forward.

Cardew surely realised that the proposed agenda would only serve to alienate Kelly even more, to drive him further away. Is this what he intended? Kelly was an anarchist whose ideas had to be 'wiped out'. This was Cardew's intractable message to all reactionaries, subversives and revisionists.

From the 11 to the 15 December Cardew was at the Bradford College of Art for a second visit that year, this time with an agreed, overtly political agenda which included a number of lectures: 'The communist artist'; 'The battle in the realm of ideas'; 'The situation in Ireland' (on which there are extensive notes in his Journal). In the notes for his Bradford visit Cardew begins:

> For our production, a choice of themes: 1) To go out fact-finding, to produce a work to reflect a local struggle. 2) To uncover the contradictions within the College, thus to attack bourgeois ideology at its constant source in the education system. 3) To take the theme where the struggle is breaking out into the open, Ireland, and point out the relationship with the situation there and our situation here. 4) To produce a work on Manchester Martyrs, as part of the background to the Irish situation, and on the basis of this to institute discussion on the current situation.[39]

He goes on to describe the changing, revolutionary situation throughout the world, with China in a leading position. The scale of these events, he remarks, is such that it has even reached the Scratch Orchestra: 'one of the most elitist, most obscure, most idealistic and most individualistic groups in the avant-garde'. (The redeeming features he once acknowledged in the Scratch Orchestra have been swept away, no longer viable; the old Scratch is now completely beyond the pale.) An important stage has been reached when artists and intellectuals are beginning to desert the avant-garde and bourgeois ideology in general to join the revolutionary movement and place themselves under the leadership of a revolutionary party: the Communist Party of England (Marxist-Leninist). He also lists those 'treacherous' groups and parties on the Left which subvert the revolutionary movement into harmless byways, or reactionary blind alleys; the Communist Party of Great Britain's 'Peaceful Road to Socialism' is cited as a particularly impoverished and disingenuous revisionist manifestation. The rank and file of such organisations is misled:

> It is for the leadership that we reserve our hatred. [...] The expression 'social fascist' characterises these leaders: socialist in words, fascist in deeds.[...] We must proclaim proletarian ideology. [...] We must go amongst the masses who are ultimately the only source of artistic inspiration.[40]

And so forth. The content and language is unequivocal.

Subsequent music rehearsals involving drumming, and a TV programme on religion in Northern Ireland, did little to generate enthusiasm amongst the students; in terms of numbers the response seems to have been very poor. How could it have been otherwise? It was as if he had learnt nothing from his experiences earlier in the year, at Bradford and in particular at the Cardiff College of Art. We need not rehearse the same arguments and counter-arguments again but essentially Cardew was unable to capture either the minds or the souls of his young charges, however much some of them may have admired him and warmed to him, and to socialist ideas, over the three days. The substance and especially, I believe, the *tone* of his message, on each occasion, was alienating, and this led to resentment and, from some, downright hostility; the gulf between them became unbridgeable. It was as if Cardew the believer, or rather, the convert, had been rendered insensible, through his own certainties, to the physical, mental and emotional needs and limitations (their human vulnerability) of those he was addressing and whom he wished to reach. Perhaps his lack of patience was forced upon him by a lack of time (just three days), and by the students' apparent refusal, or inability, to recognize the irrefutability, the down-to-earth commonsense of the *Communist Manifesto*. Yet the problem for the students was probably not their equivocal attitude towards the desirability of socialism. The real issue was the *means* by which, according to Cardew and his comrades, these time-honoured and inspiring *ends* were to be achieved. For the students, the sacrifices demanded of them beggared belief: change yourself and follow me, the Party, Mao Tse-Tung.[41] Abandon your self-indulgent attempts at art and join the greatest movement of all: the emancipation of the poor and oppressed peoples of the world. Such an equivocalness, at the time, Cardew would not have countenanced, nor comprehended. Doubt, in any case cannot be an excuse for inaction:

'Above all: how does one act?' I believe the students' response had both a positive and a negative side; ironically, Cardew's 'tone' may have provided excuses for those for whom the studio was a haven, and art an escape.

The following miscellaneous notes on Mao's philosophical essays are extracted from the 1972 Journal. Described as 'unused', they were probably intended for one of Cardew's College lectures and demonstrate how he would apply his lively and creative intelligence to philosophical matters, how he would bring abstract philosophical theses to life, subjecting them to sharp scrutiny and testing their relevance to the imperatives of everyday reality.

Mao's essay 'On Practice' formed the basis for more general philosophical discussion: materialism versus idealism, being and consciousness, the continuity between matter and consciousness, the origin of ideas, the dialectic of theory/practice, and the 'relativity' of Marxism (absolute and relative truth). Cardew summarises points and occasionally comments, amplifies and questions:

> Is it true to say that music is pushed forward by its internal contradictions? I don't think so. That would be like saying that the evolution of Man's big toe proceeds according to its internal contradictions. The problem here is one of 'categories' – the ability to correctly delimit 'relative wholes'.[42]

Earlier in the same entry, commenting on Mao's thesis 'In each thing contradiction is present from beginning to end,' he writes:

> Difficulty. What is a thing? Is there a contradiction in a sheet of paper or a mountain? No – these things are expressions, details, phenomena representative of larger matters: the development of the paper industry, the development of the earth's crust.

And a little further on there are also extensive notes on Engels' *Anti-Dühring*.

Cardew's study was never 'academic'; that is, study for its own sake. He always attempted to refer the philosophical points made to concrete, everyday situations, particularly in the field of music. ('When the contradictions in the Id Group are resolved it will cease to exist' – an interestingly Zen-like formulation – he wrote somewhere.) Referring to Mao's thesis of the relationship between the general and the particular character of contradiction ('law: particular to general, *then* general to particular') Cardew comments:

Think of an example in music, e.g. interpretation: first physical mastery of detail, then grasp of large form, then in the light of this large form other details – not necessarily the physically difficult – need study and so on… [Mao's essay] ends by summing up the universality and particularity of 'Contradiction' in terms of absolute and relative, general and individual character. This is the 'quintessence'.[43]

Cardew then refers to the next section of Mao's essay: 'The Principal Contradiction and the Principal Aspect of a Contradiction'. He never allows these ideas to remain dormant, latent; rather, he drags them out into the harsh light of potential practice, of the actual situation in England, and in Ireland, applying Mao's thesis not only to aspects of national and international conflict, but also to personal, individual conflicts:

At every level there is a principal contradiction and a principal aspect of it. International, national, within the revolutionary front, within a study group, within one man's thought or action. They are all related.[44]

Elsewhere the danger of mechanical materialism is addressed:

True, in history material determines mental, and being determines consciousness – but never forget the reaction of the mental (consciousness) on the material: 'An idea grasped by the masses becomes a material force.' [45]

There is also an interesting, philosophical rationalisation of the need for revolution under the heading 'Antagonism':

Chiefly – it is not the only form in the struggle of opposites. Contradiction can often be resolved non-antagonistically. Why is it that the class struggle cannot be resolved to produce socialism without antagonism – open revolution? (Is it true to say that the classes are fundamentally in contradiction to one another, but that this contradiction can be resolved without antagonism? It never has been, but is there a real reason why not?) Well, the image of the bomb as a contradiction is good. The contradiction in a bomb is resolved when a new condition – ignition – is present, through explosion. Of course, the bomb can be kept away from ignition and defused, and the contradiction no longer exists. Two points: 1) the elements of a bomb have no will to resist whatever the bomb expert does with them, and 2) such a non-antagonistic resolution of the contradiction does not bring about change in the world, does not flood it with new energy. Lin Piao's aphorism that Mao Tse-tung Thought is a spiritual atom bomb is a fair description of the facts. We must ensure that it is not defused by bomb disposal experts.[46]

At the end of his commentary Cardew concludes that the study and application of the law of contradiction teaches us two important lessons: that we can 'demolish dogmatism' and that we can organize our practical experience into principles.

If Cardew's position was often embattled during this period, he was still capable of generating and sustaining enthusiasm for unorthodox music-making from a wide range of musicians and non-musicians. A. J. Adamson, a participant in Cardew's workshop at the Birmingham Arts Laboratory on 9 December, accompanied by a small contingent of Scratch members, described the occasion with considerable enthusiasm. The programme included works by Keith Potter, Jolyon Laycock, Dave Jackman (*Georgina Cries*) and Cardew himself (Paragraph 7 of *The Great Learning*).[47]

I think perhaps the most impressive feature of the sound-workshop was its sense of freedom of expression, and yet unity of purpose.[...] The social climate was extremely pleasant, and I feel much of the credit must go to Cardew himself, who remained throughout completely relaxed and always helpful. [48]

The problem for Cardew with these sorties into venues such as the Birmingham Arts Lab was the fact that, with respect to the repertoire, he did not share the enthusiasm of the majority of the participants. Indeed, much to the bewilderment and consternation of those present, he would often use the occasion to expose the 'reactionary content' of the material offered.[49] This phase, the critique of contemporary bourgeois art in which musical works and forms of music-making were consciously exposed to public criticism, culminated in the publication of *Stockhausen Serves Imperialism* and to all intents and purposes was abandoned in the second half of the decade where the emphasis was on creating new works imbued with revolutionary, communist content. Of course, the latter was a task he had already begun; the Journals mention a concert with János Négyesy in Munich on 5 December which included Cardew's *The East is Red* for violin and piano. However, there are occasional frustrated references in the journals to the slow development of 'music for the masses' within the Scratch Orchestra, which is still on a low level, compared to the performances of his transcription of the Chinese national anthem with Négyesy, a professional violinist (who was also an 'anti-communist'), which would certainly have been on a very high level. But this was not the arena where he wished to be 'successful'.

Meanwhile, and for Cardew of far greater import, the ongoing, day-to-day confrontation with the forces of the (bourgeois) state – specifically the police and the judiciary – was the object of continuous analysis and strategy building, and it was incumbent upon all Party members and supporters to contribute their physical presence in a variety of situations. On 16 December Cardew duly presented himself at Camberwell Court in support of comrades who had been arrested. In a somewhat unexpected turn of events a man from Sotheby's, the art dealers, on a different case, offered to pay their bail – a fee of £5, which the comrades accepted. However, this generous gesture was opposed by the police on the grounds of the nature of the offence, the intention to disrupt the court proceedings, and the fact that the accused were liable to commit further offences. There was talk of explosives, petrol bombs and live ammunition but no written statements were offered. Furthermore, because of an administrative error the usual search was not completed. No bail was granted, however, and the comrades were remanded in custody for a week, after which they would receive legal aid to assist them in their presentation of case material. Cardew comments: 'The question to ask: What led the police to raid this house? This brings out the politics'.[50]

Compositions 1971-2

During the summer of 1971 it was as if for the first time Cardew had been overtaken by events; he was no longer the helmsman utilising 'the interplay of natural forces and currents to steer a course'; rather he was at the mercy of elements to which, nevertheless, he felt ineluctably drawn. These had been unleashed by a cumulative chain of events which had impacted upon him both artistically and psychologically and which had left him temporarily in a state of disorientation and uncertainty, particularly with respect to the trajectory of his compositional development. For now it was the demands of a more specific, political agenda, as opposed to those of a broader social context, that he had to meet.

His music had already moved away from formal composition and modernism, so that there are overlaps between his earlier music-making (with the Scratch Orchestra and in *The Great Learning*) and his first essays in political music: *10,000 nails in the coffin of Imperialism* would not be out of place in the *Nature Study Notes*; and the bacchanalian ending of *Fight Sterilization,* with its dancing and improvising, recalls the Scratch Orchestra's renderings of the invitations to collective music-making provided by Alvin Curran or Frederic Rzewski's *Les Moutons de Panurge*. Like much of the music of *The Great Learning* the monody *Soon* is modally based, whilst one of the *Three Bourgeois Songs* is taken from the Odes in Paragraph 5. And the 'violence' of the drumming in Paragraph 2 would occasionally be invoked as an expression of

17. Summer, 1970 (l-r) Svend Bayer (pottery student), Emily, Stella, Cornelius, Walter and Horace

18. Cardew at the prepared piano

19. With The Scratch Orchestra in Cornwall, 1970 (photo by Alec Hill)

20. AMM (l-r) Keith Rowe, Cardew, Lou Gare and Eddie Prévost

21. Outdoor event with AMM

22. The Cottage at Alexandra Palace, 1971

23. The Scratch Orchestra tour of the north-east, 1971

24. Cardew with home-made percussion, early 1970s

revolutionary upheaval. The view at the time was that it was the function, rather than the nature, of the Scratch Orchestra repertoire that had to be re-orientated, its activities skewed in the direction of revolutionary politics. Nobody, not even Cardew, would have contemplated the necessity for the creation of an entirely new repertoire to supplant the existing one.

The manuscript of *Octet '71* is neat and obviously represents a complete and final version, with the date 5 April 1971. It is an enigmatic work: intangible, 'uncatchable', to use Cardew's expression, its provenance unknown; and the fact that, as far as we know, its one and only performance was at the memorial concert in 1982 must be due at least partly to the difficulty of assembling the instrumental forces involved (as in *Octet 1959*). Why those particular instruments, including alto flute and a banjo? As far as we know there was no commission. So was it simply a 'sound' conjured up by a wayward imagination and realised compositionally in the teeth of the almost certain prospect of relative obscurity? A purely conceptual instrumentation. Then there is the arcane title: *Octet '71* (Cardew's third 'Octet'), for a piece scored for ten instruments. Although like other conundrums in Cardew's compositional output it might well have been the inescapable consequence of some characteristic Cardew-esque 'logic', which further scrutiny of the journals may one day explain.[51] The Octet itself is subtly humorous: the wind quartet and harp play slow, sustained sounds, with the tuba, oboe and clarinet dropping out early on. The flute and harp are left to continue the slow tread of the music alone, while the strings, guitar and banjo are each assigned a gentle melodic phrase (marked 'no hurry') with which, increasingly, the proceedings are punctuated (Ex.14.1).

But there is a nagging, unresolved thought which I am unable to discard, particularly as very few of Cardew's pieces can be considered to stand alone, to have been wilfully left out on a limb.[52] Could *Octet '71* be a compressed instrumental version of the ten Odes from Paragraph 5? There is a close, though not exact, analogy to Paragraph 5 in the way that the entrances and exits of the ten parts of the Octet are staggered; moreover, the rich profusion of melodic material in the Odes might well have provided Cardew with all he needed for the instrumental parts of the Octet.[53] *The Great Learning* was still very much on his mind; February had seen the first printing and there would be a second printing in June. Be that as it may, *Octet '71*'s other claim to fame is that it was Cardew's last composition with no political content, or as he would have described it, his last 'bourgeois' piece.

Ex.14.1. From *Octet '71*.

Music for a film entitled 'Strindberg' is another enigma; efforts to trace its origin have failed to unearth any information, despite the fact that on the first page, which outlines the music sections, the name of the well-known Swedish actor Max von Sydow appears: 'Max von Sydow driving in Stockholm'. The music, consisting of two stretches, thirteen minutes and sixteen minutes, was completed on the 19 July 1971 and appears to have been 'written' for AMM, together with some instrumental solo parts: flute, concertina, xylophone, and two cellos (one played by Cardew, the other, possibly, by Keith Rowe). Cardew gives more general instructions to the improvising musicians, while solo instrumentalist parts are written out conventionally. Perhaps the score never reached the recording studio; there are no recollections of a recording session.

Sometime in the early seventies, in 1970 or 71, just before I was due to leave for the United States, Cardew casually passed a piece of manuscript paper to me. On it, in pencil, he had written a few chords and an ornamented base line; he had also added some performance instructions. I assumed it was for piano and when I asked him for a title he suggested *Unintended Piano Music*. I took it with me to America where it received its first performance. I never heard him perform the piece, nor did he ever mention it to me; but then during the seventies he had other concerns.

Fight Sterilization! (moral and physical) by the lackeys of Imperialism, for chorus, solo trumpet, solo trombone, and a band of miscellaneous instruments, was written in August 1971 and was Cardew's first independently-conceived political piece, written during the Scratch 'discontent' period when his attitude towards the political developments would still have been ambivalent. The instrumental introduction features freely chosen but preferably flat key scales in descending sequences, together with unpitched instruments and sound sources in rhythmic unison which continue throughout the song. Girls' voices with trumpet in unison sing a simple, sequentially driven phrase: 'I want a child', which is answered by men's voices, with trombone in unison, with a similarly constructed phrase of marginally greater melodic interest. In answer to the girls' plea 'but who will look after it [the child]', the comforting reply, in four-part (SATB) harmony is: Karl Marx, Lenin, Stalin, Mao Tse-tung, the latter's name sung four times.

The piece ends with a sequence of 'lively dancing' and instrumental improvisation. The feeble text is unattributed but may well have been provided by Cardew himself. The idea for the piece probably relates to the Third World female sterilization programmes which were receiving considerable publicity at that time. But it was an inauspicious beginning to Cardew's career as a political composer.

'Soon' was written in September 1971 as a unison song for unaccompanied voice(s) (Ex.14.2). The words are based on an open letter Mao Tse-tung wrote on 5 January 1930: 'A single spark can start a prairie fire'. Cardew's choice of this particular text was certainly quite conscious, it did not fall arbitrarily into his lap. All the poetic imagery is taken from the last paragraph of Mao's letter: the 'high tide of revolution', the 'ship' and its 'mast-head', the sun's 'shimmering rays' and the child 'turning restlessly in its mother's womb'.

'Soon' is a sturdy monody, not lacking in plasticity and elegance, which gives off an air of optimism and indomitability. One could say that it expresses certainty (inevitability) rather than the necessity for struggle; it proclaims a glorious future. The insistent high Es inspired us in the Scratch Orchestra to strive for, and attain, the vocal heights; Cardew had chosen that particular pitch, I am sure, with the forces at his disposal in mind. It was written for the Scratch Orchestra and we enjoyed singing it, which we did with gusto. And we sang the whole song, ignoring Cardew's note at the end that 'bars 6, 12-18, 35 may be omitted in community singing'. Just as Mao, in his letter, was criticizing certain pessimistic views which existed in the Party at that time, so Cardew was chivvying along the faint-hearted and the feeble-minded amongst the members of the Scratch Orchestra.

Ex.14.2. *Soon.*

The instructions to *10,000 nails in the coffin of Imperialism,* written in October 1971, read as follows:

A Large resonant space.

Everyone has a block of wood, some nails and a good hammer.

Each person draws a line on his sheet of dots, and plays any dots he reads while his eye is travelling that line as hammer strokes.

To finish, a leader – it can be someone different for each slogan – calls out the first slogan in natural rhythm.

Then everyone repeats it in the rhythm given. And so on.

Finally the rhythm is played once more as unison hammer strokes, with one shout as indicated

Duration: five minutes or so before the slogans.

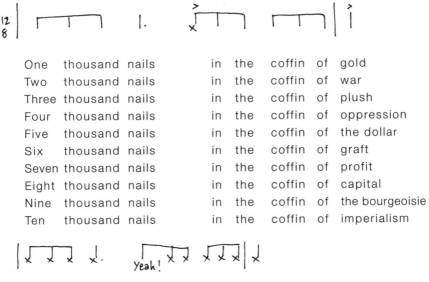

One	thousand	nails	in	the	coffin	of	gold
Two	thousand	nails	in	the	coffin	of	war
Three	thousand	nails	in	the	coffin	of	plush
Four	thousand	nails	in	the	coffin	of	oppression
Five	thousand	nails	in	the	coffin	of	the dollar
Six	thousand	nails	in	the	coffin	of	graft
Seven	thousand	nails	in	the	coffin	of	profit
Eight	thousand	nails	in	the	coffin	of	capital
Nine	thousand	nails	in	the	coffin	of	the bourgeoisie
Ten	thousand	nails	in	the	coffin	of	imperialism

x = hammer stroke

Ex.14.3. *10,000 nails in the coffin of Imperialism.*

Sweet FA is a collectively written opera in five acts for a chorus of thirty-two voices, five speakers, flute, oboe, clarinet, tuba, tubular bells, five drums, cello, and stereo tape playback equipment. Cardew's own version of the opera, written towards the end of 1971 in the aftermath of the debacle in Newcastle, falls between two stools: on the one hand it demands musical expertise far beyond the capabilities of the Scratch Orchestra;

on the other its parochialism (despite its pretensions to universality) would make it decidedly unattractive to a professional group. What is interesting is the extent to which Cardew draws on his own earlier music, in particular *The Great Learning*, as well as the general Scratch Orchestra repertoire, to provide musical substance for the work. In the entr'acte before the intermission a 'hissing and booing chorus', which is dispersed amongst the audience, recalls the 'compositions' from Paragraph 5, and the work ends with a long stretch of Paragraph 7 ('The solid cannot be swept away as trivial and nor can trash be established as solid') – except that Cardew actually provides the pitches to be sung, in each individual case, by the sixteen solo singers – a curious detraction from the original. In Act 3 an ambitious section for twenty-four singers (each with his/her own part) derives melodically, with its descending scales, from Ode Machine 4, and Cardew's creation for the opening scene of Act 4 might be perceived as a throwback to AMM and his spatial experiments, which would magically transform the performance area:

Act 4. Stockton-on-Tees. The Arts Centre

Scene: White rope (or a material that floresces in ultraviolet light) is suspended to outline a cube as large as the stage can hold.[54]

Cardew also sets challenging tasks for the choreographer of the dances (which also incorporate mime) that are an integral part of the opera. In Act 3, for example:

Ballet 1. A group of three men, a woman and a child are gathered round a guitar and some drums at one side of the stage. The grown-ups try and get the child to participate, both gymnastically and in playing the instruments.

But his attempts to represent the 'hippie' culture with some jaunty little popular tunes indicates just how remote from the world of popular music Cardew was. Moreover, it was an omen of the difficulties which lay ahead: the espousal of a totally new musical language would present as many, if not more problems than that of a new ideology. Perhaps this was one of the reasons why he was to persevere with the musical styles he had adopted for *The Great Learning*, up to and including its revised version for the Promenade concerts the following year.

1972 saw only one original instrumental composition, *The East is Red,* and even that was based on musical material emblematic of a culture, and its political and national aspirations, of which, at least artistically, Cardew had little or no direct experience. Apart from the revisions of Paragraph 2 of *The Great Learning* there were also routine arrangements for chorus and small ensemble of Verdi's 'Va Pensiero' ('Chorus of Hebrew Slaves' from the opera *Nabucco*), the 'Red Flag', and a traditional Tibetan melody, 'Golden Mountain in Peking'.[55]

The East is Red, for violin and piano, was composed in 1972 and was first performed on 5 December 1972 by János Négyesy and the composer at the Studio for New Music, Munich. It begins with a flourish — fast ascending scales on both instruments which then state the theme simply in unison. In the following variations the unaltered tune is a constant present but ingeniously ornamented and embellished; the writing, especially for the violin, is florid and virtuosic, and Cardew's use of chromaticisms and altered chords enhances the character of the piano accompaniment. The flowing nature of the music serves to maintain the momentum throughout. F major predominates, although in the middle of the piece there is a change of character, *dolce*, and the piano presents the theme in E flat major. Towards the end the violin falls silent and a thunderous sequence of huge chords on the piano provides for an heroic rendering of the theme (Ex.14.4).[56] Remarkably, in view of its profusion of musical content, *The East is Red* is a mere three and a half minutes in duration.

Ex.14.4.

Here Cardew reflects on the reception of a performance of *The East is Red* in Berlin:

This virtuoso piece, depicting the transformation of a simple folk tune into a solemn national anthem and then showing the lilt of the folk tune within that, was played in a concert of modern music in the British Centre, Berlin on 10 February [1973]. The audience responded enthusiastically and the piece was played again; the other pieces were received with sighs and groans. The critics could make nothing of it: one could not make out whether it was ironic, and another could not detect any critique of socialism in the piece. Was I backward to compose it? Were the people backward to enjoy it? This is nonsense. There is nothing to be gained by restricting the productive activity of artists.[57]

A month or two later Cardew again takes up the theme of the reception of music:

Music (culture) supports, backs up the social consciousness of its audience (which is also its indirect producer). Thus when we try and write revolutionary music for the usual audience we're faced with the insurmountable problem of giving it a form that backs up the (bourgeois) class consciousness of the audience. If we succeed, then the revolutionary content is turned around to serve the bourgeois (in its ideas and cultural milieu) audience.[58] If we fail, then the revolutionary content remains but does not touch the audience – you get the negative reaction either on the grounds that it's bad music, or on the grounds that it is an attack on the audience (on their bourgeois consciousness). Music *cannot* be my career as a revolutionary artist.

What about the 'progressives' in the audience? The above suffers from 'logic'. [Added later, as an afterthought? JT.][59]

Notes and references

1　The Crepaz family had become acquainted with the work of Cardew and the Scratch Orchestra through me. I had been the recipient of their generous hospitality on a number of occasions in Solbad Hall. Their concert agency, Galerie Santa Barbara, which was run by themselves and their young children, started up in September 1968.

2　Christian Wolff: *Cues: Writings and Conversations,* Cologne: MusikTexte,1998, p.358.

3　Michael Nyman, 'Cage/Cardew', *Tempo* magazine 107, December 1973, pp.34-5.

4　I remember Cage laughing during a performance in Bremen by Frederic Rzewski and myself of some of Cardew's later political music. It was probably the two-piano work *Boolavogue*. As I recall, it was not a mocking response; I believe Cage genuinely found something funny about the music. I can say no more.

5　Christian Wolff: *Cues: Writings and Conversations,* (MusikTexte) 1998, p.256. In fact, as mentioned above, it *was* recorded.

6　Ibid, p.496.

7　Ibid, pp.104-6.

8　In today's money (2006) around 50 Euros each.

9　Ezra Read was famous in the early part of the twentieth century for his piano tutor. My father, Alan, was one of thousands who learnt the piano with Ezra Read's tutor.

10　In Solbad Hall 'Bells Across the Meadow' was adopted briefly as a kind of signature tune, a piano piece abstracted from a volume of compositions by Albert Ketelby – an English composer (1875-1959) whom one or two Scratch members, such as Christopher Hobbs, took under their wing. The Scratch, or some members, waxed sentimental. Cardew did not approve; he probably thought it flippant. I had already performed the piece on the piano in Cornwall (with the Scratch Orchestra); I remember Catherine Williams standing on the stage next to the piano, dressed elegantly in black and wearing a red rose.

11　At a Soft Machine/Intermodulation concert at the Royal Albert Hall, London in 1972 Harris released locusts in a free interpretation of La Monte Young's *Piano Piece for David Tudor No.3*: 'most of them were very old grasshoppers.' At a free concert in Hyde Park around the same time, the Rolling Stones had released butterflies.

12　This is a straight translation of one part of the interview at the Crepaz home on 5 April 1994.

13　In fact, even people within his 'immediate circle' were always conscious of that 'certain distance'.

14　My son Jasper, aged seven, was in this group. The Scratch Orchestra, and Liz Hay in particular, looked after him and delivered him safely to his mother.

15　One Italian newspaper headline read ' Revolution as aperitif'.

16　Relations between Carraro and myself were strained for some time after the event but we have long ago buried the hatchet and are once again good friends.

17　This summary of Cardew's text was composed on the basis of the original, which is now missing (March 2003).

18　Sue Gittins and myself were the two 'lead singers'; from time to time Bryn Harris cruelly recalls my renditions which, unfortunately, have survived on tape.

19　Jrnl. 1971/72, undated but almost certainly from the early part of !972.

20　From a letter from the American singer Joan La Barbara, dated 31 July 1972.

21　*25 years from Scratch,* p.36.

22   Ibid, p.36.

23   LaBarbara, ibid.

24   Ibid.

25   *Scratch Music*, p.14.

26   According to Psi Ellison Cardew expressed regret that he, Ellison, did not practice, or even use, the violin he possessed. Ellison felt that Cardew would like to have insisted that everybody 'performed' on an instrument, that he wanted to make 'musicians' out of the whole Orchestra. Ellison thought this was absurd and in fact most Scratch members resisted; they were content with their 'non-musician' status; they regarded what they were doing as 'making music'. This may have been Cardew's view in the later years; I do not believe that such an idea would have entered his head at any time prior to the politicisation of the Scratch Orchestra.

27   *Scratch Music*, p.12.

28   Ibid, p.16.

29   Ibid, p.9.

30   Ibid.

31   Jrnl. 25 February 1965.

32   Gerrard Winstanley (Digger), from *A Radical Reader*, ed. by Christopher Hampton (Harmondsworth, Middx: Penguin Books, 1984), p. 231.

33   Bertolt Brecht, *The Measures Taken* (London: Methuen, 1977), p.28.

34   From an open letter of 1930 to 'pessimistic' comrades, *Selected Works of Mao Tse-tung* (Peking: Foreign Languages Press, 1975), vol.I, p.119.

35   From a recorded interview with the author on 9 July 1996.

36   Jrnl 1972, undated but towards the end of 1972.

37   From a letter from Bernard Kelly to CC, dated 1 November 1972.

38   From a letter from CC to Bernard Kelly, dated 8 November 1972.

39   Jrnl. 10 December 1972.

40   Ibid.

41   The cult of Mao Tse-Tung encapsulated the problem of the 'single deity' – what Nietzsche described as 'the most monstrous of human errors', because it closed off the viability of other spaces, other aims. Many Party members and supporters, certainly in the first half of the decade, were in thrall to Mao: the 'single deity'. I believe that Cardew's convictions, which I still hesitate to label 'beliefs' however unshakeable they appeared at that time, were based essentially on Marxist *philosophy,* whose most authoritative practitioners, in the judgement of the CPE(M-L), were Stalin, Lenin and Mao Tse-tung. If he eulogised them excessively and irrationally, unlike some of his comrades he never lost sight of the fact that, whatever their remarkable attributes, they were, like all of us, mere mortals.

42   Jrnl. 1972. Cardew notes in an index at the beginning of the Journal: 'On Contradiction misc. notes *(unused)*'.

43   Ibid.

44   Ibid.

45   Ibid.

46   Ibid.

47   According to a footnote in *Stockhausen Serves Imperialism* the Scratch Orchestra had vetoed Cardew's proposal to include Wolff's *Accompaniments* in the Birmingham programme

for reasons which will be discussed in the chapter on *Stockhausen Serves Imperialism*.

48   From the magazine *Contact*, no.4.

49   Despite these strong reservations he still felt able to support a proposal to reorganize the Experimental Music Catalogue.

50   Jrnl. 1972, 16 December.

51   Not a few of the titles of Cardew's compositions have a touch of humour: *Bun for Orchestra*, because 'a bun is something you give to elephants at the zoo and that is how I feel when I give my pieces to an orchestra to play' and/or because a bun is 'filling but not substantial'. It may also refer back to his schooldays in Canterbury where the doughty bun was a perennial teatime feature.

52   We have seen, for example, how the second *Winter Potato* is a version of *Autumn 60,* and how several pieces are versions or realisations of parts of *Treatise.*

53   We have already noted in the chapter on *The Great Learning* that Cardew had conceived the idea of a Symphonic Ode Machine, an instrumental version of the Odes, sometime during 1971, the year of the completion of the *Octet.*

54   From the score of *Sweet FA.*

55   Dave Smith's arrangement of 'Golden Mountain of Peking' featured a three-part canon. According to Smith this was the only arrangement of his which managed to pass Party censorship.

56   János Négyesy describes *The East is Red* as a 'magic piece', recalling that after every performance members of the audience would be both bewildered and exhilarated: 'It comes and it goes and you think: what happened.' In Cardew's view, what was startling about the piece was that it dealt with 'fact'; the 'fact' being the People's Republic of China and its culture as symbolized by its national anthem.

57   Jrnl. January-April 1973, undated. Eddie Prévost questions whether the anthem *The East is Red* is in any sense at all a revolutionary or proletarian work of art. Is it not more to do with creating an ideology for the emergent state? This was probably Cardew's own view.

58   Analogously, we may contrast the reception of the (bourgeois) revolutionary content of Beethoven's ninth symphony (for example, the clear reference of the Alla Marcia section in the Finale to the French Revolutionary march) in the climate of Metternich's Vienna with its reception at the Royal Festival Hall in our time. The rich and complex psychological states it represents are ironed out, made irrelevant, and the music fits smugly with the demands of an average culture.

59   Jrnl. April 1973-February 1974, 11 July 1973.

Cornelius Cardew a life unfinished

15

AMM versus Mao Tse-Tung Thought 1971–73

In describing what befell AMM in the early seventies there is a conceptual leap which may well create an air of unreality for many readers. That the group's artistic and social identity should have suffered outright rejection from within, from two of its own musicians, and that its achievements, its whole ethos, should have been the object of a hostile, uncompromising critique from the same quarter is, as Cardew himself admitted, a measure of the hold AMM music had exerted over Keith Rowe and himself.

From the formation of the Scratch Orchestra in the summer of 1969 Rowe and Cardew, and to a much lesser extent Prévost and Gare, were involved in two contiguous music-making activities, and it was the hardening of the demands of one of these which was to bring about the partial dissolution of the other. As we have seen, the political rumblings in the Scratch Orchestra began to surface during the summer of 1971, at a time when AMM had reached an artistic peak of maturity. Yet there had been no concomitant growth of political involvement within AMM itself; rather it was the fallout of the politicisation of the Scratch Orchestra which ultimately took its toll of AMM.

After the trauma of the events in the Northeast with the Scratch Orchestra Cardew might have welcomed the respite which an AMM tour in the US, mainly New England, in October/November 1971, would seem to have offered; but the presence of Keith Rowe ensured that the debate pursued its relentless course, and criticism, or rather critical analysis, of the AMM begins to find expression in Cardew's own writings, including those which purported to seek and promote engagements.

On the social side, a recurrent theme is of course that music must attract an audience, and hold it by communicating with it. This communication concentrates of course on emotional response rather than intellectual appreciation. The fact that most 'modern music' plays to dwindling audiences may be responsible for some of our 'phases of exploration' with regard to the audience. The violent bludgeoning of the audience with huge masses of sound, the mantra-like repetition of beautiful sounds that leads to psychological submission, and the development of an intimate private language amongst ourselves that tended to leave potential listeners in the dark – I see these as explorations of escape routes from the 'dwindling audience' situation caused by the increasing intellectualisation of modern music. The aim of our music is to go forward *with* the audience. AMM can show that a constructive spirit and a mood of optimism result from the harmonious working together of spirited individuals. It shows that in spontaneous music-making (as in all other spheres) conflicts can arise, the constructive resolution of which provides taking-off points for further enterprises. It realises that the proper music for human beings is not the music of the spheres or birdsong or the sound of a steam hammer, but the dynamic combination of rhythm and melody (which certainly may *refer* to all these other things) that produces a physical and emotional response in a social context. Only on the foundation of such a response can the mind be stimulated in a meaningful way. The exact nature of the stimulus that the mind receives from the physical and emotional response to the music is dependent on the audience.[1]

One can sense a shift of position here; by confining his argument within the sphere of 'contemporary music' and the avant-garde Cardew contrives to compare AMM music favourably with 'modern music' and its 'dwindling audiences' whilst at the same time initiating criticism of the group from within. By focusing on the question of audience response he is able both to exploit the Achilles heel of contemporary music – its disaffected audience – and to infiltrate prescriptive solutions, as he does with his reference to the primacy of melody and rhythm – 'formal music' – and with the downgrading or marginalisation of 'informal' sound (such as 'the steam hammer'). These criticisms fly in the face of an aesthetic which he himself had helped to forge and develop in AMM, as we have seen in Cardew's own contrasting definitions of the history of music and the history of sound. And it is clearly to this 'informal' sound – 'violent bludgeoning' and 'mantra-like repetition' – that he is referring in his strictures regarding the manipulation and control of audience response, although, ironically, it was precisely a certain predictability of response that he sought in his later political music.[2]

Crucially, this radical shift of emphasis away from 'informal' sound left Keith Rowe in an extremely vulnerable position – as we shall see in our brief discussion of the recordings that have survived from the Dutch tour in 1973. The discrete intervals and intervallic dissonances, the phrasing still dominated by vocal and instrumental influence, the broad, formal schemes of symphonic music, had been replaced in Rowe's contributions to AMM by the creation of vast, all-embracing soundscapes, with phrasing unfettered by received historico-theoretical constraints, and characterised by the subtlest microtonal inflections. Rowe may have been operating outside the boundaries of conventional Western musical practices but what he created did meet Cardew's new demands; it did elicit 'physical and emotional response in a social context'.

It is hard to accept Cardew's thesis in the above quotation – if a thesis can be extracted at all; it comes perilously close to saying that the musician's role is simply to satisfy the listener's expectations. Of course, much music does just this, but what Cardew and Rowe had achieved with their fellow musicians in AMM was to create an entirely new musical agenda in which the audience was invited to participate in the expansion of musical horizons and the discovery of new musical, and human, relations. Cardew's text, uncharacteristically for an AMM member, prescribes and circumscribes, and was an insidious prelude to a canonicity whose artistic tenets, at least as they were represented by its adherents, would find no purchase in AMM. In any case, they had already begun to find political expression in another context: the Scratch Orchestra. As Eddie Prévost has pointed out:

> Such external agendas are dangerous precisely because they are orthodoxies; in that they have a fixed view of the world and ultimately insist upon particular social settings and intellectual conformity. In other words, they, having once invented themselves, become reactionary forces and intolerant to the process of 'self-invention'.[3]

In the above text, it seems to me, Cardew had already embarked on the road to orthodoxy; its reasonable tone cannot conceal the destructive consequences of its implications, especially for Rowe, whose single-mindedness and audacious talent Cardew had found so inspirational.

On a visit to Cologne in January 1972 for a concert which was recorded by West German radio, part of the long journey by road was enlivened by an ongoing argument between Eddie Prévost and Keith Rowe, whose commitment to AMM was by now beginning to wane. What irked Prévost was that whilst Rowe would materialize for a paid engagement in Germany, unlike Cardew he now hardly ever took part in the domestic, informal sessions in which aesthetic and social issues were worked through and which, Prévost insisted, were an essential and integral part of AMM's ongoing musical quest. It must have been a difficult occasion for Cardew – he himself now riven by doubts and making music in the presence, as it happened, of his old mentor, Karlheinz Stockhausen.

For Keith Rowe the problem had become insoluble: the uncompromising nature of Party demands on the one hand, and the moral basis of his commitment to AMM on the other, could not be reconciled.[4] The political model into which Rowe had invested more and more of his lifeblood was a highly centralised one; but AMM was unassimilable by any ideology. The kind of music-making AMM was engaged in did not, could not, reflect this model, and it became impossible to continue with it. In AMM the music was *you*; there could be no half-measures, no escape clauses, no self-deception. Rowe's predicament was extreme because, creatively, he had no where else to go; artistically, he was suffering from an acute sense of displacement. Finally, he made his decision; Art was relegated to, at best, an epiphenomenal status; the meta-musical revolution was to be sacrificed on the altar of a revelatory, apocalyptic ideology which raised the stakes to dizzying heights; 'self-invention', the humanistic quintessence and *raison-d'être* of AMM music-making was superseded by the 'personal salvation' of religious mythology which was promised by the Maoist world revolution.

For many people the abolition of capitalism was indeed both necessary and desirable; and they recognised that a price would have to be paid – although from the comfort of their armchairs they hoped that a deal would be negotiated in gentlemanly fashion and would be paid for painlessly, in instalments, possibly after their deaths. The Maoists poured scorn on these symptoms of bourgeois hypocrisy; 'Revolution is the main trend in the world today' was the watchword provided by Chairman Mao (which Cardew was later to set to music) and the price, the Maoists insisted, would have to be paid in blood. By the end of 1971 both Rowe and Cardew had reached this position; they sought cataclysms. Rowe's break with AMM was brutal, unconditional, and under the circumstances inevitable. It also occurred over a relatively short space of time, bearing in mind the importance which was attached in some of Cardew's later pronouncements to the need firstly to *absorb* the ideas, thereby ensuring a durability of commitment. Like many of his political comrades Rowe had come to exhibit an existential hostility to any manifestation that had not received the Party's seal of approval, that did not pass the supreme test of Party political correctness, whatever private doubts they may have harboured.[5] The 'correct line' was the catchword which was most frequently enunciated in those days, with due gravity and reverence, without which all aspirations, all activity, was destined for bourgeois oblivion.[6]

Cardew's severance from AMM took longer and was less distressing than Rowe's; rather, he allowed his membership to lapse, to peter out. During the second half of 1971, after the Scratch Orchestra tour of the Northeast, and especially during AMM's aforementioned visit to the US, where they were constantly in close proximity, Rowe had belaboured Cardew with an uncompromising critique of his musical activities. At the heart of the analysis lay the irreconcilability of the aesthetic and social tenets of the Scratch Orchestra and AMM with the political models which Rowe and, by now, Cardew espoused. These one-sided discussions certainly contributed to Cardew's politicisation; his well-practised gift of sophistry may have served him well in intellectual pastimes, exercises which sharpen the wits without disturbing the mind, but he could not withstand the ferocity and, above all, the moral purity of Rowe's critique, and he could no longer skirt its implications. Membership of both AMM and the Scratch Orchestra, as they then were, could not consort with communist revolutionary praxis. Either they changed or he must formally countermand his allegiance to them. In fact, a confluence of factors occasioned Cardew's politicization; some were external, as he was caught up in the stormy currents of contemporary politics; others were related to an inner struggle, a matrix of problems and concerns he had addressed with his compositions from the late sixties – in particular *The Great Learning*. If the latter can be regarded as the culmination of Cardew's contribution to the avant-garde, it was also the chrysalis from which pertinent and radical ideas emerged to serve those final revolutionary years when he espoused communism.

In his dealings with the Scratch Orchestra Cardew's behaviour had been shot through with contradictions; he had been lax, liberal, and uncharacteristically woolly-minded.[7] To repair these omissions it was necessary for him to make his position clear and to try to carry the Scratch Orchestra with him, or to abandon it to its own devices. From the perspective of his Maoist comrades the conjunctive facts of Cardew's experiences with both the AMM and the Scratch Orchestra added up, irrefutably, to a damning narrative of petit bourgeois individualism, anarchism and escapism, which could no longer be tolerated. After their own quaint fashion the Scratch Orchestra and AMM, like gadflies, may have achieved some nuisance value, but the prevailing mores of monopoly capitalist society remained unthreatened; genuine revolutionary change was attendant on much sterner stuff. Such was the essence of Rowe's long tirades and I shall return to some of the important issues raised here in later chapters.

Whatever the impact Rowe's lengthy and uncompromising expositions had made, Cardew continued to show up at AMM gigs, deigning to perform. However, he showed less commitment and eventually stopped participating altogether.[8] But in the history of AMM there has been continuous playing irrespective of public performances, which more often than not, certainly in the early years, were regarded as a kind of fortuitous by-product of its private music-making. So that when Rowe, and later Cardew, driven by their political imperatives and the need to abjure all contact with 'bourgeois' art, simply dropped out of the informal playing sessions, it was tantamount to leaving the group altogether. As they later admitted, during the period of politicization public performances were used consciously and solely for political purposes. For it was in the public arena, in the full glare of public exposure and scrutiny – rather than within the confines of someone's living room or in an empty room over a pub – that a new, revolutionary music could begin to be forged.

Discussions did take place between the two 'factions', at Cardew's house in Barnes, during which the ethical norms which inform AMM's music-making were summarily dismissed as irrelevant to the urgent priorities of the class struggle; AMM music was therefore meaningless and ultimately reactionary. While Rowe and Cardew inveighed against all manifestations of non-proletarian art Gare and Prévost remained obdurate under the scathing attacks that their erstwhile colleagues unleashed on their beliefs. As Eddie Prévost perceived at the time, AMM were expected to abandon their musical practice, in an act of redemption, for the ideological gratification of a peripheral, if ambitious, political group. Prévost and Gare were enjoined to submit to Party discipline or to sink into the mire of bourgeois culture. There was no political or ideological debate within AMM (unlike the Scratch Orchestra) until it was too late – when Prévost and Gare were presented with a *fait accompli*. Such a preposterous ultimatum inevitably intensified their estrangement and feelings of hostility both towards the political doctrine in question and its supporters. The group's very existence was now in a parlous situation; Christopher Hobbs had already left the group, in May 1971; Prévost and Gare, benighted impenitents, had been put under the political microscope and found wanting. AMM was now in a state of disarray.

What confronted Prévost and Gare, when the political agenda was finally put on the table, were not the fairly circumscribed demands for party political commitment with which, eventually, some accommodation might have been reached – as was the case with most political groups. Rather it was an apocalyptic, revolutionary ideology which assumed access to every aspect of personal existence, with a political agenda in which the dialectic of morality and action is met head on. It posited the creation of the New Man through revolutionary action (just as AMM sought 'self-invention' through 'meta-musical' practice), determined by Marxist-Leninist or, rather, Maoist ideology and controlled by the Party, whose noble, if quixotic, aim was the emancipation of the 'working and oppressed peoples' of the whole world – to which end it demanded, if necessary, the sacrifice of life itself. In fact, the demand for self-sacrifice was overriding; without it the heights of proletarian emancipation could not be reached.

Thus, there was neither time nor space on the revolutionary agenda for AMM music; as such it was a hindrance, a waste of revolutionary time. More, its content and ethos were considered 'counter-revolutionary', rendered inconsequential by a crippling inability to distinguish the wood from the trees. The way in which AMM sought to manifest and interpret the subtle refinements of its relations within and without its sound-world were denounced as self-indulgent escapism. In the opinion of the Party élite the trajectory and purpose of a genuinely 'revolutionary' Art required a much broader sweep, and a simpler, more direct message: 'The main thing is to learn how to think crudely. Crude thinking (*Das plumpe Denken*) is the thinking of great men', Berthold Brecht had said with a forthrightness which Cardew would have admired.[9] And his elaboration of this characteristically provocative thesis found resonance in the substance of the critique of AMM which Cardew and Rowe were to formulate and exploit during their confrontational sessions with Eddie Prévost and Lou Gare.[10] In the Journals for 1972 Cardew scribbles: 'AMM Frankfurt (ceases).' On the next page he identifies the date, 26 March, and writes: 'AMM at Frankfurt Jazz Festival (last play together).' For a time AMM continued to function as two duos which performed separately one after the other: Gare and Prévost, Rowe and Cardew. But by the time of a tour of the Netherlands, in January 1973, the disjunction of AMM was complete, although Gaudeamus, who were sponsoring the concerts, had understandably billed them as one group: AMM music.

What then was the true function of this 'revolutionary' music proffered by Cardew and Rowe? If it was to inspire the audience through its revolutionary ardour, more often than not it failed; after all the expectant listener was hearing, *experiencing,* AMM music. What it did, it seems to me, was to give succour to the musicians; for at times the music reveals a certain tentativeness, born perhaps of a sudden loss of nerve or a flash of self-doubt which appears momentarily to compromise the performers – musicians whose bold, experimental ethos was dependent above all on self-belief. Perhaps what the audience was witnessing was a deeply personal, and painful, process of extraction or exorcism – a public 'remoulding of their bourgeois world-outlook', a musical purge unleashed and legitimised by an exclusive, unyielding political agenda which prescribed the representation of its interpretation of Chairman Mao's thoughts in all artistic manifestations. Listening to the recordings now, and recalling these arguments, it is as if, at certain moments in the music, we can identify the problems and dilemmas which beset the performers; we can pinpoint the terrible constraints under which their music-making laboured.

In fact, in a strange way the music was enriched by the cluster of ambivalent and contradictory feelings, an inner tangle of tensions and energies, which they carried within them. The concern of the two revolutionaries was to try and transform the sound material which constituted AMM music, no less. Many derivative devices were tried out, and dismissed: they would play tapes of *The East is Red* and other Maoist songs, for example, or, having looked up the schedule of the programmes in *The People's Daily*, they would tune in to Radio Tirana and provide discreet improvised accompaniments.[11] This politico/artistic ploy – an interesting throw-back to the early days when the songs used were by the Beach Boys – was eventually abandoned; aesthetically, it was no different to AMM's earlier use of radio music and was therefore ideologically unsound. The frenzied banalities of the last section of the *Yellow River Piano Concerto*, the apotheosis of revolutionary optimism, feature prominently in most sets from the Dutch tour, but its revolutionary message is subverted by an irreverent accompaniment of grunts and squeaks; the music comes over more as a Scratch Orchestra interpretation of a Popular

Classic – utterly, and one might say, delightfully incongruous.

Cardew's advantage was that he was able to draw on a number of diverse sources in terms of musical language and style; the gestural quality of the jagged piano rhythms and clusters which he occasionally executes, for example, suggests that the piano music of the European avant-garde was still in his fingers. More often than not, however, his contributions are couched within a diatonic, politically-correct framework; after a radio rendering of *The East is Red* towards the end of one of the sets he plays a staunchly diatonic, chorale-like piece which is quite startling. Clearly articulated dotted rhythms, rhythmic flourishes, repetition, are all used to express resoluteness and tenacity, while the stirring, jangling tremolos create an heroic quality. There are echoes and reminiscences of revolutionary songs and allusions to the Beethovenian heroic style, for in every performance he was anxious to rise to the revolutionary occasion; the idea was always to emulate the spirit of the Chinese revolutionary music, to strive towards the indomitable. But in these expressions of solidarity with the transistor radio, in their forthrightness and earnestness, Cardew's contributions came perilously close to parody of the very music which was the source of his inspiration. At least, that was the perception of a good percentage of his audience which, however broadly sympathetic to Chairman Mao's Thoughts, still maintained some reservations and even a degree of scepticism.

And how did Rowe approach the problem? Clearly, compared to Cardew, he did not have access to the wide range of musical resources which the classical heritage offered. What he did was always achieved with consummate artistry: the soaring, euphoric melodic lines he would weave with his guitar, and the wild, exhilarating inventiveness of his electronics were – are – his forte. Yet through his uncompromising political commitment during the early seventies his artistic self-belief was undermined. He continued to play experimentally, the expedient of the transistor radio his only musical concession to the revolutionary theme; perhaps it was his intention 'to reflect the alienation and contradictions inherent in industrial society' whilst the joyful broadcasts from his transistor represented the Maoist solution – a strategy which would certainly have been summarily dismissed by the Party as bourgeois sophistry. For if his radio contribution is abstracted, the revolutionary content – such as it was – evaporates. In any case the Chinese revolutionary music was transformed by the context into which it was transplanted; for all the modifications and changes of material, Rowe and Cardew were still operating within the old AMM aesthetic which could not be adapted to serve the political agenda.

Initially, and by default, Cardew and Rowe were using forms of music-making with which they had become familiar over a relatively long period, so that the new political correctives created a cramping disability and, as a consequence, an eviscerated music, even if, at the time, they regarded them as a necessary corrective to their bourgeois indulgences with the Scratch Orchestra and the AMM. In any case, this was a transitional period of intense politicisation; neither had had any political schooling of any kind and were relatively unfamiliar even with the great musical contributions to political art of figures like Hanns Eisler. Certainly, the Party-political language used, especially by Rowe, the fervour and the pressure for rapid change in people's attitudes and behaviour, the comrades' sheer importunity, were for many alienating and ultimately counter-productive. Eddie Prévost has suggested that in fact there was a certain degree of disingenuousness and that another deeper agenda prevailed at the time; he imputes an impurity of motive which, historians have shown, has tarnished the pursuit of many noble causes. The 'subjectivism' that the comrades constantly attacked in part explains Cardew's and Rowe's own blind espousal of every dot and comma of Party doctrine. For Cardew this doctrine embodied the idea of an 'authority', an elite, to which he himself had always subscribed and belonged – whether as part of a self-confident middle-class artistic family, as member of a male public school, as part of an artistic avant-garde that was mapping out the future of all artistic endeavour, or as a member of a Central Committee of a political party that would emancipate 'the working and oppressed peoples of the world'. As we have seen with his role in the Scratch Orchestra and his choice of a Confucian text for his *magnum opus*, Cardew remained conscious of the need for leadership and authority and, moreover, of his own destiny to fill that particular role.

Listening some thirty years later to the tapes that have survived from the ill-fated Dutch tour, one is struck by both the originality and the eccentricity of the music of the Cardew/Rowe revolutionary duo; at its best there is excitement, tension, movement – a feeling of urgency and intent. Yet what is perhaps most significant is its enduring AMM-ness, even if the imaginations were forced to function within a much narrower frame of references; there is a sense of strain and stress, a profound unease generated by the contradictions of form and content in their music-making. In fact, the bounds of Party orthodoxy were all-too-frequently exceeded – even if by default; the approved subject-matter emitting from the radio would run the gauntlet of AMM music's rigorous demands, for which the transistor's exclusive political message was no match, rendered superfluous by the sheer aural imagination, the exalted tone, of this or that particular imposition of the sound material – the ideologically-inspired orchestral and choral music incorporated aesthetically and all-too-often heretically into the texture.

In the Netherlands the other half of AMM reacted with dignity and resolve to the antics of the revolutionaries. In the Amsterdam set Gare's tenor saxophone weaves an elaborate tapestry and there are beautifully managed, long silences. A rarefied section, with Gare blowing long, quiet tones and Prévost adding a discreet, sparse accompaniment, is vintage AMM. Occasionally, the influence of jazz becomes marked; the musicians seem comfortable with this and the music remains natural and convincing – familiar ground on which Gare, in particular, could express himself freely and self-confidently, with considerable inventiveness and aplomb. And Prévost plays with admirable fluency, executing the feral and the exquisite with so much dispatch. Performing in the shadow of criticism and rejection by their erstwhile colleagues and close friends, they were the upholders of a kind of music-making which they cherished and which was under threat – music which for them embodied an artistic truth untainted by ideological strictures, and they responded to the challenge with flair and imagination.[12]

In 1976, on a hot summer's day, an attempt was made to reconstitute the original AMM, and a 'rehearsal' session was held in Cardew's flat in Camden with the same four musicians. In Lou Gare's opinion the result was 'total rubbish' and he phoned Prévost to say that he saw no future in the collaboration.[13] Cardew showed no interest but by that time Rowe's political imperatives no longer held sway and for a time he and Prévost began to perform together as AMM III and produced a Duo LP for JAPO/ECM.

Such was the political episode in the AMM. However, unlike the case of the Scratch Orchestra and Cardew's life and career as a whole, despite its disruptive influence at the time the politics had no lasting effect on AMM – by which I mean that, ultimately, AMM music survived. It has also developed and changed. But whereas for Cardew and the Scratch Orchestra Marxism-Leninism had cataclysmic consequences, as we shall see in the subsequent chapters, AMM music resisted the sacrifices and changes demanded of it by an alien political agenda drawn up by people for whom the status of art was purely utilitarian.

Notes and references

1   From a hand-written, undated text from the Journals. Almost certainly an introduction to an AMM concert in the US in the autumn of 1971.

2   Interestingly, in the later AMM – in fact, after Cardew's death – many of these criticisms were taken to heart; there are rarely long sections of violent, bludgeoning sound; nor do we indulge in mantra-type repetitions. As for our 'private' language, if it *is* private it would seem nevertheless that a great many people have succeeded in cracking the code. Certainly, we are much more at ease with the references to tonality and with the discrete rhythmicisation of melodic phrases – the kind of approach which can be heard, and admired, in the recordings – if and when they are released – from the Dutch tour in 1973.

3   *No Sound Is Innocent*, p.24.

4   The increasing frequency of the concept and reality of 'Party' and 'Party Line' in the context of Cardew's political life, in this and subsequent chapters, requires an attempt at definition: the' Party' was the Revolutionary Communist Party of England (Marxist-Leninist), later the Revolutionary Party of Britain (Marxist-Leninist), and the 'Party Line' was the embodiment of its political philosophy which could be gleaned, in part, from the pages of its publication *Workers' Weekly*.

5   I remember one occasion when I mentioned the writings of Christopher Caudwell to Rowe; following the Party line he dismissed them. When I asked him if he had read anything by Caudwell he said he had not.

6   'In retrospect, I see their (Cardew's and Rowe's) attitude and actions as a kind of moral bullying. "Political commitment" is not sufficient to explain the hectoring and violent language used against "friends"'. Email communication from EP to JT, March 2005.

7   It was not only the communists who had taken him to task for 'liberalism'; some of his musical friends and colleagues, including, as we have seen, the American singer Joan LaBarbara, had criticised his laissez-faire approach to Scratch Orchestra inadequacies and excesses.

8   Eddie Prévost recalls an occasion at the King's Head pub in East Acton, west London, in March 1972: 'Lou [Gare] and I shared a weekly residency with Evan Parker and Paul Lytton. Keith was not involved. Cornelius, although not expected, arrived and joined Lou and I; we had already started playing. I seem to recall Lou flourishing his handkerchief over the piano keys (dusting them off) and nodding an invitation for Cornelius to join us. The gig got a great review in the *Melody Maker*. Cornelius must have been mulling over just what his relationship with AMM was. I think that this was the last time that he and Lou ever played together in public.' Email communication to JT, sometime in 2003.

9   Walter Benjamin, *Understanding Brecht*, p.81.

10   Eddie Prévost has provided a robust rejoinder to my interpretation here. He argues that Cardew's 'post-AMM analysis is anything but "crude thinking" in the Brechtian manner. He [Cardew] adopted a politically informed artistic line that is uninspiringly similar to every other Marxist-Leninist approach on the issue of music/art in a pre/revolutionary situation. It was propagandist. Rather than thinking crudely you could say that he was guilty of not thinking'. Email communication to JT, March 2002.

11   It could have been the case that these radio intercessions were more apparent than real. In other words, certain themes and programmes could have been pre-recorded so as not to risk releasing politically inappropriate material into the proceedings.

12   In the sleeve notes for the 1994 CD reissue of *To Hear and Back Again* (Matchless MRCD03) Martin Davidson puts this view into sharper perspective: 'The absence of Rowe's swirling veil meant that this duo was the most naked version of AMM – there was nothing for Gare and Prévost to hide behind or amongst. It was also the AMM with the most jazz-like sound, revealing that this highly original pair of individuals had long absorbed their early influences of Sonny Rollins and Max Roach. However, as before, the methodology was unlike jazz – absolutely nothing (melody, harmony, rhythm, tempo) was predetermined.' The LP contained recordings from 1974, whilst material from June 1973 and April 1975 was included on the CD. Incus EP1, *AMM at the Roundhouse*, carried material from August 1972; that entire performance has subsequently been released on CD, again as *AMM at the Roundhouse* (Anomalous Records ICES 01).

13   In his note of June 2003 Gare refers to the *AMM at the Roundhouse* CD thus: 'When Eddie and Keith tried to get it together again with the four of us I could not go back after the freedom of the duo'.

16
Berlin 1973-74

We also firmly believe that to be 'free' in humiliation will only bring disgrace forever, but to fight for truth, though in chains, is to lead a life full of honour.[1]

At the beginning of April 1973 Cardew abandoned the substantial, linen-bound, hard-backed writing books (7 by 9 inches, sometimes larger), initially for a smaller, red plastic-covered Chinese diary commemorating the twentieth anniversary of the China Ocean Shipping Agency, and subsequently, up to February 1976, he used small, regular, soft-backed note books. The note books from the seventies contain relatively few personal or speculative musings (which often have little or no connection with music), such as abound in the earlier Journals. The later Journals include drafts for talks, speeches, political analyses, study notes on reading the Marxist classics, expenditure lists, occasional names and addresses – in short the contents are more critical, more calculating, concerned exclusively with matters of political import. And conversely there is less spontaneity, less open vulnerability.[2] However, in these later Journals there are occasions of self-analysis, when Cardew lapses into an almost confessional mode (à la Wittgenstein), which are often revelatory in ways which he himself might well not have recognised; but in measuring the degree of negligence, or misjudgement, or self-delusion in his actions, and sometimes in his (private) thoughts, he would be doing so in relation to an unshakeable and stark criterion: in what way and to what extent did his actions serve, or harm, the Party and the revolution. Of course, in the early years too, despite the apparent anarchy, there were also criteria which were applicable, and encouraging, to the spontaneity and recklessness of certain thoughts and actions, and to the *modus vivendi* of which they were a defiant and daring expression. For example, I recall that the philosophical maxim: '*l'acte gratuit*',[3] whose very essence covers a multitude of sins, was fashionable amongst young males of an artistic bent in London in the fifties, and in relation to which I remember Cardew once commenting on the need 'to learn the art of letting people down'.[4]

On 8 January 1973 Cardew left for Berlin to take up an 'artist in residence' position as part of the Künstlerprogramm of the German Academic Exchange Service (Deutscher Akademischer Austauschdienst). The financial inducement would have been paramount – he was still in dire straits – and the arrangement was flexible. There seems to have been no great demands on his physical presence although presumably it was taken for granted by the authorities that the artist would make some kind of contribution to musical life in the city as well as using the relatively favourable conditions provided to produce new work. The approximate dates of his presence in Berlin were: 8-24 January 1973; the second half of February and the second half of March; all of April; the second half of May; most of the second half of the year, and a week at the beginning of January 1974. Roughly 9 months altogether. Of course, during these periods he would occasionally absent himself for a few days, normally connected with a performing engagement.

Prior to his departure a lecture at Morley College to an American College choir on 6 January is noted in the Journals. It is hard to imagine what the content of his lecture might have been: a diatribe directed at US Imperialism would have been counterproductive although, as we have seen with his Art School visits, his revolutionary ardour could render him indifferent to the particular expectations and needs of his audience; perhaps the most likely choice would have been an illustrated talk on Irish Republicanism and the musical culture which has always been an integral part of the anti-colonial movement. We know that at that time Cardew was studying the history of Irish music and the Journals list books on the subject which were to be found on the shelves of the Central Music Library in Victoria.

Matters concerning the ideological welfare and progress of the Scratch Orchestra followed him to Berlin. In a lengthy letter (Cardew heads it 'Jan 73?'), which seems to have been written in the wake of a Scratch meeting after the Birmingham Arts Lab concert the previous December, Carole Finer, who at the time was a lecturer in typography at the London College of Printing, complains that some members are 'using' the Scratch Orchestra; they only make an appearance when, in their view, the occasion warrants it: a prestigious concert hall (such as the Promenade concert at the Albert Hall), an art gallery, the performance of works by noted composers. She expresses the view that there should be much more thought, more sense of purpose, more serious research, before the Scratch Orchestra accepts engagements. She suggests that the Id Group is responsible for the deterioration in morale: through lack of time and perhaps a waning belief in the Orchestra's potential for radical change and effective politicisation.[5]

The brief notes in the Journals, usually venues and dates, suggest fitful appearances in Berlin, at least initially, although it is conceivable that events are recorded at which he was not present. He certainly participated in a Scratch Orchestra concert at a London Polytechnic on 9 February.[6] On this occasion political songs were interspersed with talks on China, Ireland and bourgeois culture generally; a discussion ensued – by that time the standard Scratch format. Of the ten songs six were from China: 'This reflects the fact that China is the most progressive state in the world today. The leadership of Chairman Mao, how natural it is that the Chinese people, and revolutionaries in other countries, should revere him.'.[7] The Irish songs were particularly apposite: four Party supporters had recently been arrested during a demonstration against the British presence in Ireland. 'Why were they arrested? Because they touched British Imperialism's sore spot: Ireland. What is the true importance of the Irish situation? A nation that oppresses another cannot itself be free.[8]

The Journals note a 'lecture' at Hillside Comprehensive School in Holloway, north London, on 6 February, and on 10 February a programme of 'Chinese Revolutionary Songs' with the singer Jessica Cash at Warwick University. At the school there seems to have been little written preparation; in the January/April 1973 Journal Cardew had scribbled down a few points relating to the politics of art, the importance of dialectical materialism, and the conflict between religion and science. Perhaps his idea was to engage the students in an off-the-cuff discussion. A lecture at the Bradford school of art on 12 February is noted (with a question mark), and on the same day, apparently, a visit to the Leeds School of Art ('talk only') with members of the Scratch Orchestra: Rod and Joy Eley, Michael Parsons, Bryn Harris and Penny Jordan. The Bradford lecture, if it took place, may have been a taster for his five-day philosophy course scheduled for the following month. On 14 February a lecture at the Chelsea College of Art coincided with a performance of Cardew's *The East is Red* by violinist János Négyesy and pianist Manfred Reuthe at the British Centre in Berlin.

Cardew's commitment to communism or, more accurately, to Maoist doctrine, was by this time unequivocal, and he was now ready to embark on a new stage. This was demonstrated in a letter to the editors of *WEDNR*[9], taking them to task for serious shortcomings which, in his perception, were compromising the effectiveness of the paper. (In his letter he claimed to have read over a hundred issues.) This was a sensible tactic; such criticism of the Party made at a public meeting would have been given short shrift; the response was invariably *ad hominem* – the foolhardy dissenter denounced for holding and attempting to disseminate 'incorrect', bourgeois ideas. Lenin's dictum that the Party needed members with integrity, who would represent a minority 'line' and argue for it, whilst democratically accepting and working for the majority decision, would have been construed as a step too far; even impartial questioning (from the floor), let alone expressions of outright dissent, was given short shrift.

An air of intimidation pervaded Party-sponsored meetings such that people were reluctant even to ask questions, let alone express the mildest criticism. But a letter could be read in private and its contents given due consideration, especially if it emanated from a source of proven seriousness and political rectitude. Acceptance of criticism and subsequent changes in tactics, however limited and marginal, could not involve loss of Party face in a public arena. In his bid to join (eventually) the Party elite Cardew was certainly cognisant of these factors. In essence his criticism related to the 'abstract' nature of the paper:

> The paper is not too intellectual, it is too abstract. It should be more intellectual in a better sense, more intelligent. Political line is not an abstraction, it is held by people.[10]

Cardew's objection was that the articles which appeared in the paper, including a surfeit of reprints from *Peking Review*, did not enhance its status among ordinary English working people, to whom such concerns were remote; there was not enough detailed analysis of *their* situation. The solemn advice for people to study should be accompanied by guidelines on what and how to study. The selection of articles seemed arbitrary and it was therefore difficult to glean what exactly the Party wanted to communicate. And in a telling sentence he wrote: 'The existence of the Party implies an authority; if this authority is not felt it indicates a lack of leadership, and the Party cannot play the part of vanguard.' Nor was the Party leader himself, George Malcolm, spared: 'Malcolm seemed to advance the notion of a daily paper as a long-cherished dream now become reality. Almost as though it was an end in itself.' Cardew's stricture claimed that the Party failed to 'communicate the decisions of the Party, leaving them as a "mystery" that the readers have to solve'. One admires both the boldness and the subtlety of this letter; it did not criticise the Party's aims, it fully supported the Party's ideological stand against imperialism and revisionism. But there was clearly a new agenda; Cardew was trying to create a space for himself within the Party elite, where he felt he belonged. And in due course he was to achieve this aim.

Meanwhile, Scratch Orchestra meetings continued at the Recreation Ground venue in Winchester Road, Swiss Cottage. By now a significant minority of original Scratch members had embraced the political agenda, so that when a Party representative attended a meeting and contended that the group should now be acting under the authority of the Party there was no dissenting voice, or rather, there was no public expression of dissent. Cardew himself was unequivocal:

> To see all our work in the context of the overall strategy of the Party. Not subjectively

to put our own problems first and attach exaggerated importance to them. To deal collectively with the problems of revolutionary work that we encounter as individuals. (This spreading of the revolution on a one to one basis is important.) To develop the theory of proletarian culture commensurately to our present needs. To unite with the Party and with the masses.[11]

Unsurprisingly, Cardew's music-making in the early seventies led to fractures and schisms. For people such as David Jackman, Psi Ellison, Judy Euren, Stefan Szczelkun, to name a handful of Scratch Orchestra members, the idea of creating 'proletarian art' – that is, of submitting to demands based on what they considered to be criteria crudely formulated by a small group of people, a self-appointed 'revolutionary elite', for whom they felt neither sympathy nor respect, was deeply alien. And even for those for whom the politics was inspirational, and gave meaning to their artistic endeavours, it was a daunting task and one which they approached circumspectly – a lack of orientation and of self-belief conspiring to compromise and undermine all aspects of their music-making. The Party demanded a glassy-eyed optimism from its followers and supporters – a consequence of the crude determinism which underpinned its political philosophy at the time – and in his desire to satisfy these demands there is no doubt that these ideological constraints constituted a negative influence on Cardew's own musical experiments.[12] What was missing was the *humanity* which the listener and the participant experience in the revolutionary songs of Brecht and Eisler – stirring songs such as 'Solidarity Song' and the 'United Front Song', utterly without gloss or pretension, which were occasionally performed at Party events and which dug deep at the nerve ends, awakening and sharpening the sensibilities in a way which also managed to convey the enormity of what was actually being proposed, of the task ahead. Inspiring, but never comforting.

Cardew recognized the timidity from which 'progressive composers' often suffered and attributed it to a 'fear of making mistakes':

The only way to combat our mistakes is to make them and bring them out into the open so that it becomes a matter in the objective world, and not a subjective future. Self-criticism – a protracted process.[13]

It is interesting that Cardew still felt that it was incumbent upon himself, as a musician, to offer criticism and advice, to assume leadership. A contribution to the debate surrounding Cardew's role in the Scratch Orchestra from Michael Chant stated what others had preferred to conjecture – that the Scratch Orchestra was Cardew's 'composition'. Chant highlighted the issue of Cardew's changing relationship to the

Scratch Orchestra in a way which seemed to emphasize the need for a resolution:

Notes for Cornelius (possible subtitle? – the obvious)

The Leader question

The old Scratch Orchestra was a composition by C. Cardew. The new Scratch? People in the new Scratch naturally glance up to refer to the composition when in doubt. There is still the temptation to perform the composition – and how are people to behave when pages of the score are missing?

Its not only that the need for self reliance has to be cultivated, but that we understand that there is a need for Scratch (what that need is).

The position of Cornelius as the leader of the Scratch must be normalised (?). Or alternatively the situation must be faced and the leader done away with.[14]

By this time Chant himself had become committed to Marxism-Leninism (or, to be precise, to the CPE (M-L), one of several Parties claiming authenticity), and therefore the question of 'leadership', of political authority and guidance, would have been of paramount importance in relation to the Scratch Orchestra's ongoing politicization. Clearly, like his Party mentors he was uneasy in respect of the ideological residue from the old Scratch Orchestra and the influence not only of Cardew the communist – that was acceptable – but more insidiously of the old Cornelius, from whom Scratch members had learnt so much and to whom, at that point in time, they owed far more than to the Communist Party of England (Marxist-Leninist), even if some of them were now deeply immersed in the task of 're-moulding their world outlook'. That is what Chant is referring to in the third paragraph. The influence that Cardew had exerted over them – which in my view was neither malign nor even excessive – was certainly more profound than that which had been exerted over him by his erstwhile mentors: Cage and Stockhausen. He had shared his life with the Scratch Orchestra.

Chant's reference to 'the need for self-reliance' illustrates an irony which others in the Scratch Orchestra have picked up on over the years. For it is argued that 'self-reliance' was a quality, a virtue, that the old Scratch Orchestra, in its messy, muddled but always principled way, possessed and nurtured effectively and consequentially in the early days, weeks and months of its existence, but which was undermined and corrupted into self-doubt, a sense of inadequacy, and finally into obedience: serve the people by serving the Party. The Party, the inner circle, may have been 'self-reliant', but it had no friends, rather followers and supporters it browbeat or manipulated into a reliance on itself. The nature of the 'need for Scratch' (Chant) was defined and determined by the Party on a take-it-or-leave-it basis. By the 'normalisation' of Cardew's position as leader Chant presumably meant that the new situation, the Party hegemony, had to be recognised. And within that hegemony Cardew was rather low down the pecking-order, though not as low down as the ordinary Scratch foot-soldier who, however, was unlikely at this new stage to refer to Cardew as their 'leader'. They knew that he recognised and abided by Party authority and discipline, that he was taking his orders. And some of them followed suit.[15] For Cardew, the creation of a music, or rather a musical culture, to 'serve the people', the Party, the revolution, was now the only worthy objective for an artist in our time. And in class society the question of 'for whom' remained fundamental. By the mid-seventies his revolutionary credentials were impeccable; he had recognised the 'necessity for change', the need to make a stand, to break with the old (bourgeois) world and its false consciousness. Both outside and within the Party he was considered a man to be reckoned with.

From 19 to 23 March 1973 Cardew was back at the Bradford School of Art to teach (Marxist) philosophy; the decision to jettison music and art reflects the inconclusive nature of his two visits in February and December of the previous year. His desire to awaken political consciousness and to create 'a happy, positive atmosphere' had not been fulfilled. The situation had been blighted by ongoing public rows with members of staff and in the second visit attendance had been depressingly low. As we have seen, the messianic content, the implications of the huge sacrifices that were demanded and, in particular, the *tone* of Cardew's message had alienated the students. On the third visit there had to be 'rectification' but no compromise; the chosen strategy (presumably after discussion with Party comrades whose advice Cardew would have sought as a matter of course) seems to have been a sensible one: to take nothing for granted in terms of the students' political knowledge and understanding; to unravel and define concepts and ideas in down-to-earth language (to avoid 'Party-speak'); to appeal to common sense and the desire for fair play and justice in the world; and, crucially, to objectify the role of the student and the art they were producing, to encourage them to shed what he considered to be the chronic self-delusion from which most of the students appeared to be suffering; to consider the *social* function of art.

The January-April 1973 Journals contain the Bradford agenda in note form, undated. It begins:

What is politics?

What is economic base?
What is Imperialism? (Plunder)
What is Imperialist culture? (Things)

Clearly, this was the *aide-mémoire*, with key words and lines of argument, which he used in his introductory talk to the students. Other concepts and issues included 'proletarian revolution' and its desirability, the necessity and justification for revolutionary violence ('in Africa, South America, Vietnam, Ireland, the people have reached the stage of armed struggle'), the cultural superstructure and the necessity to engage in struggle within and against it, the need for the 'battle of ideas', the proletarian Cultural Revolution (with reference to China), and so forth.

Cardew was never a political 'consumer', by which I mean that he read the Marxist classics creatively, imaginatively, and critically – just as he had always read. He would question a Marxist thesis, a Maoist 'thought', and then perhaps leave the issue unresolved for further reflection and investigation, so that his Journal entries were often in question form:

If revolutionary content cannot stand up in a bourgeois environment, then what hope is there of revolution? [...] In the dialectical unity of theory and practice we insist on the primacy of practice. In the dialectical unity of form and content we insist on the primacy of content. [...] No, see On Contradiction: theory *can* be the principal aspect under certain circumstances. So I suppose so can form. How do things stand today? In ordinary language: Theory can be *ahead* of practice (*must* be?).[16]

At one point in the notes the following headings appear: 'Two questions that occupy me at present: The necessity of building the Party. The possibilities of Revolutionary Culture'.[17] Were these concerns divulged to the students or were they salutary reminders to himself as to the true nature and purpose of his presence in Bradford? His notes do show evidence of a concern for the relationship of the 'revolutionary movement' to students in general:

Students, should we unite with them?
Or should they unite with us?
Which line in fact contributes to party-building?

Attitude to a student audience.
a) we're on their side.

b) but they must change their side (class stand)
This is a problem.

On whose initiative do we gain access to the student audience?
a) on their initiative (student unions etc.) (bourgeois initiative)
b) on the initiative of the revolutionary movement.
Propaganda produced at the request of the bourgeoisie is almost bound to be *for* the bourgeoisie.[18]

On the basis of his experience at Art schools as a visiting tutor Cardew would have been sceptical about the possibility of making inroads and gaining lasting support in the student movement as a whole. The Party's view was that the 'revolutionary idea' could be packaged by the media establishment as an attractive and chic alternative life style to the young, to be consumed and shed according to the dictates of fashion: subscribing to 'left' magazines and broadsheets, parading Che Guevara T-shirts, sprinkling conversation with Marxist sound-bites – rather than submitting to the arduous, unglamorous and unrelenting demands of a serious political commitment. In Enver Hoxha's words:

Today, the phenomena of decay and degeneration of bourgeois culture are becoming more and more pronounced. Its 'isms', which grow like mushrooms, are the clearest symptoms of this decay. Every day 'new' major and minor schools of thought appear like innumerable religious sects and heresies. Nevertheless, they have a common philosophical basis – idealism – with all its endless refinements.[19]

On a sheet of paper, undated but certainly long before he had read a word of Enver Hoxha, or even Marx, Cardew had noted: 'Artistic thinking these days is an endless process of finessing. Without interest'. A decade or so later the German artist Gerhard Richter made a similar observation: '...a mindlessly proliferating activity that is becoming ever less committed'.[20]

At Bradford, and at the Cardiff School of Art, Cardew may have been fighting a losing battle for the hearts and minds of the young. And yet, as we have seen, despite the infrequency and brevity of his visits (although Bradford had offered him a follow-up visit), he invariably made an impact in his meetings and collaborations with fellow artists. The students (and staff) at Cardiff and Bradford would have taken something of him away with them – although perhaps not in the form that he would have preferred at the time – and it might even have been the case that at some critical juncture the memory of

Cardew may have surfaced to play a significant role in the trajectory of their lives. Moreover, there appears to have been no falling away of interest in Cardew as a leading protagonist on the cultural scene in England; invitations followed to lecture at the Hornsey School of Art on 27 March and at the Brighton College of Education on the next day.

Certainly, his Marxism had widened the cultural sphere in which he operated; issues which in the past would have evoked merely a brief, passing comment were now the subject of political scrutiny. For example, in the January-April 1973 Journal Cardew provides a page of notes under the heading 'Clarify the bourgeois character of copyright'. He begins: 'As Trollope shows; when the author is dependent on the success of his work, then the demand for truth in the work gets eroded'. Similarly, private enterprise may initially provide what people need; but the criterion of profitability becomes paramount and private enterprise then has to provide what people do not need and create a demand for it. The 'bourgeois' imagines that he spontaneously desires something which the 'market' conveniently, if not beneficently, provides.[21] Cardew argues that the problem for the petit bourgeois artist who tries to circumvent the corruptive influence of the market is that he/she misses out on 'the struggle for production – the frontier of progress in their particular field':

> They renounce the constant day-to-day handling of the material of their art – hence they become over-theoretical and cannot reach the masses. They revert to the dilettantism of the Enlightenment, patronage, etc. They fail to confront the new situation. They gain the freedom to speak the truth, at the price of not being able to speak it to anyone.[22]

Between 1 and 9 April Cardew was back in Berlin ('with Stella'). On 7 April he directed the Ensemble Musik Projekte Berlin in a concert comprising three works – Frederic Rzewski's *Coming Together* and *Attica* (both 1972) and Christian Wolff's *Accompaniments* (1972), followed by a discussion in which both works were put to the sword by Cardew's trenchant, Marxist-Leninist criticism. By now this had become an obligatory feature of all concerts in which he was involved in an organisational, as well as artistic, capacity. The event is documented in *Stockhausen Serves Imperialism* and is discussed below in a chapter of the same title.

April also saw the publication, in the no.4 issue of the Chinese Journal *Red Flag*, of an article by Chu Lan entitled 'Deepen the criticism of the bourgeois theory of human nature'. The cornerstone of the article is a quotation from Chairman Mao:

> Is there such a thing as human nature? Of course there is. But there is only human nature in the concrete, no human nature in the abstract. In class society there is only

human nature of a class character; there is no human nature above classes. We uphold the human nature of the proletariat and of the masses of the people, while the landlord and bourgeois classes uphold the human nature of their own classes, only they do not say so but make it out to be the only human nature in existence.[23]

And further on, on the same page:

'The fundamental point of departure for literature and art is love, love of humanity.' Now to love may serve as a point of departure, but there is a more basic one. Love as an idea is a product of objective practice.

In other words an infant does not 'love' its mother because she is its (biological) mother but because she is the person who succours it, attends to its needs, feeds and cuddles it. Thus, even the most universal of human sentiments – love – is contingent upon the criterion of 'objective practice'. 'There will be genuine love of humanity – after classes are eliminated all over the world'.[24] This became a key text in the Maoist canon and was often referred to in Scratch Orchestra meetings and discussions concerned with cultural matters, particularly in view of its specifically musical references.

Officially, and briefly, Cardew's first address in Berlin was bei Fink, Herrnhuterweg 16, Neuköln, a working-class district of Berlin. He subsequently moved to Regensburgerstrasse 9, bei Kaehr, in Schöneberg, where he rented a basement room. An undated letter to Sheila Kasabova, soon after his arrival in Berlin, demonstrates how his politics impinges upon the nature of his personal relations and, exceptionally, how it emboldens him to criticise his mentor Wittgenstein.

Thinking of our relationship I keep thinking of Lenin's 'There *is* an absolute *in* the relative', which Chairman Mao quotes in 'On Contradiction'. I think that an intimacy such as ours would produce a kind of 'exclusive' relationship. But Lenin's remark and what Mao says about it sets my mind at rest (at least on that point). I'm still struggling with philosophy. I've brought Lenin's 'Materialism and Empirio-Criticism'. It's not so difficult as I thought it would be. What Lenin says is clear, it's the views he is attacking that are so 'profoundly' confusing. And all his opponents seem to have been relegated to the 'dustbin of history' anyway, which is a comfort. What's interesting is that they seem to be chewing on the same kind of thing as Wittgenstein. I think he too must have been trying to merge Materialism and Idealism, to harmonise them, hence obscuring the absolute struggle between them. Just like the Trade Unions obscure the absolute struggle between labour and capital – under their belligerence they are conciliatory.

I must confess at the moment I feel sort of 'blinded' or 'bowled over' with the brilliance of Lenin and Chairman Mao, and that's no good. Blinded or bowled over people are not a very substantial support for leading comrades, and I must learn to stand on my own feet.

On his arrival in Berlin, and while he was looking for more permanent accommodation, Cardew was invited by the Hungarian violinist János Négyesy to stay with him in his apartment in Charlottenburg.[25] Négyesy describes their first meeting:

He looked very British to me, he even had a tweed jacket on. Our first dinner was basically 'Mr.Cardew' and 'Mr. Négyesy' – until he disappeared into his room and came back with a thick book asking if he could read some parts of it to me. Not knowing what book he had in his hands, I said: 'Of course'. It was *Das Kapital* by Karl Marx. I replied: 'Mr. Cardew, please, don't even open this book, not to mention reading it to me! I had the pleasure of studying the theory of Marxism-Leninism at the Liszt Academy – ending it with a state exam – and I had the privilege to experience the reality of it – just by stepping out of the classroom – in Budapest.' I accused him of being a 'salon communist'. After spending a few days in my apartment in Charlottenburg Cornelius told me that he wanted to live with the people. I replied: 'Fine, I'll drive you to Neuköln. That is the closest place to the people here in West Berlin'. He was back very soon, complaining bitterly: 'It was so awful there, I rented a room – it had no heat and no bathroom! Next door were two sailors, always drunk and loud. Prostitutes were walking under my window all night, doing business. No phone, no privacy. Terrible!' I did not say anything. He was right, but they were the people Cornelius was looking for.[26]

During the years I spent with Cornelius I learned how deep his belief was in justice and equality. His active political life in West Berlin showed me – especially in the Künstlerhaus Bethanien protests – how seriously he was fighting for the people's rights.[27]

Zoltan Peszko, the Hungarian composer/conductor whom Cardew had known from his Rome days and their studies with Petrassi, recalls the conditions in Regensburgstrasse as 'ascetic', unsurprisingly in view of Cardew's predispositions, and for a time felt sorry for Cardew – that is, until he discovered that the Westerner Cardew's stipendium was considerably larger than his own. But Peszko liked Cardew and as he had contacts at Zerboni publishers in Milan suggested that his English friend should send them some of his compositions; Petrassi, too, sent references. Zerboni responded positively and requested recent works. A few months later, on a visit to Milan, Peszko was shown the 'composition' that Cardew had sent: a piece of paper torn out of a school exercise book across which he had inscribed a Maoist slogan. Cardew later told Peszko that it had been his intention to shock the publisher, that his interest was now music and politics, and the 'class struggle'. His aim was to demolish links with the content of contemporary bourgeois music, and with a cultural system he regarded as a cruel and cynical fraud in which the unwary, in George Steiner's words, can be 'caught in the net of old values, of the grammars that can condescend or enslave'.[28] The 'graffiti' he sent to Zerboni exemplified his rejection of all the conventions of contemporary (bourgeois) musical discourse.

A single, hand-written sheet, undated but almost certainly from around this time, succinctly summarizes Cardew's political agenda:

What are the themes that any artist worth his salt has to tackle today?
Fascism
War

Revolution
Socialism

Are there other themes? Yes – human relationships, the family, work, science.

But in the present circumstances these are subsidiary and should be linked to the 4 main themes.

How should these themes be treated? Positively – so that the artist can actually take up his real role as an instrument of enlightenment and progress, as a factor for uniting the ordinary working people to take up their destiny and exert themselves for the forward march of humanity.

Go into the themes in more detail. Underlying all of them is the crisis, the class struggle. Democracy. Peace. The working class. The Social Order. Military in art. Sensitivity in art.
Breadth in art.

Scientificness in art. Partisanship in art. Truth and Objectivity in art.

The references to 'human relationships' and 'the family', against a background of his own personal problems at that time, are an impelling reminder of the hierarchical nature of his thought (and feeling); the 'themes' of fascism, war, revolution and socialism constitute Mao's 'principal contradiction': monopoly capitalism impinges on 'human relationships' – threatening, undermining, distorting, destroying. Ultimately, it is only through the eradication of capitalism and imperialism that the truly *human* potential of such relationships can be realized. To believe and act otherwise is to engage in a futile exercise in self-deception, with bitter and depressing consequences. Cardew concludes: the all-embracing and fathomless relation of art to the *realities* of human life (the 'military', the 'scientific', the 'partisan' and so on) has been impoverished and disfigured within the context of bourgeois culture.

Such weighty issues would doubtless have been given due consideration by the 'study group' formed in Berlin and whose first meeting, as noted in the Journals, was on 27 May. According to Cardew they were 'a motley selection springing from the concert and discussion I put on in April. Despite a revisionist member we start from Yenan [Mao Tse-tung's Talks at the Yenan Forum]'. More pressing were the rehearsals of the Ives sonatas with Négyesy, which continued unabatedly, whenever he was in Berlin and for several months; there were occasions when they would work on the pieces for five or six hours during the day. Négyesy recalls that there was little discussion; from the very first rehearsal they enjoyed a mutual approach to the music, both in general and in matters of detail. And during the first part of the month Cardew had been in Rome participating in a Symposium on 'Music of the Fifties'. A note in the Journals reads: 'Play 3 W.Pots (Winter Potatoes) and talk.'[29] A draft of the talk, which was as abrasive, scathing, and unrelenting as one had come to expect, appears in the red, plastic Chinese diary; most of the content is duplicated in *Stockhausen Serves Imperialism,* to which the following chapter is devoted. ('In the avant-garde the fifties were productive and now we are unproductive and some people are worried about this. But let's get it straight. The avant-garde has made the transition from illusion to disillusion. This is a very good thing'.[30])

Meanwhile, on Fridays in London, the Morley group continued to meet; many were also Scratch Orchestra members but it managed to lead a relatively autonomous existence, although, as would have been expected, the content of the course mirrored the changes that the Scratch Orchestra had undergone and it was no longer an 'experimental music' class.[31] This came to the attention of the Principal, Barry Till, who sat in on a class. He observed that there was no music, only discussion, and that the proceedings bore no relation to what was in the prospectus; he was therefore considering closing the class. All this was conveyed to Cardew in a letter, dated 23 May, from Michael Chant, by then a comrade-in-arms, who also reported on the group's 'successful' presentation on the theme of Ireland at the London School of Economics. Significantly, Chant makes the point that 'the most positive aspect was the further consolidation of the Scratch Orchestra around the political line of the Party'. In his reply, dated 29 May, Cardew informs Chant that he will attend the Morley classes on 8 and 15 June, where next year's class can be discussed, and that he intends to submit a proposal: 'a sort of course in Irish History through Music'. Referring to the situation at Morley Cardew writes: 'You may want to struggle with Barry Till for the retention of the class in its present shape. I don't know whether we could prevail or not.' [32]

On the same day, in ideologically more neutral language, Cardew wrote to Michael Parsons (who had resigned from the Morley class at the end of 1972) suggesting that the Morley class be reconstituted and outlining his proposal for the Irish music course: Parsons would be responsible for musical research while Michael Chant and Alec Hill should keep a watchful eye on the 'political line':

As far as I've studied so far there is hardly an aspect of the Irish struggle that doesn't have its musical reflection. It should be possible to produce an anthology of Irish music with a Historical Materialist commentary that would help to dispel some of the widespread ignorance of the background to the Irish struggle now.

The aim of the course would be to integrate more with other students at Morley College, drawing in new people, or it could be run independently of Morley if the authorities place more restrictions on the group's activities. The letter also reflects Cardew's self-doubt in relation to the Scratch Orchestra as a whole:

This is all tentative. My ideas and suggestions are often treated with a certain amount of scepticism and suspicion, and from a position of absence I don't want to sway things my way against a lot of opposition. However, the idea seems sufficiently important to me that I will probably press on with it independently of Morley – with your help if you are interested.

Cardew treated Michael Parsons respectfully and with discretion; he knew Parsons did not subscribe to the Party and its political line. Nevertheless, it was deemed important to maintain a positive relation with the 'progressive liberals' – at least at this stage. In the letter he seems to be adopting a more confidential, heart-to-heart tone, as if he were hoping to gain a measure of mutual understanding, solidarity, even complicity from Parsons.

Already two months earlier Cardew had made 'a clear statement of the orientation and present tasks' of the Morley group in which he defined the common ground: 'trying to change society and genuinely to serve people'.[33] Only through revolution and the overthrow of imperialism, he asserted, could this be achieved. He also insisted, which he did on every formal and semi-formal occasion, on the necessity to build and support a revolutionary Party. The assumption was that the group would consolidate around the Party line – that is, under Party authority – and would produce and perform songs at Party functions. Cardew described the Morley class as a

> Music Workshop in the service of the working and oppressed people of England and the whole world. Our aim is to forge revolutionary music, as an integral part of the revolutionary movement. The tasks of a revolutionary music group are three: 1) Criticism of the bourgeois and attacking the fascist lines in music. 2) Strengthening and consolidating our own proletarian revolutionary line. 3) The creation and performance of new music[...]. Our work cannot but advance with the advance of the revolutionary movement. With the Great Proletarian Cultural Revolution and the revolution in Peking Opera, everyone is quite clear about the function of music in a socialist country and its role in the prevention of the restoration of capitalism.

In a handwritten afterthought Cardew reminds himself:

> We should not be worried whether our musicians and artists are 'revolutionaries'. That is up to them (as it is up to every individual). As long as they are not anti-communist we should make them feel welcome and encourage their activities and initiatives.

Cardew gave much thought to the question of the relationship of the artist to the Party. In the same month, March 1973, in another criticism of the 'Morley College Scratch', type-written on a single sheet, he writes:

> We do not struggle in a proletarian politically conscious way to establish the correct relationship between our artistic organization and the Party. Our reasons for wanting to play to the Party are based on the employee mentality.[34] This line has the effect of liquidating the role of revolutionary art as a contributory factor to the growth of the mass movement.

And as an afterthought he notes:

Art is not politics. The Party will not organise creative work. Ever. My mistake; to expect directives from the Party.

This may well have been a positive conclusion to draw, but it placed enormous responsibility on his own shoulders – that of implementing the Party line in the manifold cultural activities over which the Party felt it could exercise varying degrees of control. Cardew was now a 'commissar', and it was his job to keep members and supporters of the Party on the straight and narrow. Of course, he had been used to assuming authority and giving guidance in the old Scratch Orchestra, but as a Party activist he was now much more self-conscious, his 'man-management' more rigorous, more demanding, more inquisitorial. Moreover, the Party agenda necessitated ongoing *self-criticism,* a dictate to which he was particularly vulnerable in view of the ideological baggage he had inherited, the 'bourgeois world-outlook' which would occasionally blur the purity of vision of the true revolutionary ('fight self – repudiate revisionism' was the oppressive watchword at the time). He had to become a tougher task-master but at the same time without alienating people and thus losing their support for the Party – something, in view of its modest numbers, the Party could ill afford. His own creative work was also under scrutiny, and under attack, too, from a number of sources, which I shall consider in a later chapter. Support for Irish Republicanism and the Peoples' Republic of China were the main sources of inspiration: song arrangements such as 'Ireland belongs to the Irish People', 'Stand up and Fight', 'Long Live Chairman Mao', and *Piano Album 1973* – most of these were completed and performed during the first part of 1973, in a variety of venues and with sharply contrasting responses.

For most of the second half of the year Cardew was in Berlin, making occasional visits home to the family when he would also be able to catch up with Party news and with the ongoing situation regarding the politicisation of the Scratch Orchestra. In the Journal April 1973-February 1974 there is a report of a hearing at the Marylebone Magistrates' Court on 14 June. According to Cardew the police had framed Party comrades, planting cannabis in their flat. The police had previously provoked the comrades who were then charged with intent to cause a breach of the peace. The magistrate's wish, according to Cardew's notes, was to make the police case watertight by eliminating its weakest charges.

In relation to the Scratch Orchestra (or what was left of it) Cardew was still pushing for it to adopt a Leninist democratic centralist structure. At a meeting comprising fifteen people on 15 June he put forward the reasons for a 'Scratch committee' in what was now a familiarly dogmatic fashion. His notes read:

In order to be active we have to be organized. A committee is the prime necessity for organising anything. Discussion as to whether we need a committee is useless. If we want to do anything we must have a committee.

The Leninist model is made clear in his note on the 'Authority of the Committee':

The committee makes decisions, puts forward its reasons, and these are discussed. If there is general acceptance, the decision is implemented by all. Minorities have to swallow their reservations and submit to the authority of the majority.

This clearly demonstrates how far away from the original Scratch Orchestra ethos the political group had moved. Such a committee would never have been accepted; indeed, it would never have entered the Scratch imagination. The flaws in what is routinely described by political analysts as the 'Leninist' model are obvious.[35] What happens, for example, if there is no 'general acceptance'? How would such an impasse be resolved 'democratically'? In practice a committee's decisions can be steamrollered through because the time allowed for discussion is (intentionally) inadequate. The committee knows the agenda and is therefore well prepared; others can only react spontaneously without the benefit of reflection and consideration. The response is mostly individual; individuals can be picked off by an intransigent, united committee, and they have no choice but to submit to the authority of that committee – that is, to the authority of the Party. From start to finish, the Party pulls the strings.[36] Over the next six weeks there was much debate and considerable 'struggle' on this question. Generally, in a mirror image of the Party, whose position brooked no opposition, all dissent was summarily dismissed as the expression of petit bourgeois sentiments and hang-ups, under the insidious influence of a corrupt ideology. The advice to these confused souls was usually couched in words which have become part of Maoist mythology: that they should 'remould their world-outlook.' Such was the situation in the new Scratch Orchestra.

On 26 June, at the Berlin Philharmonic, the Berliner KonzertChor under Fritz Weisse performed Paragraphs 7 and 2 of *The Great Learning*. Cardew appears to have had little input, apart from assisting in rehearsals; perhaps an agreement had been reached with the Philharmonic and the conductor whereby his influence was restricted. He may not even have attended the concert. As we shall see, his intervention in a performance of two Paragraphs in Berlin the following year created a depressing experience for both participants and audience. A more congenial engagement awaited him two weeks later when on 6 July he travelled to Hamburg to rehearse arrangements of nine songs from China with the German singer, Geeske Hof-Helmers. On the next day he and

Ms. Hof-Helmers, together with János Négyesy, were in Bremen at the Serenadenhof, a café popular with tourists and perhaps a somewhat incongruous choice of venue for a concert which included Ed Fulton's *Violin Music 5*, Cardew's *The East is Red,* and the nine Chinese songs. On the next day, 8 July, he returned to Berlin.

On that same day, in southeast London, the Morley class was closed, as had been threatened by the principal Barry Till, and the group was trying to galvanize support amongst the students there. Penny Jordan, a member of the class who had also been Cardew's student at the Royal Academy, produced a leaflet, The Unjust Closure of Our Evening Class, for distribution:

> The reasons he (Barry Till) gave were as follows: 1) Although attendance was reasonable some of those attending had not paid their fees – this was immediately rectified. 2) The teachers listed in the brochure were not in fact teaching the class – this was because our meetings were chaired in rotation by students and 'teachers' alike. 3) the content of the workshop did not correspond to the notice in the brochure – this was not true. The real reason for his closing the class is not any of those given, but a desire to suppress the serious discussion of political issues in any connection within the College. In this he is carrying out the educational policy of the ruling class.

Such minor set-backs would have been met with ever greater resolve; efforts would have been redoubled and the group would have participated in Party celebrations for China's National Day on 1 October, as well as the SACU (Society for Anglo-Chinese Understanding) one-day event (performing songs), with boundless enthusiasm and commitment.

In August a Scratch programme was agreed upon: 1. Investigation, analysis and repudiation of various manifestations of bourgeois culture; 2. Production of new political songs and arrangements for existing songs – as requested, in particular, by the Party – to be performed at Party rallies and socials; 3. Development of own creative work – although because this was considered to be the most problematic area, it should therefore have the least emphasis at this stage. According to Hugh Shrapnel's circular letter (in Cardew's absence Shrapnel had taken over the administrative duties), 'a summary of the Scratch meeting we had on Monday 13th August',

> these 3 areas also clarify the question of the relationship to the Party. Only (2) comes under the direct leadership of the Party, and it is this aspect of our work through which we want to approach the Party. For the rest of our work we shall consider ourselves as a separate group, not under direct discipline of the Party.

In fact, this was a rather naive assumption; the Party's directives hung heavily over every aspect of the (Scratch) group and controlled – that is, subverted, every activity. Moreover, this would have been in accordance with the objectives of Cardew and the more hard-line supporters. The Party, in its wisdom, had expressed the desire for newly-composed instrumental accompaniments for the revolutionary songs at meetings. Shrapnel also mentions a play, 'with revolutionary content', by Scratch member Frances Rifkin, and proposes the favoured, Party-approved procedure that extracts should be performed 'with a view to criticising it, changing it, with the Scratch as a whole perhaps eventually making a contribution, such as songs, etc.'. In the same letter Shrapnel also moots the idea of re-naming the Scratch Orchestra, which it was generally agreed was a redundant and misleading nomenclature.

Back in Germany, between 24 and 26 August, the 1973-74 Journals note a concert in Bonn for Josef-Anton Riedl by Cardew and myself with a programme of Cardew's recent piano pieces and arrangements of Chinese Revolutionary songs. The books for summer reading are also listed: these include Marx's *Critique of Political Economy*, Hegel on Aesthetics, books on Irish history, and the *History of the CPSU (Bolsheviks)*. For September the Journals list a 'study programme' which includes the English Cromwellian Revolution and unspecified works by Lenin and Hegel. With respect to the socialist education from which, in his youth, he had been protected, Cardew's thirst for knowledge and understanding was insatiable. These works were not simply read; they were annotated and copious notes were made in the Journals and note-books; there is much evidence of serious, detailed study. In the 1973-74 Journals there are extensive, painstaking notes, over fifty pages, and in great detail, on Irish history. These were culled from various sources, including T.A. Jackson's *Ireland Her Own,* and James Connolly's *Labour in Irish History*. The latter contains important material judging from the number of quotes from it in the Journals; and with each chapter Cardew was at pains to identify and analyse the present effects of past history. A.L. Lloyd's book *Folk Music in England* was an important source, and there are also notes on Werth's *Musical Uproar in Moscow*. The Journal contains lists of Soviet books, music and periodicals from the Stalin era; Zhdanov's views on music were of particular interest to Cardew.[37] At the time he was also completing his book *Stockhausen Serves Imperialism* and attending a German short course, at the Goethe Institute at the DAAD expense, for which, on 11 November, he received his Kleines Deutsches Sprachdiplom. Christmas was spent back home with the family and an old friend from Germany, Klaus Koch.

An entry in the Journals dated 12 September 1973 states briefly: 'Bethanien begins'. Presumably this refers to the beginning of the campaign, in which Cardew was prominent, to save a Berlin hospital. Around a year later, in the September 1974 Journal, Cardew describes the background to the campaign in some detail. Lengthy though it is, it may well have formed part of the introduction to his recital programme for Bristol, York and Oxford in October 1974:

Bethanien is the name of an old hospital complex in one of the poorest quarters of Berlin. In 1970, after £1m. had been invested in renovation work, the hospital was closed, and since then the buildings have been empty − heated and renovated but empty. The Berlin City Senate has plans to develop this again − Kreuzberg − from a working class district (now inhabited largely by immigrant Turkish workers) into a bourgeois district with luxury flats and expensive shops and palatial parks and motorways. 80% of the present population would be constrained to move out into concrete jungles on the edge of the city. Plans like this aren't restricted to Berlin. They are rolling in most metropolitan areas of the capitalist world. The technique employed is not pretty: the first stage is to 'dry-out' the area, as the planners say. Close hospitals, post offices, and other public amenities, worsen the transportation and inform the landlords of their plans, so that they stop doing any repairs or improvements to their properties (because of imminent compulsory purchase orders, etc.). At this stage of seediness many inhabitants move out voluntarily. Then the planners take steps to make the area attractive to capital investment. Announce plans for civic centres, motorway links etc. In Kreuzberg they had the grand idea of converting the Bethanien ex-hospital into an Artists' Centre − obviously they felt they should build on the somewhat Bohemian tradition of the area.

Since by this time the health services in the area had plummeted to the point that for instance one doctor specialising in children's health was responsible for 10,000 children (as compared with 1 doctor to 1200 children in other parts of the city), the decision to open an artists' centre in a well-heated and equipped hospital evoked a storm of protest. Local community groups and left-wing political groups in the area supported this protest and a strong mass movement under the leadership of the KPD (German Communist Party) developed. The main targets were of course the local governments' urban renewal plans, government health policy, and the construction capitalists who stood to make vast profits from the development. The focal point of the campaign was Bethanien, and gradually a number of artists with a stake in the future artists' centre were drawn into the campaign on the side of the people. I was one of these, and I worked as an activist in the campaign for 6 months, thus drawing down on myself the bitter hatred of my employers − the DAAD(German Academic Exchange Service), who were heavily implicated in the proposed artists' centre.[38]

Michael Heardter, the then general Secretary of the Akademie der Künste, and from 1973 to 1999 the Director of the Künstlerhaus Bethanien, understandably puts a somewhat different, though equally plausible, gloss on the story, recalling that Cardew was 'not much of a friend of the Bethanien'. The campaign certainly made it more difficult for him to establish the Artists' Centre; some important figures (including the German artist Rebecca Horn) refused invitations, not wanting to get involved in the controversy.

Heardter maintains that the majority of artists in Berlin at the time supported the Künstlerhaus; even those who campaigned *for* the children's hospital, such as the composer Erhard Grosskopf, were not necessarily against the Artists' Centre. In fact, Grosskopf argued that the two institutions were not only both desirable but also mutually beneficial. It is very unlikely, however, that Cardew would have conceded this; he saw the art that was being produced and proposed as a pernicious and degenerate manifestation of bourgeois culture and would have opposed it irrespective of the children's clinic. In fact, the campaign continued for some time and when, in 1975, after the Künstlerhaus Bethanien had officially opened, there were local elections in Kreuzberg, core members of the Communist party stood as candidates with the aim of overturning the decision; they were unsuccessful and the campaign died out. And yet, the song which Cardew wrote for the Bethanien campaign lives on in the memory of many who were involved, even if, curiously, few of them have any memories of Cardew himself. Erhard Grosskopf, a musical comrade from that time, has suggested that the participants in the Bethanien campaign may have enjoyed singing the song but they would not have been interested in knowing the name of the composer.

Cardew's sojourns in Berlin may have been sporadic but, according to Grosskopf, he did show considerable commitment: co-organising and attending meetings, demonstrations and concerts, leading discussions, and rehearsing choirs whenever he was available. He also managed to compose, among other works, pieces from the two *Piano Albums* and the *Thälmann Variations* during his time in Berlin. Grosskopf recalls that at the time Cardew held an extremely 'hard-line' position; his own work, *Looping,* written for the British group Gentle Fire*,* contained a text by Mao, his treatment of which was severely criticized by Cardew: too 'aesthetic'; the translations too 'poetic'; and the music altogether too 'abstract'. In his criticism and dismissal of the avant-garde Cardew was unequivocal.

Almost a year after Cardew's departure from Berlin, on 16 December 1974, he returned to take part in a particularly memorable event: a politically-inspired concert at the Quartier Latin, a large space normally associated with the underground rock scene. The programme consisted of Cardew's *Thälmann Variations* and works by Grosskopf,

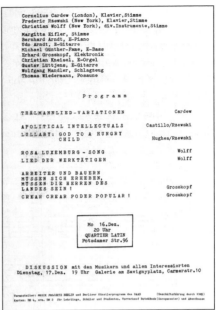

Rzewski (with texts), and Wolff (including his *Rosa Luxemburg – Song*). The DAAD had unwittingly funded the event which was explicitly in support of the Bethanien campaign and therefore diametrically opposed to the aims of the DAAD and the Berlin arts establishment. Grosskopf had received the cheque just hours before the directors noticed the poster for the event which, in a gesture of disarming candour, he had displayed in their office. The concert attracted between eight hundred and a thousand people; at one point somebody from the audience jumped onto the stage and began to rouse the whole audience to repeat, in hushed tones, the phrase: 'the people, united, will never be defeated'. It was one of the defining moments of the event. Journalists from leading newspapers criticised the participants, branding them as *nützliche Idioten* (useful idiots), that is, as 'puppets' of the German Marxist-Leninist Party.[39]

Christian Kneisel, who participated as a keyboard player in the Quartier Latin concert and who later secured the post of secretary of the Music section at the Akademie der Künste (a position he held until 2001), recalls that during that period in Berlin, from the late sixties to the mid-seventies, it was virtually impossible for a foreign band to perform in the city unless it was aligned to a particular 'cause', usually anti-Vietnam war and invariably anti-American (Berlin attracted a significant number of 'draft-dodgers'). The 1971-72 Pink Floyd concerts were in fact benefits for the German Communist Party, but

Frank Zappa's show in the late sixties, with no such 'sponsorship', had been successfully disrupted by leftist/anarchist, SDS students (Sozialistische Deutsche Studenten Bund)[40] with Zappa himself shouting his own self-revealing, counter-revolutionary slogan: 'What we want is not revolution, but evolution'.

Cardew himself contributed to the anti-Vietnam war campaign with a setting of words which were probably provided by German comrades: 'Lied der Anti-Imperialisten' (Ex.16.1). The march-like character recalls Eisler's political songs, which Cardew knew well and had often sung; the last five bars of the refrain end the song on a note of militant optimism:

Ex.16.1

Almost every week there were big demonstrations against the US and the West German government, particularly in Berlin and Frankfurt. There were violent clashes with the police and the situation was often close to civil war, compounded by the fact that the RAF (Rote Armee Fraktion) were still active at the time. And, inevitably, the various leftist groups would often fight amongst themselves. Some of the musicians who supported the SDS, for example, felt uneasy about performing with the likes of Cardew and other Maoist supporters of the KPDAO (Aufbau Organisation) Marxist-Leninist group. There were also artistic divergences which, as we have seen, were also the subject of much debate in the Scratch Orchestra in England. In essence the argument ran that a popular 'people's music' already existed (rock music) and that the experiments by the Maoists to forge a new popular music, based on Chilean, American or Chinese workers' songs, as in the Quartier Latin concert, were irrelevant and conceptually flawed. Yet the early seventies saw many collaborations between forms of 'high' and 'low' art, between classical and avant-garde composers and rock musicians – some of them 'stars'. According to Kneisel Cardew himself 'improvised' with Tangerine Dream in one of their Berlin concerts.[41] The State's reaction was characteristically heavy-handed; under a piece of legislation known as the 'Berufsverbot' it became impossible for somebody who had been a member of a communist party, or was a known, leftist activist/sympathizer, to secure or hold down a job as a 'civil servant' with even the most minor administrative responsibilities.

Cardew officially relinquished his position as artist in residence at the DAAD on 15 January 1974. The next day he left Berlin to join Steve Reich and his musicians for a month tour in the United States (17 January – 16 February). In an undated note in his Journal, a small green note-book with the dates 5.3.74 – 9.4.74 written in pencil on the front and drawing far less attention to itself than previous, weightier journals, Cardew makes a point with reference to specific pieces by Howard Skempton and Steve Reich:

Mystical composers seek an archetype.
Skempton Drum No.1
pg [Philip Glass] 1 + 1
Reich Clapping music? [42]

On the next line Cardew draws a comparison: 'This is like their closest approach to the word of God, the simple and unique source of all multiplicity'.[43]

Meanwhile, the Scratch Orchestra had been invited to contribute to an event at the Institute of Contemporary Arts on 25 January. Cardew himself provided a draft of a talk entitled Art to Serve the People, which the Scratch Music group completed and presented. The relatively short talk, which was no more than a statement of the Party cultural line, began with a brief history of the Scratch Orchestra and proceeded under a series of headings: Our Society is a Class Society; The Monopoly Capitalist System, by its very nature, must inevitably lead to its own destruction; What has Art to do with Politics?; How can Art serve the People? Following the talk the audience were invited to take part in a discussion in which a number of complementary issues were raised: art for art's sake; the relationship of form and content; the way in which bourgeois culture is used to deceive and oppress the people, and to divert their struggles; revolutionary art from past and present struggles.[44]

Just two days after his return from the tour with Steve Reich, on 18 February, Cardew joined forces with another English communist composer, Bernard Stevens,[45] for a joint talk at the Royal Holloway College in Egham, Surrey. This had been organized by Scratch Orchestra member Brian Dennis, who was on the staff of the College. Stevens, a likeable man who taught composition at the Royal College of Music, was from an older generation of communists, tainted no doubt with 'revisionism', but in relation to musical matters there would have been much common ground.

Cardew had returned home to a war-torn Britain in which the working class, not for the first, or the last time, had been cast in the role of 'the enemy within'.[46] On 4 February the miners had voted to strike by a huge majority and a three-day week had been introduced. The Prime Minister, Edward Heath, responded with an election on 28 February to settle the question blazoned across the front page of every newspaper in the country: Who Governs Britain? The Communist Party of England (Marxist-Leninist) put up two candidates: Carol Reakes in Battersea North, and Ekins Brome in Lambeth Central. Place and time of meetings, mainly open air, were announced during the day through the Party's loudspeaker van and an impressive Communist Manifesto, comprehensive in the range and scope of its message, was distributed in the streets – its main target the treacherous Labour Party:

> The periods of Labour Government are always characterised by more repressive legislation being developed against the working class, all in the name of 'labour', and the Labour Party fully supports imperialist policies of the British monopoly capitalist class at home and abroad. It was the Labour Party who in the name of 'labour' sent the British Imperialist army into Ireland in 1969 to massacre Irish working people.

However, the Party's prognosis went largely unheeded, and with 37% of the votes cast the Labour Party was duly elected.

On 5 March a concert at the Purcell Room, organized by Cardew, included his *Three Bourgeois Songs* and arrangements of nine Chinese songs, convincingly rendered by Jane Manning and accompanied with verve and panache by the composer himself. Four Proletarian Songs were performed by People's Liberation Music (PLM)[47], Cardew's arrangement of *The East is Red* was sung by a small chorus with piano accompaniment, and some solo piano pieces based on Irish themes from Cardew's *Piano Album 1973* were rather ineptly performed by myself.[48]

The concert turned out to be a watershed in Cardew's musical career; according to Laurie Baker it was the first time that Cardew had heard PLM and he was 'on the edge of his seat'. On 23 March a PLM rehearsal had been arranged at Baker's house in Shepherds Bush; on answering the doorbell at the appointed hour he found Cardew waiting on the doorstep. Apparently, I had sent Cardew as my replacement, an offer he gladly accepted. At the time my professional teaching and piano commitments, which involved frequent visits out of London and abroad, made it difficult to appear on a regular basis with PLM and it had been agreed that eventually a replacement should be found, although it appears that I had not given any indication of whom that replacement might be. In fact, over the years there were few changes in personnel in PLM; Vicky Silva was the vocalist, Laurie Baker played bass guitar, the drummer was John Marcangelo (who was also well versed in popular piano style) and occasionally, at a later stage, oboist Hugh Shrapnel and pianist Dave Smith would participate. As for the new member, it was a huge leap from performing Stockhausen and Cage at Darmstadt to performing *Long Live Chairman Mao* in the Students' Union bar. Nevertheless, he joined Vicky Silva as a lead singer in the band and brought with him a new impetus and wealth of ideas. 'He could sing/play in any circumstances, in the rain on the back of a truck or when being pelted by fascists or under attack by the State, [and] he became more central as time went on'.[49] For Cardew it was the beginning of a musical education which he claimed he never had. Rather than Karlheinz Stockhausen it was John Marcangelo, keyboard player and composer with PLM, who could teach him the rudiments of a compositional style which would serve his political ambitions.

Cardew appears to have spent most of the rest of March in England. The journals note a lecture at the City University in London on 7 March, an invitation to Birmingham University music department the next day, a recording (unspecified) for the Chinese section of the BBC on 16 March, and from 22 to 24 March there is mention of a Working People's Conference under the title: 'The present 'crisis' is caused by the monopoly capitalist system'. On 20 March he was with PLM at the Chapter Arts Centre in Cardiff and on the 27 he was back in Berlin attending a performance of Paragraphs 1 and 2 of *The Great Learning* at the Berlin Philharmonic Hall.

I decided to accept the engagement with the proviso that I would write a relatively comprehensive article describing the nature of the piece and what I thought about it, and distribute this article to the concert audience and attempt to have the article used on all subsequent occasions when the piece might be brought before the public, e.g. in broadcasts, etc.[50]

This event and Cardew's criticism of the work are discussed in the chapter 'Stockhausen Serves Imperialism'.

The Journals note the marriage of Scratch Orchestra members Michael Chant and Carole Finer on 4 April; Chant had pursued his bride-to-be with quiet determination for several months, a relationship which had been monitored by some Scratch members with discretion and varying degrees of expectation. And on the next day the acquisition of a new car is logged. On 6 April the Journals summarise a talk on the Indian (Naxalbari/Maoist) revolution, and on 27 April a meeting was held in St. John's Church Brixton around opposition to the Labour Party's 'social contract' and on the need for the Afro-Caribbean community to organise against both class and race oppression. The Journals also mention the possibility of working with the National Union of Students (NUS). Cardew made detailed notes on the development of the working class and its institutions during the nineteenth century and the Journals show evidence of an in-depth study of social history and political theory going back to ancient Greece when the situation of women, children and old people (he remarks) might be compared favourably to that of life under the yoke of nineteenth-century capitalism, where people were forced to work ten hours a day in appalling conditions.

On 12 April, in a report on 'mass work' [51] Cardew noted that there was wide-spread disillusionment with the policies of all parties, that people regarded themselves as the victims of politicians' lies and deceit. The report was supplemented with constant references to the Marxist classics, along with pertinent quotations. Cardew's friend and comrade, Peter Devenport, who frequently accompanied Cardew on mass work, recalled in conversation with me years later that Cardew wanted complete clarity in his own mind on all the issues which might arise; he would then be quite uncompromising. There would be no courting of popularity, no side-tracking, no blurring of definitions – so that when he said 'socialism' he wanted his interlocutors to know exactly what he meant, what he *envisaged*, concretely, by a socialist society. And he would demand from them the same clarity in expressing their ideas; there could be neither fudge nor trade-off. Cardew would never gloss over anything in order to reach a compromise (this was a predisposition, a character trait, which applied throughout his life); he would be happy to leave a situation in a state of total non-agreement.[52] Cardew was sceptical of 'conversions' – that is, people who seemed, rather too easily, to espouse the cause. Fundamentally, the basis of change must be *internal*; the argument should provide favourable conditions for the change to be effected and to have lasting consequences, but it is practical involvement in the struggle against injustice and oppression ('the act of finding out') that creates the best possible external conditions for the internal development of an individual's (political) consciousness.

In the Journals, on 9 April, there is what appears to be a formal recognition of a change of name: the Scratch Orchestra became Red Flame Proletarian Propaganda Team (RFPPT). It was agreed that the name 'Scratch Orchestra', with its anarchistic associations, and its quaintness, should be jettisoned in favour of a more politically explicit title. Was this the seal of death, the final nail in the Scratch Orchestra's coffin? Or had the Scratch Orchestra finally grown up? Had it simply developed and gained a maturity that imposed social and political responsibilities which it had previously refused to recognise? While it had not been amongst the front-runners of political activism in Britain, the Scratch Orchestra had nevertheless spawned a social and artistic radicalism many of whose protagonists, especially from within its own ranks, and even today, have not succumbed to the crude blandishments of corporate business and the hypocrisy and wheeler-dealing of 'third way' politics which continues to find eager converts amongst self-aware artists and chastened revolutionaries. So how could the newly-fledged Red Flame Proletarian Propaganda Team, for whom the Party was the gravity centre of its whole existence, its *raison d'être*, announce its inauguration? How could it demonstrate peremptorily and categorically its allegiance to the revolutionary agenda? Cardew, always quick to respond to initiatives, was first to make a contribution, a sketch of the outline of a short play with music:

> Project could be: either a series of sketches unified by the political line or: a long thing on one subject.
> It is to be primarily for a working-class audience, where possible in a struggle situation: sit-ins, lock-outs, picketing, etc.
> It could raise funds for the strikers. It needs to be mobile and flexible…

> The monopoly capitalist class would be presented as static visual material – paintings, photographs of board meetings, headlines, which a commentator could dissect like a lecturer exposing their true character.

> Working class characters should carry all (or virtually all) the action.
> The hero: a Labour voter who takes up communism.
> Supporting hero: educated girl communist.
> Villain: a Trotskyite who tries to divert the hero from his path […].

> Note: *any* research material can be integrated with this project from the point of view of how it raises the hero's consciousness.
> The project needs a dramatic climax. [53]

Yet many from the political wing of the old Scratch Orchestra were still discouraged by the close links to the Party, and had no desire to become part of an official Party organ. They were understandably disquietened by the fact that many talented people had given up creative work and felt it would be better to remain independent of the Party whom even sympathisers mistrusted. They argued that the Scratch Orchestra should continue its own development (and under its own name), and that if a prescribed, that is, subordinate relationship with the Party were formed it would frustrate the Scratch Orchestra's development. The Scratch Orchestra should clarify its own ideas on art whether or not the Party 'approved'. However, Cardew's Leninist enthusiasm for the idea of affiliation to the Party, of working under the guidance of the Party and submitting to its criticism, was undiminished by Scratch scepticism and trepidation. A Journal entry is characteristically clear and uncompromising:

1. Revolutionary Art is a powerful weapon in the hands of the masses, to prepare the ground ideologically.
2. All Art is geared to definite political lines.
3. Art for Whom.[54]

Much has been written, and spoken, of the irrelevance, indeed the obscenity of artistic endeavour in the light of the unspeakable banalities of twentieth century history. Whereas many in the Scratch Orchestra baulked at the implications and perceived consequences of the Maoist agenda, Cardew was overwhelmed, intoxicated by the Hegelian prospect of life beyond art, life without need of the *semblance* of beauty, by the idea of a new human consciousness as yet undreamed of. Tucked away in the back cover of a Journal is a sheet of notes on Hegel's Aesthetics. It ends:

A question to be discussed: Art in the sense that it developed with the bourgeoisie to its great heights; will Art in this sense be carried over and developed by the Proletariat in its own interests? Or will the mode of Art associated with bourgeois philosophy (Hegel) pass away with the bourgeoisie? IMPORTANT. [55]

Hanns Eisler, too, refers to this in an extemporaneous talk, 'Thoughts on Form and Content, to the Composers and Musicologists Union of the German Democratic Republic on 9 March 1962', his last public appearance:

I would like you to acquire a taste for Hegel, and consequently for Marx too. Just let me quote from memory: 'It is possible that in a society finally freed, art will die away. Philosophy will take its place.' That is a prodigious sentence. Is it an impertinence of the philosopher towards us artists? Hegel means that with the progressing consciousness of man – and here we should amplify him by adding a mankind finally freed and at the highest stage of material and cultural development – the production of art might be more inclined to die away than increase.[56]

This is the utopia in pursuit of which Cardew was willing to sacrifice not only his own life, but also the lives of his family and comrades. Small wonder that few could follow him. To follow was to trudge the streets of the most deprived parts of London, to suffer abuse on street corners, to be threatened with violence on doorsteps, to be constantly in danger and at risk, to spend hours in libraries studying the 'human condition', to be on call for the revolution twenty four hours a day, to be accountable to the Party, to be remorselessly critical of oneself and of one's own actions and their consequences for the revolutionary cause, and to be intoxicated with the idea of a new world, a new planet. Cardew refused to (over)protect or to exclude his family from any part of his own life, whatever feelings of insecurity and even trauma may occasionally have overtaken them. And, as the family themselves acknowledge, there were always huge compensations; Cardew taught the children to be free and adventurous, to be alive to the world around them.

He always spoke to children with respect; he never talked down to them – a common adult foible; he was never condescending or patronising. In a letter to Michael Parsons he describes his attitude towards writing music for children:

> I didn't send the Children's Pieces – somehow it didn't seem worth it yet. I felt I'd approached the problem from the wrong end: taking richness and vitality away from grown-up music and giving it to children as an empty shell. Instead, a child has embryonic richness and vitality which grows into grown-up music, and this should be the starting point for children's pieces.[57]

Stella Cardew recalls that for many years they had been a happy family. The emotional complexity of their estrangement in the early seventies was compounded by the dissolution of the Scratch Orchestra and her husband's disappearance into a maelstrom of unrelenting political activism. Apart from the marital crisis, losing touch with his erstwhile friends was painful and deleterious to his emotional stability. Moreover, the relationship with his lover Sheila had become fraught and vulnerable and he had written to her from Berlin asking her to visit him there. They had already met, by chance, in January in New York while he was performing with Steve Reich and had spent a weekend together.[58] But she declined and refused to change her mind when he wrote to tell her that Stella had asked for a divorce. Cardew had written many letters to Stella during this period but in a protracted state of anguish and despair at home in Barnes she destroyed them all.

Cardew's relationship with Sheila had also reached a crisis point; somehow he wanted to find a delicate equilibrium which would obviate the necessity for the abandonment of his family. But when he suggested, by way of 'compromise', that Sheila should visit him at home, for 'secretarial' work, Stella was appalled. Her surface tractability belied a toughness of spirit which would express itself when her integrity, her selfhood, was threatened. There would be terrible rows and in her fury Stella would throw plates and other missiles. But Cardew would never enter into discussion; his few proposals were not negotiable and, according to his wife, he was devious and manipulative. He would not come to bed, would not sleep, though he would spend hours just playing the cello. Sometimes it would appear as if he had left, but he would return and there would be tears and the cycle would recommence and Stella would resume her plate-throwing and Cardew would accuse his wife of derangement and brutality.

Stella recalls that 'he would never face up to personal problems'[59]; during the latter part of their own relationship, when the domestic tension was mounting, he was evasive, dissembling, and often silent when words, however fallible, could have helped to breach the deadlock. Insofar as the family's needs coincided with his own he could be an inspiring partner, father, step-father, and Stella to this day can still bask in the memory of profound

Cornelius Cardew a life unfinished

happiness and unity, even though his chronic infidelity caused her pain and, when he was away from home for longer periods, created unsettling and portentous visions of rupture. Throughout their relationship abandonment was to be her portion and she would be left to bewail her fate in letters.

Finally he packed his things. Horace and Walter had been sent away for a week to their grandmother and when they returned their father told them he had left for good. By 6 May he had made a detailed list of domestic out-goings, presumably in preparation for his departure. On 10 May 1974, three days after his thirty-eighth birthday, which Stella, in a last-ditch attempt to salvage their marriage, had celebrated with her husband, the Journals note tersely: 'Leave Elm Grove Road. Scratch dissolved'.

Regarding the dissolution of the Scratch Orchestra there are widely differing interpretations, with dates ranging from the 'discontent' meetings in 1971 to its re-naming in 1974. I am unable to declare myself for one date or another. For each individual Scratch member the Orchestra 'died' or 'metamorphosed' at a different time and for different reasons.

> Surely we were trying to make folk music. A music born out of our experiences as individuals in the urban, industrial state. Just as people made music when they came together in our agrarian history. We were getting places. Finding alternatives to the classical modes of notation and instrumentation. Finding direct ways of expression through making the problem of relating, the focus. Working out new strategies to keep the spontaneity and brilliance alive. What did it matter that people could remember it, respect it, like it, and so on, so long as they could do it and feel the powerful effect of being empowered.
>
> Surely it is better to express one's own life than to be continually experiencing someone else's expression of that same life.
>
> Cornelius was heading for another consensus music, only this time, believed in, and believed by the political grouping of one sort or another.
>
> By now, if we had kept it up, relating, expressing and exploring, the Scratch Orchestra would be a force to be reckoned with. We would have a vibrant and effective tool for change. Instead we have a memory of a beginning whose initiator lost the way. Thanks Cor, but let's use the memory to begin again.[60]

Michael Chant, who has remained a communist activist to this day, detects no demise, rather change and continuity:

> One can enumerate, for example, some of the preoccupations which were

characteristic of the Scratch. How to function as a collective and the relation of the individual to the collective, how to function in the public sphere, and hence to raise the question, 'For Whom?', how to develop culture which has a democratic or progressive content as opposed to the demands of the establishment that culture be self-serving or part of an 'industry', how to develop a mass culture, where at the same time each individual found their place and made their contribution, how to give a crucial place to the people in the culture that is produced, and recognise the diversity of their cultures, how to join the activity of professional cultural workers with amateurs, especially the youth. These are some of the preoccupations that come to mind when considering the Scratch Orchestra in its whole development. [61]

Interestingly, many of these issues were also highlighted by Gerhard Crepaz when I interviewed him in 1994 (see Chapter 14). And it is true to say that Scratch Orchestra members, to this day, and in a wide variety of manifestations, carry these ideals around with them, etched in their consciousness, a guiding and critical force in the lives they lead, the art they make. At the end of his essay on the Scratch Orchestra Michael Parsons provides a fitting epitaph:

> More important, however, than any significance it may have for theorists, historians and musicologists, and over and above its musical failures and achievements, it should always be remembered that for those who participated in it, the Scratch Orchestra was primarily an adventure in collaborative discovery and invention, a social laboratory for the sharing and testing of ideas, for the forging of relationships, for the disruption and re-evaluation of inherited values, and for the realization of conceptual possibilities.[62]

When he left his family Cardew moved into modest bed and breakfast accommodation in Westbourne Grove, then a depressing area of west London near Paddington, which would have resonated sympathetically with the trappings of his personal life at that time. The domestic traumas had afflicted him profoundly; moreover, the turmoil of his private life, its upheavals, and the pain he had caused family and friends, impinged upon his political activities and judgements. And the reverse would have been true; we know how bitter Stella Cardew felt about the disruption to family life caused by her husband's political commitments. And whilst he would not have sought any kind of justification for his actions in respect of his family and friends, it would certainly have been his view at the time that his own personal feelings (and probably those of others, too) could only be brought to the surface, rationalised and rendered meaningful in relation, existentially, to an exclusive, subsumptive political reality. This is demonstrated in an entry in the Journals headed Fight Self – Repudiate Revisionism, a confessional which reflected a practice common in China at the time, and in particular during the Cultural Revolution, and which may well have been prompted by an article in *Peking Review* no.12. An elderly Professor of Philosophy had likewise confessed to a 'bourgeois world outlook' and had proclaimed the possibility and necessity for the individual to change in accordance with the Party line and the 'objective laws of history'.

In countless cases I've been guided by self in dealings with the Party.

Thinking it was generous of me to contribute.

Thinking it was silly about the cheques.

Setting my own thoughts up against the Party's line.

Using the opportunity of Chris Coleman's criticism to air my views.

Being negligent about security – not thinking that my recklessness can damage the Party.

Having a passive attitude of relying on the masses and then having no proper regard for the Party.

In whose interest is it for people to sit and wait for the revolution in its own good time? The bourgeoisie.

The interests of the Party are for revolution soon.

To be passive about relying on the masses means revising the revolutionary aspect of Marxism.

It led me to take an evasive attitude in the dialectic of conscious activity in relation to economic development independent of man's will.

Here my line of asking for more work on the Imperialist contradictions indicates that I regarded the weakness of the enemy as the leading factor, and the strength of the Party as secondary. This was defeatist and pessimistic, and would become objectively harmful if it continued. It's an expression of a bourgeois world outlook. This outlook expresses itself more seriously in intellectual twisting and turning. Evasiveness.

Setting myself up against the Party by having a negative critical attitude to Party utterances.

My appreciation of what I considered 'good articles' was also bourgeois – 'appreciative'.

My attitude has been to protect my bourgeois individuality and led to laziness in coming forward for intellectual work.

Showing off a false cheerfulness – preoccupation with secondary issues which interest me personally: petit bourgeois culture.

Carol's (Reakes) criticism is just.[63]

Thus my attitude has been manifested in practice, and my change of attitude must also be manifested in practice.

'Man's will' is impotent to change the laws of history. But it is a potent force for pushing history forward.

Marxism-Leninism has pushed history forward in accordance with its objective laws – in the only way it can go.

To have a negative, critical attitude to Marxism-Leninism is to side with reaction.[64]

Significantly, Cardew's two great mentors, Wittgenstein and Lenin, had also felt the need to eschew personal gratification, and to subjugate sensuous impulses (in Lenin's case aesthetic impulses, too). In Lenin's, and Cardew's, chosen worlds discipline, denial, self-abnegation, duty, service and sacrifice reigned. The effect of music on Lenin, through its intrinsic meanings and associational references, its 'vagrancy', was so powerful that he literally could not bear it; he would break down and even, on occasions, ask to be permitted to leave the company. In fact, Lenin's self-denial extended into many other areas as well: skating, Latin, chess, and the visual arts. There is the story that when Lenin and Krupskaya were in exile together they would attend the theatre or the cinema every night, and in the middle of each performance Lenin would get up and leave, thereby simultaneously both satisfying and denying his craving for aesthetic fulfilment. Lenin's talents, his most significant contributions to Marxism, lay in the field of revolutionary practice, in his supreme organizational abilities, and in his grasp of the nature of the state. Whereas art troubled him and he could not come to terms with its potency and the debilitating effect it had on him. Lenin did not object to art because it was 'bourgeois' but because it was art. Hanns Eisler discussed the subject with characteristic candour and insight. One of his favourite quotes was from *The Damnation of Music* by the philosopher Me-Ti, 600 years BC:

If the nobles of the country really have the welfare of the people at heart, they should prevent and forbid music wherever it makes an appearance. For the fact that the people practise music has four disadvantages. The hungry are not fed, the cold are not clothed, the homeless are not sheltered and the desperate find no consolation.[65]

But Eisler would alter the last phrase to 'and the desperate *do* find consolation'. Typically, Eisler identified a fundamental problem which, as we have seen, Lenin encountered and could not come to terms with:

Music and poetry can turn individuals and masses away from necessity – in some cases the necessity of acceptance, in others the necessity of self-sacrifice in the cause of social advancement – towards sensuousness, toward individual gratification, toward play, toward childhood.[66]

Like Wittgenstein Cardew thought a lot about himself. On things that mattered they were their own fiercest critics. Wittgenstein wrote to Russell: 'Perhaps you regard this thinking about myself as a waste of time – but how can I be a logician before I am a human being! Far the most important thing is to settle accounts with myself.'[67] For Wittgenstein philosophy was a kind of confessional; without this crucial element it would fail: 'If anyone is unwilling to descend into himself, because this is too painful, he will remain superficial in his writing.'[68] Pride was the greatest obstacle to lasting philosophical achievement, not lack of intelligence. At one stage Wittgenstein had had the idea of publishing a refutation of the ideas of the *Tractatus* alongside it, just as Cardew had criticised and denounced the content of his earlier works on occasions of their performances.

Red Flame Proletarian Propaganda Team (RFPPT) continued to meet on a regular basis, including several meetings in May which Cardew refers to in his Journal in some detail. There seems to have been ongoing disagreement revolving mostly around the nature of the group's relationship with the Party, which seems to have been unimpressed with the 'cultural workers' artistic achievements (in particular its singing) and sceptical of its ambitions. In the cultural field generally the Party still seemed to favour critical work[69]; it saw no virtue in the group's 'opera project' and recommended that it should shed its illusions and abandon its grandiose notions, at this stage, of 'serving the Party' through its artistic pretensions, which, it suggested, had actually held up the revolutionary work. The Party argued that there was nothing to be gained by writing an opera; the time for that would be when a membership of fifty thousand people had been built. Cardew, however, seems to have disagreed, dismissing the idea of a moratorium on creative work as a 'bourgeois line'. The RFPPT was unequivocal: the Party was downgrading artistic work to the extent that it was considered at best an irrelevance, at worst a time-consuming nuisance.

At an RFPPT meeting on 26 May cultural issues were laid aside and 'the history of the Communist movement and its lessons for today' constituted the agenda. Agreement was reached on the need to investigate 'revisionist' ideas, especially those originating in the Labour Party, which were detracting from support for revolutionary politics. How could Marxism best be used to combat these ideas? Revisionism was considered to be the subtle technique which the bourgeoisie favoured to destroy Marxism. Revisionists were everywhere – including SACU (Society for Anglo-Chinese Understanding), although this did not prevent the Red Flame group from contributing a programme of songs for a SACU meeting.[70] The revisionist thesis, according to the Maoists, was based on the idea that the proletariat should strive to achieve the same benefits, the same life-style, as the bourgeoisie; in other words, a bourgeois world, with bourgeois culture, without the aggravation of an exploited proletariat. The whole populace would develop an appreciation of 'high', Western culture: ballet, opera, Shakespeare, and so forth.

There are invariably harsh words for the Labour Party, including a scathing polemic against the iniquitous 'social contract' (the origin of Cardew's song 'Smash the Social Contract'), through which workers were invited to share and participate in 'helping the bourgeoisie to run its capitalist enterprises'.[71]

In what sense is it opportunistic to want to win people over on demonstrations to our line? Essence of opportunism: to lose sight of the main line and objective and get side-tracked (in fact to side-track the revolution)? Inspiration. What about our Manifesto? That says show good things are going to be. What does it say about how we are going to achieve it?[72]

Occasionally there are injunctions, culled from the canon, addressed to himself:

We must have faith in the masses and we must have faith in the Party. These are two cardinal principles. If we doubt these principles we shall accomplish nothing.[73]

In his Journal notes Cardew stresses the need to use Marxism-Leninism 'to inject life into your art.' Professionals, that is, professional musicians, should develop contacts and build the influence of the Party in their professional circles; Marxist-Leninists should recognize their responsibility to lead.

Party is not a chance organisation. Faith in the Party is a scientific matter. Against 'doubtism' – leads to general support, not particular support – i.e., anti-Party. Support for the Party not a question of choice; it's a question of necessity.[74]

Two decades ago (and quoted in chapter 2), Cardew had raised the issue of doubt: 'Doubt begets thought; thought bedims the eye. [...] People free of doubt are bold.'[75] And the juxtaposition of 'faith' and 'science' here is problematic, not least for Marxists. I have already referred to it briefly in another context; the argument can be characterised as follows: We must act decisively because we know we are right. We must act decisively, even though we may not be right. The latter is more difficult to act upon; it is easier, and therefore more dangerous, to act on the basis of *certainty.*

Despite his discouraging experiences he continued his relationship with Art Schools whenever the opportunity arose, although his tactics seemed to have remained much the same: his introductory remarks invariably blunt, polemical and provocative. With reference to Art School education in a talk at Falmouth School of Art he wrote:

> In whatever job you land you will diffuse intellectual confusion, and fierce competitive individualism – these are the attributes on which capitalist society depends for its very existence… What jobs do art students do in fact? Hyde Park railings (maximum degradation of skills); Woolworths landscapes (ditto); Advertising industry (maximum identification with capitalist ideology). […] Art career (buy it with a few years poverty).[76]

And finally a clinching quote from the *Communist Manifesto*:

> The bourgeoisie has stripped of its halo every profession previously looked up to with reverent awe. It has converted the priest, the lawyer, the poet, the physician, the scientist into its paid wage-labourers.[77]

In a letter to Rod Eley, which was apparently not sent – the stamped envelope was simply addressed c/o Progressive Books and Periodicals – Cardew refers to his marriage break-up without giving much away:

> While working on the book (*Stockhausen Serves Imperialism*) my family situation became intolerable and I've moved out – nothing to do with the book at all, of course. And I'm generally quite happy.[78]

He refers to a 'useful conference a couple of weeks ago' when the idea of a bulletin was put forward, and mentions that he is about to start a manual job for 'ready cash'. There is also reference to the Scratch Orchestra: 'The Scratch (now changed to Red Flame) has been meandering a bit. Unresolved contradictions'. And to Keith Rowe: 'Keith is back in London, politically wandering, but otherwise his same old self. (That's not possible, but you can guess what I mean)', which suggests that Rowe was already out of favour with the Party. The letter also informs Eley that Cardew is to join PLM and that he wants to become more active in the musicians' union, where the Trotskyites are particularly vociferous. The plan is that he and Laurie Baker will try 'to form a picture of how the various organisations of musicians fit together and overlap'. Together with the letter Cardew encloses a copy of a project entitled Concert Series – Proletarian Music, an ambitious series of concerts of militant working-class music from various countries and from different historical periods, including music from the Soviet Union after the October Revolution; the German Workers' Movement from 1918-33; the history and musical culture of the Irish National Liberation Struggle from 1609 to the present; socialist composers in England 1926-45; and music reflecting the proletarian revolutionary movement in England today.

Under the aegis of Victor Schonfield's Music Now Cardew spent considerable time and energy during 1974 promoting the series; yet it never materialised, at least in its original format. In a letter to Alan Bush the following year he writes:

> As for our proletarian music concert series, it is on the shelf for the time being I'm afraid. The Arts Council announced it might be interested in sponsoring the two folk concerts, and then turned them down on the basis that it does not support folk music on principle! Also, the collective that was planning the series became rather uncertain and hesitant, and I myself also feel that the problem of how and what to organise in terms of concert activity is a very open question. But I certainly mean to return to it![79]

Which he did, in the following years although, as we shall see, the issues of the nature of 'concert activity' and that of 'venue' were always contentious. Regarding the Arts Council withdrawal of support, the most likely explanation is certainly not the one proffered. Rather, Council officers had got wind of the real agenda of Cardew's proposal and immediately looked for excuses; the feebleness of the explanation, as in this case, was immaterial. Alan Bush himself had previously expressed reservations about the series:

> I cannot imagine that it could possibly attract any public at all. If you yourself had a public for your avant-garde music, they will now turn their backs on you. The working-class of Britain seem particularly to dislike songs of proletarian struggle. It is not possible to persuade a choir of Welsh miners to sing the 'Internationale' at rallies of the Morning Star.[80]

One can imagine Cardew's response to an inveterate 'revisionist', even though he certainly felt a lot of affection, and admiration, for Bush. The resigned negativity towards the working-class, the pessimism, were revisionist traits which tarnished and discredited his political line, or rather the line of the official Communist Party of Great Britain. And yet the following month Bush writes enthusiastically about a project with the Birmingham Folk Centre:

Live performances on stage of Ewan MacColl's Radio Ballad 'The Big Hewer', largely to mining audiences (we played at the South Wales Miners' Gala last Saturday, and we are playing at the Yorkshire Miners' Gala this coming Saturday) and the response is tremendous.[81]

In July Cardew moved to Carleton Road, Tufnell Park, in north London. He rented a small, white room – which resembled a monk's cell – at the back of an Edwardian house, part of a flat in which he shared the kitchen. The conditions were Spartan – just a bed, a table, and a television for when his sons visited him; visually, apart from two or three modern Chinese communist paintings on the wall, it was unengaging. A pleasant view onto a sloping garden with a pear tree provided a therapeutic contrast. The manual job referred to in the letter to Eley was in a paint factory where the conditions were dire.[82]

Throughout July the Red Flame group stuttered on; on the back of an envelope, dated 19 July, Cardew summed up a recent meeting: 'Activities suspended pending further winding up meeting in September'. At the end of his note Cardew added: 'Are we taking a line of no-struggle?' Written along the side of the envelope is another afterthought: 'I suppose I've had the line of waiting and watching – sinisterly "biding my time". No – keep to objective facts. No speculation.' Beginning with the May Day demonstration, when the Party had been widely distributing a Mayday leaflet (in the north of the country too, including Manchester and Liverpool), there was intense political activity throughout the summer. Carole and Michael Chant spent several months in Newcastle, and Cardew, at the behest of the Party, spent some time in the Midlands, working in a shoe factory.

Sheila Kasabova, who had been involved in local socio-political issues in north London, was now becoming drawn to Marxism-Leninism. But her anarcho-socialist, anti-authoritarian political leanings could not be jettisoned so easily, despite Cardew's unrelenting criticisms. She recalls an occasion, during the summer of 1974, when they were walking along the canal at Camden and discussing the large Irish family she had become involved with – mother and nine children, no father. Instead of sending the children into care, a 'free school' called Freightliners had been set up (which her own daughter Anna attended), sited on waste land with deserted stables and old railway tracks. Cardew dismissed them as a 'lumpen proletariat' family who were beyond the pale. His attitude angered Sheila who insisted that these were just the kind of people she wanted to work with. 'Bad politics' was Cardew's response and they agreed to differ.

However, their tiff did not deter him from asking Sheila if she would live with him (or rather if he could live with her) on his return from the Midlands. She was unwilling, or unable, to give him the immediate answer that he demanded, even though she had already informed her husband George that she was leaving him. She was unsure about going straight into another relationship, living with another person. Cardew was also struggling with the notion of 'bourgeois' (romantic) love at this time; he and Sheila had very strong feelings for one another. What was the nature of this love? How did it fit in with his blossoming love for the Party? There was something within him which recognised love for the Party as a higher relationship, and he wanted to give himself to this ideal. It was a very difficult time for both of them. They parted and for the time being the matter remained unresolved.

On 29 July, in what appears to be a self-addressed directive, Cardew takes stock of the current stage of the revolutionary strategy, in particular in relation to the need for unity. But its rhetorical opening suggests that it is a text to be delivered, to be read out, rather than simply read – like the officer's pep-talk before battle, or the manager's crack of a whip at half-time in a crucial match, with the emphasis on the need for commitment, for clarity of purpose and above all, for *spirit*. But how is this passion and determination, this *spirit*, instilled? Even professional soldiers may falter if total conviction, *belief*, is lacking. For although it may not be difficult to see off, philosophically and politically, the bogus democracy of the bourgeois 'one man, one vote' system, the problem that remains for many of us is our scepticism in relation to the 'correct line' (or more precisely, the *application* of theory to practice), and its formulation by an omniscient Central Committee:

What does it mean to unite the Marxist-Leninists? On what basis? The main thing is the *spirit*: *desire* to unite. No formula can suffice. Absolute adherence to the real world – this is essential. Struggle is absolute. Marxism-Leninism is the concrete analysis of concrete conditions. Unity is on the basis of political line. It's no good working and uniting begrudgingly.

Raise contradictions from the point of view of resolving them. Persist; don't be half-hearted. Don't raise them from the point of view of individualism, or from the point of view of splitting.
1. Spirit of Unity.
2. Basis of political line.
3. Raising contradictions from the point of view of resolving them.

Unity is not abstract, general or egalitarian. We mean Unity behind the Central Committee.

We don't give freedom to an incorrect line.
Unity requires conscious effort.

Full right of the Central Committee to decide policy.
Full right of the local comrades to implement policy.[83]

Such expressions of ideological certainty and purpose, invariably pertaining to 'the Party' and 'the Party line' occur with monotonous regularity in these later chapters. They beg the same questions, over and over, although I am not sure that the (petit bourgeois) justification for *inaction*, through feelings of uncertainty and scepticism, by those of us who were not Party activists, is ultimately more tenable. Is it not rather the case that these feelings provide us with a convenient alibi for our acceptance and quietism, for our *complicity* in 'crimes against the poor and oppressed people of the world'? So I give Cardew his head, following him, from a discreet distance, to the end. Often, as the reader will already have noticed, and perhaps with some irritation, I insert these axiomatic and intractable texts and extracts with a minimum of comment; the context in which they appear, I choose to presume, provides them with a degree of viability, if not acceptability. Of course, this depends entirely on the predispositions of the reader. But occasionally, as in the present instance, I feel, not the obligation, rather the expediency to adjust the focus, to let it rest critically on a word, a political 'sound-bite', and to allow scrutiny and moments of consideration of such utterances to take their course. The above text combines passion, boldness, resilience and pragmatism, which together stamp it, in my view, with the mark of authenticity, and of probity. It may also be regarded as misguided and foolhardy in what it appears to prescribe, which embodies risk and danger, and not only of a physical nature. My own relation to the text is unstable, unresolved; my feelings vacillate between outrage and admiration; for many readers it will be preposterous, unworthy. And even if one decides to give Cardew the benefit of the doubt, and one 'reads up' on Marxism-Leninism, there is still no guarantee that it will provide, as Cardew maintains, 'the concrete analysis of concrete conditions'. In relation to Cardew's own private cosmology, I believe that there *were* zones of doubt, but the Party refused to engage with doubt and this attracted and nurtured the authoritarian streak which several close friends, like Ilona Halberstadt, David Jackman and Psi Ellison, identified in him. In their view his authoritarian strain was pervasive; as a personality, however sensuous he was and however spontaneous he could be, he was always implicitly critical of people, identifying faults, limitations, inconsistencies, and so forth; in his letters to Ilona this moralizing vein occasionally surfaces; later it would be exploited politically.

During the seventies, as part of a return to the rhetoric of nineteenth-century *laissez-faire* for the first time since the end of the Second World War, an agenda of sustained vilification of working people was adopted: that the working-class, and in particular members of trade unions, were unreliable, rapacious, untrustworthy, insensitive to the sufferings of their fellow beings. A typical and constant image in the media during that period (especially in the newspapers), etched into the memory of its readers by means of gory, visual examples, was that of the 'thinking individual' (in union parlance the 'scab') versus the 'mindless, thuggish mob' (striking trade unionists). Whereas, it was proclaimed, capital had been reformed, and cleansed, the workers remained backward, intransigent and ungrateful. Moreover, as if to demonstrate their trust in international capital the Government had surrendered its notional control over Britain's economy to the overseers of the International Monetary Fund, an act which served only to confirm the view that politics was mere 'shadow-play', and that by corollary voting itself was a fruitless exercise. Perhaps for the first time the contention that Western democracy was a 'bogus democracy' began to obtain a degree of currency amongst the populace at large. A disillusionment with the political process, which since the end of the war had never been seriously challenged, now began to take hold.[84]

The Party's response to this new, confrontational phase was undaunted, but measured and exhaustive, and Cardew's new-style note books, for all their insubstantial physical appearance and occasional indecipherableness, provide the patient researcher with interesting material. A typical week in August 1974, for example, involved selling the Party newspaper outside the main gate of the GEC factory between 6.45 and 7.30 am, as well as detailed investigation of chosen companies and their activities in a particular area: 'Investigation should advance in the direction of analysis of industry'.[85] This would have necessitated consultation of a number of sources, including the *Financial Times*, government statistics and surveys, local economic reviews and more general books: capital ownership, the role of merchant banking, takeovers, land ownership, import/export details, employment and union structures, etc. would all have been subject to revolutionary scrutiny. And this was done on a countrywide scale. A visit to Rochdale in Lancashire involved the survey of a street, the class structure of the town, its race policies, and interviewing workers, mainly Irish, employed on construction sites. Party members and supporters in the same area also reported on industrial action at the glass manufacturers Pilkington Bros Ltd in St Helens. There were many interviews with workers and much anti-establishment, 'progressive' sentiment was expressed: need for unions, but unions are weak; fragmentation of communities; poor quality of life of working people; victimisation of individuals who speak out against fascism and racism. The work and study was painstaking and conscientious: lists of streets to visit were made; the picture had to be both broad and detailed. Subsequently, on the basis of this study, a seminar was held by the Party on the economic and political situation in the northwest of England.

For Cardew, for all his militancy and unflagging devotion to the cause, there is no doubt that the personal trauma that he was experiencing at this time – his separation from Stella and his sons, the breaking up of the Scratch Orchestra and the loss of many friends – had left him in a state of acute vulnerability. In this respect the Party's role was crucial, for it embodied powerful feelings and ideas: it was representative of an ideology which could illuminate a path (the 'shining path') through and out of his chaotic condition, out of the moral morass which engulfed him.[86] As we have seen, it had taken a long time for his political commitment to attain that state of irreversibility which was to follow him to his grave. For many months, and on a regular basis, he would meet high-ranking Party comrades for lengthy discussions in which every conceivable issue would have been raised, including those, one may speculate, where private and political imperatives were in conflict.

In the Journals Cardew includes a rare personal entry, headed 'About Sheila' (none of these later Journals, or rather note books, accommodate more than three months of entries, most of them considerably less), although the content is analysed, predictably, in political terms:

1. One recurrent theme – that maybe it would be good if you decide against me. It would remove a barrier to my full-hearted participation in the political work. Thus after Rally today I do not stick around for social exchange with comrades because I want to fly to you. (And it's an *immediate* thought, so even while with them I'm not participating fully.)

Error: this makes my decision dependent on an outside force – passive.

2. That you are bent on tormenting and exploiting me over a long period. Same error: that I'm somehow incapable of initiative.

Is my desire for you a desire for a bourgeois base from which to (hum-hum) engage in pol? [politics] Just as with the family?

The right course: to continue to struggle over political line rather than to struggle to gain the objective of 'possession' of you – to win you for me, instead of win you for the revolution and thus be genuinely united. [87]

Clearly, his relationship with Sheila was suffering and one senses an obsessiveness, reflecting a depth of feeling for Sheila which is undeniable. An entry in the same note book returns to this perceived contradiction between domestic and political life:

Making love to anyone at all does nothing at all for loneliness. What is needed is a fundamentally different attitude to relationships.

What's happening? I'm failing to develop any social life. Hence putting pressure on Sheila too much and making myself dependent on her. Preparing the ground for just the same as with Stella.
Should I leave London? [88]

But there is no reference to the role of the Party in relation to the inadequacy of his social life; the status of the Party remains inviolable. And there had been more self-criticism in an earlier entry: 'Bad tendency: Because "Revolution is the main trend" one can just sit back and wait'.

In the same entry Cardew reflects on the increasing militancy of the Trade Union membership which is held in check by 'revisionist' and social democratic leadership. The Party must develop its line within the Trade Union movement. It must take 'a lead' in the struggle for the 'correct line'. 'We have to bring people to Branch meetings, and make the meetings more lively'. Cardew's view was that the low level of political debate at meetings was the way in which the Trade Unions were kept tied to the Labour Party. On the last day of the month (September) he attended a Musicians' Union meeting for which he took the minutes. They make interesting reading: a detailed analysis of the MU negotiations with the BBC for new rates of pay and, more generally, reference to the transparency of the (ideological) conflict between the various and disparate elements within the Union: in particular Trotskyite 'adventurism' (nationalisation of the entertainment industry *now*), versus the measured, conservative response of the Union leadership, represented by Bernard Parris and Tom Barton ('our members don't want to take over the pubs and clubs, and the BBC'), 'old hands' who were used to deflecting or absorbing and neutralising criticism.

'Does nationalisation improve the workers' lot', one of them asked, claiming, somewhat disingenuously, that nationalisation will only be viable under socialism. In a discussion on the merits of the case for 'amalgamation' with other unions in the entertainment industry, such as the actors' union Equity (in which, at the time, the Trotskyite Workers Revolutionary Party was a strong presence), what appears to be Cardew's contribution (although there is no clear indication of authorship) argued against the Trotskyite demand for 'amalgamation now'. The essence of his argument was that the Workers Revolutionary Party's demands were at that point in time divisive. Moreover, it would probably not lead to a greater degree of democracy and rank-and-file participation. Cardew (that is, the Party he represented) stressed the need to develop the unity of the working class as a whole. This meant developing the strength of unions (in the entertainment industry) individually as well as creating facilities for effective cooperation. A strong MU would have the majority of practising musicians as members, with a large proportion participating actively in Union affairs on the basis of a high level of 'class-consciousness'. And non-union members had to be mobilised. Then, with a sideswipe at Trotskyite tactics:

> Because unity cannot be built by waving a magic wand, like the word 'amal-gamation', but by a conscious process of struggle in which the relation between the rank and file and our elected representatives must be a relationship of solidarity. To condemn the actions of our elected representatives as 'totally inadequate' is a ludicrous slander and divisive tactics.[89]

It was a clever speech: criticising and isolating the 'Trots', stressing the need for unity, emphasising the fact that this would be a protracted process ('conscious process of struggle'), and defending the (elected) leadership without endorsing its political line. There was a certain *gravitas,* an ideological *weight*, about Cardew's contribution to the discussion; he was not proposing a panacea, rather that 'working class unity' was the *sine qua non*, that without it nothing of substance – that is, nothing lasting – could be accomplished. The accuracy of the preamble to the Trotskyite motion at the MU meeting, the contextualisation of the debate, could not be questioned: the iniquitous effect of the Social Contract, the huge cuts imposed on the Arts Council, opera, the National Theatre, and the BBC, the disappearance of municipal orchestras, the use of 'canned' music to supplant live music, and so forth. Such a state of affairs, it was argued, with the Labour Party embracing the imminent reality of the corporate take-over of the country, demanded an urgent response and precipitous action. However, for Cardew's Party, to stampede members opportunistically into action, however debilitating the political and social climate had become, was a counter-productive and therefore disastrous tactic: 'he who can keep his head in the presence of a tiger is qualified to come to his deed in due hour', Cardew might have recalled; his old mentor, Confucius, still had wise advice to impart to the rebel apostate.

As a performing musician Cardew was still in demand and in October (19-21) the Journals mention piano recitals in Bristol, Oxford and York, probably of the recent piano music, *Piano Album 1973* and *Piano Album 1974*, which he was to record soon after for the Cramps record company in Milan. Around this time, late autumn of 1974, Cardew received a telephone call from Peter Devenport, a second year student at the Royal College of Music. A number of College students, including Ian McQueen, Peter West, Avril Anderson, Robert Coleridge and Devenport himself, were interested in Cardew's work and wanted to invite him to give an illustrated talk at the RCM. Cardew suggested that he, Devenport, should visit him at his temporary accommodation in Acklam Road, Ladbroke Grove to discuss the idea. Cardew's room was right on the Westway motorway; Devenport recalled the gongs hanging on the wall which reverberated every time a lorry went by, and as a consequence of which it was decided to go to a pub. Hardly had they settled into their pints than Cardew set down his agenda for discussion: 'Why do you want to put on a concert of my music? Is it because you want to serve the working people or not?' Not surprisingly, Devenport was absolutely dumbstruck by Cardew's opening gambit and had no idea how to respond. They finally agreed on a programme of two concerts: the first was to include, among other works, *Octet '61* and Paragraph 2 of *The Great Learning,* and according to a 'cryptic note' in Robert Coleridge's Journal, this was reported back to Devenport's fellow students at the RCM on 21 November.[90]

In December a meeting with the Director of the RCM, David Willcocks, was arranged, ostensibly to get permission for the Cardew concert to go ahead. According to Devenport and Coleridge Cardew had agreed to collaborate with Willcocks on some carol arrangements, although there is a divergence as to the exact nature of the 'collaboration'. Devenport seemed to be suggesting that Cardew, anonymously, was ghosting Willcocks' arrangements, whereas Coleridge understood that Cardew was simply being employed as a copyist. Given the dire straits of his finances either version could claim authenticity. Finally, a date for the concert, in around two months time, was agreed: 5 March 1975.

Sheila Kasabova, née Muir, was born in Madras, India on the 12 April 1938, seven years after her brother Stephen. Her father, David Muir, the son of a Scottish Presbyterian minister, had been posted there as a young civil servant and subsequently became the deputy Indian High Commissioner in South Africa where the family spent most of the war years. Her mother, Mary, was born in Edinburgh, as was her father, and had studied graphic design at Edinburgh College of Art.

One day in 1944, in Cape Town, together with her mother and brother (her father had already returned to India), Sheila, aged six, found herself sitting in the back of their chauffeur-driven car on their way to the port and on to a troop ship bound for Britain and eventually to Scotland, where her maternal grandmother was dying of cancer. Due to the wartime restrictions the parents had not been allowed to divulge their plans. It was an experience, a traumatic severance, which affected her deeply; young as she was, a welter of feelings consumed her – anxiety, fear, sense of loss, resentment. For she had grown to love South Africa; it had become her home and she felt strongly attached to many people there, not least to her parents' black servants. South Africa was where Sheila became 'alive to the world' and where she still, to this day, feels spiritually at home. The family stayed in Scotland until Sheila was ten, by which time she had grown attached to Scotland, and then left again, this time to go to Weybridge in Surrey, England, where she felt an acute sense of displacement and alienation. Initially her parents had gone without her and her brother – for a divorce, she thought, because they seemed so distant from one another, and their relationship, through incompatibility and a lack of love, had descended into sadness. However, the children rejoined their parents and have remained in England ever since.

Sheila failed her eleven-plus grammar school entrance examination and rather than suffering the embarrassment, the social inadvisability, of their daughter attending the local secondary modern school, her parents, in defiance of their religious denomination, sent her to a nearby convent school in Weybridge. Sheila can still recall her first day – sitting in a circle with the other children, praying. They were told to put their hands together and to keep their eyes closed, and this was accompanied by a graphic description of Christ on the Cross. Despite the caveats and threats, which tend to accompany religious indoctrination, Sheila opened her eyes and looked around to see all the children with closed eyes. She recalls her state of incomprehension from which the nuns were never able to awaken her during her distressing time at the school. She remained a lonely, unhappy misfit, a fish out of water.

The Weybridge nuns, cloned in a culture informed by the strategy of imperialist conquest and religious conversion, reviled the black heathens of Africa. Tainted by association Sheila was an unregenerate pagan, and made conscious of the fact that she would never see the face of God. She was excluded from her 'O' level English literature class for challenging the bible's theory of the origin of man and therefore for being possessed of the devil; she was suffering from a moral disorder and might infect other girls in the class. For this shameless defamation of the Christian faith she was banished from the classroom to the corridor outside where she would hide behind the various plaster-cast saints to escape the notice of other nuns. Her only solace were the various animals which populated the surrounding countryside – including a pony which she bought with the fifty pounds she had been left by her grandmother and which she had persuaded her mother to allow her to keep.

Sheila left school at fifteen and worked for a year breaking in and looking after horses. Her father wanted her to go to Paris but she refused. Her mother wanted her to go to art school which she also refused, mainly as acts of rebellion towards both parents. However, she finally decided to follow her mother's advice and attended Guildford art school for a year before moving on to the Central School of Arts and Crafts in London, where she studied mural painting. On successfully completing the course she taught for eighteen months in a girls' secondary modern school in east London where it became apparent that the school's assessments and expectations of their pupils and her own convictions and belief in the girls' worth and potential were irreconcilable. She decided to quit education and found work as a picture researcher in the burgeoning industry of the coffee-table book where, in 1963, as previously described, she met Cardew.

Number 7 Agar Grove was built in the eighteen-nineties and was owned by the architect Barnaby Milburn, an acquaintance of Sheila Kasabova. Sheila and her daughter Anna had moved in, initially just for a few weeks, and from 6 November 1974 on a more permanent basis. Three weeks later, on 26 November, Cardew joined them and they were to remain there until 1979. It was a large building, plain but beautiful, with a substantial-looking, solid slab frontage. Steps led up and through doors into their living room which was clean but higgledy-piggledy; eclectic. Initially, the accommodation arrangements were fluid: two rooms on the third floor, both of which leaked, were designated for Sheila, Anna and Cornelius, and after around four months they were also granted possession of the front room on the ground floor, which was formally Mr. Milburn's bedroom (which he rarely used), and which functioned felicitously for the family as a sitting room. It was a commodious room, in a sorry state of repair, although with a faded elegance; two huge windows with large shutters reached down to the floor and in the summer the honeysuckle outside enveigled its way through windows into the room; the walls were painted a sand colour. The room hosted a shabby old leather sofa, an antiquated fire place, an elegant Edwardian hat and coat stand, a maroon haircord carpet which had seen better days, a handle-less door which had been stripped, and Barnaby Milburn's single bed. A single bulb with no shade provided sufficient light. There were books and various musical instruments, including a piano painted white which Cardew had rented from Markson's in nearby Kentish Town. A Michael Cardew teapot, his exquisite cups, and other objects, enhanced and refined the trestle table which Sheila had bought Cornelius for his compositional work. In general, although dilapidated, with the occasional missing floorboard, the furniture was aesthetically appropriate and the room served its purpose. Cardew wrote his music and practised, the children played their instruments, and PLM would occasionally meet and rehearse there. A paraffin heater failed to alleviate the extreme cold. (According to Frederic Rzewski it was the coldest room he had ever slept in.) The toilet had neither light nor door; a piece of green cloth over the doorway provided a less than adequate degree of privacy. And when it rained, and the rain came in, the lights in the hallway had to be turned off. Using the toilet, therefore, had to be approached circumspectly and skilfully. Cardew never spent money on clothes or furnishings or the like. Nor did he ever feel the need to apologise to visitors for whatever condition they encountered on their arrival, whether fortuitous or expected.[91] He spurned comfort and possessions, or rather the acquisition of possessions; those that he had he cherished, investing them with a kind of totemic significance. Of course, many of these objects were part of his family inheritance – especially from his father's pottery. But there was no sentimentality. Cornelius Cardew was economical, thrifty, never wasteful, and yet he was an extremely generous man.

During the week (not at weekends) the room had to be vacated, but not until midnight, when Barnaby Milburn would return to claim his bed. Financially it was agreed that there would be no rent, but gas, electricity and water would be paid for by his tenants. Despite the primitive conditions the years at Agar Grove were happy ones.[92] On the second floor there were sitting tenants: an old Irish lady (who died while Cardew and Sheila were still there) and her middle-aged son Gus, who had discharged himself from the British army. Anna was particularly impressed with their large television set and would spend as much time as her mother would allow watching programmes with Gus. *Come Dancing* was a particular favourite with both of them, as it was for millions of others around the country.[93]

There were always people in the house; there was a convivial atmosphere with much discussion, as there was in all the Cardew households. Sheila recalls that Keith Rowe was a frequent visitor and he and she would go for walks and have long talks about many things, including communism and the Party. From September 1974 to July 1976 Sheila was a full-time student of Political Sociology at the Polytechnic of North London.[94] With his partner at college Cardew would clean and cook; beef stew was a favourite, learnt from his father and cooked in Michael Cardew's pot. Sometimes he would look after Anna and other children from the school and the neighbourhood; children were always welcome. Occasionally, his sons would visit – Walter, the younger, rather than Horace, who tended to keep a distance from his father and his new family. Sheila recalls that Cardew's separation from his two sons caused him great distress and after speaking to them on the phone he would break down and weep; the intensity of his reaction was so extreme that it horrified her. He was also deeply concerned about his friends' responses both to his abandonment of Stella and to his deepening involvement in the Party; many of them had broken off contact.[95]

Nevertheless, the Party, with its uncompromising demands, continued to control every aspect of his life and, it has to be said, he submitted himself to the authority and discipline consciously and willingly. The appalling plight of the 'human condition' and the prodigious task of emancipation to which he and his comrades had committed themselves cast all other problems into the shadows. Moreover, the devastation, physical and mental, which capitalism inflicted upon working people was all around him; he had no need to visit Third World countries. He had only to walk around the streets of his neighbourhood, to look into the eyes of the people he encountered; the degradation of human life, the stripping away of human potential, the cash nexus which distorts human relations – such manifestations of the system were at every street corner and between.

As a musician Cardew sought a rapport with working people by undergoing a kind of social training which he believed would help him to integrate and to feel more comfortable in a working class milieu. Thus he would spend many hours attempting to assimilate the piano style appropriate to accompanying pub singers. Fred Bryne was one such artiste who sang 'standards' from the forties and fifties in the Earl of Essex pub in Islington. Cardew enjoyed working with Fred although it did not come naturally to him; for all his practice he always felt inadequate, worried that he would not be up to scratch for Fred. And, of course, he was unable to respond to 'requests'. He did not know the repertoire and even if a tune were hummed or sung to him he would not have been able to transform it spontaneously into pub-piano style. The money, too, minimal though it was, was much needed; but that usually depended on the evening's takings, or on the whim of the landlord. On one occasion he was paid with a pair of second-hand brogue shoes, but when it was found that they did not fit, some other form of remuneration, probably less stylish, was offered, and stoically, if not gratefully, accepted by Cardew. The job with Fred Bryne lasted about six months during which time they also played a few times, according to Sheila, at a pub in the Romford Road in east London. At the same time Cardew had been practicing for a recording, in March 1975, with János Négyesy of the four violin and piano sonatas by Charles Ives. These pieces presented considerable technical difficulties but they were pianistic problems with which Cardew was familiar and which he was able to surmount. There was no doubt that he felt much more confident with the Ives sonatas than with the accompaniments for Fred Bryne.

Towards the end of the year, in a somewhat doleful vein, Cardew writes of the lack of positive response from publishers. Recalling his unconventional approach to Zerboni earlier in the year, perhaps this is not surprising if, as is likely, Zerboni's account of the affair had circulated. Prospective publishers in England would have responded with circumspection on receipt of an approach from Cardew. 'I've tried a couple of other publishers since Faber, but it's hard to find one with a positive attitude. Chappell's have the scores at the moment, but heaven knows if they'll bite', he wrote to Howard Skempton.[96]

And, more positively, on the occasion of their first Christmas at Agar Grove Sheila was presented with a gift of four poems, described by Cornelius as 'little scraps and ideas of poems for you': 'Toil and Dreams', 'Anti Tao', 'Less and More', and 'The Monopoly Capitalist after the Revolution'.

'Less and More'

Talk less, take more thought
Act less, have more effect
Eat less, derive more nourishment
Sleep less, be more awake
Read less, grasp more
> Through the cracks in the present
> The future shines so sharp
> We'll penetrate the cracks
> Force the boulders apart.

> The sapling of today is the great forest of tomorrow
> Today's flickering flame is tomorrow's conflagration
> We put our shoulders to the problems
> Encourage the blaze.

Compositions 1972-74

Arrangements of Chinese songs (1973)

The arrangements of some Chinese songs are first mentioned when Cardew accompanied the singer Jessica Cash in a concert at Warwick University on 10 February 1973. The main source is a collection of Chinese 'Historical Revolutionary Songs' published by the Foreign Languages Press, Peking, in 1971. There are three groups, each comprising three songs:

1. Historical Chinese revolutionary songs:

'March of the Swords'
'Battle March'
'The Great Road'

Cardew writes:

After struggling with the question of style for a period I had the good fortune to come across a Chinese record of some of these songs. [This] group transcribes more or less faithfully the style of the accompaniments on this record. The voice does not, since the record is sung by unison chorus. Also here the words are preserved. [...] The idea is to communicate the feelings of the Chinese fighters in an integral way, not twisting and turning it to adapt it to our own need.[97]

The accompaniments are occasionally technically demanding, especially in 'Battle March', which has a virtuosic piano interlude; the lyrics are militant, sometimes bloodthirsty; they are intended to evoke pride and optimism as well as an undying love for Chairman Mao.

2. Historical songs with new words and harmonisations by Cardew:

'Graduation Song'
'Battle of Ideas'
'Newly Woken Women'

The text for 'Battle of Ideas' concerns an important issue of the time for the revolutionary movement in England: to purge ourselves of bourgeois ideas – 'the enemy inside our head; wrong ideas his weapons are; these he sends by the media to prevent revolution'. 'Newly Woken Women' is a call to women to throw off the twin yokes of male domination and bourgeois exploitation and to join the communist revolution. Cardew's accompaniment is beautifully wrought and the various points made in the text are skilfully characterised; its simplicity belies a compositional sophistication.

3. National songs from the post-revolutionary period:

'The East is Red'
'Sailing the Seas'
'Long Live Chairman Mao'

Cardew's original accompaniments are pianistic – neat and busy, they require agile hands. Unconstrained by existing arrangements these accompaniments are harmonically more ambitious; their role is more dynamic than in the previous sets.

'The East is Red' is given a suitably heroic treatment with the full range of the keyboard exploited. There is no sense of detachment, let alone irony; the music embodies a burning commitment. Cardew, typically, allows himself no safety net. At the words 'Chairman Mao loves the people, he will guide us in all we do', the music floats up into the high register, the quality is 'ethereal'. History should have persuaded Cardew that deification is a risky business; belief in a human being has to pass the acid test of viability, of infallibility (which in fact the Chairman failed). Religious faith is different; the worshipped has been placed out of reach; the revelation is on spec.

In some handwritten notes for an introductory talk to performances at two concerts in Munich Cardew describes his work on these three groups of songs. Concerning those with his own original accompaniments he makes the following observations:

An aspect which is still highly experimental is the style of these arrangements. The style in which a song is presented depends on a number of factors – on the voice that is to sing it and on the audience that are to listen to it, in particular. So it has gradually become clear that the question of style is a political question. Repeat: from the stylistic point of view the arrangements are highly experimental. A lot of work remains to be done.[98]

Three Bourgeois Songs (1972/3)

The direct, uncompromising diatonicism of most of Cardew's compositions from the early seventies is in sharp contrast to the somewhat obtuse harmonic language of the

Three Bourgeois Songs (completed 24 February 1973): 'Our Joy', 'High Heaven', and 'The Turtledove'. Nevertheless, if the tonal background is undeniable, it is rather the persistence of explicit tonal references juxtaposed with critical (?) allusions to a mid-twentieth century style associated with Benjamin Britten and Michael Tippett, which create a kind of a socio-musical 'critique' of tonality, and, most importantly for Cardew, a vehicle for 'class struggle'.

For the context of these songs was Cardew's then preoccupation with the class content of art, an aspect which had been the focal point of much of Mao Tse-tung's writings on the subject, particularly in his 'Talks at the Yenan Forum'. In an introduction to a performance of two of the *Bourgeois Songs*, 'Our Joy' and 'Turtledove', Cardew writes:

> The reason for presenting these songs is to get to grips with bourgeois thoughts, bourgeois emotions. In short, what is bourgeois ideology? [...] The first ['Our Joy'] is a love poem, supposedly written by a woman, a woman who glories in her subjection; she eulogizes the power and magnificence of her man and this automatically justifies her own existence as a mere domestic and sexual chattel. (I bet it wasn't written by a woman.)
> The second poem ['Turtledove'] again purports to have been written by a woman, this time in praise of her ruler. He is depicted as the wise, benevolent, generous and modest ruler, above all he is the mirror of nature – his way is natural, therefore destined to survive 10,000 years.
> It is not hard to see whom these sentiments serve. In the first case they serve the man, and in the second the ruler. Further they glorify the social relations that put the man or the ruler in the position they're in. For this reason, no matter whether written by the lowest serving maid, these poems are ruling class ideology. That is why Confucius selected them (along with 303 others) to be passed down for the edification of subsequent generations of serfs and slaves.
> That's the intellectual side. What about the emotional side: basically ecstatic submission, either to the power of the man, or to the eternal processes of nature whereby the master knows best just like the mother turtledove over her children.[99]

In 'The Turtledove' Howard Skempton has drawn attention to the 'effective clarification of the cooing effect [and] the subtle enmeshment of voice and piano at certain parts of the score' (Ex.16.2), all of which serves admirably to depict the discreet charm of the bourgeoisie.[100]

Ex.16.2. From 'Turtledove'.

But Cardew wants to strike a balance; the (bourgeois) woman-in-love has to have a measure of credibility – not erected Aunt Sally-like to be ridiculed and toppled. So the choice of objectifying and alienating musical materials must be circumspect; for example, the occasional awkwardness of the music is used as a ploy to demonstrate, perhaps, bourgeois instability (Ex.16.3):

Ex.16.3. From 'High Heaven'.

Cardew is writing bourgeois, not 'bourgeois' songs; he is striving to 'get to grips with bourgeois thoughts, bourgeois feelings'. But bourgeois feelings are not 'pure' feelings; they are hedged about with artificiality and hypocrisy, status and ambition, banality. This Cardew seeks to 'demonstrate' (à la Brecht) through what Michael Finnissy has described as 'the isolation and critique of 'tonal' objects'[101]. So although the music is tonal it is not innocently so. Right at the beginning of *Three Bourgeois Songs*, for example, there is a quite explicit parodical reference in the down-home ('Home on the Range') beginning of 'Our Joy' (Ex.16.4):

Ex.16.4. From 'Our Joy'.

Piano Album 1973

Piano Album 1973 consists of ten short pieces, six of which are based on Chinese themes, three on Irish folk music, and one comes from the English Labour movement. At the end of the volume Cardew states:

> I have discontinued composing music in an avant-garde idiom for a number of reasons: the exclusiveness of the avant-garde, its fragmentation, its indifference to the real situation in the world today, its individualistic outlook and not least its class character (the other characteristics are virtually products of this).[102]

And in a letter to a friend:

> I'm wrestling with piano music for John Tilbury at present, and using some of the Irish material for that too. There are some glimmers of light, but generally the problems of form in instrumental music have taken me by surprise and defeated me. *The East is Red* variations [for violin and piano] would seem to have been something of a fluke.[103]

In the early seventies, having adopted the bracing certainties of Maoism, Cardew existed on the horns of a dilemma: he had repudiated his previous music and wanted to recover an expressive language with which people were more familiar; the problem, of which he was well aware, was that he was ill-equipped to provide the kind of populist music the Party demanded.

> In taking this course a number of questions arise: What material is available, on what musical sources and traditions should we base our work? And in what style should that material be presented, bearing in mind that it must be accessible to the broad masses of so-called 'uncultured' people? The pieces I am presenting here are tentative experiments in a number of different directions, seeking provisional answers to these questions.[104]

Of the six 'Chinese' pieces in *Piano Album 1973*, 'Charge!', 'Song and Dance', 'Sailing the Sea Depends upon the Helmsman', are all staunchly diatonic, with no chromatic interventions in the interest of 'variety'; nor is there any modification of the pentatonic melodies. These are jaunty, innocent little pieces and Cardew's arrangements are 'straight'; there is no irony, no 'critique'. Occasionally, there are interpretative instructions: 'brisk', 'feather light', 'approaching from a distance', which recall Debussy's notational style in his *Preludes*. The instrumental texture is uncluttered, although towards the end of 'Charge!' the melodic line is strengthened with doublings and chordal accompaniment with a stentorian left hand. The middle section of 'Song and Dance', which is in ternary form, abandons the song, and the dancers are accompanied by a welter of on-rushing, mainly scalic, semiquavers in both hands – a brief display of pianistic virtuosity.

From a purely musical perspective 'Bring the Land a New Life', based on an aria from the Peking Opera, *Taking Tiger Mountain by Strategy*, is the odd man out. The bloodthirsty lyric, embodying 'class hatred', which Cardew provides 'to facilitate interpretation', is set to music which, to Western ears, evokes modern jazz and in particular the block-chord style of George Shearing. Cardew must have been aware of this; after all, this is exactly what he set out to do: 'tentative experiments in a number of different directions'. But the music, engaging though it is, does seem to be out of kilter with the vengeful sentiments of the protagonist and therefore derogates from Cardew's (the aria's) primary aim: to represent, in an exalted expression, a fundamental premise of Marxism-Leninism-Mao Tse-tung Thought – the class struggle (Ex.16.5). For a Western audience, therefore, the music is somewhere else, far away from Tiger Mountain, establishing its autonomy and even subverting the intended message:

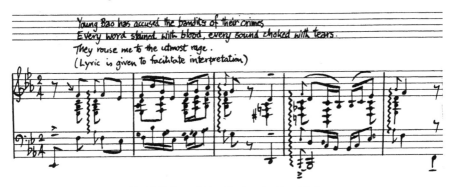

Ex.16.5. From 'Bring the hand a New Life'.

The remaining two 'Chinese' pieces, 'Soon (there will be a high tide of Revolution in our Country)' and 'Long Live Chairman Mao!' are both transcriptions of original songs by Cardew. 'Soon' is a particularly successful 'experiment': stylistically eclectic (experimental), assured, the music never falters.

With the transcriptions of the two Irish songs, 'Croppy Boy' and 'Father Murphy', Cardew is on more familiar ground and he gives the Irish folk music, which he cherished, a free rein. 'Croppy Boy' is atmospheric, beginning in a low register, 'seeking the melody' which, transposed up a tone, is re-stated more boldly in the second section. 'Father Murphy' begins with a quasi-improvisation introduction and the ensuing graceful melody is given elegant and unpretentious expression by Cardew (Ex.16.6). The drama of the story of Father Murphy, who was among the leaders of the 1798 uprising against the British, is represented in the middle section when the theme is embellished in a turbulent passage of semiquaver triplets in both hands, leading to an improvisatory coda (truncated recapitulation). Here are the opening bars of 'Father Murphy':

Ex.16.6. From 'Father Murphy'.

'Red Flag Prelude' is cast in the style of the Romantic prelude; the introduction, a four bar solo bass line followed by a two-part melody and bass line, ends with a final flourish of fast chordal movement. The 'Red Flag' melody ensues, in quadruple time and all in the bass register. The problem with the Red Flag song, as Cardew points out in the Programme notes for *Piano Album 1973*, is that it is 'sung at Labour Party rallies and has come to stand for much that is backward in the English labour movement'. Cardew's realisation is dignified and avoids sentimentality.[105]

The song 'Four Principles on Ireland' was written in response to a call by the Party to intensify the struggle for Irish liberation from British colonial rule and relates to a demonstration in East Street market in southeast London in 1972. The Party comrades who were leafleting were 'brutally attacked' by the police and several received prison sentences. Cardew subsequently wrote a song and a piano piece, 'Four Principles on Ireland', based on the Party's leaflet. In the song the musical material is effectively contrasted: the opening has a proclamatory ring about it, the music fanfare-like as each of the four principles is spelt out; the second half of the verse is based on an Irish traditional tune while the wordy text elaborates on the four principles. In the coda the music broadens out, ending with a paean to Marxism-Leninism.[106]

> I've been working quite hard. I finished the 'Four Principles on Ireland' song, though not entirely satisfactory – e.g. the melody ranges [from G below middle C to F on top line of treble clef[107]] and some of the words lack lyric force. [...] And written a new 'Long Live Chairman Mao' song which I'll sing you when I get back.[108]

'Four Principles on Ireland' is a more ambitious exercise, both compositionally and pianistically; it is quite wayward, with sudden changes of direction and character, and imbued throughout with the spirit of Irish folk music (Ex.16.7a-b). It begins:

Ex.16.7a. From 'Four Principles on Ireland'.

And ends with a jazz-like flourish, referring, perhaps, to the strong association of Ireland with the US:

Ex.16.7b

Piano Album 1974

Piano Album 1974 comprises just four pieces, three of which (possibly all four) were composed while Cardew was in Berlin and are related specifically to political campaigns in the city. *Bethanien Song* (1973), the context for which is described in this chapter in the section dealing with Cardew's Berlin period, is a piano transcription consisting of a verse and chorus played four times. The music builds up from a single-line melody with simple accompaniment to the final presentation, fortissimo, where both hands are playing in sixths and octaves in a rousing finale (Ex.16.8):

Ex.16.8. From 'Bethanien Song'.

The song, with words by the Bethanien Campaign Committee, was a popular rallying call in the neighbourhood and became part of the local folk lore (Ex.16.9). The music is steadfastly diatonic as befits a song written to be sung on demonstrations:

> I was asked to write a song for the campaign. In a few sessions of collective work
> we produced the song that I'm about to play. It has four verses. It embodies
> our demand for a children's polyclinic in Bethanien, not an artists' centre. It sings

of our children's future, threatened by the myriad abuses of capitalist society. It derides bourgeois art, exposes the politics of the social-democrat urban planners, and indicates the perspectives of revolutionary change, with the working people of all nationalities uniting to take their destiny into their own hands. The refrain runs 'Bethanien belongs to us. We will win it through struggle, led by the KPD'.[109]

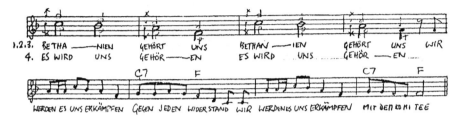

Ex.16.9. From 'Bethanien Lied'.

In his programme notes for *Piano Album 1974* Cardew writes:

The 'Red Aid Song' is also from West Berlin, where the Red Aid movement for the defence and support of political prisoners has been growing fast. Numerous arbitrary arrests and infringements of democratic rights arouse popular indignation against the bourgeois state and its repressive machinery. The communist-led Red Aid movement rallies and channels this indignation and brings it to bear against the bourgeois courts and police.[110]

The tune of the 'Red Aid Song' was whistled to Cardew by one of the cadres of the Red Aid Organisation. Here too the form is variational; in the course of the piece, which is just three pages, the theme is presented three times with ever-increasing intensity. These statements are offset by brief, pianistic interpolations thus (Ex.16.10):

Ex.16.10. From 'Red Aid Song'.

The song 'Revolution is the main trend' bears the stamp of the context in which it was written; clearly, the inspiration was Hanns Eisler's militant anti-fascist songs from the thirties and forties. The march character drives the music forward with occasional syncopations (as in Eisler), generated by the rhythm of the words, which keeps the music on its toes (Ex.16.11).

'Revolution is the main trend' was also written in West Berlin [in 1973]. [It] was intended to support the Anti-Imperialist League. This mass organisation publishes magazines and holds meetings to denounce imperialist actions – particularly those of the two superpowers – against Third World countries. The words of the song are from Mao Tse-tung's 'Statement of May 20th 1970', in which US imperialism is identified as the main enemy of the world's people.[111]

Ex.16.11. From 'Revolution is the main trend'.

The solo piano version, included in *Piano Album 1974*, stays close to the song although, freed from its accompanying role, it is prescribed a quicker tempo and from a soft but urgent beginning in the low register the music generates considerable energy and excitement, with the theme in octaves in both hands (Ex.16.12). The upward scalic movement at the end of the song, to the words 'a new upsurge in the struggle against US imperialism is now emerging throughout the world', is extended and developed harmonically to great effect in the piano piece:

Ex.16.12. From 'Revolution is the main trend' (piano version).

By contrast, the solo piano piece *The East is Red* bears little or no relation to the earlier version for violin and piano. Marked 'light' at the beginning it is a jaunty little piece in which the melody is repeated throughout, unmodified but in different registers, with an unvarying accompaniment of repeated quaver chords and busy semiquavers in the upper register.

Thälmann Variations

Cardew's *Thälmann Variations* for solo piano is one of several 'concert' compositions which he wrote during the last decade, and it is arguably the finest.[112] There is also a *Thälmann Sonata,* which is an arrangement of the *Thälmann Variations* for violin, vibraphone and marimba. It adheres closely to the original except for the first section which is somewhat shorter. The piano variations are divided into three movements, or 'sections', as Cardew calls them, and his introductory text (which is printed in the published score) emphasizes the work's programmatic character:

> These variations celebrate the proletarian hero Ernst Thälmann. [...][113] The theme of the variations is the 'Thälmann song', written in 1934. But I think the tune is an old one, hence the pastoral opening. The whole first section is loosely historical: the pastoral passages at the beginning are interrupted by a militant workers' march which leads to Hanns Eisler's tune 'Rumours of War', symbolizing the vitality that Thälmann infused into the German workers' movement. Then Charles Koechlin's 'Libérons Thälmann' is used to describe the cataclysm that overtook the German workers in 1933. The middle section comprises three slow variations: songs of sadness, warmth and dignity commemorating the countless men and women who have given their lives in the fight against fascism. Finally, a complex 'march of events' is dedicated to the present struggle of the German Communists against the re-emergence of fascism.

At the very beginning the music embodies a sense of gravitas; the voicing of the chords, with added sixths and ninths, and an almost exclusive use of root position, lends poise and focus, and creates a feeling of substantiality (Ex.16.13a).

Ex.16.13a. From *Thälmann Variations*, 1st movement.

The transition to the militant march creates excitement and anticipation and just before the presentation of the transformed 'Thälmann Lied' there is a gradual ascent into the high register; the texture becomes widely spaced and a sense of straining and striving gives the music a 'Beethovenian' (in composer Bernard Stevens' description) quality (Ex.16.13b):

Ex.16.13b

Cardew's treatment of Eisler's song, 'Heimliche Aufmarsch' ('Rumours of War'), with a sudden change of key, from A major to B flat minor, is admirable in the way that it expresses suppressed excitement and anxiety (Ex.16.13c). Firstly:

Ex.16.13c

And then in an outburst of militancy (Ex.16.13d):

Ex.16.13d

The middle section begins in G major with a succession of quiet triads in the left hand on which poignant phrases, derived from the Thälmann theme and characterised by the heroic dotted rhythm, are superimposed (Ex.16.14a):

Ex.16.14a. From 2nd section.

The second variation, in A flat major, does indeed express 'warmth and dignity', the theme embedded within the texture in the middle register, again recalling Beethoven and in particular the texture and character of the slow movement of the *Pathétique Sonata* (Ex.16.14b):

Ex.16.14b

In the first four variations of the last section, although each is characterised quite differently the initial impetus and drive does not flag (Ex.16.15a):

Ex.16.15a. From 3rd section.

Ex.16.15b

Ex.16.15c

Ex.16.15d

The work ends with the theme accompanied by thundering left hand octaves (marked 'rousing'):

Ex.16.15e

Such full-blooded treatment of the theme Cardew described as bringing 'bolshevisation to the Party', and of the *finale* in general he wrote that it represented 'continuing Thälmann's work'.[114]

In many of Cardew's later, politically-inspired pieces there is an asperity and an apparently cavalier attitude to matters of musical, and literary, taste which frequently rides roughshod over the (bourgeois) expectations of trained and cultured ears. Some of Cardew's peers, from the vantage point of their high horse, dismissed such compositions as 'I polish my rifle clean' – a piano transcription of a revolutionary song – and the short choral piece 'There is only one lie', as wilful aberrations. Others, like Cage, simply found them amusing. Such responses, from fellow musicians with whom contact was now peripheral, were probably of little consequence, but in view of the kind of public that his 'concert' music continued to attract, the question of reception, of the way an audience, individually and collectively, perceives the content of a piece of music, continued to preoccupy him:

> Music backs up, supports the social conscience of its audience (which is also its indirect producer). Thus when we try and write revolutionary music for the usual audience we're faced with the insurmountable problem of giving it a form that backs up the (bourgeois) class consciousness of the audience.[115] If we succeed then the revolutionary content is turned around to serve the bourgeois audience in its ideas and cultural milieu. If we fail, then the revolutionary content remains but does not touch the audience – you get the negative reaction either on the grounds that it's bad music, or on the grounds that it is an attack on the audience (on their bourgeois consciousness). There *cannot* be any career as a revolutionary artist.[116]

In relation to Cardew's later music the Uruguayan composer/musicologist, Coriún Aharonián, makes some interesting, and insightful, references, particularly in relation to England's 'imperial culture' and (imperial) 'scholar training':

> What becomes evident is that imperial England is, during the seventies, as provincial as Nicaragua and Albania. Only this fact can explain Cardew's lack of a stronger discussion on what he is doing. The difference is that the imperial culture acquired through the scholar training allows him to really believe he is doing something important for his historical moment. Of course, there is a lack of political background, and this can be understood if we observe for instance that, going to study in Italy in 1964, he chooses Petrassi instead of Nono as his teacher.[117]

However, the reference to 'a lack of political background' is contentious. For although Cardew was for a long time resistant and hostile to politics and politicizing, his lack of enthusiasm for Adorno and the Frankfurt school, for example, was not necessarily due to Anglo-Saxon parochialism and ignorance. We need only remind ourselves of the long sessions that Cardew spent in the studio in Cologne, and of the company he kept there, to conclude that an encounter with Adorno's ideas, to which there would have been on-going reference amongst the Studio 'inmates', would have been inescapable. And even at that time, in the early sixties and before Cardew's politicisation, Adorno's thesis of the autonomy of art – that the very existence of art is itself a form of resistance to ideological repression – would have been met with a measure of scepticism by Cardew. Moreover, it was not only Anglo-Saxons, whether through benightedness or temperament, who baulked at some of Adorno's more speculative theories: Hanns Eisler, as we have already noted, and, from a different perspective, Samuel Beckett, both took issue with Adorno on matters in which there seems to have been little willingness to compromise.[118]

As for Nono, Cardew was as familiar with the Italian's music as most; he knew Nono well in the sixties, and he knew the arguments, and in particular Nono's arguments for political music. (And, of course, Nono's public criticism of Cage, to which I have referred in chapter 5.) Perhaps it is not without significance that, according to Zoltan Peszko, it was works by Eisler, not Nono (one of the 'two tall bare trees of the Italian avant-garde establishment'), that in 1964 Cardew took to the Petrassi class for analysis and discussion. On his own admission, if we are to take it at face value, Cardew went to Petrassi 'to develop a *feeling* for the orchestra'. It is doubtful whether he had any particular interest either in Petrassi's music, or in his politics.

Unlike most contemporary leftist, political concert music (Nono, Henze, Lachenmann et al.), comfortably subsumed within the contemporary music canon of Western society, no niche could be carved out for Cardew's compositional 'experiments'.[119] Like Picasso Cardew's eclecticism signified the deliberate destruction of the unity of the personality; the *Piano Albums* are protests against the cult of originality. The fact that these pieces may or may not bear personality traits, that they represent a complete break with individualism and subjectivism, is neither here nor there; they are a *political* expression: comments, notes on reality from a political perspective. It is this, whatever their shortcomings, which determined the style or styles in which they were cast. Some of it, in particular from the song collection, was dispensable; its fate of no consequence. But we cannot leave it at that. *Tout court*: there is no excuse for writing 'bad music'. And some of it was.

By becoming utilitarian art loses its autonomy, its multiplicity of meanings; for Cardew it meant that art was to be stripped of its *status* to become a branch of politics, and the consequences in relation to his own music affected him profoundly. For the Maoists (that is, for Chairman Mao) art was the handmaid of revolution, albeit with an essential role to play:

Although man's social life is the only source of literature and art and is incomparably livelier and richer in content, the people are not satisfied with life alone and demand literature and art as well. Why? Because, while both are beautiful, life as reflected in works of literature and art can and ought to be on a higher plane, more intense, more concentrated, more typical, nearer the ideal, and therefore more universal than actual everyday life.[120]

Such a text would have resonated profoundly in Cardew, even if he were later to criticise and refute much of what Mao wrote about art. His own life, the way he approached '*being*', was indeed 'livelier and richer in content' than countless works of art. Even his espousal of politics arrived by a totally unconventional route; this is the crux. For it was a decision made in the light of his experience as an *artist*, and in relation to how he perceived music as *human activity*. And yet, paradoxically, he could speculate (with Hegel) that the role of art would not only be transformed by revolution – but that it might even be rendered superfluous, superseded by 'philosophy'. Did not John Cage say that when he wanted to listen to music he simply opened the window? In an interview in 1996 Psi Ellison encapsulated this aspect of Cardew's personality:

It felt to me that Cardew was into life before he was into music (Art). So many people are into music, into theatre, into dance, into this. You talk to them about life and they have nothing to say. But it was very different with Cardew. He made music from life, whereas I think there are a lot of artists around who've lost that connection.They keep regenerating from a musical place, a theatre place, a painting place. His resource was life.[121]

Notes and references

1 Jrnl. 5 March-9 April 1974, 8 April,[p. 55]: Cardew quotes from a Chinese revolutionary. There is an echo here of the Mexican revolutionary Zapata's famous rallying call: it is better to die on your feet than to live on your knees.

2 It appears that from 1977 onwards, on advice from the Party, Cardew did not keep any kind of Journal for fear that if it fell into the wrong hands (the police, the State) it could provide incriminating information, information of an 'evidential' nature, to the Party's enemies. Thus, for the last five years of his life there were no journals; or if there were, none have survived.

3 It was André Gide who popularised the concept of l'acte gratuit: a gratuitous act perpetrated without apparent motive.

4 I think I knew, and know, what he meant: one can make too many allowances for human anxiety and circumspection; sometimes one should just let the ordinary mortal get on with it and if necessary leave him or her in the lurch.

5 AMM too, as we have seen, had been torn asunder by the ferocity of the ideological debate. At the end of the month, from 25 to 29 January, Cardew arrived in Holland for five days of engagements with AMM, a dispiriting time which is referred to in the previous chapter.

6 Amongst Scratch Orchestra members I have interviewed there is a general consensus that such a concert took place, but a complete lack of agreement as to which Polytechnic was the venue. My own recollection is that it was in the Marylebone Road, not far from Baker Street.

7 From the programme: a single, typed sheet which was copied and distributed.

8 Ibid.

9 WEDNR stands for Workers England Daily News Release, which was the paper of the Communist Party of England (Marxist-Leninist), the forerunner Party to the Revolutionary Communist Party of Britain (Marxist-Leninist), which was founded in 1979.

10 From a letter from CC to WEDNR, dated 2 February 1973.

11 From notes written in pencil, undated but certainly early seventies, on the back of a pink sheet advertising the performance of Paragraph 5 at the Cecil Sharp House.

12 I am thinking in particular of the cheerful Chinese arrangements such as Song and Dance, Sailing the Seas Depends upon the Helmsman, and Charge!

13 Written in pencil on a single sheet of paper. Undated but certainly early seventies.

14 Hand-written in pen. Undated. Early seventies.

15 At the time of this book's completion Michael Chant remains a stalwart and active member of the same Party, the Communist Party of England (Marxist-Leninist). One of his responsibilities is running the Party's bookshop in south London.

16 Jrnl. January-April 1973. A clear reference to the authority of Mao's essay 'On Contradiction'.

17 Ibid.

18 Ibid.

19 Selected Writings of the Great Marxist-Leninist Enver Hoxha, 1971-1977, (Toronto: Norman Bethune Institute, 1978), p.351.

20 From 1975 (source mislaid): Cardew, were he alive today, would doubtless also have pointed to the fact that as the art becomes more mindlessly 'refined' the sponsors become more consciously right-wing; e.g. the involvement of Charles Saatchi, Margaret Thatcher's

ex-publicist, in contemporary 'Britart'.

21 In passing we may note that in the New World Order the word 'capitalism' has been wisely supplanted by 'market economy' or the 'free market'. 'Market' has quaint, archaic associations ('This little piggy went to market') whilst the notion of 'free' is irresistible because it is invariably followed by 'to', rarely by 'from'.

22 Jrnl. January-April 1973, undated.

23 Mao Tse-tung, 'Talks at the Yenan Forum on Literature and Art' in *Mao Tse-tung on Literature and Art* (Peking: Foreign Languages Press, 1967), p.31.

24 Ibid., p.32.

25 Walter Bauer of RIAS Berlin had introduced the two men and suggested that they should record Charles Ives' four violin and piano sonatas to commemorate the hundredth anniversary of the composer's birth – which they did. Founded by the US, DIAS (Wire Broadcasting in the American Sector), later to be known as RIAS (Radio in the American Sector), started broadcasting on 7 February 1946.

26 This was not the case. Cardew never regarded such people as being part of the revolutionary, proletarian vanguard, they were 'lumpen proletariat'.

27 Email communication from Négyesy to JT, June 2004.

28 George Steiner, *In Bluebeard's Castle* (London: Faber and Faber, 1971), p.89.

29 One assumes that at that time Cardew would have been dismissive of the objection that the *Three Winter Potatoes* were all written in the sixties.

30 Jrnl. April 1973-February 1974, p.26.

31 The Morley group included Rod and Joy Eley, Kevin Richards, Hugh Shrapnel, Adrian and Frances Rifkin, Barbara Pearce, Michael Parsons, Tim Mitchell, Penny Jordan, Alec Hill, Howard Skempton, Carole Finer, Michael Chant and Bryn Harris. The circumstances surrounding Skempton's departure from the group, around March 1973, clearly demonstrate the fact that Cardew, *in absentia*, was still regarded as the group's spokesman, its leader. It also serves as a salutary reminder of the extent to which the Party had taken control: 'Cornelius came to see me at Faber Music where I was working and we went out for a coffee. He'd returned from Berlin for a few days and somebody must have suggested that my attitude during the political discussions at Morley was hostile, and he felt obliged to ask me to resign. I think he said he'd see if Alec (Hill) could take over responsibility for the class. I don't think I was hostile. I was certainly unhappy. I remember arguing the case for improvisation (suggesting that it was the necessary roughage of a good musical diet!) and being shouted down.' Howard Skempton, email commucation to JT, 14 April 2005. In fact, Michael Parsons too, resigned, at the end of 1972.

32 According to Michael Graubart, who was Director of Music at Morley College at the time, 'he [Barry Till] was seriously worried about the political nature of the activities (inside and outside the Morley classroom) that the class was engaged in by then […]. I argued that political education and debate was a vital and legitimate part of adult education, but that what the class was doing could no longer be subsumed under the class title of Experimental Music. I would have liked the class to carry on, but under a very different name and class-description (which should have included something about discussion of the role of the arts in political activity); Barry insisted on closing it.' Email communication to JT, 10 October 2004.

33 From a paper delivered by CC to the Morley College class on 23 March 1973.

34   What does Cardew mean exactly by 'employee mentality'? Passivity, refusal to take responsibility, deference, alienation, fear (feeling of intimidation)? The irony is that the Party itself, by its high-handedness and high-mindedness, its intimidatory and manipulative approach, its self-assumed rectitude, its conspiratorial image, was mainly responsible for inculcating such a 'mentality' in its supporters and in those who attended its meetings out of a healthy political curiosity. Cardew was better equipped than most to resist these ploys and techniques but even he, as we have seen often enough, was affected and undermined by the remorseless and unforgiving nature of Party propaganda.

35   Whether Lenin should shoulder sole responsibility for it is a moot point. I suspect that most political parties avail themselves of the model on a regular basis.

36   I need to emphasise that the scenario I describe applies, in my own experience, just as appositely to 'bourgeois' political parties.

37   Andrei Zhdanov (b. 1896; d.1948) was Secretary of the Central Committee of the Soviet Union from 1946 to 1948. It was a period when considerable pressure was brought to bear, particularly in relation to the acknowledgement and implementation of socialist realism as the embodiment of the Party's demands on creative artists.

38   Jrnl. September 1974, undated, [pp.23-28].

39   This was one of the most contentious periods in the history of the Akademie der Künste, as Michael Heardter recalls. There had been considerable in-fighting between left-wing and conservative factions. Together with Nele Hertling, secretary of the Music section, and others, they had introduced much avant-garde art, performance, music, radical theatre groups, new poets, into Berlin; artists such as Günter Grass and Joseph Beuys were actively involved. Most of the artists were leftists; many of them 'gegen Kultur'. Some published critiques of the Akademie, challenging its existence and even demanding its closure.

40   The SDS was founded and led by Rudi Dutschke – friend of Adorno and the Chilean exile Gaston Salvatore – who became a hero for the younger generation. He also set up the famous Commune 1 which was used as a rehearsal space by many rock bands (including Tangerine Dream). In 1969 Dutschke was shot in the Kurfürstendamm in Berlin and survived two bullet wounds to the head. He later moved to Arhus in Denmark where he died 24 December 1979.

41   Or it might have been the group Agitation Free; my sources conflict here.

42   Perhaps the question mark was added because Cardew was not absolutely sure of its appropriateness to his polemic.

43   Further references to Cardew's attitude towards Steve Reich and his music are included in the chapter, Stockhausen Serves Imperialism.

44   These issues are raised in Stockhausen Serves Imperialism and are discussed in the chapter of the same name.

45   Bernard Stevens (1916-1983). Studied with R.O. Morris, Gordon Jacob and Arthur Benjamin, and became Professor of composition at the RCM in 1948.

46   For Cardew there were also personal matters which preoccupied him at the time. Of particular concern was the condition of his pupil Penny Jordan, who had suffered a breakdown and was in hospital. He wanted to discuss the best way – that is, the politically-correct way – of approaching her and offering her help and advice.

47   People's Liberation Music was formed by Laurie Baker, John Marcangelo, Brigid Scott

Baker, and John Tilbury in late 1972. In 1973 Cardew replaced John Tilbury and Keith Rowe also joined the group. Vicky Silva was the main vocalist. Initially it was a political rock group which supported the struggles of people around the world against oppression and exploitation; it researched songs as well as composing new ones. The band played in colleges, for workers, including street demonstrations, and for community events; over the years many left musicians participated in PLM concerts. The group continued performing until 1978 when it was dissolved under a directive from the CPE (M-L) and re-formed as the Progressive Cultural Association Band (PCA).

48   I apologized to Cardew afterwards; he was characteristically forgiving and encouraging, remarking that much of my playing had been admirable and far superior to what he himself could have managed. However, I was not to be consoled; I knew that on this occasion I had been unequal to the task (probably through insufficient preparation) and felt that I had let him down.

49   Verbal communication to JT from Laurie Baker, 12 March 2003.

50   *Stockhausen Serves Imperialism*, p.91. (*CCR*)

51   Mass work was an important part of the Party's work. It involved canvassing people on the streets and doorsteps for their opinion and, where the prognosis seemed favourable, establishing contact for further visits and meetings.

52   This 'subversion of finality' manifested itself not only in his political discussions in the seventies but also in his indeterminate music from the sixties.

53   From a hand-written sheet by Cardew, dated 9 April 1974.

54   Jrnl. 5 March-9 April, dated 5 April 1974, p.43.

55   Jrnl. April 1973-February 1974, undated.

56   Hanns Eisler, *A Rebel in Music* (Berlin: Seven Seas Books, 1978), pp. 212-3.

57   From a letter from CC to Michael Parsons, dated 29 March 1973.

58   Sheila had been visting her husband in Princeton.

59   Letter from Stella Cardew to JT, dated 19 September 2004.

60   From a letter from Psi Ellison to Stefan Szczelkun, dated 12 February 1993. This is important because it encapsulates the essence of the alternative, 'non-political' view of the Scratch Orchestra and its demise.

61   Michael Chant, 'A turning point in music history', a paper delivered at a Symposium on the Scratch Orchestra on its thirtieth anniversary, 21 November 1999. This was one of three papers published by Progressive Cultural Association, September 2002. The other two were by Richard Ascough and Michael Parsons.

62   Michael Parsons, 'The Scratch Orchestra – Performance/Interpretation'. Published in German in *Positionen* 26, February 1996 pp.8–13: 'Wer Künstler werden will, melde sich', Das London Scratch Orchestra.

63   Carol Reakes, an imposing and charismatic figure, had a great influence on Cardew and exerted considerable political/ideological pressure on him in the mid-seventies. An Englishwoman, she had studied at Trinity College Dublin from 1965-68 where her mentor had been Hardial Bains. In 1974 she returned to England to succede George Malcolm as First Secretary of the English Party (CPEML) and remained leader of the Party until the first half of 1978. She returned to Ireland in the autumn of the same year and was leader of the Irish Party until November 1979.

64   Jrnl. April 1974-July 1974, undated (probably towards the end of May), [pp.42-44]. At ld

Group meetings most people approached the notion of 'self' with a guilty conscience. The context in which 'self' was discussed was invariably negative; 'self' was associated with self-seeking, self-centredness, egotism and narcissism – in a phrase, bourgeois individualism. According to George Steiner, the theory of personality, as it develops from Hegel, through Nietzsche, to Freud, is 'essentially a theory of aggression'. The self's relation to others is seen as a negation – the self against, or in spite of, others. Hence, the 'theory of personality' is a nineteenth century theory of 'romantic', or 'bourgeois' personality in which, presumably, the twentieth century notion of 'bourgeois individualism' is rooted.

65   Hanns Eisler, *A Rebel in Music*, p.192.
66   Maynard Solomon on Lenin, from *Marxism and Art*, p.166.
67   Monk, p.97.
68   Idid, p.366.
69   Ironically, whilst the Party had dismissed the Scratch vocal endeavours, the (bourgeois) critic Peter Heyworth compared our rendering of Verdi's 'Va, pensiero' favourably to that of the Royal Opera House chorus: 'Would it be uncharitable to note that this (Scratch) homespun performance had a sense of the music's natural breath that eluded Colin Davis at Covent Garden?' From a review in the *Observer*, 2 April 1972.
70   Perhaps 'combating revisionism' was one of the reasons for Cardew's regular attendance at musicians' union meetings.
71   Jrnl. April-July 1974, dated 23 June 1974, [p.72].
72   Ibid, undated, p. 60.
73   Mao Tse-tung, 31 July 1955: On the Question of Agricultural Cooperation, from *Selected Readings from the Works of Mao Tse-tung,* (Peking: Foreign Languages Press, 1971), p.395.
74   Jrnl. April-July 1974, dated 19 May.
75   Jrnl. 20 August 1955.
76   Jrnl. April-July 1974. From notes for 'The Situation and Prospects of Art Students Today'; talk given at the Falmouth College of Art on 13 June 1974. (*CCR*)
77   Ibid.
78   From a letter from CC to Rod Eley, dated 29 June 1974.
79   From a letter from CC to Alan Bush, dated 24 February 1974.
80   From a letter from Alan Bush to CC, dated 16 May 1974.
81   From a letter from Alan Bush to CC, dated 11 June 1974.
82   At that time my partner Janice and I had a small flat in Tufnell Park Road where my Steinway grand was often a welcome distraction for Cardew. Sheila Kasabova recalls hearing him play through Irish songs, sitting at the piano, weeping.
83   Jrnl. July-August 1974, dated 29 July, pp.18-19.
84   For a comprehensive analysis of the profound changes which were heaped upon ordinary working people in the seventies I would direct the reader to *A World Still to Win, The Reconstruction of the Post-war Working Class* by Trevor Blackwell and Jeremy Seabrook (London: Faber and Faber, 1985).
85   Ibid, p.21.
86   Musically, it was the Irish rebel and folk music which was the greatest source of inspiration, partly because it was a struggle in which he could, and did, play an active part.
87   Jrnl. September 1974, dated 7 September, pp.9-10.

88 Ibid., dated 26 September 1974, p.18.

89 From the Minutes of an MU meeting on 30 September 1974.

90 Presumably, Devenport's meeting with Cardew had taken place a few days earlier, in mid-November.

91 To Keith Rowe it suggested the blindfold test where one would sense, through touch and feeling, that the owner, or resident, was somebody who was exceptionally cultured, of extraordinary perceptions, who had either lots of money, or none at all.

92 But there was also anxiety. While they were living at Agar Grove (up to July 1979) she and Cardew were on a National Front (extreme right-wing political party) hit list; their names had been seen on an NF document. When she was left alone in their ground floor flat, as she often was, and for lengthy periods, Sheila felt vulnerable and extremely nervous.

93 Many years later Sheila moved into the basement, which had been beautifully renovated.

94 Sheila Kasabova was in the same year as the Gay Rights activist Peter Tatchell, who was an occasional visitor to the flat in Agar Grove.

95 Regarding maintenance for the boys and their mother, there was no formal (legal) financial arrangement. He provided for them as and when he could.

96 Letter to HSK, 20 December 1974.

97 From an introduction to a performance of the songs, dated 26/27 June 1973.

98 Ibid. Cardew was very active in promoting Chinese revolutionary works at that time. It was not just a formal and academic meeting of minds over the positions held by the Chinese Communist artists. Cardew's own poems were influenced by Chinese forms, just as his piano writing, for a brief period, paid homage to the music which came out of the Chinese cultural revolution.

99 Jrnl. 5 March–9 April 1974, dated 5 March.

100 From Skempton's programme notes for the anniversay concert of Cardew's music at the Purcell Room in 1991.

101 Email communication from Michael Finnissy to JT, 12 October 2005.

102 From 'Programme notes for *Piano Album 1973*', as printed in the score published by the Cornelius Cardew Foundation, 1991.

103 Letter from CC to MP, 19 July 1973.

104 From 'Programme notes for *Piano Album 1973*'.

105 To the mutual benefit of both the song and New Labour, the 'Red Flag' no longer features at party conferences.

106 The reference to Mao Tse-tung – 'practise the teachings of Chairman Mao' – was omitted in later versions.

107 Cardew draws the stave here.

108 From a letter from CC to Michael Chant, dated 29 May 1973.

109 Jrnl. September 1974, undated, pp.27-28.

110 From a typewritten sheet with the heading '*Piano Album 1974* Programme notes' (June 1975).

111 Ibid. The text was subsequently replaced by a new version based on a speech by the Albanian communist leader, Enver Hoxha.

112 In a letter to Cardew dated 25 January 1976, following a performance of *Thälmann Variations* at St Pancras Town Hall, the composer Alan Bush expressed his admiration: 'I thought it was full of invention, with a range of expression and variety of effect which was most

impressive. [...] the opening statement of the theme was extremely beautiful.' And in a later correspondence, dated 25 November 1978, Bush again refers to Cardew's 'splendid [Thälmann]Variations'.

113 Ernst Thälmann was Secretary of the German Communist Party from 1927. In 1933 he was imprisoned by the Nazis. In 1944 he was murdered in Büchenwald concentration camp.

114 Jrnl. September 1974.

115 At the time Cardew questioned the thesis that there are 'universal' factors in art which make possible its impact across class lines and historical boundaries.

116 Jrnl. April 1973-February 1974, dated 11 July 1973.

117 Coriún Aharonián, 'Cardew as a basis for a discussion on ethical options', *Leonardo Music Journal*, vol.11, Cambridge (Massachusetts), 2001. Despite some reservations, which are evident in what I write here, I consider Aharonián's text as an invaluable contribution to the debate, particularly in relation to the discussion of the 'language' of political music.

118 James Knowlson describes an occasion in Frankfurt in 1961 when the head of Suhrkamp publishing house, Siegfried Unseld, had invited Beckett and Adorno to lunch. According to Unseld Adorno launched into his theory of the meaning of names in Beckett insisting that 'Hamm' in *Endgame* derives from *Hamlet*. 'Beckett said "Sorry, Professor, but I never thought of Hamlet when I invented this name". But Adorno insisted. And Beckett became a little angry.' James Knowlson, *Damned to Fame, The Life of Samuel Beckett* (London: Bloomsbury, 1996), p. 479. 'Too much Herr-Doktoring' – was Beckett's occasional reproach to his German colleagues.

119 In an email communication in March 2006 Harry Gilonis drew my attention to the fact that there were no UK public performances of Nono to mark the tenth anniversary of his death. At a piano recital at the Italian Institute dedicated to contemporary Venetian composers in 2006, ...*sofferte onde serene...* was not played, but some non-Venetians were. Most of Nono's political music has not been reissued on CD. But the reasons, we may presume, would be political, rather than musical. Unlike Cardew's later music in which he succeeded in offending the (bourgeois) musical establishment on *musical* grounds, irrespective of the political content. And in his compositional 'experiments' at that time, this was what he was striving to achieve: to create a music, like the sound of the bagpipes, that would 'strike terror into our enemy'. (Vide chapter 13.)

120 Talks at the Yenan Forum, p.19.

121 Quoted in Kathryn Gleasman Pisaro, from *Music from Scratch: Cornelius Cardew, Experimental Music and the Scratch Orchestra in Britain in the 1960s and 1970s*. Ph.D. diss., Northwestern University, US, 2001.

(*CCR*) Also found in *Cornelius Cardew A Reader*

17

Stockhausen Serves Imperialism 1974

I'm convinced that when a group of people get together and sing the 'Internationale' this is a more complex, more subtle, a stronger and more musical experience than the whole of the avant-garde put together. This is not pseudo-scientific fantasy but represents real people in the real world engaged in the most important struggle of all – the class struggle.[1]

1972 had seen the espousal of a revolutionary ideology by Cardew, followed by a period of consolidation and study. *Stockhausen Serves Imperialism*, a collection of polemical essays on cultural matters generally, but mainly with reference to music, was published in 1974 by Latimer New Dimensions London.[2] It consists of four chapters, preceded by Cardew's own brief introduction. The first chapter, written by Scratch Orchestra member Rod Eley, is a history of the Scratch Orchestra from 1969 to 1972. The second chapter, entitled 'Criticising Cage and Stockhausen', consists of three articles by Cardew (including 'On Criticism') and one by myself, each of which was commissioned by the BBC, originally as a talk. The third chapter describes and analyses 'a critical concert' in Berlin of music by Christian Wolff and Frederic Rzewski. The final chapter is entitled 'Self-Criticism: Repudiation of Earlier Works', and comprises an article, originally a talk, on *Treatise*, and one on *The Great Learning*.

In fact, the title *Stockhausen Serves Imperialism* gives a misleading impression, inflating Stockhausen's presence and importance in the book. It is not simply a polemic against Stockhausen, which forms just part of one of the four chapters; it is essentially a critique of 'bourgeois' art in general and the avant-garde, of which Cardew had been a committed and respected member, in particular. A seditious book, it was deemed worthy of a three-part review by Hans Keller in *Books and Bookmen* in 1975,[3] the ferocity of which itself raises questions and encapsulates, in an extreme expression, the reaction of incomprehension and hostility which the publication of Cardew's collection of essays provoked amongst many of his fellow musicians and even close friends (Eddie Prévost deplored 'the crass Party rhetoric and the dreary writing which pervades much of the book'.[4])

But there was also support and acclaim from some quarters: 'The savage denunciation of these composers (Cage and Stockhausen) is a great shock', wrote Howard Skempton, 'but a necessary one'. And, flying in the face of Keller's maledictory judgement: 'The aspect of Cardew's character which emerges most clearly from these pages is his passionate commitment to truth and realism. […] This book is highly recommended. We have nothing to lose but our complacency.'[5]

The composer Alan Bush was even more effusive, 'even if some of his [Cardew's] present political beliefs are quite unacceptable' (a reference to Cardew's attacks on 'soviet revisionism'):

This book is not only remarkable, it is important; as far as I know the most important book on musical theory by a British author published since Deryck Cooke's *Language of Music* appeared in 1959. It should be made compulsory reading for all university students taking musical degrees.[…] It will not be answered, *it will be ignored*, by the music critics of the national press or of most of the music periodicals, whose writings about these personalities and this subject are unprincipled where they escape total superficiality.[6]

As for a younger, 21st century audience, what may now be regarded as the 'archaisms' of the language might well create barriers, whilst the irksome tone of *certainty,* of *irrefutability,* will persuade some readers simply to disengage from the argument. For others the unequivocal language of 'class warfare' which colours the text throughout, and the brutality of its sentiment, may be unsettling: When two comrades committed suicide, in 1911, Lenin remarked: 'If you can't do any more work for the Party you must be able to face the truth and die.'[7] It was the starkness and unequivocalness, and perhaps the notion of self-sacrifice, and of *excess,* in such pronouncements which impressed Cardew.

If *Stockhausen Serves Imperialism* represents a relatively early stage of Cardew's political *engagement*, by the time the book was nearing completion he had already acquired a detailed, theoretical knowledge of the Marxist-Leninist canon; it was a period of intense study, of learning. As early as 1972 the Journals show that considerable space was devoted to notes and summaries of Marxist doctrine; much of this was concerned with basic concepts: Marx's objection to Hegel's idealism; being determines consciousness; the relation of quantitative to qualitative change; the theory of surplus value, and so forth, and again demonstrates, apart from the rigour with which he pursued his studies, the extent to which Cardew had been divorced, in his earlier years, from any political thought and debate. Marx and Lenin were for him, approaching the age of forty, new discoveries; so that first of all he had to recover lost ground, to work through and to assimilate the nineteenth/early twentieth century canon in order to be able to play his part in a new, contemporary Marxist-Leninist strategy which would provide the basis for a programme of political action. There are copious, painstakingly handwritten notes from his reading of Lenin: Lenin's article 'On Marx' is summarised, although much of the detail remains; the subject matter is dealt with comprehensively – not in note form but in a fluent, functional prose, as if he were preparing a lecture to be read, which perhaps he was. (It was around the time of his visits to the Bradford School of Art.)

With reference to Engels' oft-quoted maxim 'freedom is the appreciation of necessity'[8] Cardew registers his own response:

'Necessity is blind only in so far as it is not understood' (Engels); leads to the recognition of objective laws in nature, and of the dialectical transformation of necessity into freedom.
This is not fully clear to me.[9]

Many non-Marxist socialists have baulked at this definition of freedom with its manifold and perplexing corollaries: how, for example, can the extension of (individual) 'freedom' on the one hand, and the restraints imposed by 'civilization' on the other, be reconciled? (We presume that Cardew eventually resolved the matter to his own satisfaction.) And there were other related issues which would have engaged him, such as the problem of reconciling the objective laws of nature (an ecological awareness and programme) with the Party's demands for 'scientific progress' – that is, with political exigencies. One of the key issues which the Maoists would raise persistently at that time was the alleged neutrality of 'bourgeois' science, or indeed any science – a highly contentious position from which a number of widely differing conclusions could be drawn. In essence, for the Communist Party of England (Marxist-Leninist) accountability to the Party and its needs was an ongoing obligation from which even science could not escape. By then, however, this view of the relationship between man and nature was regarded by many Marxists as one-sided, alienating, un-scientific in fact, and was at least partly responsible for the ecological disaster areas which blighted a significant number of sites in Eastern Europe, which a more enlightened, more philosophical reading of Engels might at least have limited. Engels posited a human existence 'in harmony with the laws of nature that have become known', with the potent reminder : 'but how young the whole of human history still is, and how ridiculous it would be to attempt to ascribe any absolute validity to our present views'.[10]

Engels' *Anti-Dühring* was the subject of another of Cardew's lectures intended for the Bradford students. Again, whether used or not, Cardew's preparation is thorough and conscientious, judging from the extensive notes in the Journals. At the very beginning he reminds himself, perhaps his listeners too, of the purpose of his talk:

> 1) To summarise the content, for the benefit of those who don't have time to read the 500 page book. 2) To extol the vigour and freshness that is characteristic of all the Marxist classics. 3) To help us in our efforts to bring philosophy out of the lecture halls and libraries and apply it to our concrete problems, and place it at the service of the people.[11]

Time and again Cardew stressed the dynamic relationship of theory and practice, which was exemplified with the creation of the Scratch Orchestra. For Engels it had been important to develop a critique of Eugen Dühring precisely because he (Dühring) was claiming (falsely) to put forward materialism and socialism. Cardew seized on this to support his own Party's exposure and denunciation of various 'left-wing' publications which were circulating at the time: 'Not to do so is liberalism, and liberalism is wrong not only because it allows wrong ideas to flourish, but because it rots one's own thinking from within; it dulls it and perverts it.'[12] Cardew was dismissive of liberalism and what he regarded as its dissembling nature:

> Liberalism is just as oppressive as the religious dogma of the nineteenth century that it replaces. Liberalism is a tactic whereby the sting is taken out of the huge contradictions that run right through our cultural environment, so that we are tempted to pass them over and ignore them.[13]

Edward Thompson characterised the liberal stance in similar fashion:

> What he [the liberal intellectual] wants to say serves only too often as an intellectual gloss upon the status quo [...] and the end of politics is no longer the good life but stability – a system of checks and balances upon original sin. No matter how cynical our liberal intellectual may be about the actual conduct of our political life, he finds himself assenting to a system which silences effective dissent.[14]

Elsewhere Cardew reminds himself that dualistic thinking often masquerades as dialectics: Dualistic thinking treats of opposites as eternally divorced,

> springing either from a limited, one-sided comprehension of the dialectical nature of reality, e.g. religious good and evil, or from the conscious desire to hold back progress, to prevent the transformation of opposites into each other, to prevent the oppressed class becoming the ruling class.[15]

On the very first page of the introduction to *Stockhausen Serves Imperialism* Cardew poses two questions: the first regarding 'the relations of production in the field of music in bourgeois society', the second relating to 'the relative importance and significance of polemics such as those documented in this book in the context of the class struggles surging around us in the imperialist heartlands today'. He begins by challenging the (bourgeois) concept of the composer or writer as a 'free producer':

> In fact, a book or a composition is not an end-product, not in itself a useful commodity. The end-product of an artist's work, the 'useful commodity' in the production of which he plays a role, is ideological influence. He is as incapable of producing this on his own as a blacksmith is of producing Concorde. The production of ideological influence is highly socialised, involving (in the case of music) performers, critics, impresarios, agents, managers, etc., and above all (and this is the artist's real 'means of production') an audience.[16]

The audience – overtly, directly, subtly, unconsciously, by osmosis, as it were, spreads the message. The 'waves in the environment', the 'repercussions beyond the concert hall', referred to in the BBC broadcast in 1968, are now, some five years later, defined as 'ideological influence', with the significant enrichment of the original thesis through the crucial introduction of the idea of *socialization*.

For the remainder of this chapter – in fact it bears upon the rest of this book – I have taken the liberty for the sake of some of my readers, and at the risk of irritating others, of expatiating upon some of the Marxist, or rather Marxist-Leninist, terminology which pervades Cardew's book from cover to cover. It is not my intention to lend support to his argument, but simply to render some of the maxims and formulae, not necessarily more palatable, but more accessible, by couching them in a more neutral, and more viable language. It will also enhance understanding, if not empathy, I hope, in relation to Cardew's political profile through a greater cognisance of the context of my reflections and comments on the broader issues, and their implications, as they arise out of Cardew's polemics.

The Dictatorship of the Proletariat and Democratic Centralism

For freedom is the man that will turn the world upside down, therefore no wonder that he hath enemies.[17]

Only he is a Marxist who *extends* the recognition of the class struggle to the recognition of the *dictatorship* of the proletariat.[18]

Nowadays, at the beginning of the 21st century, to describe someone as a 'Marxist' is of no more consequence than describing him or her as a 'vegetarian', and of less significance than describing someone as an 'environmentalist' or, ironically, as an 'anti-capitalist'. The latter-day Marxist, in Cardew's opinion, is summarily characterised in Hanns Eisler's formulation in relation to the Frankfurt School:

> As far as I still read the writings of the Frankfurturists today, they suffer from one basic ill: they want simply to be cleverer than the bourgeois theorists – but they do not want to fight them. Thus, they become the star pupils of decline.[19]

To interpret the world is one thing, but to change it might be a foolhardy step too far. But Cardew was not a 'latter-day Marxist'; he was a Marxist-Leninist. And both informally and formally he would stress the incontrovertibility of the two basic, and inseparable, Leninist principles: the dictatorship of the proletariat, and democratic centralism. During the last decade it was these tenets which guided his compositional objectives, his work with the Progressive Cultural Association and, for him most importantly, his Party work.

In his political lectures to the Bradford students in March 1973 Cardew refers critically to Marx's over-optimistic calculation that after the seizure of political power by the working class the superstructure would be more or less rapidly transformed. In practice, this was not to be the case. And time and again during this period Cardew would come back to the necessity of the authority of the Party, of leadership. For there could be no 'mass democracy' without advanced ideas and guidance. Thus, the 'idea' or 'principle' of 'the dictatorship of the proletariat' is subsumed into the reality of the authority of the Communist Party, and Cardew had no qualms about that.[20]

> The central problem is the Dictatorship of the Proletariat. This dictatorship must be consolidated over a more or less long period of time; it must militantly protect itself against the infiltration of the bourgeoisie. Lenin and Stalin both took this very seriously. But the bourgeoisie succeeded in the Soviet Union despite their efforts. It is now clear that the Dictatorship of the Proletariat must be consolidated over a *long* period.
> China's great contribution to the solution of this problem is the idea of Proletarian Cultural Revolution. The working people must seize the leadership in all spheres of culture. Who did they have to seize power from? In many cases it was from Party members, who were actually agents of the bourgeoisie within the proletarian party, the Communist Party of China.[21]

The dictatorship of the proletariat was not intended to be a set of rules and regulations to encourage or inhibit modes of behaviour; rather it was perceived by the Marxist-Leninists as a 'massive social force' guided and led by themselves.

The dictatorship of the proletariat is, or rather became, a stark metaphor which already in the seventies could no longer be understood in a literal sense; and in its application as a momentous, defiant slogan it was, to say the least, counter-productive. The word 'dictatorship' enjoys no currency in the popular imagination even if one can cite countless instances, say in domestic life, and on a day-to-day basis, of dictatorial and oppressive behaviour. On the whole people have no desire either to dictate or be dictated to. Similarly, the perception of a 'proletarian' class is that of down-trodden people in faraway lands. Who in Britain, even in nineteen seventy-four, would have described themselves as 'a member of the proletariat'? Who, therefore, was the target of this Party propaganda? [22] That a political party could incorporate such a formula – the dictatorship of the proletariat – into its manifesto displayed not only a misinterpretation of the political culture of the society in which it operated, but also an infelicitous misjudgment of the very people it aimed to inspire and enlist in the struggle for emancipation. The hugely disproportionate reliance on the Chinese model and Chinese propaganda, which Cardew himself had criticised, also reflected an inability, or a (temporary?) reluctance to grasp the political nettle in their own country. Perhaps the self-aggrandizing propaganda extolling the Party and its aims was directed as much at themselves as to the oppressed working people of Wandsworth and Hackney. And the professed certainties which cluttered their arguments and speeches, their mantric repetition of arcane and 'foreign' slogans, their wide-eyedness, may have served to mask a debilitating lack of confidence and self-belief born of political immaturity, a deep-seated psychological need not necessarily in relation to the cause they had espoused, but in respect of their own concealed shortcomings.

The dictatorship of the proletariat presupposes the (more or less violent) displacement of embedded precepts, of deeply-rooted ideas in relation to 'self', to 'property', to 'social relations'; it involves the ultimate invalidating of the *mores* of a particular society; it decrees the destruction of the 'historical crib' by an historically-determined insurrection. And it establishes a new dispensation which is 'more rational', 'more just', 'more desirable', 'more necessary', but which, through its peremptoriness, presumptuousness, its utopian claims and, in particular, by its status as an unknown quantity, invokes suspicion, scepticism and hostility, even amongst those who are most likely to benefit from it. Thus the Old, simply by virtue of its time-honoured dominance, has many advantages over the New, even when the latter could boast occupancy. Hence, according to Cardew and his Marxist-Leninist comrades, the necessity for a lengthy period of uncompromising control and vigilance.

Yet behind the crassness of the metaphor (dictatorship of the proletariat) there *is* a profound (Marxist) authenticity; for from whichever side of the fence, and irrespective of demonstrable, 'objective' criteria, a profound sense of alienation *is* a condition which is endemic to class society. What the formula 'dictatorship of the proletariat' (or 'dictatorship of the bourgeoisie', for that matter) emblematizes – if we interpret it creatively and if we try to imagine its application in today's political climate, with its sharp divisions – is the 'battle of ideas': the day-to-day confrontation of irreconcilable attitudes, and for many people the struggle to protect and to consolidate, however imperfectly, an ethical code antithetical to the prevailing (dominant) *mores*. To be more specific, we may refer to the struggle to instil and safeguard values at home which are at odds with those from without which threaten to engulf us, an undertaking to which many families in Britain and elsewhere in the contemporary world have committed themselves. One teaches one's children to share, to behave modestly and with respect for others, to be considerate of others, to be honest and to say what they think, to have integrity, to cherish simple things, to be an 'individual' but not to be individualistic and selfish, to appreciate the value of something rather than simply knowing its price, and so forth. At the same time the parents are obliged to navigate their lives through an ideologically-driven economic system which to a greater or lesser extent negates these values and which dismisses them as quaint relics of a sentimental past, as outmoded, and as having no viability in the modern world.

So to protect (but not over-protect) one's charges one must be vigilant and persevering, occasionally chastising them, denying them in some way, punishing them ('one has to be cruel to be kind'). One must visit the school, monitor television programmes, insist on ethical standards in an environment where amorality is the norm. In doing so one may find oneself of necessity acting 'dictatorially' to protect what one believes is right from what one believes is wrong. And the stakes nowadays are stacked high against us. Thus, the parent is an 'outsider' representing an alien ideology but who, within his/her domain, within the confines of the home, exercises authority. She insists on a certain moral code; fights off, as well as she can, reactionary intrusions of a dominant, predatory, aggressive, individualistic culture; strives to safeguard and consolidate the moral base. And most importantly to instil an unflinching sense of self-respect, or rather *self-worth* (of far greater consequence, it seems to me, than the Dickensian notion of 'self-betterment').Cardew himself would have understood the broader definition, relating it to every domain of human commerce. He had set it to music: 'The solid cannot be swept away as trivial and nor can trash be established as solid'.

Michael Chant succinctly characterises the essence of what was, and is, the philosophical issue at hand:

Collective work and experience stands against what is being promoted on all fronts as the 'me' culture, where the issue, for example, becomes that art has importance because it expresses 'my' life, 'I' did this first, or it gratifies 'me'. This can only contribute to the general crisis of society.[23]

The key element in democratic centralism, the second Leninist principle which Cardew upheld with such single-mindedness, is the idea of a vanguard, an elite, an *authority*; and it is a political concept, the Central Committee as reification of an 'idea', which he found compelling (as well as reflecting his earlier sympathy for Confucianism).[24] Cardew's perspective was necessarily historical, contingent – to paraphrase Lenin: authority for whom, to do what, to whom. Thus, the practice of democratic centralism embodies an authority which is a key factor in the *historic* establishment and consolidation of the dictatorship of the proletariat. Democratic centralism was posited as the only means to revolutionary political power; its uncompromising nature, the 'purity' of the political programme it served, and the inherent danger, the life-threatening risks which the implementation of such an agenda presented, reflected the enormity of the task. For Cardew and his fellow cultural workers there could be no fudge; the fundamental class antagonism had to be clearly understood and represented without ambiguity, and without equivocation: 'there is only one lie, only one truth'.

Cardew was convinced that the task of overthrowing the capitalist system would of necessity involve, in Lenin's words: 'a long, stubborn and desperate war of life and death, a war demanding perserverance, discipline, firmness, indomitableness and unity of will'.[25] Cardew did not believe that revolutionary change could be achieved by peaceful means; there was too much at stake, most essentially in the domain of property relations. This deep-seated conviction explains his predisposition for discipline and incisive action, for tactics and strategy run on military lines; the ruling class (the bourgeois state) was a ruthless enemy which would stop at nothing to preserve its hegemony, its privileges. And fascism, the Marxist-Leninists claimed, would be the last throw of a degenerate, dying capitalism, when the façade of bourgeois democracy is stripped away and its true nature exposed.

Party ideologues were not the only ones to challenge the liberal notion that somehow fascism was a temporal and exclusive phenomenon, that its coexistence with bourgeois modalities and pretensions during the period of the Third Reich, for example, did not insinuate even the slightest degree of mutuality or complicity, still less of an ideological consanguinity. Yet George Steiner poses just these questions:

Not very many have asked, or pressed home the question, as to the internal relations between the structures of the inhuman and the surrounding, contemporary matrix of high civilization. [...] Why did humanistic traditions and models of conduct prove so fragile a barrier against political bestiality? In fact, were they a barrier, or is it more realistic to perceive in humanistic culture express solicitations of authoritarian rule and cruelty?[26]

However unpalatable or outlandish such a thesis may appear to some readers, it finds echoes in many of Cardew's pronouncements on (Western) bourgeois culture. We are reminded of Gandhi's celebrated retort when he was asked what he thought of Western civilisation: 'I think it would be a very good idea.'

Revisionism

During the early seventies the English Maoists, inspired and emboldened by the speeches and writings of Chairman Mao and the Albanian leader, Enver Hoxha, battled relentlessly against what was considered the most treacherous crime of all: that of 'revisionism'. The betrayal of the 'working and oppressed people of the world' by the 'revisionists' constituted the ultimate act of perfidy. Revisionism sought accommodation with capitalism; it negotiated deals and concessions which it claimed would improve the plight of the poor. The British Communist ('revisionist') Party had introduced a manifesto entitled 'The British Road to Socialism'(1951, revised 1957) – socialism via the ('bourgeois') ballot box. The socialist agenda had been diluted, if not entirely abandoned, was the maledictory verdict of the Maoists. Concomitantly, in revisionist theoretical journals the key question of class, specifically class struggle, had lost its cutting edge – its dynamic role as a necessary agent for change disparaged and marginalized.[27] In Enver Hoxha's terms:

It is precisely the militant revolutionary character of literature and art that the revisionists deny. After proclaiming that socialist realism is 'restrictive', or rejecting it as a creative method, as well as the principle of proletarian partisanship, they opened the door to the most varied reactionary and decadent trends, which led to the degeneration of their literature and art, turning them into vanguard tools of capitalist restoration. When art is the vehicle for the ideas and aims of the counter-revolution, when it becomes the mouthpiece of bureaucratised and bourgeoisified elements and is opposed to the aspirations and the struggle of the masses, it can never be true art.[28]

A pervasive theme in *Stockhausen Serves Imperialism* is that of the 'class nature' of art; this became a fundamental issue for Party cultural workers.[29] By reducing art to the ranks, by stripping it of its 'aristocratic' (exclusive) pretensions Cardew had consciously raised the stakes. And it was the 'revisionists' themselves in the person of Bob Wynn, in two articles in the *Morning Star*, who threw down the gauntlet to the Maoists:

> And I fear that the present ruling class in Britain is sometimes unwittingly aided and abetted by a few militant members of the working class who, distrusting bourgeois culture, think it wrong for workers to want to indulge in it. They believe we should be building up our own proletarian culture on an exclusive working-class basis. [...] This is nonsense. There will never be a proletarian culture in the narrow sense, any more than there has been a truly bourgeois or capitalist culture. [...] Any talk of proletarian culture, in antithesis to bourgeois culture, is the result of uncritical, un-Marxist, identification of the historic destinies of the proletariat with those of the bourgeoisie. Proletarian societies are meant to be transient.[30]

Wynn invokes the words of Lenin in support of his thesis:

> We must take the entire culture left by capitalism and build Socialism out of it. We must take all science, technology, all knowledge, all art. Without this we cannot build life in a Communist society.[31]

Wynn's second article was even more contentious; in particular, the Maoists took exception to the negative ('revisionist') attitude it expressed towards the working class:

> But it [the working class] has been deprived of all but the merest dregs of culture in the past, and is largely uneducated aesthetically. It cannot begin with nothing. It has to find some basis for that new culture. It must absorb and assimilate elements of the old culture. [...] The more the working class studies, participates, enjoys and enhances past cultures today, the easier the attainment of that Communist society will become.[32]

On behalf of the Scratch Orchestra Id Group I myself penned a refutation of Wynn's article to be sent to the *Morning Star*. Whether it was sent or published I cannot recall. The essence of our argument naturally embodied the Maoist line on culture at that time:

> The central flaw in Bob Wynn's argument, and most other errors stem from it, is his abstraction of culture from the class struggle; thus culture is idealised as a desirable property currently in the hands of the bourgeoisie.

And we used Wynn's characterisation of workers as 'uneducated aesthetically', 'deprived', devouring 'whatever trash is offered in the form of entertainment', as evidence of his anti-working class attitude. He had caricatured the working people as dupes and duffers.

For Cardew and his comrades there could be no art above classes; a totally new culture had to be forged through and out of the class struggle and it would be characterised by its class nature. It would represent, or rather serve, for however long were necessary, the dictatorship of the proletariat. Only then – when bourgeois ideology had been destroyed – could the classless society become a reality. This was, unequivocally, Cardew's position, certainly during the first half of the decade. In the 'Talks at the Yenan Forum' Mao Tse-tung pronounced:

> We deny not only that there is an abstract and absolutely unchangeable political criterion, but also that there is an abstract and absolutely unchangeable artistic criterion; each class in every class society has its own political and artistic criteria. But all classes in all class societies invariably put the political criterion first and the artistic criterion second.[33]

In the early seventies, and it jumps out at us from every page of *Stockhausen Serves Imperialism,* it was Mao, rather than Lenin, who provided Cardew and his comrades with concrete advice and guidance on matters of art and culture. Mao Tse-tung *was* an artist, an accomplished poet; by contrast Lenin was an amateur, and a rather diffident music-lover. Whilst Lenin stressed the *fact* of the role of art in the revolution, he was singularly ambivalent with regards to the nature of art and its trajectory, and thus to the complexities of its social function. The power of the classics intimidated him and he expressed incomprehension and irritation when faced with new, contemporary trends. Yet he would also re-direct his frustration to himself, his own inadequacies: 'We're both old fogies', he told Clara Zetkin; 'we won't be able to keep pace with the new art; we'll just have to come trailing along'.[34] He was wary of artists and intellectuals but also relied on them (Gorky, for example); it was as if he was formulating the cultural programme for the Revolution on the hoof. But if Lenin unambiguously proclaimed the 'freedom of the artist', the rider, 'within the framework of the needs of the revolutionary Party', was always hovering in the wings. Thus Cardew, in such matters, would invariably invoke the ultimate control of the Party, from which, except by resignation or dismissal, there was no release.

Some thirty years later I asked Michael Chant, a Party activist, still, and Cardew's close comrade, to comment on Bob Wynn's intervention in the pages of the *Morning Star*:

So, of course, the Bob Wynn articles are also of their time, but, in a word, their stand is of the character of 'politics, revolutionary – culture, bourgeois'. [...] They [the revisionists] want to prove that no radical rupture in the sphere of culture is necessary (and perhaps show a misunderstanding of the all-embracing issue of culture, identifying it with works of art). Just take the *Communist Manifesto*. In the section Proletarians and Communists, Marx and Engels discuss the issue of culture. They refer to bourgeois objections to the 'communistic modes of producing and appropriating intellectual products'. It is clear that Marx and Engels recognise the existence of 'class culture' (i.e. they do not adopt the stand of the 'revisionist' that there has never been a 'truly bourgeois or capitalist culture'). Marx and Engels say, 'Just as, to the bourgeois, the disappearance of class property is the disappearance of production itself, so the disappearance of class culture is to him identical with the disappearance of all culture.'.[35]

The Maoists' aim was to try to circumscribe bourgeois culture and to characterise it as historically antithetical to, and separate from, proletarian culture. They insisted that in the 'dictatorship of the bourgeoisie' culture has a key role to play.
Hanns Eisler identified two forms of (bourgeois) decadence:

One alien to the people and one close to them. Some of my friends believe that decadence alien to the people is the more dangerous. I consider decadence close to the people to be most dangerous.[36]

Cardew would have agreed. In relation to 'high' contemporary art, his contention was that most of it was in any case irrelevant or repugnant to the majority of the working class and that to attribute this to ignorance or lack of education is essentially patronising: a revisionist's conceit. A plumber's response to a Rothko painting is just as valid as a solicitor's to a Lowry, as both painters would doubtless have concurred.

The function of bourgeois art at this stage is not to make bourgeois art seem any brighter (that is now impossible) but to make it universal – so that pessimism, defeatism and nihilism are seen to be rooted in 'Man'.[37]

Cardew (like Eisler in the previous quote) saw the tactic of the ruling class in relation to 'bourgeois culture' generally, and its role in the ideological subjugation of the working class, as twofold: firstly, the wide-scale promotion of the image of bourgeois culture in its prime, in particular the music of the classical and romantic composers – a kind of advertising campaign: 'bourgeois is best'; and secondly, by promoting a degenerate culture *for* the working class precisely in order to emasculate it: a culture which offers bogus prescriptions, which creates unrealisable dreams, and initiates futile quests.

'John Cage: Ghost or Monster?'

In the first years of the decade criticism of bourgeois art, in particular modern art, was given a high priority by the Maoists. It was also important for 'petit bourgeois' artists (as in the Scratch Orchestra) to purge themselves of reactionary and revisionist thoughts and sentiments. Much of the criticism was therefore 'self-criticism'. Cardew himself set great store by this, analysing and criticising his own actions and motives, and repudiating his early avant-garde compositions. Ironically, the two pieces on Cage and Stockhausen included in *Stockhausen Serves Imperialism* were both commissioned by Hans Keller, who was later to contribute a hostile review of the book in *Books and Bookmen*.

> In 1972 Hans Keller of the BBC Music Section, knowing the history of my association with Cage, asked me to write an article in *The Listener* to prepare the public for some Cage performances planned for the summer. The result must have surprised him, but it seems also to have pleased him, for shortly afterwards he asked me for an introductory talk to a broadcast of Stockhausen's *Refrain*.[38]

With hindsight, in the light of his contemptuous dismissal of Cardew's political writings, Keller's action in commissioning the Stockhausen talk would seem to have been both opportunistic and mischievous – perhaps a case of killing two birds (or three in this instance) with one stone. Moreover, according to Cardew, 'punishments were also meted out inside the BBC on account of the Stockhausen broadcast which by mischance was heard by a high official of the Corporation'.[39] There were also consequences for Cardew himself: a talk, 'On Criticism', prepared around the same time, was rejected by the BBC on the grounds of its 'irrelevance', and his proposal for a broadcast round-table discussion on the theme of criticism was turned down on the grounds that it would have required 'too much work'.[40]

In his BBC talk, entitled 'John Cage; Ghost or Monster?' Cardew identifies a number of works which in his view exemplify not only Cage's compositional method and techniques but also the ideology which informs them. In *Cheap Imitation* (1970), which is based on a work by Satie, by retaining the rhythm but changing notes from the original (with the aid of the *I-Ching Book of Changes*), Cage wilfully 'contradicts the interdependence of all aspects of a structure'. [41] Furthermore, and this is really the crux of the argument between the two men, aesthetically and ideologically, Cardew insists that 'any content, as well as the dynamism that is characteristic of "saying something", is automatically lost if one aspect of the language is systematically altered'.[42] It would be hard to refute this, but whether one can then follow Cardew with his corollary of 'the resulting emptiness' is more contentious; certainly the music has changed, and not necessarily for the better, and yet the spirit (content?) of the original, at least to these ears, pervades its derivative. The issue is important because Cardew, as he often did at that time, raises the stakes and then overreaches himself; before we know where we are Cage, according to Cardew, is advocating a world devoid of human life: 'The appreciation of emptiness in art fits well with imperialist dreams of a depopulated world.'[43] For many of us this would be several steps too far. As for 'saying something', Cage would probably have suggested that his music is 'saying' no more, and no less, than Satie's; both men claimed that they conceived and approached music, in Satie's words, 'in a spirit of humility and renunciation'.[44]

Cardew develops his critique of Cage with a description of a performance in the sixties (probably in Venice on 20 September 1960) by the Austrian composer and horn player Kurt Schwertsik and himself of *Variations 1* (1958), which he regards as a key work in Cage's compositional output. All the sounds and their parameters are derived through chance operations; in Cardew's words, 'randomness is glorified as a multicoloured kaleidoscope of perceptions to which we are "omniattentive"'.[45] Cardew and Schwertsik,

> overcome with Cage's 'beautiful idea' of letting sounds be sounds (and people be people, etc., etc., in other words seeing the world as a multiplicity of fragments without cohesion), decided to do a pure performance (no gimmicks) on horn and guitar, just reading the lines and dots and notating the results and letting the sounds be themselves. The result was a desert.[46] [...] Cage calling his music 'sounds' (rather than music) therefore represents an attempt to remove it from the human sphere (categorically impossible, since the activities of human beings can never be non-human), from which he promises himself a double advantage: (a) it would absolve him from his human responsibility for his actions as a human being, and (b) it would give his music the superhuman 'objective' authority of a phenomenon of (blind, unconscious) nature. In fact, man and his thinking are themselves a part of 'nature', whose products are by no means all wise, harmonious and graceful, as can be seen from such blatant examples as the dinosaur and Cage's metaphysics.[47]

Of course, as Cage and David Tudor demonstrated, through imaginativeness, invention, musicalness, through *human agency*, the inherent formalism of the composition could be mitigated, rather than exposed and exploited (as in the case of the

Cardew/Schwertsik performance); but for whatever reason, and there was no political agenda at that time, Cardew and Schwertsik decided upon a 'pure performance' in which the sounds would be left to their own devices, with a minimum of human intervention. Since one sound is as good as another, they would have argued, each performance, irrespective of the talent, the commitment, the *intentions* of the performer, would have equal validity.[48] But if, according to Cardew, 'the one merit of such a purely formal score is that it releases the initiative of the performer'[49], were not Cardew and Schwertsik acting *en mauvais foi* by deliberately negating that 'one merit'? Perhaps. Yet the disobliging implications of Cage's philosophy persist: from the point of view of the 'omniattentive' (non-judgmental) listener, what difference can the intentions of the performers, and their 'musical' consequences, make? Again, perhaps, Cardew overreached: does such a 'formalistic' score represent, as he claimed, a 'total indifference to the seriousness of the world situation in which it occurs?'[50] Certainly, there is a quietist strand in Cage's philosophy (of which there are innumerable examples in his earlier writings) that might justify such an accusation.

Cardew also refers to what he regards as Cage's political disingenuousness, born of self-centredness and self-deception. 'What Lenin does so well (and John Russell and co., too [the Party's intellectuals]) is to expose the reactionaries' capacity to pretend, and yet apparently seriously believe that they are not pretending. This is their puppet quality.'[51] In his Diary 1966 Cage quips: 'Difference between pennilessness now and pennilessness then: now we've got unquestioned credit'. Cardew retorts: 'Who's we? John Cage and the Queen of England? It sounds as though Cage would say: Anyone can survive today provided they play the system, never mind how corrupt.'[52]

'Stockhausen Serves Imperialism'

In the fifties the serialist avant-garde, based in Darmstadt, made considerable claims for itself; it proclaimed the scientific basis of its musical experimentation, of which ideas of 'progress' and 'discovery' were a corollary; it boasted that its music led to a deepening consciousness and heightened sensitivity within the listener. Each of these claims, in Cardew's perception, gradually metamorphosed into their opposite: scientific investigation became mystical pseudo-science; the investigation of the structure of vocal sounds was applied in a totally unscientific way – in Stockhausen's *Gruppen*, for example. Consciousness and sensitivity became super-consciousness of an ever narrowing sphere, such that the human ability to cope with mathematical relationships and other complexities of performance were developed at the expense of social consciousness and the ability to communicate. And consciousness of formal problems was encouraged to the exclusion of consciousness of content. Progress and discovery at the frontiers of a new kind of music were detached, Cardew argued, from the source of all progress and discovery, namely: 'the life of the people'. Cut off from the source it withered and died and inevitably became 'a reactionary weight holding back progress'. The avant-garde had made the transition from illusion to disillusion.

Cardew's brief for his BBC talk on Stockhausen was to preface a broadcast performance of *Refrain* (1959). After the briefest introduction he comes to the point in typically robust fashion:

> The task of this article [talk] is to make clear that Stockhausen's *Refrain* is in fact – not just in my opinion – a part of the cultural superstructure of imperialism. The task falls into three parts. To expose the essential character of the musical avant-garde in general; to outline the particular development of the avant-garde in which Stockhausen plays a role; and to indicate the position and content of *Refrain* within that development.[53]

Yet despite Cardew's claim to objectivity, and irrespective of whether one agrees with him or not, it is difficult to ascribe the status of 'facts' to those which he marshals in support of his argument. That one might tend to agree with him is of course neither here nor there. That 'contemporary bourgeois music' is the contemporary musical expression of its 'death agony', that the avant-garde represents 'the collapse of imperialism and bourgeois values in general', that not only is imperialism 'rotten to the core', but 'so is its culture', that in 1959, the year of *Refrain*, Stockhausen was 'ripe' to 'take up a more definite role in the service of imperialism'[54] – all this begs too many questions, relating in particular to Cardew's highly mechanistic interpretation of the relationship between economic base and superstructure, which represents a cultural condition in a way which is too monolithic, too cut and dried.[55] I am also allowing for the strong possibility, given the context of his talk, that Cardew was wilfully using shock tactics.[56]

To accept Cardew's thesis as a generalization would be devastating enough, consigning the majority of contemporary artists to the status of 'pessimistic, degenerate symptoms of a system in decay'. And yet much of what he writes here is, if not 'fact', then certainly 'informed opinion'. For in respect of the activities of the avant-garde, Cardew was there at that time; he had first-hand knowledge (to an extent which few of his critics had) of the intellectual climate, of the tensions, of the tendencies and changes in musical fashion, of the waxing and waning of reputations. Moreover, he knew the music from the inside, as apprentice, as composer, as performer, and, as Stockhausen himself acknowledged, he knew it better than most. As for *Refrain*, Cardew had taken part in the first performance, and already some years previously, and naturally from a different perspective, had written critically of the work in his *Tempo* article 'Notation – Intepretation, etc.' His description of the score as 'a gimmick typical of Darmstadt thinking' would not have been out of place in the earlier review. In another reference to *Refrain* he comments:

> The performance itself creates a situation of intense concentration and listening for the musicians. This listening activity of the musicians communicates itself to the audience and it is this intense concentration and contemplation of sounds for their own sake that reveals the beginnings of the mystical atmosphere that Stockhausen has cultivated more and more theatrically since then.[57]

'Intense concentration and listening' may or may not be for its own sake. One may draw a distinction between the demands of stretches of music from Beethoven's last quartets with those of *Refrain,* as well as between *Refrain* and Cage's *Variations 1.* The contextualisation of these sounds, their interrelationships, their degree of immanence, in each case, is quite different.

The second half of the talk, which was intended to substantiate the claims (facts) made in the first part, comprises a brief summary of Marxist philosophy, with generous quotes from both Marx and Lenin. The reason for this is Cardew's contention that because of the Establishment's hostility to Marxism the majority of the populace is ignorant of its message. This may well have been the case, but one winces at the patronising tone which Cardew adopts as he embarks upon his enlightening discourse: 'No, my job is not to "sell" you *Refrain.* I see my job as raising the level of consciousness in regard to cultural affairs'.[58]

Just months before he died, in an interview with Paul Driver, Cardew recalled that although Stockhausen was 'arrogant' and 'doctrinaire', he 'quite liked him'. What is of importance is that the 'father figures' with whom Cardew has been associated – Stockhausen, Cage, Wittgenstein, and the communist luminaries – all represented challenging new systems at the cutting edge of contemporary intellectual thought. It was their authority and *status* in modern history that initially drew Cardew to them, although he came to question, to mistrust, the authenticity of the concept of 'status'. What was crucial was the *context* in which status is achieved, or assumed. The influence of Cage and Stockhausen was important in so far as it was the conduit to new musical horizons, but it was limited, relatively short-lived, and already by 1961, as we have seen, he was writing music which neither Stockhausen nor Cage could have conceived.

'On Criticism'

So were Cardew's aesthetic priorities, at root, 'Zhdanovist'? That is, did he subscribe to the determinist theory of direct superstructural reflection of the economic system of a given society, that the art of socialist society must mirror 'socialist reality', that a decadent bourgeois society is reflected, necessarily, in the 'footling, unwholesome, sensational, frustrating, offensive and depressing' artistic products which it spawns, as he claimed in his essay 'On Criticism' which concludes chapter 2? [59] Cardew argued that it was precisely the decadence of modern music that protected it from serious, 'objective' criticism (what Alan Bush characterised as the 'anarchy' of contemporary aesthetics); 'each artist works as he thinks fit' John Cage wrote in his 'Defence of Satie' in 1948, and evidence of 'originality' became one of the most esteemed critical virtues of a piece of music; more general, commonly-held, critical guidelines were now inapplicable and therefore redundant.

And yet one does not have to be a 'Zhdanovist', or a Marxist, to agree with Cardew's contention ('I believe I speak for the vast majority of music lovers'[60]) that the classical works of the past are infinitely superior to contemporary 'modern classical music'.[61] And, typically, his yardstick is *moral*; the criteria contentiously political: classical music is 'good', better, because it is 'effective, wholesome, moving, satisfying, delightful, inspiring, stimulating and a whole lot of other adjectives that are just as widely understood and acknowledged and just as hard to pin down with any precision'.[62] Such music corresponded to an historical period when bourgeois/capitalist society had 'brought music out of church into the realm of bourgeois art, and reached undreamed-of power and imperial glory through the upheavals of the industrial revolution, and also undreamed-of power of artistic expression'.[63]

If Cardew's polemical style in 'On Criticism' occasionally grates on liberal sensibilities, one might also be struck by an eminent reasonableness embedded within it: for example, 'good' for Cardew means, indeed always meant, promoting desired change according to people's collective needs; that one's actions should be consequential; that one should not accommodate injustice; that if needs be it is necessary to stand up and be counted; and above all that one should not indulge in self-deception.

'A Critical Concert'

The brief texts on the 'critical concert' comprise chapter 3. The concert was part of the 'Musikprojekte' series organised by the Berlin composer Erhard Grosskopf and was presented at the Berlin Academy of Arts on 7 April 1973, when Cardew was a guest of the DAAD's Berlin Artists programme. The concert consisted of Christian Wolff's *Accompaniments,* Frederic Rzewski's *Coming Together* and *Attica,* and a short talk by Cardew followed by a discussion with the audience. The audience was forewarned of the nature of the concert by a programme booklet which, besides conventional notes on the pieces and their composers, included a draft of Cardew's introductory talk and reprints of *Stockhausen Serves Imperialism*, as well as my own introduction to Cage's *Music of Changes.* Wolff describes his own piece as follows:

> [The text] is part of an account of a veterinarian and a midwife, in their own words, of their experiences in a village in the area of Yenan during and after the Cultural Revolution. It was chosen both for its concreteness and for its illustration of the principle of applying a revolutionary political orientation to immediate and practical problems, indicating that these can only be understood and dealt with within such a political framework.[64]

Writing in his Journal shortly after the concert, Cardew's revolutionary rhetoric suffers no constraints:

> When I say Proletarian criticism, class criticism, it means this: What relevance has this music to the Proletariat? Now there's nothing that doesn't have relevance to the Proletariat, including discussion amongst bourgeois and petit bourgeois music-lovers. The question is, what relevance? Does discussion and performance such as ours really mobilize people to move over to the side of the people, or does it just gratify their need for liberal debate? Are left artists going to continue to submit to the degradation of being producers of yet one more bourgeois fashion, namely left, political art? Any such tendency needs to be strongly condemned. Such artists need to be shaken, as Mao Tse-tung says, and told sharply: 'This wont do. The proletariat is not going to follow your airy-fairy notions'. In Wolff's letter his bourgeois way of working is quite clear. He had some chords lying around, somebody asked him to write a piece, he took what was to hand, combined it with an exotic literary text and Bob's your uncle. Instead, the thought uppermost in the mind of a proletarian artist is 'Serve the People'. He will look at the situation of the proletariat in his country and reflect their demands and aspirations. Their most burning objective need in the capitalist countries today is for a genuinely revolutionary party. Now is it a coincidence that the text chosen by Wolff makes no mention of a Communist Party?[65]

In his report, written with the benefit of hindsight and post-concert reflection, Cardew is rather more conciliatory in tone but makes no concession to Wolff's political line: he insists that by selecting the themes of 'sanitation and birth-control' Wolff aligns himself with 'whole armies of academics and journalists' who promote the issues of pollution and population explosion precisely to distract people's attention from the most fundamental, 'principal contradiction': capital and labour. Cardew's objection was that although this might encourage debate, it was less likely to precipitate action.

Rzewski's two pieces both relate to the uprising and 'massacre' at Attica Correctional Facility in the state of New York in September 1971. In the programme notes the composer writes: 'They reproduce personal documents [by two of the prisoners] relating to it, and attempt to heighten the feelings expressed in them by underscoring them with music.' Cardew criticises the first piece, *Coming Together*, because 'it treats of its subject in a subjective way'; although the musical style refers to popular music, the compositional method relates more to the 'hypnotic or hysterical', that is, to a negative aspect of pop music. And Cardew rejects Rzewski's choice and treatment of the text on the grounds that 'the basic ideology of the piece is anarchism'. He then devotes three paragraphs to an exposure of the bankruptcy of anarchist philosophy, an ideology which is alien to the proletariat, which 'in fact is not far removed from Mick Jagger's "I can't get no satisfaction", and contributes just as little to revolutionary change. Marxists should therefore militate against the introduction of such works amongst the masses – they get too much of this already'.[66]

In the ensuing discussion with the audience there were clearly misgivings, in particular in relation to the approach of Cardew and his Berlin comrades to the music itself, which seemed to have been presented for the sole purpose of criticism; the composers and their music had been set up. Because of this the music received less commitment from the musicians, who had been given a minimum amount of time to prepare their parts and for rehearsal. Thus, it was the overweening attitude of Cardew and his political comrades, rather than the perceived inadequacies of the music, which had served to alienate so many in the audience. At the end of the report Cardew effectively damns his own efforts: 'by not presenting the music strongly enough we failed to generate that sense of community (basis of all music-making) in which a meaningful discussion could have taken place'.[67] Instead of drawing the composers and their music into the debate, it was as if they were ostracised, paraded simply as negative examples.

A year later Cardew penned the following text on the music of Steve Reich, in whose ensemble he had performed on several occasions and with whom he had been on tour a month or two earlier. In the light of his criticisms of the music of Wolff and Rzewski there appear to be glaring inconsistencies; the Marxist-Leninist rigour which hardened his approach to the music of his two comrades-in-arms in Berlin is overtaken by a decidedly more liberal approach to the music of his employer, Steve Reich, whose socialist sympathies were probably of less artistic consequence to him (Reich) than Wolff's and

Rzewski's were to them. Might we surmise that, paradoxically, the lack of explicit political intent on the part of Reich, as opposed to the overt motives and aims of his compatriots, militated against harsher, more consequential criticism from Cardew?[68] Or could there have been other reasons? There is no indication in the Journals as to the context in which this text was to be used – if at all:

> The composer Steve Reich has been long occupied with musical techniques from outside the European tradition. He studied Nigerian drumming, later Gamelan music. Some of the musicians in his group are also seriously occupied with ethno-musicology. Reich seems to turn away from the sterile mannerisms of the dying musical tradition of Western civilisation and search for a new vitality in Oriental musical culture and the music of primitive peoples. In line with this, Reich uses a collective method in his composing, a method based on protracted handling of the material in practical sessions, trying out one thing after another until the composition begins to take shape. Only at a fairly late stage does the music get written down. In the course of these practical sessions the musicians develop techniques and perfect their coordinations to an extent that would otherwise be very difficult to achieve. Performances by Reich and his musicians often have the quality of an ensemble of perfectly coordinated parts, a smooth-running machine in which every cog fits neatly into its place. He always tries to make everything arise from *inside* the material. You could say there were 4 positive characteristics of Reich and his music. His desire to scientifically get to grips with other cultures than his own. His recognition of the bankruptcy of the Western musical avant-garde. His collective and practice-based method of composition. His discovery of new possibilities of physical (?) coordination amongst his performers.[69]

In the light of Cardew's uncompromising attitude in relation to the content and social function of the music of other composers, even and perhaps especially those like Wolff and Rzewski who were 'shuffling their feet over to the side of the people', one could say that, ideologically, Reich gets off scot-free. Perhaps Cardew did not want to antagonize his employer; after all, he desperately needed the money. Certainly one would have expected the argument to run more on the following lines: that Reich, like a true Imperialist, was plundering Third World culture, robbing it of its vitality, creating a kind of self-conscious, 'coffee-table', anodyne product which would find favour in the citadels of bourgeois art music. And to what end were Reich's musicians 'seriously occupied' with ethno-musicology? To acquire well-paid posts in ethnological music departments in American universities? How did their research help the poor and oppressed of the world who were creating the music in the first place? And whereas, according to Cardew, the music is created collectively over a relatively long period of time, Reich asserts his proprietorial rights by writing it down ('at a fairly late stage') and signing his name. As for the four positive characteristics Cardew claims that Reich's music boasted; firstly, the 'scientific' nature of his approach to 'other cultures' is a highly contentious claim; secondly, to recognise the bankruptcy of the avant-garde does not make him a 'progressive' composer – certainly no more progressive than, say, the English composer Malcolm Arnold; thirdly, his collective method of composition does not extend to waiving his 'rights' and 'privileges' as a bourgeois composer (one might argue he was exploiting his own musicians just as he was those of the Third World); and fourthly, 'making everything arise from inside the material' has been for many composers over hundreds of years a compositional imperative.

Such harsh (contrived) characterisations of Reich's music do bear comparison with the way in which Cardew criticises the music of some other composers, including Wolff and Rzewski. In fact, it was in this vein that Cardew had criticised ethnomusicology at the Rome Symposium (which is discussed below) some eighteen months earlier:

Music cannot be understood except in its social context. In any case let's think what the motive force is in ethnomusicology and related studies. Civilisation is destroying primitive man. The idea is to *take possession* of his resources. (Brazil, where they go out hunting Indians.) In order to convert the resources of primitive man – primarily his land – into bourgeois property, imperialism exterminates the people and, as a preliminary to this, it has his culture transcribed and makes this into bourgeois property too.[70]

'Problems of Notation'

Like most of the material in *Stockhausen Serves Imperialism* the first article in the final chapter was originally delivered as a talk: in this instance, on the 'problematic of today's musical notation' for an International Symposium in Rome from the 23 to the 26 October 1972. It was an opportunity, indeed the first of its kind and one which Cardew grasped with a degree of relish, to repudiate his own compositions in the public domain, with comparable severity and hostility, and the same implacability, with which he had attacked Cage and Stockhausen.

About 100 scientists, musicologists, educationalists and composers were invited (no fee, but all expenses paid, even from the remotest corners of the globe) to contribute to this 'symposium' on a non-existent problem. I participated in the symposium quite militantly, taking sides on a number of issues and refusing to vanish into thin air at the crack of any absurdly abstruse scientific or philosophical whip.[…] My own contribution took the form of a talk on my composition *Treatise*, a 200-page so-called 'graphic score' composed 1963-7, as an attempt to escape from the performance rigidities of serial music and encourage improvisation amongst avant-garde musicians.[71]

The fact that he was among scientists, musicologists, educationalists and composers – with a significant lack of both Marxist-Leninists and members of the proletariat, although doubtless with more than a sprinkling of 'revisionists' – forced him into a somewhat different mode; the style of presentation of his talk, the argumentation, was still uncompromising, militant, but there was not a single, specific mention in his talk of 'communist party', or of 'Marxism-Leninism'.

Cardew was scathing of the symposium and its priorities generally, whilst acknowledging one or two contributions of worth. The event exuded an aura of self-importance; matters of little significance, in Cardew's view, were inflated at the expense of more substantial and pressing issues: problems of notation took precedence over musical problems which in turn took precedence over social and political problems. Such an attitude (and strategy), Cardew remarked, was in fact symptomatic of bourgeois culture:

> As one of the organisers pointed out, it has been quite easy to organise this very expensive conference devoted to a very minor issue, but if you want to get money from the state to improve music education in schools you come up against complete refusal.[72]

The reference for his talk, arguably the most impressive piece in the whole book, was his own graphic score *Treatise* – a rich source of notational issues, and of musicological, philosophical, and psychological ones, too. We may agree with Cardew that a musical score is not a work of visual art and that for the composer the visual element is of merely tangential consequence; nevertheless, a musical score *can* have an impact visually.[73] And as we have seen in our discussion of *Treatise*, the compelling *visual* aspect of the work, its immediacy, is unprecedented.

> *Treatise* arbitrarily combines images of transformations that occur in the real world: images of mathematical or logical transformations (multiplication of elements, relations between pairs of dissimilar elements, presence and absence of elements), and of physical transformations (by fragmentation, exploding, squashing, bending,

melting, interpenetrating, etc.). And in amongst all these visual abstractions from reality a host of devices are used to keep the reader amused: 3-dimensional effects, pictorial effects, hints at concrete objects (trees, clouds, etc.) and enigmatic musical symbols.[74]

Cardew's eloquent description of the score of *Treatise,* albeit tinged with a sense of ironic detachment, is peremptorily disclaimed:

This fits very well with what I said about the incoherence of the liar who has lost all hope of deceiving his listeners. He is quite likely to turn then to diversionary tactics, just as a child does in a situation of embarrassment: standing on his head, singing a silly song, knocking over a jug of milk or simply pretending to be mad.[75]

Many performers (and not only musicians) would take issue with the composer here. Reading, journeying through *Treatise*, the interpreter/musician encounters a dazzling succession of visual relationships and information: challenging, perplexing, tantalizing, emotive, evocative, intimidating, *dynamic*; and they provide a formidable and exhaustive body of material and ideas (with references, for example, to nature and to industry, to birds and factories), from the arcane and abstract to the explicit, which engage the intellect and fire the (aural) imagination. Implicit throughout is the idea of *human agency,* and of human relationships, and as 'an attempt to escape from the performance rigidities of serial music and encourage improvisation amongst avant-garde musicians' *Treatise* has proved over the years to have been a successful experiment. For his part Cardew characterised *Treatise* as an 'obstacle' behind which musicians improvise ('an undefined, subjective stimulus for the interpreter') and as such 'prevents the establishment of communication between the musicians and the audience'.[76] Some improvisers would in part concur with this, but do not necessarily draw negative conclusions from their experience.[77]

In a note in *Stockhausen Serves Imperialism* Cardew refers to his work as a graphic designer, when he was obliged, through financial circumstances, to pursue music as a spare-time activity.[78] It was during one of these periods of work that he conceived and worked on *Treatise*. This, in his view, accounted for the 'escapist' nature of the 'music' and he describes it as a 'fantasy' to which, at the time, he attached 'vast importance'.

Summer changes to winter, iron ore is changed into steel, a sequence of notes can be changed into a melody, but a tree can never be changed into a saucer of milk. Not in the real world.[79]

No, of course, not in the real world – but indubitably in the artist's flight of imagination a tree *can* be transformed into a saucer of milk (we may recall the great myths and popular fairy tales, such as *Alice in Wonderland* and the extravagance and wildness of Lewis Carroll's imagination, which Cardew had admired so much). Such a licence, to allow and encourage the imagination to run riot, does not guarantee a meaningful outcome, but to claim that 'on a very fundamental level it is distorting reality, propagating lies, wrong ideas, about the world'[80], is to attach a significance to such activity that it hardly merits. We all day-dream, we all turn truth upside down, logic inside out, often involuntarily; perhaps such mental activity has a therapeutic value; it may even be the midwife of the birth of a work of art.

What might be a matter for debate is that in contemporary 'bourgeois' culture any phenomenon, however trivial, can be ring-fenced, elevated to the status of a work of art, and priced accordingly. If Cardew rejected most contemporary music as empty, superficial, solipsistic – a decorative gloss on a 'degenerate' culture – it is also demonstrable that throughout history there has always been an abundance of music of indifferent quality. Only the means for self-gratification, self-aggrandizement and self-delusion have changed; in the modern world, scaling new, unimagined heights of self-parody, of grotesquerie and barbarism, can lead the artist to instant, if short-lived, exposure to the world markets and, depending upon the degree of gullibility of critics and patrons, to substantial financial remuneration.

In his talk at the Rome Symposium Cardew grasped the nettle with aplomb; and after a few introductory words he launched into a seven-point, structured criticism (specifically planned, he informed his audience, for dealing with a work of avant-garde art), adopting a rather pedantic method of enumeration favoured by his political comrades.[81] Already by point 2 Cardew was treading dangerous ground, positing that the rightness or wrongness of ideas embodied in the score (*Treatise*) is determined in relation to 'whether they truly reflect what we know about the real world'. Less contentiously (points 3/4), he commended that the audience should examine the role of the avant-garde in music today, together with 'the cultural environment and social and economic factors which produce and mould it'. However, there would have been a palpable falling away of support and possibly attention, too, amongst his audience when he insisted that these economic and social factors could only be interpreted meaningfully within the context of the 'class struggle'. And in the course of the rest of the talk audience impartiality would have turned to disbelief, in some cases to outrage, in particular when Cardew (point 6) equated the ideas (the 'world outlook') of the avant-garde with ruling class ideology, claiming that by not challenging that class and its power the ideas of the avant-garde 'support its continued existence'. Cardew's argumentation gathered momentum and accelerated; within seconds (point 7) the ideas of the avant-garde were denounced as 'reactionary', peddling an inaccurate reflection of our knowledge of the world, its forms of expression as 'contradictory and incoherent'. The fact that the roots of all our cultural ills lie in society, Cardew argued, does not absolve the individual artist from responsibility. And echoing Marx: 'So we should say to artists, "It is not enough to decorate the world, the point is to influence it"'.[82]

By now Cardew's relation to a large proportion of his audience would have reached its nadir.[83] No *rapprochement* between the two parties would have been possible; the tight knots could not have been undone. Cardew was challenging the artist to take a political stand. Many do, or, like Cardew, claim and think they do. But taking a 'political stand' is not necessarily the same as taking a '*class* stand', which was what Cardew was demanding ('shuffling one's feet over to the side of the proletariat'). In many sections of society substantial numbers of people oppose capitalism and its values, but Cardew was dismissive of the notion of fragmented, uncoordinated forays against bourgeois ideology, which in his view amounted to no more than 'gestural politics'. Cardew was (romantically) attached to the idea of an industrial working-class vanguard, although even in the seventies, when it was still a relatively potent force, and certainly from then on, the concept of 'working-class' was in constant need of re-definition. The traditional working-class – miners, steelworkers, building workers and so forth, on whom the credibility and efficacy of some leftist strategies rested, no longer enjoyed the exclusive and crucial role which the Party had assigned to them. Cardew's ideal of the 'proletarian artist' was exclusive, limited, and threatened. In any case, his audience and fellow participants were, probably to a man/woman, 'bourgeois intellectuals' for whom he had only a limited respect.

'Criticism of *The Great Learning*'

The last section of *Stockhausen Serves Imperialism* is entitled 'Criticism of *The Great Learning*' and after a brief introduction is broken down into seven parts: The Place of Confucius in the History of China; Backward people defend Confucius against the criticism of the masses in the period of the democratic and socialist revolutions in China; Who promotes Confucius in the West and what for?; How the musical *Great Learning* came into existence; an attempt to reform the first two paragraphs of *The Great Learning*; The ideology of Reformism has a class character – a bourgeois class character; and lastly, Criticise *The Great Learning* from the standpoint of the working class. Some of these issues have already been touched upon in previous chapters. The stimulus and opportunity for such a comprehensive critique of the work was created by the occasion of a performance of Paragraphs 1 and 2 at the Berlin Philharmonic Hall in March 1974. Moreover, Cardew's involvement was conditional upon the authorities' acceptance of the critical context in which he insisted the performance should take place. His plan was that the text would also be distributed on subsequent occasions if and when the work were to appear in the public domain. 'In this way the reactionary composition can be used not only as an arena for ideological struggle but also as a carrier pigeon for revolutionary ideas.'[84] An added impetus was provided by the ongoing campaign in the People's Republic of China to expose and discredit Confucianism. By holding up his own work to analysis and criticism Cardew felt that he was participating in the 'struggle' to combat reactionary ideas and practices.

As we have seen, Cardew's initial reaction to his choice of Ezra Pound's translations wavered between insouciance and embarrassment; but by the early seventies the fact of Pound's (posthumous[85]) involvement was grist to the mill for Cardew – further proof, if proof were needed, of the reactionary nature of the philosophy of *The Great Learning.*

Pound's version is tailored to fit his idea of a 'conspiracy of intelligence' to protect Order and Civilisation against the onslaught of the 'mob'. He makes intelligence a matter of introspection. He advocates detachment: an inner sanctum of 'perfect equity' where he reclines at ease 'watching with affection' (as if through a window) the struggles of the people. His 'calm' is the calmness of intellectual superiority; his 'peace' is internal. Only along this road can one 'qualify' to take action.[86]

Referring to Pound's active support for the fascist leader Oswald Mosley in England and Mussolini in Italy, Cardew writes:

He was rabidly anti-Semitic and anti-communist and, in a period when monopoly-capitalism and imperialism were on the rampage, he chose to attribute all the evils of the world to 'usury'. Shattered by the outcome of the war he drifted more and more into visions of 'eternal light'.[87]

Pound promoted Confucianism as the necessary antidote to Western decadence and communism, and in 1937, in the magazine *The Aryan Path,* he published an article entitled 'The Immediate Need for Confucius'.[88] The unruly proletariat, too, would have been tamed and disarmed by the rigor and wisdom of Confucianism: 'There is a visible and raging need of the *Ta Hio (Great Learning)* in barbarous countries like Spain and Russia' [Pound].[89]

The Berlin concert was a watershed in Cardew's career; thereafter he was to turn his back on the avant-garde, even as an object of criticism. If he were invited to attend rehearsals and/or performances of his early works (as he was by students of the Royal College of Music the following autumn) he would express surprise and then present himself at rehearsals to make pertinent and practical observations and suggestions, usually in relation to performance; his commitment was to the performers and the task they had undertaken, rather than to the music itself – ironically the prototypical 'professional' approach about which, in the past, he had been so dismissive. Here he describes his reaction to The Great Learning concert in a way which is both disconcerting and revealing; clearly, it left a sour taste in the mouth:

> Participating in the Berlin performance of The Great Learning was a painful and – as it seemed – debilitating experience for me. Holding the view that music's main function is to bring people together, to unite them, it was a contradictory situation to have to direct a performance – which had to be a 'good' performance so that people could get to grips with its content – for the sole purpose of leading the audience, through the accompanying article, to repudiate that content. A 'good' performance is one in which the musicians and audience are totally engaged. In contravening this principle – by disengaging the audience – I had set myself the job of launching a sizeable lead balloon. I accomplished this quite successfully and it was a worried little audience that wended their way out of the hall at the end. This disturbed me; I wished I had had something better to offer, something which we could have united around. Then I reflected (on the basis of some quite concrete experience) that if I had had such a work ready it would doubtless not have been performed in those circumstances, and this depressed me still further. Later I realised the cause of these depressions: I was clinging very tenaciously to the role of the bourgeois composer.[90]

As for the abortive attempt to 'reform' The Great Learning for the BBC Promenade concert, this is described as 'a logical consequence of the fundamentally reformist attitude which informed the foundation and artistic agenda of the Scratch Orchestra: its anti-elitism, anti-intellectualism, pseudo-democracy, and utopianism:

> And in releasing the initiative of the performers we [the Scratch Orchestra] slipped into the cult of individualism. Hippy communes, mysticism, individualism – our various 'reforms' led us straight into a number of cul-de-sacs of bourgeois ideology that are being widely promoted today. […] The oppressed and exploited classes are learning in great numbers that they cannot place any faith in promises of

reform, whether these promises come from Social Democrats, Divine Light Missionaries, Revisionists or Fascists. They are learning that only through building their own organisations, the organisations of the working class, the genuine communist parties, can the reasonable course be put into practice: the course of proletarian socialist revolution. In the context of this learning, the mystical delights of *The Great Learning* are just butterflies in a blast furnace.[91]

There is much in Cardew's characterisation of the Scratch Orchestra here that one can take issue with. The charge of mysticism and individualism would be refuted by the majority of Scratch Orchestra members; if our imagination occasionally ran riot, it did not find expression in the realms of mysticism; and if there were manifestations of 'individualism' these were occasional and were somehow subsumed into the multifarious welter of Scratch activities. Whilst initially there was no intellectually-conceived or projected endgame, the Scratch Orchestra thought intelligently about what it was doing; if its 'democratic' aspirations were flawed, its attainments in respect of a collective *modus vivendi,* of socialist microcosms, were not inconsiderable. Far from being 'cul-de-sacs of bourgeois ideology' these were initiatives and enthusiasms borne out of a constant interaction of aesthetic, moral and social considerations – a survival strategy while we waited for the Party of the Proletariat to provide us with more viable options.[92]

If there is a surfeit of criticism in *Stockhausen Serves Imperialism,* there is also advice, including recommended tasks to be accomplished, and brief homilies – not exactly a programme of action, but suggestions of a fairly explicit nature, such as looking at one's own activity 'in the context of [one's] local involvement in a musical community'. Naturally, such activity is undertaken in full consciousness of its relevance and consequences in the 'class struggle'; the idea of 'local involvement' would assume a level of political consciousness and sophistication which would probably not be stimulated by accompanying the local choral society, unless the new accompanist were invited to propose and discuss new repertoire.

The Scratch Orchestra Id Group spent many hours discussing such practical measures. Mao's Yenan Forum Talks had brought us back down to earth; it was eminently *practical,* and providing the ideas were not interpreted mechanically, there was a core of common sense which we would draw upon and which would temper our more extravagant and speculative aspirations. One of many issues we discussed was Mao's insistence on the need to strike the correct balance between popularisation and raising standards, to take into account the actual needs of our (potential) audience and to serve them in the appropriate manner. To do this artists must go among the masses; they must for a long period of time unreservedly and wholeheartedly go among the masses of workers, peasants and soldiers, go into the heat of the struggle, go to the only source, the broadest and richest source, in order to observe, experience, study and analyse all the different kinds of people, all the classes, all the masses, all the vivid patterns of life and struggle, all the raw materials of literature and art.[93]

This adjuration Cardew took quite literally. In the mid seventies he did go and live in a working class area, in Leyton in east London; he observed and studied; he attempted to learn the repertoire of standards and popular songs. Like Mao, he believed that the life of the people

is always a mine of the raw materials of literature and art, materials in their natural form, materials that are crude but most vital, rich and fundamental; they make all literature and art seem pallid by comparison.[94]

At the same time, Mao recognised the need for different levels with respect to cultural dissemination, but with the proviso that if art of a 'higher level' was to be created for the cadres, the end result had to be the spiritual enrichment of the masses. Specialists (professionals) could not live in 'ivory towers', detached from the masses and from everyday reality; nor could high artistic quality preclude the possibility of reactionary political content.[95] The question in relation to any artistic endeavour therefore is *whom does it serve*. Mao described the communist attitude as 'utilitarian': 'We are proletarian revolutionary utilitarians'. 'Revolutionary utilitarianism' was a necessary stage.

In a letter to the composer/pianist Roger Smalley, probably from early 1975, Cardew writes:

The relationship between a piece of music (or work of art, etc.) and the real world is that the music is an active reflection, considered from the point of view of embodying a philosophy, of the life of the society in which the composer lives. That is, the composer lives in the real world, has views on this society – his world outlook – and this world, as viewed from the composer's *class stand*, is reflected in his music. For instance, Beethoven lived in a world where the bourgeoisie was fighting for political and ideological supremacy over the forces of feudalism and autocracy, and he reflected this struggle in his music from the standpoint of the rising bourgeoisie, coming down firmly on the side of bourgeois liberty, democracy and individualism.[96]

As Cardew's letter intimates, the Party (Maoist) line at this point in time was that Beethoven's humanitarianism was circumscribed and ultimately compromised by bourgeois 'prejudice': the brotherly love extolled in the last movement of the Ninth Symphony did not, could not, extend to those millions of people whom the bourgeoisie so brutally exploited. Just as bourgeois politicians sought to deceive the people with their 'one nation' theory, so the idea was propagated of a universal Art which appealed to, and benefited, potentially, all the people. The mythology which grew up around the Fifth Symphony – 'fate knocks on the door', and 'man's struggle with fate' – likewise reflected the determination of the German bourgeois radicals, towards the end of the eighteenth century, to sunder the feudal bonds. The Maoists interpreted the nineteenth century as an historical period when things were going from bad to worse, culminating in *fin de siècle* decadence, in 'bourgeois' impressionism, which they would contrast with the optimistic, revolutionary spirit of a contemporaneous proletarian song, such as the 'Internationale'.

Dramatic and unfathomable though it undoubtedly was for many of Cardew's associates at the time, my own view is that there is a danger in overestimating the extent to which Cardew broke with his past, wiped the bourgeois slate clean. Despite the radical change in his music-making which occurred in the early seventies, precipitated by political dialogue within the Scratch Orchestra (which itself had been fuelled, not only by the political philosophy encapsulated in Chairman Mao's little red book, but also, if to a lesser extent, by the wider political debate that developed in the aftermath of the events of 1968) – in some form or other both the ethos and praxis of Cardew's earlier music, relating in particular to works from the late sixties and also to his improvisations in AMM, survived into the last decade. There are many analogies between the ideas expressed, for example, in 'Towards an Ethic of Improvisation' (1967) and, seven years later, in the abrasive *Stockhausen Serves Imperialism*. In the former Cardew includes seven 'virtues that a musician can develop'. These 'virtues' also find expression in the later publication, where the context is explicitly political. For example, in essence the following pairs of quotes seem to be saying the same thing:

Selflessness To do something constructive you have to look beyond yourself. The entire world is your sphere if your vision can encompass it. Self-expression lapses too easily into mere documentation – 'I record that is how I feel'.[97]

What is needed is for each person to take a sober look at his own activity in the context of the world political situation, and also in the context of his local involvement in a musical community, and come to a point of readiness to work together to produce a positive atmosphere and real development.[98]

In 'Towards an Ethic' the sixth virtue is characterised:

Identification with nature Drifting through life: being driven through life; neither constitutes a true identification with nature. The best is to *lead* your life, [...] like a yachtsman to utilise the interplay of natural forces and currents to steer a course.[99]

And in the later work:

Good conditions of existence are: when your needs, physical and spiritual, are fulfilled, when you are conscious of the way you work, your productive activity, contributes to the society you live in.[100]

Shortly before his death Cardew stressed the urgent need for a music to bring people together, to demonstrate 'that life really is worth living'. In 'Towards an Ethic' he defined musicians as those who play music 'to the full capacity of their beings'. The 'seven virtues' were never abandoned; on the contrary, throughout the last decade they remained at the centre of his revolutionary quest. But as with his mentor Wittgenstein, 'all the modes of thought which had been pushed out into the transcendental penumbra are now taken in again and resettled in a more realistic way'.[101] Above all, his very praxis, as his comrades attest, embodied a timely re-definition and new understanding of the role of the individual in history. In Hanns Eisler's chamber cantata *On the Death of a Comrade* Bertolt Brecht's text is concerned with *the individual and others,* not opposed or separated, but as a unity: 'To be together without fear, that's the start. We must stay together and must not allow ourselves to be separated. [...] Truth and brotherhood shall replace the rule of lies.'[102]

Notes and references

1   Jrnl. April 1973 – February 1974, dated 8-12 May.
2   There were subsequently modifications, re-definitions and shifts of position; he had to
     come to terms with the consequences of his precipitous acceptance, and adoption, of
     the jargon, the sloganeering and dogmatizing associated with Maoism (an unfortunate
     feature of this collection), but in essence these essays represent Cardew's position in
     relation to culture, not only in the mid-seventies, but to the end of his life.
3   The review was entitled 'Thinkers of the world, Disunite!' Part 1 appeared in vol. 20, no.
     9 (June 1975), part 2 in vol. 20, no. 12 (September), and part 3 in vol. 21, no. 1 (October).
4   On re-reading *Stockhausen Serves Imperialism,* in 2005, Eddie Prévost has somewhat
     modified his original, negative appraisal.
5   *The Composer,* Spring 1975, Issue no.54, p.34.
6   From a review by Alan Bush in the *Morning Star,* 20 February 1975.
7   As quoted in *Marxism and* Art, p.165. But can we take Lenin's seemingly impatient and
     unfeeling response to the comrades' desperate act at face value? In 'bourgeois' society,
     too, suicide provokes negative, unsympathetic responses of resentment, anger, intolerance
     and an unwillingness to empathise.
8   Most references to this quotation use the formulation 'freedom is the recognition of necessity',
     although this does not seem to be borne out by what Engels actually wrote. In *Anti-Dühring*
     Engels quotes from Hegel: freedom is the insight into necessity (*die Einsicht in die
     Notwendigheit).* Lenin, quoting from the same passage, uses the phrase as quoted above
     from Cardew's Journals: 'freedom is the appreciation of necessity'.
9   Jrnl. October 1971–July 1972, undated.
10   Friedrich Engels, *Anti-Dühring* (Peking: Foreign Languages Press, 1976), p.145.
11   Jrnl.1972, undated.
12   Ibid.
13   *Stockhausen Serves Imperialism,* p.58. (*CCR*)
14   E.P. Thompson, *Writing by candlelight* (London: The Merlin Press, 1980), pp.8-9.
15   Jrnl.1972, undated.
16   *Stockhausen Serves Imperialism*, p.7.
17   Gerrard Winstanley, *A Radical Reader*, Ed. Christopher Hampton (Penguin Books Limited,
     Harmondsworth, 1984), p.232.
18   V.I. Lenin, *The State and Revolution*, chapter II: The Experience of 1848-51 (Peking: Foreign
     Languages Press, 1970), p.40. The italics are Lenin's.
19   As quoted in *Hanns Eisler A Miscellany*, compiled and edited by David Blake (Luxembourg:
     Harwood Academic Publishers, 1995), p.158.
20   In fact Marx himself never clarified the relation between the Party elite and the dictatorship
     of the proletariat. Moreover, he would often substitute the word 'rule' (*Herrschaft*) for
     'dictatorship'. In Soviet practice dictatorship of the proletariat became synomonous
     with the dictatorship of the Party, which exercised its power and authority *on behalf of* the
     proletariat.
21   Jrnl. January-April 1973, undated.
22   Moreover, from a purely political perspective, and in the wake of the revolutionary agenda
     which galvanized the students in the late sixties, reliance on the industrial working-class

to achieve revolutionary change had become a questionable strategy. Certainly, a united working-class – or large sections of it – was still capable of wreaking havoc, and this was recognized by a political establishment which waged relentless war, not just economically, but on working-class *values*, particularly as they were embodied in collective action. But at the time the Party (and Cardew) clung to the view that it was the industrial working class that would spearhead the overthrow of the 'bourgeois dictatorship'. Any deviation from this line would have been denounced as heresy.

23   M. Chant, 'A Turning Point in Music History', from the Symposium on the Scratch Orchestra in 2002.

24   In practice 'democratic centralism' was a method by which the Party exercised total control over its members. The *21 Conditions of Admission* to the Communist International (Comintern) provides clarification of the role and purpose of 'democratic centralism': 'The Communist Party will be able to fulfil its duty only if its organization is as centralized as possible, if iron discipline prevails, and if the Party centre, upheld by the confidence of the Party membership, has strength and authority and is equipped with the most comprehensive powers.' It need not be spelled out that such practices are not confined to Leninist parties. Capitalist politicians of varying hues often have recourse to 'democratic centralism' where their power and control is deemed to be under threat.

25   V.I. Lenin, *"Left-Wing" Communism, an Infantile Disorder* (Peking: Foreign Languages Press, 1965), p.6.

26   George Steiner, *In Bluebeard's Castle*, (London: Faber and Faber, 1971), p.31.

27   Disconcertingly for the 'revisionists' their abandonment of the 'class struggle' was not always reflected on the shop floor where they would occasionally find themselves in the embarrassing position of 'mediators' between bosses and a striking work force, rather than the latter's leaders.

28   Enver Hoxha, *Selected Writings of the Great Marxist-Leninist Enver Hoxha, 1971-1977* (Toronto: Norman Bethune Institute, 1978), p.122.

29   Although, as we shall see, their position was subsequently modified with the demise of Mao in the later part of the decade.

30   *Morning Star,* February 1972 – exact date of publication unknown.

31   V.I. Lenin, 'The Achievements and Difficulties of the Soviet Government' in *Lenin on Literature and Art* (Moscow: Progress Publishers, 1970), p.123.

32   *Morning Star,* February 1972 – exact date of publication unknown.

33   Mao Tse-tung, 'Talks at the Yenan Forum', *Mao Tse-tung on Literature and Art* (Peking: Foreign Languages Press, 1967), pp.29-30.

34   As quoted in *Marxism and Art,* ed. Maynard Soloman (Detroit: Wayne State University Press, 1979), pp.166-7.

35   From an email communication from Michael Chant to JT, 19 December 2003. The quotation at the end is from the *Communist Manifesto* (Peking: Foreign Languages Press, 1968), p.52. Cardew's frequent references to these issues throughout the remaining pages of this book broadly accord with Chant's thesis, and it would be as well to bear the latter's criticisms and definitions in mind.

36   Hanns Eisler, *A Rebel in Music* (Berlin: Seven Seas Books, 1978), p.190.

37   *Stockhausen Serves Imperialism*, p.19. (*CCR*)

38   *Stockhausen Serves Imperialism*, p.33. (*CCR*)

39   Ibid, p.34. (*CCR*)

40   Cardew refuted the charge of 'irrelevance'. 'I used the rejected talk as a lecture on a number of occasions and the discussions that it provoked proved its relevance'. *Stockhausen Serves Imperialism,* p.55. The affair also calls into question Keller's convoluted and anecdotal 'proof' of BBC impartiality, even-handedness and independence from what he describes as 'government interference' in his review of Cardew's book. Cardew would have retorted that there was no need for 'government interference'; by stifling the kind of debate that Cardew was proposing the BBC was simply doing the job that was expected of it. I am reminded of the BBC's rejection of E.P. Thompson's talk, 'The Segregation of Dissent', in the early sixties, a portent of that institution's ever-increasing enthusiasm for the role of 'purveyors of received wisdom'.

41   *Stockhausen Serves Imperialism*, p. 36. In Cage's defence Harry Gilonis points out that 'Cage identified a set of "modes" used by Satie and used chance to select *within* them, a procedure not wholly un-Satiesque. [...] Cage also preserved some intervallic relationships'. From a note appended to my draft of this chapter. (*CCR*)

42   Ibid, p.36. (*CCR*)

43   Ibid. (*CCR*)

44   There is another aspect which may serve to compound the debate further: Satie's original music accompanies a text ('sur des dialogues de Platon') which is clearly 'saying something'. Cage jettisoned the text and in 1969 created not only *Cheap Imitation* but also an extremely elegant arrangement for two pianos of *Socrate*.

45   *Stockhausen Serves Imperialism*, p.35. (*CCR*)

46   Ibid, p.37. (*CCR*)

47   Ibid, Note 23, p.113. (*CCR*)

48   Nevertheless, we may recall what Cardew said in a lecture in Illinois some seven years previously, and quoted in the chapter on *The Great Learning*: 'A sound made intentionally has the characteristic of being intended; the same sound made accidentally has the different characteristics of accidentalness – regardless of whether you hear it as the same or different.'

49   *Stockhausen Serves Imperialism*, pp.37-8. (*CCR*)

50   Ibid, p.38. (*CCR*)

51   Jrnl. January–April 1973, undated. Demonstrating the pervasiveness of 'chance' (and its applicability in Art), Cage recalled meeting Buckminster Fuller 'by accident' at Madrid airport – a felicitous example of the 'surface dynamism' which Cardew singles out for criticism in 'John Cage; Ghost or Monster' (p.35). The 'charm' of contingency masks a deeper grand scheme to which such 'accidents' owe their existence. The overwhelming majority of the world's starving are unlikely ever to enjoy the luxury of such a chance meeting at Madrid airport.

52   *Stockhausen Serves Imperialism,* p.38. (*CCR*)

53   Ibid, p.47. (*CCR*)

54   Ibid, pp.47-48. (*CCR*)

55   I summarise this debate, as it occurred between Cardew and the theatre director, Frances Rifkin, in a later chapter.

56   Already in chapter 4 we have seen how Cardew delineates the philosophical quagmire into which 'facts' and their exploitation can drag us: 'It is often the comment – or the

choice of context that makes a statement of fact true or false.' These 'statements of fact' in *Stockhausen Serves Imperialism* certainly demand 'explanation and comment', and, in particular, *contextualisation*. As for the question of their truth or falsity, the individual reader must decide for himself.

57 *Stockhausen Serves Imperialism,* pp.48-49. (*CCR*)
58 Ibid, p.49. (*CCR*)
59 Ibid, p.57. (*CCR*)
60 Ibid, p.56. (*CCR*)
61 In an interview for Phillipe Regniez's film on Cardew Andrew Porter referred to a review for the *Musical Times* sometime during the sixties. Cardew had observed with what reluctance the masterpieces of the past relinquished their identity. In Porter's paraphrase: 'Five notes of Chopin peep out at you from Boulez' *Structures* and speak straight to the heart; their tenacity is incredible, they refuse to die'.
62 *Stockhausen Serves Imperialism,* p.56. However, David Sladen has drawn my attention to the fact that in footnote 32 on page 115 of *Stockhausen Serves Imperialism* Cardew seems to be shedding doubt on the viability of the virtues of bourgeois music in contemporary society. As the class struggle intensifies, 'the fascination of bourgeois concerts – all that wholesomeness, delight, inspiration, etc. – is likely to grow continually paler'. (*CCR*)
63 *Stockhausen Serves Imperialism*, p.57. (*CCR*)
64 Christian Wolff, *Cues: Writings and Conversations*, p.498.
65 Jrnl. January-April 1973, undated.
66 *Stockhausen Serves Imperialism,* p.74. (*CCR*)
67 Ibid, p.77.
68 Of course, there are pieces by Reich, such as *Come Out* and *Different Trains*, which do demonstrate social awareness, but there is no political (socialist) agenda, as there is in some of Rzewski's and Wolff's works.
69 Jrnl. 5 March – 9 April 1974, undated.
70 *Stockhausen Serves Imperialism,* p.87. (*CCR*)
71 Ibid, pp.78-9. (*CCR*)
72 Ibid, p.88. (*CCR*)
73 Moreover there are correlatives which can be 'heard' in the score and 'seen' in the music, as we can experience with the pointillism of Webern and the fugal architecture of *Die Kunst der Fuge*.
74 *Stockhausen Serves Imperialism,* pp.84-85. (*CCR*)
75 Ibid.
76 Ibid.
77 I would refer the reader back to the chapter on *Treatise*.
78 *Stockhausen Serves Imperialism*, p.122, Note 53. (*CCR*)
79 Ibid, p.84. (*CCR*)
80 Ibid, p.84. (*CCR*)
81 Ibid, pp.80-81. (*CCR*)
82 Ibid, p.81. (*CCR*)
83 Thirty years on, an Italian participant, Claudio Annibaldi, recalls how deeply impressed he was listening to Cardew reading his paper (in Italian) quite impassively, ignoring the frequent and noisy interruptions, particularly by the critic Fedele D'Amico, who objected to Cardew's generalizations,

insisting that they should be supported by factual material of a more specific nature.

84   *Stockhausen Serves Imperialism*, p.91. (*CCR*)

85   Pound died in 1972.

86   *Stockhausen Serves Imperialism*, p.98. (*CCR*)

87   Ibid, p.95. (*CCR*)

88   Anthologised in *Ezra Pound: Selected Prose 1909-1965*, ed. by William Cookson (London: Faber and Faber, 1973).

89   *Stockhausen Serves Imperialism*, p.96. (*CCR*)

90   Ibid, p.102. (*CCR*)

91   Ibid, p.100-1. (*CCR*)

92   In a letter to Richard Churches (undated but probably from the late nineties) Victor Schonfield makes some thought-provoking observations and speculations regarding the Scratch Orchestra. Though never a member (Schonfield did not consider himself to be a musician, even within the limitless definition of the word adopted by the Scratch Orchestra itself), he was nevertheless its most ardent champion and promoted many of its activities for little material reward. Schonfield claims that too many people were in the Scratch Orchestra to exploit it for their own ulterior purposes (hidden agendas), including Cardew himself. My own view would be more generous; the Scratch Orchestra and its Constitution was a repository of ideas, of dreams, from which each individual could draw, according to his or her needs. This was enacted privately but as far as I recall did not involve 'exploitation' nor 'agendas' – except at the end where the 'agenda' was quite transparent.

93   Mao Tse-tung, 'Talks at the Yenan Forum', p.19.

94   Ibid, p.18. Although this seems to be contradicted by the two citations, from Mao Tse-tung and Psi Ellison, at the end of the previous chapter.

95   In a letter to the central committee of the German United Socialist Party in October 1953 Hanns Eisler refers to the need to disseminate culture on different (that is, appropriate) levels: 'I have been extremely closely associated with the German workers' movement ever since my youth. My music always was and still is nourished by it, and not just the music which is immediately accepted by the masses, but also that which is more difficult to understand and which addresses itself to a smaller audience, one that is familiar with the heritage of German music'. Albrecht Betz, *Hanns Eisler Political Musician* (Cambridge: Cambridge University Press, 1982), p.227.

96   [With emphasis added.] George Steiner alludes to this when he refers to the development of Beethoven's *tempi* in the revolutionary years as being of 'extraordinary historical and psychological interest'. *In Bluebeard's Castle*, p.19.

97   'Towards an Ethic of Improvisation', *Treatise Handbook*, p.xx. Previously quoted in chapter 5. (*CCR*)

98   *Stockhausen Serves Imperialism*, p.89. (*CCR*)

99   'Towards an Ethic of Improvisation', *Treatise Handbook*, p.xx. (*CCR*)

100 *Stockhausen Serves Imperialism*, p.61. (*CCR*)

101 Pears, p.271.

102 *Vier Kantaten*, Universal Edition 1973.

(*CCR*) Also found in *Cornelius Cardew A Reader*

18

A Revolutionary Learning Curve 1975

Fighting alongside the working class should be like eating and sleeping.[1]

On the last day of December 1974 Cardew had sent a batch of letters to a number of institutions enquiring about possible teaching vacancies: the Birmingham School of Music, Trinity College of Music, the London College of Music, the Royal Northern College of Music, and the Royal Scottish Academy of Music and Drama. The replies, in early January, were friendly, even encouraging in some cases, but no offers of posts or even of some teaching hours were forthcoming. By contrast a steady flow of invitations to lecture and perform continued to boost his schedule, and the year began with a tour of the US and Canada from 3 January to 7 February. His recital programmes included works from the two *Piano Albums* (1973 and 1974), *Thälmann Variations*, transcriptions of Albanian songs by Dave Smith, and two pieces by Michael Chant. A song, entitled 'Resistance Blues', also dates from his time – a conventional blues carrying an anti-capitalist message which may even have been written while he was on tour.

The punishing schedule began at the Chicago Musical College of Roosevelt University on 7 January, and ended, via Canada and California, on 7 February at the Philadelphia School of Music: seventeen recitals interspersed with and accompanied by lectures (including one entitled 'Bourgeois Music'), discussions, interviews (sometimes two or three on the same day), and informal talks (after rehearsals and a performance of Paragraphs 2 and 7 of *The Great Learning*), including an account of the Bethanien campaign.[2] Contacts with sympathetic, 'progressive' students were made, orders taken for Cardew's scores, and there were reunions with old friends: Richard Teitelbaum and Barbara Mayfield, Rudolf Komorous, John Adams, Gordon Mumma, Christian Wolff, Ivan Tcherepnin, Joel Chadabe, among many others. The events seem to have been well attended, generating a positive interest in both the music and the politics, although the reviews, that is the critics, almost without exception, were unanimous in their judgement: politically unconvincing and musically dull, in neither art or politics did Cardew have any currency to offer. What the critics themselves had to offer, what particular personal cosmology, and its (ideological) roots, informed their own pronouncements, were issues of which they themselves may have been only dimly aware. In his review for *The Village Voice*, dated 17 February 1975, of Cardew's recital at The Kitchen in New York, the composer Tom Johnson sided with the critics in highlighting the music's stylistic eclecticism and enervating 'lack of focus', lamenting that 'Mr Cardew's out-of-date mannerisms just didn't draw me in': the critic as arbiter of stylistic viability, and as individual consumer demanding satisfaction. Johnson also expressed surprise at what he described as Cardew's accommodating and conciliatory approach to his audience in the post-concert discussion. After the aggressiveness and political militancy of *Stockhausen Serves Imperialism* perhaps Johnson was expecting, and hoping for, a more hard-hitting debate, for inflamed passions and stern rebuttals, even conversions. Yet this may have been a deliberate ploy on Cardew's part, a more subtle induction into the ideology of Marxism-Leninism. The dialectic of extreme and unpalatable views articulated humbly in a tone of reasonableness and respect may well have had a disarming, even lasting, effect on some of his audience, although the self-deprecation which characterised some of the public utterances of the Maoists, or rather their acolytes – if indeed such an impression was imparted to Cardew's audience at The Kitchen – was often as embarrassing as it was unconvincing.

In a steady stream of letters home to Sheila he documented his travels, or more accurately, his feelings and impressions, which abound with expressions of love and yearning for his lover.

I love you so much. I'm longing to come back and embrace the future. I find myself longing for a new baby. We should talk about that more and not just let it slumber under our hearts with warm and gentle pain and excitement.[3]

Here he reflects on his own attitude towards his music-making, and on how he can develop and improve it:

In the discussion after the concert today [in San Diego, US] I was criticised for not *singing* the songs (rather than just playing them). Some criticisms come out with the regularity of clockwork – I feel much less defensive about that kind of thing now. Am shaking off the avant-garde idea of 'flawless impact' and trying to communicate struggle, flexibility, actual *thinking*, change as development and growth, and above all optimism – especially about shortcomings (ie. that they are temporary). Anyway if I do another such trip I probably *will* sing, since by that time there'll be more songs about our actual situation.[4]

The political dimension was a constant referent in his encounters and observations in the musical academia but also at airports, in Greyhound buses and during temporary escapes into the countryside.

On the Greyhound travelling all through Chicago's South Side early in the morning, seeing the vitality of the working class children waiting to get into school. Then passing the vast steel works and other huge industrial places (spouting the filthiest pollution you can imagine) on the way to Cleveland. And the Greyhound travellers as compared with the airline travellers – it shattered me first: a Chicano I spoke to just started shaking and could not speak. The people are under constant threat of harassment. But after the drunken salesmen and executives of airline travel, and The Pick-Congress Hotel – anger came back to replace fear, and a consciousness of what we're fighting for drove away that incredibly horrible floating sense of bereavement that seemed to be twisting me in half in Chicago.[5]

On a small sheet of ruled paper he notes his total net earnings, £1700, and then in some detail lists his expenses, including those incurred in England prior to departure; thus Sheila's 'labour' is calculated at 10 days @£8 = £80, and his own, at an equal rate, 3 weeks @£8 = £120. Total Expenditure £835.35. Net Earnings: £850 approx. The exactitude is as exemplary as it is revealing.

A month after his return, on 5 March, the concert arranged with the Royal College of Music students the previous term took place at the RCM. According to Robert Coleridge the programme included *Material*, Paragraph 2 of *The Great Learning* and *Autumn 60;* he could not recall a performance of *Octet' 61,* which had been included in the original draft programme.[6] Cardew himself took part in *The Great Learning* (as did the Director of the RCM, Sir David Willcocks) and came to the rehearsals. According to Devenport he could 'out-sing' everybody, presumably with length of breath and volume; his training at the Choir School in Canterbury over twenty years earlier continued to stand him in good stead. The occasion also offered some interesting anecdotal evidence of Cardew's attitude towards his earlier music. Peter Devenport recalled that in one of the rehearsals Cardew had indicated that he liked performances of his earlier music to flow: for example, in *Autumn 60* he discouraged the pointillist approach of treating each beat as an 'event in itself'. Yet by forcing a more directional mode of performance on music which often created and demanded a condition of stasis, as in many Paragraphs of *The Great Learning,* by artificially imposing an aesthetic which undermines the very essence of the music, Cardew was perpetrating an act of musical sabotage. Was he really convinced that the earlier music could be improved in some way, or redeemed, if not radically altered? Had the hard-line stance towards his earlier music, that of total rejection, softened somewhat? Probably not. We know that he regarded the attempt to transform the two paragraphs from *The Great Learning* as a failure, a mistake; and judging from his (recollected) remarks on the earlier music at rehearsals and in informal discussions it seems that they had become quite alien to him – objects spawned in a previous, less enlightened existence from which, having undergone the necessary process of expiation, he could now abrogate all responsibility. With reference to the RCM concert Coleridge recalls that Cardew seemed 'indifferent' to the earlier works, and the occasional muted prompting could even have been construed as wilfully subversive, as when he suggested a kind of 'tonal vamp' in Coleridge's (harpsichord) contribution to *Autumn 60* – a stratagem which Coleridge sensibly rejected as being 'quite out of place'. Or his indifference had led to, or coalesced with, an insensitivity, as was the case with his attitude towards his earlier pointillist music from the late fifties. For him the music was doomed to suffer the same fate as the rest of contemporary bourgeois art. The most plausible explanation of his presence at the RCM was simply that he was pleased to have made contact with young musicians who were open-minded, enthusiastic, and talented. He would have enjoyed their company and would have made the most of the opportunities to engage in political discussion with them – to which they in turn responded intelligently and sometimes positively.

The project for a recording for Thorofon Records of Charles Ives' four Sonatas for violin and piano with János Négyesy, which they had been working on in Berlin, was finally realised during the same month, 10-24 March, recorded in a church in Boswil, Switzerland. In two romantic, poetic love-letters (undated) from Boswil, on successive days, Cardew expresses his longing for Sheila. The first, 'Monday afternoon', begins:

> Big snowflakes are gently falling among the catkins. And big wet furry flakes kiss away all the tragedy from my face. I think of the scent of your skin and the spring in your long legs, it's wonderful how peace can come and sweep away all that dark turbulent confusion. The tears falling on my letter this morning were scalding. It was an effort to put it in the post, but it seems to have relieved me of some unbearable tension – I hope they are not too painful to read.

And the second, 'Tuesday afternoon', begins:

> Hello, my sweetheart, breath of my breath, soul of my soul. How I long for a long

long kiss after lunch with the sun streaming in on us and the birds singing wildly outside. I'm remembering how my breathing changes when I put my arms round you, gets light, but deep and regular, and how my heart nestles into yours.

Ives' demanding music seems to have taken its toll; on the evening before the recording sessions started, Cardew had complained of an aching wrist ('probably just nerves').

I'm just going to write to you all the time – it's the only way for me to get through. The attacks may not come again, but I know the horror of this experience won't be over until I hold you in my arms again. I feel like some medieval character – bruised and battered from fighting the devil. And I can feel you bracing your feet and holding me under the arms to prevent me sliding into the fiery furnace and in the process collecting a few slaps and scratches for your pains!… But I'm never, never going to go through this again. (Remind me!) If you can't come with me I'm going to turn the jobs down. I'd rather be on the night shift at the ABC Bakery! […]
Evening.
I went for a longish walk in the snow.[…] The woods are magical. If you touch a tree the snow comes down in a fine white dust. It just seems the most perfect equilibrium: the cold snow from the sky and the warmth rising from the earth (expressed in all the little flowers and crocuses nestling brightly in the snow).

Sheila arrived on the last day of the recording sessions so that she and Cornelius could enjoy a few days together in tranquillity – a brief holiday (an 'alchemy' in Sheila's description) which they had managed to arrange at the very last moment. They had been living together in Agar Grove for barely three months, a relatively short stretch of time during which – in a condition of emotional brittleness and susceptibility to which telephone conversations and Cardew's letters from North America bore disturbing witness – the need for both compromise and patience had to be recognised.
They set off from their accommodation, rucksacks on their backs, took a train into the mountains and booked into a small hotel. They were the only guests. The next day they climbed to a village situated higher up and had intended to sleep in a small tent which Sheila had brought with her. However, it was too cold and wet and they found a little forester's hut in the forest just below the village and decided to stay there. It was very cold, but snug. The next day they took the ski lift to the top of the mountain, where they seemed to be quite alone, and spent the day exploring a landscape of ice which, as spring began to overtake it, was dissolving around them. In the late afternoon, against local advice, they decided to climb down to the village on the one route that was open.

As dusk approached they lost their way and had to cross what seemed to be a small but forbidding frozen avalanche. Cardew made his way across, fearlessly, cutting or re-forming foot and hand holds which previous travellers had used. Sheila was terrified and halfway across the chasm was already, both physically and mentally, in a frozen condition. Cardew proffered calm words of encouragement and there were tears of relief when they were reunited on the other side. A rapid descent, on their backsides, propelled them into extremely wet, steep pastureland and they arrived in the village in darkness, covered in mud, soaking wet, extremely cold and exhausted, and in a state of quiet exhilaration. They both loved nature, responded to its overwhelming immanence, and being alone together in the mountains had been a therapeutic and intoxicating experience. Desperate for food and warmth they managed eventually to find accommodation; the inn was closed but, shocked by their condition, the landlord allowed them to stay the night. There was no heating and they had to make do with blankets and an incongruous hair dryer. Wrapped in their blankets they ate dinner, becalmed, marvelling at their good fortune, and avowing their love for each other. They left Boswil on 29 March and in a matter of a few hours were back amidst the hordes of the metropolis, back to reunite with the comrades, to rejoin the class struggle. A brief episode in Cardew's life, it was nevertheless a microcosm with all the constituent characteristics: nature, risk, danger, romance.

In fact, his restitution to political life was short-lived; within a few days, on 2 April, Cardew, Sheila and her daughter Anna were driving down to his parents at Wenford Bridge where 'struggle' of a different, domestic nature was to blight their stay. For Sheila and Anna it was their first visit to Wenford and the plan was that they should stay until 10 April. Sensing, or perhaps anticipating, the hostility to Sheila from both Michael and Mariel, Cornelius decided that by camping in a field next to the pottery a potentially confrontational situation could be avoided. His father, in particular, was singularly unwelcoming, allowing them in for tea and then virtually banishing them from the premises. The fact that it was cold, snowing, and his son was suffering from a very bad cold made no difference. A young French potter, Thiébaut Chagué, who was staying at Wenford at the time as an apprentice, was appalled by Michael's behaviour and forewarned him that he would absent himself from the supper table if Cornelius, Sheila and Anna were excluded. Bearing in mind the young man's status at the pottery, and the patrician nature and unpredictability of his master, this was a brave stance and one which could have soured his relationship with Michael Cardew and precipitated an earlier-than-planned departure from Wenford. However, to his credit, if uncharacteristically, Michael backed down; he may well have been impressed by the young Frenchman's open and challenging expression of dissent. (It may even have had deeper, disturbing ramifications for Michael, causing him to reflect more generally upon his relations with his family.) According to

Sheila Kasabova both she and her daughter subsequently got on very well with Michael Cardew. Such tensions are commonplace and perhaps unavoidable when the stability of family life has been disrupted, when a much-loved member (in this instance Stella, mother of adored grandchildren) is peremptorily excluded and a stranger introduced. Sheila also suffered hostility from Cardew's young sons, not yet in their teens, who made it clear that they resented being with her, even for the briefest periods of time. But at the end of the month, 30 April, with the news of the liberation of Vietnam, there was jubilation and celebration around the whole world, and not least in the Cardew household.

A little red memo book, dated April 1975 to February 1976, begins with the following counsel:

Less talk – more thought.
Less action, more effect.
Through the cracks in the present
the future shines so sharply.
We'll penetrate the cracks
Force the boulders apart.

A few pages on, under the title 'Building Revolutionary Mass Movement', Cardew notes: 'Wrong idea: that day-to-day struggles of the wc [working class] will inevitably lead to collapse. This leads to Trots [Trotskyites] trying to become popular in the w. [working class] movement.'[7] Cardew argues that whereas it is right to unite with people in their particular struggles, it is wrong to equate this with revolutionary work. 'It is wrong to fight *only* for the issues that come from the people.' In other words, radical change does not come about by evolution, ineluctably. Communists must raise revolutionary issues and propagate a revolutionary line where there is broad public debate – such as there was at that time (and still is) over the nature and role of the European Community:

Whether Yes or No is not the divide.
Whether revolutionary perspective is.

1. Support workers in fight against capital.
2. Support countries and peoples exploited and oppressed (in the past, too) by Britain.
3. Internationally support China and oppose SPs [superpowers].[8]

And time and again Cardew stressed the need for the Party: 'MM [the mass movement] on its own will never give rise to revolution'.[9]

Yet the desire, or need, not to lose touch with his musician friends and colleagues would occasionally surface; indeed he took every opportunity to state his case to those in the music world who, for whatever reasons, would offer him a platform. On 7 May, his thirty-ninth birthday, he returned to the RCM to give a talk on his political music, which included a tape of the solo piano version of *Thälmann Variations* (a second concert, and Cardew's third visit to the RCM, was to be much later, on 23 January the following year), and he had also received an invitation to contribute to a discussion on the 'social role of the composer' at the Aldeburgh festival on 23 June. By this time, half-way through a decade which saw his revolutionary enthusiasm harnessed to a surer theoretical grasp, as well as to a sharper practical awareness, the content of his Aldeburgh talk was predictable: the class nature of Art; the dissemination of bourgeois (ruling class) ideas and values through Art – including music; the need for artists to resist such expectations and demands and to contribute to the oppositional trends and to the establishment of a culture which genuinely 'serves the people'.

> The reason why in modern music you don't find ruling class ideas stated as clearly as [Elgar's] Pomp and Circumstance [is] because bourgeois ideas and values are largely untenable in the modern world – you get artists confusing them and mystifying them, thus screening them from attack.[10]

Howard Skempton recalls the occasion at Aldeburgh:

> Cornelius was taking part in an Aldeburgh Festival event in the Jubilee Hall at 11.00. (I remember waking at 4.00 am to catch the earliest tube.) There were only three people on the stage: Cornelius, Hugh Wood and Donald Mitchell (in the chair). The title was something like 'The Composer's Role in Society' and I think Donald, to his credit, must have instigated the event (I remember talking to him, at Faber, about *Stockhausen Serves Imperialism* following its broadcast – an interval talk during a live Aldeburgh Festival concert in 1972.)
> Cornelius was invited to speak first and gave a formal, prepared talk of extraordinary elegance and power – as you can imagine! This was high definition performance (to use Tynan's phrase[11]), with all the necessary calmness and grace. If Hugh had made any notes (you'll have to ask him!), he laid them to one side and decided instead to attack Cornelius's argument head-on. He had the authority to do this, he said, because he'd been through all this (politics) before. I'm fairly sure that he denied the composer any sort of role; and he criticized Cornelius for being

dependent on heroes (whether Stockhausen or Mao). (I remember asking Hugh, later in the day, whether he himself was dependent on Beethoven!) After these statements, the audience joined in, and I remember that the questions seemed to acknowledge, if not favour, Cornelius's position. Someone mentioned Russia, and Shostakovich, whom Hugh then discounted as a 'tenth-rate composer', a remark which Donald took exception to and which put him in the uncomfortable position of being sympathetic to neither side! I remember, this being 1975, that both Hugh and Cornelius were asked if they would accept the invitation (following the death of Arthur Bliss) to be Master of the Queen's Musicke! Cornelius said that it was a completely pointless question because there was absolutely no chance that he would be asked! I had lunch with Cornelius, Sheila and Donald. Cornelius seemed relaxed and pleased to be involved (he and Sheila had attended an open-air concert the previous evening).[12]

Later in the day I received another e-mail from Skempton:

I should amend part of the piece I sent this morning. I don't think Hugh Wood criticized Cornelius during the debate. I think it was later, in the afternoon, when he suggested to me that Cornelius was dependent on heroes (and I mentioned Beethoven).[13]

A letter from Cardew to Skempton a few weeks before the Aldeburgh event is revealing in several respects and not least in its personal references. It ends:

Could you dig up a copy of your 'The masses are the real heroes' and send it to me? I'm digging up various items with a view to 'exploiting' them as improvisation pieces, and I remember the good sentiment in your song, but I've lost my copy in the turbulence of everyday life. Say hello to M. Parsons – how is he? I miss him. Perhaps you could let me have his address and phone number.[14]

The 'turbulence' certainly refers to both his political and his personal life; even with Sheila, and the brief holiday in Boswil notwithstanding, there were questions and doubts about the nature and trajectory of their relationship. Perhaps that too was in jeopardy and may partly explain the strong sentiments towards former close friends expressed in his letter to Skempton, as if there would soon be nothing left of his past: family abandoned, friends and lovers estranged, lost. 'Politics in control' was a Party watchword; it was also the ruination of many relationships.

Natalie Gibson, née Behr, whose relationship with Cardew in the sixties is recounted above, had found him 'poetic, abstract, pure, fresh thinking, an original man, very perceptive, special'.[15] She described her dismay when she met him again, in the seventies, at St. Martin's School of Art where she was teaching. When she invited him for coffee he insisted on going to the College canteen. However, it was closed and her initial choice of the Cappucetto café around the corner in Soho prevailed. He informed her that politics was the most important thing in his life and asked her what she was doing and why. She told him she was teaching design and talked about the 'aesthetic enjoyment of a beautiful object'. There was absolutely no contact. Such discussions, unless linked to the revolutionary cause, he dismissed as self-indulgence, bourgeois escapism. Natalie Gibson recalls that Cardew was 'very serious'; all the fantasy and lightness had gone. And he seemed bitter, dissatisfied, *au fond* unhappy. That extra dimension which he always had, and which had so captivated her, was missing. He talked about the need for sacrifice, not only one's own life, but even the lives of one's children. To die for the cause. She was horrified and deeply distressed (as Sheila Kasabova had been by such discussions); she saw no virtue in it whatsoever.

Krystyna Roberts, who had been a member of the Scratch Orchestra and through her then marriage to Keith Rowe closely associated with AMM, expresses here what many in the Scratch Orchestra, indeed in the music world generally, were feeling at that time, especially in relation to his repudiation of the past:

> To me pieces like *Treatise* and *The Tiger's Mind* were not just two dimensional images, lines, notes, directions, etc.; they were people and all the flesh, sweat, love and laughter, noise, arguing etc. that had gone into the creation and the playing – so they became alive, breathing. I will never forget those times [...] and so to denounce the body, or being, or beings that were created and still exist you cannot by a declaration wipe out what is.[16]

In the May 1975 issue of *Music and Musicians* there is a revealing, yet curiously inconsequential, interview with Cardew by the composer/critic Adrian Jack. Right at the outset Cardew wisely refuses to be drawn into 'a long discussion about where the word Stalinist comes from'; thus by raising the bogey of Stalin in the first sentence of his first question Jack effectively seals off an avenue that may have yielded interesting exchanges. A more circumspect approach could have begun with a specific reference, for example to Zhdanov, which would certainly have elicited less guarded, and more challenging, responses from Cardew. Jack also repeats the common error of characterising China's cultural policy at that time as a 'blueprint' out of which a 'standard musical aesthetic' is imposed. In his reply Cardew distinguishes between a 'unified cultural programme' and the development of many different kinds of folk musics in the various national minority areas in China: 'There are many different directions. So I don't think there is a unified standard aesthetic. I don't think there can be, and I would never think of imposing it'.

The interview becomes virtually deadlocked when Cardew upholds the thesis of the decline of 'bourgeois' art, from the classics through to impressionism and the solipsism of the moderns, challenging Jack's perceived position that 'the achievements of modern composers are as satisfying as those of the classical composers'. Jack's contention that 'it's just a question of exposure', and of time, is immediately seized upon by Cardew as 'the idea that the human being is totally conditionable'. But Jack insists that in order to cultivate appreciation of the new, as well as intelligent discrimination, time and application are necessary.[17] The discussion turns *en passant* to architecture: If a magnificent building had been the home of 'a particularly vicious renaissance family', we might now appreciate it for its 'aesthetic qualities'. Cardew contends that 'you won't like it, because of what it stands for'. When Jack riposts that it is possible to 'divorce its aesthetic qualities from its function', Cardew's rejoinder is unequivocal: 'Well, I would never want to, you see'. Walter Benjamin elaborates on this theme with characteristic eloquence:

Whoever has emerged victorious participates to this day in the triumphal procession in which the present rulers step over those who are lying prostrate. According to traditional practice, the spoils are carried along in the procession. They are called cultural treasures, and a historical materialist views them with cautious detachment. For without exception the cultural treasures he surveys have an origin which he cannot contemplate without horror. They owe their existence not only to the efforts of the great minds and talents who created them, but also to the anonymous toil of their contemporaries. There is no document of civilization which is not at the same time a document of barbarism.[18]

If people are not conscious of their own culture, as a whole and from multifarious perspectives, and if they deny experiences which challenge the historical and parental crib into which they have been born, how then can they understand the culture of others? For them the oppressed people who with sweat and blood built the renaissance house have no history; for they are perceived as victims of history and therefore have no role to play in its unfolding. To enter the Tate Gallery in London, without at least a moment's reflection on the fact that the building and its contents were financed by slave-driven sugar profits, is to turn a blind eye to one of the most important foundations of Western art. But in Western society such states of denial are commonplace; moreover, they serve to produce the germs of evasion and corruption in the aesthetic and intellectual act itself, thus opening the doors to a countervailing *inhumanity*.

Jack then raises the question of 'music for the working class'.[19] Cardew agrees with Jack that 'the working class doesn't like Beethoven or Mozart', but claims that it is because 'they are the composers of the bourgeoisie'. This is not, of course, an historical reference; Cardew is alluding rather to the confinement of the classical composers to middle-class concert venues which are comparatively rarely patronized by working-class people. In other words this has more to do with social exclusion and alienation than with the ideological content of Beethoven's, or Mozart's, work. [20]

The identification of the 'class nature' of a work of art, and the extent to which this might act as a deterrent to a potential listener, was still a legitimate matter for debate, but the promiscuity of music, in particular, militated against any kind of rigid categorisation. Clearly, in his generalisations about the cultural preferences and habits of 'the working-class' Cardew was treading on dangerous ground, and the charge of condescension was made by some of his critics. He acknowledged the fact that his lack of political awareness and involvement until he was well into his thirties, rather than the disadvantages of a 'bourgeois' background, meant that there was still much ground to be made up. His recognition of this is reflected in his admission, in the Jack interview, that he and his fellow 'progressive' musicians have no access to a working-class audience:

These pieces [the *Piano Albums 1973/1974* and the *Thälmann Variations*] were written for a definite audience. It is a definite audience which comes to the Purcell Room – or the students in colleges round the country where you might get a gig. It's not an audience of workers in their work environment or even in their recreation time. It's music for a consciously culture-orientated youth. I never […] claimed it was reaching the working classes.

I acknowledge there are compositional shortcomings in these pieces, and I don't make any claims for them. The advantage of them is that they draw the attention of the listeners to social issues. If you have a concert of arrangements of Irish songs, it does draw attention to the culture of the Irish and also to their fight.

At the time Cardew had set his sights no higher, and he refers to the music of left-wing composers such as Erhard Grosskopf and Christian Wolff as 'making efforts in the right direction'. In this respect his attitude appears far more relaxed, more pragmatic: 'If I decide not to carry on writing music in the tonal idiom, it will be because I don't think it's terribly effective, not because I think there is anything wrong with it'. He also discusses the contextualisation of concerts, probably having in mind a concert in Berlin of nineteenth century 'revolutionary' music including works by Schumann, Cramer, Liszt and Chopin (I recall performing Chopin's Revolutionary Study in C minor), which would have involved research and drawn attention to the social aspects and consequences of music-making.[21]

Cardew seems now to be much more accommodating of contemporary music than he was two years ago when, as we have seen, the works by Rzewski and Wolff performed in Berlin in April 1973 received very short shrift indeed. Luigi Nono, too, another comrade-in-arms, is singled out in the Jack interview as a composer whose method of incorporating political content is 'fairly valid' – not exactly an enthusiastic endorsement of the Italian's work, but certainly a clear shift away from the dogmatic position that he had held in the early seventies. However, unlike these composers, Cardew's own political music features only the occasional residual element of modernism (as in *Mountans* for solo bass clarinet, for example). Perhaps this was because through his political activism he had found a new and wider audience which did encompass sections of the working class – an audience whose expectations were quite different to those of the culturally informed, left-wing artists and intellectuals who would attend concerts at the Purcell Room and in galleries and university departments where his old political comrades continued to concertize.

The encounter ends with a brief discussion of pop-music: Jack insists that pop-music is not part of working-class culture since it is entirely manipulated by 'middle-class exploiters'. Cardew argues that pop-music has its roots in the music of the oppressed: 'That is to say, the influence of Beethoven and Stockhausen ['bourgeois composers'] is minute.' The aim of PLM (People's Liberation Music) was to be part of a popular music that would encourage a trend which already existed. Such music, with the proliferation of new, independent record labels, would not be dependent on the mainstream media; it would be more class-conscious, anti-capitalist, and would sing of working-class heroes.

In the interview Jack is at times insulting ('the fact is that most of the audience laugh at this music') and invariably condescending ('the music you have written recently sounds almost deliberately bad. [...] Why are they [pieces from the *Piano Albums*] not better composed? You could certainly manage better, couldn't you?'). There were not a few composers at the time (as has always been the case) whom a critic such as Adrian Jack could have taken to task, drawn attention to the indifferent quality of the pieces they had written, and publicly ridiculed their music. This may occasionally have materialised in the form of a concert review but rarely, as far as I know, in a face-to-face interview. Of course, one could congratulate Jack on his bluntness, his abrasiveness, his willingness to speak his mind – but there is also a context here in which the interview needs to be understood. As spokesperson for the dominant artistic and ideological agenda of received liberal opinion (which, in his music and political activism, Cardew is challenging) Jack is speaking from a position of authority; hence, his tone is confident and aggressive. His cultural stance would have embraced the autonomy of Art; the inviability of socialist realism; the condescension towards 'the working classes' and a negativism in relation to most popular music; and, above all, the assumption of cultural pluralism and 'freedom' in the West (the artist as pioneer, as individual discoverer). In response Cardew does not defend his music; but he does refer to the generally positive response that his concerts/recitals have elicited – in the US, for example. He stresses the 'obligation to bring your individual sensibility, your passions, to bear upon your music. To deny the subjective quality of art would be to deny life'. And it was this unswerving *commitment* to the music he was performing which distinguished Cardew from many of his peers in the domains of both contemporary and classical music. Cardew's work reflected passions and imperatives of an intensity which would have embarrassed the professionals.

On 1 July the Journals note: 'PLM at Fulham Town Hall', with a line-up of Vicky Silva, Geoff Pearce, Laurie Baker, John Marcangelo, Keith Rowe, Dave Smith, and Cardew himself (playing electric piano). Just above it there is a brief entry dated 29 June: 'Leave Acklam Rd. office' – the room off Portobello Road in west London which he rented while he was still in Barnes and which he had kept on after he moved in with Sheila and Anna in Agar Grove in November 1974. By this time PLM was Cardew's main source of music-making, and there could be no questioning his total involvement in a genre in which he had had no previous experience and which served as a constant reminder of what he regarded as his musical inadequacies.

Yet he still managed to apply himself to musical composition, in this case arrangements of four songs of Christian Wolff – *A Suite of Wolff Tunes* – which recalled his tonal experimentation of two years previously. Wolff provided the tunes, with rhythmic articulations and free durations between phrases; Cardew regularized the meter and added harmonisations and accompaniments (Ex.18.1-3). Wolff's pentatonicism resembles the melodic language of some of the Ode Machines from *The Great Learning* and thus lent itself to the harmonic language, and to the pianism, of the *Three Bourgeois Songs*. 'After a Few Years' comes from a pamphlet on economics, by Rosa Luxemburg; 'Of All Things' is a text by Mao; and 'It is Said' was abstracted from a newspaper report of a miners' strike. Wolff cannot recall the provenance of the text of 'Wake Up' which, in any case, is omitted in Cardew's arrangement. The accompaniment to 'After a Few Years' consists of sequences of cadences over a repeated rhythm. In the opening Cardew steadfastly insists on the major mode in spite of the persistent minor third in Wolff's melody:

Ex.18.1a. From 'After a Few Years'.

And in the final two bars voice and accompaniment join forces to create the stark contrast between 'your enemy' and 'your friend':

Ex.18.1b. From 'After a Few Years'.

Mao's text for 'Of All Things' consists of two interlocking maxims from the communist canon:

Of all things in the world people are the most precious.
Under the leadership of the Communist Party so long as there are people every kind of miracle can be performed.

Wolff separates the phrases of the text, each of which is cast in a pentatonic mode. Cardew's setting is through-composed, beginning with a repeated bass riff under a chordal progression

Ex.18.2a. From 'Of All Things'.

and building and maintaining the momentum through ascending tremolos, which reach their apotheosis with the final words of the text:

Ex.18.2b. From 'Of All Things'.

'It is Said' recalls Eisler's *Zeitungsausschnitte* and is a more extended and elaborate composition. Wolff's setting is 'conversational', almost matter of fact, so that the words are clearly comprehensible. We are reminded of Eisler's secular cantatas, which are themselves influenced by Bach's treatment of the Evangelist in the Passions. Cardew's accompaniment is less convincing here, particularly in the solo piano postlude which reads more like an abandoned sketch.

The extant accompaniment to 'Wake Up!', with its driving rhythm and syncopations, recalls 'Revolution is the main trend', although the harmonic language is more adventurous:

Ex.18.3. From 'Wake Up!'.

On 4 August a number of songs from the PLM repertoire were recorded at a concert at the Unity Theatre in Stratford, East London. These included some of Hanns Eisler's songs, including 'Solidarity Song' and 'Song of the United Front', as well as lesser known but equally memorable songs such as 'The Peat-Bog Soldiers', composed by prisoners in Papenburg Nazi concentration camp. Together with other selected songs this collection comprised PLM's first anti-fascist song book, *Where there is Oppression there is Resistance,* and the concert marked the occasion of its publication.

The creation of new revolutionary songs was a top priority in PLM's cultural work at that time – no doubt a decree from above, from the Party: 'revolutionary intellectuals have to take revolutionary ideas into the working class'. Some of them were recorded and often featured in concerts, at meetings and at demonstrations, providing the revolutionary content alongside the time-honoured traditional and protest (especially Irish) songs. They also sought to publicise the group in locations frequented by working class people and in situations where they traditionally foregathered: such an occasion was the TUC conference in Blackpool on 2 September which Cardew, Laurie and Brigid Baker attended. They set up a stall, stayed for a few days, and tried to make contacts for future PLM engagements. The last extant Journal is the aforementioned small red memo book (April 1975 – February 1976) – the kind that can be purchased at any stationers. At one end there are six pages of names and addresses, most of them written in the contact's own hand. Many of them are from Lancashire: Manchester, Nelson, Burnley, Liverpool, Leigh, Bootle; also Leeds, the Midlands, and Scotland. Their status, membership, or in many cases ex-membership, is also noted: Trades Council, Communist Party of Great Britain, Electricians' Shop Steward, Shop Stewards' Committee, AEUW Convenor, Regional Secretaries of various unions, Teachers' and Lecturers' Union representatives, TUC Committee on the Arts. Clearly, all of these people, amongst whom there is just one woman (and this, 1975, International Women's Year!), were active in the Labour movement, and Cardew must have met them during those few days at the TUC conference. One would assume that these informal encounters, however brief, would have been of primary importance to him and had to be conducted, on his part, with a degree of circumspection. Many of these men had seen it all before – in strikes, lockouts, redundancies, dole, union meetings, chores and administration, as well as revolutionary panaceas. This had been their lives from the day they left school. They would have experienced the 'bankruptcy' of Trade Union and Labour policies, the betrayal of Socialism and disillusionment. In this latter respect Cardew and these workers would have found common ground, but where could it have gone from there? How many PLM gigs materialised and, most importantly, how many lasting contacts did he make with these comrades-in-arms?

A diverting anomaly is highlighted in another brief Journal entry which states simply: 'Sept.20: RAM – Cyril Lloyd'. Somehow or other, through oversight, or more likely through a coalescence of those typically liberal English foibles – dissimulation and hypocrisy – Cardew's name had remained on the professorial list at the Royal Academy of Music. Yet ever since the Scratch Orchestra's Newcastle debacle, and perhaps before, there seems to have been a reluctance to acknowledge Cardew's status at the RAM; he was, simply, *persona non grata.* So that when a young Welsh composer, Cyril Lloyd, was given to understand by the Academy authorities (as presumably others had been) that Mr. Cardew was 'oversubscribed' and therefore 'unavailable', the mutinous Welshman refused to be fobbed off, insisting on his right to have lessons with Cardew. And we may glean from the Journal note that the Academy authorities must have conceded. [22]

However, more bona fide engagements awaited him in Italy, noted in the Journals: 'September 24-30 Milan-Naples-Como (Autumno Musicale with Rzewski)'. Frederic Rzewski recalls a large audience of around two thousand students at the University of Milan (a concert organised by the Italian composer Sandro Melchiorre and others under the umbrella 'Cultura Populare'). Fists were raised during the singing of the 'Internationale' in which the words 'di Stalin' were added in the chorus by the militant Maoist faction and, according to Rzewski's graphic description, there were also present a number of 'hooded Spanish revolutionaries'. [23] 'Cultura Populare' was the cultural front of the CPI (M-L), Communist Party of Italy (Marxist-Leninist), which, in Cardew's opinion (as Sheila Kasabova recalls) seemed 'much more relaxed and objective about Mao'. The Italians were looking more to their own context and speculating intelligently on what might or should happen when Mao died – in stark contrast to the English Maoists, who would have viewed a future without Mao, if indeed they ever allowed themselves such an unbearable indulgence, through an ever-diminishing lens. As for the eventuality of the political demise of Chairman Mao, the inimicality of such a notion to the historical inevitability of a 'bright future' for the working and oppressed people of the world would have prohibited it from entering their revolutionary consciousness. According to Sheila Kasabova, Cardew was impressed by the Italians' approach; in particular they seemed to be grappling with cultural issues in a much freer, more open, more pragmatic, more Italian way. The admiration was mutual; Cardew was greatly respected within communist circles in Italy and people listened to him.

On 2 October 1975 Cardew began a period of employment as an evening class tutor for Goldsmiths' College Adult Studies department in New Cross, southeast London.[24] The title of the class was 'Songs for our Society' and immediately attracted a heterogeneous group of enthusiasts: among them Royal College of Music students Peter Devenport and Robert Coleridge, composer Howard Skempton (occasionally), a homeopathic nurse, a lady on day release from a mental hospital, a young German called Holger, a retired railway worker, young left-wing women – probably supporters or members of one or more of the various socialist groups, and people who were interested in contemporary China. Presumably, Cardew himself had proposed the idea of 'Songs for our Society' – a progressive-sounding catchword that would have appealed to the liberal sensibilities of those responsible for the content of the Adult Studies prospectus.

Directness of approach was Cardew's trademark and he began the first meeting in characteristic mode: with a minimum of introductory remarks he sat down at the piano and launched into 'The People United Will Never Be Defeated', a song by the Chilean composer Sergio Ortega, followed by his own 'A Law of History'. Nobody could have been left in any doubt as to the specific – or narrow, some might have objected – political agenda of 'songs for our society'. In fact, as Robert Coleridge recalls, after just one or two sessions there were already a few lapses of membership, an eventuality Cardew would have anticipated, even welcomed.

The group worked on a variety of lyrics, including poems by Mao Tse-tung, and brought them to the class every week. There was also a communal scrapbook with the title 'Lyrics', not unlike the Scratch Orchestra Documentary file, in which people could lodge material, or work in progress, or simply ideas. As with the Scratch Orchestra it was Cardew's way of emphasizing, and encouraging, a collective approach to music-making. Every session involved playing through, trying out and rehearsing material, and Cardew would lead and provoke criticism of the texts for 'reformist' or 'revisionist' tendencies, issuing caveats and offering guidelines according to the tenets of Marxism-Leninism. The content of the music, too, would occasionally come under a prescriptive scrutiny – self-indulgent, sentimental, not optimistic enough, and so forth; but there was very little purely musical, compositional or technical criticism. Nor was there any attempt at consistency; many styles and approaches were used without demur from Cardew, who was more concerned with the practicalities of arranging and preparing the music for performance. Perhaps he concluded that whereas it would be difficult, if not impossible, to raise the standard of the music submitted to a significant degree, ideological analysis and criticism could cleanse the texts of any dubious political content; and this, after all, was paramount.[25] At the end of the evening the class would adjourn to a nearby pub, usually the Goldsmiths' Tavern, occasionally the Marquis of Granby, and there would be a further two hours of intense political discussion. If the debate was occasionally heated it did not undermine the essentially congenial atmosphere which pervaded; Cardew had always been adept, from the Scratch Orchestra days, at creating and fostering a collective ethos which embraced both harmony and discord.

Eventually, a specific project was initiated: in collaboration with the theatre group Mutable Theatre Company [26] it was agreed that the 'Songs for our Society' class would compose and perform music for two short *Lehrstücke* (didactic plays) by Bertolt Brecht: *The Measures Taken,* and *The Exception and the Rule*, to be performed the following Spring, March/April 1976, at a number of venues, including the Roundhouse studio. The song writing was divided amongst the members of the group, with Cardew helping out with some of the arrangements. Jim Ward, the retired railway worker, set the 'Textile Workers' song' from *The Measures Taken,* a song about a strike, while Howard Skempton's contribution was an austere, stoical setting of 'It is Splendid', from *The Exception and the Rule,* for voice and accordion (or piano). In fact, Skempton's song was not included in the final selection; the lady on day release proffered a 'wild and free' setting of the same words which Cardew favoured, regarding its expression of 'revolutionary optimism' as more appropriate to the text and its context. Cardew's intervention may have been prompted as much by an ultra-democratic desire to encourage contributions from anonymous female composers, rather than famous male ones, as by the reasons tendered above. Or perhaps it expressed his respect for 'true naivety', as opposed to a more orthodox, compositional professionalism. As a consequence the songs varied considerably in both style and treatment (and merit), scored for those few instruments (including guitars, percussion, tin whistle, and an ex-Promenade Theatre Orchestra reed organ) which members of the class brought along to the sessions and could play with a reasonable degree of competence. In performance some of the songs were sung by the actors, others by the Goldsmiths'class 'chorus'. Little was offered in the way of criticism of the songs or suggestions for improvements; nor was anything rejected as being stylistically inappropriate, ideologically suspect or (musically) simply not good enough. One of the most (musically) successful contributions was Robert Coleridge's more extended setting of 'Song of the Rice Barge Coolies' from *The Measures Taken.*

Cardew himself provided the four Merchant's Songs from *The Exception and the Rule,* explaining that since the merchant was 'the bourgeois character in the play' he had written them in the style of Beethoven although, as Robert Coleridge has cautioned, an off-the-cuff remark at a rehearsal, which he himself dimly recollects, cannot be treated as a definitive statement of intent. Yet when Cardew finally unveiled his settings it was evident that the classical *style* – that is, Clementi and Cramer no less than Beethoven – did, in fact, inform the writing; moreover, in 'Sick Men Die' there were titillating echoes of two other bourgeois artists: Gilbert and Sullivan – much to the bemusement of the class (Ex.18.4).

Ex.18.4. From 'Sick Men Die'.

Cardew also contributed a setting of 'Change the World: It Needs It' from *The Measures Taken* for soloist and three-part women's chorus (a 'girly chorus [...] the kind of thing which could divide audience opinion' in Robert Coleridge's judgement). (Ex.18.5). Here the austerity and grandeur of Brecht's poetry, which itself, through the pressing inclusion of the idea of 'need' animates and intensifies the most famous of Marx's dicta, enshrined in stone in Highgate cemetery, suffers a double dereliction: the loss, through translation, of Brecht's language, and a musical setting eminently more suited to a happy-clappy, new-age religious meeting – a music with a Caribbean 'flavour' (reggae was in vogue at the time) which (wilfully?) trivialises Brecht's text. The latter, whatever the criticisms levelled at it from within the Goldsmiths' class – its depressing content, its contentiousness – nevertheless merited a treatment commensurate with its poetic, and political, authenticity. Instead, it was eviscerated: a sacrificial exercise in an undigested, popular music style.

Ex.18.5. From 'Change the World: It Needs It'.

Why did Cardew act in such a cavalier manner? Was it a deliberate ploy to expose and undermine a 'revisionist' text? An act of iconoclasm? A shot across the bows of the Brechtian canon? Cardew had already placed his 'reply' to the first verse of Brecht's *Song of the United Front* in the aforementioned communal scrapbook:

12/4/76
A man must have a little bite to eat?
No! Our hunger is for justice.
After a hard day's work a man deserves a bit of peace and quiet?
No! He deserves to run the country.

Next to this is a brief exchange from a TV interview with the brother of Frank Stagg, the Irish hunger-striker: 'Why did he die?' 'He hungered for justice'.

Or was it a misconceived essay in *Verfremdungseffect* (alienation effect)? We note how the voice leaps up the octave at the beginning of the phrase 'sink down in the filth' ('Versinke in Schmutz'). The question is: what effect does the musical setting have on the audience's reception of the text? And why omit the last line of the poem: 'Wer bist Du?' ('Who are you').

Bearing in mind the vehemence and single-mindedness of the Party's ongoing 'struggle' against 'revisionism', such speculative submissions cannot be dismissed out of hand. The political referents who appeared to be the closest ideologically were also (therefore) the most dangerous; Brecht would not have emerged unscathed from the discussions in the class, even if the charge of 'revisionism' in relation to, for example, *The Measures Taken* (an 'anti-revisionist' play *par excellence*), would be extremely difficult to sustain. 'Pessimism is a tool of the ruling class' Cardew had pronounced; perhaps it was this maxim which expressed the essence of his objection to Brecht's 'revisionism'.

Yet despite the fact that the German master's work is so palpably theoretically based, there is much in Brecht that Cardew would have found compelling – and not least in the *Lehrstücke*.[27]

Firstly, in its critique of 'incorrect' revolutionary attitudes and practice (in the *persona* of the 'young comrade' in *The Measures Taken*) it advances the idea that the (artistic) portrayal of the socially and politically negative can play an important role in the revolutionary movement. As we have seen in Cardew's own praxis during the early seventies the development of a critique of 'wrong ideas', in his case in relation to artistic expression (rather than, as in Brecht's case here, political behaviour), was considered an invaluable and necessary contribution.

Secondly, its didacticism: a new convention of engaging actors, musicians and audience in discussion, providing practice in dialectical thinking, thereby initiating a process of self-education; the aim to heighten class consciousness, to propagate the teaching of the Communist classics, and to promote the desirability of world revolution. In Eisler's words: 'art as an educator in class struggle' – all of which we have witnessed in the latter years of the Scratch Orchestra, in the Id Group discussions and the debates surrounding the Promenade Concert versions of Paragraphs 1 and 2 of *The Great Learning*.

Thirdly, the necessity for self-denial: in Act 2 of *The Measures Taken* the young comrade is commanded to obliterate his personal features in order to merge with the Chinese masses. In Cardew's Journals from the early seventies onwards there is constant reference to the negation of bourgeois traits, to purging bourgeois thoughts, sentiments and reactions, to the priority of remoulding one's world outlook. Moreover, the young communist in *The Measures Taken* operates incognito:

> Who would not do great things for glory; but who
> Would do them for silence?...
> And glory seeks in vain
> For the doer of great deeds.
> Step forward
> For one moment
> Unknown and hidden faces, and receive
> Our thanks![28]

And it goes further back, into the sixties; the idea of 'self-invention' was an integral part of the ethos of AMM, one in a succession of moral imperatives, a symbiotic accumulation which exemplifies in a compelling manner the line of transmission through from Cardew's early humanism, embodied in the indeterminate scores of the early sixties, to his espousal of Marxism-Leninism.

Fourthly, the Party, the apotheosis, the *sine qua non* of revolutionary progress and achievement. In *The Measures Taken* the relationship of the individual to the collective (the Party) is put under sharp scrutiny: the young comrade, convinced he is right, becomes 'an individual', thereby isolating himself from his comrades; this they see as a more serious transgression than acting mistakenly.

> Do not go the right way without us
> Without us it is
> The wrong way.
> You must stay with us![29]

The plight of the young comrade, his alienation from the Party, recalls Cardew's own, previously quoted 'confessional', 'Fight Self – Repudiate Revisionism', from the previous year, in which there are persistent, self-deprecatory references to this relationship; even the language has a Brechtian tone:

In countless cases I've been guided by self in dealings with the Party.
Setting my own thoughts up against the Party's line.
Being negligent about security – not thinking that my recklessness can damage the Party.
Having a passive attitude of relying on the masses and then having no proper regard for the Party.
Setting myself up against the Party by having a negative critical attitude to Party utterances.[30]

And so forth. 'The reflex of self-scrutiny', George Steiner wrote, 'in the name of ethical absolutes is, once more, a characteristically Western, post-Voltairian act'.[31]

In respect of the young comrade's actions, when he rejects the four agitators' (the Party's) advice, and of Cardew's self-abasement, there is also a clear reference to Lenin's *"Left-Wing" Communism, an Infantile Disorder*, which Cardew certainly would have known, and in particular to Lenin's analysis of 'petty-bourgeois revolutionism'.

This is characterized by sectarianism which leads to the isolation of the masses, often combined with a resistance to forming a political army out of those who have been deformed by capitalism. The rejection of any politics of realism or of compromise and above all of Party discipline means that this attitude becomes not only useless but damaging too. It fails to comply with that maxim for political action which requires a combination of firmly held principles with flexibility of methods.[32]

Fifthly, sacrifice: for Cardew the idea, the reality and the ineluctability, of *sacrifice* was part of his communist credo. Chris Johnstone, who directed the plays, recalls: 'I don't remember him being present at rehearsals very much. He was however clear that the idea of sacrifice in *The Measures Taken* was an important one to make clear to audiences'.[33] And in fighting, heart and soul, to the death, for a cause, an ultimate cause according to one's own cosmology, a condition of relativity is conferred upon all other aspects of one's life: 'He who fights for communism has of all virtues only one: that he fights for communism'.[34] For the four agitators the 'ends' (proletarian revolution) justify the 'means' (the sacrifice of the young comrade): a grim and malevolent precept spawned and honoured by an absolutist cast of mind. Cardew was mentally and psychologically prepared for such sacrifices, and in the remaining pages of this book the word 'sacrifice', as a moral imperative (and examples of which, by human beings in moments of supreme heroism, most readers can summon up), recurs time and again. But does the relationship between 'ends' and 'means' need to be so sharply antithetical? Is there not a *dialectical* relationship between 'ends' and 'means'? Cannot, should not, the ends also *embody* the means? And could not, therefore, a Party strategy involving the slaughter of thousands, including its own supporters, be retrospectively invalidated? Was there a viable (communist) alternative to the battle of Stalingrad? In which case could the Russians have survived, and not just physically, occupation? But even to pose such an hypothesis, speculating in sedentary, well-fed comfort; is that not itself an act of presumption, of gross condescension? For are not the 'means' determined (dictated) by cultural traditions (of resistance); the traditions of war, violence, etc. the *ultima ratio* to which western 'civilization' irrevocably resorts? Thus, in *The Measures Taken,* having shot the young comrade, the four agitators proclaim:

It is a terrible thing to kill.
We would not only kill others, but ourselves as well, if the need arose.
For violence is the only means whereby this deadly
World may be changed, as
Every living being knows.[35]

Still the question gnaws away at us and we should not flinch from asking it: Recalling that the execution of erring and psychologically 'flawed' comrades was (and still is) commonplace in the extreme circumstances of the battlefield, was there a rational, morally preferable alternative to the execution of the young comrade? In the context of *correct* political behaviour was it an *avoidable* fatality? And here we come back to the 'reality' of the play: it is this 'avoidableness' which is the crux, militating against the perceived emphasis on the use of violence and also underlining the parabolic nature of the play.[36] As Eisler said to one objector: 'Der stirbt doch gar nicht, der junge Genosse, der steht auf der Bühne...' (The young comrade does not die; he's standing there on the stage). He does not die; rather, he loses face. In other words *The Measures Taken* is not 'a tragedy'; it is a 'study text' (Lehrstück). And this in turn throws into relief the need to analyse and comprehend, from Cardew's standpoint, that is, from a Marxist-Leninist standpoint, the aetiology, not only of 'incorrect' political behaviour, but also of its 'treatment'.

These were some of the contentious issues which would have been discussed in Cardew's class at Goldsmiths and which, forty-five years earlier, had provoked such intense public controversy, both outside and within the communist movement, when *Die Massnahme,* this great synthesis of Brechtian theatre and Hanns Eisler's political music, was first performed at the Berlin Philharmonic in December 1930. Such was the fall-out, not least the work's perceived divisiveness within the working class movement itself, that it was agreed by Brecht and Eisler that the work should be withdrawn from the public domain. In 1958, two years after Brecht's death, Eisler prohibited a projected performance in London; it was not until the 1980s that permission was finally granted to perform *Die Massnahme* publicly in London.

This *cause célèbre* in itself merits lengthy documentation and discussion but I have dealt with the matter of necessity in a somewhat circumscribed and truncated manner – that is, in so far as it reflected the stage of Cardew's political development at the time and impinged upon his musical activities. In fact the 'Songs for our Society' class survived its posthumous collaboration with Brecht, continuing to function until 1977, and its subsequent activities embraced a wide range of music-making at multifarious venues.[37] So that before leaving Goldsmiths' College and 'Songs for our Society' we should recall one such occasion as experienced by Jim Ward, a stalwart member of the class. Because it is an accurate and authentic description of the kind of work that Cardew was involved in, as well as demonstrating the *fact* of his participation in the struggles of ordinary, working people, including, in this particular case, those that had been incarcerated, I reproduce Jim Ward's text in full:

Six years ago I wanted to write a song for Angela Davis[38] and bought a Penguin, *The Soledad Brother: The Prison Letters of George Jackson*.

After reading it I wrote the song 'Eleven Long Years', now called 'The Ballad of George Jackson', in June 1971. James Phillips, who sings very much like Paul Robeson, recorded the song on tape for me. Now I have been attending a class at Goldsmiths' College, New Cross: 'Songs for our Society', tutor and conductor, Cornelius Cardew.

Cornelius asked for prison songs for a singing engagement at Brixton Prison Medical Wing. I remembered that William Gallagher in his published poems *Relaxation* (November 1950) had a poem called 'Dartmoor', so with one finger at the piano I composed music for the poem, trying to see it from the viewpoint of a prisoner with a life sentence. I was encouraged by the fact that he [Cardew] had persuaded me in spite of my protests to try and compose the music for 'The Textile Workers' song' in '*The Measures Taken*' by Brecht, and my astonishment after hearing it on my cassette; by continuous replay I transcribed it.

At the next week's class they rehearsed it and then sang it in the public performance of the Brecht play.

It made me realise the hidden potential never given a chance of expression among thousands of workers, young and old. The lack of ability to write the melody line, to capture it on paper, the frustration of hours later trying to recall the tune, and finding you had lost it. This means going below the level of a mixed choir, to the individual worker; the blending and coming together of the Musicians' Union and politically conscious worker songwriters. I have sufficient evidence the latter exist from my researches which go back to 1868 and the birth of the TUC. I think that a myth has been built up by some writers, like Christopher Caudwell and Ernst Fischer, that workers do not like or write poetry.

To return to the present, C. Cardew knocked me up one Sunday morning to tell me of the engagement to sing at Brixton Prison. I was to do two songs, 'The Ballad of George Jackson' and a Hackney Folk Song 'Where the Waters Do Flow', one I wrote for the Borough's 1974 Poetry Competition. I typed fresh copies which made me late. It was a smashing experience. We performed at the end of a corridor with brightly painted walls, cells either side, facing our audience seated on chairs in the centre, with warders and hospital orderlies and staff on the right side, others watching from three tiers of balconies. We had six instrumentalists and two mikes; it was a 45 minute performance, and ended with solo performances – I was second soloist. Cornelius sang them the chorus of 'Where the waters do flow, Down in the valley, Where the waters do flow'. I introduced both songs. Whether it was the atmosphere I don't know, but I sang the ballad (first time for five years) as I've never sung before with such feeling. I had counted seven or eight black workers in the audience, the acoustics were very good and I was aware of those listening on the landings. While singing I decided to sing the third verse that had been written months later. It ended with much vocal applause.

Some of our members said it was rather strong (with its references to racist pigs and fascists in the prison service). A prisoner told me (I presume with permission) that an inmate on one of the landings above would like a copy of the ballad. I was pleased and immediately took out the new typed copy and autographed it.

It wasn't till the stereo tape cassette recording was played back in a member's home that I realised how 'strong' some of the lines were. The song was unaccompanied.

In the introduction I mentioned that George Jackson was murdered by prison warders, and talked of the racism in American prisons. The lines '...against a racist creed, The best defence is attack against a fascist breed' came over clearly. No wonder they cheered at the end. 'More, more'. It wasn't till I heard James Phillips, a black South African, sing the ballad, that I realised that one could be emotionally moved by one's own song. Is it rare? Have others had the same experience? To be apolitical where racism and fascism is, whether one realises it or not, in a multi-racial society means aiding the racists and Vorster's Apartheid.[39]

The concert, in which Eddie Prévost and Keith Rowe took part, also included some Irish songs; the enthusiastic reception given to a rendering of *Up and Over the Wall,* a song about a prison break-out, may well have reflected a high proportion of Irish prisoners. Although as Prévost recalls, with a more worldly, slightly louche perspective that advancing years tends to stimulate, 'it was my observation that many of the prison audience seemed to be mostly attentive to the presence of the women in the band!' Perhaps we should simply accept the optimistic view: that sensual arousal and revolutionary ardour are not necessarily mutually exclusive. At the end a discussion with the inmates ensued; as they were being led away the musicians followed them, continuing to talk through the bars of the cells.

Apart from the Brecht project Cardew contributed other songs to the 'Songs for our Society' repertoire, including 'Nothing to Lose but our Chains' and 'Consciously', for which he also wrote the lyrics, which are certainly among the more successful from his political songs. The latter is a militant, forceful song driven at a fast tempo by a strong feeling of revolutionary urgency and the need for 'conscious' organisation of the struggle. The Chinese imagery is still there: 'knocking out the dragon's teeth and planting them in the ground [...] the foolish old man and his sons thrust their spades into the ground'. It begins with a four bar instrumental introduction in unison:

Ex.18.6. From 'Consciously'.

'Nothing to Lose but our Chains', based on Marx's famous dictum, is an interesting essay in word setting, in that it attempts to show the same words from different, opposing standpoints: (Ex.18.7a-e). It begins in the minor mode with mock solemnity, even pathos, declaiming the demise of the capitalist system:

Ex.18.7a. From 'Nothing to Lose but Our Chains'.

Then in the major, echoing Marx – 'we have nothing to lose but our chains', although the incongruous accentuation on 'lose' does jar.

Ex.18.7b.

The ascending sequence, to the same words, followed by 'we have a world to win', is more persuasive:

Ex.18.7c.

In fact, 'we have nothing to lose' is set to three different musical phrases, the third being:

Ex.18.7d.

which in performance evokes, inappropriately, feelings and associations of sadness, resignation, yearning. Perhaps this can in part be attributed to the jazz idiom in which it is cast. On the CD the excellent pianist and bassist, Huw Warren and Laurie Baker, perform in the inimitable style of the 'jazz standard'.[40]

The coda, in E major, transforms the opening of the song so that it represents the authentic standpoint of the 'masses of the people' as they are roused to revolution by the imminent doom of capitalism ('conditions are excellent'). But in relation to the song as a whole it is too brief; disconcertingly, the music itself lacks conviction, unredeemed by a final flourish:

Ex.18.7e.

The Journals note a talk and performance at Trent Polytechnic in north London on 8 October, and PLM recordings and three concerts at Unity Theatre which saw the re-publication, with a few additions and omissions, of the anti-fascist song book of the previous August.[41] Four concerts had been scheduled – on the 3, 4, 5, and 6 November, but the final date, the sixth, had been double-booked with a play by Helena Stevens, and the PLM concert was duly cancelled. In fact, on the night/morning before the play, Unity Theatre was burnt down and neither play nor concert took place. It was a hectic time; there were many rehearsal sessions for the Unity Theatre concerts as well as meetings with Frances Rifkin's Recreation Ground and Belts and Braces theatre companies.[42]

The year, and an era, ended with another terse entry in the Journals: 'Dec.9th. Divorced from Stella'.

Notes and references

1   Jrnl. April 1975-February 1976, 25 May.
2   Roosevelt University was followed by the University of Akron, Ohio on 10 January before crossing the border, via Buffalo, to Canada: York University, Toronto, 15 January; University of Toronto, 16 January; then across to the west coast, the University of British Columbia, 20 January; the Simon Frazer University, Vancouver, 21 January; the Vancouver School of Art, 22 January; then down into California: University of California at San Diego, 23 January; Mills College, Oakland, 25 January; University of California at Santa Cruz, 28 January; and the last Californian engagement, at Stanford University, on 29 January. Then back to the east coast for a live broadcast at New York WBAI, 1 February; Dartmouth College, Hanover, 3 February; Harvard University, 4 February; The Kitchen, New York, 5 February; the State University of New York at Albany, 6 February; and finally, the Philadelphia School of Music, 7 February.
3   Letter from CC to SK, dated 15 January 1975.
4   Letter from CC to SK, dated 23 January 1975.
5   Letter from CC to SK, dated 11 January 1975.
6   Ian McQueen recalls the fortepianist Melvyn Tan (then a student at the RCM) 'walking around the canteen, ceremoniously ripping up the concert flyers!!' As recounted to Robert Coleridge sometime in 2004.
7   Jrnl. April 1975–February 1976, dated 25 May 1975.
8   Ibid.
9   Ibid.
10   Ibid, from notes entitled 'The Composer's Role'.
11   A reference to theatre critic, Kenneth Tynan.
12   Sheila Kasabova's sole recollection is of a cold, grey, windy day, and of Cardew stripping off and plunging naked into an extremely cold North Sea.
13   Two email communications from HSK to JT, 16 April 2003.
14   From a letter from CC to HSK, dated 5 June 1975. The reference to a (renewed?) interest in 'improvisation' may also have been a contrivance to re-establish links with the past, although the kind of improvisation he would have had in mind at that time would almost certainly have been in relation to his work with PLM where, within strict limits, he could elaborate the material through variational techniques. It surely could not have been 'free improvisation'.
15   From a recorded conversation with JT in the late nineties.
16   From a letter from Krystyna Roberts to EP, dated 12 June 1992.
17   We may recall that this was the point made about the sculptures which were summarily dismissed by passers-by in Cardiff during the discussion at the Art School in May 1972.
18   Walter Benjamin, 'Theses on the Philosophy of History', in *Illuminations,* ed. by Hannah Arendt (Fontana/Collins, 1979), pp. 255-266 (p.258).
19   Here the debate would have foundered on the rock of the incompatibility of the two men's perceptions of the nature and role of the 'working class'; it is unlikely that Jack would have shared Cardew's belief in the historic destiny of the working class, in its role as emancipator; nor in the crucial Marxist concept of 'class consciousness'. He (Jack) would more likely have drawn attention to its dissolution and fragmentation, and, ominously, to the waning

power and influence of the larger trade unions. The increasing categorisation and differentiation of groups within the 'working class' also necessitated further clarificatory distinctions which in turn, already in the seventies, was used to undermine the notion and practice of 'solidarity'.

20   In a school I taught in in the East End of London in the sixties the pupils contemptuously dismissed all classical music as "bleedin' opera". But I believe this designation owed more to its perceived social status than to its artistic content.

21   In one of his cardboard files I discovered nine pages of notes on 'History of Germany, 1715-1815'.

22   Shortly after the meeting with Lloyd an unspecified and so far untraceable occasion at Bristol Polytechnic on 23 September is dismissed in the Journals, colourfully, as a 'fuck up'.

23   Sheila Kasabova, who accompanied Cardew, recalls that the 'hooded Spanish revolutionaries' materialized in the Como event. Rzewski cannot recall what his and Cardew's contribution was. Furthermore he has no recollection of being in Naples. Either this event did not happen, or Cardew went there on a solo mission. In 2003, at the time of writing this footnote, Rzewski's refreshingly cynical characterisation of the young revolutionaries as 'young Molotovs who are now doctors, lawyers, and bankers (or academic composers)' may not be far from the truth, but I have no means of verifying his claim.

24   Goldsmiths' College, one of the UK's leading universities for creative studies, was founded in 1891 and has been part of the University of London since 1904.

25   If, as has been suggested, it was his intention to exploit the talents and proclivities of particular individuals in the group, he of all people was capable of generating a creative, authentic music-making with whatever means and material were at his disposal.

26   Mutable Theatre Company was formed in 1975 by Chris Johnstone and Phil Young. Their original aim was to create shows for specific communities (school children, pensioners, etc.) in the Southwark area of south-east London.

27   Lenin himself wrote of the 'British dislike of theory', and not without a grudging hint of admiration: 'With their dislike of abstract theory and their pride in their practicality, the British often pose political issues *more directly*, thus helping the socialists of other countries to discover the actual content *beneath* the husk of wording of every kind (including the 'Marxist')'. From *Lenin on Literature and Art* (Moscow: Progress Publishers, 1970), p.111.

28   Bertolt Brecht, *The Measures Taken* (London: Methuen, 1977), p.14.

29   Ibid, p.28.

30   Jrnl. April 1974-July 1974, undated (probably towards the end of May).

31   *In Bluebeard's Castle*, p.55.

32   *Hanns Eisler, Political Musician,* p.100.

33   Email communication to JT in the latter part of 2004.

34   *The Measures Taken*, p.13.

35   Ibid, p.32.

36   Eisler described *Measures Taken* as a parable; like Hans Christian Andersen and the brothers Grimm. Perhaps Shakespeare, too. But it was not universally recognised as such and to his and Brecht's chagrin was used as anti-communist propaganda.

37   According to Robert Coleridge the class was still running in the Autumn term of 1977. Nobody I have spoken to can recall when and why it finally closed. No records have

been kept at Goldsmiths' College.

38 Angela Davis (b. Birmingham, Alabama, 1944), Afro-American writer and political activist.

39 Jim Ward, 'Experiences of an Amateur Songwriter'; printed in the Workers' Music Association Bulletin, Christmas 1976.

40 The CD *We Only Want The Earth* was released on the *musicnow* label in 2001.

41 An undated, anti-fascist song in Cardew's hand (though not necessarily composed by him) and with the title 'The Enemy', or possibly 'United', has survived but does not merit our consideration; nor has anybody claimed any knowledge of it.

42 Belts and Braces was one of the most prestigious political companies – like 7:84. They used political scripts, new and old, and their productions were often spectacular, popular, exciting. (For an account of Belts and Braces refer to Cathy Itzin's *Stages in Revolution*).

Cornelius Cardew a life unfinished

19

The PCA in Ireland 1976

'No nation which oppresses another can itself be free.' Karl Marx

1976 began in a militant vein with a very well attended Music of Resistance concert, equally militantly advertised by Keith Rowe's poster, at the St Pancras Town Hall, London, on 22 January. The programme consisted of four items: Cardew's *Thälmann Variations* (played by Frederic Rzewski), Rzewski's *Coming Together/Attica* and *No Place to Go but Around,* and piano transcriptions of three arias from the Chinese opera *The Red Lantern* by Yin Cheng-tsung. Together with Rzewski and Cardew, who recited the text in *Coming Together,* Laurie Baker, John Marcangelo, Evan Parker and Paul Rutherford also took part in this event which, although it was recorded by the BBC ('with very meagre resources' according to Laurie Baker), was in fact never broadcast.

The day after the Music of Resistance concert, 23 January, was the occasion of the second Cardew concert at the Royal College of Music, almost a year after the first concert. Rzewski gave a repeat performance of *Thälmann Variations,* as well as, an added bonus, Eisler's *Piano Sonata No.3*; even the Director of the RCM, David Willcocks, could not resist joining issue in the 'hard-hitting' (political) discussion which ensued and which continued afterwards, unabated, in the College canteen. Such hallowed institutions as the Royal College of Music, and Cardew's own alma mater, the Royal Academy of Music, bathed in an oppressive atmosphere of vanity and complacency, always inspired Cardew to an elegant dismissiveness of bourgeois ostentation, and to unbridled and unimpeachable expressions of commitment to the cause of the proletariat; and this occasion was no exception.[1]

On 12 February, probably due to the vicissitudes of winter rail travel, Cardew arrived late for a talk entitled 'Criteria of Art Criticism' at the Department of Fine Art at Portsmouth Polytechnic. Members of staff, in particular Fine Art lecturer Jeffrey Steele, were experiencing difficulty in holding the mainly student audience, who were beginning to show their impatience and drift away, and when he did finally arrive Cardew was in a 'rather bad mood'.[2] Perhaps he had been informed of the death, on that day, of the Irish hunger striker, Frank Stagg; this would certainly have fired his anger and intensified his negative mood, however unknowing, however innocent his audience may have been in relation to this particular event. According to Steele Cardew dealt dismissively with a number of questions, and when he, Steele, intervened to raise the issue of form and content – in this instance, the (contradictory) relationship between the virtuosic piano technique displayed in *Thälmann Variations* and the life and work of Thälmann the communist – his guest rounded on him, insisting that virtuosity-as-such was an idealist conceit and that in this case virtuosity *served* the revolutionary content of the music.[3]

A year earlier Scratch Orchestra member Stefan Szczelkun had also raised the issue of virtuosity and 'concert music', regretting Cardew's dismissal of all Scratch music-making. And in a letter to Cardew, dated 25 January 1976, a few days after the St Pancras Town Hall concert, which he had attended and enjoyed, Szczelkun contrasted the informality of Scratch activity – in terms of venues and modes of music-making, and the potential of sophisticated musical notations such as *The Great Learning,* in which nobody is excluded and which encourages participation – with the virtuosic works by Cardew and Rzewski performed by a musical elite at the St Pancras Town Hall. The Scratch modes of music-making, in Szczelkun's opinion, were a more direct, grassroot challenge to bourgeois social relations, and a more powerful musical 'carriage' of revolutionary ideas, both for the performers and for the audience. Szczelkun saw the danger, well-founded, that the St Pancras Town Hall music could and would be absorbed by the establishment (Radio 3 exposure) and rendered harmless. 'Please don't reject lessons of Scratch' he concluded.[4]

On 15 February an augmented PLM band (Baker, Cardew, Rowe, Tony Hicks, Alec Hill, Geoff Pearce, Vicky Silva and Dave Smith) performed at a conference in Nottingham, an Afro Association event in which Frances Rifkin's Recreation Ground Theatre Company participated. It was also the occasion of the first public performance of Cardew's new song 'A Law of History' (to a text by Mao Tse-tung), used later as the basis for a larger ensemble work: *Vietnam's Victory.* And just over a month later, on 20 March, in a huge protest against rising unemployment, people from all over the country descended upon London on a 'Right to Work' march. PLM performed on the back of their van from

Shepherds Bush to the Royal Albert Hall, the live music much appreciated. Requests were made by the marchers that they should play at the final rally inside the Royal Albert Hall but, for whatever reason, this did not materialise.

Between 1 March and 17 April *The Measures Taken* and *The Exception and the Rule* were toured with the Mutable Theatre Company and 'Songs for our Society', ending with a run, 13-17 April, at the Roundhouse Downstairs in Chalk Farm.[5] The plays were performed in a downstairs space, rather than in the main upstairs auditorium, and the musicians were on a platform behind the audience. After every performance a discussion ensued; Robert Coleridge, who participated as keyboard player in the performances, recalls that 'responses to the music (varied) hugely from people who loved it and returned to hear it again to people who found it counter-revolutionary and probably a bit amateur'.[6]

Cardew missed most of the performances, including those at the Roundhouse; for part of the time he was away in Italy – three concerts for MLS (a leftist student group, according to Rzewski, possibly 'Movimento di Liberazione Studentesca'): in Siena (5 April), Brescia (9 April), and Milan (10 April, with Rzewski). From 19-26 April he was in Germany, and on 23 April he and Jànos Nègyesy appeared in an ambitious duo recital at Amerika Haus in Berlin. The concert, which was under the auspices of Amerika Haus and the DAAD, included the third and fourth sonatas for violin and piano by Charles Ives (which they had recorded the year previously in Switzerland) as well as Morton Feldman's *Vertical Thoughts 2* and a work for solo violin by the American composer Maurice Weddington. On 1 May Cardew was back amongst the proletariat in London with PLM, participating in a Mayday march from Charing Cross to Hyde Park.

The Progressive Cultural Association (PCA) was founded by the Communist Party of England (Marxist-Leninist) on 7 March 1976 and was officially inaugurated in a concert at Acklam Hall in west London on 2 May. The aim was that the PCA should be organised and expanded, along with all other 'genuinely progressive culture', under the Party's leadership to 'consciously develop culture around the Party's line, and thus maximise our effectiveness in the service of the people'. A leaflet introducing the PCA announced a series of monthly public meetings and workshops; these included a talk on the class nature of the British documentary film movement; a speaker from ZANU on the struggle for national liberation in Zimbabwe (Rhodesia); a talk on the history of the actors' union, Equity, and the Musicians' Union; a 'class analysis' of the history of the theatre; and a talk by a representative of the Communist Party of England (Marxist-Leninist) on 'the present stage of the revolution in Britain'. This auspicious event consisted of performances by People's Liberation Music (PLM) and Recreation Ground, which performed two plays: *United We Stand,* an anti-racist play by Party member Chris Coleman, and *Seeing Red,* a play about communists leading a trade union struggle, written collectively by Frances Rifkin, Sarah Boyes and Sue Granville.

Like most of Recreation Ground's activities *Seeing Red,* which was toured extensively and successfully, fell foul of Party ideologues for its 'revisionism'. Yet Frances Rifkin was to remain a member of PCA for another two years – her independence of spirit, her refusal to allow her artistic judgements to be compromised, militated against a cosy, subservient relationship with the Party and opened a vein of mistrust. She did acquire a patina of acceptance from the Party but she was prevented from visiting what was perceived as her political indulgencies on the PCA, which prevailed upon its members to expose the vagaries of bourgeois existence and to expunge all traces of revisionism. The Party ordained; the artist ministered. The Party issued into artistic life and spread about it an air of certitude, of authority and virtue. The inner machinations of the PCA, like all Party-run or Party-initiated organisations, were shrouded in mystery.

United We Stand, first published in the Irish Marxist-Leninist Party journal *Nua Chultúr,* is set in an English industrial city and, in the words of the introduction to the play, concerns 'the British Government's use of racism against the Irish people, both in order to try and divide the workers in England and so smash their struggles and also to attack the Irish national liberation struggle itself – under the hoax of attacking "terrorism".' The play is a dramatisation of a political line. For the Party, at that time, art was prescriptive; there was no educative process; the Party presided over apodeictic sessions of indoctrination. For the artist this meant to espouse meliorism and to depict faithfully the tenor of life under a revolutionary proletarian dispensation. *United We Stand* was a facsimile of life as the Party saw it, or rather as it wanted it to be seen. The aim was to 'inform', to present the Party line on Ireland with clarity and conviction in a way which could be more 'influential', more irresistible, than an article in a journal. In evaluating the play the cold recognition and acceptance of its political correctness was all that mattered; the possibility of false readings could not be countenanced. PCA member Hugh Shrapnel stalwartly praised the play's potency: 'I recall that the play was very effective dramatically, well written with good characterisation – individual people the audience could identify with, so that the political message came over strongly'.[7]

Nevertheless, to return briefly to our discussion of the *Lehrstücke,* Coleman's play, for all its solid virtues, does not, in my view, *engage* the mind of his audience in the way that Brecht does with, for example, his tightly argued critique of false revolutionary consciousness in *The Measures Taken*, although the argumentative, agnostic listener might well have taken issue with some of the premises in Coleman's play – a response which could be viewed as a measure of the play's strengths. Perhaps, after all, what manifests itself here is an historico/cultural difference: the German propensity for theoretical thought (Kant, Marx) as opposed to Anglo-Saxon mistrust of, and impatience with, abstract theory (as a brake, an unnecessary constraint on *practice*) and, to repeat Lenin's words, 'their pride in their practicality'.

PLM's contribution to the event included a performance of Cardew's song 'A Law of History' (which had received its first performance the previous February), sung by Vicky Silva with the composer at the piano (Ex.19.1a-c). 'A Law of History' (1975) is a song to words from the last paragraph of Mao Tse-tung's Statement of May 20th, 1970: 'People of the World, Unite and Defeat the US Aggressors and all their Running Dogs'. It begins quasi-recitative with a highly expressive, pentatonic, ascending line played on the piano. The first statement, 'a weak nation can defeat a strong, this is a law of history', is solidly cast in four-bar phrases over chord changes derived from jazz:

Ex.19.1a. From 'A Law of History'.

A middle section raises the tempo; the busy accompaniment, beginning with fast triplets, enhances the sense of revolutionary urgency and optimism: 'Facts prove that a just cause enjoys abundant support.'

Ex.19.1b.

The song, in ternary form, returns to a modified version of the first section and ends with the pentatonicism of the very opening with voice and piano in unison:

Ex.19.1c.

Hugh Shrapnel, who was present at this inaugural concert, comments:

This caused quite a stir in these revolutionary circles because it was the first revolutionary 'art' song, that is, the first song to be written in a relatively complex and developmental musical idiom. This represented a real breakthrough from the simple folk-like tunes of the revolutionary songs hitherto performed at Party gatherings and rallies. Possibly, some of the party comrades found the musical idiom too 'sophisticated' and therefore 'bourgeois'; I personally think this is yet another example of Cor's extraordinary capacity to break out and make a decisive leap into something new.[8]

Soon after this event, in April, Cardew completed his *Vietnam Sonata*. The following text appears on the first page of the score:

This Sonata celebrates the resplendent victory of May 1975. The outside movements are based on two songs I wrote in connection with the Vietnam war. The first – entitled 'Law of History' – describes how the people of a small country can defeat aggression by a big country, if only they dare to rise in struggle, take up arms and grasp in their own hands the destiny of their country. The song which provides the music for the final Presto is entitled 'Revolution is the main trend in the world today'.
The middle movement, which may be played on its own, illustrates the principle that a just cause enjoys abundant support. The three themes of this Rondo are: 'The Song of the National Liberation Front of South Vietnam' (symbolizing self-reliance), the Albanian song 'To Heroic Vietnam' (symbolizing the fraternal support of the socialist countries), and 'The People of Vietnam', a song written by members of the Kreuzberg Vietnam Committee in West Berlin (symbolizing the internationalism and solidarity of the democratic people in the imperialist heartlands).

The opening of the Sonata stays close to the song; the theme is played an octave higher against a low bass line (Ex.19.2a). A left-hand cadenza leads to the lively middle section ('innumerable facts prove that a just cause enjoys abundant support'), marked 'quick, sharp', in which much of the triplet figuration from the song accompaniment is used and developed, with sequences of repeated chords sustaining the momentum and with fragments of the melodic line from the song highlighted (Ex.19.2b).

Ex.19.2a. From The *Vietnam Sonata*, 1st movement.

Ex.19.2b.

In the return of the first section the second phrase of the theme is presented in a characteristically pianistic transformation, and this is followed by a highly dissonant section, treated canonically, in which the harmonic synchronisation between the hands is disrupted (Ex.19.2c):

Ex.19.2c.

The movement ends with five improvisatory phrases (preceded by the indication 'freely'), specific in character and separated by pause marks, the first of which is marked 'like a flash of lightning'.

The strong impetus which drives the second movement (four pages of which were composed, with skill and conviction, by Dave Smith) creates the impression of both turmoil and resolve (Ex.19.3a-c). Again there is a feel for voicings, often unconventional, and for contrast of register and articulation: 'legatissimo' in middle register, and 'staccatissimo' in high register are indicated. Occasionally there are stylistic allusions to the classics, to Bach and Beethoven: sequential passages and imitative counterpoint with interesting rhythmic displacements (Ex.19.3a):

Ex.19.3a. From The *Vietnam Sonata*, 2nd movement.

And there are passages of a wilful brutishness (shades of Ives?):

Ex.19.3b.

The rather pallid Kreuzberg Vietnam Committee contribution is enlivened with fast flourishes and glissandi which introduce a new dimension into the musical style:

Ex.19.3c.

The third movement is an ingenious transcription of the song 'Revolution is the main trend in the world today'; each verse is characterised pianistically. The opening bars of the song (previously quoted) are cast in toccata style ('presto leggiero') beginning (Ex.19.4a):

Ex.19.4a. From The *Vietnam Sonata*, 3rd movement.

Similarly, the melody of the phrase from the song beginning 'a new upsurge in the struggle against US imperialism' is embedded within the texture of the piano work, and marked by the composer (Ex.19.4b):

Ex.19.4b.

And the movement/work ends with a modified version of the opening, 'Revolution is the main trend' marked *prestissimo possibile*.

In the *Vietnam Sonata* there are multiple references to a wide variety of music: 'The Yellow Submarine', 'Back in the USSR' and the 'standards' from his apprenticeship playing in London pubs with Fred Bryne vying and jostling for space and presence with the 'alla Marcia' of late Beethoven. (And speaking of marches, let us not forget the inestimable influence of Hanns Eisler.) There is a palpable, Beethovenian sense of strain (cf. *Thälmann Variations*) in stretches of the music, but never at the expense of flair and poetry, as well as a fair share of the unexpected. In such matters Cardew's attitude was essentially pragmatic; it was immaterial to him whether or not he was conscious of these sources when composing the music.

In the same year he wrote a companion piece, *Vietnam's Victory*, another work based on the song 'A Law of History' – this time a weighty, effectively written transcription for brass ensemble. The same harmony and much of the accompanimental counterpoint from the song is used although there is some modification in the length and ordering of the sections.

For quite different reasons Keith Rowe, too, regards 1976 as an important year for Cardew. On 1 April Cardew was persuaded, by Rowe, to take part in a Concert of Music which took place at the Drill Hall in Chenies Street WC1; the other participants included Eddie Prévost, the flautist John Wesley-Barker and the Brazilian double-bassist Marcio Mattos. Rowe called it a 'hidden' AMM concert (to a sizeable audience nevertheless), reflected also in the poster of a yellow Sc**amm**ell truck (a yellow lorry was a common early AMM image). Perhaps it was an attempt on Rowe's part to breathe life into the idea of reviving AMM although, curiously, Lou Gare was not asked to take part.

The following month, on 14 May, Cardew was in Antwerp for an International Festival of New Music, at a performance venue of extreme luxuriousness ('ultra-bourgeois' in Keith Rowe's description). Some months previously Cardew had telephoned Rowe regarding a proposal for a programme consisting of Rzewski's *Attica* and extracts from *Treatise* and had asked his advice in respect of possible co-performers. Rowe suggested saxophonist Evan Parker and drummer Dennis Smith and recalls that Cardew seemed neither enthusiastic nor embarrassed about the prospect. Sheila Kasabova accompanied them and they drove to Antwerp in a Volkswagen van.

At the rehearsal Cardew armoured himself with a supreme indifference, an offhandedness, deflecting exegetic questions about *Treatise* to Rowe, who was directing the performance. *Treatise* still enjoyed currency in the world of contemporary music as a masterpiece of graphic notation, a classic; for Cardew it was a token of bourgeois ephemerality, although he would have discharged his musical duties with consummate professionalism. Rzewski's *Attica* was included perhaps as a dubiously political counterweight to the abstract *Treatise*, as a sop to the revolutionary sensibilities of the times; it, too, we may recall, had received short shrift from Cardew in *Stockhausen Serves Imperialism*. So why did Cardew agree to take part? It may well have been for purely financial reasons; in this respect his situation was desperate, but no more than was usual. Could it have been an expression of tolerance towards his friends' and colleagues' unknowing complicity with bourgeois reaction, a propitiatory gesture towards a work, *Treatise*, he had forsworn publicly and in print?

Rowe's importunacy survived into the summer months when, from an understandable desire to revive and nourish a unique way of making music, he initiated an attempt to reconstitute AMM, and in June the group began to play together in Agar Grove; perhaps he felt that such music-making would encourage Cardew to abandon, at least temporarily, his revolutionary enthusiasms for more quietist (musical) solutions. There were a few sessions; Prévost recalls that Cardew's contributions were mainly melodic and of a tonal or modal nature, as if he were attempting to infiltrate the language and style of his later piano works into the improvisations (although this in itself did not necessarily negate the inclusive ethos of AMM music-making). But Gare was not convinced – he felt that

Cardew's contributions lacked commitment, 'heart' – and his lack of enthusiasm had a dissuasive effect on both Cardew and Prévost. The project foundered and in the New Year Gare and his family left London for Devon where they still live.

From the 27 to the 30 May Cardew returned to Boswil, Switzerland, invited on to the jury of an International Competition for composers. The jury included the Hungarian Marxist musicologist János Maróthy, the Italian composer Luca Lombardi, the Swiss composer Klaus Huber, the French pianist Gérard Frémy, the Dutch bass-clarinettist Harry Spaarnay (who also took part in the performances) and Cardew himself. The theme chosen for the seminar, 'Der Komponist als Mitarbeiter (variously translated as 'Composer as Co-worker', or 'Composer as Collaborator'), which was held at the Alte Kirche in Boswil, itself presented a problem of interpretation, both semantically and ideologically. The British contingent from the Royal College of Music, which included Robert Coleridge, Ian McQueen, Peter Devenport, Robert Kyr and Claire van Kampen, responded by submitting a portfolio of compositions which it was intended should be performed as one work. Some of these had already been performed at a Composers' Group concert at the RCM and subsequently underwent varying degrees of revision, a process which continued in the library at Boswil right up to the day of performance. Amongst them were tonal and modernist settings of two texts – one by the recently deceased Mao Zedong, the other by Victor Jara, who had been brutally murdered three years earlier in the coup in Chile which overthrew President Allende.

From the start the jury was split: the majority were supporters, protagonists, noted performers of twentieth century music, and there was considerable opposition to Cardew's view that what the RCM group had offered represented a progressive way forward for the contemporary composer. Certainly, the British students produced the most explicitly political work, interpreting the seminar theme partly as the composer working alongside 'the people' (hence the choice of texts), and partly as composers working together to create a multi-authorial work – the independently written pieces being woven into an overall continuity creating, at least in theory, a single, unified work. Various approaches were explored for collaboration between composers and performers – such as group improvisation within a given broad framework – and between the composers themselves: in the RCM group, for example, Coleridge took the melody of McQueen's modernist setting of Victor Jara's song text 'Manifesto' and reharmonised it in a tonal, more 'popular' style.

In the jury meetings Cardew fought hard for the 'political' music with some measure of success; Kyr, McQueen, Coleridge and van Kampen were invited to attend and assist in the rehearsals for the finals between 17 and 21 November. The RCM group were awarded the second prize as well as an additional 'special jury prize' – an invitation to go back to Boswil in July for further work on their project, although according to Ian McQueen, corroborated by Coleridge, 'nothing emerged out of our three weeks there'.

Robert Coleridge sums up:

> The event does however show Cor encouraging and supporting students who he felt were raising the right issues at that time [...] Ours was the only really political piece at Boswil (as I recall, the rest mostly reflected various modernist and avant-garde tendencies of the time), and its presence there and at the ICA [the following December] sparked some discussion and soul-searching which I am sure did affect a few people, even if they never became active and committed revolutionaries like Pete [Devenport] and Cor.[9]

The British contribution was also performed in a Swiss ISCM concert in Zürich just before their return to London, where it was included in a concert by Greg Rose's Singcircle at the ICA on 5 December.

In June Cardew started working for Diagram Visual Information Ltd, a publishing house in Chenies Street in central London – employment which he desperately needed and for which he was more than adequately qualified.[10] Bruce Robertson had been Art Director at Aldus Books during Cardew's stints there in the sixties and had recognised his talent and aptitude as a graphic designer. In terms of Cardew's long association with publishing this revival of the relationship, albeit on the basis of financial exigency (as it usually was), might also be construed as, as it were, 'payback time'. For just as the opportunities and experience afforded him at Aldus Books had aided, inspired and influenced his work on *Treatise* fifteen or so years earlier, now Diagram Visual Information was reaping the benefits of his years of creative experimentation with graphic scores: *Octet '61, Memories of You, Treatise, Schooltime Compositions* and *The Great Learning*. According to Robertson, Cardew was both skilful and conscientious and seemed to enjoy his work as much as anybody in the organisation. However, Robertson recalls that Cardew would invariably arrive late for work, with a demeanour of total unconcern, and then, according to his indulgent employer, would spend considerable time on the phone, speaking in a low voice and in an obviously coded language.

Cardew worked together with Ruth Midgley, who was Managing Editor, as Associate Designer, scheming diagrams, among other tasks, for an extremely intricate and challenging book entitled *Comparisons*, which was published in 1980:

This was a complex way of expressing units of number, a visual attempt to explain logorhythmic scales, all aspects of measurement: a basic encyclopaedia of numeration. Cor worked day after day visualizing it and loved the challenge.[11]

In Midgley's words: 'Cor was a stimulating and sometimes dazzling work companion, who used his great intellect and creativity to invigorate every page'.[12] Cardew had also been involved in research for a book entitled *Man's Body*, published in 1977 by Paddington Press, and worked as Co-Art Director on a publication entitled *Sports Comparisons*, which appeared in 1982. And there were translating commissions from other sources, including a German book on Impressionist Art. All this with ever-increasing, round-the-clock, heedless demands on his time and level of commitment from the Party at which he would never baulk, whatever his personal circumstances.

The likes of Cardew, and they were few, were the prop and mainstay of the Party. One lunchtime Sheila Kasabova found him asleep, through sheer exhaustion, on a small patch of grass just off the pavement on Tottenham Court Road, a very busy part of London. It has been suggested that Cardew enjoyed, indeed needed, the sedative of a routine in at least one area of his life which, in the main, was fraught with uncertainty and in a constant state of turmoil. This may well have been the case, but at the time there was an overriding need, purely and simply, for a regular, if modest, income to provide for Sheila and Anna, to contribute to the upbringing of his two sons, and, of course, to transfer amounts into the Party's coffers well in excess of normal 'Party dues'. In this respect the translation commissions, which occupied him right up to the time of his death, were just as important as his employment at Diagram Visual Information. They were among a number of things he took on, not out of a particular interest but to boost his families' fragile finances. Yet, as Sheila Kasabova recalls, he never complained, making the best of whatever opportunities presented themselves and applying himself conscientiously to the task in hand.

More encouragingly, the summer months of 1976 also saw performances of *Vietnam's Victory* and his arrangement of Handel's *Sound the Alarm* by the Royal Academy of Music Brass Group under Sidney Ellison, in July, and a visit to Brixton prison by the Goldsmiths 'Songs for our Society' class on 8 August (described above by Jim Ward).

A week later, in Birmingham, on 15 August maoist, that is, First Secretary of the Communist Party of England (Marxist-Leninist), Carol Reakes, delivered a talk to the Progressive Cultural Association with the unequivocal title: 'Politics in Command' – a rallying cry at a time when every single aspect of cultural work had to support the Party line, had to wave a banner, shout a slogan. This particular occasion may well have been in response to an ongoing 'struggle' which had been concentrating the minds of the members of the PCA for some time. According to Peter Devenport there had been meetings and discussions in an upstairs room at the Princess Alice pub in Forest Gate in east London where Frances Rifkin had put forward Engels' view that while man's cultural and artistic life did, of course, reflect the economic development and changing modes of production of the necessities of life, at times it could build up a momentum propelled by its own internal contradictions which bore little or no relation to the economic base of the society which produced it. Rifkin insisted that this was a very important point; between social developments and art there is a dialectic relationship as well as a causal (or parallel) sequence.

Cardew opposed Rifkin, insisting that it was essential to maintain a clarity of definition, that a clear line of demarcation should be drawn between bourgeois and Marxist theories of art and culture, and that this was made necessary by the ongoing ideological struggle against the insidious and pervasive influence of bourgeois culture. Moreover, in Engels' letter to W. Borgius (possibly one of Rifkin's sources) there is what might be construed as a loophole which a Jesuitical cast of mind could seize upon:

Political, juridical, philosophical, religious, literary, artistic, etc., development is based on economic development. But all these react upon one another and also upon the economic basis. It is not that the economic situation is *cause, solely active*, while everything else is only passive effect. There is, rather, interaction on the basis of economic necessity, which *ultimately* always asserts itself.[13]

The word 'ultimately' is of course crucial here (Engels himself italicises it); how far along the time continuum do we place it? At what point, and how, does the base, authoritatively and palpably, determine the superstructure, thereby attesting its *historicity*?[14]

The issue for Cardew, and the Party, was that the bourgeoisie upheld the notion of the *immanence* of art (the notion of 'ultimately' thus rendered incongruous), maintaining that culture could transcend social and economic conditions and could therefore boast a relative autonomy.[15] Cardew insisted that it was the duty of Marxists to argue strongly for an opposing, and possibly more fundamental (Maoist) view: that *all* culture is determined by the economic base. ('In the world today all culture, all literature and art belong to definite classes and are geared to definite political lines. There is in fact no such thing as art for art's sake, art that stands above classes or art that is detached from or independent of politics.'[16]) Cardew probably recognised the validity of Rifkin's argument – it was, after all, an issue over which there continues to be considerable debate, and not only within the Marxist tradition – but was convinced that it was an unnecessary concession to bourgeois ideologues, or more dangerously, a kind of bourgeois Trojan horse which would lead to further obfuscatory and time-wasting debate within communist circles in general and within the PCA in particular. True, Rifkin was running a professional, left-wing theatre company, but Cardew was responsible for implementing the tactics and strategy for revolution. In essence his opposition to Rifkin would have been implacable; moreover it would have echoed the revolutionary caveat that 'the superstructure is often the refuge of the pseudo-revolutionary dialectician, who is Marxist in all but two things: the theory of the state and the desire to change the world'.[17] The question of *class* – class struggle, class stand, etc. had become the cornerstone of Cardew's political cosmology and moreover a conscious denial of his previous existence: 'You think class is so important, but actually individuals are the most important', he remarked to his (Marxist) friend Ilona Halberstadt, sometime in the late fifties/early sixties. As we have seen in his attitude towards 'the individual' and 'class', he held two diametrically opposed views quite dogmatically at different periods of his life. But what is interesting is the *authority* which he conferred on these views, both of which, of course, were gross simplifications. He did not understand the relationship between the 'individual' and 'class', the 'individual' and 'the state', because for most of his life he had given it no thought whatsoever, at least not in political or sociological terms.

Perhaps comrade Reakes' talk on the subject was coincidental, but such ongoing debates would have been reported to her and to other high-ranking Party members, and discussed, and a formal contribution from a political heavyweight, such as the General Secretary, would certainly have served to strengthen the Party line within the PCA. According to Hardial Bains the propagation of Mao Zedong Thought ('Put Mao Tse-tung Thought in Command of Everything'[18]) was still regarded as the *sine qua non* for revolutionary advance and ultimate victory; and comrade Reakes, a protégée of Hardial Bains, was an eloquent and persuasive purveyor of the Chairman's thoughts. She had also been the object of an unbridled attack some years earlier, in Ireland, by a 'renegade' Marxist-Leninist, Brendan McSweeny, who had given vent to his fury in a letter to the Irish Party:

There was a time when perhaps the Internationalists [Irish] had potential but whatever existed was destroyed when Carol Reakes, that dogmatic, dictatorial, anti-intellectual, pragmatic philistine, finally took over [...]. Behind the façade of the proletarian party of Ireland lies a small, irrelevant and insignificant group, led by the most ignorant and arrogant people I have ever met [...]. You [the Party] through deceit used a large number of good Irish people, drained them of their money, their health and energies, and their idealism.[19]

And in our conversation in September 2003 Keith Rowe echoed McSweeny's tirade: 'Most of us, even to this day, support the basic Party line. But its implementation led literally to people dying and to the artistic death of people. It was awful. Unnecessary.' Greater Marxist-Leninists than Carol Reakes have suffered similar abuse and, in any case, it is not for this writer to pass judgement on her here and now; what is undeniable, however, is the influence she exerted, for better or for worse, on Cardew.[20]

A holiday on the Isle of Wight offered a brief but welcome respite from the travails of politics and revolution. On 23 August Cardew, with Sheila and Anna and his two sons, Keith Rowe and his two daughters, his friend Tanya and her two daughters, headed south, in two cars, and took the ferry across from Lymington to Yarmouth, a small town in the northwest of the island. Sheila's friend Amelia Fell, daughter of the historian A.J.P. Taylor, had invited them and they camped next to the family house, The Mill, which belonged to her father. Rowe recalls that Cardew seemed to be in his element: away from London, and from politics, he was relaxed, open, his demeanour and behaviour irresistibly reminiscent of the Scratch camping tours when all his material needs would be carefully deposited in a wooden fruit tray, not forgetting, as a separate item, his shaving mirror.[21] Politics and art were discussed, but not in a confrontational manner; Party statements and replies set in concrete replaced by questions and responses; inflexibility giving way to accommodation and subtlety; expressions of certainties giving way to an inquiring mode. Rowe comments: 'The Party lacked the imagination to deal with the extremely talented people that were willing to work with it.'[22] Cardew would have sniffed at 'extremely talented people'; such people abound and he would have riposted with reference to the depressing abundance of *wasted* talent. If 'talent' refuses to accept the need for revolutionary sacrifice and discipline then why should the Party waste its creative faculties on people with 'bourgeois hang-ups'? Such was the proletarian logic with which Cardew would have dispatched these 'extremely talented people' – with a proletarian flea in their ear.

That same summer, probably after the trip to the Isle of Wight, Sheila Kasabova recalls a return visit to Wenford with Cornelius, his two sons, and Anna, for a family holiday. Michael Cardew rose to the occasion and tried to create a congenial atmosphere; when Horace began to behave in an unpleasant manner towards Anna at the dinner table one evening, he rebuked his grandson reminding him that 'Anna is your sister; you should treat her accordingly', referring him to the African family tradition. However, Mariel's arrival at the pottery for the firing somehow exposed her son's vulnerability, and when Cardew, Sheila and Anna (without the boys) finally left, Sheila recalls that Cornelius sat in the car and wept. She sensed an unresolved contradiction in the relationship between

Cornelius and his mother. Perhaps Mariel had still not been able to come to terms with the replacement of Stella by Sheila within the family constellation. Or was it the fact of leaving his sons behind? This occasion, so graphically and movingly described by Sheila, was in stark contrast to his politico-musical life, the extraordinary and unreasonable demands of which he endured stoically and without question, although not, on occasions, without tears.

On their return to London Cardew immediately resumed his musical responsibilities with PLM, and on 3 September, together with a Chilean Exiles Theatre group, the band played at a social in Southall, west London, in support of the Chilean people's struggle against the fascist dictatorship which had taken over their country. It was one of several performances around that time expressing solidarity with the Chilean people. Yet even these occasions, memorable though they were, were completely overshadowed by the announcement, on 9 September, of the death of Mao Tse-tung, an event which reverberated around the world. If the politicians in the West responded to the news with varying degrees of ambivalence, there was no doubt that for millions Mao's death was seen as a catastrophic blow. The following week, on 20 September, Cardew and Sheila Kasabova, with Keith Rowe, attended a commemorative meeting at the Conway Hall in central London organised by the Party.

Within a few days Cardew was at the Venice Bienale, as a 'jobbing musician', to participate (with Frederic Rzewski) in a performance of Cage and Lejaren Hiller's *HPSCHD*.[23] He would have had no qualms about his participation (it was an engagement prompted by purely financial considerations) and would have entered the performance arena in a spirit of disinterestedness, as much observer as participant. This was a bourgeois audience which, as he had once characterised it to me in his inimitable way, 'had learnt to take their medicine'. He and Rzewski would have drawn sympathetic young Italian musicians into their conversational circle during their stay, accompanied by much eating and drinking and late nights. Rzewski comments:

I have no clear memory of the performance, but I do remember going to see a rehearsal of *Einstein on the Beach* [by Philip Glass] and sitting there with Cornelius for a couple of hours until we both got tired. Cornelius observed at one point that the show was full of charged symbols (like a train) which created the impression that the images and actions meant something, whereas they were actually empty of content.[24]

But the audience he reached out to as a communist musician awaited him the following month in Northern Ireland where PLM would perform for Nationalists and Republicans in support of their struggle against the British occupation forces.

On PLM's 1976 Irish tour Cardew also gave some solo performances and lectures. These took place towards the end of October and were coordinated with the PLM schedule. According to extant posters there seems to have been one at the Bricklayers and Stonemasons Hall, Dublin, on 28 October, and at Trinity College [Dublin] Junior Common Room the following day. Cardew also lectured/performed at the Magee College in Derry and the Royal Irish Academy of Music in Dublin, at both of which, due to inadequate efforts to publicise his visits, attendance was poor. The fee for the Magee College performance was paid for by the Arts Council of Great Britain; this was added to the kitty for the whole tour and shared with the other musicians.

In Cork, at the Music Department of University College, his illustrated talk entitled 'New music that meets the social and political needs of our time' was received warmly. After a lively discussion Aloys Fleischmann, head of music, rebutted Cardew's views but in an informal discussion after the concert he

> reminisced about his experiences as a child during the Anglo-Irish wars. In particular he recalled a British teacher of literature at Cork in those days, a venerable professor named Stockley, whose support for the cause of Irish independence was so strong that he incurred the hatred of the authorities. They sent a squad of Black and Tans gunning for him and he only escaped by a lucky accident.[25]

Cardew himself made the point that it was not only intellectuals who had supported Irish Independence, that there had been a long tradition in the British working class movement, going back to the Chartists for whom, in the 1840s, Irish Independence had been one of the key issues.

The PLM concerts, between 26 October and 3 November, were sponsored by the Culture and Art for National Independence Study Group (CANISG); the aim was to promote friendship between English and Irish working people in their struggle against British Imperialism. Along with Cardew the group included Brigid and Laurie Baker, Keith Rowe and Hugh Shrapnel. Ex-Scratch Orchestra member Rod Eley also contributed, but independently of PLM. They performed in Dublin on 28 October and again on 3 November on the steps outside Trinity College (a popular venue which had to be booked), and in Cork on 29 October. On 1 November they performed at the Andersonstown Community Centre, a Republican stronghold in Belfast, which happened to be the day of republican lawyer Máire Drumm's funeral.[26] Apart from CANISG, the Irish Prisoners Defence Club had also been involved in setting up this particular event:

> The Republican audience was lively and good-humoured; there were many families with children present and the music was warmly applauded. This homely

atmosphere was brutally broken when, during a performance of 'Lid of me Granny's Bin', towards the end of our programme, four armed British soldiers stormed in and started harassing some of the audience; however we kept on playing (it was scary!). They left fairly soon, possibly because of our presence (if it had come out in the press, it would have been politically embarrassing for both the British army in the North and the British Government). The Republicans were very friendly and hospitable and after the concert/social we were invited back to one of their homes where they regaled us with hair-raising stories of their escapes from the H block, which included one by helicopter (this giving rise to a song 'The Helicopter Song' or 'The Provie Birdie' by a group called The Wolfe Tones).[27]

During this period, from 24 October to 12 December, an ambitious series of concerts devised by Cardew in collaboration with the Institute of Contemporary Arts took place at the Institute's venue in the Mall. By using his contacts in the music world and the artistic establishment in general Cardew was seeking a consensus, a broader agenda, within which space for political content could be created. The first two concerts, on 24 and 31 October, featured six English 'experimental composers', all to a greater or lesser degree associated with the Scratch Orchestra: Christopher Hobbs and John White; Michael Parsons and Howard Skempton; Dave Smith and John Lewis. PLM performed on the 7 November, arriving by ferry from Ireland and reaching London just in time to set up and play. Understandably, the Irish theme, 'Support the Irish people', was retained in a programme which included historical Irish songs, Irish instrumental music and new songs reflecting the Irish struggle for national independence. The latter appeared in a collection entitled *We Only Want the Earth*, the second song book published by People's Liberation Music. The concert on the 28 November involved a ten piece instrumental group directed by Cardew, the vocal group Singcircle, directed by Gregory Rose, and included the aforementioned Boswil piece by the RCM students. There was also music by Erhard Grosskopf (*for Whom?*), Christian Wolff (*Wobbly Music*), Frederic Rzewski (*Struggle Song*), and John Marcangelo (*Sound and Rumour*) – the latter as part of a larger joint project by Marcangelo and Laurie Baker to commemorate the fiftieth anniversary of the 1926 General Strike.[28] In a heated discussion with the audience after the concert the Boswil compositions in particular, according to Robert Coleridge, 'came in for some heavy criticism'. By now the responses and objections to the new political music had become predictable: in essence, the 'preaching' and 'patronising' alienated sections of the audience, and the 'revolutionary' music itself was found wanting. Of course, the negative appraisal of the music was usually not unconnected with the attitude towards the revolutionary politics, in fact, towards the introduction of *any* other disciplines in a discussion of music – something which Cardew himself would frequently draw attention to.[29]

On 5 December, the penultimate concert of the series, the Progressive Cultural Association presented a programme which included *5 Anti-fascist Songs* arranged for piano solo by Dave Smith, played by Robert Coleridge; *4 Folk Songs from North Shensi* for piano solo by Yin Cheng-tsung, played by RCM student Peter Dobson; the first and second movements of Cardew's *Vietnam Sonata* played by Claire van Kampen and the composer respectively; and songs from the 'Songs for our Society' group's repertoire.[30] The obligatory discussion ensued during which little new ground was covered and few, if any, conversions were made, either to liberalism or to Mao Tse-tung Thought. Cardew had reservations about the whole enterprise; in a letter to a German comrade in Cologne, Wolfgang Hamm, he expressed his intention not to pursue these kinds of collaboration with the avant-garde, claiming that they simply strengthened the (false) idea that a revolutionary music could be forged independently of the class struggle and dismissing the idea of a 'left-avant-garde' (Grosskopf, Wolff, Rzewski, and others) as a revisionist aberration.

On 17 December a PLM concert of mainly Irish music was recorded at the Collegiate Theatre (part of University College London).[31] Laurie Baker recalls that an adaptation of an early PLM piece, *Right to Rebel*, was performed at the Collegiate concert and that it featured 'a lot of improvisation'. This would almost certainly have been improvisation in the jazz sense, that is, 'playing the changes'. Keith Rowe recalls that improvisation, in general, was a highly contentious issue in the PCA, and that Geoff Pearce, in particular, was 'against improvisation'. Rowe compares it with the Party ethos: Party discipline = the score, from which no deviations would be brooked.

Under Cardew's stewardship the Progressive Cultural Association (of which, somewhat reluctantly, he was secretary) had become a centre where left-wing artists and musicians could work together and discuss the theoretical and practical problems of developing a new culture 'in the service of the people'. PCA members included the PLM musicians and there were actors from Recreation Ground as well as individual writers, poets, artists and film makers who were loosely associated with the Party. There was dialogue and 'the battle of ideas', with socialism at the centre; a collaborative struggle towards a new and positive creativity. Unsurprisingly, it was not all plain sailing; many of the artists found the Party's cultural agenda too circumscribed, and oppressively prescriptive; one such 'fellow-traveller', Chris Johnstone of Mutable Theatre Company, who had been introduced into the PCA by Frances Rifkin, insisted on asking 'awkward' questions, thereby sealing his fate as an unwanted bourgeois interloper.

Cardew worked tirelessly and selflessly, taking responsibility for the bulk of the administrative work just as he had done in the Scratch Orchestra. He quickly identified a number of problems: in setting up various study groups too much time was spent on discussion of organisational matters and not enough on political struggle – that is, on the need to establish a 'correct' political line. There had also been a corresponding decentralisation and consequent weakening of Party influence and discipline which in Cardew's view was a dangerous development that required urgent attention and incisive action. The repercussions of Carol Reakes' speech in Birmingham the previous August were still taking their toll. The struggle to impose Mao Tse-tung Thought on all aspects of the cultural agenda – in other words, to bring everything under Party control – preoccupied Cardew. It was not easy; there was reluctance and resistance from a number of sources, and if he was drawing closer to the inner (Party) elite an increasing alienation from some rank and file supporters was the heavy price he had to pay.

Individuals, such as ex-Scratch member Alec Hill, would throw the occasional party at which records of current hits would provide a counterweight to the prevailing musical orthodoxy and the body's rhythms were re-discovered; but, as in the Scratch Orchestra, there were no bacchic extremes. Politics was never far beneath the surface although thoughts, rather than behaviour, would occasionally become disorderly. People would feel free to visit their indulgences on the occasion in a harmless manner, such as political throwaways of a risqué nature. But none of this seemed to have any purchase. Certainly there was never the chance of recapturing that dizzying sense of total possibility which characterised the sixties. One or two comrades, sipping beer, would present a smiling negativity like strict, not entirely approving parents – for this was not the ideal example of life under proletarian dispensation. And yet, we can recall that even in the pre-political days of the Scratch Orchestra Cardew discountenanced what he regarded as lightweight behaviour. Not that he lacked a sense of humour, of irony, but it would surface in unexpected contexts, and in situations where it would manifest itself in a more subtle guise.

The list of commitments during 1976 (a 'hectic period' in Laurie Baker's words) gives a clear indication of Cardew's prodigious contribution to Party and non-Party cultural work: practicing and directing rehearsals for concerts with PLM and other groups, concerts and recordings, travels abroad, composing, talks, workshops, study groups, demonstrations, marches, meetings, preparing and printing song sheets and song books, leafleting, administrative and organisational duties, and so on. PLM engagements were usually on a modest scale ('no job too small'): the Camden Tenants Association, Newham Action (related to a conference and workshops on industry, housing, racism, education, health and transport in October 1976), Waltham Forest Trades Council (also October), and so forth. When and wherever there was a perceived need in a working-class community PLM would never stint in its offer of solidarity. And it was usually much appreciated. At that time there was generally a proliferation of agitprop events, some weeks taking up a whole page of *Time Out.*[32] Demanding and exhausting though many of these activities were, there was much conviviality and, one should say, an *optimism* which sustained weary legs and minds in the relentless struggle with Capital.

Notes and references

1   In the Journals, dated 26 January 1976, "'SUGAR' Film music with Elgar Howarth" is noted, although Howarth himself has no recollection of this. Sheila Kasabova recalls Cardew working on the music in the living room at Agar Grove but has no recollection of a recording or performance. Nor has any evidence of either film or music subsequently come to light. It could have been the same film, sponsored by the General Dental Council and directed by Terence Macartney-Filgate, with Cardew's music, which had the title *Why Dentistry?*, but which has been impossible to track down.

2   In the early seventies James Allen was a part-time lecturer in History of Film at the Portsmouth College of Art. He got to know Cardew who was a visiting lecturer. When Allen became unwell, living in a tiny box room in Crouch End, Cardew was very supportive. On one occasion he sent Allen a telegram inviting him to Agar Grove. Allen had no phone.

3   Steele remained unconvinced and on another occasion questioned Cardew's use of the language of Hymns Ancient and Modern, and of rock music, describing them as two 'highly influential and corruptive musical genres closely associated with the working class'. Ironically, similar reservations were expressed, particularly in relation to rock music, by Albanian and Canadian comrades.

4   There were several members of the Orchestra, including Szczelkun himself, who, while broadly supportive of its eventual 'politicisation', nevertheless maintained that the Scratch Orchestra 'could only work within the middle class'.

5   According to Devenport and Shrapnel's list of songs, in August of 1976 Cardew wrote the song 'Proud Indians' to a text by Geronimo Sehmi, who was a member of Mutable Theatre Company. At the time of publication of this book the song remains undiscovered, although I dimly recall hearing a cassette recording of it.

6   Email communication from Robert Coleridge to JT, April 23 2003.

7   Email communication from HS to JT, mid-2003.

8   Email communication from HS to JT, April 2003.

9   Email communication from Robert Coleridge to JT, 20 July 2003.

10   Diagram Visual Information, jointly owned by Robert Chapman and Bruce Robertson, has been a registered partnership since 1960 and was incorporated in 1967.

11   Bruce Robertson, in a recorded conversation with JT on 6 November 1991.

12   Email communication from Ruth Midgley to Bruce Robertson, August 2004.

13   Letter from Friedrich Engels to W. Borgius, as quoted in *Marxism and Art*, ed. Maynard Soloman (Detroit: Wayne State University Press, 1979), p.33.

14   It is true that history provides compelling support for the thesis that the economic base is primary, that politics is the concentrated expression of economics and the superstructure protects the economic base: for example, whereas today money-lenders are the pillars of society, in the time of Shakespeare money-lending was not only a crime but also a sin. Another example: nowadays, in the era of imperialism and overproduction, self-indulgence, profligacy and waste have superseded the Victorian virtues of self-discipline, thrift and hard work.

15   In Marx's *A Contribution to the Critique of Political Economy*, there is reference to art's ability to transcend the historical moment.

16   Mao Zedang, 'Talks at the Yenan Forum', p.25.

17   *Marxism and Art,* p.543.
18   Hardial Bains, 'Combat this growing Fascism' speech from 1970 (Toronto: Norman Bethune Institute, 1976), p.15.
19   Letter from Brendan McSweeny to the Communist Party of Ireland (M-L), 16 December 1973.
20   I myself met Carol Reakes on a personal, non-Party basis only two or three times. She used our flat in Tufnell Park Road for a short period, as Cardew had done. I found her pleasant and considerate.
21   Rowe recalls that he himself forgot his shaving equipment; by the end of holiday he had a significant growth which he has never shaved off.
22   From a recorded conversation between KR and JT, 8 September 2003.
23   Cardew refers to his participation in a performance of *HPSCHD* in *Stockhausen Serves Imperialism*, pp.39-40. *(CCR)*
24   Email communication from Frederic Rzewski to JT, 28 April 2003.
25   From *Nua Chultúr*, Vol.1, no.3, Journal of the Culture and Art for National Independence Study Group (CANISG), the cultural wing of the Communist Party of Ireland (Marxist-Leninist). This issue would have appeared in November or December 1976.
26   Máire Drumm, Vice-President of Sinn Féin, was shot dead by Loyalist paramilitaries on 28 October 1976 while she was a patient in the Mater Hospital in Belfast
27   From an email from HS to JT sometime during the late nineties.
28   According to Baker, the Arts Council of Great Britain had agreed to fund the pressing of an LP record of the General Strike piece but subsequently withdrew their offer on the grounds that they didn't like it, although the project was important enough for them to attempt (unsuccessfully) to seize the master tape.
29   Robert Coleridge made the following pertinent observation: 'What I do find striking is the way that once (in the seventies) some people would seem to be upset by the idea that music wasn't some pure world which could transcend social reality; now [2003] new musicology, taking ideas from literary theory, sociology, ethnomusicology, gender studies etc, is addressing all these problems within the universities – albeit not really from a revolutionary communist perspective.' Email correspondence to JT, 7 October 2003.
30   According to the programme I had been scheduled to perform all the piano music but for reasons which I cannot recall I was indisposed.
31   A saxophonist, Jessie, joined the band for the occasion; a friend of Keith Rowe, she was involved in left-wing politics and subsequently, with her partner, went to Mozambique. The rendering of Eisler's *United Front Song* from this occasion was later included in the CD *We Only Want the Earth*.
32   *Time Out* was started by Tony Elliot in August 1968 as a guide to 'alternative' London. I remember him phoning me at our flat in Highbury and asking what the 'music experimentalists' were planning for the following week. It was beneficial for us and I suppose it also enhanced the status of *Time Out* as an indispensable journal for those interested in the 'avant-garde'.

(CCR) Also found in *Cornelius Cardew A Reader*

20
Maoist Apotheosis 1977–78

From a compositional perspective 1977 began encouragingly, and in April Cardew completed a new work, *Mountains*, for bass clarinet solo, written for the Dutch bass-clarinettist Harry Sparnaay. In a letter dated 4 July 1977, responding to Cardew's technical queries, Sparnaay appears helpful and even enthusiastic about some sections, although he complains that the triplets at the end are 'hardly possible'. *Mountains* is a set of five variations on the opening theme of the Gigue from Bach's *Partita VI* for solo keyboard in which Cardew fuses avant-garde instrumental techniques with elements of traditional music (Ex.20.1-5). At the very beginning there is a quotation of a poem by Mao Tse-tung:

Mountains!
Piercing the blue of heaven, your barbs unblunted!
The skies would fall
But for your strength supporting.[1]

After the opening statement of Bach's theme, and its inversion, the first variation, 'bowling along', is a modal transformation extended through motivic repetition, to which is added another version of the theme in a higher register, creating a two-part counterpoint. The minor key returns with the theme in diminution (upper part) and in augmentation (the lower part).

Ex.20.1. From *Mountains*.

For the second variation Cardew quite unexpectedly introduces a graphic element into the score (shades of *Treatise*):

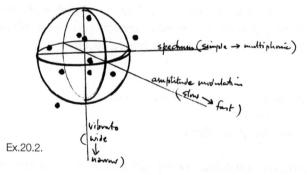

Ex.20.2.

and invites the performer to select (improvise) a different quality/character for each of ten given tones:

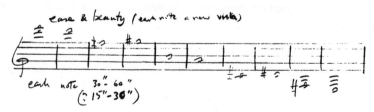

Ex.20.3.

The graphic element is carried over into the third, cadenza-like variation; the notes of the opening theme, transposed down an octave, are linked by ascending and descending diminished chord arpeggios whose contours clearly delineate 'mountains'.

Ex.20.4.

The final variation, marked 'exuberant', unleashes a torrent of atonal semi-quavers; the music accelerates, suddenly changes direction ('new growth'), gives free rein to the motivic components of Bach's theme ('fantasy'), and ends with a blistering succession of repeated Gs.

Ex.20.5.

Such assignments, which were all too rare, offered him a kind of (political) asylum; that is, his creativity would be rekindled, albeit temporarily, by the renewed challenges of (relatively) abstract composition. For Cardew's compositional art had been dwarfed and compromised, his talents freeze-dried, by the sacrificial demands of the Party. Party-scripted art was valorised according to strictly political yardsticks. 'One perfectly straightforward factor is that I don't compose *enough* to be very familiar with the craft', he had written some months earlier.[2] But in the same letter he continues:

One thing I'm realizing: the psychological formation of the avant-gardist (who *conceals* the things he actually wants to communicate) is very difficult to break out of, and working with PLM is one kind of social practise that is helping to chip away at this problem. In groups the problem for the 'composer' (individual creator) is to learn to work with other people.

And you learn that as a person, not a composer, and I'm persevering.

The issue of Irish independence was one which PLM had taken up with passion and resolve, and in May of 1977 they returned to Ireland for a tour which took them to Dublin, Limerick, Galway, Cork, Belfast, and which included engagements in two Technical Colleges. Cardew, Laurie Baker, and Hugh Shrapnel were joined by Geoff Pearce in the absence of Keith Rowe. The two occasions in Belfast were particularly memorable – for the republican hospitality which the English musicians enjoyed after their performance, and also for their encounters with the RUC, and with the army. The concert at the Labour Club, a Trade Union venue, attracted barely a handful of people, but included an old lady who expressed enthusiasm for the music and stayed on at the end of the concert to chat to the musicians. Shrapnel attributed the low turnout to a recent bomb scare: 'it very much resembled a war-time situation; the streets were deserted'[3]. After leaving the venue Geoff Pearce takes up the story:

> Within a couple of minutes the van we were all travelling in was stopped by the police. We were told to follow one police Landrover whilst another came up behind. We were led into the compound of the nearest police station which resembled the German POW camps you see in old films but much smaller. Armed guards and lots of barbed wire. We were separated and interrogated. It wasn't a big station so they had to use what space was available. I was taken to the police 'social club' with a billiard table in it. There were always two or three police with me asking the questions, one of whom continually brandished a rifle and played with it taking aim at various items in the room including myself. I assume it wasn't loaded but it was a little unnerving. They basically wanted to know who we were, what we had been doing and why we were there. After something like one and a half to two hours, having made their calls to England to check things out, they let us go. Within a minute of leaving the compound, we drove straight into an army road block. They made us sit in the van whilst a machine gun was set in the middle of the road in front of the van and trained on us (this *was* loaded) whilst they checked out our story that the police had only just released us after questioning. Ten or fifteen minutes later they let us go. We got back to our various lodgings without further incident.

1976 had seen a proliferation of racist propaganda in the tabloids; much was made, in particular, of the so-called Heathrow Asians 'scandal'[4]; less prominently featured was the exponential rise in the number of attacks (some of them fatal) on ethnic minority groups, in particular Asians. It was these developments which served to intensify the Party's anti-fascist activity (PLM frequently performed at anti-fascist events and demonstrations), drawing Cardew into the anti-racist struggle and establishing his reputation as a supporter and defender of the Asian communities. The militant song 'The Enemy' was one of his many contributions, with some adventurous harmonies and a surprising but effective change of metre in the middle of the chorus (Ex.20.6):

Ex.20.6. From 'The Enemy'.

Racism was a critical issue underlying the dispute at the film-processing laboratories at Grunwick in northwest London in the summer of 1977. Ostensibly a demand for union recognition, it became a *cause célèbre* which succeeded in galvanising large sections of the labour movement: a group of low-paid Asian women wanting to unionise and the employers hell-bent on preventing it. Sheila Kasabova and some friends were already frequenting the site to express solidarity with the women. Cardew, however, was wary of a so-called 'movement' led by the 'labour aristocracy' and infiltrated by Trotskyite 'opportunists'; the Party's reservations, likewise, were based on the leading role played by the TUC leadership, which, in its view, was manifestly striving to defuse the situation by stage-managing a 'dignified show of strength' (i.e. of weakness): mollification rather than confrontation. Eventually, however, Cardew decided that as a musician and supportive trade unionist he should make a contribution to the Asian women's struggle, and on the very first day that he joined the picket line he grabbed hold of a policeman's arm, whacked it, and was arrested. Undeterred, on the morning of the Grunwick 'day of action', 11 July, which included a rally in the nearby Roundwood Park, Cardew and his comrades took up their positions on the 6 am picket. To rally their spirits they sang songs, including the 'Internationale' which was shown on lunchtime TV news, the unknowing reporter commenting: 'Some people are singing the Russian national anthem'.

Frances Rifkin recalls that while the demonstrators (which included the miners' leaders) were on their way to the rally at Roundwood Park, vulnerable people on the picket line were left to fend for themselves at the hands of the police and the snatch groups. And the 'scab' bus went through. Rifkin and others managed to get to the front of the march to inform the leaders what was happening. They were dismissive; in fact, she recalls that they were hostile and abusive, intent only on reaching the park for the rally.

Despite her many fundamental differences with the Party, Rifkin shared its contempt for 'revisionist' politics. Having adopted 'the parliamentary road to socialism' they (the 'revisionists') could always be guaranteed to go to the brink and then to back off – ultimately to 'toe the bourgeois line'. At an anti-fascist demonstration, for example, rather than opposing the fascists directly, physically preventing them from holding a meeting, the 'revisionists' would lead their demonstrators elsewhere, thus ensuring that what they were protesting against actually took place. Rifkin calls it (still) 'a betrayal': 'no wonder that Cardew was so contemptuous of the revisionists'.[5] She herself would join the picket line at Grunwick and recalls the violence of the police attacks – or rather, elements within the police force, in particular the 'Special Patrol Group' (SPG). On one occasion a group of policemen from Limehouse in the East End intervened to protect them from an assault by the SPG whom they (the Limehouse officers) thought were acting with a 'disproportionate' degree of violence.

On 16 July a Grunwick Benefit concert, organised by the local Trades Council, the Grunwick support committee and Banner Theatre company,[6] took place at the Assembly Hall of the White Horse Hotel in Willesden. PLM opened the proceedings at 7.15 pm to a virtually empty hall, but by the time Banner Theatre went on stage (at around 8.30 pm), with its *Saltley Gates Show*, numbers had swollen and they were playing to a packed house. In his post-event analysis Cardew concludes:

> Brigid [Scott Baker] took the view that we'd been out-manoeuvred, but there may be a more prosaic explanation. Or it may have been Brigid that did the manoeuvring, so that Laurie [her bass guitarist husband] and our drummer could get away at 7.45 and do their paid gigs![7]

At the end of the event, in what appears to have been an unfortunate tactical error, bearing in mind the contrasting reception received by Banner Theatre, a rendering of Cardew's Grunwick song (Cardew's words to an Irish melody: 'The Rising of the Moon'), minus bass guitar and drums, failed to enhance PLM's popularity. What they should

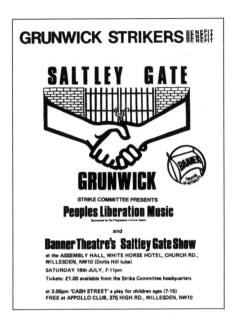

GRUNWICK STRIKERS BENEFIT BENEFIT

SALTLEY GATE

GRUNWICK

STRIKE COMMITTEE PRESENTS

Peoples Liberation Music
Sponsored by the Progressive Cultural Assoc.

and

Banner Theatre's Saltley Gate Show

at the ASSEMBLY HALL, WHITE HORSE HOTEL, CHURCH RD.,
WILLESDEN, NW10 (Dollis Hill tube)
SATURDAY 16th JULY, 7-11pm
Tickets: £1.00 available from the Strike Committee headquarters

at 3.00pm 'CASH STREET' a play for children ages (7-15)
FREE at APPOLLO CLUB, 375 HIGH RD., WILLESDEN, NW10

have done, according to Cardew, was to call for a discussion of the play that was performed, at the same time launching a struggle over the leadership of the picket.

I think the revisionist line (in the play and on the picket) is expressed in their use of the [word] 'mass': 'mass action', 'massive show of strength', etc., with the underlying implication: individual = violent = ultra-left = terrorist vs. mass = peaceful (as though the State will fade away when the masses rise).[8]

Moreover, by allowing themselves to be drawn in, PLM were thereby tarnished with the revisionist brush. Cardew commented ruefully:

The revisionists opportune on the revolutionary culture (to improve their image), and we opportune on the revisionist movement on the spurious pretext that 'at least everyone in the hall has a copy of our songsheet' (Brigid).[9]

And the subject of 'revisionism' surfaced again in a play centred around the strike which Recreation Ground had commissioned from the Irish playwright and TV writer Caroline Swift, and for which Cardew had agreed to provide the music (the songs). An anti-racist play entitled *Resistance* was produced, directed by Rifkin, and which, inevitably, bearing in mind the relation between Rifkin and the Party, was later denounced as 'revisionist' by the Party. Already during the creation of the play, as recollected by Rifkin, there had been much discussion and vociferous dissent, especially, one would assume, from the composer. According to Frances Rifkin Cardew and Caroline Swift 'loathed each other': his revolutionary rigour and arrogance versus her liberalism – an Irishwoman who was against revolution. Yet they collaborated successfully on the songs: her lyrics, his music. But why did Cardew get involved in the first place? Perhaps, given his ongoing financial difficulties, even a minimal fee provided sufficient inducement, but he also recognised the importance of maintaining contact and collaborating with working musicians and actors.[10]

Cardew's antagonism towards Francis Rifkin was based primarily on the fact that she represented another (opposing?) line in the PCA, where he (the Party) was virtually unchallenged. Moreover, while others accommodated themselves to a *modus vivendi* in relation to Party dicta the combative Rifkin would argue and fight. At the same time, as we have noted, Rifkin admired the strong anti-fascist stand of the Party and, not least, the importance they ascribed to culture; for example, Cardew's painstaking research into Irish rebel songs. Both Rifkin and Cardew took culture, cultural analysis, the battle of ideas, very seriously; it was this which drew Rifkin into the Party orbit and, initially, Cardew too. In this respect they were compatible.

In his report on the Musicians' Union Biennial Conference in Loughborough on 12-14 July (he and Laurie Baker were still active in the Union) Cardew refers to the various contributions to the Grunwick debate by himself and other comrades who attended the Conference:

> We can learn things from the Grunwick struggle. Firstly, we can learn about the nature of the capitalist state. Part of the state is the police and legal system which is supposed to protect all of us from crime. But in fact the legal system is there to protect the capitalists. If there was any proper justice, Ward and his cronies would have been in jail long ago. Enticing a picket into the factory and then beating him up is a crime. So is intentionally running down a picket with your Jaguar. But these criminals are still at large. These people who cry out for the rule of law, themselves acknowledge no law. The state is in their hands and they manipulate it as they please.[11]

Cardew also draws attention to the complicity and encouragement of the Labour government in relation to the deployment of the police and their assaults on the strikers.

When the mass picket started, we saw what it was like, and we wrote a song for the Grunwick picket, and I went down at seven one morning and sang it with the pickets. A few minutes later the busload of scabs drove up and the police started assaulting us and I was dragged off to the police station and charged with assault. That's their logic: they assault you, and then charge you with assault. One NATSOPA official put it very well last Monday: he said 'I am supposed to have crushed a policeman's hand with my kidney'. Under these conditions, there is no alternative for the people but to fight and hit back. If we don't we'll be slaughtered.[12]

'Class', and the reality of 'class struggle', was the cornerstone of all Cardew's writings and actions at that time, in whatever area of concern, whether political or cultural, and his report ends with a reference to the Arts debate and in particular to the position adopted by the TUC and the Labour Party:

The reports of the TUC and Labour Party are attempts to paper over the terrific struggles that are going on in this field of ideas and culture, and have been going on over the last few years with particular intensity. According to them, something abstract called 'art' is to be taken out of the hands of the privileged few and distributed amongst everyone in society, and by this method this 'art' itself will also be stimulated and improved. They omit to mention that the 'man' who is the political subject of all this art, has little in common with the working people in Britain today. He is an abstraction left over from the 19th century, the bourgeois individual. The point is that the different classes in society produce their own culture. As we progressively recognise that we are aligned with the working class in the struggles that are going on, so we must come to realise that there is such a thing as working class culture – which the TUC report explicitly denies – and that it is our business to see that this culture develops and thrives and plays its proper role in the struggles to come.[13]

The MU conference also provided the background for Cardew's new song, 'Smash the Social Contract'. With reference to the Social Contract debate Cardew denounced this 'so-called contract' as a 'manoeuvre to impose wage-cuts on workers while the rich enrich themselves further'. And in a response to a point made from the floor he argued:

The Social Contract is not dead – if you don't hit it it won't fall – and even when we hit it it will be resurrected in one guise or another until we establish a new economic system – that is, a socialist economic system in which the working people take over the ownership of the means of production. And that is a long hard fight. The revolutionary spirit of the working class is to reject the Social Contract unconditionally, and say no to the class compromise that it represents, that compromise that is acted out for us in the negotiations between the TUC and the Government.[14]

'There is such a thing as working class culture' – a proclamation denied not only by the TUC report, but by a host of 'neo-revisionist' sociologists. But what did Cardew mean by 'working class culture'? Clearly, artistic activity and its artefacts are only part of a concept which, as Richard Hoggart has pointed out, indicates 'activities, relationships, and processes', handed down, invariably, by tradition. For Cardew and his Party 'culture' relates to *social forms*, to *mores*; the idea of 'comradeship', for example, is an aspect of proletarian culture, and therefore is the kind of *relationship between people* which provides the foundation on which new revolutionary culture can be built.

PCA upholds the line that culture embraces not only literature and art, song, theatre and film, but also social form. The work of developing a new revolutionary culture is not merely a question of producing new songs, stories, etc., but is an entire question of generating a new spiritual, cultural and social environment in which men and women of our bright red socialist future will grow strong and firm.[15]

So at least in theory, and after a shaky and unpromising start, the Party had begun to recognise the need to engage as *revolutionaries* (that is, not with a reformist agenda) with a whole range of experience – family, gender and sexuality, morality, education, vast areas of lived daily reality – which had been marginalized by many leftist parties and groups in their quest for more circumscribed political advances and influence based on an unshakeable belief that only through an intensification of the struggle *at the point of production* could real progress towards socialism and the transformation of society be achieved.[16] In essence the Party fundamentalists would have agreed with this – that without the seizure and control of the economic base, and the 'dictatorship of the proletariat', the transformation into a socialist society was unattainable. Yet, at the same time, it recognized that even those once-secret havens, the heart and the imagination, the human psyche itself, were no longer safe from the insidious and corrupting influence of bourgeois ideology which had to be exposed and attacked, rather than opportunistically exploited, as was the case, it argued, with the Trotskyite groups. The Party's view was that the 'working class culture' that was foisted upon the populace was essentially reactive, that it was about making life at best less unbearable (which in itself contributed to its 'popularity'); more importantly, it depicted life as essentially unchangeable except by the hand of fate, through external forces: bingo, winning the pools, a TV game show, etc. The terms, as laid out by bourgeois society, were clear: abandon all relationships with an irrelevant and vanquished past; act individually; compete, be a winner, or a loser.[17]

But if, during the seventies, this collective expression of dissent was a manifestation of working class culture, what and where was working class art? Where was a progressive popular music to which the masses would respond positively, which would contribute towards satisfying their needs, towards raising consciousness, inspiring them to ever more purposeful, more determined action? Were a few isolated examples to be found subsumed within the plethora of trash? Was it recognised? Or was its message lost? Yes, popular music did occasionally express dissent, though much of it was confused, unfocused and therefore unlikely to create a lasting effect. As for Cardew's new song, 'Smash the Social Contract' sounds more like 'having fun' (Ex.20.7). Perhaps cheerfulness can go hand in hand with militancy, like those Second World War songs which were sung in the factories ('Praise the Lord and pass the ammunition'). Or perhaps it relates to the music hall tradition, or even to the Salvation Army repertoire? So what culture is Cardew drawing on here? Because of this stylistic ambivalence many of his songs do not engage in 'struggle' with reality. They do not 'reflect their [the British workers] sentiment to fight tooth and nail for the just demands of the working class'; they lack a dialectic. Too often they *project* a psychological condition (say of blissful, proletarian happiness) into the future. Or they express a kind of yearning, as in the more successful 'A Law of History', which also expresses militancy.

Ex.20.7. From 'Smash the Social Contract'.

Arguably, art and art forms are more vulnerable in the sense that whereas it has been comparatively easy to appropriate and subvert working class 'art' – music, film (TV), books, etc., in other words, marketable artefacts – to take over and subvert a *culture* is more difficult, an altogether much more complex undertaking. This is why, Cardew would have reasoned, there were/are culturally-rooted residues in surviving working class communities which are authentic and progressive (and I refer to this in my discussion of Cardew's attitude towards folk music in the sections on his later music). If we recall the content of the British TV programmes of yesteryear, of yesterdecade, and if we compare them with the current menu on the same channels, the thesis that the 'dumbing-down' of the populace is an integral part of the world strategy of Pax Americana is hard to gainsay. But to sink into despondency, to acknowledge an enervating feeling of powerlessness, Cardew warned the doubters and the faint-hearted, is precisely what our rulers seek to create ('pessimism is a tool of the ruling class'). In fact, it is more rational, more natural, to see ordinary people in a positive light. As Frederic Rzewski has pointed out:

Humans are perfectly all right the way they are. Mostly they get along fine, without anyone telling them how to do it. They tend not to bump into one another walking on the street. They feed, nurse, and help each other. Most of their transactions happen easily, quickly, unconsciously, efficiently, and without money.[18]

Of course, Cardew would have objected to Rzewski's all-embracing reference to 'humans', rather than to members of conflicting classes, and the question was often raised: is Cardew not idealising, romanticising the working class? Is there a *scientific* justification for claiming a *moral* superiority for the working class? Have not the toilers themselves been brutalised, physically and psychologically, their imaginations crippled, by monopoly capitalism? Do they not yearn and clamour for greater material abundance and improved life-chances? To become 'bourgeois'? If so, can *false consciousness* really be negated through revolutionary action? Transformed into its opposite? Can working people deliver themselves from a state of permanent insecurity and frustration, from mindless consumption and spiritual self-denial, from desperate dreaming and escapism and the belief in the life-changing power of lottery numbers, from ultimate self-effacement, to which condition, at every waking moment, they are forced to accommodate?

Well, yes they can, would have been Cardew's retort. And experiences from every part of the globe provide compelling examples of not just 'politicisation through struggle', but, more importantly, of profound *cultural* shifts. Miners' wives who became involved in the 1984-5 strike in Britain, for example, have written and spoken about the way that the nature and modality of their everyday existence, including beliefs, habits, routines, attitudes, underwent radical scrutiny and upheaval during and in the wake of the strike:

'We've all changed. Some of us never went out *anywhere,*' says Brenda Halliwell from Oakdale (in Gwent, South Wales). 'It's opened my eyes to a lot of things, nuclear power and Greenham Common. It was just a name to me, I never bothered till we met the Greenham Common women from Hackney who were supporting us. They never pushed it, they just answered our questions. And then we got to thinking, what's it like, we'd love to go and see it for ourselves. I admire them, they're brave women. I went and I'd like to go again. The women I met are marvellous.'

Do they know, these women from the coalfields, that the Greenham network thinks they're marvellous, too? Brave women.[19]

Cardew's attitude towards the Musicians' Union lacked the assiduity of his other political commitments; as a consequence he and his two comrades, Laurie Baker and Geoff Pearce, had been ill-prepared for the Loughborough conference, and had entered the debate extemporaneously and without a co-ordinated strategy. Yet neither Cardew nor Baker was without influence: Baker's untiring and conscientious work for the Central London Branch Committee had enhanced his standing in the Union while Cardew wielded a degree of influence through his professional status and from the fact that his uncle, Phil Cardew, had been active in the MU after the war, as a communist, and had gained considerable respect from fellow musicians. Cardew's considered view was that their activity in the Musicians' Union was 'relatively less important' than their work in the industrial unions (at Grunwick, for example, despite Party reservations), and in the PCA. Nevertheless it was decided that during the ensuing months he, Pearce and Baker should devote their energies to persuading the Union to lay charges against those MU members who flagrantly promoted racism or fascism (surely an insignificant number?), with a view to 'raising issues of music and ideology within the MU and promoting consciousness of the class nature of culture'. And as we shall see, the interview in *Rolling Stone* magazine the previous year with David Bowie would provide them with an effective test case.

These issues of working class culture were thrown into sharp relief by the shenanigans which led up to and surrounded the Queen's 25th Jubilee on 7 July. An article written by Peter Devenport entitled 'National Chauvinism in Classical Music in Britain', which appeared in the second issue of the PCA's *Cogs and Wheels* magazine in March of the following year, referred to the upsurge of national chauvinism in response to the silver jubilee and to the publication of songs of gross chauvinist sentiment. A 'Royal' edition of the *Musical Times* appeared and all the British music magazines had carried related articles. Academic institutions, too, had clambered onto the bandwagon, with the Guildhall School of Music and Drama organising a 'Music Trail' following the route of Queen

Elizabeth II's Coronation procession. Composers from the so-called National School –
Parry, Stanford, Vaughan Williams, Bliss, Walton and others – were promoted as well
as the theory that such music, characterised by its 'pastoral' quality, was clearly inspired
by the landscape of Britain. An illustration on the front cover of the *Radio Times* depicted
the Royal Albert Hall in the idyllic setting of an English field, with an English brook running
peacefully and contentedly by its side.

Devenport's article highlighted the fact that it was Sir Edward Elgar who received the
most attention – all his potboilers were included in the celebrations and other songs
of dubious artistic merit were dug up and revived. Most of the selected works, such
as 'Land of Hope and Glory', extolled British Imperialism as a 'liberating' force and
included such paeans as *Imperial March, Crown of India, Empire March*, and *Pageant
of Empire*. Elgar had been close to the Royal family and throughout his life had glorified
the monarchy in his music with an enthusiasm which few of his contemporaries in the
field of music could match. The depth of his commitment, his devotion and zeal, was
unfathomable, as is attested by his propaganda pieces for that most infamous imperialist
bloodbath, the First World War: *The Spirit of England, Fringes of the Fleet* and *Carillon*.
The libretto for *Caractacus* was provided by Harry Arbuthnot Acworth and is set, ostensibly,
in ancient Britain. The final scene begins with a premonitory call: "Britons, alert! and fear
not", and the noble cause of British imperialism is given powerful expression in the
following stanzas, from which I quote:

> But gird, gird your loins for fight,

> And ever your dominion
> From age to age shall grow
> O'er peoples undiscover'd,
> In lands we cannot know;

> And where the flag of Britain
> Its triple crosses rears,
> No slave shall be for subject,
> No trophy wet with tears.

Small wonder that Sir Edward received honours such as no other English musician,
then or since, has enjoyed in so short a time. (Queen Victoria herself was the dedicatee
of *Caractacus*.) And small wonder, too, that Cardew and his comrades took the
opportunity to vent their contempt both on the streets and in print. Even Elgar's friend,
A.J. Jaeger ('Nimrod' in the *Enigma Variations*), was moved to criticise the 'excessive

jingoism' of *Caractacus*.[20]

Of course, this was very much the culture within which Cardew had been educated – at public school and the Royal Academy of Music – and he would have been familiar with its various manifestations during the Jubilee celebrations. His mentor, Lenin, encapsulated what would have been Cardew's response to the gushing complicity of the musical establishment:

> Those who seek to serve the proletariat must unite the workers of all nations, and unswervingly fight bourgeois nationalism, *domestic* and foreign. The place of those who advocate the slogan of national culture is among the nationalist petty bourgeois, not among the Marxists.[21]

During the summer months of 1977 the PCA sponsored a number of informal meetings with PLM and Fight Back (an anti-racist reggae band based in south London) at the Eagle and Child pub in Forest Gate, East London, each of which adopted a particular theme; these included Ireland, anti-racism, and anti-monarchy (relating, in particular, to the extravagant antics surrounding the Jubilee). In response to the increase in racially-motivated attacks during the seventies a broad-based anti-racist movement had gathered momentum and many such meetings were held in towns and cities around the country, with commensurate State response. On 29 July the East London People's Democratic Front meeting at the Co-Op Hall in Ilford, called to oppose fascist attacks in East London,

> was attacked and broken up by the police They smashed down the door of the hall and arrested seven of the eighty people present, all of whom defended themselves militantly. When local people came into the street to protest at the violence and brutality shown by the police, they were threatened with police dogs and racist insults. Afterwards several locals came to the meeting which was held in another hall.[22]

In August an anti-racist concert preceded an impressive anti-fascist march in Lewisham (in response to a National Front march under the slogan 'Stop the Muggers'); in an exemplary display of militancy Cardew and another comrade led part of the demonstration against the instructions of the police who, right from the outset, had contrived to control

the demonstration and neutralise any effect and consequence it might have had. Cardew refused to go where he was told and encouraged others to act with him; there was a struggle and he was manhandled and arrested. Since he had previously been arrested and bound over imprisonment was automatic, although not immediate.

On 5 October a concert entitled Music for Socialism, involving various Left groups and including PLM and Fight Back, took place at the Battersea Town Hall. Fight Back was part of the West Indian Defence Committee which continued to resist PCA's overtures for closer links. The importunate dogma of many of PLM's lyrics and what was perceived as their simplistic and sectarian message, compounded by the air of correctitude which members and supporters of the CPE (M-L) (whose musical mouthpiece it was) exuded in their social intercourse, bred resentment amongst fellow musicians. The concert attracted an audience of no more than fifty or so people – a depressing turn-out, one would have thought, considering the invocatory nature of its title. The PLM verdict on the event was that it 'went well'; for the Maoists, putting on a brave face was part and parcel of revolutionary politics.

And a year later there is little evidence that Cardew had learnt the lessons that such experiences provide:

> In our experience in PCA, trained artists too often *impose* their conception of art – of what art is, and what standards to apply to it – on the people. The point is to serve the people as a *person* – to apply ourselves to solving whatever problems may be facing them – rather than as an artist. By standing shoulder to shoulder with the working people in battle, by sharing weal and woe with them, we will then be in a position to make some art that is of the people and for the people.[23]

Despite their outward show of solidarity there were still considerable tensions between individual Party and PCA members and supporters. Cardew clearly had reservations about Laurie Baker's contributions in some areas, however well-intended; in relation to advertising the 'Punk is fascist' event on 21 October, for example, he complained that Baker was 'messing it up'.[24] There is no doubt that difficulties in communication, and the tensions generated by such problems, arose from the fact that Cardew subjected others to the same stringent, critical analysis that he applied to himself: the same moral and politically-correct high ground had to be aspired to by all. He was an unrelenting task-master, but unlike others he would never demand as much of his friends and comrades as he did of himself.

Yet it seems to me, as a (relative) outsider, that the essence of these problems derived from a single, unresolved issue: that of the relationship of the PCA to the Party.[25] In a brief PCA report the last two paragraphs contain the following 'unequivocal' statements:

> The PCA was *set up and led by the Party* in order to organise and maximise the political effectiveness of the cultural work that is springing up from the struggles of the masses. And, *further to transmit the Party's line to the masses. Under the leadership of the Party* it is part of the whole democratic process... At the same time, the PCA *is not an organisation of the Party*. Those leading the PCA are not necessarily under the discipline of the Party.[26]

How could the Party 'set up and lead' an organisation (the PCA), one asks oneself, and then in the same breath, as it were, deny that it was 'an organisation of the Party'? More, how could a revolutionary Party 'set up and lead ' an organisation and then allow it to discipline itself? I believe Cardew was well aware of this contradiction, which is why he fought tooth and nail in the PCA committee to bring the Association formally and without equivocation under Party control. Of course, there were those in the PCA who were uneasy, but at the risk of losing members this is what Cardew insisted should be the *de facto* relationship between the PCA and the CPE (M-L).

On 10 October Cardew took part in a concert (one of a series) at the Air Gallery in Shaftesbury Avenue, in London's West End. These forays into the world of the avant-garde were rare, but Cardew seldom missed the opportunity when it arose. Of course, his reputation, both as former avant-gardist and communist militant, ensured that he could still attract an audience. In his introduction he dismissed the series as of little importance, 'in the sense that it does not raise any of the important issues facing the people in society today, and is totally divorced from the great struggles that the working people are engaging in in the real world'.[27] The thrust of Cardew's talk, on this occasion, was an appeal to the 'petit bourgeois' composers, musicians and artists to 'come forward and actively support the revolution'. Cardew was unequivocal; if you fail to support the liberation struggle you are supporting Imperialism. By doing nothing, by turning a blind eye, you are condoning evil; there is no middle course. Nor was 'engagement' enough; engaged artists he dismissed as being 'two a penny'. The fact that a number of old and close friends were in the audience, including Howard Skempton, Dave Smith, Michael Parsons, Benedict Mason, Michael Nyman and Jeffrey Steele, made it all the more challenging. For these friends had followed, one might even say monitored, his politicisation – they had argued the issues with him in the latter days of the Scratch Orchestra, and subsequently; and yet, despite an ungrudging degree of solidarity with him, both moral and practical, they had resisted his demands to join him. That so many of these 'petit bourgeois' individuals seemed unable to commit themselves to the revolutionary cause was a political 'issue' which Cardew had decided to open up to discussion. He claimed there were three basic reasons why people were 'holding back':

1. The overall effort of the bourgeoisie to hold you back.
2. The specific bourgeois line of pacifism, of 'no harm in people getting on with whatever cultural pursuits they fancy.'
3. The character of the petit bourgeoisie, the social class to which most of us belong.[28]

Cardew elaborated on these themes and concluded with a denunciation of the

total bankruptcy and degeneracy of new bourgeois art. For an artist to serve the people, he has to make a radical break with avant-gardism. This is not a question of style, it is a question of the basic ideology of avant-gardism – that you are 'advanced', and hence speak to an elite, and hence cannot be integrated with the masses of the people.[29]

Most of Cardew's contribution to the event at the Air Gallery has survived on cassette; some of the contributions from the audience in the earlier, more formal part of the occasion are intelligible, but of the cut and thrust of the debate proper, in which there are heated exchanges between Cardew and his audience, much is lost. Nevertheless, the recording is an invaluable document, affording us the opportunity to relive one of many occasions during the seventies when Cardew transforms a discussion about musical aesthetics into a rallying call to revolutionary action, and the venue becomes a battlefield. Just as the audience for *The Great Learning* at Cheltenham, almost ten years earlier, from confronting the music had in the end confronted itself, it was now Cardew's momentous purpose that his musical activity should not just 'make waves in the environment' but should have *political* repercussions 'beyond the concert hall'. In the following extract I pick up the discussion soon after the point when Cardew invites comments and questions from the audience. In response to a loaded reference to Mao's 1957 speech, 'Let a hundred flowers blossom, let a hundred schools of thought contend', Cardew counters robustly that if amongst them there are 'poisonous weeds' then these cannot be allowed to prevail. And with a dramatic gesture he rounds on Bruce Russell's abstract paintings, fortuitously exhibited around the space [30]:

This painting here is a poisonous weed. I don't think there is any doubt about it. There is nothing progressive about it. It's not about anything that's of interest to the working people.

It's just rubbish. We don't want to have this kind of blossoming weed. We want to develop revolutionary blossoms of all different types. [Protests from audience] These paintings have no relevance to the working people of this country. I don't have to analyse them to find that out. I just have to look at them and see that every one is the same with different colours. [A chorus of protest objecting, as far as one can detect, to Cardew's caricature of 'abstraction', and in response to a suggestion that, under the circumstances, the painter should have been given the opportunity to introduce his paintings in the same way that Cardew has introduced his music.] Because these paintings are painted in an avant-garde language any amount of explanation you gave them wouldn't elucidate to the working people that they had any relevance to their struggle. [More vociferous protests including the point that if Cardew had not been given the opportunity to discuss his works with the audience they too could have been dismissed as 'pretty meaningless music'.] Well, I challenge that. Read what the artist has to say about his paintings – these paintings actually exist in the world and I say they are reactionary. Do you say they are progressive? If so, say why… [Nobody leaps to the defence of the paintings.] The basic thing about an abstract painting of this type is that you look at it and try to think what it can be and then various people look at it and one person says what I like about it is this, and another says I like this. Everybody sees something different in it. Somebody sees this as clouds and this as sea. [Further uproar, attack led vehemently by painter Jeffrey Steele, but very difficult to determine precisely what is being said; there is no microphone in the audience. Cardew and his audience were unnecessarily at cross purposes here; the audience's vociferous objection to his vulgar characterisation ('clouds' and 'sea') of abstraction was justified but could have been circumvented by a less disingenuous analysis on Cardew's part. To Steele:]

You asked for this. You are trying to split these political ideas and insist on analysing the form, not the content. The essence of these things is that everybody can think what they like about them. That it is entirely a matter of opinion what it means, and that's the idea that the bourgeoisie spread throughout the world. It is a matter of opinion that the revolution is going on or not: some people think there's going to be a revolution and some people don't think there's going to be a revolution. Some people think the working class is progressive, some people think the working class is dying out. So, what is the working class? In capitalist society they say there isn't such a thing. These kinds of rubbishy ideas are given as a matter of opinion. Everybody has a right to their opinion. However, what we say is you've got to get to the heart of things and find out what actually is the case. And when I play this music I'm saying to you what actually is the case. This music is about Thälmann. It uses the materials that developed culturally around Thälmann, around the issue of Thälmann, and how he fought against the fascists before the second world war, and nobody is going to tell me any different.[31]

For all his virtues – he was an incisive thinker and a formidable conversationalist possessed of a fleetness of mind – Cardew was not an authoritative public speaker, a view which, I suggest, is supported by this particular talk at the Air Gallery. He spoke with intensity but did not always control or project his subject matter effectively. Moreover, unlike his piano-playing, with its famed near-perfect balance of commitment and detachedness, he had no reserves to call on; he was too emotionally involved in what he was saying, or rather, he could not harness the excess of emotional energy in the most expedient manner. Yet the directness of his delivery, for all its shortcomings, did echo the compelling quality of his piano-playing (his recordings of Ives are exemplary examples of this). It was as if he were not sure whether he was having a conversation with one or two people – where he could insert some lubricant 'you knows' and 'etcetera etceteras' – or whether he was addressing an audience, a crowd of people, where precision and economy of expression is of the essence. Occasionally, as in conversation, his voice would dip, or trail off, creating, if briefly, an inconclusive, or rather indecisive, impression. At Scratch Orchestra meetings his verbal communications, even with thirty or forty people present, were conversational, intimate, avuncular in style.

In a sense, at the Air Gallery his delivery was too extempore. Yet he had the ability to seize upon a situation and to transform it (as in Scratch Orchestra concerts) or to dramatise it, as he showed by confronting the unfortunate Bruce Russell's paintings. He was unafraid of taking up extreme, threatening positions to which logical argument and reasoning might, inexorably, have led, and he would cut through and expose, mercilessly, attempts to obfuscate and to intellectualise. Like his mentor Lenin, he was able to expose pretence and self-delusion; and he recognised, perhaps most importantly, that 'a thought must be crude to come into its own in action'.[32]

But to return to the offending paintings at the Air Gallery, if we reflect upon Cardew's outburst my impression is that this had little to do with the art works themselves; the issue at hand was not 'abstraction', non-representational Art, but *receptivity*. What he was objecting to, I suggest, was a *symbolic* (intellectualising) interpretation of what was essentially a visual experience. (I refer the reader back to the quotation from Susan Sontag in Chapter 10.)[33] Throughout his life Cardew recognised and responded to the physicality, the authenticity, of a *purely* visual response. 'The visual is an image of distance and non-possession. The idea of space and quietness, thinking, seeing, attending, keeping still, not seizing [...] [34] His own music had an extraordinary sense of *materiality* (think of the very beginning of *The Great Learning*). And he understood as well as anybody that there were (purely) aural, musical, pianistic aspects of his *Thälmann Variations* which affected the reception of the music; from Cardew's (Marxist) standpoint they were part of the 'superstructure', while the essential content, the 'base', was Thälmann's anti-fascist life; together they expressed (part of) the interdependent relationship of form and content.

Regarding the problem of 'content' in music, which Cardew addressed in militant fashion at the Air Gallery, a measure of agreement with his audience could have been reached, even if many would have baulked at Cardew's insistence on the hierarchical base/superstructure relation. If particular circumstances and events inspired the creation of a piece of music, is it not reasonable to propose that these circumstances are therefore, whether overtly or subliminally, part of the music? And why should not the composer divulge this information to his audience, either verbally or in a programme note? If a piece of music was composed in a concentration camp (as was the case with Messiaen's *Quatuor pour la fin du temps*) or in the heat of the struggle against fascism (as was some of Eisler's music), is it not reasonable to assume that somehow these extreme circumstances inform the music? Some would say no, but few composers deny the influence on their work of the world around them.[35] Of course, music is promiscuous; moreover, all music has 'a programme'. In other words, it is *about* something, or some things, even if not all the 'aboutness' in a piece of music is intended by its creator. As was/is the case with the multiple meanings generated, by accident or by design, by the musicians of AMM.

Perhaps Cardew feared a rapprochement with an audience (at least the majority of them) to whose 'world-outlook' he was so implacably opposed. We have already seen, in the case of Frances Rifkin, even when concessions to the 'revisionists' could be granted without compromising fundamental, Marxist-Leninist tenets, Cardew was reluctant to do so. With Marxism-Leninism Cardew scented a victory over uncertainty; he was no longer satisfied with 'the truce of a brief but brilliant enlightenment'. In the last decade he lived within, and thrived on, a subsuming reality of unchallengeable *certainties,* and I have referred to this, semi-autobiographically, in an earlier chapter. Can one act only on the basis of certainty? Is an (political) action somehow compromised if it is accompanied by uncertainty? Can even the slightest degree of scepticism, say on the battlefield, crucially undermine commitment and therefore put lives at risk? For Cardew, the threat posed by 'abstraction' was its vulnerability to speculation; to unresolved ambivalence and 'bourgeois' indulgence. It appeared to sit well with the idea that 'everything is a matter of opinion'. Thus, rather than opposing capitalism artists might more gainfully merely question the 'fact'of its existence.

Cardew was deeply sceptical of the 'fashionable socialism' of the day, and of 'arm-chair' socialists: people who embraced socialism as one would embrace a religion – as a safety-net[36], cheering from the sidelines, assuaging feelings of middle-class guilt, supporting the socialist cause rather than fighting for socialist revolution.[37] Proletarian Art had to be tough, direct and, where necessary, 'crude'('plump'); it was meant to discompose and if necessary antagonize the left-liberal intelligentsia who, while bemoaning the capitalist system, would accommodate to it, use it to further their personal ambitions. They would still seek refuge in 'beautiful ideas, elegance of manner, logical completeness, formal perfection…' They still hankered after commissions and fame within the bourgeois art establishment, at galleries and festivals, and would close off their minds when the intellectual going got tough, when the questions about art became unanswerable because the answers were unthinkable.

The shadow of Mao Tse-tung hung heavily over the proceedings on that October day in 1977; so I feel no apologies are required for allowing the Great Leader to have the last word in my discussion of the Air affair. For it needs to be said that re-reading Mao's aforementioned text (and, indeed, many other of his texts) is an enlightening and sobering reminder of the Chairman's pragmatism and reasonableness. Mao was not the first 'great leader' whose thoughts and intentions were misunderstood, misinterpreted, revised, deformed, subverted, cynically and opportunistically distorted, perverted, mutilated – with the result that all manner of wrongs have been heaped upon him, that he alone bears the responsibility for the excesses of his 'followers'. Can the 'thoughts of Chairman Mao' really be blamed for the costive utterances and half-baked policies of the Communist Party of England (Marxist-Leninist) or even for the extraordinary behaviour of some of the Red Guards? Scrutiny of the 'Hundred Flowers' text reveals a less dogmatic and certainly far more measured approach than Cardew's 'performance' at the Air Gallery:

Questions of right and wrong in the arts and sciences should be settled through free discussion in artistic and scientific circles and through practical work in these fields. They should not be settled in summary fashion… Ideological struggle is not like other forms of struggle. The only method to be used in this struggle is that of painstaking reasoning and not crude coercion… What is needed is scientific analysis and convincing argument. Dogmatic criticism settles nothing.[38]

Mao, towards the end of his life, might well have echoed Marx: If this is Maoism, I'm no Maoist.[39]

The autumn of 1977 also saw the publication of the first issue of the aforementioned *Cogs and Wheels,* Journal of the Progressive Cultural Association, No.1. Described as 'a magazine for all working and progressive people' its contents include an article entitled 'Punk Rock is Fascist'[40], a motion against fascism put forward by Baker and Cardew at a Musicians' Union meeting, a play – *Down with the Monarchy,* revolutionary songs, and a selection of poems by a young, fifteen year-old Cypriot supporter of the Communist Party of England (Marxist-Leninist) as an example of 'the new vigorous, revolutionary culture springing up from the youth in this country'. Discussions, or rather 'struggles', over the nature of the Journal had been preoccupying the editorial committee from as far back as April; the bone of contention, inevitably, was the extent to which the Party exercised control over its contents. Whereas Cardew and Carole Rowe (who were responsible for the introductory editorial) had argued that the magazine should be strictly monitored by the Party, others, notably Keith Rowe and Frances Rifkin, had grown increasingly impatient with what they regarded as the hackneyed and bovine arguments of the Party ideologues, had begun to rebel against aspects of the 'Party line' on artistic issues, and had sought, unsuccessfully, to advance the thesis of the desirability of maintaining a certain distance from the Party in such matters – a stance which would result, ultimately, in their political undoing.

In a typewritten report headed 'Progressive musicians take a stand against punk rock' a PCA meeting held at the Eagle and Child pub in Forest Gate, on 21 October, under the slogan "Punk Rock is Fascist", is described enthusiastically.[41] This was a debut occasion for Bright Future, a new rock trio led by guitarist and Party supporter Geoff Pearce who wanted to form a group that was more 'youth and rock' orientated. Pearce recalls that Cardew was very supportive, discussing and commenting on the ideas and Pearce's lyrics. The set began with a rendering of Woody Guthrie's Second World War song 'Dig a Hole', followed by the Beatles' 'Get Back' with new anti-fascist lyrics. Other songs included 'Four Anti-Fascist Slogans', and a song, after Marx, entitled 'Gravediggers of the Bourgeoisie', written in the aftermath of the police attack on the meeting in Ilford at the end of July.

The various performances were preceded by a thirty-minute talk (which I summarise below) by a PCA representative, on this occasion Cardew himself, in which it was posited that pop music in general was used consistently as 'a major ideological weapon to distort reality and confuse the youth about the issues in society', and that punk rock, in particular, was part of an increasingly reactionary trend in which support for racism and fascism was becoming ever more blatant. Recent history had provided some instructive precedents: Elvis Presley, for example, with his rebellion against 'middle class values', was promoted precisely at the time when McCarthyism raged in America, while genuine rebellion was denounced and repressed under the banner of 'un-American activities'.

Similarly, as the militant anti-imperialist upsurge was in full swing during the late sixties, the imperialists launched their 'peace and love' culture. In the seventies, an era of extreme economic difficulty for the imperialists, when anti-democratic, fascist methods were introduced as a way of dealing with the crisis, a not insignificant number of pop stars and groups openly flaunted fascist ideas and slogans, reflecting a cultural degeneracy which in turn fuelled the fascist demagogic calls for 'cleaning up the country'. Punk was also promoted as an expression of the 'generation gap'; thus the older generation was blamed for the present ills in society, along with 'mismanagement', 'bureaucracy', 'corruption' in local councils, and so forth. For all its alleged 'rebelliousness' Punk received not only publicity but also financial backing, with The Clash, for example, signing a lucrative recording contract with CBS. Such was the Party's analysis.

The problem for the critics, and the sociologists, was the ambivalence at the heart of the punk phenomenon: 'White Riot' (The Clash's first single) may have been concerned (according to some commentators) with an exasperated demand for a white riot to react against the situation in which all the power is in the hands of those rich enough to buy it, but the fascists had always used this argument. Joe Strummer was no racist and his public utterances certainly betrayed 'leftist' sympathies; yet students at Lanchester Polytechnic in Coventry vetoed payment to The Clash because 'they thought 'White Riot' was fascist.'[42] And in any case, in the popular music industry at the time, a predisposition to right-wing demagoguery was not confined to punks; similar views to those denounced by Cardew in his talk had also been expressed in the 'main-stream' press: early in 1976 David Bowie had attracted considerable publicity for expressing fascist views in an interview in *Rolling Stone* magazine. Although he was said to have retracted his statements after much adverse coverage in the music press, the retraction received relatively little publicity. And in August of the same year, as Jon Savage recalls, "a drunken Eric Clapton made a speech in favour of Enoch Powell at a concert in Birmingham, his debt to black Blues guitarists or Reggae artists forgotten." [43] Punk polarised black and white; few black people went to punk concerts.[44]

At a meeting of the Central London Branch of the Musicians' Union in September 1976 a number of musicians, including Cardew and Laurie Baker, had decided to take up the issue by demanding David Bowie's expulsion from the Union. Their initial motion was debated and narrowly defeated; some members voted against it on the grounds that 'draconian' measures such as expulsion and slogans such as 'Fascists have no right to speak' (adopted by the National Union of Students in 1974) only serve to make martyrs of the fascists and intensify their commitment.[45] However, an amended motion was carried by an overwhelming majority:

When a musician declares publicly that he or she is 'very interested in fascism' and that 'Britain could benefit from a fascist leader' he or she is influencing public opinion through the massive audiences of young people that such musicians have access to. Such behaviour is detrimental to the interests of the Union, since it prepares the ground for a political system in which the Trade Union movement can be smashed, as it was in Nazi Germany. This Central London Branch therefore proposes that any member who uses his or her professional standing or his or her stage act or records to promote fascism or any other undemocratic party or political system, should be actively opposed.[46]

Cardew and his comrades were sceptical with regards to the meaning, implications, and most importantly, the efficacy of the phrase 'actively opposed'; they would also have questioned the definition of 'undemocratic party', and if their own credentials as a 'democratic' party were regarded by many as suspect they would have fought their corner with tenacity and conviction: 'dictatorship of the proletariat' versus 'bourgeois democracy'. After all, in Britain 'bourgeois democracy', in the grotesque form of the election of Margaret Thatcher, was about to usher in a long, bleak period for millions of people in the country.

Prone as the Maoists may have been to hyperbole in relation to what they described as the reactionary and noxious role of the imperialist 'superstructure', they were certainly correct in their perception of Fascism as a serious threat at that time – as were other less ideologically motivated groups and individuals. By 1976 the National Front was the fourth largest political party in Britain and considerable media attention was lavished upon right-wing politicians and fascist ideologues such as the Conservative MP Enoch Powell and the leader of the National Front, Martin Webster, whose legitimacy was sanctioned and enhanced through frequent invitations to air their views. Unreported or played down was the fact that there had been an exponential rise in the number of attacks on Asians. The National Front was recruiting in the sub-culture, and for the punks and their liberal supporters in the media to argue that they were part of a counter-culture of 'dissent' and even, in some cases, to boast left-wing credentials, was, to many of its opponents, a preposterous conceit. To claim that the punks were highlighting and drawing attention to working-class alienation was sociological quackery; one could hear their language, though richer and more colourful, and observe their Hogarthean antics, though more extreme, on many streets in any British city on a Saturday night. A brief visit to one of the poor estates which blighted the social landscape throughout the country was sufficient to become fully informed of the way many people were (and still are) forced to lead their lives. It was hardly necessary to dress a few of them in eye-catching garb, put them on a platform with a guitar between their legs and call it music, or art, or (lumpen) proletarian rebellion. Yet such an orthodoxy has persisted beyond the millennium.[47]

The professed links between the punks and organisations such as Rock against Racism and the Anti-Nazi League were tenuous, usually ambiguous, and therefore questionable. (The Sex Pistols, for example, never performed at a Rock against Racism event, presumably because this would have undermined their single-minded cultivation of an image of cynicism.) The claim of ambiguity in relation to punk politics was lent support by drawing attention to the juxtaposition of the swastika and other Nazi symbols with the hammer and sickle and pictures of Karl Marx on punk uniforms, just as the German Nazis before them, in the thirties, had described themselves as a national 'socialist' party and had opportunistically exploited leftist rhetoric ('fleece the rich', 'social justice for all', etc.) in their propaganda. Roger Sabin has commented on "its political 'ambiguity'(which) left ample space for right-wing interpretation."[48] And a little further on: 'As we've noted, mainstream culture was racist, and punk was bound to pick up on this to some degree. After all, the movement was born out of the same political recession that had produced the rise in far right activity, and subcultures have historically mimicked their parent cultures as well as rebelled against them.'[49] Such commentators had little doubt that seventies punk sowed the seeds for a more aggressive and overtly fascist music scene, if short-lived, in the eighties. And yet not everyone on the left took this view, not even in the Communist Party of England (Marxist-Leninist). Laurie Baker recalls many anti-fascist events during the late seventies in which 'punk' youth participated and who demanded to know who was labelling them as fascists. One should differentiate between the disenfranchised youth who dressed in punk style and the later, openly racist and nihilist, wing of punk, Oi!, which was also at some pains to distinguish itself from punk 'proper'. In any case, according to Baker, the slogan 'Punk Rock is Fascist' was dropped from Party propaganda.

In November 1977 the Party-approved programme, which the PCA had adopted and urged its members to support, consisted of three popular music groups: PLM, the West Indian band Fight Back (still a reluctant bedfellow), and Geoff Pearce's Rock trio Bright Future; a new documentary film entitled Dare to Struggle, Dare to Win; and an anti-fascist play – United We Stand. As part of this programme two tours (two duos) of Ireland were agreed, including Dublin and Cork, for November/December, organised by CANISG (Culture and Art for National Independence Study Group), the cultural wing of the Communist Party of Ireland (Marxist-Leninist).[50] Cardew and Geoff Pearce left for Dublin on 18 November, while Laurie Baker and Hugh Shrapnel followed later on 4 December, and with a different itinerary. However, the Irish comrades were clearly unprepared for Cardew and Pearce who performed just one, under-rehearsed concert, and then returned home. Disappointed and frustrated though they were by the inadequate arrangements

25. Anna, Sheila, Cornelius: Cornwall, Spring 1975

26. Mid-seventies: on a demonstration in London

27. Cardew in Berlin 1973-74

28. Internationalist Youth Concerts: Birmingham 1980

29. Cardew leading demonstration in central London, 1980

30. Demonstration against racist attacks in east London, circa 1980

31. Cardew and Sheila's living room in Leyton, early 1980s

32. Cardew's funeral, December 1981

in Ireland, Cardew and Pearce were nevertheless reluctant to criticise their Irish comrades. Cardew's generous view was that perhaps they themselves could have been more proactive, could have somehow outwitted circumstances. 'In retrospect', he writes, somewhat ambiguously, 'I think this was another symptom of the air of 'lordly detachment' that comes from our first report.'[51] We can presume, therefore, that at the unprepared and only rehearsal in Dublin Cardew would have quickly assessed the situation, begun rolling himself a cigarette, and adopted the untroubled air of a man who had seen it all before.

Meanwhile in England the situation regarding the two rebel apostates – Frances Rifkin and Keith Rowe – had provoked lengthy discussion involving several of the Party heavyweights whose knowledge and experience in artistic matters would have been at best rudimentary, and their contributions to the debate therefore nugatory. At two PCA meetings, on 25/26 October, by which time comrade Chris Coleman was no longer chairman of PCA, it was finally decided to expel Rowe from the leading group, but to retain Rifkin, despite her waywardness. (Brigid Scott-Baker was also relieved of her Party affiliation – one of several such admonitions she had received[52].) She, Rifkin, should be interviewed and her attitude and progress (her 'line') monitored. According to Hugh Shrapnel Cardew was very unhappy about this turn of events and yet, for all his disquiet, he continued to display a self-eclipsing and unfathomable complicity; his loyalty to the Party line was unassailable, and his Jesuitical cast of mind invaluably adept at redeploying the arguments to accommodate changes (some, like the reassessment of Mao, of considerable magnitude): thus the problem with Frances Rifkin was her reluctance to bring her theatre group Recreation Ground, based in the borough of Camden, under PCA committee/Party discipline, reflecting an unwillingness on her part to implement the Party line. Cardew writes in his report:

The two main issues that came out [of his talks with Frances Rifkin] were: 1. The need to earn 'professional' respect, and achieve high artistic standards, and 2. The issue of supporting opportunist theatre groups (eg Red Ladder) on a TU [Trade Union] basis – defending their right to an Arts Council grant of umpteen thousand.

This is connected with her difficulty over reports. She wants to hold onto the problems rather than solve them. She likes flitting in and out of Party circles, but does not wish to commit herself intellectually or organisationally in a proper partisan way. Eg, from a partisan point of view, opportunist theatre is an enemy force [53] – they go around the country spouting counter-revolutionary politics to working class audiences – so that the question of 'standing by them in their struggle to get money from the state' simply doesn't arise.[54]

Cardew then proposes that she should be suspended from the Party committee until she agrees 'to adopt a genuinely revolutionary line', in other words, to toe the Party line. Regarding Keith Rowe Cardew simply notes: 'I'm persisting in the struggle for discipline in his leadership of the Visual Arts group (which is quite large and lively). He is still quite surly – seems to avoid contact.' [55]

For the Party the enforcement and development of both discipline and commitment was absolutely essential, even when it opened a vein of resentment and created psychological obstructions in the lines of communication with its supporters. Such requirements allowed of no inflexion; a comrade and Cardew's close friend, Peter Devenport, who consistently failed to keep appointments, was sent a peremptory, formal communication asking for an explanation; the excuse of 'mitigating circumstances' cut no ice with the Party.

Of course, compelling examples of the importance Cardew attached to discipline, or rather to self-discipline, in his compositions and in his music-making in the pre-communist days, have been cited at regular intervals throughout these pages. And his ability to be extraordinarily focused on the task at hand – any task, whether a contribution to AMM music or the drawing up of a political plan of action – is also a quality to which there have been many references. At the same time he had the ability to compartmentalise his life, physically and emotionally. Sheila Kasabova recalls that if he took a day off, an all-too-rare occurrence, and they decided to do something or go somewhere quite unrelated either to music or politics, the moment he climbed into the car he would mentally switch off and, likewise, on their return, he would switch back again, more or less instantaneously, into Party mode. So that in his reports he could refer to Sheila with a somewhat unnerving detachment:

> JB and SK's [Sheila Kasabova] commitment to EL [East London] work is limited, though JB's support for Party is much more wholehearted. They should be encouraged but not 'pushed', and the current level of their commitment should be respected.[56]

A more dramatic scenario provided further evidence of Cardew's ability to act swiftly, coolly, and as expediently as the situation demanded. Sheila Kasabova recalls an occasion when she and Cardew were at Green Street market in Forest Gate distributing leaflets advertising a concert. They had planned to spend a rare weekend away together, with Anna, at Sheila's cottage in Cowley, Bedfordshire, and were due to leave at 6 pm.[57] However, the Party needed leafleteers and bill-stickers that evening, and Cardew, dutifully and without his partner's consent, had offered their services. Sheila and another Party supporter were putting up posters and Cardew was the 'look-out'. Suddenly, with a screeching of brakes, the police arrived. Sheila dropped the bucket and fled; within a few minutes a public house materialized and she ran in, straight past Cardew who, quite correctly, showed no reaction. Nor did he offer to pay when on ordering a drink she realised she had no money. Within minutes she was apprehended by the police and bundled into the back of a van. Four hours later, at about 2 am, Sheila, Cornelius and Anna finally set off for the cottage where they spent a very enjoyable week-end, with barely a mention of the preceding events. It was, after all, all in a day's work.

The People's Democratic Front (PDF) was set up by the CPE (M-L) as a popular front 'to defend the rights of working people and national minorities' in East London and other cities, including Birmingham and Manchester.[58] Cardew himself had been very influential in setting up the PDF in East London and assumed responsibility for its programme of action. This involved picketing, especially at the courts, printing and distribution of leaflets, canvassing, and taking part in, and sometimes leading, demonstrations against racist attacks by the then main fascist group, the National Front.[59] On 14 November, when the Post Office workers went on strike for a shorter working week, Cardew and other comrades joined the demonstration which succeeded in blocking the whole of central London and made the front page of the London *Evening Standard*.

At the same time, as a musician, composer and performer, he was active in gathering together groups of musicians and artists to support the Party's work even if, as Sheila Kasabova recalls, the purely political work always took precedence. In fact, when Cardew made an unsuccessful attempt to consolidate the East London group on the basis of support for the Party, it had been Kasabova's fear that such a development would lead eventually to the total abandonment of his cultural work. On one occasion (one of many) there was a heated discussion, emotionally highly charged and with Sheila reduced to tears – as was so often the case in these situations. A comrade who was present opined that Sheila was right to air her reservations and differences. Cardew conceded, but with bad grace, describing her reservations as 'amorphous' and 'subjective'. One detects here, admittedly from a considerable distance, a conduct, a manner, which was both patronizing and expedient on the part of both men. And it was because of Cardew's insistence on 'total struggle' (so that interpersonal relations, mediated by ideology, were subject to the same relentless scrutiny and criticism as political activity *per se*) that a visitor to Agar Grove would sometimes experience a palpable and pervasive tension. Yet Cornelius and Sheila enjoyed a close, loving relationship and he treated her daughter Anna (Tiggy) as his own; he once said to his close friend and comrade Peter Devenport: 'Perhaps I am a romantic artist, perhaps I will die poor in a garret – but I won't be alone!'[60] According to Devenport, who lodged with Cardew and Sheila for several months from late 1977 and again when they moved to Leyton, and was therefore able to observe them at close quarters, as it were, and in a domestic setting, Cardew convinced him that he was a devoted partner/lover/father. Devenport would often accompany him when he went to Barnes to see his sons Horace and Walter and on the journey home they would discuss at length the boys' problems and development, at home and at school. An undated letter to Ilona Halberstadt in 1959 already demonstrates the problematic nature of Cardew's attitude towards 'relationships':

Your trust is irrespective of me.
About that I have never before thought. Now it seems to me that to be in a relationship – like 'trusting' – I must separate myself from the world, whereas really I think I would like not only to be in, but also of and with the world. Thus you can see, if you are following me through all my inefficiencies, that all relationship is in some sense, and in some degree inimical. And to trust is to emphasise rather than reduce this.
This is too difficult to tell.
But Dear Ilona, I find this is all very serious.

One of the projects initiated by the PCA was an in-depth study of a number of classical composers and involved, among others, Michael Chant, Keith Rowe, Adrian Rifkin, Hugh Shrapnel and, of course, Cardew himself. Here, Cardew sets out the group's ambitious brief:

In deciding what to study in our particular field we should be guided by the trends, the currents and cross-currents of the present-day cultural environment. In terms of classical music these trends are fairly stable – the greatest 'geniuses' of bourgeois music are promoted year-in, year-out and monopolise vast chunks of music-lovers' time and consciousness. In studying them we should proceed in an opposite manner to the bourgeois music historians. We should study them in relation to the social and political history of their time. We should study the progress of the class struggle of that time and see how these composers viewed them (their subjective attitude), as well as what role they played in them objectively. We should demystify their heroic isolation and uniqueness, and show how they built on achievements that were handed down to them. We should be able to show in fact that music history too (as part of the overall history of mankind) is made with the masses as the motive force. We should show how the ideologies of the contending classes of their time are embodied in their music, and how and on whom they exerted their ideological influence, and discover whether and how this influence has changed with social, technical and other changes that have come about since they wrote. We should study whether their contributions to the development of musical language have remained current or become obsolete. And we should study whether these composers looked forward or backward in relation to the advanced thinking and discoveries of their time. We should challenge the basic concepts and point of view that the bourgeoisie has put forward and is putting forward on questions of the history of music.[61]

On Beethoven the (Party) line was that Beethoven was a bourgeois revolutionary and did not support the emancipation of the working class. Cardew referred to an editorial in the *Daily Telegraph*:

The next day, celebrating the fact that Beijing Radio had announced that it would celebrate the 150th anniversary (26 March) of Beethoven's death by broadcasting excerpts from the Fifth Symphony, the *Daily Telegraph* asked the question in it's editorial: 'Is it by coincidence that liberty and Beethoven and the bourgeoisie are associated in the mind?' implying correctly, if 'liberty' is understood to refer to the liberty of the bourgeoisie rather than liberty in the abstract – the answer 'No'.[62]

Cardew then pointed out that the *Daily Telegraph* linked this news with a further 'encouraging' development in China in which intellectuals who had been 'oppressed' by the so-called 'Gang of Four' (which included Mao's wife, Jiang Qing, and three other leaders of the 'left' movement in Chinese politics) had been elevated from the lowly position to which they had been assigned, whilst their 'oppressors' had been arrested:

Unity is our point of departure, and proceeding from the desire to achieve unity, we should patiently and carefully educate the intellectuals, remoulding them and help them to really shift their stand over to the side of the proletariat. In this way, unity is strengthened. All intellectuals who really wish to serve the socialist cause should be trusted, and we must improve our relations with them, help them solve various problems that must be solved so as to enable them to apply their talents in a positive way, work devotedly and willingly at their tasks and at the same time remould their world outlook.[63]

This softening and dilution of the Chinese Party's attitude towards intellectuals provoked Cardew's scorn; in a direct reference to this passage from *Peking Review* he asked, with heavy irony:

On what basis can the fighters for socialist revolution unite with bourgeois living composers who 'wish to serve the socialist cause'? What attitude can those fighting for socialism have towards Beethoven, as the most prominent representative of bourgeois classical music? [64]

And continuing in similar vein:

Compare this sweetness and light with Mao's statements of 1942: "Then does not Marxism destroy the creative mood? Yes, it does. It definitely destroys creative moods that are feudal, bourgeois, petty-bourgeois, liberalistic, individualist, nihilist, art-for-art's sake, aristocratic, decadent and pessimistic, and every other creative mood that is alien to the masses of the people and to the proletariat. So far as proletarian artists are concerned, should not these kinds of creative moods be destroyed? I think they should; they should be utterly destroyed. And while they are being destroyed, something new can be constructed." [65]

Cardew then tarred the Chinese Party with the revisionist brush:

In 1970, on the 200th anniversary of Beethoven's birth, the Socialist Unity Party of West Germany (puppet of the revisionist, or 'new bourgeois', regime in East Germany) issued a record of Beethoven's 5th symphony, and today the same work is broadcast in China. [66]
Consider these facts in relation to a very clear-cut statement in the Chinese journal *Red Flag* in 1974 (reprinted in *Hsinhua*, April 25 1974): 'classical on the one hand... reactionary effect'. [67]

And from a talk the following year:

[So] not only is this culture hostile by the mere fact of being a privilege that working people don't have access to; it is hostile by virtue of its content and ideology. Bourgeois plays and operas are not about the lives of working people and they don't express their aspirations and hopes: they are about individuals whether heroic or miserable – wrestling with their inner contradictions, agonising over subjective states, or blandly deal in abstractions. So this whole field of bourgeois culture (including classical music) is foreign to the working class, and is a burden on their backs. It is parasitic in the sense that without the productive labour of the workers there would be no surplus value out of which to make and distribute this high-flown culture. In short it is reactionary and oppressive.[68]

Yet history informs us that Cardew and the Maoists were already being left behind in the great Marxist-Leninist debate – even if, at a later date they, too, were to abandon the discredited Chairman. Disconcertingly, the Albanian Party now claimed, in an heretically 'abstract' formulation, that these (classical) composers were part of the cultural heritage of mankind.[69] Yet Cardew and his wilfully phillistine comrades in the PCA were still upholding the English Party's ill-considered, half-baked 'theories' of musical history (based on an unenlightened reading of Mao's provocative thesis ('Does not Marxism destroy the creative mood?') – from which Cardew defiantly and anachronistically quotes – which demanded that *all* bourgeois art should be subjected to criticism and exposure, including the 'masterpieces' of the eighteenth and nineteenth centuries. Hugh Shrapnel recalls 'trying to put in a good word for Mozart by saying he rebelled against the straitjacket of the feudal aristocracy and brought a new humanity and expression into music but was derided for succumbing to bourgeois ideology by trying to present Mozart as being a "champion of the people".'[70]

Is it the (bourgeois) *content* of Beethoven's music that is 'foreign' and harmful to the working class (and if so, how), or is it its *role* in contemporary, capitalist society which is the essential bone of contention? And to compound the dilemma: is it not true that Beethoven's music is equally 'alien' to the young, contemporary 'bourgeois'? Perhaps not harmful, but certainly irrelevant. Or is it, as the 'revisionists' aver, simply a question of 'education'? Or is it generational? Is listening to classical music a pleasure one can (tends to) discover late in life? Conversely, is it possible for classical music-lovers to turn away from classical music in later life? The case of Lenin and music (art) is illuminating; one wonders whether Cardew gave this the consideration it merited. The psychological effect of art, and in particular music, on the founder of Marxism-Leninism has often been remarked upon. But was it the 'bourgeois' content of Beethoven's music that caused him such mental and physical distress? Or was it the immanent meanings, the complex matrix of associational references – in short, was it his profound love of and need for *Art* that was the source of such an oceanic, uncontrollable emotional response? Lenin himself answered the question:

I don't know of anything better than the [Beethoven's] 'Appassionata', I can listen to it every day. Amazing, superhuman music! I always think with a pride that may be naïve: look what miracles people can perform![71]

Cardew's own views tended to fluctuate in his texts and interviews; sometimes, temporarily removing his Party hat and allowing the informality of the occasion to take over, he would express doubt and ambivalence (*vide* the Adrian Jack interview). To return to Beethoven one might venture two considerations: if Historical Materialism determines that the bourgeois revolution was both necessary and inevitable, and therefore desirable (?), it seems unreasonable to criticise Beethoven for not expressing a pie in the sky desire for the 'emancipation' of the working class at the beginning of the nineteenth century; there were no Marxist parties in Vienna in 1800. Furthermore, amidst the euphoria of nineteenth-century bourgeois triumphalism and optimism Beethoven expressed profound disillusionment (beginning with his rejection of Napoleon). Nineteenth-century 'bourgeois man' was a quite different animal to the modern bourgeois man of the new millennium when quietism and cynicism have overtaken idealism (however limiting and self-serving that may have been during the Romantic period). Does Beethoven's music, especially the later music, 'harmonise' with the sensibilities of the modern bourgeois?

To quote Thomas Mann on Beethoven's bourgeois, contemporary admirers: 'In the works of the last period they stood with heavy hearts before a process of dissolution, or alienation, of a mounting into air no longer familiar or safe to meddle with.'[72] Beethoven's own words attest to a positive, rather than a patronising attitude towards 'the masses'. And, hypothetically (speculatively), might not the intrinsicality, especially in the late quartets, of the intimate references to folk music ('the people') pre-figure, however insubstantially, the kind of world that Cardew himself was fighting for? Perhaps these hermetic works, with their transcendent quality, and for all their 'bourgeois' provenance, will survive (and nourish?) the 'dictatorship of the proletariat', and will one day assume their exalted position amongst the artistic repertory of the classless society.

Cardew also made a considerable number of notes on Bach (a composer with whom he had great empathy right from his schooldays); all the main sources were referred to.[73] This was done in a systematic and painstaking way, the chronology of Bach's musical activities throughout his life duly noted and discussed in relation to contemporary developments in science and philosophy. The material was intended for an (as yet undiscovered) talk on Bach for the PCA. Cardew was as aware as anyone of the enduring, if problematic, links with the 'incomparable human creativity' of the past, but the exigencies of the Party's revolutionary programme disallowed, overruled even the acknowledgment of such inexpedient truths.

On 15 December a 'Defence' concert at the Earl of Essex pub in East London was organised by the PCA in support of comrades who were on trial at the Redbridge Court the next day. A militant leaflet distributed in streets and factory plants by the East London

People's Democratic Front states:

> In particular it [the concert] draws attention to the vicious attack carried out by
> the police, assisted by fascists, on an anti-fascist meeting held at the Co-op Hall,
> Ilford Lane, on 29 July. In the fight that followed, seven Comrades of the Communist
> Party of England (Marxist-Leninist) were arrested. The state thinks that if it brings
> these Comrades into Court it can whitewash its attack on them, and give it the
> appearance of being 'legal'. But in fact it is the Comrades who have been
> dominating the courtroom and ruthlessly exposing the evidence of the police as
> a bundle of lies and concoctions. This phoney trial is continuing on 16 December,
> and we call on all progressive people to come to Redbridge Court that day and
> support the Comrades.[74]

The concert was introduced by Cardew, as the defence campaign representative,
against a backcloth with the slogan: 'Uphold Active Resistance to all attacks by the
monopoly capitalist class'. Bright Future provided the music, including a new song for
the campaign by Geoff Pearce, and the film *Dare to Struggle, Dare to Win* was screened.
There followed a discussion, more songs, and the evening ended with a spirited rendering
of the 'Internationale'.

The report of a visit to an Asian doctor's surgery in Ilford, as well as a discussion of
the Defence Concert and the picket at Redbridge Court, provide good examples of the
way Cardew and his comrades tried to encourage the local people to take a stand against
racism:

> At a doctor's surgery near the Co-Op Hall (the one with NF written on the door)
> we asked to see the doctor. His assistant would not let us, but took the line
> that he wasn't going to do anything about the graffiti. An Indian girl in the waiting
> room asked to see the leaflet and then everyone took one. Then we went and
> bought a felt tip pen and crossed out the graffiti – at which the assistant said
> 'Now I expect we'll get a brick through the window'. He also said there were two
> other surgeries in Woodlands Road, both plastered with racist slogans.
> This assistant was a bit red-faced about the whole thing, but anti-racist. We could
> have handled the whole thing a lot better. a) We should have got the people talking
> – all nationalities were there – about 10 people, and b) we should have
> encouraged <u>them</u> to wipe out the graffiti.[75]

What emerges clearly in his report on the Defence Concert is the extraordinary level
of responsibility that Cardew took upon himself and, moreover, his unwillingness to blame

anyone but himself for any perceived shortcomings in the organisation of the event: the lack of a satisfactory arrangement for the children; the fact that new people were not properly welcomed and integrated; that due to the fact that the PCA committee had not been properly mobilised (by whom?). Cardew had to run the concert single-handedly; that there was not enough time for discussion; and that he himself had failed to brief anyone to write a report of the concert for *Workers Weekly*. As for the Redbridge picket and demonstration, Cardew again subjected himself to 'self-criticism' in a situation where there were multiple failings all round. The crux of the matter was that for Cardew the revolution was *at the very centre* of his life. Few of his comrades, if any, gave evidence of a similar, all-consuming commitment, so that, for example, a talk on pop music by the 'pop study group' did not materialise. Even a relatively stalwart member such as Geoff Pearce claimed he had not had the time 'to tackle it'. And an annual report still waited to be drawn up. The PCA had been in existence for nearly two years. It should have been a sobering thought for the Party elite that without Cardew's unflagging efforts, intellectually and physically, little, if anything, would have been achieved.

The latter months of the year had been a period of intense, unremitting political activity. Hectic, one might say, except that Cardew always gave the impression of equanimity, whether such excessive and relentless demands on his talents and energies emanated from the Party or, in earlier times, from a particularly complicated musical score. But there were rewards, and not least the number of letters he had received throughout the year, from around the country, and mainly from the younger generation, expressing interest in the PCA and wanting to establish contact. Many of these were from foreigners resident in Britain or from ethnic minority and non-English groups (Malaysian, Indian, Welsh, among others). Somehow or other the existence of a 'progressive cultural association', perhaps even the nature of its work and its aims, had reached a small but not insignificant portion of the very people Cardew wanted to reach. As the New Year approached this would have given him cheer.

Notes and references

1 1 *Mao Tse-tung Poems*: the third of *Three Short Poems – to the tune of Shih Liu Tzu Ling* (1934-35) (Peking: Foreign Languages Press, 1976).

2 From a letter to the German magazine *Berliner Hefte, Zeitschrift für Kultur und Politik*, 5 October 1976.

3 In an email correspondence from Rod Eley to JT, dated 8 July 2005, Eley writes: 'I think the bomb scare was the usual concoction to make sure the audience didn't come or went away, but in fact I don't think Vipond [David Vipond: Irish Marxist-Leninist party member] and his wife Blaithnaid were able to muster much interest from the Labour Club, which was actually the last place in Belfast where nationalists and unionists, protestants and catholics, whatever you want to call the sectarian divide, could mix freely. But the circles were aging fast and withering away, i.e. the old trade union and socialist movement, in the face of the sectarian divide and the body count from the bombing campaign, etc.' Rod Eley, an Englishman who eventually became General Secretary of the Irish Marxist-Leninist Party, was living in Belfast at the time and probably had a more reliable grasp of the situation.

4 The Heathrow Asians 'scandal' refers to one of the more pernicious myths invented at the time (still nurtured and exploited by the media), that people who arrived in Britain, in particular from the sub-continent, were granted a *rite de passage* and proceeded to live the life of Riley on the backs of the indigenous Britons. This particular incident referred to the situation in Uganda, where General Idi Amin had given notice to Uganda's 70,000 Asians to leave the country within 3 months. 'Since most of them were British citizens this greatly embarrassed the British Government....caught between the evident obligation to allow British citizens into Britain, and the clamour against allowing them in if they were numerous and black'. Peter Calvocoressi, *World Politics since 1945* (London, New York: Longman, 1996), p.664.

5 Frances Rifkin, from a recorded interview with JT, 14 April 2004.

6 Banner Theatre Company, founded by Charles Parker in the mid-seventies, is a Socialist multi-media theatre company which has been performing in the West Midlands and nationally for over thirty years.

7 From a typewritten PCA Report on Grunwick Day of Action, 11 July 1977.

8 Ibid.

9 Ibid.

10 At the end of April he had applied himself energetically to the task of securing engagements for a projected tour of Germany in the autumn (October/November) of 1977. A considerable number of letters were dispatched detailing repertoire (mainly his own works) and a proposal for a lecture entitled 'Gesellschaftliche Rolle der Komponisten' (the Social Role of the Composer). There was a small measure of success but a thick wad of replies (sixteen) stapled together and labelled 'Duds' reflects also the negative and disheartening consequences of the exercise. The extant correspondence suggests that there were engagements in Lüneberg, Essen and possibly Freiburg during November, although there is no hard evidence to show that these lectures/concerts actually materialized.

11 From Cardew's typewritten Report on the MU Biennial Conference, Loughborough, July 12-14, 1977.

12 Ibid.

13   Ibid.

14   Ibid.

15   "From the General Resolution of the First Revolutionary Conference of Progressive Cultural Association, as printed in *Cogs and Wheels,* No.3, August 1978.

16   Of course some of these areas, in particular equality for women and a whole raft of issues affecting women, had been taken up, relatively successfully, by movements with strong 'reformist' impulses, such as the mainstream feminist movement.

17   The notion of 'losing' is the natural and essential spawn of a competitive culture. Nowadays, therefore, it has acquired a broader signification, which includes stigmatisation. For example, 'losing' is not only about 'failure'; it also encompasses anti-social behaviour. To be a 'loser' is to be an outcast, a psychological cripple. In the year 2003, in Canterbury, England, I noticed a maledictory message on the city's litter bins: a person who negligently disposes of litter in the street was branded 'a loser'.

18   From *'LITTLE BANGS* – towards a nihilist theory of improvisation', a lecture delivered on 31 March 2000, in Frankfurt, Germany).

19   *The Cutting Edge – Women and the Pit Strike,* ed. by Vicky Seddon (London: Lawrence and Wishart, 1986), p.277.

20   Edward Elgar, *Complete Edition, Vol. 5,* ed.by Robert Anderson and Jerrold Northrop Moore. (London: Novello, 1985), Foreword, p.ii.

21   V.I. Lenin, 'Critical Remarks on the National Question' in *Lenin on Literature and Art* (Moscow, Progress Publishers, 1970), p.85.

22   From a typewritten sheet advertising a PCA 'anti-fascist concert' at the Eagle and Child pub in Forest Gate on 12 August 1977.

23   From 'Role of the composer in the class struggle'. Undated, but probably 1978. (*CCR*)

24   This may well have been because of what Baker considered to be an over-simplification of the relation of Punk Rock to fascism. In his experience many rank-and-file 'punks' were decidedly anti-racist.

25   According to the PCA Constitution there were two levels of membership: 'Associate membership is open to all who support the aims of the organisation. Full membership is open to those associate members who actively participate in the implementation of the aims. The PCA functions by means of a Committee which is elected by the full members. …The role of the Committee is to lead politically, ideologically, and practically.'

26   From a typewritten, undated 'PCA Report'. All italics added by JT.

27   From a cassette recording of the discussion by Benedict Mason. The music was recorded by Dave Smith.

28   Ibid.

29   Ibid.

30   Bruce Russell (b.1946), British abstract painter.

31   From Benedict Mason's cassette recording.

32   Walter Benjamin, from a review by Walter Benjamin of the *Dreigroschenroman*. Cf. *Versuche über Brecht*, Frankfurt 1966, p.90. As quoted in Hannah Arendt's *Introduction to Benjamin's Illuminations* (Fontana/Collins, 1979), p.15.

33   Perhaps it is precisely those 'abstract' paintings that lack a compelling (visual) presence which invite a consolatory act of interpretation, by way of compensation, as it were. There is always plenty to discuss after experiencing a mediocre piece of art, or music; it is the

masterpiece which does away with the argument altogether, that reduces us to silence.

34   Murdoch, *Metaphysics as a Guide to Morals* (London: Penguin Books, 1992), p.462.

35   "The illusion is that art is for the sake of art, that it has nothing to do with the rest of the world – art is over *here*, politics is over *there*. For me, that's not true. I believe politics is into everything." Max Roach, American musician, from an interview in March 1985, as quoted in Graham Lock, *Chasing the Vibrations* (Exeter, Devon: Stride Publications, 1994), p.86.

36   It reminds me of the early sixties when I was studying in Warsaw: Party functionaries would also attend church – just to be on the safe side.

37   Although it must be said, in the last years it seemed as if he had begun to accept these different levels of commitment.

38   Mao Tse-tung, 'On "Let a hundred flowers blossom, let a hundred schools of thought contend"', in *Selected Readings from the Works of Mao Tse-tung* (Peking: Foreign Languages Press, 1971), pp.462-468.

39   The Albanians were predictably less charitable in their interpretation of Mao's metaphor: "….it led to Chinese diplomats dancing rock and roll at the US embassy…..there is only one artistic method: socialist realism." From a speech by the leader of the Albanian delegation at the 10th anniversary of the Canadian Party.

40   Geoff Pearce thinks he may have been the author of this article, but is not sure. Nor is anybody else I have asked.

41   It was eventually decided, because of a certain level of harassment of the landlord, to leave the Eagle and Child pub and find alternative venues for PCA concerts and events.

42   Jon Savage, *England's Dreaming: Sex Pistols and Punk Rock* (London: Faber and Faber, 1994), p.243. Perhaps the students had seen the photos of The Clash wearing swastika armbands.

43   Ibid, p.242-3.

44   'A quarter of a century on, it is widely understood that punk has been among the most influential of youth movements. Less freely admitted is the fact that this influence was entirely malign. Not that this is any sort of revelation. Even at the time, many of those broadly sympathetic to the counter-revolution understood that there was no excuse, except mental illness, for the sort of blank, negative anger that the Sex Pistols sold.' (Deborah Orr, *Independent on Sunday*, Section 12, 12 October 2003).

45   The Party disputed this: "The spuriousness of this argument was demonstrated in 1973 when anti-fascist students threw [the British psychologist] [Hans] Eysenck (notorious for his fascist theories of race and intelligence) off the stage when he was lecturing at the London School of Economics. This has not made Eysenck a martyr. On the contrary, he is now completely discredited – research has shown that the data on which many of his theories rested were fraudulently assembled." From 'A Motion against Fascism' in *Cogs and Wheels* No.1, p.14.

46   Ibid, pp.14-15.

47   Harry Gilonis demurs: Punk 'was unequivocally empowering to the semi-skilled, and excluded, just as the Scratch was. And there were, immediately post-punk, a lot of interesting challenges to traditional song structures, instrumentation, group hierarchies, etc.' Email communication to JT sometime at the beginning of 2006. Punk was also, in Gilonis's view, 'the product of an ill-informed urge to annoy elders and betters – the Bill Grundys of this world'. Ibid.

48   Roger Sabin, *Punk Rock: so what* (London and New York: Routledge, 1999), p.199.

49   Ibid, p.212.

50   CANISG also produced a publication entitled *Nua-Chultúr,* which comprised revolutionary poems, songs, cartoons, articles on Irish cultural and political issues, and which had probably been the inspiration for the English Party's *Cogs and Wheels.*

51   From a typewritten report: PCA Dublin visit of 18 November.

52   On more than one occasion the Party seems to have experienced difficulty with Brigid Scott-Baker's outspokenness, one of her many virtues. On one May Day in the late seventies, possibly 1979, she was standing on the Embankment brandishing a Party banner. The PLM truck was a little way away and there was a problem with the technical equipment which comrade Brigid normally operated and understood. However, the Party had banned her, for some political indiscretion, and she was not allowed to be on the truck. Brigid Scott-Baker was one of the Party's most valuable assets; but they did not know it. Or rather her independent spirit was considered a threat. In this they may well have been correct.

53   These 'opportunist' groups to which Cardew refers produced lively, often humorous, agit-prop theatre which had begun to build up a reputation in left-wing circles.

54   From a typewritten PCA Report, dated 29 November 1977.

55   Ibid.

56   From a typewritten Report on PCA EL [East London] work, dated 1 November 1977.

57   Ownership of the cottage was shared between Sheila Kasabova and Richard and Victoria Gibson, who lived in the Shetlands. It was quite isolated, surrounded by fields, and had no electricity – for Cardew and his family a minor deprivation; it must have felt like home from home.

58   At the request of the Party Hugh Shrapnel had moved to Birmingham, where he taught and did factory work until 1981.

59   This included the aforementioned anti-racist demonstration in Lewisham in August 1977 which to all intents and purposes eliminated the National Front in that area. It was, according to the CPE (M-L), a vindication of the revolutionary, as opposed to, 'peaceful', road to socialism.

60   Oral communication from PD to JT sometime in the nineties.

61   From a paper entitled PCA 'High' Bourgeois music Study Group. Draft Orientation.

62   From an undated (probably 1977) two-page, handwritten text entitled 'Beethoven (1770-1827): dead or alive?'

63   From *Peking Review*, under sub-heading, 'Pressurising and Attacking the Intellectuals', 18 March 1977, p.20.

64   From 'Beethoven (1770-1827): dead or alive?'

65   Mao Tse-tung, *Mao Tse-tung on Literature and Art*, p.36.

66   The fact that the 'revisionist' parties had so enthusiastically adopted Beethoven 's Fifth as a rallying call was for Cardew incontestable evidence of the work's incompatibility with 'proletarian revolution' (As we have seen, in the 'Songs for our Society' class at Goldsmiths in 1975 Cardew had cast the Merchant's songs in Beethovenian/classical style as the merchant was the 'bourgeois character in the play').

67   From 'Beethoven (1770-1827): dead or alive?'

68   From an undated talk, probably 1978, entitled 'Role of the Composer in the Class Struggle'. Some of these issues arose in the interview with Adrian Jack in the May 1975 issue of

Music and Musicians and have been discussed above.

69   Even more disconcertingly, 'a direct lift from Lenin' – as Harry Gilonis observed.

70   Email correspondence from HS to JT, June 13 2003.

71   Maxim Gorky, from *Lenin on Literature and Art* (Moscow: Progress Publishers, 1970), pp. 246-47.

72   Thomas Mann, *Dr.Faustus* (London: Secker and Warburg, 1976), p.52.

73   In the previously mentioned recorded conversation sometime in the early nineties Kurt Schwertsik remarked: "Cornelius also had the traditional side – he played the *Well-Tempered Clavier* with great equanimity. Unlike Cage, who didn't have it, and the Europeans, who denied it".

74   From a leaflet entitled 'Fight back Against Government and Nazi Organised Racist and Fascist Attacks'.

75   From a typewritten PCA EL [east London] report, dated 17 December 1977.

(*CCR*) Also found in *Cornelius Cardew A Reader*

Cornelius Cardew a life unfinished

21
The God that Failed 1978

The dismantling of Mao Tse-tung's reputation and influence had already begun informally, even before his death. Thereafter the process gathered momentum and 1978 saw the beginning of a period of refutation during which Mao's theories, both political and cultural, were publically and systematically criticised, in particular by the Albanian Party of Labour under Enver Hoxha, who, for Cardew and his comrades, became the new leader of the International Marxist-Leninist Communist movement. Yet in England, under the stewardship of Carol Reakes, the Maoist orthodoxy persisted, with ever-decreasing tolerance, reaching its apotheosis in the ill-fated Conference in Birmingham in April, which is discussed below.

Frances Rifkin and Laurie Baker were just two of those (Party supporters) who fell foul of the Party's ongoing programme of ideological purification. The Party disapproved of what they considered to be Recreation Ground's wayward and promiscuous politics and therefore could not entertain their presence in the Progressive Cultural Association. Its reliance on Arts Council, Trade Union and Labour Party funding compromised any relation it might seek to revolutionary politics:

> 'Opportunist theatre'… expresses 'militancy' but the political line is 'counter-revolutionary'; opportunist theatre is dangerous because it *sounds* revolutionary and therefore can influence people who harbour revolutionary sentiments.[1]

Rifkin claimed that Recreation Ground had been misrepresented and slandered, that it was nonsense to label its actors as 'careerist', 'opportunist', when they were working, relatively speaking, for a pittance. Actors joined Recreation Ground because they wanted to work, to *act*, and they believed in the kind of theatre that Recreation Ground represented; a subsequent commitment to a prescriptive, political agenda was not necessarily something they had anticipated or welcomed.

Shortly after a PCA meeting, on 13 January, at which 'the issue of FR's [Frances Rifkin] commitment to PCA' was discussed, Cardew contacted two Recreation Ground members, Brian Davey and Dave Statham:

> I had talks with Dave and Brian separately at RG [Recreation Ground] and clarified PCA/RG relations, and discussed how they could get active in PCA. Talked about opportunist theatre and advised them to get active in Theatre Study Group.[2]

In the circumstances that prevailed it would be reasonable to suspect that Cardew's aim was to cast doubts on Frances Rifkin's integrity and to undermine her authority. In fact, Rifkin knew nothing of these approaches; in her view, then and now, such actions demonstrated how 'manipulative', 'unscrupulous', 'unkind', and 'monomaniacal' comrade Cardew was. And those who occupied the upper reaches of the Party hierarchy were, according to Rifkin, of the same ilk.[3] And yet, paradoxically, at meetings of the Actors' Union, Equity, she would uphold the political line of the CPE(M-L). She recalls that the Trotskyists would try to inveigle Union members into joining either the Socialist Workers' Party (SWP) or the Workers' Revolutionary Party (WRP). By contrast, the CPE(M-L) would try to unite the Union, and thereby strengthen it; their Party 'line' was that the Union and the Party were separate. Rifkin agreed with this and attempted, with a measure of success, to implement it at Union meetings.

Laurie Baker's indiscretion was of a different order which, if not resolved, was more amicably mediated. He had proposed that the PCA should develop contacts with traditional and folk-orientated groups such as brass bands and steel bands. Cardew's dismissal of such ventures probably emanated from a higher (Party) authority: 'I think he (Baker) is still on a small business platform here; he has the illusion that you can commercially, or professionally, engage such bands to play revolutionary music.'[4] Was Cardew, the Party dogmatist, jumping to conclusions here? One would assume that it had not been Baker's intention to propose that the bands should play revolutionary music; rather that they should play their own music as part of a 'broad front' policy. Like Recreation Ground these bands would not have been under PCA leadership; nor would the members have expressed anything more than, perhaps, a grudging acceptance of a shared platform with the PCA. If they could have been persuaded to include Cardew's *Vietnam's Victory* (for brass ensemble), for example, in their programme, this would have been no more than a token gesture, even if it turned out to be a musically satisfying experience. Just as actors joined Recreation Ground because they wanted to act, musicians joined steel bands and brass bands because they wanted to make music: it was cultural recreation. As for the 'small business' platform, if that is what it was, of course the Party was opposed to all such 'petit bourgeois initiatives'; it was individualistic and its practitioners were often politically 'reactionary' (vide Marx's characterisation in the *Communist Manifesto*) – proud of their achievement of separating themselves from the working class into which they had been born and justifying it by referral to their own superior qualities: thrift, hard work, sacrifice, determination, intelligence, and so forth. As far as the Party was concerned, such initiatives as Baker was proposing, such aspirations, merely deflected from the central issue of the overthrow of the capitalist system.

During all these discussions, in which he alternated between Jesuitic equivocation and a more direct, censorious approach, Cardew insisted that in any situation, work or recreational, the CPE(M-L) Party line, represented the straight and narrow path from which there could be no deviation. In this respect PCA meetings, though without the same degree of severity and concentration, would have resembled the Party's public meetings, as I recall them, in the early seventies: a moral court of enquiry where an atmosphere of nervous acquiescence prevailed, and where an innocent rejoinder from a supporter would only serve to demonstrate his or her deeply-entrenched bourgeois world-outlook, which could be re-moulded only by 'mass work' ('shuffling their feet over to the side of the people') under the guidance of the Party. Morally, the Party would brook no infraction of its code, no departure from what they had imagined to themselves as working-class morality. Party ideologue Cardew saw the world through the prism of Party consciousness; he was the ultimate referent, a model; and this, matched by his untiring activism, his 'street credibility', made him a 'shining example' for which he would receive both reward and, ultimately, punishment. His ascent within the Party hierarchy had become irresistible; it was now only a matter of time before he would be invited to join the Party's inner circle.

But if the trappings persisted, the 'content' of Maoism was now under critical scrutiny; sanctioned by the Party a critique began to unfold and much of an East London group meeting, which Cardew and Sheila Kasabova attended, was taken up with a discussion of the now discredited 'three worlds' theory.[5] One can understand, if not sympathise with, the Party's dilemma: they, more than anybody, were tarred with the Maoist brush and were therefore in a vulnerable position; they had uttered the Chairman's name in hushed, reverential tones; they had pronounced his inviolable thoughts with the ardour and wide-eyed conviction of members of a religious sect. Tactically, the Party elite had to be extremely circumspect; aspects of Mao's theories could be criticised, but the veil of secrecy, the discipline, the *control*, had to be maintained and safeguarded. The means through which power was wielded over the few supporters they had mustered so far could not be challenged. The Party monolith could not be allowed to be broken up.

So that when a new 'mass work' programme was drawn up, including a list of individuals and their responsibilities, Cardew took some members to task: 'He is the problematic one. He is all for Marxist-Leninist principles, but when it comes to giving up some evenings to mass work, he hesitates.'[6] Then, in a rare token of leniency, Cardew concedes: 'Actually, he is courting, so it's understandable'.[7] No such indulgence is granted to his own family when, taking up the theme of love and relationships, Sheila Kasabova objects to Cardew's suggestion that he and she should work (for the Party) on alternate Saturdays: 'Can't we have one family evening a week at least'?[8] Cardew's unrelenting response typifies his attitude to domestic matters:

> Trouble is she sees EL [East London] programme as a threat to her 'normal' life. I tried to collectivise the issue – which included Anna's (Sheila's daughter) participation in the Red Guards – but it ended in tears and despair lasting well into the next day. We probably will alternate. Her agreeing to sell WW [*Workers' Weekly*] in the market is a big breakthrough.[9]

As for Anna's participation in the Red Guards, this was an absurd proposal which Anna's father, George Kasabov, would certainly have vetoed, and with Sheila's consent.[10] As we have seen in countless situations throughout his life, Cardew had always revelled in the obligations and challenges of domestic, family life; and yet, in the political years, when it cut across the demands of the Party, as it often did, it would metamorphose from a paradigmatic relationship of love and affection, sharing and understanding, into a 'bourgeois life style' – a maledictory catchphrase which provided a defensive weapon against powerfully instinctive and subversive feelings.

Cardew's PCA report, dated 15 to 22 January, is written in an unusually personal vein and reads more like one of the earlier Journals. It also reveals the prodigious extent of his day-to-day commitment: on 15 January he is present at a Social at Recreation Ground at which the Party documentary film, *Dare to Struggle, Dare to Win,* is shown and discussed; this is followed by talks with the East London group in relation to the PCA committee. The next day (and at least twice a week) he leaves home at 5 am, in the dark and cold, driving across London to arrive in time for the morning shift at Ford's at Dagenham where he and a few comrades manage to sell nine copies of *Workers' Weekly*.[11] On 17 January he attends another (anti-racist) meeting with the East London group. On the 18th he is teaching. On the 19th he is back at Ford's billsticking. Late that evening he has talks with the Visual Arts group about banners for a forthcoming event;

this was taking longer than had been anticipated because, according to Sheila Kasabova and Keith Rowe, their work was being disrupted by unreasonable Party demands; they argue and Cardew gets his way. On 20 January there is a PCA meeting at 8 am for which Cardew arrives late because his alarm did not go off. In the evening he returns to Forest Gate for anti-racist, anti-fascist committee meetings to discuss recruiting progress, among other things, with the East London comrades. He looks through the contents of the new, second issue of *Cogs and Wheels* and assesses the financial situation; he seems to be able to hold an extraordinary amount of information in his head. He leaves notes for some people to carry out this, and to ensure that other people carry out that. He appears to have assumed overall responsibility; one is reminded of the Scratch Orchestra. On 21 January he is with a few comrades in Kilburn, in northwest London, for 'mass work' (selling *Workers' Weekly*, leafleting for a 'Bloody Sunday' concert in support of the Irish struggle on 29 January, engaging passers-by). As usual, somebody fails to turn up; the pace, the mental and physical demands, are relentless. Cardew then lists 'some problems': one of the members of the Visual Arts group, Prudence Stevenson, Sheila Kasabova's friend, has decided to drop out 'because of the Party'. Cardew is convinced, however, that the source of the problem is her husband, Drew – a leftist who is profoundly sceptical of the CPE (M-L)'s viability. Cardew visits them. The husband insists that the Party is not a mass party, does not have mass support; nor is it creating alternative structures to replace those of bourgeois society; it denies the importance of the contribution of the Women's Movement. The discussion gets 'rather heated'. Cardew describes Prudence and her husband condescendingly as being 'at a low political level' – an opinion his notes do not bear out. He reflects that he should have been 'more patient'. One gets the impression that he was discomposed by the criticisms, however familiar he undoubtedly was with both the letter and the spirit of the argument. And lest, in this welter of detail, it may have temporarily escaped our consciousness, we should remind ourselves that all or most of this activity occurred before or after his day job at Diagram Visual Information Ltd.

The above report (15-22 January), from which I have abstracted considerable detail, is an accurate reflection of Cardew's daily existence over an extended period – a *way of life* which, I believe, from time to time he needed to objectify, through verbal description, in order to retrieve, if momentarily, some *personal* space in a situation where he was beholden to others, by which we understand to the *cause,* for every moment of his waking hours. He was under enormous stress, mentally and physically. And we can add to this roster of duties and obligations: Party meetings and discussions on policy; the shoe-string delegations he would lead to various parts of the world; working on Party articles; preparing talks and speeches for meetings; an evening rehearsal for an imminent concert. And always the threats and reality of danger. The Party was dangerous, or rather

– because of its refusal to compromise its principles, particularly in the struggle against fascism and racism – one might say that it *courted* danger. The demands were unremitting, relentless, prodigious. For Cardew this was what 'being a communist' meant.

From his childhood, everything had an element of danger in it. In Nature and Art he sought and found danger, and purity. He led an extremely demanding, hard life; he chose a stoical existence. What sustained him in that last decade? The *truth* of Marxism-Leninism? A loving partner? At home, in a brief, quiet moment, he sits at the piano. What does he play? His Irish folk song arrangements? What about 'art'? Bourgeois masterpieces? Bryn Harris recalls staying over at Elm Park Road on many occasions when he had missed the last train back to Bracknell. Cardew would often play his out-of-tune Broadwood and nearly always Bach, especially the *Toccata, Adagio and Fugue*. For certain not Feldman, not Cage. There is now an unbridgeable remoteness from this music.

During 1977/78 Cardew's compositional output was at a low ebb: a ten minute piece for solo bass clarinet (*Mountains*) and a few routine songs.[12] The above mentioned 'Ford Workers Song' was written by Cardew and Devenport for a Ford strike, which included a march by the Dagenham plant workers, on which PLM was playing (Ex.21.1). Cardew and Devenport sat up the night before in Cardew's house in Agar Grove writing it. Cardew came up with the three repeated notes at the beginning, a stylistic feature which he liked and which I have referred to in my discussion of the earlier music.

Ex.21.1. From the 'Ford Workers' Song'.

Of even more (political) consequence was the observation that Keith Rowe's disaffection was growing – a state of mind which, according to Cardew, betrayed his 'petit bourgeois opposition to democratic centralism'. Rowe was critical of the Party's high-handed behaviour, which he blamed for Prudence Stevenson's departure, and resented the fact that a Visual Arts group project could be held up at any time, under intolerable pressure from the Party, and with no explanation or justification. Rowe recalls that throughout his association with the Party, demands would be made and, more often than not, met, however unreasonable: for example, he would be told to drive to Birmingham from London, and would have to wait outside, or in the car, while a meeting took place. He would subsequently bring the comrades back to London in the early hours with just a few hours remaining before driving across the capital to his 'day job'. In effect, as a supporter, all one's waking hours would be subject to Party control, and to censure.[13]

As the Party's belief in its own immortality increased, so did its demand for unquestioning acceptance and loyalty from its rank and file. Expressions of an enquiring, as opposed to a submissive nature, were treated harshly, and in discussion the mildest hint of scepticism would receive short shrift. A psychological diagnosis of the Party's behaviour – and by 'Party' we are referring to a self-appointed elite, a handful of people – might suggest that it had its roots in a deep and unconscious sense of insecurity, of vulnerability, particularly in the light of the deeply unsettling effect (for some traumatic) of the exposure of Mao's fallibility, and that in order to assuage such feelings the *other* should suffer. The relation of the Party to its satellite groups and supporters had long been a bone of contention, although apart from Keith Rowe and Frances Rifkin few were willing to express open dissent. Some opted for the relative comfort of silent acquiescence while others quietly drifted away into 'petit bourgeois nihilism'. The PCA constitution might have stated that

the PCA is not an organisation of the Party. Those leading the PCA are not necessarily Party members; also, PCA members are not necessarily under the discipline of the Party. PCA membership does not bring a member under discipline of the Party: PCA is a mass organisation of the people.[14]

But PCA members were always conscious of the fact that the Association *was* a creature of the Party, *was* subject to Party discipline, and for some its status *vis-à-vis* the Party was a source of considerable discomfort and self-questioning. The occasional personal asides in Cardew's notes and reports show that he was also preoccupied with problems which resided at home:

Anna has been ill this week; I have discovered that I have a £100 overdraft; SK [Sheila] has been depressed every day except one. I urgently have to find work; besides which I have to find time to write 20 mins of orchestral music for a gig on 22 February when I go to Norway.[15]

The 29 January East London concert/meeting was not, according to Cardew, a success. (Nor for that matter did the planned release of a record of PLM music materialise on Laurie and Brigid Scott-Baker's new Unity Records label). Part of the problem was the fact that the PCA committee showed little commitment to the East London group;

most of them lived and worked in another part of town, as did Cardew at that time.

> Why wasn't it packed out? My impression of the week is that we spent too much time on things and not enough on people… Altogether I see considerable passivity on the part of the PCA committee. They don't regard these events as their responsibility. The whole PCA struggle over line has cleared the air, but left me in a quite embattled position. Only HS [Hugh Shrapnel] can be fully counted on. LB [Laurie Baker] is positive but his head is full of dubious schemes. There is something in MS [name not remembered] that can be developed but she is crippled by illness. This committee has to be united and galvanised into action in support of the East London work. Meanwhile my work in ELPF [East London People's Front] is virtually at a standstill, and I can't see how to take it up. I can do plenty of work in ELPF but I don't have the spirit of leading it. Three things are undermining me: not living in East London, a heavy bourgeois work programme over the next month, and the problems of leading PCA![16]

Reading Cardew's reports one is struck by his extraordinary grasp not only of the broader perspective of strategy and tactics, but also of the minutest detail. It was a gift which had served him compositionally: the immensity of *The Great Learning*, the vastness of *Treatise*, their complexity, their breadth and scope splintered by a superabundance of homeopathic detail: the dots and points, specks and motes – the crumbs of a transient musical existence. And then the Scratch Orchestra and the extraordinary, ordinary, warts-and-all people who came together with subtle and challenging demands, fragile yet resilient, creative yet down-to-earth, biddable yet subversive and ungovernable, mercurial and wayward yet dependable. Small wonder then that in the later years, as a political activist, his ability to empathise (despite his strictness) – to fathom the shortcomings of his comrades, to address and overcome their weaknesses – came to represent a kind of *moral* ascendancy which in turn earned him enormous respect: volunteers would fail to show up, so that agreed tasks would be unfulfilled; comrades would arrive late, well after the agreed time; 'promises' to do or to provide this and that were broken. The reasons were various; we have seen how the Party elite drove its supporters with little or no concern for their individual well-being, and some simply could not stand the pace. There were different levels of commitment: some Party workers and supporters harboured reservations, some were occupied with 'other things', some were trying to nurture relationships; not surprisingly, then, some Party members and rank-and-file supporters did look as if they had suffered multiple deprivations. Cardew was profoundly aware of all these contingencies, and as if to compensate on behalf of his comrades he would make superhuman demands of himself.

So he would chivvy them along, help, advise, direct, rectify and sometimes cover for their mistakes; he himself was extremely quick-witted, he could improvise appropriate responses in difficult and unexpected situations (as he had in AMM), such as encounters with the police and confrontations with fascists. Above all he *led*. The cost was high. And the fruits of his endeavours? The tangible results? At an early morning appearance with comrades at a factory, a Ford plant, an office block or a market, half a dozen copies of *Workers' Weekly* might be sold, some leaflets distributed, occasionally abuse would be directed at them. Yet who knows what effect his demeanour, his behaviour, his actions had on those people with whom he established brief, sometimes fleeting contact. Such intangible effects may well have been more durable, of more lasting consequence than a disposable broadsheet. We know that long before he decided to devote his life to 'the struggle for socialism' an encounter with him, of whatever category and duration, would leave a lasting imprint. Cardew did not hide his disappointments, although he never indulged them: at the above-mentioned East London concert 'financial loss' was suffered through lack of audience; elsewhere, at another meeting, there was a disheartening 'lack of broad masses'; a very limited response to 'mass work' was noted, and so forth. Yet, echoing Chairman Mao (still), small beginnings can lead to momentous consequences. If the enormity of the task weighed heavily upon him, his resolve did not weaken. At the end of the 30 January report he wrote: 'Organise our basic steady programme very firmly: Mass work, Study Groups, PCA Players, Contact work, Dues'.

Despite the palpable reluctance on the part of its members, Cardew clearly recognised the need for the PCA to establish a base in East London and to that end he and his comrades continued to make concerted efforts to secure PCA affiliation to the Newham Arts Council music panel. They were also seeking Council assistance to find suitable premises, with unpromising responses from various Council officials. Finally in February, at his own family's expense (income and expenses were shared; there were no separate accounts), Cardew rented a small office in the High Road in Ilford which also functioned as a kind of mental and physical refuge for those, mainly Asians, who were under attack from the National Front; a cheque for £187.50, signed by Sheila Kasabova, was sent (which probably covered three months rent). But the undertaking proved to be financially unrealistic and the rental was not renewed. And so it went on.

A hand-written letter from Norway, dated 29 January 1978, beginning 'we hereby invite you to come to the Bergen UNM festival 1978 as a special guest composer and lecturer', offered a (much-needed) fee of £500 plus expenses, although the letter does read more like a first approach than a confirmation. '20 mins of orchestral music for a gig on 22 February' Cardew had scribbled down in his PCA report; the time scale of barely three weeks is hard to fathom. Robert Coleridge recalls that a Norwegian youth orchestra and choir were involved; the programme consisted of Cardew's arrangement of his song 'Consciously', Rzewski's *Struggle Song,* Hugh Shrapnel's arrangement of his own song 'The Azanian People Will Win', Robert Coleridge's *Long was the Night,* and Dave Smith's arrangement for voice and piano of an Albanian Partisan song, 'Eagle of the Guerillas', which, in turn, was arranged for voice and orchestra, presumably by Cardew. The fact that neither the visit to Norway, nor the 'orchestra music' received further mention, at least in the extant documentation (apart from a poor-quality cassette recording), was yet another indication of the ease with which non-Party musical engagements were relegated to the recesses of his mind and to a brief reminder in a PCA report that time had to be found, somehow, to write and copy twenty minutes of music.

A by-election in Ilford North on 1 March 1978 (where the fascist National Front were standing) precipitated a flurry of activity in the area: cultural events were organized in support of the Party-sponsored East London People's Front candidate – including a concert at the Methodist Hall in Ilford Lane on the eve of the election – and at the beginning of the campaign, on 25 February, PCA rented a truck and drove around the locality advertising the concert and urging people to come out and oppose the National Front march/demonstration which was scheduled to take place on that same day, an occasion recalled by Hugh Shrapnel:

> I remember it was pretty cold… I remember crowds of people about, it was an electrifying and very tense atmosphere. The police were pretty vicious and I recall them shoving us forward and actually kicking us…a police officer jumped on the truck to try and arrest us, only to be pushed off! [17]

Shrapnel was arrested but on his appearance in court, perhaps because of the relatively high rank of the police officer he had ejected from the truck, the said officer did not materialise and the case was dismissed. On that same occasion Shrapnel recalls walking along the street with fellow musicians; the police were literally hard on their heels, stamping on them from behind; this kind of police harassment was common. During the election campaign the East London People's Front candidate, Carole Rowe, the election agent, Ranjit Panesar, and numerous supporters were arrested for 'holding a meeting in the street' while Mr. Panesar was taken to court on charges of 'threatening words and behaviour.' In fact, as many as twenty arrests of Party election workers, including Cardew, were made during the election campaign. [18]

However, despite the problems, and certainly as part of the measures to overcome them, March saw the publication of the second issue of *Cogs and Wheels*, the contents including a transcript of an excellent talk entitled 'Reject the Imperialist Consumer Culture' (contributed by Carol Reakes and Alan Evans), the article 'National Chauvinism in Classical Music in Britain' (referred to previously), a new play – *Hit Back Tit forTat,* later re-named *Fight Back*, and new songs and poems of 'active resistance'. March also saw Cardew's departure to Dortmund for an agit prop festival organised by the KPD (M-L) (Communist Party of Germany (Marxist-Leninist)).

The mantra of 'party leadership', and its inviolability, permeated the First Revolutionary Conference of the Progressive Cultural Association which took place in Birmingham during the weekend of 1 and 2 April. The PCA had been in existence for two years and now the aim of the Party and its more zealous supporters within the Association, including Cardew, was to bring it under even tighter control. 'Politics in Command', the rallying call from Carol Reakes' talk to the PCA in Birmingham on 15 April 1976, two years earlier, was still the overriding theme and it was she who was mainly responsible for calling the conference, the preparations for which, according to Hugh Shrapnel, went as far back as the meetings the previous October when Keith Rowe was expelled from the leading group committee and Frances Rifkin was cautioned. Even Cardew did not escape the criticism which issued forth from the Conference platform, presumably for a laxity of discipline towards back-sliders, for not driving his charges hard enough, although one cannot be sure – an indication of the specious grasp of human realities which the Party elite exhibited in discharging their fantasies onto a man who still believed that 'loyalty (obedience) to the Party' was the discipline above all others in which one must excel.

    The main speech – there was also a contribution from the Irish (CPI M-L) delegation – was delivered by Comrade Reakes herself, at that time General Secretary of the Party, who outlined the tasks which the PCA was expected to undertake. Accompanying her on the platform was a suitably chastened Cardew, whose status in the bourgeois music world seemed to impress the upper echelons of the Party, his political foibles notwithstanding, considerably more than it did his friends and colleagues from the political and musical rank-and-file. In her speech Comrade Reakes stressed the necessity of laying down a clear line of demarcation between bourgeois culture and a 'genuine proletarian culture' based on revolutionary politics. Furthermore it was important that the distinction should be drawn between the 'working class' culture supported by Trotskyists and revisionists, masquerading as 'rebellious' culture, and the revolutionary proletarian culture of the Marxist-Leninists. Pop music, soap operas, TV games, Bingo, and so forth, were all part of the bogus 'working-class' culture through which the bourgeoisie and its revisionist and Trotskyite allies subverted the spiritual health of the working people: 'The monopoly capitalist class use culture to say to the workers that 'life is void' and then proceed to fill up this "void" with the most decadent bourgeois values'.[19] The Party's aim (and therefore that of the PCA) was to combat what it perceived as the twin evils of imperialist culture: degeneracy and nihilism.

> Our task as revolutionaries is to take this message to the working class with enormous enthusiasm, with electric amplification, drums or anything else, and tell the workers to come and support the Party, join the Party, build it and oppose social democracy and we will have a revolution. Cultural work will only flourish if it takes up this path and songs, plays, etc. are written celebrating this issue, putting it to the workers and convincing them that it is the way forward. To take any message short of this is to fall short of the needs of the revolution and would be trying to hide the good news that exists in the British revolution.[20]

Art as a recruitment agency. Spreading 'the good news' was, and still is, the banner which religious groups and evangelical sects take up in their quest to make converts and to save souls. And in the more extravagant examples of political propaganda there are often strong religious overtones, with compelling and congruent imagery, as well as the practice of time-honoured inquisitorial methods in pursuit of obedience and loyalty through fear and insecurity. In brief, the main task of the revolutionary cultural movement was twofold:

1) to mobilise and organise the broad masses of the people *against* monopoly capitalism and opportunism [that is, the Trade Unions leadership, the Labour Party, the Revisionists, and the Trotskyists] and *for* Marxism-Leninism and proletarian socialist revolution.
2) to build the Party, strengthen and consolidate it.[21]

Cardew believed in a *revolutionary* culture; the Party's dictum was that there could be no revolutionary culture without revolutionary politics and that therefore the cultural activity of the PCA could not be detached from the revolutionary *political* activity of the Party. The PCA should 'always serve the Party and not itself'. So that when the PCA recruited cultural workers it was recruiting for the Party. Furthermore, it was stressed that the cultural workers must ensure that the Party programmes provided a rich and vigorous cultural life, that they should be presented with imagination and flair – even if the latter attributes, because they tended to emanate from more speculative, more unruly zones of human behaviour, would create a *frisson* of nervousness in Party circles which could only be dissipated by the restoration of more stolid, and less flighty, virtues.

After the conference Cardew and Sheila Kasabova went camping across the border in Wales; Sheila recalls that Cardew was extraordinarily tense, yet unwilling to discuss the matter; he seemed defensive and it took at least twenty-four hours before he was able to unwind. This was unusual; normally he was extremely adept at switching off – and on – from Party responsibilities into holiday mode and vice versa. On this occasion he made frequent phone-calls, driving some distance from the camp-site to the nearest phone box. He was clearly concerned about Party matters but would not divulge the reasons for his discomfort, even to his partner. The veil of secrecy which protected all Party matters was scrupulously maintained.

The Birmingham Conference speech was reported at length in *Cogs and Wheels* no.3, from which a pivotal passage relating to the question of 'ideological transformation' bears citation, not only in relation to the Party's ongoing struggle against 'Trotskyism' – a frequent term of abuse in Party rhetoric – but also to the rigorous, demanding process of *self-invention*, and of 're-moulding one's world outlook'.

The Trotskyites say that it is possible to maintain all our bourgeois prejudices up to the time of the working class revolution and that, somehow or other, when the working class takes over power, we will have a socialist state without any ideological change in our thinking. This is the formula for a fascist state because the proletarian state is being created *now* in embryo by all the people in Britain who take up the issue of revolution and participate in revolutionary activity, consciously transforming our own ideological outlook to become part of the new socialist men and women. That is what is happening *now*, and if this ideological transformation doesn't take place alongside our revolutionary programme there won't be a revolution because 'revolutionaries' who have merely read the right books and are well versed in Marxist-Leninist jargon, but who have maintained every kind of bourgeois prejudice, bourgeois thought and idea, are not going to be able to sustain a revolution. […] There will only be a revolution where new people have a completely new spirit to create something completely new and fantastic; by people who have the spirit of the proletariat throughout the world. For this to happen a tremendous amount of sacrifice has to occur.[22]

Thus at Christmas and the New Year, to combat liberalism and as a conscious mark of disrespect, or rather of non-recognition of reactionary, bourgeois culture, the Party would organize study programmes of the Marxist-Leninist classics which were open to comrades, supporters and friends. Throughout Christmas day, for example, instead of Christmas pudding and the Queen's speech a Marxist text would be studied and discussed over cheese and pickle sandwiches. And Cardew would be tireless in preparing material and leading discussions, as well as providing everybody with adequate and suitably proletarian sustenance.

The Conference has to be seen in the context of the shifting ideological sands, prefiguring a destabilisation (and 'rectification') in the Maoist (Marxist-Leninist) parties. It was already of some significance that the Chinese Party's 'three worlds' theory, which was regarded as a non-Marxist-Leninist theory, was now attributed to Mao's successor, the neo-revisionist Teng Hsiao Ping, rather than to Mao himself, reflecting perhaps a reluctance, understandably, at this stage and in this particular political arena, to confront the issue of Mao's legacy (and 'mistakes'). Indeed, while a quotation from Mao Tse-Tung appeared on the front cover of *Cogs and Wheels* no.2, published just six months earlier in March, neither in the Birmingham Conference speech, nor in any other contribution to *Cogs and Wheels* no.3, was there any mention of Mao Tse-Tung, whether favourably or critically. Mao was now, officially, *persona non grata.* The 'bastion of socialism in the world today', according to Comrade Reakes as quoted in *Cogs and Wheels* no.3 in August 1978, five months after the Conference, was now the People's Socialist Republic of Albania. Perhaps the Party judged that the aura of a conference, addressed by the General Secretary, and the gravitas associated with such an event, would inhibit public expression of disquiet, even dissent, amongst Party supporters at a time of crisis; it was decided simply to close ranks. At that time there could be no clean-cut incision to remove that part of the disease which was particularly malignant (Maoism); the wound would be messy and the body, despite all precautions, would be vulnerable for a time.

On 25 March 1978 the CPE (M-L) had organised a demonstration in the Sparkhill area of Birmingham to commemorate the 1916 Easter Uprising. Since 1974 no such Irish event had occurred in Birmingham; the silence was broken.[23] Around six weeks earlier, on 18 February, the Party had led a demonstration to stop a National Front meeting in Digbeth town hall where, according to several of the demonstrators, fighting was deliberately engineered by the police. The Easter Uprising march had barely started when the police attacked the demonstration. There were many arrests, at first under the Prevention of Terrorism Act but subsequently changed to 'threatening behaviour', for which the slogan 'British Imperialism Get Out of Ireland' was presented as evidence. In such situations Cardew was always in the forefront, in a leading position, with a megaphone, encouraging people to follow him rather than obeying the police, and militantly shouting slogans and instructions: 'death to the fascists' and 'this way, follow me' and so forth. And if the police attempted to manhandle him he would resist and reply in kind. Not surprisingly, he won his spurs with such performances of his street credibility

– demonstrations of defiance, fearlessness and leadership in the face of the enemy.

In June, in a round-robin letter to friends and colleagues in the music world Cardew appealed for donations towards the fines that had been imposed:

Over the past few months the band I work with (now called 'Band of the PCA') has been attacked by the police on three occasions. Firstly on the anti-fascist demonstration of the East London People's Front from Ilford to Barking in September 1977, secondly during the Ilford North By-election, and thirdly on the Party demonstration to commemorate the Easter Uprising in Birmingham on 25 March. On two of these occasions I was arrested and hauled up before the courts like a criminal. In Birmingham I was picked up simply because I refused to give my name and address.[24] The reason I refused was because I was so angry at the brutal way the police had attacked the demonstration. For this I was handed a one-month prison sentence suspended for two years, plus a three-figure fine! And these sentences were handed out under the Public Order Act of 1936, which we are told was put through in order to oppose Mosley's Blackshirts, [25] but which actually was used against the anti-fascists, and is being used thus today. [...] The conclusion to be drawn from these and lots of other instances is that the State is out to get anybody who stands up for justice, takes a stand against fascism, supports the cause of Irish freedom, and resists harassment by the police.[26]

Positive responses were forthcoming although at least two people, Victor Schonfield and the critic Dominic Gill, questioned why Cardew had not opted for imprisonment, rather than asking friends, some of them as poor as himself, to pay his fines. In fact, paying a fine was not an alternative to imprisonment; as we shall see, the issue of fines and imprisonment was to arise again in 1980/81.

But it was in the light of events which were rapidly unfolding on the global stage that the leaders of the English Marxist-Leninist Party had to assess the situation regarding their own credibility, particularly in relation to the meagre band of members and supporters it had managed to enlist. Thus in September 1978, galvanised no doubt by criticisms of some of Mao's key policies and philosophical conceits by the Albanian Party of Labour, the First Congress of the CPE (M-L) itself initiated an investigation into Mao Tse-tung Thought. And following comrade Reakes' return to Ireland a new General Secretary was elected: John Buckle.[27]

On the basis of its investigation the Party's conclusion was not that Mao was an ogre;

on the contrary, he was a great revolutionary who had led his people out of feudalism. But his political philosophy was not Marxist-Leninist; he was not a dialectical materialist, which is why a stable socialist base was never established in China.[28] Nor, therefore, was Mao Tse-Tung Thought applicable to the world communist movement, a judgement which Mao himself acknowledged. The Party's consensus (and Cardew would certainly have been part of this process of reassessment) was/is that Maoism had had adverse consequences for the thinking and functioning of Marxist-Leninist Parties around the world – and none more so than itself, one might add.[29]

But can the Chairman be held wholly responsible for this state of affairs? Should not the English 'Maoists' shoulder at least part of the blame for applying Mao Tse-tung Thought mechanically and dogmatically? For example, should blame for the fact that domestic human relations were rendered unstable and fraught by accusations of insidious manifestations of traits of the class enemy (such that normal human conduct became impossible) be laid solely at the feet of Chairman Mao? And in the light of their adulation of the Chairman, which in the early seventies knew no bounds, could not this latest manoeuvre be considered as the ultimate political *volte face?*[30] Even today, some thirty years on, such questions provoke conflicting responses, but there is no doubt that this was a momentous time for Cardew, culminating in the Autumn of 1978, and perhaps coinciding with the above-mentioned First Congress, when he was elected onto the Central Committee of the Party, something he would have regarded as a great honour.

Criticisms of Mao Tse-tung began to emerge in the minutes of PCA meetings towards the end of 1978 and earlier the following year. Yet a continuing state of ambivalence was reflected in some of the decisions made at the Birmingham conference (and later upheld) when, despite his conspicuous absence and the burgeoning criticism, Mao's position as guiding ideologue, particularly in relation to cultural matters, still seemed, at least outwardly and albeit temporarily, unassailable. For the Party the problem was both tactical and psychological: to jettison much of the Maoist baggage, with which they were ineluctably encumbered, but at the same time not to relinquish *control*. If the *letter* of the Conference could be questioned in part, the *spirit*, in particular that of discipline and obedience to the Party line, had to be re-emphasised. Thus, to the chagrin of many of its members, the still 'relative' autonomy of the PCA was challenged at the Conference, and annulled. From the platform the General Secretary argued that it was wrong for the PCA to organise 'separate programmes' running parallel with Party work; there had to be much more liaison before embarking on an initiative (in other words, more Party control) in order to achieve total integration. The end result of the Conference was, in effect, to create a moratorium on all cultural activity; this included Cardew's work on classical music (including Songs for Our Society and his own compositions), the literature and painting groups (including Stella Cardew's political paintings), and Stuart Monroe's films. The PCA was thus decimated. And with the bit between its teeth Conference also decided to dissolve all the existing bands which had operated under the aegis of the PCA: People's Liberation Music, Fight Back Band, Bright Future, and ordained that a new PCA band, the PCA Players, should be formed 'to serve the concrete needs of the revolution and develop the Culture of the Barricades'.[31] This was transparently a tactic to facilitate Party control over all cultural affairs; and the knock-on effect for the PCA was catastrophic – to the extent that much of its hard-won support from a number of talented artists was now lost.

This was the sad result of the absurd Maoist idea that all culture had to be overt political propaganda in the crudest sense. This mechanical and superficial line on the role of culture in society was a barrier to the development of vital and progressive culture.[32]

Having survived the crisis, and following the publication of *Cogs and Wheels* no.3, it was agreed at a general meeting of the PCA on 12 October that the issues raised at the Birmingham conference should also be discussed with supporters and more casual contacts, and that copies of the new *Cogs and Wheels* should be shown to 'old contacts', including Rowe and Rifkin, and their stand 'reassessed'. A report noted: 'FR [Frances Rifkin] was upset by C&W3 play – thought it attacked her as a 'police socialist' and got subjective. Must be seen as she has some bone to pick with us.'[33] The offending play, *Destroy the Old to Build the New,* includes a character called 'opportunist woman' which clearly represented Frances Rifkin and her 'incorrect' ideas. Was the Party genuinely inviting criticism from Rowe and Rifkin, and other 'old contacts', or simply giving them the opportunity to recant and return to the fold? What was the reason for contacting them? The reality of an embarrassing number of defections from rank-and-file supporters could not be taken lightly. Yet as Keith Rowe recollects:

The ultimate arbiter in these matters was not in the English Party, who were ideologically the poor relations. It was the Canadians (Hardial Bains). The *Cogs and Wheels* issue would go to the Party and then to the Canadians for approval. Hardial Bains was the games master, at the centre, constructing and manipulating this puzzle/game.[34]

The London Branch of the PCA, in particular, was unequivocal, clearly set on consolidating support for the Conference line and dealing with problems as defined by the Conference. One of these 'problems' was a decimated PLM (re-named the PCA band), consisting of Baker, Cardew, Shrapnel, (Chris)Thompson and Hamilton[35], which now seemed to be more of an ad-hoc ('scratch') band; there were few rehearsals and minimal organisation. However, one of Cardew's reports describes the music as 'strong', and at a demonstration at Ford's Chris Thompson's song 'Oppose all attempts' came out 'loud and clear' on TV news. In his report of 12 October the Theatre and Film group fares less well, with Cardew again complaining about the lack of 'strong practical leadership': many ideas, a lot of potential, projects lying dormant. And a comrade is criticised for not fighting to promote the Conference line, for half-heartedness. Despite reservations expressed by others, Cardew was still intent on ensuring that the decisions of the Conference should be upheld in all the various committees.

An interesting point emerges in Cardew's report of a PCA General Council meeting on 15 October:

> Issue of classical culture in view of various Albanian articles and news – how they translate Dickens, Mark Twain, etc. EH's [Enver Hoxha] speech about supporting what is revolutionary, democratic and progressive in the classics, and how this culture has a role in educating the masses and resisting the effect of degenerate imperialist culture. Proletariat builds on the achievements of past epochs, etc. Some investigation of the Marxist-Leninist classics on this issue would be useful, especially to combat revisionist distortions of this question.[36]

But how could Beethoven, for example, be used progressively when so much had been done to exclude him, as we have seen, by crudely caricaturing his music and characterising him as a champion of bourgeois liberty? Cardew was clearly conscious of the pitfalls in this area of debate, and of the Party's vulnerability, but he argued that the (Party) line of a 'radical breach' with bourgeois culture was not out of kilter with the Albanian leader's speech, ending his report with an unconvincing, almost desperate, reference, in the context, to Marxist dialectics: 'but it is a question of things turning into their opposite' – as if he were conscious that his thesis needed bolstering. What does this mean? That the accumulated achievements of bourgeois culture, at a certain point in history, are transformed, by proletarian revolution, and subsumed into proletarian culture? This is not such an outrageous idea, to which the promiscuous history of Beethoven's Ninth convincingly attests. The Albanian communists were more positive towards the art of the past, seeing it as part of a cultural tradition, of a cultural heritage of mankind. The crucial point is: irrespective of his role during the early part of the nineteenth century, what *role* does Beethoven's music play today? On reflection Mao's dictum that 'all art is geared to definite political lines' does have a contemporary validity: 'geared to' does not necessarily refer to content; rather it highlights the function, and the exploitation, of art, and its subsequent status in the class struggle.

At the same meeting Cardew publicly stated that his, and Laurie Baker's, workloads were excessive and because of this they could not function efficiently. In his summing-up Cardew made his position clear: 'For me it is a question of <u>either</u> holding all necessary meetings, <u>or</u> doing some actual work', adding the rider that 'since Conference took place I think we are beginning to inch forward on this front'. Such an admission, in effect a complaint, from Cardew was in itself remarkable, but it may also have been a ploy to shame his comrades in the PCA to a greater level of commitment and to accept a larger share of the work load. He had even taken Laurie Baker to task with a pointed reference to his 'position in the Party', suggesting that Baker's attitude to the Party was 'ambivalent, less than wholehearted [...] He seems to be actually willing to let things slide, while acknowledging that it is wrong'. And, as we have already seen in relation to PLM, he again criticised Baker for his failure to organise rehearsals and 'to actually <u>lead</u> the music work'.

One of the criticisms levelled at Mao Tse-tung after 1976, when he was finally removed from his pedestal, was that he had attributed too much importance to the role of art in the revolution, and that he had 'misquoted' Lenin, to boot. Mao's idea of 'cogs and wheels' in the revolutionary movement overemphasised the role of culture. What Lenin said was that Party literature was a 'cog and a *screw*' in the whole revolutionary mechanism.[37] It was Lenin's intention that 'Party literature' should embody, in myriad forms, the ideals of socialism, so inspiringly propounded in the *Communist Manifesto.* This is why it was called '*Party* literature' and why it was inseparable from the struggle for a new and just society. The Party would *control* publishing and distribution centres but it would not, according to Lenin, control writers:

> There is no question that literature is least of all subject to mechanical adjustment or levelling, to the rule of the majority over the minority. There is no question, either, that in this field greater scope must undoubtedly be allowed for personal initiative, individual inclination, thought and fantasy, form and content.[38]

In a report from a PCA executive meeting on 17 November the question of the malign influence of Mao's line on literature and art in the most recent issue of *Cogs and Wheels* is raised.[39] The jettisoning of Mao Tse-tung Thought had become a matter of some urgency in the Party, and Cardew had begun to re-read, and to re-assess 'Talks at the Yenan Forum'. Thus the question was posed: 'Does Mao overemphasise literature and art'? Possibly. Unlike Lenin, Mao was himself an artist, a poet. In his article 'Party Organisation and Party Literature' Lenin discusses the Party's whole propaganda work, including newspapers, reviews, books, as well as literature on science, philosophy and art. Cardew's inference is that, like the revisionists, Mao separated art from culture, thus 'distorting' their essential interdependence. However, in a generous concession, he notes that Mao's view 'that art must provide "help" to other revolutionary work' is echoed by Enver Hoxha.[40]

Having (re)read through *Cogs and Wheels* no.3 Cardew opined that it 'expresses very well how the cultural work has to be an integral part of the revolutionary process, but we should be seeking a new title for our magazine because of the association of Cogs and Wheels with Mao'.[41] The title itself was now contentious. One can imagine that the PCA executive must have had a field day (and night) struggling with the ideological implications of the relationship between a cog and a wheel, as opposed to that of a cog and a screw. The die was cast: from now on every nut and bolt of the Chairman's utterances would be subject to the severest scrutiny.

Thus, at a PCA Executive meeting at the end of the year, December 16, the General Secretary made the breathtaking observation, and presumably with a straight face, that whereas in China the masses were 'over regimented', in Albania 'everyone is happy – which is what socialism is for'. Admittedly with the benefit of hindsight, such quaintly expressed, ideological conceits did not bode well for the future of a Party based, by its own admission, on the science of Marxism-Leninism. 'Everyone is happy – which is what socialism is for' would more appropriately be placed at the end of a fairy-tale, or a sermon, rather than at a meeting of dialectical materialists. Again, as in the early part of the seventies, one senses the need for a projected model, a prescriptive 'utopia', just as one experiences in the music, and the text, at least to these ears and sensibilities, for *We Sing for the Future*.

When Cardew does take issue with Mao the impression given is more of a semantic exercise in nit-picking than the disclosure of substantive ideological differences: Mao's quotation of a couplet from a poem by Lu Hsun, for example, is deemed 'questionable':

'Fierce-browed, I coolly defy a thousand pointing fingers,
Head-bowed, like a willing ox I serve the children.[42]

Cardew demurs: 'being oxen for the working people. No mention of *leading*'.[43] Elsewhere Mao cautions (the artists and intellectuals) that integrating with the masses involves 'pain and friction'. Cardew objects primly: 'Emphasises this rather than the joy of liberation from alien petit bourgeois ideas and influences'.[44] Mao describes base areas as 'revolutionary new-democratic society under proletarian leadership'. Cardew disapproves: 'Not as Dictatorship of the Proletariat'?? '[45]

The emphasis was now on defeating bourgeois culture and its various manifestations *in general* in the context of revolution and 'long after', and this would be led by the Party (not the PCA) and implemented by the masses (not the cultural workers). What role then, one asks, did the PCA and its cultural workers have to play? Certainly, the Party's hounding and denunciation of bourgeois culture was relentless. An article by the South London Revolutionary Youth (organ of the Party) entitled 'Down with Imperialist Propaganda for Fascism', reviewing Stanley Kubrick's 1971 film *Clockwork Orange,* dismissed the film as 'part of a general trend in imperialist films which are increasingly promoting degenerate, self-centred life-style and fascist violence as ideological preparation for fascism'. (Of course, there were also bourgeois critics, including some on the far right politically, who took objection to the film.) Other films were attacked for their glamorisation of the police force: arbitrary ('fascist') violence and propaganda for the justification for the police to 'bend the rules' and live beyond the law to protect the system. In such films people were invariably depicted as helpless victims or passive onlookers. Hardial Bains, the leader of the Canadian Marxist-Leninist Party, had characterised the role of the reactionary intellectuals in the propagation of contemporary bourgeois culture thus:

> The strata which has come forward to serve the big bourgeoisie are the scholar despots, a section of the petty bourgeoisie, decadent artists, actors and actresses, writers, singers, musicians, painters, etc. They follow the life style and social practice which best serve the interests of the big bourgeoisie, which is characterized by:
>
> 1. Eclecticism in attitude or general outlook,
> 2. Detachment from the real problems of the people (especially the working people),
> 3. Isolation from the real, material world,
> 4. Parasitism in life style and parasitism on the labours of the working people,
> 5. Exuberance about decay – heading towards total decay.
> [...] The core of this is bourgeois individualism, the festering "ego", and complete opposition to anything healthy.[46]

In the late seventies Cardew became a fully-fledged Party functionary and as such spread about him an aura of political correctness. Of course, all such bourgeois comforts and privileges that he had enjoyed in his previous existence had to be abjured, but that presented no difficulty to Cardew; in this respect his bohemian upbringing in Cornwall stood him in good stead. A regimen of proletarian fare was self-imposed and he was respectably and appropriately accoutred – ennobled, on occasions, by a proletarian suit.

Like all revolutionary parties, the CPE (M-L) was censorious; cast in the mode of intolerance it belaboured all expressions of non-conformity and would even treat genuine doubt (on political and ideological matters) with a minimum degree of patience. Woe betide he or she who derogated from the paths of proletarian righteousness: habitual infringements of party discipline were tantamount to a kind of recidivism. Cardew himself nursed a strong inner need to signal his allegiance to the working class, and it was his political convictions which emboldened him to talk to people who were neither musicians nor intellectuals, people whom he would encounter for the first time in doorstep confrontations and discussions on inner London housing estates. In such 'mass work', according to Peter Devenport, Cardew would not flinch, nor compromise; he would demand maximum clarity of line – no blurring of definitions, no fudge. When he uttered the word 'socialism' he wanted his interlocutors to know exactly what he meant, and in turn expected them to tell him precisely and without equivocation what their own position was. He would be quite content to abandon a discussion, on any topic, on a complete lack of agreement; he would never gloss over an argument in order to reach a dubious 'resolution'.

In a recorded interview Brigid Scott Baker recalls the dockers' strike which began towards the end of 1978. There were four comrades, including Cardew and Scott Baker, who was driving. I reproduce her account here more or less verbatim:

We went to Liverpool, it was a big picket down on the docks and we talked to pickets and had the paper [*Workers' Weekly*] [...] We may have stayed with comrades somewhere in Liverpool, [went] to the picket again and crossed the Pennines in the evening. I remember this as all the roads were being closed and we crossed behind a snow-plough. Police were just taking people out of cars, it was so bad. There were banks of snow, it was all pretty hairy. That was the thing then, we just did stuff, a bit like the Scratch Orchestra! We stayed somewhere in Sheffield, or Leeds. We went to the University students union and I asked if someone could put us up and the student was so pleased to have us as nobody had ever used his crash pad. We were going to Hull docks; there was a picket there. Cor wanted to look at the new bridge as it took into account the curve of the earth so we drove to look at it on the way. We went to Avonmouth [Bristol] and some other places where there were dockers in unlikely locations. Cor's idea was to get the workers to put us up – a bunch of hopeless looking people. Cor used to wear those walking boots all the time and I don't think any of us were particularly 'well dressed'. When he tried this strategy it failed miserably so I got us crash pads from local students and this was what we did everywhere.

At Avonmouth (I think this was the last port of call, or maybe we went to Southampton on the way back) Cor was trying to get one of the pickets to take us home and I remember a conversation with this guy and him saying that he would really like to take us home but his wife would have a fit (or words to that effect), that he couldn't just turn up with a load of people. I don't think Cor understood that at all so the conversation went on for some time!

[Laurie Baker, who was present at the interview commented, 'he [Cardew] had a romantic illusion about the working class, too much Chinese literature'.]

We ended up in a crash pad in a huge house on the edge of a hill in Bristol and it was freezing and there was a double bed in the room and really it was as if there was no glass in the windows. It was so cold with the wind and the snow. We all started off sleeping in different places; we put on more clothes to keep warm and ended up with all the sleeping bags on the double bed, huddled together, trying to keep warm. It was so cold I don't think anyone slept much. They were students so I don't think they had any heating at all![47]

As an artist who was perceived to be part of the stormy currents of contemporary political history Cardew continued to be invited to academic institutions; in the university music departments, in particular, he would be in embattled mood and his adamantine, uncompromising stance would infuriate above all those who felt a basic sympathy with his political views (as we have seen in our discussion of his Air Gallery concert the previous year): the pseudo-revolutionaries, as he would have dismissed us, 'who were Marxist in all but two things: the theory of State and the desire to change the world.'[48] Cardew saw the development of music as inseparable from the struggle of ordinary people against privilege, injustice, systematised greed and exploitation. He regarded participation in the class struggle as paramount. His note books reveal the depth of his study of Marxism-Leninism and, more importantly, the way he applied these principles to his everyday life. His activities reached heroic proportions: twenty-four hours a day refining his political and musical ideas: composing, arranging, lecturing, touring, organising, discussing, analysing and demonstrating, for which he was imprisoned. And it was he who was instrumental in setting up the PCA to help artists organise and focus their work.

Yet an episode earlier in the year, involving Keith Rowe, indicated that there was still an amount of unwieldy and unwanted furniture in his mind which created problems in his relationships, in particular with old friends. And in this instance there was an added complication: Rowe, whose crusading zeal in the early seventies had done much to politicise Cardew, was now a rebel apostate, a former insider who had departed the fold. At one of their sporadic meetings, over a number of years, in an Italian café (more an ice-cream parlour) just along the road from Goodge Street tube station, and close to the office where Cardew worked, Rowe recalls that Cardew seemed to be behaving with undue formality. Finally he produced a letter from the PCA, dated 22 April 1978, just three weeks after the Birmingham Conference, which he described as being 'of serious import'. He proceeded to read it through to Rowe, in the manner of a riot act, as Rowe recollects, elucidating and amplifying the content as was deemed necessary. It begins as follows:

Dear Keith Rowe,
For some time now you have consistently opposed, in theory and practice, the line of the PCA as a revolutionary organisation to develop revolutionary culture in the service of the revolutionary movement in this country. What is more serious is that you have refused to carry out your responsibility and come to PCA committee meetings to put forward your views and sort out differences. [...] You've attacked the PCA by putting forward a totally spurious line that there is "no democracy" in the PCA, and that your views "wouldn't be represented" in the PCA committee. This is a complete distortion of what is meant by proletarian democracy, and is in fact cold war anti-communism.
The PCA committee recently met to review the situation and [...] it was decided to expel you from the committee and suspend you from all work in the PCA until your stand towards PCA is sorted out. [...] It boils down to a question of class stand: whether the PCA is to develop culture to serve the proletariat and masses, or serve the bourgeoisie.

The letter was signed by Cardew (Secretary of the PCA). Rowe recalls that he 'just put the letter in his bag', without folding it and putting it back into the envelope, and they continued their conversation on other matters: baroque music, visual art – perhaps something Cardew and the Party needed help with. In fact, as late as 1979 Rowe and Cardew together designed the logo for the Party-sponsored International Sports and Culture Festival on a table in that same café, as well as numerous posters for concerts, including the one in Camden in December 1981. Rowe's political demise and exclusion appears to have had no bearing on such tasks, to either man.[49]

But to return to the meeting between Rowe and Cardew in April of 1978, it was as if Cardew had feared that Rowe might pierce the carapace of Party political artifice that he, Cardew, had erected for the purpose of that particular encounter, and which he was unable, and unwilling (?), to sustain once his duty had been discharged. Even though any residual feelings from the Scratch Orchestra days and before had been effectively repressed, in Rowe's presence Cardew may well have felt vulnerable. And the situation was compounded by the fact that Rowe had been over the years, perhaps still was, a true soul-mate, arguably Cardew's closest friend. Of course, much of this came from Cardew's deep admiration for Rowe the musician, but there was more; their meetings continued – despite Rowe's political estrangement – and his influence on Cardew, perhaps as a nagging conscience, continued undiminished to the end.

There has been frequent reference in these pages to 'the Party' or the 'Revolutionary Party', and it begins to attain an almost mythological status. And yet what, or who, concretely, was 'the Party'? I recall discussing this very issue with Keith Rowe on that sunny afternoon in London on 8 September 2003, along with many other questions on which I was seeking his responses. In respect of the particular communist party under discussion, during a brief historical period in the recent past, what was its work and what was its effect; what changes, if any, did it bring about? Rowe and I had similar reservations, similar unanswered (and unanswerable?) questions: Was it anything more than a series of 'incestuous meetings'? Was it some kind of esoteric 'glass bead game'?

At the end of 1978, despite his changing, diminishing *persona*, Mao Tse-tung still hovered implacably over the political landscape; in China thousands of people every day travelled sometimes vast distances to pay homage to him, and in other parts of the world liberation movements were/are still named after him. It would therefore be foolhardy, indeed presumptuous, on my part to attempt to offer even a broad assessment of his achievements, and his failures. However, in the context of this book, the extent to which Mao's political legacy and its manifold repercussions throughout the world influenced Cardew and the English 'Maoists', during the seventies and since, needs to be addressed, and from the perspective of those members, supporters, activists for whom Mao Tse-Tung Thought had been both an inspiration and a moral guide for nearly a decade.

Hardial Bains' article, entitled 'Centenary of the Birth of Mao Zedong', originating in an International Seminar held in Coventry, England, 2-3 January 1994, provides us with a later assessment, of Mao's contribution to the international Communist movement. Apart from its Marxist-Leninist authenticity,[50] another important reason for quoting from Hardial Bains' text is based on the influence that he exerted on the CPE (M-L), which later became the Revolutionary Communist Party of Britain (Marxist-Leninist), up to his untimely death in 1997. Hardial Bains became Cardew's mentor and played an important role in his political development and achievements. During the last three or four years of Cardew's life the two men developed a close relationship, a fact born out by the formal tributes that Bains paid to Cardew on various occasions following the latter's death. The following is a summary of comrade Bains' assessment of Mao's legacy:

As leader of a long revolutionary war, which culminated in the establishment of the People's Republic of China in 1949, Mao Zedong remains one of the great revolutionary figures of the twentieth century. His subsequent errors were crucial to the extent that they undermined the impetus for world revolution which the Chinese achievements had inspired: the 'theory of three worlds', which aim was to create a new world equilibrium, resulted in a complete separation of the Chinese leadership from the needs of the international revolutionary movement and from the (Marxist-Leninist) theory on which it was built. World issues were seen and acted upon narrowly from a purely Chinese perspective – that is, how does a particular strategy accord with the needs of the Chinese. The Chinese 'model' was promoted as an 'exception', the result of which was that internationalism and solidarity with the working classes of countries around the world was abandoned; conciliation and collaboration with the bourgeoisie, under certain circumstances, was necessary. Mao Zedong Thought had therefore very little relevance to the world proletariat. The Chinese Communist Party would ally itself with the US against the Soviet Union or vice versa according to what suited their needs.[51] Mao Zedong did not participate in world political affairs as a world (revolutionary) leader and statesman; he participated in these affairs as a Chinese leader.

> Mao Zedong Thought as a doctrine does not pertain to the conditions for the complete emancipation of the working class. It falls short of proclaiming itself as such since it has at its centre the glorification of China. In a way it is a reaction against Eurocentrism, but not a theory which can demolish it. Caught in this way with the spirit of Sino-centrism, Mao Zedong Thought could not possibly assume that internationalist character which could provide it with the status of a doctrine of the world proletariat.[52]

With all due respect to comrade Bains, attention had been drawn at least twenty years earlier to Chairman Mao's political aberrations by a variety of anti-imperialists, including the Irish anarchist Bernard Kelly, whose letter to Cardew (quoted in Chapter 15) was written as far back as 1972, and in which at least part of Hardial Bains' analysis was given colourful and theatrical representation. Such criticisms received short shrift from the Chairman's acolytes; not surprisingly, in his reply to Kelly Cardew chose not to address the issue. It was not, at that time, even a matter of giving Mao the benefit of the doubt, because doubt had been ruled out by certainty, by *belief*. As we shall see, as we approach the end of the decade it was to take a little longer for these assessments and criticisms to find expression, in a tangible way, in Cardew's own political *modus operandi*.

Notes and references

1 From an unsigned text entitled 'Opportunist Theatre'; undated (probably 1978), part typed (with atrocious spelling!), part handwritten by Cardew; probably a transcript.

2 From a typewritten PCA Report, dated 13 January, 1978.

3 There is a further twist in the tale of the stand-off between PCA and Recreation Ground: when the latter had its grant withdrawn for performing for the IRA Provisionals in Belfast, Belts and Braces theatre company accused it of jeopardising precious grant money by taking risks beyond what was sensible. In the light of such evidence, the charge of 'careerism' levelled at Recreation Ground seems to have been wide of the mark.

4 From Cardew's typewritten PCA Report, dated 13 January 1978.

5 The 'three worlds' theory, attributed to Mao Tse-tung, divided the world, politically, into three main areas: 1. The two superpowers: the US and the Soviet Union; 2. The Western industrialised countries; 3. The developing countries. This resulted in the Communist Party of China aligning itself with various pro-US reactionary regimes, such as Pinochet in Chile, and the Shah of Iran, as well as a rapprochement with the US. It was criticised and rejected by Enver Hoxha and various Marxist-Leninist and leftists parties around the world.

6 From Cardew's typewritten PCA Report, dated 13 January 1978.

7 Ibid.

8 Ibid.

9 Ibid.

10 The 'Little Red Guards', organised and run by comrades and supporters, was a kind of Maoist equivalent of the Cubs and Brownies. Both engaged in creative activity, which included games, music, plays, sports and camping, but whereas the Cubs and Brownies were expected to swear allegiance to God and Queen (as I recall from my own daughters' brief membership) the Little Red Guards were encouraged to oppose theism and privilege.

11 He even managed, with Devenport, to produce a song: 'Ford Workers' Song' (1978) which PLM performed on a march by striking Ford workers. Dalwinder Atwal, a Ford worker, recalls that sometimes Cardew would be 'smuggled' into the factory to attend meetings in the canteen.

12 Not a few songs were written collectively, such that in many cases the issue of individual authorship does not arise. In my listing of Cardew's songs I have therefore been quite conservative, only ascribing authorship to him where there is clear evidence (usually word-of-mouth evidence from those comrades close to him at the time) that a song (though usually not the lyrics) was his own individual creation.

13 In our conversation sitting outside a café in Euston on 8 September 2003, Rowe recalled a domestic occasion when he was roundly denounced by a member of the inner elite for re-heating pasta from the night before: this was unhygienic and therefore incorrect behaviour. Of course, it is arguable that everything is 'political', but Rowe reflected on the manner in which, hypothetically, millions of such examples of 'incorrect behaviour' might be addressed: whether routinely or creatively, intelligently or imaginatively, crudely or sensitively.

14 From the previously mentioned 'PCA Report', Chapter 20, fnt. 26.

15 From Cardew's PCA report, dated 15-22 January.

16 From Cardew's PCA report, dated 30 January 1978. According to Laurie Baker it was Carol Reakes who had originally referred to his 'dubious schemes' so disparagingly.

17 Hugh Shrapnel, from a recorded conversation with JT, 9 July 1996.

18 The engagement in Norway during the election campaign excluded Cardew from candidacy, which he had set his sights on; Carole Rowe was selected in his place.

19 From Carol Reakes' National Executive speech at the First Revolutionary Conference of the Progressive Cultural Association, as reported in *Cogs and Wheels* No. 3, 1/2 April 1978.

20 Ibid.

21 Ibid.

22 Ibid.

23 On 21 November 1974 twenty-one people were killed by bomb attacks in two pubs near the centre of Birmingham. Six Irishmen were sentenced to life imprisonment but the convictions were overturned by the Court of Appeal in March 1991.

24 From this time on, according to Brigid Scott Baker, Cardew rarely wrote anything down. Somehow he managed to retain information in his head. In Birmingham, while the Band were playing on the truck, he had had his briefcase with him (he was going to a meeting afterwards) with addresses and other information which he would not have wanted the police to get sight of.

25 Oswald Mosley (1896-1980) was the founder of the British Union of Fascists (1932); the members of his organisation were called Blackshirts.

26 From a letter dated 1 June 1978.

27 Experienced political commentators and cynics might have drawn attention to the fact that 'a change at the top' is often a ploy to ensure more of the same. Dazzled by the vaunted *figura* of a 'new leader' the people are thus blinded to the consequences, to the political reality, of an act of accession conceived and hatched from behind closed doors. Cardew would have dismissed such a stratagem as 'bourgeois politics'.

28 Michael Chant has elegantly characterised Mao's dialectical 'one divides into two' theory – that the bourgeois headquarters therefore resided within the Communist Party – as 'to a point Marxist-Leninist, but with an admixture of Confucianism and other Chinese philosophy'.

29 Mao Tse-tung Thought, now described as the 'monkey on the back' of Marxism-Leninism – in the words of a previous disciple – was severed from the canon. A characteristically extreme response from his erstwhile admirers and an undeserved fate, particularly in the light of his philosophical essays, such as 'On Practice' and 'On Contradiction', which won praise from no less a (Marxist-Leninist) critic than Bertolt Brecht.

30 Other commentators, from further afield, including the Uruguayan composer/musicologist Coriún Aharonián, have also challenged the presumption of these reformed Maoists, suggesting that what Mao was proposing in terms of revolutionary culture was misinterpreted; worse still, that these distortions were then imposed mechanically on a situation which was quite different to that which Mao faced in mid-century China.

31 Shortly after the Conference a PCA meeting was held at Carol Reakes' flat in Sutton Coldfield, attended by Hugh Shrapnel, Cardew, Geoff Pearce and one or two others, and at which a Party directive was delivered. Pearce recalls: "Involvement in PLM and Bright Future was to cease. We were asked to respond. Cor and Hugh agreed with the party line. I did not respond until everyone else had spoken. I was then asked by Carol (Reakes) what my view was. I told them I thought it was a really bad idea. I was immediately out of there

and out of the PCA. There was no room for discussion." Email correspondence from Geoff Pearce to JT sometime during 2004.

32 Email correspondence from Hugh Shrapnel to JT, 14 April 2003. According to Shrapnel, in the same email, "this ridiculous approach was soon repudiated and the PCA went on to do valuable work in developing progressive culture over the next few years."

33 From Cardew's handwritten Theatre and Film Committee report, dated 14 October 1978.

34 From the 8 September 2003 conversation between KR and JT. At a PCA Executive meeting on 16 December 1978 it was noted that a letter was to be sent to Canada 'explaining *Cogs and Wheels* 3. Internal document only'.

35 Nobody can recall Hamilton's other name(s).

36 From Cardew's hand-written report of a PCA General Council meeting in Birmingham, dated 15 October. Regarding the 'revisionist distortions' let me refer the reader back to Michael Chant's contribution on this issue in the chapter 'Stockhausen Serves Imperialsm'.

37 'Party Literature' – an invidious term guaranteed to raise the hackles of the liberal reader. Lenin used the term 'in contradistinction to bourgeois customs, to the profit-making, commercialised bourgeois press, to bourgeois literary careerism and individualism, "aristocratic anarchism" and drive for profit'. V.I. Lenin, 'Party Organization and Party Literature' in *On Literature and Art* (Moscow: Progress Publishers, 1970), p.23.

38 Ibid, p.24.

39 The report makes for interesting reading, not least because it begins, unprecedentedly, with a criticism of Cardew 'for not having prepared agenda', presumably from the General Secretary, who was present on this occasion.

40 The Albanian leader described cultural workers as 'auxiliaries' in the revolutionary movement, which might be interpreted, in relation to Mao's perception, as a down-grading of their status.

41 Typewritten, untitled sheet, dated 20 December 1978.

42 Quoted in *Mao Tse-tung on Literature and Art* (Peking: Foreign Languages Press, 1967), p.39.

43 From an undated text, probably 1978/79, entitled 'Cog & Screw'. [My emphasis added.]

44 Ibid.

45 Ibid.

46 Hardial Bains, *Combat This Growing Fascism* (Toronto: Norman Bethune Institute, 1976), pp.7-8.

47 From a recorded interview in Hugh Shrapnel's garden in Ladywell, southeast London, on 15 September 2005.

48 *Marxism and Art*, ed. Maynard Soloman (Detroit: Wayne State University Press, 1979), p.543.

49 In our conversation in Euston on 8 September 2003, not far from the café where Rowe and Cardew used to meet, Rowe mused that the pleasure derived from the work must have been enhanced by the fact that he was not obliged to attend meetings!

50 I resort to the word 'authenticity' advisedly; some might say that Hardial Bains' Marxist-Leninist credentials are questionable. I have heard and seen him described as a charlatan, and as a genius. What is not in doubt is that Cardew held him in great esteem, which is why comrade Bains features prominently in the latter stages of this book.

51 The infamous meeting of Mao Zedong and Richard Nixon in Peking in 1972, apart from

causing dismay and criticism in many left-wing circles, was also the inspiration for an opera by John Adams, *Nixon in China* (1987).

52   Hardial Bains, 'Centenary of the Birth of Mao Zedong,' inserted into a 'Thematic Report' which was based on issues raised during an International Seminar held in Coventry, England, 2-3 January 1994. The title of the Seminar was 'The Retreat of Revolution and the Tasks of the Communist and Workers' Movement'.

22
Hardial Bains and the Canadians 1979

'I have always striven to write music that serves Socialism. This was often a difficult and contradictory exercise, but the only worthy one for artists in our time.'[1]

In Britain the so-called 'winter of discontent' (1978-9) had been announced by the media even before it had begun – with a tanker-drivers' dispute and a lorry-drivers' strike which presaged 'the removal of the life-support system of the nation' and furnished the rampant tabloids with 'nation held to ransom' headlines.

> The Shakespearean phrase already hinted at the epic spectacle it was to become. It was to be a tragi-comedy, of didactic purpose, which would demonstrate conclusively that the working class had not changed. We were shown that working people are venal, and stupid, and also lacking in human decency.[2]

The strategy was to fragment, undermine and ultimately to break down working class resistance by launching a sustained, relentless attack on the ethos, the moral viability, of *solidarity*, all demonstrations of which were cynically identified in the media with 'mob rule'. Thus on television news programmes an 'informed', *individual*, browbeaten housewife would be shown bravely confronting (that is, crudely abusing) a 'selfish', 'mindless', *collectivist* mob (that is, a picket line). This was the persistent leitmotif which pervaded the media at that time. As essential social structures fractured and crumbled, public servants in all walks of life were berated and reviled in the media for their insatiable greed, unreliability, cruelty and insensitivity to the sufferings of others. And, not to be upstaged and deprived of easy spoils, the liberal intelligentsia weighed in: in his review of *Stockhausen Serves Imperialism* Hans Keller denounced the 'new left's commitment to violent collectivism, its regression to infantile depersonalisation and dehumanisation [...] As a result, multiple regressions to group and gang behaviour under quasi-parental protection are taking place'.[3] As Blackwell and Seabrook recall:

The myth that there is kindness, charity and compassion among ordinary working people was going to be shattered before our very eyes. 'Heartless', 'callous', 'cruel', 'without mercy', 'pitiless' were the key words, as we were invited to watch the working class of this country in the process of forfeiting even its sense of common humanity.[4]

Effectively, the seventies tolled the death-knell of the mixed economy, a system 'exposed' as the essential cause of Britain's ills. Now was the moment to 'release market forces, for all the world as though these were a caged species, endangered by their long years of captivity in a socialist zoo'.[5] The background to this onslaught was the sundering of a section of the working class from the mainstream, some of whom were now moving into more salubrious and above all safer accommodation – just rewards, they felt, and justifiably, for their efforts, for their long hours, for overtime, and for the wives' part-time contributions in supermarkets and on the assembly-lines. Left behind were the poor – a threatening, disenfranchised underclass, ever-increasing in numbers, which both preyed on itself and offered what scant comforts they could to each other. Socialism, or socialist aspirations, was a fool's paradise out of which the populace had to be shaken with a heady dose of old-fashioned, laissez-faire liberalism. Governmental control of the economy, which in any case had long been the subject of extreme scepticism among the government's constituents, was formally surrendered to the custodians of the International Monetary Fund (IMF).

The 'impoverishment of the rich' was the watchword taken up by the Press to underline and highlight the injustices in the world; the captains of industry were threatening to emigrate for the lack of 'incentives' to remain in Britain. Meanwhile, pop stars intoxicated their fans with fleeting visits from their tax-exile. Small wonder that during the seventies there was much anger, frustration, cynicism, bitterness and despair in all areas of society. There was also criticism, protest and resistance, which did force changes of tactics, if not strategy, on the government: the battle outside the gates of the Saltley coal depot in 1972, the use of the Industrial Relations Act to imprison the dockers who became known as 'the Pentonville Five' and the campaign to free them, and the heroic struggle of low-paid Asian women for unionisation at Grunwick's photographic processing plant in the late seventies.

Like all the leftist Parties and groups at that time the CPE (M-L) entered the fray, grinding its political axe, taking the invincible message of Marxism-Leninism into the working-class heartlands. So that when the steel workers went on strike in 1980, a strike which lasted fourteen weeks, a small group of Party members and supporters, including Cardew, were assigned the responsibility of going up to Sheffield to discuss the issues arising from and within the strike with the steelworkers. Once a week they would drive up to Sheffield – a hazardous and unpredictable journey during an extremely cold winter, and in a vehicle that was prone to breaking down. They would join the pickets at the steel factories, sell *Workers' Weekly* and disseminate the Party line, listen attentively to the workers' views, and arrange to meet them at a pub for further discussion in the evening. The comrades would also visit the university and housing estates to discuss the strike with students and local people, stressing its importance and wider significance. After a long day they would drive back to London, stopping off for coffee on the motorway to keep themselves awake.[6]

Time and again, in my interviews and conversations with people who knew Cardew, there is one attribute that is constantly singled out – Cardew as 'enabler': his ability to inspire people to believe in themselves, and to surpass their own expectations by transcending their self-imposed limitations – as he did in the Scratch Orchestra, encouraging us through music-making to mine our own feelings and to rescue the untenanted and the discarded from oblivion. In this respect alone he has achieved a mythological status. And in the seventies, as we have seen, as a revolutionary fighter and leader he was inspirational, exhorting his political comrades to ever-greater militancy and resolve in the struggle against the rich and the powerful.

Hakim Adi, a young student at the time, remembers an occasion when he and Cardew arrived back at Adi's flat in London in the early hours of the morning. Cardew made himself comfortable on the settee but informed Adi that at some point he would have to go home, assuring him that he would be back at 5 am in time for them to drive to Ford's together to join the picket. Adi had no idea why Cardew had to return home, but he was, and still is, astonished by Cardew's energy and commitment at a time when he was already in his forties. For Adi Cardew was a truly inspirational figure who led by example and would carry all his much younger comrades along with him. Cath Walker, an art student at the time, recalls:

> He was very thoughtful and measured in his approach, although on demonstrations and marches he would energetically deliver condemnation of the fascist state and the ruling class. I worked alongside him during those times, organising pickets, typing and running off leaflets, making banners, fly-posting and selling *Workers Weekly* at Upton Park market and outside Ford's in Dagenham. I 'looked up' to Cornelius as he was an exceptional person, accessible, and very influential to many at the time. He would talk, and indeed talked, to anyone, whether it was a professional of some kind, undaunted by authority, or to any person on the street. Although I only knew him for a few years, it seems that he achieved so much. I couldn't help marvelling on many occasions, particularly after a busy day 'on the march' or a picket line, how he would deliver an articulate speech, sing and play at an evening meeting without the slightest hint of the day's skirmishes.[7]

The English Party maintained close links with the fraternal Irish Party and in a letter dated 6 January to CANISG, the cultural wing of the Irish Party, the PCA again raised the perennial issue of the relationship between the cultural work and the Party leadership, stressing that all cultural activities should 'concretely consolidate the comrades around the Party's line and take that line to the masses'. (There are echoes here of the Scratch Orchestra's Draft Constitution; it too constituted an agenda, socio-artistic in this case, within which its members orbited and which they too 'took to the masses'.) To that end it was imperative that communist cultural workers should produce songs which related to the revolutionary conditions in the contemporary world, and to the Party's work, as well as new songs about the past, about the history and traditions of the British working class and the international communist movement. The Party's view was that since, inevitably, many of the historical working-class songs reflected the political lines of the various mass movements from which they had sprung – anarcho-syndicalism, reformism, spontaneism and so on – it would be counter-revolutionary to promote such songs in contemporary performance: presentation of historical songs should not be allowed to degenerate into 'history-as-such' (see below). Rather, it was necessary to analyse the events on which the songs were based in the light of subsequent Marxist-Leninist theory for a clearer, more objective, more *scientific,* understanding. Similarly, 'broad front' songs were acceptable up to a point but, as Cardew insisted, 'there is an urgent need for "Party Songs" that not only popularise the Party's *line* but also the fact that it is the *Party's* line, and the necessity and principles of building and strengthening the Party to lead the revolution'.[8] The Party's First Congress (the previous autumn) had also taken the irrevocable decision that all references to Mao Tse-Tung Thought in the songs should be eradicated; the words of songs written in the Maoist period needed therefore to be scrutinised, edited, and, if necessary discarded altogether.

In his pamphlet *Necessity for Change! The Dialectic Lives!* Hardial Bains devotes a section to the concept of 'history-as-such':

> The particular prejudices of a society, transmitted through parents and social institutions, constitute the *historical crib* into which we are born. Like the womb of the mother, it provides us with everything we need. Our purpose and our goal are defined, that is, how to receive nourishment and how to be grateful for it. The historical crib gives us a perspective with which to look at the world and the people in it, including ourselves. We only see those things which can be correlated with that perspective. [...] We create history-as-such when we eliminate all experiences which do not agree with the historical crib. [...] History-as-such provides comfort to the individual only to the extent that one is alive in its context. But the moment a person goes toward an historical analysis of the situation, the

so-called history of the 'various classes of people who have usurped power by force' blocks the way and threatens the individual through its culture and heritage.[9]

George Steiner makes the same point, although without the dynamic extrapolation with which Bains concludes his exposition:

We 'undergo' much of reality, sharply filtered and pre-sensed, through the instant diagnostic sociology of the mass media. No previous society has mirrored itself with such profuse fascination.[10]

But, we may ask, what precisely is mirrored? And to what end?

Despite the waves of optimism in the wake of Carol Reakes' departure and its re-organisation under the leadership of the new General Secretary of the Party, John Buckle, the PCA had still not fully recovered from the battering it had received at the Birmingham conference the previous year. Thus, for example, there seems to have been little or no liaison between Laurie Baker, who was ostensibly leading the new band, and Peter Devenport, who had organised a singing group. Baker's leadership of the PCA band continued to be a bone of contention; it was not 'getting together'. Recalling how enthusiastic and prolific the PLM band had been only six months earlier must have been frustrating for Baker, who had consistently opposed its disbandment by the then Party leadership. It would have been galling for Cardew too, even if he, as much as anybody, had endorsed the necessity for a more Party-controlled cultural orientation.

Moreover, despite the fact that barely two months earlier Cardew had praised its contribution to the 'revolutionary process', the reservations about *Cogs and Wheels* no.3 seem to have intensified; its (Maoist) line on art and literature was now judged to have been in opposition to that of Lenin, and letters relating to the issue were sent to the Canadian and Irish comrades – although it is difficult to judge whether the aim was simply to inform, or whether the English comrades were seeking opinions and advice from the two 'senior' Parties. This was clearly all part of the process of expelling Mao Tse-Tung Thought from the Marxist-Leninist canon while at the same time affirming the contributions of those long-serving luminaries of exemplary pedigree. Thus, Laurie Baker's Party-proscribed task was to extract important quotations from Stalin's writings on culture for PCA scrutiny and edification, whilst another comrade was responsible for reading and reporting on Enver Hoxha's writings on the 'bourgeois classics' and folk culture.

In his response to a letter from Cardew Julian Silverman, an old friend and music journalist working for *Time Out*, furnished further evidence of the emergence of Albania as the new 'bastion of socialism' for Marxist-Leninists at that time. Silverman, not entirely without condescension, demurs:

> Apart from the crucial fact that they have abolished capitalism and 'landlordism' – what does this poor backward chauvinistic police-state [Albania], with its continual uncoverings of massive 'plots against the state' etc. have to do with Marx' or Lenin's ideas of international workers' democracy, the withering away of the state, etc?[11]

He then makes the reasonable, if opportunistic, point that if Cardew wants to make provocative statements he should at least provide some arguments and explanations to back them up. If the Albanian system is to be admired, if it is held up as a model, what are the lessons it can teach the British workers and how can it inspire them to follow suit? 'Do you want to win people over, or do you want to be the only one who's right'?[12]

At the risk of misjudging Cardew's response, but in the light of our by now considerable knowledge of his 'political line', or rather that aspect of it which was unwavering, we may conjecture that the crux of his response would have been to refer to Silverman's 'revisionist' glossing over of the key issue of the 'dictatorship of the proletariat' (following the overthrow of the 'dictatorship of the bourgeoisie'), and to the necessity for vigilance and struggle over a relatively long period of time to ensure that the old order is not restored. This would have been the all-important lesson that the Albanian model could 'teach the British workers', and, as we have seen, it was an issue to which Cardew returned over and over again.

This exchange had originated in Silverman's request to Cardew for a text previewing a concert of his early music at the ICA on Sunday 28 January, comprising a first half of *February Pieces, Solo with Accompaniment, Winter Potatoes,* and *Autumn 60,* followed by an interval and a second half consisting of Paragraph 3 from *The Great Learning,* in which a large number of students from Goldsmiths' College took part (recruited by myself; I was teaching at Goldsmiths' at the time). Cardew duly obliged, and in characteristically uncompromising form he ends:

> In this context it is not only irrelevant but downright reactionary to persist in the intricate conceits of avant-gardism. Artists with revolutionary aspirations have to make a thoroughgoing break with the past, gather around the Party's organisation for revolutionary culture, the Progressive Cultural Association (PCA), and use their

talents to assist in building the revolutionary mass movement, consciously aimed at the overthrow of the existing order.[13]

Silverman responded:

I didn't feel I could put up very good arguments for including it [in *Time Out*] in the end because, firstly, you don't say anything about the music, and that is what we are inviting people to listen to. Secondly, while you might say that the music doesn't interest you any more and there are more important things, you don't explain why: e.g. why the fight for socialism is relevant, what a *Time Out* reader might gain from it, what role – if any – you think music has to play in the struggle and/or after victory, [and] some examples – perhaps – of what you are doing at present and why etc.[14]

When Silverman subsequently wrote a piece in *Time Out* attacking the Albanian Party of Labour, and Josef Stalin to boot, Cardew was outraged and Silverman was denounced as a 'bourgeois', a 'reformist' and a 'counter-revolutionary'. It was, to all intents and purposes, the end of a relationship.

In fact, the concert attracted around two hundred people and was well received. The performers in Paragraph 3 enjoyed the experience and must have found Cardew's talk at the end disconcerting, if not depressing: having stated at the outset that he had no desire to discuss the music that had just been played, Cardew continued in the somewhat avuncular manner of Chairman Mao's *Yenan Talks*:

So I'm going to talk a bit about politics, about the situation in the country, and what the Party's line on it is. Now anyone who says they're not interested in this and would rather talk about the interval of a major 6th, or about Confucius, or the Scratch, is just burying their head in the sand, because actually the situation in the country is very serious, is developing very rapidly, and is fraught with all kinds of dangers (as well as all kinds of possibilities for revolutionary action). Does this mean that the avant-garde in general *can't* discuss the major 6th, Confucius, and the Scratch? Of course not – we should discuss these things in proportion to our general or specialized interest in them, *but*: we should discuss them in the context of, and with due regard for their relevance to, the political situation in the country. Certainly amongst musical comrades and the Party, there's plenty of discussion as to whether the major 6th is the best interval to start a new anti-fascist song with, etc., and whether certain notes should be bunched up or widely spaced, etc.[15]

It was all too reminiscent of the aforementioned concert of parts of *The Great Learning* at the Berlin Philharmonic nearly five years previously. At the ICA, too, the performers and audience had been totally engaged, and resented Cardew's attempts, through a political intervention, to disengage them, to cast doubt on the legitimacy, the authenticity, of their *experience* of the music. He had committed the same mistake; it was a lesson he had still not learnt. Even old musician friends did not speak out in his support; after all, he had just publicly renounced a part of his history, of himself, which they still admired and respected. And yet, and yet, and this is the crux: were we, his friends, simply seeking alibis to avoid taking that 'very crude, inchoate road' which he had embarked upon because, in Phillip Guston's agonised words (previously quoted), he 'wanted to be complete again [...] to be whole between what [he] thought and what [he] felt'. Were we not refusing to engage with him because the answers to the questions he posed were unthinkable? And were they unthinkable because we lacked the moral stature to acknowledge the reality of their implications? To say the least, was there not an inkling of recognition of the incongruity, as Cardew saw it, between that event at the ICA on 28 January 1979, and the 'winter of discontent' which had engulfed and threatened millions of people around the country and in relation to which the Institute of Contemporary Arts stood as a monument of supreme irrelevance.[16]

Of course there was some sympathy in the audience with his political agenda: twenty people signed a petition, relating to a court case, upholding the principle that 'Nazis have no right to organise', and after the concert seven or eight Goldsmiths' students, who had expressed interest in what he had to say, accompanied him for a meal. But to visit Goldsmiths' and talk to the student body there, a thought which had entertained him briefly, would only have happened 'if the Party think it's a good idea'. No independent ('political') initiative was permissible.

Thus, when a violinist from East Berlin, Götz Bernau, wrote to Cardew requesting a short piece for solo violin to be included in a concert at the British Centre in West Berlin on 21 March, Cardew was duty bound to inform the Party that 'this would mean taking a couple of days off work next week' (presumably from Diagram Visual Information) and to ask for permission. Finally, permission presumably granted, Cardew responded, and within a relatively short space of time sent two copies of *Arbeiterlied* (*The Worker's Song*) to Berlin. One of them was for the violinist's comments and improvements, where appropriate, which Götz was requested to return, together with a recording of a rehearsal performance, in the knowledge that recordings of concerts by radio stations were (and still are) notoriously hard to come by after the event.[17]

The Worker's Song is based on two contrasting themes: 'The Coal Owner and the Pitman's Wife', a 19th century Durham miners' song which was re-written by members of the PCA as 'The Worker's Song' in 1978, and 'Our Party's First Congress', written by Cardew in the same year (Ex.22.1-3). Here there is no flirtation with 'modernism, such as the experimental notations which appeared albeit briefly in *Mountains*. The material is strongly reminiscent of folk style throughout whilst incorporating traditional techniques from the baroque/classical repertoire – that is, 'The Workers Song' is cast in a synthesis of traditional violin styles.

The 'lyrical' opening (the folk song), expressing the plight of the workers, their strife and hardship, is peremptorily overtaken by the militant optimism of the succeeding set of six variations, a mood which prevails throughout the rest of the piece (Ex.22.1):

Ex.22.1. From *The Worker's Song*.

The technically demanding final section begins with the two themes in counterpoint, one *pizzicato*, the other *arco,* rendered even more difficult by Cardew's direction to 'preserve the character of the 2 tunes': the 'lyrical' and the 'militant'. (Ex.22.2):

Ex.22.2.

In the virtuosic coda the first theme returns in the tonic major. The dynamic drops to *pianissimo* but the tempo increases (*presto*) and the vitality of the music is maintained right up until the last flourish (Ex.22.3):

Ex.22.3.

The Worker's Song was Cardew's sole instrumental work from 1979; the rest of his output that year were songs, beginning with 'The Founding of the Party' which was written to celebrate the founding of the Revolutionary Communist Party of Britain (Marxist-Leninist) in March of that year (Ex.22.4). This was a revised version – with just a few minimal adjustments to the text – of the aforementioned 'Our Party's First Congress'. It is a sturdy song with a rousing chorus which the Party faithful, with few exceptions, could learn, remember, and enjoy. Along with the 'Internationale' it was invariably sung at the end of Party gatherings – such would have been its anthemic status.

Ex.22.4. From 'The Founding of the Party'.

For the Party the role of music was not to cast doubt, or inhibit action; rather it was to inculcate a reassuring feeling of certainty, to inspire and galvanise so that at the end of a meeting the mood was joyful and the hearts and minds of Party members and supporters were infused with confidence and optimism. In other words, and this is the crux, the music enhances their abilities, and their determination, to fulfil their duties and obligations to the Party, to revolution and the overthrow of Imperialism; it had no other function. Cardew opposed *Kulturpessimismus* or what George Steiner has called 'a new stoic realism'.

So perhaps carping over Cardew's text, which would have been subject to modification and revision in the light of criticism and advice from high-ranking Party ideologues, is a pointless exercise which only petit bourgeois critics such as myself would deem necessary. On the other hand, there is no doubt that the large mouthfuls of vowels and consonants which abound in every line of the 'lyric' disrupt the flow of the melody, rendering it difficult to sing and thus, I submit, detracting from the affective response of the singer (and the listener) to the *content* of the music. In all the performances I have attended the singer appeared to be struggling against the odds; but there was never a winner, and in the battle between text and music the two antagonists would grind out yet another goalless draw. Too often, in his desire for social definition, for political rectitude, Cardew the musician allowed himself to be compromised. 'Our music (the Party's line, etc.) is the *embodiment* of the best traditions of the British working class', he proclaimed.[18]

In March the controversy surrounding *Cogs and Wheels* no.3 was finally put to rest when the offending number was withdrawn from circulation. Cardew tabulates the reasons:

1. Relation of PCA to the Party: *Cogs and Wheels* 3 still (tacitly) keeps them apart, so that PCA 'takes its cue' from the Party, etc.

2. One-sided opposition to professionalism.

3. Underplays the role of form.

4. Implies that revolutionaries have to take up culture in order to propagate the Party [...] thus gives an exaggerated role to culture.

5. Attack on Recreation Ground Theatre was correct, but sectarian if widely distributed.

6. Reveals details of committees, etc., i.e., organisational details.[19]

Such admissions and corrections of past 'errors' may well have introduced a feel-good (or feel-better) sentiment into Party circles. Yet the degree of alienation from those 'bourgeois' living composers who 'wish to serve the socialist cause' (as at the ICA concert), and the gulf between them and Cardew was still considerable; the panacea of proletarian revolution failed to convince. The Marxist-Leninists had wrapped themselves up again in robes of comforting certainty and a spurious optimism; but the rest, the majority, had not yet been able to cast off the well-worn hand-me-downs of a worldly scepticism.

In essence the 1 March report constituted at least a partial retraction of statements made at the Birmingham conference the previous year and which were reported in *Cogs and Wheels* no.3. All of these 'errors' were attributed to the malign influence of Mao Tse-Tung Thought.[20] A necessary and practical first step was agreed: that the much criticised title *Cogs and Wheels* should be replaced by *Proletarian Culture,* a forthright and unequivocal message to potential readers proposed by Laurie Baker. The aim now was to reject the dogmatism and sectarianism which had bedevilled the Party's line on culture and to recognize the need to assimilate everything 'progressive and democratic' in history – including, presumably, bourgeois writers such as Balzac, from whom, Engels wrote, one could learn more about French society 'than from all the professional historians, economists and statisticians of the period together'.[21]

The sceptic, now, and then, might well interpret the 'dogmatism' which the Party opposed as, in many cases, simply a refusal to accept the Party line; Cardew himself, by this time an established member of the Central Committee of the Party, demanded acceptance, commitment, and implementation in respect of Party directives from members and supporters alike.[22] Thus, whilst the Party had indeed initiated an investigation of bourgeois, classical culture, such a programme had to be under strict Party discipline: the masterpieces of the past had to be studied, somewhat speculatively, in relation to the conditions of the dictatorship of the proletariat – that is, in a projected (desired) context. And in any case, at that particular pre-revolutionary juncture the propagation of the classics was not a priority for a Marxist-Leninist party. Of far greater urgency was to encourage the British working class to have pride in *their* history, *their* traditions –

as opposed to the national chauvinism of British Imperialism – whilst refuting the notion of superior and inferior peoples and stressing the idea of national characteristics and the unique contribution of the people of every country. As Enver Hoxha, the new Marxist-Leninist leader, wrote:

> The imperialist bourgeoisie has always tried to denigrate or eliminate the cultural traditions of small countries and the national features of their art and culture. This is one of the ways to carry out their cultural aggression and to subjugate the people. The reactionary bourgeois concept of the 'internationalisation' of culture and art, the idea that 'the stage of national schools has already been superseded' aims to eliminate the cultures of other peoples.[23]

As we have seen, with his reference to the dissipation and internationalisation of folk music in a lecture in September 1967, Cardew had argued on much the same lines long before he became a fighter for the proletarian cause. But even within the correct political context the use of folk music had to be approached circumspectly.

For an outsider, mindful of the exalted, seemingly unassailable position that Chairman Mao had occupied barely a year ago, the relative ease with which his thoughts were expelled from the canon was hard to comprehend. One wants to ask: what then had been the relationship between the heady sentiments of adulation and trust, and the philosophical and political *naiveté* which, after almost a decade, had finally been recognised?[24] Whatever the answers to this and other questions might be, in the wake of the departure of Carole Reakes (a comrade by now tarred with the Maoist brush), and with the adoption of a new General Secretary, John Buckle, the Party entered upon a period of 'rejuvenation and optimism', on both political and cultural fronts, with an outward show of equanimity and resoluteness.

This new mood was reflected both organisationally and by militant action. On 16 March 1979 the Party was re-named the Revolutionary Communist Party of Britain (Marxist-Leninist) and at the end of May the Party decided that the PCA, as a 'mass organisation', with its General Council, its Executive Council, its committees and branches, should be radically overhauled. It had become bureaucratic, unwieldy, and the art that had been produced – short plays for mass work, and songs such as the 'Ford Workers Song' – had been merely provisional, tending towards a suspect brand of populism. It was finally decided to streamline the PCA so that a central council of cultural activists, led directly by a National Executive, should plan, lead, and organise all the Party's cultural work, assuming responsibility for the cultural aspect of all Party events, conferences, rallies, and so forth. Cultural workers would also be charged with organising cultural activities and events in their particular area and enlisting assistance as and when required. The central council, which, in its public *persona*, according to one report, bore the quaint title 'The London Frescobaldi Society', consisted of Baker, Cardew, Devenport, Shrapnel and Thompson, and was overseen by the Party leader, John Buckle.[25] The structure would therefore be reduced to one central body which would decide what was necessary in the towns and cities of the various geographical areas in which the Party had begun to establish a number of People's Fronts.[26]

A *cause célèbre* in March was the case of the four Virk brothers who in April 1977, nearly two years previously, had been attacked by a gang of drunken racists while they were repairing their car. The Indians defended themselves and in doing so not only inflicted considerable injuries on their attackers, but, in the view of the Party, also provided the State with a convenient pretext for sending them down for long prison terms: three months, two years, three years and seven years respectively. The East London People's Front, led by Cardew, was actively involved in demanding freedom for the Virk brothers, denouncing the 'Government and Nazi organized racist attacks', and in March 1979 a special issue of East London People's News appeared in support of the appeal against the sentences which the Indian brothers had lodged. The paper drew attention to the discrepancy between the sentences of racists and those defending themselves against daily racist harassment and attacks. Racists were invariably given light sentences or bail or simply a few admonishing words from the judge. The paper provided a number of examples, naming names, insisting that 'there can be no appealing to the government, a government which organises racist attacks, operates racist laws and builds up a racist police force. It is also clear therefore that we can rely only upon ourselves, and develop our own self-defence'.[27] Satnam Atwal, an Indian Party supporter, recalls Cardew leading a group of demonstrators from the Angel tube station to the Court of Appeal. The police persistently disrupted the demonstration by stopping the marchers and attempting to force them to change the planned route, thereby preventing them from reaching the court. Cardew called on the demonstrators to ignore the demands of the police and was promptly arrested.

As a necessary consequence of the recent proliferation of Party activities, and of its geographical expansion, comrades, and supporters, were now being urged to move to parts of the country where the Party was beginning to establish bases and consolidate its presence. Hugh Shrapnel, for example, was persuaded to move to Birmingham;

others moved to Newcastle, Wales, and the Midlands. All this necessitated a considerable amount of planning and organisation, and in some cases upheaval. However, when it was suggested that Cardew and his family should uproot and settle in Glasgow Sheila's refusal was point-blank. A second proposal was put forward, and agreed upon, and on 15 July, by which time the flat in Agar Grove had deteriorated to such an extent that it constituted a danger to its residents, Cardew, Sheila Kasabova and her daughter Anna moved into number 28, Leyton Park Road, a modest three-bedroomed house in East London – a location that was handily placed, from a Party perspective, in relation to the Ford plant in Dagenham. A small van was hired to transport their few possessions, although on the day of the move Anna was sick with a temperature and stayed in bed until the moment of departure.[28] Sheila Kasabova recalls that she and Cornelius viewed the move to Leyton positively; they settled in and soon made friends.

The summer months saw an accumulation of demonstrations and protests in defence of the Asian communities. Southall in west London hosted several meetings and Cardew himself led a demonstration against 'State attacks' on Asians on 2 June. The Canadian Party leader, Hardial Bains, was in the UK and spoke at conferences at the Dominion cinema in Southall, and in Coventry and Bradford, on the problems facing the Indian communities abroad. He also addressed a meeting in Coventry on the theme of 'modern revisionism', including Mao Tse-Tung Thought and the 'three world theory'. Following the departure of Carol Reakes in the autumn of 1978, Bains seems to have taken an even more active part in shaping and guiding the British Party. According to Frances Rifkin, Hardial Bains' speeches were long and (at least for her) uninspiringly routine; moreover, no allowance was made for the fact that there were women with children at these occasions.[29] Rifkin recalls that there were certain issues, such as arranged marriages and homosexuality, which were not discussed in the Party; for example, should arranged marriages or, more contentiously, female genital mutilation be accepted as part of a national culture in which the Party had no right to interfere, or should the latter at least have been debated as a humanitarian issue beyond the bounds of nationalist autonomy and independence? Such issues were not debated, at least not publicly; the Party neither initiated nor welcomed open discussion.

Sheila Kasabova recalls that such formalities as adherence to Party etiquette remained inviolable, and that at one Party function (there may have been more), for whatever reason, the Central Committee table was served special, or at least different, food. Moreover, she would be separated from her partner, and since these social events were so rare it irked her that she could not spend the evening in his company. The elitism seemed to be endemic; there was no way that it could be mitigated, or reined in. However, we have to remind ourselves that such occasions were *official* Party functions and therefore Party protocol had to be observed. Family status and personal relationships were *never* referred to; as far as possible such relationships were kept secret; they certainly would not have been publicly acknowledged.

In October/November 1979, in a joint venture with the Canadian Cultural Workers' Committee, the PCA was invited to tour Canada for a period of around six weeks as part of a festival organised by the Communist Party of Canada (Marxist-Leninist): the Second All-Canada National Youth Festival. The PCA delegation was led by Cardew and included Peter Devenport, Laurie Baker, Chris Thompson, Hugh Shrapnel and the Canadian Penny Wright, who was resident in London. The itinerary embraced venues throughout Canada, including Toronto, Edmonton, Vancouver, Regina, Winnipeg, Thunder Bay, Guelph and Montreal, as well as many small towns and villages.

From the outset the demands on the British contingent were considerable and expectations were high, as if their revolutionary commitment and resilience were on trial. No sooner had they set foot on Canadian soil than poems and lyrics were presented for the British comrades to set to music. And they rose to the occasion, working through the night in a small office where a piano had been installed and where Hardial Bains would join them, elucidating the revolutionary content of the texts, many of which he himself had written or sanctioned. Moreover, comrade Bains had decreed that all the songs presented in the concerts should be new; no old or re-cycled material was permitted. In response the PCA produced more than twenty songs, most of which were written during the first week. Tired and exhausted though they were, the British comrades found the atmosphere exhilarating; to be free to devote themselves to these tasks, without distraction, was a unique experience. At meetings which took place in the afternoon, renderings of the songs were given and comments and criticism invited. Bains himself was delighted with the results and quipped that whereas in 1964 the British bourgeoisie had sent over the Beatles, fifteen years later 'the British working class had sent us the PCA'.

PCA's participation began formally on 30 September at a meeting in Toronto at which Hardial Bains, whose *persona* loomed large throughout the Festival, presented his Party's proposals for the coming week: as well as the production and rehearsal of new song material there would also be regular discussions relating to cultural matters. These meetings would be held every evening at 10pm and would provide the opportunity to expose and denounce Maoist, Trotskyite and revisionist errors and distortions; Lenin's writings on culture were held up as the correct cultural orientation. Details of the Internationalist concert at the end of the week, 7 October, would also be discussed and a final programme hammered out.

Hugh Shrapnel recalls one of the rehearsals during which Cardew was behaving in such an intolerable manner that he (Shrapnel) eventually walked out 'in a huff'. Shrapnel reflected that Cardew 'could sometimes be difficult to work with'; his political zeal would occasionally lead to his behaving in a dictatorial fashion.[30] Perhaps on this occasion there were underlying tensions associated with the politics, or with the meretricious music he had undertaken to perform against his better (musical) judgement, which provoked deep frustration and resentment in him. In 1977 Cardew had written in irreproachable Partyspeak:

> When we set up our own state of the Dictatorship of the Proletariat we aim to replace bourgeois culture with our new proletarian culture, so that in the course of time all our concert halls, record libraries, socials and dances, and the as yet uninvented social forms in which music will play a part, all these will be filled with proletarian music, and bourgeois music will have become past history from which we will have liberated ourselves and which will no longer have the capacity to sit on our backs and force us to be obedient slaves and lackeys of the exploiters. That this transformation will be neither short nor easy has been indicated by the ferocity and complexity of the class struggles in China since the start of the Cultural Revolution in 1966.[31]

Could these words have come back to haunt him during that rehearsal? Was this the 'new proletarian culture'which would joyously ring out in all the concert halls across the length and breadth of the country? Deep within him could it have been this unthinkable prospect which tormented him and drove his behaviour? Or was it simply because his musicians could not rise to the heights which the occasion demanded?

Comrade Bains' inaugural address covered a wide range of issues: he broached philosophical questions of idealism (that 'everything is subject to interpretation') versus historical materialism, and provided a spirited defence of the Soviet Union under Stalin. Anecdotal evidence of Stalin's irrational and inhuman behaviour was ridiculed and a refreshingly unorthodox theory of Trotsky's death was put forward by another Canadian comrade. And the following evening a not inconsiderable part of the discussion dealt with the discredited Mao Tse-Tung, and in particular with what were considered to be the late Chairman's erroneous theories in the field of culture. A Canadian comrade declared:

> During the 'cultural revolution' Mao also gave the line of making a complete break with everything of the past, with all tradition, and building an entirely new 'proletarian' culture. We also gave this line. But in fact this is an expression of conservatism, of reaction. Society cannot simply come to an end and restart.[32]

The historian of Maoism may duly register this admission, but the misjudgement to which the Canadian comrade was confessing on behalf of his Party, in a five-word sentence, several years after the event, was glaringly obvious at the time to thousands of observers and commentators, and not all of them hostile. More importantly, it had disastrous and possibly lasting consequences. Exorcism is a painful and traumatic experience, it is said; Mao Tse-Tung's 'unscientific' and therefore heretical thoughts had eaten into the souls of his erstwhile disciples and every insidious vestige of influence had to be expunged.

Yet Cardew was more circumspect, more even-handed, in his criticisms of Mao, occasionally drawing attention to a positive side of the Chairman's legacy: 'Good aspect of Maoism – his Puritanism was not such a bad influence in [the] heartlands of the sixties.'[33] He may have had the Scratch Orchestra in mind; as we have seen, the wild flights of fancy to which the Scratch Orchestra was prone were tempered by a degree of restraint, even detachment, although the source of such a disposition, at least in the formative months of the Orchestra, could hardly be ascribed to the influence of Chairman Mao – more to the benign equanimity of the presence of Cardew.

The issue of 'cogs and wheels', which had so troubled the British comrades, was also raised:

How can we use culture as an instrument the way Mao says? If the Party takes offensives, then we will have victories. Where do cogs and wheels fit in? How does culture assist in the promotion of political line? It can only disrupt the work.[34]

Yet it is difficult to square this objection with Lenin's dictum that 'literature must become *part* of the common cause of the proletariat [...] must become a component of organised, planned and integrated Social-Democratic Party work'.[35] Was this not an acknowledgement of the positive role literature (culture) was expected to play in the revolutionary scheme of things? Mao was being criticised for having over-estimated the role of culture to the extent that culture was used to supplant the political role of the Party. In fact, what Mao said was that 'to defeat the enemy we must rely primarily on the army with guns. But this army alone is not enough; we must also have a *cultural* army, which is absolutely indispensable for uniting our ranks and defeating the enemy'.[36] And when the Canadian Party insisted that 'it is necessary for the Party cultural workers to produce propagandistic culture for the Party [which] is addressed not at mobilising the masses, but to the comrades'[37] – is this not what Mao was saying in the previous citation?

Mao's general thesis, previously upheld vigorously by his followers, that 'all culture, all literature and art belong to definite classes and are geared to definite political lines' was now dismissed as a crudely reductionist formula. So that when comrade Bains directed that 'revolutionaries should show the way that intellectual development relates to the social practice and economic base of society'[38], eschewing any mention of 'class' except by inference ('social practice'), this might well be construed as a modification, or rather a dilution, of the original line, with its emphasis on 'class', and 'class struggle', materially and in the realm of ideas. A retreat from the thesis of the *class content* of culture might even have signalled a retreat from partisanship, from militancy, especially when the Canadian party seemed now to have adopted the following formulation: that 'the consciousness of the people will reflect the economic base, i.e. it will be bourgeois ideology dominant in society [...] [that] for millions of workers culture is, under capitalism, merely the training to act as an automaton [...] that in class society the motive of production of the ruling class denies any access to workers to the best traditions of mankind, etc.'[39] Is this not a mechanistic, one-sided interpretation – a retreat from dialectics? In relation to previous pronouncements does it not too compliantly characterise the workers as dupes and victims? For a Marxist-Leninist Party should they not be perceived rather as *dynamic* fighters who, under the correct leadership, present a (potential) threat to existing social relations, to the prevailing (bourgeois) ethos?

Let us take just one more example of the peremptory and, in a sense, pedantic rebuttal of 'Maoism' from a session which took place towards the end of the tour. During a discussion it was claimed (by the Canadian comrades) that 'language which exists in very well-developed ideological form has no class character. Stalin denounced the idea that the working class has its own language'.[40] Another Canadian comrade claimed: 'Mao Zedong's theory of the imprint of class is a serious attack on scientific culture.'[41] Certainly one would concur with the view that the theory, and not least the way it was applied, pervasively, in Canadian Maoist publications, was crudely reductionist. As we have seen, time and time again, 'class' and 'class struggle' was *the* key tenet of Marxist-Leninist ideology to which Cardew himself referred, routinely and unyieldingly.[42] Yet the *fact* (rather than the theory) of the 'imprint of class' does not violate the scientific method; it is neither fanciful nor speculative. On the contrary, staying with the example of language, and the way it is actually used in practice – that is, in speech, the class imprints are often striking: consider, for example, the mode of delivery that has developed within a tradition of giving orders, in which confidence, clarity and a sense of authority are of the essence; and compare it with the reactive utterances which emanate from within a tradition of accepting and carrying out orders, in which a tug of the forelock and an inarticulate vocal expression of compliance is all that is required. The characteristic use of language is a *cultural* expression; it is not a linguistic issue; and it is in the *use* of language, in myriads of subtle ways, that the indelible trace of class manifests itself. Cardew was aware of the subtle tonalities of *class,* even if he had not reached the stage of a clarity of objectification, of formulation of the way in which, in all human commerce, such tonalities served to embed, to strengthen and project the power relations of the Western social order, and which operate just as insinuatingly and corruptively in the art of music.

The reader may well already be exasperated by my refusal to let sleeping (Maoist) dogs lie, but in his last interview, shortly before his death, Cardew was still expressing the need (personal and collective?) to cast off their residual influences ('We are in recovery from Maoism'[43]) Thus the collective guilt is purged by transference; Mao alone bears sole responsibility for the exegetic limitations and transgressions of his erstwhile followers. As for my frequent references to, and reliance on, Hardial Bains and his Party, this is a reflection of the esteem, and the awe, in which Bains was held by the British comrades. And yet, in artistic matters, left to their own devices, the erring hand of Mao having been cast off, the Canadian comrades appear woefully out of their depth. Nor could comrade Lenin, with his ambivalence in relation to artistic matters, as we have seen, provide guidance. Lenin wisely refused to be drawn into making pronouncements on artistic matters: 'I don't claim to be an expert in the arts' he once said to Lunacharsky. 'Since you're a People's Commissar you ought to be enough of an authority yourself'.[44] There is little or no hard evidence to suggest that the Canadians, and Hardial Bains in particular, made a similar appeal to the British Commissar, despite his expertise and experience in artistic matters. Perhaps Cardew himself was as much to blame; it was as if he lacked the confidence in his own ability to write music of a high standard which would serve the proletarian revolution. This may have created a certain reluctance on his part to offer criticism and prescriptive advice.[45]

So the Canadians floundered, suggesting, on the one hand, that culture is for 'leisure time', and that the Party should provide people with 'healthy things': 'we should create very popular tunes', they concluded, 'propagandist music, using the same technique as advertising. Tunes that people can hum. We should not worry about if it is classical music'.[46] And conversely: 'In the Oct.7th Variety show there were indications of disco dancing, hints of it, etc. We have to be very firm. Ideological sharpness is crucial. When writing songs, you cannot liberalise/soften the line'.[47] So if culture can 'only disrupt the [political] work', small wonder that it should have been down-graded. Judging by the lyrics they provided, with which the British musicians dutifully engaged, in respect of the art of music the Canadian comrades had nugatory talent and little understanding. Nevertheless, at the end of the tour proper, after the British delegation had returned home, Cardew stayed on for another week or so to transcribe all the songs. The following year, 1980, an anthology of seventy-eight mainly Canadian revolutionary songs and poems was published by the Canadian Cultural Workers' Committee under the title *We Sing for the Future.*

Writing music that serves the proletarian revolution; this was the 'difficult and contradictory task' which the Canadians, undeterred by their own ineptitude in artistic matters, had set their British comrades during their collaborations. In 1979, for the most part, Cardew's compositional output was dominated, and controlled, by the needs and demands of the Canadian Party. Apart from the *Workers' Song*, a modest seven minutes in duration, which he wrote in England for a professional German violinist, Cardew's contribution amounted to a handful of songs, most of which were written in haste at the behest of the Canadians during the October/November tour.

Invariably, the songs are extended by virtue of repetition: in 'Revisionist Somersaults and the Opportunist Opposition' (which appears in the aforementioned anthology) the brevity and uneventfulness of the melody is a blessing, except that there are ten verses; the crude lyric is provided with music which is appropriately routine – an exemplary model of the political abuse of the art of music, as in the glamorised 'political' musicals which occasionally visit London's West End. How can this be explained – by which I mean, what was Cardew *thinking* at the time? I quote just the first verse (Ex.22.5):

Ex.22.5. From 'Revisionist Somersaults and the Opportunist Opposition'.

'An Opportunist Has Come Back Home' (also included in the anthology) is an endless, turgid, sectarian tract attacking a 'revisionist' who has betrayed the Party (Ex.22.6). The text is spoken and sung; the music is interspersed with, and accompanies, speech, alternating with a sung chorus (Ex.22.6):

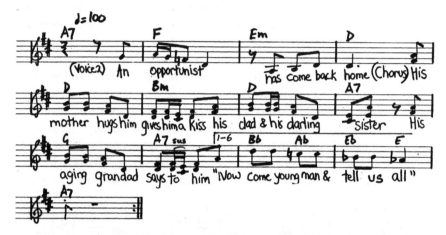

Ex.22.6. From 'An Opportunist Has Come Back Home'.

This is the full extent of Cardew's musical offering; it serves the whole text, which is of extraordinary length, doubtless uncut and unabridged. Here, towards the beginning, Voice 1 describes the young man:

Oh beautiful sight! What a striking pose!
Oh look at his Russian greatcoat,
The Mao badge on his lapel,
His Castroite fatigues,
And this is not all! Oh yes!
Voice II
An opportunist has come back home.

'Somebody spilled the Beans' was a song hurriedly put together by Hardial Bains and Cardew for the occasion of a sectarian confrontation involving the Canadian Marxist-Leninists in Nathan Phillips Square in Toronto on 14 October 1979. This took place during the period of the youth festival although, Cardew apart, the British contingent played no part in this particular event.

In stark contrast 'The Workers of Ontario' is arguably Cardew's finest political song and bears comparison with Hanns Eisler's songs, from which Cardew drew considerable inspiration (Ex.22.7). The song exalts the courage and determination of the workers of Ontario in the face of capitalist exploitation and revisionist compromise: 'Our ideology is Marxism-Leninism, we're workers and like workers everywhere our aspiration is for socialism ushered in by violent revolution'. Again, the Canadian cultural workers' text shows scant respect for the needs of melody. Nevertheless, the music flows, underpinned and driven by a livelier harmonic activity and exploiting the expressive possibilities afforded in the chorus by the minor tonality. Cardew even allows himself the luxury of a reference to a Romantic masterpiece: the first two bars of the middle section, in E major, are a quote from the beginning of the middle section of the slow movement of Chopin's *Piano Sonata No.2*. Bass guitarist Laurie Baker recalls the genesis of the song:

> I can remember Cornelius writing 'Workers of Ontario'; he was looking at this poem that had just been written. We all looked at the poems and chose what we wanted to do. He sat at the table with a manuscript for about an hour, then got up and went over to the Fender piano and hit a couple of notes and then sat down again. The PCA and the Canadian Cultural Workers would always have a discussion about the content and character of each new song. Frederick, a Canadian comrade, told us that the workers of Ontario liked yodelling, so when Cornelius wrote it he had this in mind.[48]

Cardew went through his first version with Baker, introducing some chromatic elements in the bass line to produce a more flowing effect. Baker recalls that it did not take long: 'I was astonished to see somebody write like this and he only checked one thing on the piano. I'd never seen anyone do that so quickly before.'[49]

'Great Indian People', with words and music by Cardew, was another song produced in 1979. It was written for a series of rallies in Britain in support of the revolutionary struggle in India but was never used.

Towards the end of the Canada tour, while the British contingent continued on to Quebec, Cardew stayed in Toronto and composed 'We Sing for the Future'. The idea was to present a song which would somehow sum up all the collective work of the previous weeks. And when Cardew eventually arrived in Quebec most of the brief rehearsal time was spent on the new song which received a spirited and convincing performance by a small chorus accompanied by piano and bass at the final concert that same evening. The words of the song were written by Hardial Bains; Cardew told Peter Devenport that Bains would declaim his poem in an expressive mode derived from Indian poetry and Cardew would compose fitting music, an inevitably long drawn out process. However, when it came to artistic matters the evidence suggests that comrade Bains, for all his incontestable qualities as a charismatic and courageous leader, was out of his depth.

Ex.22.7. 'The Workers Of Ontario'.

And it was Cardew's heresy that as a musician of stature, bourgeois or proletarian, he stood by, turning a deaf ear to the multiple nullifications with which Party ideologues and their compliant supporters wilfully compromised artistic aspiration and endeavour. Brecht took such people to task in his inimitable fashion:

> Art is not capable of translating official conceptions of art into works of art. Only boots can be made to measure. Besides, the taste of many politically-educated people is poor, and hence no criterion. Socialist Realism should not be treated as a style, and anyone lacking the aesthetic education to appreciate this stands in need of such training, and should undergo it, before taking up administrative work. It is particularly regressive to oppose Socialist Realism to critical realism and thereby brand it as an *uncritical realism*.[50]

Thus, Cardew's appealing, flowing music for 'We Sing for the Future' is forced to accommodate 'lyrics' of an overbearing nature, which – even if they do encapsulate the conviction that the international working class holds the future in its hands, fighting together for a new and better world – are an affront to the art of melody (Ex.22.8). Comrade the late John Maharg also drew attention to these unsingable texts: '"In utter chaos the old order spews out unlimited decadence and parasitism". You don't just make political statements for texts to music. [...] Its painful to listen to as well.'[51]

The slogan 'politics in command' meant that the Party always oversaw and provided 'suitable material' – that is, ill-contrived political tracts alien to any artistic representation. Cardew had no serious contact with artists or poets. There was no Brecht, no Joris Ivens, no John Heartfield, no Piscator – all of whom had been of immeasurable importance for Hanns Eisler. And if such artists had materialised, the individuality of their contributions would have been perceived as too independent, too challenging, and therefore a threat to Party control. The index of 'renegade' artists and scientists which had accumulated throughout the seventies, and included such luminaries as Christopher Caudwell and Noam Chomsky, had deprived Party members and supporters of a range of collaborative work which would have been of immense value to the cause.

But what of Cardew's 'appealing' music? Several connoisseurs of the English song tradition have drawn attention to a certain kinship between the chorus of 'We Sing for the Future' with the 'Eton Boating Song' (Ex.22.9)[52]:

Ex.22.8. From 'We Sing for the Future'.

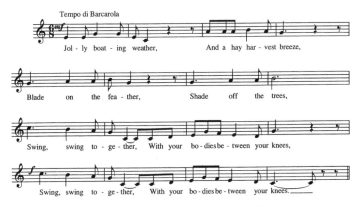

Ex.22.9. From the 'Eton Boating song'.

There is a certain emotional flabbiness about the music; it exudes a complacency steeped in an unshakeable sense of rectitude and infallibility common to both Etonians and certain Marxist-Leninists. Who is Cardew trying to reach? Is it then a throwback to his days as a chorister, or, subsequently, to his experiences at a public school highly conscious of its traditional legacy?[53] Or is he involuntarily reaching back to a subconscious past? And when the Party comrades stood on the platform and sang so ingenuously 'we sing for the future' – indeed when Cardew set those words – was the belief in historical ascent still unassailable? Did the reality of the threat of the arbitrary extermination of millions not give them pause to (re)consider? Would this have been 'revisionism'? It certainly would have challenged the bright-eyed faith which inspires so many Party songs. 'Realistic artists represent the *contradictions* in people and their relationships to each other and show the conditions needed for this development.'[54] Moreover, if there can be no real socialist construction under capitalism, then revolutionary art under capitalism must of necessity be destructive. And how is this destructiveness sustained without imaginative (artistic) reference to purpose and aims, to the 'bright future'? An unequivocal separation of ends (glorious victory) from means (unrelenting struggle), it seems to me, is bad dialectics and, as I shall suggest in due course, it was Cardew's failing that projections of this 'bright future' in works such as *We Sing for the Future* were, and remain, unconvincing: insubstantial, artless, and not infrequently embarrassing in performance. 'For socialist realism the task is to interpret the present in the light of the future', Andrei Zhdanov proclaimed.[55] But it is because the future, for Zhdanov, was so rigorously determined, binding the artist hand and foot, that it is such a terrible statement, and one which is, to quote Sartre, 'pregnant with consequence'.

Our prime responsibility is towards the people. And I go further and say: primarily we are responsible to the people of the future, secondarily to the people of the present and thirdly to the people of the past (who bequeathed to us our 'material' in the sense we're discussing). In other words: without a vision of the future development, we cannot serve the needs of the present. Or truly interpret the past. (This is far too grandiose a statement.)[56]

Was the Party therefore not compromised by its fundamentally a-historical position? We are reminded, again, of Eisler:

Perhaps the artist's task [...] is to see the past correctly and clearly and to [...] link it up to the future. Anyone who does not do this will supply an *untrammelled unctuous optimism* which doesn't sound right and makes no sense. The future cannot be conveyed in an undialectical way.[57]

When Hanns Eisler proclaimed that he had always striven to write music which would 'serve Socialism', it was not a confession of Party loyalty, especially – although it would have to have been a matter of 'last resort' – if he felt that the latter was incompatible with the former. By contrast Cardew allowed himself all too readily to be served and advised by Party ideologues whose grasp of music and its reception was misconceived, if not perverse.

In the seventies Cardew's musical priorities demanded not only more traditionally-based compositional methods; more importantly, they presupposed another context, in which music, and all other human activities, found expression and meaning. But he allowed this context to overrule the intrinsic demands of content; he was heedless of the 'reality principle' – in this case, of the imperatives of the composer's craft. Thus, the exigencies of a politically revolutionary agenda created distortive emphases which were woven into the fabric of his polictics – a heedless continuum of political rectitude: no deviations, no surprises, but a granite-like ineluctability driven by the logic of historical materialism. 'We should see all our work in the context of the overall strategy of the Party. Not subjectively to put one's own problems first and attach exaggerated importance to them'.[58] 'We have to be Party people. Partyism is an art', he jotted down in some hand-written notes dated 18 November 1979. Cardew was never one to baulk at the challenge of squaring the circle.

How did the PCA delegates respond, with hindsight and a little breathing space, to their experiences in Canada? First of all, the Canadians, from Hardial Bains to the rank-and-file Party supporters, were unstinting with their hospitality: paying all their British guests' expenses, from air tickets to meals, ferrying them often throughout the night to their concert venues, putting them up in their apartments and houses when and where necessary – endless acts of kindness and solicitude. Overall, the consensus was that the trip had helped to consolidate the British Party's work; the line on culture and political education was 'sharper'. Among the most invaluable souvenirs of their visit to Canada, Cardew and the PCA delegation brought back eight sheets of foolscap with the title: Notes from Canada October 1979. These summarised the whole gamut of issues raised and discussed during the Festival: Science, Philosophy, History, Culture, Music, Form and Content, and so forth, and has provided edifying material on which the above observations and comments are mainly based.

The minutes of the PCA Canada delegation meeting in London on 18 November contain the usual expressions of self-congratulatory optimism: that Marxism-Leninism is the 'highest development of human knowledge' (Cardew), and that 'cultural workers working together [are] bound to solve problems'. 'The best traditions of the past have given rise to us, the Marxist-Leninists', they had heard Hardial Bains proclaim in Canada.[59] However, when a comrade who had not been to Canada observed that 'lots of problems [were] sorted out in Canada' Cardew cautioned that 'comrades should be careful how they discuss the issues'. This is ambiguous; one assumes that he was suggesting that however 'successful' the visit to Canada was, its importance and relevance for the British comrades should not be over-estimated. Ultimately, problems would be 'sorted out' under the concrete conditions existing in Britain and under the leadership of the Party – not in Canada, however authoritative, however irresistible the discourses of Hardial Bains had been. Was Cardew beginning to assert his (the British Party's) independence? And yet, as we have seen, it was through his deference to Bains, to the slogan 'politics first', art in the service of ideology, that his considerable aesthetic judgement had been so painfully compromised. According to Sheila Kasabova, when Cardew returned home from Canada he would occasionally break down in tears. Everything the British comrades did was vetted and censored by the Canadian Party (by Hardial Bains). The PCA, as the political 'junior partner', took its line from the Canadians; a pecking order was observed so that even in artistic matters it appears that Cardew deferred to Hardial Bains. How else can one explain the acceptance and accommodation of texts which displayed such an implacable hostility to the art of melody?[60] Yet Cardew accepted it; it was politically correct and therefore it was his duty to overcome and expel the remnants of his former bourgeois self through self-abnegation and submission.

And because of the lack of clarity as to what precisely the pre-revolutionary role of culture should be (Party songs for Marxist-Leninists and/or songs based on 'advertising music' for the uninitiated?), the PCA work came to a halt, or at least into a temporary state of abeyance. After the 1979 Canadian tour Cardew's contributions during the next two years were modest: a transcription of his song 'A Law Of History' for brass quintet (*Vietnam's Victory*), a solo piano piece, *We Sing for the Future*, the two-piano piece *Boolavogue* – a commission which he accepted without great enthusiasm and which, in fact, he did not complete – and a handful of songs of varying merit, most of them commissioned by the Canadians when he returned to Canada in the spring of 1980.

The individual contributions by comrades at the 18 November meeting are preceded by an initial, that of their adopted (for security reasons) name.[61] E, the main contributor, is certainly Ernest (Cardew), a cardewesque choice with a roster of positive associations, not least in its (modified) adjectival form: serious, intent, committed, solemn, concentrated, and so forth. Not a fashionable name, rarely chosen then or now by parents (although Victor Schonfield gave the name to one of his sons), it betokens a solidness, even uprightness, certainly dependability – attributes admired in working class culture. Perhaps the communist hero of one of his piano works was also at the back of Cardew's mind: Ernst Thälmann.[62]

With the preliminaries disposed of Ernest immediately grasped the nettle, raising the issue of 'class and art'. For the Maoists it had been essential to establish the immanence of 'class' and aspects of 'class struggle' in all human commerce. Now there appeared to be a retreat from this position; the development of musical language, and even of the Western symphony orchestra, for example, were (according to Ernest) 'above class' Such a statement would have received short shrift from the Party.[63] Similarly (quoting Cardew again), 'a good scientist devotes himself to science; raises level of human knowledge on this front'[64] – a clear rupture with the Maoist theory of the 'two lines' (Two Lines on Medicine, Two Lines on Natural Science) which had dominated the two-day conference 'Seek Truth to Serve the People' during the heady days of December 1971. The class analysis of art was now deemed 'restrictive' although Cardew added the caveat that 'we (should) avoid going in the opposite direction'.[65] A comrade concurred, insisting that the 'bourgeoisie holds back science [which] can't develop again until socialism'.[66]

The subtlety and incontestability of the role of 'class' in all human relations has been the subject of some of the most original thinkers since Marx. As we have seen, during the seventies Cardew's Party had wilfully and disastrously closed its collective mind to a body of political, philosophical and artistic work of a remarkable range and depth, and as a consequence its post-Maoist utterances on art and culture were invariably equivocal, blighted by ignorance and confusion. It was as if they had been engulfed by an existential anxiety to explode the late Chairman's every thesis, to impugn his every thought – a condition which, paradoxically, in its obsessiveness and exclusivity, served only to limit and circumscribe, rather than to free and broaden, their vision of the nature and purpose of art. Thus, according to the Canadians, whilst the Maoists had claimed that form was 'not important', Lenin had insisted 'that in order to change the content, you have first to give up the form'.[67] If they had read Brecht they would have encountered, and perhaps, like the German Marxist, would have adopted, a more flexible, more practical attitude to the past, would have studied many of the old forms of poetry, story, drama, theatre, and would only have abandoned them, like Brecht, when they began to get in the way of what he/they wanted to say.

A distinction now was being drawn, according to the new Party orthodoxy, between a revolutionary culture which arises on the basis of the necessity, under capitalism, to 'create the conditions for socialist culture, for revolution and the dictatorship of the proletariat', and a 'socialist culture' which flourishes on the basis of a socialist economic base. Moreover, Cardew seemed to be proposing that culture should have a broader remit in the Party's work, and should be on a higher level (a united front with progressive artists?); at the same time, following Hardial Bains, he was now resolutely opposed to the idea of 'using culture to mobilize people for revolution'. Perhaps the reasons had little or nothing to do with ideology; for the songs, with their doctrinaire and unsingable texts, had succeeded in alienating all but the most devoted Party members and supporters. And it may well have been the eventual realisation and admission of this stark and unpalatable truth, even if it were not publicly acknowledged, that had brought about the new Party line in cultural matters. And with an irony that may have escaped their notice such songs had appeared in abundance amongst the twenty-five or so new songs which Comrade Bains had commissioned and which were rapturously received by the Party faithful. One must presume that this was strictly material for internal consumption only: 'Mainly Party culture is what we are producing; it is for activists and friends – may have some influence outside.'[68]

Time and again, as manifested in the Canadian reports, the scientist Bains had made the unequivocal demand that 'our culture must be a scientific culture'. (A syllogism defined the Party's relation to science: The Party bases itself on science; science in its analysis of the material world is correct; the Party is correct.) Comrade Bains' injunction is less contentious if one bears in mind that Bains was not necessarily referring to 'art' and artistic activities, which are only part of the wider concept of 'culture'. Whereas 'culture' may be susceptible to 'scientific analysis', one suspects that, like his mentor Wittgenstein, Cardew still held the view that the aesthetic creations of the human mind enjoy a precious immunity from even the most penetrating 'scientific' scrutiny; Wittgenstein had exposed the inherent limitations of science through reference to its conservatism:

> In fact, nothing is more *conservative* than science. Science lays down railway tracks. And for scientists it is important that their work should move along those tracks.[69]

But for Cardew the all-embracing and fathomless relation of art to the *realities* of human life (the 'military', the 'scientific', the 'partisan' and so on) had been impoverished and disfigured within the context of bourgeois culture, and the way in which art reflected reality was, *scientifically*, still relatively uninvestigated. On a torn piece of paper, from a small note-book, Cardew scribbled and elaborated on the theme of 'scientific culture':

> A culture of oppression, a culture that describes or bemoans the oppression of the working class is not yet scientific culture, however realistic it may be. Scientific culture is a culture of the *liberation* of the working masses. Spontaneously the masses resist oppression and strive for progress and freedom, and this too produces culture. Scientific culture begins where this movement for freedom and progress becomes conscious of its goals, when it is guided by the [word unclear] science of Marxism-Leninism. [...] And the culture, both that produced by the

special stratum of artists and writers, and that produced amongst the working people for their enjoyment, will be a culture of proletarian class character, of socialist content, international because of the universality of the science of Marxism-Leninism, and national in form because of the varied historical developments that the nations have gone through. So much for the general picture.

The issue of the 'national character' had been brought up by Comrade Bains in Canada and was considered of importance for the British comrades: the need for the British working class to have pride in its own history, as well as respect for the international working class. At the same time, echoing Bains, it was important to recognize that some of the most reactionary cultural trends, for example, the Beatles, had originated in Britain. One of the (Party) explanations attributed this situation to the degeneracy of the English 'revisionists': soap operas such as *Till Death Do Us Part*, and *Coronation Street*, which purported to be realistic portrayals of working-class life and attitudes, were the work of 'revisionists'.[70] Cardew himself refers to this in the 18 November meeting: 'Important' he notes, heavily underlined.

Cardew's pre-eminent role in PCA meetings is evident from the extant notes: despite reservations in relation to some aspects of it, as we have seen, he was implementing a Party cultural programme which bore the stamp of Comrade Hardial Bains, with whom he worked closely in the last years of his life – both driven by the same imperatives, the same revolutionary certainties. The communist movement embodied a whole set of traditions, modes of behaviour, which were upheld and applied to each and every social and political eventuality; and when Cardew became a communist, and a leading Party member, he took these 'traditions' on board – lock, stock, and barrel; he did not pick and choose. It may well have been the case, as Sheila Kasabova attests, that in respect of the fundamental tenets of Marxism-Leninism Cardew suffered mental agony – forced to struggle against reactionary, 'bourgeois' modes of thinking which stubbornly refused to vacate his mind and which continued to subvert a correct political orientation. But the central principle of 'democratic centralism' – the subordination, in practice, of all the individual Party members to the Central Committee (of which, by then, he himself was a member) – would eventually have ripped away the remaining vestiges of a liberal (bourgeois) conscience, even if, in modern times, ironically, Lenin's doctrine has been enthusiastically and unsentimentally adopted by governments and rulers of all political persuasions and is no longer confined to the Parties of the proletariat. Politicians, whatever their individual dispositions, must, through lying teeth, publicly and convincingly represent the Party line.

Like so many 'converts', whether religious or political, Cardew became one of the Party's most zealous, most loyal, most orthodox adherents. And then allowed himself to be led, too easily, by the Party, whose perceived rectitude became his Achilles heel. During the latter part of the decade, in particular, Cardew was weighed down by the lava accretions of duty heedlessly imposed upon him against which, eventually, as we have seen, he did protest – but only in order to take on other duties and responsibilities. It was as if, through an undying allegiance to the Party, he had willingly conspired in the transmutation of his own singularity, of his own self. Such that, for example, he would accept, and propagate, a cultural policy which in some respects was crass (and which, according to Sheila Kasabova, he would not in truth endorse) by somehow redeploying the arguments and thus becoming even further entrenched, and more profoundly, distressingly, alienated.

One of the more undesirable aspects of 'collective decision-making' is that people pull rank; they claim 'superior political insight', that they are privy to certain information that lesser comrades do not have; that they are on a 'higher political level'. They thus exploit and abuse the *loyalty* that rank-and-file members feel, as well as the necessity for discipline and secrecy. If a comrade is hesitant or dogmatic he or she runs the risk of being marginalized, demoted, or even expelled. Long-standing friendships become vulnerable, dispensable, and bitter battles emerge that may go on for long periods of time. In the RCPB (M-L) this problematic situation was compounded by the fact that it had virtually no experienced and mature comrades. Most of them, even amongst the leaders, were not long out of university. Why then did Cardew, and others, let things go, when their frustration and unhappiness was so palpable? The most persuasive reason is that in the late seventies, in particular, there was a widespread feeling that radical change was not only desirable but possible. Cardew, and others, worked twenty-four hours a day in pursuit of this ideal, the revolutionary cause which the Party embodied, and were prepared to make huge personal sacrifices.

On 25 November the PCA took part in a 20,000-strong demonstration against racist attacks in London, followed three days later by an even bigger demonstration to protest against the harsh economic measures the Government was introducing. And on 12 December Cardew led a demonstration in support of Zimbabwe by the London branch of the Party. Four days later Cardew's report lists the Party's priorities in the cultural field, an agenda for us to bear in mind as we continue to track and monitor his activities during the coming months:

1. Investigation into British national culture.
2. Develop the critique of Mao's line on culture.
3. Party guidelines for PCA work:
   a) what is scientific culture.
   b) populism.
   c) further critique of *Cogs and Wheels*.
   d) class character of Art.[71]

'The Year of Stalin' ended uncompromisingly with a rally and conference organised by the Party to celebrate the great leader's hundredth anniversary. It took place on 21-23 December at, somewhat incongruously perhaps, the German YMCA in Craven Terrace, off the Bayswater Road. Rehearsals were required as well as the need for appropriate songs and poems to be selected. This was the occasion when, appropriately, the decision to form the Stalin youth brigade was announced. The plans for the publication of a new magazine, *Proletarian Culture*, were also on the agenda, while the inability of Bob and Paul (Laurie Baker and Peter Devenport) to pool their artistic and organisational resources provoked yet another briefly assertive entry in Cardew's notes: 'a real problem on this front'.[72]

Notes and references

1 Hanns Eisler, from an open letter to the Composers' Union of the German Democratic Republic, printed in the newspaper *Neues Deutschland* on 24 February 1957.

2 Trevor Blackwell and Jeremy Seabrook, *A World Still to Win* (London: Faber and Faber, 1985), p.145.

3 Hans Keller, 'Thinkers of the world, disunite! 3', *Books and Bookmen*, Vol. 21, no. 1 (October 1975), p.57.

4 Blackwell and Seabrook, *A World Still to Win*, p.145.

5 Ibid., p.133.

6 On a separate occasion, in March 1977, coming back from a concert for striking hotel workers in Oxford, Cardew did fall asleep at the wheel and drove into the parapet of a bridge. It was a salutary warning, an indication of their physical, and mental, condition, and of the limits to which they were driving themselves for the cause of proletarian revolution.

7 From an email communication to JT in February 2006.

8 From the aforementioned PCA letter to CANISG, dated 6 January 1979.

9 Hardial Bains, *Necessity for Change! The Dialectic Lives!* (Ottawa: Communist Party of Canada (Marxist-Leninist), 1998), pp. 30-33.

10 George Steiner, *In Bluebeard's Castle* (London: Faber and Faber, 1971), p.67.

11 Letter from Julian Silverman to CC, dated 24 January 1979.

12 Ibid.

13 Cardew's undated, typewritten text, entitled 'Why Look Back', must have been written around 20 January.

14 Letter from Julian Silverman to CC, dated 24 January 1979.

15 From Cardew's talk at the end of a concert of his music at the ICA on 28 January 1979.

16 I suspect that Cardew would have taken issue with my characterisation ('supreme irrelevance') of the ICA here. He would probably have insisted that the ICA's role was more *dynamic,* as a promoter of reaction and degeneracy.

17 So far, I have found no evidence of a response from Götz or his wife.

18 A handwritten note at the bottom of a typed letter to 'Kevin' (surname not known), dated 11 May 1980.

19 From Cardew's handwritten report, dated 1 March 1979. In a letter dated 11 May 1980 Cardew returned to the issue of the 1978 Conference and *Cogs and Wheels 3*: "We consider the basic orientation of the Conference – that the Party leads the cultural work as it leads all other aspects of the revolutionary work – to have been correct. But there are several repercussions of Maoism in the Conference Resolutions, in particular the line of *Cogs and Wheels*, which a) philistinely treats *all* culture as propaganda and b) overstresses the role of culture in transmitting the Party's line."

20 In a brazen *volte face*, all the comrades were now being encouraged to re-read the Yenan talks – in order to refute them. At the same time study of Marxist-Leninist classics was urged: Lenin's *On Party Organisation and Party Literature*, in particular, was prescribed as essential reading.

21 As quoted in *Marxism and Art*, ed. Maynard Soloman (Detroit: Wayne State University Press, 1979), p.11.

22   Invoking 'unity and discipline' is a time-honoured ploy for stifling dissent in all political parties and groups.

23   Enver Hoxha, *Selected Writings*, p.350.

24   I recall an observation by one Party member that the jettisoning of Mao Zedong Thought seemed to have caused more concern and confusion outside than inside Party circles. Some years later, by way of explanation, or excuse, he suggested that these issues and responses were 'of their time'.

25   Hugh Shrapnel does not recall the adoption of the title; perhaps it was discarded or, more likely, was used for bookings of public venues.

26   In email communications to me in the winter of 2003 Hugh Shrapnel recalled that the aim of these initiatives was not necessarily recruitment to the Party, or to Marxism-Leninism, but rather to unite the people in local areas on a broad basis, to arouse them to political action on important issues such as opposition to racism and support for the Irish people. Generally, 'having cast off the shackles of Maoism', Party members and supporters felt that the Marxist-Leninist line of the Party had been strengthened and was being applied in 'a more creative way'.

27   *East London People's News*, Vol. 1, No.10, March 1979.

28   In fact, contact with Agar Grove was maintained; a one-bedroomed flat was rented by the Party for the convenience of comrades and supporters who were regularly detained by the police. Cardew shared the premises with at least twenty other revolutionaries, all of whom, when arrested, would give the same Agar Grove address.

29   Although according to Brigid Scott Baker it had been the setting up of the Little Red Guards organisation which had rescued the children from such tedium.

30   Laurie Baker, too, recalls that Cardew was a hard task-master, particularly with the conservatory-educated musicians, like Shrapnel and Devenport. And yet, in all the years I worked with him, and observed him working with others, I never witnessed such a reaction.

31   From a PCA draft orientation text on 'high bourgeois' music, undated but probably from 1977.

32   Notes from 'Discussion – Oct. 1 (evening)'. These unattributed 'notes', comprising about forty pages, and on which I draw almost exclusively, derive from discussions at various meetings during the 1979 Canadian tour. They are typed out and were possibly transcribed from recordings of the proceedings. 'Notes on Cultural Issues discussed during the visit of C.C. [Cornelius Cardew] and PCA delegations to Canada, October 1979', to which I refer below, contains a number of annotations and corrections in Cardew's hand.

33   From the handwritten (not by Cardew) minutes of the PCA Canada delegation meeting in London, 18 November 1979.

34   Notes from a discussion (evening), 1 October.

35   V.I. Lenin, *Party Organisation and Party Literature,* p.23.

36   Mao Tse-tung, *Mao Tse-tung on Literature and Art,* p.1. Emphasis added.

37   From 'Notes on Cultural Issues discussed during the visit of C.C. and PCA delegations to Canada, October 1979.'

38   Ibid.

39   Ibid.

40   From' A Discussion on Culture, 29 October.' The reference here is clearly Stalin's *Marxism and Problems of Linguistics* (Foreign Languages Press, Peking 1972).

41 Ibid.
42 Hardial Bains: 'The objective law is that class struggle necessarily leads to the dictatorship of the proletariat'. From the Minutes of the Meeting of Cultural Workers, 30 September 1979.
43 Interview with Paul Driver, 6 July 1981.
44 V.I. Lenin, On Literature and Art, p.262.
45 Such doubts, to which I refer again in the next chapter, persisted to the end.
46 Notes from a discussion (evening) in Toronto, 1 October.
47 Notes from Canada Oct '79 (CC and PCA delegations).
48 From a recorded interview in Shepherds Bush, West London, with Laurie and Brigid Baker and Chris Thompson, in March 2003.
49 Ibid.
50 Bertolt Brecht, Gesammelte Werke 19, pp. 545f. As quoted in Albrecht Betz, Hanns Eisler Political Musician, p.226.
51 From a recorded conversation with JT, 19 January 2004.
52 The Eton Boating Song is a famous English school song associated with Eton College. The melody was written by old Etonian Algernon H. Drummond; it was first performed in 1863.
53 Cardew's school friend, David Sladen, insists that Cardew never subscribed to the 'Public School ethos'. This may be so, but it does not follow that he was neither affected nor influenced by it.
54 Bertolt Brecht, as quoted in Betz, Hanns Eisler Political Musician, p.228.
55 From a speech by Jean-Paul Sartre, 'The Novel and Reality', at a Conference of European Writers in Leningrad, in the summer of 1963 (New Left Review, no. 29, January-February 1965), pp.37-40.
56 From Cardew's aforementioned letter to the German magazine Berliner Hefte, Zeitschrift für Kultur und Politik, dated 5 October 1976.
57 Betz, Hanns Eisler Political Musician, p.235. Emphasis added.
58 CC, handwritten in pencil, probably from 1973.
59 Notes from a discussion evening in Toronto, 1 October.
60 As well as a denial of Hegel's thesis that music is not meant to emphasize the text but derives from it only the universal element of its meaning.
61 This was strictly maintained, and as a principle people would be referred to by their Party name. Venues for meetings would also be given different names. People were told not to use their home phone for Party matters; family and personal affairs were not to be discussed in Party circles. Cardew himself was strongly advised not to keep a journal. In the wrong (police) hands such material could severely compromise both the individual and the Party.
62 On one occasion, perhaps more than one, when he had been arrested, Cardew gave the name Ernest to the police. However, to secure release he was usually obliged to divulge his real name. When asked why he had initially given the name Ernest, he apparently retorted that 'I just wanted to throw a bit of sand in your face'. The name also lent itself to idiosyncratic expressions of 'English humour': a comrade would ask him to 'pass the tea, Ern'.
63 And not only from the Party: Eddie Prévost, an unlikely bed-fellow, argues that 'it must be

more than coincidence that the terminology used in orchestral life so mirrors a mode of capitalist production – the factory. The composer retains the property rights to the music through copyright and property protection legislation, which is enforced and collected by publishers and agents. The conductor acts like a managing director of a factory to bring his work force in line to make the product. Even his sub-lieutenants (leaders of the various instrumental sections) are called 'foremen'. Another factory-like feature is the division of labour in which parts of the production are shared out amongst the work force. Thus the parts are produced almost to a point of (audible) independence within the total production. This is especially so of a large symphonic work where it is impossible for the musicians to hear all the contributions of others – echoes here perhaps of a Marxian sense of a worker's alienation from the goods produced.' From *Minute Particulars*, p.150.

64   From the minutes of the 18 November meeting.
65   Ibid.
66   Ibid.
67   From Notes from Canada, October 1979 (CC and PCA Delegations).
68   A contribution from Cardew in the minutes of the PCA Canada delegation meeting in London, 18 November 1979.
69   Monk, p. 486.
70   The 'revisionists' would have described *'Til Death Us Do Part* as a satire on 'false consciousness'; the Party, no doubt, would have dismissed this as sophistry, pointing to the fact that the bigot Alf Garnett became a kind of anti-hero, and that in fact viewers were encouraged to sympathise and identify with him.
71   From Cardew's handwritten report of a PCA meeting on 16 December 1979.
72   From a handwritten sheet of notes from the 16 December meeting.

Cornelius Cardew a life unfinished

23
Arrests and Imprisonment 1980

'The capitalist system is a prison
The mass of humanity having to get out
to the air, to the light, to learn
to build a future.'
'Every revolution has thrown open the prisons.'[1]

Labour having been emasculated, the time was now ripe, as the new decade was ushered in, for Capital to be exalted and freed. Previously a stigma had been attached to it; people generally mistrusted it; certainly in state schools it was comparatively rare for a young person to announce that he or she were 'going into business'. Such ambitions, if and where they existed, would have been guarded discreetly. So for the capitalists and their representatives in the media in particular, the first stage was to elevate business to a status of neutrality; business was neither good nor bad, such a judgment being contingent upon the nature of the business, its methods and aims. Business was amoral. In Britain it was the new, crusading prime minister Margaret Thatcher who took the process a stage further, thereby effecting a qualitative change of image. Business ('honest money') was not only necessary, it was a positive expression of human nature: acquisitiveness, competitiveness, individualism were 'natural' and therefore 'good' – except when such qualities manifested themselves in Trade Unionists and other destabilizing elements ('the enemy within'), whether individually or collectively. And many were sucked into the quicksands of the new political culture with its combative slogan of 'looking after number one', and its deep mistrust and dislike of 'johnny foreigner' – which also included those who inhabited the European mainland, and whose beaches and bars were fast becoming economically and culturally transformed by hundreds of thousands of British holiday makers. The dream was to 'set up business on your own', 'be your own man (or woman)'; some ventures flourished briefly, more fell by the wayside leaving the dreamers disillusioned and broke. Few were untouched by the Thatcher decade of greed; if some bought it, others – an initially credulous majority – were sceptical but powerless to escape the consequences: a breakdown of the social fabric, an irreversible decline in social services, record bankruptcies and levels of crime, and a widening of the gap between rich and poor with one in five children living below the official poverty level. Of course, there were high-profile manifestations of dissent: on 9 March, a huge demonstration took place in London against the policies of the government, and during March and April meetings against war preparations were held in twenty-five cities across the length and breadth of the country. But Thatcher, like an evangelist driven and sustained by the certainties of her creed, ignored or rode roughshod over all opposition. And when she finally met her nemesis, in 1990, it was too late; irreparable damage had been done.

Against this background, at the beginning of the eighties there seems to have been a corresponding shift in the tactics of Cardew and his comrades – an acknowledgement of the need to respond proactively, on the cultural as well as the political level, to the increasing intensity of capital's assault on working people. The stratagem of using contacts in the Establishment and in the musical and artistic world in general, virtually abandoned at the end of 1976, was revived, and PCA members were now being encouraged to re-establish contact with old friends and colleagues. It was also deemed important to encourage initiatives to start groups and mount concerts and events with progressive content, such as a production at Goldsmiths' College of Brecht/Eisler's collaboration based on Maxim Gorky's *The Mother*, one of the models of revolutionary artistic practice. For the Party the 'degenerate literature' that was now being produced in the Soviet Union was a 'sobering lesson': 'It shows how thoroughly the revolutionary Soviet Union of Lenin and Stalin has been turned into its opposite – a fascist dictatorship.'[2] The aim was to involve and unite artists in and around an event organized on a political basis, but which was broadly based and on terms which the invited artists would be able to accept. There was also discussion of the possibility of mobilizing West Indian musicians to make a contribution; there had already been abortive attempts (previously mentioned) but it was hoped that through the offices of the West Indian members and supporters of the Party relations could be revived and a positive outcome achieved. The PCA band, too, was expected to resolve its differences and become a regular feature on demonstrations, as it had been before the 1978 Birmingham conference. A new song book was being prepared while the successor to the journal *Cogs and Wheels* had been placed 'on ice for a while'.

In an unlikely change of tack Cardew himself was enjoined (by the General Secretary of the Party, no less) to apply himself to composition, to pursue musical engagements at home in Britain, and to re-establish his position in the profession, thereby extending and widening his (and the Party's) influence.[3] For the Party Cardew's class background and education was neither an encumbrance nor an embarrassment; moreover, his reputation as a leading composer of international status was still (just) intact. Shortly before his death in 2004 comrade John Maharg reminded me that the Central Committee as a whole came from the middle classes; they were 'more educated'. But there was more to it than that; they had also been trained to organize, to assume responsibility, to *lead*; as we have seen, leadership was a quality which Cardew demonstrated authoritatively and in response to a diversity of challenges throughout his life. After all, it was within the public school system that future ministers and captains of industry were being nurtured and groomed. Cardew's relationship to his Party expressed a mutual need, and one might argue that both needs were grounded as much in human psychology as in political expediency. Curiously, this new 'line', in relation to Cardew's role in the public domain, was not made known to other PCA members. Yet if he had been successful – for example, through commissions and a higher profile in Establishment venues – one would assume that this would not have escaped the notice of musician comrades such as Hugh Shrapnel, Peter Devenport, Laurie Baker, among others. One senses a loosening up, in some respects, although the insistence on central Party control would have been as immutable as ever.

Cardew's decision to study at King's College, University of London, on a Master of Music course in musical analysis (a letter of application was dispatched on New Year's Day) would not have been taken unilaterally; it would have been necessary to convince his comrades on the Central Committee that this extremely time-consuming commitment would ultimately benefit the Party. Of course, arguments in favour would have carried weight simply by virtue of his status, of the respect in which he was held at all levels in the Party hierarchy, but there would have had to be a certain amount of re-organization of the Party's already over-stretched (human) resources; in order to facilitate his study it would have been necessary to relieve Cardew of some of his more menial, administrative duties. His extant notes, some typed, some handwritten, relating to the PCA, demonstrate an extraordinary prolificacy which would have been impossible to emulate. Regarding his duties as member of the Party's Central Committee, naturally I have had no access to information concerning the precise nature and extent of this activity, but we can reasonably assume that the demands that were made of him in this capacity would have been herculean, and unremitting. It was an impenetrable world, shrouded in secrecy, which Cardew inhabited in those later years, so that as far as his Party (Central Committee) commitments were concerned we have to make do with remembered and recorded observations of him on a day-to-day basis. For Cardew the Party's noble aim, the emancipation of the poor and oppressed of the world, seemed viable, but the path was long, tortuous, and strewn with sacrifices, some self-imposed, others imposed from the highest authority, the Party. But who were these high-ranking comrades? What was their moral status? Were they characters of steel who could resist under enormous pressure, and survive? What imprint, if any, have they made on human history? Will the Communist Party of Great Britain (Marxist-Leninist) live to fight another day, or will it too suffer the 'enormous condescension of posterity' as a footnote to history?

As for the relation between his Party work and his obligations to his families, there was often considerable tension. It was not possible for him to make any decision autonomously; as we have seen, a planned family weekend would have been subject to cancellation, and at the last minute, by Party decree. But there is no doubt that the music faculty at King's would have been both astonished and delighted by his presence as part of the student body. Some four months later, on 8 May, a letter from the head of the department, Dr. Arnold Whittall, confirmed acceptance for the Course 'provided that the University is prepared to waive the regulations in respect of an initial degree' [which Cardew did not have]. The Academic Council of the University duly obliged and Cardew was enrolled as a student from the coming autumn term, 1980.

Relations with the Canadians continued to flourish and a delegation of PCA cultural workers, led by General Secretary John Buckle, Cardew, and Chris Thompson, was invited to Canada, from 27 March to 9 April, to participate in the celebrations for the tenth anniversary of the Canadian Party. Other PCA members who were part of the delegation included Laurie Baker, Peter Devenport, John Maharg, Stuart and Charlotte Monroe, Penny Wright, and there were also two or three non-PCA members. The Party's brief to the delegation, hand-written by Cardew the day before departure, is an instructive document and appears to have covered every eventuality. The role and function of the delegation, indeed its deportment and behaviour, is prescribed precisely and on the basis of ideological rectitude – rather like young novices invited to attend seminars at the Vatican:

> Is a Party Delegation. P. [Party] is [the] vanguard of British working class. Delegation is not a collection of individuals, is a delegation of the class. Delegation should conduct itself as a body representing the British working class. *Discipline.* Everything goes through [the] delegation. Problems, queries, complaints, suggestions. No giving of views on arrangements outside delegation. If there are things to be raised with the comrades or others, must be raised with delegation leaders. Must be sorted out *in* the delegation, and then everyone follow decision. At the same time, uphold Party line, and talk about it as fully as you can. Don't hold back.
>
> On social occasions etc., or with comrades you are staying with.
>
> Don't answer questions you don't know the answers to. Say 'don't know', or 'I'll ask'.
>
> Don't give [your] own views, give Party line, and nothing else. Unless on certain

things it is appropriate to give views, in which case make it clear that is what they are.

Also ask freely – but don't ask or answer organizational questions.

Uphold Party, Party's work, Party's history. Avoid subjectivism on work here as result of achievements there. Coming back with such sentiment is very disruptive, and quite incorrect.

Contribution of the cultural workers has been most important and will be. Canadian comrades value it highly. Uphold this – no mean contribution – take it seriously and work hard.

D [John Buckle] leads; when not there, E [Cardew] leads; then Chas [Chris Thompson].[4]

Such were the behavioural strictures which were binding upon the British delegation: a *modus operandi,* from which they would not have strayed, that also reflected the self-discipline which the Party's inner circle, members of the Central Committee and including the General Secretary, demanded of itself.[5] The ideological strait-jacket, 'made in Canada', for which they had been fitted, was to be worn on all occasions, both public and private.

The 'celebrations' to which the PCA had been invited did not embrace the notion of entertainment, although the idea of 'leisure time' and 'recreation' was now being promoted by the Canadian Party. One might speculate as to whether the delegates from Albania and Germany, for example, had exercised the same degree of self-conscious, revolutionary rigour in their preparations for the event. The British Party (including the higher echelons) was still in thrall to the Canadians, or rather to Hardial Bains; like the eager and ambitious pupils at school they were doubtless anxious to impress their teacher and to receive his praise and encouragement. This they duly received and not least, it would appear, in cultural matters – performing and recording a number of songs which were enthusiastically received by the Canadian comrades. These included Hugh Shrapnel's 'A Naxalite in Birmingham', and 'Lament of the Petit Bourgeois Democrat', in which text and music are locked together in a mutually exclusive struggle for survival. The preparation of the songs for a PCA performance at an Internationalist rally of Marxist-Leninist parties in Montreal on 30 March received the same detailed attention. In a text entitled 'Points to deal with (singers)', divided into three sub-sections – Criticism, Political level, and Discipline, Cardew delineates the preparatory tasks necessary for an ideologically and musically successful presentation.

Back in England a meeting was held in London on 4 May to report on the Party delegation's visit to Canada. Entertainment was provided at the end with musical contributions from Cardew and others. And on the previous day *Workers' Weekly* had announced the first issue of *Voice of the Youth,* a new magazine edited by Cardew.

On 10 May a 'Hands off Iran' demonstration in central London, followed by a picket at the US embassy and a rally in Hyde Park, again saw Cardew in a leading role, undeterred by the constraints which had been imposed upon him by the courts.[6] And two days later, in contrasting circumstances but with the same unyielding agenda, Cardew was back in academia with a lecture/recital for which the following text was used, either as a programme note, or perhaps as a verbal introduction:

1. Cultural workers like everyone else should get organised and prepare for the revolutionary storms ahead. Why? Because thinking people, enlightened people, have the responsibility to place themselves on the side of progress, not reaction.
2. Cultural workers should see themselves as *scientists* and strive to place their work on a scientific footing and push forward the frontiers of human knowledge.
The revolutionaries also strive to do this, but mainly they work night and day developing strategy and tactics to hasten the victory of the revolution and establish socialism – because we know that *only then* will the conditions be created for great advances in science and culture, in the cause of humanity in general.
Composers should compose, critics criticise, etc., but they too should take up the advanced ideas of our epoch, the enlightened ideas of Marxism-Leninism, and with this outlook give voice to the democratic and revolutionary aspirations of the working people in militant, clear, profound and moving works. The rich, the reactionaries in our society should be given no peace; they should be hounded and denounced from all sides, and the struggles of the workers should be praised, made conscious of their goal, etc. Cultural workers have an important contribution to make in this.[7]

What would the music students at Brighton have made of this? Certainly, some would have baulked at its prescriptive, condescending tone; others would have been switched off by its presumptive, moralistic tenor, its display of petty headmastership. To be labelled 'cultural workers' probably jarred with some, and to equate cultural workers with scientists would have been even more contentious, especially if they perceived that the term 'cultural worker', according to Cardew's definition, also embraced musicians and artists in general. In such situations Cardew normally had two options: the softly-softly approach, or the take-it-or-leave-it approach. On this occasion (possibly following Party guidelines) he opted for the latter. It was not his brief, one suspects, to be 'persuasive'; the tactic was rather to storm the citadel of bourgeois academia, take and maintain control of the agenda, and not to allow liberals and reactionaries to hijack the proceedings by giving them more space than necessary. A debate will allow the sceptics and cynics to undermine or to sanitize your message. Be conscious of the time factor; challenge your audience. At the bottom of his sheet of paper three names and addresses (presumably of students) were scrawled, with the reminder: 'PCA send info'.

At a PCA committee meeting on 24 May again the need to expand the singing group is emphasized, as is the desirability of professional involvement. Vicky Silva, who had performed regularly with PLM in the mid-seventies but who had ultimately failed the test of political correctness, is mentioned as a possible participant in a series of 'New Culture' concerts in south and east London, and a composers group with Cardew, Devenport, Baker, Robert Coleridge and Dave Smith is proposed, with commissions for new works. On 8 June a 'New Culture' concert with the PCA singers and West Indian musicians took place in south London and included three songs by Shrapnel and one by Cardew. The Canadian texts, of an unsurpassable political and literary crassness, demonstrate to what extent the talented British musicians were prepared to stoop in order to serve their Canadian mentors. Here is an extract from 'Castro's Baggy Pants', which Hugh Shrapnel set:

Yes there is some space in these baggy pants.
I am not entirely a bigot.
I am not just a sold-out lackey
Of Soviet social-imperialism.
Oh you imperialist buggers,
Look! Come to your senses.

There is a lot of space,
Three hundred billion dollars worth –
My baggy pants
Have unlimited scope
For accommodation.[8]

Perhaps such 'lyrics' explain the reference in Cardew's notes on a PCA committee meeting early in July to the singers 'demand for discussion on New Culture, the Party's line, more summing up of events, etc.' In fact, around this time, in June, the PCA produced another song book, *Make the Rich Pay*, which boasted a majority of new songs written by Canadian, West Indian, Albanian and English comrades (including just two by Cardew – 'The Party's First Congress' and 'Smash the Social Contract'), all of which would have passed the censor in terms of the political relevance and correctitude of their content.

Cardew was still active in the Musicians' Union, agitating for strike action against the BBC – who had issued a plan to close down five of its eleven staff orchestras – and helping to organize picketing of the BBC, at the TV Centre in particular, beginning 1 June, not only by MU members but by the Trade Union movement as a whole. A ballot had shown that strike action was unanimously supported by members of all eleven orchestras. Such activity could have enhanced his Union credentials when, on 12 June, he returned to Sheffield for a meeting to celebrate the 110th anniversary of the birth of Lenin. The venue was the Brown Cow pub in Wicker, on the northeast outskirts of Sheffield, where during the steel strike the previous winter Cardew had held discussions with the steel workers and had no doubt maintained contact with some of them.[9]

This was a quite different audience to the one he had addressed the previous month in Brighton. At the University the language of his talk was appropriately formal, but in Sheffield, as befitted the occasion and the subject matter, each and every phrase was hewn from the rock of the Leninist canon:

Lenin, the great theoretician and revolutionary leader, defended and elaborated the principles of scientific socialism and proletarian internationalism first elaborated by Marx and Engels, and developed the theory and tactics of the proletarian revolution and the dictatorship of the proletariat in the new conditions of imperialism.[10]

How would this paean to Lenin have been received? Did the working class in Sheffield, even the most 'advanced' members, respond to Cardew's call? Certainly the last section of the talk, couched in a more 'neutral' style, would have struck a sympathetic chord: 'This 1980 strike brought important lessons on the role of the Trade Union leaders in thwarting the militant actions of the workers, and collaborating with the state to suppress their struggle'.[11] This was a specific and timely reference to a struggle which profoundly affected the lives of the steel workers and which reminded them, confrontationally, of the fact of their betrayal. Some may even have acknowledged the panacean revolutionary quest that Leninism represented, its ideological irreproachability, but surely to most of his audience it would have seemed too remote, too exotic, for them to have contemplated its implementation in Sheffield. Perhaps Cardew was aware of this; perhaps he had hoped that the talk would have attracted a few more enlightened members of the political vanguard (a few seasoned, and therefore difficult 'revisionists') with whom he could have forged more lasting and consequential links. And there were other contacts in Yorkshire the Party wanted to develop; it had been proposed that during the summer a study group should visit Leeds to talk to small farmers in the area and to exchange views on the current political and economic situation.

The trip to Sheffield also served to demonstrate that, despite the renewed emphasis on his role in cultural matters, Cardew's political responsibilities as Central Committee member would still have been given an unchallengeable priority. During this period the extant reports adumbrate ambitious plans for launching new programmes: setting up Regional 'cells', which would also recommend people for Party membership (a 'Regional Secretaries' conference was planned, to be followed some weeks later with a full conference), preparing a programme of action for Youth, broadening all aspects of Party work and encouraging the 'masses' to participate. Despite their sanguine response to questions relating to Party membership, it was clear that the still relatively small numbers of activists and supporters was a matter of ongoing concern to the Party leaders. In the copious notes for all this information each individual is referred to by an initial, either of their real name, or of their Party name, and some of them I have been unable to identify. Sometimes, individual cases are discussed and analysed in the notes – a Party supporter or member who is ailing, or backsliding in some way. Occasionally a reference to the minutes of meetings provides an indication of the kind of issue which the Party felt it necessary to address: that the Indian comrades and supporters must come under Party leadership, that they could not simply be left to their own devices, for example, was an edict which emanated from the highest Party authority. Or the issue of terrorism would surface at Party meetings, usually informally; the Party was consistently opposed to terrorism – terrorism as a substitute for 'mobilizing the masses'; or rather, terrorism as a consequence of the lack of mobilisation and Marxist-Leninist leadership. The Party held (and still holds) the view that in reformist politics there is little or no attempt to mobilise people; this leads inevitably to petit bourgeois pessimism, which can turn to 'adventurism'. Without correct leadership, which must create an intensification of the class struggle, then inevitably 'terrorism raises its head'.

Meanwhile, racist attacks in East London were increasing to the extent that in July 1980 a Pakistani People's Organisation was formed, and on 2 August a demonstration in east London denounced the racist murder (for a £5 bet) of an Asian man, Akhtar Ali Baig. On 20 July an Indian (Marxist-Leninist) Party organiser in Oldham, Sreeleeka Kazi, died in hospital three and a half months after sustaining injuries when she was hit by a motor-cyclist while on a visit in south London. She was struck as she was going through the garden gate and died from massive brain damage; the motorcyclist sustained minor injuries. There was a minimal, inconclusive inquest; the victim's husband sued for compensation which allowed the case to be reopened. The family were then able to ask for new evidence to be taken into account. It came to light, for example, that the rider was a British soldier, about to return to Ireland. How did it happen that he rode his motorcycle on to the pavement and at the gate? It was as if some intention was involved. What was of particular significance in the Sreeleeka Kazi case was the amount of circumstantial evidence that the police had chosen to withhold.

As she lay dying, comrades and friends would visit Sreeleeka in hospital and play tapes of music, in particular those of Cardew singing. Although she was unconscious, when she heard his voice she would react with slight changes of movement and breathing; sometimes she would shed tears.

Earlier in the year, on 6 March, together with Paul Cana, a supporter of Hind Mazdoor Lehar (Indian Workers'Association), Cardew had appeared at Bow Street Magistrates' Court in connection with the demonstration supporting the aforementioned Virk brothers in June of the previous year. Cana was fined £50 for assault; Cardew was remanded in custody for one week in Pentonville, the magistrate declaring that he 'must go and defend communism in prison for a while'.[12] The person who appeared in the same court before Cardew was a young Irish neighbour from Stratford Villas, not far from Agar Grove, who came from a family which the police seemed to have continually in its sights. He was surprised but cheered to see Cardew and immediately proffered him some useful information and advice concerning Pentonville, which he knew intimately: the inmates, how to acquire something, how to sell your cigarettes, and so forth. However, immediately on release, on 13 March, Cardew was back in Bow Street where he was fined £200 with £200 pounds costs for a previous offence: again, obstructing the police. He was bound over for £1000; Adah Kay, a close friend, stood bail.

In a letter dated 12 July from Alan Bush, the veteran communist composer, Bush refers to Cardew's imprisonment and subsequent fine. Cardew had written asking for a contribution and a letter of support to the court. Bush was rightly sceptical on two counts:

> It is not clear to me (either) what conceivable help my 'admirable' letter could have been. I will certainly send some money to help pay these fines, but I am not very enthusiastic about sending it to East London People's Front, as I have had experience of such organisations disappearing in bankruptcy, in which case the money goes to the creditors and does nothing towards the fined individuals.

Between 19 July and 3 August 1980 the PCA sent a three-man delegation, including Cardew, to the Fourth International Youth Camp in Trier, West Germany – one of the oldest towns in central Europe. To save money they drove; for most of the time Cardew had a raging toothache for which he incessantly ate peanuts, theorizing that they would somehow act as a substitute for fillings. They stopped to rest just once in a lay-by outside a petrol station in Amsterdam; this apart the journey was non-stop. When they arrived at the camp they discovered that they did not have enough money to pay the camping fees; they were all broke. Somehow, probably through the Canadian comrades, the matter was resolved.

Right from the outset the German comrades had to stave off attempts by the authorities to stop the camp from taking place. This they had circumvented by mobilizing considerable local support in the surrounding villages and farms and even from a local mayor, as well as enlisting the assistance of a legal representative and ensuring that there was media presence. The Germans were much more involved in 'united front' politics and had learnt the need for compromise and tactical awareness. Eventually, the state authorities backed down and the camp went ahead as planned. At the other end of the political spectrum gate-crashers and 'saboteurs', in particular a group of Turkish Maoists, created difficulties of a different order. There was disagreement on how to handle this – from compromise to outright physical expulsion – but finally a solution was agreed upon.

The British delegation – defiantly, if anachronistically, designated the Stalin Youth Brigade – had impeccable musical credentials; it comprised Party members Cardew, aged 44, Devenport, in his mid-twenties, and Party supporter Shrapnel, aged 33.[13] However, despite its artistic prowess, it had not received an official invitation and had only participated through the offices of the Canadian and Irish Parties. The Stalin Youth Brigade was thus very much the poor relation, reliant on the Canadians for its viability, and this despite the quality of the original songs they presented and Cardew's work with the international choir.

Before departure from London Cardew had written a speech, presumably outlining the objectives of the British delegation's participation, which he submitted to the Party National Executive for criticism. The Party line for participation in the Youth Camp was decreed as follows: 'To present concerts or whatever with the Canadians, and participate fully in the various activities that will be organised, such as choirs, etc. But above all we must work very hard on the material for the IYC (International Youth Concerts)'.[14] The original plan had been to spend some time preparing for these concerts which were to take place in England the following August. In Trier there appears to have been some objections, presumably from other delegations, and the IYC work was jettisoned in favour of a more general contribution to the cultural life in the camp.

With characteristic vigour and determination, and a little help from the Canadian delegation, Cardew set up an international choir which attracted a large number of people. This was in fact an important unifying act since the proceedings consisted in general of individual countries presenting their own material, with the attendant problems of language. Shrapnel recalls Cardew exhorting the choir to ever greater heights of vocal achievement by inspiring accounts and images of the heroic struggles of the proletariat and working people. The British delegation also put together an international song book ('against superhuman odds' according to Cardew), gathering together all the songs which the various delegations had brought from their own countries. In short, the international choir was an unqualified success. Peter Devenport recalled a talented young Turkish song writer and *saz* player, Nadine Borra; after Cardew's death, in conversation with Devenport, Borra reflected on what a tremendous impact Cardew had made on him, impressing upon him the importance of studying the classical and folk traditions of his country and on this basis to develop his own music.

Cardew introduced the participants to more advanced musical settings – such as 'Hands Off Iran', with words by Cardew to music by Shrapnel. Iran was a major political issue at the time; the Iranian people had overthrown the Shah and the US was threatening to invade and depose the new revolutionary government. The situation had generated much discussion and debate in the camp and Cardew asked Shrapnel to write a song on Iran for performance by the international choir. Unlike the Albanians, Shrapnel recalls that the Germans did not like 'Hands Off Iran'; they felt it was much too 'classical', and the idiom was old-fashioned. The Germans themselves were striving to uphold and develop the tradition of Hanns Eisler and performed several of his settings of Bertolt Brecht's poems. Yet Cardew's efforts and initiatives certainly served to raise the overall standard of the singing and performance. As one of the few groups attempting to break new ground on the cultural front (despite the misgivings of their hosts), the Stalin Youth Brigade provided a 'firm rallying point for the New Culture'. A carapace of Marxist-Leninist ideology, untainted and impenetrable, shielded the SYB from the pernicious influence of 'revisionism', and on a scorching afternoon its three members, possibly accompanied by a few sympathisers, marched around the camp singing and shouting slogans, rallying an audience for the Anglo-Canadian presentation later in the day at which a speech, presumably spiced with adulatory references to Comrade Stalin, was followed by three songs: 'Song for the British Working Class', 'The Worker's Song', and 'J.V. Stalin'. The Canadian contribution, whose militant delivery failed to mitigate its incomprehensibility, also suffered from the discomforting truth that the Canadians' singing left much to be desired.[15] Moreover, the sheer verbal artlessness of the texts, with their cumbersome demands, made it impossible for willing participants to join in. By contrast, the Germans, with their cultural permissiveness, were considered in this respect 'opportunistic'. The opposing factions agreed to differ, concurring that much discussion on the matter was required and leaving it at that. Ironically, it was the more traditional songs which were the most popular, in particular the Turkish, Spanish, Danish, and Portuguese (especially) contributions; they were politically less contentious, and therefore less likely to create divisions. Thus music was both a unifying and a disjunctive factor at the camp: the use of pop music and rock'n'roll by the Germans was highly contentious, as was their engagement of 'leftist' professional musicians for the final celebrations on the 'opportunistic' grounds that it would draw other sections of the local youth into the camp

– a tactic which ensured that the 'new, living (Marxist-Leninist) proletarian culture' was relegated to an auxiliary status at the expense of a professional, non-Marxist-Leninist culture.

The Albanians, who were regarded as political and ideological models, denounced all manifestations of a 'degenerate, imperialist culture' and in this they would have been supported by the Canadians and the loyal British contingent.[16] At one point on the final evening, when Elvis Presley records were being played and 'degeneracy' was made manifest in the form of highly individualistic, exhibitionist dancing, a number of delegates walked out. Of course the Germans had heard similar arguments against jazz some fifty years earlier and argued that whereas German folk music had been polluted by its exploitation by the Nazis, rock music was regarded by contemporary youth as their own, and that the 'politically correct', Marxist-Leninist music of the Canadian and British groups would only appeal to the converted intellectuals – a generous, if ill-informed, concession by the German comrades.

The 'united front' strategy of the German hosts was highly contentious, but they were a relatively large group and had been successful in a number of militant campaigns. As Hugh Shrapnel recalls, their music was lively, intelligent, contemporary, and 'agitprop' in the best German tradition. It was not rock music but in general the Germans did not baulk at the inclusion and exploitation of elements from contemporary pop culture; their attitude to rock was more relaxed. By contrast most of the music from the other delegations was clearly folk-based, or at least folk-orientated, and, most importantly, was supported and promoted by the Albanians. Cardew was very taken with the Albanians, whose culture and music he greatly admired, and had impressed Peter Devenport, on another occasion, with an impassioned reading of Ismail Kadare's poem 'We are sons of this new age' at a Party social.

In general the British delegates tried 'to assert the presence, programme and Marxist-Leninist character of the SYB and Party'; in this they were aided by the Canadians, but because of their junior, adjunctive status, the SYB performances, which were not infrequent, would take place at the end of the evening, after the meetings and rallies. The British contingent's proposals for the final evening programme were given short shrift by the German hosts (although they contributed a 'sizeable programme' to the Canadian evening) and in speeches their presence was often not recognized by other delegations. Unsurprisingly, the issue of what constituted a 'genuine' Marxist-Leninist delegation or group provoked considerable debate; the Spanish delegation, in particular, placed obstacles to the acceptance of the Stalin Youth Brigade's participation, to the extent of crossing out their name on a poster of events. When challenged the Spaniards indicated that firstly they would have to meet, and then, in due course, would provide a 'collective' answer. No such answer was forthcoming. Presumably it was the characteristically uncompromising name of the British group which had upset Spanish (and other) sensibilities? At some point in the proceedings, in a foolhardy display of liberalism, Peter Devenport registered the view that the name did seem to create unnecessary difficulties, particularly in respect of recruiting and organizing young people. However, the Stalin Youth Brigade was eventually recognized as the official delegation from Britain, and as a Marxist-Leninist organisation to boot, with the cryptic qualification 'as far as the camp is concerned'.

In terms of numbers the Fourth International Youth Camp in Trier far exceeded anything that the British comrades could have achieved; on any one day at least seven hundred people were in the camp and overall around three thousand visitors participated in the events. Of course, this was attributed to the 'broad front' tactics of the German hosts, with the concomitant cultural 'revisionism' which so offended the purer elements: that is, the Albanians, the Canadians and, of course, the British. Hugh Shrapnel recalls: 'I have positive memories of the camp – it was exciting to be with hundreds of young people from all parts of the globe, united in their enthusiasm to build a better world'.[17]

In his report Cardew wrote, diplomatically:

It can't be said that our [Canadian and British] line on culture (or our culture) swept the camp, became dominant, etc., but we provided a firm rallying point for the New Culture, and were seen to be the only parties seriously trying to break new ground on this front.[18]

From 7-9 August three Internationalist Youth Concerts under the title 'We Sing for the Future', organized by the PCA and the Stalin Youth Brigade, were held in Manchester, Birmingham and Hampstead Town Hall in London respectively, the last of which saw the first performance of Cardew's short, a cappella choral piece, *There is only one lie*. 'Founding of the Party' and 'We Sing for the Future' were also performed along with songs from Canada, Albania, the West Indies, Turkey and India. According to the reports from previous PCA committee meetings, on 5/6 July, the intention had been to 'astonish the comrades' with a high level of music-making: a professional drummer and two talented young musicians (probably his sons, Horace and Walter) would be enlisted, 'to enhance the artistic quality', and the PCA singers would present a set of three songs in harmony – in all about forty minutes of 'new British culture'. Cardew had made arrangements of 'We Sing for the Future' and 'Founding of the Party' for alto saxophone (Horace Cardew), trombone (Walter Cardew) and Dave Smith (tenor horn) – although on this particular occasion Smith was in Albania. West Indian musicians were asked to make a twenty-minute contribution, an Indian contingent provided a short programme of songs and poems, and the Canadian cultural workers also participated. The latter were accommodated by the English comrades, including Sheila Kasabova and Cardew, and also participated in the concerts in Birmingham and Manchester.

Here Walter Cardew describes those times, beginning with his recollection of his father's

> ubiquitous green Parka and briefcase (which got run over when he left it by the wheels of the minibus – of course he never bought a new one but struggled on with that one dents and all). He was always having meetings, always busy [...]. They were very happy times for me. It was my first taste of a musical life that wasn't in school or practising at home. And the companionship and camaraderie was wonderful, particularly for a fourteen year-old boy. And I was very proud to be with Cor who obviously commanded not only respect but a great deal of genuine affection. I think his attitude to how I should be brought up was that I should be exposed to as many of the rigours of adult life as possible; be self sufficient and definitely not spoilt or pampered. I think he would have subscribed to the 'What doesn't kill you makes you stronger' idea. He actually wanted me to be named Tungsten (i.e. a very tough metal). As in many things I think Stella's common sense intervened for the best.[19]

The blanket repudiation of the past was now associated with the discredited Mao who had stated that 'on a blank sheet of paper free from any mark, the freshest and most beautiful characters can be written, the freshest and most beautiful pictures can be painted' – as if no culture had existed heretofore.[20] 'This type of culture can only be a culture of slogans, of philistinism': Cardew, representing the RCPB (M-L), made this point in a speech which he delivered at the Hampstead Town Hall concert on 9 August, an event which was attended by over two hundred people. 'When we say "new culture", "proletarian culture", we mean, as Lenin said, a culture which must assimilate and rework the best of all previous cultures.' And he went on to refer to

> the traditions of the great struggles of the Chartists, the struggles to found the Trade Unions, the great class battles of the early years of the twentieth century, and the struggles immediately after the First World War, and many others since. And not only does the British working class have its great fighting traditions of struggle, but rich cultural traditions which go along with this, for instance the culture of the miners. Much of this culture has either been suppressed, sabotaged by the social democrats, or just submerged under the weight of imperialist culture.[21]

Cardew also drew attention to the fact that the Internationalist concerts were youth concerts and elaborated on this theme:

> The youth, by nature, are for the new and against the old, ready to fight for
> everything progressive and revolutionary. They are full of energy, aspirations and
> dreams for a better life, genuine freedom and a better world. But what outlet
> do these energies and aspirations have in countries such as ours – the capitalist
> countries of the West and the formerly socialist countries of Eastern Europe?
> What prospects do the youth have in these countries? In this country increasingly
> large sections of the youth have only the prospect of the dole queue, the street
> corner, attack and harassment by the police, petty crime, drugs, detention centres.
> And of course recruitment into the armed forces to be used as cannon fodder
> by the imperialists in their squabbles with each other over raw materials, markets
> and labour. Not to mention the wholesale pessimism, mysticism, confusion
> promoted by the bourgeois cultural offerings.[22]

And his speech ended on an internationalist note – that the concerts were
above all an expression of 'the unity of working people of all lands in the struggle
for freedom, democracy and socialism'. Such rousing words would have been hard to
follow; and as far as the (relatively) uncommitted listener was concerned, who had sought
at least a measure of inspiration and enlightenment on one of those occasions in
Manchester, Birmingham or London, there could have been little or no empathy with
the texts and hardly more than a *frisson* of pleasure from a music of a disappointing
predictability.

Compositionally, 1980 was a barren year, and for the music there was no respite:
There is only one lie, for mixed chorus with optional piano accompaniment, is a setting
of another Canadian text consisting of mouthfuls of slogans, their delivery occasionally,
and uncomfortably, reminiscent of Gilbert and Sullivan (Ex.23.1a-c). Thus:

Twenty-three years of a great big lie
Of Khrushchev, Kosygin and Brezhnev
Confronts like a little mouse
The giant invincible truth
Of the international proletariat

The 'lie' here embodies 'revisionism', 'opportunism', 'imperialism', and the treacherous
politicians associated with reactionary, anti-communist programmes; the named politicians

had all been denounced as 'renegade' communists.

Ex.23.1a. From *There is only one lie.*

Perhaps it was the influence of his days in Canterbury as a chorister, as well as a consideration for the needs of the chorus, which caused Cardew to decide upon a psalmodic rendering of the text, confining the melody in both verses and chorus, in John White's words, to 'railway tracks'; in other words, the melodic lines, with few exceptions, are scalic.[23] But could it also have been his intention to exploit the 'violent negation' in the relationship between the atheistic text and the divine provenance of the music? If so, he was not entirely successful, because from the point of view of the uncommitted listener the devotional character of the music enhances, perversely, the 'devotional' nature of the text, which is a paean to the creed of Marxism-Leninism. The chorus, which is sung four times, begins in an aura of quiet reverence; it gathers momentum and in bar 8 angelic voices proclaim 'the truth', the phrase culminating on (crescendoing to) a triumphant B flat major chord ('of revolution'):

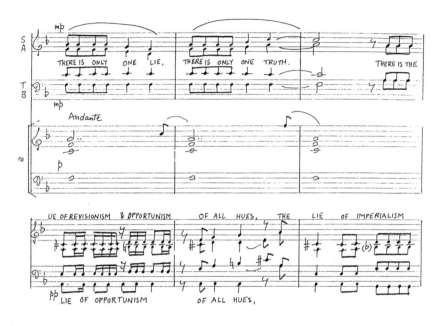

Ex.23.1b.

And at the end of the piece the defeat of 'all other imperialists and reactionaries' is set to an ecstatic cadence:

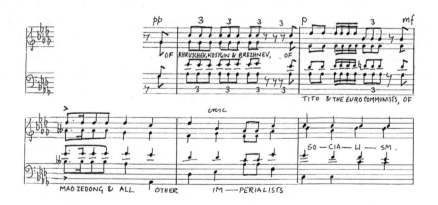

Ex.23.1c.

One asks the question: for whom was this piece written? For its categorical message will impress only the Party faithful. Perhaps that was what was needed to rally the troops for battle. To arm them with the *truth* and with the warm glow of *certainty* as they go out onto the streets of south and east London to confront fascism and the State which nurtures and protects it. While the 'uncommitted listener', unimpressed, goes home to rationalize his position, and to draw the blinds.

On 20 August, shortly after the Internationalist concerts, Cardew appeared at Newington Causeway Magistrates' Court for his part in opposing a National Front demonstration in Camberwell the previous June. Cardew denounced the court militantly, insisted he was not guilty of a crime, and was very quickly taken down. The suspended sentence of one month, which he had received in Birmingham (the Bloody Sunday demonstration in March 1978), was enforced, and the next day he was taken to Pentonville prison. Sheila and Anna went to see him in the small white cell by the court; he appeared a little shaken and Anna was clearly distressed.

Cardew was given a prison sentence of six weeks. Sheila visited him regularly and recalls that he was initially sharing a cell with an extremely unpleasant, fascist-inclined young man, who had probably been put there with him deliberately. However, he was eventually replaced and the new cell mate was a congenial companion.

My cell mate is a good character (so many good characters are in jail these days) and is at present deep in the heart of Brendan Behan's *Borstal Boy*, which turned up from somewhere. He has been to one of the Borstals that Behan was in.[24]

Cardew also made friends with the chaplain who invited him to play the organ for the service – which he did, so that he could have more contact with other prisoners; he also gave some music lessons. He even managed to achieve some creative work, drawing a staff on a sheet of paper and sketching the opening theme of the solo piano version of *We Sing for the Future*, as well as other (unidentified) melodic material (Ex.23.2).

He had also noted down some practical reminders: 'Apply to Property Officer to allow me to have the MS book and notebook that have been put in my property. Apply to Education for permission to attend Music class next Monday evening 6 p.m. Apply to take out note books'. And on a more philosophical note: 'Why are you here? Because this is where you are. This is where the future is'. The following extracts are taken from Cardew's letters to Sheila Kasabova from prison:

Ex.23.2. Extract from prison document.

Everything is broken down into tiny fragments in here, and you have to hang on to any long-term thinking like grim death.[25]

My time is divided between scrubbing floors, serving meals, playing chess, chatting, studying and reading. It's a bit like having a 'rest' in a mental hospital, except that no-one here is mad, but instead there are continual signs of real suffering and resentment. [...]
There are various good sorts in here who I haven't got space to tell you about. For some reason I've become known as a Cornishman and on exercise (walking round in a circle for an hour a day) people come up to swop stories about Cornwall.[26]

By now you've started work – so the 'Summer' is over, and here I sit. The papers say the next 2 weeks will be glorious and warm, yet here I sit. A day in the country is for me a lovely symbol of freedom; only a symbol because one is not actually trying to do anything when one spends a day in the country, and it's only when we are actually trying to do something that the dictatorship makes itself felt and we realize we are not free.[27]

Looking back over the years there is a lot of sense in what you have done since we've been together – going to those colleges and now being a teacher. It has given you a lot of self-confidence. Practical activity in the world is the one thing that stops one becoming horribly opinionated – or at least makes it more difficult to become that! And what have I done? I seem to have plucked out a lot of threads but not made a pattern out of them. Anyway, events have not made mincemeat of me (yet?), and the pattern is still there to be made.[28]

It was funny in church this morning. The only time the preacher really got attention – complete silence – was when he said 'Even when the church is dead [...] Christ can breathe life into it'. So underneath all the frivolity there is some remnant of religion among the cons.[29]

The following reflection on prison and prison life is undated:

If you want to judge a society look at its prisons, it has been said. For instance are the really big fish inside? What are the so-called crimes of those who *are* inside? Our society is oppressive, exploitative, a capitalist society. Those who rob the most rule in our society. In prison we find people who fight for freedom, and people of all walks who do not fancy being exploited.
The philosophy of 'lesser evil' which is supposed to move (?) the British public to vote Labour – is in prison raised to the heights as the philosophy of slavery, or rather the philosophy of the slave *master* who is forever turning to something, someone behind him, in order to present himself as the 'lesser evil'.
First, the 'hopelessness of fighting' is imprinted, by locks, bars, chains, barbed wire, highwalls, dogs, fascists (?).
Second, the 'incapacity to fight' is imprinted; one is stupid for not knowing a routine one has never done, underpants 6 sizes too large, food on the brink of malnutrition.

Even in such oppressive and enervating circumstances Cardew's sense of the practical did not desert him: he wanted a trade; the idea of becoming a piano-tuner appealed to him, and there is no doubt he would have excelled in that profession. Certainly he would have made a good craftsman; he could draw, he liked tools and materials. He used to enjoy making banners and designing newspapers for the Party.
Cardew was released from prison on 19 September, early in the morning; Sheila was waiting for him outside the prison. He was with an Iranian, who had also just been released; sixty-seven Iranians had been arrested at the picket of the US Embassy the previous May. He asked Sheila if she had a copy of *Workers Weekly* (which she had) to give to

the Iranian. Then they all went off together to have breakfast. Being in prison, Cardew reflected (as Sheila Kasabova recalls), 'was very much like being back at public school'.

In 1980 Cardew received three letters of substance, weighty in content and each expressing critical views of the Party: one from a veteran communist ('revisionist'), the other two from young, erstwhile supporters who were unresponsive to Party diktats and sceptical of some aspects of the Party 'line'. Two of the letters make specific reference to the aforementioned Internationalist Youth Concerts. A refreshingly blunt letter, dated 9 August, from Alan Bush, who had attended the Internationalist Youth Concert in London that same day, provides evidence that the old 'revisionist' was in fighting form, sharply critical both musically and politically:

> I purchased some literature, including especially publications by the Canadian Communist Party (Marxist-Leninist). I must admit that I am not favourably impressed with the addendum (Marxist-Leninist) in brackets to the name of any party. In fact the "ROAD OF THE PARTY" does at least admit that their prostration before the Chinese party officials (I do not say the Chinese people) was a mistake, one which they took years to perceive. It was quite obvious, from the year 1959, that the Maoists had become petty-bourgeois to a man.
> One would have thought that their support of Pakistan against Bangla-Desh, of Pinochet against Allende, and lastly their invasion of Vietnam would have had some effect on communist parties, but the Canadian Communist Party (Marxist-Leninist) was evidently one of the slowest to react – not a very good sign. [...]
> I liked nearly all the songs this afternoon, or rather the tunes and harmony of them very much indeed. I thought the texts were appalling, and ought to have been totally re-written. And I must admit that the word-setting of these awful texts were extremely amateurish, very inexpert, inartistic in fact. But they were well sung, except for the atrocious diction. I am very pleased that I came, and delighted to see such a large audience.

Cardew's belated response, dated 3 November, is equally sharp: he necessarily, if unconvincingly, refutes Bush's description of the 'appalling' texts whilst acknowledging that there is still 'a long way to go' in achieving a fitting translation of the political line, in 'rendering it in poetic images and making it broadly accessible to people'. Albania is referred to as 'the only socialist country in the world today', and the leaders of the Soviet Union are denounced as betrayers of socialism. In response to Bush's jibe aimed at the Canadians' (and, by association, British) Maoism, Cardew offers explanations of a quite breathtaking feebleness: 'many who upheld Stalin in the 1960s *wanted* Mao and the Chinese party to be Marxist-Leninist, and proceeded as if they were'. And this from a member of the Central Committee of the Revolutionary Communist party of Britain (Marxist-Leninist) for whom all political and cultural analysis must proceed according to 'scientific' guidelines. As we shall see, comrade Bush was not alone in criticising the content of the Internationalist Youth concerts, and at a PCA Executive meeting on 17 August Cardew himself refers to 'shortcomings': rushed preparations, illness, tackling the question of translating the 'line', and insisting that the way of delivering the songs must be improved ('delivery decisive'). And according to a report dated 21 September more criticisms of the concerts had filtered through: that performances were somewhat 'forced' (by which we may understand stilted, not spontaneous), too many mistakes (amateurish), and that the traditions of folk music and 'massed singing' were not well represented. The vaunted 'new British culture' may well have 'astonished the comrades' but, apart from the contribution from the West Indian contingent, it does not appear to have succeeded in engaging the ears and minds of the more discerning, less parochial, members of the audience.

In a letter, 'Dear Comrade', dated 11 May 1980, Cardew claims, or rather states, that 'in PCA as in all aspects of the Party's work, Mao Zedong Thought has been repudiated as an anti-Marxist theory'. In a belated, handwritten reply, dated 26 September 1980, Kevin, the addressee, demurs:

But in my view its [Mao Zedong Thought] defeat would have been greatly assisted by a wider discussion in the Party, and taking more account of the response of the masses. Repudiated? No, I don't think so. Firstly, although the wrong line received full publicity (and how!), the *repudiation* did *not* (and there's the sign of *another* problem: the fear of self-criticism!). Secondly, and more seriously, I don't believe the line has been repudiated fully in *practice.*[30]

There is more than a grain of truth here: the 'full publicity' Kevin was referring to was the extraordinary, quasi-religious adulation that Mao received from the British Maoists in the early part of the decade. Anyone who humbly queried one of the Great Helmsman's 'thoughts', let alone criticized one, would not have survived the remainder of the meeting. Now, most of his erstwhile disciples were distancing themselves from his every utterance – whether on philosophy, politics, or art. The main objections to the Maoist line as expressed in *Cogs and Wheels* 3 were: a) treating *all* culture as propaganda and b) overstressing the role of culture in transmitting the Party line. Kevin was questioning whether these objections materialized in actual practice.

Kevin further claimed that artistic talent was not encouraged by the Party; nor, in his view, did it manage to send competent speakers to meetings and demonstrations, and as a consequence the Party 'line' suffered. He also opined that the manner in which the 'correct line' overrode all other considerations, the way that in any cultural offering the line had to be conveyed *in toto,* was harmful.[31] Kevin was also sceptical of the level of artistic expertise that was brought to bear on cultural contributions which were sent to the Party. He suggested that it may well have been the case that very few comrades actually examined the material, and that they rejected much of it on the basis of 'conservatism' in artistic matters which proceeded from an endemic fear of ideological 'error'. In an analogous context in the German Democratic Republic some thirty years earlier, after the defeat of the Nazis, Albrecht Betz recalls that

> equipped with a handy array of theses, they (Party officials) could prescribe matters of form and content according to their own ideas; they became the administrators who provided the sketches, and it remained for the artists to colour them in.[32]

Authority, embodied in a superior, pontifical manner of criticizing, was used to compensate for, or disguise, ignorance. Such a policy stifles creative work, especially if it aims to be 'experimental' or original to any degree. As for the Party's assurance that it would offer criticism 'where appropriate' Kevin retorts:

> Comrades, what am I to say about this? It is rich irony indeed! Was not one of the main points of my last letter to you precisely that many contributions *were neither used nor returned with criticism*? Either you have chosen to ignore that complaint or you are saying that there are times when it is *neither* 'appropriate' to print *nor* to return with criticisms. If this is what you are saying, then I must say I can only conceive of one eventuality where that might be correct – are we then in the midst of such a surfeit of cultural contributions?

Unfortunately, Kevin's misgivings flew in the face of the Party's self-assessment. In the light of Hardial Bains' comments and criticisms it was claimed that the Birmingham conference two years previously had been a 'definite achievement' (in spite of the reservations expressed by some of the participants). It had established the necessity for all cultural work to be directly under Party leadership. Thus, 'wrong lines' were criticized and corrected, such as 'red or expert'(anti-professional, putting content above form), sectarianism in relation to non-communist cultural works (for example, theatre plays), and culture as propaganda and in an inappropriately pre-eminent position.

In some brief notes headed 'Kevin' Cardew noted condescendingly that Kevin had 'a good understanding on most of the points of line'. And then, in an exemplary demonstration of Party high-handedness: 'I said his criticisms go beyond what he can legitimately say and are one-sided'.[33] Kevin's letter occasionally provokes Cardew to insert question and exclamation marks (in red) in the margins, but no formal response, if there were one, has come to light.

In a report dated 4 October there was more talk of 're-launching PCA' as a 'mass organisation of cultural workers', and approaching 'progressive' professionals such as A.L. Lloyd, Greg Rose, Keith Rowe, Frederic Rzewski, Dave Smith and myself. The idea of the aforementioned 'composers group' was brought up again; the PCA was planning a concert for the following spring, in 1981, and the composers should be asked what contribution they would like to make. The report also deemed it necessary for the PCA to secure a detailed perspective of current cultural problems generally, before summing up the Party's views on ideological questions raised during the previous year. In a tentative move towards more autonomy with respect to the Party's relationship with the Canadians, Cardew maintained that issues had to be raised in relation to national traditions, that rather than summing up all the notes from Canada accumulated over the year, the PCA should appraise the response to the music that *it* had been creating. It should publish its own song books and poems and expand the singing group; more songs were needed which linked directly with British working class traditions.

The question of the kind of music which the Party would find 'useful', and would therefore sanction, was an ongoing problem which weighed heavily over the deliberations of the PCA, in particular in relation to forthcoming concerts in east and south London. In fact, on the same day, 4 October, a youth concert organised by the PCA took place in East Ham, in east London. As well as various revolutionary and anti-fascist songs the PCA band and singers also performed the 'Worker's Song', to Cardew's new lyric, and militant songs were contributed by musicians from the West Indian and Indian communities. To combat the media denigration of youth as lazy and workshy, younger Party supporters ('Voice of the Youth') produced a sketch on the bleak future which faces thousands of school leavers every year and on the need for the youth to become politically conscious:

Imperialism throws the people into crisis, war, hysteria and spiritual devastation. The programmes of these PCA concerts, which are organised regularly in various communities, are the beginnings of a genuine alternative to the cultural nightmare that is foisted particularly on the youth – for instance, concerts where such hysteria is generated that young people are trampled to death, films like *The Shining*, etc. Concerts like this one organised by the PCA, where the relationship between present and past is correctly developed, and where the positive qualities and aspirations of the youth and people are highlighted, play a role in raising and deepening the consciousness of the youth and others that the victory of revolution and socialism is not a utopian dream but a historical inevitability, the actual goal and destination of the struggles of the working people today.[34]

In the same month, October, Cardew began attending lectures at King's College, in the Strand, until, that is, he received notice that his local authority had decided against awarding him a grant. In a letter of apology, dated 3 November, Cardew informs the head of department that he will reluctantly have to withdraw from the course and apply for financial support to the Department of Education and Science in February 1981, with a view to re-joining the course the following October. The letter ends: 'Please give my apologies to Jonathan [Dunsby] and Pierluigi [Petrobelli] – all the lectures I have attended have been very stimulating.' In the meantime, to maintain contact, he offers his services as a translator for a projected musical analysis journal. There follows a brief repose, 28-31 October, at the pottery in Wenford.

The issue of Cardew's music-making is taken up by ex-PCA member Geoff Pearce, who had attended the 'We Sing for the Future' Internationalist Youth concert in Birmingham in August. He begins positively:

I felt it was a good effort, professionally performed in the light of what must have been a limited period for preparation. The variety in form and style was good, but the programme was too long.[35]

However, the theatrical projection of a glorious future under the leadership of the Party, expressed with an 'almost religious zeal' (especially from the Canadians), and the unctuous self-righteousness embodied in the on-stage, self-congratulatory back-slapping ('for being such good revolutionaries') seemed to Geoff Pearce to be utterly inappropriate and out of place in the Handsworth district of Birmingham.[36] Despite the fact that the pre-concert advertising had suggested that the event was intended for the youth and public at large, the audience was sparse and, according to Pearce, confined almost exclusively to party activists and supporters; none of the disenfranchised young people of Handsworth were there. And yet hundreds of them – militant English, Asian and Jamaican youth – had been organising against the National Front prior to the visit by

Cardew, the PCA and their Canadian comrades. 'There was little or no groundwork done in preparation for that evening and as far as I know there has been no follow up after it. I think there is nothing to be gained from this one-off approach in an area'.[37] In the absence of a political context the event was therefore a meaningless, self-indulgent exercise. In his letter to Cardew Pearce asked three questions, none of which were answered: 'Why did you put it [the Handsworth concert] on? What were you hoping to achieve by it? What did you achieve by it?'

Pearce also touched on the dilemma which had been broached in Party discussions in Canada: is the Party-produced culture (songs/poems/plays) for internal Party consumption, or for a wider audience? For if it is deemed necessary to create a Party culture which cannot yet be assimilated by the broad masses, would this not widen the gap between the Party and 'the masses'? Yet the aim is the opposite, that in due course the latter's 'taste' in music will be identified with that of the Central Committee. The Party now seems to be opposing the Maoist 'working class line': 'go amongst the masses; learn from the masses'. For the masses are ill-informed, brutalised; they must learn from the Party. Comrades should not be 'liberal about workers'; they should not harbour illusions, recalling Marx's lament that the masses do not even understand their own wretchedness. Perhaps such issues were discussed at the sixth plenum of the RCPB (M-L) which took place on 22 October, and where Cardew's presence, as member of the Central Committee, would have been obligatory.

In his handwritten notes, dated 10 and 19 November, based on a subsequent conversation between the two men, Cardew seems to have ignored most of Pearce's criticism, or rather he expresses resentment that Pearce should raise problematic issues, thereby creating 'divisions' (characterised as 'splittist'). Problems can only be solved by 'uniting with the Party'. ('Do not go the right way without us, Without us it is the wrong way, You must stay with us! You may be wrong and you may be right; therefore you must stay with us!'[38]) To unite with the Party is to carry out Party directives, right or wrong. Because *ultimately,* armed with the Party line, with the truth of Marxism-Leninism, a comrade is invincible.

Cardew picks up on the word 'nauseating' (which Pearce had used to describe the self-congratulatory posturing, the 'back-slapping') and resorts to the intimidatory Maoist technique from the early seventies of *argumentum ad hominem*: 'I said there must be something behind this word *nauseating*. None of the cultural workers allow that as an objective, natural expression. He said he would think about that, in the light also of the "Party line".'[39] But why cannot an emotive word like 'nauseating' be used in a private communication? Clearly its pungency discomposed Cardew. Condescendingly he notes: 'Overall he [Pearce] was quite jumpy. Obviously has some plan. I said "You see this is what is in the background". So he backed off – I said it was ludicrous

– [I said] that he should read *Workers Weekly* – the Party's priority, etc.'[40] So whereas the word 'nauseating' is taboo, the word 'ludicrous' is normal, acceptable currency. Moreover, there is no argument – simply reference to an authority (the Party, *Workers' Weekly*) and an intimidatory approach which serves to undermine, to induce self-doubt. 'Self-doubt' was a condition from which the Party, by its very nature, did not suffer, although throughout these latter years we have identified many examples of a Party *folie de grandeur,* of self-delusion. If, for example, 'large numbers of youth, workers and other progressive people came to participate in the concerts' in London[41], they certainly did not materialise in Birmingham.[42]

And where was musical composition at this juncture of his life? Musically, 1979/80 were the most unproductive years of his entire career. There had been nothing of substance since the violin piece, *The Worker's Song*, written early in 1979. For a composer of Cardew's stature this was a lamentable state of affairs. In a letter dated 3 November, thanking him for his contribution towards his court fines, Cardew informs Bernard Stevens that the PCA is now putting on 'regular concerts in some areas – every two months in east London, for example'. He then expresses his regret for not having contributed to the WMA (Workers' Music Association) composition contest – 'nor have I succeeded in getting any other composers in PCA to do so. Too often writing music gets put to the bottom of the list – which is not good or proper but is a fact nonetheless'. Thus, the composers and musicians of the 'genuine alternative' were unable to muster a single composition between them. In fact, just a month before his letter to Stevens Cardew had announced the completion of a new work for piano solo:

We Sing for the Future is a composition based on a song. The song is for youth, who face bleak prospects in a world dominated by imperialism, and whose aspirations can only be realised through the victory of revolution and socialism. In the framework of a solo piano piece lasting about 12 minutes, something of this great struggle is conveyed. The music is not programmatic, but relies on the fact that music has meaning and can be understood quite straightforwardly as part of the fabric of what is going on in the world.
As a reference point, here are two quatrains from the poem:

In the midst of this dying old world,
The proletarians of all lands are fighting.
The oppressed in their millions are rising,
Demanding their social and national liberation.

We bring with us from the past what is purist;
The sentiment for the liberation of man.
And from today we take Marxism-Leninism,
And the revolutionary struggles of the workers of all lands.[43]

Formally, the work is in two more or less equal parts, although their musical content differs substantially; the second part in particular exhibits a wide range of pianistic textures and makes considerable demands on the performer. The first part consists of alternating statements of the verse and chorus. At the very beginning the eight bar introduction also serves as a counter-melody to the opening line of the song (Ex.23.3).

Ex.23.3. *We Sing for the Future.*

Cardew's interest in English 16/17th century musical traditions is also evidenced here; both verse and chorus of his song recall the sturdy diatonicism (as well as tempo and time signature) of the opening of Byrd's set of variations (Ex.23.4):

Ex.23.4. William Byrd: *The Carman's Whistle.*

The first section of *We Sing for the Future* is a quite literal statement of the verse of the song, with just minimal, decorative additions. Likewise the treatment of the second section, which states the chorus. In the piano version the chorus is prescribed a faster tempo, dotted minim 88, giving it a strong forward impetus and sense of urgency enhanced by a flowing quaver movement.[44]

The third section, which is based on the first quatrain of the song, features contrapuntal devices, such as augmentation. Beginning in A major it introduces chromaticisms and key changes with each successive entry of the melody played a tone higher, in fourths, sixths and sevenths; there is a gradual crescendo and the music reaches a climax, after which, section four, the chorus returns, representing the bright future which only revolution and socialism can bring about.

The second part of the work is far more volatile and represents something of 'this great struggle'. A canon at the octave based on a rhythmicisation of the first phrase of the second quatrain of the verse (Ex.23.5)

Ex.23.5.

is followed by a passage where the same phrase is transformed by a new texture of Brahmsian richness (Ex.23.6):

Ex.23.6.

In the remaining pages Cardew explores the full range of the instrument, each register is fully exploited; the music becomes more animated, more harmonically adventurous, and more virtuosic. And quite unexpectedly a new theme is given prominence, alternating with the song material (locked in combat?), conveying the chaos and strife of the struggle, and the heroism and sacrifice which revolutionary upheaval demands (Ex.23.7):

Ex.23.7.

The song verse emerges victorious with full-blooded octaves in both hands. There can be no more resistance to the forward march of the revolutionary proletariat towards emancipation and socialism, and the piece reaches its apotheosis with the final statement of the chorus: 'We Sing for the Future' in counterpoint with the verse, which actually ends the piece (Ex.23.8):

Ex.23.8.

Sheila Kasabova recalls Cardew going over the ending of *We Sing for the Future* at home, playing the final chords over and over, as if he were dissatisfied. She recalls the final measures which to her, at the time, expressed struggle, extreme frustration, and non-resolution – although there is fulfilment on the surface, just as Party meetings would produce surface emotion and optimism. The music was certainly 'active', but for Sheila, if not for the comrades, it lacked purpose and a sense of conviction. My own response is similar.[45]

Throughout the work, but especially in the latter pages, and notwithstanding the passion and commitment of a performance such as, for example, Frederic Rzewski's,[46] there is a sense of strain, occasionally of labouring, particularly in transitional passages, which lack organicity, which seem merely to be filling the gaps between sections of greater substance (the same occurs in analogous passages in the solo violin piece, *The Worker's Song*). But is this not part of the *content* – the 'great struggle', and the 'fabric of what is going on in the world'? Could it have been Cardew's intention that this sense of strain and striving, of obstacles to be overcome, of temporary setbacks, should infuse the music, should be at its core? Or am I being too generous, too indulgent? Is this not rather a case of compositional inadequacy, a flagging of the creative powers, of an inability to sustain the musical discourse in a compelling manner? These are my own speculative musings, there may be some substance to them; others will no doubt take issue with me on one count or another. But can it all be just a matter of opinion?

I tend to agree with Cardew when at the Air Gallery, in October 1977, he launched into his attack on the 'bourgeois' notion that 'it is entirely a matter of opinion what it means, and that's the idea that the bourgeoisie spread throughout the world'. But are we not getting bogged down by Cardew's 'aboutism'? Is his agenda, which he states baldly at the beginning of his (verbal) introduction, *forcing* us to listen to the music on his (the composer's) terms? We may recall his unequivocalness at the Air Gallery event: 'And when I play this music I'm saying to you what actually is the case. This music is about Thälmann.' Here, the relation of artist to audience is both coercive and exclusive.

I recall an occasion late in 1981, at our house in Greenwich, when Cardew had come to rehearse with me – a duet, I think. He expressed his dissatisfaction with the quality of his later, political music. I cannot remember his exact words, there was no discussion as such, but he expressed disappointment and frustration. I do remember that I tried to reassure him; I argued that just as it had taken him years to develop his avant-garde music, especially in relation to his experiments with notation, so it would demand even greater commitment and probably a longer period of time to create a quite different music of the standard to which he aspired now – or words to that effect. In a sense, I suppose I am betraying a confidence. Essentially, I did share his view of his later music, but as a friend and admirer I was able to put a positive gloss on our exchange. I did not doubt his ability eventually to create music that would 'serve Socialism', but it was clear that his Party involvement, in terms of both its political demands on his time and energy, and also the malign influence of its bungling interventions and injunctions in artistic matters, was a huge obstacle, which he might never overcome. Paradoxically, the more 'successful' he became as a revolutionary leader, the more his music suffered; it was simply marginalised.

On 8/9 November Hind Mazdoor Lehar (Indian Workers Organisation) staged its first national convention with a mass rally at a school in east London. Many organizations were represented, including the East Indian Defence Committee, the PCA (with Cardew), the Irish Communist party, and Hardial Bains with some Canadian comrades. 15 November saw another anti-racist, anti-fascist concert in south London with the PCA singers accompanied by Cardew at the piano. A letter to John Fordham at *Time Out*, dated 20 November, encourages him to advertise a rally and concert for youth, Youth in Struggle for Freedom, Democracy and Socialism, on 6 December at the Trinity Community Centre in East Ham, with the caveat that 'it would probably be best if you don't send Julian Silverman!' Certainly, the renaming of the Stalin Youth Brigade as the Communist Youth Union of Britain (CYUB) on this occasion would have done little to soften Silverman's attitude towards the Communist Party of Britain (Marxist-Leninist).[47]

The event was described as a 'mass rally' which involved the PCA band and singers and included, among other items, the 'CYUB Song', a film, and a video. Again stress is laid on the need for 'professionalism', for high standards of performance – a directive which had been issued earlier in the year by comrade Bains. The instrumental line-up, which seems to have been a trio – Cardew on piano, Walter Cardew on drums, and Laurie Baker on bass guitar – would certainly have fulfilled those demands, and the PCA singers, according to the occasional mention in PCA reports, were making encouraging progress. The contents of a 'Song book for Dec 6th' are listed: 'Those Days of October', 'A Naxalite in Birmingham', 'Hands off Iran', *There is only one lie* (Cardew's sole contribution to the collection), 'Self-defence is the only way', 'The people of St. Paul's Bristol' poem, 'Our Answer is a fist', 'The comrades came the second time with red flags flying high', 'For This we Hail you', 'The most bourgeoisified of all bourgeois nations', and 'The key to our victory', all of which subsequently appeared in a new song book published by the PCA and entitled *We Sing for the Future.*

During the last months of the year Cardew was involved in a campaign to save the life of a young anti-fascist sentenced to death by the Turkish regime. Erdal Eren was a member of the Revolutionary Communist Party of Turkey and the Turkish anti-fascist youth organisation.

Cardew's letter to the Turkish authorities is characteristically militant – demanding rather than appealing, condemnatory rather than conciliatory:

I am writing to protest vehemently against the threatened execution of the young anti-fascist Erdal Eren. Such a crime as you are intending to commit arouses revulsion and condemnation throughout the world. It displays the moral and political bankruptcy of your regime.

If Erdal Eren had committed some crime then he should be tried in open court and evidence submitted in accordance with international conventions. The fact that you intend to execute him though he has not received such a trial and no evidence has been produced, is the most convincing proof that he is innocent of any crime.

In fact, Erdal Eren stands as a symbol of the heroism of young people all over the world who are fighting for freedom and democracy.

Erdal Eren must not be executed!

On 13 December 1980 the young Turk was executed. On 17 December a CYUB picket gathered outside the Turkish Embassy to denounce the murder of Erdal Eren.

ERDAL EREN

ERDAL EREN
brave anti-fascist
fighter murdered
by the fascist
regime in Turkey

To add to the family's travails, in November Sheila fell ill and almost died from an (undiagnosed) ectopic pregnancy. Both she and Cardew were desperate to have the child and Sheila had very much resented the fact that the Party did not lessen its demands on Cardew; even she, despite her ill-health, was still expected to be present at meetings and demonstrations. Cardew did his best for her, but always within the limitations which were imposed upon him. Nevertheless, after Christmas they did manage to spend a few days together at a friend's house (Patricia Mandell, who had been Sheila's colleague at Aldus Books) outside Oxford. Such opportunities would arise from time to time but were rarely indulged.

At the end of the year, in a PCA Executive report, the following summing up is recorded:

Need to deal with National traditions; more new songs required. West Indian musicians are contributing but situation is very volatile with people dropping out to be replaced by new members. Probably due to objection to CYUB (Communist

Youth Union of Britain) political agenda. Good sketches have been produced by younger members and supporters; instrumental group progressing; PCA singers have made great strides, standards rising to a more professional level. Same problem politically with some of the singers as with the West Indians. The programme of one concert a month in east London and in south London should continue and should expand to other towns. (Tour proposed 6, 7, 8 February 1981 with singers, instrumentalists, West Indians, actors, etc.) We should sing and perform items which we would encourage others (progressive and democratic performers) to sing.
Restricted view of culture is relic of Maoism.[48]

If we take this at face value it suggests that the PCA agenda set at the beginning of the year was well on course, although there is no further mention of efforts to renew old contacts and involve professional artists in PCA projects. Despite certain misgivings Sheila Kasabova recalls that for the first time over a long period she detected a 'definite shift'; there seemed to be changes and movement, and in a positive direction, as reflected in the above report: a rejuvenation of the PCA band, with more appearances at demonstrations and meetings, and an expansion of the singing group; standards and expectations seemed to be higher. And in all these developments Cardew was a centrifugal force; he not only created new initiatives, he participated fully in their implementation. And, more mundanely, he meticulously itemised all expenses, just as he had done in the Scratch Orchestra. Everything had to be done on a shoestring; the Party depended on individual financial contributions from each member, and Cardew, predictably, was one of the most generous. Sheila Kasabova, too, would often lend and give money; in any case, since they operated as a single economic unit it was the whole family that was contributing to the Party. Cardew was always, of necessity, very circumspect with money; he was aware of its indispensability and therefore never wasted it. At the same time, paradoxically, he never counted the pennies. He was neither spendthrift nor mean.

In respect of the content and conduct of Cardew's life during the last years – that is, the necessity of establishing clear priorities which could not be breached and the relationship between the different constituents – we can identify four basic areas:

Firstly, and for Cardew most importantly, his role as member of the Central Committee of the Communist Party of Britain (Marxist-Leninist).

Secondly, the Progressive Cultural Association (PCA), in which politics and culture overlapped.

Thirdly, his domestic life with Sheila and Anna, and the nurturing of his relationship with his two sons. There is no doubt that the Party's demands impinged upon these relations and were often deleterious to them. All Cardew's activities and relationships were subject to Party encroachments, to Party control and influence.

Fourthly, his day job with Diagram Visual Information which for him was routine but financially necessary and, of course, time-consuming.

Most of the material on which the last chapters of this book are based has been abstracted from PCA reports and minutes of meetings. (Cardew had long ceased to keep a diary.) These were held at fairly regular, two or three week intervals, although there were sometimes more, according to the level and intensity of political and cultural activity during any particular period. In general, whilst occasionally acknowledging shortcomings, these reports exude confidence, progress, optimism and a sense of achievement. Cardew ran the PCA and was responsible for most of the reports; those he did not write himself he would have overseen. Occasionally, he allows himself more subjective observations, usually brief, and the text succumbs to a more personal vein of expression, recalling the earlier Journals. Cardew's relation to PCA members finds eloquent expression in Hermann Hesse's work, a writer Cardew had much admired in his former, 'bourgeois' existence: 'It is the attribute of having a feeling for the nature and destiny of people, not only for my own but for those of others, too. This attribute compels me to serve others by having power over them'.[49]

Thirty years on, some of the participants who were prominent in those cultural events I have been describing retain positive memories. But at the time they were engulfed in revolutionary zeal and an ideology which provided a blinding, and deafening, certitude. I have interviewed and had discussions with one or two current senior Party members. They were as forthcoming as I had expected, though not as much as I would have liked. Their comments were guarded; I detected a wariness. Perhaps they were anxious to protect the Party and its history. They may have been suspicious of my motives in actually choosing to write the biography. Some of my questions seemed to unsettle them, in the sense that they arose from what they may have considered as a hostile agenda. A veil of secrecy has always protected the source of the Party's communications to its supporters; I have no quarrel with this. But I presume that, in any case, if its threat to the status quo had been considered real enough, it would have been infiltrated by intelligence agents, as has been the case, historically, with many left-wing parties and organisations.[50] The idea, the possibility, of a fifth column in your midst must be unsettling; a comrade trusts and relies on other comrades. Yet lurking in the recesses of your mind is the fear that your comrade is not a comrade. I sometimes wonder how Cardew dealt with this. For my own part, in the interviews I conducted I could not altogether banish the suspicion that I might be talking to a government agent. And I accept that Party members may have harboured the same suspicions about myself.

Their various statements, some of which excited my curiosity and interest, were rarely, if ever, elaborated upon: for instance, from 1979 onwards Cardew was in the leadership of the Party; he was a member of the Central Committee and candidate member of the Political Bureau, although I am not sure that I have grasped the full significance of the latter status. A Party comrade insisted that Cardew would not have reached this position through personal ambition; his contribution was to 'substantive issues' which could be 'pin-pointed', although what exactly those substantive issues were I have been unable to elicit. There can be no doubt that Cardew himself regarded these red-blooded years of unrelenting, all-consuming political activity as the most important period of his life. A Party comrade described Cardew as 'very much a political person'. He explained that as an exemplary Party member Cardew was not acting as an individual, and it was therefore difficult, if not impossible, to do justice to his life as a revolutionary communist, to his contribution to the communist movement, from a purely anecdotal point of view; there was too much substance. Nor could it be expressed by bland, generalised statements or as a sequence of events. I assumed that this was a thinly-veiled critique of what the comrade presumed would characterise, and to a degree invalidate, my own account of those days.

I also gathered information from a number of Party supporters (from the late seventies to 1981), some of whom still retain a measure of loyalty to the Party and who would not like to see it misrepresented and compromised. Some of them still maintain contact with the Party, although I did not enquire as to their current level of commitment. And there are ex-Party supporters who, with the benefit of hindsight, are now more critical of the Party's policies and of their own relationship to it during the period under discussion, although they are not necessarily hostile to the Party. Many of them agree that the Party's analyses and prognoses have been proved more correct than most, but their accounts of the time vary considerably.

While writing this biography my own inner relationship to its subject and to the Party to which he gave the last decade of his life has not been stable or consistent, and the conscientious reader would surely have noted this. Since I have been working on the book for more than twenty years this is perhaps not surprising. There have been three modes:

1) Empathy with Cardew; giving full rein to his arguments, sometimes even intervening on his behalf – as the reader would have observed and perhaps not approved, reinforcing a point in the role of sympathetic bystander. Right up to the end of his life I would occasionally, but always willingly, at his behest, take part in Party cultural events, usually playing some of his piano pieces.

2) Or I would be overtaken by scepticism of the whole 'Marxist-Leninist' project, irritated by its self-aggrandisement and dismayed by its treatment of its members and supporters,

as well as by its methods.

3) This could engender feelings of hostility and frustration in relation to some of the Party's more outrageous pretensions and, in particular, to what I perceive as a monumental self-delusion, perhaps the most devastating of all human weaknesses. As far as the 'human condition' at this point in history is concerned, and the tasks that confront us – that is, in terms of what is enshrined on Marx's tombstone in Highgate cemetery – the conclusion reached, more often than not, is that the Party was simply out of its depth.

Throughout these later pages I have found myself asking: Why those particular people? Why so few? A handful amongst millions who have assumed the mantle of leaders and saviours. How can the rest of us be so blind, so insouciant, so compliant? The Party elite had been visited by Marxism-Leninism, had received favour and empowerment. They were sanctioned (but how and by whom?) to be the vanguard who would bring about the promised land. Reading Edward Thompson's book on Blake, *Witness Against the Beast,* I was struck by the parallel between Blake's antinomianism – 'a way of breaking out of received wisdom and moralism, and entering upon new possibilities'[51] – and Cardew as 'outsider' and 'dissenter':

> The doctrine of justification by faith, in its antinomian inflexion, was one of the most radical and potentially subversive of the vectors which carried the ideas of seventeenth-century Levellers and Ranters through to the next century. [...] The doctrine of justification by faith was – and was seen to be – the more 'dangerous' heresy. And this was because it could – although it need not – challenge very radically the authority of the ruling ideology and the cultural hegemony of Church, Schools, Law and even of 'common-sense' Morality. In its essence it was exactly that: *anti*-hegemonic. It displaced the authority of institutions and of received worldly wisdom with that of the individual's inner light – faith, conscience, personal understanding of the scriptures or (for Blake) 'the Poetic Genius' – and allowed to the individual a stubborn scepticism in the face of the established culture, a fortitude in the face of the seductions or persecutions sufficient to support Christian in the face of the State or of polite learning.[52]

The 'faith', two hundred years later, is Marxism-Leninism; the 'cultural hegemony' is the dictatorship of the bourgeoisie; the scriptures are the Marxist-Leninist canon; Christian (from *Pilgrim's Progress*) is the brave communist foot-soldier. The Party is one of countless groups, sects, Parties, religions, movements, associations, societies, fraternities, supermarket chains, which seek to change the world and, in some cases, to turn it 'upside down'.

In Wittgenstein's cosmology the meaning of the world, of life, lay *outside*, in God. 'To believe in God means to see that the facts of the world are not the end of the matter'.[53] As a Communist Cardew would have attempted to locate meaning *inside*. But all meaning? Communism was a necessary *stage* in human development which, it was believed, would unlock doors to deeper perceptions, to higher levels of consciousness, which in turn would lead to further, unimaginable modes of human existence. The things people find in religion Cardew found in music and relationships. Friendships and love. Communism meant the end of exploitation of man by man, it embodied the desire to transcend alienation, to eliminate the transgressions of class society and to elevate tragedy to its purest form: the primal conflict between man and natural necessity.[54] Wittgenstein wanted to free people from 'brain-cramp'; for Cardew people were socially cramped by relationships – both to objects and to each other – which capitalism forced upon them.

For Cardew and his comrades communism was desirable, attainable, but most importantly it was *inevitable*. Such a position had profound consequences; too often the comrades failed to remind themselves that to believe in communism does not mean that 'to see that the facts of the world are the end of the matter'. The willingness to sacrifice oneself, and one's family, for example, is rendered morally unimpeachable by an aura of correctitude compounded by certainty. In the mid-seventies, Sheila Kasabova recalls, when *Chinese Literature* arrived in the post at Agar Grove she and Cornelius would sit up in bed reading from it; he would read stories aloud to her and would ask for stories to be read to him. And there would be intense and lengthy arguments about the content and quality of those stories. And one in particular: a woman who was a bare-foot doctor had gone off into the snow and cold to look after somebody's child, and to breast-feed it. But she got cut off by the snowstorm; meanwhile her own child, whom she had left behind, had perished. She was described as a heroine; what she achieved was a sacrifice of a higher order. Sheila disagreed with it fundamentally and there was a heated argument. But sacrifice was central to Cardew's moral code.[55]

It is easy to deride the Party's agenda, particularly in the light of the demise of their erstwhile leaders, and with the benefit of hindsight. Yet it is still the view of millions that the object of Marxist-Leninist rage and invective continues to command and devastate the planet. It would be just as apposite now, in 2007, a quarter of a century after Cardew's death, to list the injustices, violations and atrocities that the triumphalist capitalist system continues to heap upon the overwhelming majority of the world's population and to expose the manifold 'cultural' activities which provide gloss and embellishment, for which there are handsome rewards.

The communist view is 'dynamic'; the communist seeks to effect, to *create*, major changes of a cataclysmic nature, and in doing so changes himself and others, too; this accorded well with Cardew's own personal cosmology. For most people it seems merely desirable; more important, and certainly more practical, is to cultivate attitudes that will minimize or at least mitigate the uncontrollable and unavoidable vicissitudes of life. Most people's lives are led for them in capitalist society through deception and manipulation. Their targets and goals, if they have any, are set for them by society, authority, and by family requirements, too – although these are themselves circumscribed by societal exigencies. So we should not be surprised by Cardew's communism. Millions of people have been attracted to its ideals; many still are. For them the *Communist Manifesto* is a re-affirmation rather than a discovery. At the end, like Molly Bloom, they say Yes, yes…

David Jackman, an extremely perceptive artist/musician, felt that somewhere in Cardew fear of some kind resided, or at least something unfathomable. According to Jackman, who knew him well and had lodged with the Cardew family, he was not a joyous, nor even, perhaps, a happy man. And yet, during the Scratch Orchestra days, Cardew had given Jackman a mainly unspoken approval of what he, Jackman, was trying to achieve musically, and this was enormously beneficial; nobody had ever discussed such matters with him and he was grateful:

> I don't think I really got across to you how much I really appreciated Cornelius, the fellow himself, not his music so much – he meant a vast amount to me; one of the important people in my life, I guess. Whatever musical 'craft' I have, I learned a lot of it (absorbed it?) from the situations that he seemed to be able to generate. I guess I was lucky to have been there.[56]

It is my view that in the last tumultuous years Cardew did enjoy moments of supreme happiness – with his beloved Sheila, and with his comrades. For Cardew life was a 'tremendous force' and he lived it to the full. And in the opinion of some (including my wife Janice), in the last decade he became, at least outwardly, a much warmer, more accessible person; he formed relationships with people more easily – perhaps as a result of his political activity where he was obliged to converse and communicate with a wide spectrum of people, in particular with working-class people; initially, this had not been easy for him. But he enjoyed humour and the company of humorous people. He was a good listener and the course of action he recommended, if asked, would invariably go to the heart of the matter. And yet, in the last decade, with a cruel irony, friendships *were* destroyed, love starved, relationships compromised, undermined, sometimes torn asunder or reduced to a sterile, bitter co-existence.

We seem to be dividing up into two camps. Is it not simply the case that our perceptions and responses are influenced and shaped by our expectations, and if the original relationship is charged with an unforgettable, precious authenticity, as was the case with Nathalie Gibson, with David Jackman and others, then the residual image cannot accommodate the disruptive force of change? Hence their dismay. Just as Wittgenstein had enlisted in the Great War in the hope that it would change him, so when Cardew became a revolutionary communist he knew, or at least hoped, that he too would become a different person. And, to the deep chagrin of some of his closest and dearest friends, this was the case.

Notes and references

1   Written by Cardew in Pentonville prison on a sheet of information from the Chaplain's department.

2   From an unsourced sheet headed 'PCA Solidarity message to Rally on 60th Anniversary of October Revolution.'

3   Was the Party proposing that Cardew should somehow lead a 'double life'? Several years earlier he had insisted: 'There *cannot* be a career as a revolutionary artist' (previously quoted) and I do not think he changed his position. During 1980-81 he did nothing that would have endeared him to even the more liberal representatives of the musical establishment; there were just two instrumental compositions: one for solo piano and a two-piano work. The latter *was* a commission, but he had little heart for the project and in fact did not complete it.

4   From a single sheet, handwritten by Cardew, dated 26 March 1980.

5   Again, we are reminded of Cardew's insistence, a decade earlier, that in *The Great Learning* self-discipline is 'the most important' theme and 'is actually central to the text'.

6   We recall that in Birmingham in 1978 Cardew had received a one-month prison sentence suspended for two years.

7   From a handwritten sheet of paper headed 'Lecture/Recital Brighton University 12/5/80'.

8   From the song anthology *We Sing for the Future,* p.28. In the nineties Hardial Bains wrote several essays on Cuba which were gathered together and published in 2003 in a volume entitled *Visiting Cuba* by The New Magazine Publishing Company, Toronto. In these essays, in a complete reversal of the previous Party line, Bains extols the achievements of the Cuban revolution and its leader Fidel Castro.

9   The Wicker is a street in Sheffield; it used to have a Communist Party bookshop. The CP was very strong in Sheffield and when there were major steel works the Wicker would be a popular stopping off point for workers to have a drink on the way home.

10   From a typewritten sheet entitled '110th Anniversary of the Birth of V.I.Lenin', produced by 'The Revolutionary Communist Party of Britain (Marxist-Leninist).

11   Ibid.

12   Cardew's brief sojourn in prison had its compensations. He told Peter Devenport that it enabled him to get a whole week's sleep – something he rarely achieved outside.

13   The Stalin Youth Brigade was the precursor of the Communist Youth Union of Britain, which Cardew was to set up the following year.

14   From a report of a PCA meeting on 5/6 July 1980.

15   Yet the purity of the Canadians' political line was exemplary; even Fidel Castro had been denounced as an agent of Imperialism.

16   It is worth reminding ourselves that, according to his children, Cardew never showed the slightest interest in popular music; he never attempted to share or understand their enthusiasms. The nearest he came to an appreciation of 'popular' music was his love of jazz, a genre which he admired (he could not play jazz) from a distance, as it were, and with which, for him, perhaps only J.S.Bach could bear comparison.

17   Email communication from HS to JT, November 2003. Shrapnel recalled that there were sharp contrasts in the weather – three days of incessant rain were followed by several days of unbearable heat – and that although the diet was adequate, it was plain and

lacking in essential vitamins. As a result many of the comrades suffered from colds, coughs, loss of voice, and even influenza.

18 From a Report to NE [the National Executive] on 4th International Youth Camp, 19 July – 3 August 1980.

19 Email communication from WC to JT, 30 March 2004.

20 Mao Tse-tung, 15 April 1958: Introducing a Co-operative, from *Selected Readings from the Works of Mao Tse-tung,* (Peking: Foreign Languages Press, 1971), p.500.

21 Speech of Party representative [Cardew] at Internationalist Youth Concert, London, 9 August 1980.

22 Ibid.

23 In a remembered telephone conversation between John White and myself sometime during the early part of 2006. White also commented that the recitative-like passages and the somewhat abstruse modulations recall some of Beethoven's choral settings, for example in the *Missa Solemnis*.

24 Letter dated 14 September 1980.

25 Letter from Pentonville prison to SK, dated 20 August 1980, the day after his incarceration.

26 Letter dated 31 August 1980.

27 Letter dated 2 September 1980.

28 Ibid.

29 Letter dated 14 September 1980.

30 I have not been able to find anybody who can positively identify who Kevin was, although some have vague recollections. At the top right-hand corner of his letter is written simply 'South London' and the date. This lack of information in no way detracts from the incisiveness and sagacity of his criticism. 'Kevin's letter and reply' was important enough to be referred to by Cardew at a PCA Committee meeting on 24 May 1980. Kevin had already written to Cardew prior to 11 May, to which he refers above.

31 I have already referred to this with regard to the Canadian Party texts which the British musicians manfully attempted to set to music; the results were often disastrous.

32 Hanns Eisler, *Political Musician*, p.226.

33 From a handwritten sheet dated 21 December, which suggests that, several months on, the case of 'Kevin' had still not been laid to rest.

34 From a report, probably written by Cardew, of the Youth Concert in East Ham, dated 7 October 1980.

35 Letter from Geoff Pearce to CC dated 5 November 1980. The third of the 'three letters of substance' I refer to above.

36 Perhaps it is of significance that one of Cardew's sons, who loved him dearly, should have been his most trenchant critic. Referring to a visit to Canada, after his father's death, Walter Cardew comments: 'Certainly the Canadian comrades seemed to be perplexed by our singular failure to churn out happy-clappy folk tunes that they could sway from side to side to, determined fists clenched, brave but slightly moronic smiles fixed to their faces. I can't believe that Cor could not have been at odds with those people. But his mistake generally was, I feel, to subjugate his experience of reality to dogma and sheer Idealism in so many ways. [...] It seems clear to me that the only way to cling to those ideas is to completely neglect and deny your own experience of reality and the human condition.' Email correspondence from WC to JT, 30 March 2004.

37 Letter from Geoff Pearce to CC dated 5 November 1980.

38 Brecht, *The Measures Taken*, p.28.

39 From Cardew's hand-written notes, dated 10 November 1980.

40 Ibid.

41 From the introduction to the songbook, *We Sing for the Future* (London: Progressive Cultural Association, 1980).

42 One cannot avoid the impression of a solipsistic optimism, with a tinge of desperation, which served to justify many of the PCA's artistic endeavours: 'a very good tour in the summer with the Internationalist Youth concerts, together with the Canadian musicians' flies in the face of Geoff Pearce's description of the Birmingham concert. On many occasions the 'good response' which an event received was from Party members and supporters and a few friends and family who themselves had been exhorted to attend. This, according to Pearce, had been the situation in Handsworth. Yet there *was* an admission at the time that 'only among Indians do we have some mass following'.

43 This reads like a programme note. It was certainly penned by Cardew but regrettably I have mislaid the source.

44 The original song, because of the technical demands of the convoluted text and the absolute necessity for its comprehension, is usually sung at a much slower tempo, which tends to give the impression of scouts and guides singing round the camp fire, rather than proletarians of all lands going into battle.

45 My discussion of the song in the previous chapter raises different (though not necessarily unconnected) issues.

46 *Cornelius Cardew We Sing For The Future!* Released on New Albion Records, San Francisco, NA116 CD.

47 The invitation was also sent to the editors of *Melody Maker* and *New Musical Express*.

48 From a PCA Executive Report, 30 December 1980.

49 Hermann Hesse, *Narcissus and Goldmund* (London: Peter Owen, 1993), p.10.

50 A possibly apocryphal story tells that in one of the communist cells in Chicago every member was an intelligence agent, a fact which was unbeknown to each of them.

51 *Witness Against the Beast*, p.20.

52 Ibid, p.5.

53 Ludwig Wittgenstein, *Notebooks 1914–1916* (Oxford: Basil Blackwell, 1961), p,74e, 8.7.16.

54 Bearing in mind my own comparisons of the Maoists of the early seventies with contemporary religious sects, I cannot resist quoting from George Steiner again here: 'Nothing is more religious, nothing is closer to the ecstatic rage for justice in the prophets, than the socialist vision of the destruction of the bourgeois Gomorrah and the creation of a new, clean city for man. In their very language, Marx's 1844 manuscripts are steeped in the tradition of messianic promise. In an astounding passage, Marx seems to paraphrase the vision of Isaiah and of primitive Christianity: "Assume *man* to be *man* and his relationship to the world to be a human one: then you can exchange love only for love, trust for trust."'

55 George Steiner has elaborated on the imperative for 'sacrificial self-denial' in relation to the moral demands of Christianity, of the Sermon on the Mount and the Parables of Jesus. 'To become man, man must make himself new, and in doing so stifle the elemental desires, weaknesses and claims of the ego. Only he who can say with Pascal *le moi est haïssable,* has even begun to obey the Gospels' altruistic imperative.' *In Bluebeard's Castle*, p.39.

Clearly, there is a compelling analogy here with Cardew's communism, but we should not get carried away. Cardew would at the time, I suspect, have challenged the notions of 'elemental' desires, of 'claims of the ego', and their (implied) universality. And I think it is probably true to say that Chairman Mao's strictures on the (bourgeois) 'theory of human nature' would have continued to function as an important philosophical guideline during the rest of Cardew's life.

56   Letter from David Jackman to JT, 15 October 1996.

24

7 June Conference and Vancouver Festival 1981

Capitalism has forced us to take up arms. It has laid waste our surroundings. I no longer go off to 'commune with Nature in the woods', but accompanied by two policemen.[1]

The New Year began with a flurry of activity by the Communist Youth Union of Britain (CYUB), which included a picket at an army recruitment centre in Forest Gate, east London, and a meeting, organised by Cardew, to commemorate the life of the young Turkish revolutionary, Erdal Eren. February saw the founding of a 'democratic student front' by CYUB members who were students at the London School of Economics, and at the beginning of the month PCA mounted a series of concerts in support of a campaign in St Paul's, Bristol, where a dozen or more young West Indians had been arrested the previous year. Concerts in solidarity took place in Birmingham and London but the main event was in Bristol where Cardew and some PCA comrades from London, including the West Indian Fight Back band, performed an 'eclectic programme', as Walter Cardew recalls, which included a set of reggae songs.

In a PCA report dated 28 February Cardew again refers to the need to revive and develop associations with old musician friends:

> In the work among the cultural workers the main thing has been for me to keep up with old friends, and keep them in touch with PCA and Party developments. This has been done with John Tilbury and Dave Smith but not many others. I have written a work for two pianos [*Boolavogue*] for John T and Susan Bradshaw (another old friend) to play in a concert on 13 March. This work has had to be squeezed in and is not brilliant but better than opting out.

He is clearly feeling cut off and isolated; writing music for his friends is perhaps a way back into musical circles but one senses a certain diffidence. With regard to the PCA's activities Cardew's 28 February report is mixed: the Defence Concert (one of three) in Bristol with the West Indians was encouraging, although their progress is described as 'somewhat spasmodic', whilst the PCA singers, with a 'promising young female singer' (certainly Cardew's step-daughter Emily), acquitted themselves well at a concert in Coventry. Throughout March and April a series of meetings took place (over twenty across Britain) to oppose the British Nationality Bill; Cardew spoke at the South London meeting on 4 March. And on 13 March the PCA singers and the West Indian band accompanied a group of ten Party comrades to Brighton, where the Party had established a branch, to contribute to a 'week of action' against Imperialism, Fascism and War. The February report also mentions A.L.Lloyd, whom Cardew liked and respected, who by then was suffering from permanent ill-health: 'basically he is a "pure" folklorist, who does not like "city music" much. [...] I must find another excuse to trouble him again and spend the time to discuss politics in general with him'.[2] And around this time a student Party supporter, 'Andy', was making an anti-fascist film under the censorial eye of the Party, in the personification of comrade Cardew.

13 March saw the premiere of Cardew's *Boolavogue* at the Wigmore Hall, performed by Susan Bradshaw and myself, in a concert for two pianos entitled 'The Boulez Connection'. The three-movement work had been commissioned by New Macnaghten Concerts and the concert also featured Cardew's earlier music, including *Two Books of Study for Pianists,* and works by Pierre Boulez and Richard Rodney Bennett. On 18 March, as part of his strategy to re-integrate into the professional music world, Cardew sent a letter of application to rejoin the Master of Music Analysis course at King's College – presumably in anticipation of an award from the Department of Education and Science. On his application form he makes no bones about his political agenda:

There are several reasons for taking this course. 1. to investigate the new methods of musical analysis from the point of view of whether they have any scientific validity. 2. to investigate what has been thought and written on the British national tradition in music. 3. to work on the Marxist concept of artistic 'realism' as applied to music, and especially look into the music of 'socialist realism'.

There is no doubt that he was looking forward to the opportunity not only to study Western classical music in depth, albeit from the circumscribed perspective of 'analysis', but also to sharpen his wits in one of the citadels of 'bourgeois ideology'.

Boolavogue and national traditions

Boolavogue was described by Cardew in the programme notes for the first performance as 'attempts at handling folk material in classical terms; in particular they give expression to the passion and drive of the working people's struggle against the barbarity of national oppression and wage-slavery'.[3] It is in three movements, and I recall that while Susan Bradshaw and I were rehearsing the first movement we were also encouraging him to provide us with the remainder of the piece. When a second and third movement finally arrived, they had the appearance of work under pressure – which, by his own admission, it was. In fact, the projected fourth and final movement never materialised. 'More time is needed to do something decent in this field', he wrote.[4]

In the first movement the ternary melody, 'Boolavogue', is introduced by piano 1; piano 2 accompanies with ornamented tenths, in stepwise movement (Ex.24.1a-b).

Ex.24.1a. From the first movement of *Boolavogue*.

The second statement of the theme shows a dramatic metamorphosis; the lyrical theme is cast impressively in an heroic mode, punctuated by the occasional trumpet-like motif, and accompanied by an insistent rhythmic figure in piano 2.

Ex.24.1b.

In the ensuing section the texture becomes more complex, with sweeping scale-patterns divided between the two pianos. An element of 'struggle' is created through the introduction of conflicting elements, dissonant and syncopated accompanying figures which serve as a disruptive influence on the music. The section dissolves and the movement ends with a final quiet variant of the theme.

The graceful second movement, in which the politics seems to be in limbo, is cast in the form of a *moto perpetuo*; running semiquavers prevail, modulating freely and sometimes to unexpected regions, where the music leaves the comfort zone and the flow is momentarily destabilized.

The third movement begins with an arrangement of the 'Internationale'; the main musical material consists of variations on the 'Blackleg Miner', a militant miners' song from 1844 which was written as a warning to working class traitors ('scabs' or 'blacklegs') who at that time were being imported into the coalfields from other parts of the country (Ex.24.2a-d). And yet Cardew refers to it quite dismissively: 'the opportunists, who lose no opportunity of presenting, e.g. the 'Blackleg Miner' (which has nothing to do with revolution) as "working class culture"'.[5]

The theme appears first in the second piano:

Ex.24.2a. From the third movement *Boolavogue*.

And then with rhythmic syncopations in the accompaniments in both pianos:

Ex.24.2b.

The second section uses a technique common amongst the early English virginalists: the practice of 'divisions' where the beat is divided into smaller notes and the successive figurations are used cumulatively to build and sustain climaxes. The contrasting middle section, too, captures the spirit of the Renaissance virginal music:

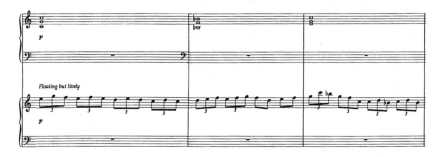

Ex.24.2c.

In the extended coda the repeated quaver chords and driving scalic passages in the left hand create a rousing finale:

Ex.24.2d.

Some years earlier Cardew had been asked about his attitude towards the material, folk or classical, he was using. He replied:

My attitude is pragmatic. I'm a shocking musical fornicator, and worst of all, my consciousness of such factors is very low. When the musicologist's hair is standing on end in horror, I'm just beginning to enjoy myself. 'Fidelity to the material' is such a floating, relative idea – I find it useless.[6]

Be that as it may, his concern for the English national tradition became increasingly evident in the later years, not only in his speeches and conversations, but also in his music. Arrangements of songs such as the 'Blackleg Miner' reflect his commitment to folk and popular music, while the two solo piano works, *Boolavogue* and *We Sing for the Future*, clearly reveal a debt to English sixteenth and seventeenth-century art music.

This had been a relatively long process during which Cardew had survived the tortuous PCA (Party) debates on 'bourgeois art' and its viability for revolutionary cultural work; he came to believe in the continuity of culture, that contemporary culture had to assimilate and rework the best of the past. And yet, in relation to the use of folk music he showed considerable wariness. When the *Berliner Hefte* raised the question of the 'consciousness of the population' Cardew replied:

I've heard there are now over 3000 'Folk clubs' in England (presumably including Scotland and Wales). Obviously every gradation between philistinism and connoisseurship can be found – and that's just it: they are not centres of the expression of a genuine or progressive culture 'of the people', but an entertainment genre. [...] My opinion is that English folk music is non-existent in the consciousness of the population. (What the hell is this 'consciousness of the population' anyway?) England is an oppressor of other nations, so its 'national consciousness' is bound to be chauvinistic. We have to work for a 'proletarian consciousness'. Irish folk music is quite different. An unbroken cultural tradition of resistance, the people are still responding to every development in their struggle with songs and poems. Our (English) folk music is feudal. Our 'popular' culture has been and is being appropriated by the bourgeoisie day by day. Our proletarian culture has been systematically smashed up and its one of our jobs to rediscover it as part of our history. I don't know in detail how the culture of the Chartist movement has been suppressed, but the flowering of Trade Union culture in the period of maximum militancy, 1890-1926, was suppressed by the TU leadership itself (as far as I've gathered from a retired worker who has made it his business to collect proletarian songs and poems of that period).[7]

A year earlier, in a revealing letter to Sheila Kasabova from North America, where he had been on tour, Cardew described his response to some South American folk music in which the theme is love, love as it finds expression in a Chilean working class community. The poignancy, and irony, of Cardew's thoughts would not have escaped the recipient of his letter, for in the day-to-day struggle in his homeland love was a luxury which he could enjoy only in the bosom and within the confines of his family, and even then, as we have seen, such feelings were considered vulnerable, prey to bourgeois ideology and thus potentially treacherous to the revolutionary cause.

He [Richard Teitelbaum] also played me a tape of Angel Parra's concert here [Toronto, Canada]. He is a Chilean singer. It was very striking, very emotional, like love songs for the people. In one song he talks about his father (an engine driver) – mining the earth and stoking heaven. He remembers the things his father taught him as a child and the last thing was:
'Justice is the people,
and Woman is love'.
It struck me warm and strong, working man's sentiment, not chauvinistic. I wish you could have heard it. The 'Justice is the people' is such a good image, and then to have woman as symbol of love could be kind of backward, but somehow his warmth and the family feeling he was talking about raised it above that. I'm thinking a lot about love and all its different forms. And inside I'm feeling a piece of some sort edging into all that turbulence.[8]

Did that 'piece' materialise in the way that Cardew felt it at the time? The letter was written at the beginning of 1975; the only, or at least the most likely, contender would be 'A Law of History', but we can only speculate. In any case, on his return to London he would have immediately thrown himself back into the fray and into the harsh realities of class struggle.

The worker's culture can only be centred in the class struggle. Out of the experiences and needs of the class struggle will be evolved those new elements which will bring about a true revival of art.[9]

The old 'revisionist' Alan Bush ends his essay 'Marxism and music' thus, with a revolutionary flourish which Cardew could not have faulted. And in a text relating to the writing and performance of songs, Cardew devotes a section to the 'political level' of songs and lyrics:

This cannot be too high. Our culture should present the most profound and scientific truths to the people (whether comrades or masses) on every social and political issue, whether personal, national or international. And we must strive to present the ideas in the most lucid way, illustrating them with the day-to-day life experience of the people, but never compromising or falsifying our science, which is the science of reality. Good realist art can be appreciated on many levels – and we should aim to create this kind of realism.[10]

But what is 'good realist art'? And what are its roots? For when we come to discuss the nature and role of working class art, poetry and music, and its potential in the political arena, there are deep-seated problems, many of which have been raised and discussed in greater or lesser detail throughout this book. Brass band music at one end of the working class spectrum and punk rock at the other, to posit just two of the genres which have enjoyed a following within working class groups and communities, would have been rejected by Cardew and his comrades on the grounds of paternalism in the case of the former, and nihilism in the case of the latter. This is not surprising since the Party was suspicious of all artistic manifestations – most of which are neither party-political nor scientific. Moreover, art is notoriously promiscuous and tends to resist long-term relationships; it is difficult to harness and control works of art – that is, to circumscribe their field of operation and influence. The Party did not want art; it wanted only those cultural artefacts which would serve its needs. It demanded of its cultural work that it should be 'educational', that it should expose the iniquities of monopoly capitalism and expound the Marxist-Leninist solution. Cardew's political songs were not 'art'; they were largely political tracts set to music, and music *per se* is not art. In Cardew's revolutionary circles art was a political red herring.

In his talk 'Role of the composer in the class struggle' Cardew argues:

The idea that artists can make a purely *cultural* contribution to the revolution is a bourgeois idea; it rests on the conception of the artist as a special individual with a special way of looking at the world. This is why the revisionists love Beethoven so much: his contribution to the bourgeois revolution was purely cultural: he didn't go out to fight for it, he just wrote music for it. And the revisionists try to make out that the same is true of the proletarian revolution – that you can make your contribution from an armchair or from a notebook. But as I have said: this revolution is different, and it is very often the artists who stand in the way of revolutionary art and oppose it; and the revolutionary fighters have to brush aside their cultural comrades in order to produce the revolutionary art.[11]

This seems to be expressing a moral imperative, or perhaps (for many) a dilemma, from which Cardew never shrank. For still within living memory of many of us is the terrible and compelling image of talented violinists putting aside their violins, pianists closing their piano-lids and drummers putting away their sticks, to 'brush aside' other cultural comrades in an ultimate act of sacrifice. Many of them (have) lost their lives in appalling circumstances.

And yet, more than sixty years later, in a 'civilisation' where starvation, torture and mass-murder are endemic, the 'bourgeois' can still use art, as Iris Murdoch posits, as 'a spurious short cut to "instant wisdom"'[12], as an alibi, a haven, a temporary escape from the harsh realities of the consequences of the mendacious ideology into which we are subsumed. 'The written text seems to "do it for us", and need not be diligently assimilated or transformed into our own personal understanding and practice'.[13] Art as a substitute for action, especially good action. Is not the staging of a 'cultural debate' at a learned institution – where all too often such atrocities (especially contemporary ones) surface as a passing conceit, or, more substantively, in contributions circumscribed by the academic obligation to career mobility – therefore a degenerate act, an obscenity?[14] Indeed, as I labour over this book, I can imagine that Cardew would give me the same advice that, forty years ago, Frederic Rzewski gave him while he was struggling with *Treatise:* 'Abandon it!' Except that Cardew would have added: 'And join the revolution!'

And the prospect of revolution provided uplifting occasions, such as the Second Anniversary, on 5 April, of the Revolutionary Communist Party of Britain (Marxist-Leninist), when Cardew chaired 'a joyous revolutionary rally and celebration', followed by a banquet, to mark the event. On the negative side, during the first part of 1981, very few, if any, new songs of quality had been produced, and none by Cardew; moreover, disconcertingly, one or two of the PCA groups seem to have been on the verge of collapse. There were also oblique references in the reports to the objections to Party policy mentioned above by Kevin and Geoff Pearce; clearly, such criticisms continued to rankle, the issues raised unresolved. And they were unresolved because they were never fully acknowledged, let alone confronted. Walter Cardew has commented on the Party's chronic inability to unite with people on even the broadest issues: 'The Party could only do business with its own kind'.[15] Thus, an initiative would invariably become a Party 'front', and its high-handedness often created resentment, alienation, and ultimately total withdrawal.

In a letter to Howard Skempton, dated 8 April, in which Cardew invites his old friend for a meal at his home in Leyton, Cardew refers back to a conversation at the Wigmore Hall the previous month: 'It seems wrong that we don't meet ever. The trouble is that I get very little time to go to concerts – and they're not that brilliant anyway!' And then in a reference, it seems, to the idea of a musical drama he continues, 'I haven't got round to re-reading [D.H. Lawrence's] *The Virgin and the Gypsy* yet. I periodically scratch my brain for what is the appropriate dramatic subject for these stirring times. There seems to be a shortage of progressive writers'. Skempton recalls:

> I am pleased to be reminded of this letter. The reference to a musical drama concerns a conversation Cornelius and I had after the *Boolavogue* première (I remember Cornelius cajoling Susan [Bradshaw] to join us all for a drink). I told Cornelius that I was thinking of writing an opera based on D.H. Lawrence's *The Virgin and the Gipsy.* Without hesitation, Cornelius said that it was 'a terrible idea' (I can hear him saying it). His letter suggests that he might have modified this view! [16]

26 April saw the founding of a Trade Union Revolutionary Opposition group which Cardew attended as a representative of the People's Democratic Front. Delegations from other countries attended and Cardew's knowledge of German was put to good use with the German-speaking contingent. A few days later May Day was celebrated in traditional fashion with a meeting and concert at Hampstead Town Hall, and in a PCA report dated 2 May Cardew notes that 'a minor breakthrough is in prospect with the agreement of John T. to organise a concert at Goldsmiths on the afternoon of June 6th in support of the June 7th conference'.

The main work in the concert was Eisler's cantata, *The Mother,* to Brecht's adaptation of Gorky's novel; Cardew's *Boolavogue* was performed as well as works by 'progressive' composers Hugh Shrapnel, Howard Skempton and Ian McQueen. In fact Cardew's perception of the political context was not entirely accurate; as far as the Goldsmiths' contingent was concerned the concert was a memorial for the victims of a fire in New Cross, and most of the participants, and indeed the audience, would have had little or no knowledge of the 7 June Conference against Racism and Fascism, whatever its relative significance, and however germane the aims of the Conference were to the implications of the New Cross deaths. [17] Cardew's professed aim, as we have seen, was to 're-start' the PCA on a broader basis, with people like Dave Smith, Keith Rowe and myself, as part of a progressive, anti-capitalist, democratic, popular culture:

> Not that we want to point to this or that example of it today, but PCA exists to foster it and create it on the basis of the people's struggles. Of course, there is the risk of losing PCA [...] but JT and myself are there to fight that, just as JT and KR fought in the Scratch to bring everyone round to the Party. However, the problem of fitting it in is quite serious. I have set myself a target of doing four days

a week at least in the office [Diagram Visual Information Ltd], in order to get my finances back on some footing.[18]

There is an element of self-deception here, which also relates to the (perceptual) hijacking of the Goldsmiths concert ('in support of the June 7th conference') to serve the needs of the Party – a wish expressed as a fact or a *fait accompli*. And 'risking' the PCA and Party influence by a more open artistic agenda and then relying upon revisionists like myself and renegades like Keith Rowe to fight against the possibility of PCA extinction – this was surely a highly dubious strategy. Perhaps it was subjectively motivated; at the beck and call of people (such as Hardial Bains) who had down-graded the art of music to a political accessory, Cardew the musician was, I suspect, suffering acute deprivation. At that time my own relationship to the PCA was as 'supporter' or, more accurately, on the basis of a close friendship which went back many years. I do not recall being a member of PCA – at best a sleeping partner. Cardew would phone me, make overtures regarding participation in a concert, to which I would normally respond positively. Why was my involvement essentially passive? The explanation is three-fold: firstly, on a practical level, I was frequently out of London; blocks of teaching at the Falmouth School of Art in the mid-seventies and subsequently, through the late seventies, a regular three-day-a-week stint at the Welsh College of Music and Drama. Secondly, my equivocalness was rooted in a deep-seated scepticism, previously referred to, in relation to the Party's ability to achieve even partial success in pursuit of its aims; such an agenda, according to my own understanding of the relations of power and wealth in the world, required men and women of an extraordinary calibre. Those comrades I had met, like most of us, fell far too short of the necessary stature. Except, possibly, his political *naiveté* and inexperience notwithstanding, Cardew: a personage who inhabited a different space and who seemed to be possessed of an overwhelming immanence – an individual who could, just conceivably, have been instrumental in affecting the course of human history. And thirdly, to return to my own insufficiencies: a surfeit of human weaknesses which I all-too-compliantly accommodated: self-indulgence; faint-heartedness in the face of adversity, of overwhelming odds; a lack of the necessary mental and physical stamina (of staying power); and, crucially, a lack of vision, of a utopian perspective for which the present, *now*, could be relegated to the category of *means*.

In an interview with Paul Driver, which appeared in the *Guardian* as an article entitled 'Social Harmony' on 6 June 1981, Cardew identifies Maoism as the *bête noire* which continues, four years on, to bedevil the Party's cultural policy:

The problem now is two-fold: to get rid of Maoism, the approach of simple indoctrination – we're having to swallow a lot of what we once stated very categorically – and to build a material basis for composition out of traditions such as British folk-song, choral-singing, urban culture.

What must be done [...] is to create the material conditions out of which a composer can produce a piece that grapples with the profound issues of the social struggle, one that would show what a tremendous force life is.

If I could see that there was a big piece to do, that would hit the nail on the head, I'd start looking for a writer (though good writers are notoriously hard to find). What we want is a socialist society where everyone takes part in artistic production. In the meantime writing propaganda songs is still useful and necessary – provided of course they are true.[19]

But in truth it was neither lack of text, nor lack of inspiration, which prevented Cardew from applying himself to composition, even on a relatively modest scale; for despite the scaling down of his responsibilities it was the demands made on him as a member of the Party's Central Committee, as well as his PCA work, including administration, which were devouring his time and sapping his energy.

When Driver suggests that Cardew might also be suffering from thwarted ambition, Cardew objects, echoing both Schoenberg (composers as 'fighters') and Hans-Werner Henze (composers as 'competitors in the same market'): 'You can't look at things like that. It's all part of "false consciousness". A bourgeois composer has to fight for his existence, make it over his fellow composers, create a new brand.' By contrast, Hanns Eisler, who previously might have been considered to be too closely associated with 'revisionist' Marxism (along with Brecht), is now regarded, felicitously, as 'a very important figure': 'Eisler's music has stirring qualities; it has survived; it is used'. And Cardew compares Eisler's qualities to the 'detachedness' of Stravinsky and the 'subjectivism' of Schoenberg. When the discussion turns to Mao's thesis of the class nature of all art, which led to the production of ultra-propagandistic songs to the exclusion of a more broadly-based art, Cardew argues that, in any case, 'people are not won over by songs or explanations, but by actual struggle, by awareness of oppression by the bourgeois state, by the ever-present threat to living standards – in short, by an awareness of the *political reality*'.

Driver attempts to steer the conversation along musical tracks, eliciting from Cardew, significantly, a more conciliatory attitude towards his earlier music: thus, the problem with *The Great Learning* is its 'mystical basis'; it is still 'a useful piece in education'. But Cardew still insists that the political framework, within which all artistic decisions are made, whether consciously or not, must be referred to: the need, in particular, to counter the strong reformist strain in British politics, and not least in the trade union movement where, whether resolved in victory or defeat, struggles are 'always taken in the direction of reformism'. Hence the necessity of Marxist-Leninist revolutionary leadership – an inviolable principle which formed the background, still, of every discourse which Cardew undertook. The Party's aim is to build a revolutionary opposition within the unions in order to raise the consciousness of working people, to show that the debilitating limitations of reformism result inevitably in despair and disillusionment. Whilst the objective conditions for revolution are good, Cardew argues, the subjective conditions – the resoluteness and confidence to effect radical change – are lacking.

Driver's article is based on what must have been Cardew's last public interview. Towards the end, in an already self-acknowledged *volte face*, he unequivocally rejects 'doctrinal' music, art that indoctrinates:

We want pieces [of music] that are about life and show the tremendous force life is, and how it is expressing itself. Songs should be the expression of the living experience of people, but the expression of struggle and in very concrete images. The whole Marxist conception is against having doctrinal works of art…

We are back with Engels and his paean to the objectivity of the art of the bourgeois Balzac. Of course, there would be no lack of demand for 'propaganda songs', but what Cardew sought was a mutually-beneficial development and accumulation of such material alongside music of a 'progressive' but less circumscribed content. One senses a freeing up of language (of thought?) in Cardew's last, valedictory (as it were) public utterances; the images and metaphors could just as fittingly refer to some of his pre-political music: *Treatise*, AMM, *The Great Learning*, even the earlier indeterminate music; all these 'show the tremendous force life is, and how it is expressing itself'. They, too, point to an inexhaustible human potential, to a creative and collaborative future where people manage and determine their own lives. And in their imaginative projection of music-making in a new society might serve to inspire and sustain us when, in the coming years, the going gets tough. In the *18th Brumaire* Marx wrote: 'The social revolution of the 19th century cannot draw its poetry from the past, but only from the future.'

On 7 June, at the Conway Hall in central London, Cardew chaired the Conference against Racism and Fascism; he was also a key member of the organising committee. The event, which drew a packed audience of around five hundred people, was sponsored by over one hundred organisations and individuals; these included many Asian, African and Afro-Caribbean groups, trade unionists, teachers, academics and students, women's groups, political groups, church groups, residents' committees (including a Jewish group), youth clubs, arts organisations, and immigrant organisations – an impressive cross-section of the populace, or rather that considerable part of it that identified the rising tide of racism and fascism as a real threat to the lives of many people across the country. Representatives of many of these organisations were present at the Conference and some delivered speeches. There were also speeches by representatives of fraternal delegations from Germany, Canada, India and the Surinamese workers in the Netherlands.

An eighteen-point Declaration condemned 'the murderous and criminal activities of the nazi gangs and their promotion of racist and fascist politics and ideology'. It also insisted that it was 'essential to deprive these racists and fascists of the right to speak and organise'. It condemned the British Nationality Bill,[20] 'the racist speeches of Thatcher and other politicians', the leaders of the Labour Party and Trade Unions for their 'openly chauvinist, racist stands and policies', and 'stands firmly against all forms of discrimination against the national minority people'. It also opposed those who tried 'to pacify the struggles of the people for their rights, who try to take the initiative in the struggle out of the hands of the people and put it in the hands of the police, the state, and the various parties of the rich, in order to liquidate the struggle'.

In essence the Declaration was abstracted from the Party manifesto and embraced other areas of social and foreign policy: thus, it demanded the right of all working people to a means of livelihood, to decent housing, education, living standards, and condemned the 'increasing attempts to restrict the political rights of the people'. And, with political foresight, and ever relevant, it drew attention to

the danger which this ruling class is presenting to the lives, liberties and democratic rights of the people in Britain, as well as throughout the world, (which) is further seen in the extent to which the British government is tying the fate and future of the people to the war chariot of the Pentagon generals, and is, alongside the governments in Washington, Moscow and those of other warmongering powers, arming to the teeth, preparing for war and so gravely endangering the lives of millions upon millions of people on a world-wide scale.[21]

It also demanded Britain's withdrawal from NATO and 'an end to British colonial rule in Ireland'.

The Conference declared that in order to achieve these aims it was necessary to begin the work of building and organising a 'broad front'. In the light of the increasing danger which threatened the rights and liberties of the people and the burgeoning resistance which was being developed by the people against this danger, it considered that the establishment of such an organisation was an urgent necessity at that time.

To this end, the Conference took the decision to establish 'the National Organising Committee of People's Democratic Front (PDF)', whose central feature was: 'Unity in Action against Racism, Fascism, War, Imperialism and Reaction'. The immediate tasks of the PDF were: to set up local committees in communities and localities throughout Britain, to prepare for a First Congress of the PDF, to publish a regular national newspaper, to begin to organise various national 'agitations', and to establish a national headquarters to direct, assist and coordinate the work.

The Party was playing for high stakes; this was an ambitious strategy – a bid for revolutionary leadership on a national scale no less. It was dynamic, proactive and dangerous. And in this political universe from which nothing was excluded and in which no sacrifice was too great, Cardew would have had few equals: he was fearless but calculating, impassioned but controlled, energetic but calm, both spontaneous and circumspect, intuitive and cerebral, imaginative and measured. For his comrades he seemed indefatigable.

The Declaration presented the issues: that it was useless to depend on the state authorities and institutions and to 'plead' with Parliament to defend the rights of the people – especially the rights of the national minority communities.[22] For these Marxist-Leninists self-defence was the only way, with the people relying on their own strengths, taking the initiative into their own hands, building fighting organisations 'to defend themselves, and to defend their democratic rights and freedoms from racist and fascist attacks'. Self-defence was the main, compelling theme of the 7 June Conference, a strategy based on the recognition of the State not as a neutral arbiter but as a hostile force created by the rich and powerful to serve its own needs, a force whose *raison d'être* was therefore inimical to the struggles and aspirations of working people. In St Paul's, Bristol, in 1980; in Brixton, London, in 1981; in the 25,000-strong march in London in response to the reaction of the state in the wake of the Deptford fire-bombing; in the large demonstrations in Coventry against murder and attacks by nazi gangs; and in the march by thousands of people against the British 'Nationality' Bill – such resistance did manifest itself in a way that shook the authorities. And the media would duly characterise such demonstrations as 'race riots', denigrating self-defence as 'vendettas' and 'feuds' by national minority groups to 'settle scores'.

The Organising Committee of the People's Democratic Front argued that more than anything the state feared independent action by people – that is, action that state organisations did not themselves initiate and could not control; that the aim of the state was to disarm the people, ideologically, politically and organisationally, so that the rich and powerful could pursue their reactionary policies. This idea of independent, anti-authoritarian, mass action would have fed the anarcho-libertarian strain in Cardew's nature (just as he had forged an artistic and aesthetic autonomy, independent of the received music authority in the sixties); but now, intellectually, he also recognised the limitations of such action, that without the perspective of irreversible, revolutionary change, it was doomed to failure. And for such change a revolutionary *authority* – ideologically, politically, and culturally – was a *sine qua non*. This Janus-like quality, as we have seen, enabled Cardew to embrace the imperatives of opposites – the turmoil of revolution and the iron discipline of the 'dictatorship of the proletariat', without which the revolution cannot survive. 'The solid cannot be swept away as trivial', it states unequivocally in *The Great Learning*. The Conference concluded:

> We can have no faith in this kind of 'democracy', in the 'democracy' in Britain, the United States, the Soviet Union, China and so on. [...] The life experience of the people shows that their rights have never been handed to them on a silver platter, that the defence of their rights and the extension of them has only come about through vigorous struggle, sacrifice and unity. [...]
>
> The task which confronts the anti-racist, anti-fascist forces in this Conference today is to advance their struggle for the democratic rights and freedoms of the people. It is to make this struggle against racism, fascism, war and reaction broader, deeper, more conscious, more organised and planned. And to achieve this there is an urgent necessity to build an organised form, an organisation which genuinely unites all sections of the people in struggle, in action in defence of their rights and against racism, fascism, war, reaction and imperialism.
>
> This is the task we have set in this Conference today. In carrying out this task, we have no false euphoria or expectations of any easy victories in relation to the grave problems which confront people, the difficulties to be overcome and the sacrifice which has to be made. But neither are we pessimistic or fatalistic before the attempts of the ruling class to inculcate an atmosphere of fear and powerlessness in the face of the onrush of racism, fascism and war.
>
> The very fact that the British and other reactionary powers have racism as a preferred policy, are developing fascism and preparing for war, shows not their strength but their weakness, in the face of their deepening crisis and the rising struggles of the people.[23]

Buoyed by the positive atmosphere which had begun to envelop the Party at every level – People's Democratic Front branches had been set up in Nottingham and in Birmingham, and a new, June/July issue of *Voice of Youth* had also come out – Cardew took up his next assignment with characteristic aplomb, leading the PCA delegation at the First International Sports and Cultural Festival against Racism, Fascism and Imperialist

War, organised by the Canadian Party, and which took place in Vancouver from 27 July to 5 August. A broad-based 'people's festival' – in which 50,000 people from many different countries (including India, Pakistan, Britain, Denmark and Germany) participated, in the events or as spectators – it received no financial support from the state (indeed had not applied for such support), relying on contributions from the organisers and participants themselves. The large numbers ensured a high profile for the Festival which was launched in Robson Square in the city centre.

There was a wide range of sports, including soccer, basketball and kabbadi, which attracted an impressive number of participants and spectators, and many cultural events, including the Jugnu Bhangra dancers from Gravesend, in Kent, England, and concerts by the PCA and the Canadian Cultural Workers. Again, as at the Festival in 1979, the PCA was responsible for providing new songs (to Canadian lyrics), as well as established ones – including Laurie Baker's 'Streets of Britain', sung by Cardew, 'H-Block song', and 'People of St Paul's Bristol', a song by the West Indian group Fight Back. The British participants included Cardew, his son Walter and step-daughter Emily, Laurie Baker, Chris Thompson, Peter Devenport, Hugh Shrapnel, and Penny Wright.

Cardew's 'The Festival' was the Festival's theme song, the inspiration for which were some 'catchy' Irish dances written for guitar by a rather 'sullen and taciturn' Irish schoolteacher, a Party supporter who was living in London. The Festival opened with Cardew's arrangements of the music which were interspersed with his own rousing refrain (Ex.24.3):

Ex.24.3.

And Hugh Shrapnel contributed some variational material, based on Cardew's theme, for the ad hoc instrumental ensemble which had been assembled.

> The variations were in a kind of mock classical style (I had Haydn in mind), and rather tongue in cheek. The music was overall quite jolly, but looking back I seem to remember it as being rather embarrassingly 'happy-clappy'. [24]

There may well have been advantages for the British Party from such closeness to an experienced, revolutionary Party of some standing – Cardew himself had developed good relations with many of the Canadian cultural workers, and in particular with their leader, Hardial Bains – but it also exposed a contradiction at the core of the RCPB (M-L)'s cultural programme which threatened to negate its current optimism. It was difficult to see how its recently adopted cultural strategy of a 'broad front' could be reconciled with the cultural politics of the Canadian Party (as exemplified the previous year at the international youth camp in Trier), whose doctrinaire, hidebound texts the PCA musicians had struggled to accommodate. As we have seen, such products had already succeeded in alienating many of the West Indian musicians the PCA had recruited in London – unless, which has already been mooted, the strategy was to develop two cultural strands: one for the consumption of the Party faithfuls, the other to attract and involve sympathisers and fellow-travellers. The examples of 'Party Art', in particular those works to which the Canadians contributed, but also, it has to be said, some of Cardew's own songs, demonstrated subordination to an oppressive conformity and to a system of dogmatic, and philistine, vetting.

The Canadian Party leader was impressed, and possibly intrigued, by Cardew, revolutionary artist; and the latter, according to Sheila Kasabova, may have allowed himself to be flattered by this. Hardial Bains had great leadership qualities: charisma, and an impressive, larger-than-life personality; Cardew was the only English comrade who might eventually have measured up to him in stature. But on the evidence of his contribution to the cultural relics that have survived, Comrade Bains, the Marxist-Leninist scientist, for all his wide-ranging experience, had much to answer for.

Immediately on his return from Canada Cardew embarked on preparations for the Communist Youth Union of Britain summer camp (25 August to 1 September) in Bakewell, in the Peak District of Derbyshire. As was often the case with these communal projects, for which his experience with the Scratch Orchestra stood him in good stead, Cardew was the main organiser. And just as he had done prior to the Scratch Orchestra northeast tour, he went to Bakewell a week or two before the camp began to look at the site and plan the location of the tents. The projected events included a sports tournament, excursions, a cultural festival of revolutionary songs, music and dance, discussions and speeches, and a final banquet.

If the atmosphere was more relaxed, more ludic, than was the case with the adult equivalents, such as the recent International Sports and Cultural Festival, the priority of the political agenda, with its seven-point manifesto, was made manifest by the ubiquitous banners with their insistent slogans: 'Youth Against Racism, Fascism and War', 'An Injury to One is an Injury to All', 'No to Whitelaw's Attacks on Youth', 'Culture in the Service of the People', and 'Workers of All Countries Unite'. Nor was there any respite from Party speeches, delivered by authoritative and well-meaning adults at the beginning and end of the week, the content of which the majority of the young participants – most of whom were Party offspring and their friends – would already have had imprinted indelibly in their consciousness. Even the three 16-millimetre films which Cardew hired – *Lenin in October, Three Songs of Lenin*, and *Battleship Potemkin* – hardly fell into the category of entertainment, however gripping, however salutary their subject matter indubitably was; except that, unfortunately, they did not materialise. On 9 September Cardew penned a humble letter to Educational and TV Films Ltd informing them that because of the primitive conditions (deep in the countryside with only a small petrol generator to supply power) it had not been possible to show the films. Cardew asked whether, under these mitigating circumstances, the hire fee might be waived or whether just a nominal amount would be acceptable, even though such a gesture would 'go against nearly every principle of business practice', he acknowledged, with a somewhat overweight irony. The reply from Educational and TV Films Ltd has not come to light.

Walter Cardew, who, as we have seen, could be quite critical of his father's initiatives, recalls enjoying Bakewell very much, especially the beautiful countryside and the fact that there was much music-making. Clearly, the summer camp was a great success; Cardew senior would have been in his element, and his enthusiasm would have been transmitted to his young charges. As I often observed during my long association with him, he had a marvellous gift with children and young people: discreetly observant, his presence subtly reassuring, sensitive to their relationships with each other, always ready to offer wise advice and guidance when appropriate, encouraging them to express themselves with imagination, to try things they had never done before. It was probably the best education they would ever receive.

On his return from Canada Cardew had received a letter from the Department of Education and Science, dated 6 August 1981, informing him that he had been awarded a one-year State Studentship. He duly re-entered the Master of Music course at King's College and took no time in establishing his Marxist-Leninist credentials. On 5 October a circular to students, staff and lecturers 'who care for the future of our society' announced the opening of the 'Lenin Club' for fortnightly discussion sessions and other appropriate activities. Interested parties were requested to contact Cardew, c/o Socialist Society.

We may speculate on Cardew's attitude towards the course and its demands: he would have responded with a cynical curiosity to its claims of a scientific methodology and may even have been intrigued by such claims although, in those latter years, he would have found the reductionism of analysis hard to come to terms with. When the class was asked to comment on the opening of Beethoven's *Sonata Pathétique* Cardew's 'subjective' referral to the overwhelming *dramatic* impact, as I recall him telling me, received short shrift from the lecturer; such a response betrayed a dereliction of the scientific, or at least, objective criteria which should form the basis of the analytical approach. In the analysis classes 'text' is perceived in the form of *object* of contemplation, not as an extension of human 'being', not as sensuous, human activity. Cardew had allowed his *musicalness* to intervene, to assert itself, whereas the professional analyst must of necessity place his volatile and sometimes perverse musical instinct (spontaneous responses) into voluntary confinement. This, throughout his musical career, Cardew had never achieved, nor even attempted. Rather he had sought to *release* music; firstly, from the constraints of tradition and convention, and finally to *appropriate* it for proletarian revolution, the one contributing to his reputation as a maverick, the other to his 'involuntary confinement' at Her Majesty's pleasure. I suspect also that he would have viewed musical academia's lofty disinterestedness with respect to political matters rather as compliancy with the status quo (any status quo) – comparable to membership of the police or the armed forces.

Cardew was arrested several times; the last occasion was on 27 October 1981 in the Strangers' Gallery in the House of Commons, with another comrade, Hakim Adi, during the final reading of the British Nationality Bill. As soon as Enoch Powell began to speak Cardew got up, shouted 'this house stinks of racism', and threw leaflets denouncing the 'racist legislation' down into the chamber – for which he and his accomplice were manhandled by ushers and the police and ejected from the gallery. The Strangers' Gallery is appointed with tiered wooden benches and Cardew had been at the front; when the police removed him they pulled him up very roughly and damaged his hands. The two offenders were subsequently detained at a police station until the early hours of the morning (until the Commons had risen) and formally banned from the House of Commons for the next seven years. Adi recalls that in such situations Cardew was always outwardly calm and in control, exuding a self-confidence which rubbed off onto those who were with him. He would always resist physically when arrested, which impressed his comrades, and showed little or no respect for the police; experience had taught him not to trust them. His comrade and friend John Maharg recalled that at trials Cardew always spoke impressively, with clarity and militancy.

On almost every occasion Cardew's arrests were for 'obstruction', that is, physical resistance. For example, during a National Front march the police would try to ensure that, firstly, the fascists were able to march through an area, and secondly that they would be able to express their ideology freely and publicly. The aim of the Marxist-Leninists was to prevent this: 'Nazis have no right to organise' was their slogan, and they were often successful, as we have seen – in Lewisham, for example. In a letter to a friend,

'David', thanking him for a supportive letter to the court, Cardew refers to the huge number of arrests of anti-fascists ('342 trials arising from the Southall events of last April', for example[25]):

> What it boils down to is that in the present stage of fascisation [sic] in this country, to oppose fascism or racism is a criminal offence. No less fascist are the arrests of the workers on picket lines now going on. So it is a matter of principle to oppose these developments, and they are being opposed by large numbers of people. But the real issue in society is not just to 'oppose' fascism or racism, but overthrow the whole system that gives rise to these things.[26]

Cardew's perception of fascism would have been more comprehensive than the jack-booted Nazi stereotype; it would have been historically researched and he would have been conscious of the influence of social, economic and cultural factors on its various manifestations around the globe, just as he would have been aware of its universal, defining characteristics: the key role of corporate power, the obsession with crime and punishment, the exploitation of fear (national security) as a tactic for control of the populace; the virtually unlimited power of the police, particularly the secret police; the emasculation of the trade unions; rampant cronyism in business and government circles; control and censorship of the media; the identification of scapegoats (in particular immigrants and ethnic minorities); a disproportionate amount of funding for the military and the routine recourse to military solutions rather than negotiation; the glamorization of violence and aggressivity; the downgrading of human rights. We could go on.

But to return to the House of Commons, the People's Democratic Front, which had organised the demonstration, drew attention to the fact that whilst 'notorious racist ministers such as (William) Whitelaw and (Timothy) Raison, as well as the 'fascist Enoch Powell', were allowed, if not encouraged, to speak freely and shamelessly in favour of the Bill, those 'genuinely democratic forces' who publicly denounced the legislation were treated harshly and their protests suppressed. The House of Commons intervention was the culminating act after a series of meetings in various cities, which had begun in March, on the theme: 'Oppose the British Nationality Bill', 'Oppose Racism and Fascism'. And on 31 October, as part of a 'day of action' highlighting the chronic unemployment which blighted the whole area, the CYUB picketed West Ham police station, protesting against harassment and attacks on the local youth. The momentum that had been building up continued throughout the latter part of the year: on 6 November there was a Party-organised rally at the Conway Hall to commemorate the 40th anniversary of the Party of Labour of Albania, and in the same month the Brighton branch of the Party joined forces with other anti-fascist organisations to oppose a National Front march through the town.

On 21 November a rally at a school in Southall in west London, which attracted around 150 people, was organised by the People's Democratic Front to celebrate the success of the First International Sports and Cultural Festival in Vancouver and to launch preparations for the second Festival to be hosted by the PDF in Britain the following year. As chairman and representative of the National Organising Committee of the PDF, Cardew delivered the opening address; this was followed by a short programme of songs: 'Death to Fascism', 'Hail Ireland's Glorious Martyrs', 'Bold Revolt', and 'The Festival', following which representatives of the Pakistan People's Association, the Indian Sports and Culture Federation, the PCA, and the Afro-Caribbean Defence Committee, gave messages of support to the Rally, which was also addressed by comrade Hardial Bains. Both Cardew and Bains emphasised that the Sports and Culture festivals which had been initiated by the Marxist-Leninist parties were diametrically opposed to those promoted by the bourgeoisie and the imperialists:

Comrade Bains explained how the bourgeoisie and reactionaries hate such festivals of the people; they do not want the masses of people to unite in struggle against racism, fascism, war and imperialism; they do not want the people to develop their life all-sidedly, to advance their cultural life. He pointed out that the bourgeoisie and their governments want to instil in the people a mentality of inferiority, whereby they cannot carry out any activity without the bourgeoisie, but should emulate the 'cultured' members of society – the bourgeoisie and reactionaries. But what is this 'culture' which they are calling upon the people to follow? It is a 'culture' of a dying class, a culture of decadence, pornography, money-making, a backward and reactionary culture. And the people reject this 'culture', this culture that goes directly against their aspirations and life, a 'culture' which does so much damage to their youth.[27]

At the beginning of the eighties there was a buoyant, optimistic feeling in the Revolutionary Communist Party of Britain (Marxist-Leninist) and a surge of confidence; moreover, it had begun to recognize that flexibility of means need not undermine firmness of principle and had begun to jettison much of the baggage which had seriously compromised its relations with potential supporters. The comrades were learning, if belatedly, to reach out to people in a leavening way, which lent a genuine *viability* to the Party – something it had previously never been able to achieve. So even among those who had preferred to keep the Party at a discreet distance, and who had maintained a degree of scepticism in relation to its avowed aims and achievements, there was recognition of a palpable upsurge of support for the RCPB (M-L), particularly in respect of its stand against fascism.

The 7 June Conference against Racism and Fascism had been an impressive achievement, bringing together a large number of groups, organisations and associations from a wide spectrum of British society. Cardew himself had taken up the anti-fascist struggle with enthusiasm and determination; he liked to be out on the streets: as fighter, propagandist, orator and musician. John Buckle, too, was finding his feet, gaining experience of leadership, and consolidating his position as General Secretary.

But if the Party was now reaching out to people, it was still cautious in respect of the tactic of a 'united front' which the German comrades had adopted in the Youth Festival in Trier, much to the consternation of the Albanian delegation. In the *figura* of Hardial Bains, the Canadian Party still wielded considerable influence within and over the British Party. Above all, the unchallengeable leadership of the Party had to be maintained and strengthened. As we have seen, the doctrinaire stance on many issues by the Canadians, and particularly in relation to cultural matters, had alienated not a few of the British comrades and supporters, and, we might speculate, may well have created a degree of tension in the relationship between the two parties at a higher level.

On 28 November, a week after the rally to celebrate the Sports and Culture Festival, the newly-formed East London and Kent Committee of People's Democratic Front was demonstrating against racist attacks on the national minority community in East London, and specifically against the recent attacks in which fire bombs were used. In Birmingham there had been similar attacks, and the Birmingham Committee of PDF, together with Hind Mazdoor Lehar (Indian Workers' Association) had organised a picket outside a court in Oldbury where two Indian brothers had been charged with 'assault' and 'causing actual bodily harm' to the police. According to the defendants it was the police themselves who had launched a racist attack on them. There were many such incidents throughout the country and Cardew and his Party and supporters were often at the cutting edge: 'Self Defence is the Only Way' was the implacable slogan of the People's Democratic Front.

On his return from a conference in France, where preparations had begun for the next Anti-Fascist International Youth Camp, Cardew met a few friends and comrades for a rehearsal at his house in Leyton. He was very tired, but calm and relaxed, and again expressed his admiration for the Albanian delegation which had contributed to the discussions in France: how tactically adept they were at uniting the various elements against the imperialists, and how invaluable they were in their ability to obviate unnecessary argument. Upholding Party policy, Cardew had not told Sheila he was going to France, although she knew when he was going abroad because he always polished his shoes. Generally, most of the comrades that evening, as on most evenings, were exhausted from Party work; yet, as Peter Devenport recalled, there was 'a strong feeling of excitement and optimism'.

On 5 December a Women's Conference preceded an anti-fascist concert 'They shall not Pass', which took place at Clarence Way Hall in Camden, north London and was attended by over one hundred and fifty people, including many members of London's ethnic groups. It was a dual commemoration: the 45th anniversary of the battle of Cable Street,[28] and the beginning of the Spanish Civil War. The programme included militant songs from around the world by the PCA singers, and traditional Irish music and dance performed by The Hole in the Wall Band. Benjamin Zephaniah read his verse and a satirical group, National Interest also participated. I myself played two of Cardew's piano transcriptions of Irish traditional melodies and a fifteenth century *Hornpype* by Hugh Aston. Cardew had persuaded me to lend my Steinway grand piano for the event, which I agreed to, I must confess, against my better judgement and with a degree of trepidation. I knew that the precious instrument would be transported from Deptford in southeast London to north London by a team of non-professional volunteers; moreover, the idea of insuring the operation would have been dismissed as being too costly. Cardew accompanied at the piano and sung; it was a far cry from the international festivals of contemporary music where he had begun his career, but it was the destination he had consciously chosen, and which he reached by 'forcing his music into life'. The next day, 6 December, an anti-fascist conference, which Cardew chaired – 'Build the Unity of the People in Action against Racism and Fascism' – was held in Fairholt House at the City of London Polytechnic in Whitechapel, and in the evening an Albanian film was screened at the Bishopsgate Institute.

Cardew had even found the time to discuss with Keith Rowe a projected performance of *Treatise* in Bristol the following March, as well as the possibility of a return to free improvisation, to AMM. Perhaps these small concessions which were elicited from him did presage more, as Rowe perceived it; certainly, in the early seventies they would have been inadmissible – a bourgeois Trojan horse driven into the proletarian heartlands to spread decadence and confusion. Now, perhaps, it was part of the Party's tactical change: the 'broad front'; Cardew had recently acknowledged the educational usefulness of parts of *The Great Learning*, for example. But it was not, in my view, a change of heart, which is how Rowe interpreted Cardew's response. Michael Chant, a comrade who was close to Cardew, concurs; the fact that Cardew no longer spent time and energy attacking his earlier works and other cultural activities which did not 'serve the revolutionary cause' did not necessarily represent a radical change of opinion, a double *volte face*, it was simply that there were other more important things to do.

Notes and references

1   Bertolt Brecht, *Poems 1913-1956*, ed. by John Willett and Ralph Manheim with the co-operation of Erich Fried (London: Methuen, 1979), pp.458-59.
2   PCA report, dated 28 February 1981.
3   'Boolavogue', the title of the song on which the first movement is based, is a small town in the southeast of Ireland which was the site of an uprising against the British in 1798. In fact, 'Boolavogue' is based on a song by P. J. McCall and was for generations known as 'Youghal Harbour'.
4   From a PCA report dated 29 March 1981.
5   From the aforementioned letter to comrade Kevin, dated 11 May 1980. One might accept that the 'Blackleg Miner' 'has nothing to do with revolution', but surely the issue of 'blacklegging' is an integral part of working class culture?
6   From a handwritten response, dated 5 October 1976, written on the back of a letter (unsigned) which Cardew received from *Berliner Hefte, Zeitschrift für Kultur und Politik*, dated 24 July 1976. In it Cardew deals with a list of questions on the subject of folk music.
7   Ibid.
8   Letter from CC to SK, dated 18 January 1975.
9   Alan Bush, *In My Eighth Decade and other essays* (London, Kahn and Averill, 1980), p.31.
10 From a hand-written text from March 1980.
11 Transcribed from a handwritten text, probably from 1978. (See *CCR* p.267)
12 Iris Murdoch, *Metaphysics as a Guide to Morals*, p.19.
13 Ibid.
14 I am reminded of Hannah Arendt's reference to 'the customary academic suspicion of anything that is not guaranteed to be mediocre' in her introduction to Walter Benjamin's *Illuminations*, p.8.
15 Email communication from WC to JT, 30 March 2004.
16 From an email contribution from HSK to JT, March 2004. Skempton abandoned the idea of a 'musical drama', but he did write 'The Gipsy Wife's Song' in 1983 for mezzo soprano, flute, oboe, vibraphone and piano.
17 On 18 January 1981 a fire broke out at a party in New Cross, in south-east London. Thirteen black teenagers died in what at the time was thought to have been a racist attack, although subsequent investigations seem to suggest that the fire could have been started within the party. The case remains unsolved.
18 From a PCA Report dated 2 May 1981. This was the same 'united front' tactic of the German comrades which the PCA and the Canadians had criticised so trenchantly in Trier the previous year. But Cardew would have argued that within the confines of a Marxist-Leninist camp it was quite inappropriate to provide a platform for the expression of a culture which, however popular, ultimately 'served imperialism'. Making compromises and concessions in the context of a 'broad front' in society at large was of a different order.
19 This extract is taken from a cassette copy of the recording of the interview, in Leyton at the beginning of June, which Paul Driver kindly forwarded to me.
20 The British Nationality Act defined five categories of British nationality: British citizen, British dependent territories citizen, British overseas citizen, British subject and British protected person – with different rights for each. Thus only someone possessing British *citizenship*

had the right of abode in the UK. The Party characterised the Act as providing the British state 'with a new definition of nationality based on race, colour or creed – in contravention even of the UN Declaration of Human Rights – which will be used as the criterion for defining and removing the basic rights of the people, withdrawing the democratic rights of the national minority people on the grounds that they are not really citizens of British nationality, as part of, and as a spearhead for, the withdrawal of democratic rights of all people'. Workers' Weekly: 28 November 1981, p.5.

21 The Declaration was printed in *Workers' Weekly* on 13 June 1981.

22 Already in the seventies 'searching for illegal immigrants' had become a pretext for harassment, abuse, attack and imprisonment.

23 From *Workers' Weekly*, 13 June 1981.

24 From an email communication from HS to JT sometime during 2005.

25 Southall, in west London, is home to a large Asian community.

26 Typed letter to 'David' (surname unknown) dated 14 March 1980.

27 A Report from *Workers Weekly*, 28 November 1981, p.7. Laurie Baker still regards this as the beginning of a new mass culture in Britain. And the First and Second International Sports and Culture Festivals in Canada were important developments in this respect.

28 In the spring of 1936 Oswald Mosley targeted the East End as a focal point for BUF (British Union of Fascists) activity. The planned fascist parade through the East End was intended to be a show of strength. The battle of Cable Street took place on Sunday, 4 October 1936 between Mosley's Blackshirts and the local Jewish people and various left-wing and communist groups. Most of the media sympathised with the Jewish community and sided with them against the BUF. The Labour, Communist and Trades Union movement responded with a campaign to 'fight against fascism'. On the day of the march thousands of anti-fascist demonstrators blocked the route of the BUF who were forced to abandon their march.

(*CCR*) Also found in *Cornelius Cardew A Reader*

Cornelius Cardew a life unfinished

25

12/13 December 1981

It had been snowing and was very cold. Cardew was due in Birmingham that day, Saturday 12 December, to report to the Party's Central Committee on his meeting the previous week with the French Marxist-Leninists. Sheila was hoping that the trains from London to Birmingham would be cancelled; she feared that because of the severe weather conditions Cardew might become marooned in Birmingham. Cardew went out to make a call to British Rail from an outside call-box (the Party decreed that no calls should be made from home) and was informed that the trains were running normally. He returned to the house, said good-bye and left. Sheila began to feel anxious, doom-laden, and was overtaken by a sense of impending loss, of deep sadness, and found herself in tears. Within a few minutes, and for no apparent reason, Cardew returned and went back into the bedroom. He told her how much he loved her, and left again.The whole day and the evening went by. Sheila occupied herself to help the time pass more quickly, but despite being busy a feeling of anxiety prevailed. Finally, at around 11 pm, she went to bed.

> I wasn't really asleep, because I never really went to sleep until Cor came in and he never normally came in until 2 or 3 and I used to sort of drift. And we had these two storage tins downstairs, and perhaps because of the change of temperature, when the central heating went off the tins must have contracted or expanded just underneath our bedroom and there was this loud bang of exploding tin which really startled me. And then about ten minutes, fifteen minutes, or twenty minutes later, around 2 am, the doorbell rang and it was the police. A man and a woman. And I have never ever let the police in before; I've always firmly stood my ground. I went downstairs and I just let them in. There were lots of times when the police came to our house and every time I would ask for a search warrant.

On this occasion they just walked in and they said: 'We need to come in, we need to talk to you.' [...] They asked me where 'Mr Cardew' was, and I said I didn't know. And they asked if he had been on a journey and I said that's possible. And they asked if he had been on a journey to Birmingham and I said well why are you asking me. And they said 'well, he's had an accident'. And I think I said 'is he dead', and they said 'yes'. And I said 'well, why did you ask me about Birmingham?'[1] They asked if he had been on the motorway and I said no and then they asked again if he had been on a journey to Birmingham. And I asked them why they'd said that and they said 'well, because we found a ticket in his pocket, a return ticket from Birmingham'. And then they just told me that he had been killed by a car on the bridge by Leyton tube station. And I think I asked them again to say it to me, and I never for a moment believed he wasn't dead because I knew that if Cornelius was alive he was alive and if he was dead he was dead. He couldn't be in between; he wasn't somebody to be in between. And I asked them to go; I didn't want them in the house. And the woman said 'can I stay' and I said 'no'. And then I didn't know what to do; I knew that I had to phone somebody and I realised I didn't know where Cor was. I'd wanted to get rid of the police so quickly; I didn't want to break down in front of them. I didn't want them in the house. So I thought, well, I could go down the road to the phone box to ring, and I knew that theoretically I should be ringing Chris Coleman because of his position in the Party and I had better do that. That's what Cor would have expected me to do. But he was in Edinburgh, and so then I rang Michael Chant.[2]

Sheila phoned from home and broke Party rules; she recalls that she could not face going out to a public phone box. Moreover, she was not prepared to leave Anna alone in the house. She sat in the sitting room, staring out of the window into the dark, waiting for Michael. She cannot remember her sensations at that time. Numbness. Except that she was dreading Anna coming downstairs, hearing her footsteps, and having to put it into words to her. Michael Chant finally arrived. The next thing Sheila can recall is later in the morning when Carole Chant (Michael's wife) arrived. Anna's father called to pick up his daughter and take her away, and Carole drove Sheila to Camden to be with close friends. Sheila recalls telling Carole that she must drive over the bridge by the tube station or she would never go over the bridge again. They did not stop or look. Sheila stayed with her friends in Camden overnight and returned home the next day.

Michael Chant formally identified Cardew's body at Walthamstow public mortuary on Sunday the 13 December. Sheila went to the morgue with her friend Adah Kay and Mariel Cardew to look at the body. Mariel came by tube wearing her slippers and carrying a little basket with marmalade and various goodies. It was what she had planned to bring for their lunch together that Sunday.[3] Because Mariel was slow they arrived late, ten minutes after the appointed time. The people at the morgue were 'vile' – rude and officious even to the extent of initially not allowing them entry. They said 'you are too late [...] you shouldn't look at him; he's in too bad a shape'. Sheila and Mariel insisted and were taken to the slab where he had been laid out. Sheila recalls:

It was horrible; it was so murky, everywhere that Cornelius would not have wanted to be – a police morgue. It was dirty, and I don't mean the dirt of physical matter, it was the dirt of the business they do; it was like that. I felt very sad and also very angry. Except for his chin there was gross disfigurement, his face frozen in a terrible demonic look. Terror. Later the body was taken to the Co-op funeral parlour where they said they would 'do a job on him, tidy him up'. They did make him look a lot better but he still looked terrible. I asked that he be buried wrapped in the banner of the last demonstration he had led. It had been a fortnight earlier, a local demonstration against fascist attacks. Quite a few people went to see him. Penny Wright, a nurse, saw the body and said he had been killed instantaneously. Only his face was visible, the rest of his body was covered.[4]

Initially, the police seemed disinterested or, perhaps, feigned disinterest. They told Sheila that the inquest would not be held for some weeks, perhaps a month or more. This upset her because it meant that the funeral would have to be delayed. However, this decision was reversed, with no explanation, and the inquest was opened and then adjourned on the 15 December 1981. Cause of death was given as multiple injuries and the coroner concluded that the death was accidental. The body was released for burial.

The Funeral 22 December 1981

Sheila Kasabova recalls:

First of all, during the morning, close friends and relatives gathered together at our house in Leyton. The coffin was covered in red material, decorated with the hammer and sickle on the corners. I remember sitting in our living room in Leyton with a number of close women comrades sewing it, and how doing this seemed to offer us some relief through this collective homage to Cor. The hearse arrived and we followed it to Manor Park cemetery. It was bitterly cold, thick snow and ice covered the cemetery terrain. A large number of people, between one hundred and fifty and two hundred, came to pay their respects; many were grief-stricken, some were weeping uncontrollably.[5]

As we entered the Chapel Alan Brett was playing movements from Bach's unaccompanied cello suites. Comrade Chris Coleman introduced the proceedings: Mariel Cardew spoke. Then I spoke. Then we all sang 'In the Dawn'. Towards the end of the short service there was banging on the door by the next group of mourners, impatient to bury their own. A peremptory cutting-off, just as his life had been ended. The hearse was carried out of the chapel by Cornelius's younger brother Ennis, his son Horace and two comrades. Because of the ice on the ground the coffin was then handed over to undertakers to carry it to the grave, with comrades in front and behind carrying red flags. We duly filed out and followed the hearse to the place of burial. Sheila said a few words of farewell and we sang 'Immortal Sacrifice' and the 'Internationale'. We then went to Manor Park library where the Party had put together an exhibition of photos representing Cornelius's life. There was food and the PCA singers performed. Michael Cardew was there; he seemed composed. But Sheila recalls: 'Michael was very distraught when I met him at Mariel's two days before the funeral. He had driven up from Cornwall and when I came into the room he fell into my arms and wept'.

The structure and symbolism of the funeral, with the red flags flying and the testimony of the photos, exemplified Cardew's communist beliefs, but at the same time in a most profound way it captured and integrated the feelings of a very wide range of people. In a letter to Sheila Kasabova the singer Jane Manning wrote: 'As a Christian I found yesterday's ceremony deeply moving and memorable in so many ways, especially for the intimate and personal quality so often lacking in church services. Everyone was united in expressing their love for Cornelius and their devotion to all he stood for.'[6]

The Inquest

On 21 January 1982 the inquest was reopened. Sheila Kasabova attended with comrade Chris Coleman. It was brief, minimal. There were six witnesses: the mini cab driver who was the first on the scene, the doctor who had certified the death, Michael Chant who had identified the body, and three police witnesses. The police failed to produce any forensic evidence, which was described as 'pending'. The coroner described the main injuries to the head and to the left leg but was unable to demonstrate how the injuries related to each other. Nor could he explain the distance between the injuries. There was a massive injury to the head causing disintegration of the right side of the skull, and laceration of the right side of the brain. These injuries were given as the cause of death.

The right leg had been practically severed high up, and below this the femur was fractured. There were various other more superficial injuries. The coroner could not give an accurate description of how all these injuries had been sustained. He was able to say that this injury was sustained because of that, and another possibly because of this, but seemed uncertain as to how the two main areas of injury, sustained simultaneously, could be linked. He brought the proceedings to an unsatisfactory conclusion, saying that he had no experience of injuries sustained in such severe weather conditions. However, in a coroner's court one cannot intervene and ask for further explanation and clarification. A verdict of accidental death was returned.

In an extraordinary, if not disturbing, prevision/precognition of his end Cardew wrote at the back of his 1952/54 Journals (he would have been seventeen or eighteen years of age) the following paragraph:

> My Epitaph.
> I have an insane desire to be an unsolved mystery. The only difficulty is to find a murderer clever enough to carry this out. Not only clever, for escaping justice, but with enough wit to get my epitaph engraved with the following: he died as he had lived .. an unsolved mystery

The unanswered questions

Another unexplained fact was that there was very little blood on the clothes (which were eventually returned to Sheila from the police), despite the fact that his leg had been almost severed. The main injury was a massive blow to the head, one side of which was smashed, completely destroyed. So whence the disfigurement, the severed leg, the demonic look? And contrary to normal police practice there were no photographs. In such circumstances, a hit-and-run driver, shouldn't the police have photographed the body at the scene of the incident? At the inquest the police produced photographs of the scene of the incident taken on the 18 December when the weather conditions were quite different. By this time Sheila and many others were haunted by the idea of assassination. Could somebody have pushed him out of a car when he was already dead, or pushed him out and run over him, or simply driven into him? But do any of these theories correspond to the actual injuries he sustained?

And what of the circumstances surrounding the surmised moment of death? Between 1 and 1.30am two men in a taxicab office heard a loud bang outside in the street. One of the men, a mini-cab driver, ran out and saw a body lying on the other side of the road opposite their premises. He saw a car, a Renault, brake and skid into a bus layby at the bottom of the hill; the driver (or a passenger) got out and was looking back up. He/she would have seen the person standing over the body. The car lights were immediately switched off, perhaps to avoid identification of the number plates; the person got back into the car which was then driven down a one-way street in the wrong direction.[7]

A cursory examination told the mini-cab driver that the person was dead; the body was cold. This young Asian was the closest thing to a witness. He told his colleague there was no point in calling for an ambulance – just get the 'meat-wagon'. He was now standing on the brow of the hill, anxious lest somebody should drive over the body. For around five minutes there were no other cars and no pedestrians. Then a car travelling at great speed approached from the Walthamstow direction and almost hit him, swerving away just in time. There was a lot of ice on the pavement and on the road; the conditions were very dangerous. The car then slowed right down. The immediate area was well lit. The young man assumed they were going to get out to see what had happened. But they drove away. Can any significance be attached to this second car? Did they drive off when they saw the extent of the accident and did not want to get involved? Or, less likely perhaps, were they accomplices who were reconnoitring to confirm that the mission had been accomplished? The ambulance eventually arrived, later than anticipated, and Cardew was taken to Whipps Cross hospital, where he was pronounced dead.

Cardew was, in Sheila Kasabova's words, extremely sure-footed: aware, alert, even if he were tired; physically and mentally he was always very much in tune with the material world around him. He was not the kind of person who would make a mistake. And the lighting was good. Yet it would appear that he was walking with, rather than against, the traffic. Why? Moreover, if you are walking home from Stratford on that side of the road you walk past open playing fields; it is much colder. And wanting to get home and out of the bitter cold would also draw you to the other side of the road and to the turning into Leyton Park Road. And there was another anomaly, something domestic which assumed a significance for Sheila which has not diminished with the passage of time: in his briefcase, which was eventually returned to her, considerably damaged, were his thick socks which he had evidently not been wearing at the time of his death. Cardew had always suffered terribly from the cold, from chilblains, and he had especially taken these thick socks for protection against the cold. 'Its one of those silly little things which remains in your head – why was he not wearing his thick socks?' It was freezing, and since the trains from Stratford to Leyton were not running, he would have had to walk that part of the journey – a distance of around two miles on a bitter night. So having taken his thick socks, why did he not put them on? Sheila cannot make sense of this. It was unlike him.

In the wake of the tragedy, after some days had elapsed, Sheila Kasabova had asked the police what they were doing to apprehend the perpetrator of the crime. They informed her that they had put up accident boards and had circulated a radio message through the metropolitan police network giving details of the accident. However, they had given the wrong car colour, despite the fact that flakes of paint found on Cardew's briefcase had matched fragments of turquoise paint and glass which had been found at the site of his death the following day and which had been sent for forensic testing.

The police also told Sheila that they were making enquiries at all the local garages to see if a car with a missing or broken wing mirror or/and windscreen had been taken in for repairs; there had been a lot of broken glass at the scene of the incident. They told her that they had found no leads. Sheila then approached several local garages; none of them had been contacted by the police. In the hope of receiving further information a local paper was asked by the police to run an article on Cardew's death; but the article contained several inaccuracies: Cardew was described as 'Brian Cardew, a local teacher', for example. It contained nothing of significance.

Sheila felt that there was also a lack of initiative on the part of the Party in the aftermath of Cardew's death; she, and she alone it seemed, had been left with the main responsibility of carrying out the investigative work. Perhaps this was because the Party had come to the conclusion that the most likely explanation was that Cardew's death had been a tragic accident.

In terms of the funeral arrangements and the service itself the comrades had been very supportive, but they seemed reluctant to recognise and discuss what Sheila regarded as a clear obligation to establish the truth of what happened on that fateful morning. They said, or they implied, that it was necessary to tread carefully; they posited the hypothesis that the wrong person, perhaps someone from the Asian community, might well be selected by the police as a scapegoat. Sheila was singularly unimpressed by the Party's arguments and justifications for what she perceived as their inaction. She was disturbed by this; some Party supporters were also bemused and critical of the Party's stance.

During this period, the early eighties, there had been an increase in Nazi activity in East London and the Party was known for its militant opposition to it. Cardew himself had been prominently involved and would certainly have been regarded by the fascists as a 'traitor' to the 'white community'. Two years later John Buckle, the leader of the Party, along with other Marxist-Leninist leaders, was killed in a plane crash in Spain. A tardy investigation into the disaster has still not provided a satisfactory explanation. In this context the possibility that Cardew was assassinated cannot be ruled out. Could the State have been involved? As John Maharg, an old comrade and friend of Cardew, said: 'MI5 are quite ruthless; people don't realise it. And they kill pre-emptively'.[8]

The aftermath

During the following four years Sheila persisted in her investigations. In the summer of 1982 she approached Michael Mansfield, QC, a prominent barrister whom she and Cardew had met at a party only a few weeks prior to his death. When she described the facts surrounding the incident Mansfield was of the opinion that there were aspects of the case, in particular the way the police had subsequently dealt with it, which might have suggested that this was not just another death caused accidentally by a hit-and-run driver, citing the minimal evidence produced by the police at the inquest as one instance which would support this thesis.

In an article by Edward Fox in *The Independent* Magazine, entitled 'Death of a Dissident', Fox quotes Mansfield: 'He [Cardew] was a very political animal, and that's rare among musicians'. And on Cardew's death: 'I would not be surprised if agents of the state decided his time had come.'[9] Mansfield suggested three possible areas of investigation that Sheila could pursue:

Firstly, she should try to obtain a copy of the original notes made by the doctor who had certified the death at Whipps Cross Hospital, stressing that notes jotted down in the margins sometimes reveal further information which would not necessarily be disclosed in the final, official documentation. Sheila duly went to Whipps Cross hospital, alone, and asked to see the notes. At first the hospital administration simply refused, because she could not prove she was married to Cardew. (She wasn't.) A lengthy discussion and argument ensued; finally, the clerk went to get the file, brought it back, showed it to Sheila, but refused to allow her to read the contents. She then took it away. Sheila left, appalled by the attitude and behaviour of the hospital employee.

Secondly, Mansfield recommended that she should try to make contact with the ambulance men who had taken the body. This, too, proved to be an extremely frustrating exercise. She had to make numerous phone calls before an appointment to visit the ambulance station could be agreed. And when she arrived at the appointed hour she was informed that the men were not available as they were now on different shifts. To compound her frustration, on a subsequent return visit she was informed that they had been moved to another station. However, she did ascertain that the ambulance crew had also been given wrong information on the night of the 13 December. They had been instructed to go to the wrong place and arrived at the hospital later than would have been expected; in fact, their base at Whipps Cross was not far away from the scene of the 'accident'. Sheila persisted until finally, towards the end of 1982, she received an admonitory visit from an official from the Ambulance Service. He told her that what she was doing was irregular, that if she wanted to speak to the ambulance men she would have to provide the Ambulance Service with a solicitor, who would be present at the meeting, and for whom she would have to pay, indicating a fee which was totally beyond Sheila's means. The meeting ended unsatisfactorily and Sheila was thoroughly frustrated and angered by the intimidatory nature of the visit. Perhaps it was insensitivity, rather than intimidation, on the part of a bureaucrat trained to put observance before sentiment, who was 'doing his job', protecting his men from an 'interfering member of the public'. Sheila had been traumatised and was in need of a manner couched in understanding and sympathy. The encounter was doomed.[10]

Thirdly, Mansfield suggested that Sheila should contact the solicitor Gareth Pierce. Initially, Ms. Pierce agreed to take up the case but subsequently never seemed to be available when Sheila tried to contact her. Nor did Sheila get back to Michael Mansfield. All of the undertakings which he had suggested had been plagued by problems; nothing had been straightforward. Perhaps he had underestimated the difficulties she would encounter; but she felt she had been unequal to the task.

Two years after the event Sheila Kasabova and a Party comrade went back to the scene, knocked on people's doors, talked to people in shops and garages, went back to the police. She achieved nothing – except that the two Asians, the 'witnesses', maintained their initial claim: that Cardew was cold, and he was dead. He therefore must have been walking for some time in the cold.[11] Sheila also continued to question the police, asking for updates on the case, but was always informed that nothing new had emerged. On one occasion she asked for the broken wing mirror which had been found at the scene of the incident, but was told by the police that, unfortunately, it had been lost in a 'clear out' at the station.

On Cardew's death few, if any, of the obituaries were generous; as representatives of musical officialdom and guardians of good taste, most of the critics had always belaboured Cardew's work. He discomposed them, challenging the basis on which they pronounced their judgements, and not only critics – audiences, too, as we saw with *The Great Learning* at Cheltenham. In terms of their lesser cosmologies he was of marginal significance, his political adventures and utopian fallacies a disfigurement of whatever talent he might have possessed. Thus he was mythologized and dismissed. But he would not have wanted his restitution, after his death, to composer status.[12] It is significant that during the last years many of his younger comrades were unaware of his musical prestige. When he died, an unregenerate communist, the only encomiums were from abroad: Marcello Panni, the Italian composer/conductor, who made Cardew's acquaintance in Italy, regarded Cardew as 'a poet among careerists, who was not interested in money, career, or fame'; the Swiss composer, Thomas Kessler, who got to know Cardew in Berlin, described him as '*ein Vorbild*' (a model, a kind of hero figure); Christian Wolff, too, referred to what he regarded as Cardew's most important quality: his 'exemplary character'. More recently, younger English critics have warmed to Cardew's later music. In the pilot issue of *Resonance* magazine Ed Baxter wrote:

Cardew was right to take a stance [...] he was wise to stake out the social dimension to his music. [...] His purpose was [...] to fight a corner and to express something human, faced with what Phil Ochs called 'the terrible heartless men' who still run our lives. [...] Listening to them now I am overwhelmed, rendered inarticulate and revitalised. Great stuff. The newspaper is full of details of how long 'Starlight Express' has been running. It's all quite clear. 'There's only one lie, there's only one truth.' Whey hey hey![13]

Cardew understood that too often the song is invalidated by the culture that sings it.

So he drew lines and dared people to cross them; and few could. Keith Rowe recalls a brown cup Cardew used to drink his coffee out of while he was living in Barnes. The cup, which had been made by his father, was badly chipped. Yet it was somehow still intact and useable. It has been said that if you cracked a Bernard Leach cup then it was ruined, finished. But with a Cardew cup you could crack it, break bits off, bury it and dig it up years later and still drink out of it. Cardew himself was like this, and it was this indestructibility which Cardew the political activist attributed to the working class.[14]

In the preceding pages, from time to time, the notion of 'failure' has surfaced; it was an idea which preoccupied and fascinated Cardew. Failure and Utopia, were the two most constant themes throughout his life's work. As was once said about Philip Guston, his gamble was to find 'a way to "fail" hugely' – except that Cardew did not need to seek a way; he was able to grasp, at every turn, what was intrinsic to life, and to art. Works like *Treatise* and *The Great Learning*, with which his artistic creativity reached its apogee, not to mention the Scratch Orchestra, have achieved mythological status.

In his *Critique of Judgement* Immanuel Kant calls into question the primacy of the experience of art in relation to the experience of nature; Cardew, too, in the last decade, abandoned 'a chamber where are to be found those beauties that minister to vanity or to any social joys'. But he did not turn to 'the beautiful in nature in order to find, as it were, delight for his spirit.' Rather it was to the ill-formed, to the ugly, and to the temporal he turned; to the dispossessed, to the starving, to the victims against whose suffering and degradation no work of art, according to his own moral imperatives, could claim precedence, to the average inhabitant of the planet for whom to be 'human' is a condition of unbearable and unremitting suffering.

> And yet your report shows us what is
> Needed to change the world:
> Anger and tenacity, knowledge and indignation
> Swift action, utmost deliberation
> Cold endurance, unending perseverance
> Comprehension of the individual and comprehension of the whole:
> Taught only by reality can
> Reality be changed.[15]

Cardew's Art was Life was Politics was… Art? Or was it a loss of faith? In music? In art? Joyce's desiderata for an artist's life: silence, exile, cunning, were anathema to Cardew.[16] His self-sacrificing response to moral demand, the commitment to make oneself new, is an imperative that has been stated and re-stated innumerable times in the course of Western history, culminating in the last century in the rise of messianic socialism, where yet again men strove to come to terms with, and accomplish, the monumental tasks, both spiritual and material, which had been set them. Nor was there a fall-back position, no question of 'failing better' – only, in George Steiner's words, the 'insistence of the ideal continued, with a terrible tactless force': transcendence or betrayal.

Notes and references

1 Whenever Cardew was stopped by the police, whatever the occasion, within seconds the police knew who he was: his full name and date of birth, his address, his record, etc. So the police would have known immediately at the time of the accident who it was.
2 This is Sheila Kasabova's verbatim account, which I recorded during September 2005.
3 There had always been varying degrees of tension between Cardew and his mother. Recently, there had seemed to be a rapprochement, a kind of reconciliation; they began to see more of each other and Mariel had agreed to visit Cornelius, Sheila and Anna for lunch, for the first time – although she had allowed them both to visit her on occasions.
4 From the aforementioned recording.
5 Ibid.
6 Letter from Jane Manning to SK, dated 23 December 1981.
7 Neither the car nor the driver was ever found.
8 I recall the late Peter Devenport telling me in conversation that in 1979, or 1980, the Metropolitan Police report for London had cited the Communist Party of Britain (Marxist-Leninist), a relatively tiny group, as the most dangerous political organisation in London. I have been unable to substantiate this.
9 Edward Fox, *The Independent* Magazine, 9 May 1992, pp. 24-29.
10 In a letter subsequent to his visit the Ambulance Service official wrote that he had asked the crew in question but they were unable to help in any way, adding that he was sorry that they could not be of any further assistance.
11 An Irish friend told Sheila Kasabova that it is shared knowledge within the Irish community that it is not uncommon for political activists to be assassinated by cars, that it was not at all unusual – in fact to her it was utterly feasible. What was of particular significance in the Sreeleeka Kazi case mentioned above was the amount of circumstantial evidence that the police had chosen to withhold. And this may well have been the case at the inquest into Cardew's death where the circumstances likewise had raised profound suspicions.
12 Harry Gilonis recalls that Cardew once said that 'being a composer is a posthumous award', but I personally never saw or heard this.
13 *Resonance* Magazine, Vol.1 No1, November 1992.
14 Rowe recalls that Cardew once pointed to a picture of a tree by Corot and, 'in a way the Party could never have understood', described it as an expression, or image, of the working class.
15 From the very end of Brecht's *The Measures Taken,* p.34.
16 When he became a communist, and in fact before, Cardew (like Kant) questioned the 'supremacy' of Art in relation to, for example, nature. I often think that Cardew's whole life was 'a work of Art' which rendered Art itself irrelevant. Hegel talked about the possibility of life beyond Art. Cardew was the nearest to this of anybody I have ever known, although I am sure many such 'meta-artists' exist in the world.

Cornelius Cardew a life unfinished

Appendix 1
From AMM's booklet for The Crypt record

Hui-sze said to Kwang-sze: 'I have a large tree which men call Ailantus Glandulosa, or the "fetid tree". Its trunk swells out to a large size, but is not fit for a carpenter to apply his line to it. When he looks up at its smaller branches they are so twisted and crooked that they cannot be made into rafters and beams, when he looks down to its root, its trunk is divided into so many rounded portions that neither coffin nor shelf could be made from it. Lick one of its leaves and your mouth feels torn and wounded. The mere smell of them makes a man frantic, as if intoxicated, for more than three whole days on end. Though it were planted in the most convenient spot beside the road no builder would turn his head to look at it. Now your words, Sir, are great, but of no use; all unite in putting them away from them.'

Kwang-sze replied: 'Can it be that you have never seen the pole-cat, how it crouches waiting for the mouse, ready to leap this way or that, high or low, till one day it lands plump on the spring of a trap and dies in the snare? And what about the Yak, so large that it is like a cloud hanging in the sky? It maintains this vast bulk but would be quite incapable of catching a mouse. You, Sir, have a large tree and are troubled because it is of no use; why do you not plant in the realm of Nothing Whatever, or in the wilds of the unpastured desert? There you might saunter idly by its side, or in the enjoyment of untroubled ease sleep and dream beneath it. Neither bill nor axe would shorten its existence; there would be nothing to injure it. What is there in its uselessness to cause you distress?' (Kwang-Sze I and IV)

Appendix 2
Cardew: 'The Story of Agatha' (1967)

This account is really a sexual reminiscence – generally speaking a disgusting class of narrative. Since it fringes on Galactic Data and Research, however, my conscience has overstruggled my repulsion and I have decided to enword it for the benefit of whosoever may find interest or profit in it. My concern for such purely hypothetical beings is not entirely philanthropic. I am assuming that anyone who finds interest or profit in my story is for that reason alone a member of what I call my tribe. Again a purely hypothetical collection. Scattered throughout the Universe I imagine a sparse collection of individuals who own the same beliefs and observe the same rituals as I do myself. Part of the dream is that we shall be reunited – in pairs, groups or as a whole. Reunited is wrong, for members all start from different points, with different backgrounds, different skins, different languages, etc. So a meeting is an end rather than a beginning, and rarely lasts long – communication is on a primeval level of mere recognition since the divergent cultures of the members makes a sophisticated interchange impossible. And it could never be protracted because no community (of the tribe) exists to support such a relationship, so I guess one just shakes hands and passes on – it seems inadequate somehow.

However, my tribe has nothing to do with my story, only with the telling of it. The story concerns an expedition to a system whose name and number are unimportant. Conditions on one planet approximated to our own and that was sufficient reason for the foundation of the expedition. I accepted my appointment to the post of psychometric suggestibility counter class AM(M) in silence assuming that some error was responsible and not wishing to negate it by admitting my total lack of qualifications. I later heard from a high-up eccentric on the Commission of the Expedition that I had been included for the specific purpose of 'smelling' the planet. Whether I actually succeeded in smelling it to the satisfaction of my superiors and if so how they extracted the smell-data from me afterwards (or at the time) are points that are still completely obscure to me. Perhaps this story is the revelation the Commission has been waiting for; I certainly seemed to get a real whiff of the planet through the events I am about to describe.

As soon as I stepped out on the planet I felt a great surge of joy at having a body to be alive in. Something to do with the air probably: just like home only more so. The expedition quickly made contact with the locals, a dignified and rustic race with no technology and no desire for it. They subsisted in about all regions of the planet in similar, very slightly interdependent communities. The expedition's dome, in which we disported ourselves amongst all our research paraphernalia and in which I had my small appointed space, was probably the nearest thing to a community centre, or village, that the planet had ever seen. I progressively spent less and less time in the dome, however, finding no profitable employment amongst the gadgetry. I preferred to walk about the erratic network of lanes that served the countryside, sniffing the local flora, and I soon found that the locals spent much of their time in similar pursuit.

It was in chance meetings on these strolls that I made the acquaintance of two locals whom I shall call Gladys and Agatha for the sake of convenience in narrative. I prefer to make them feminine and leave my own sex in doubt rather than declare myself a man and leave their sex in doubt. In fact I never formed a precise idea of the biological make-up of the race: I am certain there were more than two sexes, but the differences between them were much subtler than in our own species. I do not even know if Gladys and Agatha were of the same sex.

When I first came upon Gladys she was walking some distance ahead of me, moving in the same direction as I. She walked with a beautiful irregular random rhythm; her walk seemed phrased. As I came closer the colour of her skin changed, gradually but more and more markedly. I reached her at the end of a phrase; she was at rest when I finally touched her, and at my touch her colour instantaneously reverted to normal. At that moment the colour of a blue roadside flower seemed to jump out at me – it was the exact colour she had changed to, and at the instant that she reverted the flower leapt up to fill the empty space in the spectrum. We proceeded and I began to learn the rhythm of her walk. Our subsequent walks were like marvellously pleasant exercises in counterpoint. Walking was her language (or rather one of her languages, for I later found that she had several) and I came to understand it. After some time our intertwined phrasing brought us to her home: a very natural home, a sort of cave, but with a fire and a hole for smoke to escape, and various utensils for concocting the liquids that formed Gladys' only sustenance. I suppose the preparation and consumption of these liquids were another of her languages, but I never attempted to master it; for it quickly transpired that she was a musician and the language of her music required very little learning on my part. She had six instruments; three of them stringed and three of them for blowing. She bowed the stringed instruments with her arm (the arms of these creatures were provided with a rather rough ridge, slightly elastic, on the inside) and applied the wind instruments to an aperture like a navel in her body through which she breathed. I used to pluck the stringed instruments and later found a trick of blowing the wind instruments orally.

So after a walk we would come to Gladys' home, share some of her liquid (which I found mildly intoxicating) and then each selecting an instrument we would sit before the fire and play, often for a very long time, never tiring and yet sometimes resting singly to listen to the eloquence of the other. Inspired by hers, I found more eloquence in myself than I had dreamt was there and sometimes after listening to me silently for a while she would take up her smallest stringed instrument and start bowing a high note very quietly. This produced an extaordinary effect on me – I found myself executing passages where I really did not know what I was saying, as though recounting adventures that I had never experienced. Whether blowing or plucking, the music seemed to go beyond my control and I moved towards a state of unconsciousness until she gradually came down off her high note. Afterwards she would walk-dance me back to the dome. She would never come right up to it on account of her colour changing in its proximity as it had on the occasion of my first meeting her. I came to regard this colour change as a symptom of some kind of embarrassment towards our species and its works, quickly negated in the case of myself (surely she was of my tribe) but never overcome in relation to the generality of our kind.

And how did I first meet Agatha? The chronology of my acquaintance with Agatha is all confused. I never really understood any of her languages – colour changing was one of her most fluent, to judge by the speed at which she 'spoke' it. All these terms are wickedly metaphoric. Could love have been the language we had in common? We certainly communicated. She had one faculty which I never detected in any other of her species: Agatha could sing. I used to lie for hours with my ear glued to her navel listening to an endless stream of melody. I used to use strands of it as best I could when playing with Gladys and if Agatha was there you would notice her colours brighten and change in tune with her own melodies. If Agatha participated in our music it was always with her colours, she would never sing with us. Her singing was an unconscious utterance that she had no control over. Perhaps it was at Gladys' house that I first met Agatha. I am sure they were acquainted long before I knew either of them.

I suppose 'garrulous' is the only word to describe Agatha's activity with colour. She was never the colour that I had come to regard as the norm in Gladys. Only her eyes never changed colour – they were always a light and lustrous brown when Gladys and I were playing. Agatha would move around mysteriously, sometimes huddling up before the fire, sometimes elongating herself between and around us, all the while displaying strange colours which would often seem to influence the music. Once while Gladys was sitting silent I got carried away by the play of colours. Agatha was probably responding to the play of notes equally. On this occasion when Gladys brought in her high drone I actually did gently and gradually lose consciousness, the while dimly aware of peculiar movements and mixtures of language amongst the two of them, accompanied by a sensation of envelopment. When I came to, Agatha was a truly amazing sight, radiant with colours winking on and off and glowing all over her lovely body. She was tendering me a cup of a liquid that I had never tasted before. That night I had to walk back under the stars to the dome alone, as Gladys and Agatha were so involved in a complex celebratory interchange as to exclude all else.

The next day they both had presents for me. Gladys gave me an instrument which I treasure and use to this day, and Agatha gave me a baby! I could not exactly take possession of it as it was still attached to its mother by a long liana-like cord, but the gesture with which Agatha handed it to me left no room for doubt as to whose it was. A beautiful gift, a sweet friendly organism that I had no difficulty in relating to. It was generally spherical but quite intricate in structure, and remained for a long time attached to its mother by the cord (I do not know how long this attachment lasted as I did not witness its termination). It perforce accompanied us on all our subsequent walks, requiring very little tending, rolling about and bouncing playfully around us, miraculously refraining from tangling us in its cord. It was with us the day big drops of rain drove us into a beautiful wood and it was playing amongst the flowers beside my lover's head as she showed me the possibility of our making love – demonstrated in fact what had happened during my unconsciouness that night preceding her gift to me. That half-sheltering hollow in the wood harbouring the wavering column of my Agatha as she showed me the way. As I penetrated her I saw the eyes change; the vortical facets that usually rendered them kaleidoscopic dissolved into a pure band of reflection, with the lovely brown overlaid with the bright green of trees and the deep blue of the sky. And reflected in her eyes I saw the stars of the galaxy in their strange configurations and picked out my home star. And indeed in that action I was really home, wriggling a bit and stretching myself as might be to test the dimensions of some house unvisited since childhood.

Since I returned with the expedition I have never again experienced the sensation of home, though it is at home I sit, day by day, amongst many relics and emblems of a familiar past.

Shortly after my return I took up my instrument – Gladys' gift – and sent a letter:

Dear Agatha,

To this message – though it was sent to its destination on the brightest beam of the most powerful transmitters our science can provide – I received no reply.

Appendix 3
Firelighting Component from Paragraph 5 of The Great Learning

The following inspirational text is from the book of Kwang-Sze, XIV. 3, translated from the Chinese by James Legge.

Pei-măn Khăng asked Hwang-Tî, saying, 'You were celebrating, O Tî, a performance of the music of Hsien-khih, in the open country near the Thungthing lake. When I heard the first part of it I was afraid; the next made me weary; and the last perplexed me. I became agitated and unable to speak, and lost my self-possession.' The Tî said, 'It was likely that it should so affect you! It was performed with (the instruments of) men, and all attuned according to (the influences of) Heaven. It proceeded according to (the principles of) propriety and righteousness, and was pervaded by (the idea of) the Grand Purity.

'The Perfect Music first had its response in the affairs of men, and was conformed to the principles of Heaven; it indicated the action of the five virtues, and corresponded to the spontaneity (apparent in nature). After this it showed the blended distinctions of the four seasons, and the grand harmony of all things; – the succession of those seasons one after another, and the production of things in their proper order. Now it swelled, and now it died away, its peaceful and military strains clearly distinguished and given forth. Now it was clear, and now rough, as if the contracting and expanding of the elemental processes blended harmoniously (in its notes). These notes then flowed away in waves of light, till, as when the hibernating insects first begin to move, I commanded the terrifying clash of thunder. Its end was marked by no formal conclusion, and it began again without any prelude. It seemed to die away, and then it burst into life; it came to a close and then it rose again. So it went on regularly and inexhaustibly, and without the intervention of any pause: – it was this which made you afraid.

In the second part (of the performance), I made it describe the harmony of the Yin and Yang, and threw round it the brilliance of the sun and moon. Its notes were now short and now long, now soft and now hard. Their changes, however, were marked by an unbroken unity, though not dominated by a fixed regularity. They filled every valley and ravine; you might shut up every crevice, and guard your spirit (against their entrance), yet there was nothing but gave admission to them. Yea, those notes resounded slowly, and might have been pronounced high and clear. Hence the shades of the dead kept in their obscurity; the sun and moon, and all the stars of the zodiac, pursued their several courses. I made (my instruments) leave off, when (the performance) came to an end, and their (echoes) flowed on without stopping. You thought anxiously about it, and were not able to understand it; you looked for it, and were not able to see it; you pursued it, and were not able to reach it. All-amazed, you stood in the way all open around you, and then you leant against an old rotten dryandratree and hummed. The power of your eyes was exhausted by what you wished to see; your strength failed in your desire to pursue it, while I myself could not reach it. Your body was but so much empty vacancy while you endeavoured to retain your self-possession: – it was that endeavour that made you weary.

'In the last part (of the performance), I employed notes that did not have that wearing effect. I blended them together as at the command of spontaneity. Hence they came as if following one another in confusion, like a clump of plants springing from one root, or like the music of a forest produced by no visible form. They spread themselves all around without leaving a trace (of their cause); and seemed to issue from deep obscurity where there was no sound. Their movements came from nowhere; their home was in the deep darkness; – conditions which some would call death, and some life; some, the fruit, and some, (merely) the flower. Those notes, moving and flowing on, separating and shifting, and not following any regular sounds, the world might well have doubts about them, and refer them to the judgment of a sage, for the sages understand the nature of this music, and judge in accordance with the prescribed (spontaneity). While the spring of that spontaneity has not been touched, and yet the regulators of the five notes are all prepared; – this is what is called the music of Heaven, delighting the mind without the use of words. Hence it is said in the eulogy of the Lord of Piâo, "You listen for it, and do not hear its sound; you look for it and do not perceive its form; it fills heaven and earth; it envelopes all within the universe." You wished to hear it, but could not take it in; and therefore you were perplexed.

'I performed first the music calculated to awe; and you were frightened as if by a ghostly visitation. I followed it with that calculated to weary; and in your weariness you would have withdrawn: I concluded with that calculated to perplex and in your perplexity you felt your stupidity. But that stupidity is akin to the Tâo; you may with it convey the Tâo in your person, and have it (ever) with you.'

Literary works

Poems

Toil and Dreams (1974)

The Monopoly Capitalist after the Revolution (1976)

To Survey the Stars (1976)

Less and More (1976)

The Revolution is Spring 9 August (1978)

We spurn the Theory of 3 Worlds (1978)

First Congress (1978)

Working Committee (1978)

On Hearing the Message From the Irish Party 10 September (1978)

A Matter of Principle (undated)

No Title (undated)

Sons of the New Age (undated).Unattributed, probably by Cardew

Cornelius Cardew a life unfinished

Primary Sources

Cardew Estate: Cardew's Journals and Correspondence, including the two ledgers (1961-64), Lectures, Interviews and Conversations. Compositions: Peters Edition, Universal Edition, Danny Dark Records, Novello and Canadian Cultural Workers' Committee (CCWC). Original Manuscripts, Journals and Correspondence are lodged in the British Library. The British Music Information Centre in Lincoln House, London, contains a variety of Cardew scores. Many can be viewed and downloaded via the website www.bmic.co.uk and are all available for perusal by visitors to the BMIC library. Papers pertaining to the Scratch Orchestra are in the private collection of Richard Ascough. For an extensive collection of Cardew's published writings I would refer the reader to the Cardew Reader, published by Copula, an imprint of Matchless Recordings and Publishing. Its contents are listed below. The editor, Edwin Prévost, writes:

This Reader includes most of Cornelius Cardew's published writings. Many were published in newspapers and periodicals. Others appeared in books. We have also included a number of Cardew's lectures and talks. These have been mostly drawn from his notes.

'Unity of Musical Space', *New Departures*, Summer No.1 1959

'Notation – Interpretation, etc.', *Tempo*, No.58, Summer 1961

'Report on Stockhausen's *Carré* – Part 1', *Musical Times* Vol.102, No.1424, pp.619-622, October 1961

'Report on Stockhausen's *Carré* – Part 2', *Musical Times*, November 1961

'The American School of John Cage', a radio programme on Earle Brown, Morton Feldman and Christian Wolff, broadcast on Westdeutscher Rundfunk, 27 December 1962

'Autumn 60', a lecture given to the Cambridge University *Heretics' Society*, transcribed from note books. Entry dated 5 September 1962

'In re La Monte Young', *New Departures* No.4 1962

'Piano (Three Hands) – Morton Feldman', *Accent* No.4 Autumn 1962, Leeds College of Art and School of Architecture

Darmstadt 1964 'New Music has found its feet', *Financial Times*, 31 July 1964. Reprinted in the *Musical Times*, September 1964 as 'Modern Music has found its feet but on what low ground'

'Cage and Cunningham', *Musical Times*, September 1964

Rome Letter 'Nuova Consonanza', *Financial*

Times, 25 May 1965

'Composed Laughter', *New Statesman,* 10 December 1965

'Stockhausen in London', *Musical Times,* Vol.107, No.1475, pp.43-47, January 1966

'Introduction to *Four Works*', Universal Edition 1966

'Yoko Ono', *Financial Times*, 29 September 1966

'One Sound: LaMonte Young', *Musical Times,* Vol.107, No.1485, pp.959-960

'Stockhausen's *Plus-Minus*' and 'The Sounds of La Monte Young', *London Magazine,* April 1967

Sextet – *The Tiger's Mind, Musical Times*, Vol.108, No.14935, pp.618-619, June 1967

'Sitting in the dark', *Musical Times*, Vol.109, No.1501, pp.233-234, March 1968

'A Scratch Orchestra: draft constitution', *Musical Times*, pp.617-619, June 1969

'The Rite: Advice', *Pages* No.2 Winter 1970

Treatise Handbook, published by Edition Peters (Hinrichsen Edition Ltd), 1971. Original publication also includes *Bun No.2* and *Volo Solo*.

A talk for BBC radio (not broadcast). Probably 1971.

Scratch Music 1972, *New Dimensions,* Latimer, London 1972

Stockhausen Serves Imperialism, *New Dimensions*, Latimer, London 1974

'The Situation and Prospects of Art Students Today', a talk given at Falmouth College of Art on 13 June 1974 and again at the School of the Art Institute of Chicago on 8 January 1975

'Cornelius Cardew – interviewed by Adrian Jack' *Music and Musicians*, Vol.23, May 1975

'A note on Frederic Rzewski', *Musical Times,* Vol.117, No.1598, p.32, January 1976

'Struggle Sounds', *Time Out*, 16 January 1976

'Wiggly Lines and Wobbly Music', *Studio International*, Vol.192, No.984, pp.249-255, November/December 1976

'Role of the composer in the class struggle', transcribed from a handwritten text, delivered as a talk – probably 1978

'Speech of Party representative at Internationalist Youth Concert', London, 9 August 1980

Programme notes for *Piano Album 1973*, Cornelius Cardew Foundation, 1991

Selected Secondary Sources

Books, films, broadcasts, theses, essays, articles, reviews, programmes, letters and interviews. I apologize for the parochial limitations of the following selection, almost exclusively from the United Kingdom and North America. Of course, around the world people have been performing, recording and writing about Cardew, but to incorporate this material would have extended my brief beyond the realms of possibility. Perhaps such endeavours have already been undertaken and in years to come there will be a universal compilation of Cardew scholarship. This selection also includes the 'commentaries' listed in the Cardew Reader.

Aharonián, Coriún, 'Cardew as a basis for a discussion on ethical options', *Leonardo Music Journal*, vol.11, Cambridge (Massachusetts), 2001

Anderson, Virginia, *British Experimental Music: Cornelius Cardew and His Contemporaries*, Master of Music thesis, The University of Redlands, California, August 1983

Anderson, Virginia, recorded interview with Bryn Harris, 15 April 1983

Austin, Larry, 'Forum Improvisation', Reprint from *Perspectives of New Music,* Fall-Winter 1982, Spring-Summer 1983, Vol. 21, Nos. 1 & 2, 27-33

Bains, Hardial, *Combat This Growing Fascism* (Toronto: Norman Bethune Institute, 1976)

Barrett, Richard, 'Cornelius Cardew' in Finnissy, M. & Wright, R. (eds.) *New Music 87*, Oxford University Press, 1987 (*CCR*)

Barry, Malcolm, 'Bedford, Cardew and Henze', *Music and Musicians*, May 1979

Bedford, David, 'an appreciation', *Performance* magazine, April-May 1982

Bedford, David and Cardew, Cornelius, 'A Conversation', *Musical Times*, Vol.107, No.1477, pp.198-200, 202, March 1966

Boenisch, Hanne, *Cornelius Cardew and the Scratch Orchestra – Journey to the North Pole*, a film produced with support from the Munich Academy for Film and Television, and Bavarian Television, Munich, in 1971/72

Bradshaw, Susan, 'Cornelius Cardew (1936-1981)', *Tempo*, New Series, No.140, March 1982

Bright, Greg, *Visual Music* (London: Latimer, 1975)

Cardew, Cornelius, interviewed by Keith Potter: 'Some Aspects of a Political Attitude', *Contact 10,* Winter 1975-76

Cardew, Michael, *A Pioneer Potter* (Oxford: Oxford University Press, 1989)

Churches, Richard, *From Improvisation to Revolution; a History of* the Scratch

Orchestra (1969-1972) – *its Origins and Development up to and including the Period of Discontent* (Unpublished)

Connolly, Justin, 'Cardew's *Great Learning*', *Tempo* no. 86, Autumn 1968

Cook, Nicholas, *Music, Imagination and Culture*, (Oxford: Clarendon Press, 1999)

Dennis, Brian, 'Music in Our Time', *Musical Times*, Vol.111, No.1534, December 1970

Dennis, Brian, 'Cardew's *The Great Learning*', *Musical Times*, Vol.112, No.1546, pp.1066-1068, November 1971 (*CCR*)

Dennis, Brian, 'Intermodulation, Scratch Orchestra', *Musical Times*, No.1538, pp.355-363, April 1971

Dennis, Brian, 'Cardew's *Treatise* (mainly the visual aspects)', *Tempo* No.177, June 1991 (*CCR*)

Dusman, Linda J., 'The Individual as Structure in Cornelius Cardew's *The Great Learning*: Paragraph 7, *Interface*, Vol.16 (1987), pp.201-217

Eley, Rod, 'A History of the Scratch Orchestra, 1969-72', in *Stockhausen serves Imperialism*

Eno, Brian, 'Generating and Organising Variety in the Arts', *Studio International*, Vol.192, No.984, pp.270-283, November-December 1976

Feldman, Morton, *Give My Regards to Eighth Street: Collected Writings of Morton Feldman*, (ed. B.H. Friedman) (Cambridge, MA: Exact Change, 2000)

Feldman, Morton, *Morton Feldman Essays* (Kerpen, Germany: Beginner Press, 1985)

Fowler, Luke, *Pilgrimage from Scattered Points*, a film funded by the Dewar Arts Award, 2006

Fox, Christopher, 'Cornelius Cardew 1936-1981', CD notes: *Cornelius Cardew chamber music 1955-64*, Matchless Recordings MRCD45, 2001 (*CCR*)

Hampshire, Sophie, 'Language, Representation and Rules: a study of Wittgenstein's theories of language and their relevance to visual art and music'. Undergraduate Thesis for the London Institute (1991).

Hobbs, Christopher, 'Cardew as Teacher', *Perspectives of New Music*, Vol.xvii, January 1981

Hobbs, Christopher, 'Cardew' in Vinton, John (ed.) *Dictionary of Twentieth Century Music* (London: Thames and Hudson,1974)

Hopkins, G.W., '3 Winter Potatoes', *Musical Times*, Vol.108, No.1494, p.739, August 1967

Jack, Adrian, 'Cornelius Cardew' (interview), *Music and Musicians*, May 1975

Karlgren, Bernhard, *The Book of Odes* (Stockholm: Museum of Far Eastern Antiquities, 1950)

Keller, Hans, a conversation with Cardew in a BBC *New Comment* programme, 19 September 1963

Keller, Hans, 'Thinkers of the world, disunite!' *Books and Bookmen,* Part 1 in Vol.20, No.9 (June 1975), part 2 in Vol.20, No.12 (September), and part 3 in Vol.21, No.1 (October)

Larner, Gerald, 'Cheltenham', *Musical Times,* Vol.109, No.1509, pp.1033-1040, September 1968

Lukoszevieze, Anton, 'Cornelius Cardew – Early Works' from CD notes: *Cornelius Cardew chamber music 1955-64*, Matchless Recordings MRCD45, 2001 (*CCR*)

Mann, William, 'Arts Laboratory', *Musical Times*, Vol.105, No.1501, pp.249-255, March 1968

Northcott, Bayan, 'Modern Proms', *Music and Musicians*, Vol.21, No.3, November 1972

Nyman, Michael, 'believe it or not melody rides again', *Music and Musicians*, Vol.20, No.2, p.28, October 1971

Nyman, Michael, 'Cardew's *The Great Learning*', *London Magazine*, Vol.11, No.5, p.134, December 1971/January 1972 (*CCR*)

Nyman, Michael, 'Cage/Cardew', *Tempo*

No.107, December 1973

Nyman, Michael, *Experimental Music* (London: Studio Vista, 1974, reprinted Cambridge: Cambridge University Press, 1999)

Parsons, Michael, 'Avant-garde operas?', *Musical Times*, Vol.109, No.1503, pp.446-452, May 1968

Parsons, Michael, 'Sounds of Discovery', *Musical Times*, Vol.109, No.1503, pp.429-430, May 1968

Parsons, Michael 'Cardew' In *New Grove Dictionary of Music and Musicians* (London: Macmillan,1980), (update in *Grove Music Online*, 2007)

Parsons, Michael, *The Scratch Orchestra and Visual Arts*; Leonardo Music Journal Vol.11, 2001. German translation: *Das Scratch Orchestra und die visuellen Künste;* Positionen 45/46, November 2000 / February 2001.

Parsons, Michael, *The Scratch Orchestra: 25th Anniversary*, in Resonance, Volume 3 No.1, Winter 1994

Parsons, Michael, Skempton, Howard, Smith, Dave, Tilbury, John, contributors to the programme for the first complete performance of *The Great Learning* at the Union Chapel in north London, July 1984 (*CCR*)

Phillips, Jill, 'New Music' *Musical Times*, Vol.110, No.1513, April 1969

Phillips, Tom (interview), *Studio International*, Vol.192, No.984, pp.290-296, November/December 1976

Potter, Keith, 'Boulez and Stockhausen, Bennett and Cardew', *Musical Times*, Vol.122, No.1657, pp.170-171, March 1981

Pound, Ezra, *The Cantos of Ezra Pound* (London: Faber and Faber, 1987)

Prévost, Edwin, 'Improvisation', Cornelius Cardew Memorial Concert programme, 16 May 1982 (*CCR*)

Prévost, Edwin, *No Sound is Innocent* (Harlow UK: Copula, 1995)

Prévost, Edwin, *Minute Particulars* (Harlow UK: Copula, 2004)

Prevost, Edwin, and Rowe, Keith, 'AMM: Eddie Prevost, Keith Rowe', *Perspectives of New Music*, Fall-Winter 1982, Spring-Summer 1983, Vol. 21 Nos. 1 & 2

Progressive Cultural Association (PCA), 'Cornelius Cardew – Composer, Communist and Fighter for the People's Cause', in the Cornelius Cardew Memorial Concert Programme, 16 May 1982

Regniez, Phillipe, Film: *Cornelius Cardew 1936 – 1981* (Arts Council of Great Britain, 1986)

Richards, Sam, *john cage as...* (Charlbury, Oxford: Amber Lane Press, 1996)

Ryan, David, 'Cornelius Cardew – Four Indeterminate Works', CD notes: *Cornelius Cardew chamber music 1955-64*, Matchless Recordings MRCD45, 2001 (amended October 2005) (*CCR*)

Schwertsik, Kurt, '...*for* CORNELIUS CARDEW', *Tempo*, New Series, No.140, March 1982

Skempton, Howard 'A Tribute to Cornelius Cardew', *Tempo*, New Series, No.140, March 1982

Smalley, Roger, 'Unconventional Conventions', *Musical Times*, Vol.108, No.1497, pp.1029-1030, November 1967

Smalley, Roger, 'A beautiful score', *Musical Times*, Vol.109, No.1503, May 1968

Smalley, Roger, 'The New Music' (in Music Reviews), *Musical Times*, Vol.113, No.1552, pp.593-595, June 1972

Smalley, Roger, Experimental Music, *Musical Times*, Vol.116, No.1583, pp.23-26, January 1975

Souster, Tim 'Three Music Now programmes', *Tempo*, No.89, Summer 1969

Szczelkun, Stefan, letter to Brian Dennis, July 6 1994

Szczelkun, Stefan, *Noisegate,* Vol.1, No.10 (London ISSN 1367613X, 2002)

Taylor, Timothy, 'Moving in Decency: The Music and Radical Politics of Cornelius Cardew', *Music and Letters*, Vol.79, No.4, pp.555-576, November 1998

Tilbury, John, *Ark* 45 [Royal College of Art magazine] Winter 1969

Tilbury, John and Parsons, Michael, 'The Contemporary Pianist', *Musical Times*, Vol.110, No.1512, pp.150-152, February 1969

Tilbury, John, 'The Experimental Years: A View from the Left', *Contact*, No.22, pp.16-21, Summer 1981

Tilbury, John, 'Cornelius Cardew', *Contact*, No.26, pp.4-12, Spring 1983 (*CCR*)

Tilbury, John, 'Cornelius Cardew', *Grove Music Online*, ed. L. Macy (www.grovemusic.com)

Tilbury, John, 'The Music', in the Cornelius Cardew Memorial Concert Programme, 16 May 1982

Tilbury, John, 'John Tilbury's Volo Solo', Macnaghten Concerts, London, 1970-1

Tilbury, John, 'Some Reflections on Cardew's John Cage: Ghost or Monster?', *Leonardo Music Journal*, Vol.8, pp.66-68, 1998 (*CCR*)

White, John, from a Radio Programme on the Scratch Orchestra on BBC Radio 3, 27 September 1987

Wolff, Christian, from 'Dedications', in Cornelius Cardew Memorial Concert Programme, 16 May 1982

Wolff, Christian, 'Briefly on Cornelius Cardew and John Cage', *Cues, Writings and Conversations* (Cologne: Edition MusikTexte 1998) (*CCR*)

'25 Years from Scratch', programme from event at the ICA in London on 20 November 1994

Visual Anthology (London: Experimental Music Catalogue, 1974)

(*CCR*) Also found in *Cornelius Cardew A Reader*

List of Compositions

The publisher for an individual work is indicated as follows: Peters Edition (PE). Universal Edition (UE). Danny Dark Records (DDR), Canadian Cultural Workers' Committee (CCWC).

With reference to the political songs written during the seventies, these were sung solo or by unison voices. Most of them were provided with piano accompaniments which may or may not have been used. Furthermore, in relation to the authorship of some of these songs a problem arises from the fact that not a few of them were written collectively – such that a song attributed to Cardew may have features which were suggested by a colleague, and vice versa. Where this has been established by those concerned I have noted it in my discussions of the music.

The British Music Information Centre in Lincoln House, London, contains a variety of Cardew scores. Many can be viewed and downloaded via the website www.bmic.co.uk and all are available for perusal by visitors to the Bmic Library.

1948
Chorale: 'On Another's Sorrow', setting of a poem by William Blake. Date, c.1948, according to Seth Cardew, but may be a little later

1952
Prometheus Unbound
for small ensemble and voices

1953
Three Early English Lyrics
for treble voice, clarinet and viola

1954
Canto VII (Ezra Pound)
for unaccompanied tenor
First String trio * (PE)
Introduction, Theme and Variations and Coda for two pianos
Kyrie for two sopranos and ensemble
Little Suite for piano solo
Six Variations in F on a Swiss Air for piano solo
Songs for counter tenor with guitar accompaniment
Two Mirror Studies for cello solo
Variations for two pianos

1955
Fantasia for 2 pianos
Piano Pieces for piano solo
Piano Sonata No.1
Recitative and Aria for piano solo
Second String Trio (PE)
Short Pieces for piano duet (for Ruth)
Three Rhythmic Pieces for Trumpet
and Piano
Three Short Piano Pieces for piano solo
Variations (or *Viola sextet*)
    for viola, flute, clarinet, bassoon, horn
    and double bass

1956
Duets for Ruth for two pianos
Fantasy for mezzo soprano and string quartet
First Rhythmic study for mechanically
    controlled instrument
Flute and String Trio (incomplete)
Mikrokosmos for Orchestra
Piano Sonata No.2
Study for mezzo-soprano, vibraphone and
    guitar

1957
Quintet 1957 (transparencies only)
Septet with Percussion
String trio (for Seth's birthday)
Untitled piece for piano solo
'Voice from Thel's Grave' (from William
    Blake's 'The Book of Thel') for voice and
    piano

1958
Piano Sonata No.3
Two Books of Study for Pianists (PE)

1959
Ansatz for two pianos
February piece I (PE)
Octet 1959 (PE)

1960
Arrangement for Orchestra (PE)

Autumn 60 (UE)
February piece II (PE)
February piece III (PE)
Third Orchestral Piece (PE)

1961
February Pieces (complete) (PE)
First Movement for String Quartet (PE)
for Stella for solo guitar
Octet '61 for Jasper Johns (PE)

1962
Ah Thel for mixed chorus with optional piano
    accompaniment. Published by Novello
Movement for Orchestra (PE)

1964
Bun No.2 for Orchestra (PE)
Material for any ensemble of harmony
    instruments (UE)
Memories of You for piano solo (UE)
Solo with Accompaniment for any solo
    instrument and accompanist(s) (UE)

1965
Bun for Orchestra No.1 (PE)
Three Winter Potatoes for piano solo (UE)
Volo Solo for virtuoso performer(s) on any
    instrument(s) (PE)

1967
Sextet—The Tiger's Mind (PE)
Treatise (1963-67) (PE)

1968
Film music for *Who is Oscar Niemeyer,*
    directed by William Brayne, produced by
    Allan King Associates.
Schooltime Compositions
Schooltime Special
The Great Learning Paragraph 1 (DDR)

1969
The Great Learning Paragraphs 2, 6 and 7
    (DDR)

1970
The Great Learning Paragraphs 3, 4 and 5
  (DDR)
Unintended Piano Music

1971
Fight Sterilization! (moral and physical) by the
  lackeys of Imperialism for chorus, solo
  trumpet, solo trombone, and a band of
  miscellaneous instruments
Octet '71 for alto flute, oboe, clarinet, tuba,
  harp, guitar, banjo, violin, viola and cello
'Soon' for unaccompanied voice(s).
  Text, 'A single spark can start a prairie
  fire', by Mao Tse-tung
Strindberg film music
10,000 nails in the coffin of Imperialism
  for an unspecified number of performers
Sweet FA Opera in five Acts for a chorus of
  32 voices, 5 speakers, flute, oboe,
  clarinet, tuba, tubular Bells, 5 drums, cello,
  and stereo tape playback equipment

1972
The East is Red for violin and piano (DDR)
Three Bourgeois Songs
  for voice and piano (DDR)

1973
'Bethanien Lied'. Words by the Bethanien
  campaign committee. Music by Cardew
'Four Principles on Ireland'.
  Words and music by Cardew
'Lied der Anti-Imperialisten'. Text in German
'Long Live Chairman Mao'. Text probably
  from a Chinese source. Music by Cardew
Piano Album 1973 (DDR)
Statement of May 20th 1970' ('Revolution is
  the main trend in the world today').
  Text by Mao Tse-tung

1974
Piano Album 1974 (DDR)
Thälmann Sonata
  for violin and percussion (DDR)

Thälmann Variations for piano solo (DDR)

1975
'A Law of History'. Words and music by Cardew
A Suite of Wolff Tunes arr. Cardew:
  'It is Said', 'Of All Things', 'After a Few
  Years', 'Wake Up'
'Consciously'.
  Words and music by Cardew
'Nothing to Lose but our Chains', or
  'Chains', or 'Winning the World'.
  Words and music by Cardew
'Resistance Blues'.
  Words and music by Cardew

1976
Four songs from Brecht's Exception and the
  Rule: 'The Weak Lag Behind', 'Sick Men Die',
  'This is How', 'That's How It Should Be'.
One song, 'Change the World', from
  Brecht's Measures Taken
'United' (or 'The Enemy').
  Date uncertain
Vietnam Sonata for solo piano.
  (Part of the second movement,
  was composed by Dave Smith.)
Vietnam's Victory for Brass Quintet

1977
Mountains for bass clarinet solo
'Smash The Social Contract'.
  Words and music by Cardew

1978
'Ford Workers song'.
  Written by Cardew and Peter Devenport
'Our Party's First congress'.
  Words and music by Cardew
  (see 'The Founding of the Party'.)
Pakistan for oboe solo
  (date conjectural)

1979
'Great Indian People' for solo voice.
  Words and Music by Cardew

'I want my rights – "Husband Right" and
  "Father Right" ' Canadian Text (CCWC)
'Revisionist Somersaults and the
  Opportunist Opposition'
  Canadian Text (CCWC)
'The Founding of The Party'
  (Revision of 'Our Party's First Congress').
  Words and music by Cardew
The Worker's Song for solo violin (DDR)
'We are the Workers of Ontario'
  Canadian Text (CCWC)
'We Sing For The Future'
  Canadian Text (CCWC)
  'An Opportunist has come back home'
  Canadian Text (CCWC)

1980
'CYUB Song'.
  Words and music by Cardew and Peter
  Devenport
There is only one lie for SATB and piano
  accompaniment.
  Canadian Text (CCWC)
We Sing for the Future for piano solo (DDR)

1981
Boolavogue for two Pianos (DDR)
'The Festival'
  Canadian Text (CCWC)
'Somebody spilled the beans'
  Author of text not known (CCWC)

Arrangements
In the seventies Cardew wrote a number
of arrangements. These included Verdi's
'Chorus of Hebrew Slaves' from *Nabucco*;
'Golden Mountain in Peking' – a traditional
Tibetan melody; 'The Red Flag', a small
group of revolutionary Chinese songs;
an Albanian song – 'The Little Partisan';
Peter Devenport's song – 'The Dream
of the Old Generations is Young and
Fresh'; Alec Hill's setting of Mao Tse-tung's
text – 'The Proletariat seeks to transform
the world'; and some Canadian and Irish
songs. Some of these are referred to in
the previous pages. They are mainly quite
functional, with little or no elaboration,
and were written for a particular (political)
occasion, or campaign, using whatever
forces were available.

Cardew Discography

Cornelius Cardew *Chamber Music 1955-64*
Apartment House Ensemble
*Solo with Accompaniment, Three Rhythmic
Pieces for Trumpet and Piano, Autumn '60*
(two versions), *Material* (two versions),
*Second String Trio, Piece for Guitar
(for Stella), Memories of You, Octet '61
for Jasper Johns*
Recorded 2001
Matchless Recordings MRCD 45

Piano Avant-Garde
David Tudor: piano
Includes Cardew's *Piano Sonata No 3* (1958)
hatART CD 618

Cornelius Cardew piano music 1959-70
John Tilbury: piano (Eddie Prévost:
percussion guests on last track)
*February Piece 1959, February Piece 1960,
February Piece 1961, Volo Solo, Unintended
Piano Music, Winter Potato No 1, Winter
Potato No 2, Winter Potato No 3, Material,
Treatise* (excerpt). Recorded 1996
Matchless Recordings MRCD29

Cornelius Cardew, *Material*
Ensemble conducted by Art Lange
Autumn 60, Treatise (pages 21 & 22), *Memories
of You, Material, Octet for Jasper Johns*

Recorded 2001
hat [now] ART CD 150

Rara Leo Brouwer (guitar)
Includes Cardew's *Material*
Deutsche Grammophon DGG Echo 20/21

*Cornelius Cardew – Memorial Concert
First Movement for String Quartet, Octet '71,
Treatise* (excerpt), *The Great Learning,*
(Paragraph I), 'The Turtledove' (from *Three
Bourgeois Songs*), *The Workers' Song,
Thälmann Variations*, 'Croppy Boy',
'Watkinson's Thirteens', 'Smash the Social
Contract', *There is only one lie*, 'We Sing
for the Future'
Performed by a variety of Cardew's friends
and colleagues 16 May 1982
Impetus double LP IMP 28204

Recordings of *Treatise*

Historische Aufnahmen 1968-1998
Ensemble Neue Horizonte Bern
One single page of *Treatise,*
performed by Peter Streiff (vcl, perc, zither)
Musiques Suisses MGB CTS-M 76.
[Second CD, 3rd track (3:17)]

Goodbye 20th Century
Sonic Youth (Kim Gordon, Thurston Moore,
Lee Ranaldo, Steve Shelley) plus Takehisa
Kosugi, Jim O'Rourke and William Winant.
Instrumentation unspecified
Compilation of many 20th century avant
garde works includes a short extract from
Treatise (p.183)
Double LP and double CD
Sonic Youth Records SYR4

Combine+Laminates+Treatise '84
AMM (Eddie Prévost/Keith Rowe/John Tilbury)
a concert recorded at Arts Club, Chicago,
25 May 1984. Two improvisations and a
32:07 extract from *Treatise*
Matchless Recordings MRCD26

Treatise
1998 recording of complete score performed
by ensemble conducted by Art Lange
hat[now]ART CD 2-122 double CD

Unspecified extract from *Treatise*
performed by Formanex in issue 1 of the
'revue texte/son/image' *Plastic*
recorded in April 2000 at the Formanex
studio, Blockhaus DY.10, Nantes

Live in extrapool "treatise"
FORMANEX Christophe Havard: electroacoustic devices; Emmanuel Leduc: electronic
devices, feedback; Julien Ottavi: electroacoustic
devices, feedback; Anthony Taillard: guitar
Treatise pp.43, 67-69, 71, 83-85, 111-116
recorded live (in Nijmegen) 2000
ENTROPIC CD egbc 002

Treatise
FORMANEX
No personnel or instrumentation listed
but similar to other CD, plus Laurent Dailleau
(theremin, computer). Two unspecified
extracts, recorded 2002
fibrr records FIBRR 004

AMM – FORMANEX
AMM: Eddie Prévost (percussion), Keith Rowe
(guitar, electronics), John Tilbury (piano)
Formanex: Christophe Havard: soprano & tenor
saxophones, amplified objects; Emmanuel
Leduc: electronics; Julien Ottavi: percussion
and electronics; Anthony Taillard: guitar and
bass plus Laurent Dailleau: theremin, aks
analogue synthesizer; John White: bass
trombone, piano
Recorded live 2002
fibrr records 006

AMPLIFY 2002: balance box set.
Seven Guitars live in Tokyo, 2002
Treatise pages 82-84, played by Keith Rowe:
guitar, electronics with Tetuzi Akiyama:
amplified acoustic guitar; Oren Ambarchi:
guitar, electronics; Toshimaru Nakamura:
electric guitar; Yoshihide Otomo: electric
guitar; Burkhard Stangl: electric & acoustic
guitars and Taku Sugimoto: electric guitar.
Extract from *Treatise* lasts 38:25
One CD in a 7-CD set
Erstwhile 033-040

Treatise
Yorkshire COMA Ensemble,
dir. John Tilbury
Treatise pp.1-14, 16-19, 42-44, 63-64, 84-
85, 89, 91, 150, 168, 183, 187-193 & 190
COMA COMALCD002

Low Dynamic Orchestra
Kjell Nordeson, percussion; Sten Sandell,
piano/harmonium; Amit Sen, cello;
Peter Söderberg, lute/theorbo/
guitar; Stefano Scodanibbio, double bass.
CD released 2006; contains an extract
from *Treatise* (3:45)
Alice Musik ALCD 026

AMM

'Live at the Royal College of Art', 28 March 1966 (6:24 extract) Cardew/Lou Gare/ Eddie Prévost/Keith Rowe/Lawrence Sheaff One track on compilation CD *Not necessarily 'English Music'* Electronic Music Foundation EMF CD 036

AMMMusic -1966 Cornelius Cardew, piano, cello and transitor radio; Lou Gare, tenor saxophone and violin; Eddie Prévost, percussion; Keith Rowe, electric guitar and transistor radio, Lawrence Sheaff, cello, accordion, clarinet and transistor radio Elektra 256 EUK 7256 Rereleased as a CD with additional material in 1989 ReR Megacorp ReRAMMCD

Live Electronic Music (1968) treated excerpts from the Crypt concert (see later entry). This LP also features Musica Elettronica Viva. Mainstream MS-5002

An afflicted man's musica box A compilation album released in 1982. Contains AMM track 'Commonwealth Institute 20 April 1967'. No personnel/instrumentation listed United Dairies UD012

AMM – The Crypt 12 June 1968 (1981) 2 LP box set – Matchless Recordings MR5. Re-released as a double CD *The Crypt – 12th June 1968 the complete session* Matchless Recordings MRCD05

LAMINAL An AMM thirty years retrospective three CD box set. Cardew appears, with Gare, Hobbs, Prévost and Rowe, on the first CD: *The Aarhus Sequences* which was recorded in 1969 Matchless Recordings MRCD31

The Great Learning

Cornelius Cardew: The Great Learning The Scratch Orchestra Paragraphs 2 and 7. The Scratch Orchestra/Conductor Cornelius Cardew. Recorded on February 15/16 1971 at Chappell Studio, London Deutsche Grammophon 2561 107

The Great Learning Paragraphs 1, 2 and 7 Paragraph 1 from the London Cardew memorial concert at the Queen Elizabeth Hall 16 May 1982. Paragraphs 2 and 7 reissue of the Deutsche Grammophon recordings organ of Corti (Corti 21)

Bedford: Two Poems; Cardew: The Great Learning CD re-release of the material first issued on DG 2561 107 plus David Bedford's *Two Poems for Chorus on Words of Kenneth Patchen* Deutsche Grammophon 471 572-2

'Ode Machine No.2' arr Rowe appears on *A Dimension of Perfectly Ordinary Reality* (7:28); '73, an improvisation by Rowe, includes a version of a page of *Treatise* Matchless Recordings MRCD19

Bloody Amateurs Unknown Public compilation CD includes two extracts from *The Great Learning* Para. 3 (1:58) & Par. 4 (2:25) from the first complete performance at the Almeida Festival in 1984 CD UP14

The Scratch Orchestra

London, 1969 The Scratch Orchestra Two sections from the first Scratch Orchestra concert given at Hampstead Town

Hall, London on 1 November 1969.
Issued as a 10" EP in a limited edition of
100 copies in November 1999.
Die Stadt DS23

'Pilgrimage from scattered points on the
surface of the body to the brain, the inner
ear, the heart and the stomach' (7:15 extract)
The Scratch Orchestra, recorded London,
1970. One track on compilation
Not necessarily 'English Music'
Electronic Music Foundation EMF CD 036

Thurston Moore/John Tilbury
*Concerto for Guitar and Posthumous
Scratch Orchestra* (12:20), on a compilation
CD given away with *Resonance* magazine
Performers: Moore on guitar plus live tape
manipulation by Tilbury, Sophie Hampshire,
Bryn Harris and Michael Parsons
RESONANCE RES CD

Late Piano Music

Cornelius Cardew Piano Music:
'The Croppy Boy', 'Father Murphy', 'Four
Principles on Ireland', 'Charge', 'Bethanien
Song', 'Red Flag Prelude', 'Soon', 'Revolution
is the Main Trend', *Thälmann Variations*,
Boolavogue, Sing for the Future. Performed
by Cornelius Cardew (1-9), Andrew Bottrill
(11) and the duo of Andrew Ball and John
Tilbury (10) Music Now BLCD 011

'Four Principles on Ireland' and other pieces
(1974)
Cornelius Cardew: piano
'The Croppy Boy', 'Father Murphy', *Four
Principles on Ireland*, 'Charge', 'Song and
Dance', 'Sailing the Seas depends on the
Helmsman', 'Bethanien', 'Bring the Land a
New Life', 'The East is Red', 'Red Flag
Prelude', 'Soon (there will be a high tide of
revolution in our country)', 'Long Live

Chairman Mao', 'Revolution is the Main
Trend Today'
Originally released as an LP in 1975
Cramps CRSLP 6106
Later re-released as a CD
Ampersand Ampere CD07

We Sing For The Future!
Frederic Rzewski: piano
We Sing for the Future and *Thälmann
Variations* and two cadenzas by F.R.
Recorded 2001
New Albion Records NA 116 CD

Thälmann Variations
Cornelius Cardew: piano
Thälmann Variations, 'Bethanien Song',
'The Red Flag', 'Soon', 'Croppy Boy',
'Father Murphy', 'Four Principles on Ireland'
January 1975 concert recording in New York
Matchless Recordings LP MR10

Instrumental Music

Vietnam's Victory for brass ensemble
Unspecified musicians, mostly from
Goldsmiths' College, London. Conducted by
Dave Smith
On the compilation CD *ReR Quarterly Vol. 4,
No. 1*, 1994
ReR CD 0401

The Edge Of The World
Ian Mitchell: bass clarinet
Includes Cardew's *Mountains* for solo bass
clarinet with works by Christopher Hobbs,
Dave Smith, John White, Barney Childs
Black Box CD BBM1052

Songs

We Only Want The Earth
PLM tapes and songs
Cornelius Cardew/Peoples' Liberation Music
Includes six songs by Cardew: 'Revolution is
the Main Trend', 'Nothing to Lose but our
Chains', 'Smash the Social Contract', 'Law
of History', 'Four Principles on Ireland',
'Watkinson's Thirteens'
MNCD 004

Consciously, Cornelius Cardew
Peoples Liberation Music/Fight Back
Band/and others.
Includes five songs by Cardew:
'Consciously', 'We are the Workers of
Ontario', 'CYUB Song ', 'The Founding of
the Party', 'We Sing for the Future', as well
as 'The Blackleg Miner', which Cardew used
in *Boolavogue*
MNCD 009

Walter and Sabrina: We Sing For The Future
Contains a version of 'We Sing for the
Future' (Cornelius Cardew;
arr. W.Cardew/S.Moore)
Danny Dark Records CD DD1120

Arrangements by Cardew

Not necessarily 'English Music'
(compilation double-CD)
One track *Battle March* (02.07) Cornelius
Cardew piano, Jane Manning voice
Recorded at the Purcell Room, London
5 March 1974
Electronic Music Foundation EMF CD 036

Cardew performing other music

Eddie Prévost, *Silver Pyramid* Music Now
Ensemble: including Gare, Cardew, Prévost,
Rowe and others, directed by Rowe.
Recorded at The Roundhouse, London as
part of a Music Now Festival on 4 May 1969
Matchless Recordings MRCD40

Charles Ives, Four Violin Sonatas (1975)
János Négyesy violin, Cardew, piano
2 LP box set.
Thorofon ATHK 136/7

Steve Reich, Drumming
Steve Reich and Musicians
Includes Cardew on marimba/glockenspiel
Recording: Hamburg Musikstudio I, 1/1974
Deutsche Grammophon DGG 427 428-2
Vinyl catalogue number 2740 106

Morton Feldman
a compliation CD in which Cardew (piano)
and János Négyesy (violin) perform *Vertical
Thoughts 2*
Editions RZ, CD 1010

Cardew documentary

BBC Documentary on Cornelius Cardew
available for free download at
http://www.ubu.com/sound/cardew.html

Cornelius Cardew a life unfinished

Index

Compositions in italics, standing alone, are by Cardew. Compositions by other composers are placed under the composer's name. Songs by Cardew are also in inverted commas followed by his name in brackets. Articles, reviews etc. by Cardew are in inverted commas. Page numbers in bold indicate a substantial entry.

Ashley, Robert 409
She was a Visitor 571, 612

Astaldi, Francesca 186-7, 207, 222 fnt 26, 272-3, 281 fnt 77
Centro Internazionale di Danza 285
Cardew's improvisations 186

A Suite of Wolff Tunes 784-87

Attwood, Tony 587-8
In the Shadow of Westway 588

Atwal, Satnam 916

Austin, Larry 196, 222 fnt 27

Autumn 60 44, 86, 93, 103, 105-115, 121 fnt 57, 128, 132, 139, 151-2, 154,166 fnt 43, 177, 190, 204, 218, 231, 234, 236, 250, 254, 259, 263, 267, 272, 276-7, 773-4

avant-garde (European and American) 53-5, 57, 68, 70, 72-3, 75, 80, 83, 85, 90, 93-4, 96-7, 99, 101, 118 fnt 43, 120 fnt 56, 136, 138, 144, 147, 150, 162, 165 fnt 5, 174, 179-81, 187-9, 195-6, 206, 211, 221 fnt 16, 334, 343, 351, 357, 361, 363, 365, 605, 607-8, 616-7, 627-8

B

Babbitt, Milton 192

Bach, Johann Sebastian 30, 38, 424, 833, 864, 1018
Partita no. 6 in E minor 831
Toccata, Adagio and Fugue 411, 878

Bains, Hardial 557-8, 597 fnt 9, 821, 830 fnt 18, 889, 893, 897-8, 901 fnts 46,50, 52, 907, 917-9, 922, 924-5, 928-33, 945, 964, 973-4, 983 fnt 8, 998, 1005, 1009, 1010
assessment of Mao Zedong's contribution, 897-98
Necessity for Change! The Dialectic Lives! 558, 906

Baker, Laurie 419, 682, 694, 726 fnt 6, 728 fnt 47, 729 fnt 49,

805-6, 824-7, 830 fnt 28, 834, 838, 843, 846, 853-4, 856, 868 fnt 24, 870 fnt 52, 873-5, 879-80, 889, 891, 896, 899 fnt 16, 900 fnt 24, 907, 914, 918, 925, 936, 937 fnts 29, 30, 938 fnts 46, 48
Right to Rebel 826

Banner Theatre company 836, 867 fnt 6
Saltley Gates Show 836

Barthes, Roland
Image-Music-Text (1977) 166 fnt 25, 376 fnt 57, 515 fnts 64 & 66

Bauermeister, Mary 75-6, 83, 86-7, 95, 132-3

BBC (British Broadcasting Corporation) 337, 342, 347, 349, 374 fnt 38, 401, 407, 411, 414, 421, 423, 573, 577, 581, 590, 592-5, 733, 737, 746, 749, 761, 768 fnt 40, 948

Beckett, Samuel 121 fnt 91, 724, 732 fnt 118
Molloy 54, 117 fnt 13

Bedford, David 156, 167 fnt 53, 196, 207, 212, 216, 219, 249, 254, 230 fnt 66

Beethoven, Ludwig van 31, 73, 202, 418-20, 428, 720-1, 750, 763-4, 770 fnt 96, 779, 782-3, 790, 813, 815, 861-4, 870 fnts 62, 64, 66, 67, 890, 995
Appassionata Sonata 863
Sonata Pathétique 721, 1016

Bennett, Richard Rodney 18, 29, 30-2, 35, 40, 47, 59, 64, 68, 71, 82, 89, 91, 117 fnt 21

Benjamin, Walter 554-5, 561, 781, 801 fnt 18

Berio, Luciano 179, 211, 317, 332 fnt 78

Berlin
Akademie der Künste 678-9, 728 fnt 39
Bethanien 668, 676-9, 716-7
Deutscher Akademischer Austauschdienst 658, 677
Kreuzberg 677-8

Kreuzberg Vietnam Committee 811, 814

Berlin, Isaiah 34

Bernau, Götz 910

'Bethanien Lied' 716-7

Biel, Michael von
Book for Three 177 197-8, 205, 207, 223 fnt 41

'Blackleg Miner' folk song 991, 993, 1012 fnt 5

Blake, William 35-6, 42, 46, 48 fnt 25, 133, 161, 167 fnt 55, 195, 339, 368, 454, 979
antinomianism 979
The Book of Thel 35, 46, 161
Voice from Thel's grave 35, 46
The Marriage of Heaven and Hell 48 fnt 25

Boehmer, Konrad 54

Boenisch, Hanne 432, 467 fnt 54, 475-6, 563-5, 598 fnt 17
– *see also under* 'interviews'

Boolavogue 930, 987-9, 991, 993, 997, 1012 fnt 3

Boulez, Pierre 31, 55, 61, 66, 80, 117 fnt 23, 119 fnt 58, 139, 141, 189, 217, 345
Le Marteau sans Maître 71, 109
Structures I (for two pianos) 30, 45-6, 90, 93

Bowie, David 843, 854

Boyle, Mark 213, 224 fnt 59, 283, 332 fnt 74
The Sensual Laboratory, Journey to the Surface of the Earth 224 fnt 59

Bradford College of Art 571, 581, 599 fnt 25, 627, 658, 663

Bradshaw, Susan 30, 48 fnt 6, 480, 481 fnt 6, 987-8, 997

Brecht, Bertolt 650, 661, 790-93, 796, 798, 802 fnts 28, 36, 926, 931, 938 fnts 50, 54
'crude thinking' 650, 655 fnt10
The Measures Taken 792, 808
The Exception and the Rule 790, 807
The Mother 598 fnt 14, 600 fnt 51, 997

Cornelius Cardew a life unfinished

Other books published by Copula

No Sound is Innocent
AMM and the Practice of Self-Invention, Meta-Musical Narratives
and other essays, Edwin Prévost 1995 ISBN 0-9525492-0-4

Minute Particulars
Meanings in music-making in the wake of hierarchial realignments
and other essays, Edwin Prévost 2004 ISBN 0-9525492-1-2

Cornelius Cardew – A Reader
A collection of Cornelius Cardew's published writings with commentaries
and responses from Richard Barrett, Christopher Fox, Brian Dennis,
Anton Lukoszevieze, Michael Nyman, Eddie Prévost, David Ryan,
Howard Skempton, Dave Smith, John Tilbury and Christian Wolff
ISBN 0-9525492-2-0

Matchless Recordings and Publishing has a sizeable catalogue of recordings
that feature many of the musics which inform and are discussed in the books
above. Also available is Cardew's score *The Great Learning*.

For details of these and other related items please write or go to:
www.matchlessrecordings.com